BLACKSTONE'S

CRIMINAL PRACTICE

BLACKSTONE'S

CRIMINAL PRACTICE

2021

SUPPLEMENT 3

GENERAL EDITORS

DAVID ORMEROD CBE, QC (HON)

BARRISTER, BENCHER OF MIDDLE TEMPLE,
PROFESSOR OF CRIMINAL JUSTICE,
UNIVERSITY COLLEGE LONDON

DAVID PERRY QC

BARRISTER, 6KBW COLLEGE HILL

FOUNDING EDITOR

HIS HONOUR PETER MURPHY

SUPPLEMENT EDITOR

WILLIAM HAYS

BARRISTER, 6KBW COLLEGE HILL

CONTRIBUTORS

PARAMJIT AHLUWALIA, DUNCAN ATKINSON QC, ALEX BAILIN QC,
DIANE BIRCH OBE, HHJ JONATHAN COOPER, HHJ JOHANNAH CUTTS QC,
ANAND DOOBAY, ANTHONY EDWARDS, HHJ STEVEN EVERETT,
RUDI FORTSON QC, DANIEL GODDEN, HHJ MARTIN EDMUNDS QC,
KATHERINE HARDCASTLE, WILLIAM HAYS, MICHAEL HIRST,
LAURA C. H. HOYANO, PETER HUNGERFORD-WELCH, PAUL JARVIS,
ADRIAN KEANE, SALLY KYD, KARL LAIRD, MICHAEL LEREGO QC,
RICHARD MCMAHON QC, ALEXANDER MILLS, VALSAMIS MITSILEGAS,
TIM MOLONEY QC, REBECCA NIBLOCK, AMANDA PINTO QC,
HH PETER ROOK QC, RICHARD D. TAYLOR, MARK TOPPING, MARTIN WASIK CBE

OXFORD
UNIVERSITY PRESS

OXFORD
UNIVERSITY PRESS

Great Clarendon Street, Oxford, OX2 6DP,
United Kingdom

Oxford University Press is a department of the University of Oxford.
It furthers the University's objective of excellence in research, scholarship,
and education by publishing worldwide. Oxford is a registered trade mark of
Oxford University Press in the UK and in certain other countries

Impression: 1

Published in the United States of America by Oxford University Press
198 Madison Avenue, New York, NY 10016, United States of America

British Library Cataloguing in Publication Data
Data available

ISBN 978–0–19–886962–7

Printed in Italy by
L.E.G.O. S.p.A.

Introduction

Paragraphing

For the 2021 Edition we have changed the paragraphing for the Criminal Procedure Rules and the Criminal Practice Directions to follow the numbering of the primary instruments and make navigation more intuitive for the user.

Criminal Procedure Rules 2020: Paragraphs are prefixed R so that R2.1 in this Supplement is the text of Criminal Procedure Rule 2.1.

Criminal Practice Directions: Paragraphs are prefixed CPD so that CPD.26A in this Supplement is the text of Criminal Practice Direction Part 26, Jurors, Subsection A, Introduction.

Sentencing Guidelines: Paragraphs are prefixed SG and then ordered and numbered to cover the Overarching Guidelines, followed by the Magistrates' Court Sentencing Guidelines, and then each Offence Type.

Contents

This Supplement is the third of three cumulative updating supplements to *Blackstone's Criminal Practice 2021*. It includes updates to the text of *Blackstone's Criminal Practice 2021* taking account of legislative developments and leading cases since the publication of the 2021 edition. These updates are included at the start of the Supplement and follow the headings and the paragraph numbering used in the 2021 edition.

This Supplement contains the complete text of the Criminal Procedure Rules 2020 (SI 2020 No. 759) as amended by the Criminal Procedure (Amendment) Rules 2021 (SI 2021 No. 40) which came into force on 8 February 2021, save for the following which came into force on 5 April 2021:

(a) r. 6(a) and (b);
(b) r. 9(a) to (h), (k), (l) and (m)(ii);
(c) r. 10;
(d) r. 17(c)(i);
(e) r. 20;
(f) r. 21;
(g) r. 22;
(h) r. 23(b) and (c);
(i) r. 24;
(j) r. 25; and
(k) r. 30(b).

The Criminal Procedure Rules 2020 replaced the Criminal Procedure Rules 2015 (SI 2015 No. 1490, as amended).

The Supplement also contains the Criminal Practice Directions October 2015 (as amended April 2016, November 2016, January 2017, April 2018, October 2018, April 2019, October 2019, May 2020 and November 2020); and the Sentencing Guidelines as at 6 May 2021.

The Criminal Practice Directions are included after the relevant Criminal Procedure Rules and set as shaded text to differentiate the Rules and Practice Directions. The Criminal Practice Directions included are the Directions issued in October 2015 as amended and are stated as at 1 April 2021. Please note that this does mean that the Practice Directions still make reference to the Criminal Procedure Rules 2015.

The Sentencing Guidelines reflect the text as set out on the Sentencing Council website. Previous PDF versions of Guidelines are now included on that website for archive purposes only by the Council and we have amended the Guidelines in this Supplement to reflect the official statement of the Guidelines which means that some previous explanatory material has been excised. The approach taken in the Supplement is that the Overarching Guidelines are set out first from SG1 to SG9, followed by the Magistrates' Court Sentencing Guidelines at SG10 and then the Sentencing Guidelines by Offence Type. For a more detailed note on the treatment and order of the Sentencing Guidelines please see SG0-1 ***et seq.***

The approach we have taken is to include all Sentencing Guidelines triable on indictment only and triable either way in the Offence Types. Offences triable summarily only are included in the Magistrates' Court Sentencing Guidelines along with a cross-reference for any offences triable either way to the location of that guideline within the Offence Types.

In this supplement, a table of offences is included at **SG0-2** which lists all of the offence-specific guidelines in alphabetical order indicating where the standard steps apply.

Covid-19 Updating

We are publishing a digital Special Supplement to provide for information on any temporary and special laws and regulations and procedural changes related to managing Covid-19. Please visit the *Blackstone's Criminal Practice 2021* companion website at www.oup.com/blackstones/criminal to download the latest update.

Blackstone's Briefing and Fortnightly Updates

Please visit the Blackstone's Criminal Practice 2021 companion website at www.oup.com/blackstones/criminal to register for e-mail updates or to download the latest updates.

Blackstone's Briefing includes analysis of key developments and feature articles.

If you have any queries, please contact blackstonescriminal@oup.com.

Contents

Table of Cases

Table of Statutes

Table of Statutory Instruments

Table of Practice Directions

Table of Codes of Conduct

Table of Guidelines

Table of Protocols and Circulars

Table of International Treaties and Conventions and other Legal Instruments

Table of European Legislation

SUPPLEMENT TO PART A
CRIMINAL LAW

NOVUS ACTUS INTERVENIENS

Conduct of the Victim

Kennedy (No. 2) [2007] UKHL 38, [2008] 1 AC 269, was distinguished in *Field* [2021] EWCA Crim 380. In this case, D appealed against his conviction for the murder of V, a lonely man whom he had seduced and pretended to befriend, while covertly drugging him to simulate illness and plotting his death for the purpose of inheritance under V's will. The prosecution case was that D had finally tricked V into drinking a large quantity of malt whisky which, in conjunction with the drug, caused or substantially contributed to his death, perhaps hastened by smothering (as to alternative explanations of this kind, see **A1.40** in the main work). In his summing-up, the trial judge had directed the jury that: **A1.35**

> If it is proved that, with intent to kill, [D] gave [V] drink then, even if [V] agreed to drink it, it would be open to you to conclude that the giving was a cause of death, unless [V]'s decision was informed in that he knew that the drink being offered to him was intended to cause his death.

The Court of Appeal approved this direction. The distinction is that in *Kennedy*, V knew what he was doing. If, in *Field*, V had known he was taking a fatal cocktail of whisky and drugs, the case could only have been one of assisting or encouraging suicide, but by convicting D of murder, the jury had clearly rejected that possibility. They found, in other words, that V's act of drinking was not a free, voluntary and informed decision such as to break the chain of causation. See also (in the context of negligent causation) *Rebelo* [2021] EWCA Crim 306 (noted in this supplement at **B1.66**).

CAUSATION ISSUES AND ALTERNATIVE EXPLANATIONS

Morby (1882) 8 QBD 571; *Misra* [2004] EWCA Crim 2375, [2005] 1 Cr App R 21 (328) and *Sellu* [2016] EWCA Crim 1716, [2017] 1 Cr App R 24 (349) were considered by the Court of Appeal in *Broughton* [2020] EWCA Crim 1093. In this case, D supplied his girlfriend, V, with a cocktail of controlled drugs, including 2CP, ketamine and MDMA (Ecstasy), which she took in his presence in woodland adjacent to a rock festival site. She experienced a violent reaction, but D did not call for medical assistance, even after phoning members of V's family, who begged him to do so. Instead, he video-recorded V's trip as her condition deteriorated. She died. **A1.40**

V had voluntarily consumed the drugs, so this could not be advanced as a case of constructive manslaughter by unlawful administration (*Kennedy (No. 2)* [2007] UKHL 38, [2008] 1 AC 269 (see **A1.36** in the main work)), but at his trial D was convicted *inter alia* of manslaughter by gross negligence as a result of his subsequent neglect.

On appeal, the central issue was whether D's conduct, however negligent, was proved to have caused or at least contributed to V's death, and it was concluded that the prosecution evidence on this was deficient. There was evidence that the neglect had drastically reduced her chances of survival, but that alone could not suffice. Such has been the law at least since *Morby*, in which D failed to secure medical treatment for his child, who then died of smallpox. Medical experts in that case had testified that treatment would not necessarily have saved the child, but would have improved his chances of survival, and that was held to be insufficient. So it was in *Broughton*. The exact cause of V's death could not be determined, and the only expert witness to address the causation issue concluded:

> In view of the lack of previously documented deaths from 2CP, the combined effect of three stimulant drugs and the unknown mechanism that resulted in [V's] death, it is not possible to state beyond reasonable doubt that earlier medical intervention would have been able to save [V's] life once she had ingested the 2CP.

This case was not, said Lord Burnett, analogous to *Gian* [2009] EWCA Crim 2553, in which the experts merely struggled to exclude a theoretical or hypothetical alternative explanation for V's death; nor was it one in which there was evidence, other than the expert evidence, from which a jury could still conclude that causation was proved. At best, V might have had a 90 per cent chance of survival if given prompt medical intervention, but that still left room for reasonable doubt. D's manslaughter conviction was quashed.

Section A2 Mens Rea

STRICT LIABILITY

The Imposition of Strict Liability

A2.23 In *R (Highbury Poultry Farm Produce Ltd) v Telford Magistrates' Court* [2020] UKSC 39, [2020] 1 WLR 4309, the Supreme Court considered two offences under the Welfare of Animals at the Time of Killing (England) Regulations 2015 (SI 2015 No. 1782), reg. 30(1)(g), involving the contravention, by slaughterhouse operators, of articles of Regulation (EC) 1099/2009, on the protection of animals. Although the Supreme Court upheld the conclusion of the Divisional Court that the two offences in question imposed strict liability, it did so by a different route. While the Divisional Court had reached its conclusion as a matter of domestic law, Lord Burrows, in delivering the single unanimous judgment of the Supreme Court, held that the question of whether the provision imposed strict liability was dictated by the correct interpretation of Regulation (EC) 1099/2009 as a matter of EU law (partly because not to do so would undermine the objective of harmonisation). It was further held that EU law does not prohibit the imposition of strict liability and that the Regulation properly interpreted, applying EU law principles of statutory interpretation, did impose strict liability. Lord Burrows also noted (at [55]) that, had it been correct to apply domestic law, he 'would have agreed with the Divisional Court's view that the presumption of *mens rea* or culpability was here rebutted'. Reference was also made (at [36]) to *Blackstone's Criminal Practice 2020*, para. A2.22, in relation to strict liability often being regarded as less problematic in relation to regulatory offences, such as the offences in this case.

Pwr v DPP [2020] EWHC 798 (Admin), [2020] 2 Cr App R 11 (165), provides another illustration of the imposition of strict liability, in this case under the TA 2000, s. 13. The offence covers one who 'wears, carries or displays an article, in such a way or in such circumstances as to arouse reasonable suspicion that he is a member or supporter of a proscribed organization'. The presumption of *mens rea* was displaced: no intention to arouse reasonable suspicion, or knowledge that the (PKK) flag being carried would give rise to such suspicion, was required, although D must act deliberately in the sense that D must know that D is wearing, carrying or displaying the article in question. It was relevant in interpreting the offence as one of strict liability that other offences in the legislation had words expressly requiring *mens rea* and carried more serious penalties. The offence was also compatible with Article 10 of the ECHR protecting freedom of expression, the restriction being proportionate to the public interest in combating terrorist organisations, notwithstanding the offence being one of strict liability. Permission to appeal to the Supreme Court was granted on 6 November 2020.

Damji [2020] EWCA Crim 1774 concerned breaches of a restraining order contrary to the Protection from Harassment Act 1997, s. 5(5), by referring to two named individuals on Twitter. The subsection creating the offence required D to have acted 'without reasonable excuse', which Carr LJ said 'provides for what could be described as "the middle ground" between full *mens rea* and strict liability (as explored in *Blackstone's Criminal Practice 2021* at A2.23 and A3.6)' (at [46]). The inclusion of this fault element meant there was 'no need to read into the statute any words importing a requirement of knowledge or additional *mens rea*' (at [47]).

Section A3 General Defences

DEFENCES DENYING BASIC ELEMENTS OF LIABILITY

Mistake and Inadvertence: Offences Satisfied by Negligence

Damji [2020] EWCA Crim 1774 concerned breaches of a restraining order contrary to the Protection from Harassment Act 1997, s. 5(5), by referring to two named individuals on Twitter. The subsection creating the offence required D to have acted 'without reasonable excuse', which Carr LJ said 'provides for what could be described as "the middle ground" between full *mens rea* and strict liability (as explored in *Blackstone's Criminal Practice 2021* at A2.23 and A3.6)' (at [46]). The inclusion of this fault element meant there was 'no need to read into the statute any words importing a requirement of knowledge or additional *mens rea*' (at [47]). **A3.6**

DEFENCES INVOLVING OTHER EXCUSES AND JUSTIFICATIONS

Necessity

In *Thacker* [2021] EWCA Crim 97, Lord Burnett CJ said (at [100]) that the comments of Lord Hoffmann in *Jones* [2006] UKHL 16, [2007] 1 AC 136 (see **A3.56** in the main work), about the limits on claims of justification in relation to acts of self-help, civil disobedience or protest, were not to be confined to the defence of prevention of crime but also applied to necessity and duress of circumstances. The judge had therefore on the facts correctly refused to let any of the defences of necessity, duress of circumstances or prevention of crime go to the jury. **A3.47**

Coercion and Compulsion

The argument that s.45 of the Modern Slavery Act 2015 was retrospective and provided defences to offences committed before the commencement date (31 July 2015) was rejected in *CS* [2021] EWCA Crim 134. **A3.54**

Section A5 Inchoate Offences

STATUTORY CONSPIRACY

Parties to Conspiracies and Acquittal of Other Alleged Conspirators

In *Gates* [2021] EWCA Crim 66, D and his co-defendants were charged with conspiring 'together with others unknown' to supply cocaine. D was convicted, but his co-defendants were each acquitted on that particular charge, and on appeal it was submitted that D's conviction should be quashed as inconsistent with their acquittals. **A5.50**

As explained in the main work, the conviction of one defendant on a conspiracy charge may be inconsistent with the acquittal of another, based on identical evidence (*Longman* (1980) 72 Cr App R 121), but in this case, said the Court of Appeal, the acquittal of the co-defendants left open the possibility that D conspired (as alleged in the indictment) with other persons unknown. There was also ample evidence specific to D on which a jury could properly have concluded that he must have conspired with someone, if not with his co-defendants. This evidence included a large quantity of cocaine-contaminated cash found in D's possession, for which he could offer no credible explanation. His conviction was upheld.

CONSPIRACY TO DEFRAUD

Indictment and Procedure

A5.66 In *Bermingham* [2020] EWCA Crim 1662, the Court of Appeal advised that, where the gist of a charge of conspiracy to defraud is that the defendants deliberately acted in a way that unlawfully prejudiced the economic or financial interests of others, the indictment should make it clear that intent and not merely recklessness is required. Fulford LJ said (at [110]):

> For the avoidance of doubt, indictments in the future would be better framed in this context using, for instance, the expression 'thereby intending to prejudice the economic interests of others' rather than 'thereby intending that the economic interests of others may be prejudiced'.

Mens Rea

A5.69 The revised dishonesty test established by *Ivey v Genting Casinos (UK) Ltd* [2017] UKSC 67, [2018] AC 391 and *Barton* [2020] EWCA Crim 575, [2020] 2 Cr App R 7(93), was applied in the context of a charge of conspiracy to defraud in *Bermingham* [2020] EWCA Crim 1662. Following *Barton*, the Court of Appeal in that case rejected a submission that the offence of conspiracy to defraud lacked certainty and could lead to the conviction of a defendant who did not realise at the relevant time that what he or she was doing was wrong. Quoting from *Barton*, Fulford LJ observed (at [102]) that:

> The test of dishonesty formulated in *Ivey* remains a test of the defendant's state of mind — his or her knowledge or belief — to which the standards of ordinary decent people are applied.

This subjective limb of the *Ivey* test, he added, 'gives a substantial measure of protection from the application of an objective test unrelated to the state of mind of the defendant under consideration'.

Section A7 Human Rights

SENTENCE

Retroactive Penalties

A7.92 When passing sentence, the court is not concerned with the release regime that will apply in the event that it imposes upon D an immediate term of imprisonment. It follows that where the release regime is changed during the period of D's incarceration — with the result that D will have to spend longer in custody before being released than either D or the court expected at the time the sentence was imposed — the continued detention is not a breach of Article 7 of the ECHR. There is an important distinction to be drawn between the imposition of a penalty that is harsher than the maximum penalty that was available to the court at the time the offence was committed, and the subsequent administration of a penalty that is not harsher than the maximum penalty that was available to the court at the time the offence was committed. The former may infringe Article 7 but the latter will not, even if it results in an increase in the length of time D will spend in custody pursuant to the sentence of imprisonment lawfully imposed (*R (Khan) v Secretary of State for Justice* [2020] EWHC 2084 (Admin), [2020] 1 WLR 3932).

Section A8 Territorial and Extra-territorial Jurisdiction

INTRODUCTION

The possibility that a suspected offender could be prosecuted for extra-territorial offences under English law does not mean that the Secretary of State should refuse or deny a request for the sharing of evidence with another country in accordance with a treaty providing for Mutual Legal Assistance (MLA). In *R (Elgizouli) v Secretary of State for the Home Department* [2020] EWHC 2516 (Admin), both the US and UK authorities were interested in the prosecution of British citizens who were suspected of murdering captives (including both British and US citizens) in Syria. The US authorities provided an assurance that the death penalty would not be imposed if the UK acceded to their MLA request. Giving the judgment of the Divisional Court, Dame Victoria Sharp P agreed (at 67]) with a submission that: **A8.1**

> The absence of a CPS charging decision does not preclude the sharing of evidence with the US for the use in their investigation and/or prosecution. It is perfectly legitimate for two countries to be investigating individuals at the same time and parallel investigations are not uncommon.

She added (at [68]):

> The question as to which was the better forum for a prosecution … was not the question before the Secretary of State. She was being asked to provide material that would assist in a contemplated US prosecution, pursuant to a treaty that provided for material to be shared between prosecuting authorities in such circumstances.

SUPPLEMENT TO PART B OFFENCES

Section B1 Homicide and Related Offences

LOSS OF CONTROL

Burden of Proof and Role of Jury

The need for a sufficient evidential basis for each and every one of the three components of the defence is again illustrated by the decision in *Dawson* [2021] EWCA Crim 40. D1 and D2 had both denied any involvement in the killing and did not therefore put forward loss of control but there was evidence that V had been extremely irritating and troublesome to them over a period of years. The trial judge had declined to leave loss of control to the jury, ruling that there was not sufficient evidence of a qualifying trigger constituting 'circumstances of an *extremely* grave character' causing 'a *justifiable* sense of being seriously wronged' (emphasis added). The Court of Appeal agreed on this point but said that quite apart from this second component, there was not even sufficient evidence of the first component — actual loss of self-control — and this was itself sufficient reason not to leave the defence to the jury. The killing was quite brutal but Fulford VP reiterated (at [23]), in the light of previous case law, that the: **B1.32**

> ... sustained and gratuitously violent nature of the assault did not, standing alone, provide sufficient evidence of loss of control. It is important in this context to emphasise that attacks leading to death can be unnecessarily brutal and prolonged for a wide range of reasons that do not involve loss of control.

There was no other evidence in this case of loss of self-control so there was insufficient evidence to put the defence to the jury on this first component, quite apart from the lack of a sufficiently grave qualifying trigger.

MANSLAUGHTER BY GROSS NEGLIGENCE

The Need for a Serious and Obvious Risk of Death

The issue of causation was the focus of the decision in *Broughton* [2020] EWCA Crim 1093, [2021] 1 Cr App R 3 (25), where it was emphasised that the question was whether the death resulted from conduct of D at, or following, the time when there was a serious and obvious risk of death. D had supplied drugs to his girlfriend (V) at a festival from which she experienced a bad trip and ultimately died. Although clearly the supply of the drugs could not ground a conviction for manslaughter since V had voluntarily taken them, D was initially convicted of gross negligence manslaughter on the basis of his failure to summon medical assistance. The only relevant medical evidence was to the effect that had D summoned aid at the time when the risk of death had become obvious, there was a 90 per cent chance that V would have survived but it could not be said for certain that V would not have died anyway. The Court of Appeal quashed the conviction, saying the case should not have gone to the jury following a submission of no case to answer, since there was no evidence on which the jury could be sure that V would not have died anyway. It was not enough that D's negligence deprived V of a significant or substantial chance of survival; it had to be proved to the criminal standard that it was the cause of death, in the sense of, but for D's breach of duty, V would not have died. **B1.66**

Reference was made to the correct principle being established in *Morby* (1882) 8 QBD 571, where a conviction was quashed because the medical evidence went no further than saying that the child (who died of smallpox) might have been saved had medical help been summoned, not that he would have been saved. Lord Burnett CJ summed up the position in *Broughton* as follows (at [100]–[101]):

> In the context of causation in this very sad case the task of the jury was to ask whether the evidence established to the criminal standard that, with medical intervention as soon as possible after [V's] condition presented a serious and obvious risk of death, she would have lived. In short, had the prosecution excluded the realistic possibility that, despite such treatment, [V] would have died?

> In our judgment none of Professor Deakin's descriptive language achieved that. Even his description of a 90% chance of survival at 21.10, were medical help available, leaves a realistic possibility that she would not have lived.

There was no other evidence on which the jury could rely to show that the negligence was the cause of death, and the conviction was quashed.

The prosecution in *Broughton* was based on D's failure to seek medical attention rather than the fact that D had been the supplier of the drug since:

(a) such supply is not a dangerous unlawful act for the purposes of unlawful act manslaughter (see **B1.58 to B1.60** in the main work), and

(b) there was no suggestion that it was grossly negligent to supply the drug nor that it was not V's free and voluntary decision to ingest the drugs.

Rebelo [2021] EWCA Crim 306, in contrast, illustrates the exceptional situation where there can be a causal link between grossly negligent supply of a highly toxic substance (DNP) via the internet and the subsequent death of V. The issue turned on whether V's addiction and mental health issues meant that her decision to take the fatal capsules of DNP was not 'fully free, voluntary and informed'. If the jury had concluded that it was or *might have been* 'fully free, voluntary and informed', V's death would flow from her own decision and D could not be said to have caused it. However, if the jury were sure that the decision was *not* 'fully free, voluntary and informed', as their verdict indicated, that meant that the grossly negligent supply was the cause of V's death with no intervening voluntary act to break the chain. The conviction for gross negligence manslaughter was therefore upheld. It should be noted that this was an unsuccessful appeal against conviction at a second trial following a previous appeal (*Rebelo* [2019] EWCA Crim 633) which quashed convictions at the first trial for both unlawful act manslaughter (quashed because no unlawful and dangerous act) and gross negligence manslaughter (misdirection on causation at first trial but retrial ordered).

Section B2 Non-fatal Offences Against the Person

WOUNDING OR CAUSING GRIEVOUS BODILY HARM WITH INTENT

Sentence

B2.76 **Knives** In *Summerville* [2020] EWCA Crim 944, D stabbed V three times with a large kitchen knife, causing wounds to V's right shoulder and to the left of his back and a laceration to V's left upper eyelid. The Court of Appeal held that the harm was somewhat above that which is normal in a s. 18 attack, but not so significantly as to justify moving this case from category 2 to category 1 (*Fa Xue* [2020] EWCA Crim 587, [2020] 2 Cr App R (S) 49 (350) considered).

FALSE IMPRISONMENT

Sentence

B2.102 In *Flanagan* [2020] EWCA Crim 1117, a sentence of three years' imprisonment for false imprisonment following a late guilty plea was held to be manifestly excessive. D struck his partner in front of their young children, pinned her to the floor and prevented her from leaving their home. While the incident was serious, particularly as D admitted similar previous conduct, the degree of injury inflicted was modest. A sentence of 27 months' imprisonment was substituted.

Section B3 Sexual Offences

RAPE

Sentencing Guidelines

Life Imprisonment: Automatic and Discretionary Life Sentences In a conjoined appeal with *A-G's Refs (Nos. 688 of 2019 (McCann) and 5 of 2020 (Sinaga))* [2020] EWCA Crim 1676, [2021] 4 WLR 3, the Court of Appeal upheld 53 concurrent life sentences for offences of assault by penetration (together with 37 concurrent determinate sentences for sexual assault) in respect of the applicant Shah who as a medical general practitioner had carried out multiple unnecessary breast, vaginal and rectal examinations on vulnerable young women and girls. The most serious aggravating feature of the applicant's offending was the gross breach of trust. He had persuaded his victims to submit to internal examinations, deceived his colleagues and falsified patients' records. The applicant's thinking was distorted to such an extent that he sought to normalise prolific offending in gross breach of trust. In her sentencing remarks the judge observed that the breach of trust was at least as serious as the use of violence. The offending had had serious adverse psychological impact on some of the complainants. Given the applicant's denial of sexual motivation and lack of insight into his own behaviour, the judge had concluded that 'it is possible that he could seek to put himself in a position when he can again groom women' (see [46]). The Court of Appeal held that the judge had been entitled to find that the fact that the applicant would not practise again was insufficient to protect the public given, amongst other factors, the scale and persistence of the offending over a period spanning just over four years (90 sexual offences perpetrated against 24 women, four of whom were under 18). The circumstances of the offending did not preclude the real possibility of the applicant finding other opportunities to commit serious sexual offences. It was open to the judge to determine that the applicant was dangerous and there were no reliable assessments as to the length of time he would remain a danger. He had demonstrated attitudes which needed to be examined. His risk and the trigger factors needed to be explored before the danger he posed could be safely managed. While the results of the Offender Assessment System placed him at a low risk of re-offending, the technical assessment tools are not binding upon a judge (*Almoshaweh* [2016] EWCA Crim 1910). Here the tools did not account for the prolific nature of the applicant's offending. The judge's conclusion that the applicant is dangerous was unimpeachable as was her decision that the criteria for a life sentence were made out. She had recognised that a life sentence was one of last resort but such a disposal was necessary in this case. B3.25

The Court also observed that it was unimpressed by the submission that the 'restrained' nature of the offences provided the applicant with mitigation, given that more 'overt' sexual offending risked complaint being made to the authorities. Furthermore, good character as a mitigating factor was to a significant extent outweighed by the way he used his standing as a doctor, which in part depended upon his good character, to perpetrate these offences.

In *A-G's Refs (Nos. 688 of 2019 (McCann) and 5 of 2020 (Sinaga))* [2020] EWCA Crim 1676, [2021] 4 WLR 3, the Solicitor-General applied for leave to refer the sentences of two unconnected prolific sexual offenders to the Court of Appeal on the grounds that their multiple life sentences with minimum terms of 30 years were unduly lenient. McCann had been convicted of 37 counts including seven of rape, seven of kidnapping and ten of false imprisonment, while Sinaga had been convicted of 136 offences of rape in relation to 44 victims as well as counts in respect of other sexual offences. The Solicitor-General submitted that the scale and nature of the offending called for whole life tariffs to be attached to the life sentences. The Court of Appeal, Lord Burnett CJ giving judgment, reviewed the authorities and cited Treacy LJ in *Andrews* [2015] EWCA Crim 883, [2015] 2 Cr App R (S) 40 (317), who had observed (at [35]): 'Although the door is not conclusively closed to the imposition of a whole life order in serious cases, not involving homicide, the practice of this court to date has been against the imposition of such a sentence in a non-homicide cases'. The Court concluded that the decisions leave open the possibility that a whole life term could be attached to a discretionary life sentence, but took the view that there is a principled reason for reserving the B3.26

most serious cases to murder, save in the most exceptional circumstances. Rejecting the Solicitor-General's submission, the Court decided that the offending in these cases, very serious though it was, did not call for either to receive a whole life sentence.

The Court did, however, raise the minimum sentences in both cases to 40 years. In *McCann* the offending involved a large number of offences committed over a short time span with gratuitous sadistic violence, while in *Sinaga* the extent of the offending was unique in involving the humiliation of victims, health risks and extensive planning. In the collective experience of the Court the cases of *McCann* and *Sinaga*, albeit very different on the individual facts, came within the category of the most serious cases involving campaigns of rape to be tried in England and Wales. The judges had no guidance available from the Court of Appeal in cases of similar severity, in particular multiple sexual and associated offending at a level not previously encountered. Both cases were paradigms of the circumstances that justify a departure from the usual position of fixing the requisite custodial period as half of the determinate sentence. A custodial period of two-thirds was necessary to ensure that the proper requirements of punishment were met for unique cases rather than by reference to the release provisions for an extended sentence.

SEXUAL ASSAULT

Elements

B3.69 In *A-G's Ref (No. 1 of 2020)* [2020] EWCA Crim 1665, [2021] 1 Cr App R 15 (291), the A-G, pursuant to the CJA 1972, s. 36, referred a point of law which had arisen in trial proceedings for an opinion of the Court of Appeal. After a trial D had been acquitted of sexual assault by the jury. It was common ground that D, while travelling on a train, had kissed on the lips without her consent V, a fellow passenger. At trial D stated that the kiss had not been sexual. Rather it had been a friendly reassuring gesture. The trial judge accepted submissions that it was a necessary ingredient of the offence for the prosecution to prove that D intended the touching to be sexual. The Court of Appeal disagreed. The statutory ingredients of an offence under the SOA 2003, s. 3, did not contain the requirement that D intended the touching to be 'sexual'. The presumption of *mens rea* only applies if the plain meaning of the words in the offence-creating provision are ambiguous (*Lane* [2018] UKSC 36, [2018] 2 Cr App R 35 (606)). The scheme of the Act is that whenever an offence is committed against a victim by sexual touching, proof of a sexual intention as part of the *mens rea* is not required. The judge had blurred the distinction between D's intention and the possible relevance of D's purpose to the determination of whether his action was 'sexual' under s. 78(b).

Section B4 Theft, Handling Stolen Goods and Related Offences

ROBBERY AND ASSAULT WITH INTENT TO ROB

Sentence

B4.70 In *Davis* [2020] EWCA Crim 1066, a sentence of eight and a half years' imprisonment imposed following a guilty plea to robbery in which shop staff were threatened at knife point, was reduced to seven years to reflect the fact that although it had been sentenced as a professionally planned commercial robbery, it was a less sophisticated commercial robbery with aggravating features. An adjustment was also made to reflect the fact that a co-defendant had received the same custodial term yet had been sentenced for two offences of robbery, both of which had been committed on licence.

Actus Reus

Dawson (1976) 64 Cr App R 170, *Clouden* [1987] Crim LR 56 and *P v DPP* [2012] EWHC 1657 Admin, [2013] 1 WLR 2337, were considered in *Martins* [2021] EWCA Crim 223, in which the issue on appeal was whether D and his accomplice could properly be said to have committed robbery by snatching V's phone and keys from his hands. Upholding D's conviction, Holroyde LJ said: **B4.73**

> 19. We think it clear that robbery does not necessarily require direct physical contact between robber and victim. Often of course it will, but it is in our view established that the indirect use of force on a person can be sufficient. For example, where a robber wrenches a bag away from the grasp of his victim it is open to the jury … to find that the robber had used force on a person. We respectfully agree with the observation of the learned authors of Smith, Hogan and Ormerod's *Criminal Law*, 15th edn at section 19.1.2.1 that:
>
> > '… it will be robbery where, for example, a struggle, even a fleeting one, takes place for possession of a handbag or where an earring is snatched tearing the lobe of the ear.'
>
> 20. There will however sometimes be cases in which a jury could not properly find that the actions of a thief amounted to the use of force on any person, for example if an opportunist thief intervened to snatch a bank note which one person was passing to another. On a submission of no case to answer being made in relation to a charge of robbery, it will be for the judge to decide whether the evidence taken at its highest is such that a jury could properly find that defendant had used force on the victim.

Section B5 Fraud and Blackmail

THE OFFENCE OF FRAUD

Dishonesty in Fraud Cases

The revised dishonesty test established by *Ivey v Genting Casinos (UK) Ltd* [2018] UKSC 67, [2018] AC 391 and *Barton* [2020] EWCA Crim 575, [2020] 2 Cr App R 7 (93) was applied in the context of a charge of conspiracy to defraud in *Bermingham* [2020] EWCA Crim 1662. Following *Barton*, the Court of Appeal in that case rejected a submission that the offence of conspiracy to defraud lacked certainty and could lead to the conviction of a defendant who did not realise at the relevant time that what he or she was doing was wrong. Quoting from *Barton*, Fulford LJ observed (at [102]) that: **B5.11**

> The test of dishonesty formulated in *Ivey* remains a test of the defendant's state of mind — his or her knowledge or belief — to which the standards of ordinary decent people are applied.

This subjective limb of the *Ivey* test, he added, 'gives a substantial measure of protection from the application of an objective test unrelated to the state of mind of the defendant under consideration'.

BLACKMAIL

Sentencing Guidelines

Murphy [2019] EWCA Crim 438, [2019] 2 Cr App R (S) 13 (101), was considered by the Court of Appeal in *Berkeley* [2021] EWCA Crim 158. This was a very serious case of blackmail in which V had been assaulted by intruders in his own home, threatened and abducted at gunpoint, before being ransomed for £34,000 in cash, which was never recovered. D, if not one of the original abductors, was clearly a major player in the subsequent ransom negotiations. Having been acquitted on other charges, he fell to be sentenced for the blackmail demand alone, but as Goose J explained: **B5.50**

B

Part B Offences

> 12. … [D's] participation in the blackmail was against the obvious background of false imprisonment, and [this] could not be ignored in sentencing the applicant. He was not making demands for money in a vacuum; he was part of the negotiation in obtaining £34,000 and the threat that [V] would not be released if payment was not made.
>
> 13. We are satisfied that the judge was entitled to find [D] as having high culpability, for an offence which caused serious harm and, in absence of sentence guideline, inevitably sentence … was required to be towards the top of the sentencing range available.

Goose J then adopted this dictum from *Murphy*:

> The typical case of blackmail falls somewhere between robbery and simple theft in terms of seriousness. Relevant factors include the nature of the demand, the victim's ability to meet that demand, the nature of the threat to the victim should the demand not be met, the anguish and fear which the victim would usually experience, and the extent to which that anguish and fear was intended.

A sentence of 12 years' imprisonment was upheld.

Section B7 Company, Commercial and Insolvency Offences

FINANCIAL SERVICES OFFENCES

Misleading Statements and Impressions

B7.25 In the Financial Services Act 2012, s. 93(8B)(b), the words 'IP completion day' (implementation period completion day) replace the words 'exit day' (Financial Services and Economic and Monetary Policy (Consequential Amendments) (EU Exit) Regulations 2020 (SI 2020 No. 1301), reg. 3(1)). 'IP completion day' is defined as 11 p.m. on 31 December 2020 in the European Union (Withdrawal Agreement) Act 2020, s. 39, and the Interpretation Act 1978, s. 5 and sch. 1, para. 1.

OFFENCES CONCERNING COMPANY INSOLVENCY AND LIQUIDATION

Procedure in Summary Proceedings

B7.42 In the Insolvency Act 1986, s. 431(1), the words 'Parts AI to VII' replace the words 'Parts I to VII' with effect from 26 June 2020 (Corporate Insolvency and Governance Act 2020, sch. 3, para. 27).

Insolvency and Winding Up

B7.43 The Corporate Insolvency and Governance Act 2020 contains provisions to introduce flexibility into insolvency law and temporarily suspend parts of insolvency law during the Covid-19 pandemic.

SCHEDULE OF OFFENCES UNDER THE INSOLVENCY ACT 1986

B7.75 Section 224(2) of the SA 2020 has replaced s. 78(2) of the PCC(S)A 2000.

SENTENCING: INSOLVENCY AND BANKRUPTCY OFFENCES

B7.76 In *Hilsdon* [2021] EWCA Crim 52, the Court of Appeal imposed a sentence of eight months' imprisonment for an offence of removing £20,000 from D's bank account when bankrupt and 12 months' consecutive for nine further offences consisting of taking part in the management of a company while bankrupt, breaches of a bankruptcy restriction order and obtaining credit. The Court refused to suspend the sentence. D had traded unlawfully for over four years, causing losses said to have been over £280,000.

Section B10 Terrorism, Piracy and Hijacking

SUBSTANTIVE OFFENCES UNDER THE TERRORISM ACT 2000

Membership of a Proscribed Organisation

Sentence The Court of Appeal considered the effect of s. 1(2) of the Terrorist Offenders (Restriction of Early Release) Act 2020 on young offenders in *Scothern* [2020] EWCA Crim 1540, [2021] 1 WLR 1735. In June 2020, following a trial, a member of the proscribed group, National Action, was sentenced to 18 months' detention in a young offender institution for offences contrary to the TA 2000, s. 11. At the latest point that he was a member of the organisation, he was only 16. When he came to be sentenced, he was 19 years old. The sentencing judge concluded that if he had been 18 at the time of his offending, the relevant starting point would have been a sentence of five years' imprisonment. However, because he had only been 16 at the time of the offence, section 6 of the *Sentencing Children and Young People* guideline (see **SG8-8**) applied and suggested that the appropriate starting point should be the sentence which is likely to have been imposed on the date at which the offence is committed. In D's case that was a two-year detention and training order and, after taking into account all relevant aggravating and mitigating factors, the sentence settled upon was a detention and training order of 18 months' duration. That sentence was challenged upon appeal on two bases. First, that the sentencing judge had failed to give sufficient weight to D's mitigation. Second, that the imposition of 18 months' detention in a young offender institution was a breach of the ECHR, Article 7(1), and therefore a breach of the HRA 1998, s. 6(1). The first ground of appeal was refused. The second ground was based on the early release provisions enacted under the CJA 2003, s. 247A, in respect of terrorist prisoners serving determinate sentences. **B10.35**

Section 247A of the 2003 Act was inserted by the Terrorist Offenders (Restriction of Early Release) Act 2020, s. 1(2). The effect of that provision is that a 'terrorist prisoner' who has not been released on licence is not automatically released at the halfway point of the custodial term (as provided for by s. 244(1) of the 2003 Act) but instead serves two-thirds of the custodial term and is then only released if considered suitable for release by the Parole Board or, if not released earlier, at the end of the custodial term. The provisions apply to a terrorist prisoner regardless of the date of sentence and therefore have retrospective effect. However, in this case, the Court of Appeal decided that s. 247A did not apply in respect of a detention and training order. The primary reasoning for that conclusion was:

(a) the CJA 2003, s. 237(1), provides a definition of what comprises a 'fixed-term sentence', which does not include someone who is subject to a detention and training order (at [41]);
(b) the PCC(S)A 2000, s. 101(12A) (repealed by the SA 2020, sch. 28, para. 1, with effect from 1 December 2020), contrasts a fixed-term prisoner with an individual who is subject to a detention and training order: 'Section 243 of the Criminal Justice Act 2003 (persons extradited to the United Kingdom) applies in relation to a person sentenced to a detention and training order as it applies in relation to a fixed-term prisoner, with the reference in subsection (2A) of that section to section 240ZA being read as a reference to subsection (8) above' (at [42]).

Section 247A of the Act had in practice, however, been applied to D's sentence by the prison authorities. He had been refused parole and was likely to remain in custody for the whole 18 months of the detention and training order. Accordingly, the Court allowed the appeal to the extent that it reduced the sentence to one of nine months' detention and training order.

Collection of Information

Elements In *Dunleavy* [2021] EWCA Crim 39, the Court of Appeal upheld convictions under the TA 2000, s. 58, after a trial judge had withdrawn the defence of reasonable excuse from the jury. The Court acknowledged that a judge should only withdraw a defence of reasonable excuse under s. 58(3) if, as a matter of law, no jury could accept it (*Y (A)* [2010] EWCA Crim 762, [2010] 2 Cr App R 15 (106)) but concluded (at [47]): **B10.69**

B

Part B Offences

> We are left in no doubt that the judge was right to decide that the explanations or excuses advanced by the applicant could never be regarded as reasonable. To use the example of Lord Rodger's in *R v G* [[2009] UKHL 13, [2010] 1 AC 43] at [79], possessing a document or record of a kind likely to be useful to a person committing or preparing an act of terrorism for the purposes of carrying out a bank robbery is a purpose which is not connected with terrorism, but it could not constitute a reasonable excuse. Similarly, it could never amount to a reasonable excuse to possess documents of the kind with which we are concerned in the present case when the purpose, even if only in part, was to distribute them to others known to have a terrorist ideation. This would be the case even if it was believed that the recipients did not intend to act on those beliefs at that particular moment, but only in the event of some contingency. It would never be reasonable, therefore, to provide a record of information of a kind likely to be useful to a person committing or preparing an act of terrorism to someone who was known to adhere to a terrorist ideology (save perhaps in the most exceptional circumstances of which it is presently difficult to conceive).

D suffered from autistic spectrum disorder. The Court explained the relevance of that condition to the defence of reasonable excuse in the context of s. 58 by reference to *G* (see **B10.69** in the main work) in the following way (at [49]):

> As in *R v G*, there can be no question of the applicant's ASD making it reasonable for him to possess the information for a particular purpose when it would not be reasonable for anyone else to do so (see *R v G* at [88]). Notwithstanding G's paranoid schizophrenia, the House of Lords determined that 'on no view could a desire to wind up prison officers … be a reasonable excuse for collecting and recording the information' (see [87]). This conclusion is not to undermine the potential relevance, when a case is left to the jury, of factors such as the accused's age, background, associates and way of life, the circumstances in which the information was collected or recorded, and the length of time it was in the defendant's possession. A mental illness or like condition cannot make an unreasonable excuse reasonable, but it is a potentially relevant factor when considering whether to accept the excuse advanced by the defendant. Relying on the example set out in *R v G* (at [81]), someone who suffers from a condition which tends to cause memory lapses can rely on evidence to this effect to explain why there was a failure, for instance, to take a disk found on a train to the police in the way the individual claimed he or she had intended.

SENTENCING FOR OFFENCES COMMITTED IN A TERRORIST CONTEXT

B10.116 Changes to the release provisions for prisoners serving determinate sentences were made by the Terrorist Offenders (Restriction of Early Release) Act 2020 and the Release of Prisoners (Alteration of Relevant Proportion of Sentence) Order 2020 (SI 2020 No. 158, in force 1 April 2020). Those changes require prisoners serving fixed-term sentences for terrorist offences or serious sexual or violent offences to serve two-thirds of their sentence before being considered for release.

In *Shaikh* [2021] EWCA Crim 45, the Solicitor General sought to refer, as unduly lenient, a life sentence for a terrorist offender. The Solicitor General challenged the setting of the minimum term by reference to half of the notional determinate term, seeking to contend that by reason of the Terrorist Offenders (Restriction of Early Release) Act 2020 and the Release of Prisoners (Alteration of Relevant Proportion of Sentence) Order 2020 the discretionary life sentence should now habitually be two-thirds of the notional determinate sentence. Both prisoners had been convicted under the TA 2006, s. 5, and both had been given discretionary life terms. Their minimum terms had been fixed at one half of the notional determinate sentence they would have received had they not been found to be dangerous. The Court of Appeal rejected the argument of the Solicitor General that the Terrorist Offenders (Restriction of Early Release) Act 2020 required the court to have regard to the length of time served by those serving determinate sentences. Thus courts sentencing terrorist prisoners to discretionary life sentences should continue to have primary regard to half of the determinate equivalent in assessing the minimum term.

Section B12 Offences Relating to Weapons

POSSESSING ETC. FIREARM OR AMMUNITION WITHOUT FIREARM CERTIFICATE

Firearm Certificates: General Matters

In relation to the safe storage of firearms, see the *Firearms Security Handbook 2020* (20 January 2021, tinyurl.com/vpapphs). **B12.42**

Note **B12.48** (in the main work and in this supplement) in respect of firearms that, from 22 March 2021, are no longer 'antique firearms'. There is a transitional period of six months from that date. Section 1(1)(a) of the FA 1968 does not apply (pursuant to the Policing and Crime Act 2017 (Commencement No. 11 and Transitional Provisions) Regulations 2021 (SI 2021 No. 282), reg. 3(2)) in relation to the *possession* of the firearm in the following cases:

(a) by the person where—
  (i) the person has applied before the end of the transitional period for a firearm certificate under section 26A of the 1968 Act or to vary such a certificate under section 29 of the 1968 Act, and
  (ii) either that application is still being processed or any appeal in respect of it has not been determined;
(b) by the persons responsible for the management of a museum and their servants, where—
  (i) in respect of that museum an application has been made before the end of the transitional period for a museum firearms licence or to vary such a licence under the Schedule to the [F(A)A 1988], and
  (ii) that application is still being processed;
(c) by the person or their servants where—
  (i) the person has applied before the end of the transitional period to register as a firearms dealer under section 33 of the 1968 Act, and
  (ii) either that application is still being processed or any appeal in respect of it has not been determined.

In respect of the transfer of a former antique firearm (and save where the transferor carries on a business as a firearms dealer and the sale or transfer is for the purposes of the business (reg. 4(2)), s. 1(1)(a) of the FA 1968 does not apply, in the case of transferors, in relation to the *possession* of the firearm (reg. 4(3)):

(a) by the transferor;
(b) by the persons responsible for the museum's management or their servants, where the transferor is a museum to which the Schedule to the 1988 Act applies, or
(c) by the servants of the transferor, where the transferor carries on the business of a firearms dealer and is registered as such under the 1968 Act.

In respect of transferees, s. 1(1)(a) of the FA 1968 does not apply in relation to the possession, purchase or acquisition of the firearm (reg. 4(6)):

(a) by the transferee, where
  (i) the transferee has applied before the end of the transitional period for a firearm certificate in relation to the possession of the firearm under section 26A of the 1968 Act or to vary such a certificate under section 29 of the 1968 Act, and
  (ii) either that application is still being processed or any appeal in respect of it has not been determined, or
(b) by the persons responsible for the management of a museum and their servants where
  (i) an application has been made in respect of that museum before the end of the transitional period for a museums firearms licence or to vary such a licence under the Schedule to the 1988 Act, and
  (ii) that application is still being processed.

Where, immediately before the commencement date (22 March 2021) a person has in his or her possession a firearm that ceases to be an antique firearm, an application by the person for a certificate (or for the renewal of a certificate) under s. 1 or 2 of the FA 1968 in respect of possession of the firearm may not be refused on the ground that the person does not have a good reason for having the firearm in his or her possession (PCA 2017, s. 126(6), (7)).

EXEMPTIONS AND DEFENCES FOR THE PURPOSES OF THE FIREARMS ACT 1968, s. 1

Antique Firearms

B12.48 The Antique Firearms Regulations 2021 (SI 2021 No. 215), in force from 22 March 2021:

(a) make specifications as to the conditions set out in s. 58(2B), (2C) and (2D) of the FA 1968;
(b) provide (for the purposes of s. 58(2B)) a description of cartridges (now obsolete) for which the firearm's chamber or chambers had been designed for use;
(c) provide (for the purposes of s. 58(2C)) a description of firearms' propulsion systems; and
(d) specify (as an additional condition for the purposes of s. 58(2A)(b)), that a firearm must be manufactured before 1 September 1939 in order to be an antique firearm.

These provisions must be read together with the PCA 2017, s. 126, which inserts subsections (2A) to (2H) into s. 58 of the FA 1968 and makes certain consequential amendments to that Act, and which came into force on 22 March 2021 (see SI 2021 No. 282) but subject to the transitional arrangements set out in the PCA 2017, s. 126(4) to (8), and the additional (shorter) transitional provisions in SI 2021 No. 282. See also Circular 001/2021: *Antique Firearms Regulations 2021 and the Policing and Crime Act 2017 (Commencement No. 11 and Transitional Provisions) Regulations 2021* (11 March 2021).

OFFENCES RELATING TO SHOT GUNS

Possessing etc. Shot Gun without Shot Gun Certificate

B12.52 Note **B12.48** (in the main work and in this supplement) in respect of firearms that, from 22 March 2021, are no longer 'antique firearms'. There is a transitional period of six months from that date with the result that s. 2(1) of the 1968 Act does not apply (pursuant to SI 2021 No. 282, reg. 3(3)) in relation to the possession of the firearm in the following cases:

(a) by the person where—
  (i) the person has applied before the end of the transitional period for a shot gun certificate under section 26B of the 1968 Act, and
  (ii) either that application is still being processed or any appeal in respect of it has not been determined;
(b) by the persons responsible for the management of a museum and their servants where—
  (i) in respect of that museum an application has been made before the end of the transitional period for a museum firearms licence or to vary such a licence under the Schedule to the 1988 Act, and
  (ii) that application is still being processed;
(c) by the person or their servants where—
  (i) the person has applied before the end of the transitional period to register as a firearms dealer under the 1968 Act, and
  (ii) either that application is still being processed or any appeal in respect of it has not been determined.

In respect of the transfer of a former antique firearm (and save where the transferor carries on a business as a firearms dealer and the sale or transfer is for the purposes of the business (reg. 4(2)), s. 2(1) of the FA 1968 does not apply, in the case of transferors, in relation to the *possession* of the firearm (reg. 4(3)):

(a) by the transferor;
(b) by the persons responsible for the museum's management or their servants, where the transferor is a museum to which the Schedule to the 1988 Act applies, or

(c) by the servants of the transferor, where the transferor carries on the business of a firearms dealer and is registered as such under the 1968 Act.

In respect of transferees, s. 2(1) of the FA 1968 does not apply to the possession, purchase or acquisition of the firearm (reg. 4(7)):

(a) by the transferee, where
  (i) the transferee has applied before the end of the transitional period for a shot gun certificate in relation to the possession of the shot gun under section 26B of the 1968 Act, and
  (ii) either that application is still being processed or any appeal in respect of it has not been determined, or
(b) by the persons responsible for the management of a museum and their servants, where
  (i) an application has been made in respect of that museum before the end of the transitional period for a museum firearms licence or to vary such a licence under the Schedule to the 1988 Act, and
  (ii) that application is still being processed.

POSSESSING OR DISTRIBUTING PROHIBITED WEAPONS OR AMMUNITION

Offence in Respect of Prohibited Weapons and/or Ammunition

From 22 March 2021, the expression 'antique firearm' is defined by the FA 1968, s. 58(2A), noting the conditions set out in s. 58(2B) to (2C) (inserted by the PCA 2017, s. 126; see SI 2021 No. 282 and SI 2021 No. 215). Accordingly, certain firearms may cease to be 'antique firearms'. In such cases, and pursuant to the PCA 2017, s. 126(5), s. 5 of the FA 1968 does not apply in relation to the *possession* of the firearm by a person *unless* (a) the person carries on a business as a firearms dealer, and (b) the firearm is in his or her possession for the purpose of the business. **B12.61**

However, under SI 2021 No. 282, there is a six-month transition period beginning on 22 March 2021 so that the FA 1968, s. 5(1), (1A) and (2A)(c), do not apply in relation to the *possession* of the firearm by a person who carries on a business as a firearms dealer and possesses the firearm for the purposes of the business, *and* who has applied for authorisation of the Secretary of State in accordance with s. 5 of the 1968 Act before the end of the transitional period and that application is still being processed (reg. 3(4)).

Similarly, where, during the transitional period, a person ('the transferor') *sells or transfers* the firearm to another person ('the transferee'), then (unless the transferor carries on a business as a firearms dealer and the sale or transfer is for the purposes of the business (reg. 4(2)), in the case of transferors, s. 5(1) and (2A)(c) of the 1968 Act do not apply in relation to the *possession for sale or transfer* of the firearm (and s. 5(2A)(b) does not apply in relation to its *sale or transfer*: reg. 4(4)):

(a) by the transferor;
(b) by the persons responsible for the museum's management or their servants, where the transferor is a museum to which the Schedule to the 1988 Act applies, or
(c) by the servants of the transferor, where the transferor carries on the business of a firearms dealer and is registered as such under the 1968 Act.

In respect of transferees, s. 5 of the FA 1968 does not apply in relation to the possession, purchase or acquisition of the firearm by the transferee unless (reg. 4(5)):

(a) the transferee carries on a business as a firearms dealer, and
(b) the firearm is in his or her possession or is purchased or acquired for the purposes of the business.

Where the transferee makes an application during the transitional period for a firearm certificate under the FA 1968, s. 26A, or to vary such a certificate under s. 29, the application may not be refused on the ground that the person does not have good reason for having the firearm in his or her possession (reg. 4(8)).

BUSINESS, EXPORT AND OTHER TRANSACTIONS INVOLVING FIREARMS AND AMMUNITION

Either-way Offences

B12.133 Note B12.48 (in the main work and in this supplement) in respect of firearms that, from 22 March 2021, are no longer 'antique firearms' (FA 1968, s. 58(2B) to (2C), inserted by the PCA 2017, s. 126; see SI 2021 No. 282 and SI 2021 No. 215). There is a transitional period of six months from that date. In respect of the transfer of a former antique firearm (and save where the transferor carries on a business as a firearms dealer and the sale or transfer is for the purposes of the business (SI 2021 No. 282, reg. 4(2)), s. 3(1)(b) of the 1968 Act does not apply in relation to the *possession* of the firearm (reg. 4(3)), and s. 3(1)(a), (b) and (2) of the 1968 Act do not apply in relation to the *sale or transfer* of the firearm (reg. 4(4)):

(a) by the transferor;
(b) by the persons responsible for the museum's management or their servants, where the transferor is a museum to which the Schedule to the 1988 Act applies, or
(c) by the servants of the transferor, where the transferor carries on the business of a firearms dealer and is registered as such under the 1968 Act.

MAKING OR POSSESSION OF EXPLOSIVE UNDER SUSPICIOUS CIRCUMSTANCES

Lawful Object

B12.260 *Copeland* [2020] UKSC 8, [2020] 2 WLR 681 was considered in *Flint* [2020] EWCA Crim 1266, [2021] 1 Cr App R 8 (168). The Court of Appeal held (at [39]) that the trial judge ought not to have directed the jury that the breach of the Explosives Regulations 2014 (SI 2014 No. 1638) was determinative of the issue of whether or not, on a balance of probabilities, D had a lawful object. As highlighted in *Fegan* [1972] NI 80, (1971) 78 Cr App R 189, the absence of a certificate, permit or other authority may well be evidence of whether there was a lawful object, but its absence was not necessarily incompatible with an explosive substance being possessed for a lawful object. The Court in *Flint* stated by way of a postscript (at [56]):

> It is a central element of the majority decision in *Copeland* that an otherwise lawful objective (such as experimentation) which involves obvious risk to other people, or their property, from the use of the explosive substance will lead to the inference that the object of the accused was mixed, and therefore was not (wholly) lawful. Further, if the defendant knew that his or her proposed use of the explosive substance in his possession would injure others or cause damage to their property, or was reckless regarding this risk, the object would be tainted by that unlawfulness inherent in the way the object was being pursued, thereby rendering it impossible to establish the defence.

The Court added (at [57]):

> All cases differ on their facts, but we emphasise, therefore, that given the obvious risks with using explosive substances, any experimentation involving them which gives rise to a risk of harm to other people or their property, or other unlawfulness such as causing a public nuisance, will not be capable of coming within the scope of the lawful object defence.

As to whether it would be open to a judge to withdraw from the jury a defence that was founded on the second limb of the Explosive Substances Act 1883, s. 4, on the grounds that experimentation gave rise to a risk of harm to persons or their property ('or other unlawfulness'), see the commentary to *Flint* at [2021] Crim LR 126.

SENTENCING FOR FIREARMS OFFENCES

See the sentencing guideline, *Firearms Offences* (see SG34-1), with effect from 1 January 2021. **B12.137**

Section B14 Offences Against the Administration of Justice

PERJURY IN A JUDICIAL PROCEEDING

Wilfulness

In *R (Purvis) v DPP* [2020] EWHC 3573 (Admin), the Divisional Court examined the concept of wilfulness as it relates to the offence of perjury, and emphasised that where a witness's evidence is shown to be untrue, the issue may not be simply whether that witness was (a) dishonest and lied or (b) made an honest mistake. Wilfulness may include 'being reckless as to whether or not the statement was true' and the Court took this to include failing to give thought to that question. Moreover (at [42]): **B14.9**

> Proof of motive is not necessary for an offence of perjury, but it may be of forensic relevance if the question being considered is whether a witness deliberately lied. However, it is of less forensic relevance if the issue is whether the witness failed to give any thought to whether or not the statement he was making was true.

Despite the reference to 'giving no thought', the Court cannot have meant to restore an objective, *Caldwell*-type definition of wilful recklessness, given that such a definition was firmly rejected in *A-G's Ref (No. 3 of 2003)* [2004] EWCA Crim 868, [2005] QB 73 (see A2.13 in the main work). If however D deliberately testifies as to something D knows full well might not be true, such recklessness may properly be described as wilful perjury.

PERVERTING THE COURSE OF JUSTICE

Definition

In *R (Purvis) v DPP* [2020] EWHC 3573 (Admin), Garnham LJ, giving the judgment of the Divisional Court, said (at 54]): **B14.29**

> There is, it might be thought, an obvious difference between the mental element required for perjury and for perverting the course of justice. As discussed above, perjury is made out by proof that the person concerned wilfully makes a statement 'which he knows to be false or does not believe to be true.' Perverting the course of justice requires conduct which is intended to pervert.

Such intent cannot be established by 'incompetence, muddle and [D's] failure to appreciate the significance of what he had done' (at [57]).

CONTEMPT OF COURT IN RESPECT OF CRIMINAL PROCEEDINGS

Nature of Contempt

The distinction between civil and criminal contempt was considered by MacDonald J, sitting in the Court of Protection, in *P v Griffith* [2020] EWCOP 46. The case involved the 'deliberate and calculated' forgery of a court order, an act which he described as one that 'strikes at the very heart of the due administration of justice'. The learned judge quoted Lord Toulson in *Director of the SFO v O'Brien* [2014] UKSC 23, [2014] AC 1246: **B14.84**

> The question whether a contempt is a criminal contempt does not depend on the nature of the court to which the contempt was displayed; it depends on nature of the conduct. To burst into a court room and disrupt a civil trial would be a criminal contempt just as much as if the court had been conducting a criminal trial. Conversely, disobedience to a procedural order of a court is not in itself

> a crime, just because the order was made in the course of criminal proceedings. To hold that a breach of a procedural order made in a criminal court is itself a crime would be to introduce an unjustified and anomalous extension of the criminal law. 'Civil contempt' is not confined to contempt of a civil court. It simply denotes a contempt which is not itself a crime.

In sentencing the contemnor to 12 months' immediate imprisonment, MacDonald J noted that the object of the sentence was:

> To mark the disapproval of the court of her deliberate and calculated actions and to deter others from acting in a similar fashion, rather than to ensure future compliance with orders of the court….

As to contempt by breach of procedural orders made by a criminal court, see *Taktouk* [2020] EWCA Crim 1325 (at **B14.99** in this supplement).

Jurisdiction and Procedure: the Crown Court

B14.91 In *Re An Improper Disclosure Issue (Hamilton)* (19 November 2020 unreported), the Court of Appeal considered (but did not finally decide) whether there had been a contempt of court when counsel for the appellants copied to a journalist confidential material disclosed to them following a reference by the CCRC. This was not a disclosure to which the CPIA 1996, ss. 17 and 18, could apply, but it was submitted that counsel were nevertheless under a duty to respect the confidentiality of the disclosed material, and Holroyde LJ held (at [21]) that it was a contempt issue, not merely one for the Bar Standards Board:

> If there be such a duty … and if there be here a breach of it, then that would, on the face of it, be a civil contempt of court, which is a matter for the court.

Penalties for Contempt

B14.99 In *Taktouk* [2020] EWCA Crim 1325, D appealed against a sentence of seven months' imprisonment imposed for 14 breaches of restraint and disclosure orders made under the POCA 2002 in the context of a private prosecution for fraud. These breaches included withdrawals from bank accounts subject to the order, failure to disclose the existence of other accounts which were then discovered by the prosecution, and failure to disclose other relevant names and transactions in witness statements. In monetary terms, the breaches related to transactions or accounts worth approximately £55,000.

Dismissing D's appeal against this sentence, Simler LJ, noting that there are no sentencing guidelines for cases of this kind, referred (at [19]) to *Baird* [2011] EWCA Crim 459, [2011] 2 Cr App R (S) 78 (451), in which the Court of Appeal upheld a sentence of 18 months' imprisonment where there were five admitted breaches, and to *Patel* [2017] EWCA Crim 820, where there were three admitted breaches concerning continuous failures to give disclosure and the Court upheld penalties of 12 months' imprisonment, a fine of £330,000 with a further three years' imprisonment if there was a default, and costs of £9,300. Simler LJ stated:

> Although in some cases sentences of imprisonment are imposed in cases of this kind to secure compliance with disclosure orders and orders of that kind made in the public interest, that is not the only legitimate purpose of sentencing. The court may well be justified in imposing sentences to punish and deter.

Section B16 Revenue, Customs and Social Security Offences

VAT FRAUDS

The amendments made to s. 72 of the Value Added Tax Act 1994 were brought into effect at 11 p.m. on 31 December 2020, the 'IP completion day': see the Interpretation Act 1978, s. 5 and sch. 1, para. 1; the European Union (Withdrawal Agreement) Act 2020, s. 39; and the Finance Act 2016, Section 126 (Appointed Day), the Taxation (Cross-border Trade) Act 2018 (Appointed Day No. 8, Transition and Saving Provisions) and the Taxation (Posttransition Period) Act 2020 (Appointed Day No. 1) (EU Exit) Regulations 2020 (SI 2020 No. 1642), reg. 7. **B16.8**

CUSTOMS AND EXCISE: INTRODUCTION

The changes made by the Taxation (Cross-border Trade) Act 2018 were brought into force at 11 p.m. on 31 December 2020, the 'IP completion day'; see the Interpretation Act 1978, s. 5 and sch. 1, para. 1; the European Union (Withdrawal Agreement) Act 2020, s. 39, and SI 2020 No. 1642, reg. 4. **B16.11**

IMPROPER IMPORTATION AND EXPORTATION OF GOODS

Improper Importation of Goods

Procedure, Evidence and Penalties When the Offensive Weapons Act 2019 is brought into force the categories of weapons set out in the FA 1968, s. 5(ag) and (ba) (see **B12.61** in the main work), are added to those for which the importation carries life imprisonment (Offensive Weapons Act 2019, ss. 54 and 56 and sch. 2, para. 2). **B16.28**

Offences in Relation to Exportation of Prohibited or Restricted Goods

Procedure and Penalties When the Offensive Weapons Act 2019 is brought into force the enhanced maximum penalty of life imprisonment applies to the exportation of the categories of weapons set out in the FA 1968, s. 5(ag) and (ba) (Offensive Weapons Act 2019, ss. 54 and 56 and sch. 2, para. 3). **B16.35**

Elements The Export Control (Amendment) (EU Exit) Regulations 2020 (SI 2020 No. 1502) amend the Export Control Order 2008 (SI 2008 No. 3231). **B16.36**

FRAUDULENT EVASION OF DUTY ('SMUGGLING')

Sentencing

When the Offensive Weapons Act 2019 is brought into force the enhanced maximum penalty of life imprisonment applies to smuggling the categories of weapons set out in the FA 1968, s. 5(ag) and (ba) (Offensive Weapons Act 2019, ss. 54 and 56 and sch. 2, para. 4). **B16.42**

Untrue Declarations

In *Nurse v Republic of Trinidad and Tobago* [2019] UKPC 43, [2021] AC 1, the Privy Council decided (at [39] and [50]) that s. 212(a) of the Trinidad and Tobago Customs Act, which contains language similar to s. 167(3) of the Customs and Excise Management Act 1979, creates offences of strict liability (see **A2.24** in the main work). This is because those who import or export goods are in a position to ensure that the correct goods are consigned. **B16.52**

Counterfeiting Documents

The words 'counterfeits or falsifies' in the Customs and Excise Management Act 1979, s. 168(1), involve a requirement of knowledge of the falsity (*Nurse v Republic of Trinidad and Tobago* [2019] UKPC 43, [2021] AC 1 at [28]). **B16.53**

SENTENCING GUIDELINES FOR REVENUE FRAUD

B16.56 In *Banach* [2020] EWCA Crim 422, the Court of Appeal upheld a sentence of ten and a half years' imprisonment upon a lorry driver of previous good character following his plea of guilty to importing 44 kilograms of Class A drugs.

Section B19 Offences Related to Drugs

CONTROLLED DRUGS

'Substances and Products' Specified as Controlled Drugs in Class A, B or C

B19.9 Practitioners should be alert to the likelihood that, from a date to be announced, the following drug substances are reclassified from Class C to Class B in the MDA 1971, sch. 2, namely, *Gamma-hydroxybutyrate* (GHB), *gamma-butyrolactone* (GBL) and *1,4-butanediol* (1,4-BD) (letter, Home Secretary, 20 November 2020).

SENTENCING GUIDELINES FOR OFFENCES UNDER THE MISUSE OF DRUGS ACT 1971

Forfeiture and Confiscation

B19.147 Revisions made to certain sentencing guidelines for drug offences (including offences under the PSA 2016) came into effect on 1 April 2021 (see **SG35-1** ***et seq.***).

Guideline Structure and Approach

B19.148 In *Bailey* [2020] EWCA Crim 1719, the Court of Appeal made a number of general observations (at [33]–[38]) concerning the application of the 'totality principle' and the sentencing guideline, *Totality* (see **SG4-1**). Whether a judge has applied 'totality' is a question of substance and not form. Sentencing remarks are not intended to amount to a test of drafting but to be succinct explanations of the facts and matters that have affected the judge's judgement as to the sentence to be imposed. Totality is designed to ensure that the sentencing exercise is not formulaic and that the final sentence is just and proportionate. Totality is not about reducing sentences as opposed simply to getting to the correct final sentence. The imposition of consecutive sentences is not, in itself, indicative that totality has not been adequately considered. A judge is not obliged to refer expressly, in the sentencing remarks, to the stages set out in the guideline in relation to determinate sentences (see **SG4-4**).

Section B22 Modern Slavery, Trafficking and Immigration Offences

SLAVERY, SERVITUDE AND FORCED OR COMPULSORY LABOUR

Procedure and Sentence

B22.3 No sentencing guideline is in place in relation to modern slavery offences. A consultation in relation to offences under the Modern Slavery Act 2015, ss. 1, 2, 4 and 30, closed on 15 January 2021.

HUMAN TRAFFICKING

Sentence

B22.8 No sentencing guideline is in place in relation to modern slavery offences. A consultation in relation to offences under the Modern Slavery Act 2015, ss. 1, 2, 4 and 30, closed on 15 January 2021.

CONSIDERATIONS PRIOR TO PROSECUTION OF VICTIMS OF TRAFFICKING OR SLAVERY

In *VCL and AN v UK* (2021) Appln. 77587/12, 16 February 2021, the ECtHR held unanimously that there had been a violation of both Articles 4 and 6(1) of the ECHR. The cases concerned the prosecution of two Vietnamese youths, found following police raids on cannabis farms. Both had pleaded guilty in 2009 to the offences concerning production of cannabis. **B22.17**

The ECtHR considered that any decision on whether to prosecute a potential victim of trafficking should, insofar as possible, only be taken once a trafficking assessment had been made by a qualified person. That was particularly important where children were concerned (at [161]). While prosecutors might not be bound by the findings of a trafficking assessment, they would need clear reasons, consistent with the definition of trafficking contained in the Palermo Protocol and Anti-Trafficking Convention, for disagreeing with it (at [162] and [181]).

In *VCL and AN v UK*, neither applicant had been referred at the time to the Competent Authority for a trafficking assessment. The ECtHR considered that the State had not fulfilled its duty under Article 4 to take operational measures to protect the applicants, either initially, as potential victims of trafficking, or subsequently, as persons recognised by the Competent Authority to be victims of trafficking.

While criminal defence lawyers should undoubtedly be alert to indicators of trafficking, their failure to recognise or act upon such indicators cannot by itself absolve the State and its agents of their responsibility to do so (at [198]). The State is under a positive obligation under Article 4 both to protect victims of trafficking and to investigate potential trafficking. A defendant, especially a minor, cannot be required to self-identify as a victim of trafficking or be penalised for failing to do so (at [199]).

Although both applicants had entered unequivocal guilty pleas, there had been no waiver of their rights under Article 6, as there had been no assessment of whether they were trafficked and if that could impact criminal liability. As a result, those guilty pleas had not been made in 'full awareness of the facts'.

The ECtHR found that the reasons given by the CPS for disagreeing with the Competent Authority were inadequate and inconsistent with the definition of trafficking in international law. The ECtHR considered that the Court of Appeal had not considered the case through the prism of the State's positive obligations under Article 4 but had rather restricted itself to a relatively narrow review, which would penalise victims of trafficking for not initially identifying themselves as such and allow the authorities to rely on their own failure to fulfil their duties under Article 4.

Abuse of Process for Cases Following the Modern Slavery Act 2015

Subsequent to *DS* [2020] EWCA Crim 285, [2021] 1 WLR 303, the Court of Appeal confirmed in *A* [2020] EWCA Crim 1408, [2021] 4 WLR 16, that the abuse of process jurisdiction is no longer necessary to fill a 'lacuna' for cases following enactment of the Modern Slavery Act 2015. See also the *Crown Court Compendium* (December 2020), ch. 18-6. **B22.19**

The Court in *A* went on to consider that Parliament's decision to legislate by sch. 4 to the 2015 Act reflected the balance struck by Parliament between preventing perpetrators of serious criminal offences from evading justice and protecting genuine victims of trafficking from prosecution (at [62]). Further, that in serious criminal cases to which sch. 4 applies, the common-law defence of duress/necessity and the four-stage approach to prosecution decisions set out in the CPS guidance (see **B22.22** in the main work) provide appropriate safeguards (with express regard at stage four to the public interest).

B

Part B Offences

Cases in which duress and the s. 45 defence are not available, but where it would not be in the public interest to prosecute on the basis of a victim of trafficking's status, will be rare. The seriousness of the offence in such circumstances will require an even greater degree of continuing compulsion and the absence of any reasonably available alternatives to the defendant before it is likely to be in the public interest not to prosecute an individual suspected of an offence to which sch. 4 applies (at [64]).

National Referral Mechanism

B22.20 In *DPP v M* [2020] EWHC 3422 (Admin), [2021] 1 WLR 1669, the Divisional Court considered that the conclusive grounds decision by the Single Competent Authority was admissible evidence, in determining whether D was a victim of criminal exploitation in relation to s. 45 of the Modern Slavery Act 2015 (see also **B22.29** in this supplement).

B22.21 In *H v DPP* [2021] EWHC 147 (Admin), a 17-year-old had pleaded guilty in the youth court to possession of a knife and possession with intent to supply of heroin and cocaine. He had been sentenced in the Crown Court, but later discovered that a defence under s. 45 of the Modern Slavery Act 2015 would have been available to him. The remedy available here was through an application to the CCRC, not s. 142 of the MCA 1980, which was designed to correct mistakes in a magistrates' court which only affected its own determinations and not to set aside sentences imposed by the Crown Court.

Guidance

B22.22 Despite the CPS guidance of 30 April 2020, subsequent to *DS* [2020] EWCA Crim 285, [2021] 1 WLR 303, the CPS published a news item on 9 October 2020 indicating that:

> The CPS position is that a case should not be dropped because a suspect or defendant had claimed they were the victim of modern slavery and had received a positive decision from the NRM as these decisions are based on a balance of probabilities….
>
> If cases have been dropped after a positive National Referral Mechanism decision was made it should be because of other factors which on their own, or together, mean that there is not a reasonable prospect of conviction.
>
> There may be other aspects of the case that a prosecutor is required to take into account when deciding whether to commence or continue a prosecution which are entirely unrelated to the National Referral Mechanism, for example witness withdrawal, medical evidence or other guilty pleas.

STATUTORY DEFENCE UNDER THE MODERN SLAVERY ACT, s. 45

B22.25 Schedule 4 to the Modern Slavery Act 2015 excludes certain offences from the scope of the defence under s. 45. In *A* [2020] EWCA Crim 1408, [2021] 4 WLR 16, the Court of Appeal considered (at [65]) that sch. 4 was not in conflict with the international obligations imposed by the Council of Europe Convention on Action Against Trafficking (ECAT) and/or Directive 2011/36/EU on preventing and combating trafficking in human beings and protecting its victims ([2011] OJ L101/1).

The Modern Slavery Act 2015, s. 45, does not have retrospective effect. In *CS* [2021] EWCA Crim 134, the Court of Appeal considered there was nothing to indicate that Parliament intended that the defence under s. 45 should be available in respect of offences committed by victims of trafficking before the Act came into force on 31 July 2015.

Nexus

B22.29 Section 45(1)c of the Modern Slavery Act 2015 provides that for adults, compulsion be 'attributable to slavery or relevant exploitation'. Under s. 45(5), relevant exploitation is defined as being 'attributable to the exploited person being, or having been, a victim of human trafficking'.

In terms of appeals, decisions of the Single Competent Authority have been admitted in evidence pursuant to the Criminal Appeal Act 1968, s. 23 (see also **B22.20** in this supplement).

In determining if D was a victim of criminal exploitation in relation to s. 45, the Divisional Court in *DPP v M* [2020] EWHC 3422 (Admin), [2021] 1 WLR 1669, considered that the conclusive grounds decision by the Single Competent Authority was admissible evidence. D was a 15-year-old boy of good character found in possession of a hunting knife, heroin and cocaine with others known to have gang affiliations and many drug convictions. At trial, a s. 10 admission referencing the positive conclusive grounds decision was included. The stated case concerned whether D had discharged the evidential burden, given that D had not given evidence at trial, nor given an account of exploitation in police interview.

Simler LJ concluded that the Single Competent Authority had expertise in relation to those issues, and (at [54]) that:

> The judge was entitled to consider the findings and assess the extent to which they were supported by the evidence. Insofar as appropriate, she would have been able to reduce the weight she gave to the findings. However that is a question of weight rather than the admissibility. In fact the SCA decision was based on a proper evidential foundation and it was not contradicted by other material available to the judge.

In *DPP v M* the Court decided that a conclusive grounds decision is admissible in a criminal trial (see the *Crown Court Compendium* (December 2020), para. 18-29). The Court commented (at [55]): 'As the facts of this case amply demonstrate, a conclusive grounds decision will not be determinative in the criminal context any more than it is in tribunal proceedings.'

The Court went on to emphasise that a conclusive grounds decision would not be determinative in the criminal context any more than it was in (immigration) tribunal proceedings.

In *BTT* [2021] EWCA Crim 4, the Court of Appeal reflected that it was not necessary to determine whether the decision of the Divisional Court in *DPP v M* was correct, as leave was refused. The Court did highlight (as was the case in *GS* [2018] EWCA Crim 1824, [2019] 1 Cr App R 7 (84)) that the Court in *BTT* was 'not to be taken as determining that the decisions of the Competent Authority or the Upper Tribunal would be admissible at any trial'. However, in *BTT*, the Court did consider that in practical terms any 'admissibility difficulties would be very likely to be resolved by admissions'.

The Statutory Guidance of April 2020 states (at para. 17.6) that 'the decision of the SCA as to whether a person had been trafficked for the purposes of exploitation is not binding on the Court or the CPS. Unless there was evidence to contradict or significant evidence that had not been considered, it is likely that the criminal courts will abide by the decision.' Contrast this with the statutory defence under the Immigration and Asylum Act 1999, s. 31 (at **B22.86** in the main work).

County Lines Offending

Indicators of county lines exploitation within the Ministry of Justice guidance of October 2019 were referred to in *A* [2020] EWCA Crim 1408, [2021] 4 WLR 16 (at [53]). **B22.30**

SUPPLEMENT TO PART C
ROAD TRAFFIC OFFENCES

Section C3 Offences Relating to Driving Triable on Indictment

MANSLAUGHTER

Sentence

In *Long* [2020] EWCA Crim 1729, [2021] 4 WLR 5, the trial judge had followed the sentencing guideline for unlawful act manslaughter (see **SG25-2**), placing the case in the highest category of culpability and finding a number of aggravating factors that increased the starting point, before considering mitigating circumstances relating to age and maturity (learning difficulties in relation to two co-defendants). The defendants had been acquitted of murder after the death of a police officer, who had been caught in a rope as the defendants fled the scene of a quad bike theft, and had been dragged behind the car driven by D1, causing his death. The Court of Appeal refused the A-G's application to refer as unduly lenient the extended sentence of 19 years against D1, comprising 16 years' detention followed by a three-year licence period, and sentences of 13 years' detention imposed on his two co-defendants for manslaughter. The Court of Appeal confirmed that the judge was right to follow the guidelines as he did, and found no basis on which to conclude that the sentences were unduly lenient. **C3.6**

CAUSING DEATH BY DANGEROUS DRIVING

Elements

The prosecution must consider very carefully following the police investigation into a fatal collision, and make a charging decision on the evidence available. In *Wangige* [2020] EWCA Crim 1319, [2021] RTR 7 (115), an appeal against the judge's decision not to stay a prosecution for causing death by dangerous driving for abuse of process was allowed. D had already served a sentence in relation to four charges arising out of a fatal collision and no new facts had come to light two years later when the more serious charge was brought. Rather, following the inquest into V's death, the prosecution had sought an additional expert report which questioned the speed at which D was driving as estimated from CCTV footage. The Court of Appeal held that as D had already been prosecuted for offences arising out of the same incident based on substantially the same facts, and in the absence of the prosecution establishing special circumstances to justify fresh proceedings as per *Phipps* [2005] EWCA Crim 33 (see **C3.41** in the main work), the prosecution should have been stayed (for more on abuse of process arguments generally, see **D3.89** ***et seq.***, especially **D3.96**, in the main work). **C3.9**

Sentence

Where D has engaged in an impromptu race with another driver, resulting in a fatal collision between the other driver and a third party, each offender was equally culpable and it was appropriate to sentence them on the same basis. It was not a mitigating factor for D that his co-defendant was also racing (*Fettah* [2020] EWCA Crim 320, [2020] 2 Cr App R (S) 25 (189)). **C3.19**

In *Ravikumar* [2020] EWCA Crim 1217, the Court of Appeal found a sentence to be unduly lenient where numerous mitigating factors were outweighed by the aggravating feature that four counts of causing serious injury by dangerous driving arose from the same episode of bad driving. It was not open to the judge to conclude that the balancing of aggravating and mitigating factors should result in a downward movement from the guideline starting point. Rather, it should have resulted in an upward movement.

CAUSING DEATH BY CARELESS DRIVING WHEN UNDER THE INFLUENCE OF DRINK OR DRUGS

Sentence

C3.26 Where D was a taxi driver with a cannabis habit, and was found to be three times over the prescribed limit for cannabis, the fact that his carelessness did not constitute much more than 'momentary inattention' led to the Court of Appeal describing the sentence as 'stiff', but did not result in it being judged to be manifestly excessive. A period of imprisonment of four years, six months was upheld (*Adebisi* [2020] EWCA Crim 1446).

CAUSING DEATH BY CARELESS, OR INCONSIDERATE, DRIVING

Elements

C3.29 In *Adeluwoye* [2020] EWCA Crim 856, the role of the expert witness was considered. D had caused the death of a motorcyclist when he had moved into the outside lane of a dual carriageway at the last minute, in order to make use of a gap in the central reservation to turn right. V had been approaching from behind in the outside lane, ahead of other vehicles that had moved off from a set of traffic lights, and was unable to avoid colliding with the rear of D's car. The collision reconstruction experts had agreed that V's motorcycle might have been 'masked' by other traffic so that D was unable to see V when he claimed to have looked in his mirror and over his shoulder. In convicting D of causing death by careless driving, the jury must have rejected this evidence. Counsel sought to draw a general proposition from the case of *Brennan* [2014] EWCA Crim 2387, [2015] 1 Cr App R 14 (161) (see **B1.20** in the main work) that the jury can only reject expert evidence with good reason (an approach endorsed by the Supreme Court in *Golds* [2016] UKSC 61, [2017] 1 Cr App R 18 (273)). The Court in *Adeluwoye* was clear that whether expert witness evidence can be rejected by the jury is dependent on the nature of the expert evidence. In this case, the opinion of the experts was not an issue falling exclusively within their expertise, and it was open to the jury to conclude that despite their view, V's motorbike was visible to D, at least for a significant period. The conviction was upheld.

DANGEROUS DRIVING

Sentence

C3.45 In *Simpson-Etheridge* [2020] EWCA Crim 1276, the in-car police footage of the pursuit which lasted three minutes showed that this was not the worst example of dangerous driving, meaning that 24 months was not the correct starting point, and it should have been 18 months. It was also wrong of the judge to have sentenced D to four months consecutive for driving whilst disqualified as this led to double counting, and the sentence for that offence should run concurrently. Conversely, in *Williams* [2020] EWCA Crim 1140, the Court of Appeal upheld 24 months as a starting point, despite the driving not being the worst imaginable, on the basis that D had a long record of driving offences and the previous sentences had apparently had no effect in dissuading him from continuing to flout the law. He put other road users at risk by continuing to drive whilst disqualified and it was right that the court use prison as a last resort to take him off the road.

The notion that disqualification is intended to protect the public and not to further punish the offender, was reiterated in *Mongan* [2020] EWCA Crim 1536. The offender was only 18 and, citing *Parkin* [2020] EWCA Crim 614, [2021] RTR 11 (180), it was held that the period of disqualification imposed by the judge was deemed to be excessive and likely to impede rehabilitation. A period of disqualification for four years was reduced to one of two years.

Section C5 Drink-Driving and Drug-Driving Offences

DRIVING, OR BEING IN CHARGE, WITH ALCOHOL CONCENTRATION ABOVE PRESCRIBED LIMIT

Admissibility of Specimens

Challenging the Specimen Evidence In *Ali v DPP* [2020] EWHC 2864 (Admin), [2020] 4 WLR 146, it was confirmed that if D wishes to challenge the reliability of the evidential breath machine there is a legal burden on D to rebut the presumption on the balance of probabilities. If D adduces relevant evidence that the reading was not reliable, it is necessary for the prosecution then to prove to the criminal standard that the reading was reliable. **C5.44**

Section C7 Sentencing

DISQUALIFICATION GENERALLY

Length of Disqualification

In *Downes* [2020] EWCA Crim 1773, the Court of Appeal reinforced the principle that a period of disqualification cannot commence at a future date and added that there must be precision when identifying the offences attracting disqualification and the exact periods applicable to each such offence. **C7.36**

In *Austin* [2020] EWCA Crim 1269, disqualification for ten years for an offence of causing death by careless, or inconsiderate, driving contrary to the RTA 1988, s. 2B (see C3.27 in the main work), was upheld because, although long, D's past driving-related offending and psychiatric issues, including PTSD, meant D presented a real risk to others on the road. **C7.37**

In *Rai* [2020] EWCA Crim 1453, it was stressed that disqualification is not intended as a further punishment, so a period longer than what is mandatory may not be required, and the length must not impede an offender's rehabilitation, which is particularly relevant for a young offender.

SUPPLEMENT TO PART D
PROCEDURE

Section D1 Powers of Investigation

DETENTION AND TREATMENT OF SUSPECTS

Detention Time-limits

In *XX's Application for Habeas Corpus* [2019] NIQB 31, the term 'medical treatment' under the Police and Criminal Evidence (Northern Ireland) Order 1989 (SI 1989 No. 1341 (NI 12)), art. 42(4), was considered (which is in exactly the same terms as the PACE 1984, s. 41(6)). It was held that the term 'medical treatment' encompassed psychiatric/psychological/mental-state assessment/examination/interview and/or treatment. Furthermore, the fact that medical treatment was not actually administered in hospital to the arrested person did not result in the disapplication of art. 42(4). D1.67

INTERROGATION OF SUSPECTS

An Interview Protocol between the National Police Chiefs' Council, Crown Prosecution Service, Law Society, the Criminal Law Solicitors' Association and the London Criminal Courts Solicitors' Association was issued on 2 April 2020 and updated on 24 April 2020 to provide guidance to investigators and prosecutors in deciding whether a suspect should be interviewed as part of a police investigation during the Covid-19 pandemic. The purpose of the protocol was to introduce alternative ways for interviews to take place to ensure that those participating were less at risk. Due to the discretionary terms in which the protocol is drafted there are no immediate consequences if an interview takes place in breach of it. However, the necessary protections are found in PACE Codes C and H and Home Office Circular 34/2007 which set out the obligations on custody officers to undertake a risk assessment and implement actions judged to be necessary. If a custody officer is to disregard the protocol, it will need to be a considered, rational and documented decision. It is axiomatic that a failure to provide a safe environment for those involved in the interview would be a relevant consideration in determining whether an adverse inference should be drawn under the CJPO 1994, s. 34. The protocol sets out a cascading decision-making process in deciding whether and how an interview ought to take place with the options being: D1.80

(1) a completely virtual interview;
(2) a partially virtual interview;
(3) parties in physical attendance with PPE;
(4) a written statement under caution;
(5) a charge without interview.

It should be noted however that many of the functions of appropriate adults require them to be physically present and cannot be carried out remotely. For example, an appropriate adult would still need to be physically present when samples were taken or when an interview was conducted.

On 17 June 2020 the Home Office attempted to regularise the position by issuing a short consultation which concluded on 3 July 2020 in relation to amendments to Codes C and E which would authorise the remote interviewing of suspects and allow for legal advice to be provided during police interviews by way of live link or telephone. On 2 February 2021 the response published by the Home Office confirmed that it would not seek to amend Codes C and E in the manner proposed. Instead, the Home Office confirmed that it would seek to increase compliance with the existing interview protocol.

Serious Fraud and other Serious Crime

D1.94 The Supreme Court in *R (KBR Inc.) v Director of the SFO* [2021] UKSC 2, [2021] 2 WLR 335, allowed the appeal against the Divisional Court decision of *R (KBR Inc.) v Director of the SFO* [2018] EWHC 2368 (Admin), [2019] 2 WLR 267, on the basis that the CJA 1987, s. 2(3), did not have extraterritorial effect. In addition, it was found that the Divisional Court's creation of an implied requirement that the power pursuant to the CJA 1987, s. 2(3), could only be used if there was a 'sufficient connection' between the company served and the jurisdiction, without defining what would constitute such a connection, would be inherently uncertain and would involve illegitimately re-writing the statute.

SEARCH OF THE PERSON

Search at the Police Station

D1.97 *Pile v Chief Constable of Merseyside Police* [2020] EWHC 2472 (QB), was, in the words of Turner J, an appeal 'to establish the liberty of inebriated English subjects to be allowed to lie undisturbed [in a police cell] overnight in their own vomit-soaked clothing'. The issue was whether the police had the power to remove the claimant's outer clothing while providing her with a clean dry outfit. Turner J noted that the alternative was to leave her 'to marinade overnight in her own bodily fluids'. The claimant submitted that none of the factors listed in the PACE 1984, s. 54(4), applied and due to the operation of s. 54(6C) no power of seizure arose and the removal of her clothes was unlawful. The Divisional Court found that the claimant's reliance on s. 54 was entirely misplaced. The power to remove her outer clothes existed pursuant to the PACE 1984, s. 39(1), which established a duty on the custody officer to ensure that 'all persons in police detention at that station are treated in accordance with [the] Act and any code of practice'. It was further provided at Code C, para. 8.5 that: 'If it is necessary to remove a detainee's clothes for the purposes of investigation, for hygiene, health reasons or cleaning, removal shall be conducted with proper regard to the dignity, sensitivity and vulnerability of the detainee and replacement clothing of a reasonable standard of comfort and cleanliness shall be provided'. In addition, the Court found that the behaviour of the claimant amounted to 'exceptional circumstances' which justified the departure from the requirements laid out in Code C, Annex A, para. 11(c), in relation to the conduct of strip searches. A further ground of appeal that it was a breach of the ECHR, Article 8, to place the claimant in a CCTV-monitored cell was similarly rejected.

BIOMETRIC IMPRESSIONS AND SAMPLES

Retention or Destruction of Biometric Data

D1.117 In *Gaughran v UK* (2020) Appln. 45245/15 (13 February 2020), the ECtHR found that the indefinite retention of the personal data (DNA profile, fingerprints and photograph) of D who had a spent conviction in Northern Ireland for driving with excess alcohol was a breach of the ECHR, Article 8. The Court's judgment largely reflected the dissenting judgment of Lord Kerr in *Gaughran v Chief Constable of the Police Service of Northern Ireland* [2015] UKSC 29, [2016] AC 345 (at [50]–[103]). The ECtHR found that the powers of retention were exercised indiscriminately, without reference to either the seriousness of the offence or the need for indefinite retention. Furthermore, there was a lack of any relevant safeguards including an absence of any real possibility for review. The ECtHR noted that the UK was an outlier in the Council of Europe in terms of permitting indefinite retention and therefore the margin of appreciation available to the UK had been narrowed. The Court held for the first time, contrary to earlier decisions by the Commission, that the taking and retention of custody photographs amounted to an interference with Article 8(1) (*S v UK* (2009) 48 EHRR 50 (1169) was not concerned with the retention of photographs).

POWERS TO PHOTOGRAPH SUSPECTS

D1.119 See D1.117 in this supplement.

ENTRY AND SEARCH UNDER WARRANT

In *R (C) v DPP* [2020] EWHC 2967 (Admin), [2020] 4 WLR 158, permission was refused to bring a claim for judicial review against a European Investigation Order ('EIO') which was submitted by the NCA to the authorities in France on 11 March 2020 to access material obtained through investigation of the EncroChat system of communication. The issue was whether the conditions precedent for validating the EIO pursuant to reg. 7(1)(a) and (b) of the Criminal Justice (European Investigation Order) Regulations 2017 (SI 2017 No. 730) were met. It was common ground that the EIO in this case did not request the transfer of evidence in relation to any specific offence(s). Regulation 7 states that: **D1.147**

> (1) If it appears to a designated public prosecutor—
> (a) that an offence has been committed or that there are reasonable grounds for suspecting that an offence has been committed, and
> (b) proceedings have been instituted in respect of the offence in question or it is being investigated, the prosecutor may make an order under this regulation.
>
> (2) A designated public prosecutor in England and Wales and Northern Ireland may, at the request of a designated investigating authority, validate an order under this regulation where it appears to the prosecutor that the conditions in paragraph (1) are satisfied.
>
> (3) An order under this regulation is an order specifying one or more investigative measures to be carried out in a participating State ('the executing State') for the purpose of obtaining evidence for use either in the investigation or the proceedings in question or both.
>
> (4) But an order under this regulation may only be made or validated if it appears to the designated public prosecutor that—
> (a) it is necessary and proportionate to make or validate the order for the purposes of the investigation or proceedings in question;
> (b) the investigative measures to be specified in the order could lawfully have been ordered or undertaken under the same conditions in a similar domestic case (see regulation 11), and
> (c) where the order is for an investigative measure in relation to which specific provision is made in Chapter 2 of this Part, any conditions imposed by virtue of such provision are satisfied.

It is apparent that the legislation covers both 'proceedings' and 'investigations' (reg. 7(1)(b)). The court found that the purpose of an 'investigation' is to determine whether an offence has been committed. It was held that a designated public prosecutor did not have to identify a particular offence related to a specified set of facts at the time the EIO was validated in order to satisfy reg. 7(1)(a).

It should be noted that an EIO can no longer be issued in light of the UK's departure from the EU on 31 December 2020. See also **D1.199, F2.33** and **F2.34** in this supplement.

Search Warrant Issued by Judge

The Application *R (Jordan) v Chief Constable of Merseyside Police* [2020] EWHC 2274 (Admin) was an application to judicially review the issue of a search warrant. D asserted public interest immunity (PII) in respect of part of the application. The Administrative Court stated that the general effect of a PII claim, if upheld, is that the relevant material becomes inadmissible for all purposes and cannot be relied on by any party or the court. This differs fundamentally from a closed material procedure (CMP). In a CMP the court can, in reaching its substantive decision, consider and rely upon material that has been withheld from one or more parties (*R (Haralambous) v St Albans Crown Court* [2018] UKSC 1, [2018] AC 236; *Al-Rawi v Security Service* [2011] UKSC 34, [2012] 1 AC 531 at [30]–[40]). **D1.167**

The Court held (at [13]) that the applicable principles in a search warrant case where a PII application is made are as follows:

(a) Before any question of a CMP arose, it was necessary to consider whether to uphold the PII claim. That involved determination of all three issues identified in *R v Chief Constable of West Midlands Police ex parte Wiley* [1995] 1 AC 274, at pp. 280–281 (and see

Metropolitan Police Commissioner v Bangs [2014] EWHC 546 (Admin); *R (Haralambous) v St Albans Crown Court*).

(b) As to the first *Wiley* question — was the PII material relevant to an issue — any material which could arguably support the pleaded, or as yet unpleaded, grounds of challenge would be relevant. However, it did not follow that every piece of information before the issuing authority would *ipso facto* pass the test (e.g., where there was more than one basis for the warrant and the issuing authority made clear that one or more of the bases advanced had not been relied on).

(c) The second question in *Wiley* is whether the disclosure of that evidence would cause harm to the public interest. If so, then pursuant to the third *Wiley* question, the court must balance the public interest in the administration of justice against the harm to the public interest that would be occasioned by making an order for disclosure. This requires two calibrated fact-specific assessments.

(d) In answering the third question, the court must assess the *extent* of any damage that would be caused to the public interest by making an order for disclosure. It will sometimes be obvious that there is a serious risk of grave damage (such as revealing the identity of an informer). In other cases, the extent of that damage may be low, or the damage feared may not be grave.

(e) Any assessment of the damage to the public interest in the administration of justice required a close focus on the issues in the case and the nature of the closed material. It should not be assumed that because the court could conduct a CMP there was no such damage: any proceeding precluding adversarial scrutiny represented a fundamental derogation from common-law standards of fairness. The Court expressly disagreed with the proposition by Marcus Smith J in *Competition and Markets Authority v Concordia International RX (UK) Ltd* [2018] EWHC 3448 (Ch), [2019] Lloyd's Rep FC 183, that a higher standard of cogency was required in any argument asserting PII if that material was to be considered in a CMP.

The Court set out (at [34]) the procedure to be adopted in resolving claims to PII in search warrant cases:

(a) If the court grants permission to apply for judicial review, the court should give directions for two separate hearings to take place: (i) a hearing to determine the PII claim; and (ii) a substantive hearing to determine the application for judicial review.

(b) In the PII hearing, the court should consider representations by both parties in 'open' proceedings before considering any further representations by the party asserting PII in 'closed' proceedings in the subject's absence. So far as possible, purely legal matters should be resolved in the 'open' proceedings (*Metropolitan Police Commissioner v Bangs*).

(c) If the PII claim is upheld in whole or in part, the court should give directions dealing with: (i) the timeframe within which the defendant must disclose and the claimant must respond to any new material; (ii) whether the case is sufficiently exceptional that it is necessary to invite the A-G to appoint a special advocate to represent the interests of the claimant in the CMP (*R (Terra Services Ltd) v NCA* [2020] EWHC 130 (Admin), [2020] 1 WLR 1149; *Competition and Markets Authority v Concordia International RX (UK) Ltd* [2018] EWCA Civ 1881, [2019] 1 All ER 699).

(d) At the substantive hearing, the open hearing should take place first, with the closed hearing following. The claimant's representatives should be available to return for a short further open hearing in case anything emerges from the closed hearing on which it is necessary to invite further open submissions. If no special advocate is present, counsel for the public authority has a special obligation to assist the court by identifying any points arising from the closed material which might arguably support the claimant or undermine the defence. Counsel seeking such an order 'must put on his defence hat and ask himself what, if he were representing the defendant or a third-party with the relevant interest, he would be saying to the judge, and, having answered that question, that is what he must tell the judge' (*Re Stanford International Bank Ltd* [2010] EWCA Civ 137, [2011] Ch 33).

(e) After the substantive hearing, open and closed judgments should be prepared. To the utmost extent possible, care should be taken to identify in the open judgment every conclusion that has been reached in whole or in part on the basis of evidence referred to in the closed judgment (*Bank Mellat v HM Treasury (No. 2)* [2013] UKSC 38, [2014] AC 700, at [68]).

In the substantive hearing of *R (Jordan) v Chief Constable of Merseyside Police* [2020] EWHC 2408 (Admin), the Administrative Court held that the correct approach when considering a challenge to a search warrant on the ground of non-disclosure was to begin by asking two questions:

(a) Did the applicant fail to disclose something which he or she was legally obliged to disclose?
(b) If so, was the non-disclosure material?

In relation to question (b) the Court reformulated the test set out in *R (Mills) v Sussex Police* [2014] EWHC 2523 (Admin), [2015] 1 WLR 2199 and *R (Dulai) v Chelmsford Magistrates' Court* [2012] EWHC 1055 (Admin), [2013] 1 WLR 220, as 'might the information that should have been given to the magistrate reasonably have led him or her to refuse to issue the warrant?'. It was held that the court must focus on the information that should have been given to the magistrate, not merely the information that *it is alleged* should have been given. The Court accepted that a different approach may be required where the non-disclosure is part of a deliberate attempt to mislead the issuing authority. In those circumstances, the court may quash the warrant even if the non-disclosure was not material.

If questions (a) and (b) are both answered in the affirmative then the court must consider the Senior Courts Act 1981, s. 31(2A), which states that 'The High Court (a) must refuse to grant relief on an application for judicial review… if it appears to the court to be highly likely that the outcome for the applicant would not have been substantially different if the conduct complained of had not occurred'. The Court concluded that once it was established that there was a material non-disclosure which could reasonably have led the magistrate to refuse to grant the warrant, it would be difficult to see on what basis the court could nonetheless conclude that it is 'highly likely' that the warrant would have been granted so that s. 31(2A) applied.

INTERCEPTION OF COMMUNICATIONS AND SURVEILLANCE

Interception of Communications

A [2021] EWCA Crim 128 concerned the admissibility of material obtained from the EncroChat mobile phone system. The key issue in the appeal was whether at the relevant time the communications were 'being transmitted' or were 'stored in or by the telecommunication system' pursuant to the IPA 2016, s. 4. The Court of Appeal found that they were 'stored' and that s. 4(4)(b) extended 'to all communications which are stored on the system, whenever that might occur'. On that basis the harvesting amounted to interception but, pursuant to s. 6(1)(c), was rendered lawful by the Targeted Interference Warrants issued under s. 99. **D1.199**

It should be noted that while the appeal proceeded on an agreed basis that the mobile phones were part of a 'public telecommunications system', the Court expressed doubt as to whether this was correct. See also **D1.147**, **F2.33** and **F2.34** in this supplement.

Surveillance and Covert Human Intelligence Sources

The Covert Human Intelligence Sources (Criminal Conduct) Act 2021 was passed on 1 March 2021. The main body of the Act is not yet in force. The Act creates a procedure by which a separate authorisation can be granted for a CHIS to engage in criminal conduct (see the RIPA 2000, s. 29(6ZA), inserted by the Covert Human Intelligence Sources (Criminal Conduct) Act 2021, s. 1(4)). **D1.200**

The RIPA 2000, s. 26(8A) (inserted by the Covert Human Intelligence Sources (Criminal Conduct) Act 2021, s. 1(3)), states that:

In this Part references to criminal conduct in the course of, or otherwise in connection with, the conduct of a covert human intelligence source are references to any conduct that—

(a) disregarding this Part, would constitute crime, and
(b) consists of, is in the course of, or is otherwise in connection with, the conduct of a covert human intelligence source.

The list of 'persons designated' to 'have the power to grant criminal conduct authorisations' is extensive and includes 'any police force', the NCA, the SFO, any of the intelligence services or any of Her Majesty's forces, HMRC, the Department of Health and Social Care, the Home Office, the Ministry of Justice, the Competition and Markets Authority, the Environment Agency, the FCA, the Food Standards Agency, the Gambling Commission (Covert Human Intelligence Sources (Criminal Conduct) Act 2021 ss. 1(5) and 4).

The type of criminal conduct which can be authorised is defined by the RIPA 2000, s. 29(B)(8) (inserted by the Covert Human Intelligence Sources (Criminal Conduct) Act 2021, s. 1(5)), as:

The conduct that is authorised by a criminal conduct authorisation is any conduct that—

(a) is comprised in any activities—
(i) which involve criminal conduct in the course of, or otherwise in connection with, the conduct of a covert human intelligence source, and
(ii) are specified or described in the authorisation;
(b) consists in conduct by or in relation to the person who is so specified or described as the covert human intelligence source to whom the authorisation relates; and
(c) is carried out for the purposes of, or in connection with, the investigation or operation so specified or described.

A criminal conduct authorisation may not be granted unless it is believed to be both necessary and proportionate to what is sought to be achieved (RIPA 2000, s. 29B(4)). For an authorisation to be 'necessary' it must be (a) in the interests of national security; or (b) for the purpose of preventing or detecting crime or of preventing disorder; or (c) in the interests of the economic well-being of the UK (s. 29B(5)). Furthermore, a person must take into account 'whether what is sought to be achieved by the authorised conduct could reasonably be achieved by other conduct which would not constitute crime' (s. 29B(6)). This is 'without prejudice to the need to take into account other matters so far as they are relevant (for example, the requirements of the Human Rights Act 1998)' (s. 29B(7)).

The Covert Human Intelligence Sources (Criminal Conduct) Act 2021, s. 2, will further amend the RIPA 2000 by inserting s. 29C which sets out specific safeguards in relation to the grant of juvenile criminal conduct authorisations.

The Intelligence Services Act 1994, s. 5, entitles the Secretary of State (subject to meeting certain statutory conditions) to issue a warrant authorising the UK intelligence agencies to take such action as is 'specified in the warrant in respect of any property so specified or in respect of wireless telegraphy so specified'. It was held by the Administrative Court in *Privacy International v Investigatory Powers Tribunal* [2021] EWHC 27 (Admin), that a warrant issued under s. 5 will be lawful if it is sufficiently specific for the property concerned to be objectively ascertainable on the face of the warrant.

D1.201 The decision of the Divisional Court in *R (Bridges) v Chief Constable of South Wales Police* [2019] EWHC 2341 (Admin), [2020] 1 Cr App R 3 (52) was overturned by the Court of Appeal (Civil Division) in *R (Bridges) v Chief Constable of South Wales Police* [2020] EWCA Civ 1058, [2021] 1 Cr App R 4 (51), holding that:

(a) the interference with the claimant's Article 8(1) rights was not 'in accordance with the law' for the purposes of Article 8(2) as there was no clear guidance on where AFR Locate could be used and who could be put on a watchlist. This meant that the discretion afforded to police officers was too broad to meet the standard required by Article 8(2);
(b) the 'data protection impact assessment', which had been produced pursuant to the Data Protection Act 2018, s. 64, was deficient insofar as it was written on the basis that Article 8 was not infringed;

(c) the Chief Constable of South Wales Police had failed to take reasonable steps to make inquiries about whether the AFR Locate software had bias on grounds of sex or race which contravened its Public Sector Equality Duty pursuant to the Equality Act 2010, s. 149.

Section D2 The Decision to Prosecute and Diversion

THE DECISION TO PROSECUTE

The *Director's Guidance on Charging* was revised in December 2020 (6th edn, tinyurl.com/h5tdxkza). The new edition was published on the same day as the A-G's Guidelines on Disclosure 2020 and the Criminal Procedure and Investigations Act (CPIA) Code of Practice 2020 and incorporates these documents, as well as reflecting the Code for Crown Prosecutors 2018 and the Magistrates' Court (Transforming Summary Justice) and Crown Court (Better Case Management) initiatives. The revised *Guidance* largely consolidates principles set out in the last edition, but with a new focus on the early management of disclosure, and the need for expedition. **D2.1**

The Tests for Deciding Whether to Charge

Public Interest Stage The CPS has issued interim guidance for use by prosecutors during the Covid-19 pandemic (14 April 2020, tinyurl.com/y8hkrf6x). The guidance states that, when applying the public interest test, 'prosecutors should do so in the context of the ongoing impact on the criminal justice system of the Covid-19 pandemic'. This is relevant to both the charging decision for new cases and the review of existing ('live') cases. **D2.12**

JUDICIAL REVIEW OF PROSECUTION DECISIONS

Decision to Prosecute The same standard of review in abuse of process applications arising from challenges to decisions to prosecute applies to the Health and Safety Executive as to those made by the CPS or other prosecutorial bodies (*Connors Building & Restoration Ltd* [2020] EWCA Crim 868). **D2.21**

Decision Not to Prosecute Where there are alternative routes by which an offence may be made out, a decision-maker must consider the sufficiency of the available evidence in relation to each of the alternative routes. In *R (L) v DPP* [2020] EWHC 1815 (Admin), the Divisional Court quashed a decision not to prosecute where there was no evidence that the decision-maker had taken this approach. **D2.22**

Where applicants for judicial review of a decision not to prosecute have all the information necessary to challenge the rationality of that decision, an application for disclosure of documents will be refused (*R (Bullock) v DPP* [2020] EWHC 2259 (Admin)).

ALTERNATIVES TO PROSECUTION

Simple Cautions (Adults)

Procedure for Administering Simple Caution and its Consequences In *R (RD) v Secretary of State for Justice* [2020] EWCA Civ 1346, [2021] 1 WLR 262, the Court of Appeal (Civil Division) held that the requirement within the Rehabilitation of Offenders Act 1974 (Exceptions) Order 1975 (SI 1975 No. 1023) for applicants to become a police officer to disclose a reprimand received as a youth is compatible with the ECHR, Article 8. **D2.28**

D

Part D Procedure

DETENTION FOLLOWING CHARGE

Detention of Children after Charge

D2.52 In *Archer v Commissioner of Police of the Metropolis* [2020] EWHC 1567 (QB), [2020] 2 Cr App R 23 (357), the Divisional Court held that the detention of a youth under the PACE 1984, s. 38(1)(b)(ii), on the basis that it was necessary for his own protection was not incompatible with Article 5(1)(c) and (3) of the ECHR. Note that this decision is subject to appeal.

Section D3 Courts, Parties and Abuse of Process

ABUSE OF PROCESS: THE POWER TO STAY PROCEEDINGS

Delay

D3.73 The authorities on delay in the context of abuse of process were reviewed in *Hewitt* [2020] EWCA Crim 1247, where the Court of Appeal upheld the refusal of a stay despite the fact that the allegations related to events that occurred in 1982 to 1983 (reported to the police in 2014). The Court concluded that, despite the passage of time and serious shortcomings in disclosure by the prosecution, the defence had nonetheless 'an unusual wealth of material' on which to cross-examine the complainant 'robustly and effectively'; moreover, the inconsistencies in the complainant's evidence were 'fully explored'. The Court also noted a number of reasons which would have justified the jury finding the complainant's evidence to be credible (at [188]). Furthermore, the judge had 'summarised the evidence fully and fairly' and had 'identified the issues very clearly' (at [189]). The Court also noted that the jury were 'plainly a discerning and diligent jury': they had sent a total of 32 notes to the judge during the course of the trial and had reached 'mixed' verdicts, thereby (said the Court) demonstrating 'the care with which they examined and analysed the evidence'. The Court expressed itself 'quite satisfied' that the jury faithfully discharged their duty of evaluating the evidence, and that the conviction was therefore safe (at [189]).

Manipulation of Procedure

D3.102 *Beedie* [1998] QB 356 was followed in *Wangige* [2020] EWCA Crim 1319, [2021] RTR 7 (115) (see also **C3.9** in this supplement). The Court of Appeal reiterated (at [42]) that:

> ... no person should be punished twice for an offence arising out of the same, or substantially the same, set of facts. Second, there should be no sequential trials for offences on an ascending scale of gravity.

In the instant case, it was held that the second set of proceedings should have been stayed as an abuse of process because (see [62]), as regards the primary facts:

> ... nothing had changed between the first charging decision and the subsequent charging decision. What had changed was that a different expert opinion, making a different analysis of the issue of speed and reaching a different conclusion on the evidence, had been obtained.

Furthermore, the 'substance' of the charges that D faced in the magistrates' court could not be divorced from the 'substance' of the more serious charge of causing death by dangerous driving, since these offences all arose out of the 'same incident' (at [63]). The facts had not changed; what had changed was the evaluation of the evidence in relation to those facts (at [66]).

The Court rejected the argument that 'special circumstances' meant that the proceedings should be allowed to continue, holding (at [79]):

> ... a change in position on charging made solely by reference to the new expert report obtained following initial conviction and sentence and founded on the same facts that were in existence at the time of the first charging decision cannot, in the circumstances of this case, amount to a special circumstance sufficient to justify refusing to grant a stay.

The Court clarified (at [81], emphasis in original) that:

> … we are *not* saying that the obtaining of fresh expert, or other, evidence designed to correct an error or oversight or omission relevant to a first charging decision can *never* sufficiently constitute a special circumstance. Ultimately, all will depend on the particular circumstances of the particular case. What we do say is that on such a scenario very close scrutiny indeed is called for before it may properly be adjudged that a second prosecution may fairly proceed.

Section D6 Classification of Offences and Determining Allocation (Mode of Trial)

INTRODUCTION

References throughout this section to the PCC(S)A 2000, s. 3, the power to commit for sentence to the Crown Court, should be read as references to the SA 2020, s. 14 (see **D23.30** in this supplement). **D6.1**

Section D12 Arraignment and Pleas

AUTREFOIS ACQUIT AND AUTREFOIS CONVICT

Scope of the Pleas

Findings that Cannot Form Basis for Plea of Autrefois Acquit For a recent example of the application of *Beedie* [1998] QB 356, where D sought to argue that a prosecution for human trafficking was barred by autrefois convict in relation to an earlier conviction for drug offences which also involved the exploitation of trafficked children, see *Wabelua* [2020] EWCA Crim 783, [2020] 1 Cr App R (S) 3 (13). Holroyde LJ observed (at [14]) that the later prosecution concerned 'a distinct form of criminality involving different conduct at a different time'. **D12.26**

CHANGE OF PLEA

From Guilty to Not Guilty

Discretion to Allow a Change The guidance for vacating a guilty plea in *Drew* [1985] 2 All ER 1061 was revisited in *Tierney-Campbell* [2020] EWCA Crim 1194. In that case, D had pleaded guilty to the unlawful wounding with intent of V who later died. D sought to appeal against his conviction for the offence under the OAPA 1861, s. 18. The Court restated the principle that an accused who has admitted facts that constitute an offence by an unambiguous and deliberately intended plea of guilty, cannot ordinarily appeal against conviction because a conviction founded on D's own voluntary confession in open court is rarely unsafe. Where, as here, D sought to argue that the plea was entered following erroneous legal advice, the facts must be so strong as to show that the plea of guilty was not a true acknowledgment of guilt. This required the advice to be fundamental to the plea, or alternatively if it can be shown that, with the benefit of correct advice, there would probably have been an acquittal. **D12.95**

Section D15 Trial on Indictment: General Matters and Pre-trial Procedure

CUSTODY TIME-LIMITS

D15.7 The Prosecution of Offences (Custody Time Limits) (Coronavirus) (Amendment) Regulations 2020 (SI 2020 No. 953) have been amended by the Prosecution of Offences (Custody Time Limits) (Coronavirus) (Amendment) Regulations 2021 (SI 2021 No. 91). The 2020 Regulations extended the length of the custody time-limit period, in the light of the Covid-19 pandemic. The 2021 Regulations return the length of the custody time-limit to its pre-pandemic duration in the case of those under the age of 18 when first remanded into custody.

The pandemic, and the limitations it has imposed on the ability of the Crown Court to list trials, is also recognised as capable of amounting to a good and sufficient cause for the extension of custody time-limits (*R (DPP) v Crown Court at Woolwich* [2020] EWHC 3243 (Admin), [2021] 1 Cr App R 11 (223)).

PRE-TRIAL DISCLOSURE OF THIRD-PARTY MATERIAL

D15.79 The Criminal Procedure (Amendment) Rules 2021 (SI 2021 No. 40) amend CrimPR Part 3 to include at r. 3.3 a requirement that parties alert the Crown Court to related family proceedings, and at r. 3.5 the Court has the power to request information from those proceedings.

Section D18 Trial on Indictment: Procedure between Close of Defence Case and Retirement of Jury

SUMMING-UP

Preliminary and General Matters

D18.21 A new edition of the *Crown Court Compendium* was published in December 2020.

Standard Directions

D18.28 **Separate Consideration of Counts and Defendants** In *Adams* [2019] EWCA Crim 1363, the Court of Appeal emphasised that where D faced multiple counts, the jury should be given clear direction as to whether, and if so in what way, evidence relating to one count was admissible in relation to their consideration of any other. Where there was no cross-admissibility between counts this had to be made clear.

D18.32 **Other Standard Directions** In *Gabbana* [2020] EWCA Crim 1473, [2020] 4 WLR 160, the Court of Appeal repeated the observations of the Supreme Court in *Mitchell* [2016] UKSC 55, [2017] AC 571, to the effect that the criminal standard of proof could apply to an individual element of the prosecution case, such as disputed bad character evidence, even though each individual strand of evidence might not suffice to justify a conviction. The Court considered that trial judges should include a reference to the criminal standard in a bad character direction.

Section D19 Trial on Indictment: Procedure Relating to Retirement of the Jury and Verdict

VERDICT OF GUILTY OF AN ALTERNATIVE OFFENCE

Judge's Judgment in Directing Jury as to Alternative Offences

In *M* [2019] EWCA Crim 1094, the Court of Appeal, having considered *Coutts* [2006] UKHL 39, [2007] 1 Cr App R 6 (60), made clear that there was no requirement that a lesser alternative always be left to the jury whenever it was a possibility. It involved consideration of factors such as the evidence adduced or to be adduced at trial, whether the leaving of an alternative will assist or complicate the jury's task, and whether the leaving of the alternative will be fair to D or otherwise. **D19.58**

RETURNING THE VERDICT

Correcting a Verdict

Where the Verdict is Incorrect In *RN* [2020] EWCA Crim 937, the Court of Appeal addressed, on particular and unusual facts, the proper approach where an issue is raised as to whether a verdict has been correctly returned. The jury had returned not guilty verdicts on two counts on the indictment against D, whose discharge was ordered. However, information then rapidly came to the notice of the judge which suggested that the jury had reached their verdicts on the basis of a misunderstanding of the approach that they should take. The judge then directed the jury to continue considering their verdicts, and D was then convicted. The Court of Appeal concluded that there was no valid reason for concluding that the original not guilty verdicts were mistaken, and the verdicts should not have been reopened and further deliberation permitted. **D19.75**

Section D21 Summary Trial: General and Preliminary Matters

JURISDICTION TO TRY CASES SUMMARILY

Transfer of Cases between Magistrates' Courts

The reference to the PCC(S)A 2000, s. 10, should be read as a reference to the SA 2020, s. 28: **D21.6**

Sentencing Code (Sentencing Act 2020, s. 28)

(1) Subsection (2) applies where—
   (a) a person aged 18 or over has been convicted by a magistrates' court ('the convicting court') of a relevant offence ('the present offence'),
   (b) it appears to the convicting court that some other magistrates' court ('the other court') has convicted the offender of another relevant offence in respect of which the other court has not—
      (i) passed sentence on the offender,
      (ii) committed the offender to the Crown Court for sentence, nor
      (iii) dealt with the offender in any other way, and
   (c) the other court consents to the offender's being remitted to it under this section.

(2) The convicting court may remit the offender to the other court to be dealt with in respect of the present offence by the other court instead of by the convicting court.

(3) In subsection (1), 'relevant offence', in relation to the convicting court or the other court, means an offence which is punishable by that court with—
   (a) imprisonment, or
   (b) driving disqualification.

...

(4) Where the convicting court remits the offender to the other court under this section the other court may deal with the offender in any way in which it could deal with the offender if it had convicted the offender of the present offence ...

Part D Procedure

(5) The power conferred on the other court by subsection (4) includes, where applicable, the power to remit the offender under this section to another magistrates' court in respect of the present offence.

(6) Where the convicting court has remitted the offender under this section, the other court may remit the offender back to the convicting court; and where it does so subsections (4) and (5) (so far as applicable) apply with the necessary modifications.

Section D22 Summary Trial: The Course of the Trial

SETTING ASIDE A CONVICTION FOR REHEARING BEFORE DIFFERENTLY CONSTITUTED BENCH

Use of s. 142 where Accused Pleaded Guilty

D22.76 The power to set a conviction aside under the MCA 1980, s. 142(2), was considered in *Wilson v CPS* [2020] EWHC 820 (QB). It was reiterated that s. 142 is 'generally and correctly described as a "slip rule" and should not be used in a situation beyond those akin to a mistake' (at [30]). Moreover, the jurisdiction to vacate a plea of guilty 'should be exercised sparingly and only in clear cases'. However, if it can be established that the accused 'pleaded guilty without understanding elements of the offence, or without intending to admit that he was guilty of what was alleged', then it might be appropriate to allow withdrawal of the guilty plea (at [31]). The Court added (at [32]) that legal representation 'may be a relevant factor', in that it will be more difficult for an accused to change an unequivocal plea of guilty if there has been 'representation by experienced criminal [representatives]'.

In *H v DPP* [2021] EWHC 147 (Admin), the Divisional Court reaffirmed that s. 142(2) can be used to vacate guilty pleas only in cases where the nature of the mistake or error justifies its use. Lord Burnett CJ (at [20]) said that an argument that a defendant failed to adduce evidence which might have led to an acquittal, or otherwise failed to pursue a defence that it is later asserted was available, 'is not something that falls within s. 142(2) of the 1980 Act'. The Court also confirmed that (as was held in *RD* [2019] EWCA Crim 1545 (at [33])), where there has been a committal for sentence and the Crown Court has passed sentence for the offence(s) in question, s. 142(2) has no application. Section 142 goes no further than enabling a magistrates' court or youth court 'to intervene when the impact of an order only affects its own determinations' (at [12]).

Section D23 Sentencing in the Magistrates' Court

COMMITTAL FOR SENTENCE

Committal under the Powers of Criminal Courts (Sentencing) Act 2000, s. 3

D23.30 References to the PCC(S)A 2000, s. 3 (the power to commit for sentence to the Crown Court where the accused pleads guilty to, or is convicted of, an either-way offence) should be read as references to the SA 2020, s. 14.

Sentencing Code (Sentencing Act 2020, s. 14)

(1) This section applies where—
  (a) on the summary trial of an offence triable either way a person aged 18 or over is convicted of the offence, and
  (b) the court is of the opinion that—
    (i) the offence, or
    (ii) the combination of the offence and one or more offences associated with it,
  was so serious that the Crown Court should have the power to deal with the offender in any way it could deal with the offender if the offender had been convicted on indictment.

This is subject to the provisions mentioned in subsection (4).

(2) The court may commit the offender in custody or on bail to the Crown Court for sentence in accordance with section 21(2).
(3) For powers of the court, where it commits a person under subsection (2), also to commit in respect of other offences, see section 20.
(4) For offences in relation to which this section does not apply see sections 17D and 33 of the Magistrates' Courts Act 1980 (exclusion in respect of certain offences where value involved is small).
(5) This section applies to a corporation as if—
(a) the corporation were an individual aged 18 or over, and
(b) in subsection (2) the words 'in custody or on bail' were omitted.

Committal for Sentence under the Powers of Criminal Courts (Sentencing) Act 2000, s. 4

References to the PCC(S)A 2000, s. 4 (committal for sentence where the accused pleads guilty to one or more either-way offences but not guilty to others and is sent to the Crown Court for trial in respect of the latter), should be read as references to the SA 2020, s. 18. **D23.42**

Sentencing Code (Sentencing Act 2020, s. 18)

(1) Where a magistrates' court—
(a) has convicted an offender aged 18 or over of an offence triable either way following an indication of a guilty plea, and
(b) has sent the offender to the Crown Court for trial for one or more related offences,
it may commit the offender in custody or on bail to the Crown Court to be dealt with in respect of the offence in accordance with section 21(2).
(2) For offences in relation to which subsection (1) does not apply, see section 17D of the Magistrates' Courts Act 1980 (cases where value involved is small).
(3) Where a magistrates' court—
(a) convicts an offender aged 18 or over of an offence triable either way following an indication of a guilty plea, and
(b) is still to determine to send, or whether to send, the offender to the Crown Court for trial under section 51 or 51A of the Crime and Disorder Act 1998, for one or more related offences,
it must adjourn the proceedings relating to the offence until after it has made those determinations.
(4) Where the court—
(a) commits the offender under subsection (1) to the Crown Court to be dealt with in respect of the offence, and
(b) in its opinion also has power under section 14(2) or is required under section 15(2) to commit the offender to the Crown Court to be dealt with in respect of the offence,
the court may make a statement of that opinion.
(5) For powers of the court, where it commits a person under subsection (1), also to commit in respect of other offences, see section 20.
...
(7) For the purposes of this section—
(a) 'related offence' means an offence which, in the opinion of the court, is related to the offence, and
(b) one offence is related to another if, were they both to be prosecuted on indictment, the charges for them could be joined in the same indictment.
(8) In doing anything under or contemplated by this section, the court is not bound by any indication of sentence given in respect of the offence under section 20 of the Magistrates' Courts Act 1980 (procedure where summary trial appears more suitable).
(9) Nothing the court does under this section may be challenged or be the subject of any appeal in any court on the ground that it is inconsistent with an indication of sentence.

Hearing in the Crown Court following a Committal under the Powers of Criminal Courts (Sentencing) Act 2000, s. 3 or s. 4

Powers of Crown Court References to the PCC(S)A 2000, s. 5 (powers of the Crown Court following committal for sentence under the PCC(S)A 2000 s. 3, 3A, or 4; SA 2020, s. 14, 15 or 18) should be read as references to the SA 2020, s. 21. **D23.46**

Sentencing Code (Sentencing Act 2020, s. 21)

(1) This section applies where an offender is committed by a magistrates' court for sentence under—
   (a) section 14(2) (committal for sentence on summary trial of offence triable either way),
   (b) section 15(2) (committal for sentence of dangerous adult offenders), or
   (c) section 18(1) (committal for sentence on indication of guilty plea to offence triable either way).

(2) The Crown Court—
   (a) must inquire into the circumstances of the case, and
   (b) may deal with the offender in any way in which it could deal with the offender if the offender had been convicted of the offence on indictment before the court.

This is subject to subsections (4) and (5).

...

(4) Subsection (5) applies where a magistrates' court—
   (a) commits an offender under section 18(1) to be dealt with in respect of an offence ('the offence'), but
   (b) does not make a statement under section 18(4) (statement of power to commit under section 14(2) or 15(2)).

(5) Unless the offender is convicted before the Crown Court of at least one of the offences for which the magistrates' court has sent the offender for trial (see section 18(1)(b))—
   (a) subsection (2)(b) does not apply, and
   (b) the Crown Court may deal with the offender for the offence in any way in which the magistrates' court could have dealt with the offender for it.

Other Committal Powers

D23.49 **Dangerous Offenders** References to the PCC(SA) 2000, s. 3A (committal for sentence in the case of dangerous offenders) should be read as references to the SA 2020, s. 15.

Sentencing Code (Sentencing Act 2020, s. 15)

(1) This section applies where—
   (a) on the summary trial of a specified offence (see section 306) triable either way a person aged 18 or over is convicted of the offence, and
   (b) the court is of the opinion that an extended sentence of detention in a young offender institution or of imprisonment (see section 266 or 279) would be available in relation to the offence.

(2) The court must commit the offender in custody or on bail to the Crown Court for sentence in accordance with section 21(2).

(3) For powers of the court, where it commits a person under subsection (2), also to commit in respect of other offences, see section 20.

(4) In doing anything under or contemplated by this section, the court is not bound by any indication of sentence given in respect of the offence under section 20 of the Magistrates' Courts Act 1980 (procedure where summary trial appears more suitable).

(5) Nothing the court does under this section may be challenged or be the subject of any appeal in any court on the ground that it is inconsistent with an indication of sentence.

(6) Nothing in this section prevents the court from committing an offender convicted of a specified offence to the Crown Court for sentence under section 14 or 18 if the provisions of that section are satisfied.

Conditional Discharge

D23.51 The reference to the PCC(S)A 2000, s. 13(5), should be read as a reference to the SA 2020, sch. 2, para. 5(4).

Community Order

D23.52 The reference to the CJA 2003, sch. 8, para. 9(6), should be read as a reference to the SA 2020, sch. 10, para. 10(3); and the reference to the CJA 2003, sch. 8, para. 7(1), as a reference to the SA 2020, sch. 10, para. 8(1).

Suspended Sentence Order

The reference to the CJA 2003, sch. 12, para. 8(6), should be read as a reference to the SA 2020, sch. 16, para. 10(3); the reference to the CJA 2003, sch. 12, para. 6(1), as a reference to the SA 2020, sch. 16, paras. 3, 8(1); and the reference to the CJA 2003, sch. 12, para. 11(2), as a reference to the SA 2020, sch. 16, para. 11(2). **D23.53**

Committal under the Powers of Criminal Courts (Sentencing) Act 2000, s. 6

References to the PCC(S)A 2000, s. 6 (power to commit for sentence where a 'primary' power of committal has been exercised) should be read as references to the SA 2020, s. 20. **D23.55**

Sentencing Code (Sentencing Act 2020, s. 20)

(1) This section applies where a magistrates' court ('the committing court') commits an offender to the Crown Court under—
  (a) sections 14 to 19 (committal for sentence for indictable offences),
  (b) paragraph 5(4) of Schedule 2 (further offence committed by offender given conditional discharge order),
  (c) paragraph 24(2) of Schedule 10 (committal to Crown Court where offender convicted of further offence while community order is in force),
  (d) paragraph 11(2) of Schedule 16 (committal to Crown Court where offender commits further offence during operational period of suspended sentence order),
  (e) section 43 of the Mental Health Act 1980 (power of magistrates' courts to commit for restriction order),
  (f) section 6(6) or 9(3) of the Bail Act 1976 (committal to Crown Court for offences of absconding by person released on bail or agreeing to indemnify sureties in criminal proceedings), or
  (g) the Vagrancy Act 1824 (incorrigible rogues),
  to be sentenced or otherwise dealt with in respect of an offence ('the relevant offence').
(2) Where—
  (a) the relevant offence is an indictable offence, and
  (b) the committing court has power to deal with the offender in respect of another offence,
  the committing court may also commit the offender to the Crown Court to be dealt with in respect of the other offence in accordance with section 23.
(3) It is immaterial for the purposes of subsection (2) whether the court which convicted the offender of the other offence was the committing court or another court.
(4) Where the relevant offence is a summary offence, the committing court may commit the offender to the Crown Court to be dealt with, in accordance with section 23, in respect of—
  (a) any other offence of which the committing court has convicted the offender which is punishable with—
    (i) imprisonment, or
    (ii) driving disqualification, or
  (b) any suspended sentence in respect of which it falls to the committing court to deal with the offender by virtue of paragraph 11(1) of Schedule 16.

...

(6) A committal to the Crown Court under this section is to be in custody or on bail as the case may require.

References to the PCC(S)A 2000, s. 7 (powers of the Crown Court in respect of offences committed under the PCC(S)A, s. 6; SA 2020, s. 20) should be read as references to the SA 2020, s. 23.

Sentencing Code (Sentencing Act 2020, s. 23)

(1) Subsection (2) applies where under section 20(2) or (4)(a) (committal for sentence in certain cases where offender committed in respect of another offence) a magistrates' court commits a person to be dealt with by the Crown Court in respect of an offence.
(2) The Crown Court—
  (a) must inquire into the circumstances of the case, and
  (b) may deal with the offender for the offence in any way in which the magistrates' court could have dealt with the offender (assuming it had convicted the offender of the offence).

D

Part D Procedure

(3) Subsection (4) applies where under section 20(4)(b) a magistrates' court commits a person to be dealt with by the Crown Court in respect of a suspended sentence.

(4) The powers under paragraphs 13 and 14 of Schedule 16 (power of court to deal with suspended sentence) are exercisable by the Crown Court.

Section D24 Trial of Children and Young People

References in this section to the PCC(S)A 2000, s. 91 (detention where a child or young person is convicted of a certain serious offences) should be read as references to the SA 2020, s. 249:

Sentencing Code (Sentencing Act 2020, s. 249)

(1) A sentence of detention under section 250 is available where a person aged under 18 is convicted on indictment of an offence listed in the following table—

Offences punishable with imprisonment for at least 14 years

(a) an offence which—
  (i) is not an offence for which the sentence is fixed by law, and
  (ii) is punishable in the case of a person aged 21 or over with imprisonment for 14 years or more;

Sexual offences

(b) an offence under any of the following provisions of the Sexual Offences Act 2003—
  (i) section 3 (sexual assault);
  (ii) section 13 (child sex offences committed by children or young persons);
  (iii) section 25 (sexual activity with a child family member);
  (iv) section 26 (inciting a child family member to engage in sexual activity);

Offences related to firearms

(c) an offence (other than one within paragraph (a)) which—
  (i) is listed in Schedule 20 (firearms offences to which minimum sentence applies), and
  (ii) was committed when the offender was aged 16 or over.

The SA 2020, s. 250, defines a 'sentence of detention' for this purpose as 'a sentence requiring the offender to be detained for the period specified in the sentence'.

DETERMINING PLACE OF TRIAL OF CHILDREN AND YOUNG PEOPLE

Guidance on the Decision-making Process in s. 91 Cases

D24.34 **Power to Commit for Sentence** In *R (BB) v West Glamorgan Youth Court* [2020] EWHC 2888 (Admin), the Divisional Court emphasised the importance of applying the guidance given by Sir Brian Leveson P in *R (DPP) v South Tyneside Youth Court* [2015] EWHC 1455 (Admin), [2015] 2 Cr App R (S) 59 (411) (at [29]–[31]), adding that it is 'incumbent on those appearing before a youth court making an allocation decision to ensure that the court is aware of the principles set out in *South Tyneside Youth Court*'. The Court observed (at [14]) that:

> The practical outcome of this guidance as to the interrelationship between the allocation provision and the general power to commit for sentence is that it is only rarely that a Youth Court should send a child or young person for trial. Cases in which a defendant under 15 is sent for trial pursuant to [the CDA 1998, s.51A(3)(b),] should be very rare.

The Court also underlined (at [16]) the importance of following the Sentencing Council's guideline, *Sentencing Children and Young People* (see **SG8-1**), when evaluating the likely sentence. Assuming that the magistrates have sufficient information to allow them to do so, before deciding that a custodial sentence is likely they should first consider whether, taking account of D's age, individual circumstances, and involvement in the offences, no sentence other than custody would be appropriate (at [17]).

COMMITTAL FOR SENTENCE

Committal under the Powers of Criminal Courts (Sentencing) Act 2000, s. 3B

D24.57 References to the PCC(S)A 2000, s. 3B (committal for sentence of young offenders in respect of certain serious offences) should be read as references to the SA 2020, s. 16.

Sentencing Code (Sentencing Act 2020, s. 16)

(1) This section applies where—
(a) on the summary trial of an offence within paragraph (a) or (b) of the table in section 249(1) (offences punishable with imprisonment for 14 years or more and certain sexual offences), a person is convicted of the offence,
(b) the person is aged under 18 at the time of conviction, and
(c) the court is of the opinion that—
(i) the offence, or
(ii) the combination of the offence and one or more offences associated with it,
was such that the Crown Court should have power to deal with the offender by imposing a sentence of detention under section 250.
(2) The court may commit the offender in custody or on bail to the Crown Court for sentence in accordance with section 22(2).
(3) For powers of the court, where it commits a person under subsection (2), also to commit in respect of other offences, see section 20.

Committal for Sentence: Related Offences Sent for Trial

References to the PCC(S)A 2000, s. 4A (committal for sentence on indication of guilty plea by child or young person with related offences) should be read as references to the SA 2020, s. 19. **D24.59**

Sentencing Code (Sentencing Act 2020, s. 19)

(1) Where—
(a) a magistrates' court—
(i) has convicted a person aged under 18 of an offence following an indication of a guilty plea, and
(ii) has sent the person to the Crown Court for trial for one or more related offences, and
(b) the offence falls within paragraph (a) or (b) of the table in section 249(1) (offences punishable with imprisonment for 14 years or more and certain sexual offences),
the court may commit the offender in custody or on bail to the Crown Court to be dealt with in respect of the offence in accordance with section 22(2).
(2) Where a magistrates' court—
(a) convicts a person aged under 18 of an offence mentioned in paragraph (a) or (b) of the table in section 249(1) following an indication of a guilty plea, and
(b) is still to determine to send, or whether to send, the person to the Crown Court for trial under section 51 or 51A of the Crime and Disorder Act 1998 for one or more related offences,
it must adjourn the proceedings relating to the offence until after it has made those determinations.
(3) Where the court—
(a) commits the offender under subsection (1) to the Crown Court to be dealt with in respect of the offence, and
(b) in its opinion, also has power so to commit the offender under section 16(2) or 17(2),
the court may make a statement of that opinion.
(4) For powers of the court, where it commits a person under subsection (1), also to commit in respect of other offences, see section 20.
...
(6) For the purposes of this section—
(a) 'related offence' means an offence which, in the opinion of the court, is related to the offence, and
(b) one offence is related to another if, were they both to be prosecuted on indictment, the charges for them could be joined in the same indictment.

Committal for Sentence: Dangerous Offenders

References to the PCC(S)A 2000, s. 3C (committal for sentence of dangerous young offenders) should be read as references to the SA 2020, s. 17. **D24.60**

Sentencing Code (Sentencing Act 2020, s. 17)

(1) This section applies where—
(a) on the summary trial of a specified offence (see section 306) a person aged under 18 is convicted of the offence, and

(b) the court is of the opinion that an extended sentence of detention under section 254 would be available in relation to the offence.

(2) The court must commit the offender in custody or on bail to the Crown Court for sentence in accordance with section 22(2).

(3) For powers of the court, where it commits a person under subsection (2), also to commit in respect of other offences, see section 20.

(4) Nothing in this section prevents the court from committing a person convicted of a specified offence to the Crown Court for sentence under section 16 or 19 if the provisions of that section are satisfied.

Powers of Crown Court Following Committal for Sentence

D24.62 References to the PCC(S)A 2000, s. 5A (powers of the Crown Court following committal for sentence) should be read as references to the SA 2020, s. 22(1) and (2).

Sentencing Code (Sentencing Act 2020, s. 22)

(1) This section applies where an offender is committed by a magistrates' court for sentence under—

(a) section 16(2) (committal for sentence of young offenders on summary trial of certain serious offences),

(b) section 17(2) (committal for sentence of dangerous young offenders), or

(c) section 19(1) (committal for sentence on indication of guilty plea by child or young person with related offences).

(2) The Crown Court—

(a) must inquire into the circumstances of the case, and

(b) may deal with the offender in any way in which it could deal with the offender if the offender had been convicted of the offence on indictment before the court.

This is subject to subsections (4) and (5).

TRIAL OF CHILDREN AND YOUNG PEOPLE ON INDICTMENT

Reporting Restrictions

D24.77 **Excepting Directions** In *KL* [2021] EWCA Crim 200, Dame Victoria Sharp P (at [67]) summarised the relevant principles as follows:

(1) The general approach to be taken is that reports of proceedings in open court should not be restricted unless there are reasons to do so which outweigh the legitimate interests of the public in receiving fair and accurate reports of criminal proceedings and in knowing the identity of those in the community who have been guilty of criminal conduct.

(2) The fact that the person before the court is a child or young person will normally be a good reason for restricting reports of the proceedings in the way permitted by the legislation; and it will only be in rare cases that a direction under section 45(3) of the 1999 Act will not be given or, having been given, will be discharged.

(3) The reason why removal of a restriction will be rare is the very great weight that the court must give to the welfare of a child or young person. In practical terms, this means that the power to dispense with anonymity must be exercised with 'very great care, caution and circumspection' ...

(4) However, the welfare of the child or young person will not always trump other considerations. Even in the Youth Court, where the regime requires that proceedings should be held in private, with the public excluded, the court has power to lift restrictions. When a juvenile is tried on indictment in the Crown Court there is a strong presumption that justice takes place in open court and the press may report the proceedings.

(5) The decision for the trial judge is a case specific and discretionary assessment where, guided by the above considerations, a balance falls to be struck between the interests of the child and the wider public interest in open justice and unrestricted reporting.

(6) When considering a challenge to an excepting direction made by the Crown Court by way of judicial review, the Divisional Court will 'respect the trial judge's assessment of the weight to be given to particular factors, interfering only where an error of principle is identified, or the decision is plainly wrong' ...

(7) To this standard public law approach must be added the conventional public law requirements that: (i) a fair process should be adopted by the judge in considering an application to remove a restriction; and (ii) the judge should give reasons sufficient to explain why the balance has come

down in favour of removal of the restriction. This latter point is particularly important because the judge's reasons are the only indicator that the parties (and a reviewing court) will have to satisfy themselves that the judge has indeed performed a lawful balancing exercise.

Appeals against Orders In *KL* [2021] EWCA Crim 200, the Court of Appeal confirmed that, for the purposes of the SCA 1981, s. 29(3), the making of an excepting direction after conviction is not a matter relating to trial on indictment and is therefore amenable to judicial review (at [53]). However, the Court went on to hold that the Court of Appeal 'does not enjoy a concurrent jurisdiction with the Divisional Court to entertain freestanding appellate challenges to excepting directions'. Rather, it has a 'limited power' to consider an excepting direction as an ancillary matter when dealing with an appeal against conviction and/or sentence. The Court emphasised that this power is ancillary to an appeal: it does not exist unless and until leave to appeal has been granted, and it can never be invoked as the basis for an appeal to the Court of Appeal (at [60]). **D24.78**

SENTENCING POWERS AND PROCEDURE IN THE YOUTH COURT

Sending to Another Youth Court

The reference to the PCC(S)A 2000, s. 8, should be read as a reference to the SA 2020, s. 25(1) and (3). **D24.99**

Sentencing Code (Sentencing Act 2020, s. 25)

(1) This section applies where a person aged under 18 is convicted by or before a court ('the convicting court') of an offence other than homicide.

...

(3) If the convicting court is a youth court, it may remit the offender to another youth court.

Sentencing Powers where Accused Attains the Age of 18 after Finding of Guilt

Remission to an Adult Magistrates' Court The reference to the PCC(S)A 2000, s. 9, should be read as a reference to the SA 2020, s. 27. **D24.101**

Sentencing Code (Sentencing Act 2020, s. 27)

(1) Subsection (2) applies where a person who appears or is brought before a youth court charged with an offence subsequently reaches the age of 18.

(2) The youth court may, at any time after conviction and before sentence, remit the offender for sentence to a magistrates' court other than a youth court ('the adult court').

(3) Where an offender is remitted under subsection (2), the adult court may deal with the offender in any way in which it could deal with the offender if it had convicted the offender of the offence.

SENTENCING PROCEDURE AND POWERS IN THE CROWN COURT

Remission to the Youth Court

The reference to the PCC(S)A 2000, s. 8, should be read as a reference to the SA 2020, s. 25(1) and (2). **D24.104**

Sentencing Code (Sentencing Act 2020, s. 25)

(1) This section applies where a person aged under 18 is convicted by or before a court ('the convicting court') of an offence other than homicide.

(2) If the convicting court is the Crown Court, it must remit the offender to a youth court acting for the place where the sending court sat, unless satisfied that it would be undesirable to do so. The 'sending court' is the magistrates' court which sent the offender to the Crown Court for trial.

...

(8) Where an offender is remitted to a youth court under this section, that court may deal with the offender in any way in which it could deal with the offender if it had convicted the offender of the offence.

SENTENCING PROCEDURE AND POWERS IN THE ADULT MAGISTRATES' COURT

D24.108 The reference to the PCC(S)A 2000, s. 8, should be read as a reference to the SA 2020, s. 25.

Sentencing Code (Sentencing Act 2020, s. 25)

(1) This section applies where a person aged under 18 is convicted by or before a court ('the convicting court') of an offence other than homicide.

...

(4) If the convicting court is a magistrates' court other than a youth court—
   (a) it may remit the offender to a youth court, and
   (b) must do so unless subsection (5) applies.

(5) This subsection applies where the convicting court—
   (a) would be required by section 85(1)(a) to make a referral order if it did not remit the offender to a youth court, or
   (b) is of the opinion that the case is one which can properly be dealt with by means of—
      (i) an order for absolute discharge or an order for conditional discharge,
      (ii) a fine, or
      (iii) an order (under section 376) requiring the offender's parent or guardian to enter into a recognizance to take proper care of, and exercise proper control over, the offender,

   with or without any other order that the court has power to make when making an order for absolute discharge or an order for conditional discharge.

...

(8) Where an offender is remitted to a youth court under this section, that court may deal with the offender in any way in which it could deal with the offender if it had convicted the offender of the offence.

Section D25 Behaviour Orders: Civil Injunctions, CBOs, CPNs, PSPOs, Closure Notices, Closure Orders, SCPOs, VOOs, STROs, KCPOs and SPOs

CRIMINAL BEHAVIOUR ORDERS

Power to Make CBOs

D25.17 In *Brain* [2020] EWCA Crim 457, [2020] 2 Cr App R (S) 34 (237), the Court of Appeal emphasised that in considering whether to make a CBO the court at first instance is not entitled to take into account conduct that took place before 20 October 2013.

Terms of a CBO

D25.24 In *Brain* [2020] EWCA Crim 457, [2020] 2 Cr App R (S) 34 (237), the Court of Appeal held that a blanket ban on D using any internet-based social networking sites was too wide because it interfered with D's ability to carry out his employment. Accordingly it was amended to permit D to access social networking sites only for employment-related purposes.

Section D26 Appeal to the Court of Appeal (Criminal Division) Following Trial on Indictment

COMMONLY OCCURRING ERRORS RAISED ON APPEAL

Inconsistent Verdicts and Jury Irregularities

In *Gates* [2021] EWCA Crim 66, the Court of Appeal dealt with an appeal arising out of a conviction for conspiracy. D was the only person convicted of the alleged conspiracy by the jury. Some defendants pleaded guilty to substantive offences and others were acquitted by the jury. D alleged that the position rendered the verdict on him 'inconsistent' and his conviction unsafe. The Court of Appeal observed that the prosecution had always alleged that the conspiracy was an 'open' conspiracy, with persons unknown. Accordingly, there was no inconsistency in the verdict because it was open to the jury to conclude that D had conspired with a 'person or persons unknown'. **D26.28**

Section D27 Procedure on Appeal to the Court of Appeal (Criminal Division)

HEARING OF AN APPEAL

Practice in Usual Case

The question of whether an appellant has the right to argue orally all grounds of appeal on which leave has been given was considered in *Hamilton v Post Office* [2021] EWCA Crim 21. The proceedings were in connection with a number of conjoined appeals referred to the Court of Appeal by the CCRC which were founded on concerns about miscarriages of justice caused by prosecutions based on unreliable accounting software used by Post Office Ltd. The CCRC had referred the cases on two grounds. The respondents conceded the vast majority of the referred cases on the first ground without conceding the second ground. Three of the appellants whose cases had been conceded on the first ground of appeal claimed the right to argue the second ground even if the Court of Appeal quashed their convictions on the second ground. The Court of Appeal concluded that: **D27.22**

(a) It could not properly *dismiss* an appeal against conviction without first considering all the grounds of appeal (at [29]).
(b) There is a well-established practice that the court will sometimes allow an appeal against conviction on one ground without deciding, or hearing argument upon, another ground or grounds (at [32]) (see, e.g., *Berry (No. 3)* (1994) 99 Cr App R 88; *Mandair* [1995] 1 AC 208; *Mears* [2011] EWCA Crim 2651; *Sadeer* [2018] EWCA Crim 3000).
(c) In performing its statutory duty under the Criminal Appeal Act 1968, s. 2, the court must resolve all matters which are necessary to determine whether the convictions are unsafe but is not required to resolve matters which are not necessary to that resolution (at [33]).
(d) It follows that it will be for the court to decide to what extent it needs to hear submissions about a particular ground of appeal before finding that a conviction is unsafe. The court has the right and duty to regulate the way in which appeals are conducted before it. In all cases, therefore, it is for the court to decide whether it needs to hear argument on all grounds and, if so, in what sequence and in what degree of detail. Those will, necessarily, be case-specific decisions (at [33]).

The Court set out a non-exhaustive list of factors which may need to be taken into account when considering whether it is necessary or desirable in the interests of justice that a further ground should be determined, including (at [36]):

i) The article 6 rights of the appellant;
ii) The overall importance to the parties and to the public of the further ground, bearing in mind that the appeal will in any event be successful;
iii) The furtherance of the overriding objective in accordance with the Criminal Procedure Rules;

iv) Whether the additional ground raises issues of particular importance in relation to the character and/or reputation of the appellant and/or of a witness or other person concerned in the proceedings;
v) Whether the additional ground relates to an issue which should be resolved in order to maintain public confidence in the criminal justice system;
vi) Whether the additional ground raises a legal issue which may be important in other cases;
vii) The desirability of an appellant, even though his or her appeal will in any event succeed, being able to seek appropriate vindication;
viii) The time and expense which will be involved in determining the additional ground, and the extent to which the court's resources will be taken up, bearing in mind the interests of appellants in other, unrelated cases who wish their appeals to be heard;
ix) Whether determination of the additional ground would give rise to undesirable delay to the instant appeal, or to other cases which are in some way linked to it or affected by it;
x) Whether determination of the additional ground is necessary in order to establish the proper basis on which a retrial of an appellant would be conducted;
xi) Whether any party may have a collateral reason for wishing to argue, or to avoid having to argue, the additional ground, and if so, the legitimacy (or otherwise) of that reason.

Section D32 Public Funding

ADVICE AND ASSISTANCE, ADVOCACY ASSISTANCE AND REPRESENTATION ORDERS

Applying for a Representation Order in a Magistrates' Court and the Crown Court

D32.8 In calculating the amount of a capital contribution under reg. 28(4) of the Criminal Legal Aid (Contribution Orders) Regulations 2013 (SI 2013 No. 483) the 'amount or value of an individual's specified capital' is a single figure representing the aggregate of the amounts or values of the individual resources. There is no justification for the netting of a supposedly negative value on one resource against a positive value on another resource (*R (Lipman) v Director of Legal Aid Casework* [2020] EWHC 2668 (Admin)).

TOPPING UP CRIMINAL LEGAL AID FEES

D32.23 It should be noted that the Legal Aid Agency's *Criminal Legal Aid Manual* (10th edn), para. 9.5.3, indicates that even in the magistrates' courts a legally aided defendant may not privately instruct an advocate and that in any event this would lead to a reassessment of the defendant's means.

Section D33 Costs

PROSECUTION COSTS

Power to Make Order for Prosecution Costs from Central Funds

D33.23 The decision in *Somaia* [2019] EWHC 1227 (QB), [2019] 2 Cr App R 24 (253) was reversed by the Court of Appeal (Civil Division) in *Mirchandani v Lord Chancellor* [2020] EWCA Civ 1260, [2021] 1 Cr App R 7 (136). Private prosecutors seeking to enforce, in the civil courts, a confiscation order obtained in indictable proceedings, may obtain under s. 17 their costs of doing so.

SUPPLEMENT TO PART E
SENTENCING

Section E1 Sentencing: General Provisions

OVERVIEW OF SENTENCING CODE PROVISIONS

The Sentencing Act 2020 came into force (the 'commencement date') on 1 December 2020 (Sentencing Act 2020 (Commencement No. 1) Regulations 2020 (SI 2020 No. 1236)). **E1.1**

When re-sentencing an offender care must be taken in applying s. 402 of the Code. That section states that whenever a court has power to re-sentence an offender for an offence, the court may deal with the offender in any way in which it could deal with the offender if the offender had just been convicted by or before it of the offence. One implication of this is that if the sentencing powers of the court have been enhanced by statute at some point between the date of conviction of the offender and the date of re-sentencing, the additional powers of the court are available at re-sentencing. However, s. 402 is subject to the key application provision of s. 2 (set out in **E1.1** in the main work), which makes it clear that the Code only applies if the relevant conviction was on or after the commencement date (i.e. 1 December 2020). Section 402 also states that if the court is re-sentencing an offender who was aged under 18 when convicted, the re-sentencing court must deal with that offender as if he or she were the same age as when in fact convicted. Finally, of course, it must be borne in mind that Crown Court judges are subject to magistrates' courts powers if the original order was made by the lower court.

SENTENCING GUIDELINES

In *Long* [2020] EWCA Crim 1729, [2021] 4 WLR 5, a case involving the manslaughter of a police officer by three teenage offenders, the A-G applied to refer as unduly lenient sentences of 19 years in respect of one offender and 13 years in respect of the two others, arguing that the judge had erred in *failing to depart* from the applicable manslaughter guideline. The Court of Appeal said that an application on such a basis was 'unusual', and that no proper criticism could be made of the judge's approach to sentence or of his application of the guideline. **E1.5**

REQUIRED REDUCTIONS IN SENTENCE

Reduction in Sentence for a Guilty Plea

In *Hodgin* [2020] EWCA Crim 1388, [2020] 4 WLR 147, D was charged with conspiracy to burgle, a matter triable only on indictment. At the magistrates' court the Better Case Management form was completed by D's solicitor, and indicated 'likely guilty plea'. D was sent for trial, and at the PTPH admitted involvement in some of the burglaries. The sentencing judge observed that D's indication of 'likely guilty plea' was meaningless, but that D was entitled to a 25 per cent credit for admitting guilt at the PTPH. The Court of Appeal observed that where an indictable-only offence has been charged, and so it is not procedurally possible for D to enter a plea of guilty at the magistrates' court, there must instead be an *unequivocal indication* of D's intention to plead guilty. The Court approved the earlier decision in *Davids* [2019] EWCA Crim 553 [2019] 2 Cr App R (S) 33 (243), where the Court said that, when entering 'likely to be guilty pleas on a basis' on the Better Case Management form, D was keeping his options open and this was not an indication such as to entitle D to full credit for plea. The Court in *Hodgin* noted that in *Hewison* [2019] EWCA Crim 1278 an unofficial version of the Better Case Management form had apparently been used in the magistrates' court, and it was stressed that only the official version, approved by the Criminal Procedure Rule Committee, should be used. **E1.9**

In *Hussain* [2020] EWCA Crim 1514, D was charged with wounding with intent. In August there was discussion between counsel as to a potential plea to an offence under the OAPA 1861, s. 20, but that was not acceptable to the Crown and in September D simply entered a plea of not guilty to s. 18. By October the Crown had changed its position, and did accept a guilty plea to s. 20. D was accorded 10 per cent credit for plea, the judge applying the Sentencing Council's guideline, *Reduction in Sentence for a Guilty Plea*, para. F3 (see **SG5-7** in this supplement), and the decision in *West* [2019] EWCA Crim 497, [2019] 2 Cr App (S) 27 (209). The Court of Appeal upheld the decision of the judge, and said that D could have retained a greater credit for plea if he had made an unequivocal indication at an earlier stage of not guilty to s. 18 but guilty to s. 20, irrespective of the Crown's position at that time. See also *Bannergee* [2020] EWCA Crim 909, [2020] 2 Cr App R (S) 55, where the Court of Appeal took the same line in relation to D's failure to enter a prompt guilty plea to assault occasioning actual bodily harm to an indictment which charged s. 18 and s. 20 offences in the alternative. The Crown later accepted a plea to the s. 47 offence when it became clear that the injury caused to V had been less serious than initially thought. The fact that the Crown would not have accepted a plea of guilty to the lesser offence at the earlier stage was 'beside the point and irrelevant'. In *Stickells* [2020] EWCA Crim 1212, the Court of Appeal summarised the position thus (at [27]):

> The critical question is when and in what circumstances the defendant first indicates his intention to plead guilty to the offence in question and the mere fact that it has not been charged does not mean that full credit for plea will be preserved until it is. The position is most clear where there is a recognised alternative to the charged defence ... In such cases it is for the defendant to indicate his intention to plead to the lesser offence and in some cases it may be necessary for him to enter that plea to demonstrate the seriousness and irrevocability of that stated intention.

On the facts of *Stickells* itself, however, a case involving domestic violence, D pleaded guilty at the PTPH to two of the three offences charged, namely theft and taking a conveyance, but denied an offence of false imprisonment although he had accepted, initially at police interview, many of the facts underlying that charge. Following a change of representation, seven days later the parties agreed that a guilty plea would be entered to a new charge, of controlling and coercive behaviour. When the matter was re-listed, D pleaded guilty to that offence. The judge ordered a 20 per cent reduction for the guilty plea in relation to that matter, which had been 'denied initially and is now accepted'. The Court of Appeal said that the charge of coercive and controlling behaviour was not a straightforward alternative to a charge of false imprisonment and, although full credit was not appropriate in all the circumstances, the reduction given had been too small, and it was increased to 25 per cent.

The Court in *Hodgin* observed that in a case where a *Newton* hearing is set down for hearing and prepared for, but does not in the event proceed, the sentencing judge has discretion to decide what reduction, if any, should be made from the credit to which D would otherwise be entitled.

The Court of Appeal in *Williamson* [2020] EWCA Crim 1085, [2021] 1 Cr App R (S) 29 (223), held that where D was charged with conspiracy to rob, but had absconded before his initial appearance before the magistrates' court and was at large for several months, before being arrested on a warrant and pleading guilty at the PTPH, D could have no complaint that the credit accorded for his guilty plea was 10 per cent rather than 25 per cent. The Court added that if D has received a lesser discount for that reason the court should not impose an additional penalty for the Bail Act offence.

AGGRAVATING FACTORS

Previous Convictions

E1.15 The SA 2020, s. 65(4) to (6), make it clear that if proceedings for the current offence were instituted before 'IP completion day' (11 p.m. on 31 December 2020), 'relevant previous conviction' in this context means a previous conviction by a court in the UK or a previous conviction in another EU Member State of a 'relevant offence', or a previous conviction or finding of guilt of a Member State service offence (see the Taking Account of Convictions (EU Exit) (Amendment) Regulations (SI 2020 No. 1520)). In respect of proceedings instituted after that date, 'relevant previous conviction' means a previous conviction by a court in the UK or a previous conviction of a service offence within the meaning of the Armed Forces Act 2006.

In *Fothergill* [2019] EWCA Crim 2236, [2020] 2 Cr App R (S) 4 (21), the Court of Appeal approved the judge's decision to move up one category within the *Theft* guideline (see **SG33-1**) to reflect D's 'extensive previous convictions for similar offending' while also managing to keep the sentence proportionate to the offending.

DUTY TO GIVE REASONS FOR, AND EXPLAIN EFFECT OF, SENTENCE

The Court of Appeal in *Beckett* [2020] EWCA Crim 914, [2021] 1 Cr App R (S) 15 (123), said that although brevity in sentencing remarks was desirable (in line with the decision in *Chin-Charles* [2019] EWCA Crim 1140, [2020] 1 Cr App R (S) 6 (40); see **E1.24** in the main work), the judge's sentencing remarks in this case had been too brief and, in failing to refer to the applicable sentencing guideline while passing a sentence which fell outside that guideline, the judge had failed to comply with the SA 2020, s. 52 (then the CJA 2003, s. 174). **E1.24**

In *Bailey* [2020] EWCA Crim 1719, the Court of Appeal said that, in respect of the issue of totality (see **E13.22** in the main work), whether a judge had applied totality was a matter of substance rather than form, and it was not necessary that the judge should use the phrase 'just and proportionate' from the *Totality* guideline (see **SG4-1**). Sentencing remarks were not intended to amount to a test of drafting — they were intended to be succinct explanations of the facts and matters that had affected the judgement regarding the sentence to be imposed.

Failure to Comply

In *Rose* [2021] EWCA Crim 155, the judge imposed a determinate sentence of nine years for an offence of aggravated burglary. When announcing sentence the judge said that D would be required to serve half of the sentence in custody and would then be released on licence. That was incorrect, because by virtue of the Release of Prisoners (Alteration of Relevant Proportion of Sentence) Order 2020 (SI 2020 No. 158) D would be required to serve two-thirds of the sentence in custody (see **E13.26** in the main work). The error quickly came to light, and the judge reduced the sentence to seven years under the slip rule, saying that D had a 'legitimate expectation' that he would serve just half the sentence indicated. The Court of Appeal said that when a judge made a mistake of this kind no legitimate expectation arises requiring a reduction in the sentence. The sentence was therefore now unduly lenient, and was put back up to nine years. **E1.25**

Section E12 Community Orders

POWER TO MAKE A COMMUNITY ORDER

Community Order Requirements

The Court of Appeal in *Gregson* [2020] EWCA Crim 1529 found that the SA 2020, s. 208(10), had not been complied with (no requirement imposed for the purpose of punishment), and the exceptions in s. 208(11) did not apply, in a case where a community order with a rehabilitation activity requirement and an alcohol treatment requirement had been imposed for an offence of wounding with intent. The sentence was for that reason therefore unduly lenient, and was adjusted by inserting an additional requirement of 200 hours' unpaid work. **E12.9**

Unpaid Work Requirement In *Gregson* [2020] EWCA Crim 1529, the Court of Appeal referred to the problem of the probation service finding it difficult to provide unpaid work for offenders during a lockdown phase of the Covid-19 pandemic. The Court said that the best approach, if unpaid work was not available at the time of sentencing, was to order the work to be carried out within 12 months, as and when such work became available. **E12.11**

E12.24 **Alcohol Abstinence and Monitoring Requirement** The alcohol abstinence and monitoring requirement became generally available across Wales from 21 October 2020 and across England from 31 March 2021 but, even so, may not be ordered by a court unless the necessary arrangements, as specified by the Secretary of State, are in force in the local area (SA 2020, s. 207(1) and (2)). Monitoring is carried out by means of a transdermal electronic tag, which is a device fitted to an offender's leg to measure the level of alcohol contained in sweat. The tag does not provide curfew or tracking capability.

Section E13 Custodial Sentences: General Provisions

DETERMINATE CUSTODIAL SENTENCES AND EARLY RELEASE PROVISIONS

Relevance to Sentence of Early Release Provisions etc.

E13.27 In addition to the authorities cited in **E13.27** in the main work, see now *Rose* [2021] EWCA Crim 155, considered at **E1.25** in this supplement.

Section E14 Suspended Sentences

IMPOSITION OF REQUIREMENTS

E14.7 With regard to the alcohol abstinence and monitoring requirement see further E12.24 in this supplement.

Section E15 Custodial Sentences: Detention and Custody of Offenders under 18

DETENTION UNDER THE SENTENCING CODE (SA 2020, s. 250) (FORMERLY PCC(S)A 2000, s. 91)

Sentencing Principles

E15.7 In *Robinson* [2020] EWCA Crim 866, [2020] 2 Cr App R (S) 48 (345), the Court of Appeal made clear the continuing application of the principle stated in *AM* [1998] 1 All ER 874 that where an offender falls to be sentenced for an offence or offences which do qualify for a sentence under the SA 2020, s. 250 (formerly the PCC(S)A 2000, s. 91), and another offence or offences which do not, a term of detention commensurate with the seriousness of all the offences should be passed under s. 250 only on those offences which do qualify, and the court should order no separate penalty on those which do not.

Section E16 Life Sentences, Extended Sentences, Serious Terrorism Sentences and Custodial Sentences for Certain Offenders of 'Particular Concern'

EFFECT OF LIFE SENTENCE: MINIMUM TERM OR WHOLE LIFE ORDER

In addition to the authorities cited in **E16.31** in the main work, see now the case of *A-G's Refs (Nos. 688 of 2019 (McCann) and 5 of 2020 (Sinaga))* [2020] EWCA Crim 1676, [2021] 4 WLR 3, where the Court of Appeal said that the whole life minimum term should be reserved for cases of murder, except in the most exceptional circumstances, such as a plan to commit mass murder which did not succeed only because of some fortuitous intervening event. **E16.31**

Section 323(2)(b) (formerly s. 82A(3)(c))

In *Shaikh* [2021] EWCA Crim 45, the Court of Appeal noted that, as a result of the Terrorist Offenders (Restriction of Early Release) Act 2020 (see **E13.26** in the main work), an offender convicted of a qualifying terrorism offence and who received a determinate sentence would, rather than being released at the halfway point of that sentence, now be considered for early release at the two-thirds point of that sentence. The Solicitor General argued that, in the case of an offender convicted of a qualifying terrorism offence and receiving a life sentence, the minimum term should be set at two-thirds (rather than half) of the nominal determinate sentence. The Court of Appeal rejected that argument, observing that the only early release provision referred to in s. 323(2)(b) was the CJA 2003, s. 244(1) (release at the half-way point), and that to accede to the Solicitor-General's application would create a new rule in respect of qualifying terrorist offenders, and a policy change of that kind was a matter for Parliament. The Court noted that matters may be different in respect of the Release of Prisoners (Alteration of Relevant Proportion of Sentence) Order 2020 (SI 2020 No. 158) (see **E13.26** in the main work), since that Order stipulates that in cases to which the Order applies the definition of 'relevant custodial period' must be read as 'two-thirds' rather than 'one half'. **E16.34**

More generally, using a higher proportion than half of the nominal determinate sentence to fix the minimum term in a life sentence case had been done only rarely in the past, to address a particular feature of the offender or his or her sentencing history. Thus, in *A-G's Refs (Nos. 688 of 2019 (McCann) and 5 of 2020 (Sinaga))* [2020] EWCA Crim 1676, [2021] 4 WLR 3, the Court of Appeal held that life sentences with minimum terms of 30 years were unduly lenient in respect of 'two of the most serious multiple rape cases ever to be tried in England and Wales', and raised the minimum term to be served in the case of each offender to 40 years, a figure representing two-thirds of the nominal determinate sentence of 60 years. Lord Burnett CJ said (at [95]) that these 'were paradigms of the circumstances which justified a departure from the usual position of fixing the requisite custodial period at a half of the determinate term … to ensure that the proper requirements of punishment were met for their unique crimes'.

Section E19 Confiscation Orders

GENERAL

The Process: A Summary

The Court of Appeal held in *Westbrook* [2020] EWCA Crim 1243, [2020] 4 WLR 138 (at [39]), that there is nothing in the POCA 2002, s. 6(5), or any other section which suggests that a 'confiscation order' is invalid (in the sense of being a nullity) unless made in writing. The fact that, e.g., the CrimPR contemplate that a formal order will be drawn up and a copy sent to the parties does not mean that an order solemnly made by a judge has no legal existence unless and until drawn up in a formal written document. In this regard, orders made by judges under the POCA 2002 are no different from any other orders. The fact that there may be administrative **E19.4** delays or failures in resulting or drawing up the order does not mean that no order exists or came into existence when uttered by the judge.

As for the importance of the judge providing reasons to explain how he or she had approached and resolved issues in confiscation proceedings that were critical to the judge's conclusions, see *Ayensu* [2020] EWCA Crim 1569.

MAKING OF CONFISCATION ORDER

Stage Two — Determination of Benefit from Criminal Conduct

E19.25 **Individual Benefit** The Court of Appeal held in *Munir* [2020] EWCA Crim 1549, citing *May* [2008 UKHL 28, [2008] 1 AC 1028; *Sivaraman* [2008] EWCA Crim 1736, [2009] 1 Cr App R (S) 80 (469), and *Allpress* [2009] EWCA Crim 8, [2009] 2 Cr App R (S) 58 (399), that a defendant who receives property solely on behalf of another, who cannot be said to be receiving it for his or her own benefit, whether sole or joint, does not obtain such property for the purposes of s. 76(4) of the POCA 2002. The Court added that a person who receives property solely by way of possession on behalf of another and without obtaining a proprietary interest does not obtain the benefit of the value of the property within the meaning of the 2002 Act (at [15]). In *Munir*, D contended that since he was a mere custodian of controlled drugs, they did not constitute his property and thus their street value was not a 'benefit' to him. The Court concluded that D was (on the basis of his basis of plea) 'a mere custodian who did not receive the property for his own benefit whether jointly or solely. He received possession merely as a bailee' (at [16]). The Court reasoned (at [17], emphasis in original):

> A bailee has physical control of property by virtue of his possession. That physical control means that he may in fact sell it, or otherwise deal with it in a way which is contrary to the terms on which he has agreed to hold it. So, for example, a drug runner carrying out a delivery from a dealer to the user has physical control, so as to be able to sell it elsewhere or consume it himself, were he brave enough to do so. Section 76(4), however, focuses on *obtaining* property, and requires assessment of the circumstances governing what role the defendant was to play when he received the property. The mere fact that he received possession, and therefore physical control, is insufficient to amount to the obtaining of property as a benefit to him, recognised by s.76(4), if he was obtaining possession solely on behalf of another. It is for this reason that Lord Bingham observed that a mere custodian or courier would not ordinarily be treated as obtaining property. The fact that the obtaining of possession carries with it some degree of control does not alter the position. Of course, if he subsequently takes it upon himself to use his possessory control to obtain an actual benefit by, for example, selling the property for his own ends, he will at that stage obtain a benefit recognised by the 2002 Act which will be represented by the benefit which he obtains by selling it. But unless and until he does so, his mere possessory interest when holding the property is not a recognised benefit.

Note, by way of contrast, that in *Elsayed* [2014] EWCA Crim 333, [2014] 1 WLR 3916, the Court had rejected D's account that he was a 'mere temporary custodian'. In *Munir*, the Court remarked that the offences to which D pleaded guilty were possession of a controlled drug with intent to supply it (MDA 1971, s. 5(3)) and not ones of conspiracy (at [18]). Practitioners may therefore wish to contrast *Munir* with a case such as *Mejia* [2009] EWCA Crim 1940.

E19.26 **Pecuniary Advantage** The Court of Appeal held in *Ryder* [2020] EWCA Crim 1110 that the saving of costs, by failing to remove contaminated waste that was stored on a site owned and controlled by the appellants, in breach of the Environmental Permitting (England and Wales) Regulations 2010 (SI 2010 No. 675), can be a pecuniary advantage and thus a 'benefit' from criminal conduct (citing *Morgan* [2013] EWCA Crim 1307, [2014] 1 WLR 3450; *Rory J Holbrook Ltd* [2015] EWCA Crim 1908).

E19.28 **'As a result of'** *Sumal and Sons (Properties) Ltd v Newham London Borough Council* [2012] EWCA Crim 1840, [2013] 1 WLR 2078; *Palmer* [2016] EWCA Crim 1049, [2017] 4 WLR 15; *Hussain* [2014] EWCA Crim 2344 and *Del Basso* [2010] EWCA Crim 1119, [2011] Cr App R (S) 41 (268), were considered in *R (Haringey London Borough Council) v Roth* [2020] EWCA Crim 967, [2020] 4 WLR 130. D had obtained benefit, namely, the receipt of rents for 12 flats, as a result of or in connection with his criminal conduct in failing, for 53 months, to comply with remedial action required in an enforcement notice (contrary to the Town and

Country Planning Act 1990, s. 179(1) and (2)). See also *Bajaj* [2020] EWCA Crim 1111 as another example of problems that can arise when determining the value of benefit in respect of certain regulatory statutory regimes.

Stage Four — Determination of the Available Amount

For an example of the difficulties that can arise when, at the time that a confiscation order is made, the value of assets held by a defendant are 'agreed' on the mistaken assumption that it would be open to a court under the POCA 2002, s. 23, to reduce that value if it was subsequently shown that the assets did not exist at that time (consider *Younis* [2008] EWCA Crim 2950, [2009] 2 Cr App R (S) 34 (247)), see *Blackledge* [2020] EWCA Crim 1108. **E19.50**

Cramer (1992) 13 Cr App R (S) 390 (cited in the main work) was applied in *Lowther* [2020] EWCA Crim 1387, [2020] 4 WLR 152, which held that the costs of sale of any properties included in the benefit figure fell to be deducted against the defendant's realisable assets in calculating the 'available amount' (at [54]). There was no requirement to reduce the amount of the benefit figure, since at the benefit stage the market value of the property was what somebody would be prepared to pay for it on the open market, not the net proceeds of sale which the defendant would obtain from its sale (at [57], having cited, at [56], *Pattison* [2007] EWCA Crim 1536, [2008] 1 Cr App R (S) 51 (287)).

Third-party interests *Hilton* [2020] UKSC 29, [2020] 1 WLR 2945, was considered in *Forte* [2020] EWCA Crim 1455, [2021] 4 WLR 26. The Court of Appeal remarked that where the real issue at the confiscation stage is a third-party interest in property, then it may be convenient to deal with it under the POCA 2002, s. 10A, 'even if it is a significant issue' (at [11]): **E19.57**

> We doubt if the Supreme Court intended to give case management guidance to the Crown Court judges of England and Wales on the management of proceedings of this kind. Many of those judges will see an advantage in having one contested hearing at which all issues are resolved, rather than two contested hearings in each such case. If that is their view, then they are not inhibited from taking that course.

The proper classification of proceedings under s. 10A, as well as in respect of (i) the burden of proof; (ii) the standard of proof; and (iii) what the proper approach should be where a person could have given evidence in his or her own case, but elected not to, was that which applies to civil proceedings (at [14]–[15]).

In *Bevan* [2020] EWCA Crim 1345, [2021] 4 WLR 19, the prosecution contended, in relation to the s. 10A procedure, that under the principles of *Stack v Dowden* [2007] UKHL 17, [2007] 2 AC 432 and *Jones v Kernott* [2011] UKSC 53, [2012] 1 AC 776, the appraisal — when searching for the presumed intention of the parties as to their respective interests in property — has to be across the whole course of dealings, taking an objective viewpoint. The Court of Appeal did not doubt this to be right but added that the matter (on the facts in *Bevan*) was 'overtaken by the acceptance at the hearing below' and by the finding of the trial judge; that the mutual agreement from the outset was that there be equal ownership in the equity of the property, and that never altered (at [14]). The Court observed that although there are cases where the underlying beneficial interest can be at variance with the ostensible legal title (e.g., *Reid* [2019] EWCA Crim 690), the prosecution identified no statutory or other provision (where the tainted gift provisions were not invoked) whereby the legal and equitable rights could be adjusted in D's case, under the POCA 2002, Part 2, so as to cause such interests to be adjusted away from the legal and beneficial ownership and the parties' mutual agreement. The prosecution's argument was essentially one of 'fairness' or 'public policy', with regard to depriving a criminal of the proceeds of his or her criminality, as a means for altering the otherwise clear and established legal and equitable entitlements of the relevant owners. In any event, the argument was contrary to the decision in *Gibson v Revenue and Customs Prosecution Office* [2008] EWCA Civ 645, [2009] QB 348, which, although decided under the Drug Trafficking Act 1994, was equally applicable in the context of confiscation proceedings under the POCA 2002 (at [37]–[42]).

Stage Five — Proportionality

E19.61 **Proportionality and Abuse of Process** The Court of Appeal held in *Andrewes* [2020] EWCA Crim 1055 that, on the issue of proportionality, it is clear that the issue of disproportionality, by reference to the POCA 2002, s. 6(5), is to be assessed by reference to the making of a confiscation order: it is not to be assessed by reference to the amount of benefit (at [77]). The Court usefully explained the notion of 'proportionality' in the context of Part 2 of the POCA 2002, in terms of what the word 'disproportionate' does and does not connote. Thus, in respect of what 'disproportionality' does *not* connote (see [79]):

(1) It does not reintroduce by the 'back door' the notion of a residual judicial discretion. Section 6(5) is plainly founded on the lead judgment in *Waya* [2012] UKSC 51, [2013] 1 AC 294, which is specific on the point (at [24]). Moreover, in the POCA 2002, s. 10, limitations on the making of the criminal lifestyle statutory assumptions are permitted where there would be a 'serious risk of injustice' if the assumptions in question were made. But 'serious risk of injustice' is not the language of s. 6(5).
(2) An assessment of disproportionality is not to be made by a balancing of factors and competing interests in the way that may be appropriate in some public law or procedural law or family law contexts (see, e.g., *Morrison* [2019] EWCA Crim 351, [2019] 2 Cr App R (S) 25 at [67]).
(3) Disproportionality cannot, for these purposes, properly be assessed by reference to the proportion which the available amount bears to the benefit. Such an approach would be arbitrary and would be contrary to the scheme and purpose of the 2002 Act.

As to what the word 'disproportionality' *does* connote (see [80]–[86]):

(1) The answer is given by posing the notional question 'disproportionate to what?' The authorities, particularly *Waya*, make it clear that the assessment of disproportionality is made by reference to the aim of the 2002 Act, which is to deprive criminals of the proceeds of their criminality (at [81]).
(2) Where the criminal lifestyle provisions, or the tainted gift provisions, have been applied correctly, the outcome will only exceptionally be capable of being adjudged disproportionate. This is because the statutory provisions on criminal lifestyle (which also include an entitlement to disapply the assumptions) and on tainted gifts, are themselves geared to the objective of depriving criminals of the proceeds of their crimes (at [82]).
(3) The Supreme Court, in the cases of *Waya* and *Harvey* [2015] UKSC 73, [2017] AC 105, has eschewed approaching the issue of proportionality in confiscation proceedings under the 2002 Act in the way taken in the civil courts. Cases such as *de Freitas v Permanent Secretary of Ministry for Agriculture, Fisheries, Lands and Housing* [1999] 1 AC 69 and (post-*Waya*) *Bank Mellat v HM Treasury (No. 2)* [2013] UKSC 38, [2014] AC 700, are neither cited nor discussed in those cases. Rather, the underpinning for the assessment of whether the making of the confiscation order in the recoverable amount is disproportionate to the achievement of depriving criminals of the proceeds of crime, is indicated by reference to whether such an order will constitute a double recovery from (or a double penalty on) D: neither would achieve expropriation of the proceeds of D's crime (at [84]). A confiscation order is not designed to be a punishment, but is restorative, in the sense of requiring D to disgorge, to the extent possible, the product of the criminality (at [85]).
(4) The Supreme Court contemplated the possibility of cases of disproportion that are 'analogous' to those of the goods or money entirely restored to V (at [89]), e.g., *Sale* [2013] EWCA Crim 1306, [2014] 1 Cr App R (S) 60 (381); *King* [2014] EWCA Crim 621, [2014] 2 Cr App R (S) 54 (437); *Reynolds* [2017] EWCA Crim 1455, [2018] 4 WLR 33.
(5) Where disproportionality is being assessed by reference to arguments raised as to restoration (in whole or in part), the court ordinarily will need to be satisfied that the postulated restoration has been lawful.

As to the application of the concept of proportionality in respect of the turnover or gross profits of a business, it was stated in *R (Haringey London Borough Council) v Roth* [2020] EWCA Crim 967, [2020] 4 WLR 130 (per Davis LJ, at [58]):

> As stressed in cases such as *Waya*, the focus of the confiscation legislation is on what is obtained: not on what is retained. There may be some instances (of which *Sale* ..., is an example) where the vast majority of a particular business undertaking is lawful; and therefore it may, depending on the circumstances, be disproportionate to make a confiscation order in the amount of the entire turnover or gross profits of the business for the relevant period, when only a small part of its operation was tainted by the criminality in question. On the other hand, there will be cases where the entirety of the relevant turnover or gross profits can properly and proportionately be the subject of a confiscation order: see, for example, the discussion by Fulford LJ, giving the judgment of the court, in *King*.

Postponement

The principles to be derived from authorities such as *Guraj* [2016] UKSC 65, [2017] 1 WLR 22, and see *Johal* [2013] EWCA Crim 647, [2014] 1 WLR 146, make plain that, in the absence of specific evidence of unfairness to D, an advocate seeking to quash a confiscation order on the basis of delay beyond the two-year time-limit 'faces at least something of an uphill task' (*Ahmed* [2020] EWCA Crim 1396, per Coulson LJ at [14]). The Court of Appeal rejected the submission that because exceptional circumstances had not been the subject of an express finding at the last moment before the two-year period expired, that was fatal to the validity of the POCA 2002 proceedings thereafter. On the facts in *Ahmed*, even if time was not extended prospectively, it was properly extended retrospectively in accordance with the principles set out in *Johal*. Not only was a finding of exceptional circumstances permissible, it was all but inevitable. **E19.68**

ENFORCEMENT, RECONSIDERATION AND APPEALS

Reconsideration

Inadequacy *Younis* [2008] EWCA Crim 2950, [2009] 2 Cr App R (S) 34 (247), was cited in *Blackledge* [2020] EWCA Crim 1108. **E19.82**

Appeals

In *Ryder* [2020] EWCA Crim 1110, the Court of Appeal held that there could be no sensible reason to deprive D, who has an interest in property, of all right of challenge (by way of an appeal to the Court of Appeal) to a POCA 2002, s. 10A, determination. The Explanatory Notes to the Serious Crime Act 2015 (that inserted s. 10A into the 2002 Act) expressly contemplate such a right of appeal (at [46]). There was no reason to 'delimit' the wording of the POCA 2002, s. 31(5), which is broad (i.e., that it permits an appeal at the instance of 'a person who the Court of Appeal thinks is or may be a person holding an interest in the property, if' (s. 32(5)(b)) 'it appears to the Court of Appeal to be arguable that giving effect to the determination would result in a serious risk of injustice to the person' (s. 31(7)). **E19.83**

For a case in which adherence with the CrimPR was discussed, see *Court* [2021] EWCA Crim 242 (in this instance, CrimPR Part 39).

Section E20 Recommendation for Deportation

POWER TO RECOMMEND FOR DEPORTATION

Following the departure of the UK from the EU, at the end of the transition period (31 December 2020) the UK Borders Act 2007 was amended by the Immigration, Nationality and Asylum (EU Exit) Regulations 2019 (SI 2019 No. 745), which provided that, in s. 32, after 'British citizen' there is inserted 'or an Irish citizen', and that s. 33 is amended so as to create an additional exception to automatic deportation for persons lawfully resident in the UK before exit day, and where the offence occurred before that date. **E20.1**

Section E21 Exclusions and Disqualifications

SLAVERY AND TRAFFICKING PREVENTION ORDERS

E21.39 The Court of Appeal in *Wabelua* [2020] EWCA Crim 783, [2021] 1 Cr App R (S) 3, provided helpful guidance as to the principles which apply to the making of any STPO. The Court stressed the importance of the necessity test, not only to the making of the order itself, but also to the individual terms of the order. In many cases where the relevant risk is identified it will be necessary to make a STPO, but in determining whether an order is needed in a particular case the court must consider whether the risk is sufficiently addressed by the nature and length of the sentence imposed, and by the ability of a chief officer of police to apply for an order if it becomes necessary in the future. The terms of the STPO must be reasonable, proportionate and clear. The Court added that a draft order must always be provided to the court and to defence advocates in good time before the sentencing hearing.

Section E24 Rehabilitation of Offenders

EXCEPTIONS TO THE ACT

E24.5 The declarations of incompatibility in respect of P and Gallagher (multiple convictions) and G (reprimand) have been addressed, and appropriate amendments made, by the Police Act 1997 (Criminal Record Certificates: Relevant Matters) (Amendment) (England and Wales) Order 2020 (SI 2020 No. 1364), which came into force on 28 November 2020.

SUPPLEMENT TO PART F
EVIDENCE

Section F1 General Principles of Evidence in Criminal Cases

RELEVANCE

Delayed Complaints

Further to the *Crown Court Compendium*, ch. 20-1, see also the updated CPS legal guidance, *Rape and Sexual Offences* (19 October 2020, tinyurl.com/y2j265j3). **F1.15**

CIRCUMSTANTIAL EVIDENCE

Lies

In *Lucas* [1981] QB 720 at p. 724, Lord Lane CJ observed that: 'The jury should in appropriate cases be reminded that people sometimes lie, for example, in an attempt to bolster up a just cause, or out of shame or out of a wish to conceal disgraceful behaviour from their family'. Although the three potential explanations for the lie are a useful way of illustrating why a lie may not be supportive of guilt, a formula of this kind should only be used, as Lord Lane stated, 'in appropriate cases'. The examples given are not a magic formula to be deployed in every case regardless of the circumstances. Reference to them may be misleading, for example because shame may be an irrelevant consideration or there may be no relevant family. The judge should concentrate particularly on any explanation that has been given for the lie and direct the jury that they need to consider whether there may have been an innocent reason for the lie, using general examples only if that will assist (per Fulford LJ in *Wainwright* [2021] EWCA Crim 122 at [33]). **F1.25**

Section F2 Evidence Unlawfully, Improperly or Unfairly Obtained and the Discretion to Exclude Evidence

PACE 1984, s. 78

Overview

In *Boxall* [2020] EWCA Crim 688, relying on *Twigg* [2019] EWCA Crim 1553, [2019] 1 WLR 6533, it was said, *per curiam*, that exercise of the judgement under the PACE 1984, s. 78, although sometimes described as a discretion, is more properly described as an evaluative decision in ensuring that there is a fair trial in accordance with the ECHR, Article 6. **F2.7**

Application to Evidence Obtained Unlawfully, Improperly or Unfairly

'The Fairness of the Proceedings' The test under s. 78 will not normally be satisfied simply on the basis that the evidence in question is to be given by a witness whose credibility is open to challenge. Save exceptionally, issues relating to credibility, however far-reaching, are for advocates to investigate in cross-examination and otherwise and for the jury to resolve. Challenges to credibility are entirely different from those that are based on substantive unreliability or unjust prejudice, for instance because there has been a breach of the provisions of the PACE 1984 or the Codes of Practice or some other impropriety by those who obtained the evidence (per Fulford LJ in *Thomasson* [2021] EWCA Crim 114 at [31]). **F2.14**

Undercover Operations In *Sutherland v HM Advocate for Scotland* [2020] UKSC 32, [2020] 2 Cr App R 25 (401), where entrapment was not in issue, the question arose whether the obtaining of evidence from D by undercover operations carried out by individuals acting on their own initiative and the use of such evidence at trial interferes with D's rights under the ECHR, Article 8 (respect for private life and correspondence). An adult member of a 'paedophile hunter' group, acting as a decoy, created a false profile on an online dating app in order to attract communications from those with a sexual interest in children. D entered into **F2.18**

F

Part F Evidence

communications with the decoy, who said that he was aged 13. Copies of the communications were passed to the police and introduced at D's trial. It was held that there had been no interference with D's rights under Article 8 by reason of either the collection of the evidence of the communications or the use of the evidence at trial.

F2.23 **Undercover Operations after Commission of the Offence** Further to *King* [2012] EWCA Crim 805, see also *Bond* [2020] EWCA Crim 1596 where evidence of a covertly recorded conversation between co-accused, obtained in breach of the surveillance provisions of the RIPA 2000, was held to have been properly admitted. The officers had acted in good faith, relying on an authority apparently properly given. They had not sought to circumvent the rights of the co-accused. The evidence had not been obtained through oppression, inducement, misrepresentation, entrapment or lies; what the co-accused had said, they said of their own free will.

F2.24 Further to *Khan* [2013] EWCA Crim 2230, see also *Bond* [2020] EWCA Crim 1596, considered at **F2.23** in this supplement.

INTERCEPTIONS OF COMMUNICATIONS

F2.33 In *A* [2021] EWCA Crim 128 at [18], it was doubted, *obiter*, whether handsets ordinarily form part of a public telecommunications 'system' for the purposes of the IPA 2016.

F2.34 A communication intercepted at the time of its transmission must be distinguished from one recovered from storage, e.g. storage on a handset; the former will be inadmissible, but the latter admissible, provided that an appropriate warrant was in place (see *A* [2021] EWCA Crim 128 and the IPA 2016, s. 4(4) and the exception to s. 56 in sch. 3, para. 2).

Section F3 Burden and Standard of Proof and Presumptions

BURDEN OF PROOF

Incidence of the Legal Burden: the Human Rights Act 1998

F3.36 **Regulatory Offences** *Davies v Health and Safety Executive* [2002] EWCA Crim 2949 was followed in *AH Ltd* [2021] EWCA Crim 359.

STANDARD OF PROOF

Usual Direction where Legal Burden on the Prosecution

F3.49 In *Broughton* [2020] EWCA Crim 1093, [2021] 1 Cr App R 3 (25), it was said (at [100]): 'It is unhelpful to attempt to contrast scientific certainty (put at 100%) with a different figure for legal certainty. Human beings asked whether they are sure of something do not think in those terms.' However, in *Broughton*, expert opinion evidence on the issue of causation, cast in percentage terms, led to the conclusion that the criminal standard could not be met. The charge was gross negligence manslaughter and the prosecution, in order to establish guilt, had to make the jury sure that at the time when V's condition was such that there was a serious and obvious risk of death, D was grossly negligent in failing to obtain medical assistance and that such assistance would have saved her life. The only evidence dealing with causation was that of an expert who gave evidence that had medical assistance been available there was a 90 per cent chance of survival. It was held that this evidence was not capable of establishing causation to the criminal standard and therefore, applying the test in *Galbraith* [1981] 1 WLR 1039, the case should have been withdrawn from the jury.

PRESUMPTIONS

Presumption as to Working of Mechanical and Other Instruments

F3.59 In *DPP v Marrable* [2020] EWHC 566 (Admin), it was held that:

(a) a TRUCAM device approved by the Secretary of State for the purposes of speed measurement is presumed to be accurate and reliable;
(b) the evidence required to rebut the presumption is evidence of a technical nature that the device was not operating correctly or evidence that the device was not operated correctly; and
(c) in order to rebut the presumption, although D's opinion of his or her speed, by itself, is insufficient, it may suffice if supported by unopposed evidence of a printout from a GPS tracking device that has been fitted to D's vehicle.

In *Ali v DPP* [2020] EWHC 2864 (Admin), [2020] 4 WLR 146, it was confirmed that a breath specimen machine is presumed to be reliable; that an accused against whom the presumption operates has an evidential burden to adduce sufficient relevant evidence to the contrary; and that if such evidence is adduced, the burden is on the prosecution to establish, to the criminal standard, that the machine is reliable.

Section F5 Corroboration and Care Warnings

CARE WARNINGS

An Accomplice who is a Co-accused

Jones [2003] EWCA Crim 1966, [2004] 1 Cr App R 5 (60), was distinguished in *Binoku* [2021] EWCA Crim 48, where there was no need to give a direction is respect of a co-accused whose evidence had not undermined the case of the accused. **F5.13**

Section F6 Examination-in-chief

PREVIOUS COMPLAINTS

The conditions set out in the CJA 2003, s. 120(4) and (7), do not have to be met where evidence of a complaint is introduced not as evidence of what was stated but for some other reason, e.g. as evidence of the complainant's inconsistency (*KH* [2020] EWCA Crim 1363 at [53]–[55]). Nor do the conditions need to be met if the evidence of complaint is introduced in order to rebut an allegation of recent fabrication and is admissible under the CJA 2003, s. 120(2), as evidence of what was stated (*KH* at [60]–[64]). **F6.32**

Section F7 Cross-examination and Re-examination

CROSS-EXAMINATION: GENERAL CONSIDERATIONS

Role of the Judge during Cross-examination

It is not the judge's function to cross-examine, but not every departure from good practice, in this respect, will render the trial unfair. However, there comes a point when such a departure is so gross or so persistent or so irremediable that the trial becomes unfair and a conviction has to be quashed (*Binoku* [2021] EWCA Crim 48). **F7.6**

Useful guidance is also to be found in the civil authorities. They establish that judicial interventions, during cross-examination, should be as infrequent as possible. They also establish that although trial judges are now much more proactive and interventionist than they used to be, interventions during the giving of evidence, as opposed to during final submissions, generate a risk of their descent into the arena, which should be assessed not by whether it gives rise to an appearance of bias in the eyes of the fair-minded observer, but by whether it renders the trial unfair. Those who are unrepresented present the court with well-known challenges.

The judge's conduct must take account of the fact that those appearing in person are unlikely to be equipped, as professional advocates generally are, to withstand a degree of judicial pressure (*Serafin v Malkiewicz* [2020] UKSC 23, [2020] 1 WLR 2455). As to those appearing in person, see also the *Equal Treatment Bench Book* (February 2021), ch. 1.

In *Mustafa* [2020] EWCA Crim 1723, the Court approved the following principles as set out by the Court of Appeal (Civil Division) in *Serafin v Malkiewicz* [2019] EWCA Civ 852 at [108]–[110] under the heading 'The principle of fairness':

(1) It is a fundamental tenet of the administration of law that all those who appear before the courts are treated fairly and that judges act — and are seen to act — fairly and impartially throughout the trial.
(2) It is a duty of a judge to intervene in the course of witness evidence 'to ask questions which clarify ambiguities in answers previously given or which identify the nature of the defence, if this is unclear' (per Rose LJ in *Tuegel* [2000] 2 Cr App R 361).
(3) It is wrong for a judge 'to descend into the arena and give the impression of acting as advocate' (per Lord Parker CJ in *Hamilton* (9 June 1969 unreported), cited in *Hulusi* (1973) 58 Cr App R 378 at p. 382).

In *Mustafa*, the scale and content of the judicial interventions were held to be inimical to the adversary system, leading to the conclusion that D had not been fairly tried. The conviction was therefore quashed, notwithstanding that the judge's summing-up was beyond criticism and that there was ample evidence to sustain a conviction.

RULES GOVERNING CONDUCT OF CROSS-EXAMINATION

Cross-examination as to Credit

F7.21 Concerning false assumptions about complainants in sexual cases and further to the *Crown Court Compendium*, ch. 20-1, see also the updated CPS legal guidance, *Rape and Sexual Offences* (19 October 2020, tinyurl.com/y2j265j3).

PROTECTION OF COMPLAINANTS IN PROCEEDINGS FOR SEXUAL OFFENCES

Rationale

F7.26 Evidence or questioning about the complainant's sexual behaviour which involves speculation or is simply irrelevant to any issues in the case will be inadmissible on ordinary evidential principles (*T* [2021] EWCA Crim 318).

The Restriction

F7.28 It is submitted that 'the complainant' in the YJCEA 1999, s. 41, means the complainant as specified in the indictment and therefore does not cover a different complainant in a previous trial, as was suggested by the trial judge in *Philo-Steele* [2020] EWCA Crim 1016 (at [60]).

Sexual identity and sexual orientation may suggest sexual activity or constitute sexual experience and therefore in appropriate circumstances may fall within the definition of 'sexual behaviour' in s. 42(1)(c) (*T* [2021] EWCA Crim 318).

Previous False Complaints

F7.30 Where it is alleged that the complainant has made a previous false complaint of a sexual offence and the court has granted leave to cross-examine under the CJA 2003, s. 100(4), it may also be necessary to make an application under s. 41. There are two principal possibilities. First, the accused may wish to rely on the false allegation not only in relation to the credibility of the accused but for some other reason that is covered by s. 41. Second, the questions and evidence may stray outside the narrow confines of whether a previous allegation was false and into matters relating to the complainant's sexual behaviour, although it is likely that the wider questions and evidence will fall foul of s. 41(4) (*Fichardo* [2020] EWCA Crim 667 at [35]).

In *Garaxo* [2005] EWCA Crim 1170, it was held that there would be a proper evidential basis for asserting that a previous complaint was false if there was material such that, depending on the answers given by the complainant in cross-examination, 'the jury could have been satisfied that the previous complaint was untrue' (at [14]). In *Fichardo* [2020] EWCA Crim 667, it was observed at [30] that the phrase 'depending on the answers given by the complainant in cross-examination' cannot be relied upon as permitting speculative cross-examination in the hope that the complainant might admit a previous falsehood. See also, *sed quaere*, the Court's further observation, *obiter*, that in cases where the complainant is cross-examined and denies having made the suggested false allegation, the jury should be directed that the burden is on the accused to prove on the balance of probabilities that the allegation was made and is false. **F7.31**

Section 41(3)(a): A Relevant Issue Other than Consent

The example in (b) (per Lord Hope in *A (No. 2)* [2001] UKHL 25, [2002] 1 AC 45 at [79]), that the complainant had a motive to fabricate the evidence, calls for care. In some circumstances, the evidence of sexual behaviour may be properly admissible, even where this brings into play questions of credibility, but not where it is, in truth, an obfuscation of the real or main purpose to undermine a complainant's credibility (*T* [2021] EWCA Crim 318). **F7.37**

As to the example in (d), that principle cannot apply where there is no similarity between the other sexual activity and the sexual activity as alleged in the case; nor can it apply where the sexual activity alleged in the case is so unexceptional that someone of the complainant's age could be expected to know about it, e.g. an attempt to remove underwear in order to touch the complainant (*Philo-Steele* [2020] EWCA Crim 1016 at [45] and [49]).

Section F8 Documentary Evidence and Real Evidence

PROOF OF PUBLIC AND JUDICIAL DOCUMENTS

Births, Deaths and Marriages

Although age may be proved by inference from appearance, it is difficult to assess the age of young people in the absence of documentary evidence, especially the closer the person is to 18 years; physical attributes and demeanour are fragile material on which to base an assessment of age (*R (AB) v Kent County Council* [2020] EWHC 109 (Admin) at [43]). **F8.24**

REAL EVIDENCE

Photographs, Video Recordings and Films

Admissibility as Hearsay or Real Evidence In *Thomasson* [2021] EWCA Crim 114, it was confirmed that the reasoning in *Cook* [1987] QB 417 and *Constantinou* (1989) 91 Cr App R 74 has been superseded by the definition of a 'statement' in the CJA 2003, s. 115(2), which includes 'a representation made in a sketch, photofit or other pictorial form'. It was held that 'other pictorial form' plainly covers E-Fit pictures. **F8.61**

Section F9 Public Policy

GENERAL PRINCIPLES

Where a PII certificate has been issued by a senior official, such as a permanent under-secretary of state, it carries no less force than a certificate issued by a minister (*R (Dunn) v Secretary of State for Foreign and Commonwealth Affairs* [2020] EWHC 3010 (Admin)). **F9.3**

Concerning *Balfour v Foreign and Commonwealth Office* [1994] 2 All ER 588, in relation to cases concerning national security, see also *R (Dunn) v Secretary of State for Foreign and Commonwealth Affairs*, which is considered in this respect at **F9.11** in this supplement.

HEADS OF PUBLIC INTEREST IMMUNITY

National Security, Diplomatic Relations and International Comity

F9.11 Despite what was said in *Balfour v Foreign and Commonwealth Office* [1994] 2 All ER 588, it is submitted that where there is a ministerial or departmental certificate that disclosure will cause serious harm to national security, it is more accurate to say, not that it is 'conclusive', but that it is likely to carry such weight as to be almost always conclusive. In *R (Dunn) v Secretary of State for Foreign and Commonwealth Affairs* [2020] EWHC 3010 (Admin), the Divisional Court gave such a certificate 'substantial weight' but reached its own view, on the usual balance of competing interests, that the PII claim should succeed.

Section F10 Privilege

LEGAL PROFESSIONAL PRIVILEGE

Legal Advice Privilege

F10.24 **Joint Interest Legal Professional Privilege** Joint privilege is a principle of procedure and evidence rather than trust law. Under the principle, no privilege attaches to communications between solicitor and client as against persons having a joint interest with the client in the subject matter of the communication. Thus there is no privilege as between partners, a company and its shareholders or trustee and beneficiary (*Dawson-Damer v Taylor Wessing LLP* [2020] EWCA Civ 352, [2020] 3 WLR 1).

Section F11 Opinion Evidence

EXPERT OPINION EVIDENCE

Competence of Expert Witnesses

F11.4 Further to *Pabon* [2018] EWCA Crim 420 at [77], see also *Byrne* [2021] EWCA Crim 107 at [101]: 'the Crown must take all necessary steps to ensure that inappropriate expert witnesses are not called in criminal trials'.

F11.5 For a further example of expertise derived from experience, see also *Byrne* [2021] EWCA Crim 107 (experience in the financial, commodity and carbon credit markets).

Matters Calling for Expertise

F11.8 Further to *Calland* [2017] EWCA Crim 2308, see *Turner* [2020] EWCA Crim 1241, where it was held that, concerning attribution of a particular mobile phone to a particular person, a non-expert may give evidence of data relating to the frequency with which a number used a mast and the position of the mast relative to that person's home address, but whether the mast serves the address requires the evidence of an expert in radio frequency.

The findings of a decision-maker of the Home Office Single Competent Authority that a person has been trafficked for the purposes of exploitation are admissible as expert evidence. The factors relevant to trafficking and exploitation are not necessarily within the knowledge of the ordinary person; the decision-maker has the necessary expertise to assess the significance of such factors present in a particular case and to give context to them by reference to their wider expertise of other cases (*DPP v M* [2020] EWHC 3422 (Admin), [2021] 1 WLR 1669, currently on appeal to the Supreme Court). See further **B22.29** in this supplement.

In *Land* [1998] 1 Cr App R 301, a case of possession of indecent photographs of children, it was held, *obiter* (at [306]), that expert evidence is inadmissible on the question whether a photograph depicts a person under the age of 16, because it is not an issue outside the normal experience and knowledge of the jury. In *RT* [2020] EWCA Crim 1343, [2021] 1 Cr App R 14 (282), in which it was unnecessary to decide whether expert evidence is admissible on the age of a person shown in a photograph or film in the normal case where the subject's face is shown, it was held that such evidence is admissible where the photograph or film shows only the lower half of the subject's body. **F11.9**

Duty of Lawyers

Further to *Pabon* [2018] EWCA Crim 420, see also *Byrne* [2021] EWCA Crim 107, considered at F11.4 in this supplement. **F11.36**

Content of Expert's Report

The justification for applying to introduce expert evidence must be set out in sufficient detail in the report. If the opinion in the report is of a general nature and fails to focus on the specific issues in the case, it will be inadmissible and the judge should not hold a *voir dire* to allow the expert to raise new issues or provide greater detail on the issues raised in the report (*Dunleavy* [2021] EWCA Crim 39). **F11.40**

Function and Weight of Expert Evidence

Further to *DPP v Wynne* [2001] EWHC 21 (Admin), see *Ali v DPP* [2020] EWHC 2864 (Admin), [2020] 4 WLR 146, where it was held that the district judge had been entitled to reject the unchallenged evidence of an expert concerning the calibration of a breath specimen machine on the grounds that it was speculative: he had not examined the machine or its calibration records but based his opinion on a document that was 20 years old and did not refer to a specific device. **F11.42**

Section F12 Admissibility of Previous Verdicts

RELEVANCE AND ADMISSIBILITY OF PREVIOUS NON-JUDICIAL FINDINGS

Where there has been a non-judicial finding on a fact that is in issue in subsequent criminal proceedings, the finding may be relevant and admissible but will not be conclusive. Thus a Home Office conclusion that a person was a victim of human trafficking will not bind a criminal court. The court will bear the finding very much in mind, but will examine the cogency of the evidence that was relied upon and subject it to forensic examination. It does not follow from the fact that an individual fits the profile of a victim of trafficking that he or she is necessarily the victim of trafficking (*BTT* [2021] EWCA Crim 4). See further B22.29 and F11.8 in this supplement. **F12.24**

Section F13 Character Evidence: Evidence of Bad Character of Accused

EVIDENCE OF BAD CHARACTER UNDER THE CJA 2003

Notice Requirements

In *Grieves* [2020] EWCA Crim 1703, a defence witness was being cross-examined as to whether D had pressured her to give false evidence, which she denied, and she was then asked whether he had been violent towards her in the past. The Court of Appeal noted that it was unfortunate that the question had been put without any application to adduce evidence of bad character **F13.3** having been made (see further, as to the effect of a surprise revelation of bad character, **F13.86** in this supplement).

Bad Character

F13.10 **'Has To Do With' Alleged Facts** In *Byrne* [2021] EWCA Crim 107, the Court of Appeal endorsed what was said in *McNeill* [2007] EWCA Crim 2927 about the need to construe the words 'has to do with the alleged facts of the offence' in the CJA 2003, s. 98(a), in light of the overall context of the bad character provisions in the Act and the restrictions or protections they contain. The context was an application by a co-accused under the gateway in s. 101(1)(e) which is intended to provide an appropriate level of protection for the person against whom bad character evidence is sought to be adduced by a co-accused (see **F13.66** ***et seq.*** in the main work). The charges concerned conspiracy to defraud by a company, and the evidence related to the misconduct of the accused against whom the application was made in relation to a different company, which was said to show his knowledge of relevant matters. The evidence did not have a sufficient nexus with the matter charged to be admissible under s. 98(a) and admissibility fell to be decided under s. 101(1)(e) (see further **F13.68** in this supplement).

EVIDENCE OF BAD CHARACTER ADDUCED BY PROSECUTION TO PROVE GUILT OR UNTRUTHFULNESS

CJA 2003: Admissibility under s. 101(1)(d)

F13.39 **Propensity as an Issue** In *CN* [2020] EWCA Crim 1028, the accused were convicted of murder. V had suffered multiple stab wounds and the medical evidence suggested that more than one weapon could have been involved, but no knives were found. D3 admitted stabbing V but claimed it was in self-defence. D1 and D2 denied stabbing. Both had previous convictions for possession of knives that were admitted as evidence of propensity, and evidence was given of an incident two weeks before in which one had held a knife and the other had threatened to stab V. On appeal it was contended that eye-witnesses to the attack who testified to the participation of D1 and D2 did not clearly state that they had seen either youth use a knife. The prosecution did not specifically allege that either had in fact stabbed — the case was put on the broader ground that they had actively participated in the attack with the necessary intention for murder. On appeal it was contended that the lack of specificity in the prosecution case and the testimony of the eye-witnesses meant that the evidence of propensity should not have been admitted. The Court of Appeal disagreed: it was wrong to 'restrict the judge's parameters to consideration of individual eyewitness accounts' (at [18]). Looking at the evidence as a whole, including the scientific evidence of the possible use of multiple weapons, the judge was justified in seeing the bad character evidence as probative of a central issue in the case, and it could not be said that it was introduced to 'bolster' a weak prosecution case.

F13.40 **Demonstrating Propensity** In *Gabbana* [2020] EWCA Crim 1473, [2020] 4 WLR 160, the Court of Appeal considered that the principles regarding the standard of proof laid down by the Supreme Court in *Mitchell* [2016] UKSC 55, [2017] AC 571, apply for the purposes of evidence admitted under any gateway in the CJA 2003, s. 101, where a disputed issue as to bad character arises for the jury to determine. In *Gabbana* the disputed evidence concerned deposits and withdrawals from D's accounts, and whether they were suggestive of criminal activity and hence of bad character. The application was made under s. 101(1)(f) on the ground that D had given the false impression that his income derived from a compensation payment. The judge's direction complied with the *Mitchell* principles in that the jury would have understood that the matter of whether the money came from a legitimate source was for them to decide, and that it was necessary for them to be sure that it did not before treating the evidence as displaying criminal propensity.

EVIDENCE OF BAD CHARACTER ADDUCED BY A CO-ACCUSED

CJA 2003: Evidence of Bad Character Going to Matter in Issue Between Co-Accused

Substantial Probative Value In *Byrne* [2021] EWCA Crim 107, D1 and D2 were directors of a company and both were alleged to have been involved in a conspiracy to defraud. D2's defence was that D1 was, and he was not, involved with the day-to-day running of the company. D1 sought to introduce an undertaking made by D2 under the Company Director Disqualification Act 1986 arising from misconduct in relation to a company which had operated a similar business model, which was said to suggest a level of knowledge and involvement inconsistent with D2's defence. The Court of Appeal held, applying *Phillips* [2011] EWCA Crim 2935, [2012] 1 Cr App R 25 (332), that the trial judge had correctly ruled that, while the issue of D2's involvement was an important one between D1and D2, the undertaking was not of substantial probative value in resolving it. It was not akin to a conviction nor did it amount to an admission of relevant knowledge on the part of D2, and no further evidence was available to resolve the issue. The Court held (at [145]): **F13.68**

> There is a difference between a court being asked to admit bad character evidence which itself has substantive probative value in relation to a matter of substantial importance, as opposed to evidence which, even taken as a whole, is equivocal or inadequate. In the former case the fact that evidence meeting the test for admissibility under gateway (e) may give rise to satellite litigation does not provide a basis for its exclusion. Instead, the potential problem of satellite litigation is a matter for case management so that the matter is dealt with proportionately, applying, for example, the guidance in Phillips at [59]. In the latter case, the CJA 2003 does not envisage that the lack of substantive probative value may be cured by satellite litigation.

EVIDENCE OF BAD CHARACTER TO CORRECT FALSE IMPRESSION OR COUNTER ATTACK ON ANOTHER'S CHARACTER

Examples of False Impression

In *Biffa Waste Services Ltd* [2020] EWCA Crim 827, the appellant company had been convicted of transporting contaminated waste material intended for export to a paper recycling facility in China. The contested issue at trial was whether the contaminants exceeded the permissible level. In his evidence-in-chief, the company's chief operating officer testified both to the awards won by the company in relation to health and safety and to its charitable works, and went on to assert that the company took its moral responsibility to protect the environment extremely seriously. The Court of Appeal held that there could be no objection to the judge's decision that this gave a false impression of the company's environmental track record, as it was apt to suggest that it would be at odds with its business standards and ethics for it to have committed environmental offences when in fact there were 14 previous convictions for environmental regulatory offences. It was not possible to justify the evidence given by the chief operating officer on the basis that it was necessary in order to put forward the appellant's defence to the allegation that the waste had not been sorted at all. The judge had been careful to exclude evidence of further health and safety offences that were not necessary to correct the specific false impression. **F13.81**

'Attack on Another Person's Character'

In *Yayare* [2020] EWCA Crim 1314, [2020] 4 WLR 156, the Court of Appeal rejected an argument that D's bad character should not be put in evidence unless it appeared that D was the 'author' of the attack. A police officer who had led the investigation into violent incidents involving a group of men had given evidence of identification of D based on many hours of observation of CCTV images. In cross-examination it was suggested that she had not made a dispassionate and impartial assessment of the evidence; that she had not told the truth about the time she had spent viewing the footage; and that she did not care whether she had made a correct identification because she was so invested in the case that she simply wanted a result. 'In summary, the suggestion was that she was intent on getting a conviction and keeping her **F13.84** reputation intact' (at [101]). The CJA 2003, s. 106, makes it clear that the introduction of D's bad character is not dependent on either D giving evidence or having 'personal knowledge' of the matters that constitute the attack. Instead, it is sufficient that D's advocate asks questions in order to elicit evidence that the witness has behaved, or is disposed to behave, in a reprehensible way. Although D's previous offences related to previous incidents of violence, evidence of them provided context to the allegations against the police officer and they were not so prejudicial as to require the exercise of the judge's discretion under s. 101(3).

F13.86 **'Attack'** Where the court is taken by surprise by a revelation about the character of the accused made by a witness under cross-examination, the judge must consider the nature and extent of any prejudice to the defence, taking account of the importance of the evidence and its likely effect, in the context of the case as a whole, and the extent to which it can be corrected by a direction to ignore it. In *Grieves* [2020] EWCA Crim 1703, it was suggested to a defence witness that D had pressured her to lie, and she was then asked, without a bad character application having been made, whether D had been violent towards her in the past. She agreed that he had. The assertion went only to a marginal matter in the case, and although it should not have been solicited, and occasioned some prejudice, the judge understandably took the view that the matter could be dealt with by a clear and firm direction to disregard it.

Section F14 Admissibility of Evidence of Accused's Good Character

MEANING OF GOOD CHARACTER

Absolute and Effective Good Character

F14.7 **Effective Good Character** In *KH* [2020] EWCA Crim 1363, the Court of Appeal once again stressed the importance of the discretion of the trial judge in deciding how to formulate a modified good character direction. D1 and D2 were tried for serious sexual offences involving D2's underage daughter. The offences were over 30 years old. D2 was of good character but D1 had a conviction for theft from around the time of the alleged sexual offending. The defence put the conviction in evidence, so the trial judge was bound to deal with it. She treated D1 as a man of effective good character and said that the fact that he had not committed any offences similar to those with which he was now charged may mean that he was less likely to have committed the offences with which he was now charged. She then directed the jury that they were entitled to take the conviction into account when assessing D1's credibility. The Court of Appeal rejected the criticism of the credibility limb: the direction was within the trial judge's discretion. Further, if defence advocates do not take a point on the character direction at trial and/or if they agree with the judge's proposed directions which are then given, these are 'good indications that nothing was amiss' (citing *Hunter* [2015] EWCA Crim 631, [2015] 1 WLR 5367 at [98]).

Section F15 Character Evidence: Evidence of Bad Character of Persons Other than the Accused

CJA 2003, s.100: GATEWAYS TO ADMISSIBILITY

Evidence of Substantial Probative Value in Relation to Matter in Issue of Substantial Importance

F15.16 **Matters Relevant to Assessment of Probative Value** *Mohammed* [2021] EWCA Crim 201 was an unusual case in that the probative value of the evidence of bad character derived from an argument about coincidence rather than the nature of the previous offence. D had been convicted of two sexual assaults. The description of the attacker and his bicycle was very similar to that provided by other victims of similar assaults in the vicinity that remained unsolved. A mobile phone had been found at the scene of one of the offences of which D was convicted, which V thought might have been used in the assault to simulate a metal weapon. Some years later DNA on the phone was matched to S. S fitted the description of the attacker, and the Court of Appeal admitted the DNA evidence as fresh evidence, together with evidence of S's bad character relating to a caution for committing an act outraging public decency by behaving indecently in public with a sex worker. S had a mountain bike with him at the time of his arrest. Although this offence, being consensual, was different in nature, it helped to rebut the coincidence that S, a man who matched the description of the attacker, and who rode a bicycle, had innocently dropped his mobile phone at the scene of an assault committed by another man who might then have used it in connection with the assault. Although S's caution was not of itself determinative of his guilt, it was of substantial probative value and further 'grist to the mill' of the appeal.

Bad Character Evidence Consisting of Unproven Allegations *Braithwaite* [2010] EWCA Crim 1082, [2010] 2 Cr App R 18 (128), was considered in *A* [2020] EWCA Crim 1687. D was convicted of the murder by stabbing of a friend, V. D's defence was that V had suddenly attacked him with a knife, compelling him to defend himself. Evidence of a caution against V for possessing a knife was admitted under the CJA 2003, s. 100, as was a similar caution against D. D appealed, contending that further evidence of the bad character of V was wrongly excluded, including evidence that he had the nickname 'Stabber' and that he had been disruptive and violent at school. The trial judge had carefully examined V's school records and determined that there was nothing that suggested serious violence, and that the application was essentially 'mud-slinging'. The nickname was unsubstantiated hearsay of no substantial probative value. The Court of Appeal agreed, adding that what was said in the school records was not to be taken as proved and, as in *Braithwaite*, involved a degree of assertion. The submission regarding V's nickname was 'completely hopeless' in that it would have invited the jury to speculate as to what V had done, if anything, to earn it. **F15.21**

Section F16 The Rule against Hearsay: General Principles

DEFINITION OF 'STATEMENT'

Hearsay and Mechanically Produced Evidence

In *Thomasson* [2021] EWCA Crim 114, the Court of Appeal confirmed that *Cook* [1987] QB 417 has been reversed by the CJA 2003, s. 115(1). In *Cook* the Court had held that the production of a photofit likeness was analogous to a photograph. This was always a misclassification, enabling the depiction to avoid the operation of the hearsay rule. E-Fit images, like sketches and photofits, are now clearly 'statements' to which the hearsay provisions of the CJA 2003 may apply. **F16.11**

Section F17 Exceptions to the Rule against Hearsay (Excluding Confessions)

INTRODUCTION

Notice

In *Turner* [2020] EWCA Crim 1241, the Court of Appeal declined to decide whether the notice procedure technically applies to evidence admitted by agreement of the parties. The evidence in question had not been disputed at trial and it was too late for the objection based on hearsay to be raised on appeal. **F17.5**

HEARSAY EXCEPTIONS: (2) HEARSAY ADMISSIBLE IN THE INTERESTS OF JUSTICE

Section 114(1)(d) Benefiting Defence

F17.41 *Finch* [2007] EWCA Crim 36, [2007] 1 WLR 1645, was considered in *Williams* [2021] EWCA Crim 226, where the evidence concerned a letter written after trial by a co-accused confessing to an offence for which D was convicted. The Court of Appeal considered that the provisions of the PACE 1984, s. 76A (see **F18.29** in the main work), could be applied to such a case where the co-accused were jointly tried, whether or not they were charged with the same offence. In such a case it is not necessary to fall back on the provisions of s. 114(1)(d).

In *Thomasson* [2021] EWCA Crim 114, the Court of Appeal confirmed that the hearsay rule applies to E-Fit images (see **F16.11** in this supplement). It was held not to be in the interests of justice for the defence to introduce an image compiled by V in the wake of a shooting in order that police officers investigating the crime could be asked to confirm that they had not considered it a likeness of D. V, who testified for the prosecution, subsequently claimed to have recognised a newspaper photograph of D as the man who was an accomplice of the shooter. The E-Fit was admitted by agreement under the CJA 2003, s. 119 (see **F7.56** in the main work), as the basis for cross-examination of the witness herself, but the Court held (at [47]) that it could not be used for the purpose of inviting the officers' perceptions because 'the risk would simply have been too great that the jury would have been misled by undetected human error. If the route to admissibility was via section 114(1) (d), we are confident it would not have been in the interests of justice for it to have been admitted.'

POWER TO STOP TRIAL WHERE CASE BASED ON HEARSAY

F17.99 *Riat* [2012] EWCA Crim 1509, [2013] 1 All ER 349 was applied in *RT* [2020] EWCA Crim 1343, [2021] 1 Cr App R 14 (282). D was tried for serious sexual offences against his two nephews, one of whom, TS, had committed suicide before the trial began. TS's recorded evidence was admitted under the CJA 2003, s. 116(2)(a), and an application under the CJA 2003, s. 125, on the grounds that the evidence was so unconvincing that a conviction would be unsafe was rejected. The trial judge had carefully considered whether an admittedly incorrect statement by TS in which he identified himself as the victim of an assault on a 'sex tape' was necessarily a lie, or might have been attributable to honest mistake. He had also identified material capable of both testing and of supporting TS's account. The Court of Appeal concluded (at [23]):

> The judge's decision on whether TS' hearsay evidence was 'unconvincing' within the meaning of s. 125 required an assessment of the relevant potentially reliable evidence as a whole. The judge was right to rule that the hearsay evidence did not 'fall foul of the *Riat* test' and that he should reject the defence application under s. 125.

Section F19 Evidence of Identification

VISUAL IDENTIFICATION

Identification Evidence and Identification Issues

F19.3 In *Thomasson* [2021] EWCA Crim 114, D sought to have the evidence of an identifying witness excluded as unfairly prejudicial under the PACE 1984, s. 78. Although the defence submitted that there were weaknesses and inconsistencies in the identification, the principal basis on which they sought exclusion was that the witness was malicious and lacked credibility. This was not, said Fulford LJ (at [26]), an argument based on the *Turnbull* guidelines, 'in the sense that the evidence depended solely on a fleeting glance or … a longer observation of the individual in difficult conditions'. Moreover (at [31]):

> There was no suggestion that there had been impropriety on the part of the prosecuting authorities as to the way this evidence was obtained. Therefore, the admissibility challenge was not based on the suggested unreliability of the identification evidence, for instance because it had been obtained unlawfully, improperly or unfairly. Nor was it suggested that the appellant had, for some other reason, been unjustly prejudiced in relation to this evidence.

The credibility of the identifying witness was a proper issue for the jury to consider and counsel was able to explore this and other weaknesses in the prosecution case during cross-examination. There was no proper basis for exclusion under s. 78.

Supporting Evidence

Mutually Supportive Identifications In *Dickens* [2020] EWCA Crim 1661, D was identified by V's widow (nearly a year after the event) as the getaway driver in a murder case. Another eyewitness had independently identified D's workmate, H, as the actual killer. Each of the accused relied upon an alibi, which would have placed them together at their usual workplace. The trial judge directed the jury that it was open to them to consider these identifications mutually supportive, and the Court of Appeal upheld that direction. Fulford LJ said (at [73]): **F19.14**

> If two witnesses identify two different individuals who were not only known to each other, but each claimed that at the time the offence was being committed they were in the same place at some distance from the scene of the crime, this constitutes a potential unexplained 'odd coincidence' within the terms of *Turnbull* that can be supporting evidence for the identification of each accused. Furthermore, by analogy with the position in *Weeder* (1980) 71 Cr App R 228, there is no requirement that the jury must first be sure that one of the identifications is correct before they consider whether it provides support for the identification by the other witness. ... *Jones (Terence)* [1992] Crim LR 365 confirms that association between two individuals who are separately identified is relevant to whether the identification is accurate, and it can support the identification evidence.

CCTV, VIDEO AND OTHER IMAGES

LT [2019] EWCA Crim 58 was considered in *Crampton* [2020] EWCA Crim 1334, [2019] 1 Cr App R 30 (405). This was yet another case involving a witness (in this instance, the complainant in a historical sexual abuse case) who had already made an informal Facebook identification of the alleged offender by the time she contacted the police. **F19.19**

The complainant (a child at the time of the offence) remembered the first name of her attacker, but 25 years later was she given a possible second name (that of D, who had lived nearby at the time) and she then searched for and found an image of him on Facebook, which she took to show the police when she made her complaint. She had some support from her mother, but neither was invited to view a (VIPER) video identification parade, even though D asked for one.

The trial judge regarded this omission as a breach of Code D. Despite the risk that the witnesses would simply have picked out the image of the man they had recently identified on Facebook, even if he was the wrong man, the judge was not satisfied that the exercise would have been pointless or futile; but even if there was a breach of Code D, it did not in his judgment require the exclusion of the Facebook identification evidence, which was supported by other (mostly circumstantial) evidence.

The Court of Appeal dismissed D's appeal against conviction. The Court was not convinced that the failure to hold a video parade had prejudiced D in any material way, and in any event the judge had weighed the various consideration in the balance. He had quite reasonably concluded that the Facebook identification was properly supported by other evidence, and had fully directed the jury as to its strengths and weaknesses.

Smith (Dean) [2008] EWCA Crim 1342 was considered in *Yaryare* [2020] EWCA Crim 1314, [2020] 4 WLR 156, as to which see **F19.20** in this supplement.

Photographic and Video Evidence at Trial

F19.20 Although a witness (such as a police officer) who has made a careful study of CCTV footage may be qualified to explain and interpret that footage to a court or jury as an expert witness, even to the extent of expressing an opinion on the identities of those involved (*Clare* [1995] 2 Cr App R 333, *Abnett* [2006] EWCA Crim 3320), objections may be raised where no record (or an inadequate record) was kept of the circumstances and conditions under which that witness viewed the footage and identified or recognised the individuals. PACE Code D, para 3.36, lists the matters that should be recorded.

In *Yaryare* [2020] EWCA Crim 1314, [2020] 4 WLR 156, a police officer (B) studied CCTB footage of three violent and related incidents and gave opinion evidence as to the participants and the roles they had played. She thereby incriminated a number of defendants, but it was submitted that her evidence ought to have been excluded as unreliable and unfairly prejudicial, because she had not provided any statement setting out why she had arrived at her conclusions until long after she had commenced viewing the CCTV footage and she had failed to maintain a satisfactory log while viewing it.

Fulford LJ referred to *Smith (Dean)* [2008] EWCA Crim 134, in which the Court of Appeal said:

> 67. A police officer asked to view a CCTV is not in the same shoes as a witness asked to identify someone he has seen committing a crime. But … safeguards which [PACE Code D] is designed to put in place are equally important in cases where a police officer is asked to see whether he can recognise anyone in a CCTV recording. The mischief is that a police officer may merely assert that he recognised someone without any objective means of testing the accuracy of such an assertion. Whether or not Code D applies, there must be in place some record which assists in gauging the reliability of the assertion. …
>
> 68. Absent any such check as would be available had a witness described the commission of an offence and recollected his description of the offender, it is important that the police officer's initial reactions to the recording are set out and available for scrutiny. Thus, if the police officer fails to recognise anyone on first viewing but does so subsequently those circumstances should be noted. The words that officer uses by way of recognition may also be of importance. If an officer fails to pick anybody else out that also should be recorded, as should any words of doubt. Furthermore, it is necessary that if recognition takes place a record is made of what it is about the image that is said to have triggered the recognition.
>
> 69. Absent any such record, it will not be possible to assess the reliability of the recognition.

In *Yaryare*, the Court took the view that Code D applied and that B had failed properly to follow it, but sympathised with her plight. Fulford LJ said:

> 90. … From a practical point of view it may be unrealistic to expect an officer to note all of his or her passing thoughts whilst watching CCTV footage time and again. Any conclusions in a case such as the present are likely to emerge incrementally, and the fine detail of an improving or changing recognition may be difficult to record in a log.

The Court was also satisfied that the breaches of Code D were not, in all the circumstances, such as would require the exclusion of her evidence:

> 91. For each of the appellants, [B] explained the reasons for her recognition of them by reference to the relevant features of their appearance, and the jury, as in *Lariba* [2015] EWCA Crim 478, were able, from the footage and the stills, to see exactly what the witness saw from these permanent images. Moreover, given the relative good quality of the images, they were able to assess whether a recognition made from them was one on which they could rely even though they were not making an identification of their own. … It is to be regretted that [B] failed to apply the relevant parts of Code D and the guidance given in *Smith*, and we accept that the appellants and the jury were put at a disadvantage as a result, but given the extent of the opportunities to test and assess the reliability of the recognition evidence, and in the particular circumstances of this case, we consider that this expert evidence which it is accepted was *prima facie* admissible did not fall to be excluded under PACE s. 78.

DNA EVIDENCE

Evaluating DNA Matches

In *Gabriel* [2020] EWCA Crim 998 the three appellants were monozygotic triplets, which meant that their DNA was indistinguishable as between each other. Each was alleged to have participated in a conspiracy to possess a firearm with intent to endanger life. DNA from one of them was found on the muzzle of the firearm in question; but even if the jury could be sure that it got there through handling of the gun in the course of the conspiracy, rather than by (say) secondary transference, that evidence alone could not possibly have sufficed to identify any one of them as being responsible. The DNA could just as easily have been attributed to one of the others. **F19.30**

The DNA evidence, however, did not stand alone. There was also a great deal of mobile phone and cell-site analysis that showed repeated contact between each of the appellants (allegedly acting as or for the vendors) and other alleged conspirators, such as the buyer, the broker and the courier, each of whom were convicted at an earlier trial. The DNA merely added something to a case that was (as Irwin LJ put it at [36]) 'in its fundamentals founded on the mobile phone and cell-site evidence':

> 38. … It would operate to rebut any suggestion that what had happened was all by way of coincidence… There was no unfairness in allowing it to be put before the jury. Indeed, it might have been a very surprising outcome if the jury were deprived of all knowledge of the fact that the DNA of at least one of the appellants, as alleged conspirators, had been found on one of the firearms which were the subject of the conspiracy.

Innocent Explanations for DNA Matches

In *Jones* [2020] EWCA Crim 1021, [2020] 2 Cr App R 26 (424), D's DNA was found (along with other DNA) on the firing pin of an improvised explosive device or grenade that had apparently been left under the potential victim's car. There was clear evidence of a conspiracy to plant the grenade, and if secondary transfer could not be ruled out, the DNA on the firing pin would have been highly incriminating, whether there was evidence that D himself had planted the grenade or not. But in contrast to *Gabriel* [2020] EWCA Crim 998 (see **F19.30** in this Supplement) mobile phone analysis could not prove D's involvement in the conspiracy, and although the agreed expert evidence was that direct deposit is an inherently more probable explanation for the presence of DNA on any object, direct deposit could not be proved in this case with any degree of certainty. There was no proven physical or temporal link between D and the device, and in contrast to *Tsekiri* [2017] EWCA Crim 40, [2017] 1 Cr App R 32 (479), there was no expert evidence to the effect that secondary transfer was improbable in the particular circumstances of the case. **F19.31**

> 22. … the DNA results do not help to determine how long ago the DNA was deposited, the order in which DNA from different individuals was deposited or, as a logical consequence, whether [D] was the last person to touch the safety pin before it was recovered.

In the Court's view, the fact that D had connections with the locality, which the trial judge interpreted as strengthening the prosecution case, actually had the opposite effect, because 'if D lived in the north of Scotland or the west of Cornwall, the risk of innocent secondary transfer might be thought to be very much lower'. His conviction was quashed.

Although the Court considered that the case turned largely on its own facts, it also issued this general guidance (at [35]) as to the inferences that might be drawn from a suspect's failure to explain how DNA might innocently have been deposited:

> 35. … There are many circumstances where it may be reasonable to expect an individual to put forward a case in relation to the presence of their DNA, not because they can be expected to analyse the science or the detailed material on which the scientific conclusions were based. Such an expectation may arise, for example, because the presence of their DNA may be explained by some connection or contact, or because the opportunity for direct transfer can be precluded or shown to be unlikely, or because the facts mean that the presence of their DNA at least calls for explanation.

Section F20 Inferences from Silence and the Non-production of Evidence

OUT-OF-COURT SILENCE UNDER THE 1994 ACT

Facts which Should Have Been Mentioned

F20.17 Dicta in *Argent* [1997] 2 Cr App R 27 were considered in *Black* [2020] EWCA Crim 915. In *Argent* the Court of Appeal had identified that case as a straightforward one where facts could be expected to be mentioned (it concerned a fatal stabbing where it was clear that D had been identified by eye-witnesses). The Court drew a contrast with a case of fraud or conspiracy with more complex interlocking facts, where it might not be expected that an immediate response would be forthcoming. In *Black*, D sought to rely on this distinction. He had been interviewed about conspiracy to commit fraud against the purchasers of solar panels marketed by him, who had been promised repayment of the cost of their purchases in addition to the savings made on their electricity bills. D's defence was that he believed at all times that arrangements were in place to repay the purchasers. His failure to mention this at interview was held not to fall within the class of case envisaged in *Argent* because D had been given adequate disclosure before interview and 'had lived through events': he knew what promises had been given, and the level of investments that had been made in order to meet them. It was therefore a case where the jury could be invited to consider drawing an inference under the CJPO 1994, s. 34.

The drawing of an otherwise permissible inference might be frustrated by the way in which a case is presented. In *Jones (William Francis)* [2020] EWCA Crim 1021, [2020] 2 Cr App R 26 (424), a crucial issue was whether the finding of D's DNA on a home-made explosive device might have been attributable to innocent indirect transfer. The agreement between the experts in the case was unnecessarily broad in that it included an observation that it was 'not realistic' to expect anyone to be able to account for indirect transfer. In light of that agreement the Court of Appeal observed that it was hard to see how it could have been argued that such an explanation could have been expected from D at interview, whereas in fact there are many circumstances where it may be reasonable to expect individuals to put forward a case in relation to the presence of their DNA: not because they can be expected to analyse the science or the detailed material on which the scientific conclusions were based, but because they would be aware of facts pointing to an alternative explanation. The Court was 'sceptical' as to whether it was wise to reach an agreement between experts in such broad terms.

Direction as to Permissible Inferences

F20.25 **Direction where s. 34 Applicable** The statement in *Petkar* [2003] EWCA Crim 2668, [2004] 1 Cr App R 22 (270) that there must be a case that 'clearly called for an answer' on the prosecution case as it stood at the time of interview was approved in *Black* [2020] EWCA Crim 915. Although this requirement was not set out in the wording of s. 34, it would be wrong to draw an inference against D if nothing has been said or shown to D at the police interview to call for an answer.

Black, and the suggested s. 34 direction from the *Crown Court Compendium* (July 2020) set out in the main work, were considered in *Dybicz* [2020] EWCA Crim 1047. The failure of the trial judge in that case to follow the direction verbatim was not to be criticised: the question was whether the terms in which the judge directed the jury were correct in law and sufficient in the circumstances of the case. In *Dybicz* the judge's detailed instructions to the jury had conveyed the substance of the suggested direction. A related criticism, that the trial judge had failed to curtail cross-examination of D as to his reasons for failing to deal with specific matters, was also rejected (at [29]):

> A judge when summing up will be obliged to identify to the jury the specific matters which it is alleged the defendant failed to mention, and the inference or inferences which they are being invited to draw from that failure. It may therefore be appropriate, and indeed necessary, for the prosecution to investigate details in cross-examination of a defendant.

Relationship with *Lucas* Direction on Lies In *Wainwright* [2021] EWCA Crim 122, the Court of Appeal considered the authorities in the main work including *Rana* [2007] EWCA Crim 2261, *Hackett* [2011] EWCA Crim 380, [2011] 2 Cr App R 3 (35) and *Spottiswood* [2019] EWCA Crim 949. The Court emphasised that *Hackett* was concerned with a straightforward situation where D had failed to mention matters on which he later relied, by telling in interview what was contended to be a lie, and by giving the same explanation for his failure to mention a fact and for what was contended to be a lie. In such a case it is preferable to give a single direction — appropriately modified, if necessary — to combine the *Lucas* and s. 34 directions, where it is feasible and convenient to do so. It is ultimately a question for the judge to determine whether a dual direction or two separate directions best fits the facts and circumstances of the case. The fact that the prosecution were advocating only a s. 34 direction and the defence only a *Lucas* direction did not mean that the judge had to make a choice between them. On the facts of *Wainwright*, two separate issues arose as to the lies told in D's first police interview, and his failure to raise the matter of coercion relied on at trial over the course of that and a subsequent interview, so that the judge's decision to give separate directions was 'entirely sustainable'. In a postscript, the Court emphasises the importance of sharing proposed directions with counsel in advance to allow any concerns to be addressed. **F20.26**

CRIMINAL PROCEDURE RULES AND CRIMINAL PRACTICE DIRECTIONS

Criminal Procedure Rules 2020 (SI 2020 No. 759 (L. 19)) and Criminal Practice Directions

The following text reproduces the Criminal Procedure Rules 2020 (as amended by the Criminal Procedure (Amendment) Rules 2021 (SI 2021 No. 40)) and the Criminal Practice Directions. The Criminal Procedure (Amendment) Rules 2021 came into force on 8 February 2021, save for the following which came into force on 5 April 2021:

(a) r. 6(a) and (b);
(b) r. 9(a) to (h), (k), (l) and (m)(ii);
(c) r. 10;
(d) r. 17(c)(i);
(e) r. 20;
(f) r. 21;
(g) r. 22;
(h) r. 23(b) and (c);
(i) r. 24;
(j) r. 25; and
(k) r. 30(b).

The Rules and the Practice Directions have been designed and structured to provide, in combination, an effective procedural framework, a key part of which has been arranging the Practice Directions so as to correspond so far as practicable with the related parts of the Criminal Procedure Rules. We have integrated the 2020 Rules (as amended by the 2021 Amendment Rules) and the Practice Directions so far as possible and have included the eleventh amendment to the Practice Directions which has effect from 16 November 2020. At present the Practice Directions reference the Criminal Procedure Rules 2015 and those references have been included unedited. The text of the Rules is presented as laid, accompanied by a corresponding paragraph number (e.g., **R3.26** indicates **Rule 3.26; Commencement of preparatory hearing**). The text of the Practice Direction is displayed in grey boxes which, where possible, follow the text of the associated Rules. We have adopted a paragraph structure with the prefix CPD followed by the number used in the Practice Direction itself, or the Roman numeral section where there is no sequential numbering.

CRIMINAL PRACTICE DIRECTIONS GENERAL MATTERS

CPD I General matters A CPD.0A

0A.1 The Lord Chief Justice has power, including power under section 74 of the Courts Act 2003 and Part 1 of Schedule 2 to the Constitutional Reform Act 2005, to give directions as to the practice and procedure of the criminal courts. The following directions are given accordingly.

0A.2 These Practice Directions came into force on October 5, 2015 [2015] EWCA Crim 1567. Amendment Number 1 [2016] EWCA Crim 97 was issued by the Lord Chief Justice on 23rd March 2016 and came into force on the 4th April 2016. Amendment Number 2 [2016] EWCA Crim 1714 was issued by the Lord Chief Justice on 16th November 2016 and came into force on 16th November 2016. Amendment Number 3 [2017] EWCA Crim 30 was issued by the Lord Chief Justice on 31st January 2017 and came into force on 31st January 2017. Amendment Number 4 [2017] EWCA Crim 310 was issued by the Lord Chief Justice on 28th March 2017 and came into force on 3rd April 2017. Amendment Number 5 [2017] EWCA Crim 1076 was issued by the Lord Chief Justice on 27th July 2017 and came into force on 2nd October 2017. Amendment Number 6 [2018] EWCA Crim 516 was issued by the Lord Chief Justice on 21st March 2018 and came into force on 2nd April 2018. Amendment Number 7 [2018] EWCA Crim 1760 was issued by the Lord Chief Justice on 26th July 2018 and came into force on the 1st October 2018. Amendment Number 8 EWCA [2019] Crim 495 was issued by the Lord Chief Justice on 28th March 2019 and came into force on the 1st April 2019; Amendment Number 9 [2019] EWCA Crim 1603 was issued by the Lord Chief Justice on 10th October 2019 and came into force on 14th October 2019; Amendment Number 10 was issued by the Lord Chief Justice on 12th May 2020 and came into force on the 13th May 2020. Amendment Number 11 was issued by the Lord Chief Justice on 29th October 2020 and came into force on the 16th November 2020.

0A.3 Annexes D and E to the Consolidated Criminal Practice Direction of 8th July, 2002, [2002] 1 W.L.R. 2870; [2002] 2 Cr. App. R. 35, as amended, which set out forms for use in connection with the Criminal Procedure Rules, remain in force. See also paragraph I 5A of these Practice Directions.

0A.4 These Practice Directions supplement many, but not all, Parts of the Criminal Procedure Rules, and include other directions about practice and procedure in the courts to which they apply. They are to be known as the Criminal Practice Directions 2015. They came into force on 5th October, 2015. They apply to all cases in all the criminal courts of England and Wales from that date.

0A.5 Consequent on the rearrangement of the Criminal Procedure Rules in the Criminal Procedure Rules 2015, S.I. 2015/1490:

(a) the content of these Practice Directions is arranged to correspond. Within each division of these Directions the paragraphs are numbered to correspond with the associated Part of the Criminal Procedure Rules 2015. Compared with the Criminal Practice Directions given in 2013, as amended, the numbering and content of some divisions is amended consequentially, as shown in this table:

Derivations	
Divisions of 2015 Directions	*Divisions of 2013 Directions*
I General matters II Preliminary proceedings III Custody and bail IV Disclosure V Evidence VI Trial VII Sentencing VIII Confiscation and related proceedings [empty] IX Appeal X Costs [Criminal Costs Practice Direction] XI Other proceedings XII General application XIII Listing	I General matters; II Preliminary proceedings 16A–C II Preliminary proceedings 9A, 10A, 14A–B III Custody and bail IV Disclosure V Evidence VI Trial VII Sentencing VIII Confiscation and related proceedings [empty] X Appeal XI Costs [Criminal Costs Practice Direction] II Preliminary proceedings 6A, 17A–F; IX Contempt of court XII General application XIII Listing

(b) the text of these Practice Directions is amended:

(i) to bring up to date the cross-references to the Criminal Procedure Rules and to other paragraphs of these Directions which that text contains, and

(ii) to adopt the abbreviation of references to the Criminal Procedure Rules ('CrimPR') for which rule 2.3(2) of the Criminal Procedure Rules 2015 provides.

0A.6 In all other respects, the content of the Criminal Practice Directions 2015 reproduces that of the Criminal Practice Directions 2013, as amended.

NOTE ON STATUTORY POWERS

The Criminal Procedure Rule Committee noted that in making the Rules listed in the first column of this table, it exercises also the powers listed in the corresponding entry in the second column—

Rule	*Power*
2.4, 2.5, 2.6, 2.7, 2.8 and 2.9	Section 67B(1) of the Courts Act 2003[1]
3.16	Section 86A(2) of the Courts Act 2003[2]
3.21	Section 86A(2) of the Courts Act 2003
3.32	Section 77(1) of the Senior Courts Act 1981[3]
4.1 and 4.12	Section 12(1) and (3) of the Road Traffic Offenders Act 1988[4]
5.5	Section 32(1) of the Criminal Appeal Act 1968[5]
Part 8	Section 48(1) of the Criminal Law Act 1977[6]
Part 10	Section 2 of the Indictments Act 1915[7] and section 2(6) of the Administration of Justice (Miscellaneous Provisions) Act 1933[8]
14.6	Section 5B(9) of the Bail Act 1976[9]
16.4	Section 9(2A) of the Criminal Justice Act 1967[10]
19.3	Section 81(1) of the Police and Criminal Evidence Act 1984[11] and section 20(3) of the Criminal Procedure and Investigations Act 1996[12]
20.4	Section 132(4) of the Criminal Justice Act 2003[13]

Rule	*Power*
Part 23	Sections 37(5) and 38(6) and (7) of the Youth Justice and Criminal Evidence Act 1999[14]
24.11	Section 174(4) of the Criminal Justice Act 2003[15]
24.14	Section 12(7ZA) of the Magistrates' Courts Act 1980[16]
25.16	Section 174(4) of the Criminal Justice Act 2003
28.4	Section 155(7) of the Powers of Criminal Courts (Sentencing) Act 2000[17]
29.4	Section 2 of the Commissioners for Oaths Act 1889[18]
33.7, 33.37, 33.39 and 33.40	Section 91 of the Proceeds of Crime Act 2002[19]
33.47	Section 52(1) of the Senior Courts Act 1981[20]
34.11	Sections 73(2) and 74(2), (3) and (4) of the Senior Courts Act 1981[21]
36.8	Section 87(4) of the Senior Courts Act 1981[22]
37.6	Section 49(1) of the Criminal Justice Act 2003
38.9	Section 73(2) of the Criminal Justice Act 2003
40.8	Section 159(6) of the Criminal Justice Act 1988[23]
42.14, 42.18, 42.19 and 42.20	Section 91 of the Proceeds of Crime Act 2002
44.2	Section 30(1) of the Criminal Justice Act 2003[24] and section 2 of the Commissioners for Oaths Act 1889[25]
45.6 and 45.7	Section 52(1) of the Senior Courts Act 1981
47.4 and 47.10; 47.24 and 47.30	Paragraph 15A of Schedule 1 to the Police and Criminal Evidence Act 1984[26]
47.4 and 47.11 to 47.16 inclusive	Paragraph 10(2) of Schedule 5, paragraph 14(2) of Schedule 5A, paragraph 4(1) of Schedule 6 and paragraph 5(1) of Schedule 6A to the Terrorism Act 2000[27]
47.4 and 47.17 to 47.22 inclusive	Sections 351(2), 362(2), 369(2) and 375(1) of the Proceeds of Crime Act 2002[28]
47.4 and 47.23	Section 157(9) of the Extradition Act 2003[29]
47.24 and 47.31	Paragraph 11(5) of Schedule 5 to the Terrorism Act 2000[30]
47.24 and 47.32	Section 352(8) of the Proceeds of Crime Act 2002[31]
47.24 and 47.33	Section 160(10) of the Extradition Act 2003[32]
47.35 and 47.38	Section 59(13) of the Criminal Justice and Police Act 2001[33]
47.49	Section 74(3) of the Senior Courts Act 1981[34]
47.66 to 47.71 inclusive	Sections 11(1) and 18(2) of the Crime (Overseas Production Orders) Act 2019[35]
48.16	Section 19 of the Criminal Procedure and Investigations Act 1996[36]
50.17	Section 67 of the Senior Courts Act 1981[37]
50.23	Sections 36A(4), 36B(3), 118A(4) and 118B(3) of the Extradition Act 2003[38]
50.30	Sections 19(3) and 66(1) of the Senior Courts Act 1981[39]

[1] 2003 c. 39; section 67B was inserted by section 3 of, and paragraph 32 of the Schedule to, the Courts and Tribunals (Judiciary and Functions of Staff) Act 2018 (c. 33).

[2] 2003 c. 39; section 86A was inserted by section 162 of the Policing and Crime Act 2017 (c. 3).

[3] 1981 c. 54; section 77 was amended by section 15 of, and paragraph 11 of Schedule 2 to, the Criminal Justice Act 1987 (c. 38), section 168 of, and paragraph 18 of Schedule 9 to, the Criminal Justice and Public Order Act 1994 (c. 33), section 41 of, and paragraph 54 of Schedule 3 to, the Criminal Justice Act 2003 (c. 44) and article 3 of, and paragraphs 11 and 13 of the Schedule to, SI 2004/2035. It is further amended by section 31 of, and paragraph 11 of Schedule 1 and Schedule 2 to, the Prosecution of Offences Act 1985 (c. 23) with effect from a date to be appointed.

[4] 1988 c. 53; section 12 was amended by article 3 of, and paragraphs 29 and 30 of the Schedule to, S.I. 2004/2035.

[5] 1968 c. 19.

[6] 1977 c. 45; section 48 was amended by paragraph 190 of Schedule 8 to the Courts Act 2003 (c. 39).

Criminal Procedure Rules and Criminal Practice Directions

[7] 1915 c. 90; section 2 was amended by section 19 of the Criminal Justice Administration Act 1956 (c. 34) and sections 56 and 109 of, and paragraph 67 of Schedule 8 and Schedule 11 to, the Courts Act 2003 (c. 39).
[8] 1933 c. 36; section 2(6) was amended by Part IV of Schedule 11 to the Courts Act 1971 (c. 23), paragraph 1 of the Schedule to S.I. 2004/2035 and section 82 of the Deregulation Act 2015 (c. 20).
[9] 1976 c. 63; section 5B(9) was inserted by section 30 of the Criminal Justice and Public Order Act 1994 (c. 33) and amended by paragraph 183 of Schedule 8 to the Courts Act 2003 (c. 39).
[10] 1967 c. 80; section 9(2A) was inserted by section 80 of the Deregulation Act 2015 (c. 20).
[11] 1984 c. 60; section 81 was amended by paragraph 286 of Schedule 8 to, the Courts Act 2003 (c. 39).
[12] 1996 c. 25; section 20(3) was amended by paragraph 378 of Schedule 8 to, the Courts Act 2003 (c. 39).
[13] 2003 c. 44; section 132 was amended by article 3 of, and paragraphs 45 and 51 of the Schedule to, S.I. 2004/2035.
[14] 1999 c. 23; section 37(5) and section 38(6), (7) were amended by section 109 of, and paragraph 384 of Schedule 8 to, the Courts Act 2003 (c. 39).
[15] 2003 c. 44; section 174 was substituted by section 64 of the Legal Aid, Sentencing and Punishment of Offenders Act 2012 (c. 10).
[16] 1980 c. 43; section 12(7ZA) was inserted by section 81 of the Deregulation Act 2015 (c. 20).
[17] 2000 c. 6; section 155(7) was amended by article 3 of, and paragraphs 39 and 43 to, S.I. 2004/2035.
[18] 1889 c. 10; section 2 was amended by section 59 of, and paragraph 15 of Schedule 11 to, the Constitutional Reform Act 2005 (c. 4).
[19] 2002 c. 29; section 91 was amended by section 109(1) of, and paragraph 410 of Schedule 8 to, the Courts Act 2003 (c. 39).
[20] 1981 c. 54; section 52 was amended by section 31 of, and Part II of Schedule 1 to, the Prosecution of Offences Act 1985 (c. 23), section 4 of the Courts and Legal Services Act 1990 (c. 41), article 3 and paragraphs 11 and 12(a) of the Schedule to S.I. 2004/2035 and section 59 of, and paragraph 26 of Schedule 11 to, the Constitutional Reform Act 2005 (c. 4).
[21] 1981 c. 54; section 73(2) was amended by article 3 of, and paragraphs 11 and 12(b) of the Schedule to, S.I. 2004/2035. Section 74(2) and (3) was amended by article 3 of, and paragraphs 11 and 12(c) of the Schedule to, S.I. 2004/2035.
[22] 1981 c. 54; section 87(4) was amended by articles 2 and 3 of, and paragraphs 11 and 17 of the Schedule to, S.I. 2004/2035.
[23] 1988 c. 33; section 159(6) was amended by S.I. 2004/2035.
[24] 2003 c. 44; section 30 was amended by article 3 of, and paragraphs 45 and 46 of the Schedule to, S.I. 2004/2035.
[25] 1889 c. 10; section 2 was amended by section 59 of, and paragraph 15 of Schedule 11 to, the Constitutional Reform Act 2005 (c. 4).
[26] 1984 c. 60; paragraph 15A of Schedule 1 was inserted by section 82 of the Deregulation Act 2015 (c. 20).
[27] 2000 c. 11; paragraph 10 of Schedule 5 was amended by section 109(1) of, and paragraph 389 of Schedule 8 to, the Courts Act 2003 (c. 39) and it is further amended by section 65 of, and paragraph 9 of Schedule 4 to, the Courts Act 2003 (c. 39), with effect from a date to be appointed. Paragraph 4 of Schedule 6 was amended by section 109(1) of, and paragraph 390 of Schedule 8 to, the Courts Act 2003 (c. 39). Schedule 6A was inserted by section 3 of, and paragraph 1(1) and (3) of Part 1 of Schedule 2 to, the Anti-terrorism, Crime and Security Act 2001 (c. 24).
[28] 2002 c. 29.
[29] 2003 c. 41; section 157(9) was inserted by section 174 of the Anti-social Behaviour, Crime and Policing Act 2014 (c. 12).
[30] 2000 c. 11; paragraph 11(5) of Schedule 5 was inserted by section 82 of the Deregulation Act 2015 (c. 20).
[31] 2002 c. 29; section 352(8) was inserted by section 82 of the Deregulation Act 2015 (c. 20).
[32] 2003 c. 41; section 160(10) was inserted by section 174 of the Anti-social Behaviour, Crime and Policing Act 2014 (c. 12).
[33] 2001 c. 16; section 59(13) was inserted by section 82 of the Deregulation Act 2015 (c. 20).
[34] 1981 c. 54; section 74(3) was amended by article 3 of, and paragraphs 11 and 12(c) of the Schedule to, S.I. 2004/2035. The Act's title was amended by section 59(5) of, and paragraph 1 of Schedule 11 to, the Constitutional Reform Act 2005 (c. 4).
[35] 2019 c. 5.
[36] 1996 c. 25; section 19 was amended by section 109 of, and paragraph 377 of Schedule 8 to, the Courts Act 2003 (c. 39), section 331 of, and paragraphs 20 and 34 of Schedule 36 to, the Criminal Justice Act 2003 (c. 44) and section 15 of, and paragraph 251 of Schedule 4 to, the Constitutional Reform Act 2005 (c. 4).
[37] 1981 c. 54.
[38] 2003 c. 41; sections 36A, 36B, 118A and 118B were inserted by section 161 of the Anti-social Behaviour, Crime and Policing Act 2014 (c. 12).
[39] 1981 c. 54

Criminal Procedure Rules Part 1 The Overriding Objective

R1.1 The overriding objective

1.1 (1) The overriding objective of this procedural code is that criminal cases be dealt with justly.

(2) Dealing with a criminal case justly includes—

(a) acquitting the innocent and convicting the guilty;
(b) treating all participants with politeness and respect;
(c) dealing with the prosecution and the defence fairly;
(d) recognising the rights of a defendant, particularly those under Article 6 of the European Convention on Human Rights;
(e) respecting the interests of witnesses, victims and jurors and keeping them informed of the progress of the case;
(f) dealing with the case efficiently and expeditiously;
(g) ensuring that appropriate information is available to the court when bail and sentence are considered; and
(h) dealing with the case in ways that take into account—

(i) the gravity of the offence alleged,
(ii) the complexity of what is in issue,
(iii) the severity of the consequences for the defendant and others affected, and
(iv) the needs of other cases.

The duty of the participants in a criminal case R1.2

1.2 (1) Each participant, in the conduct of each case, must—
(a) prepare and conduct the case in accordance with the overriding objective;
(b) comply with these Rules, practice directions and directions made by the court; and
(c) at once inform the court and all parties of any significant failure (whether or not that participant is responsible for that failure) to take any procedural step required by these Rules, any practice direction or any direction of the court. A failure is significant if it might hinder the court in furthering the overriding objective.
(2) Anyone involved in any way with a criminal case is a participant in its conduct for the purposes of this rule.

The application by the court of the overriding objective R1.3

1.3 The court must further the overriding objective in particular when—
(a) exercising any power given to it by legislation (including these Rules);
(b) applying any practice direction; or
(c) interpreting any rule or practice direction.

Criminal Practice Directions Part 1 The Overriding Objective

CPD I General matters 1A: The Overriding Objective CPD.1A

1A.1 The presumption of innocence and an adversarial process are essential features of English and Welsh legal tradition and of the defendant's right to a fair trial. But it is no part of a fair trial that questions of guilt and innocence should be determined by procedural manoeuvres. On the contrary, fairness is best served when the issues between the parties are identified as early and as clearly as possible. As Lord Justice Auld noted, a criminal trial is not a game under which a guilty defendant should be provided with a sporting chance. It is a search for truth in accordance with the twin principles that the prosecution must prove its case and that a defendant is not obliged to inculpate himself, the object being to convict the guilty and acquit the innocent.

1A.2 Further, it is not just for a party to obstruct or delay the preparation of a case for trial in order to secure some perceived procedural advantage, or to take unfair advantage of a mistake by someone else. If courts allow that to happen it damages public confidence in criminal justice. The Rules and the Practice Direction, taken together, make it clear that courts must not allow it to happen.

Criminal Procedure Rules Part 2 Understanding and Applying the Rules and Powers of Authorised Court Officers

Understanding and applying the rules

When the Rules apply R2.1

2.1 (1) In general, the Criminal Procedure Rules apply—
(a) in all criminal cases in magistrates' courts and in the Crown Court;
(b) in extradition cases in the High Court; and
(c) in all cases in the criminal division of the Court of Appeal.
(2) If a rule applies only in one or some of those courts, the rule makes that clear.
(3) These Rules apply on and after 5th October, 2020, but unless the court otherwise directs, they do not affect a right or duty existing under the Criminal Procedure Rules 2015[1].
(4) The following rules temporarily have effect as described beneath, subject to paragraphs (5) and (6) of this rule—
(a) in this Part, rules 2.2 (Definitions), 2.7 (Exercise of functions of the Crown Court) and 2.8 (Exercise of functions of a magistrates' court) as if they were amended by rule 5 of the Criminal Procedure (Amendment No. 2) (Coronavirus) Rules 2020[2] ('the Coronavirus Rules');

[1] S.I. 2015/1490; amended by S.I. 2016/120, 2016/705, 2017/144, 2017/282, 2017/755, 2017/915, 2018/132, 2018/847, 2019/143, 2019/908, 2019/1119, 2020/32, 2020/417.
[2] S.I. 2020/417.

Criminal Procedure Rules and Criminal Practice Directions

(b) in Part 3 (Case management)—
(i) rules 3.2 (The duty of the court), 3.3 (The duty of the parties) and 3.5 (The court's case management powers) as if they were amended by rule 6(a), (b) and (c) respectively of the Coronavirus Rules,
(ii) rule 3.8 (Case preparation and progression) as if it were amended by rule 6(d) of the Coronavirus Rules (which amended rule 3.9 of the Criminal Procedure Rules 2015), and
(iii) rule 3.10 (Directions for commissioning medical reports, other than for sentencing purposes) as if it were amended by rule 6(e) of the Coronavirus Rules (which amended rule 3.28 of the Criminal Procedure Rules 2015);
(c) in Part 5 (Forms and court records), rule 5.4 (Duty to make records) as if it were amended by rule 7 of the Coronavirus Rules;
(d) in Part 14 (Bail and custody time limits), rule 14.18 (Exercise of court's powers: extension of live link bail) as if it were amended by rule 8 of the Coronavirus Rules;
(e) in Part 18 (Measures to assist a witness or defendant to give evidence)—
(i) the heading to the Part as if it were amended by rule 9(a) of the Coronavirus Rules,
(ii) rules 18.1 (When this Part applies), 18.2 (Meaning of 'witness'), 18.4 (Decisions and reasons), 18.23 (Exercise of court's powers), 18.24 (Content of application for a live link direction), 18.25 (Application to discharge a live link direction, etc.) and 18.26 (Representations in response) as if they were amended by rule 9(b) to (h) respectively of the Coronavirus Rules, and
(iii) the note at the end of the Part as if it were amended by rule 9(i) of the Coronavirus Rules;
(f) in Part 24 (Trial and sentence in a magistrates' court), rule 24.11 (Procedure if the court convicts) as if it were amended by rule 10 of the Coronavirus Rules;
(g) in Part 25 (Trial and sentence in the Crown Court), rule 25.16 (Procedure if the court convicts) as if it were amended by rule 11 of the Coronavirus Rules;
(h) in Part 28 (Sentencing procedures in special cases), rule 28.8 (Directions for commissioning medical reports for sentencing purposes) as if it were amended by rule 12 of the Coronavirus Rules;
(i) in Part 47 (Investigation orders and warrants) the rules listed in rule 13 of the Coronavirus Rules as if they were amended by that rule; and
(j) in Part 50 (Extradition), rules 50.3 (Exercise of magistrates' court's powers) and 50.17 (Exercise of High Court's powers) as if they were amended by rule 14 of the Coronavirus Rules.

(5) The temporary amendments to rules 3.10 (Directions for commissioning medical reports, other than for sentencing purposes) and 28.8 (Directions for commissioning medical reports for sentencing purposes) to which paragraph (4) of this rule refers cease to have effect when paragraph 6 of Schedule 8 to the Coronavirus Act 2020[3] expires.

(6) The other temporary amendments to which paragraph (4) of this rule refers cease to have effect when section 53 (and Schedule 23), section 54 (and Schedule 24) and section 55 (and Schedule 25) of the Coronavirus Act 2020 expire.

[Note. The rules replaced by the first Criminal Procedure Rules (the Criminal Procedure Rules 2005[4]) were revoked when those Rules came into force by provisions of the Courts Act 2003, the Courts Act 2003 (Consequential Amendments) Order 2004 and the Courts Act 2003 (Commencement No. 6 and Savings) Order 2004[5]. The first Criminal Procedure Rules reproduced the substance of all the rules they replaced.

The Criminal Procedure (Amendment No. 2) (Coronavirus) Rules 2020 made temporary amendments to the Criminal Procedure Rules 2015 in consequence of modifications to statutory provisions made by the Coronavirus Act 2020.]

R2.2 Definitions

2.2 (1) In these Rules, unless the context makes it clear that something different is meant:
'advocate' means a person who is entitled to exercise a right of audience in the court under section 13 of the Legal Services Act 2007[6];
'authorised court officer' has the meaning given by rule 2.4;

[3] 2020 c. 7.
[4] S.I. 2005/384; amended by S.I. 2006/353, 2006/2636, 2007/699, 2007/2317, 2007/3662, 2008/2076, 2008/3269 and 2009/2087.
[5] S.I. 2004/2066.
[6] 2007 c. 29.

'business day' means any day except Saturday, Sunday, Christmas Day, Boxing Day, Good Friday, Easter Monday or a bank holiday;

'court' means a tribunal with jurisdiction over criminal cases. It includes a judge, recorder, District Judge (Magistrates' Court), lay justice and, when exercising their judicial powers, the Registrar of Criminal Appeals, and an authorised court officer;

'court officer' means the appropriate member of the staff of a court;

'justices' legal adviser' means a person authorised under section 28 of the Courts Act 2003[7] to give advice about law to justices of the peace;

'legal representative' means:

(i) the person for the time being named as a party's representative in any legal aid representation order made under section 16 of the Legal Aid, Sentencing and Punishment of Offenders Act 2012[8], or

(ii) subject to that, the person named as a party's representative in any notice for the time being given under rule 46.2 (Notice of appointment, etc. of legal representative: general rules) provided that person is entitled to conduct litigation in the court under section 13 of the Legal Services Act 2007;

'live link' means an arrangement by which a person can see and hear, and be seen and heard by, the court when that person is not in the courtroom;

'Practice Direction' means the Lord Chief Justice's Criminal Practice Directions, as amended, and 'Criminal Costs Practice Direction' means the Lord Chief Justice's Practice Direction (Costs in Criminal Proceedings), as amended;

'public interest ruling' means a ruling about whether it is in the public interest to disclose prosecution material under sections 3(6), 7A(8) or 8(5) of the Criminal Procedure and Investigations Act 1996[9]; and

'Registrar' means the Registrar of Criminal Appeals or a court officer exercising a function of the Registrar.

(2) Definitions of some other expressions are in the rules in which they apply.

[Note. The glossary at the end of the Rules is a guide to the meaning of certain legal expressions used in them.]

References to legislation, including these Rules **R2.3**

2.3 (1) In these Rules, where a rule refers to an Act of Parliament or to subordinate legislation by title and year, subsequent references to that Act or to that legislation in the rule are shortened: so, for example, after a reference to the Criminal Procedure and Investigations Act 1996[10] that Act is called 'the 1996 Act'; and after a reference to the Criminal Procedure and Investigations Act 1996 (Defence Disclosure Time Limits) Regulations 2011[11] those Regulations are called 'the 2011 Regulations'.

(2) In the courts in which these Rules apply—

(a) unless the context makes it clear that something different is meant, a reference to the Criminal Procedure Rules, without reference to a year, is a reference to the Criminal Procedure Rules in force at the date on which the event concerned occurs or occurred;

(b) a reference to the Criminal Procedure Rules may be abbreviated to 'CrimPR'; and

(c) a reference to a Part or rule in the Criminal Procedure Rules may be abbreviated to, for example, 'CrimPR Part 3' or 'CrimPR 3.5'.

Powers of authorised court officers

Exercise of court's functions by authorised court officers: general rules **R2.4**

2.4.—(1) This rule and rules 2.5, 2.6, 2.7, 2.8 and 2.9 provide for the exercise of relevant judicial functions within the meaning of section 67A of the Courts Act 2003[12]—

(a) in a court in which these Rules apply;

(b) by a person authorised for the purpose by the Lord Chief Justice under section 67B of that Act[13].

[7] 2003 c. 39; section 28 is substituted by section 3 of, and paragraph 26 of the Schedule to, the Courts and Tribunals (Judiciary and Functions of Staff) Act 2018 (c. 33).

[8] 2012 c. 10.

[9] 1996 c. 25; section 7A was inserted by section 37 of the Criminal Justice Act 2003 (c. 44).

[10] 1996 c. 25.

[11] S.I. 2011/209.

[12] 2003 c. 39; section 67A is inserted by section 3 of, and paragraph 32 of the Schedule to, the Courts and Tribunals (Judiciary and Functions of Staff) Act 2018 (c. 33).

[13] 2003 c. 39; section 67B is inserted by section 3 of, and paragraph 32 of the Schedule to, the Courts and Tribunals (Judiciary and Functions of Staff) Act 2018 (c. 33).

(2) In this rule and in rules 2.5, 2.6, 2.7, 2.8 and 2.9—
(a) 'authorised court officer' means any such person;
(b) a reference to an authorised court officer who is legally qualified is a reference to one who has such qualifications as are for the time being prescribed by regulations made under section 28(3) of the Courts Act 2003.

(3) No court officer may—
(a) authorise a person's committal to prison;
(b) authorise a person's arrest (but that exclusion does not apply to the issue of a warrant of arrest, whether or not endorsed for bail, to secure that a person attends court proceedings relating to an offence of which the person has been accused or convicted in a case in which no objection is made by or on behalf of that person to the issue of the warrant);
(c) grant or withhold bail, except to the extent that rule 2.6 or rule 2.8 allows;
(d) adjudicate on guilt, or on the act or omission with which a defendant is charged, except to the extent of—
(i) acquitting a defendant against whom the prosecutor offers no evidence,
(ii) convicting a defendant who pleads guilty, or
(iii) giving a prosecutor permission to withdraw a case;
(e) determine the admissibility of evidence;
(f) set ground rules for the conduct of questioning where rule 3.8(6), (7) (directions for the appropriate treatment and questioning of a witness or the defendant) applies;
(g) make findings of fact for the purpose of sentence, defer or pass sentence, impose a penalty or commit a defendant to the Crown Court for sentence;
(h) make an order for a party or other person to pay costs, unless that party or person agrees;
(i) make any other order consequent upon acquittal, conviction or a finding that the accused did the act or made the omission charged, except to the extent that rule 2.8 allows;
(j) vary, discharge, remit, remove, revoke, review or suspend a sentence, penalty or other order consequent on acquittal or conviction, except to the extent that rule 2.8 allows;
(k) order the search, confiscation, restraint, detention or seizure of property except to the extent that rule 2.8 allows;
(l) determine an appeal or reference to an appeal court, or an application for permission to appeal or refer, except to the extent that rule 2.6 allows; or
(m) determine an allegation of contempt of court.

(4) An authorised court officer may exercise a relevant judicial function for which rule 2.5, 2.6, 2.7, 2.8 or 2.9 provides—
(a) only subject to the same conditions as apply to its exercise by the court or person whose function it is; and
(b) where a party affected by the exercise of that function is entitled to make representations before its exercise, only if each such party has had a reasonable opportunity to make such representations—
(i) in writing, or
(ii) at a hearing (whether or not that party in fact attends).

(5) Unless the context makes it clear that something different is meant, provision in rule 2.5, 2.6, 2.7, 2.8 or 2.9 permitting the exercise of a relevant judicial function by an authorised court officer includes a power to decline to exercise that function.

[Note. Under section 67A of the Courts Act 2003, 'relevant judicial function' means a function of a court to which the general duty of the Lord Chancellor under section 1 of that Act applies and a judicial function of a person holding an office that entitles the person to exercise functions of such a court, but does not include in a court in which Criminal Procedure Rules apply—
(a) any function so far as its exercise involves authorising a person's committal to prison; or
(b) any function so far as its exercise involves authorising a person's arrest, except the issue of a warrant of arrest (whether or not endorsed for bail) to secure that a person attends court proceedings relating to an offence of which the person has been accused or convicted in a case in which no objection is made by or on behalf of that person to the issue of the warrant.

Under section 67B of the 2003 Act, in a court in which Criminal Procedure Rules apply the Rules may provide for the exercise of relevant judicial functions by persons who are appointed under section 2(1) of that Act and who satisfy any requirements specified in the Rules as to qualifications or experience. Such a person may exercise such a function only if authorised to do so by the Lord Chief Justice.

Section 28 of the 2003 Act provides for persons authorised by the Lord Chief Justice to give advice to justices of the peace about matters of law. Such a person may be authorised for that purpose only if appointed under section 2(1) of that Act and possessed of such qualifications as may be prescribed by regulations made under section 28. See also rule 2.2 (Definitions).]

Exercise of functions of the Court of Appeal R2.5

2.5.—(1) This rule provides for the exercise by an authorised court officer of relevant judicial functions of—

(a) the criminal division of the Court of Appeal; and
(b) the Registrar of Criminal Appeals.

(2) Subject to rule 2.4, an authorised court officer may exercise—

(a) any function of the criminal division of the Court of Appeal that may be exercised by the Registrar of Criminal Appeals; and
(b) any other judicial function of the Registrar.

(3) Where an authorised court officer exercises a function of the court—

(a) the same provision as that made by section 31A(4) or section 31C(3), as the case may be, of the Criminal Appeal Act 1968[14] applies as if that function had been exercised by the Registrar; and
(b) rule 36.5 (Renewing an application refused by a judge or the Registrar) applies.

[Note. See also rule 2.4, which makes general rules about the exercise of judicial functions by authorised court officers.

For the functions of the criminal division of the Court of Appeal that may be exercised by the Registrar of Criminal Appeals, see sections 31A and 31B of the Criminal Appeal Act 1968[15]*. For other functions of the Registrar, see section 21 of that Act*[16]*.*

Sections 31A(4) and 31C(3) of the 1968 Act provide for the reconsideration by a judge of a decision by the Registrar to which those provisions apply.]

Exercise of functions of the High Court R2.6

2.6.—(1) This rule provides for the exercise by an authorised court officer of relevant judicial functions of the High Court in relation to its jurisdiction under the Extradition Act 2003[17].

(2) An authorised court officer may exercise any such function of the High Court to which the rules in Section 3 of Part 50 apply (Extradition; Appeal to the High Court), subject to—

(a) rule 2.4; and
(b) paragraph (3) of this rule.

(3) No court officer may—

(a) grant or withhold bail;
(b) impose or vary a condition of bail; or
(c) reopen a decision which determines an appeal or an application for permission to appeal, unless paragraph (4) applies.

(4) If making a decision to which the parties have agreed in writing, an authorised court officer may—

(a) give or refuse permission to appeal;
(b) determine an appeal;
(c) grant or withhold bail; or
(d) impose or vary a condition of bail.

(5) Paragraph (6) of this rule—

(a) applies where a party wants a judge to reconsider a decision made by an authorised court officer;
(b) does not apply where such an officer agrees to postpone the date on which the required period for extradition begins under section 36(3) of the Extradition Act 2003[18].

(6) Such a party must—

(a) apply for such a reconsideration as soon as reasonably practicable, and in any event no later than the earlier of—
    (i) the next hearing before a judge, or
    (ii) the fifth business day after the date on which notice of the decision is served on the applicant;

[14] 1968 c. 19; section 31A was inserted by section 6 of the Criminal Appeal Act 1995 (c. 35) and amended by sections 87 and 109 of, and Schedule 10 to, the Courts Act 2003 (c. 39) and paragraphs 86 and 88 of Schedule 36 to the Criminal Justice Act 2003 (c. 44). Section 31C was inserted by section 87 of the Courts Act 2003 (c. 39) and amended by sections 47 and 149 of, and paragraphs 1 and 12 of Schedule 8 and part 3 of Schedule 28 to, the Criminal Justice and Immigration Act 2008 (c. 4).
[15] 1968 c. 19; section 31B was inserted by section 87 of the Courts Act 2003 (c. 39).
[16] 1968 c. 19.
[17] 2003 c. 41.
[18] 2003 c. 41; section 36 was amended by section 40 of, and paragraph 81 of Schedule 9 to, the Constitutional Reform Act 2005 (c. 4).

(b) unless the application is made at a hearing, serve the application on—
(i) the court officer, and
(ii) each other party (if any) affected by the decision; and
(c) in the application—
(i) specify the decision in issue,
(ii) explain why it is appropriate for the decision to be reconsidered and what decision the applicant thinks would be appropriate, and
(iii) ask for a hearing, if one is wanted, and explain why it is needed.

(7) The judge may determine the application—
(a) at a hearing (which may be in public or private), or without a hearing;
(b) in the absence of—
(i) the applicant,
(ii) each other party (if any) affected by the decision.

(8) But the judge must not determine the application in the absence of an affected party unless that party has had—
(a) such notice as the nature and urgency of the application permits; and
(b) a reasonable opportunity to make representations.

[Note. See also—
(a) rule 2.4, which makes general rules about the exercise of judicial functions by authorised court officers;
(b) rule 2.10, which provides for extension of the time limit under this rule;
(c) rule 3.6 (Application to vary a direction); and
(d) rule 50.18 (Case management in the High Court).

For the functions of the High Court for which this rule provides, see the introductory note to Section 3 of Part 50. See also rule 50.30 for the constitution of the High Court when exercising the powers to which that Section of that Part applies.

Under section 36 of the Extradition Act 2003, where an extradition order has been made under Part 1 of the Act and the outcome of an appeal by the defendant is that he or she is to be extradited then (a) the defendant must be removed to the requesting territory within 10 days starting with the day on which the decision of the relevant court on the appeal becomes final or proceedings on the appeal are discontinued, unless (b) the requesting authority and the High Court agree to postpone that starting date.]

R2.7 Exercise of functions of the Crown Court

2.7.—(1) This rule provides for the exercise by an authorised court officer of relevant judicial functions of the Crown Court in a criminal cause or matter.

(2) Subject to rule 2.4 and to paragraph (3) of this rule, an authorised court officer may—
(a) determine an application to extend a time limit set by a rule or by a judge, including a time limit for the conduct of confiscation proceedings, unless the effect would be—
(i) to affect the date of any hearing that has been fixed, including a trial, or
(ii) significantly to affect the progress of the case in any other way;
(b) give a live link direction under section 57B, 57E or 57F of the Crime and Disorder Act 1998[19] (Use of live link at preliminary hearings where accused is in custody; Use of live link in sentencing hearings; Use of live link in certain enforcement hearings);
(c) exercise the court's functions listed in rule 23.2 (Appointment of advocate to cross-examine witness) and select such an advocate as that rule describes (but a court officer may not decline to select such an advocate where that rule applies).

(3) An authorised court officer may not exercise a function of the court in a case in which a judge so directs.

(4) Paragraph (5) of this rule applies where a party or an advocate appointed under rule 23.2 (Appointment of advocate to cross-examine witness) wants a judge to reconsider a decision made by an authorised court officer.

(5) Such a party or advocate must—
(a) apply for such a reconsideration as soon as reasonably practicable, and in any event no later than the earlier of—
(i) the next hearing before a judge, or
(ii) the tenth business day after the date on which notice of the decision is served on the applicant;
(b) unless the application is made at a hearing, serve the application on—

[19] 1998 c. 37; sections 57A to 57E were substituted for section 57 as originally enacted by section 45 of the Police and Justice Act 2006 (c. 48). Sections 57B and 57E were amended, and section 57F was inserted, by section 106 of the Coroners and Justice Act 2009 (c. 25).

(i) the court officer, and
(ii) each other party (if any) affected by the decision; and
(c) in the application—
(i) specify the decision in issue,
(ii) explain why it is appropriate for the decision to be reconsidered and what decision the applicant thinks would be appropriate, and
(iii) ask for a hearing, if one is wanted, and explain why it is needed.

(6) The judge may determine the application—
(a) at a hearing (which may be in public or private), or without a hearing;
(b) in the absence of—
(i) the applicant,
(ii) each other party (if any) affected by the decision.

(7) But the judge must not determine the application in the absence of an affected party unless that party has had—
(a) such notice as the nature and urgency of the application permits; and
(b) a reasonable opportunity to make representations.

[Note. See also—

(a) rule 2.4, which makes general rules about the exercise of judicial functions by authorised court officers;
(b) rule 2.10, which provides for extension of the time limit under this rule; and
(c) rule 3.6 (Application to vary a direction).

For the constitution and powers of the Crown Court, see the note to rule 25.1 (Trial and sentence in the Crown Court; When this Part applies).]

Exercise of functions of a magistrates' court **R2.8**

2.8.—(1) This rule provides for the exercise by an authorised court officer of relevant judicial functions of a magistrates' court in a criminal cause or matter.

(2) Subject to rule 2.4 and to paragraph (12) of this rule, an authorised court officer may—
(a) fix, cancel or vary the date, time or place for a hearing, including a trial, or adjourn a hearing;
(b) adjourn, remit or transfer proceedings from one local justice area to another;
(c) determine an application to extend a time limit set by a rule or by the court, unless the effect would be—
(i) to affect the date of any hearing that has been fixed, including a trial, or
(ii) significantly to affect the progress of the case in any other way;
(d) issue a summons at the request of a public prosecutor, or under section 16B of the Magistrates' Courts Act 1980[20] (Cases not tried in accordance with section 16A) or section 83 of that Act[21] (Process for securing attendance of offender);
(e) give a prosecutor permission to withdraw a case;
(f) grant bail where the defendant already is on bail and—
(i) the conditions, if any, to which that bail is subject will remain the same, or
(ii) bail conditions will be varied or imposed with both parties' agreement;
(g) give consent for another magistrates' court to deal with a defendant for an offence in respect of which the defendant, when an adult, was discharged conditionally;
(h) order a convicted defendant to produce his or her driving licence;
(i) require a statement of the defendant's assets and other financial circumstances;
(j) amend an attendance centre order to—
(i) vary the day or hour specified in that order for the defendant's first attendance, or
(ii) substitute an alternative centre;
(k) amend the local justice area or responsible officer named in an order of the court;
(l) amend a sentence or order by requiring it to be completed in Northern Ireland or Scotland;
(m) extend the time for service of a statutory declaration to which applies—
(i) rule 44.2 (Statutory declaration of ignorance of proceedings), or
(ii) rule 29.4 (Statutory declaration to avoid fine after fixed penalty notice);

[20] 1980 c. 43; section 16B was inserted by section 48 of the Criminal Justice and Courts Act 2015 (c. 2).
[21] 1980 c. 43; section 83 was amended by articles 46 and 47 of S.I. 2006/1737 and sections 97(2) and 106 of, and Part V (table 8) of Schedule 15 to, the Access to Justice Act 1999 (c. 22).

(n) fix a later time at which a defendant must attend court for the purposes of an enquiry or hearing under section 82 of the Magistrates' Courts Act 1980[22] (Restriction on power to impose imprisonment for default);
(o) conduct a means enquiry;
(p) make a collection order;
(q) issue a warrant of control;
(r) extend the time for payment of a fine or sum to which Part 30 (Enforcement of fines and other orders for payment) applies;
(s) vary an order for the payment by instalments of such a fine or sum;
(t) make a transfer of fine order;
(u) make a disclosure order under section 125CA Magistrates' Courts Act 1980[23] (Power to make disclosure order) for the purposes of securing the execution of a warrant;
(v) make an attachment of earnings order;
(w) make or withdraw an application for deductions to be made from a defendant's benefit payments; and
(x) take any step listed in paragraph 38 of Schedule 5 to the Courts Act 2003[24] (range of further steps available against defaulters).

(3) In addition to the functions listed in paragraph (2), subject to rule 2.4 and to paragraph (12) of this rule an authorised court officer who is legally qualified may exercise the other functions of a magistrates' court listed in paragraphs (4) to (11).

(4) In connection with the rules about general matters (Parts 1 to 6)—
(a) exercising the powers to which section 50 of the Crime and Disorder Act 1998[25] (Early administrative hearings) refers, where that section applies and subject to the restrictions that it contains;
(b) giving, varying or revoking a live link direction under Part IIIA of the Crime and Disorder Act 1998[26] (Live links for accused's attendance at certain preliminary, sentencing and other hearings);
(c) determining an application to extend a time limit set by a rule or by the court;
(d) giving, varying or revoking an order for separate or joint trials in respect of two or more defendants or two or more offences, if all parties agree;
(e) giving, varying or revoking directions for the conduct of proceedings, including—
(i) the timetable for the case,
(ii) the attendance of the parties,
(iii) the service of documents (including summaries of any legal arguments relied on by the parties),
(iv) the manner in which evidence is to be given, insofar as this rule makes no other provision and except the making, varying or revocation of a witness anonymity order;
(f) determining an application under rule 5.7(5) (supply to a party of information or documents from records or case materials; information to which paragraph (4) of that rule does not apply) where—
(i) rule 5.7(6) applies (information about the grounds on which an order was made, or a warrant was issued, in the absence of the party or person applying for that information), and

[22] 1980 c. 43; section 82 was amended by section 77 of, and paragraph 52 of Schedule 14 to, the Criminal Justice Act 1982 (c. 48), sections 61 and 123 of, and paragraphs 1 and 2 of Schedule 8 to, the Criminal Justice Act 1988 (c. 33), section 55 of and paragraph 10 of Schedule 4 to the Crime (Sentences) Act 1997 (c. 43), paragraph 220 of Schedule 8 to the Courts Act 2003 (c. 39), section 62 of, and paragraphs 45 and 51 of Schedule 13 to, the Tribunals, Courts and Enforcement Act 2007 (c. 15) and section 179 of the Anti-social Behaviour, Crime and Policing Act 2014 (c. 12) and section 54 of, and paragraphs 2 and 3 of Schedule 12 to, the Criminal Justice and Courts Act 2015 (c. 2). It is further amended by paragraphs 58 and 63 of Part II of Schedule 7 to the Criminal Justice and Court Services Act 2000 (c. 43) and Part 7 of Schedule 37 to the Criminal Justice Act 2003 (c. 44), with effect from dates to be appointed.

[23] 1980 c. 43; section 125CA was inserted by section 28 of the Domestic Violence, Crime and Victims Act 2004 (c. 28) and amended by section 62 of, and paragraphs 45 and 60 of Schedule 13 to, the Tribunals, Courts and Enforcement Act 2007 (c. 15).

[24] 2003 c. 39; paragraph 38 of Schedule 5 was amended by articles 2, 4 and 26 of S.I. 2006/1737, section 62 of, and paragraphs 148 and 149 of Schedule 13 to, the Tribunals, Courts and Enforcement Act 2007 (c. 15), section 80 of the Criminal Justice and Immigration Act 2008 (c. 4) and section 88 of the Legal Aid, Sentencing and Punishment of Offenders Act 2012 (c. 10).

[25] 1998 c. 37; section 50 was amended by section 106 of, and Schedule 15 to, the Access to Justice Act 1999 (c. 22), sections 41 and 332 of, and paragraphs 15 and 16 of Schedule 3 and Part 4 of Schedule 37 to, the Criminal Justice Act 2003 (c. 44), regulation 8 of S.I. 2006/2493 and section 39 of, and paragraphs 46 and 47 of Schedule 5 to, the Legal Aid, Sentencing and Punishment of Offenders Act 2012 (c. 10). It is further amended by section 3 of, and paragraphs 20 and 22 of the Schedule to, the Courts and Tribunals (Judiciary and Functions of Staff) Act 2018 (c. 33).

[26] 1998 c. 37; Part IIIA was substituted by section 45 of the Police and Justice Act 2006 (c. 48).

(ii) no notice of objection under that paragraph is given within the time for which that paragraph provides;

(g) imposing a reporting restriction under section 45 of the Youth Justice and Criminal Evidence Act 1999[27] (identity of a person under 18) where there is no objection to the order;

(h) giving permission for proceedings to be recorded; and

(i) asking a court security officer to remove a person from a courtroom.

(5) In connection with the rules about preliminary proceedings (Parts 7 to 12)—

(a) issuing a summons and giving directions for service;

(b) under section 4 of the Summary Jurisdiction (Process) Act 1881[28], endorsing a summons or warrant issued by a court in Scotland;

(c) giving a prosecutor permission to withdraw a charge;

(d) dismissing a prosecution where the prosecutor offers no evidence;

(e) amending a charge; and

(f) sending a defendant to the Crown Court for trial where the only condition for sending is—

(i) that prescribed by section 51(2)(a), of the Crime and Disorder Act 1998[29] (offence triable only on indictment other than one in respect of which notice is given under section 51B or 51C of that Act[30]), or

(ii) the service of a notice under section 51B or 51C of that Act (prosecutor's notice requiring sending for trial in a case of serious or complex fraud or a case in which a child is to be called as a witness).

(6) In connection with the rules about custody and bail (Parts 13 and 14)—

(a) issuing or withdrawing a warrant for a person's arrest to secure that the person attends court proceedings relating to an offence of which the person has been accused or convicted in a case in which no objection is made by or on behalf of that person to the issue of the warrant; and

(b) granting bail where—

(i) the defendant is present,

(ii) the prosecutor agrees to the grant of bail, and

(iii) the conditions, if any, to which that bail will be subject will remain the same as before, or will be varied or imposed with the parties' agreement.

(7) In connection with the rules about evidence (Parts 16 to 23)—

(a) requiring a person who has made a written statement to attend before the court to give evidence;

(b) issuing a witness summons and giving directions for its service; and

(c) exercising the court's functions listed in rule 23.2 (Appointment of advocate to cross-examine witness) and appointing such an advocate as that rule describes (but a court officer may not decline to appoint such an advocate where that rule applies).

(8) In connection with the rules about trial (Parts 24 to 27)—

(a) convicting a defendant who has pleaded guilty;

(b) requesting a pre-sentence report where a defendant pleads guilty; and

(c) directing the commissioning of a medical report.

(9) In connection with the rules about appeal (Parts 34 to 44)—

(a) stating a case for the opinion of the High Court where the decision under appeal was made by an authorised court officer; and

(b) requiring the appellant to enter into a recognizance under section 114 of the Magistrates' Courts Act 1980[31] on an application to state a case for the opinion of the High Court.

[27] 1999 c. 23.

[28] 1881 c. 24.

[29] 1998 c. 37; section 51 was substituted by paragraphs 15 and 18 of Schedule 3 to the Criminal Justice Act 2003 (c. 44) and amended by section 52 of the Criminal Justice and Courts Act 2015 (c. 2).

[30] 1998 c. 37; sections 51B and 51C were inserted by paragraphs 15 and 18 of Schedule 3 to the Criminal Justice Act 2003 (c. 44). Section 51B was amended by section 50 of, and paragraph 69 of Schedule 4 to, the Commissioners for Revenue and Customs Act 2005 (c. 11), paragraphs 46 and 48 of Schedule 5 to the Legal Aid, Sentencing and Punishment of Offenders Act 2012 (c. 10) and article 3 of, and paragraphs 14 and 15 of Schedule 2 to, S.I. 2014/834. Section 51C was modified by section 63 of, and paragraph 36 of Schedule 6 to, the Serious Crime Act 2007 (c. 27) and amended by regulations 8 and 9 of S.I. 2016/244.

[31] 1980 c. 43; section 114 was amended by section 90 of, and paragraphs 95 and 113 of Schedule 13 to, the Access to Justice Act 1999 (c. 22) and section 109 of, and paragraph 235 of Schedule 8 to, the Courts Act 2003 (c. 39). It is further amended by section 3 of, and paragraphs 5 and 7 of the Schedule to, the Courts and Tribunals (Judiciary and Functions of Staff) Act 2018 (c 33).

(10) In connection with the rules about costs (Part 45)—
(a) making or varying an order for a party to pay costs, if both parties agree;
(b) making or varying an order for another person to pay costs, if that person agrees; and
(c) making a costs order to which rule 45.4 (Costs out of central funds) applies.
(11) In connection with the rules about other proceedings (Parts 46 to 50)—
(a) making a legal aid representation order on an appeal against a refusal of legal aid (but a court officer may not decline to make such an order); and
(b) determining an application for a change of legal representative.
(12) An authorised court officer who is not a justices' legal adviser may not exercise a function of the court in a case in which a District Judge (Magistrates' Courts), a lay justice or a justices' legal adviser so directs.

[Note. See also—

(a) rule 2.4, which makes general rules about the exercise of judicial functions by authorised court officers; and
(b) rule 3.6 (Application to vary a direction).

Under section 148 of the Magistrates' Courts Act 1980[32]*, the expression 'magistrates' court' means any justice or justices of the peace acting under any enactment or by virtue of their commission or under the common law. For a court's power to try an allegation of an offence, see the note to rule 24.1 (Trial and sentence in a magistrates' court; When this Part applies).*

Under section 50 of the Crime and Disorder Act 1998[33]*, where a defendant has been charged with an offence at a police station the magistrates' court before whom he or she appears or is brought for the first time in relation to the charge may consist of a single justice; and where on such an occasion the powers of a single justice are exercised by an authorised court officer that court officer may not remand the defendant in custody or, without the consent of the prosecutor and the defendant, remand the defendant on bail on conditions other than those (if any) previously imposed.*

Under section 8B(3) of the Magistrates' Courts Act 1980[34]*, a magistrates' court may discharge or vary (or further vary) a pre-trial ruling within the meaning of section 8A of that Act*[35] *if the court has given the parties an opportunity to be heard and if, among other things, there has been a material change of circumstances since the ruling was made or, if a previous application has been made, since the application (or last application) was made.*

Under section 53(4) of the Courts Act 2003[36]*, a court security officer acting in the execution of that officer's duty may remove any person from a courtroom at the request of a judge or a justice of the peace.]*

R2.9 Exercise of functions of a District Judge (Magistrates' Courts) in extradition cases

2.9.—(1) This rule provides for the exercise by an authorised court officer of relevant judicial functions of a District Judge (Magistrates' Courts) in a case to which Part 50 (Extradition) applies.
(2) Subject to rule 2.4, an authorised court officer who is legally qualified may—
(a) fix, cancel or vary the date, time or place for a hearing, including an extradition hearing; and
(b) determine an application to extend a time limit set by a rule or by the court, unless the effect would be—
(i) to affect the date of any hearing that has been fixed, including an extradition hearing, or
(ii) significantly to affect the progress of the case in any other way.
(3) An authorised court officer who is not a justices' legal adviser may not exercise a function of the court in a case in which a District Judge (Magistrates' Courts) or a justices' legal adviser so directs.

32 1980 c. 43; section 148 was amended by section 109 of, and paragraph 248 of Schedule 8 to, the Courts Act 2003 (c. 39).
33 1998 c. 37; section 50 was amended by section 106 of, and Schedule 15 to, the Access to Justice Act 1999 (c. 22), sections 41 and 332 of, and paragraphs 15 and 16 of Schedule 3 and Part 4 of Schedule 37 to, the Criminal Justice Act 2003 (c. 44), regulation 8 of S.I. 2006/2493 and section 39 of, and paragraphs 46 and 47 of Schedule 5 to, the Legal Aid, Sentencing and Punishment of Offenders Act 2012 (c. 10). It is further amended by section 3 of, and paragraphs 20 and 22 of the Schedule to, the Courts and Tribunals (Judiciary and Functions of Staff) Act 2018 (c. 33).
34 1980 c. 43; section 8B was inserted by section 45 of, and Schedule 3 to, the Courts Act 2003 (c. 39) and amended by paragraph 51 of Schedule 3, and Part 4 of Schedule 37, to the Criminal Justice Act 2003 (c. 44).
35 1980 c. 43; section 8A was inserted by section 45 of, and Schedule 3 to, the Courts Act 2003 (c. 39) and amended by SI 2006/2493 and paragraphs 12 and 14 of Schedule 5 to the Legal Aid, Sentencing and Punishment of Offenders Act 2012 (c. 10).
36 2003 c. 39.

[Note. See also—

(a) rule 2.4, which makes general rules about the exercise of judicial functions by authorised court officers;
(b) rule 3.6 (Application to vary a direction); and
(c) rule 50.4 (Case management in the magistrates' court and duty of court officer).]

Court's power to extend time under rule 2.6 or rule 2.7 **R2.10**

2.10.—(1) The court may extend (even after it has expired) a time limit under rule 2.6 (Exercise of functions of the High Court) or rule 2.7 (Exercise of functions of the Crown Court).

(2) A party who wants an extension of time must—

(a) apply when serving the application for which it is needed; and
(b) explain the delay.

Criminal Procedure Rules Part 3 Case Management

General rules

When this Part applies **R3.1**

3.1 (1) Rules 3.1 to 3.15 apply to the management of each case in a magistrates' court and in the Crown Court (including an appeal to the Crown Court) until the conclusion of that case.

(2) Rules 3.16 to 3.18 apply in a magistrates' court unless—

(a) the court sends the defendant for trial in the Crown Court; or
(b) the case is one to which rule 24.8 or rule 24.9 applies (Written guilty plea: special rules; Single justice procedure: special rules).

(3) Rules 3.19 to 3.34 apply where—

(a) the defendant is sent to the Crown Court for trial;
(b) a High Court or Crown Court judge gives permission to serve a draft indictment; or
(c) the Court of Appeal orders a retrial.

[Note. Rules that apply to procedure in the Court of Appeal are in Parts 36 to 42 of these Rules.

A magistrates' court may send a defendant for trial in the Crown Court under section 51 or 51A of the Crime and Disorder Act 1998[1]. See Part 9 for the procedure on allocation and sending for trial.

Under paragraph 2(1) of Schedule 17 to the Crime and Courts Act 2013[2] and section 2 of the Administration of Justice (Miscellaneous Provisions) Act 1933[3], the Crown Court may give permission to serve a draft indictment where it approves a deferred prosecution agreement. See Part 11 for the rules about that procedure and Part 10 for the rules about indictments.

The procedure for applying for the permission of a High Court judge to serve a draft indictment is in rule 10.9 (Application to a High Court judge for permission to serve a draft indictment).

[1] 1998 c. 37; section 51 was substituted by paragraphs 15 and 18 of Schedule 3 to the Criminal Justice Act 2003 (c. 44) and amended by section 59 of, and paragraph 1 of Schedule 11 to, the Constitutional Reform Act 2005 (c. 4). Section 51A was inserted by paragraphs 15 and 18 of Schedule 3 to the Criminal Justice Act 2003 (c. 44) and amended by section 49 of, and paragraph 5 of Schedule 1 to, the Violent Crime Reduction Act 2006 (c. 38) and paragraph 6 of Schedule 21 to the Legal Aid, Sentencing and Punishment of Offenders Act 2012 (c. 10).

[2] 2013 c. 22.

[3] 1933 c. 36; section 2 was amended by Part IV of Schedule 11 to, the Courts Act 1971 (c. 23), Schedule 5 to, the Senior Courts Act 1981 (c. 54), Schedule 2 to the Prosecution of Offences Act 1985 (c. 23), paragraph 1 of Schedule 2 to the Criminal Justice Act 1987 (c. 38), paragraph 10 of Schedule 15 to the Criminal Justice Act 1988 (c. 33), paragraph 8 of Schedule 6 to the Criminal Justice Act 1991 (c. 53), Schedule 1 to the Statute Law (Repeals Act 1993, paragraph 17 of Schedule 1 to the Criminal Procedure and Investigations Act 1996 (c. 25), paragraph 5 of Schedule 8 to the Crime and Disorder Act 1998 (c. 37), paragraph 34 of Schedule 3 and Part 4 of Schedule 37 to the Criminal Justice Act 2003 (c. 44), paragraph 1 of the Schedule to S.I. 2004/2035, section 12 of, and paragraph 7 of Schedule 1 to, the Constitutional Reform Act 2005 (c. 4), sections 116 and 178 of, and Part 3 of Schedule 23 to, the Coroners and Justice Act 2009 (c. 25), paragraph 32 of Schedule 17 to the Crime and Courts Act 2013 (c. 22) and section 82 of the Deregulation Act 2015 (c. 20).

The Court of Appeal may order a retrial under section 8 of the Criminal Appeal Act 1968[4] *(on a defendant's appeal against conviction) or under section 77 of the Criminal Justice Act 2003*[5] *(on a prosecutor's application for the retrial of a serious offence after acquittal). Section 8 of the 1968 Act, section 84 of the 2003 Act and rules 27.6 and 39.14 require the arraignment of a defendant within 2 months.]*

R3.2 **The duty of the court**

3.2 (1) The court must further the overriding objective by actively managing the case.
(2) Active case management includes—
(a) the early identification of the real issues;
(b) the early identification of the needs of witnesses;
(c) achieving certainty as to what must be done, by whom, and when, in particular by the early setting of a timetable for the progress of the case;
(d) monitoring the progress of the case and compliance with directions;
(e) ensuring that evidence, whether disputed or not, is presented in the shortest and clearest way;
(f) discouraging delay, dealing with as many aspects of the case as possible on the same occasion, and avoiding unnecessary hearings;
(g) encouraging the participants to co-operate in the progression of the case; and
(h) making use of technology.
(3) The court must actively manage the case by giving any direction appropriate to the needs of that case as early as possible.
(4) Where appropriate live links are available, making use of technology for the purposes of this rule includes directing the use of such facilities, whether an application for such a direction is made or not—
(a) for the conduct of a pre-trial hearing, including a pre-trial case management hearing;
(b) for the defendant's attendance at such a hearing—
(i) where the defendant is in custody, or where the defendant is not in custody and wants to attend by live link, but
(ii) only if the court is satisfied that the defendant can participate effectively by such means, having regard to all the circumstances including whether the defendant is represented or not; and
(c) for receiving evidence under one of the powers to which the rules in Part 18 apply (Measures to assist a witness or defendant to give evidence).
(5) Where appropriate telephone facilities are available, making use of technology for the purposes of this rule includes directing the use of such facilities, whether an application for such a direction is made or not, for the conduct of a pre-trial case management hearing—
(a) if telephone facilities are more convenient for that purpose than live links;
(b) unless at that hearing the court expects to take the defendant's plea; and
(c) only if—
(i) the defendant is represented, or
(ii) exceptionally, the court is satisfied that the defendant can participate effectively by such means without a representative.

[Note. In relation to the defendant's attendance by live link at a pre-trial hearing, see sections 46ZA and 47 of the Police and Criminal Evidence Act 1984[6] *and sections 57A to 57D and 57F of the Crime and Disorder Act 1998*[7]*.*

[4] 1968 c. 19; section 8 was amended by Section 12 of, and paragraph 38 of Schedule 2 to, the Bail Act 1976 (c. 63), section 56 of, and Part IV of Schedule 11 to, the Courts Act 1971 (c. 23), section 65 of, and paragraph 36 of Schedule 3 to, the Mental Health (Amendment Act 1982 (c. 51), section 148 of, and paragraph 23 of Schedule 4 to, the Mental Health Act 1983 (c. 20), section 43 of the Criminal Justice Act 1988 (c. 33), section 168 of, and paragraph 19 of Schedule 10 to, the Criminal Justice and Public Order Act 1994 (c. 33), section 58 of the Access to Justice Act 1999 (c. 22), sections 41 and 332 of, and paragraph 43 of Schedule 3 to, and Part 4 of Schedule 37 to, the Criminal Justice Act 2003 (c. 44) and section 32 of, and paragraph 2 of Schedule 4 to, the Mental Health Act 2007 (c. 12).

[5] 2003 c. 44.

[6] 1984 c. 60; section 46ZA was inserted by section 46 of the Police and Justice Act 2006 (c. 48) and amended by section 107 of the Coroners and Justice Act 2009 (c. 25). Section 47 was amended by sections 27, 29 and 168 of, and Schedule 11 to, the Criminal Justice and Public Order Act 1994 (c. 33), section 46 of the Crime and Disorder Act 1998 (c. 37), section 109 of, and paragraph 283 of Schedule 8 to, the Courts Act 2003 (c. 39), sections 12 and 28 of, and paragraphs 1 and 10 of Schedule 1 and paragraphs 1 and 6 of Schedule 2 to, the Criminal Justice Act 2003 (c. 44), sections 10 and 46 of, and paragraphs 1, 6 and 11 of Schedule 6 to, the Police and Justice Act 2006 (c. 48) and section 1 of the Police (Detention and Bail Act 2011 (c. 9).

[7] 1998 c. 37; sections 57A to 57E were substituted for section 57 as originally enacted by section 45 of the Police and Justice Act 2006 (c. 48). Section 57A was amended by section 109 of the Coroners and Justice Act 2009 (c. 25) and section 105 of, and paragraphs 36 and 39 of Schedule 12 to, the Legal Aid, Sentencing and Punishment of Offenders Act 2012 (c. 10). Sections 57B, 57C and 57D were amended by section 106 of the Coroners and Justice Act 2009 (c. 25). Section 57F was inserted by section 109 of the Coroners and Justice Act 2009 (c. 25).

In relation to the giving of evidence by a witness and the giving of evidence by the defendant, see section 32 of the Criminal Justice Act 1988[8]*, sections 19, 24 and 33A of the Youth Justice and Criminal Evidence Act 1999*[9] *and section 51 of the Criminal Justice Act 2003*[10]*. Part 18 (Measures to assist a witness or defendant to give evidence) contains relevant rules.]*

The duty of the parties **R3.3**

3.3 (1) Each party must—
(a) actively assist the court in fulfilling its duty under rule 3.2, without or if necessary with a direction; and
(b) apply for a direction if needed to further the overriding objective.
(2) Active assistance for the purposes of this rule includes—
(a) at the beginning of the case, communication between the prosecutor and the defendant at the first available opportunity and in any event no later than the beginning of the day of the first hearing;
(b) after that, communication between the parties and with the court officer until the conclusion of the case;
(c) by such communication establishing, among other things—
(i) whether the defendant is likely to plead guilty or not guilty,
(ii) what is agreed and what is likely to be disputed,
(iii) what information, or other material, is required by one party of another, and why, and
(iv) what is to be done, by whom, and when (without or if necessary with a direction);
(d) reporting on that communication to the court—
(i) at the first hearing, and
(ii) after that, as directed by the court;
(e) alerting the court to any reason why—
(i) a direction should not be made in any of the circumstances listed in rule 3.2(4) or (5) (The duty of the court: use of live link or telephone facilities), or
(ii) such a direction should be varied or revoked.
(f) alerting the court to any potential impediment to the defendant's effective participation in the trial; and
(g) alerting the court to any related family proceedings or anticipated such proceedings as soon as reasonably practicable after becoming aware of them.

Case progression officers and their duties **R3.4**

3.4 (1) At the beginning of the case each party must, unless the court otherwise directs—
(a) nominate someone responsible for progressing that case; and
(b) tell other parties and the court who that is and how to contact that person.
(2) In fulfilling its duty under rule 3.2, the court must where appropriate—
(a) nominate a court officer responsible for progressing the case; and
(b) make sure the parties know who that is and how to contact that court officer.
(3) In this Part a person nominated under this rule is called a case progression officer.
(4) A case progression officer must—
(a) monitor compliance with directions;
(b) make sure that the court is kept informed of events that may affect the progress of that case;
(c) make sure that he or she can be contacted promptly about the case during ordinary business hours;
(d) act promptly and reasonably in response to communications about the case; and
(e) if he or she will be unavailable, appoint a substitute to fulfil his or her duties and inform the other case progression officers.

[8] 1988 c. 33; section 32 was amended by section 55 of the Criminal Justice Act 1991 (c. 53), section 29 of, and paragraph 16 of Schedule 2 to, the Criminal Appeal Act 1995 (c. 35), section 62 of the Criminal Procedure and Investigations Act 1996 (c. 25), section 67 of, and Schedule 6 and paragraph 3 of Schedule 7 to, the Youth Justice and Criminal Evidence Act 1999 (c. 23) and article 3 of, and paragraphs 24 and 26 of the Schedule to S.I. 2004/2035.
[9] 1999 c. 23; section 24 was amended by paragraph 385 of Schedule 8 to, and Schedule 10 to, the Courts Act 2003 (c. 39) and section 102(1) of the Coroners and Justice Act 2009 (c. 25). Section 33A was inserted by section 47 of the Police and Justice Act 2006 (c. 48).
[10] 2003 c. 44.

R3.5 **The court's case management powers**

3.5 (1) In fulfilling its duty under rule 3.2 the court may give any direction and take any step actively to manage a case unless that direction or step would be inconsistent with legislation, including these Rules.

(2) In particular, the court may—

(a) nominate a judge, magistrate or justices' legal adviser to manage the case;

(b) give a direction on its own initiative or on application by a party;

(c) ask or allow a party to propose a direction;

(d) receive applications, notices, representations and information by letter, by telephone, by live link, by email or by any other means of electronic communication, and conduct a hearing by live link, telephone or other such electronic means;

(e) give a direction—

(i) at a hearing, in public or in private, or

(ii) without a hearing;

(f) fix, postpone, bring forward, extend, cancel or adjourn a hearing;

(g) shorten or extend (even after it has expired) a time limit fixed by a direction;

(h) require that issues in the case should be—

(i) identified in writing,

(ii) determined separately, and decide in what order they will be determined;

(i) specify the consequences of failing to comply with a direction.

(j) request information from a court dealing with family proceedings by—

(i) making the request itself, or

(ii) directing the court officer or a party to make the request on the criminal court's behalf; and

(k) supply information to a court dealing with family proceedings as if an application had been made under rule 5.8(7) (Supply to the public, including reporters, of information about cases) by—

(i) supplying the information itself, or

(ii) directing the court officer or a party to supply that information on the criminal court's behalf.

(3) A magistrates' court may give a direction that will apply in the Crown Court if the case is to continue there.

(4) The Crown Court may give a direction that will apply in a magistrates' court if the case is to continue there.

(5) Any power to give a direction under this Part includes a power to vary or revoke that direction.

(6) If a party fails to comply with a rule or a direction, the court may—

(a) fix, postpone, bring forward, extend, cancel or adjourn a hearing;

(b) exercise its powers to make a costs order; and

(c) impose such other sanction as may be appropriate.

[Note. Depending upon the nature of a case and the stage that it has reached, its progress may be affected by other Criminal Procedure Rules and by other legislation. The note at the end of this Part lists other rules and legislation that may apply.

See also rule 3.8 (Case preparation and progression).

The court may make a costs order under—

(a) section 19 of the Prosecution of Offences Act 1985[11]*, where the court decides that one party to criminal proceedings has incurred costs as a result of an unnecessary or improper act or omission by, or on behalf of, another party;*

(b) section 19A of that Act[12]*, where the court decides that a party has incurred costs as a result of an improper, unreasonable or negligent act or omission on the part of a legal representative;*

[11] 1985 c. 23; section 19 was amended by section 166 of the Criminal Justice Act 1988 (c. 33), section 45 of, and Schedule 6 to, the Legal Aid Act 1988 (c. 34), section 7 of, and paragraph 8 of Schedule 3 to, the Criminal Procedure (Insanity and Unfitness to Plead Act 1991 (c. 25), section 24 of, and paragraphs 27 and 28 of Schedule 4 to, the Access to Justice Act 1999 (c. 22), sections 40 and 67 of, and paragraph 4 of Schedule 7 to, the Youth Justice and Criminal Evidence Act 1999 (c. 23), section 165 of, and paragraph 99 of Schedule 9 to, the Powers of Criminal Courts (Sentencing Act 2000 (c. 6), section 378 of, and paragraph 107 of Schedule 16 to, the Armed Forces Act 2006 (c. 52), section 6 of, and paragraph 32 of Schedule 4 and paragraphs 1 and 5 of Schedule 27 to, the Criminal Justice and Immigration Act 2008 (c. 4) and paragraphs 22 and 23 of Schedule 5, and paragraphs 1 and 5 and Part 4 of Schedule 7, to the Legal Aid, Sentencing and Punishment of Offenders Act 2012 (c. 10).

[12] 1985 c. 23; section 19A was inserted by section 111 of the Courts and Legal Services Act 1990 (c. 41).

(c) section 19B of that Act[13]*, where the court decides that there has been serious misconduct by a person who is not a party.*

Under some other legislation, including Parts 19, 20 and 21 of these Rules, if a party fails to comply with a rule or a direction then in some circumstances—

(a) the court may refuse to allow that party to introduce evidence;
(b) evidence that that party wants to introduce may not be admissible;
(c) the court may draw adverse inferences from the late introduction of an issue or evidence.

See also—

(a) section 81(1) of the Police and Criminal Evidence Act 1984[14] *and section 20(3) of the Criminal Procedure and Investigations Act 1996*[15] *(advance disclosure of expert evidence);*
(b) section 11(5) of the Criminal Procedure and Investigations Act 1996[16] *(faults in disclosure by accused);*
(c) section 132(5) of the Criminal Justice Act 2003[17] *(failure to give notice of hearsay evidence).]*

Application to vary a direction **R3.6**

3.6 (1) A party may apply to vary a direction if—
(a) the court gave it without a hearing;
(b) the court gave it at a hearing in that party's absence; or
(c) circumstances have changed.
(2) A party who applies to vary a direction must—
(a) apply as soon as practicable after becoming aware of the grounds for doing so; and
(b) give as much notice to the other parties as the nature and urgency of the application permits.

Agreement to vary a time limit fixed by a direction **R3.7**

3.7 (1) The parties may agree to vary a time limit fixed by a direction, but only if—
(a) the variation will not—
(i) affect the date of any hearing that has been fixed, or
(ii) significantly affect the progress of the case in any other way;
(b) the court has not prohibited variation by agreement; and
(c) the court's case progression officer is promptly informed.
(2) The court's case progression officer must refer the agreement to the court if in doubt that the condition in paragraph (1)(a) is satisfied.

Case preparation and progression **R3.8**

3.8 (1) At every hearing, if a case cannot be concluded there and then the court must give directions so that it can be concluded at the next hearing or as soon as possible after that.
(2) At every hearing the court must, where relevant—
(a) if the defendant is absent, decide whether to proceed nonetheless;
(b) take the defendant's plea (unless already done) or if no plea can be taken then find out whether the defendant is likely to plead guilty or not guilty;
(c) set, follow or revise a timetable for the progress of the case, which may include a timetable for any hearing including the trial or (in the Crown Court) the appeal;
(d) in giving directions, ensure continuity in relation to the court and to the parties' representatives where that is appropriate and practicable; and
(e) where a direction has not been complied with, find out why, identify who was responsible, and take appropriate action.
(3) In order to prepare for the trial, the court must take every reasonable step—
(a) to encourage and to facilitate the attendance of witnesses when they are needed; and
(b) to facilitate the participation of any person, including the defendant.
(4) Facilitating the participation of the defendant includes finding out whether the defendant needs interpretation because—
(a) the defendant does not speak or understand English; or
(b) the defendant has a hearing or speech disorder.

[13] 1985 c. 23; section 19B was inserted by section 93 of the Courts Act 2003 (c. 39).
[14] 1984 c. 60; section 81(1) was amended by section 109(1) of, and paragraph 286 of Schedule 8 to, the Courts Act 2003 (c.39).
[15] 1996 c. 25; section 20(3) was amended by section 109(1) of, and paragraph 378 of Schedule 8 to, the Courts Act 2003 (c.39).
[16] 1996 c. 25; section 11 was substituted by section 39 of the Criminal Justice Act 2003 (c. 44) and amended by section 60 of the Criminal Justice and Immigration Act 2008 (c. 4).
[17] 2003 c. 44.

(5) Where the defendant needs interpretation—
(a) the court officer must arrange for interpretation to be provided at every hearing which the defendant is due to attend;
(b) interpretation may be by an intermediary where the defendant has a speech disorder, without the need for a defendant's evidence direction;
(c) on application or on its own initiative, the court may require a written translation to be provided for the defendant of any document or part of a document, unless—
(i) translation of that document, or part, is not needed to explain the case against the defendant, or
(ii) the defendant agrees to do without and the court is satisfied that the agreement is clear and voluntary and that the defendant has had legal advice or otherwise understands the consequences; and
(d) on application by the defendant, the court must give any direction which the court thinks appropriate, including a direction for interpretation by a different interpreter, where —
(i) no interpretation is provided,
(ii) no translation is ordered or provided in response to a previous application by the defendant, or
(iii) the defendant complains about the quality of interpretation or of any translation.
(6) Facilitating the participation of any person includes giving directions for the appropriate treatment and questioning of a witness or the defendant, especially where the court directs that such questioning is to be conducted through an intermediary.
(7) Where directions for appropriate treatment and questioning are required, the court must—
(a) invite representations by the parties and by any intermediary; and
(b) set ground rules for the conduct of the questioning, which rules may include—
(i) a direction relieving a party of any duty to put that party's case to a witness or a defendant in its entirety,
(ii) directions about the manner of questioning,
(iii) directions about the duration of questioning,
(iv) if necessary, directions about the questions that may or may not be asked,
(v) directions about the means by which any intermediary may intervene in questioning, if necessary,
(vi) where there is more than one defendant, the allocation among them of the topics about which a witness may be asked, and
(vii) directions about the use of models, plans, body maps or similar aids to help communicate a question or an answer.

[Note. Part 18 (Measures to assist a witness or defendant to give evidence) contains rules about an application for a defendant's evidence direction under (among other provisions) sections 33BA and 33BB of the Youth Justice and Criminal Evidence Act 1999[18]*.*

Where a trial in a magistrates' court will take place in Wales, a participant may use the Welsh language: see rule 3.18. Where a trial in the Crown Court will take place in Wales and a participant wishes to use the Welsh language, see rule 3.34.]

R3.9 Ground rules hearing

3.9 (1) This rule applies where the court exercises the powers to which rule 3.8(6) and (7) apply (directions for appropriate treatment and questioning of a witness or defendant).
(2) At a pre-trial case management hearing convened for the purpose—
(a) the parties and any intermediary must—
(i) attend, unless the court otherwise directs, and
(ii) actively assist the court in setting ground rules and giving directions;
(b) the court must—
(i) discuss proposed ground rules and directions with the parties and any intermediary,
(ii) set ground rules for the conduct of questioning of the witness or defendant, as applicable, and
(iii) give such other directions as may be required to facilitate the effective participation of that witness or defendant; and
(c) despite rule 3.14(b) (court officer's duty to make a record of directions), the court may require the parties—
(i) to make a record of those ground rules and directions, and
(ii) to serve that record on each other, on any intermediary and on the court officer.

[18] 1999 c. 23; sections 33BA and 33BB are inserted by section 104 of the Coroners and Justice Act 2009 (c. 25), with effect from a date to be appointed.

(3) In setting such ground rules and giving such directions, the court must have regard to—
(a) any intermediary's report;
(b) the parties' representations; and
(c) such other information or advice as the court requires.
(4) The ground rules for questioning set by the court may include any listed in rule 3.8(7)(b).
(5) The directions given by the court may include any about—
(a) the timetable for the submission of proposed questions;
(b) the timetable for the trial, including the taking of breaks during proceedings;
(c) seating arrangements in the court room for the defendant, the defendant's advocate and legal representative, any intermediary and any parent, guardian or other companion of the defendant; and
(d) any explanation to be given to the jury, if there is one, of—
(i) the witness' or the defendant's communication needs and behaviour, as applicable, and
(ii) the role of the intermediary, if there is one.

[Note. See also rule 3.16 (Pre-trial hearings in a magistrates' court: general rules) and rule 3.21 (Pre-trial hearings in the Crown Court: general rules).]

Directions for commissioning medical reports, other than for sentencing purposes **R3.10**

3.10 (1) This rule applies where, because of a defendant's suspected mental ill-health—
(a) a magistrates' court requires expert medical opinion about the potential suitability of a hospital order under section 37(3) of the Mental Health Act 1983[19] (hospital order without convicting the defendant);
(b) the Crown Court requires expert medical opinion about the defendant's fitness to participate at trial, under section 4 of the Criminal Procedure (Insanity) Act 1964[20]; or
(c) a magistrates' court or the Crown Court requires expert medical opinion to help the court determine a question of intent or insanity,
other than such opinion introduced by a party.
(2) A court may exercise the power to which this rule applies on its own initiative having regard to—
(a) an assessment of the defendant's health by a mental health practitioner acting independently of the parties to assist the court;
(b) representations by a party; or
(c) observations by the court.
(3) A court that requires expert medical opinion to which this rule applies must—
(a) identify each issue in respect of which the court requires such opinion and any legislation applicable;
(b) specify the nature of the expertise likely to be required for giving such opinion;
(c) identify each party or participant by whom a commission for such opinion must be prepared, who may be—
(i) a party (or party's representative) acting on that party's own behalf,
(ii) a party (or party's representative) acting on behalf of the court, or
(iii) the court officer acting on behalf of the court;
(d) where there are available to the court arrangements with the National Health Service under which an assessment of a defendant's mental health may be prepared, give such directions as are needed under those arrangements for obtaining the expert report or reports required;
(e) where no such arrangements are available to the court, or they will not be used, give directions for the commissioning of an expert report or expert reports, including—
(i) such directions as can be made about supplying the expert or experts with the defendant's medical records,
(ii) directions about the other information, about the defendant and about the offence or offences alleged to have been committed by the defendant, which is to be supplied to each expert, and
(iii) directions about the arrangements that will apply for the payment of each expert;
(f) set a timetable providing for—
(i) the date by which a commission is to be delivered to each expert,

[19] 1983 c. 20; section 37(3) was amended by sections 1 and 55 of, and paragraphs 1 and 7 of Schedule 1 and Schedule 11 to, the Mental Health Act 2007 (c. 12).

[20] 1964 c. 84; section 4 was substituted, together with section 4A, for section 4 as originally enacted, by section 2 of the Criminal Procedure (Insanity and Unfitness to Plead Act 1991 (c. 25), and amended by section 22 of the Domestic Violence, Crime and Victims Act 2004 (c. 28).

(ii) the date by which any failure to accept a commission is to be reported to the court,
(iii) the date or dates by which progress in the preparation of a report or reports is to be reviewed by the court officer, and
(iv) the date by which each report commissioned is to be received by the court; and
(g) identify the person (each person, if more than one) to whom a copy of a report is to be supplied, and by whom.

(4) A commission addressed to an expert must—
(a) identify each issue in respect of which the court requires expert medical opinion and any legislation applicable;
(b) include—
(i) the information required by the court to be supplied to the expert,
(ii) details of the timetable set by the court, and
(iii) details of the arrangements that will apply for the payment of the expert;
(c) identify the person (each person, if more than one) to whom a copy of the expert's report is to be supplied; and
(d) request confirmation that the expert from whom the opinion is sought—
(i) accepts the commission, and
(ii) will adhere to the timetable.

[Note. See also rule 28.8 (Directions for commissioning medical reports for sentencing purposes).

The court may request a medical examination of the defendant and a report under—

(a) section 4 of the Criminal Procedure (Insanity) Act 1964, under which the Crown Court may determine a defendant's fitness to plead;
(b) section 35 of the Mental Health Act 1983[21]*, under which the court may order the defendant's detention in hospital to obtain a medical report;*
(c) section 36 of the 1983 Act[22]*, under which the Crown Court may order the defendant's detention in hospital instead of in custody pending trial or sentence;*
(d) section 37 of the 1983 Act[23]*, under which the court may order the defendant's detention and treatment in hospital, or make a guardianship order, instead of disposing of the case in another way (section 37(3) allows a magistrates' court to make such an order without convicting the defendant if satisfied that the defendant did the act or made the omission charged);*
(e) section 38 of the 1983 Act[24]*, under which the court may order the defendant's temporary detention and treatment in hospital instead of disposing of the case in another way;*
(f) section 157 of the Criminal Justice Act 2003[25]*, under which the court must usually obtain and consider a medical report before passing a custodial sentence if the defendant is, or appears to be, mentally disordered;*

21 1983 c. 20; section 35 was amended by sections 1(4) and 10(1) and (2) of, and paragraphs 1 and 5 of Schedule 1 to, the Mental Health Act 2007 (c. 12) and section 208(1) of, and paragraphs 53 and 54 of Schedule 21 to, the Legal Services Act 2007 (c. 29).

22 1983 c. 20; section 36 was amended by sections 1(4), 5(1) and (2) and 10(1) and (3) of, and paragraphs 1 and 6 of Schedule 1 to, the Mental Health Act 2007 (c. 12) and section 208(1) of, and paragraphs 53 and 55 of Schedule 21 to, the Legal Services Act 2007 (c. 29).

23 1983 c. 20; section 37 was amended by sections 55 and 56 of, and paragraph 12 of Schedule 4 and Schedule 6 to, the Crime (Sentences Act 1997 (c. 43), section 67 of, and paragraph 11 of Schedule 4 to, the Youth Justice and Criminal Evidence Act 1999 (c. 23), paragraph 90 of Schedule 9 to the Powers of Criminal Courts (Sentencing Act 2000 (c. 6), section 304 of, and paragraphs 37 and 38 of Schedule 32 to, the Criminal Justice Act 2003 (c. 44), sections 49 and 65 of, and paragraph 2 of Schedule 1 and Schedule 5 to, the Violent Crime Reduction Act 2006 (c. 38), sections 1, 4, 10, 55 and paragraphs 1 and 7 of Schedule 1, and Part 1 of Schedule 11 to, the Mental Health Act 2007 (c. 12), sections 6 and 149 of, and paragraph 30 of Schedule 4, and Schedule 28 to, the Criminal Justice and Immigration Act 2008 (c. 4), sections 122 and 142 of, and paragraph 1 of Schedule 19 and paragraph 2 of Schedule 26 to, the Legal Aid, Sentencing and Punishment of Offenders Act 2012 (c. 10) and section 28 of, and paragraph 1 of Schedule 5 to, the Criminal Justice and Courts Act 2015 (c. 2). It is further amended by section 148 of, and paragraph 8 of Schedule 26 to, the Criminal Justice and Immigration Act 2008 (c. 4) with effect from a date to be appointed.

24 1983 c. 20; section 38 was amended by section 49(1) of the Crime (Sentences Act 1997 (c. 43), sections 1(4) and 10(1) and (5) of, and paragraphs 1 and 8 of Schedule 1 to, the Mental Health Act 2007 (c. 12) and section 208(1) of, and paragraphs 53 and 56 of Schedule 21 to, the Legal Services Act 2007 (c. 29).

25 2003 c. 44; section 157 was amended by section 38 of the Health and Social Care Act 2012 (c. 7).

(g) *section 207 of the 2003 Act*[26] *(in the case of a defendant aged 18 or over), or section 1(1)(k) of the Criminal Justice and Immigration Act 2008*[27] *(in the case of a defendant who is under 18), under which the court may impose a mental health treatment requirement.*

For the purposes of the legislation listed in (a), (c), (d) and (e) above, the court requires the written or oral evidence of at least two registered medical practitioners, at least one of whom is approved as having special experience in the diagnosis or treatment of mental disorder. For the purposes of (b), (f) and (g), the court requires the evidence of one medical practitioner so approved.

Under section 11 of the Powers of Criminal Courts (Sentencing) Act 2000[28]*, a magistrates' court may adjourn a trial to obtain medical reports.*

Part 19 (Expert evidence) contains rules about the content of expert medical reports.

For the authorities from whom the court may require information about hospital treatment or guardianship, see sections 39 and 39A of the 1983 Act[29]*.*

The Practice Direction includes a timetable for the commissioning and preparation of a report or reports which the court may adopt with such adjustments as the court directs.

Payments to medical practitioners for reports and for giving evidence are governed by section 19(3) of the Prosecution of Offences Act 1985[30] *and by the Costs in Criminal Cases (General) Regulations 1986*[31]*, regulation 17 (Determination of rates or scales of allowances payable out of central funds), regulation 20 (Expert witnesses, etc.) and regulation 25 (Written medical reports). The rates and scales of allowances payable under those Regulations are determined by the Lord Chancellor.]*

Hearing to inform the court of sensitive material R3.11

3.11 (1) This rule applies where the prosecutor has, or is aware of, material—
(a) the revelation of which to the public or to the defendant the prosecutor thinks would give rise to a real risk of serious prejudice to an important public interest;
(b) to which the prosecutor does not think the obligation to disclose prosecution material applies, under Part I of the Criminal Procedure and Investigations Act 1996; but
(c) of the existence of which the prosecutor thinks it necessary to inform the court to avoid—
(i) potential unfairness to the defendant in the conduct of the trial,
(ii) potential prejudice to the fair management of the trial, or
(iii) potential prejudice to that public interest.

(2) Such a prosecutor must—
(a) ask for a hearing so to inform the court; and
(b) notify the defendant of that request only to such extent, if any, and at such time, if at all, as the court directs.

(3) At or before the hearing the prosecutor must—
(a) explain—
(i) why the hearing is necessary, and
(ii) why it is necessary for the hearing to take place in the defendant's absence;
(b) explain to what extent, if any, and when, if at all, the defendant should be informed—
(i) of the hearing, and
(ii) of the material of which the prosecutor wants to inform the court; and
(c) provide or describe the material to the court—

[26] 2003 c. 44; section 207 was amended by article 4(2) of, and paragraph 7 of Schedule 5 to, S.I. 2009/1182, article 14(a and (b of, and Part 1 of Schedule 5 to, S.I. 2010/813, section 72 of the Health and Social Care Act 2012 (c. 7), section 73 of the Legal Aid, Sentencing and Punishment of Offenders Act 2012 (c. 10) and section 62 of, and paragraph 48 of Schedule 5 to, the Children and Social Work Act 2017 (c. 16).

[27] 2008 c. 4.

[28] 2000 c. 6.

[29] 1983 c. 20; section 39 was amended by sections 2(1) and 5(1) of, and paragraph 107 of Schedule 1 and Schedule 3 to, the Health Authorities Act 1995 (c. 17), section 2(5) of, and paragraphs 42 and 46 of Schedule 2 to, the National Health Service Reform and Health Care Professions Act 2002 (c. 17), section 31(1) and (2) of the Mental Health Act 2007 (c. 12), article 3 of, and paragraph 13 of the Schedule to, S.I. 2007/961 and section 55 of, and paragraphs 24 and 28 of Schedule 5 to, the Health and Social Care Act 2012 (c. 7). Section 39A was inserted by section 27(1) of the Criminal Justice Act 1991 (c. 53).

[30] 1985 c. 23; section 19(3) was amended by section 166 of the Criminal Justice Act 1988 (c. 33), section 7 of, and paragraph 8 of Schedule 3 to, the Criminal Procedure (Insanity and Unfitness to Plead Act 1991 (c. 25), sections 40 and 67 of, and paragraph 4 of Schedule 7 to, the Youth Justice and Criminal Evidence Act 1999 (c. 23), section 165 of, and paragraph 99 of Schedule 9 to, the Powers of Criminal Courts (Sentencing Act 2000 (c. 6) and section 378 of, and paragraph 107 of Schedule 16 to, the Armed Forces Act 2006 (c. 52).

[31] S.I. 1986/1335; regulation 17 was amended by regulations 2 and 13 of S.I. 2008/2448, regulation 20 was amended by regulations 2 and 14 of S.I. 2008/2448 and by regulations 4 and 7 of S.I. 2012/1804, and regulation 25 was amended by regulations 2 and 10 of S.I. 2009/2720.

(i) only to the extent needed to achieve the purpose for which the hearing is convened, and
(ii) in such manner as the court directs.

(4) Unless the court otherwise directs—
(a) any such hearing—
(i) must be in private, and
(ii) must take place in the defendant's absence;
(b) the court officer must not give notice to anyone other than the prosecutor of—
(i) the court's decision on the request for a hearing,
(ii) the arrangements for any such hearing, and
(iii) any directions given at such a hearing; and
(c) the court officer may—
(i) keep any written representations or material received under this rule, or
(ii) arrange for the whole or any part to be kept by some other appropriate person, subject to any conditions that the court may impose.

R3.12 Readiness for trial or appeal

3.12 (1) This rule applies to a party's preparation for trial or appeal, and in this rule and rule 3.13 'trial' includes any hearing at which evidence will be introduced.
(2) In fulfilling the duty under rule 3.3, each party must—
(a) comply with directions given by the court;
(b) take every reasonable step to make sure that party's witnesses will attend when they are needed;
(c) make appropriate arrangements to present any written or other material; and
(d) promptly inform the court and the other parties of anything that may—
(i) affect the date or duration of the trial or appeal, or
(ii) significantly affect the progress of the case in any other way.
(3) The court may require a party to give a certificate of readiness.

R3.13 Conduct of a trial or an appeal

3.13 In order to manage trial or an appeal, the court—
(a) must establish, with the active assistance of the parties, what are the disputed issues;
(b) must consider setting a timetable that—
(i) takes account of those issues and any timetable proposed by a party, and
(ii) may limit the duration of any stage of the hearing;
(c) may require a party to identify—
(i) which witnesses that party wants to give evidence in person,
(ii) the order in which that party wants those witnesses to give their evidence,
(iii) whether that party requires an order compelling the attendance of a witness,
(iv) what arrangements are desirable to facilitate the giving of evidence by a witness,
(v) what arrangements are desirable to facilitate the participation of any other person, including the defendant,
(vi) what written evidence that party intends to introduce,
(vii) what other material, if any, that person intends to make available to the court in the presentation of the case, and
(viii) whether that party intends to raise any point of law that could affect the conduct of the trial or appeal; and
(d) may limit—
(i) the examination, cross-examination or re-examination of a witness, and
(ii) the duration of any stage of the hearing.

[Note. See also rules 3.5 (The court's case management powers) and 3.8 (Case preparation and progression).]

R3.14 Duty of court officer

3.14 The court officer must—
(a) where a person is entitled or required to attend a hearing, give as much notice as reasonably practicable to—
(i) that person, and
(ii) that person's custodian (if any);
(b) where the court gives directions, promptly make a record available to the parties.

[Note. See also rule 5.7 (Supply to a party of information or documents from records or case materials).]

Court's power to vary requirements under this Part R3.15

3.15 (1) The court may—
(a) shorten or extend (even after it has expired) a time limit set by this Part; and
(b) allow an application or representations to be made orally.
(2) A person who wants an extension of time must—
(a) apply when serving the application or representations for which it is needed; and
(b) explain the delay.

Preparation for trial in a magistrates' court

Pre-trial hearings in a magistrates' court: general rules R3.16

3.16 (1) A magistrates' court—
(a) must conduct a preparation for trial hearing unless—
(i) the court sends the defendant for trial in the Crown Court, or
(ii) the case is one to which rule 24.8 or rule 24.9 applies (Written guilty plea: special rules; Single justice procedure: special rules);
(b) may conduct a further pre-trial case management hearing (and if necessary more than one such hearing) only where—
(i) the court anticipates a guilty plea,
(ii) it is necessary to conduct such a hearing in order to give directions for an effective trial, or
(iii) such a hearing is required to set ground rules for the conduct of the questioning of a witness or defendant.
(2) At a preparation for trial hearing the court must give directions for an effective trial.
(3) At a preparation for trial hearing, if the defendant is present the court must—
(a) satisfy itself that there has been explained to the defendant, in terms the defendant can understand (with help, if necessary), that the defendant will receive credit for a guilty plea;
(b) take the defendant's plea or if no plea can be taken then find out whether the defendant is likely to plead guilty or not guilty; and
(c) unless the defendant pleads guilty, satisfy itself that there has been explained to the defendant, in terms the defendant can understand (with help, if necessary), that at the trial—
(i) the defendant will have the right to give evidence after the court has heard the prosecution case,
(ii) if the defendant does not attend, the trial is likely to take place in the defendant's absence, and
(iii) where the defendant is released on bail, failure to attend court when required is an offence for which the defendant may be arrested and punished and bail may be withdrawn.
(4) A pre-trial case management hearing must be in public, as a general rule, but all or part of the hearing may be in private if the court so directs.
(5) The court—
(a) at the first hearing in the case must require a defendant who is present to provide, in writing or orally, his or her name and date of birth; and
(b) at any subsequent hearing may require such a defendant to provide that information by those means.

[Note. At the first hearing in a magistrates' court the court may, and in some cases must, send the defendant to the Crown Court for trial, depending upon (i) the classification of the offence, (ii) the defendant's age, (iii) whether the defendant is awaiting Crown Court trial for another offence, (iv) whether another defendant charged with the same offence is awaiting Crown Court trial, and (v) in some cases, the value of property involved. See also Part 9 (Allocation and sending for trial).

Under section 11 of the Magistrates' Courts Act 1980[32]*, where the defendant does not attend the trial, where the defendant is at least 18 years old, and subject to some exceptions, then the court must proceed in his or her absence unless it appears to the court to be contrary to the interests of justice to do so. Where the defendant does not attend the trial and he or she is under 18 then, again subject to some exceptions, the court may proceed in his or her absence.*

[32] 1980 c. 43; section 11 was amended by section 123 of, and paragraph 1 of Schedule 8 to, the Criminal Justice Act 1988 (c.Â 33), section 168 of, and paragraph 39 of Schedule 10 to, the Criminal Justice and Public Order Act 1994 (c. 33), section 119 of, and paragraph 39 of Schedule 8 to, the Crime and Disorder Act 1998 (c. 37), paragraphs 25 and 26 of Schedule 32 to the Criminal Justice Act 2003 (c. 44), section 54 of the Criminal Justice and Immigration Act 2008 (c. 4) and sections 48 and 50 of, and paragraphs 2 and 4 of Schedule 11 to, the Criminal Justice and Courts Act 2015 (c. 2).

Under sections 8A and 8B of the Magistrates' Courts Act 1980[33]*, a pre-trial ruling about the admissibility of evidence or any other question of law is binding unless it later appears to the court in the interests of justice to discharge or vary that ruling.*

Under section 86A of the Courts Act 2003[34]*, Criminal Procedure Rules must specify stages of proceedings at which the court must require the information listed in rule 3.16(5) and may specify other stages of proceedings when such requirements may be imposed. A person commits an offence if, without reasonable excuse, that person fails to comply with such a requirement, whether by providing false or incomplete information or by providing no information.]*

R3.17 Place of magistrates' court trial

3.17 The court officer must arrange for a magistrates' court trial to take place in a courtroom provided by the Lord Chancellor, unless—
- (a) the court otherwise directs; or
- (b) the case is one to which rule 24.9 (Single justice procedure: special rules) applies.

[Note. See section 3 of the Courts Act 2003[35] *and section 16A of the Magistrates' Courts Act 1980*[36]*.*

In some circumstances the court may conduct all or part of the hearing outside a courtroom. The members of the court may discuss the verdict and sentence outside the courtroom.]

R3.18 Use of Welsh language at magistrates' court trial

3.18 Where a magistrates' court trial takes place in Wales—
- (a) any party or witness may use the Welsh language; and
- (b) if practicable, at least one member of the court must be Welsh-speaking.

[Note. See section 3 of the Courts Act 2003[37] *and section 22 of the Welsh Language Act 1993*[38]*.]*

Preparation for trial in the Crown Court

R3.19 Service of prosecution evidence

3.19 This rule applies where—
- (a) a magistrates' court sends the defendant to the Crown Court for trial; and
- (b) the prosecutor serves on the defendant copies of the documents containing the evidence on which the prosecution case relies.

(2) The prosecutor must at the same time serve copies of those documents on the Crown Court officer.

[Note. See the Crime and Disorder Act 1998 (Service of Prosecution Evidence) Regulations 2005[39]*. The time for service of the prosecution evidence is prescribed by regulation 2. It is—*

- *(a) not more than 50 days after sending for trial, where the defendant is in custody; and*
- *(b) not more than 70 days after sending for trial, where the defendant is on bail.]*

R3.20 Application to dismiss offence sent for Crown Court trial

3.20 (1) This rule applies where a defendant wants the Crown Court to dismiss an offence sent for trial there.

(2) The defendant must—
- (a) apply in writing—
  - (i) not more than 20 business days after service of the prosecution evidence, and
  - (ii) before the defendant's arraignment under rule 3.32 (Arraigning the defendant on the indictment);
- (b) serve the application on—
  - (i) the Crown Court officer, and
  - (ii) each other party; and
- (c) in the application—

33 1980 c. 43; section 8A was inserted by section 45 of, and Schedule 3 to, the Courts Act 2003 (c. 39) and amended by SI 2006/2493 and paragraphs 12 and 14 of Schedule 5 to the Legal Aid, Sentencing and Punishment of Offenders Act 2012 (c. 10). Section 8B was inserted by section 45 of, and Schedule 3 to, the Courts Act 2003 (c. 39) and amended by paragraph 51 of Schedule 3, and Part 4 of Schedule 37, to the Criminal Justice Act 2003 (c. 44).

34 2003 c. 39; section 86A was inserted by section 162 of the Policing and Crime Act 2016 (c. 3).

35 2003 c. 39.

36 1980 c. 43; section 16A was inserted by section 48 of the Criminal Justice and Courts Act 2015 (c. 2).

37 2003 c. 39.

38 1993 c. 38.

39 S.I. 2005/902; amended by S.I. 2012/1345.

(i) explain why the prosecution evidence would not be sufficient for the defendant to be properly convicted,
(ii) ask for a hearing, if the defendant wants one, and explain why it is needed,
(iii) identify any witness whom the defendant wants to call to give evidence in person, with an indication of what evidence the witness can give,
(iv) identify any material already served that the defendant thinks the court will need to determine the application, and
(v) include any material not already served on which the defendant relies.

(3) A prosecutor who opposes the application must—
(a) serve notice of opposition, not more than 10 business days after service of the defendant's notice, on—
(i) the Crown Court officer, and
(ii) each other party; and
(b) in the notice of opposition—
(i) explain the grounds of opposition,
(ii) ask for a hearing, if the prosecutor wants one, and explain why it is needed,
(iii) identify any witness whom the prosecutor wants to call to give evidence in person, with an indication of what evidence the witness can give,
(iv) identify any material already served that the prosecutor thinks the court will need to determine the application, and
(v) include any material not already served on which the prosecutor relies.

(4) The court may determine an application under this rule—
(a) at a hearing, in public or in private, or without a hearing; and
(b) in the absence of—
(i) the defendant who made the application, and
(ii) the prosecutor, if the prosecutor has had at least 10 business days in which to serve notice opposing the application.

(5) The court may—
(a) shorten or extend (even after it has expired) a time limit under this rule; and
(b) allow a witness to give evidence in person even if that witness was not identified in the defendant's application or in the prosecutor's notice.

[Note. Under paragraph 2 of Schedule 3 to the Crime and Disorder Act 1998[40]*, on an application by the defendant the Crown Court must dismiss an offence charged if it appears to the court that the evidence would not be sufficient for the applicant to be properly convicted.]*

Preparation for trial in the Crown Court

Pre-trial hearings in the Crown Court: general rules R3.21

3.21 (1) The Crown Court—
(a) may, and in some cases must, conduct a preparatory hearing where rule 3.22 applies;
(b) must conduct a plea and trial preparation hearing; and
(c) may conduct a further pre-trial case management hearing (and if necessary more than one such hearing) only where—
(i) the court anticipates a guilty plea,
(ii) it is necessary to conduct such a hearing in order to give directions for an effective trial, or
(iii) such a hearing is required to set ground rules for the conduct of the questioning of a witness or defendant.

(2) At the plea and trial preparation hearing the court must—
(a) satisfy itself that there has been explained to the defendant, in terms the defendant can understand (with help, if necessary), that the defendant will receive credit for a guilty plea;
(b) take the defendant's plea in accordance with rule 3.24 (Arraigning the defendant on the indictment) or if no plea can be taken then find out whether the defendant is likely to plead guilty or not guilty;
(c) unless the defendant pleads guilty, satisfy itself that there has been explained to the defendant, in terms the defendant can understand (with help, if necessary), that at the trial—
(i) the defendant will have the right to give evidence after the court has heard the prosecution case,
(ii) if the defendant does not attend, the trial may take place in the defendant's absence,

[40] 1998 c. 37; paragraph 2 of Schedule 3 was amended by paragraphs 15 and 20 of Schedule 3, paragraph 73 of Schedule 36 and Part 4 of Schedule 37 to the Criminal Justice Act 2003 (c. 44) and SI 2004/2035.

(iii) if the trial takes place in the defendant's absence, the judge may inform the jury of the reason for that absence, and
(iv) where the defendant is released on bail, failure to attend court when required is an offence for which the defendant may be arrested and punished and bail may be withdrawn; and
(d) give directions for an effective trial.
(3) A pre-trial case management hearing—
(a) must be in public, as a general rule, but all or part of the hearing may be in private if the court so directs; and
(b) must be recorded, in accordance with rule 5.5 (Recording and transcription of proceedings in the Crown Court).
(4) Where the court determines a pre-trial application in private, it must announce its decision in public.
(5) The court—
(a) at the first hearing in the Crown Court must require a defendant who is present—
(i) to provide, in writing or orally, his or her name and date of birth, or
(ii) to confirm that information by those means, where the information was given to the magistrates' court which sent the defendant for trial; and
(b) at any subsequent hearing may require such a defendant to provide or confirm that information by those means.

[Note. See also the general rules in the first section of this Part (rules 3.1 to 3.15) and the other rules in this section.

The Practice Direction lists the circumstances in which a further pre-trial case management hearing is likely to be needed in order to give directions for an effective trial.

There are rules relevant to applications which may be made at a pre-trial hearing in Part 6 (Reporting, etc. restrictions), Part 14 (Bail and custody time limits), Part 15 (Disclosure), Part 17 (Witness summonses, warrants and orders), Part 18 (Measures to assist a witness or defendant to give evidence), Part 19 (Expert evidence), Part 20 (Hearsay evidence), Part 21 (Evidence of bad character), Part 22 (Evidence of a complainant's previous sexual behaviour) and Part 23 (Restriction on cross-examination by a defendant).

On an application to which Part 14 (Bail and custody time limits) applies, rule 14.2 (exercise of court's powers under that Part) may require the defendant's presence, which may be by live link. Where rule 14.10 applies (Consideration of bail in a murder case), the court officer must arrange for the Crown Court to consider bail within 2 business days of the first hearing in the magistrates' court.

Under section 40 of the Criminal Procedure and Investigations Act 1996[41]*, a pre-trial ruling about the admissibility of evidence or any other question of law is binding unless it later appears to the court in the interests of justice to discharge or vary that ruling.*

Under section 86A of the Courts Act 2003[42]*, Criminal Procedure Rules must specify stages of proceedings at which the court must require the information listed in rule 3.21(5). A person commits an offence if, without reasonable excuse, that person fails to comply with such a requirement, whether by providing false or incomplete information or by providing no information.]*

R3.22 Preparatory hearing

3.22 (1) This rule applies where the Crown Court—
(a) can order a preparatory hearing, under—
(i) section 7 of the Criminal Justice Act 1987[43] (cases of serious or complex fraud), or
(ii) section 29 of the Criminal Procedure and Investigations Act 1996[44] (other complex, serious or lengthy cases);
(b) must order such a hearing, to determine an application for a trial without a jury, under—
(i) section 44 of the Criminal Justice Act 2003[45] (danger of jury tampering), or

41 1996 c. 25.
42 2003 c. 39; section 86A was inserted by section 162 of the Policing and Crime Act 2017 (c. 3).
43 1987 c. 38; section 7 is amended by paragraph 30 of Schedule 9 to the Criminal Justice and Public Order Act 1994 (c. 33), sections 72 and 80 of, paragraph 2 of Schedule 3 to, and Schedule 5 to, the Criminal Procedure and Investigations Act 1996 (c. 25) and sections 45 and 310 of, and paragraphs 52 and 53 of Schedule 36 to, the Criminal Justice Act 2003 (c. 44).
44 1996 c. 25; section 29 is amended by sections 45, 309 and 310 of, and paragraphs 65 and 66 of Schedule 36 to, the Criminal Justice Act 2003 (c. 44) and section 16 of the Terrorism Act 2006 (c. 11).
45 2003 c. 44.

(ii) section 17 of the Domestic Violence, Crime and Victims Act 2004[46] (trial of sample counts by jury, and others by judge alone); and

(c) must order such a hearing, under section 29 of the 1996 Act, where section 29(1B) or (1C) applies (cases in which a terrorism offence is charged, or other serious cases with a terrorist connection).

(2) The court may decide whether to order a preparatory hearing—

(a) on an application or on its own initiative;

(b) at a hearing (in public or in private), or without a hearing; and

(c) in a party's absence, if that party—

(i) applied for the order, or

(ii) has had at least 10 business days in which to make representations.

[Note. See also section 45(2) of the Criminal Justice Act 2003 and section 18(1) of the Domestic Violence, Crime and Victims Act 2004.

At a preparatory hearing, the court may—

(a) require the prosecution to set out its case in a written statement, to arrange its evidence in a form that will be easiest for the jury (if there is one) to understand, to prepare a list of agreed facts, and to amend the case statement following representations from the defence (section 9(4) of the 1987 Act, section 31(4) of the 1996 Act); and

(b) require the defence to give notice of any objection to the prosecution case statement, and to give notice stating the extent of agreement with the prosecution as to documents and other matters and the reason for any disagreement (section 9(5) of the 1987 Act, section 31(6), (7), (9) of the 1996 Act).

Under section 10 of the 1987 Act[47], and under section 34 of the 1996 Act[48], if either party later departs from the case or objections disclosed by that party, then the court, or another party, may comment on that, and the court may draw such inferences as appear proper.]

Application for preparatory hearing **R3.23**

3.23 (1) A party who wants the court to order a preparatory hearing must—

(a) apply in writing—

(i) as soon as reasonably practicable, and in any event

(ii) not more than 10 business days after the defendant pleads not guilty; and

(b) serve the application on—

(i) the court officer, and

(ii) each other party.

(2) The applicant must—

(a) if relevant, explain what legislation requires the court to order a preparatory hearing; or

(b) explain—

(i) what makes the case complex or serious, or makes the trial likely to be long,

(ii) why a substantial benefit will accrue from a preparatory hearing, and

(iii) why the court's ordinary powers of case management are not adequate.

(3) A prosecutor who wants the court to order a trial without a jury must explain—

(a) where the prosecutor alleges a danger of jury tampering—

(i) what evidence there is of a real and present danger that jury tampering would take place,

(ii) what steps, if any, reasonably might be taken to prevent jury tampering, and

(iii) why, notwithstanding such steps, the likelihood of jury tampering is so substantial as to make it necessary in the interests of justice to order such a trial; or

(b) where the prosecutor proposes trial without a jury on some counts on the indictment—

(i) why a trial by jury involving all the counts would be impracticable,

(ii) how the counts proposed for jury trial can be regarded as samples of the others, and

(iii) why it would be in the interests of justice to order such a trial.

Application for non-jury trial containing information withheld from a defendant **R3.24**

3.24 (1) This rule applies where—

(a) the prosecutor applies for an order for a trial without a jury because of a danger of jury tampering; and

46 2004 c. 28.

47 1987 c. 38; section 10 is amended by section 72 of, and paragraph 5 of Schedule 3 to, the Criminal Procedure and Investigations Act 1996 (c. 25), and paragraphs 52 and 55 of Schedule 36 to the Criminal Justice Act 2003 (c. 44).

48 1996 c. 25; section 34 is amended by paragraphs 65 and 68 of Schedule 36 to the Criminal Justice Act 2003 (c. 44).

(b) the application includes information that the prosecutor thinks ought not be revealed to a defendant.

(2) The prosecutor must—
(a) omit that information from the part of the application that is served on that defendant;
(b) mark the other part to show that, unless the court otherwise directs, it is only for the court; and
(c) in that other part, explain why the prosecutor has withheld that information from that defendant.

(3) The hearing of an application to which this rule applies—
(a) must be in private, unless the court otherwise directs; and
(b) if the court so directs, may be, wholly or in part, in the absence of a defendant from whom information has been withheld.

(4) At the hearing of an application to which this rule applies—
(a) the general rule is that the court will receive, in the following sequence—
(i) representations first by the prosecutor and then by each defendant, in all the parties' presence, and then
(ii) further representations by the prosecutor, in the absence of a defendant from whom information has been withheld; but
(b) the court may direct other arrangements for the hearing.

(5) Where, on an application to which this rule applies, the court orders a trial without a jury—
(a) the general rule is that the trial will be before a judge other than the judge who made the order; but
(b) the court may direct other arrangements.

R3.25 Representations in response to application for preparatory hearing

3.25 (1) This rule applies where a party wants to make representations about—
(a) an application for a preparatory hearing;
(b) an application for a trial without a jury.

(2) Such a party must—
(a) serve the representations on—
(i) the court officer, and
(ii) each other party;
(b) do so not more than 10 business days after service of the application; and
(c) ask for a hearing, if that party wants one, and explain why it is needed.

(3) Where representations include information that the person making them thinks ought not be revealed to another party, that person must—
(a) omit that information from the representations served on that other party;
(b) mark the information to show that, unless the court otherwise directs, it is only for the court; and
(c) with that information include an explanation of why it has been withheld from that other party.

(4) Representations against an application for an order must explain why the conditions for making it are not met.

R3.26 Commencement of preparatory hearing

3.26 At the beginning of a preparatory hearing, the court must—
(a) announce that it is such a hearing; and
(b) take the defendant's plea under rule 3.32 (Arraigning the defendant on the indictment), unless already done.

[Note. See section 8 of the Criminal Justice Act 1987[49] *and section 30 of the Criminal Procedure and Investigations Act 1996*[50]*.]*

R3.27 Defence trial advocate

3.27 (1) The defendant must notify the court officer of the identity of the intended defence trial advocate—
(a) as soon as practicable, and in any event no later than the day of the plea and trial preparation hearing; and
(b) in writing, or orally at that hearing.

[49] 1987 c. 38.
[50] 1996 c. 25.

(2) The defendant must notify the court officer in writing of any change in the identity of the intended defence trial advocate as soon as practicable, and in any event not more than 5 business days after that change.

Application to stay case for abuse of process R3.28

3.28 (1) This rule applies where a defendant wants the Crown Court to stay the case on the grounds that the proceedings are an abuse of the court, or otherwise unfair.
(2) Such a defendant must—
(a) apply in writing—
(i) as soon as practicable after becoming aware of the grounds for doing so,
(ii) at a pre-trial hearing, unless the grounds for the application do not arise until trial, and
(iii) in any event, before the defendant pleads guilty or the jury (if there is one) retires to consider its verdict at trial;
(b) serve the application on—
(i) the court officer, and
(ii) each other party; and
(c) in the application—
(i) explain the grounds on which it is made,
(ii) include, attach or identify all supporting material,
(iii) specify relevant events, dates and propositions of law, and
(iv) identify any witness the applicant wants to call to give evidence in person.
(3) A party who wants to make representations in response to the application must serve the representations on—
(a) the court officer; and
(b) each other party,

not more than 10 business days after service of the application.

Application for joint or separate trials, etc. R3.29

3.29 (1) This rule applies where a party wants the Crown Court to order—
(a) the joint trial of—
(i) offences charged by separate indictments, or
(ii) defendants charged in separate indictments;
(b) separate trials of offences charged by the same indictment;
(c) separate trials of defendants charged in the same indictment; or
(d) the deletion of a count from an indictment.
(2) Such a party must—
(a) apply in writing—
(i) as soon as practicable after becoming aware of the grounds for doing so, and
(ii) before the trial begins, unless the grounds for the application do not arise until trial;
(b) serve the application on—
(i) the court officer, and
(ii) each other party; and
(c) in the application—
(i) specify the order proposed, and
(ii) explain why it should be made.
(3) A party who wants to make representations in response to the application must serve the representations on—
(a) the court officer; and
(b) each other party,
not more than 10 business days after service of the application.
(4) Where the same indictment charges more than one offence, the court may exercise its power to order separate trials of those offences if of the opinion that—
(a) the defendant otherwise may be prejudiced or embarrassed in his or her defence (for example, where the offences to be tried together are neither founded on the same facts nor form or are part of a series of offences of the same or a similar character); or
(b) for any other reason it is desirable that the defendant should be tried separately for any one or more of those offences.

[Note. See section 5 of the Indictments Act 1915[51]*. Rule 10.2 (The indictment: general rules) governs the form and content of an indictment.*

Any issue arising from a decision under this rule may be subject to appeal to the Court of Appeal. Part 37 (Appeal to the Court of Appeal against ruling at preparatory hearing), Part 38 (Appeal to the Court of Appeal against ruling adverse to prosecution) and Part 39 (Appeal to the Court of Appeal about conviction or sentence) each contains relevant rules. The powers of the Court of Appeal on an appeal to which Part 39 applies are set out in sections 2, 3 and 7 of the Criminal Appeal Act 1968[52]*.]*

R3.30 Order for joint or separate trials, or amendment of the indictment

3.30 (1) This rule applies where the Crown Court makes an order—
(a) on an application under rule 3.29 applies (Application for joint or separate trials, etc.); or
(b) amending an indictment in any other respect.
(2) Unless the court otherwise directs, the court officer must endorse any paper copy of each affected indictment made for the court with—
(a) a note of the court's order; and
(b) the date of that order.

R3.31 Application for indication of sentence

3.31 (1) This rule applies where a defendant wants the Crown Court to give an indication of the maximum sentence that would be passed if a guilty plea were entered when the indication is sought.
(2) Such a defendant must—
(a) apply in writing as soon as practicable; and
(b) serve the application on—
(i) the court officer, and
(ii) the prosecutor.
(3) The application must—
(a) specify—
(i) the offence or offences to which it would be a guilty plea, and
(ii) the facts on the basis of which that plea would be entered; and
(b) include the prosecutor's agreement to, or representations on, that proposed basis of plea.
(4) The prosecutor must—
(a) provide information relevant to sentence, including—
(i) any previous conviction of the defendant, and the circumstances where relevant, and
(ii) any statement of the effect of the offence on the victim, the victim's family or others; and
(b) identify any other matter relevant to sentence, including—
(i) the legislation applicable,
(ii) any sentencing guidelines, or guideline cases, and
(iii) aggravating and mitigating factors.
(5) The hearing of the application—
(a) may take place in the absence of any other defendant; and
(b) must be attended by—
(i) the applicant defendant's legal representatives (if any), and
(ii) the prosecution advocate.

R3.32 Arraigning the defendant on the indictment

3.32 (1) In order to take the defendant's plea, the Crown Court must—
(a) obtain the prosecutor's confirmation, in writing or orally—
(i) that the indictment (or draft indictment, as the case may be) sets out a statement of each offence that the prosecutor wants the court to try and such particulars of the conduct constituting the commission of each such offence as the prosecutor relies upon to make clear what is alleged, and
(ii) of the order in which the prosecutor wants the defendants' names to be listed in the indictment, if the prosecutor proposes that more than one defendant should be tried at the same time;
(b) ensure that the defendant is correctly identified by the indictment or draft indictment;

[51] 1915 c. 90; section 5 was amended by section 12 of, and paragraph 8 of Schedule 2 to, the Bail Act 1976 (c. 63), section 31 of, and Schedule 2 to, the Prosecution of Offences Act 1985 (c. 23) and section 331 of, and paragraph 40 of Schedule 36 to, the Criminal Justice Act 2003 (c. 44).
[52] 1968 c. 19; section 2 was amended by section 2 of the Criminal Appeal Act 1995 (c. 35). Section 3 was amended by section 316 of the Criminal Justice Act 2003 (c. 44). Section 7 was amended by sections 43 and 170 of, and Schedule 16 to, the Criminal Justice Act 1988 (c. 33) and paragraph 44 of Schedule 36 to the Criminal Justice Act 2003 (c. 44).

(c) satisfy itself that there has been explained to the defendant, in terms the defendant can understand (with help, if necessary), each allegation against him or her; and
(d) in respect of each count—
(i) read the count aloud to the defendant, or arrange for it to be read aloud or placed before the defendant in writing,
(ii) ask whether the defendant pleads guilty or not guilty to the offence charged by that count, and
(iii) take the defendant's plea.

(2) Where a count is read which is substantially the same as one already read aloud, then only the materially different details need be read aloud.
(3) Where a count is placed before the defendant in writing, the court must summarise its gist aloud.
(4) In respect of each count in the indictment—
(a) if the defendant declines to enter a plea, the court must treat that as a not guilty plea unless rule 25.10 applies (Defendant unfit to plead);
(b) if the defendant pleads not guilty to the offence charged by that count but guilty to another offence of which the court could convict on that count—
(i) if the prosecutor and the court accept that plea, the court must treat the plea as one of guilty of that other offence, but
(ii) otherwise, the court must treat the plea as one of not guilty; and
(c) if the defendant pleads a previous acquittal or conviction of the offence charged by that count—
(i) the defendant must identify that acquittal or conviction in writing, explaining the basis of that plea, and
(ii) the court must exercise its power to decide whether that plea disposes of that count.
(5) In a case in which a magistrates' court sends the defendant for trial, the Crown Court must take the defendant's plea—
(a) not less than 10 business days after the date on which that sending takes place, unless the parties otherwise agree; and
(b) more than 80 business days after that date, unless the court otherwise directs (either before or after that period expires).

[Note. See section 6 of the Criminal Law Act 1967[53]*, section 77 of the Senior Courts Act 1981*[54] *and section 122 of the Criminal Justice Act 1988*[55]*. Part 10 contains rules about the content and service of indictments: see in particular rule 10.2 (The indictment: general rules).*

Under section 6(2) of the 1967 Act, on an indictment for murder a defendant may instead be convicted of manslaughter or another offence specified by that provision. Under section 6(3) of that Act, on an indictment for an offence other than murder or treason a defendant may instead be convicted of another offence if—

(a) the allegation in the indictment amounts to or includes an allegation of that other offence; and
(b) the Crown Court has power to convict and sentence for that other offence.]

Place of Crown Court trial **R3.33**

3.33 (1) Unless the court otherwise directs, the court officer must arrange for a Crown Court trial to take place in a courtroom provided by the Lord Chancellor.
(2) The court officer must arrange for the court and the jury (if there is one) to view any place required by the court.

[Note. See section 3 of the Courts Act 2003[56] *and section 14 of the Juries Act 1974*[57]*.*

In some circumstances the court may conduct all or part of the hearing outside a courtroom.]

Use of Welsh language at trial **R3.34**

3.34 Where a Crown Court trial will take place in Wales and a participant wishes to use the Welsh language—

[53] 1967 c. 58; section 6 was amended by paragraph 41 of Schedule 36 to the Criminal Justice Act 2003 (c. 44) and section 11 of the Domestic Violence, Crime and Victims Act 2004 (c. 28).
[54] 1981 c. 54; section 77 was amended by section 15 of, and paragraph 11 of Schedule 2 to, the Criminal Justice Act 1987 (c. 38), section 168 of, and paragraph 18 of Schedule 9 to, the Criminal Justice and Public Order Act 1994 (c. 33), section 41 of, and paragraph 54 of Schedule 3 to, the Criminal Justice Act 2003 (c. 44) and article 3 of, and paragraphs 11 and 13 of the Schedule to, SI 2004/2035. It is further amended by section 31 of, and paragraph 11 of Schedule 1 and Schedule 2 to, the Prosecution of Offences Act 1985 (c. 23) with effect from a date to be appointed.
[55] 1988 c. 33.
[56] 2003 c. 39.
[57] 1974 c. 23; section 14 was amended by paragraph 173 of Schedule 8 to the Courts Act 2003 (c. 39).

(a) that participant must serve notice on the court officer, or arrange for such a notice to be served on that participant's behalf—
(i) at or before the plea and trial preparation hearing, or
(ii) in accordance with any direction given by the court; and
(b) if such a notice is served, the court officer must arrange for an interpreter to attend.

[Note. See section 22 of the Welsh Language Act 1993[58].]

Other provisions affecting case management
Case management may be affected by the following other rules and legislation:

Criminal Procedure Rules
Part 8 Initial details of the prosecution case
Part 9 Allocation and sending for trial
Part 10 The indictment
Part 15 Disclosure
Parts 16 – 23: the rules that deal with evidence
Part 24 Trial and sentence in a magistrates' court
Part 25 Trial and sentence in the Crown Court

Regulations
The Prosecution of Offences (Custody Time Limits) Regulations 1987[59]
The Crime and Disorder Act 1998 (Service of Prosecution Evidence) Regulations 2005[60]
The Criminal Procedure and Investigations Act 1996 (Defence Disclosure Time Limits) Regulations 2011[61]

Acts of Parliament
Sections 10 and 18, Magistrates' Courts Act 1980[62]: powers to adjourn hearings
Sections 128 and 129, Magistrates' Courts Act 1980[63]: remand in custody by magistrates' courts
Sections 19 and 24A, Magistrates' Courts Act 1980[64] and sections 51 and 51A, Crime and Disorder Act 1998[65]: allocation and sending for trial
Section 2, Administration of Justice (Miscellaneous Provisions) Act 1933[66]: procedural conditions for trial in the Crown Court

58 1993 c. 38.

59 S.I. 1987/299; amended by sections 71 and 80 of, and paragraph 8 of Schedule 5 to, the Criminal Procedure and Investigations Act 1996 (c. 25) and S.I. 1989/767, 1991/1515, 1995/555, 1999/2744, 2000/3284, 2012/1344.

60 S.I. 2005/902; amended by S.I. 2012/1345.

61 S.I. 2011/209.

62 1980 c. 43; section 10 was amended by section 59 of, and paragraph 1 of Schedule 9 to, the Criminal Justice Act 1982 (c. 48), section 68 of, and paragraph 6 of Schedule 8 to, the Criminal Justice Act 1991 (c. 53) and section 47 of the Crime and Disorder Act 1998 (c. 37). Section 18 was amended by section 59 of, and paragraph 1 of Schedule 9 to, the Criminal Justice Act 1982 (c. 48), section 68 of, and paragraph 6 of Schedule 8 to, the Criminal Justice Act 1991 (c. 53), section 49 of the Criminal Procedure and Investigations Act 1996 (c. 25), and paragraphs 1 and 4 of Schedule 3 to the Criminal Justice Act 2003 (c. 44).

63 1980 c. 43; section 128 was amended by section 59 to, and paragraphs 2, 3 and 4 of Schedule 9 to, the Criminal Justice Act 1982 (c. 48), section 48 of the Police and Criminal Evidence Act 1984 (c. 60), section 170(1) of, and paragraphs 65 and 69 of Schedule 15 to, the Criminal Justice Act 1988 (c. 33), section 125(3) of, and paragraph 25 of Schedule 18 to, the Courts and Legal Services Act 1990 (c. 41), sections 49, 52 and 80 of, and Schedule 5 to, the Criminal Procedure and Investigations Act 1996 (c. 25), paragraph 75 of Schedule 9 to the Powers of Criminal Courts (Sentencing) Act 2000 (c. 6) and paragraph 51 of Schedule 3 and Part 4 of Schedule 37 to the Criminal Justice Act 2003 (c. 44). It is modified by section 91(5) of the Legal Aid, Sentencing and Punishment of Offenders Act 2012 (c. 10). Section 129 was amended by paragraph 51 of Schedule 3 to the Criminal Justice Act 2003 (c. 44).

64 1980 c. 43; section 19 was substituted by paragraphs 1 and 5 of Schedule 3 to the Criminal Justice Act 2003 (c. 44) and amended by sections 144, 177 and 178 of, and paragraph 4 of Schedule 17, paragraph 80 of Schedule 21 and Part 5 of Schedule 23 to, the Coroners and Justice Act 2009 (c. 25).

65 1998 c. 37; section 51 was substituted by paragraphs 15 and 18 of Schedule 3 to the Criminal Justice Act 2003 (c. 44) and amended by section 59 of, and paragraph 1 of Schedule 11 to, the Constitutional Reform Act 2005 (c. 4). Section 51A was inserted by paragraphs 15 and 18 of Schedule 3 to the Criminal Justice Act 2003 (c. 44) and amended by section 49 of, and paragraph 5 of Schedule 1 to, the Violent Crime Reduction Act 2006 (c. 38) and paragraph 6 of Schedule 21 to the Legal Aid, Sentencing and Punishment of Offenders Act 2012 (c. 10).

66 1933 c. 36; section 2 was amended by Part IV of Schedule 11 to, the Courts Act 1971 (c. 23), Schedule 5 to, the Senior Courts Act 1981 (c. 54), Schedule 2 to the Prosecution of Offences Act 1985 (c. 23), paragraph 1 of Schedule 2 to the Criminal Justice Act 1987 (c. 38), paragraph 10 of Schedule 15 to the Criminal Justice Act 1988 (c. 33), paragraph 8 of Schedule 6 to the Criminal Justice Act 1991 (c. 53), Schedule 1 to the Statute Law (Repeals) Act 1993, paragraph 17 of Schedule 1 to the Criminal Procedure and Investigations Act 1996 (c. 25), paragraph 5 of Schedule 8 to the Crime and Disorder Act 1998 (c. 37), paragraph 34 of Schedule 3 and Part 4 of Schedule 37 to the Criminal Justice Act 2003 (c. 44), paragraph 1 of the Schedule to S.I. 2004/2035, section 12 of, and paragraph 7 of Schedule 1 to, the Constitutional Reform Act 2005 (c. 4), sections 116 and 178 of, and Part 3 of Schedule 23 to, the Coroners and Justice Act 2009 (c. 25), paragraph 32 of Schedule 17 to the Crime and Courts Act 2013 (c. 22) and section 82 of the Deregulation Act 2015 (c. 20).

Sections 8A and 8B, Magistrates' Courts Act 1980[67]*: pre-trial hearings in magistrates' courts*
Section 7, Criminal Justice Act 1987[68]*; Parts III and IV, Criminal Procedure and Investigations Act 1996: pre-trial and preparatory hearings in the Crown Court*
Section 9, Criminal Justice Act 1967[69]*: proof by written witness statement*
Part 1, Criminal Procedure and Investigations Act 1996[70]*: disclosure.]*

Criminal Practice Directions Part 3 Case Management

CPD I General matters 3A: Case Management CPD.3A

3A.1 CrimPR 1.1(2)(e) requires that cases be dealt with efficiently and expeditiously. CrimPR 3.2 requires the court to further the overriding objective by actively managing the case, for example:

a) When dealing with an offence which is triable only on indictment the court must ask the defendant whether he or she intends to plead guilty at the Crown Court (CrimPR 9.7(5));
b) On a guilty plea, the court must pass sentence at the earliest opportunity, in accordance with CrimPR 24.11(9)(a) (magistrates' courts) and 25.16(7)(a) (the Crown Court).

3A.2 Given these duties, magistrates' courts and the Crown Court therefore will proceed as described in paragraphs 3A.3 to 3A.28 below. The parties will be expected to have prepared in accordance with CrimPR 3.3(1) to avoid unnecessary and wasted hearings. They will be expected to have communicated with each other by the time of the first hearing; to report to the court on that communication at the first hearing; and to continue thereafter to communicate with each other and with the court officer, in accordance with CrimPR 3.3(2).

3A.3 There is a Preparation for Effective Trial form for use in the magistrates' courts, and a Plea and Trial Preparation Hearing form for use in the Crown Court, each of which must be used as appropriate in connection with CrimPR Part 3: see paragraph 5A.2 of these Practice Directions. Versions of those forms in pdf and Word, together with guidance notes, are available on the Criminal Procedure Rules pages of the Ministry of Justice website.

Case progression and trial preparation in magistrates' courts

3A.4 CrimPR 8.3 applies in all cases and requires the prosecutor to serve:

i. a summary of the circumstances of the offence;
ii. any account given by the defendant in interview, whether contained in that summary or in another document;
iii. any written witness statement or exhibit that the prosecutor then has available and considers material to plea or to the allocation of the case for trial or sentence;
iv. a list of the defendant's criminal record, if any; and
v. any available statement of the effect of the offence on a victim, a victim's family or others.

The details must include sufficient information to allow the defendant and the court at the first hearing to take an informed view:

i. on plea;
ii. on venue for trial (if applicable);
iii. for the purposes of case management; or
iv. for the purposes of sentencing (including committal for sentence, if applicable).

[67] 1980 c. 43; section 8A was inserted by section 45 of, and Schedule 3 to, the Courts Act 2003 (c. 39) and amended by SI 2006/2493 and paragraphs 12 and 14 of Schedule 5 to the Legal Aid, Sentencing and Punishment of Offenders Act 2012 (c. 10). Section 8B was inserted by section 45 of, and Schedule 3 to, the Courts Act 2003 (c. 39) and amended by paragraph 51 of Schedule 3, and Part 4 of Schedule 37, to the Criminal Justice Act 2003 (c. 44).

[68] 1987 c. 38; section 7 was amended by section 168(1) of, and paragraph 30 of Schedule 9 to, the Criminal Justice and Public Order Act 1994 (c. 33), section 80 of, and paragraph 2 of Schedule 3 and Schedule 5 to, the Criminal Procedure and Investigations Act 1996 (c. 25) and sections 45 and 310 of, and paragraphs 52 and 53 of Schedule 36 to, the Criminal Justice Act 2003 (c. 44). The amendment made by section 45 of the Criminal Justice Act 2003 (c. 44) is in force for certain purposes; for remaining purposes it has effect from a date to be appointed.

[69] 1967 c. 80; section 9 was amended by section 56 of, and paragraph 49 of Schedule 8 to, the Courts Act 1971 (c. 23), section 168 of, and paragraph 6 of Schedule 9 to, the Criminal Justice and Public Order Act 1994 (c. 33), section 69 of the Criminal Procedure and Investigations Act 1996 (c. 25), regulation 9 of, and paragraph 4 of Schedule 5 to, S.I. 2001/1090, paragraph 43 of Schedule 3 and Part 4 of Schedule 37 to the Criminal Justice Act 2003 (c. 44), section 26 of, and paragraph 7 of Schedule 2 to, the Armed Forces Act 2011 (c. 18) and section 80 of the Deregulation Act 2015 (c. 20). It is further amended by section 72 of, and paragraph 55 of Schedule 5 to, the Children and Young Persons Act 1969 (c. 54) and section 65 of, and paragraph 1 of Schedule 4 to, the Courts Act 2003 (c. 39), with effect from dates to be appointed.

[70] 1996 c. 25.

Defendant in custody

3A.5 If the defendant has been detained in custody after being charged with an offence which is indictable only or triable either way, at the first hearing a magistrates' court will proceed at once with the allocation of the case for trial, where appropriate, and, if so required, with the sending of the defendant to the Crown Court for trial. The court will be expected to ask for and record any indication of plea and issues for trial to assist the Crown Court.

3A.6 If the offence charged is triable only summarily, or if at that hearing the case is allocated for summary trial, the court will forthwith give such directions as are necessary, either (on a guilty plea) to prepare for sentencing, or for a trial.

Defendant on bail

3A.7 If the defendant has been released on bail after being charged, the case must be listed for the first hearing 14 days after charge, or the next available court date thereafter when the prosecutor anticipates a guilty plea which is likely to be sentenced in the magistrates' court. In cases where there is an anticipated not guilty plea or the case is likely to be sent or committed to the Crown Court for either trial or sentence, then it must be listed for the first hearing 28 days after charge or the next available court date thereafter.

Guilty plea in the magistrates' courts

3A.8 Where a defendant pleads guilty or indicates a guilty plea in a magistrates' court the court should consider whether a pre-sentence report — a stand down report if possible — is necessary.

Guilty plea in the Crown Court

3A.9 Where a magistrates' court is considering committal for sentence or the defendant has indicated an intention to plead guilty in a matter which is to be sent to the Crown Court, the magistrates' court should request the preparation of a pre-sentence report for the Crown Court's use if the magistrates' court considers that:

(a) there is a realistic alternative to a custodial sentence; or
(b) the defendant may satisfy the criteria for classification as a dangerous offender; or
(c) there is some other appropriate reason for doing so.

3A.10 When a magistrates' court sends a case to the Crown Court for trial and the defendant indicates an intention to plead guilty at the Crown Court, then that magistrates' court must set a date for a Plea and Trial Preparation Hearing at the Crown Court, in accordance with CrimPR 9.7(5)(a)(i).

Case sent for Crown Court trial: no indication of guilty plea

3A.11 In any case sent to the Crown Court for trial, other than one in which the defendant indicates an intention to plead guilty, the magistrates' court must set a date for a Plea and Trial Preparation Hearing, in accordance with CrimPR 9.7(5)(a)(ii). The Plea and Trial Preparation Hearing must be held within 28 days of sending, unless the standard directions of the Presiding Judges of the circuit direct otherwise. Paragraph 3A.16 below additionally applies to the arrangements for such hearings. A magistrates' court may give other directions appropriate to the needs of the case, in accordance with CrimPR 3.5(3), and in accordance with any standard directions issued by the Presiding Judges of the circuit.

Defendant on bail: anticipated not guilty plea

3A.12 Where the defendant has been released on bail after being charged, and where the prosecutor does not anticipate a guilty plea at the first hearing in a magistrates' court, then it is essential that the initial details of the prosecution case that are provided for that first hearing are sufficient to assist the court, in order to identify the real issues and to give appropriate directions for an effective trial (regardless of whether the trial is to be heard in the magistrates' court or the Crown Court). In these circumstances, unless there is good reason not to do so, the prosecution should make available the following material in advance of the first hearing in the magistrates' court:

(a) A summary of the circumstances of the offence(s) including a summary of any account given by the defendant in interview;
(b) Statements and exhibits that the prosecution has identified as being of importance for the purpose of plea or initial case management, including any relevant CCTV that would be relied upon at trial and any Streamlined Forensic Report;
(c) Details of witness availability, as far as they are known at that hearing;
(d) Defendant's criminal record;
(e) Victim Personal Statements if provided;
(f) An indication of any medical or other expert evidence that the prosecution is likely to adduce in relation to a victim or the defendant;
(g) Any information as to special measures, bad character or hearsay, where applicable.

3A.13 In addition to the material required by CrimPR Part 8, the information required by the Preparation for Effective Trial form must be available to be submitted at the first hearing, and the parties must complete that form, in accordance with the guidance published with it. Where there is to be a contested trial in a magistrates' court, that form includes directions and a timetable that will apply in every case unless the court otherwise orders.

3A.14 Nothing in paragraph 3A.12-3A.13 shall preclude the court from taking a plea pursuant to CrimPR 3.9(2)(b) at the first hearing and for the court to case manage as far as practicable under Part 3 CrimPR.

Exercise of magistrates' court's powers

3A.15 In accordance with CrimPR 9.1, sections 49, 51(13) and 51A(11) of the Crime and Disorder Act 1998, and sections 17E, 18(5) and 24D of the Magistrates' Courts Act 1980 a single justice can:

a) allocate and send for trial;
b) take an indication of a guilty plea (but not pass sentence);
c) take a not guilty plea and give directions for the preparation of trial including:
   i. timetable for the proceedings;
   ii. the attendance of the parties;
   iii. the service of documents;
   iv. the manner in which evidence is to be given.

Case progression and trial preparation in the Crown Court

Plea and Trial Preparation Hearing

3A.16 In a case in which a magistrates' court has directed a Plea and Trial Preparation Hearing, the period which elapses between sending for trial and the date of that hearing must be consistent within each circuit. In every case, the time allowed for the conduct of the Plea and Trial Preparation Hearing must be sufficient for effective trial preparation. It is expected in every case that an indictment will be lodged at least 7 days in advance of the hearing. Please see the Note to the Practice Direction.

3A.17 In a case in which the defendant, not having done so before, indicates an intention to plead guilty to his representative after being sent for trial but before the Plea and Trial Preparation Hearing, the defence representative will notify the Crown Court and the prosecution forthwith. The court will ensure there is sufficient time at the Plea and Trial Preparation Hearing for sentence and a Judge should at once request the preparation of a pre-sentence report if it appears to the court that either:

(a) there is a realistic alternative to a custodial sentence; or
(b) the defendant may satisfy the criteria for classification as a dangerous offender; or
(c) there is some other appropriate reason for doing so.

3A.18 If at the Plea and Trial Preparation Hearing the defendant pleads guilty and no pre-sentence report has been prepared, if possible the court should obtain a stand down report.

3A.19 Where the defendant was remanded in custody after being charged and was sent for trial without initial details of the prosecution case having been served, then at least 7 days before the Plea and Trial Preparation Hearing the prosecutor should serve, as a minimum, the material identified in paragraph 3A.12 above. If at the Plea and Trial Preparation Hearing the defendant does not plead guilty, the court will be expected to identify the issues in the case and give appropriate directions for an effective trial. Please see the Note to the Practice Direction.

3A.20 At the Plea and Trial Preparation Hearing, in addition to the material required by paragraph 3A.12 above, the prosecutor must serve sufficient evidence to enable the court to case manage effectively without the need for a further case management hearing, unless the case falls within paragraph 3A.21. In addition, the information required by the Plea and Trial Preparation Hearing form must be available to the court at that hearing, and it must have been discussed between the parties in advance. The prosecutor must provide details of the availability of likely prosecution witnesses so that a trial date can immediately be arranged if the defendant does not plead guilty.

Further case management hearing

3A.21 In accordance with CrimPR 3.13(1)(c), after the Plea and Trial Preparation Hearing there will be no further case management hearing before the trial unless:

(i) a condition listed in that rule is met; and
(ii) the court so directs, in order to further the overriding objective.

The directions to be given at the Plea and Trial Preparation Hearing therefore may include a direction for a further case management hearing, but usually will do so only in one of the following cases:

(a) Class 1 cases;
(b) Class 2 cases which carry a maximum penalty of 10 years or more;

(c) cases involving death by driving (whether dangerous or careless), or death in the workplace;
(d) cases involving a vulnerable witness;
(e) cases in which the defendant is a child or otherwise under a disability, or requires special assistance;
(f) cases in which there is a corporate or unrepresented defendant;
(g) cases in which the expected trial length is such that a further case management hearing is desirable and any case in which the trial is likely to last longer than four weeks;
(h) cases in which expert evidence is to be introduced;
(i) cases in which a party requests a hearing to enter a plea;
(j) cases in which an application to dismiss or stay has been made;
(k) cases in which arraignment has not taken place, whether because of an issue relating to fitness to plead, or abuse of process or sufficiency of evidence, or for any other reason;
(l) cases in which there are likely to be linked criminal and care directions in accordance with the 2013 Protocol.
(m) cases in which a substantial quantity of unused prosecution material has been disclosed, or will be disclosed, or in which the disclosure of such material raises complex questions of law or procedure.

3A.22 If a further case management hearing is directed, a defendant in custody will not usually be expected to attend in person, unless the court otherwise directs.

Compliance hearing

3A.23 If a party fails to comply with a case management direction, that party may be required to attend the court to explain the failure. Unless the court otherwise directs a defendant in custody will not usually be expected to attend. See paragraph 3A.26-3A.28 below.

Conduct of case progression hearings

3A.24 As far as possible, case progression should be managed without a hearing in the courtroom, using electronic communication in accordance with CrimPR 3.5(2)(d). Court staff should be nominated to conduct case progression as part of their role, in accordance with CrimPR 3.4(2). To aid effective communication the prosecution and defence representative should notify the court and provide details of who shall be dealing with the case at the earliest opportunity.

Completion of Effective Trial Monitoring form

3A.25 It is imperative that the Effective Trial Monitoring form (as devised and issued by Her Majesty's Courts and Tribunals Service) is accurately completed by the parties for all cases that have been listed for trial. Advocates must engage with the process by providing the relevant details and completing the form.

Compliance courts

3A.26 To ensure effective compliance with directions of the courts made in accordance with the Criminal Procedure Rules and the overriding objective, courts should maintain a record whenever a party to the proceedings has failed to comply with a direction made by the court. The parties may have to attend a hearing to explain any lack of compliance.

3A.27 These hearings may be conducted by live link facilities or via other electronic means, as the court may direct.

3A.28 It will be for the Presiding Judges, Resident Judge and Justices' Clerks to decide locally how often compliance courts should be held, depending on the scale and nature of the problem at each court centre.

CPD.3B **CPD I General matters 3B: Pagination and Indexing of Served Evidence**

3B.1 The following directions apply to matters before the Crown Court, where
(a) there is an application to prefer a bill of indictment in relation to the case;
(b) a person is sent for trial under section 51 of the Crime and Disorder Act 1998 (sending cases to the Crown Court), to the service of copies of the documents containing the evidence on which the charge or charges are based under Paragraph 1 of Schedule 3 to that Act; or
(c) a defendant wishes to serve evidence.

3B.2 A party who serves documentary evidence in the Crown Court should:
(a) paginate each page in any bundle of statements and exhibits sequentially;
(b) provide an index to each bundle of statements produced including the following information:
i. the name of the case;
ii. the author of each statement;
iii. the start page number of the witness statement;
iv. the end page number of the witness statement.

(c) provide an index to each bundle of documentary and pictorial exhibits produced, including the following information:
   i. the name of the case
   ii. the exhibit reference;
   iii. a short description of the exhibit;
   iv. the start page number of the exhibit;
   v. the end page number of the exhibit;
   vi. where possible, the name of the person producing the exhibit should be added.

3B.3 Where additional documentary evidence is served, a party should paginate following on from the last page of the previous bundle or in a logical and sequential manner. A party should also provide notification of service of any amended index.

3B.4 The prosecution must ensure that the running total of the pages of prosecution evidence is easily identifiable on the most recent served bundle of prosecution evidence.

3B.5 For the purposes of these directions, the number of pages of prosecution evidence served on the court includes all

(a) witness statements;
(b) documentary and pictorial exhibits;
(c) records of interviews with the defendant; and
(d) records of interviews with other defendants which form part of the served prosecution documents or which are included in any notice of additional evidence,

but does not include any document provided on CD-ROM or by other means of electronic communication.

CPD I General matters 3C: Abuse of Process Stay Applications

CPD.3C

3C.1 In all cases where a defendant in the Crown Court proposes to make an application to stay an indictment on the grounds of abuse of process, written notice of such application must be given to the prosecuting authority and to any co-defendant as soon as practicable after the defendant becomes aware of the grounds for doing so and not later than 14 days before the date fixed or warned for trial ('the relevant date'). Such notice must:

(a) give the name of the case and the indictment number;
(b) state the fixed date or the warned date as appropriate;
(c) specify the nature of the application;
(d) set out in numbered sub-paragraphs the grounds upon which the application is to be made;
(e) be copied to the chief listing officer at the court centre where the case is due to be heard.

3C.2 Any co-defendant who wishes to make a like application must give a like notice not later than seven days before the relevant date, setting out any additional grounds relied upon.

3C.3 In relation to such applications, the following automatic directions shall apply:

(a) the advocate for the applicant(s) must lodge with the court and serve on all other parties a skeleton argument in support of the application, at least five clear working days before the relevant date. If reference is to be made to any document not in the existing trial documents, a paginated and indexed bundle of such documents is to be provided with the skeleton argument;
(b) the advocate for the prosecution must lodge with the court and serve on all other parties a responsive skeleton argument at least two clear working days before the relevant date, together with a supplementary bundle if appropriate.

3C.4 All skeleton arguments must specify any propositions of law to be advanced (together with the authorities relied upon in support, with paragraph references to passages relied upon) and, where appropriate, include a chronology of events and a list of dramatis personae. In all instances where reference is made to a document, the reference in the trial documents or supplementary bundle is to be given. Paragraphs XII D.17 to D.23 of these Practice Directions set out the general requirements for skeleton arguments.

3C.5 The above time limits are minimum time limits. In appropriate cases, the court will order longer lead times. To this end, in all cases where defence advocates are, at the time of the preliminary hearing or as soon as practicable after the case has been sent, considering the possibility of an abuse of process application, this must be raised with the judge dealing with the matter, who will order a different timetable if appropriate, and may wish, in any event, to give additional directions about the conduct of the application. If the trial judge has not been identified, the matter should be raised with the Resident Judge.

CPD.3D **CPD I General matters 3D: Vulnerable People in the Courts**

3D.1 In respect of eligibility for special measures, 'vulnerable' and 'intimidated' witnesses are defined in sections 16 and 17 of the Youth Justice and Criminal Evidence Act 1999 (as amended by the Coroners and Justice Act 2009); 'vulnerable' includes those under 18 years of age and people with a mental disorder or learning disability; a physical disorder or disability; or who are likely to suffer fear or distress in giving evidence because of their own circumstances or those relating to the case.

3D.2 However, many other people giving evidence in a criminal case, whether as a witness or defendant, may require assistance: the court is required to take 'every reasonable step' to encourage and facilitate the attendance of witnesses and to facilitate the participation of any person, including the defendant (CrimPR 3.9(3)(a) and (b)). This includes enabling a witness or defendant to give their best evidence, and enabling a defendant to comprehend the proceedings and engage fully with his or her defence. The pre-trial and trial process should, so far as necessary, be adapted to meet those ends. Regard should be had to the welfare of a young defendant as required by section 44 of the Children and Young Persons Act 1933, and generally to Parts 1 and 3 of the Criminal Procedure Rules (the overriding objective and the court's powers of case management).

3D.3 Under Part 3 of the Rules, the court must identify the needs of witnesses at an early stage (CrimPR 3.2(2)(b)) and may require the parties to identify arrangements to facilitate the giving of evidence and participation in the trial (CrimPR 3.11(c)(iv) and (v)). There are various statutory special measures that the court may utilise to assist a witness in giving evidence. CrimPR Part 18 gives the procedures to be followed. Courts should note the 'primary rule' which requires the court to give a direction for a special measure to assist a child witness or qualifying witness and that in such cases an application to the court is not required (CrimPR 18.9).

3D.4 Court of Appeal decisions on this subject include a judgment from the Lord Chief Justice, Lord Judge in *R v Cox* [2012] EWCA Crim 549, [2012] 2 Cr App R 6; *R v Wills* [2011] EWCA Crim 1938, [2012] 1 Cr App R 2; and *R v E* [2011] EWCA Crim 3028, [2012] Crim LR 563.

3D.5 In *R v Wills*, the Court endorsed the approach taken by the report of the Advocacy Training Council (ATC) 'Raising the Bar: the Handling of Vulnerable Witnesses, Victims and Defendants in Court' (2011). The report includes and recommends the use of 'toolkits' to assist advocates as they prepare to question vulnerable people at court: http://www.advocacytrainingcouncil.org/vulnerable-witnesses/raising-the-bar

3D.6 Further toolkits are available through the Advocate's Gateway which is managed by the ATC's Management Committee: http://www.theadvocatesgateway.org/

3D.7 These toolkits represent best practice. Advocates should consult and follow the relevant guidance whenever they prepare to question a young or otherwise vulnerable witness or defendant. Judges may find it helpful to refer advocates to this material and to use the toolkits in case management.

3D.8 'Achieving Best Evidence in Criminal Proceedings' (Ministry of Justice 2011) describes best practice in preparation for the investigative interview and trial: www.cps.gov.uk/publications/docs/best_evidence_in_criminal_proceedings.pdf

CPD.3E **CPD I General matters 3E: Ground Rules Hearings to Plan the Questioning of a Vulnerable Witness or Defendant**

3E.1 The judiciary is responsible for controlling questioning. Over-rigorous or repetitive cross-examination of a child or vulnerable witness should be stopped. Intervention by the judge, magistrates or intermediary (if any) is minimised if questioning, taking account of the individual's communication needs, is discussed in advance and ground rules are agreed and adhered to.

3E.2 Discussion of ground rules is required in all intermediary trials where they must be discussed between the judge or magistrates, advocates and intermediary before the witness gives evidence. The intermediary must be present but is not required to take the oath (the intermediary's declaration is made just before the witness gives evidence).

3E.3 Discussion of ground rules is good practice, even if no intermediary is used, in all young witness cases and in other cases where a witness or defendant has communication needs. Discussion before the day of trial is preferable to give advocates time to adapt their questions to the witness's needs. It may be helpful for a trial practice note of boundaries to be created at the end of the discussion. The judge may use such a document in ensuring that the agreed ground rules are complied with.

3E.4 All witnesses, including the defendant and defence witnesses, should be enabled to give the best evidence they can. In relation to young and/or vulnerable people, this may mean departing radically from traditional cross-examination. The form and extent of appropriate cross-examination will vary from case to case. For adult non vulnerable witnesses an advocate will usually put his case so that the witness will have the opportunity of commenting upon it and/or answering it. When the witness is young or otherwise vulnerable, the court may dispense with the normal practice and impose restrictions on the advocate 'putting his case' where there is a risk of a young or otherwise vulnerable witness failing to understand, becoming distressed or acquiescing to leading questions. Where limitations on questioning are necessary and appropriate, they must be clearly defined. The judge has a duty to ensure that they are complied with and should explain them to the jury and the reasons for them. If the advocate fails to comply with the limitations, the judge should give relevant directions to the jury when that occurs and prevent further questioning that does not comply with the ground rules settled upon in advance. Instead of commenting on inconsistencies during cross-examination, following discussion between the judge and the advocates, the advocate or judge may point out important inconsistencies after (instead of during) the witness's evidence. The judge should also remind the jury of these during summing up. The judge should be alert to alleged inconsistencies that are not in fact inconsistent, or are trivial.

3E.5 If there is more than one defendant, the judge should not permit each advocate to repeat the questioning of a vulnerable witness. In advance of the trial, the advocates should divide the topics between them, with the advocate for the first defendant leading the questioning, and the advocate(s) for the other defendant(s) asking only ancillary questions relevant to their client's case, without repeating the questioning that has already taken place on behalf of the other defendant(s).

3E.6 In particular in a trial of a sexual offence, 'body maps' should be provided for the witness' use. If the witness needs to indicate a part of the body, the advocate should ask the witness to point to the relevant part on the body map. In sex cases, judges should not permit advocates to ask the witness to point to a part of the witness' own body. Similarly, photographs of the witness' body should not be shown around the court while the witness is giving evidence.

CPD I General matters 3F: Intermediaries CPD.3F

Role and functions of intermediaries in criminal courts

3F.1 Intermediaries facilitate communication with witnesses and defendants who have communication needs. Their primary function is to improve the quality of evidence and aid understanding between the court, the advocates and the witness or defendant. For example, they commonly advise on the formulation of questions so as to avoid misunderstanding. On occasion, they actively assist and intervene during questioning. The extent to which they do so (if at all) depends on factors such as the communication needs of the witness or defendant, and the skills of the advocates in adapting their language and questioning style to meet those needs.

3F.2 Intermediaries are independent of parties and owe their duty to the court. The court and parties should be vigilant to ensure they act impartially and their assistance to witnesses and defendants is transparent. It is however permissible for an advocate to have a private consultation with an intermediary when formulating questions (although control of questioning remains the overall responsibility of the court).

3F.3 Further information is in *Intermediaries: Step by Step* (Toolkit 16; The Advocate's Gateway, 2015) and chapter 5 of the *Equal Treatment Bench Book* (Judicial College, 2013).

Links to publications

- https://www.theadvocatesgateway.org/images/toolkits/16-intermediaries-step-by-step-2019.pdf
- https://www.judiciary.gov.uk/wp-content/uploads/2013/11/5-children-and-vulnerable-adults.pdf

Assessment

3F.4 The process of appointment should begin with assessment by an intermediary and a report. The report will make recommendations to address the communication needs of the witness or defendant during trial.

3F.5 In light of the scarcity of intermediaries, the appropriateness of assessment must be decided with care to ensure their availability for those witnesses and defendants who are most in need. The decision should be made on an individual basis, in the context of the circumstances of the particular case.

Intermediaries for prosecution and defence witnesses

3F.6 Intermediaries are one of the special measures available to witnesses under the Youth Justice and Criminal Evidence Act 1999 (YJCEA 1999). Witnesses deemed vulnerable in accordance with the criteria in s.16 YJCEA are eligible for the assistance of an intermediary when giving evidence pursuant to s. 29 YJCEA 1999. These provisions do not apply to defendants.

3F.7 An application for an intermediary to assist a witness when giving evidence must be made in accordance with Part 18 of the Criminal Procedure Rules. In addition, where an intermediary report is available (see 3F.4 above), it should be provided with the application.

3F.8 The Witness Intermediary Scheme (WIS) operated by the National Crime Agency identifies intermediaries for witnesses and may be used by the prosecution and defence. The WIS is contactable at wit@nca.x.gsi.gov.uk / 0845 000 5463. An intermediary appointed through the WIS is defined as a 'Registered Intermediary' and matched to the particular witness based on expertise, location and availability. Registered Intermediaries are accredited by the WIS and bound by Codes of Practice and Ethics issued by the Ministry of Justice (which oversees the WIS).

3F.9 Having identified a Registered Intermediary, the WIS does not provide funding. The party appointing the Registered Intermediary is responsible for payment at rates specified by the Ministry of Justice.

3F.10 Further information is in *The Registered Intermediary Procedural Guidance Manual* (Ministry of Justice, 2015) and *Intermediaries: Step by Step* (see 3F.3 above).

Link to publication

- http://www.theadvocatesgateway.org/images/procedures/registered-intermediary-procedural-guidance-manual.pdf

Intermediaries for defendants

3F.11 Statutory provisions providing for defendants to be assisted by an intermediary when giving evidence (where necessary to ensure a fair trial) are not in force (because s.104 Coroners and Justice Act 2009, which would insert ss. 33BA and 33BB into the YJCEA 1999, has yet to be commenced).

3F.12 The court may direct the appointment of an intermediary to assist a defendant in reliance on its inherent powers (*C v Sevenoaks Youth Court* [2009] EWHC 3088 (Admin)). There is however no presumption that a defendant will be so assisted and, even where an intermediary would improve the trial process, appointment is not mandatory (*R v Cox* [2012] EWCA Crim 549). The court should adapt the trial process to address a defendant's communication needs (*R v Cox* [2012] EWCA Crim 549). It will rarely exercise its inherent powers to direct appointment of an intermediary but where a defendant is vulnerable or for some other reason experiences communication or hearing difficulties, such that he or she needs more help to follow the proceedings than her or his legal representatives readily can give having regard to their other functions on the defendant's behalf, then the court should consider sympathetically any application for the defendant to be accompanied throughout the trial by a support worker or other appropriate companion who can provide that assistance. This is consistent with CrimPR 3.9(3)(b) (see paragraph 3D.2 above); consistent with the observations in *R v Cox* (see paragraph 3D.4 above), *R (OP) v Ministry of Justice* [2014] EWHC 1944 (Admin) and *R v Rashid* [2017] EWCA Crim 2; and consistent with the arrangements contemplated at paragraph 3G.8 below.

3F.13 The court may exercise its inherent powers to direct appointment of an intermediary to assist a defendant giving evidence or for the entire trial. Terms of appointment are for the court and there is no illogicality in restricting the appointment to the defendant's evidence (*R v R* [2015] EWCA Crim 1870), when the 'most pressing need' arises (*OP v Secretary of State for Justice* [2014] EWHC 1944 (Admin)). Directions to appoint an intermediary for a defendant's evidence will thus be rare, but for the entire trial extremely rare, keeping in mind paragraph 3F.12 above.

3F.14 An application for an intermediary to assist a defendant must be made in accordance with Part 18 of the Criminal Procedure Rules. In addition, where an intermediary report is available (see 3F.4 above), it should be provided with the application.

3F.15 The WIS is not presently available to identify intermediaries for defendants (although in *OP v Secretary of State for Justice* [2014] EWHC 1944 (Admin), the Ministry of Justice was ordered to consider carefully whether it were justifiable to refuse equal provision to witnesses and defendants with respect to their evidence). 'Non-registered intermediaries' (intermediaries appointed other than through the WIS) must therefore be appointed for defendants. Although training is available, there is no accreditation process for non-registered intermediaries and rates of payment are unregulated.

3F.16 Arrangements for funding of intermediaries for defendants depend on the stage of the appointment process. Where the defendant is publicly funded, an application should be made to the Legal Aid Agency for prior authority to fund a pre-trial assessment. If the application is refused, an application may be made to the court to use its inherent powers to direct a pre-trial assessment and funding thereof. Where the court uses its inherent powers to direct assistance by an intermediary at trial (during evidence or for the entire trial), court staff are responsible for arranging payment from Central Funds. Internal guidance for court staff is in *Guidance for HMCTS Staff: Registered and Non-Registered Intermediaries for Vulnerable Defendants and Non-Vulnerable Defence and Prosecution Witnesses* (Her Majesty's Courts and Tribunals Service, 2014).

3F.17 The court should be satisfied that a non-registered intermediary has expertise suitable to meet the defendant's communication needs.

3F.18 Further information is in *Intermediaries: Step by Step* (see 3F.3 above).

Ineffective directions for intermediaries to assist defendants

3F.19 Directions for intermediaries to help defendants may be ineffective due to general unavailability, lack of suitable expertise, or non-availability for the purpose directed (for example, where the direction is for assistance during evidence, but an intermediary will only accept appointment for the entire trial).

3F.20 Intermediaries may contribute to the administration of justice by facilitating communication with appropriate defendants during the trial process. A trial will not be rendered unfair because a direction to appoint an intermediary for the defendant is ineffective. 'It would, in fact, be a most unusual case for a defendant who is fit to plead to be so disadvantaged by his condition that a properly brought prosecution would have to be stayed' because an intermediary with suitable expertise is not available for the purpose directed by the court (*R v Cox* [2012] EWCA Crim 549).

3F.21 Faced with an ineffective direction, it remains the court's responsibility to adapt the trial process to address the defendant's communication needs, as was the case prior to the existence of intermediaries (*R v Cox* [2012] EWCA Crim 549). In such a case, a ground rules hearing should be convened to ensure every reasonable step is taken to facilitate the defendant's participation in accordance with CrimPR 3.9. At the hearing, the court should make new, further and/ or alternative directions. This includes setting ground rules to help the defendant follow proceedings and (where applicable) to give evidence.

3F.22 For example, to help the defendant follow proceedings the court may require evidence to be adduced by simple questions, with witnesses being asked to answer in short sentences. Regular breaks may assist the defendant's concentration and enable the defence advocate to summarise the evidence and take further instructions.

3F.23 Further guidance is available in publications such as *Ground Rules Hearings and the Fair Treatment of Vulnerable People in Court* (Toolkit 1; The Advocate's Gateway, 2015) and *General Principles from Research — Planning to Question a Vulnerable Person or Someone with Communication Needs* (Toolkit 2(a); The Advocate's Gateway, 2015). In the absence of an intermediary, these publications include information on planning how to manage the participation and questioning of the defendant, and the formulation of questions to avert misunderstanding (for example, by avoiding 'long and complicated questions ... posed in a leading or 'tagged' manner' (*R v Wills* [2011] EWCA Crim 1938, [2012] 1 Cr App R 2)).

Links to publications

- https://www.theadvocatesgateway.org/images/toolkits/1-ground-rules-hearings-and-the-fair-treatment-of-vulnerable-people-in-court-2019.pdf
- https://www.theadvocatesgateway.org/images/toolkits/2-general-principles-from-research-policy-and-guidance-planning-to-question-a-vulnerable-person-or-someone-with-communication-needs-2019.pdf

Intermediaries for witnesses and defendants under 18

3F.24 Communication needs (such as short attention span, suggestibility and reticence in relation to authority figures) are common to many witnesses and defendants under 18. Consideration should therefore be given to the communication needs of all children and young people appearing in the criminal courts and to adapting the trial process to address any such needs. Guidance is available in publications such as *Planning to Question a Child or Young Person* (Toolkit 6; The Advocate's Gateway, 2015) and *Effective Participation of Young Defendants* (Toolkit 8; The Advocate's Gateway, 2013).

Links to publications

- https://www.theadvocatesgateway.org/images/toolkits/6-planning-to-question-a-child-or-young-person-141215.pdf
- https://www.theadvocatesgateway.org/images/toolkits/8-effective-participation-of-young-defendants-2017.pdf

3F.25 For the reasons set out in 3F.5 above, the appropriateness of an intermediary assessment for witnesses and defendants under 18 must be decided with care. Whilst there is no presumption that they will be assessed by an intermediary (to evaluate their communication needs prior to trial) or assisted by an intermediary at court (for example, if / when giving evidence), the decision should be made on an individual basis in the context of the circumstances of the particular case.

3F.26 Assessment by an intermediary should be considered for witnesses and defendants under 18 who seem liable to misunderstand questions or to experience difficulty expressing answers, including those who seem unlikely to be able to recognise a problematic question (such as one that is misleading or not readily understood), and those who may be reluctant to tell a questioner in a position of authority if they do not understand.

Attendance at ground rules hearing

3F.27 Where the court directs questioning will be conducted through an intermediary, CrimPR 3.9 requires the court to set ground rules. The intermediary should be present at the ground rules hearing to make representations in accordance with CrimPR 3.9(7)(a).

Listing

3F.28 Where the court directs an intermediary will attend the trial, their dates of availability should be provided to the court. It is preferable that such trials are fixed rather than placed in warned lists.

Photographs of court facilities

3F.29 Resident Judges in the Crown Court or the Chief Clerk or other responsible person in the magistrates' courts should, in consultation with HMCTS managers responsible for court security matters, develop a policy to govern under what circumstances photographs or other visual recordings may be made of court facilities, such as a live link room, to assist vulnerable or child witnesses to familiarise themselves with the setting, so as to be enabled to give their best evidence. For example, a photograph may provide a helpful reminder to a witness whose court visit has taken place sometime earlier. Resident Judges should tend to permit photographs to be taken for this purpose by intermediaries or supporters, subject to whatever restrictions the Resident Judge or responsible person considers to be appropriate, having regard to the security requirements of the court.

CPD.3G **CPD I General matters 3G: Vulnerable Defendants**

Before the trial, sentencing or appeal

3G.1 If a vulnerable defendant, especially one who is young, is to be tried jointly with one who is not, the court should consider at the plea and case management hearing, or at a case management hearing in a magistrates' court, whether the vulnerable defendant should be tried on his own, but should only so order if satisfied that a fair trial cannot be achieved by use of appropriate special measures or other support for the defendant. If a vulnerable defendant is tried jointly with one who is not, the court should consider whether any of the modifications set out in this direction should apply in the circumstances of the joint trial and, so far as practicable, make orders to give effect to any such modifications.

3G.2 It may be appropriate to arrange that a vulnerable defendant should visit, out of court hours and before the trial, sentencing or appeal hearing, the courtroom in which that hearing is to take place so that he or she can familiarise him or herself with it.

3G.3 Where an intermediary is being used to help the defendant to communicate at court, the intermediary should accompany the defendant on his or her pre-trial visit. The visit will enable the defendant to familiarise him or herself with the layout of the court, and may include matters such as: where the defendant will sit, either in the dock or otherwise; court officials (what their roles are and where they sit); who else might be in the court, for example those in the public gallery and press box; the location of the witness box; basic court procedure; and the facilities available in the court.

3G.4 If the defendant's use of the live link is being considered, he or she should have an opportunity to have a practice session.

3G.5 If any case against a vulnerable defendant has attracted or may attract widespread public or media interest, the assistance of the police should be enlisted to try and ensure that the defendant is not, when attending the court, exposed to intimidation, vilification or abuse. Section 41 of the Criminal Justice Act 1925 prohibits the taking of photographs of defendants and witnesses (among others) in the court building or in its precincts, or when entering or leaving those precincts. A direction reminding media representatives of the prohibition may be appropriate. The court should also be ready at this stage, if it has not already done so, where relevant to make a reporting restriction under section 39 of the Children and Young Persons Act 1933 or, on an appeal to the Crown Court from a youth court, to remind media representatives of the application of section 49 of that Act.

3G.6 The provisions of the Practice Direction accompanying Part 6 should be followed.

The trial, sentencing or appeal hearing

3G.7 Subject to the need for appropriate security arrangements, the proceedings should, if practicable, be held in a courtroom in which all the participants are on the same or almost the same level.

3G.8 Subject again to the need for appropriate security arrangements, a vulnerable defendant, especially if he is young, should normally, if he wishes, be free to sit with members of his family or others in a like relationship, and with some other suitable supporting adult such as a social worker, and in a place which permits easy, informal communication with his legal representatives. The court should ensure that a suitable supporting adult is available throughout the course of the proceedings.

3G.9 It is essential that at the beginning of the proceedings, the court should ensure that what is to take place has been explained to a vulnerable defendant in terms he or she can understand and, at trial in the Crown Court, it should ensure in particular that the role of the jury has been explained. It should remind those representing the vulnerable defendant and the supporting adult of their responsibility to explain each step as it takes place and, at trial, explain the possible consequences of a guilty verdict and credit for a guilty plea. The court should also remind any intermediary of the responsibility to ensure that the vulnerable defendant has understood the explanations given to him/her. Throughout the trial the court should continue to ensure, by any appropriate means, that the defendant understands what is happening and what has been said by those on the bench, the advocates and witnesses.

3G.10 A trial should be conducted according to a timetable which takes full account of a vulnerable defendant's ability to concentrate. Frequent and regular breaks will often be appropriate. The court should ensure, so far as practicable, that the whole trial is conducted in clear language that the defendant can understand and that evidence in chief and cross-examination are conducted using questions that are short and clear. The conclusions of the 'ground rules' hearing should be followed, and advocates should use and follow the 'toolkits' as discussed above.

3G.11 A vulnerable defendant who wishes to give evidence by live link, in accordance with section 33A of the Youth Justice and Criminal Evidence Act 1999, may apply for a direction to that effect; the procedure in CrimPR 18.14 to 18.17 should be followed. Before making such a direction, the court must be satisfied that it is in the interests of justice to do so and that the use of a live link would enable the defendant to participate more effectively as a witness in the proceedings. The direction will need to deal with the practical arrangements to be made, including the identity of the person or persons who will accompany him or her.

3G.12 In the Crown Court, the judge should consider whether robes and wigs should be worn, and should take account of the wishes of both a vulnerable defendant and any vulnerable witness. It is generally desirable that those responsible for the security of a vulnerable defendant who is in custody, especially if he or she is young, should not be in uniform, and that there should be no recognisable police presence in the courtroom save for good reason.

3G.13 The court should be prepared to restrict attendance by members of the public in the courtroom to a small number, perhaps limited to those with an immediate and direct interest in the outcome. The court should rule on any challenged claim to attend. However, facilities for reporting the proceedings (subject to any restrictions under section 39 or 49 of the Children and Young Persons Act 1933) must be provided. The court may restrict the number of reporters attending in the courtroom to such number as is judged practicable and desirable. In ruling on any challenged claim to attend in the courtroom for the purpose of reporting, the court should be mindful of the public's general right to be informed about the administration of justice.

3G.14 Where it has been decided to limit access to the courtroom, whether by reporters or generally, arrangements should be made for the proceedings to be relayed, audibly and if possible visually, to another room in the same court complex to which the media and the public have access if it appears that there will be a need for such additional facilities. Those making use of such a facility should be reminded that it is to be treated as an extension of the courtroom and that they are required to conduct themselves accordingly.

CPD I General matters 3H: Wales and the Welsh Language: Devolution Issues CPD.3H

3H.1 These are the subject of Practice Direction: (Supreme Court) (Devolution Issues) [1999] 1 WLR 1592; [1999] 3 All ER 466; [1999] 2 Cr App R 486, to which reference should be made.

CPD I General matters 3J: Wales and the Welsh Language: Applications for Evidence to be Given in Welsh CPD.3J

3J.1 If a defendant in a court in England asks to give or call evidence in the Welsh language, the case should not be transferred to Wales. In ordinary circumstances, interpreters can be provided on request.

CPD.3K **CPD I General matters 3K: Wales and the Welsh Language: Use of the Welsh Language in Courts in Wales**

3K.1 The purpose of this direction is to reflect the principle of the Welsh Language Act 1993 that, in the administration of justice in Wales, the English and Welsh languages should be treated on a basis of equality.

General

3K.2 It is the responsibility of the legal representatives in every case in which the Welsh language may be used by any witness or party, or in any document which may be placed before the court, to inform the court of that fact, so that appropriate arrangements can be made for the listing of the case.

3K.3 Any party or witness is entitled to use Welsh in a magistrates' court in Wales without giving prior notice. Arrangements will be made for hearing such cases in accordance with the 'Magistrates' Courts' Protocol for Listing Cases where the Welsh Language is used' (January 2008) which is available on the Judiciary's website: https://www.judiciary.gov.uk/publications/mags-cts-protocol-for-listing-cases-in-welsh-language/. See also CrimPR 24.14.

3K.4 If the possible use of the Welsh language is known at the time of sending or appeal to the Crown Court, the court should be informed immediately after sending or when the notice of appeal is lodged. Otherwise, the court should be informed as soon as the possible use of the Welsh language becomes known.

3K.5 If costs are incurred as a result of failure to comply with these directions, a wasted costs order may be made against the defaulting party and / or his legal representatives.

3K.6 The law does not permit the selection of jurors in a manner which enables the court to discover whether a juror does or does not speak Welsh, or to secure a jury whose members are bilingual, to try a case in which the Welsh language may be used.

Preliminary and plea and case management hearings

3K.7 An advocate in a case in which the Welsh language may be used must raise that matter at the preliminary and/or the plea and case management hearing and endorse details of it on the advocates' questionnaire, so that appropriate directions may be given for the progress of the case.

Listing

3K.8 The listing officer, in consultation with the resident judge, should ensure that a case in which the Welsh language may be used is listed

(a) wherever practicable before a Welsh speaking judge, and
(b) in a court in Wales with simultaneous translation facilities.

Interpreters

3K.9 Whenever an interpreter is needed to translate evidence from English into Welsh or from Welsh into English, the court listing officer in whose court the case is to be heard shall contact the Welsh Language Unit who will ensure the attendance of an accredited interpreter.

Jurors

3K.10 The jury bailiff, when addressing the jurors at the start of their period of jury service, shall inform them that each juror may take an oath or affirm in Welsh or English as he wishes.

3K.11 After the jury has been selected to try a case, and before it is sworn, the court officer swearing in the jury shall inform the jurors in open court that each juror may take an oath or affirm in Welsh or English as he wishes. A juror who takes the oath or affirms in Welsh should not be asked to repeat it in English.

3K.12 Where Welsh is used by any party or witness in a trial, an accredited interpreter will provide simultaneous translation from Welsh to English for the jurors who do not speak Welsh. There is no provision for the translation of evidence from English to Welsh for a Welsh speaking juror.

3K.13 The jury's deliberations must be conducted in private with no other person present and therefore no interpreter may be provided to translate the discussion for the benefit of one or more of the jurors.

Witnesses

3K.14 When each witness is called, the court officer administering the oath or affirmation shall inform the witness that he may be sworn or affirm in Welsh or English, as he wishes. A witness who takes the oath or affirms in Welsh should not be asked to repeat it in English.

Opening / closing of Crown Courts

3K.15 Unless it is not reasonably practicable to do so, the opening and closing of the court should be performed in Welsh and English.

Role of Liaison Judge

3K.16 If any question or problem arises concerning the implementation of these directions, contact should in the first place be made with the Liaison Judge for the Welsh language through the Wales Circuit Office:

HMCTS WALES / GLITEM CYMRU
3rd Floor, Churchill House / 3ydd Llawr T Churchill
Churchill Way / Ffordd Churchill
Cardiff / Caerdydd
CF10 2HH
029 2067 8300

CPD I General Matters 3L: Security of Prisoners at Court CPD.3L

3L.1 High-risk prisoners identified to the court as presenting a significant risk of escape, violence in court or danger to those in the court and its environs, and to the public at large, will as far as possible, have administrative and remand appearances listed for disposal by way of live link. They will have priority for the use of video equipment.

3L.2 In all other proceedings that require the appearance in person of a high-risk prisoner, the proceedings will be listed at an appropriately secure court building and in a court with a secure (enclosed or ceiling-high) dock.

3L.3 Where a secure dock or live link is not available the court will be asked to consider an application for additional security measures, which may include:
(a) the use of approved restraints (but see below at 3L.6);
(b) the deployment of additional escort staff;
(c) securing the court room for all or part of the proceedings;
(d) in exceptional circumstances, moving the hearing to a prison.

3L.4 National Offender Management Service (NOMS) will be responsible for providing the assessment of the prisoner and it is accepted that this may change at short notice. NOMS must provide notification to the listing officer of all Category A prisoners, those on the Escape-list and Restricted Status prisoners or other prisoners who have otherwise been assessed as presenting a significant risk of violence or harm. There is a presumption that all prisoners notified as high-risk will be allocated a hearing by live link and/or secure dock facilities. Where the court cannot provide a secure listing, the reasons should be provided to the establishment so that alternative arrangements can be considered.

Applications for use of approved restraints

3L.5 It is the duty of the court to decide whether a prisoner who appears before them should appear in restraints or not. Their decision must comply with the requirements of the European Convention on Human Rights, particularly Article 3, which prohibits degrading treatment, see *Ranniman v Finland* (1997) 26 EHRR 56.

3L.6 No prisoner should be handcuffed in court unless there are reasonable grounds for apprehending that he will be violent or will attempt to escape. If an application is made, it must be entertained by the court and a ruling must be given. The defence should be given the opportunity to respond to the application: proceeding in the absence of the defendant or his representative may give rise to an issue under Article 6(1) of the European Convention on Human Rights: *R v Rollinson* (1996) 161 JP 107, CA. If an application is to be made ex parte then that application should be made inter partes and the defence should be given an opportunity to respond.

Additional security measures

3L.7 It may be in some cases that additional dock officers are deployed to mitigate the risk that a prisoner presents. When the nature of the risk is so serious that increased deployment will be insufficient or would in itself be so obtrusive as to prejudice a fair trial, then the court may be required to consider the following measures:
(a) reconsider the case for a live link hearing, including transferring the case to a court where the live link is available;
(b) transfer the case to an appropriately secure court;
(c) the use of approved restraints on the prisoner for all or part of the proceedings;
(d) securing the court room for all or part of the proceedings; and
(e) the use of (armed) police in the court building.

3L.8 The establishment seeking the additional security measures will submit a Court Management Directions Form setting out the evidence of the prisoners identified risk of escape or violence and requesting the courts approval of security measures to mitigate that risk. This must be sent to the listing officer along with current, specific and credible evidence that the security measures are both necessary and proportionate to the identified risk and that the risk cannot be managed in any other way.

3L.9 If the court is asked to consider transfer of the case, then this must be in accordance with the Listing and Allocation Practice Direction XIII F.11-F.13 post. The listing officer will liaise with the establishment, prosecution and the defence to ensure the needs of the witnesses are taken into account.

3L.10 The Judge who has conduct of the case must deal with any application for the use of restraints or any other security measure and will hear representations from the Crown Prosecution Service and the defence before proceeding. The application will only be granted if:

(a) there are good grounds for believing that the prisoner poses a significant risk of trying to escape from the court (beyond the assumed motivation of all prisoners to escape) and/or risk of serious harm towards those persons in court or the public generally should an escape attempt be successful; and

(b) where there is no other viable means of preventing escape or serious harm.

High-risk prisoners giving evidence from the witness box

3L.11 High-risk prisoners giving evidence from the witness box may pose a significant security risk. In circumstances where such prisoners are required to move from a secure dock to an insecure witness box, an application may be made for the court to consider the use of additional security measures including:

(a) the use of approved restraints;

(b) the deployment of additional escort staff or police in the courtroom or armed police in the building. The decision to deploy an armed escort is for the Chief Inspector of the relevant borough: the decision to allow the armed escort in or around the court room is for the Senior Presiding Judge (see below);

(c) securing the courtroom for all or part of the proceedings;

(d) giving evidence from the secure dock; and

(e) use of live link if the prisoner is not the defendant.

CPD.3M **CPD I General Matters 3M: Procedure for Application for Armed Police Presence in the Royal Courts of Justice, Crown Courts and Magistrates' Court Buildings**

3M.1 This Practice Direction sets out the procedure for the making and handling of applications for authorisation for the presence of armed police officers within the precincts of any Crown Court and magistrates' court buildings at any time. It applies to an application to authorise the carriage of firearms or tasers in court for security purposes. It does not apply to officers who are carrying CS spray or PAVA incapacitant spray, which is included in the standard equipment issued to officers in some forces and therefore no separate authorisation is required for its carriage in court. Likewise, no separate authorisation is required for officers carrying tasers as part of their operational equipment where they are attending court on routine court business or to give evidence. If, however, the carrying of tasers is part of a tactical deployment for security purposes then an application must be made in accordance with the following provisions to ensure the court is aware of the arrangements sought.

3M.2 This Practice Direction applies to all cases in England and Wales in which a police unit intends to request authorisation for the presence of armed police officers in the Crown Court or in the magistrates' court buildings at any time and including during the delivery of prisoners to court.

3M.3 This Practice Direction allows applications to be made for armed police presence in the Royal Courts of Justice.

Emergency situations

3M.4 This Practice Direction does not apply in an emergency situation. In such circumstances, the police must be able to respond in a way in which their professional judgment deems most appropriate.

Designated court centres

3M.5 Applications may only be made for armed police presence in the designated Crown Court and magistrates' court centres (see below). This list may be revised from time to time in consultation with the Association of Chief Police Officers (ACPO) and HMCTS. It will be reviewed at least every five years in consultation with ACPO armed police secretariat and the Presiding Judges.

3M.6 The Crown Court centres designated for firearms deployment are:
- (a) Northern Circuit: Carlisle, Chester, Liverpool, Preston, Manchester Crown Square & Manchester Minshull Street.
- (b) North Eastern Circuit: Bradford, Leeds, Newcastle upon Tyne, Sheffield, Teesside and Kingston-upon-Hull.
- (c) Western Circuit: Bristol, Winchester and Exeter.
- (d) South Eastern Circuit (not including London): Canterbury, Chelmsford, Ipswich, Luton, Maidstone, Norwich, Reading and St Albans.
- (e) South Eastern Circuit (London only): Central Criminal Court, Woolwich, Kingston and Snaresbrook.
- (f) Midland Circuit: Birmingham, Northampton, Nottingham and Leicester.
- (g) Wales Circuit: Cardiff, Swansea and Caernarfon.

3M.7 The magistrates' courts designated for firearms deployment are:
- (a) South Eastern Circuit (London only): Westminster Magistrates' Court and Belmarsh Magistrates' Court.

Preparatory work prior to applications in all cases

3M.8 Prior to the making of any application for armed transport of prisoners or the presence of armed police officers in the court building, consideration must be given to making use of prison video link equipment to avoid the necessity of prisoners' attendance at court for the hearing in respect of which the application is to be made.

3M.9 Notwithstanding their designation, each requesting officer will attend the relevant court before an application is made to ensure that there have been no changes to the premises and that there are no circumstances that might affect security arrangements.

Applying in the Royal Courts of Justice

3M.10 All applications should be sent to the Listing Office of the Division in which the case is due to appear. The application should be sent by email if possible and must be on the standard form.

3M.11 The Listing Office will notify the Head of Division, providing a copy of the email and any supporting evidence. The Head of Division may ask to see the senior police officer concerned.

3M.12 The Head of Division will consider the application. If it is refused, the application fails and the police must be notified.

3M.13 In the absence of the Head of Division, the application should be considered by the Vice-President of the Division.

3M.14 The relevant Court Office will be notified of the decision and that office will immediately inform the police by telephone. The decision must then be confirmed in writing to the police.

Applying to the Crown Court

3M.15 All applications should be sent to the Cluster Manager and should be sent by email if possible and must be on the standard form.

3M.16 The Cluster Manager will notify the Presiding Judge on the circuit and the Resident Judge by email, providing a copy of the form and any supporting evidence. The Presiding Judge may ask to see the senior police officer concerned.

3M.17 The Presiding Judge will consider the application. If it is refused the application fails and the police must be informed.

3M.18 If the Presiding Judge approves the application it should be forwarded to the secretary in the Senior Presiding Judge's Office. The Senior Presiding Judge will make the final decision. The Presiding Judge will receive written confirmation of that decision.

3M.19 The Presiding Judge will notify the Cluster Manager and the Resident Judge of the decision. The Cluster Manager will immediately inform the police of the decision by telephone. The decision must then be confirmed in writing to the police.

Urgent applications to the Crown Court

3M.20 If the temporary deployment of armed police arises as an urgent issue and a case would otherwise have to be adjourned; or if the trial judge is satisfied that there is a serious risk to public safety, then the Resident Judge will have a discretion to agree such deployment without having obtained the consent of a Presiding Judge or the Senior Presiding Judge. In such a case:
- (a) the Resident Judge should assess the facts and agree the proposed solution with a police officer of at least Superintendent level. That officer should agree the approach with the Firearms Division of the police.
- (b) if the proposed solution involves the use of armed police officers, the Resident Judge must try to contact the Presiding Judge and/or the Senior Presiding Judge by email and telephone. The Cluster Manager should be informed of the situation.

(c) if the Resident Judge cannot obtain a response from the Presiding Judge or the Senior Presiding Judge, the Resident Judge may grant the application if satisfied:
 (i) that the application is necessary;
 (ii) that without such deployment there would be a significant risk to public safety; and
 (iii) that the case would have to be adjourned at significant difficulty or inconvenience.

3M.21 The Resident Judge must keep the position under continual review, to ensure that it remains appropriate and necessary. The Resident Judge must make continued efforts to contact the Presiding Judge and the Senior Presiding Judge to notify them of the full circumstances of the authorisation.

Applying to the magistrates' courts

3M.22 All applications should be directed, by email if possible, to the Office of the Chief Magistrate, at Westminster Magistrates' Court and must be on the standard form.

3M.23 The Chief Magistrate should consider the application and, if approved, it should be forwarded to the Senior Presiding Judge's Office. The Senior Presiding Judge will make the final decision. The Chief Magistrate will receive written confirmation of that decision and will then notify the requesting police officer and, where authorisation is given, the affected magistrates' court of the decision.

Urgent applications in the magistrates' courts

3M.24 If the temporary deployment of armed police arises as an urgent issue and a case would otherwise have to be adjourned; or if the Chief Magistrate is satisfied that there is a serious risk to public safety, then the Chief Magistrate will have a discretion to agree such deployment without having obtained the consent of the Senior Presiding Judge. In such a case:
(a) the Chief Magistrate should assess the facts and agree the proposed solution with a police officer of at least Superintendent level. That officer should agree the approach with the Firearms Division of the police.
(b) if the proposed solution involves the use of armed police officers, the Chief Magistrate must try to contact the Senior Presiding Judge by email and telephone. The Cluster Manager should be informed of the situation.
(c) if the Chief Magistrate cannot obtain a response from the Senior Presiding Judge, the Chief Magistrate may grant the application if satisfied:
 (i) that the application is necessary;
 (ii) that without such deployment there would be a significant risk to public safety; and
 (iii) that the case would have to be adjourned at significant difficulty or inconvenience.

3M.25 The Chief Magistrate must keep the position under continual review, to ensure that it remains appropriate and necessary. The Chief Magistrate must make continued efforts to contact the Senior Presiding Judge to notify him of the full circumstances of the authorisation.

CPD.3N **CPD I General Matters 3N: Use of Live Link and Telephone Facilities**

3N.1 Where it is lawful and in the interests of justice to do so, courts should exercise their statutory and other powers to conduct hearings by live link or telephone. This is consistent with the Criminal Procedure Rules and with the recommendations of the President of the Queen's Bench Division's *Review of Efficiency in Criminal Proceedings* published in January 2015. Save where legislation circumscribes the court's jurisdiction, the breadth of that jurisdiction is acknowledged by CrimPR 3.5(1), (2)(d).

3N.2 It is the duty of the court to make use of technology actively to manage the case: CrimPR 3.2(1), (2)(h). That duty includes an obligation to give directions for the use of live links and telephone facilities in the circumstances listed in CrimPR 3.2(4) and (5) (pre-trial hearings, including pre-trial case management hearings). Where the court directs that evidence is to be given by live link, and especially where such a direction is given on the court's own initiative, it is essential that the decision is communicated promptly to the witness: CrimPR 18.4. Contrary to a practice adopted by some courts, none of those rules or other provisions require the renewal of a live link direction merely because a trial has had to be postponed or adjourned. Once made, such a direction applies until it is discharged by the court, having regard to the relevant statutory criteria.

3N.3 It is the duty of the parties to alert the court to any reason why live links or telephones should not be used where CrimPR 3.2 otherwise would oblige the court to do so; and, where a direction for the use of such facilities has been made, it is the duty of the parties as soon as practicable to alert the court to any reason why that direction should be varied CrimPR 3.3(2)(e) and 3.6.

3N.4 The word 'appropriate' in CrimPR 3.2(4) and (5) is not a term of art. It has the ordinary English meaning of 'fitting', or 'suitable'. Whether the facilities available to the court in any particular case can be considered appropriate is a matter for the court, but plainly to be appropriate such facilities must work, at the time at which they are required; all participants must be able to hear and, in the case of a live link, see each other clearly; and there must be no extraneous noise, movement or other distraction suffered by a participant, or transmitted by a participant to others. What degree of protection from accidental or deliberate interception should be considered appropriate will depend upon the purpose for which a live link or telephone is to be used. If it is to participate in a hearing which is open to the public anyway, then what is communicated by such means is by definition public and the use of links such as Skype or Facetime, which are not generally considered secure from interception, may not be objectionable. If it is to participate in a hearing in private, and especially one at which sensitive information will be discussed – for example, on an application for a search warrant – then a more secure service is likely to be required.

3N.5 There may be circumstances in which the court should not require the use of live link or telephone facilities despite their being otherwise appropriate at a pre-trial hearing. In every case, in deciding whether any such circumstances apply the court will keep in mind that, for the purposes of what may be an essentially administrative hearing, it may be compatible with the overriding objective to proceed in the defendant's absence altogether, especially if he or she is represented, unless, exceptionally, a rule otherwise requires. The principle that the court always must consider proceeding in a defendant's absence is articulated in CrimPR 3.9(2)(a). Where at a pre-trial hearing bail may be under consideration, the provisions of CrimPR 14.2 will be relevant.

3N.6 Such circumstances will include any case in which the defendant's effective participation cannot be achieved by his or her attendance by such means, and CrimPR 3.2(4) and (5) except such cases from the scope of the obligation which that rule otherwise imposes on the court. That exception may apply where (this list is not exhaustive) the defendant has a disorder or disability, including a hearing, speech or sight impediment, or has communication needs to which the use of a live link or telephone is inimical (whether or not those needs are such as to require the appointment of an intermediary); or where the defendant requires interpretation and effective interpretation cannot be provided by live link or telephone, as the case may be. In deciding whether to require a defendant to attend a first hearing in a magistrates' court by live link from a police station, the court should take into account any views expressed by the defendant, the terms of any mental health or other medical assessment of the defendant carried out at the police station, and all other relevant information and representations available. No single factor is determinative, but the court must keep in mind the terms of section 57C(6A) of the Crime and Disorder Act 1998 (Use of live link at preliminary hearings where accused is at police station) which provides that 'A live link direction under this section may not be given unless the court is satisfied that it is not contrary to the interests of justice to give the direction.'

3N.7 Finally, that exception sometimes may apply where the defendant's attendance in person at a pre-trial hearing will facilitate communication with his or her legal representatives. The court should not make such an exception merely to allow client and representatives to meet if that meeting can and should be held elsewhere. However, there will be cases in which defence representatives reasonably need to meet with a defendant, to take his or her instructions or to explain events to him or her, either shortly before or immediately after a pre-trial hearing and in circumstances in which that meeting cannot take place effectively by live link.

3N.8 Nothing prohibits the member or members of a court from conducting a pre-trial hearing by attending by live link or telephone from a location distant from all the other participants. Despite the conventional view that the venue for a court hearing is the court room in which that hearing has been arranged to take place, the Criminal Procedure Rules define 'court' as 'a tribunal with jurisdiction over criminal cases. It includes a judge, recorder, District Judge (Magistrates' Court), lay justice and, when exercising their judicial powers, the Registrar of Criminal Appeals, a justices' clerk or assistant clerk.' Neither CrimPR 3.25 (Place of trial), which applies in the Crown Court, nor CrimPR 24.14 (Place of trial), which applies in magistrates' courts, each of which requires proceedings to take place in a courtroom provided by the Lord Chancellor, applies for the purposes of a pre-trial hearing. Thus for the purposes of such a hearing there is no legal obstacle to the judge, magistrate or magistrates conducting it from elsewhere, with other participants assembled in a courtroom from which the member or members of the court are physically absent. In principle, nothing prohibits the conduct of a pre-trial hearing by live link or telephone with each participant, including the member or members of the court, in a different location (an arrangement sometimes described as a 'virtual hearing'). This is dependent upon there being means by which that hearing can be witnessed by the public – for example, by public attendance at a courtroom or other venue from which the participants all can be seen and heard (if by live link), or heard (if by telephone). The principle of open justice to which paragraph 3N.17 refers is relevant.

3N.9 Sections 57A to 57F of the Crime and Disorder Act 1998 allow a defendant who is in custody to enter a plea by live link, and allow for such a defendant who attends by live link to be sentenced. In appropriate circumstances, the court may allow a defendant who is not in custody to enter a plea by live link; but the same considerations as apply to sentencing in such a case will apply: see paragraph 3N.13 beneath.

3N.10 The Crime and Disorder Act 1998 does not allow for the attendance by live link at a contested trial of a defendant who is in custody. The court may allow a defendant who wishes to do so to observe all or part of his or her trial by live link, whether she or he is in custody or not, but (a) such a defendant cannot lawfully give evidence by such means unless he or she satisfies the criteria prescribed by section 33A of the Youth Justice and Criminal Evidence Act 1999 and the court so orders under that section (see also CrimPR 18.14–18.17); (b) a defendant who is in custody and who observes the trial by live link is not present, as a matter of law, and the trial must be treated as taking place in his or her absence, she or he having waived the right to attend; and (c) a defendant who has refused to attend his or her trial when required to do so, or who has absconded, must not be permitted to observe the proceedings by live link.

3N.11 Paragraphs I 3D to 3G inclusive of these Practice Directions (Vulnerable people in the courts; Ground rules hearings to plan the questioning of a vulnerable witness or defendant; Intermediaries; Vulnerable defendants) contain directions relevant to the use of a live link as a special measure for a young or otherwise vulnerable witness, or to facilitate the giving of evidence by a defendant who is likewise young or otherwise vulnerable, within the scope of the Youth Justice and Criminal Evidence Act 1999. Defence representatives and the court must keep in mind that special measures under the 1999 Act and CrimPR Part 18, including the use of a live link, are available to defence as well as to prosecution witnesses who meet the statutory criteria. Defence representatives should always consider whether their witnesses would benefit from giving evidence by live link and should apply for a direction if appropriate, either at the case management hearing or as soon as possible thereafter. A defence witness should be afforded the same facilities and treatment as a prosecution witness, including the same opportunity to make a pre-trial visit to the court building in order to familiarise himself or herself with it. Where a live link is sought as a special measure for a young or vulnerable witness or defendant, CrimPR 18.10 and 18.15 respectively require, among other things, that the applicant must identify someone to accompany that witness or defendant while they give evidence; must name the person, if possible; and must explain why that person would be an appropriate companion for that witness. The court must ensure that directions are given accordingly when ordering such a live link. Witness Service volunteers are available to support all witnesses, prosecution and defence, if required.

3N.12 Under sections 57A and 57D or 57E of the Crime and Disorder Act 1998 the court may pass sentence on a defendant in custody who attends by live link. The court may allow a defendant who is not in custody and who wishes to attend his or her sentencing by live link her or him by such means. Factors of which the court will wish to take account in exercising its discretion include, in particular, the penalty likely to be imposed; the importance of ensuring that the explanations of sentence required by CrimPR 24.11(9), in magistrates' courts, and in the Crown Court by CrimPR 25.16(7), can be given satisfactorily, for the defendant, for other participants and for the public, including reporters; and the preferences of the maker of any Victim Personal Statement which is to be read aloud or played pursuant to paragraph VII F.3(c) of these Practice Directions.

Youth defendants

3N.13 In the youth court or when a youth is appearing in the magistrates' court or the Crown Court, it will usually be appropriate for the youth to be produced in person at court. This is to ensure that the court can engage properly with the youth and that the necessary level of engagement can be facilitated with the Youth Offending Team worker, defence representative and/or appropriate adult responsible for the youth's care. The court should deal with any application for use of a live-link on a case-by-case basis, after consultation with the parties and the Youth Offending Team. Such hearings that may be appropriate, include, onward remand hearings at which there is no bail application or case management hearings, particularly if the youth is already serving a custodial sentence.

3N.14 It rarely will be appropriate for a youth to be sentenced over a live link. However, notwithstanding the court's duties of engagement with a youth, the overriding welfare principle and the statutory responsibility of the youth offending worker to explain the sentence to the youth, after consultation with the parties and the Youth Offending Team, there may be circumstances in which it may be appropriate to sentence a youth over the live-link: a) If the youth is already serving a custodial sentence and the sentence to be imposed by the court is bound to be a further custodial sentence, whether concurrent or consecutive; b) If the youth is already serving a custodial sentence and the court is minded to impose a non-custodial sentence which will have no material impact on the sentence being served; c) The youth is being detained in a secure establishment at such a distance from the court that the travelling time from one to the other will be significant so as to materially affect the welfare of the youth; d) The youth's condition – whether mental or otherwise – is so disturbed that his or her production would be a significant detriment to his or her welfare.

3N.15 Arrangements must be made in advance of any live link hearing to enable the youth offending worker to be at the secure establishment where the youth is in custody. In the event that such arrangements are not practicable, the youth offending worker must have sufficient access to the youth via the live link booth before and after the hearing.

Conduct of participants

3N.16 Where a live link is used, the immediate vicinity of the device by which a person attends becomes, temporarily, part of the courtroom for the purposes of that person's participation. That person, and any advocate or legal representative, custodian, court officer, intermediary or other companion, whether immediately visible to the court or not, becomes a participant for the purposes of CrimPR 1.2(2) and is subject to the court's jurisdiction to regulate behaviour in the courtroom. The substance and effect of this direction must be drawn to the attention of all such participants.

Open justice and records of proceedings

3N.17 The principle of open justice to which CrimPR 6.2(1) gives effect applies as strongly where electronic means of communication are used to conduct a hearing as it applies in other circumstances. Open justice is the principal means by which courts are kept under scrutiny by the public. It follows that where a participant attends a hearing in public by live link or telephone then that person's participation must be, as nearly as may be, equally audible and, if applicable, equally visible to the public as it would be were he or she physically present. Where electronic means of communication are used to conduct a hearing, records of the event must be maintained in the usual way: CrimPR 5.4. In the Crown Court, this includes the recording of the proceedings: CrimPR 5.5.

CPD I General matters 3P: Commissioning Medical Reports CPD.3P

General observations

3P.1 CrimPR 24.3 and 25.10 concern procedures to be followed in magistrates' courts and in the Crown Court respectively where there is doubt about a defendant's mental health and, in the Crown Court, the defendant's capacity to participate in a trial. CrimPR 3.28 governs the procedure where, on the court's own initiative, a magistrates' court requires expert medical opinion about the potential suitability of a hospital order under section 37(3) of the Mental Health Act 1983 (hospital order without convicting the defendant), the Crown Court requires such opinion about the defendant's fitness to participate at trial, under section 4 of the Criminal Procedure (Insanity) Act 1964, or either a magistrates' court or the Crown Court requires such opinion to help the court determine a question of intent or insanity.

3P.2 Rule 3.28 governs the procedure to be followed where a report is commissioned at the instigation of the court. It is not a substitute for the prompt commissioning of a report or reports by a party or party's representatives where expert medical opinion is material to that party's case. In particular, those representing a defendant may wish to obtain a medical report or reports wholly independently of the court. Nothing in these directions, therefore, should be read as discouraging a party from commissioning a medical report before the case comes before the court, where that party believes such a report to be material to an issue in the case and where it is possible promptly to commission it. However, where a party has commissioned such a report then if that report has not been received by the time the court gives directions for preparation for trial, and if the court agrees that it seems likely that the report will be material to what is in issue, then when giving directions for trial the court should include a timetable for the reception of that report and should give directions for progress to be reviewed at intervals, adopting the timetable set out in these directions with such adaptations as are needed.

3P.3 In assessing the likely materiality of an expert medical report to help the court assess a defendant's health and capacity at the time of the alleged offence or the time of trial, or both, the court will be assisted by the parties' representations; by the views expressed in any assessment that may already have been prepared; and by the views of practitioners in local criminal justice mental health services, whose assistance is available to the court under local liaison arrangements.

3P.4 Where the court requires the assistance of such a report then it is essential that there should be (i) absolute clarity about who is expected to do what, by when, and at whose expense; and (ii) judicial directions for progress with that report to be monitored and reviewed at prescribed intervals, following a timetable set by the court which culminates in the consideration of the report at a hearing. This is especially important where the report in question is a psychiatric assessment of the defendant for the preparation of which specific expertise may be required which is not readily available and because in some circumstances a second such assessment, by another medical practitioner, may be required.

Timetable for the commissioning, preparation and consideration of a report or reports

3P.5 CrimPR 3.28 requires the court to set a timetable appropriate to the case for the preparation and reception of a report. That timetable must not be in substitution for the usual timetable for preparation for trial but must instead be incorporated within the trial preparation timetable. The fact that a medical report is to be obtained, whether that is commissioned at a party's instigation or on the court's own initiative, is never a reason to postpone a preparation for trial or a plea and trial preparation hearing, or to decline to give the directions needed for preparation for trial. It follows that a trial date must be set and other directions given in the usual way.

3P.6 In setting the timetable for obtaining a report or reports the court will take account of such representations and other information that it receives, including information about the anticipated availability and workload of medical practitioners with the appropriate expertise. However, the timetable ought not be a protracted one. It is essential to keep in mind the importance of maintaining progress: in recognition of the defendant's rights and with respect for the interests of victims and witnesses, as required by CrimPR Part 1 (the overriding objective). In a magistrates' court account must be taken, too, of section 11 of the Powers of Criminal Courts (Sentencing) Act 2000, which limits the duration of each remand pending the preparation of a report to 3 weeks, where the defendant is to be in custody, and to 4 weeks if the defendant is to be on bail.

3P.7 Subject, therefore, to contrary judicial direction the timetable set by the court should require:

(a) the convening of a further pre-trial case management hearing to consider the report and its implications for the conduct of the proceedings no more than 6 – 8 weeks after the court makes its request in a magistrates' court, and no more than 10 – 12 weeks after the request in the Crown Court (at the end of Stage 2 of the directions for pre-trial preparation in the Crown Court);

(b) the prompt identification of an appropriate medical practitioner or practitioners, if not already identified by the court, and the despatch of a commission or commissions accordingly, within 2 business days of the court's decision to request a report;

(c) acknowledgement of a commission by its recipient, and acceptance or rejection of that commission, within 5 business days of its receipt;

(d) enquiries by court staff to confirm that the commission has been received, and to ascertain the action being taken in response, in the event that no acknowledgement is received within 10 business days of its despatch;

(e) delivery of the report within 5 weeks of the despatch of the commission;

(f) enquiries into progress by court staff in the event that no report is received within 5 weeks of the despatch of the commission.

3P.8 The further pre-trial case management hearing that is convened for the court to consider the report should not be adjourned before it takes place save in exceptional circumstances and then only by explicit judicial direction the reasons for which must be recorded. If by the time of that hearing the report is available, as usually should be the case, then at that hearing the court can be expected to determine the issue in respect of which the report was commissioned and give further directions accordingly. If by that time, exceptionally, the report is not available then the court should take the opportunity provided by that hearing to enquire into the reasons, give such directions as are appropriate, and if necessary adjourn the hearing to a fixed date for further consideration then. Where it is known in advance of that hearing that the report will not be available in time, the hearing may be conducted by live link or telephone: subject, in the defendant's case, to the same considerations as are identified at paragraph 3N.6 of these Practice Directions. However, it rarely will be appropriate to dispense altogether with that hearing, or to make enquiries and give further directions without any hearing at all, in view of the arrangements for monitoring and review that the court already will have directed and which, by definition therefore, thus far will have failed to secure the report's timely delivery.

3P.9 Where a requirement of the timetable set by the court is not met, or where on enquiry by court staff it appears that the timetable is unlikely to be met, and in any instance in which a medical practitioner who accepts a commission asks for more time, then court staff should not themselves adjust the timetable or accede to such a request but instead should seek directions from an appropriate judicial authority. Subject to local judicial direction, that will be, in the Crown Court, the judge assigned to the case or the resident judge and, in a magistrates' court, a District Judge (Magistrates' Courts) or justice of the peace assigned to the case, or the Justices' Clerk, an assistant clerk or other senior legal adviser. Even if the timetable is adjusted in consequence:

(a) the further pre-trial case management hearing convened to consider the report rarely should be adjourned before it takes place: see paragraph 3O.13 [*sic*: 3P.8] above;

(b) directions should be given for court staff henceforth to make regular enquiries into progress, at prescribed intervals of not more than 2 weeks, and to report the outcome to an appropriate judicial authority who will decide what further directions, if any, to give.

3P.10 Any adjournment of a hearing convened to consider the report should be to a specific date: the hearing should not be adjourned generally, or to a date to be set in due course. The adjournment of such a hearing should not be for more than a further 6 – 8 weeks save in the most exceptional circumstances; and no more than one adjournment of the hearing should be allowed without obtaining written or oral representations from the commissioned medical practitioner explaining the reasons for the delay.

Commissioning a report

3P.11 Guidance entitled 'Good practice guidance: commissioning, administering and producing psychiatric reports for sentencing' prepared for and published by the Ministry of Justice and HM Courts and Tribunals Service in September 2010 contains material that will assist court staff and those who are asked to prepare such reports:

http://www.ohrn.nhs.uk/resource/policy/GoodPracticeGuidePsychReports.pdf

The guidance includes standard forms of letters of instruction and other documents.

3P.12 CrimPR 3.28 requires the commissioner of a report to explain why the court seeks the report and to include relevant information about the circumstances. The HMCTS Guidance contains forms for judicial use in the instruction of court staff, and guidance to court staff on the preparation of letters of instruction, where a report is required for sentencing purposes. Those forms and that guidance can be adapted for use where the court requires a report on the defendant's fitness to participate, in the Crown Court, or in a magistrates' court requires a report for the purposes of section 37(3) of the Mental Health Act 1983.

3P.13 The commission should invite a practitioner who is unable to accept it promptly to nominate a suitably qualified substitute, if possible, and to transfer the commission to that person, reporting the transfer when acknowledging the court officer's letter. It is entirely appropriate for the commission to draw the recipient's attention to CrimPR 1.2 (the duty of the participants in a criminal case) and to CrimPR 19.2(1)(b) (the obligation of an expert witness to comply with directions made by a court and at once to inform the court of any significant failure, by the expert or another, to take any step required by such a direction).

3P.14 Where the relevant legislation requires a second psychiatric assessment by a second medical practitioner, and where no commission already has been addressed to a second such practitioner, the commission may invite the person to whom it is addressed to nominate a suitably qualified second person and to pass a copy of the commission to that person forthwith.

Funding arrangements

3P.15 Where a medical report has been, or is to be, commissioned by a party then that party is responsible for arranging payment of the fees incurred, even though the report is intended for the court's use. That must be made clear in that party's commission.

3P.16 Where a medical report is requested by the court and commissioned by a party or by court staff at the court's direction then the commission must include (i) confirmation that the fees will be paid by HMCTS, (ii) details of how, and to whom, to submit an invoice or claim for fees, and (iii) notice of the prescribed rates of fees and of any legislative or other criteria applicable to the calculation of the fees that may be paid.

Remand in custody

3P.17 Where the defendant who is to be examined will be remanded in custody then notice that directions have been given for a medical report or reports to be prepared must be included in the information given to the defendant's custodian, to ensure that the preparation of the report or reports can be facilitated. This is especially important where bail is withheld on the ground that it would be otherwise impracticable to complete the required report, and in particular where that is the only ground for withholding bail.

CPD I General matters 3Q: Failure to Comply with Requirement to Give Name, Date of Birth And Nationality CPD.3Q

3Q.1 Section 86A of the Courts Act 2003 requires a magistrates' court and the Crown Court to require a defendant to provide his or her name, date of birth and nationality in the circumstances and at the times set out in CrimPR 3.13(5) and 3.27(5). Section 86A(3) of the Act makes it an offence for the defendant without reasonable excuse to fail to comply with such a requirement, whether by providing false or incomplete information or by providing no information. A person guilty of such an offence is liable on summary conviction to imprisonment for a term not exceeding 6 months, or to a fine, or both. It follows that a prosecution for failure to comply with a section 86A requirement may be brought by any of the procedures for which CrimPR Part 7 provides (Starting a prosecution in a magistrates' court) in the same way as any other allegation of a summary offence.

3Q.2 It does not follow, however, that every such allegation first must be reported to the police. Where the defendant's conduct evinces guilt, especially if the defendant refuses altogether to give the information required, such conduct undermines the administration of justice and the authority of the court. In principle, it should be dealt with at once. Section 86A(6) of the Act provides that, 'The criminal court before which a person is required to provide his or her name, date of birth and nationality may deal with any suspected offence under subsection (3) at the same time as dealing with the offence for which the person was already before the court'. In such a case, therefore, a magistrates' court may invite the prosecutor to institute proceedings orally, there and then, pursuant to section 1 of the Magistrates' Courts Act 1980 and CrimPR Part 7, and may there and then try the alleged offence in accordance with the rules in CrimPR Part 24 (Trial and sentence in a magistrates' court). A defendant should be allowed a reasonable opportunity to reflect and to take legal advice, from a duty solicitor if the defendant has no legal representative in the prosecution for the main offence. After that, unless the defendant then pleads guilty the prosecutor must call such evidence as may be convenient and sufficient, in the prosecutor's view, formally to prove the allegation; and the defendant may present evidence, for example of reasonable excuse, and may make representations in accordance with those rules.

3Q.3 Given that the Act expressly contemplates a prompt determination by the court before which there occurs an ostensible failure to comply with a section 86A requirement, rarely will it be necessary or appropriate to adjourn the trial of that allegation to a differently constituted court unless there emerges such a dispute of fact about what has occurred in the sight and hearing of the court as to disqualify the first bench from determining that dispute with perceived impartiality. In that rare event the trial of the allegation must be heard, the same day, by a different bench.[1] In any other event the constitution before whom the alleged offence under section 86A(3) has occurred usually should try the allegation, usually the same day.

3Q.4 If in the circumstances contemplated in the preceding paragraph a different bench convicts the defendant of the section 86A(3) offence, and if the defendant is convicted by the first bench of the offence for which the defendant was already before the court, then the court which passes sentence for that main offence should pass sentence also under section 86A(3). However, an offence under section 86A(3) is one that stands apart from the proceedings in the course of which it was committed the seriousness of which can be reflected by an appropriate and, generally, separate penalty.

3Q.5 Whether an alleged contravention of a section 86A requirement is dealt with the same day or later, after investigation by the police, no member of the court before whom the alleged contravention occurs should participate in the proceedings as the complainant or as a witness. Nor will it be appropriate to invite the defendant's representative, if any, to give evidence of what that representative may have witnessed in the court room. It is unexceptionable for court staff, including a legal adviser in a magistrates' court, to be asked to give evidence of what has taken place.

3Q.6 The offence contrary to section 86A(3) of the 2003 Act is one to which the time limit imposed by section 127 of the Magistrates' Courts Act 1980 applies, namely that a magistrates' court may not try an information unless that information was laid within 6 months from the time when the offence was committed. Where the court does not adopt the procedure described in paragraphs 3Q.2 and 3Q.3 above the alleged offence must be reported promptly to allow it to be investigated and, if appropriate, prosecuted in time.

CPD.3R

CPD I General matters 3R: Hearing to Inform the Court of Sensitive Material

3R.1 CrimPR 3.29 (Hearing to inform the court of sensitive material) governs the procedure that must be followed where a prosecutor has, or is aware of, sensitive material to which the prosecutor does not think the obligation to disclose applies but of the existence of which the prosecutor thinks it necessary to inform the court in order to mitigate the risks listed in that rule.

[1] The risk is that a constitution which witnesses a defendant's refusal to give the information required will not be perceived to adjudicate impartially on a contention that, as a matter of fact, and against the prosecution evidence, the defendant was not asked for the information or did not refuse to give it. If that were the defence then the court would, of course, offer the defendant a renewed opportunity to comply with the requirement and only if that further opportunity were declined would the prosecution for the section 86A(3) offence be adjourned to a different bench. Such circumstances may be expected to arise only wholly exceptionally.

3R.2 Examples of such material were given by the Court of Appeal in *R* v *Ali* [2019] EWCA Crim 1527. Examples include information about the activities of a defendant or witness, or about a person to whom the evidence in the case refers, or information to the effect that the prosecution evidence omits matters irrelevant to the trial, derived from observations, for example, which is of sensitivity in some other respect. These are, however, only examples and other material may come within the scope of the rule.

3R.3 In the Crown Court a hearing to which rule 3.29 applies must be recorded: CrimPR 5.5 (Recording and transcription of proceedings in the Crown Court). It is very likely that the hearing will be conducted in private (see CrimPR 3.29(4)) and very likely that it will take place in a private room rather than in the courtroom. The recording therefore should be made using a suitable and suitably secure device, and it should be stored securely. In some circumstances that may require arrangements for the storage of the recording to be dealt with in accordance with CrimPR 3.29(4)(c)(ii) (storage by an appropriate person other than the court officer). Such storage arrangements are likely also to apply to any written material provided to the court under CrimPR 3.29(3)(c).

Criminal Procedure Rules Part 4 Service of Documents

When this Part applies R4.1

4.1 (1) The rules in this Part apply—
(a) to the service of every document in a case to which these Rules apply; and
(b) for the purposes of section 12 of the Road Traffic Offenders Act 1988[1], to the service of a requirement to which that section applies.
(2) The rules apply subject to any special rules in other legislation (including other Parts of these Rules) or in the Practice Direction.
(3) In this Part, 'the relevant court office' means—
(a) in relation to a case in a magistrates' court or in the Crown Court, an office—
(i) at which that court's business is administered, and
(ii) the address or electronic address of which is advertised by the Lord Chancellor at the date of service as that at which that type of document must be served;
(b) in relation to an application to a High Court judge for permission to serve a draft indictment—
(i) in London, the Queen's Bench Listing Office, Royal Courts of Justice, Strand, London WC2A 2LL,
(ii) elsewhere, the office at which court staff administer the business of any court then constituted of a High Court judge, and
(iii) in either case, the electronic address which is advertised by the Lord Chancellor at the date of service as that at which such an application must be served;
(c) in relation to an extradition appeal case in the High Court—
(i) the Administrative Court Office, Royal Courts of Justice, Strand, London WC2A 2LL, and
(ii) the electronic address which is advertised by the Lord Chancellor at the date of service as that at which that type of document must be served; and
(d) where the recipient is the Registrar of Criminal Appeals—
(i) the Criminal Appeal Office, Royal Courts of Justice, Strand, London WC2A 2LL, and
(ii) the electronic address which is advertised by the Lord Chancellor at the date of service as that at which that type of document must be served.

[Note. Section 12 of the Road Traffic Offenders Act 1988 allows the court to accept the documents to which it refers as evidence of a driver's identity where a requirement to state that identity has been served under section 172 of the Road Traffic Act 1988[2] or under section 112 of the Road Traffic Regulation Act 1984[3].]

Methods of service R4.2

4.2 (1) A document may be served by any of the methods described in rules 4.3 to 4.6 (subject to rules 4.7 and 4.10), or in rule 4.8.
(2) Where a document may be served by electronic means under rule 4.6, the general rule is that the person serving it must use that method.

[1] 1988 c. 53; section 12 was amended by article 3 of, and paragraphs 29 and 30 of the Schedule to, S.I. 2004/2035.
[2] 1988 c. 52; section 172 was substituted by section 21 of the Road Traffic Act 1991 (c. 40) and amended by paragraph 24 of Schedule 3 to the Vehicle Excise and Registration Act 1994 (c. 22) and the Statute Law (Repeals) Act 2004 (c. 14).
[3] 1984 c. 27; section 112 was amended by section 102 of, and Schedule 17 to, the Local Government Act 1985 (c. 51) and section 4 of, and paragraph 6 of the Schedule to, the Parking Act 1989 (c. 16).

R4.3 Service by handing over a document

4.3 (1) A document may be served on—

(a) an individual by handing it to him or her;

(b) a corporation by handing it to a person holding a senior position in that corporation;

(c) an individual or corporation who is legally represented in the case by handing it to that legal representative;

(d) the prosecution by handing it to the prosecutor or to the prosecution representative; and

(e) the court officer or the Registrar of Criminal Appeals by handing it to a court officer with authority to accept it at the relevant court office.

(2) If an individual is under 18, a copy of a document served under paragraph (1)(a) must be handed to his or her parent, or another appropriate adult, unless no such person is readily available.

(3) Unless the court otherwise directs, for the purposes of paragraph (1)(c) or (d) (service by handing a document to a party's representative) 'representative' includes an advocate appearing for that party at a hearing.

[Note. Some legislation treats a body that is not a corporation as if it were one for the purposes of rules about service of documents. See for example section 143 of the Adoption and Children Act 2002[4].]

R4.4 Service by leaving or posting a document

4.4 (1) A document may be served by addressing it to the person to be served and leaving it at the appropriate address for service under this rule, or by sending it to that address by first class post or by the equivalent of first class post.

(2) The address for service under this rule on—

(a) an individual is an address where it is reasonably believed that he or she will receive it;

(b) a corporation is its principal office, and if there is no readily identifiable principal office then any place where it carries on its activities or business;

(c) an individual or corporation who is legally represented in the case is that legal representative's office;

(d) the prosecution is the prosecutor's office;

(e) the court officer or the Registrar of Criminal Appeals is the relevant court office.

[Note. In addition to service in England and Wales for which these rules provide, service outside England and Wales may be allowed under other legislation. See—

(a) section 39 of the Criminal Law Act 1977[5] (service of summons, etc. in Scotland and Northern Ireland);

(b) section 1139(4) of the Companies Act 2006[6] (service of copy summons, etc. on company's registered office in Scotland and Northern Ireland);

(c) sections 3, 4, 4A and 4B of the Crime (International Co-operation) Act 2003[7] (service of summons, etc. outside the United Kingdom) and rules 49.1 and 49.2; and

(d) section 1139(2) of the Companies Act 2006 (service on overseas company).]

R4.5 Service by document exchange

4.5 (1) This rule applies where—

(a) the person to be served—

(i) has given a document exchange (DX) box number, and

(ii) has not refused to accept service by DX; or

(b) the person to be served is legally represented in the case and the legal representative has given a DX box number.

(2) A document may be served by—

(a) addressing it to that person or legal representative, as appropriate, at that DX box number; and

(b) leaving it at—

(i) the document exchange at which the addressee has that DX box number, or

(ii) a document exchange at which the person serving it has a DX box number.

4 2002 c. 38.

5 1977 c. 45; sub-section (1) was substituted by section 331 of, and paragraph 6 of Schedule 36 to, the Criminal Justice Act 2003 (c. 44). Sub-section (3) was amended by section 83 of, and paragraph 79 of Schedule 7 to, the Criminal Justice (Scotland) Act 1980 (c. 62).

6 2006 c. 46.

7 2003 c. 32; sections 4A and 4B were inserted by section 331 of, and paragraph 16 of Schedule 36 to, the Criminal Justice Act 2003 (c. 44).

(3) Where the person to be served under this rule is the court officer, the address for service is the relevant court office.

Service by electronic means R4.6

4.6 (1) This rule applies where—
(a) the person to be served—
(i) has given an electronic address and has not refused to accept service at that address, or
(ii) is given access to an electronic address at which a document may be deposited and has not refused to accept service by the deposit of a document at that address; or
(b) the person to be served is legally represented in the case and the legal representative—
(i) has given an electronic address, or
(ii) is given access to an electronic address at which a document may be deposited.
(2) A document may be served—
(a) by sending it by electronic means to the address which the recipient has given; or
(b) by depositing it at an address to which the recipient has been given access and—
(i) in every case, making it possible for the recipient to read the document, or view or listen to its content, as the case may be,
(ii) unless the court otherwise directs, making it possible for the recipient to make and keep an electronic copy of the document, and
(iii) notifying the recipient of the deposit of the document (which notice may be given by electronic means).
(3) Where the person to be served under this rule is the court officer, the address for service is the relevant court office.
(4) Where a document is served under this rule the person serving it need not provide a paper copy as well.

Documents that must be served by specified methods R4.7

4.7 (1) An application or written statement, and notice, under rule 48.9 alleging contempt of court may be served—
(a) on an individual, only under rule 4.3(1)(a) (by handing it to him or her); and
(b) on a corporation, only under rule 4.3(1)(b) (by handing it to a person holding a senior position in that corporation).
(2) For the purposes of section 12 of the Road Traffic Offenders Act 1988[8], a notice of a requirement under section 172 of the Road Traffic Act 1988[9] or under section 112 of the Road Traffic Regulation Act 1984[10] to identify the driver of a vehicle may be served—
(a) on an individual, only by post under rule 4.4(1) and (2)(a); and
(b) on a corporation, only by post under rule 4.4(1) and (2)(b).

Service by person in custody R4.8

4.8 (1) A person in custody may serve a document by handing it to the custodian addressed to the person to be served.
(2) The custodian must—
(a) endorse it with the time and date of receipt;
(b) record its receipt; and
(c) forward it promptly to the addressee.

Service by another method R4.9

4.9 (1) The court may allow service of a document by a method—
(a) other than those described in rules 4.3 to 4.6 and in rule 4.8; and
(b) other than one specified by rule 4.7, where that rule applies.
(2) An order allowing service by another method must specify—
(a) the method to be used; and
(b) the date on which the document will be served.

Documents that may not be served on a legal representative R4.10

4.10 Unless the court otherwise directs, service on a party's legal representative of any of the following documents is not service of that document on that party—
(a) a summons, requisition, single justice procedure notice or witness summons;

[8] 1988 c. 53; section 12 was amended by article 3 of, and paragraphs 29 and 30 of the Schedule to, S.I. 2004/2035.
[9] 1988 c. 52; section 172 was substituted by section 21 of the Road Traffic Act 1991 (c. 40) and amended by paragraph 24 of Schedule 3 to the Vehicle Excise and Registration Act 1994 (c. 22) and the Statute Law (Repeals) Act 2004 (c. 14).
[10] 1984 c. 27; section 112 was amended by section 102 of, and Schedule 17 to, the Local Government Act 1985 (c. 51) and section 4 of, and paragraph 6 of the Schedule to, the Parking Act 1989 (c. 16).

(b) notice of an order under section 25 of the Road Traffic Offenders Act 1988[11];
(c) a notice of registration under section 71(6) of that Act[12],
(d) notice of a hearing to review the postponement of the issue of a warrant of detention or imprisonment under section 77(6) of the Magistrates' Courts Act 1980[13],
(e) notice under section 86 of that Act[14] of a revised date to attend a means inquiry;
(f) any notice or document served under Part 14 (Bail and custody time limits);
(g) notice under rule 24.15(a) of when and where an adjourned hearing will resume;
(h) notice under rule 28.5(3) of an application to vary or discharge a compensation order;
(i) notice under rule 28.10(2)(c) of the location of the sentencing or enforcing court;
(j) a collection order, or notice requiring payment, served under rule 30.2(a); or
(k) an application or written statement, and notice, under rule 48.9 alleging contempt of court.

R4.11 **Date of service**

4.11 (1) A document served under rule 4.3 or rule 4.8 is served on the day it is handed over.
(2) Unless something different is shown, a document served on a person by any other method is served—
(a) in the case of a document left at an address, on the next business day after the day on which it was left;
(b) in the case of a document sent by first class post or by the equivalent of first class post, on the second business day after the day on which it was posted or despatched;
(c) in the case of a document served by document exchange, on the second business day after the day on which it was left at a document exchange allowed by rule 4.5;
(d) in the case of a document served by electronic means—
(i) on the day on which it is sent under rule 4.6(2)(a), if that day is a business day and if it is sent by no later than 2.30pm that day (or 4.30pm that day, in an extradition appeal case in the High Court or 5pm that day if it is an application for permission to refer a sentencing case to which Part 41 (Reference to the Court of Appeal of point of law or unduly lenient sentencing) applies),
(ii) on the day on which notice of its deposit is given under rule 4.6(2)(b), if that day is a business day and if that notice is given by no later than 2.30pm that day (or 4.30pm that day, in an extradition appeal case in the High Court, or 5pm that day if it is an application for permission to refer a sentencing case to which Part 41 (Reference to the Court of Appeal of point of law or unduly lenient sentencing) applies), or
(iii) otherwise, on the next business day after it was sent or such notice was given; and
(e) in any case, on the day on which the addressee responds to it, if that is earlier.
(3) Unless something different is shown, a document produced by a computer system for dispatch by post is to be taken as having been sent by first class post, or by the equivalent of first class post, to the addressee on the business day after the day on which it was produced.
(4) Where a document is served on or by the court officer or the Registrar of Criminal Appeals, 'business day' does not include a day on which the relevant court office is closed.

R4.12 **Proof of service**

4.12 The person who serves a document may prove that by signing a certificate explaining how and when it was served.

R4.13 **Court's power to give directions about service**

4.13 (1) The court may specify the time as well as the date by which a document must be—
(a) served under rule 4.3 (Service by handing over a document) or rule 4.8 (Service by person in custody); or
(b) sent or deposited by electronic means, if it is served under rule 4.6.
(2) The court may treat a document as served if the addressee responds to it even if it was not served in accordance with the rules in this Part.

[11] 1988 c. 53; section 25 was amended by section 90 of, and paragraphs 140 and 142 of Schedule 13 to, the Access to Justice Act 1999 (c. 22), section 165 of, and paragraph 118 of Schedule 9 to, the Powers of Criminal Courts (Sentencing) Act 2000 (c. 6) and section 109 of, and paragraph 311 of Schedule 8 to, the Courts Act 2003 (c. 39).
[12] 1988 c. 53; section 71(6) was amended by section 109 of, and paragraph 317 of Schedule 8 to, the Courts Act 2003 (c. 39).
[13] 1980 c. 43; section 77(6) was substituted by section 109 of, and paragraph 218 of Schedule 8 to, the Courts Act 2003 (c. 39).
[14] 1980 c. 43; section 86 was amended by section 51(2) of the Criminal Justice Act 1982 (c. 48) and section 97(3) of the Access to Justice Act 1999 (c. 22).

CRIMINAL PROCEDURE RULES PART 5 FORMS AND COURT RECORDS

Forms

Applications, etc. by forms or electronic means R5.1

5.1 (1) This rule applies where a rule, a practice direction or the court requires a person to—
(a) make an application or give a notice;
(b) supply information for the purposes of case management by the court; or
(c) supply information needed for other purposes by the court.
(2) Unless the court otherwise directs, such a person must—
(a) use such electronic arrangements as the court officer may make for that purpose, in accordance with those arrangements; or
(b) if no such arrangements have been made, use the appropriate form set out in the Practice Direction or the Criminal Costs Practice Direction, in accordance with those Directions.

Forms in Welsh R5.2

5.2 (1) Any Welsh language form set out in the Practice Direction, or in the Criminal Costs Practice Direction, is for use in connection with proceedings in courts in Wales.
(2) Both a Welsh form and an English form may be contained in the same document.
(3) Where only a Welsh form, or only the corresponding English form, is served—
(a) the following words in Welsh and English must be added:
"Darperir y ddogfen hon yn Gymraeg / Saesneg os bydd arnoch ei heisiau. Dylech wneud cais yn ddi-oed i (swyddog y llys) (rhodder yma'r cyfeiriad)
This document will be provided in Welsh / English if you require it. You should apply immediately to (the court officer) (address)"; and
(b) the court officer, or the person who served the form, must, on request, supply the corresponding form in the other language to the person served.

Signature of forms R5.3

5.3 (1) This rule applies where a form provides for its signature.
(2) Unless other legislation otherwise requires, or the court otherwise directs, signature may be by any written or electronic authentication of the form by, or with the authority of, the signatory.

[Note. Section 7 of the Electronic Communications Act 2000[1] provides for the use of an electronic signature in an electronic communication.]

Court records

Duty to make records R5.4

5.4 (1) For each case, as appropriate, the court officer must record, by such means as the Lord Chancellor directs—
(a) each charge or indictment against the defendant;
(b) the defendant's plea to each charge or count;
(c) each acquittal, conviction, sentence, determination, direction or order;
(d) each decision about bail;
(e) the power exercised where the court commits or adjourns the case to another court—
(i) for sentence, or
(ii) for the defendant to be dealt with for breach of a community order, a deferred sentence, a conditional discharge, or a suspended sentence of imprisonment, imposed by that other court;
(f) the court's reasons for a decision, where legislation requires those reasons to be recorded;
(g) any appeal;
(h) each party's presence or absence at each hearing;
(i) any consent that legislation requires before the court can proceed with the case, or proceed to a decision;
(j) in a magistrates' court—
(i) any indication of sentence given in connection with the allocation of a case for trial, and
(ii) the registration of a fixed penalty notice for enforcement as a fine, and any related endorsement on a driving record;
(k) in the Crown Court, any request for assistance or other communication about the case received from a juror;
(l) the identity of—

[1] 2000 c. 7.

(i) the prosecutor,
(ii) the defendant,
(iii) any other applicant to whom these Rules apply,
(iv) any interpreter or intermediary,
(v) the parties' legal representatives, if any, and
(vi) the judge, magistrate or magistrates, justices' legal adviser or other person who made each recorded decision;

(m) where a defendant is entitled to attend a hearing, any agreement by the defendant to waive that right; and
(n) where interpretation is required for a defendant, any agreement by that defendant to do without the written translation of a document.

(2) Such records must include—
(a) each party's and representative's address, including any electronic address and telephone number available;
(b) the defendant's date of birth, if available; and
(c) the date of each event and decision recorded.

[Note. For the duty to keep court records, see sections 5 and 8 of the Public Records Act 1958[2]*.*

Requirements to record the court's reasons for its decision are contained in: section 5 of the Bail Act 1976[3]*; section 47(1) of the Road Traffic Offenders Act 1988*[4]*; sections 20, 33A and 33BB of the Youth Justice and Criminal Evidence Act 1999*[5]*; section 174 of the Criminal Justice Act 2003*[6]*; and rule 6.8.*

The prosecution of some offences requires the consent of a specified authority. Requirements for the defendant's consent to proceedings in his or her absence are contained in sections 23 and 128 of the Magistrates' Courts Act 1980[7]*.*

In the circumstances for which it provides, section 20 of the Magistrates' Courts Act 1980[8] *allows the court to give an indication of whether a custodial or non-custodial sentence is more likely in the event of a guilty plea at trial in that court.]*

R5.5 Recording and transcription of proceedings in the Crown Court

5.5 (1) Where someone may appeal to the Court of Appeal, the court officer must—
(a) arrange for the recording of the proceedings in the Crown Court, unless the court otherwise directs; and
(b) arrange for the transcription of such a recording if—

[2] 1958 c. 51; section 5 was amended by sections 67 and 86 of, and paragraph 2 of Schedule 5 to, the Freedom of Information Act 2000 (c. 36); and section 8 was amended by sections 27 and 35 of, and Schedule 2 to, the Administration of Justice Act 1969 (c. 58), section 1 of, and paragraph 19 of Schedule 2 to, the Administration of Justice Act 1970 (c. 31), section 56 of, and Schedule 11 to, the Courts Act 1971 (c. 23), section 152 of, and Schedule 7 to, the Senior Courts Act 1981 (c. 54) and sections 56 and 59 of, and Schedule 11 to, the Constitutional Reform Act 2005 (c. 4).

[3] 1976 c. 63; section 5 was amended by section 65 of, and Schedule 12 to, the Criminal Law Act 1977 (c. 45), section 60 of the Criminal Justice Act 1982 (c. 48), paragraph 1 of Schedule 3 to the Criminal Justice and Public Order Act 1994 (c. 33), paragraph 53 of Schedule 9 to the Powers of Criminal Courts (Sentencing) Act 2000 (c. 6), section 129(1) of the Criminal Justice and Police Act 2001 (c. 16), paragraph 182 of Schedule 8 to the Courts Act 2003 (c. 39), paragraph 48 of Schedule 3, paragraphs 1 and 2 of Schedule 36, and Parts 2, 4 and 12 of Schedule 37 to the Criminal Justice Act 2003 (c. 44) and section 208 of, and paragraphs 33 and 35 of Schedule 21 to, the Legal Services Act 2007 (c. 27).

[4] 1988 c. 53.

[5] 1999 c. 23; section 20(6) was amended by paragraph 384(a) of Schedule 8 to the Courts Act 2003 (c. 39); section 33A was inserted by section 47 of the Police and Justice Act 2006 (c. 48). Section 33BB is inserted by section 104(1) of the Coroners and Justice Act 2009, with effect from a date to be appointed.

[6] 2003 c. 44; section 174 was substituted by section 64 of the Legal Aid, Sentencing and Punishment of Offenders Act 2012 (c. 10).

[7] 1980 c. 43; section 23 was amended by section 125 of, and paragraph 25 of Schedule 18 to, the Courts and Legal Services Act 1990 (c. 41) and paragraphs 1 and 8 of Schedule 3 to the Criminal Justice Act 2003 (c. 44). Section 128 was amended by section 59 to, and paragraphs 2, 3 and 4 of Schedule 9 to, the Criminal Justice Act 1982 (c. 48), section 48 of the Police and Criminal Evidence Act 1984 (c. 60), section 170(1) of, and paragraphs 65 and 69 of Schedule 15 to, the Criminal Justice Act 1988 (c. 33), section 125(3) of, and paragraph 25 of Schedule 18 to, the Courts and Legal Services Act 1990 (c. 41), sections 49, 52 and 80 of, and Schedule 5 to, the Criminal Procedure and Investigations Act 1996 (c. 25), paragraph 75 of Schedule 9 to the Powers of Criminal Courts (Sentencing) Act 2000 (c. 6) and paragraph 51 of Schedule 3 and Part 4 of Schedule 37 to the Criminal Justice Act 2003 (c. 44). It is modified by section 91(5) of the Legal Aid, Sentencing and Punishment of Offenders Act 2012 (c. 10).

[8] 1980 c. 43; section 20 was amended by section 100 of, and paragraph 25 of Schedule 11 to, the Criminal Justice Act 1991 (c. 53), paragraph 63 of Schedule 9 to the Powers of Criminal Courts (Sentencing) Act 2000 (c. 6) and paragraphs 1 and 6 of Schedule 3 to the Criminal Justice Act 2003 (c. 44).

(i) the Registrar wants such a transcript, or
(ii) anyone else wants such a transcript (but that is subject to the restrictions in paragraph (2)).

(2) Unless the court otherwise directs, a person who transcribes a recording of proceedings under such arrangements—
(a) may only supply a transcript of a recording of a hearing in private to—
(i) the Registrar, or
(ii) an individual who was present at that hearing;
(b) if the recording of a hearing in public contains information to which reporting restrictions apply, may only supply a transcript containing that information to—
(i) the Registrar, or
(ii) a recipient to whom that supply will not contravene those reporting restrictions; but
(c) subject to paragraph (2)(a) and (b), must supply any person with any transcript for which that person asks—
(i) in accordance with the transcription arrangements made by the court officer, and
(ii) on payment by that person of any fee prescribed.

(3) A party who wants to hear a recording of proceedings must—
(a) apply—
(i) in writing to the Registrar, if an appeal notice has been served where Part 36 applies (Appeal to the Court of Appeal: general rules), or
(ii) orally or in writing to the Crown Court officer;
(b) explain the reasons for the request; and
(c) pay any fee prescribed.

(4) If the Crown Court or the Registrar so directs, the Crown Court officer must allow that party to hear a recording of—
(a) a hearing in public; and
(b) a hearing in private, if the applicant was present at that hearing.

[Note. See also section 32 of the Criminal Appeal Act 1968[9]*.*

For the circumstances in which reporting restrictions may apply, see the provisions listed in the note to rule 6.1. In summary, reporting restrictions prohibit the publication of the information to which they apply where that publication is likely to lead members of the public to acquire the information concerned.]

Custody of case materials **R5.6**

5.6 Unless the court otherwise directs, in respect of each case the court officer may—
(a) keep any evidence, application, representation or other material served by the parties; or
(b) arrange for the whole or any part to be kept by some other appropriate person, subject to—
(i) any condition imposed by the court, and
(ii) the rules in Part 34 (Appeal to the Crown Court) and Part 36 (Appeal to the Court of Appeal: general rules) about keeping exhibits pending any appeal.

Supply to a party of information or documents from records or case materials **R5.7**

5.7 (1) This rule—
(a) applies where—
(i) a party wants information, or a copy of a document, from records or case materials kept by the court officer (for example, in case of loss, or to establish what is retained), or
(ii) a person affected by an order made, or warrant issued, by the court wants such information or such a copy; but
(b) does not apply to—
(i) a recording arranged under rule 5.5 (Recording and transcription of proceedings in the Crown Court),
(ii) a copy of such a recording, or
(iii) a transcript of such a recording.

(2) Such a party or person must—
(a) apply to the court officer;
(b) specify the information or document required; and
(c) pay any fee prescribed.

(3) The application—
(a) may be made orally, giving no reasons, if paragraph (4) requires the court officer to supply the information or document requested; but

[9] 1968 c. 19.

Criminal Procedure Rules and Criminal Practice Directions

(b) must be in writing, unless the court otherwise permits, and must explain for what purpose the information is required, in any other case.

(4) The court officer must supply to the applicant party or person —

(a) a copy of any document served by, or on, that party or person (but not of any document not so served); and

(b) by word of mouth, or in writing, as requested—

(i) information that was received from that party or person in the first place,

(ii) information about the terms of any direction or order directed to that party or person, or made on an application by that party or person, or at a hearing in public, and

(iii) information about the outcome of the case.

(5) If the court so directs, the court officer must supply to the applicant party or person, by word of mouth or in writing, as requested, information that paragraph (4) does not require the court officer to supply.

(6) Where the information requested is about the grounds on which an order was made, or a warrant was issued, in the absence of the party or person applying for that information—

(a) that party or person must also serve the request on the person who applied for the order or warrant;

(b) if the person who applied for the order or warrant objects to the supply of the information requested, that objector must—

(i) give notice of the objection not more than 10 business days after service of the request (or within any longer period allowed by the court),

(ii) serve that notice on the court officer and on the party or person requesting the information, and

(iii) if the objector wants a hearing, explain why one is needed;

(c) the court may determine the application for information at a hearing (which must be in private unless the court otherwise directs), or without a hearing; and

(d) the court must not permit the information requested to be supplied unless the person who applied for the order or warrant has had at least 10 business days (or any longer period allowed by the court) in which to make representations.

(7) A notice of objection under paragraph (6) must explain—

(a) whether the objection is to the supply of any part of the information requested, or only to the supply of a specified part, or parts, of it;

(b) whether the objection is to the supply of the information at any time, or only to its supply before a date or event specified by the objector; and

(c) the grounds of the objection.

(8) Where a notice of objection under paragraph (6) includes material that the objector thinks ought not be revealed to the party or person applying for information, the objector must—

(a) omit that material from the notice served on that party or person;

(b) mark the material to show that it is only for the court; and

(c) with that material include an explanation of why it has been withheld.

(9) Where paragraph (8) applies—

(a) a hearing of the application may take place, wholly or in part, in the absence of the party or person applying for information; and

(b) at any such hearing, the general rule is that the court must consider, in the following sequence—

(i) representations first by the party or person applying for information and then by the objector, in the presence of both, and then

(ii) further representations by the objector, in the absence of that party or person

but the court may direct other arrangements for the hearing.

R5.8 Supply to the public, including reporters, of information about cases

5.8 (1) This rule—

(a) requires the supply and publication of information about cases with regard to the importance of—

(i) dealing with criminal cases in public, and

(ii) allowing a public hearing to be reported to the public;

(b) applies where a member of the public, including a reporter, wants information about a case from the court officer;

(c) requires the court officer to publish information about cases due to be considered by the court; but

(d) does not apply to—

(i) a recording arranged under rule 5.5 (Recording and transcription of proceedings in the Crown Court),
(ii) a copy of such a recording, or
(iii) a transcript of such a recording.

(2) A person who wants information about a case from the court officer must—
(a) apply to the court officer;
(b) specify the information requested; and
(c) pay any fee prescribed.

(3) The application—
(a) may be made orally, giving no reasons, if—
(i) paragraph (4) requires the court officer to supply the information requested, and
(ii) the information is to be supplied only by word of mouth; but
(b) must be in writing, unless the court otherwise permits, and must explain for what purpose the information is required, in any other case.

(4) The court officer must supply to the applicant—
(a) any information listed in paragraph (6), if—
(i) the information is available to the court officer,
(ii) the supply of the information is not prohibited by a reporting restriction, and
(iii) the trial has not yet concluded, or the verdict was not more than 6 months ago; and
(b) details of any reporting or access restriction ordered by the court.

(5) The court officer must supply that information—
(a) by word of mouth; or
(b) in writing, including by—
(i) written certificate or extract, or
(ii) such arrangements as the Lord Chancellor directs.

(6) The information that paragraph (4) requires the court officer to supply is—
(a) the date of any hearing in public, unless any party has yet to be notified of that date;
(b) each alleged offence and any plea entered;
(c) the court's decision at any hearing in public, including any decision about—
(i) bail, or
(ii) the committal, sending or transfer of the case to another court;
(d) whether the case is under appeal;
(e) the outcome of the case;
(f) the identity of—
(i) the prosecutor,
(ii) the defendant,
(iii) the parties' representatives, including their addresses, and
(iv) the judge, magistrate or magistrates, or justices' legal adviser by whom a decision at a hearing in public was made; and
(g) such other information about the case as is required by arrangements made under paragraph (5)(b)(ii).

(7) If the court so directs, the court officer must—
(a) supply to the applicant, by word of mouth or in writing (including by written certificate or extract), other information about the case; or
(b) allow the applicant to inspect or copy a document, or part of a document, containing information about the case.

(8) The court may determine an application to which paragraph (7) applies—
(a) at a hearing, in public or in private; or
(b) without a hearing.

(9) Where a case is due to be heard in public, the court officer must—
(a) publish the information listed in paragraph (10) if—
(i) the information is available to the court officer, and
(ii) the publication of the information is not prohibited by a reporting restriction; and
(b) publish that information for no longer than 5 business days—
(i) by notice displayed somewhere prominent in the vicinity of a court room in which the hearing is due to take place, and
(ii) by such arrangements as the Lord Chancellor directs, including arrangements for publication by electronic means, but only to the extent needed to comply with paragraph (1)(a).

(10) The information that paragraph (9) requires the court officer to publish is—
(a) the date, time and place of the hearing;
(b) the identity of the defendant; and
(c) such other information as it may be practicable to publish concerning—

(i) the type of hearing,
(ii) the identity of the prosecutor,
(iii) the identity of the court,
(iv) the offence or offences alleged, and
(v) whether any reporting restriction applies.

(11) Where a case is ready to be tried without a hearing under rule 24.9 (Single justice procedure: special rules), the court officer must—
(a) publish the information listed in paragraph (12) if—
(i) the information is available to the court officer, and
(ii) the publication of the information is not prohibited by a reporting restriction; and
(b) publish that information for no longer than 5 business days—
(i) by such arrangements as the Lord Chancellor directs, including arrangements for publication by electronic means, but
(ii) only to the extent needed to comply with paragraph (1)(a).

(12) The information that paragraph (11) requires the court officer to publish is—
(a) the identity of the defendant;
(b) the identity of the prosecutor;
(c) the offence or offences alleged; and
(d) whether any reporting restriction applies.

[Note. Rule 5.8(4) requires the court officer to supply on request the information to which that paragraph refers. On an application for other information about a case, rule 5.8(3)(b), (7) and (8) apply and the court's decision on such an application may be affected by—
(a) any reporting restriction imposed by legislation or by the court (Part 6 lists the reporting restrictions that might apply);
(b) Articles 6, 8 and 10 of the European Convention on Human Rights, and the court's duty to have regard to the importance of—
(i) dealing with criminal cases in public, and
(ii) allowing a public hearing to be reported to the public;
(c) the Rehabilitation of Offenders Act 1974[10] (section 5 of the Act[11] lists sentences and rehabilitation periods);
(d) section 18 of the Criminal Procedure and Investigations Act 1996[12], which affects the supply of information about material, other than evidence, disclosed by the prosecutor;
(e) Part 3 of the Data Protection Act 2018[13] (sections 43(3) and 117 of which make exceptions for criminal proceedings from some other provisions of that Act); and
(f) sections 33, 34 and 35 of the Legal Aid, Sentencing and Punishment of Offenders Act 2012[14], which affect the supply of information about applications for legal aid.]

R5.9 Supply of written certificate or extract from records for use in evidence, etc

5.9 (1) This rule applies where legislation—
(a) allows a certificate of conviction or acquittal, or an extract from records kept by the court officer, to be introduced in evidence in criminal proceedings; or
(b) requires such a certificate or extract to be supplied by the court officer to a specified person for a specified purpose.

(2) A person who wants such a certificate or extract must—
(a) apply in writing to the court officer;
(b) specify the certificate or extract required;
(c) explain under what legislation and for what purpose it is required; and
(d) pay any fee prescribed.

(3) If the application satisfies the requirements of that legislation, the court officer must supply the certificate or extract requested—
(a) to a party; and
(b) unless the court otherwise directs, to any other applicant.

10 1974 c. 53.
11 1974 c. 53; section 5 was amended by section 15 of, and paragraphs 77 and 78 of Schedule 4 to, the Constitutional Reform Act 2005 (c. 4) and by sections 126 and 139 of, and paragraph 2 of Schedule 21 to, the Legal Aid, Sentencing and Punishment of Offenders Act 2012 (c. 10).
12 1996 c. 25.
13 2018 c. 12.
14 2012 c. 10.

[Note. Under sections 73 to 75 of the Police and Criminal Evidence Act 1984[15]*, a certificate of conviction or acquittal, and certain other details from records to which this Part applies, may be admitted in evidence in criminal proceedings.*

Under section 115 of the Crime and Disorder Act 1998[16]*, information from records to which this Part applies may be obtained by specified authorities for the purposes of that Act.*

Under section 92 of the Sexual Offences Act 2003[17]*, a certificate which records a conviction for an offence and a statement by the convicting court that that offence is listed in Schedule 3 to the Act is evidence of those facts for certain purposes of that Act.*

A certificate of conviction or acquittal, and certain other information, required for other purposes, may be obtained from the Secretary of State under sections 112, 113A and 113B of the Police Act 1997[18]*.*

This rule applies where certificates or extracts from court records are required for use in evidence or for some other purpose specified in legislation. Where this rule does not apply, information about a case may be obtained under rule 5.8.]

Criminal Practice Directions Part 5 Forms and Court Records

CPD I General matters 5A: Forms CPD.5A

5A.1 The forms at Annex D to the Consolidated Criminal Practice Direction of 8th July 2002 [2002] 1 WLR 2870; [2002] 2 Cr App R 35, or forms to that effect, are to be used in the criminal courts, in accordance with CrimPR 5.1.

5A.2 The forms at Annex E to that Practice Direction, the case management forms, must be used in the criminal courts, in accordance with that rule.

5A.3 The table at the beginning of each section of each of those Annexes lists the forms and:
(a) shows the Rule in connection with which each applies;
(b) describes each form.

5A.4 The forms may be amended or withdrawn from time to time, or new forms added, under the authority of the Lord Chief Justice.

CPD I General matters 5B: Access to Information Held by the Court CPD.5B

5B.1 Open justice, as Lord Justice Toulson re-iterated in the case of *R (Guardian News and Media Ltd) v City of Westminster Magistrates' Court* [2012] EWCA Civ 420, [2013] QB 618, is a 'principle at the heart of our system of justice and vital to the rule of law'. There are exceptions but these 'have to be justified by some even more important principle'. However, the practical application of that undisputed principle, and the proper balancing of conflicting rights and principles, call for careful judgments to be made. The following is intended to provide some assistance to courts making decisions when asked to provide the public, including journalists, with access to or copies of information and documents held by the court, or when asked, exceptionally, to forbid the supply of transcripts that otherwise would have been supplied. It is not a prescriptive list, as the court will have to consider all the circumstances of each individual case.

[15] 1984 c. 60; section 73 was amended by section 90(1) of, and paragraphs 125 and 128 of Schedule 13 to, the Access to Justice Act 1999 (c. 22), paragraph 285 of Schedule 8 to the Courts Act 2003 (c. 39) and paragraph 13 of Schedule 17 to the Coroners and Justice Act 2009 (c. 25); and section 74 was amended by paragraph 85 of Schedule 36, and Part 5 of Schedule 37, to the Criminal Justice Act 2003 (c. 44) and paragraph 14 of Schedule 17 to the Coroners and Justice Act 2009 (c. 25).

[16] 1998 c. 37; section 115 was amended by paragraphs 150 and 151 of Schedule 7 to the Criminal Justice and Court Services Act 2000 (c. 43), paragraph 35 of Schedule 1 to S.I. 2000/90, section 97 of the Police Reform Act 2002 (c. 30), paragraph 25 of Schedule 1 to S.I. 2002/2469, section 219 of the Housing Act 2004 (c. 34), section 22 of, and paragraphs 1 and 7 of Schedule 9 to, the Police and Justice Act 2006 (c. 48), paragraph 29 of the Schedule to S.I. 2007/961, section 29 of the Transport for London Act 2008 (c. i), paragraph 13 of Schedule 2 to S.I. 2008/912, paragraphs 109 and 111 of Schedule 2 to S.I. 2010/866 and paragraphs 83 and 90 of Schedule 5 to the Health and Social Care Act 2012 (c. 7).

[17] 2003 c. 42.

[18] 1997 c. 50; section 112 was amended by section 50 of the Criminal Justice and Immigration Act 2008 (c. 4), sections 93, 97 and 112 of, and Part 8 of Schedule 8 to, the Policing and Crime Act 2009 (c. 26) and sections 80 and 84 of the Protection of Freedoms Act 2012 (c. 9). Section 113A was added by section 163(2) of the Serious Organised Crime and Police Act 2005 (c. 15), modified by regulation 4 of S.I. 2010/1146, and amended by paragraph 14 of Schedule 9 to the Safeguarding Vulnerable Groups Act 2006 (c. 47), section 50 of the Criminal Justice and Immigration Act 2008 (c. 4), sections 97 and 112 of, and Part 8 of Schedule 8 to, the Policing and Crime Act 2009 (c. 26), sections 80 and 115 of, and paragraphs 35 and 36 of Schedule 9 and Part 5 of Schedule 10 to, the Protection of Freedoms Act 2012 (c. 9), articles 2 and 3 of S.I. 2009/203 and articles 36 and 37 of S.I. 2012/3006. Section 113B was added by section 163(2) of the Serious Organised Crime and Police Act 2005 (c. 15), modified by regulations 5 to 7 of S.I. 2010/1146, and amended by paragraph 14 of Schedule 9 to the Safeguarding Vulnerable Groups Act 2006 (c. 47), paragraph 149 of Schedule 16 to the Armed Forces Act 2006 (c. 52), section 50 of the Criminal Justice and Immigration Act 2008 (c. 4), sections 97 and 112 of, and Part 8 of Schedule 8 to, the Policing and Crime Act 2009 (c. 26), sections 79, 80, 82 and 115 of, and paragraphs 35 and 37 of Schedule 9 and Parts 5 and 6 of Schedule 10 to, the Protection of Freedoms Act 2012 (c. 9), articles 2 and 4 of S.I. 2009/203, regulation 8 of S.I. 2010/1146 and articles 36, 37 and 39 of S.I. 2012/3006.

5B.2 It remains the responsibility of the recipient of information or documents to ensure that they comply with any and all restrictions such as reporting restrictions (see Part 6 and the accompanying Practice Direction).

5B.3 For the purposes of this direction, the word document includes images in photographic, digital including DVD format, video, CCTV or any other form.

5B.4 Certain information can and should be provided to the public on request, subject to any restrictions, such as reporting restrictions, imposed in that particular case. CrimPR 5.5 governs the supply of transcript of a recording of proceedings in the Crown Court. CrimPR 5.8(4) and 5.8(6) read together specify the information that the court officer will supply to the public; an oral application is acceptable and no reason need be given for the request. There is no requirement for the court officer to consider the non-disclosure provisions of the Data Protection Act 1998 as the exemption under section 35 applies to all disclosure made under 'any enactment … or by the order of a court', which includes under the Criminal Procedure Rules.

5B.5 If the information sought is neither transcript nor listed at CrimPR 5.8(6), rule 5.8(7) will apply, and the provision of information is at the discretion of the court. The following guidance is intended to assist the court in exercising that discretion.

5B.6 A request for access to documents used in a criminal case should first be addressed to the party who presented them to the court or who, in the case of a written decision by the court, received that decision. Prosecuting authorities are subject to the Freedom of Information Act 2000 and the Data Protection Act 1998 and their decisions are susceptible to review.

5B.7 If the request is from a journalist or media organisation, note that there is a protocol between the NPCC, the CPS and the media entitled 'Publicity and the Criminal Justice System':
www.cps.gov.uk/publications/agencies/mediaprotocol.html
www.cps.gov.uk/publication/publicity-and-criminal-justice-system
There is additionally a protocol made under CrimPR 5.8(5)(b) between the media and HMCTS:
www.newsmediauk.org/write/MediaUploads/PDF%20Docs/Protocol_for_Sharing_Court_Documents.pdf
This Practice Direction does not affect the operation of those protocols. Material should generally be sought under the relevant protocol before an application is made to the court.

5B.8 An application to which CrimPR 5.8(7) applies must be made in accordance with rule 5.8; it must be in writing, unless the court permits otherwise, and 'must explain for what purpose the information is required.' A clear, detailed application, specifying the name and contact details of the applicant, whether or not he or she represents a media organisation, and setting out the reasons for the application and to what use the information will be put, will be of most assistance to the court. Applicants should state if they have requested the information under a protocol and include any reasons given for the refusal. Before considering such an application, the court will expect the applicant to have given notice of the request to the parties.

5B.9 The court will consider each application on its own merits. The burden of justifying a request for access rests on the applicant. Considerations to be taken into account will include:

i. whether or not the request is for the purpose of contemporaneous reporting; a request after the conclusion of the proceedings will require careful scrutiny by the court;
ii. the nature of the information or documents being sought;
iii. the purpose for which they are required;
iv. the stage of the proceedings at the time when the application is made;
v. the value of the documents in advancing the open justice principle, including enabling the media to discharge its role, which has been described as a 'public watchdog', by reporting the proceedings effectively;
vi. any risk of harm which access to them may cause to the legitimate interests of others; and
vii. any reasons given by the parties for refusing to provide the material requested and any other representations received from the parties.

Further, all of the principles below are subject to any specific restrictions in the case. Courts should be aware that the risk of providing a document may reduce after a particular point in the proceedings, and when the material requested may be made available.

Documents read aloud in their entirety

5B.10 If a document has been read aloud to the court in its entirety, it should usually be provided on request, unless to do so would be disruptive to the court proceedings or place an undue burden on the court, the advocates or others. It may be appropriate and convenient for material to be provided electronically, if this can be done securely.

5B.11 Documents likely to fall into this category are:

i. Opening notes;
ii. Statements agreed under section 9 of the Criminal Justice Act 1967, including experts' reports, if read in their entirety;
iii. Admissions made under section 10 of the Criminal Justice Act 1967.

Documents treated as read aloud in their entirety

5B.12 A document treated by the court as if it had been read aloud in public, though in fact it has been neither read nor summarised aloud, should generally be made available on request. The burden on the court, the advocates or others in providing the material should be considered, but the presumption in favour of providing the material is greater when the material has only been treated as having been read aloud. Again, subject to security considerations, it may be convenient for the material to be provided electronically.

5B.13 Documents likely to fall into this category include:

i. Skeleton arguments;
ii. Written submissions;
iii. Written decisions by the court.

Documents read aloud in part or summarised aloud

5B.14 Open justice requires only access to the part of the document that has been read aloud. If a member of the public requests a copy of such a document, the court should consider whether it is proportionate to order one of the parties to produce a suitably redacted version. If not, access to the document is unlikely to be granted; however open justice will generally have been satisfied by the document having been read out in court.

5B.15 If the request comes from an accredited member of the press (see *Access by reporters* below), there may be circumstances in which the court orders that a copy of the whole document be shown to the reporter, or provided, subject to the condition that those matters that had not been read out to the court may not be used or reported. A breach of such an order would be treated as a contempt of court.

5B.16 Documents in this category are likely to include:

i. Section 9 statements that are edited.

Jury bundles and exhibits (including video footage shown to the jury)

5B.17 The court should consider:

i. whether access to the specific document is necessary to understand or effectively to report the case;
ii. the privacy of third parties, such as the victim (in some cases, the reporting restriction imposed by section 1 of the Judicial Proceedings (Regulation of Reports) Act 1926 will apply (indecent or medical matter));
iii. whether the reporting of anything in the document may be prejudicial to a fair trial in this or another case, in which case whether it may be necessary to make an order under section 4(2) of the Contempt of Court Act 1981.

The court may order one of the parties to provide a copy of certain pages (or parts of the footage), but these should not be provided electronically.

Statements of witnesses who give oral evidence

5B.18 A witness statement does not become evidence unless it is agreed under section 9 of the Criminal Justice Act 1967 and presented to the court. Therefore the statements of witnesses who give oral evidence, including ABE interview and transcripts and experts' reports, should not usually be provided. Open justice is generally satisfied by public access to the court.

Confidential documents

5B.19 A document the content of which, though relied upon by the court, has not been communicated to the public or reporters, nor treated as if it had been, is likely to have been supplied in confidence and should be treated accordingly. This will apply even if the court has made reference to the document or quoted from the document. There is most unlikely to be a sufficient reason to displace the expectation of confidentiality ordinarily attaching to a document in this category, and it would be exceptional to permit the inspection or copying by a member of the public or of the media of such a document. The rights and legitimate interests of others are likely to outweigh the interests of open justice with respect these documents.

5B.20 Documents in this category are likely to include:
i. Pre-sentence reports;
ii. Medical reports;
iii. Victim Personal Statements;
iv. Reports and summaries for confiscation.

Prohibitions against the provision of information

5B.21 Statutory provisions may impose specific prohibitions against the provision of information. Those most likely to be encountered are listed in the note to CrimPR 5.8 and include the Rehabilitation of Offenders Act 1974, section 18 of the Criminal Procedure and Investigations Act 1996 ('unused material' disclosed by the prosecution), sections 33, 34 and 35 of the Legal Aid, Sentencing and Punishment of Offenders Act 2012 ('LASPO Act 2012') (privileged information furnished to the Legal Aid Agency) and reporting restrictions generally.

5B.22 Reports of allocation or sending proceedings are restricted by section 52A of the Crime and Disorder Act 1998, so that only limited information, as specified in the statute, may be reported, whether it is referred to in the court room or not. The magistrates' court has power to order that the restriction shall not apply; if any defendant objects the court must apply the interests of justice test as specified in section 52A. The restriction ceases to apply either after all defendants indicate a plea of guilty, or after the conclusion of the trial of the last defendant to be tried. If the case does not result in a guilty plea, a finding of guilt or an acquittal, the restriction does not lift automatically and an application must be made to the court.

5B.23 Extradition proceedings have some features in common with committal proceedings, but no automatic reporting restrictions apply.

5B.24 Public Interest Immunity and the rights of a defendant, witnesses and victims under Article 6 and 8 of the European Convention on Human Rights may also restrict the power to release material to third parties.

Other documents

5B.25 The following table indicates the considerations likely to arise on an application to inspect or copy other documents.

Document	Considerations
Charge sheet Indictment	The alleged offence(s) will have been read aloud in court, and their terms must be supplied under CrimPR 5.8(4)
Material disclosed under CPIA 1996	To the extent that the content is deployed at trial, it becomes public at that hearing. Otherwise, it is a criminal offence for it to be disclosed: section 18 of the 1996 Act.
Written notices, applications, replies (including any application for representation)	To the extent that evidence is introduced, or measures taken, at trial, the content becomes public at that hearing. A statutory prohibition against disclosure applies to an application for representation: sections 33, 34 and 35 of the LASPO Act 2012.
Written decisions by the court, other than those read aloud in public or treated as if so read	Such decisions should usually be provided, subject to the criteria listed in CrimPR 5.8(4)(a) (and see also paragraph 5B.31 below).
Sentencing remarks	Sentencing remarks should usually be provided to the accredited Press, if the judge was reading from a prepared script which was handed out immediately afterwards; if not, then permission for a member of the accredited Press to obtain a transcript should usually be given (see also paragraphs 5B.26 and 29 below).
Official recordings	See CrimPR 5.5.
Transcript	See CrimPR 5.5 (and see also paragraphs 5B.32 to 36 below).

Access by reporters

5B.26 Under CrimPR Part 5, the same procedure applies to applications for access to information by reporters as to other members of the public. However, if the application is made by legal representatives instructed by the media, or by an accredited member of the media, who is able to produce in support of the application a valid Press Card (http://www.ukpresscardauthority.co.uk/) then there is a greater presumption in favour of providing the requested material, in recognition of the press' role as 'public watch dog' in a democratic society (*Observer and Guardian v United Kingdom* (1992) 14 EHRR 153, Times November 27, 1991). The general principle in those circumstances is that the court should supply documents and information unless there is a good reason not to in order to protect the rights or legitimate interests of others and the request will not place an undue burden on the court *R* (*Guardian News and Media Ltd*) at [87]. Subject to that, the paragraphs above relating to types of documents should be followed.

5B.27 Court staff should usually verify the authenticity of cards, checking the expiry date on the card and where necessary may consider telephoning the number on the reverse of the card to verify the card holder. Court staff may additionally request sight of other identification if necessary to ensure that the card holder has been correctly identified. The supply of information under CrimPR 5.8(7) is at the discretion of the court, and court staff must ensure that they have received a clear direction from the court before providing any information or material under rule 5.8(7) to a member of the public, including to the accredited media or their legal representatives.

5B.28 Opening notes and skeleton arguments or written submissions, once they have been placed before the court, should usually be provided to the media. If there is no opening note, permission for the media to obtain a transcript of the prosecution opening should usually be given (see below). It may be convenient for copies to be provided electronically by counsel, provided that the documents are kept suitably secure. The media are expected to be aware of the limitations on the use to which such material can be put, for example that legal argument held in the absence of the jury must not be reported before the conclusion of the trial.

5B.29 The media should also be able to obtain transcripts of hearings held in open court directly from the transcription service provider, on payment of any required fee. The service providers commonly require the judge's authorisation before they will provide a transcript, as an additional verification to ensure that the correct material is released and reporting restrictions are noted. However, responsibility for compliance with any restriction always rests with the person receiving the information or material: see CPD I General Matters 6B beneath.

5B.30 It is not for the judge to exercise an editorial judgment about 'the adequacy of the material already available to the paper for its journalistic purpose' (*Guardian* at 82) but the responsibility for complying with the Contempt of Court Act 1981 and any and all restrictions on the use of the material rests with the recipient.

Written decisions

5B.31 Where the Criminal Procedure Rules allow for a determination without a hearing there may be occasions on which it furthers the overriding objective to deliver the court's decision to the parties in writing, without convening a public hearing at which that decision will be pronounced: on an application for costs made at the conclusion of a trial, for example. If the only reason for delivering a decision in that way is to promote efficiency and expedition and if no other consideration arises then usually a copy of the decision should be provided in response to any request once the decision is final. However, had the decision been announced in public then the criteria in CrimPR 5.8(4)(a) would have applied to the supply of information by the court officer; and ordinarily those same criteria should be applied by the court, therefore. Moreover, where considerations other than efficiency and expedition have influenced the court's decision to reach a determination without convening a hearing then those same considerations may be inimical to the supply of the written decision to any applicant other than a party. Reporting restrictions may be relevant, for example; as may the considerations listed in paragraph 5B.9 above. In such a case the court should consider supplying a redacted version of the decision in response to a request by anyone who is not a party; or it may be appropriate to give the decision in terms that can be supplied to the public, supplemented by additional reasons provided only to the parties.

Transcript

5B.32 CrimPR 5.5 does not require an application to the court for transcript, nor does the rule anticipate recourse to the court for a judicial decision about the supply of transcript in any but unusual circumstances. Ordinarily it is the rule itself that determines the circumstances in which the transcriber of a recording may or may not supply transcript to an applicant.

5B.33 Where reporting restrictions apply to information contained in the recording from which the transcript is prepared then unless the court otherwise directs it is for the transcriber to redact that transcript where redaction is necessary to permit its supply to that applicant. Having regard to the terms of the statutes that impose reporting restrictions, however, it is unlikely that redaction will be required frequently. Statutory restrictions prohibit publication 'to the public at large or any section of the public', or some comparable formulation. They do not ordinarily prohibit a publication constituted only of the supply of transcript to an individual applicant. However, any reporting restrictions will continue to apply to a recipient of transcript, and where they apply the recipient must be alerted to them by the endorsement on the transcript of a suitable warning notice, to this or the like effect:

> 'WARNING: reporting restrictions may apply to the contents transcribed in this document, particularly if the case concerned a sexual offence or involved a child. Reporting restrictions prohibit the publication of the applicable information to the public or any section of the public, in writing, in a broadcast or by means of the internet, including social media. Anyone who receives a copy of this transcript is responsible in law for making sure that applicable restrictions are not breached. A person who breaches a reporting restriction is liable to a fine and/or imprisonment. For guidance on whether reporting restrictions apply, and to what information, ask at the court office or take legal advice.'

5B.34 Exceptionally, court staff may invite the court to direct that transcript must be redacted before it is supplied to an applicant, or that transcript must not be supplied to an applicant pending the supply of further information or assurances by that applicant, or at all, in exercise of the judicial discretion to which CrimPR 5.5(2) refers. Circumstances giving rise to concern may include, for example, the occurrence of events causing staff reasonably to suspect that an applicant intends or is likely to disregard a reporting restriction that applies, despite the warning notice endorsed on the transcript, or reasonably to suspect that an applicant has malicious intentions towards another person. Given that the proceedings will have taken place in public, despite any such suspicions, cogent and compelling reasons will be required to deny a request for transcript of such proceedings and the onus rests always on the court to justify such a denial, not on the applicant to justify the request. Even where there are reasons to suspect a criminal intent, the appropriate course may be to direct that the police be informed of those reasons rather than to direct that the transcript be withheld. Nevertheless, it may be appropriate in such a case to direct that an application for the transcript should be made which complies with paragraph 5B.8 above (even though that paragraph does not apply); and then for the court to review that application with regard to the considerations listed in paragraph 5B.9 above (but the usual burden of justifying a request under that paragraph does not apply).

5B.35 Some applicants for transcript may be taken to be aware of the significance of reporting restrictions, where they apply, and, by reason of such an applicant's statutory or other public or quasi-public functions, in any event unlikely to contravene any such restriction. Such applicants include public authorities within the meaning of section 6 of the Human Rights Act 1998 (a definition which extends to government departments and their agencies, local authorities, prosecuting authorities, and institutions such as the Parole Board and the Sentencing Council) and include public or private bodies exercising disciplinary functions in relation to practitioners of a regulated profession such as doctors, lawyers, accountants, etc. It would be only in the most exceptional circumstances that a court might conclude that any such body should not receive unredacted transcript of proceedings in public, irrespective of whether reporting restrictions do or do not apply.

5B.36 The rule imposes no time limit on a request for the supply of transcript. The assumption is that transcript of proceedings in public in the Crown Court will continue to be available for as long as relevant records are maintained by the Lord Chancellor under the legislation to which CrimPR 5.4 refers.

CPD.5C **CPD I General matters 5C: Issue of Medical Certificates**

5C.1 Doctors will be aware that medical notes are normally submitted by defendants in criminal proceedings as justification for not answering bail. Medical notes may also be submitted by witnesses who are due to give evidence and jurors.

5C.2 If a medical certificate is accepted by the court, this will result in cases (including contested hearings and trials) being adjourned rather than the court issuing a warrant for the defendant's arrest without bail. Medical certificates will also provide the defendant with sufficient evidence to defend a charge of failure to surrender to bail.

5C.3 However, a court is not absolutely bound by a medical certificate. The medical practitioner providing the certificate may be required by the court to give evidence. Alternatively the court may exercise its discretion to disregard a certificate which it finds unsatisfactory: *R v Ealing Magistrates' Court ex parte Burgess* [2001] 165 JP 82.

5C.4 Circumstances where the court may find a medical certificate unsatisfactory include:

(a) where the certificate indicates that the defendant is unfit to attend work (rather than to attend court);

(b) where the nature of the defendant's ailment (e.g. a broken arm) does not appear to be capable of preventing his attendance at court;
(c) where the defendant is certified as suffering from stress/anxiety/depression and there is no indication of the defendant recovering within a realistic timescale.

5C.5 It therefore follows that the minimum standards a medical certificate should set out are:
(a) the date on which the medical practitioner examined the defendant;
(b) the exact nature of the defendant's ailments;
(c) if it is not self-evident, why the ailment prevents the defendant attending court;
(d) an indication as to when the defendant is likely to be able to attend court, or a date when the current certificate expires.

5C.6 Medical practitioners should be aware that when issuing a certificate to a defendant in criminal proceedings they make themselves liable to being summonsed to court to give evidence about the content of the certificate, and they may be asked to justify their statements.

Criminal Procedure Rules Part 6 Reporting, etc. Restrictions

General rules

When this Part applies **R6.1**

6.1 (1) This Part applies where the court can—
(a) impose a restriction on—
(i) reporting what takes place at a public hearing, or
(ii) public access to what otherwise would be a public hearing;
(b) vary or remove a reporting or access restriction that is imposed by legislation;
(c) withhold information from the public during a public hearing;
(d) order a trial in private; or
(e) allow there to take place during a hearing—
(i) sound recording, or
(ii) communication by electronic means.

(2) This Part does not apply to arrangements required by legislation, or directed by the court, in connection with—
(a) sound recording during a hearing, or the transcription of such a recording; or
(b) measures to assist a witness or defendant to give evidence.

[Note. The court can impose reporting restrictions under—
(a) section 4(2) of the Contempt of Court Act 1981[1] *(postponed report of public hearing);*
(b) section 11 of the Contempt of Court Act 1981 (matter withheld from the public during a public hearing);
(c) section 58 of the Criminal Procedure and Investigations Act 1996[2] *(postponed report of derogatory assertion in mitigation);*
(d) section 45 of the Youth Justice and Criminal Evidence Act 1999[3] *(identity of a person under 18);*
(e) section 45A of the Youth Justice and Criminal Evidence Act 1999[4] *(identity of a witness or victim under 18);*
(f) section 46 of the Youth Justice and Criminal Evidence Act 1999[5] *(identity of a vulnerable adult witness);*
(g) section 82 of the Criminal Justice Act 2003[6] *(order for retrial after acquittal); or*
(h) section 75 of the Serious Organised Crime and Police Act 2005[7] *(identity of a defendant who assisted the police).*

[1] 1981 c. 49.
[2] 1996 c. 25.
[3] 1999 c. 23.
[4] 1999 c. 23; section 45A was inserted by section 78 of the Criminal Justice and Courts Act 2015 (c. 2).
[5] 1999 c. 23.
[6] 2003 c. 44.
[7] 2005 c. 15.

There are reporting restrictions imposed by legislation that the court can vary or remove, under—

(a) *section 49 of the Children and Young Persons Act 1933*[8] *(youth court proceedings);*
(b) *section 8C of the Magistrates' Courts Act 1980*[9] *(pre-trial ruling in magistrates' courts);*
(c) *section 11 of the Criminal Justice Act 1987*[10] *(preparatory hearing in the Crown Court);*
(d) *section 1 of the Sexual Offences (Amendment) Act 1992*[11] *(identity of complainant of sexual offence);*
(e) *section 37 of the Criminal Procedure and Investigations Act 1996*[12] *(preparatory hearing in the Crown Court);*
(f) *section 41 of the Criminal Procedure and Investigations Act 1996*[13] *(pre-trial ruling in the Crown Court);*
(g) *section 52A of, and paragraph 3 of Schedule 3 to, the Crime and Disorder Act 1998*[14] *(allocation and sending for trial proceedings);*
(h) *section 47 of the Youth Justice and Criminal Evidence Act 1999*[15] *(special measures direction);*
(i) *section 141F of the Education Act 2002*[16] *(restrictions on reporting alleged offences by teachers);*
(j) *section 71 of the Criminal Justice Act 2003*[17] *(prosecution appeal against Crown Court ruling); and*
(k) *section 4A of, and paragraph 1 of Schedule 1 to, the Female Genital Mutilation Act 2003*[18] *(identity of person against whom a female genital mutilation offence is alleged to have been committed).*

There are reporting restrictions imposed by legislation that the court has no power to vary or remove, under—

(a) *section 1 of the Judicial Proceedings (Regulation of Reports) Act 1926*[19] *(indecent or medical matter);*
(b) *section 2 of the Contempt of Court Act 1981*[20] *(risk of impeding or prejudicing active proceedings).*

[8] 1933 c. 12; section 49 was substituted by section 49 of the Criminal Justice and Public Order Act 1994 (c. 33) and amended by section 45 of the Crime (Sentences) Act 1997 (c. 43), section 119 of, and paragraph 1 of Schedule 8 to, the Crime and Disorder Act 1998 (c. 37), section 165 of, and paragraph 2 of Schedule 9 to, the Powers of Criminal Courts (Sentencing) Act 2000 (c. 6), paragraph 2 of Schedule 32 to, the Criminal Justice Act 2003 (c. 44), sections 208 and 210 of, and paragraphs 15 and 19 of Schedule 21, and Schedule 23 to, the Legal Services Act 2007 (c. 29) and section 6 of, and paragraphs 1, 3 and 100 of Schedule 4 to, the Criminal Justice and Immigration Act 2008 (c. 4). It is further amended by section 48 of, and paragraphs 1 and 3 of Schedule 2 to, the Youth Justice and Criminal Evidence Act 1999 (c. 23), section 74 of, and paragraph 5 of Schedule 7 to, the Criminal Justice and Court Services Act 2000 (c. 43) and sections 6 and 149 of, and paragraphs 1 and 3 of Schedule 4 and Schedule 28 to, the Criminal Justice and Immigration Act 2008 (c. 4), with effect from dates to be appointed.

[9] 1980 c. 43; section 8C was inserted by section 45 of, and Schedule 3 to, the Courts Act 2003 (c. 39) and amended by paragraphs 12 and 15 of Schedule 5 to the Legal Aid, Sentencing and Punishment of Offenders Act 2012 (c. 10).

[10] 1987 c. 38; section 11 was amended by paragraphs 1 and 6 of Schedule 3 to the Criminal Procedure and Investigations Act 1996 (c. 25), section 24 of, and paragraphs 38 and 40 of Schedule 4 to, the Access to Justice Act 1999 (c. 22), section 311 of, and paragraph 58 of Schedule 3 and Part 4 of Schedule 37 to, the Criminal Justice Act 2003 (c. 44) and section 40(4) of, and paragraph 46 of Schedule 9 to, the Constitutional Reform Act 2005 (c. 4).

[11] 1992 c. 34; section 1 was amended by section 48 of, and paragraphs 6 and 7 of Schedule 2 to, the Youth Justice and Criminal Evidence Act 1999 (c. 23).

[12] 1996 c. 25; section 37 was amended by section 24 of, and paragraph 49 of Schedule 4 to, the Access to Justice Act 1999 (c. 22), section 311 of the Criminal Justice Act 2003 (c. 44) and section 40(4) of, and paragraph 61 of Schedule 9 to, the Constitutional Reform Act 2005 (c. 4).

[13] 1996 c. 25; section 41 was amended by section 311 of the Criminal Justice Act 2003 (c. 44).

[14] 1998 c. 37; section 52A was inserted by paragraphs 15 and 19 of Schedule 3 to the Criminal Justice Act 2003 (c. 44) and amended by paragraphs 46 and 47 of Schedule 5 to the Legal Aid, Sentencing and Punishment of Offenders Act 2012 (c. 10). Paragraph 3 of Schedule 3 was amended by section 24 of, and paragraphs 53 and 55 of Schedule 4 to, the Access to Justice Act 1999 (c. 22), paragraphs 68 and 71 of Schedule 3 to the Criminal Justice Act 2003 (c. 44) and paragraphs 46 and 50 of Schedule 5 to the Legal Aid, Sentencing and Punishment of Offenders Act 2012 (c. 10).

[15] 1999 c. 23; section 47 was amended by section 52 of, and paragraph 37 of Schedule 14 to, the Police and Justice Act 2006 (c. 48).

[16] 2002 c. 32; section 141F was inserted by section 13 of the Education Act 2011 (c. 21).

[17] 2003 c. 44; section 71 was amended by section 40(4) of, and paragraph 82 of Schedule 9 to, the Constitutional Reform Act 2005 (c. 4) and paragraph 65 of Schedule 5 to the Legal Aid, Sentencing and Punishment of Offenders Act 2012 (c. 10).

[18] 2003 c. 31; section 4A and Schedule 1 were inserted by section 71 of the Serious Crime Act 2015 (c. 9).

[19] 1926 c. 61; section 1 was amended by sections 38 and 46 of the Criminal Justice Act 1982 (c. 48), paragraph 2 of Schedule 8 to the Family Law Act 1996 (c. 27) and paragraph 8 of Schedule 27 to the Civil Partnership Act 2004 (c. 33). It is further amended by paragraph 7 of Schedule 26 to the Criminal Justice Act 2003 (c. 44), with effect from a date to be appointed.

[20] 1981 c. 49; section 2 was amended by paragraph 31 of Schedule 20 to the Broadcasting Act 1990 (c. 42).

Access to a youth court is restricted under section 47 of the Children and Young Persons Act 1933[21]*. See also rule 24.2 (Trial and sentence in a magistrates' court – general rules).*

Under section 36 of the Children and Young Persons Act 1933[22]*, no-one under 14 may be present in court when someone else is on trial, or during proceedings preliminary to a trial, unless that person is required as a witness, or for the purposes of justice, or the court permits.*

The court can restrict access to the courtroom under—

- *(a) section 8(4) of the Official Secrets Act 1920*[23]*, during proceedings for an offence under the Official Secrets Acts 1911 and 1920;*
- *(b) section 37 of the Children and Young Persons Act 1933*[24]*, where the court receives evidence from a person under 18;*
- *(c) section 75 of the Serious Organised Crime and Police Act 2005*[25]*, where the court reviews a sentence passed on a defendant who assisted an investigation.*

The court has an inherent power, in exceptional circumstances—

- *(a) to allow information, for example a name or address, to be withheld from the public at a public hearing;*
- *(b) to restrict public access to what otherwise would be a public hearing, for example to control disorder;*
- *(c) to hear a trial in private, for example for reasons of national security.*

Under section 9(1) of the Contempt of Court Act 1981[26]*, it is a contempt of court without the court's permission to—*

- *(a) use in court, or bring into court for use, a device for recording sound;*
- *(b) publish a recording of legal proceedings made by means of such a device; or*
- *(c) use any such recording in contravention of any condition on which permission was granted.*

Under section 41 of the Criminal Justice Act 1925[27]*, it is an offence to take or attempt to take a photograph, or with a view to publication to make or attempt to make a portrait or sketch, of any judge, juror, witness or party, in the courtroom, or in the building or in the precincts of the building in which the court is held, or while that person is entering or leaving the courtroom, building or precincts; or to publish such a photograph, portrait or sketch.*

Section 32 of the Crime and Courts Act 2013[28] *(Enabling the making, and use, of films and other recordings of proceedings) allows for exceptions to be made to the prohibitions imposed by section 9 of the 1981 Act and section 41 of the 1925 Act.*

By reason of sections 15 and 45 of the Senior Courts Act 1981[29]*, the Court of Appeal and the Crown Court each has an inherent power to deal with a person for contempt of court for disrupting the proceedings. Under section 12 of the Contempt of Court Act 1981*[30]*, a magistrates' court has a similar power.*

See also—

- *(a) rule 5.5, under which the court officer must make arrangements for recording proceedings in the Crown Court;*

[21] 1933 c. 12; section 47 was amended by Parts II and III of Schedule 7 to the Justices of the Peace Act 1949 (c. 101), paragraph 40 of Schedule 11 to the Criminal Justice Act 1991 (c. 53), sections 47(7) and 120(2) of, and Schedule 10 to, the Crime and Disorder Act 1998 (c. 37) and paragraphs 15 and 18 of Schedule 21 to the Legal Services Act 2007 (c. 29). It is further amended by paragraph 2 of Schedule 4 to the Youth Justice and Criminal Evidence Act 1999 (c. 23), with effect from a date to be appointed.
[22] 1933 c. 12; section 36 was amended by section 73 of, and Part III of Schedule 15 to, the Access to Justice Act 1999 (c. 22).
[23] 1920 c. 75; section 8 was amended by section 32 of the Magistrates' Courts Act 1980 (c. 43).
[24] 1933 c. 12; section 37 was amended by paragraphs 15 and 16 of Schedule 21 to the Legal Services Act 2007 (c. 29) and is further amended by paragraph 2 of Schedule 4 to the Youth Justice and Criminal Evidence Act 1999 (c. 23), with effect from a date to be appointed.
[25] 2005 c. 15.
[26] 1981 c. 49.
[27] 1925 c. 86; section 41 was amended by section 56(4) of, and Part IV of Schedule 11 to, the Courts At 1971 (c. 23), sections 38 and 46 of the Criminal Justice Act 1982 (c. 48) and section 47 of the Constitutional Reform Act 2005 (c. 4).
[28] 2013 c. 22.
[29] 1981 c. 54.
[30] 1981 c. 49; section 12 was amended by section 78 of, and Schedule 16 to, the Criminal Justice Act 1982 (c. 48), section 17(3) of, and Part I of Schedule 4 to, the Criminal Justice Act 1991 (c. 53); section 65(3) and (4) of, and paragraph 6(4) of Schedule 3 to, the Criminal Justice Act 1993 (c. 36) and section 165 of, and paragraph 83 of Schedule 9 to, the Powers of Criminal Courts (Sentencing) Act 2000 (c. 6).

(b) Part 18, which applies to live links and other measures to assist a witness or defendant to give evidence;
(c) rule 45.10, which applies to costs orders against a non-party for serious misconduct; and
(d) Part 48, which contains rules about contempt of court.]

R6.2 Exercise of court's powers to which this Part applies

6.2 (1) When exercising a power to which this Part applies, as well as furthering the overriding objective, in accordance with rule 1.3, the court must have regard to the importance of—
(a) dealing with criminal cases in public; and
(b) allowing a public hearing to be reported to the public.
(2) The court may determine an application or appeal under this Part—
(a) at a hearing, in public or in private; or
(b) without a hearing.
(3) But the court must not exercise a power to which this Part applies unless each party and any other person directly affected—
(a) is present; or
(b) has had an opportunity—
(i) to attend, or
(ii) to make representations.

[Note. See also section 121 of the Magistrates' Courts Act 1980[31] *and rule 24.2 (general rules about trial and sentence in a magistrates' court).]*

R6.3 Court's power to vary requirements under this Part

6.3 (1) The court may—
(a) shorten or extend (even after it has expired) a time limit under this Part;
(b) require an application to be made in writing instead of orally;
(c) consider an application or representations made orally instead of in writing; and
(d) dispense with a requirement to—
(i) give notice, or
(ii) serve an application.
(2) Someone who wants an extension of time must—
(a) apply when making the application or representations for which it is needed; and
(b) explain the delay.

Reporting and access restrictions

R6.4 Reporting and access restrictions

6.4 (1) This rule applies where the court can—
(a) impose a restriction on—
(i) reporting what takes place at a public hearing, or
(ii) public access to what otherwise would be a public hearing; or
(b) withhold information from the public during a public hearing.
(2) Unless other legislation otherwise provides, the court may do so—
(a) on application by a party; or
(b) on its own initiative.
(3) A party who wants the court to do so must—
(a) apply as soon as reasonably practicable;
(b) notify—
(i) each other party, and
(ii) such other person (if any) as the court directs;
(c) specify the proposed terms of the order, and for how long it should last;
(d) explain—
(i) what power the court has to make the order, and
(ii) why an order in the terms proposed is necessary;
(e) where the application is for a reporting direction under section 45A of the Youth Justice and Criminal Evidence Act 1999[32] (Power to restrict reporting of criminal proceedings for lifetime of witnesses and victims under 18), explain—
(i) how the circumstances of the person whose identity is concerned meet the conditions prescribed by that section, having regard to the factors which that section lists; and

[31] 1980 c. 43; section 121 was amended by section 61 of the Criminal Justice Act 1988 (c. 33), section 92 of, and paragraph 8 of Schedule 11 to, the Children Act 1989 (c. 41), section 109 of, and paragraph 237 of Schedule 8 and Schedule 10 to, the Courts Act 2003 (c. 39).
[32] 1999 c. 23; section 45A was inserted by section 78 of the Criminal Justice and Courts Act 2015 (c. 2).

(ii) why such a reporting direction would be likely to improve the quality of any evidence given by that person, or the level of co-operation given by that person to any party in connection with the preparation of that party's case, taking into account the factors listed in that section; and

(f) where the application is for a reporting direction under section 46 of the Youth Justice and Criminal Evidence Act 1999[33] (Power to restrict reports about certain adult witnesses in criminal proceedings), explain—

(i) how the witness is eligible for assistance, having regard to the factors listed in that section, and

(ii) why such a reporting direction would be likely to improve the quality of the witness' evidence, or the level of co-operation given by the witness to the applicant in connection with the preparation of the applicant's case, taking into account the factors which that section lists.

[Note. Under section 45A(10) or section 46(9) of the Youth Justice and Criminal Evidence Act 1999, if the conditions prescribed by those sections are met the court may make an excepting direction dispensing, to any extent specified, with the restrictions imposed by a reporting direction made under those sections.]

Varying or removing restrictions **R6.5**

6.5 (1) This rule applies where the court can vary or remove a reporting or access restriction.

(2) Unless other legislation otherwise provides, the court may do so—

(a) on application by a party or person directly affected; or

(b) on its own initiative.

(3) A party or person who wants the court to do so must—

(a) apply as soon as reasonably practicable;

(b) notify—

(i) each other party, and

(ii) such other person (if any) as the court directs;

(c) specify the restriction; and

(d) explain, as appropriate, why it should be varied or removed.

(4) A person who wants to appeal to the Crown Court under section 141F of the Education Act 2002[34] must—

(a) serve an appeal notice on—

(i) the Crown Court officer, and

(ii) each other party;

(b) serve on the Crown Court officer, with the appeal notice, a copy of the application to the magistrates' court;

(c) serve the appeal notice not more than 15 business days after the magistrates' court's decision against which the appellant wants to appeal; and

(d) in the appeal notice, explain, as appropriate, why the restriction should be maintained, varied or removed.

(5) Rule 34.11 (Constitution of the Crown Court) applies on such an appeal.

[Note. Under section 141F(7) of the Education Act 2002, a party to an application to a magistrates' court to remove the statutory restriction on reporting an alleged offence by a teacher may appeal to the Crown Court against the decision of the magistrates' court. With the Crown Court's permission, any other person may appeal against such a decision.]

Trial in private **R6.6**

6.6 (1) This rule applies where the court can order a trial in private.

(2) A party who wants the court to do so must—

(a) apply in writing not less than 5 business days before the trial is due to begin; and

(b) serve the application on—

(i) the court officer, and

(ii) each other party.

(3) The applicant must explain—

(a) the reasons for the application;

(b) how much of the trial the applicant proposes should be in private; and

(c) why no measures other than trial in private will suffice, such as—

(i) reporting restrictions,

(ii) an admission of facts,

[33] 1999 c. 23.

[34] 2002 c. 32; section 141F was inserted by section 13 of the Education Act 2011 (c. 21).

(iii) the introduction of hearsay evidence,
(iv) a direction for a special measure under section 19 of the Youth Justice and Criminal Evidence Act 1999,
(v) a witness anonymity order under section 86 of the Coroners and Justice Act 2009, or
(vi) arrangements for the protection of a witness.

(4) Where the application includes information that the applicant thinks ought not be revealed to another party, the applicant must—
(a) omit that information from the part of the application that is served on that other party;
(b) mark the other part to show that, unless the court otherwise directs, it is only for the court; and
(c) in that other part, explain why the applicant has withheld that information from that other party.

(5) The court officer must at once—
(a) display notice of the application somewhere prominent in the vicinity of the courtroom; and
(b) give notice of the application to reporters by such other arrangements as the Lord Chancellor directs.

(6) The application must be determined at a hearing which—
(a) must be in private, unless the court otherwise directs;
(b) if the court so directs, may be, wholly or in part, in the absence of a party from whom information has been withheld; and
(c) in the Crown Court, must be after the defendant is arraigned but before the jury is sworn.

(7) At the hearing of the application—
(a) the general rule is that the court must consider, in the following sequence—
(i) representations first by the applicant and then by each other party, in all the parties' presence, and then
(ii) further representations by the applicant, in the absence of a party from whom information has been withheld; but
(b) the court may direct other arrangements for the hearing.

(8) The court must not hear a trial in private until—
(a) the business day after the day on which it orders such a trial, or
(b) the disposal of any appeal against, or review of, any such order, if later.

R6.7 Representations in response

6.7 (1) This rule applies where a party, or person directly affected, wants to make representations about an application or appeal.
(2) Such a party or person must—
(a) serve the representations on—
(i) the court officer,
(ii) the applicant,
(iii) each other party, and
(iv) such other person (if any) as the court directs;
(b) do so as soon as reasonably practicable after notice of the application; and
(c) ask for a hearing, if that party or person wants one, and explain why it is needed.
(3) Representations must—
(a) explain the reasons for any objection; and
(b) specify any alternative terms proposed.

R6.8 Order about restriction or trial in private

6.8 (1) This rule applies where the court—
(a) orders, varies or removes a reporting or access restriction; or
(b) orders a trial in private.
(2) The court officer must—
(a) record the court's reasons for the decision; and
(b) as soon as reasonably practicable, arrange for notice of the decision to be—
(i) displayed somewhere prominent in the vicinity of the courtroom, and
(ii) communicated to reporters by such other arrangements as the Lord Chancellor directs.

Sound recording and electronic communication

R6.9 Sound recording and electronic communication

6.9 (1) This rule applies where the court can give permission to—
(a) bring into a hearing for use, or use during a hearing, a device for—

(i) recording sound, or
(ii) communicating by electronic means; or
(b) publish a sound recording made during a hearing.
(2) The court may give such permission—
(a) on application; or
(b) on its own initiative.
(3) A person who wants the court to give such permission must—
(a) apply as soon as reasonably practicable;
(b) notify—
(i) each party, and
(ii) such other person (if any) as the court directs; and
(c) explain why the court should permit the use or publication proposed.
(4) As a condition of the applicant using such a device, the court may direct arrangements to minimise the risk of its use—
(a) contravening a reporting restriction;
(b) disrupting the hearing; or
(c) compromising the fairness of the hearing, for example by affecting—
(i) the evidence to be given by a witness, or
(ii) the verdict of a jury.
(5) Such a direction may require that the device is used only—
(a) in a specified part of the courtroom;
(b) for a specified purpose;
(c) for a purpose connected with the applicant's activity as a member of a specified group, for example representatives of news-gathering or reporting organisations; or
(d) at a specified time, or in a specified way.

Forfeiture of unauthorised sound recording **R6.10**

6.10 (1) This rule applies where someone without the court's permission—
(a) uses a device for recording sound during a hearing; or
(b) publishes a sound recording made during a hearing.
(2) The court may exercise its power to forfeit the device or recording—
(a) on application by a party, or on its own initiative; and
(b) provisionally, despite rule 6.2(3), to allow time for representations.
(3) A party who wants the court to forfeit a device or recording must—
(a) apply as soon as reasonably practicable;
(b) notify—
(i) as appropriate, the person who used the device, or who published the recording, and
(ii) each other party; and
(c) explain why the court should exercise that power.

[Note. Under section 9(3) of the Contempt of Court Act 1981[35]*, the court can forfeit any device or recording used or made in contravention of section 9(1) of the Act.]*

CRIMINAL PRACTICE DIRECTIONS PART 6 REPORTING, ETC. RESTRICTIONS

CPD II Preliminary proceedings 6A: Unofficial Sound Recording of Proceedings **CPD.6A**

6A.1 Section 9 of the Contempt of Court Act 1981 contains provisions governing the unofficial use of equipment for recording sound in court.
Section 9(1) provides that it is a contempt of court:
(a) to use in court, or bring into court for use, any tape recorder or other instrument for recording sound, except with the permission of the court;
(b) to publish a recording of legal proceedings made by means of any such instrument, or any recording derived directly or indirectly from it, by playing it in the hearing of the public or any section of the public, or to dispose of it or any recording so derived, with a view to such publication;
(c) to use any such recording in contravention of any conditions of leave granted under paragraph (a).
These provisions do not apply to the making or use of sound recordings for purposes of official transcripts of the proceedings, upon which the Act imposes no restriction whatever.

[35] 1981 c. 49.

Criminal Procedure Rules and Criminal Practice Directions

6A.2 The discretion given to the court to grant, withhold or withdraw leave to use equipment for recording sound or to impose conditions as to the use of the recording is unlimited, but the following factors may be relevant to its exercise:
(a) the existence of any reasonable need on the part of the applicant for leave, whether a litigant or a person connected with the press or broadcasting, for the recording to be made;
(b) the risk that the recording could be used for the purpose of briefing witnesses out of court;
(c) any possibility that the use of the recorder would disturb the proceedings or distract or worry any witnesses or other participants.

6A.3 Consideration should always be given whether conditions as to the use of a recording made pursuant to leave should be imposed. The identity and role of the applicant for leave and the nature of the subject matter of the proceedings may be relevant to this.

6A.4 The particular restriction imposed by section 9(1) (b) applies in every case, but may not be present in the mind of every applicant to whom leave is given. It may therefore be desirable on occasion for this provision to be drawn to the attention of those to whom leave is given.

6A.5 The transcript of a permitted recording is intended for the use of the person given leave to make it and is not intended to be used as, or to compete with, the official transcript mentioned in section 9(4).

6A.6 Where a contravention of section 9(1) is alleged, the procedure in section 2 of Part 48 of the Rules should be followed. Section 9(3) of the 1981 Act permits the court to 'order the instrument, or any recording made with it, or both, to be forfeited'. The procedure at CrimPR 6.10 should be followed.

CPD.6B **CPD II Preliminary proceedings 6B: Restrictions on Reporting Proceedings**

6B.1 Open justice is an essential principle in the criminal courts but the principle is subject to some statutory restrictions. These restrictions are either automatic or discretionary. Guidance is provided in the joint publication, *Reporting Restrictions in the Criminal Courts* issued by the Judicial College, the Newspaper Society, the Society of Editors and the Media Lawyers Association. The current version is the fourth edition and has been updated to be effective from May 2015.

6B.2 Where a restriction is automatic no order can or should be made in relation to matters falling within the relevant provisions. However, the court may, if it considers it appropriate to do so, give a reminder of the existence of the automatic restriction. The court may also discuss the scope of the restriction and any particular risks in the specific case in open court with representatives of the press present. Such judicial observations cannot constitute an order binding on the editor or the reporter although it is anticipated that a responsible editor would consider them carefully before deciding what should be published. It remains the responsibility of those reporting a case to ensure that restrictions are not breached.

6B.3 Before exercising its discretion to impose a restriction the court must follow precisely the statutory provisions under which the order is to be made, paying particular regard to what has to be established, by whom and to what standard.

6B.4 Without prejudice to the above paragraph, certain general principles apply to the exercise of the court's discretion:
(a) The court must have regard to CrimPR Parts 6 and 18.
(b) The court must keep in mind the fact that every order is a departure from the general principle that proceedings shall be open and freely reported.
(c) Before making any order the court must be satisfied that the purpose of the proposed order cannot be achieved by some lesser measure e.g., the grant of special measures, screens or the clearing of the public gallery (usually subject to a representative(s) of the media remaining).
(d) The terms of the order must be proportionate so as to comply with Article 10 ECHR (freedom of expression).
(e) No order should be made without giving other parties to the proceedings and any other interested party, including any representative of the media, an opportunity to make representations.
(f) Any order should provide for any interested party who has not been present or represented at the time of the making of the order to have permission to apply within a limited period e.g., 24 hours.
(g) The wording of the order is the responsibility of the judge or Bench making the order: it must be in precise terms and, if practicable, agreed with the advocates.
(h) The order must be in writing and must state:
(i) the power under which it is made;
(ii) its precise scope and purpose; and
(iii) the time at which it shall cease to have effect, if appropriate.

(i) The order must specify, in every case, whether or not the making or terms of the order may be reported or whether this itself is prohibited. Such a report could cause the very mischief which the order was intended to prevent.

6B.5 A series of template orders have been prepared by the Judicial College and are available as an appendix to the Crown Court Bench Book Companion; these template orders should generally be used.

6B.6 A copy of the order should be provided to any person known to have an interest in reporting the proceedings and to any local or national media who regularly report proceedings in the court.

6B.7 Court staff should be prepared to answer any enquiry about a specific case; but it is and will remain the responsibility of anyone reporting a case to ensure that no breach of any order occurs and the onus rests on such person to make enquiry in case of doubt.

CPD I General Matters 6C: Use of live text-based forms of communication (including *Twitter*) from court for the purposes of fair and accurate reporting **CPD.6C**

6C.1 This part clarifies the use which may be made of live text-based communications, such as mobile email, social media (including *Twitter*) and internet-enabled laptops in and from courts throughout England and Wales. For the purpose of this part these means of communication are referred to, compendiously, as 'live text-based communications'. It is consistent with the legislative structure which:

(a) prohibits:
  (i) the taking of photographs in court (section 41 of the Criminal Justice Act 1925);
  (ii) the use of sound recording equipment in court unless the leave of the judge has first been obtained (section 9 of the Contempt of Court Act 1981); and

(b) requires compliance with the strict prohibition rules created by sections 1, 2 and 4 of the Contempt of Court Act 1981 in relation to the reporting of court proceedings.

General Principles

6C.2 The judge has an overriding responsibility to ensure that proceedings are conducted consistently, with the proper administration of justice, and to avoid any improper interference with its processes.

6C.3 A fundamental aspect of the proper administration of justice is the principle of open justice. Fair and accurate reporting of court proceedings forms part of that principle. The principle is, however, subject to well-known statutory and discretionary exceptions. Two such exceptions are the prohibitions, set out in paragraph 6C.1(a), on photography in court and on making sound recordings of court proceedings.

6C.4 The statutory prohibition on photography in court, by any means, is absolute. There is no judicial discretion to suspend or dispense with it. Any equipment which has photographic capability must not have that function activated.

6C.5 Sound recordings are also prohibited unless, in the exercise of its discretion, the court permits such equipment to be used. In criminal proceedings, some of the factors relevant to the exercise of that discretion are contained in paragraph 6A.2. The same factors are likely to be relevant when consideration is being given to the exercise of this discretion in civil or family proceedings.

Use of Live Text-based Communications: General Considerations

6C.6 The normal, indeed almost invariable, rule has been that mobile phones must be turned off in court. There is however no statutory prohibition on the use of live text-based communications in open court.

6C.7 Where a member of the public, who is in court, wishes to use live text-based communications during court proceedings an application for permission to activate and use, in silent mode, a mobile phone, small laptop or similar piece of equipment, solely in order to make live text-based communications of the proceedings will need to be made. The application may be made formally or informally (for instance by communicating a request to the judge through court staff).

6C.8 It is presumed that a representative of the media or a legal commentator using live text-based communications from court does not pose a danger of interference to the proper administration of justice in the individual case. This is because the most obvious purpose of permitting the use of live text-based communications would be to enable the media to produce fair and accurate reports of the proceedings. As such, a representative of the media or a legal commentator who wishes to use live text-based communications from court may do so without making an application to the court.

6C.9 When considering, either generally on its own motion, or following a formal application or informal request by a member of the public, whether to permit live text-based communications, and if so by whom, the paramount question for the judge will be whether the application may interfere with the proper administration of justice.

6C.10 In considering the question of permission, the factors listed in paragraph 6A.2 are likely to be relevant.

6C.11 Without being exhaustive, the danger to the administration of justice is likely to be at its most acute in the context of criminal trials e.g., where witnesses who are out of court may be informed of what has already happened in court and so coached or briefed before they then give evidence, or where information posted on, for instance, *Twitter* about inadmissible evidence may influence members of the jury. However, the danger is not confined to criminal proceedings; in civil and sometimes family proceedings, simultaneous reporting from the courtroom may create pressure on witnesses, by distracting or worrying them.

6C.12 It may be necessary for the judge to limit live text-based communications to representatives of the media for journalistic purposes but to disallow its use by the wider public in court. That may arise if it is necessary, for example, to limit the number of mobile electronic devices in use at any given time because of the potential for electronic interference with the court's own sound recording equipment, or because the widespread use of such devices in court may cause a distraction in the proceedings.

6C.13 Subject to these considerations, the use of an unobtrusive, hand-held, silent piece of modern equipment, for the purposes of simultaneous reporting of proceedings to the outside world as they unfold in court, is generally unlikely to interfere with the proper administration of justice.

6C.14 Permission to use live text-based communications from court may be withdrawn by the court at any time.

CPD.6D **CPD I General matters 6D: Taking Notes in Court**

6D.1 As long as it does not interfere with the proper administration of justice, anyone who attends a court hearing may quietly take notes, on paper or by silent electronic means. If that person is a participant, including an expert witness who is in the courtroom under CrimPR 24.4(2)(a)(ii) or 25.11(2)(a)(ii), note taking may be an essential aid to that person's own or (if they are a representative) to their client's effective participation. If that person is a reporter or a member of the public, attending a hearing to which, by definition, they have been admitted, note taking is a feature of the principle of open justice. The permission of the court is not required, and the distinctions between members of the public and others which are drawn at paragraphs 6C.7 and 6C.8 of these Practice Directions do not apply.

6D.2 However, where there is reason to suspect that the taking of notes may be for an unlawful purpose, or that it may disrupt the proceedings, then it is entirely proper for court staff to make appropriate enquiries, and ultimately it is within the power of the court to prohibit note taking by a specified individual or individuals in the court room if that is necessary and proportionate to prevent unlawful conduct. If, for example, there is reason to believe that notes are being taken in order to influence the testimony of a witness who is due to give evidence, perhaps by briefing that witness on what another witness has said, then because such conduct is unlawful (it is likely to be in contempt of court, and it may constitute a perversion of the course of justice) it is within the court's power to prohibit such note taking. If there is reason to believe that what purports to be taking notes with an electronic device is in fact the transmission of live text-based communications from court without the permission required by paragraph 6C.7 of these Practice Directions, or where permission to transmit such communications has been withdrawn under paragraph 6C.14, then that, too, would constitute grounds for prohibiting the taking of such notes.

6D.3 The existence of a reporting restriction, without more, is not a sufficient reason to prohibit note taking (though it may need to be made clear to those who take notes that the reporting restriction affects how much, if any, of what they have noted may be communicated to anyone else). However, if there is reason to believe that notes are being taken in order to facilitate the contravention of a reporting restriction then that, too, would constitute grounds for prohibiting such note taking.

CPD.6E **CPD I General matters 6E: Access to Courts**

Proceedings before the Crown Court

6E.1 The right of the public to access court rooms to observe proceedings is a fundamental part of open justice, and good practice will ensure that the public are able to view proceedings quietly, and without causing interruption, as far as is possible.

6E.2 However, as observed in *R (O'Connor) v Aldershot Magistrates' Court* [2017] 1 WLR 2833 'The right to attend a public court hearing and to enter the court building for that purpose is not unqualified.' The court has an inherent power to restrict public access to the courtroom where it is necessary to do so in the interests of justice, for example to prevent disorder.

6E.3 During criminal proceedings in a Crown Court there are some specific parts of proceedings whereby it may be appropriate for a judge to restrict movement in the public gallery. As observed by Bean LJ in *R (on the application of Ewing) v Isleworth Crown Court* [2019] EWHC 288 (Admin) this is to ensure that during 'these sensitive moments, generally of brief duration, it is necessary for the court to be still so that the process can take place without distraction and in a manner which preserves the dignity and solemnity of the proceedings'. It is expected that during the following parts of the proceedings, access may be restricted to prevent comings and goings in the public gallery:

I. Arraignment;
II. Empanelling and swearing in of the jury;
III. Oath taking or affirmation;
IV. Return of verdict by a jury;
V. Passing of sentence by a Judge.

6E.4 In the *Ewing* judgment the Administrative Court made clear that it would be unlawful to issue a blanket policy that restricted access during other parts of the proceedings. Unless the judge has specifically directed restrictions to access to the public gallery for good reason in a particular case, then at all other times, it is expected that the public can enter and leave the courtroom as they require, provided they do so quietly and without disrupting proceedings.

Criminal Procedure Rules Part 7 Starting a Prosecution in a Magistrates' Court

When this Part applies **R7.1**

7.1 (1) This Part applies in a magistrates' court where—

(a) a prosecutor wants the court to issue a summons or warrant under section 1 of the Magistrates' Courts Act 1980[1];

(b) a prosecutor with the power to do so issues—

(i) a written charge and requisition, or

(ii) a written charge and single justice procedure notice under section 29 of the Criminal Justice Act 2003[2]; or

(c) a person who is in custody is charged with an offence; or

(d) the prosecutor alleges an offence against a defendant who is due to attend, or attends, the court in response to another allegation.

(2) In this Part, 'authorised prosecutor' means a prosecutor authorised under section 29 of the Criminal Justice Act 2003 to issue a written charge and requisition or single justice procedure notice.

[Note. Under section 1 of the Magistrates' Courts Act 1980, on receiving a formal statement (described in that section as an 'information') alleging that someone has committed an offence, the court may issue—

(a) a summons requiring that person to attend court; or

(b) a warrant for that person's arrest, if—

(i) the alleged offence must or may be tried in the Crown Court,

(ii) the alleged offence is punishable with imprisonment, or

(iii) the person's address cannot be established sufficiently clearly to serve a summons or requisition.

The powers of the court to which this Part applies may be exercised by a single justice of the peace.

Under section 29 of the Criminal Justice Act 2003, a prosecutor authorised under that section may issue a written charge alleging that someone has committed an offence, and either—

(a) a requisition requiring that person to attend court; or

(b) a notice that the single justice procedure under section 16A of the Magistrates' Courts Act 1980[3] and rule 24.9 of these Rules applies.

[1] 1980 c. 43; section 1 was amended by section 68 of, and paragraph 6 of Schedule 8 to, the Criminal Justice Act 1991 (c. 53), sections 43 and 109 of, and Schedule 10 to, the Courts Act 2003 (c. 39), section 31 of, and paragraph 12 of Schedule 7 to, the Criminal Justice Act 2003 (c. 44) and section 153 of the Police Reform and Social Responsibility Act 2011. It is further amended by paragraphs 7 and 8 of Schedule 36 to, the Criminal Justice Act 2003 (c. 44), with effect from a date to be appointed.

[2] 2003 c. 44; section 29 has been brought into force for certain purposes only (see S.I. 2007/1999, 2008/1424, 2009/2879, 2010/3005, 2011/2188, 2012/825 and 2014/633). It was amended by section 50 of, and paragraph 130 of Schedule 4 to, the Commissioners for Revenue and Customs Act 2005 (c. 11), section 59 of, and paragraph 196 of Schedule 4 to, the Serious Organised Crime and Police Act 2005 (c. 15), section 15 of, and paragraph 187 of Schedule 8 to, the Crime and Courts Act 2013 (c. 22), S.I. 2014/834 and section 46 of the Criminal Justice and Courts Act 2015 (c. 2).

[3] 1980 c. 43; section 16A was inserted by section 48 of the Criminal Justice and Courts Act 2015 (c. 2).

Section 30 of the 2003 Act[4] *contains other provisions about written charges, requisitions and single justice procedure notices.*

A person detained under a power of arrest may be charged if the custody officer decides that there is sufficient evidence to do so. See sections 37 and 38 of the Police and Criminal Evidence Act 1984[5]*.]*

R7.2 **Application for summons, etc.**

7.2 (1) A prosecutor who wants the court to issue a summons must—
(a) serve on the court officer a written application; or
(b) unless other legislation prohibits this, present an application orally to the court, with a written statement of the allegation or allegations made by the prosecutor.
(2) A prosecutor who wants the court to issue a warrant must—
(a) serve on the court officer—
(i) a written application, or
(ii) a copy of a written charge that has been issued; or
(b) present to the court either of those documents.
(3) An application for the issue of a summons or warrant must—
(a) set out the allegation or allegations made by the applicant in terms that comply with rule 7.3(1) (Allegation of offence in application or charge); and
(b) demonstrate—
(i) that the application is made in time, if legislation imposes a time limit, and
(ii) that the applicant has the necessary consent, if legislation requires it.
(4) As well as complying with paragraph (3), an application for the issue of a warrant must—
(a) demonstrate that the offence or offences alleged can be tried in the Crown Court;
(b) demonstrate that the offence or offences alleged can be punished with imprisonment; or
(c) concisely outline the applicant's grounds for asserting that the defendant's address is not sufficiently established for a summons to be served.
(5) Paragraph (6) applies unless the prosecutor is—
(a) a public authority within the meaning of section 17 of the Prosecution of Offences Act 1985[6]; or
(b) a person acting—
(i) on behalf of such an authority, or
(ii) in that person's capacity as an official appointed by such an authority.
(6) Where this paragraph applies, as well as complying with paragraph (3), and with paragraph (4) if applicable, an application for the issue of a summons or warrant must—
(a) concisely outline the grounds for asserting that the defendant has committed the alleged offence or offences;
(b) disclose—
(i) details of any previous such application by the same applicant in respect of any allegation now made, and
(ii) details of any current or previous proceedings brought by another prosecutor in respect of any allegation now made; and
(c) include a statement that to the best of the applicant's knowledge, information and belief—
(i) the allegations contained in the application are substantially true,
(ii) the evidence on which the applicant relies will be available at the trial,

[4] 2003 c. 44; section 30 has been brought into force for certain purposes only (see S.I. 2007/1999, 2008/1424, 2009/2879, 2010/3005, 2011/2188, 2012/825 and 2014/633). It was amended by article 3 of, and paragraphs 45 and 46 of the Schedule to, S.I. 2004/2035 and section 47 of the Criminal Justice and Courts Act 2015 (c. 2).

[5] 1984 c. 60; section 37 was amended by section 108(7) of, and Schedule 15 to, the Children Act 1989 (c. 41), sections 72 and 101(2) of, and Schedule 13 to, the Criminal Justice Act 1991 (c. 53), sections 29(4) and 168(3) of, and Schedule 11 to, the Criminal Justice and Public Order Act 1994 (c. 33), section 28 of, and paragraphs 1 and 2 of Schedule 2 to, the Criminal Justice Act 2003 (c. 44), section 23(1) of, and paragraphs 1 and 2 of Schedule 1 to, the Drugs Act 2005 (c. 17) and sections 11 and 52 of, and paragraph 9 of Schedule 14 to, the Police and Justice Act 2006 (c. 48).
Section 38 was amended by section 108(5) of, and paragraph 53 of Schedule 13 to, the Children Act 1989 (c. 41), section 59 of the Criminal Justice Act 1991 (c. 53), sections 24, 28 and 168(2) of, and paragraph 54 of Schedule 10 to, the Criminal Justice and Public Order Act 1994 (c. 33), section 57 of the Criminal Justice and Court Services Act 2000 (c. 43), section 5 of, and paragraph 44 of Schedule 32 and paragraph 5 of Schedule 36 to, the Criminal Justice Act 2003 (c. 44), section 23 of, and paragraphs 1 and 3 of Schedule 1 to, the Drugs Act 2005 (c. 17) and paragraph 34 of Schedule 11 to the Legal Aid, Sentencing and Punishment of Offenders Act 2012 (c. 10).

[6] 1985 c. 23; section 17 was amended by section 40 of, and paragraph 41 of Schedule 9 to, the Constitutional Reform Act 2005 (c. 4) and paragraphs 1 and 4 and Part 4 of Schedule 7 to the Legal Aid, Sentencing and Punishment of Offenders Act 2012 (c. 10).

(iii) the details given by the applicant under paragraph (6)(b) are true, and
(iv) the application discloses all the information that is material to what the court must decide

(7) Where the statement required by paragraph (6)(c) is made orally—
(a) the statement must be on oath or affirmation, unless the court otherwise directs; and
(b) the court must arrange for a record of the making of the statement.

(8) An authorised prosecutor who issues a written charge must notify the court officer immediately.

(9) A single document may contain—
(a) more than one application; or
(b) more than one written charge.

(10) Where an offence can be tried only in a magistrates' court, then unless other legislation otherwise provides—
(a) a prosecutor must serve an application for the issue of a summons or warrant on the court officer or present it to the court; or
(b) an authorised prosecutor must issue a written charge, not more than 6 months after the offence alleged.

(11) Where an offence can be tried in the Crown Court then—
(a) a prosecutor must serve an application for the issue of a summons or warrant on the court officer or present it to the court; or
(b) an authorised prosecutor must issue a written charge, within any time limit that applies to that offence.

(12) The court may determine an application to issue or withdraw a summons or warrant—
(a) without a hearing, as a general rule, or at a hearing (which must be in private unless the court otherwise directs);
(b) in the absence of—
(i) the prosecutor,
(ii) the defendant; and
(c) with or without representations by the defendant.

(13) If the court so directs, a party to an application to issue or withdraw a summons or warrant may attend a hearing by live link or telephone.

[Note. In some legislation, including the Magistrates' Courts Act 1980, an application for the issue of a summons or warrant is described as an 'information' and serving an application on the court officer or presenting it to the court is described as 'laying' that information.

The time limits for serving or presenting an application and for issuing a written charge are prescribed by section 127 of the Magistrates' Courts Act 1980[7] and section 30(5) of the Criminal Justice Act 2003[8].

In section 17 of the Prosecution of Offences Act 1985 'public authority' means (a) a police force as defined by that Act, (b) the Crown Prosecution Service or any other government department, (c) a local authority or other authority or body constituted for purposes of the public service or of local government, or carrying on under national ownership any industry or undertaking or part of an industry or undertaking, or (d) any other authority or body whose members are appointed by Her Majesty or by any Minister of the Crown or government department or whose revenues consist wholly or mainly of money provided by Parliament.

Part 46 (Representatives) contains rules allowing a member, officer or employee of a prosecutor, on the prosecutor's behalf, to—

(a) serve on the court officer or present to the court an application for the issue of a summons or warrant; or
(b) issue a written charge and requisition.

See Part 3 for the court's general powers of case management, including power to consider applications and give directions for (among other things) the amendment of an allegation or charge and for separate trials.

See also Part 32 (Breach, revocation and amendment of community and other orders). Rule 32.2(2) (Application by responsible officer) applies rules 7.2 to 7.4 to the procedure with which that rule deals.

The Practice Direction sets out a form of application for use in connection with rule 7.2(6).]

Allegation of offence **R7.3**

7.3 (1) An allegation of an offences in an application for the issue of a summons or warrant or in a charge must contain—

[7] 1980 c. 43.
[8] 2003 c. 44; section 30(5) was amended by section 47 of the Criminal Justice and Courts Act 2015 (c.2).

(a) a statement of the offence that—
(i) describes the offence in ordinary language, and
(ii) identifies any legislation that creates it; and
(b) such particulars of the conduct constituting the commission of the offence as to make clear what the prosecutor alleges against the defendant, including the value of any damage or theft alleged where that value is known and where it affects the exercise of the court's powers.

(2) More than one incident of the commission of the offence may be included in the allegation if those incidents taken together amount to a course of conduct having regard to the time, place or purpose of commission.

(3) Where rule 7.1(1)(d) applies (additional allegation in existing prosecution), the prosecutor must—
(a) set out the additional allegation in terms that comply with paragraph (1);
(b) as soon as practicable—
(i) serve the additional allegation on the court officer and the defendant, or
(ii) present the additional allegation orally to the court, with a written statement of that allegation;
(c) demonstrate that the allegation is made in time, if legislation imposes a time limit; and
(d) demonstrate that the prosecutor has the necessary consent, if legislation requires it.

[Note. In some circumstances the court may allow the prosecutor to amend an allegation of an offence, including to allege a different offence. In those circumstances the allegation may be amended after any time limit for prosecuting the different offence has expired if the amendment is based on substantially the same facts as the allegation first made. See Part 3 for the court's general powers of case management, including power to consider an application and give directions for (among other things) the amendment of an allegation.]

R7.4 Summons, warrant and requisition

7.4 (1) A summons, warrant or requisition may be issued in respect of more than one offence.

(2) A summons or requisition must—
(a) contain notice of when and where the defendant is required to attend the court;
(b) specify each offence in respect of which it is issued;
(c) in the case of a summons, identify—
(i) the court that issued it, unless that is otherwise recorded by the court officer, and
(ii) the court office for the court that issued it; and
(d) in the case of a requisition, identify the person under whose authority it is issued.

(3) A summons may be contained in the same document as an application for the issue of that summons.

(4) A requisition may be contained in the same document as a written charge.

(5) Where the court issues a summons—
(a) the prosecutor must—
(i) serve it on the defendant, and
(ii) notify the court officer; or
(b) the court officer must—
(i) serve it on the defendant, and
(ii) notify the prosecutor.

(6) Where an authorised prosecutor issues a requisition that prosecutor must—
(a) serve on the defendant—
(i) the requisition, and
(ii) the written charge; and
(b) serve a copy of each on the court officer.

(7) Unless it would be inconsistent with other legislation, a replacement summons or requisition may be issued without a fresh application or written charge where the one replaced—
(a) Was served under rule 4.4 (Service by leaving or posting a document) ; but
(b) is shown not to have been received by the addressee.

(8) A summons or requisition issued to a defendant under 18 may require that defendant's parent or guardian to attend the court with the defendant, or a separate summons or requisition may be issued for that purpose.

[Note. Part 13 contains other rules about warrants.

Section 47 of the Magistrates' Courts Act 1980[9] *and section 30(5) of the Criminal Justice Act 2003 make special provision about time limits under other legislation for the issue and service of a summons or requisition, where service by post is not successful.*

Section 34A of the Children and Young Persons Act 1933[10] *allows, and in some cases requires, the court to summon the parent or guardian of a defendant under 18.]*

Criminal Practice Directions Part 7 Starting a Prosecution in a Magistrates' Court

CPD II Preliminary proceedings 7A: First Court Attendance after Charge and Detention **CPD.7A**

7A.1 A defendant who has been kept in police detention after being charged with an offence must be brought before a magistrates' court as soon as practicable and in any event no later than the first subsequent court sitting: section 46 of the Police and Criminal Evidence Act 1984. If no magistrates' court is due to sit on the day on which the defendant is charged, or on the next day which is not a Sunday, Christmas Day or Good Friday, then the Act requires the police custody officer to inform the court's designated officer of the defendant's detention, and requires the designated officer to arrange for a magistrates' court to sit.

7A.2 The 1984 Act thus imposes duties on the police and on HM Courts and Tribunals Service. In *R (on the application of H (A Child)) v Clerk to Teesside Justices* [2000] 10 WLUK 532 the High Court observed,

> "it is incumbent on justices and their clerks, however busy their courts may be, to ensure that they are able to receive persons in custody up to the end of normal court hours, at least, in order to comply with section 46 …, unless some exceptional circumstance intervenes to make that impossible in any particular case".

7A.3 To comply with those duties arrangements must be made to allow courts to receive such defendants during the course of a sitting day if the available time allows for the hearing of all cases to be concluded by 4.30pm, or later if, and only if, some disability or vulnerability of the defendant so requires. In practice, to allow sufficient time for consultation with a legal representative and for the subsequent hearing, the defendant must have been brought to the court building, or given access to a live link to the court, by no later than 3.30pm. To that end, Judicial Business Groups must ensure that effective practical arrangements have been made between police forces, HMCTS, the Crown Prosecution Service and prisoner escort contractors for the prompt transmission of information about defendants held for production before the court.

7A.4 On a Saturday or bank holiday normal court hours may differ from court to court based on likely caseload. Those hours must be determined by the HMCTS Head of Legal Operations in consultation with the judiciary and other agencies. In accordance with the court's observations in the *Teesside Justices' Clerk* case, all magistrates' courts should sit until at least 11.30 a.m. to receive defendants to whom these directions apply unless arrangements have been made for such defendants to be dealt with by another court, either by attendance in person or by live link.

7A.5 For the purposes of section 46 of the 1984 Act the designated officer is the HMCTS Director of Operations, by whom the exercise of that statutory function is delegated to members of court staff. When informing such a delegate of a defendant's detention the police custody officer must at the same time supply the following, usually by electronic means:

(a) confirmation that:
   (i) the defendant has been charged,
   (ii) the case file is complete and available,
   (iii) any interpreter required is available,
   (iv) any appropriate adult or local authority officer responsible for the defendant's care has been notified and is available,
   (v) the defendant's legal representative has been notified and is available, and
   (vi) the CPS or other relevant prosecuting authority has been notified;

(b) the custody officer's proposal for the means by which the defendant should attend court, whether by live link or in person, and, if the latter, then whether by police transport or by prisoner escort contractor transport; and

[9] 1980 c. 43; section 47 was amended by section 109(1) of, and paragraph 207 of Schedule 8 to, the Courts Act 2003 (c. 39).
[10] 1933 c. 12; section 34A was inserted by section 56 of the Criminal Justice Act 1991 (c. 53) and amended by section 107 of, and paragraph 1 of Schedule 5 to, the Local Government Act 2000 (c. 22).

(c) details of:
(i) any physical or mental disability or other vulnerability (whether by reason of age or other circumstance) of the defendant of which police officers are aware, in particular where any such might be thought to make the use of live link inappropriate, and
(ii) the expected time of arrival at court, if the defendant is to be brought to court in person.

No court should be expected to hear a case in respect of which such information is missing or incomplete, or in respect of which such arrangements have not been made.

7A.6 The designated officer's delegates must liaise with staff at the court buildings to which defendants in police detention may be brought. Each such delegate must be sufficiently experienced to be able to assess, swiftly and accurately, the availability of courts sitting in those buildings, and of sufficient seniority to take the decisions required by these directions. Each must be in a position to assess
(i) the availability of court members, of legal advisers, of prosecutors and of the other staff needed to deal with an unexpected case,
(ii) the potential effect of an unexpected case on other cases awaiting hearing that day, including the risk of a less urgent case being adjourned, perhaps not for the first time, in consequence of accommodating the unexpected hearing,
(iii) the likely length of the unexpected hearing, and
(iv) the significance of the age and any disability or other vulnerability of the unexpected defendant.

7A.7 The delegate to whom a police custody officer reports a defendant's detention must decide whether, and if so how, when and where, to accommodate that defendant's case within the period to which paragraph 7A.3 or 7A.4 refers, having regard to the availability and content of the information to which paragraph 7A.5 refers and to the considerations listed in paragraph 7A.6. The decision must be informed by the views of those court members and legal advisers who may be affected, as listing is a judicial responsibility and function. It may be necessary for the delegate to take such steps as arranging for the unexpected case to be heard by live link; reorganising courts sitting in the court building to which the defendant is due to be brought; adjourning other cases; calling upon additional resources; or making arrangements with the delegate at another court building for the unexpected case to be heard by a court sitting there, by live link if appropriate. It may be necessary for the court that hears the unexpected case to impose a timetable for representations or to restrict the decisions that will be taken immediately. If it will not be possible to hear within the period to which paragraph 7A.3 or 7A.4 refers every case due to be heard that day at the court building to which the defendant is to be brought then every effort must be made to ensure that the cases of all defendants in custody, whether in that court building or attending by live link, still can be heard within that period. The delegate for that building must ensure that the police, the staff responsible for the court's own cells and the relevant prisoner escort contractor all are aware of the arrangements that have been made. If the prosecuting authority is not the CPS then that delegate must ensure that that other authority will arrange for a representative to attend, in person or by live link, to assist the court.

7A.8 If after conducting the assessment required by paragraph 7A.6 and taking the steps to which paragraph 7A.7 refers the designated officer's delegate finds it impossible to accommodate an unexpected case within the period to which paragraph 7A.3 or 7A.4 refers then arrangements must be made to hear the case on the next sitting day and the police custody officer must promptly be so informed.

Criminal Procedure Rules Part 8 Initial Details of the Prosecution Case

R8.1 **When this Part applies**

8.1 This Part applies in a magistrates' court.

R8.2 **Providing initial details of the prosecution case**

8.2 (1) The prosecutor must serve initial details of the prosecution case on the court officer—
(a) as soon as practicable; and
(b) in any event, no later than the beginning of the day of the first hearing.
(2) Where a defendant requests those details, the prosecutor must serve them on the defendant—
(a) as soon as practicable; and
(b) in any event, no later than the beginning of the day of the first hearing.
(3) Where a defendant does not request those details, the prosecutor must make them available to the defendant at, or before, the beginning of the day of the first hearing.

Content of initial details R8.3

8.3 Initial details of the prosecution case must include—
(a) where, immediately before the first hearing in the magistrates' court, the defendant was in police custody for the offence charged—
(i) a summary of the circumstances of the offence, and
(ii) the defendant's criminal record, if any; or
(b) where paragraph (a) does not apply—
(i) a summary of the circumstances of the offence,
(ii) any account given by the defendant in interview, whether contained in that summary or in another document,
(iii) any written witness statement or exhibit that the prosecutor then has available and considers material to plea, or to the allocation of the case for trial, or to sentence,
(iv) the defendant's criminal record, if any, and
(v) any available statement of the effect of the offence on a victim, a victim's family or others.

Use of initial details R8.4

8.4 (1) This rule applies where—
(a) the prosecutor wants to introduce information contained in a document listed in rule 8.3; and
(b) the prosecutor has not—
(i) served that document on the defendant, or
(ii) made that information available to the defendant.
(2) The court must not allow the prosecutor to introduce that information unless the court first allows the defendant sufficient time to consider it.

Criminal Practice Directions Part 8 Initial Details of the Prosecution Case

CPD II Preliminary proceedings 8A: Defendant's Record CPD.8A

Copies of record

8A.1 The defendant's record (previous convictions, cautions, reprimands, etc) may be taken into account when the court decides not only on sentence but also, for example, about bail, or when allocating a case for trial. It is therefore important that up to date and accurate information is available. Previous convictions must be provided as part of the initial details of the prosecution case under CrimPR Part 8.

8A.2 The record should usually be provided in the following format:

Personal details and summary of convictions and cautions — Police National Computer ['PNC'] Court/Defence/Probation Summary Sheet;
Previous convictions — PNC Court/Defence/Probation printout, supplemented by Form MG16 if the police force holds convictions not shown on PNC;
Recorded cautions — PNC Court/Defence/Probation printout, supplemented by Form MG17 if the police force holds cautions not shown on PNC.

8A.3 The defence representative should take instructions on the defendant's record and if the defence wish to raise any objection to the record, this should be made known to the prosecutor immediately.

8A.4 It is the responsibility of the prosecutor to ensure that a copy of the defendant's record has been provided to the Probation Service.

8A.5 Where following conviction a custodial order is made, the court must ensure that a copy is attached to the order sent to the prison.

Additional information

8A.6 In the Crown Court, the police should also provide brief details of the circumstances of the last three similar convictions and/or of convictions likely to be of interest to the court, the latter being judged on a case-by-case basis.

8A.7 Where the current alleged offence could constitute a breach of an existing sentence such as a suspended sentence, community order or conditional discharge, and it is known that that sentence is still in force then details of the circumstances of the offence leading to the sentence should be included in the antecedents. The detail should be brief and include the date of the offence.

8A.8 On occasions the PNC printout provided may not be fully up to date. It is the responsibility of the prosecutor to ensure that all of the necessary information is available to the court and the Probation Service and provided to the defence. Oral updates at the hearing will sometimes be necessary, but it is preferable if this information is available in advance.

General rules

R9.1 **When this Part applies**

9.1 (1) This Part applies to the allocation and sending of cases for trial under—
(a) sections 17A to 26 of the Magistrates' Courts Act 1980[1]; and
(b) sections 50A to 52 of the Crime and Disorder Act 1998[2].
(2) Rules 9.6 and 9.7 apply in a magistrates' court where the court must, or can, send a defendant to the Crown Court for trial, without allocating the case for trial there.
(3) Rules 9.8 to 9.14 apply in a magistrates' court where the court must allocate the case to a magistrates' court or to the Crown Court for trial.

[Note. A magistrates' court's powers to send a defendant to the Crown Court for trial are contained in section 51 of the Crime and Disorder Act 1998[3].

The exercise of the court's powers is affected by—

(a) the classification of the offence (and the general rule, subject to exceptions, is that an offence classified as triable on indictment exclusively must be sent for Crown Court trial; an offence classified as triable only summarily must be tried in a magistrates' court; and an offence classified as triable either on indictment or summarily must be allocated to one or the other court for trial: see in particular sections 50A, 51 and 51A of the 1998 Act[4] and section 19 of the Magistrates' Courts Act 1980[5];
(b) the defendant's age (and the general rule, subject to exceptions, is that an offence alleged against a defendant under 18 must be tried in a magistrates' court sitting as a youth court: see in particular sections 24 and 24A of the 1980 Act[6];
(c) whether the defendant is awaiting Crown Court trial for another offence;
(d) whether another defendant, charged with the same offence, is awaiting Crown Court trial for that offence; and
(e) in some cases (destroying or damaging property; aggravated vehicle taking), whether the value involved is more or less than £5,000.

The court's powers of sending and allocation, including its powers (i) to receive a defendant's indication of an intention to plead guilty (see rules 9.7, 9.8 and 9.13) and (ii) to give an indication of likely sentence (see rule 9.11), may be exercised by a single justice: see sections 51 and 51A(11) of the 1998 Act, and sections 17E, 18(5) and 24D of the 1980 Act[7].]

R9.2 **Exercise of magistrates' court's powers**

9.2 (1) This rule applies to the exercise of the powers to which rules 9.6 to 9.14 apply.
(2) The general rule is that the court must exercise its powers at a hearing in public, but it may exercise any power it has to—
(a) withhold information from the public; or
(b) order a hearing in private.

[1] 1980 c. 43; sections 17A, 17D, 17E, 18 to 21 and 23 to 26 were inserted or amended by Schedule 3 to the Criminal Justice Act 2003 (c. 44).
[2] 1998 c. 37; sections 50A to 52 were inserted or amended by Schedule 3 to the Criminal Justice Act 2003 (c. 44).
[3] 1998 c. 37; section 51 was substituted by paragraphs 15 and 18 of Schedule 3 to the Criminal Justice Act 2003 (c. 44) and amended by section 59 of, and paragraph 1 of Schedule 11 to, the Constitutional Reform Act 2005 (c. 4).
[4] 1998 c. 37; section 50A was inserted by paragraphs 15 and 17 of Schedule 3 to the Criminal Justice Act 2003 (c. 44). Section 51A was inserted by paragraphs 15 and 18 of Schedule 3 to the Criminal Justice Act 2003 (c. 44) and amended by section 49 of, and paragraph 5 of Schedule 1 to, the Violent Crime Reduction Act 2006 (c. 38) and paragraph 6 of Schedule 21 to the Legal Aid, Sentencing and Punishment of Offenders Act 2012 (c. 10).
[5] 1980 c. 43; section 19 was substituted by paragraphs 1 and 5 of Schedule 3 to the Criminal Justice Act 2003 (c. 44) and amended by sections 144, 177 and 178 of, and paragraph 4 of Schedule 17, paragraph 80 of Schedule 21 and Part 5 of Schedule 23 to, the Coroners and Justice Act 2009 (c. 25).
[6] 1980 c. 43; section 24 was amended by paragraph 47 of Schedule 14 to the Criminal Justice Act 1982 (c. 48), sections 17, 68 and 101 of, and paragraph 6 of Schedule 8 and Schedule 13 to, the Criminal Justice Act 1991 (c. 53), paragraph 40 of Schedule 10, and Schedule 11, to the Criminal Justice and Public Order Act 1994 (c. 33), sections 47 and 119 of, and paragraph 40 of Schedule 8, to the Crime and Disorder Act 1998 (c. 37), paragraph 64 of Schedule 9 to the Powers of Criminal Courts (Sentencing Act 2000 (c. 6), section 42 of, and paragraphs 1 and 9 of Schedule 3, and Part 4 of Schedule 37, to the Criminal Justice Act 2003 (c. 44) and sections 49 and 65 of, and paragraph 1 of Schedule 1 and Schedule 5 to, the Violent Crime Reduction Act 2006 (c. 38). Section 24A was inserted by paragraphs 1 and 10 of Schedule 3 to the Criminal Justice Act 2003 (c. 44).
[7] 1980 c. 43; section 17E was inserted by paragraphs 1 and 3 of Schedule 3 to the Criminal Justice Act 2003 (c. 44). Section 18 was amended by section 59 of, and paragraph 1 of Schedule 9 to, the Criminal Justice Act 1982 (c. 48), section 68 of, and paragraph 6 of Schedule 8 to, the Criminal Justice Act 1991 (c. 53), section 49 of the Criminal Procedure and Investigations Act 1996 (c. 25), and paragraphs 1 and 4 of Schedule 3 to the Criminal Justice Act 2003 (c. 44). Section 24D was inserted by paragraphs 1 and 10 of Schedule 3 to the Criminal Justice Act 2003 (c. 44).

(3) The general rule is that the court must exercise its powers in the defendant's presence, but it may exercise the powers to which the following rules apply in the defendant's absence on the conditions specified—
  (a) where rule 9.8 (Adult defendant: request for plea), rule 9.9 (Adult defendant: guilty plea) or rule 9.13 (Young defendant) applies, if—
    (i) the defendant is represented, and
    (ii) the defendant's disorderly conduct makes his or her presence in the courtroom impracticable; and
  (b) where rule 9.10 (Adult defendant: not guilty plea) or rule 9.11 (Adult defendant: allocation for magistrates' court trial) applies, if—
    (i) the defendant is represented and waives the right to be present, or
    (ii) the defendant's disorderly conduct makes his or her presence in the courtroom impracticable.

(4) The court may exercise its power to adjourn—
  (a) if either party asks; or
  (b) on its own initiative.

(5) Where the court on the same occasion deals with two or more offences alleged against the same defendant, the court must deal with those offences in the following sequence—
  (a) any to which rule 9.6 applies (Prosecutor's notice requiring Crown Court trial);
  (b) any to which rule 9.7 applies (sending for Crown Court trial, without allocation there), in this sequence—
    (i) any the court must send for trial, then
    (ii) any the court can send for trial; and
  (c) any to which rule 9.14 applies (Allocation and sending for Crown Court trial).

(6) Where the court on the same occasion deals with two or more defendants charged jointly with an offence that can be tried in the Crown Court then in the following sequence—
  (a) the court must explain, in terms each defendant can understand (with help, if necessary), that if the court sends one of them to the Crown Court for trial then the court must send for trial in the Crown Court, too, any other of them—
    (i) who is charged with the same offence as the defendant sent for trial, or with an offence which the court decides is related to that offence,
    (ii) who does not wish to plead guilty to each offence with which he or she is charged, and
    (iii) (if that other defendant is under 18, and the court would not otherwise have sent him or her for Crown Court trial) where the court decides that sending is necessary in the interests of justice

  even if the court by then has decided to allocate that other defendant for magistrates' court trial; and
  (b) the court may ask the defendants questions to help it decide in what order to deal with them.

(7) After following paragraph (5), if it applies, where the court on the same occasion—
  (a) deals with two or more defendants charged jointly with an offence that can be tried in the Crown Court;
  (b) allocates any of them to a magistrates' court for trial; and
  (c) then sends another one of them to the Crown Court for trial,

the court must deal again with each one whom, on that occasion, it has allocated for magistrates' court trial.

[Note. See sections 50A, 51, 51A and 52 of the Crime and Disorder Act 1998[8] *and sections 17A, 17B, 17C, 18, 23, 24A, 24B and 24C of the Magistrates' Courts Act 1980*[9]*.*

Under sections 57A to 57E of the 1998 Act[10]*, the court may require a defendant to attend by live link a hearing to which this Part applies.*

[8] 1998 c. 37; section 52 was amended by paragraphs 68 and 69 of Schedule 3 to the Criminal Justice Act 2003 (c. 44).

[9] 1980 c. 43; sections 17A, 17B and 17C were inserted by section 49 of the Criminal Procedure and Investigations Act 1996 (c. 25). Section 17A was amended by paragraph 62 of Schedule 9 to the Powers of Criminal Courts (Sentencing Act 2000 (c. 6) and paragraphs 1 and 2 of Schedule 3 to the Criminal Justice Act 2003 (c. 44). Section 23 was amended by section 125 of, and paragraph 25 of Schedule 18 to, the Courts and Legal Services Act 1990 (c. 41) and paragraphs 1 and 8 of Schedule 3 to the Criminal Justice Act 2003 (c. 44). Sections 24A, 24B and 24C were inserted by paragraphs 1 and 10 of Schedule 3 to the Criminal Justice Act 2003 (c. 44).

[10] 1998 c. 37; sections 57A to 57E were substituted for section 57 as originally enacted by section 45 of the Police and Justice Act 2006 (c. 48), and amended by sections 106, 109 and 178 of, and Part 3 of Schedule 23 to, the Coroners and Justice Act 2009 (c. 25). Section 57A was further amended by paragraphs 36 and 39 of Schedule 12 to the Legal Aid, Sentencing and Punishment of Offenders Act 2012 (c. 10).

Where a defendant waives the right to be present then the court may nonetheless require his or her attendance by summons or warrant: see section 26 of the 1980 Act[11]*.*

Under section 52A of the 1998 Act[12]*, reporting restrictions apply to the proceedings to which rules 9.6 to 9.14 apply.*

Part 46 contains rules allowing a representative to act on a defendant's behalf for the purposes of these Rules. Part 3 contains rules about the court's powers of case management.]

R9.3 Matters to be specified on sending for trial

9.3 (1) Where the court sends a defendant to the Crown Court for trial, it must specify—
(a) each offence to be tried;
(b) in respect of each, the power exercised to send the defendant for trial for that offence; and
(c) the Crown Court centre at which the trial will take place.
(2) In a case in which the prosecutor serves a notice to which rule 9.6(1)(a) applies (notice requiring Crown Court trial in a case of serious or complex fraud), the court must specify the Crown Court centre identified by that notice.
(3) In any other case, in deciding the Crown Court centre at which the trial will take place, the court must take into account—
(a) the convenience of the parties and witnesses;
(b) how soon a suitable courtroom will be available; and
(c) the directions on the allocation of Crown Court business contained in the Practice Direction.

[Note. See sections 51 and 51D of the Crime and Disorder Act 1998[13]*.]*

R9.4 Duty of justices' legal adviser

9.4 (1) This rule applies—
(a) only in a magistrates' court; and
(b) unless the court—
(i) includes a District Judge (Magistrates' Courts), and
(ii) otherwise directs.
(2) On the court's behalf, a justices' legal adviser may—
(a) read the allegation of the offence to the defendant;
(b) give any explanation and ask any question required by the rules in this Part; and
(c) make any announcement required by the rules in this Part, other than an announcement of—
(i) the court's decisions about allocation and sending,
(ii) any indication by the court of likely sentence, or
(iii) sentence.
(3) A justices' legal adviser must—
(a) assist an unrepresented defendant;
(b) give the court such advice as is required to enable it to exercise its powers; and
(c) if required, attend the members of the court outside the courtroom to give such advice, but inform the parties of any advice so given.

[Note. For the functions of a justices' legal adviser, see sections 28 and 29 of the Courts Act 2003[14]*.]*

R9.5 Duty of magistrates' court officer

9.5 (1) The magistrates' court officer must—
(a) serve notice of a sending for Crown Court trial on—
(i) the Crown Court officer, and
(ii) the parties;
(b) in that notice record—
(i) the matters specified by the court under rule 9.3 (Matters to be specified on sending for trial),
(ii) any decision by the defendant under rule 9.7 (Sending for Crown Court trial) to require Crown Court trial for low-level shoplifting,

[11] 1980 c. 43; section 26 was amended by paragraphs 1 and 12 of Schedule 3 to the Criminal Justice Act 2003 (c. 44).
[12] 1998 c. 37; section 52A was inserted by paragraphs 15 and 19 of Schedule 3 to the Criminal Justice Act 2003 (c. 44) and amended by paragraphs 46 and 47 of Schedule 5 to the Legal Aid, Sentencing and Punishment of Offenders Act 2012 (c. 10).
[13] 1998 c. 37; section 51D was inserted by paragraphs 15 and 18 of Schedule 3 to the Criminal Justice Act 2003 (c. 44) and amended by section 59 of, and paragraph 1 of Schedule 11 to, the Constitutional Reform Act 2005 (c. 4).
[14] 2003 c. 39; section 28 was amended by section 15 of, and paragraphs 308 and 327 of Schedule 4 to, the Constitutional Reform Act 2005 (c. 4).

(iii) any indication given by the defendant under rule 9.7 of intended guilty plea
(iv) any decision by the defendant under rule 9.11 (Adult defendant: allocation to magistrates' court for trial) to decline magistrates' court trial, and
(v) the date on which any custody time limit will expire;

(c) record any indication of likely sentence to which rule 9.11 applies; and
(d) give the court such other assistance as it requires.

(2) The magistrates' court officer must include with the notice served on the Crown Court officer—

(a) the initial details of the prosecution case served by the prosecutor under rule 8.2;
(b) a record of any—
(i) listing or case management direction affecting the Crown Court,
(ii) direction about reporting restrictions,
(iii) decision about bail, for the purposes of section 5 of the Bail Act 1976[15],
(iv) recognizance given by a surety, or
(v) representation order; and
(c) if relevant, any available details of any—
(i) interpreter,
(ii) intermediary, or
(iii) other supporting adult, where the defendant is assisted by such a person.

[Note. See sections 51 and 51D of the Crime and Disorder Act 1998[16]*, and section 20A of the Magistrates' Courts Act 1980*[17]*.]*

Sending without allocation for Crown Court trial

Prosecutor's notice requiring Crown Court trial **R9.6**

9.6 (1) This rule applies where a prosecutor with power to do so requires a magistrates' court to send for trial in the Crown Court—

(a) a case of serious or complex fraud; or
(b) a case which will involve a child witness.

(2) The prosecutor must serve notice of that requirement—

(a) on the magistrates' court officer and on the defendant; and
(b) before trial in a magistrates' court begins under Part 24 (Trial and sentence in a magistrates' court).

(3) The notice must identify—

(a) the power on which the prosecutor relies; and
(b) the Crown Court centre at which the prosecutor wants the trial to take place.

(4) The prosecutor—

(a) must, when choosing a Crown Court centre, take into account the matters listed in rule 9.3(3) (court deciding to which Crown Court centre to send a case); and
(b) may change the centre identified before the case is sent for trial.

[Note. Under section 51B of the Crime and Disorder Act 1998[18]*, the Director of Public Prosecutions or a Secretary of State may require the court to send a case for trial in the Crown Court if, in that prosecutor's opinion, the evidence of the offence charged—*

(a) is sufficient for the person charged to be put on trial for the offence; and
(b) reveals a case of fraud of such seriousness or complexity that it is appropriate that the management of the case should without delay be taken over by the Crown Court.

15 1976 c. 63; section 5 was amended by section 65 of, and Schedule 12 to, the Criminal Law Act 1977 (c. 45), section 60 of the Criminal Justice Act 1982 (c. 48), paragraph 1 of Schedule 3 to the Criminal Justice and Public Order Act 1994 (c. 33), paragraph 53 of Schedule 9 to the Powers of Criminal Courts (Sentencing Act 2000 (c. 6), section 129(1) of the Criminal Justice and Police Act 2001 (c. 16), paragraph 182 of Schedule 8 to the Courts Act 2003 (c. 39), paragraph 48 of Schedule 3, paragraphs 1 and 2 of Schedule 36, and Parts 2, 4 and 12 of Schedule 37 to the Criminal Justice Act 2003 (c. 44) and section 208 of, and paragraphs 33 and 35 of Schedule 21 to, the Legal Services Act 2007 (c. 27).

16 1998 c. 37; section 51 was substituted and section 51D inserted by paragraphs 15 and 18 of Schedule 3 to the Criminal Justice Act 2003 (c. 44). They were amended by section 59 of, and paragraph 1 of Schedule 11 to, the Constitutional Reform Act 2005 (c. 4).

17 1980 c. 43; section 20A was inserted by paragraphs 1 and 6 of Schedule 3 to the Criminal Justice Act 2003 (c. 44).

18 1998 c. 37; section 51B was inserted by paragraphs 15 and 18 of Schedule 3 to the Criminal Justice Act 2003 (c. 44) and amended by section 50 of, and paragraph 69 of Schedule 4 to, the Commissioners for Revenue and Customs Act 2005 (c. 11) and paragraphs 46 and 48 of Schedule 5 to the Legal Aid, Sentencing and Punishment of Offenders Act 2012 (c. 10).

Under section 51C of the Crime and Disorder Act 1998[19]*, the Director of Public Prosecutions may require the court to send for trial in the Crown Court a case involving one of certain specified violent or sexual offences if, in the Director's opinion—*

(a) the evidence of the offence would be sufficient for the person charged to be put on trial for that offence;
(b) a child would be called as a witness at the trial; and
(c) for the purpose of avoiding any prejudice to the welfare of the child, the case should be taken over and proceeded with without delay by the Crown Court.

'Child' for these purposes is defined by section 51C(7) of the 1998 Act.]

R9.7 Sending for Crown Court trial

9.7 (1) This rule applies where a magistrates' court must, or can, send a defendant to the Crown Court for trial without first allocating the case for trial there.

(2) The court must read the allegation of the offence to the defendant.

(3) The court must explain, in terms the defendant can understand (with help, if necessary)—

(a) the allegation, unless it is self-explanatory;

(b) that the offence is one for which the court, as appropriate—

(i) must send the defendant to the Crown Court for trial because the offence is one which can only be tried there or because the court for some other reason is required to send that offence for trial,

(ii) may send the defendant to the Crown Court for trial if the magistrates' court decides that the offence is related to one already sent for trial there; or

(iii) (where the offence is low-value shoplifting and the defendant is 18 or over) must send the defendant to the Crown Court for trial if the defendant wants to be tried there; and

(c) that reporting restrictions apply, which the defendant may ask the court to vary or remove.

(4) In the following sequence, the court must then—

(a) invite the prosecutor to—

(i) identify the court's power to send the defendant to the Crown Court for trial for the offence, and

(ii) make representations about any ancillary matters, including bail and directions for the management of the case in the Crown Court;

(b) invite the defendant to make representations about—

(i) the court's power to send the defendant to the Crown Court, and

(ii) any ancillary matters;

(c) (where the offence is low-value shoplifting and the defendant is 18 or over) offer the defendant the opportunity to require trial in the Crown Court; and

(d) decide whether or not to send the defendant to the Crown Court for trial.

(5) If the court sends the defendant to the Crown Court for trial, it must—

(a) ask whether the defendant intends to plead guilty in the Crown Court and—

(i) if the answer is 'yes', make arrangements for the Crown Court to take the defendant's plea as soon as possible, or

(ii) if the defendant does not answer, or the answer is 'no', make arrangements for a case management hearing in the Crown Court; and

(b) give any other ancillary directions.

[Note. See sections 51, 51A and 51E of the Crime and Disorder Act 1998[20]*, and sections 22A and 24A of the Magistrates' Courts Act 1980*[21]*.*

See also Part 6 (Reporting, etc. restrictions).]

[19] 1998 c. 37; section 51C was inserted by paragraphs 15 and 18 of Schedule 3 to the Criminal Justice Act 2003 (c. 44) and modified by section 63 of, and paragraph 36 of Schedule 6 to, the Serious Crime Act 2007 (c. 27).

[20] 1998 c. 37; section 51 was substituted, and sections 51A and 51E inserted, by paragraphs 15 and 18 of Schedule 3 to the Criminal Justice Act 2003 (c. 44). Section 51 was amended by section 59 of, and paragraph 1 of Schedule 11 to, the Constitutional Reform Act 2005 (c. 4). Section 51A was amended by section 49 of, and paragraph 5 of Schedule 1 to, the Violent Crime Reduction Act 2006 (c. 38) and paragraph 6 of Schedule 21 to the Legal Aid, Sentencing and Punishment of Offenders Act 2012 (c. 10).

[21] 1980 c. 43; section 24A was inserted by paragraphs 1 and 10 of Schedule 3 to the Criminal Justice Act 2003 (c. 44). Section 22A was inserted by section 176 of the Anti-social Behaviour, Crime and Policing Act 2014 (c. 12).

Allocation for magistrates' court or Crown Court trial

Adult defendant: request for plea R9.8

9.8 (1) This rule applies where—
(a) the defendant is 18 or over; and
(b) the court must decide whether a case is more suitable for trial in a magistrates' court or in the Crown Court.
(2) The court must read the allegation of the offence to the defendant.
(3) The court must explain, in terms the defendant can understand (with help, if necessary)—
(a) the allegation, unless it is self-explanatory;
(b) that the offence is one which can be tried in a magistrates' court or in the Crown Court;
(c) that the court is about to ask whether the defendant intends to plead guilty;
(d) that if the answer is 'yes', then the court must treat that as a guilty plea and must sentence the defendant, or commit the defendant to the Crown Court for sentence;
(e) that if the defendant does not answer, or the answer is 'no', then—
(i) the court must decide whether to allocate the case to a magistrates' court or to the Crown Court for trial,
(ii) the value involved may require the court to order trial in a magistrates' court (where the offence is one to which section 22 of the Magistrates' Courts Act 1980[22] applies), and
(iii) if the court allocates the case to a magistrates' court for trial, the defendant can nonetheless require trial in the Crown Court (unless the offence is one to which section 22 of the Magistrates' Courts Act 1980 applies and the value involved requires magistrates' court trial); and
(f) that reporting restrictions apply, which the defendant may ask the court to vary or remove.
(4) The court must then ask whether the defendant intends to plead guilty.

[Note. See section 17A of the Magistrates' Courts Act 1980[23]*.*

For the circumstances in which a magistrates' court may (and, in some cases, must) commit a defendant to the Crown Court for sentence after that defendant has indicated an intention to plead guilty where this rule applies see sections 18 and 20 of the Sentencing Act 2020[24]*.*

See also Part 6 (Reporting, etc. restrictions).]

Adult defendant: guilty plea R9.9

9.9 (1) This rule applies where—
(a) rule 9.8 applies; and
(b) the defendant indicates an intention to plead guilty.
(2) The court must exercise its power to deal with the case—
(a) as if the defendant had just pleaded guilty at a trial in a magistrates' court; and
(b) in accordance with rule 24.11 (Procedure if the court convicts).

[Note. See section 17A of the Magistrates' Courts Act 1980.]

Adult defendant: not guilty plea R9.10

9.10 (1) This rule applies where—
(a) rule 9.8 applies; and
(b) the defendant—
(i) indicates an intention to plead not guilty, or
(ii) gives no indication of intended plea.
(2) In the following sequence, the court must then—
(a) where the offence is one to which section 22 of the Magistrates' Courts Act 1980 applies, explain in terms the defendant can understand (with help, if necessary) that—
(i) if the court decides that the value involved clearly is less than £5,000, the court must order trial in a magistrates' court,

[22] 1980 c. 43; section 22 was amended by sections 38 and 170(2) of, and Schedule 16 to, the Criminal Justice Act 1988 (c. 33), section 68 of, and paragraph 6 of Schedule 8 to, the Criminal Justice Act 1991 (c. 53), section 2(2) of the Aggravated Vehicle Taking Act 1992 (c. 11) and sections 46 and 168(3) of, and Schedule 11 to, the Criminal Justice and Public Order Act 1994 (c. 33).
[23] 1980 c. 43; section 17A was inserted by section 49 of the Criminal Procedure and Investigations Act 1996 (c. 25) and amended by paragraph 62 of Schedule 9 to the Powers of Criminal Courts (Sentencing Act 2000 (c. 6) and paragraphs 1 and 2 of Schedule 3 to the Criminal Justice Act 2003 (c. 44).
[24] 2020 c. 17.

(ii) if the court decides that it is not clear whether that value is more or less than £5,000, then the court will ask whether the defendant agrees to be tried in a magistrates' court, and

(iii) if the answer to that question is 'yes', then the court must order such a trial and if the defendant is convicted then the maximum sentence is limited;

(b) invite the prosecutor to—

(i) identify any previous convictions of which it can take account, and

(ii) make representations about how the court should allocate the case for trial, including representations about the value involved, if relevant;

(c) invite the defendant to make such representations;

(d) where the offence is one to which section 22 of the Magistrates' Courts Act 1980 applies—

(i) if it is not clear whether the value involved is more or less than £5,000, ask whether the defendant agrees to be tried in a magistrates' court,

(ii) if the defendant's answer to that question is 'yes', or if that value clearly is less than £5,000, order a trial in a magistrates' court,

(iii) if the defendant does not answer that question, or the answer is 'no', or if that value clearly is more than £5,000, apply paragraph (2)(e); and

(e) exercise its power to allocate the case for trial, taking into account—

(i) the adequacy of a magistrates' court's sentencing powers,

(ii) any representations by the parties, and

(iii) any allocation guidelines issued by the Sentencing Council.

[Note. See sections 17A, 18, 19, 22 and 24A of the Magistrates' Courts Act 1980[25].

Under section 22 of the 1980 Act, some offences, which otherwise could be tried in a magistrates' court or in the Crown Court, must be tried in a magistrates' court in the circumstances described in this rule.

The convictions of which the court may take account are those specified by section 19 of the 1980 Act.

The Sentencing Council may issue allocation guidelines under section 122 of the Coroners and Justice Act 2009[26]*. The definitive allocation guideline which took effect on 1st March, 2016 provides:*

(1) In general, either way offences should be tried summarily unless—

(a) the outcome would clearly be a sentence in excess of the court's powers for the offence(s) concerned after taking into account personal mitigation and any potential reduction for a guilty plea; or

(b) for reasons of unusual legal, procedural or factual complexity, the case should be tried in the Crown Court. This exception may apply in cases where a very substantial fine is the likely sentence. Other circumstances where this exception will apply are likely to be rare and case specific; the court will rely on the submissions of the parties to identify relevant cases.

(2) In cases with no factual or legal complications the court should bear in mind its power to commit for sentence after a trial and may retain jurisdiction notwithstanding that the likely sentence might exceed its powers.

(3) Cases may be tried summarily even where the defendant is subject to a Crown Court Suspended Sentence Order or Community Order.

(4) All parties should be asked by the court to make representations as to whether the case is suitable for summary trial. The court should refer to definitive guidelines (if any) to assess the likely sentence for the offence in the light of the facts alleged by the prosecution case, taking into account all aspects of the case including those advanced by the defence, including any personal mitigation to which the defence wish to refer.

Where the court decides that the case is suitable to be dealt with in the magistrates' court, it must warn the defendant that all sentencing options remain open and, if the defendant consents to summary trial and is convicted by the court or pleads guilty, the defendant may be committed to the Crown Court for sentence.]

25 1980 c. 43; section 18 was amended by section 59 of, and paragraph 1 of Schedule 9 to, the Criminal Justice Act 1982 (c. 48), section 68 of, and paragraph 6 of Schedule 8 to, the Criminal Justice Act 1991 (c. 53), section 49 of the Criminal Procedure and Investigations Act 1996 (c. 25), and paragraphs 1 and 4 of Schedule 3 to the Criminal Justice Act 2003 (c. 44). Section 19 was substituted by paragraphs 1 and 5 of Schedule 3 to the Criminal Justice Act 2003 (c. 44) and amended by sections 144, 177 and 178 of, and paragraph 4 of Schedule 17, paragraph 80 of Schedule 21 and Part 5 of Schedule 23 to, the Coroners and Justice Act 2009 (c. 25).

26 2009 c. 25.

Adult defendant: allocation for magistrates' court trial **R9.11**

9.11 (1) This rule applies where—
(a) rule 9.10 applies; and
(b) the court allocates the case to a magistrates' court for trial.
(2) The court must explain, in terms the defendant can understand (with help, if necessary) that—
(a) the court considers the case more suitable for trial in a magistrates' court than in the Crown Court;
(b) if the defendant is convicted at a magistrates' court trial, then in some circumstances the court may commit the defendant to the Crown Court for sentence;
(c) if the defendant does not agree to a magistrates' court trial, then the court must send the defendant to the Crown Court for trial; and
(d) before deciding whether to accept magistrates' court trial, the defendant may ask the court for an indication of whether a custodial or non-custodial sentence is more likely in the event of a guilty plea at such a trial, but the court need not give such an indication.
(3) If the defendant asks for such an indication of sentence and the court gives such an indication—
(a) the court must then ask again whether the defendant intends to plead guilty;
(b) if, in answer to that question, the defendant indicates an intention to plead guilty, then the court must exercise its power to deal with the case—
(i) as if the defendant had just pleaded guilty to an offence that can be tried only in a magistrates' court, and
(ii) in accordance with rule 24.11 (Procedure if the court convicts); and
(c) if, in answer to that question, the defendant indicates an intention to plead not guilty, or gives no indication of intended plea, in the following sequence the court must then—
(i) ask whether the defendant agrees to trial in a magistrates' court,
(ii) if the defendant's answer to that question is 'yes', order such a trial, and
(iii) if the defendant does not answer that question, or the answer is 'no', apply rule 9.14.
(4) If the defendant asks for an indication of sentence but the court gives none, or if the defendant does not ask for such an indication, in the following sequence the court must then—
(a) ask whether the defendant agrees to trial in a magistrates' court;
(b) if the defendant's answer to that question is 'yes', order such a trial; and
(c) if the defendant does not answer that question, or the answer is 'no', apply rule 9.14.

[Note. See section 20 of the Magistrates' Courts Act 1980[27].

For the circumstances in which a magistrates' court may (and, in some cases, must) commit a defendant to the Crown Court for sentence after that defendant has been convicted at a magistrates' court trial, see sections 14, 15, 17 and 20 of the Sentencing Act 2020[28].

For the circumstances in which an indication of sentence to which this rule applies restricts the sentencing powers of a court, see section 20A of the 1980 Act[29]*.]*

Adult defendant: prosecutor's application for Crown Court trial **R9.12**

9.12 (1) This rule applies where—
(a) rule 9.11 applies;
(b) the defendant agrees to trial in a magistrates' court; but
(c) the prosecutor wants the court to exercise its power to send the defendant to the Crown Court for trial instead.
(2) The prosecutor must—
(a) apply before trial in a magistrates' court begins under Part 24 (Trial and sentence in a magistrates' court); and
(b) notify—
(i) the defendant, and
(ii) the magistrates' court officer.

[27] 1980 c. 43; section 20 was amended by section 100 of, and paragraph 25 of Schedule 11 to, the Criminal Justice Act 1991 (c. 53), paragraph 63 of Schedule 9 to the Powers of Criminal Courts (Sentencing Act 2000 (c. 6) and paragraphs 1 and 6 of Schedule 3 to the Criminal Justice Act 2003 (c. 44).

[28] 2000 c. 6; sections 3 and 6 were amended, and sections 3A and 3C inserted, by paragraphs 21, 22A, 23 and 28 of Schedule 3 to the Criminal Justice Act 2003 (c. 44). Section 3A was amended by section 53 of, and paragraphs 1 and 9 of Schedule 13 to, the Criminal Justice and Immigration Act 2008 (c. 4) and paragraphs 7 and 8 of Schedule 21 to the Legal Aid, Sentencing and Punishment of Offenders Act 2012 (c. 10). Section 3C was amended by paragraphs 7 and 9 of Schedule 21 to the Legal Aid, Sentencing and Punishment of Offenders Act 2012 (c. 10). Section 6 was further amended by paragraphs 90 and 91 of Schedule 32, and Parts 7 and 9 of Schedule 37, to the Criminal Justice Act 2003 (c. 44).

[29] 1980 c. 43; section 20A was inserted by paragraphs 1 and 6 of Schedule 3 to the Criminal Justice Act 2003 (c. 44).

(3) The court must determine an application to which this rule applies before it deals with any other pre-trial application.

[Note. See sections 8A and 25 of the Magistrates' Courts Act 1980[30]*. Under section 25(2B), the court may grant an application to which this rule applies only if it is satisfied that the sentence which a magistrates' court would have power to impose would be inadequate.]*

R9.13 **Young defendant**

9.13 (1) This rule applies where—
(a) the defendant is under 18; and
(b) the court must decide whether to send the defendant for Crown Court trial instead of ordering trial in a youth court.
(2) The court must read the allegation of the offence to the defendant.
(3) The court must explain, in terms the defendant can understand (with help, if necessary)—
(a) the allegation, unless it is self-explanatory;
(b) that the offence is one which can be tried in the Crown Court instead of in a youth court;
(c) that the court is about to ask whether the defendant intends to plead guilty;
(d) that if the answer is 'yes', then the court must treat that as a guilty plea and must sentence the defendant, or commit the defendant to the Crown Court for sentence;
(e) that if the defendant does not answer, or the answer is 'no', then the court must decide whether to send the defendant for Crown Court trial instead of ordering trial in a youth court; and
(f) that reporting restrictions apply, which the defendant may ask the court to vary or remove.
(4) The court must then ask whether the defendant intends to plead guilty.
(5) If the defendant's answer to that question is 'yes', the court must exercise its power to deal with the case—
(a) as if the defendant had just pleaded guilty at a trial in a youth court; and
(b) in accordance with rule 24.11 (Procedure if the court convicts).
(6) If the defendant does not answer that question, or the answer is 'no', in the following sequence the court must then—
(a) invite the prosecutor to make representations about whether Crown Court or youth court trial is more appropriate;
(b) invite the defendant to make such representations; and
(c) exercise its power to allocate the case for trial, taking into account—
(i) the offence and the circumstances of the offence,
(ii) the suitability of a youth court's sentencing powers,
(iii) where the defendant is jointly charged with an adult, whether it is necessary in the interests of justice for them to be tried together in the Crown Court, and
(iv) any representations by the parties.

[Note. See section 24A of the Magistrates' Courts Act 1980[31].

For the circumstances in which a magistrates' court may (and, in some cases, must) commit a defendant who is under 18 to the Crown Court for sentence after that defendant has indicated a guilty plea, sections 16, 17, 19 and 20 of the Sentencing Act 2020[32]*.]*

R9.14 **Allocation and sending for Crown Court trial**

9.14 (1) This rule applies where—
(a) under rule 9.10 or rule 9.13, the court allocates the case to the Crown Court for trial;
(b) under rule 9.11, the defendant does not agree to trial in a magistrates' court; or
(c) under rule 9.12, the court grants the prosecutor's application for Crown Court trial.

[30] 1980 c. 43; section 8A was inserted by section 45 of, and Schedule 3 to, the Courts Act 2003 (c. 39) and amended by SI 2006/2493 and paragraphs 12 and 14 of Schedule 5 to the Legal Aid, Sentencing and Punishment of Offenders Act 2012 (c. 10). Section 25 was amended by section 31 of, and paragraph 3 of Schedule 1 and Schedule 2, to the Prosecution of Offences Act 1985 (c. 23), paragraph 6 of Schedule 8 to the Criminal Justice Act 1991 (c. 53), paragraphs 1 and 5 of Schedule 1 to the Criminal Procedure and Investigations Act 1996 (c. 25), section 42 of the Criminal Justice Act 2003 (c. 44) and paragraphs 1 and 11 of Schedule 3, and Part 4 of Schedule 37, to the Criminal Justice Act 2003 (c. 44).

[31] 1980 c. 43; section 24A was inserted by paragraphs 1 and 10 of Schedule 3 to the Criminal Justice Act 2003 (c. 44).

[32] 2000 c. 6; sections 3B, 3C and 4A were inserted by paragraphs 21, 23 and 25 of Schedule 3 to the Criminal Justice Act 2003 (c. 44). Section 3B was amended by section 53 of the Criminal Justice and Courts Act 2015 (c. 2). Section 3C was amended by paragraphs 7 and 9 of Schedule 21 to the Legal Aid, Sentencing and Punishment of Offenders Act 2012 (c. 10). Section 6 was amended by paragraphs 21 and 28 of Schedule 3, paragraphs 90 and 91 of Schedule 32 and Parts 7 and 9 of Schedule 37 to the Criminal Justice Act 2003 (c. 44).

(2) In the following sequence, the court must—
(a) invite the prosecutor to make representations about any ancillary matters, including bail and directions for the management of the case in the Crown Court;
(b) invite the defendant to make any such representations; and
(c) exercise its powers to—
(i) send the defendant to the Crown Court for trial, and
(ii) give any ancillary directions.

[Note. See sections 21 and 24A of the Magistrates' Courts Act 1980[33] and section 51 of the Crime and Disorder 1998[34]. See also rule 9.3 (matters to be specified on sending for trial).]

CRIMINAL PRACTICE DIRECTIONS PART 9 ALLOCATION AND SENDING FOR TRIAL

CPD II Preliminary proceedings 9A: Allocation (Mode of Trial) CPD.9A

9A.1 Courts must follow the Sentencing Council's guideline on Allocation (mode of trial) when deciding whether or not to send defendants charged with 'either way' offences for trial in the Crown Court under section 51(1) of the Crime and Disorder Act 1998.

CRIMINAL PROCEDURE RULES PART 10 THE INDICTMENT

When this Part applies R10.1

10.1 This Part applies where—
(a) a magistrates' court sends a defendant to the Crown Court for trial under section 51 or section 51A of the Crime and Disorder Act 1998[1];
(b) a prosecutor wants a High Court judge's permission to serve a draft indictment;
(c) the Crown Court approves a proposed indictment under paragraph 2 of Schedule 17 to the Crime and Courts Act 2013[2] and rule 11.4 (Deferred prosecution agreements: Application to approve the terms of an agreement);
(d) a prosecutor wants to re-institute proceedings in the Crown Court under section 22B of the Prosecution of Offences Act 1985[3]; or
(e) the Court of Appeal orders a retrial, under section 8 of the Criminal Appeal Act 1968[4] or under section 77 of the Criminal Justice Act 2003[5].

[Note. See also sections 3, 4 and 5 of the Indictments Act 1915[6] and section 2 of the Administration of Justice (Miscellaneous Provisions) Act 1933[7]. Under section 2(1) of the 1933 Act, a draft indictment (in the Act, a 'bill of indictment') becomes an indictment when it is 'preferred' in accordance with these rules. See rule 10.2.

[33] 2020 c. 17.
[34] 1998 c. 37; section 51 was substituted by paragraphs 15 and 18 of Schedule 3 to the Criminal Justice Act 2003 (c. 44) and amended by section 59 of, and paragraph 1 of Schedule 11 to, the Constitutional Reform Act 2005 (c. 4).

[1] 1998 c. 37; section 51 was substituted by paragraphs 15 and 18 of Schedule 3 to the Criminal Justice Act 2003 (c. 44) and amended by section 59 of, and paragraph 1 of Schedule 11 to, the Constitutional Reform Act 2005 (c. 4). Section 51A was inserted by paragraphs 15 and 18 of Schedule 3 to the Criminal Justice Act 2003 (c. 44) and amended by section 49 of, and paragraph 5 of Schedule 1 to, the Violent Crime Reduction Act 2006 (c. 38) and paragraph 6 of Schedule 21 to the Legal Aid, Sentencing and Punishment of Offenders Act 2012 (c. 10).
[2] 2013 c. 22.
[3] 1985 c. 23; section 22B was inserted by section 45 of the Crime and Disorder Act 1998 (c. 37) and amended by paragraph 17 of Schedule 36 to the Criminal Justice Act 2003 (c. 44) and section 112 of, and Part 13 of Schedule 8 to, the Policing and Crime Act 2009 (c. 26).
[4] 1968 c. 19; section 8 was amended by Section 12 of, and paragraph 38 of Schedule 2 to, the Bail Act 1976 (c. 63), section 56 of, and Part IV of Schedule 11 to, the Courts Act 1971 (c. 23), section 65 of, and paragraph 36 of Schedule 3 to, the Mental Health (Amendment) Act 1982 (c. 51), section 148 of, and paragraph 23 of Schedule 4 to, the Mental Health Act 1983 (c. 20), section 43 of the Criminal Justice Act 1988 (c. 33), section 168 of, and paragraph 19 of Schedule 10 to, the Criminal Justice and Public Order Act 1994 (c. 33), section 58 of the Access to Justice Act 1999 (c. 22), sections 41 and 332 of, and paragraph 43 of Schedule 3 to, and Part 4 of Schedule 37 to, the Criminal Justice Act 2003 (c. 44) and section 32 of, and paragraph 2 of Schedule 4 to, the Mental Health Act 2007 (c. 12).
[5] 2003 c. 44.
[6] 1915 c. 90; section 4 was amended by section 83 of, and Part I of Schedule 10 to, the Criminal Justice Act 1948 (c. 58) and section 10 of, and Part III of Schedule 3 to, the Criminal Law Act 1967 (c. 58). Section 5 was amended by section 12 of, and paragraph 8 of Schedule 2 to, the Bail Act 1976 (c. 63), section 31 of, and Schedule 2 to, the Prosecution of Offences Act 1985 (c. 23) and section 331 of, and paragraph 40 of Schedule 36 to, the Criminal Justice Act 2003 (c. 44).
[7] 1933 c. 36; section 2 was amended by Part IV of Schedule 11 to, the Courts Act 1971 (c. 23), Schedule 5 to, the Senior Courts Act 1981 (c. 54), Schedule 2 to the Prosecution of Offences Act 1985 (c. 23), paragraph 1 of Schedule 2 to the Criminal Justice Act 1987 (c. 38), paragraph 10 of Schedule 15 to the Criminal Justice Act 1988 (c. 33), paragraph 8 of Schedule 6 to the Criminal Justice Act 1991 (c. 53), Schedule 1 to the Statute Law (Repeals) Act 1993, paragraph 17 of Schedule 1 to the Criminal Procedure and Investigations Act 1996 (c. 25), paragraph 5 of Schedule 8 to the Crime and Disorder Act 1998 (c. 37), paragraph 34 of Schedule 3 and Part 4 of Schedule 37 to the Criminal Justice Act 2003 (c. 44), paragraph 1 of the Schedule

Part 3 contains rules about the court's general powers of case management, including power to consider applications and give directions for (among other things) the amendment of an indictment and for separate trials under section 5 of the Indictments Act 1915. See in particular rule 3.29 (Application for joint or separate trials, etc.).

Under section 51D of the Crime and Disorder Act 1998[8]*, the magistrates' court must notify the Crown Court of the offence or offences for which the defendant is sent for trial. Part 9 (Allocation and sending for trial) contains relevant rules.*

A Crown Court judge may approve a proposed indictment on approving a deferred prosecution agreement. Part 11 (Deferred prosecution agreements) contains relevant rules.

A prosecutor may apply to a High Court judge for permission to serve a draft indictment under rule 10.9.

Under section 22B of the Prosecution of Offences Act 1985, one of the prosecutors listed in that section may re-institute proceedings that have been stayed under section 22(4) of that Act[9] *on the expiry of an overall time limit (where such a time limit has been prescribed). Section 22B(2) requires the service of a draft indictment within 3 months of the date on which the Crown Court ordered the stay, or within such longer period as the court allows.*

The Court of Appeal may order a retrial under section 8 of the Criminal Appeal Act 1968 (on a defendant's appeal against conviction) or under section 77 of the Criminal Justice Act 2003 (on a prosecutor's application for the retrial of a serious offence after acquittal). Section 8 of the 1968 Act and section 84 of the 2003 Act require the arraignment of a defendant within 2 months. See also rules 27.7 and 39.14.

Where a magistrates' court sends a defendant to the Crown Court for trial under section 51 or 51A of the Crime and Disorder Act 1998, in some circumstances the Crown Court may try the defendant for other offences: see section 2(2) of the Administration of Justice (Miscellaneous Provisions) Act 1933 (indictable offences founded on the prosecution evidence), section 40 of the Criminal Justice Act 1988[10] *(specified summary offences founded on that evidence) and paragraph 6 of Schedule 3 to the Crime and Disorder Act 1998 (power of Crown Court to deal with related summary offence sent to that court). An offence of theft under section 1 of the Theft Act 1968 which is low-value shoplifting under section 22A of the Magistrates' Courts Act 1980*[11] *is a summary offence unless the defendant chooses to be tried in the Crown Court.]*

R10.2 The indictment: general rules

10.2 (1) The indictment on which the defendant is arraigned under rule 3.32 (Arraigning the defendant on the indictment) must be in writing and must contain, in a paragraph called a 'count'—

(a) a statement of the offence charged that—

(i) describes the offence in ordinary language, and

(ii) identifies any legislation that creates it; and

(b) such particulars of the conduct constituting the commission of the offence as to make clear what the prosecutor alleges against the defendant.

to S.I. 2004/2035, section 12 of, and paragraph 7 of Schedule 1 to, the Constitutional Reform Act 2005 (c. 4), sections 116 and 178 of, and Part 3 of Schedule 23 to, the Coroners and Justice Act 2009 (c. 25), paragraph 32 of Schedule 17 to the Crime and Courts Act 2013 (c. 22) and section 82 of the Deregulation Act 2015 (c. 20).

[8] 1998 c. 37; section 51D was inserted by paragraphs 15 and 18 of Schedule 3 to the Criminal Justice Act 2003 (c. 44) and amended by section 59 of, and paragraph 1 of Schedule 11 to, the Constitutional Reform Act 2005 (c. 4).

[9] 1985 c. 23; section 22 was amended by paragraph 104 of Schedule 15 to the Criminal Justice Act 1988 (c. 33), section 43 of the Crime and Disorder Act 1998 (c. 37), paragraph 36 of Schedule 11 to the Criminal Justice Act 1991 (c. 53), paragraph 27 of Schedule 9 to the Criminal Justice and Public Order Act 1994 (c. 33), section 71 of the Criminal Procedure and Investigations Act 1996 (c. 25), section 67(3) of the Access to Justice Act 1999 (c. 22), section 70 of, and paragraph 57 of Schedule 3 and paragraphs 49 and 51 of Schedule 36 to, the Criminal Justice Act 2003 (c. 44), section 59 of, and paragraph 1 of Schedule 11 to, the Constitutional Reform Act 2005 (c. 4) and paragraph 22 of Schedule 12 to the Legal Aid, Sentencing and Punishment of Offenders Act 2012 (c. 10).

[10] 1988 c. 33; section 40 was amended by section 4 of, and paragraph 39 of Schedule 3 to, the Road Traffic (Consequential Provisions) Act 1988 (c. 54), section 168 of, and paragraph 35 of Schedule 9 to, the Criminal Justice and Public Order Act 1994 (c. 33), section 47 of, and paragraph 34 of Schedule 1 to, the Criminal Procedure and Investigations Act 1996 (c. 25), section 119 of, and paragraph 66 of Schedule 8 to, the Crime and Disorder Act 1998 (c. 37) and paragraph 60 of Schedule 3 and Part 4 of Schedule 37 to the Criminal Justice Act 2003 (c. 44).

[11] 1980 c. 43; section 22A was inserted by section 176 of the Anti-social Behaviour, Crime and Policing Act 2014 (c. 12).

(2) More than one incident of the commission of the offence may be included in a count if those incidents taken together amount to a course of conduct having regard to the time, place or purpose of commission.
(3) The counts must be numbered consecutively.
(4) An indictment may contain—
 (a) any count charging substantially the same offence as one for which the defendant was sent for trial;
 (b) any count contained in a draft indictment served with the permission of a High Court judge or at the direction of the Court of Appeal; and
 (c) any other count charging an offence that the Crown Court can try and which is based on the prosecution evidence that has been served, including a summary offence to which section 40 of the Criminal Justice Act 1988 applies.
(5) For the purposes of section 2 of the Administration of Justice (Miscellaneous Provisions) Act 1933—
 (a) a draft indictment constitutes a bill of indictment; and
 (b) the draft, or bill, is preferred before the Crown Court and becomes the indictment—
  (i) where rule 10.3 applies (Draft indictment generated electronically on sending for trial), immediately before the first count (or the only count, if there is only one) is read to or placed before the defendant to take the defendant's plea under rule 3.32(1)(d),
  (ii) when the prosecutor serves the draft indictment on the Crown Court officer, where rule 10.4 (Draft indictment served by the prosecutor after sending for trial), rule 10.5 (Draft indictment served by the prosecutor with a High Court judge's permission), rule 10.7 (Draft indictment served by the prosecutor on re-instituting proceedings) or rule 10.8 (Draft indictment served by the prosecutor at the direction of the Court of Appeal) applies, or
  (iii) when the Crown Court approves the proposed indictment, where rule 10.6 applies (Draft indictment approved by the Crown Court with deferred prosecution agreement).
(6) An indictment must be in one of the forms set out in the Practice Direction unless—
 (a) rule 10.3 applies; or
 (b) the Crown Court otherwise directs.
(7) Unless the Crown Court otherwise directs, the court officer must—
 (a) endorse any paper copy of the indictment made for the court with—
  (i) a note to identify it as a copy of the indictment, and
  (ii) the date on which the draft indictment became the indictment under paragraph (5); and
 (b) where rule 10.4, 10.5, 10.7 or 10.8 applies, serve a copy of the indictment on all parties.
(8) The Crown Court may extend the time limit under rule 10.4, 10.5, 10.7 or 10.8, even after it has expired.

[Note. Under section 2(6) of the Administration of Justice (Miscellaneous Provisions) Act 1933, Criminal Procedure Rules may provide for the manner in which and the time at which 'bills of indictment' are to be 'preferred'.

Under rule 3.29 (Application for joint or separate trials, etc.), the court may order separate trials of counts in the circumstances listed in that rule.]

Draft indictment generated electronically on sending for trial **R10.3**

10.3 (1) Unless the Crown Court otherwise directs before the defendant is arraigned, this rule applies where—
 (a) a magistrates' court sends a defendant to the Crown Court for trial;
 (b) the magistrates' court officer serves on the Crown Court officer the notice required by rule 9.5 (Duty of magistrates' court officer); and
 (c) by means of such electronic arrangements as the court officer may make for the purpose, there is presented to the Crown Court as a count—
  (i) each allegation of an indictable offence specified in the notice, and
  (ii) each allegation specified in the notice to which section 40 of the Criminal Justice Act 1988 applies (specified summary offences founded on the prosecution evidence).

(2) Where this rule applies—
(a) each such allegation constitutes a count;
(b) the allegation or allegations so specified together constitute a draft indictment;
(c) before the draft indictment so constituted is preferred before the Crown Court under rule 10.2(5)(b)(i) the prosecutor may substitute for any count an amended count to the same effect and charging the same offence;
(d) if under rule 3.19 (Service of prosecution evidence) the prosecutor has served copies of the documents containing the evidence on which the prosecution case relies then, before the draft indictment is preferred before the Crown Court under rule 10.2(5)(b)(i), the prosecutor may substitute or add—
(i) any count charging substantially the same offence as one specified in the notice, and
(ii) any other count charging an offence which the Crown Court can try and which is based on the prosecution evidence so served; and
(e) a prosecutor who substitutes or adds a count under paragraph (2)(c) or (d) must serve that count on the Crown Court officer and the defendant.

[Note. An 'indictable offence' is (i) an offence classified as triable on indictment exclusively, or (ii) an offence classified as triable either on indictment or summarily. See also the note to rule 9.1 (Allocation and sending for trial: When this Part applies).

Section 40 of the Criminal Justice Act 1988 lists summary offences which may be included in an indictment if the charge—

(a) is founded on the same facts or evidence as a count charging an indictable offence; or
(b) is part of a series of offences of the same or similar character as an indictable offence which is also charged.]

R10.4 Draft indictment served by the prosecutor after sending for trial

10.4 (1) This rule applies where—
(a) a magistrates' court sends a defendant to the Crown Court for trial; and
(b) rule 10.3 (Draft indictment generated electronically on sending for trial) does not apply.
(2) The prosecutor must serve a draft indictment on the Crown Court officer not more than 20 business days after serving under rule 3.19 (Service of prosecution evidence) copies of the documents containing the evidence on which the prosecution case relies.

R10.5 Draft indictment served by the prosecutor with a High Court judge's permission

10.5 (1) This rule applies where—
(a) the prosecutor applies to a High Court judge under rule 10.9 (Application to a High Court judge for permission to serve a draft indictment); and
(b) the judge gives permission to serve a proposed indictment.
(2) Where this rule applies—
(a) that proposed indictment constitutes the draft indictment; and
(b) the prosecutor must serve the draft indictment on the Crown Court officer not more than 20 business days after the High Court judge's decision.

R10.6 Draft indictment approved with deferred prosecution agreement

10.6 (1) This rule applies where—
(a) the prosecutor applies to the Crown Court under rule 11.4 (Deferred prosecution agreements: Application to approve the terms of an agreement); and
(b) the Crown Court approves the proposed indictment served with that application.
(2) Where this rule applies, that proposed indictment constitutes the draft indictment.

R10.7 Draft indictment served by the prosecutor on re-instituting proceedings

10.7 (1) This rule applies where the prosecutor wants to re-institute proceedings in the Crown Court under section 22B of the Prosecution of Offences Act 1985.
(2) The prosecutor must serve a draft indictment on the Crown Court officer not more than 3 months after the proceedings were stayed under section 22(4) of that Act[12].

R10.8 Draft indictment served by the prosecutor at the direction of the Court of Appeal

10.8 (1) This rule applies where the Court of Appeal orders a retrial.
(2) The prosecutor must serve a draft indictment on the Crown Court officer not more than 28 days after that order.

[12] 1985 c. 23; section 22(4) was amended by section 43 of the Crime and Disorder Act 1998 (c. 37).

Application to a High Court judge for permission to serve a draft indictment **R10.9**

10.9 (1) This rule applies where a prosecutor wants a High Court judge's permission to serve a draft indictment.

(2) Such a prosecutor must—
(a) apply in writing;
(b) serve the application on—
(i) the court officer, and
(ii) the proposed defendant, unless the judge otherwise directs; and
(c) ask for a hearing, if the prosecutor wants one, and explain why it is needed.

(3) The application must—
(a) attach—
(i) the proposed indictment,
(ii) copies of the documents containing the evidence on which the prosecutor relies, including any written witness statement or statements complying with rule 16.2 (Content of written witness statement) and any documentary exhibit to any such statement,
(iii) a copy of any indictment on which the defendant already has been arraigned, and
(iv) if not contained in such an indictment, a list of any offence or offences for which the defendant already has been sent for trial;
(b) include—
(i) a concise statement of the circumstances in which, and the reasons why, the application is made, and
(ii) a concise summary of the evidence contained in the documents accompanying the application, identifying each passage in those documents said to evidence each offence alleged by the prosecutor and relating that evidence to each count in the proposed indictment; and
(c) contain a statement that, to the best of the prosecutor's knowledge, information and belief—
(i) the evidence on which the prosecutor relies will be available at the trial, and
(ii) the allegations contained in the application are substantially true

unless the application is made by or on behalf of the Director of Public Prosecutions or the Director of the Serious Fraud Office.

(4) A proposed defendant served with an application who wants to make representations to the judge must—
(a) serve the representations on the court officer and on the prosecutor;
(b) do so as soon as practicable, and in any event within such period as the judge directs; and
(c) ask for a hearing, if the proposed defendant wants one, and explain why it is needed.

(5) The judge may determine the application—
(a) without a hearing, or at a hearing in public or in private; and
(b) with or without receiving the oral evidence of any proposed witness.

(6) At any hearing, if the judge so directs a statement required by paragraph (3)(c) must be repeated on oath or affirmation.

(7) If the judge gives permission to serve a draft indictment, the decision must be recorded in writing and endorsed on, or annexed to, the proposed indictment.

[Note. See section 2(6) of the Administration of Justice (Miscellaneous Provisions) Act 1933[13]*.]*

Criminal Practice Directions Part 10 The Indictment

CPD II Preliminary proceedings 10A: Preparation and Content of the Indictment **CPD.10A**

Preferring the indictment

10A.1 Section 2 of the Administration of Justice (Miscellaneous Provisions) Act 1933 allows Criminal Procedure Rules to 'make provision ... as to the manner in which and the time at which bills of indictment are to be preferred'. CrimPR 10.2(5) lists the events which constitute preferment for the purposes of that Act. Where a defendant is contemplating an application to the Crown Court to dismiss an offence sent for trial, under the provisions to which CrimPR 9.16 applies, or where

[13] 1933 c. 36; section 2(6) was amended by Part IV of Schedule 11 to the Courts Act 1971 (c. 23), paragraph 1 of the Schedule to S.I. 2004/2035 and section 82 of the Deregulation Act 2015 (c. 20).

the prosecutor is contemplating discontinuance, under the provisions to which CrimPR Part 12 applies, the parties and the court must be astute to the effect of the occurrence of those events: the right to apply for dismissal is lost if the defendant is arraigned, and the right to discontinue is lost if the indictment is preferred.

Printing and signature of indictment

10A.2 Neither Section 2 of the Administration of Justice (Miscellaneous Provisions) Act 1933 nor the Criminal Procedure Rules require an indictment to be printed or signed. Section 2(1) of the Act was amended by section 116 of the Coroners and Justice Act 2009 to remove the requirement for signature. For the potential benefit of the Criminal Appeal Office, CrimPR 10.2(7) requires only that any paper copy of the indictment which for any reason in fact is made for the court must be endorsed with a note to identify it as a copy of the indictment, and with the date on which the indictment came into being. For the same reason, CrimPR 3.22 requires only that any paper copy of an indictment which in fact has been made must be endorsed with a note of the order and of its date where the court makes an order for joint or separate trials affecting that indictment or makes an order for the amendment of that indictment in any respect.

Content of indictment; joint and separate trials

10A.3 The rule has been abolished which formerly required an indictment containing more than one count to include only offences founded on the same facts, or offences which constitute all or part of a series of the same or a similar character. However, if an indictment charges more than one offence, and if at least one of those offences does not meet those criteria, then CrimPR 3.21(4) cites that circumstance as an example of one in which the court may decide to exercise its power to order separate trials under section 5(3) of the Indictments Act 1915. It is for the court to decide which allegations, against whom, should be tried at the same time, having regard to the prosecutor's proposals, the parties' representations, the court's powers under the 1915 Act (see also CrimPR 3.21(4)) and the overriding objective. Where necessary the court should be invited to exercise those powers. It is generally undesirable for a large number of counts to be tried at the same time and the prosecutor may be required to identify a selection of counts on which the trial should proceed, leaving a decision to be taken later whether to try any of the remainder.

10A.4 Where an indictment contains substantive counts and one or more related conspiracy counts, the court will expect the prosecutor to justify their joint trial. Failing justification, the prosecutor should be required to choose whether to proceed on the substantive counts or on the conspiracy counts. In any event, if there is a conviction on any counts that are tried, then those that have not been proceeded with can remain on the file marked 'not to be proceeded with without the leave of the court or the Court of Appeal'. In the event that a conviction is later quashed on appeal, the remaining counts can be tried.

10A.5 There is no rule of law or practice which prohibits two indictments being in existence at the same time for the same offence against the same person and on the same facts. However, the court will not allow the prosecutor to proceed on both indictments. They cannot be tried together and the court will require the prosecutor to elect the one on which the trial will proceed. Where different defendants have been separately sent for trial for offences which properly may be tried together then it is permissible to join in one indictment counts based on the separate sendings for trial even if an indictment based on one of them already exists.

Draft indictment generated electronically on sending for trial

10A.6 CrimPR 10.3 applies where court staff have introduced arrangements for the charges sent for trial to be presented in the Crown Court as the counts of a draft indictment without the need for those charges to be rewritten and served a second time on the defendant and on the court office. Where such arrangements are introduced, court users will be informed (and the fact will become apparent on the sending for trial).

10A.7 Now that there is no restriction on the counts that an indictment may contain (see paragraph 10A.3 above), and given the Crown Court's power, and in some cases obligation, to order separate trials, few circumstances will arise in which the court will wish to exercise the discretion conferred by rule 10.3(1) to direct that the rule will not apply, thus discarding such an electronically generated draft indictment. The most likely such circumstance to arise would be in a case in which prosecution evidence emerging soon after sending requires such a comprehensive amendment of the counts as to make it more convenient to all participants for the prosecutor to prepare and serve under CrimPR 10.4 a complete new draft indictment than to amend the electronically generated draft.

Draft indictment served by the prosecutor

10A.8 CrimPR 10.4 applies after sending for trial wherever CrimPR 10.3 does not. It requires the prosecutor to prepare a draft indictment and serve it on the Crown Court officer, who by CrimPR 10.2(7)(b) then must serve it on the defendant. In most instances service will be by electronic means, usually by making use of the Crown Court digital case system to which the prosecutor will upload the draft (which at once then becomes the indictment, under section 2 of the Administration of Justice (Miscellaneous Provisions) Act 1933 and CrimPR 10.2(5)(b)(ii)).

10A.9 The prosecutor's time limit for service of the draft indictment under CrimPR 10.4 is 28 days after serving under CrimPR 9.15 the evidence on which the prosecution case relies. The Crown Court may extend that time limit, under CrimPR 10.2(8). However, under paragraph CrimPD I 3A.16 of these Practice Directions the court will expect that in every case a draft indictment will be served at least 7 days before the plea and trial preparation hearing, whether the time prescribed by the rule will have expired or not.

Amending the content of the indictment

10A.10 Where the prosecutor wishes to substitute or add counts to a draft indictment, or to invite the court to allow an indictment to be amended, so that the draft indictment, or indictment, will charge offences which differ from those with which the defendant first was charged, the defendant should be given as much notice as possible of what is proposed. It is likely that the defendant will need time to consider his or her position and advance notice will help to avoid delaying the proceedings.

Multiple offending: count charging more than one incident

10A.11 CrimPR 10.2(2) allows a single count to allege more than one incident of the commission of an offence in certain circumstances. Each incident must be of the same offence. The circumstances in which such a count may be appropriate include, but are not limited to, the following:

(a) the victim on each occasion was the same, or there was no identifiable individual victim as, for example, in a case of the unlawful importation of controlled drugs or of money laundering;

(b) the alleged incidents involved a marked degree of repetition in the method employed or in their location, or both;

(c) the alleged incidents took place over a clearly defined period, typically (but not necessarily) no more than about a year;

(d) in any event, the defence is such as to apply to every alleged incident. Where what is in issue differs in relation to different incidents, a single 'multiple incidents' count will not be appropriate (though it may be appropriate to use two or more such counts according to the circumstances and to the issues raised by the defence).

10A.12 Even in circumstances such as those set out above, there may be occasions on which a prosecutor chooses not to use such a count, in order to bring the case within section 75(3)(a) of the Proceeds of Crime Act 2002 (criminal lifestyle established by conviction of three or more offences in the same proceedings): for example, because section 75(2)(c) of that Act does not apply (criminal lifestyle established by an offence committed over a period of at least six months). Where the prosecutor proposes such a course, it is unlikely that CrimPR Part 1 (the overriding objective) will require an indictment to contain a single 'multiple incidents' count in place of a larger number of counts, subject to the general principles set out at paragraph 10A.3.

10A.13 For some offences, particularly sexual offences, the penalty for the offence may have changed during the period over which the alleged incidents took place. In such a case, additional 'multiple incidents' counts should be used so that each count only alleges incidents to which the same maximum penalty applies.

10A.14 In other cases, such as sexual or physical abuse, a complainant may be in a position only to give evidence of a series of similar incidents without being able to specify when or the precise circumstances in which they occurred. In these cases, a 'multiple incidents' count may be desirable. If on the other hand the complainant is able to identify particular incidents of the offence by reference to a date or other specific event, but alleges that in addition there were other incidents which the complainant is unable to specify, then it may be desirable to include separate counts for the identified incidents and a 'multiple incidents' count or counts alleging that incidents of the same offence occurred 'many' times. Using a 'multiple incidents' count may be an appropriate alternative to using 'specimen' counts in some cases where repeated sexual or physical abuse is alleged. The choice of count will depend on the particular circumstances of the case and should be determined bearing in mind the implications for sentencing set out in *R v Canavan*; *R v Kidd*; *R v Shaw* [1998] 1 WLR 604, [1998] 1 Cr App R 79, [1998] 1 Cr App R (S) 243. In *R v A* [2015] EWCA Crim 177, [2015] 2 Cr App R (S) 115(12) the Court of Appeal reviewed the circumstances in which a mixture of multiple incident and single incident counts might be appropriate where the prosecutor alleged sustained sexual abuse.

Multiple offending: trial by jury and then by judge alone

10A.15 Under sections 17 to 21 of the Domestic Violence, Crime and Victims Act 2004, the court may order that the trial of certain counts will be by jury in the usual way and, if the jury convicts, that other associated counts will be tried by judge alone. The use of this power is likely to be appropriate where justice cannot be done without charging a large number of separate offences and the allegations against the defendant appear to fall into distinct groups by reference to the identity of the victim, by reference to the dates of the offences, or by some other distinction in the nature of the offending conduct alleged.

10A.16 In such a case, it is essential to make clear from the outset the association asserted by the prosecutor between those counts to be tried by a jury and those counts which it is proposed should be tried by judge alone, if the jury convict on the former. A special form of indictment is prescribed for this purpose.

10A.17 An order for such a trial may be made only at a preparatory hearing. It follows that where the prosecutor intends to invite the court to order such a trial it will normally be appropriate to proceed as follows. A draft indictment in the form appropriate to such a trial should be served with an application under CrimPR 3.15 for a preparatory hearing. This will ensure that the defendant is aware at the earliest possible opportunity of what the prosecutor proposes and of the proposed association of counts in the indictment.

10A.18 At the start of the preparatory hearing, the defendant should be arraigned on all counts in Part One of the indictment. Arraignment on Part Two need not take place until after there has been either a guilty plea to, or finding of guilt on, an associated count in Part One of the indictment.

10A.19 If the prosecutor's application is successful, the prosecutor should prepare an abstract of the indictment, containing the counts from Part One only, for use in the jury trial. Preparation of such an abstract does not involve 'amendment' of the indictment. It is akin to where a defendant pleads guilty to certain counts in an indictment and is put in the charge of the jury on the remaining counts only.

10A.20 If the prosecutor's application for a two stage trial is unsuccessful, the prosecutor may apply to amend the indictment to remove from it any counts in Part Two which would make jury trial on the whole indictment impracticable and to revert to a standard form of indictment. It will be a matter for the court whether arraignment on outstanding counts takes place at the preparatory hearing, or at a future date.

CPD.10B **CPD II Preliminary proceedings 10B: Voluntary Bills of Indictment**

10B.1 Section 2(2)(b) of the Administration of Justice (Miscellaneous Provisions) Act 1933 and paragraph 2(6) of Schedule 3 to the Crime and Disorder Act 1998 allow the preferment of a bill of indictment by the direction or with the consent of a judge of the High Court. Bills so preferred are known as 'voluntary bills'.

10B.2 Applications for such consent must comply with CrimPR 10.3.

10B.3 Those requirements should be complied with in relation to each defendant named in the indictment for which consent is sought, whether or not it is proposed to prefer any new count against him or her.

10B.4 The preferment of a voluntary bill is an exceptional procedure. Consent should only be granted where good reason to depart from the normal procedure is clearly shown and only where the interests of justice, rather than considerations of administrative convenience, require it.

10B.5 Prosecutors must follow the procedures prescribed by the rule unless there are good reasons for not doing so, in which case prosecutors must inform the judge that the procedures have not been followed and seek leave to dispense with all or any of them. Judges should not give leave to dispense unless good reasons are shown.

10B.6 A judge to whom application for consent to the preferment of a documents submitted by the prosecutor and any written submissions made by the prospective defendant, and may properly seek any necessary amplification. CrimPR 10.3(4)(b) allows the judge to set a timetable for representations. The judge may invite oral submissions from either party, or accede to a request for an opportunity to make oral submissions, if the judge considers it necessary or desirable to receive oral submissions in order to make a sound and fair decision on the application. Any such oral submissions should be made on notice to the other party and in open court unless the judge otherwise directs.

Criminal Procedure Rules Part 11 Deferred Prosecution Agreements

When this Part applies R11.1

11.1 (1) This Part applies to proceedings in the Crown Court under Schedule 17 to the Crime and Courts Act 2013.[1]

(2) In this Part—

(a) 'agreement' means a deferred prosecution agreement under paragraph 1 of that Schedule;

(b) 'prosecutor' means a prosecutor designated by or under paragraph 3 of that Schedule; and

(c) 'defendant' means the corporation, partnership or association with whom the prosecutor proposes to enter, or enters, an agreement.

[Note. Under Schedule 17 to the Crime and Courts Act 2013, a designated prosecutor may make a deferred prosecution agreement with a defendant, other than an individual, whom the prosecutor is considering prosecuting for an offences or offences listed in that Schedule. Under such an agreement, the defendant agrees to comply with its terms and the prosecutor agrees that, if the Crown Court approves those terms, then paragraph 2 of the Schedule will apply and—

(a) the prosecutor will serve a draft indictment charging the defendant with the offence or offences the subject of the agreement;

(b) the prosecution will be suspended under that paragraph, and the suspension may not be lifted while the agreement is in force; and

(c) no-one may prosecute the defendant for the offence or offences charged while the agreement is in force, or after it expires if the defendant complies with it.

The Code for prosecutors issued under paragraph 6 of that Schedule contains guidance on the exercise of prosecution functions in relation to a deferred prosecution agreement.]

Exercise of court's powers R11.2

11.2 (1) The court must determine an application to which this Part applies at a hearing, which—

(a) must be in private, under rule 11.3 (Application to approve a proposal to enter an agreement);

(b) may be in public or private, under rule 11.4 (Application to approve the terms of an agreement), rule 11.6 (Application to approve a variation of the terms of an agreement) or rule 11.9 (Application to postpone the publication of information by the prosecutor); and

(c) must be in public, under rule 11.5 (Application on breach of agreement) or rule 11.7 (Application to lift suspension of prosecution), unless the court otherwise directs.

(2) If at a hearing in private to which rule 11.4 or rule 11.6 applies the court approves the agreement or the variation proposed, the court must announce its decision and reasons at a hearing in public.

(3) The court must not determine an application under rule 11.3, rule 11.4 or rule 11.6 unless—

(a) both parties are present;

(b) the prosecutor provides the court with a written declaration that, for the purposes of the application—

(i) the investigator enquiring into the alleged offence or offences has certified that no information has been supplied which the investigator knows to be inaccurate, misleading or incomplete, and

(ii) the prosecutor has complied with the prosecution obligation to disclose material to the defendant; and

(c) the defendant provides the court with a written declaration that, for the purposes of the application—

(i) the defendant has not supplied any information which the defendant knows to be inaccurate, misleading or incomplete, and

(ii) the individual through whom the defendant makes the declaration has made reasonable enquiries and believes the defendant's declaration to be true.

(4) The court must not determine an application under rule 11.5 or rule 11.7—

(a) in the prosecutor's absence; or

(b) in the absence of the defendant, unless the defendant has had at least 20 business days in which to make representations.

(5) If the court approves a proposal to enter an agreement—

(a) the general rule is that any further application to which this Part applies must be made to the same judge; but

[1] 2013 c. 22.

(b) the court may direct other arrangements.

(6) The court may adjourn a hearing—

(a) if either party asks, or on its own initiative; and

(b) in particular, if the court requires more information about—

(i) the facts of an alleged offence,

(ii) the terms of a proposal to enter an agreement, or of a proposed agreement or variation of an agreement, or

(iii) the circumstances in which the prosecutor wants the court to decide whether the defendant has failed to comply with the terms of an agreement.

(7) The court may—

(a) hear an application under rule 11.4 immediately after an application under rule 11.3, if the court approves a proposal to enter an agreement; and

(b) hear an application under rule 11.7 immediately after an application under rule 11.5, if the court terminates an agreement.

[Note. See paragraphs 7(4), 8(5), (6) and 10(5), (6) of Schedule 17 to the Crime and Courts Act 2013.

The Code for prosecutors issued under paragraph 6 of that Schedule contains guidance on fulfilling the prosecution duty of disclosure.]

R11.3 Application to approve a proposal to enter an agreement

11.3 (1) This rule applies where a prosecutor wants the court to approve a proposal to enter an agreement.

(2) The prosecutor must—

(a) apply in writing after the commencement of negotiations between the parties but before the terms of agreement have been settled; and

(b) serve the application on—

(i) the court officer, and

(ii) the defendant.

(3) The application must—

(a) identify the parties to the proposed agreement;

(b) attach a proposed indictment setting out such of the offences listed in Part 2 of Schedule 17 to the Crime and Courts Act 2013 as the prosecutor is considering;

(c) include or attach a statement of facts proposed for inclusion in the agreement, which must give full particulars of each alleged offence, including details of any alleged financial gain or loss;

(d) include any information about the defendant that would be relevant to sentence in the event of conviction for the offence or offences;

(e) specify the proposed expiry date of the agreement;

(f) describe the proposed terms of the agreement, including details of any—

(i) monetary penalty to be paid by the defendant, and the time within which any such penalty is to be paid,

(ii) compensation, reparation or donation to be made by the defendant, the identity of the recipient of any such payment and the time within which any such payment is to be made,

(iii) surrender of profits or other financial benefit by the defendant, and the time within which any such sum is to be surrendered,

(iv) arrangement to be made in relation to the management or conduct of the defendant's business,

(v) co-operation required of the defendant in any investigation related to the offence or offences,

(vi) other action required of the defendant,

(vii) arrangement to monitor the defendant's compliance with a term,

(viii) consequence of the defendant's failure to comply with a term, and

(ix) prosecution costs to be paid by the defendant, and the time within which any such costs are to be paid;

(g) in relation to those terms, explain how they comply with—

(i) the requirements of the code issued under paragraph 6 of Schedule 17 to the Crime and Courts Act 2013, and

(ii) any sentencing guidelines or guideline cases which apply;

(h) contain or attach the defendant's written consent to the proposal; and

(i) explain why—

(i) entering into an agreement is likely to be in the interests of justice, and

(ii) the proposed terms of the agreement are fair, reasonable and proportionate.

(4) If the proposed statement of facts includes assertions that the defendant does not admit, the application must—
(a) specify the facts that are not admitted; and
(b) explain why that is immaterial for the purposes of the proposal to enter an agreement.

[Note. See paragraphs 5 and 7 of Schedule 17 to the Crime and Courts Act 2013.]

Application to approve the terms of an agreement R11.4

11.4 (1) This rule applies where—
(a) the court has approved a proposal to enter an agreement on an application under rule 11.3; and
(b) the prosecutor wants the court to approve the terms of the agreement.
(2) The prosecutor must—
(a) apply in writing as soon as practicable after the parties have settled the terms; and
(b) serve the application on—
(i) the court officer, and
(ii) the defendant.
(3) The application must—
(a) attach the agreement;
(b) indicate in what respect, if any, the terms of the agreement differ from those proposed in the application under rule 11.3;
(c) contain or attach the defendant's written consent to the agreement;
(d) explain why—
(i) the agreement is in the interests of justice, and
(ii) the terms of the agreement are fair, reasonable and proportionate;
(e) attach a draft indictment, charging the defendant with the offence or offences the subject of the agreement; and
(f) include any application for the hearing to be in private.
(4) If the court approves the agreement and the draft indictment, the court officer must—
(a) endorse any paper copy of the indictment made for the court with—
(i) a note to identify it as the indictment approved by the court, and
(ii) the date of the court's approval; and
(b) treat the case as if it had been suspended by order of the court.

[Note. See paragraph 8 of Schedule 17 to the Crime and Courts Act 2013. See also rule 11.9 (Application to postpone the publication of information by the prosecutor).

Under paragraph 2(1) of Schedule 17 to the 2013 Act and section 2 of the Administration of Justice (Miscellaneous Provisions) Act 1933[2]*, the draft indictment to which this rule applies becomes an indictment when the court approves the agreement and consents to the service of that draft. Part 10 contains rules about indictments.*

Under paragraph 2(2) of Schedule 17 to the 2013 Act, on approval of the draft indictment the proceedings are automatically suspended.

Under paragraph 13(2) of Schedule 17 to the 2013 Act, where the court approves an agreement the statement of facts contained in that agreement is to be treated as an admission by the defendant under section 10 of the Criminal Justice Act 1967[3] *(proof by formal admission) in any criminal proceedings against the defendant for the alleged offence.]*

Application on breach of agreement R11.5

11.5 (1) This rule applies where—
(a) the prosecutor believes that the defendant has failed to comply with the terms of an agreement; and
(b) the prosecutor wants the court to decide—

[2] 1933 c. 36; section 2 was amended by Part IV of Schedule 11 to, the Courts Act 1971 (c. 23), Schedule 5 to, the Senior Courts Act 1981 (c. 54), Schedule 2 to the Prosecution of Offences Act 1985 (c. 23), paragraph 1 of Schedule 2 to the Criminal Justice Act 1987 (c. 38), paragraph 10 of Schedule 15 to the Criminal Justice Act 1988 (c. 33), paragraph 8 of Schedule 6 to the Criminal Justice Act 1991 (c. 53), Schedule 1 to the Statute Law (Repeals) Act 1993, paragraph 17 of Schedule 1 to the Criminal Procedure and Investigations Act 1996 (c. 25), paragraph 5 of Schedule 8 to the Crime and Disorder Act 1998 (c. 37), paragraph 34 of Schedule 3 and Part 4 of Schedule 37 to the Criminal Justice Act 2003 (c. 44), paragraph 1 of the Schedule to S.I. 2004/2035, section 12 of, and paragraph 7 of Schedule 1 to, the Constitutional Reform Act 2005 (c. 4), sections 116 and 178 of, and Part 3 of Schedule 23 to, the Coroners and Justice Act 2009 (c. 25), paragraph 32 of Schedule 17 to the Crime and Courts Act 2013 (c. 22) and section 82 of the Deregulation Act 2015 (c. 20).
[3] 1967 c. 80.

(i) whether the defendant has failed to comply, and
(ii) if so, whether to terminate the agreement, or to invite the parties to agree proposals to remedy that failure.

(2) The prosecutor must—
(a) apply in writing, as soon as practicable after becoming aware of the grounds for doing so; and
(b) serve the application on—
(i) the court officer, and
(ii) the defendant.

(3) The application must—
(a) specify each respect in which the prosecutor believes the defendant has failed to comply with the terms of the agreement, and explain the reasons for the prosecutor's belief; and
(b) attach a copy of any document containing evidence on which the prosecutor relies.

(4) A defendant who wants to make representations in response to the application must serve the representations on—
(a) the court officer; and
(b) the prosecutor,

not more than 20 business days after service of the application.

[Note. See paragraph 9 of Schedule 17 to the Crime and Courts Act 2013. See also rule 11.9 (Application to postpone the publication of information by the prosecutor).]

R11.6 **Application to approve a variation of the terms of an agreement**

11.6 (1) This rule applies where the parties have agreed to vary the terms of an agreement because—
(a) on an application under rule 11.5 (Application on breach of agreement), the court has invited them to do so; or
(b) variation of the agreement is necessary to avoid a failure by the defendant to comply with its terms in circumstances that were not, and could not have been, foreseen by either party at the time the agreement was made.

(2) The prosecutor must—
(a) apply in writing, as soon as practicable after the parties have settled the terms of the variation; and
(b) serve the application on—
(i) the court officer, and
(ii) the defendant.

(3) The application must—
(a) specify each variation proposed;
(b) contain or attach the defendant's written consent to the variation;
(c) explain why—
(i) the variation is in the interests of justice, and
(ii) the terms of the agreement as varied are fair, reasonable and proportionate; and
(d) include any application for the hearing to be in private.

[Note. See paragraph 10 of Schedule 17 to the Crime and Courts Act 2013. See also rule 11.9 (Application to postpone the publication of information by the prosecutor).]

R11.7 **Application to lift suspension of prosecution**

11.7 (1) This rule applies where—
(a) the court terminates an agreement before its expiry date; and
(b) the prosecutor wants the court to lift the suspension of the prosecution that applied when the court approved the terms of the agreement.

(2) The prosecutor must—
(a) apply in writing, as soon as practicable after the termination of the agreement; and
(b) serve the application on—
(i) the court officer, and
(ii) the defendant.

(3) A defendant who wants to make representations in response to the application must serve the representations on—
(a) the court officer; and
(b) the prosecutor,

not more than 20 business days after service of the application.

[Note. See paragraphs 2(3) and 9 of Schedule 17 to the Crime and Courts Act 2013.]

Notice to discontinue prosecution R11.8

11.8 (1) This rule applies where an agreement expires—
(a) on its expiry date, or on a date treated as its expiry date; and
(b) without having been terminated by the court.
(2) The prosecutor must—
(a) as soon as practicable give notice in writing discontinuing the prosecution on the indictment approved by the court under rule 11.4 (Application to approve the terms of an agreement); and
(b) serve the notice on—
(i) the court officer, and
(ii) the defendant.

[Note. See paragraph 11 of Schedule 17 to the Crime and Courts Act 2013.]

Application to postpone the publication of information by the prosecutor R11.9

11.9 (1) This rule applies where the prosecutor—
(a) makes an application under rule 11.4 (Application to approve the terms of an agreement), rule 11.5 (Application on breach of agreement) or rule 11.6 (Application to approve a variation of the terms of an agreement);
(b) decides not to make an application under rule 11.5, despite believing that the defendant has failed to comply with the terms of the agreement; or
(c) gives a notice under rule 11.8 (Notice to discontinue prosecution).
(2) A party who wants the court to order that the publication of information by the prosecutor about the court's or the prosecutor's decision should be postponed must—
(a) apply in writing, as soon as practicable and in any event before such publication occurs;
(b) serve the application on—
(i) the court officer, and
(ii) the other party; and
(c) in the application—
(i) specify the proposed terms of the order, and for how long it should last, and
(ii) explain why an order in the terms proposed is necessary.

[Note. See paragraph 12 of Schedule 17 to the Crime and Courts Act 2013.

Part 6 of these Rules contains rules about applications for a restriction on reporting what takes place at a public hearing, or public access to what otherwise would be a public hearing.]

Duty of court officer, etc. R11.10

11.10 (1) Unless the court otherwise directs, the court officer must—
(a) arrange for the recording of proceedings on an application to which this Part applies; and
(b) arrange for the transcription of such a recording if—
(i) a party wants such a transcript, or
(ii) anyone else wants such a transcript (but that is subject to the restrictions in paragraph (2)).
(2) Unless the court otherwise directs, a person who transcribes a recording of proceedings under such arrangements—
(a) must not supply anyone other than a party with a transcript of a recording of—
(i) a hearing in private, or
(ii) a hearing in public to which reporting restrictions apply; but
(b) subject to that, must supply any person with any transcript for which that person asks—
(i) in accordance with the transcription arrangements made by the court officer, and
(ii) on payment by that person of any fee prescribed.
(3) The court officer must not identify either party to a hearing in private under rule 11.3 (Application to approve a proposal to enter an agreement) or rule 11.4 (Application to approve the terms of an agreement)—
(a) in any notice displayed in the vicinity of the courtroom; or
(b) in any other information published by the court officer.

Court's power to vary requirements under this Part R11.11

11.11 (1) The court may—
(a) shorten or extend (even after it has expired) a time limit under this Part; and
(b) allow there to be made orally—
(i) an application under rule 11.4 (Application to approve the terms of an agreement), or
(ii) an application under rule 11.7 (Application to lift suspension of prosecution)

where the court exercises its power under rule 11.2(7) to hear one application immediately after another.

(2) A party who wants an extension of time must—

(a) apply when serving the application or notice for which it is needed; and

(b) explain the delay.

Criminal Procedure Rules Part 12 Discontinuing a Prosecution

R12.1 **When this Part applies**

12.1 (1) This Part applies where—

(a) the Director of Public Prosecutions can discontinue a case in a magistrates' court, under section 23 of the Prosecution of Offences Act 1985;[1] or

(b) the Director of Public Prosecutions, or another public prosecutor, can discontinue a case sent for trial in the Crown Court, under section 23A of the Prosecution of Offences Act 1985.[2]

(2) In this Part, 'prosecutor' means one of those authorities.

[Note. Under section 23 of the Prosecution of Offences Act 1985, the Director of Public Prosecutions may discontinue proceedings in a magistrates' court, before the court—

(a) sends the defendant for trial in the Crown Court; or

(b) begins to hear the prosecution evidence, at a trial in the magistrates' court.

Under section 23(4) of the 1985 Act, the Director may discontinue proceedings where a person charged is in custody but has not yet been brought to court.

Under section 23 of the 1985 Act, the defendant has a right to require the proceedings to continue. See rule 12.3.

Under section 23A of the 1985 Act, the Director of Public Prosecutions, or a public authority within the meaning of section 17 of that Act[3], may discontinue proceedings where the defendant was sent for trial in the Crown Court under section 51 of the Crime and Disorder Act 1998[4]. In such a case—

(a) the prosecutor must discontinue before a draft indictment becomes an indictment under rule 10.2(5); and

(b) the defendant has no right to require the proceedings to continue.

Where a prosecution does not proceed, the court has power to order the payment of the defendant's costs out of central funds. See rule 45.4.]

R12.2 **Discontinuing a case**

12.2 (1) A prosecutor exercising a power to which this Part applies must serve notice on—

(a) the court officer;

(b) the defendant; and

(c) any custodian of the defendant.

(2) Such a notice must—

(a) identify—

(i) the defendant and each offence to which the notice relates,

(ii) the person serving the notice, and

(iii) the power that that person is exercising; and

(b) explain—

(i) in the copy of the notice served on the court officer, the reasons for discontinuing the case,

(ii) that the notice brings the case to an end,

(iii) if the defendant is in custody for any offence to which the notice relates, that the defendant must be released from that custody, and

(iv) if the notice is under section 23 of the 1985 Act, that the defendant has a right to require the case to continue.

[1] 1985 c. 23; section 23 was amended by section 119 of, and paragraph 63 of Schedule 8 to, the Crime and Disorder Act 1998 (c. 37), paragraph 290 of Schedule 8 to the Courts Act 2003 (c. 39) and paragraph 57 of Schedule 3 to the Criminal Justice Act 2003 (c. 44).

[2] 1985 c. 23; section 23A was inserted by section 119 of, and paragraph 64 of Schedule 8 to, the Crime and Disorder Act 1998 (c. 37) and amended by paragraph 57 of Schedule 3, and Part 4 of Schedule 37, to the Criminal Justice Act 2003 (c. 44).

[3] 1985 c. 23; section 17 was amended by section 40 of, and paragraph 41 of Schedule 9 to, the Constitutional Reform Act 2005 (c. 4) and paragraphs 1 and 4 and Part 4 of Schedule 7 to the Legal Aid, Sentencing and Punishment of Offenders Act 2012 (c. 10).

[4] 1998 c. 37; section 51 was substituted by paragraphs 15 and 18 of Schedule 3 to the Criminal Justice Act 2003 (c. 44) and amended by section 59 of, and paragraph 1 of Schedule 11 to, the Constitutional Reform Act 2005 (c. 4).

(3) Where the defendant is on bail, the court officer must notify—
(a) any surety; and
(b) any person responsible for monitoring or securing the defendant's compliance with a condition of bail.

Defendant's notice to continue R12.3

12.3 (1) This rule applies where a prosecutor serves a notice to discontinue under section 23 of the 1985 Act.
(2) A defendant who wants the case to continue must serve notice—
(a) on the court officer; and
(b) not more than 25 business days after service of the notice to discontinue.
(3) If the defendant serves such a notice, the court officer must—
(a) notify the prosecutor; and
(b) refer the case to the court.

Criminal Procedure Rules Part 13 Warrants for Arrest, Detention or Imprisonment

[Note. Part 30 contains rules about warrants to take goods to pay fines, etc.]

When this Part applies R13.1

13.1 (1) This Part applies where the court can issue a warrant for arrest, detention or imprisonment.
(2) In this Part, 'defendant' means anyone against whom such a warrant is issued.

Terms of a warrant for arrest R13.2

13.2 A warrant for arrest must require each person to whom it is directed to arrest the defendant and—
(a) bring the defendant to a court—
(i) specified in the warrant, or
(ii) required or allowed by law; or
(b) release the defendant on bail (with conditions or without) to attend court at a date, time and place—
(i) specified in the warrant, or
(ii) to be notified by the court.

[Note. The principal provisions under which the court can issue a warrant for arrest are—

(a) section 4 of the Criminal Procedure (Attendance of Witnesses) Act 1965[1]*;*
(b) section 7 of the Bail Act 1976[2]*;*
(c) sections 1 and 97 of the Magistrates' Courts Act 1980[3]*; and*
(d) sections 79, 80 and 81(4), (5) of the Senior Courts Act 1981[4]*.*

See also section 27A of the Magistrates' Courts Act 1980[5] *(power to transfer criminal proceedings) and section 78(2) of the Senior Courts Act 1981*[6] *(adjournment of Crown Court case to another place).]*

Terms of a warrant for detention or imprisonment R13.3

13.3 (1) A warrant for detention or imprisonment must—
(a) require each person to whom it is directed to detain the defendant and—
(i) take the defendant to any place specified in the warrant or required or allowed by law, and
(ii) deliver the defendant to the custodian of that place; and

[1] 1965 c. 69; section 4 was amended by section 56 of, and paragraph 45 of Schedule 8 to, the Courts Act 1971 (c. 23) and sections 65, 66, 67 and 80 of, and Schedule 5 to, the Criminal Procedure and Investigations Act 1996 (c. 25).
[2] 1976 c. 63; section 7(1A) and (1B) were inserted section 198 of the Extradition Act 2003 (c. 41).
[3] 1980 c. 43; section 1 was amended by section 68 of, and paragraph 6 of Schedule 8 to, the Criminal Justice Act 1991 (c. 53), sections 43 and 109 of, and Schedule 10 to, the Courts Act 2003 (c. 39), section 31 of, and paragraph 12 of Schedule 7 to, the Criminal Justice Act 2003 (c. 44) and section 153 of the Police Reform and Social Responsibility Act 2011. It is further amended by paragraphs 7 and 8 of Schedule 36 to, the Criminal Justice Act 2003 (c. 44), with effect from a date to be appointed. Section 97 was amended by sections 13 and 14 of, and paragraph 7 of Schedule 2 to, the Contempt of Court Act 1981 (c. 47), section 31 of, and paragraph 2 of Schedule 4 to, the Criminal Justice (International Co-operation) Act 1990 (c. 5), sections 17 and 65 of, and paragraph 6 of Schedule 3 and Part I of Schedule 4 to, the Criminal Justice Act 1991 (c. 53), section 51 of the Criminal Procedure and Investigations Act 1996 (c. 25) and section 169 of the Serious Organised Crime and Police Act 2005 (c. 15).
[4] 1981 c. 54; section 80 was amended by paragraph 54 of Schedule 3 to the Criminal Justice Act 2003 (c. 44).
[5] 1980 c. 43; section 27A was inserted by section 46 of the Courts Act 2003 (c. 39).
[6] 1981 c. 54.

(b) require that custodian to detain the defendant, as ordered by the court, until in accordance with the law—
(i) the defendant is delivered to the appropriate court or place, or
(ii) the defendant is released.

(2) Where a magistrates' court remands a defendant to police detention under section 128(7)[7] or section 136[8] of the Magistrates' Courts Act 1980, or to customs detention under section 152 of the Criminal Justice Act 1988[9], the warrant it issues must—
(a) be directed, as appropriate, to—
(i) a constable, or
(ii) an officer of Her Majesty's Revenue and Customs; and
(b) require that constable or officer to detain the defendant—
(i) for a period (not exceeding the maximum permissible) specified in the warrant, or
(ii) until in accordance with the law the defendant is delivered to the appropriate court or place.

(3) Where a magistrates' court sentences a defendant to imprisonment or detention and section 11(3) of the Magistrates' Courts Act 1980[10] applies (custodial sentence imposed in the defendant's absence), the warrant it issues must—
(a) require each person to whom the warrant is directed—
(i) to arrest the defendant and bring him or her to a court specified in the warrant, and
(ii) unless the court then otherwise directs, after that to act as required by paragraph (1)(a) of this rule; and
(b) require the custodian to whom the defendant is delivered in accordance with that paragraph to act as required by paragraph (1)(b) of this rule.

[Note. Under section 128(7) of the Magistrates' Courts Act 1980, a magistrates' court can remand a defendant to police detention for not more than 3 clear days, if the defendant is an adult, or for not more than 24 hours if the defendant is under 18.

Under section 136 of the 1980 Act, a magistrates' court can order a defendant's detention in police custody until the following 8am for non-payment of a fine, etc.

Under section 152 of the Criminal Justice Act 1988, a magistrates' court can remand a defendant to customs detention for not more than 192 hours if the defendant is charged with a drug trafficking offence.]

R13.4 **Information to be included in a warrant**

13.4 (1) A warrant must identify—
(a) each person to whom it is directed;
(b) the defendant against whom it was issued;
(c) the reason for its issue;
(d) the court that issued it, unless that is otherwise recorded by the court officer; and
(e) the court office for the court that issued it.

(2) A warrant for detention or imprisonment must contain a record of any decision by the court under—
(a) section 91 of the Legal Aid, Sentencing and Punishment of Offenders Act 2012[11] (remands of children otherwise than on bail), including in particular—
(i) whether the defendant must be detained in local authority accommodation or youth detention accommodation,
(ii) the local authority designated by the court,
(iii) any requirement imposed by the court on that authority,
(iv) any condition imposed by the court on the defendant, and
(v) the reason for any such requirement or condition;

[7] 1980 c. 43; section 128(7) was amended by section 48 of the Police and Criminal Evidence Act 1984 (c. 60). It is modified by section 91(5) of the Legal Aid, Sentencing and Punishment of Offenders Act 2012 (c. 10).

[8] 1980 c. 43; section 136 was amended by section 77 of, and paragraph 58 of Schedule 14 to, the Criminal Justice Act 1982 (c. 48), section 68 of, and paragraph 6 of Schedule 8 to, the Criminal Justice Act 1991(c. 53), section 95(2) of the Access to Justice Act 1999 (c. 22) and section 165(1) of, and paragraph 78 of Schedule 9 to, the Powers of Criminal Courts (Sentencing) Act 2000 (c. 6). It is further amended by sections 74 and 75 of, and paragraphs 58 and 68 of Schedule 7, and Schedule 8 to, the Criminal Justice and Court Services Act 2000 (c. 43), with effect from a date to be appointed.

[9] 1988 c. 33; section 152 was amended by paragraphs 1 and 17 of Schedule 11 to, the Proceeds of Crime Act 2002 (c. 29) and section 8 of the Drugs Act 2005 (c. 17).

[10] 1980 c. 43; section 11(3) was amended by section 123 of, and paragraph 1 of Schedule 8 to, the Criminal Justice Act 1988 (c. 33), section 168 of, and paragraph 39 of Schedule 10 to, the Criminal Justice and Public Order Act 1994 (c. 33), section 119 of, and paragraph 39 of Schedule 8 to, the Crime and Disorder Act 1998 (c. 37), section 304 of, and paragraphs 25 and 26 of Schedule 32 to, the Criminal Justice Act 2003 (c. 44) and section 54 of the Criminal Justice and Immigration Act 2008 (c. 4).

[11] 2012 c. 10.

(b) section 80 of the Magistrates' Courts Act 1980[12] (application of money found on defaulter to satisfy sum adjudged); or
(c) section 82(1) or (4) of the 1980 Act[13] (conditions for issue of a warrant).

(3) A warrant for detention or imprisonment must include such an indication of the defendant's physical and mental health as may be needed to alert those to whom the warrant is directed—
(a) to any vulnerability of the defendant; and
(b) to any risk to others that may be posed by the defendant.

(4) The indication required by paragraph (3) may be given by reference to an accompanying document.

(5) A warrant that contains an error is not invalid, as long as—
(a) it was issued in respect of a lawful decision by the court; and
(b) it contains enough information to identify that decision.

[Note. See sections 93(7) and 102(5) of the Legal Aid, Sentencing and Punishment of Offenders Act 2012. Under section 91 of the Act, instead of granting bail to a defendant under 18 the court may—

(a) remand him or her to local authority accommodation and, after consulting with that authority, impose on the defendant a condition that the court could impose if granting bail; or
(b) remand him or her to youth detention accommodation, if the defendant is at least 12 years old and the other conditions, about the offence and the defendant, prescribed by the Act are met.

Under section 80 of the Magistrates' Courts Act 1980, the court may decide that any money found on the defendant must not be applied towards payment of the sum for which a warrant is issued under section 76 of that Act (enforcement of sums adjudged to be paid).

See section 82(6) of the 1980 Act. Under section 82(1) and (4), the court may only issue a warrant for the defendant's imprisonment for non-payment of a sum due where it finds that the prescribed conditions are met.

Under section 123 of the 1980 Act[14]*, "no objection shall be allowed to any ... warrant to procure the presence of the defendant, for any defect in it in substance or in form ...".]*

Execution of a warrant R13.5

13.5 (1) A warrant may be executed—
(a) by any person to whom it is directed; or
(b) if the warrant was issued by a magistrates' court, by anyone authorised to do so by section 125[15] (warrants), 125A[16] (civilian enforcement officers) or 125B[17] (execution by approved enforcement agency) of the Magistrates' Courts Act 1980.

(2) The person who executes a warrant must—
(a) explain, in terms the defendant can understand, what the warrant requires, and why;
(b) show the defendant the warrant, if that person has it; and
(c) if the defendant asks—
(i) arrange for the defendant to see the warrant, if that person does not have it, and
(ii) show the defendant any written statement of that person's authority required by section 125A or 125B of the 1980 Act.

[12] 1980 c. 43; section 80 was amended by section 33(1) of, and paragraph 83 of Schedule 2 to, the Family Law Reform Act 1987 (c. 42) and section 62(3) of, and paragraphs 45 and 49 of the Tribunals, Courts and Enforcement Act 2007 (c. 15).
[13] 1980 c. 43; section 82 was amended by section 77 of, and paragraph 52 of Schedule 14 to, the Criminal Justice Act 1982 (c. 48), sections 61 and 123 of, and paragraphs 1 and 2 of Schedule 8 to, the Criminal Justice Act 1988 (c. 33), section 55 of and paragraph 10 of Schedule 4 to the Crime (Sentences) Act 1997 (c. 43), paragraph 220 of Schedule 8 to the Courts Act 2003 (c. 39), section 62 of, and paragraphs 45 and 51 of Schedule 13 to, the Tribunals, Courts and Enforcement Act 2007 (c. 15) and section 179 of the Anti-social Behaviour, Crime and Policing Act 2014 (c. 12) and section 54 of, and paragraphs 2 and 3 of Schedule 12 to, the Criminal Justice and Courts Act 2015 (c. 2). It is further amended by paragraphs 58 and 63 of Part II of Schedule 7 to the Criminal Justice and Court Services Act 2000 (c. 43) and Part 7 of Schedule 37 to the Criminal Justice Act 2003 (c. 44), with effect from dates to be appointed.
[14] 1980 c. 43.
[15] 1980 c. 43; section 125 was amended by section 33 of the Police and Criminal Evidence Act 1984 (c. 60), section 65(1) of the Criminal Justice Act 1988 (c. 33), sections 95(1), 97(4) and 106 of, and Part V of Schedule 15 and Table (8) to, the Access to Justice Act 1999 (c. 22), section 109(1) of, and paragraph 238 of Schedule 8 to, the Courts Act 2003 (c. 39) and sections 62(3), 86 and 146 of and paragraphs 45 and 57 of Schedule 23 to, the Tribunals, Courts and Enforcement Act 2007 (c. 15).
[16] 1980 c. 43; section 125A was inserted by section 92 of the Access to Justice Act 1999 (c. 22) and amended by articles 46 and 52 of S.I. 2006/1737 and article 8 of, and paragraph 5 of the Schedule to, S.I. 2007/2128 and section 62 of, and paragraphs 45 and 58 of Schedule 13 to, the Tribunals, Courts and Enforcement Act 2007 (c. 15).
[17] 1980 c. 43; section 125A was inserted by section 92 of the Access to Justice Act 1999 (c. 22) and amended by articles 46 and 52 of S.I. 2006/1737 and article 8 of, and paragraph 5 of the Schedule to, S.I. 2007/2128 and section 62 of, and paragraphs 45 and 58 of Schedule 13 to, the Tribunals, Courts and Enforcement Act 2007 (c. 15).

(3) The person who executes a warrant of arrest that requires the defendant to be released on bail must—
(a) make a record of—
(i) the defendant's name,
(ii) the reason for the arrest,
(iii) the defendant's release on bail, and
(iv) when and where the warrant requires the defendant to attend court; and
(b) serve the record on—
(i) the defendant, and
(ii) the court officer.

(4) The person who executes a warrant of detention or imprisonment must—
(a) take the defendant—
(i) to any place specified in the warrant, or
(ii) if that is not immediately practicable, to any other place at which the defendant may be lawfully detained (and the warrant then has effect as if it specified that place);
(b) obtain a receipt from the custodian; and
(c) notify the court officer that the defendant has been taken to that place.

[Note. Under section 125 of the Magistrates' Courts Act 1980, a warrant issued by a magistrates' court may be executed by any person to whom it is directed or by any constable acting within that constable's police area.

Certain warrants issued by a magistrates' court may be executed anywhere in England and Wales by a civilian enforcement officer, under section 125A of the 1980 Act; or by an approved enforcement agency, under section 125B of the Act. In either case, the person executing the warrant must, if the defendant asks, show a written statement indicating: that person's name; the authority or agency by which that person is employed, or in which that person is a director or partner; that that person is authorised to execute warrants; and, where section 125B applies, that the agency is registered as one approved by the Lord Chancellor.
See also section 125D of the 1980 Act[18]*, under which—*

(a) a warrant to which section 125A applies may be executed by any person entitled to execute it even though it is not in that person's possession at the time; and
(b) certain other warrants, including any warrant to arrest a person in connection with an offence, may be executed by a constable even though it is not in that constable's possession at the time.]

R13.6 Warrants that cease to have effect on payment

13.6 (1) This rule applies to a warrant issued by a magistrates' court under any of the following provisions of the Magistrates' Courts Act 1980—
(a) section 76[19] (enforcement of sums adjudged to be paid);
(b) section 83[20] (process for securing attendance of offender);
(c) section 86[21] (power of magistrates' court to fix day for appearance of offender at means inquiry, etc.);
(d) section 136[22] (committal to custody overnight at police station for non-payment of sum adjudged by conviction).

[Note. See sections 79[23] *and 125(1) of the Magistrates' Courts Act 1980.]*

(2) The warrant no longer has effect if—
(a) the sum in respect of which the warrant was issued is paid to the person executing it;
(b) that sum is offered to, but refused by, that person; or

[18] 1980 c. 43; section 125D was inserted by section 96 of the Access to Justice Act 1999 (c. 22) and amended by sections 62 and 146 of, and paragraphs 45 and 61 of Schedule 13 to, the Tribunals, Courts and Enforcement Act 2007 (c. 15).
[19] 1980 c. 43: section 76 was amended by section 7 of the Maintenance Enforcement Act 1991 (c. 17); section 78 of, and Schedule 16 to, the Criminal Justice Act 1982 (c. 48), and section 62(3) of, and paragraphs 45 and 46 of Schedule 13 to, the Tribunals, Courts and Enforcement Act 2007 (c. 15).
[20] 1980 c. 43; section 83 was amended by articles 46 and 47 of S.I. 2006/1737 and sections 97(2) and 106 of, and Part V (table 8) of Schedule 15 to, the Access to Justice Act 1999 (c. 22).
[21] 1980 c. 43; section 86 was amended by section 51(2) of the Criminal Justice Act 1982 (c. 48) and section 97(3) of the Access to Justice Act 1999 (c. 22).
[22] 1980 c. 43; section 82 was amended by section 77 of, and paragraph 52 of Schedule 14 to, the Criminal Justice Act 1982 (c. 48), sections 61 and 123 of, and paragraphs 1 and 2 of Schedule 8 to, the Criminal Justice Act 1988 (c. 33), section 55 of and paragraph 10 of Schedule 4 to the Crime (Sentences) Act 1997 (c. 43), paragraph 220 of Schedule 8 to the Courts Act 2003 (c. 39), section 62 of, and paragraphs 45 and 51 of Schedule 13 to, the Tribunals, Courts and Enforcement Act 2007 (c. 15), section 179 of the Anti-social Behaviour, Crime and Policing Act 2014 (c. 12) and section 54 of, and paragraphs 2 and 3 of Schedule 12 to, the Criminal Justice and Courts Act 2015 (c. 2). It is further amended by paragraphs 58 and 63 of Part II of Schedule 7 to the Criminal Justice and Court Services Act 2000 (c. 43) and Part 7 of Schedule 37 to the Criminal Justice Act 2003 (c. 44), with effect from dates to be appointed.
[23] 1980 c. 43; section 79 was amended by paragraph 219 of Schedule 8 to the Courts Act 2003 (c. 39) and section 62 of, and paragraphs 45, 47 and 48 of Schedule 13 to, the Tribunals, Courts and Enforcement Act 2007 (c. 15).

(c) that person is shown a receipt for that sum given by—
(i) the court officer, or
(ii) the authority to which that sum is due.

Warrant issued when the court office is closed R13.7

13.7 (1) This rule applies where the court issues a warrant when the court office is closed.
(2) The applicant for the warrant must, not more than 72 hours later, serve on the court officer—
(a) a copy of the warrant; and
(b) any written material that was submitted to the court.

Criminal Procedure Rules Part 14 Bail and Custody Time Limits

General rules

When this Part applies R14.1

14.1 (1) This Part applies where a magistrates' court or the Crown Court can—
(a) grant or withhold bail, or impose or vary a condition of bail; and
(b) where bail has been withheld, extend a custody time limit.
(2) Rules 14.18, 14.19 and 14.20 apply where a magistrates' court can authorise an extension of the period for which a defendant is released on bail before being charged with an offence.
(3) In this Part, 'defendant' includes a person who has been granted bail by a police officer.

[Note. See in particular—
(a) the Bail Act 1976[1]*;*
(b) section 128 of the Magistrates' Courts Act 1980[2] *(general powers of magistrates' courts in relation to bail);*
(c) section 81 of the Senior Courts Act 1981[3] *(general powers of the Crown Court in relation to bail);*
(d) section 115 of the Coroners and Justice Act 2009[4] *(exclusive power of the Crown Court to grant bail to a defendant charged with murder);*
(e) section 22 of the Prosecution of Offences Act 1985[5] *(provision for custody time limits);*
(f) the Prosecution of Offences (Custody Time Limits) Regulations 1987[6] *(maximum periods during which a defendant may be kept in custody pending trial); and*
(g) sections 47ZF and 47ZG of the Police and Criminal Evidence Act 1984[7] *(extensions by court of pre-charge bail time limit).*

At the end of this Part there is a summary of the general entitlement to bail and of the exceptions to that entitlement

[1] 1976 c. 63.
[2] 1980 c. 43; section 128 was amended by section 59 to, and paragraphs 2, 3 and 4 of Schedule 9 to, the Criminal Justice Act 1982 (c. 48), section 48 of the Police and Criminal Evidence Act 1984 (c. 60), section 170(1) of, and paragraphs 65 and 69 of Schedule 15 to, the Criminal Justice Act 1988 (c. 33), section 125(3) of, and paragraph 25 of Schedule 18 to, the Courts and Legal Services Act 1990 (c. 41), sections 49, 52 and 80 of, and Schedule 5 to, the Criminal Procedure and Investigations Act 1996 (c. 25), paragraph 75 of Schedule 9 to the Powers of Criminal Courts (Sentencing) Act 2000 (c. 6) and paragraph 51 of Schedule 3 and Part 4 of Schedule 37 to the Criminal Justice Act 2003 (c. 44). It is modified by section 91(5) of the Legal Aid, Sentencing and Punishment of Offenders Act 2012 (c. 10).
[3] 1981 c. 54; section 81(1) was amended by sections 29 and 60 of the Criminal Justice Act 1982 (c. 48), section 15 of, and paragraph 2 of Schedule 12 to, the Criminal Justice Act 1987 (c. 38), section 168 of, and paragraph 19 of Schedule 9 and paragraph 48 of Schedule 10 to, the Criminal Justice and Public Order Act 1994 (c. 33), section 119 of, and paragraph 48 of Schedule 8 and Schedule 10 to, the Crime and Disorder Act 1998 (c. 37), section 165 of, and paragraph 87 of Schedule 9 and Schedule 12 to, the Powers of Criminal Courts (Sentencing) Act 2000 (c. 6), paragraph 54 of Schedule 3, paragraph 4 of Schedule 36 and Part 4 of Schedule 37 to the Criminal Justice Act 2003 (c. 44), articles 2 and 6 of S.I. 2004/1033 and section 177(1) of, and paragraph 76 of Schedule 21 to, the Coroners and Justice Act 2009 (c. 25).
[4] 2009 c. 25.
[5] 1985 c. 23; section 22 was amended by paragraph 104 of Schedule 15 to the Criminal Justice Act 1988 (c. 33), section 43 of the Crime and Disorder Act 1998 (c. 37), paragraph 36 of Schedule 11 to the Criminal Justice Act 1991 (c. 53), paragraph 27 of Schedule 9 to the Criminal Justice and Public Order Act 1994 (c. 33), section 71 of the Criminal Procedure and Investigations Act 1996 (c. 25), section 67(3) of the Access to Justice Act 1999 (c. 22), section 70 of, and paragraph 57 of Schedule 3 and paragraphs 49 and 51 of Schedule 36 to, the Criminal Justice Act 2003 (c. 44), section 59 of, and paragraph 1 of Schedule 11 to, the Constitutional Reform Act 2005 (c. 4) and paragraph 22 of Schedule 12 to the Legal Aid, Sentencing and Punishment of Offenders Act 2012 (c. 10).
[6] S.I. 1987/299; amended by sections 71 and 80 of, and paragraph 8 of Schedule 5 to, the Criminal Procedure and Investigations Act 1996 (c. 25) and S.I. 1989/767, 1991/1515, 1995/555, 1999/2744, 2000/3284, 2012/1344.
[7] 1984 c. 60; sections 47ZF and 47ZG were inserted by section 63 of the Policing and Crime Act 2017 (c. 3).

R14.2 **Exercise of court's powers: general**

14.2 (1) The court must not make a decision to which this Part applies unless—
(a) each party to the decision and any surety directly affected by the decision—
(i) is present, in person or by live link, or
(ii) has had an opportunity to make representations;
(b) on an application for bail by a defendant who is absent and in custody, the court is satisfied that the defendant—
(i) has waived the right to attend, or
(ii) was present when a court withheld bail in the case on a previous occasion and has been in custody continuously since then;
(c) on a prosecutor's appeal against a grant of bail, application to extend a custody time limit or appeal against a refusal to extend such a time limit—
(i) the court is satisfied that a defendant who is absent has waived the right to attend, or
(ii) the court is satisfied that it would be just to proceed even though the defendant is absent; and
(d) the court is satisfied that sufficient time has been allowed—
(i) for the defendant to consider the information provided by the prosecutor under rule 14.5(2), and
(ii) for the court to consider the parties' representations and make the decision required.

(2) The court may make a decision to which this Part applies at a hearing, in public or in private.

(3) The court may determine without a hearing an application to vary a condition of bail if—
(a) the parties to the application have agreed the terms of the variation proposed; or
(b) on an application by a defendant, the court determines the application no sooner than the fifth business day after the application was served.

(4) The court may adjourn a determination to which this Part applies, if that is necessary to obtain information sufficient to allow the court to make the decision required.

(5) At any hearing at which the court makes one of the following decisions, the court must announce in terms the defendant can understand (with help, if necessary), and by reference to the circumstances of the defendant and the case, its reasons for—
(a) withholding bail, or imposing or varying a bail condition;
(b) granting bail, where the prosecutor opposed the grant; or
(c) where the defendant is under 18—
(i) imposing or varying a bail condition when ordering the defendant to be detained in local authority accommodation, or
(ii) ordering the defendant to be detained in youth detention accommodation.

(6) At any hearing at which the court grants bail, the court must—
(a) tell the defendant where and when to surrender to custody; or
(b) arrange for the court officer to give the defendant, as soon as practicable, notice of where and when to surrender to custody.

(7) This rule does not apply on an application to a magistrates' court to authorise an extension of pre-charge bail.

[Note. See section 5 of the Bail Act 1976 and sections 93(7) and 102(4) of the Legal Aid, Sentencing and Punishment of Offenders Act 2012[8]*.*

Under sections 57A and 57B of the Crime and Disorder Act 1998[9]*, a defendant is to be treated as present in court when, by virtue of a live link direction within the meaning of those provisions, he or she attends a hearing through a live link.*

Under section 91 of the 2012 Act, instead of granting bail to a defendant under 18 the court may—

(a) remand him or her to local authority accommodation and, after consulting with that authority, impose on the defendant a condition that the court could impose if granting bail; or
(b) remand him or her to youth detention accommodation, if the defendant is at least 12 years old and the other conditions, about the offence and the defendant, prescribed by the Act are met.

See also rule 14.18 (Exercise of court's powers: extension of pre-charge bail).]

[8] 2012 c. 10.

[9] 1998 c. 37; sections 57A to 57E were substituted for section 57 as originally enacted by section 45 of the Police and Justice Act 2006 (c. 48), and amended by sections 106, 109 and 178 of, and Part 3 of Schedule 23 to, the Coroners and Justice Act 2009 (c. 25). Section 57A was further amended by paragraphs 36 and 39 of Schedule 12 to the Legal Aid, Sentencing and Punishment of Offenders Act 2012 (c. 10).

Duty of justices' legal adviser R14.3

14.3 (1) This rule applies—
(a) only in a magistrates' court; and
(b) unless the court—
(i) includes a District Judge (Magistrates' Courts), and
(ii) otherwise directs.
(2) A justices' legal adviser must—
(a) assist an unrepresented defendant;
(b) give the court such advice as is required to enable it to exercise its powers; and
(c) if required, attend the members of the court outside the courtroom to give such advice, but inform the parties of any advice so given.

[Note. For the functions of a justices' legal adviser, see sections 28 and 29 of the Courts Act 2003[10].]

General duties of court officer R14.4

14.4 (1) The court officer must arrange for a note or other record to be made of—
(a) the parties' representations about bail; and
(b) the court's reasons for a decision—
(i) to withhold bail, or to impose or vary a bail condition,
(ii) to grant bail, where the prosecutor opposed the grant or,
(iii) on an application to which rule 14.19 applies (Application to authorise extension of pre-charge bail).
(2) The court officer must serve notice of a decision about bail on—
(a) the defendant (but, in the Crown Court, only where the defendant's legal representative asks for such a notice, or where the defendant has no legal representative);
(b) the prosecutor (but only where the court granted bail, the prosecutor opposed the grant, and the prosecutor asks for such a notice);
(c) a party to the decision who was absent when it was made;
(d) a surety who is directly affected by the decision;
(e) the defendant's custodian, where the defendant is in custody and the decision requires the custodian—
(i) to release the defendant (or will do so, if a requirement ordered by the court is met), or
(ii) to transfer the defendant to the custody of another custodian; and
(f) the court officer for any other court at which the defendant is required by that decision to surrender to custody.
(3) Where the court postpones the date on which a defendant who is on bail must surrender to custody, the court officer must serve notice of the postponed date on—
(a) the defendant; and
(b) any surety.
(4) Where a magistrates' court withholds bail in a case to which section 5(6A)[11] of the Bail Act 1976 applies (remand in custody after hearing full argument on an application for bail), the court officer must serve on the defendant a certificate that the court heard full argument.
(5) Where the court determines without a hearing an application to which rule 14.21 applies (Application to authorise extension of pre-charge bail), the court officer must—
(a) if the court allows the application, notify the applicant; and
(b) if the court refuses the application, notify the applicant and the defendant.

[Note. See section 5 of the Bail Act 1976[12]; section 43 of the Magistrates' Courts Act 1980[13]; and section 52 of the Mental Health Act 1983[14].]

[10] 2003 c. 39; section 28 was amended by section 15 of, and paragraphs 308 and 327 of Schedule 4 to, the Constitutional Reform Act 2005 (c. 4).
[11] 1976 c. 63; section 5(6A) was inserted by section 60 of the Criminal Justice Act 1982 (c. 48) and amended by section 165 of, and paragraph 53 of Schedule 9 to, the Powers of Criminal Courts (Sentencing) Act 2000 (c. 6) and by paragraph 48 of Schedule 3, paragraphs 1 and 2 of Schedule 36, and Part 4 of Schedule 37 to the Criminal Justice Act 2003 (c. 44).
[12] 1976 c. 63; section 5 was amended by section 65 of, and Schedule 12 to, the Criminal Law Act 1977 (c. 45), section 60 of the Criminal Justice Act 1982 (c. 48), paragraph 1 of Schedule 3 to the Criminal Justice and Public Order Act 1994 (c. 33), paragraph 53 of Schedule 9 to the Powers of Criminal Courts (Sentencing) Act 2000 (c. 6), section 129(1) of the Criminal Justice and Police Act 2001 (c. 16), paragraph 182 of Schedule 8 to the Courts Act 2003 (c. 39), paragraph 48 of Schedule 3, paragraphs 1 and 2 of Schedule 36, and Parts 2, 4 and 12 of Schedule 37 to the Criminal Justice Act 2003 (c. 44) and section 208 of, and paragraphs 33 and 35 of Schedule 21 to, the Legal Services Act 2007 (c. 27).
[13] 1980 c. 43; section 43 was substituted by section 47 of the Police and Criminal Evidence Act 1984 (c. 60) and amended by paragraph 43 of Schedule 10 to the Criminal Justice and Public Order Act 1994 (c. 33) and paragraph 206 of Schedule 8 to the Courts Act 2003 (c. 39).
[14] 1983 c. 20; section 52 was amended by paragraph 55 of Schedule 3 and Schedule 37 to the Criminal Justice Act 2003 (c. 44), section 11 of the Mental Health Act 2007 (c. 12) and paragraphs 53 and 57 of Schedule 21 to the Legal Services Act 2007 (c. 29).

Bail

R14.5 Prosecutor's representations about bail

14.5 (1) This rule applies whenever the court can grant or withhold bail.
(2) The prosecutor must as soon as practicable—
(a) provide the defendant with all the information in the prosecutor's possession which is material to what the court must decide; and
(b) provide the court with the same information.
(3) A prosecutor who opposes the grant of bail must specify—
(a) each exception to the general right to bail on which the prosecutor relies; and
(b) each consideration that the prosecutor thinks relevant.
(4) A prosecutor who wants the court to impose a condition on any grant of bail must—
(a) specify each condition proposed; and
(b) explain what purpose would be served by such a condition.

[Note. A summary of the general entitlement to bail and of the exceptions to that entitlement is at the end of this Part.]

R14.6 Reconsideration of police bail by magistrates' court

14.6 (1) This rule applies where—
(a) a party wants a magistrates' court to reconsider a bail decision by a police officer after the defendant is charged with an offence; and
(b) a defendant wants a magistrates' court to reconsider a bail condition imposed by a police officer before the defendant is charged with an offence.
(2) An application under this rule must be made to—
(a) the magistrates' court to whose custody the defendant is under a duty to surrender, if any; or
(b) any magistrates' court acting for the police officer's local justice area, in any other case.
(3) The applicant party must—
(a) apply in writing; and
(b) serve the application on—
(i) the court officer,
(ii) the other party, and
(iii) any surety affected or proposed.
(4) The application must—
(a) specify—
(i) the decision that the applicant wants the court to make,
(ii) each offence charged, or for which the defendant was arrested, and
(iii) the police bail decision to be reconsidered and the reasons given for it;
(b) explain, as appropriate—
(i) why the court should grant bail itself, or withdraw it, or impose or vary a condition, and
(ii) if the applicant is the prosecutor, what material information has become available since the police bail decision was made;
(c) propose the terms of any suggested condition of bail; and
(d) if the applicant wants an earlier hearing than paragraph (7) requires, ask for that, and explain why it is needed.
(5) A prosecutor who applies under this rule must serve on the defendant, with the application, notice that the court has power to withdraw bail and, if the defendant is absent when the court makes its decision, order the defendant's arrest.
(6) A party who opposes an application must—
(a) so notify the court officer and the applicant at once; and
(b) serve on each notice of the reasons for opposition.
(7) Unless the court otherwise directs, the court officer must arrange for the court to hear the application as soon as practicable and in any event—
(a) if it is an application to withdraw bail, no later than the second business day after it was served; and
(b) in any other case, no later than the fifth business day after it was served.
(8) The court may—
(a) vary or waive a time limit under this rule;
(b) allow an application to be in a different form to one set out in the Practice Direction; and
(c) if rule 14.2 allows, determine without a hearing an application to vary a condition.

[Note. The Practice Direction sets out a form of application for use in connection with this rule.

Under section 5B of the Bail Act 1976[15]*—*

(a) where a defendant has been charged with an offence which can be tried in the Crown Court; or
(b) in an extradition case,

on application by the prosecutor a magistrates' court may withdraw bail granted by a constable, impose conditions of bail, or vary conditions of bail. See also sections 37, 37C(2)(b), 37CA(2)(b), 46A and 47(1B) of the Police and Criminal Evidence Act 1984[16]*.*

Under section 43B of the Magistrates' Courts Act 1980[17]*, where a defendant has been charged with an offence, on application by the defendant a magistrates' court may grant bail itself, in substitution for bail granted by a custody officer, or vary the conditions of bail granted by a custody officer. See also sections 37, 37C(2)(b), 37CA(2)(b), 46A and 47(1C), (1D) of the Police and Criminal Evidence Act 1984*[18]*.*

Under section 47(1E) of the Police and Criminal Evidence Act 1984[19]*, where a defendant has been released on bail by a custody officer without being charged with an offence, on application by the defendant a magistrates' court may vary any conditions of that bail. See also sections 37, 37C(2)(b), 37CA(2)(b), 46A and 47(1C) of the Act.]*

Notice of application to consider bail **R14.7**

14.7 (1) This rule applies where—
(a) in a magistrates' court—
(i) a prosecutor wants the court to withdraw bail granted by the court, or to impose or vary a condition of such bail, or
(ii) a defendant wants the court to reconsider such bail before the next hearing in the case; and
(b) in the Crown Court,
(i) a party wants the court to grant bail that has been withheld, or to withdraw bail that has been granted, or to impose a new bail condition or to vary a present one, or
(ii) a prosecutor wants the court to consider whether to grant or withhold bail, or impose or vary a condition of bail, under section 88 or section 89 of the Criminal Justice Act 2003[20] (bail and custody in connection with an intended application to the Court of Appeal to which Part 27 (Retrial after acquittal) applies).

(2) Such a party must—
(a) apply in writing;
(b) serve the application on—
(i) the court officer,
(ii) the other party, and
(iii) any surety affected or proposed; and
(c) serve the application not less than 2 business days before any hearing in the case at which the applicant wants the court to consider it, if such a hearing is already due.

[15] 1976 c. 63; section 5B was inserted by section 30 of the Criminal Justice and Public Order Act 1994 (c. 33) and amended by section 129(3) of the Criminal Justice and Police Act 2001 (c. 16), section 109 of, and paragraph 183 of Schedule 8 and Schedule 10 to, the Courts Act 2003 (c. 39) and section 198 of the Extradition Act 2003 (c. 41).

[16] 1984 c. 60; section 37 was amended by section 108(7) of, and Schedule 15 to, the Children Act 1989 (c. 41), sections 72 and 101(2) of, and Schedule 13 to, the Criminal Justice Act 1991 (c. 53), sections 29(4) and 168(3) of, and Schedule 11 to, the Criminal Justice and Public Order Act 1994 (c. 33), section 28 of, and paragraphs 1 and 2 of Schedule 2 to, the Criminal Justice Act 2003 (c. 44), section 23(1) of, and paragraphs 1 and 2 of Schedule 1 to, the Drugs Act 2005 (c. 17) and sections 11 and 52 of, and paragraph 9 of Schedule 14 to, the Police and Justice Act 2006 (c. 48). Section 37C was inserted by section 28 of, and paragraphs 1 and 3 of Schedule 2 to, the Criminal Justice Act 2003 (c. 44). Section 37CA was inserted by section 10 of, and paragraphs 1 and 8 of Schedule 6 to, the Police and Justice Act 2006 (c. 48). Section 46A was inserted by section 29 of the Criminal Justice and Public Order Act 1994 (c. 33), and amended by section 28 of, and paragraphs 1 and 5 of Schedule 2 to, the Criminal Justice Act 2003 (c. 44), sections 10 and 46 of, and paragraphs 1 and 7 of Schedule 6 to, the Police and Justice Act 2006 (c. 48) and sections 107 and 178 of, and Part 3 of Schedule 3 to, the Coroners and Justice Act 2009 (c. 25). Section 47(1B) was inserted by section 28 of, and paragraphs 1 and 6 of Schedule 2 to, the Criminal Justice Act 2003 (c. 44) and amended by section 10 of, and paragraphs 1 and 11 of Schedule 6 to, the Police and Justice Act 2006 (c. 48).

[17] 1980 c. 43; section 43B was inserted by section 27 of, and paragraph 3 of Schedule 3 to, the Criminal Justice and Public Order Act 1994 (c. 33).

[18] 1984 c. 60; section 47(1C) and (1D) were inserted by section 28 of, and paragraphs 1 and 6 of Schedule 2 to, the Criminal Justice Act 2003 (c. 44), and section 47(1C) was amended by section 10 of, and paragraphs 1 and 11 of Schedule 6 to, the Police and Justice Act 2006 (c. 48).

[19] 1984 c. 60; section 47(1E) was inserted by section 28 of, and paragraphs 1 and 6 of Schedule 2 to, the Criminal Justice Act 2003 (c. 44).

[20] 2003 c. 44; section 88 is amended by section 148 of, and paragraphs 59 and 63 of Schedule 26 to, the Criminal Justice and Immigration Act 2008 (c. 4), with effect from a date to be appointed. Section 89 was amended by section 59 of, and paragraph 1 of Schedule 11 to, the Constitutional Reform Act 2005 (c. 4). It is further amended by section 148 of, and paragraphs 59 and 63 of Schedule 26 to, the Criminal Justice and Immigration Act 2008 (c. 4), with effect from a date to be appointed.

(3) The application must—
(a) specify—
(i) the decision that the applicant wants the court to make,
(ii) each offence charged, and
(iii) each relevant previous bail decision and the reasons given for each;
(b) if the applicant is a defendant, explain—
(i) as appropriate, why the court should not withhold bail, or why it should vary a condition, and
(ii) what further information or legal argument, if any, has become available since the most recent previous bail decision was made;
(c) if the applicant is the prosecutor, explain—
(i) as appropriate, why the court should withdraw bail, or impose or vary a condition, and
(ii) what material information has become available since the most recent previous bail decision was made;
(d) propose the terms of any suggested condition of bail; and
(e) if the applicant wants an earlier hearing than paragraph (6) requires, ask for that, and explain why it is needed.

(4) A prosecutor who applies under this rule must serve on the defendant, with the application, notice that the court has power to withdraw bail and, if the defendant is absent when the court makes its decision, order the defendant's arrest.

(5) A party who opposes an application must—
(a) so notify the court officer and the applicant at once; and
(b) serve on each notice of the reasons for opposition.

(6) Unless the court otherwise directs, the court officer must arrange for the court to hear the application as soon as practicable and in any event—
(a) if it is an application to grant or withdraw bail, no later than the second business day after it was served; and
(b) if it is an application to impose or vary a condition, no later than the fifth business day after it was served.

(7) The court may—
(a) vary or waive a time limit under this rule;
(b) allow an application to be in a different form to one set out in the Practice Direction, or to be made orally; and
(c) if rule 14.2 allows, determine without a hearing an application to vary a condition.

[Note. The Practice Direction sets out a form of application for use in connection with this rule,

In addition to the court's general powers in relation to bail—
(a) under section 3(8) of the Bail Act 1976(), on application by either party the court may impose a bail condition or vary a condition it has imposed. Until the Crown Court makes its first bail decision in the case, a magistrates' court may vary a condition which it imposed on committing or sending a defendant for Crown Court trial.
(b) under section 5B of the Bail Act 1976(), where the defendant is on bail and the offence is one which can be tried in the Crown Court, or in an extradition case, on application by the prosecutor a magistrates' court may withdraw bail, impose conditions of bail or vary the conditions of bail.
(c) under sections 88 and 89 of the Criminal Justice Act 2003, the Crown Court may remand in custody, or grant bail to, a defendant pending an application to the Court of Appeal for an order for retrial under section 77 of that Act.

Under Part IIA of Schedule 1 to the Bail Act 1976(), if the court withholds bail then at the first hearing after that the defendant may support an application for bail with any argument as to fact or law, whether or not that argument has been advanced before. At subsequent hearings, the court need not hear arguments which it has heard previously.]

R14.8 Defendant's application or appeal to the Crown Court after magistrates' court bail decision

14.8 (1) This rule applies where a defendant wants to—
(a) apply to the Crown Court for bail after a magistrates' court has withheld bail; or
(b) appeal to the Crown Court after a magistrates' court has refused to vary a bail condition as the defendant wants.

(2) The defendant must—
(a) apply to the Crown Court in writing as soon as practicable after the magistrates' court's decision; and
(b) serve the application on—

(i) the Crown Court officer,
(ii) the magistrates' court officer,
(iii) the prosecutor, and
(iv) any surety affected or proposed.

(3) The application must—
(a) specify—
(i) the decision that the applicant wants the Crown Court to make, and
(ii) each offence charged;
(b) explain—
(i) as appropriate, why the Crown Court should not withhold bail, or why it should vary the condition under appeal, and
(ii) what further information or legal argument, if any, has become available since the magistrates' court's decision;
(c) propose the terms of any suggested condition of bail;
(d) if the applicant wants an earlier hearing than paragraph (6) requires, ask for that, and explain why it is needed; and
(e) on an application for bail, attach a copy of the certificate of full argument served on the defendant under rule 14.4(4).

(4) The magistrates' court officer must as soon as practicable serve on the Crown Court officer—
(a) a copy of the note or record made under rule 14.4(1) in connection with the magistrates' court's decision; and
(b) the date of the next hearing, if any, in the magistrates' court.

(5) A prosecutor who opposes the application must—
(a) so notify the Crown Court officer and the defendant at once; and
(b) serve on each notice of the reasons for opposition.

(6) Unless the Crown Court otherwise directs, the court officer must arrange for the court to hear the application or appeal as soon as practicable and in any event no later than the business day after it was served.

(7) The Crown Court may vary a time limit under this rule.

[Note. The Practice Direction sets out a form of application for use in connection with this rule.

Under section 81 of the Senior Courts Act 1981[21]*, the Crown Court may grant bail in a magistrates' court case in which the magistrates' court has withheld bail.*

Under section 16 of the Criminal Justice Act 2003[22]*, a defendant may appeal to the Crown Court against a bail condition imposed by a magistrates' court only where—*

(a) the condition is one that the defendant must—
(i) live and sleep at a specified place, or away from a specified place,
(ii) give a surety or a security,
(iii) stay indoors between specified hours,
(iv) comply with electronic monitoring requirements, or
(v) make no contact with a specified person; and
(b) the magistrates' court has determined an application by either party to vary that condition.

In an extradition case, where a magistrates' court withholds bail or imposes bail conditions, on application by the defendant the High Court may grant bail, or vary the conditions, under section 22 of the Criminal Justice Act 1967[23]*. For the procedure in the High Court, see Schedule 1 to the Civil Procedure Rules 1998 (RSC Order 79)*[24]*.]*

[21] 1981 c. 54; section 81(1) was amended by sections 29 and 60 of the Criminal Justice Act 1982 (c. 48), section 15 of, and paragraph 2 of Schedule 12 to, the Criminal Justice Act 1987 (c. 38), section 168 of, and paragraph 19 of Schedule 9 and paragraph 48 of Schedule 10 to, the Criminal Justice and Public Order Act 1994 (c. 33), section 119 of, and paragraph 48 of Schedule 8 and Schedule 10 to, the Crime and Disorder Act 1998 (c. 37), section 165 of, and paragraph 87 of Schedule 9 and Schedule 12 to, the Powers of Criminal Courts (Sentencing) Act 2000 (c. 6), paragraph 54 of Schedule 3, paragraph 4 of Schedule 36 and Part 4 of Schedule 37 to the Criminal Justice Act 2003 (c. 44), articles 2 and 6 of S.I. 2004/1033 and section 177(1) of, and paragraph 76 of Schedule 21 to, the Coroners and Justice Act 2009 (c. 25).
[22] 2003 c. 44.
[23] 1967 c. 80; section 22 was amended by section 56 of, and paragraph 48 of Schedule 8 and Schedule 11 to, the Courts Act 1971 (c. 23), section 12 of, and paragraphs 36 and 37 of Schedule 2 and Schedule 3 to, the Bail Act 1976 (c. 63), section 65 of, and Schedules 12 and 13 to, the Criminal Law Act 1977 (c. 45), paragraph 15 of Schedule 10 to the Criminal Justice and Public Order Act 1994 (c. 33), sections 17 and 332 of, and Schedule 37 to, the Criminal Justice Act 2003 (c. 44) and section 42 of, and paragraph 27 of Schedule 13 to, the Police and Justice Act 2006 (c. 48).
[24] S.I. 1998/3132; Schedule 1 RSC Order 79 was amended by S.I. 1999/1008, 2001/256, 2003/3361 and 2005/617.

R14.9 Prosecutor's appeal against grant of bail

14.9 (1) This rule applies where a prosecutor wants to appeal—
(a) to the Crown Court against a grant of bail by a magistrates' court, in a case in which the defendant has been charged with, or convicted of, an offence punishable with imprisonment; or
(b) to the High Court against a grant of bail—
(i) by a magistrates' court, in an extradition case, or
(ii) by the Crown Court, in a case in which the defendant has been charged with, or convicted of, an offence punishable with imprisonment (but not in a case in which the Crown Court granted bail on an appeal to which paragraph (1)(a) applies).
(2) The prosecutor must tell the court which has granted bail of the decision to appeal—
(a) at the end of the hearing during which the court granted bail; and
(b) before the defendant is released on bail.
(3) The court which has granted bail must exercise its power to remand the defendant in custody pending determination of the appeal.
(4) The prosecutor must serve an appeal notice—
(a) on the court officer for the court which has granted bail and on the defendant; and
(b) not more than 2 hours after telling that court of the decision to appeal.
(5) The appeal notice must specify—
(a) each offence with which the defendant is charged;
(b) the decision under appeal;
(c) the reasons given for the grant of bail; and
(d) the grounds of appeal.
(6) On an appeal to the Crown Court, the magistrates' court officer must, as soon as practicable, serve on the Crown Court officer—
(a) the appeal notice;
(b) a copy of the note or record made under rule 14.4(1) (record of bail decision); and
(c) notice of the date of the next hearing in the court which has granted bail.
(7) If the Crown Court so directs, the Crown Court officer must arrange for the defendant to be assisted by the Official Solicitor in a case in which the defendant—
(a) has no legal representative; and
(b) asks for such assistance.
(8) On an appeal to the Crown Court, the Crown Court officer must arrange for the court to hear the appeal as soon as practicable and in any event no later than the second business day after the appeal notice was served.
(9) The prosecutor—
(a) may abandon an appeal to the Crown Court without the court's permission, by serving a notice of abandonment, signed by or on behalf of the prosecutor, on—
(i) the defendant,
(ii) the Crown Court officer, and
(iii) the magistrates' court officer
before the hearing of the appeal begins; but
(b) after the hearing of the appeal begins, may only abandon the appeal with the Crown Court's permission.
(10) The court officer for the court which has granted bail must instruct the defendant's custodian to release the defendant on the bail granted by that court, subject to any condition or conditions of bail imposed, if—
(a) the prosecutor fails to serve an appeal notice within the time to which paragraph (4) refers; or
(b) the prosecutor serves a notice of abandonment under paragraph (9).

[Note. See section 1 of the Bail (Amendment) Act 1993[25]*. The time limit for serving an appeal notice is prescribed by section 1(5) of the Act. It may be neither extended nor shortened.*

For the procedure in the High Court, see Schedule 1 to the Civil Procedure Rules 1998 (RSC Order 79, rule 9) and the Practice Direction which supplements that Order. Under those provisions, the prosecutor must file in the High Court, among other things—

[25] 1993 c. 26; section 1 was amended by sections 200 and 220 of, and Schedule 4 to, the Extradition Act 2003 (c. 41), section 18 of the Criminal Justice Act 2003 (c. 44), section 15 of, and paragraph 231 of Schedule 4 to, the Constitutional Reform Act 2005 (c. 4), section 42 of, and paragraph 28 of Schedule 13 to, the Police and Justice Act 2006 (c. 48) and paragraph 32 of Schedule 11 to the Legal Aid, Sentencing and Punishment of Offenders Act 2012 (c. 10).

(a) *a copy of the appeal notice served by the prosecutor under rule 14.9(4);*
(b) *notice of the Crown Court decision to grant bail served on the prosecutor under rule 14.4(2); and*
(c) *notice of the date of the next hearing in the Crown Court.]*

Consideration of bail in a murder case R14.10

14.10 (1) This rule applies in a case in which—
(a) the defendant is charged with murder; and
(b) the Crown Court has not yet considered bail.
(2) The magistrates' court officer must arrange with the Crown Court officer for the Crown Court to consider bail as soon as practicable and in any event no later than the second business day after—
(a) a magistrates' court sends the defendant to the Crown Court for trial; or
(b) the first hearing in the magistrates' court, if the defendant is not at once sent for trial.

[Note. See section 115 of the Coroners and Justice Act 2009[26].]

Condition of residence R14.11

14.11 (1) The defendant must notify the prosecutor of the address at which the defendant will live and sleep if released on bail with a condition of residence—
(a) as soon as practicable after the institution of proceedings, unless already done; and
(b) as soon as practicable after any change of that address.
(2) The prosecutor must help the court to assess the suitability of an address proposed as a condition of residence.

Electronic monitoring requirements R14.12

14.12 (1) This rule applies where the court imposes electronic monitoring requirements, where available, as a condition of bail.
(2) The court officer must—
(a) inform the person responsible for the monitoring ('the monitor') of—
(i) the defendant's name, and telephone number if available,
(ii) each offence with which the defendant is charged,
(iii) details of the place at which the defendant's presence must be monitored,
(iv) the period or periods during which the defendant's presence at that place must be monitored, and
(v) if fixed, the date on which the defendant must surrender to custody;
(b) inform the defendant and, where the defendant is under 16, an appropriate adult, of the monitor's identity and the means by which the monitor may be contacted; and
(c) notify the monitor of any subsequent—
(i) variation or termination of the electronic monitoring requirements, or
(ii) fixing or variation of the date on which the defendant must surrender to custody.

[Note. Under section 3(6ZAA) of the Bail Act 1976[27], the conditions of bail that the court may impose include requirements for the electronic monitoring of a defendant's compliance with other bail conditions, for example a curfew. Sections 3AA and 3AB of the 1976 Act[28] set out conditions for imposing such requirements.

Under section 3AC of the 1976 Act[29], where the court imposes electronic monitoring requirements they must provide for the appointment of a monitor.]

Accommodation or support requirements R14.13

14.13 (1) This rule applies where the court imposes as a condition of bail a requirement, where available, that the defendant must—
(a) reside in accommodation provided for that purpose by, or on behalf of, a public authority; or
(b) receive bail support provided by, or on behalf of, a public authority.

26 2009 c. 25.
27 1976 c. 63; 1976 c. 63; section 3(6ZAA) was substituted, with sub-section (6ZAB), for sub-section (6ZAA) as inserted by section 131 of the Criminal Justice and Police Act 2001 (c. 16) by section 51 of, and paragraphs 1 and 2 of Schedule 11 to, the Criminal Justice and Immigration Act 2008 (c. 4) and amended by paragraphs 1 and 3 of Schedule 11 to the Legal Aid, Sentencing and Punishment of Offenders Act 2012 (c. 10).
28 1976 c. 63; section 3AA was inserted by section 131 of the Criminal Justice and Police Act 2001 (c. 16) and amended by sections 51 and 149 of, and paragraphs 1 and 3 of Schedule 11 to, and Part 4 of Schedule 28 to, the Criminal Justice and Immigration Act 2008 (c. 4) and paragraph 4 of Schedule 11 to the Legal Aid, Sentencing and Punishment of Offenders Act 2012 (c. 10).
29 1976 c. 63; section 3AC was inserted by section 51 of, and paragraphs 1 and 4 of Schedule 11 to, the Criminal Justice and Immigration Act 2008 (c. 4) and amended by paragraphs 1 and 7 of Schedule 11 to the Legal Aid, Sentencing and Punishment of Offenders Act 2012 (c. 10).

(2) The court officer must—
(a) inform the person responsible for the provision of any such accommodation or support ('the service provider') of—
(i) the defendant's name, and telephone number if available,
(ii) each offence with which the defendant is charged,
(iii) details of the requirement,
(iv) any other bail condition, and
(v) if fixed, the date on which the defendant must surrender to custody;
(b) inform the defendant and, where the defendant is under 16, an appropriate adult, of—
(i) the service provider's identity and the means by which the service provider may be contacted, and
(ii) the address of any accommodation in which the defendant must live and sleep; and
(c) notify the service provider of any subsequent—
(i) variation or termination of the requirement,
(ii) variation or termination of any other bail condition, and
(iii) fixing or variation of the date on which the defendant must surrender to custody.

R14.14 **Requirement for a surety or payment, etc.**

14.14 (1) This rule applies where the court imposes as a condition of bail a requirement for—
(a) a surety;
(b) a payment; or
(c) the surrender of a document or thing.
(2) The court may direct how such a condition must be met.
(3) Unless the court otherwise directs, if any such condition or direction requires a surety to enter into a recognizance—
(a) the recognizance must specify—
(i) the amount that the surety will be required to pay if the purpose for which the recognizance is entered is not fulfilled, and
(ii) the date, or the event, upon which the recognizance will expire;
(b) the surety must enter into the recognizance in the presence of—
(i) the court officer,
(ii) the defendant's custodian, where the defendant is in custody, or
(iii) someone acting with the authority of either; and
(c) the person before whom the surety enters into the recognizance must at once serve a copy on—
(i) the surety, and
(ii) as appropriate, the court officer and the defendant's custodian.
(4) Unless the court otherwise directs, if any such condition or direction requires someone to make a payment, or surrender a document or thing—
(a) that payment, document or thing must be made or surrendered to—
(i) the court officer,
(ii) the defendant's custodian, where the defendant is in custody, or
(iii) someone acting with the authority of either; and
(b) the court officer or the custodian, as appropriate, must serve immediately on the other a statement that the payment, document or thing has been made or surrendered.
(5) The custodian must release the defendant when each requirement ordered by the court has been met.

[Note. See also section 119 of the Magistrates' Courts Act 1980[30]*.]*

R14.15 **Forfeiture of a recognizance given by a surety**

14.15 (1) This rule applies where the court imposes as a condition of bail a requirement that a surety enter into a recognizance and, after the defendant is released on bail,—
(a) the defendant fails to surrender to custody as required, or
(b) it appears to the court that the surety has failed to comply with a condition or direction.
(2) The court officer must serve notice on—
(a) the surety; and
(b) each party to the decision to grant bail,
of the hearing at which the court will consider the forfeiture of the recognizance.
(3) The court must not forfeit the recognizance less than 5 business days after service of notice under paragraph (2).

[30] 1980 c. 43; section 119 was amended by section 77 of, and paragraph 55 of Schedule 14 to, the Criminal Justice Act 1982 (c. 48).

[Note. If the purpose for which a recognizance is entered is not fulfilled, that recognizance may be forfeited by the court. If the court forfeits a surety's recognizance, the sum promised by that person is then payable to the Crown. See also section 120 of the Magistrates' Courts Act 1980[31].]

Application to extend a custody time limit **R14.16**

14.16 (1) This rule applies where the prosecutor gives notice of application to extend a custody time limit.

(2) The court officer must arrange for the court to hear that application as soon as practicable after the expiry of—

(a) 5 days from the giving of notice, in the Crown Court; or

(b) 2 days from the giving of notice, in a magistrates' court.

(3) The court may shorten a time limit under this rule.

[Note. See regulation 7 of the Prosecution of Offences (Custody Time Limits) Regulations 1987[32].

Under regulations 4 and 5 of the 1987 Regulations[33], unless the court extends the time limit the maximum period during which the defendant may be in pre-trial custody is—

(a) in a case which can be tried only in a magistrates' court, 56 days pending the beginning of the trial;

(b) in a magistrates' court, in a case which can be tried either in that court or in the Crown Court—

(i) 70 days, pending the beginning of a trial in the magistrates' court, or

(ii) 56 days, pending the beginning of a trial in the magistrates' court, if the court decides on such a trial during that period;

(c) in the Crown Court, pending the beginning of the trial, 182 days from the sending of the defendant for trial, less any period or periods during which the defendant was in custody in the magistrates' court.

Under section 22(3) of the Prosecution of Offences Act 1985[34], the court cannot extend a custody time limit which has expired, and must not extend such a time limit unless satisfied—

(a) that the need for the extension is due to—

(i) the illness or absence of the accused, a necessary witness, a judge or a magistrate,

(ii) a postponement which is occasioned by the ordering by the court of separate trials in the case of two or more defendants or two or more offences, or

(iii) some other good and sufficient cause; and

(b) that the prosecution has acted with all due diligence and expedition.]

Appeal against custody time limit decision **R14.17**

14.17 (1) This rule applies where—

(a) a defendant wants to appeal to the Crown Court against a decision by a magistrates' court to extend a custody time limit; or

(b) a prosecutor wants to appeal to the Crown Court against a decision by a magistrates' court to refuse to extend a custody time limit.

(2) The appellant must serve an appeal notice—

(a) on—

(i) the other party to the decision,

(ii) the Crown Court officer, and

(iii) the magistrates' court officer;

(b) in a defendant's appeal, as soon as practicable after the decision under appeal; and

(c) in a prosecutor's appeal—

(i) as soon as practicable after the decision under appeal, and

(ii) before the relevant custody time limit expires.

(3) The appeal notice must specify—

[31] 1980 c. 43; section 120 was amended by section 55 of the Crime and Disorder Act 1998 (c. 37) and section 62 of, and paragraphs 45 and 56 of Schedule 13 to, the Tribunals, Courts and Enforcement Act 2007 (c. 15).

[32] S.I. 1987/299; regulation 7 was amended by S.I. 1989/767.

[33] S.I. 1987/299; regulation 4 was amended by section 71 of the Criminal Procedure and Investigations Act 1996 (c. 25) and S.I. 1989/767, 1991/1515, 1999/2744. Regulation 5 was amended by sections 71 and 80 of, and paragraph 8 of Schedule 5 to, the Criminal Procedure and Investigations Act 1996 (c. 25) and S.I. 1989/767, 1991/1515, 2000/3284, 2012/1344.

[34] 1985 c. 23; section 22 was amended by paragraph 104 of Schedule 15 to the Criminal Justice Act 1988 (c. 33), section 43 of the Crime and Disorder Act 1998 (c. 37), paragraph 36 of Schedule 11 to the Criminal Justice Act 1991 (c. 53), paragraph 27 of Schedule 9 to the Criminal Justice and Public Order Act 1994 (c. 33), section 71 of the Criminal Procedure and Investigations Act 1996 (c. 25), section 67(3) of the Access to Justice Act 1999 (c. 22), section 70 of, and paragraph 57 of Schedule 3 and paragraphs 49 and 51 of Schedule 36 to, the Criminal Justice Act 2003 (c. 44), section 59 of, and paragraph 1 of Schedule 11 to, the Constitutional Reform Act 2005 (c. 4) and paragraph 22 of Schedule 12 to the Legal Aid, Sentencing and Punishment of Offenders Act 2012 (c. 10).

(a) each offence with which the defendant is charged;
(b) the decision under appeal;
(c) the date on which the relevant custody time limit will expire;
(d) on a defendant's appeal, the date on which the relevant custody time limit would have expired but for the decision under appeal; and
(e) the grounds of appeal.

(4) The Crown Court officer must arrange for the Crown Court to hear the appeal as soon as practicable and in any event no later than the second business day after the appeal notice was served.

(5) The appellant—
(a) may abandon an appeal without the Crown Court's permission, by serving a notice of abandonment, signed by or on behalf of the appellant, on—
(i) the other party,
(ii) the Crown Court officer, and
(iii) the magistrates' court officer
before the hearing of the appeal begins; but
(b) after the hearing of the appeal begins, may only abandon the appeal with the Crown Court's permission.

[Note. See section 22(7), (8), (9) of the Prosecution of Offences Act 1985[35].]

Extension of bail before charge

R14.18 Exercise of court's powers: extension of pre-charge bail

14.18 (1) The court must determine an application to which rule 14.19 (Application to authorise extension of pre-charge bail) applies—
(a) without a hearing, subject to paragraph (2); and
(b) as soon as practicable, but as a general rule no sooner than the fifth business day after the application was served.

(2) The court must determine an application at a hearing where—
(a) if the application succeeds, its effect will be to extend the period for which the defendant is on bail to less than 12 months from the day after the defendant's arrest for the offence and the court considers that the interests of justice require a hearing;
(b) if the application succeeds, its effect will be to extend that period to more than 12 months from that day and the applicant or the defendant asks for a hearing; or
(c) it is an application to withhold information from the defendant and the court considers that the interests of justice require a hearing.

(3) Any hearing must be in private.

(4) Subject to rule 14.20 (Application to withhold information from the defendant), at a hearing the court may determine an application in the absence of—
(a) the applicant; and
(b) the defendant, if the defendant has had at least 5 business days in which to make representations.

(5) If the court so directs, a party to an application may attend a hearing by live link or telephone.

(6) The court must not authorise an extension of the period for which a defendant is on bail before being charged unless—
(a) the applicant states, in writing or orally, that to the best of the applicant's knowledge and belief—
(i) the application discloses all the information that is material to what the court must decide, and
(ii) the content of the application is true; or
(b) the application includes a statement by an investigator of the suspected offence that to the best of that investigator's knowledge and belief those requirements are met.

(7) Where the statement required by paragraph (6) is made orally—
(a) the statement must be on oath or affirmation, unless the court otherwise directs; and
(b) the court must arrange for a record of the making of the statement.

(8) The court may shorten or extend (even after it has expired) a time limit imposed by this rule or by rule 14.19 (Application to authorise extension of pre-charge bail).

[Note. For the definition of 'defendant' for the purposes of this rule and rules 14.19 and 14.20, see rule 14.1(3).

[35] 1985 c. 23; section 22(7) and (8) was amended by section 43 of the Crime and Disorder Act 1998 (c. 37).

Sections 47ZA and 47ZB of the Police and Criminal Evidence Act 1984[36] *limit the period during which a defendant who has been arrested for an offence may be on bail after being released without being charged. That period ('the applicable bail period') is—*

- *(a) 3 months from the day after the day on which the defendant was arrested (the defendant's 'bail start date') in 'an SFO case' (that is, a case investigated by the Serious Fraud Office);*
- *(b) 28 days from the defendant's bail start date in 'a standard case' (that is, 'an FCA case', meaning a case investigated by the Financial Conduct Authority, or any other non-SFO case).*

Under sections 47ZC and 47ZD of the 1984[37] *Act, in a standard case the applicable bail period may be extended on the authority of a police officer of the rank of superintendent or above until the end of 3 months from the bail start date.*

Under sections 47ZC and 47ZE of the Act[38]*, if the case is designated by a qualifying prosecutor as exceptionally complex (a 'designated case') the applicable bail period may be extended, in an SFO case, or further extended, in a standard case, on the authority of one of the senior officers listed in section 47ZE, until the end of 6 months from the bail start date.*

Under section 47ZF of the Act[39]*, on an application made before the date on which the applicable bail period ends by a member of the Serious Fraud Office, a member of staff of the Financial Conduct Authority, a constable or a Crown Prosecutor, a magistrates' court may authorise an extension of that period—*

- *(a) from a previous total of 3 months to a new total of 6 months or, if the investigation is unlikely to be completed or a police charging decision made within a lesser period, a new total of 9 months;*
- *(b) from a previous total of 6 months to a new total of 9 months or, if the investigation is unlikely to be completed or a police charging decision made within a lesser period, a new total of 12 months,*

where the conditions listed in that section are met.

Under section 47ZG of the Act[40]*, on a further such application (of which there may be more than one) a magistrates' court may authorise a further extension of the applicable bail period, on each occasion by a further 3 months or, if the investigation is unlikely to be completed or a police charging decision made within a lesser period, a further 6 months, where the conditions listed in that section are met.*

Under section 47ZL of the Act[41]*, the running of the applicable bail period does not begin (in the case of a first release on bail) or is suspended (in any other case) where—*

- *(a) the defendant is released on bail to await a charging decision by the Director of Public Prosecutions under section 37B of the Act; or*
- *(b) following arrest for breach of such bail the defendant is again released on bail.*

The court's authority therefore is not required for an extension of an applicable bail period the running of which is postponed or suspended pending a Director's charging decision. However—

- *(a) time runs in any period during which information requested by the Director is being obtained; and*
- *(b) if the Director requests information less than 7 days before the applicable bail period otherwise would end then the running of that period is further suspended until the end of 7 days beginning with the day on which the Director's request is made.*

See also section 47ZI of the Police and Criminal Evidence Act 198[42] *(Sections 47ZF to 47ZH: proceedings in magistrates' courts). The requirement for the court except in specified circumstances to determine an application without a hearing is prescribed by that section. Under that section the court must comprise a single justice of the peace unless a hearing is convened, when it must comprise two or more justices.]*

36 1984 c. 60; sections 47ZA and 47ZB were inserted by section 63 of the Policing and Crime Act 2017 (c. 3).
37 1984 c. 60; sections 47ZC and 47ZD were inserted by section 63 of the Policing and Crime Act 2017 (c. 3).
38 1984 c. 60; section 47ZE was inserted by section 63 of the Policing and Crime Act 2017 (c. 3).
39 1984 c. 60; section 47ZF was inserted by section 63 of the Policing and Crime Act 2017 (c. 3).
40 1984 c. 60; section 47ZG was inserted by section 63 of the Policing and Crime Act 2017 (c. 3).
41 1984 c. 60; section 47ZL was inserted by section 63 of the Policing and Crime Act 2017 (c. 3).
42 1984 c. 60; section 47ZI was inserted by section 63 of the Policing and Crime Act 2017 (c. 3).

R14.19 **Application to authorise extension of pre-charge bail**

14.19 (1) This rule applies where an applicant wants the court to authorise an extension of the period for which a defendant is released on bail before being charged with an offence.

(2) The applicant must—

(a) apply in writing before the date on which the defendant's pre-charge bail is due to end;

(b) demonstrate that the applicant is entitled to apply as a constable, a member of staff of the Financial Conduct Authority, a member of the Serious Fraud Office or a Crown Prosecutor;

(c) serve the application on—

(i) the court officer, and

(ii) the defendant; and

(d) serve on the defendant, with the application, a form of response notice for the defendant's use.

(3) The application must specify—

(a) the offence or offences for which the defendant was arrested;

(b) the date on which the defendant's pre-charge bail began;

(c) the date and period of any previous extension of that bail;

(d) the date on which that bail is due to end;

(e) the conditions of that bail; and

(f) if different, the bail conditions which are to be imposed if the court authorises an extension, or further extension, of the period for which the defendant is released on pre-charge bail.

(4) The application must explain—

(a) the grounds for believing that, as applicable—

(i) further investigation is needed of any matter in connection with the offence or offences for which the defendant was released on bail, or

(ii) further time is needed for making a decision as to whether to charge the defendant with that offence or those offences;

(b) the grounds for believing that, as applicable—

(i) the investigation into the offence or offences for which the defendant was released on bail is being conducted diligently and expeditiously, or

(ii) the decision as to whether to charge the defendant with that offence or those offences is being made diligently and expeditiously; and

(c) the grounds for believing that the defendant's further release on bail is necessary and proportionate in all the circumstances having regard, in particular, to any conditions of bail imposed.

(5) The application must—

(a) indicate whether the applicant wants the court to authorise an extension of the defendant's bail for 3 months or for 6 months; and

(b) if for 6 months, explain why the investigation is unlikely to be completed or the charging decision made, as the case may be, within 3 months.

(6) The application must explain why it was not made earlier where—

(a) the application is made before the date on which the defendant's bail is due to end; but

(b) it is not likely to be practicable for the court to determine the application before that date.

(7) A defendant who objects to the application must—

(a) serve notice on—

(i) the court officer, and

(ii) the applicant, not more than 5 business days after service of the application; and

(b) in the notice explain the grounds of the objection.

[Note. The Practice Direction sets out forms of application and response notice for use in connection with this rule.

See sections 47ZF (Applicable bail period: first extension of limit by the court), 47ZG (Applicable bail period: subsequent extensions of limit by the court) and 47ZJ (Sections 47ZF and 47ZG: late applications to magistrates' court) of the Police and Criminal Evidence Act 1984[43]*.*

[43] 1984 c. 60; section 47ZJ was inserted by section 63 of the Policing and Crime Act 2017 (c. 3).

The time limit for making an application is prescribed by section 47ZF(2) and by section 47ZG(2) of the 1984 Act. It may be neither extended nor shortened. Under section 47ZJ(2) of the Act, if it is not practicable for the court to determine the application before the applicable bail period ends then the court must determine the application as soon as practicable. Under section 47ZJ(3), the applicable bail period is treated as extended until the application is determined. Under section 47ZJ(4), if it appears to the court that it would have been reasonable for the application to have been made in time for it to be determined by the court before the end of the applicable bail period then the court may refuse the application.]

Application to withhold information from the defendant **R14.20**

14.20 (1) This rule applies where an application to authorise an extension of pre-charge bail includes an application to withhold information from the defendant.

(2) The applicant must—

(a) omit that information from the part of the application that is served on the defendant;

(b) mark the other part to show that, unless the court otherwise directs, it is only for the court; and

(c) in that other part, explain the grounds for believing that the disclosure of that information would have one or more of the following results—

(i) evidence connected with an indictable offence would be interfered with or harmed,

(ii) a person would be interfered with or physically injured,

(iii) a person suspected of having committed an indictable offence but not yet arrested for the offence would be alerted, or

(iv) the recovery of property obtained as a result of an indictable offence would be hindered.

(3) At any hearing of an application to which this rule applies—

(a) the court must first determine the application to withhold information, in the defendant's absence and that of any legal representative of the defendant; and

(b) if the court allows the application to withhold information, then in the following sequence—

(i) the court must consider representations first by the applicant and then by the defendant, in the presence of both, and

(ii) the court may consider further representations by the applicant in the defendant's absence and that of any legal representative of the defendant, if satisfied that there are reasonable grounds for believing that information withheld from the defendant would be disclosed during those further representations.

(4) If the court refuses an application to withhold information from the defendant, the applicant may withdraw the application to authorise an extension of pre-charge bail.

[Note. See sections 47ZH and 47ZI(5), (6), (8) of the Police and Criminal Evidence Act 1984[44] *(withholding sensitive information; proceedings in magistrates' courts: determination of applications to withhold sensitive information).]*

Summary of the general entitlement to bail and of the exceptions

The court must consider bail whenever it can order the defendant's detention pending trial or sentencing, or in an extradition case, and whether an application is made or not. Under section 4 of the Bail Act 1976[45]*, the general rule, subject to exceptions, is that a defendant must be granted bail. Under Part IIA of Schedule 1 to the Act*[46]*, if the court decides not to grant the defendant bail then at each subsequent hearing the court must consider whether to grant bail.*

Section 3 of the Bail Act 1976[47] *allows the court, before granting bail, to require a surety or security to secure the defendant's surrender to custody; and allows the court, on granting bail, to impose such requirements as appear to the court to be necessary—*

44 1984 c. 60; sections 47ZH and 47ZI were inserted by section 63 of the Policing and Crime Act 2017 (c. 3).

45 1976 c. 63; section 4 was amended by section 154 of, and paragraph 145 of Schedule 7 to, the Magistrates' Courts Act 1980 (c. 43), section 168 of, and paragraphs 32 and 33 of Schedule 10 to, the Criminal Justice and Public Order Act 1994 (c. 33), section 58 of the Criminal Justice and Court Services Act 2000 (c. 43), sections 198 and 220 of, and Schedule 4 to, the Extradition Act 2003 (c. 41), section 304 of, and paragraphs 20 and 22 of Schedule 32 to, the Criminal Justice Act 2003 (c. 44), section 42 of, and paragraph 34 of Schedule 13 to, the Police and Justice Act 2006 (c. 48), sections 6 and 148 of, and paragraphs 23 and 102 of Schedule 4 and Part 1 of Schedule 28 to, the Criminal Justice and Immigration Act 2008 (c. 4) and paragraph 19 of Schedule 7, and Schedule 8, to the Policing and Crime Act 2009 (c. 26).

46 1976 c. 63; Schedule 1, Part IIA was added by section 154 of the Criminal Justice Act 1988 (c. 33).

47 1976 c. 63; section 3 was amended by section 65 of, and Schedule 12 to, the Criminal Law Act 1977 (c. 45), section 34 of the Mental Health (Amendment) Act 1982 (c. 51), paragraph 46 of Schedule 4 to the Mental Health Act 1983 (c. 20), section 15 of, and paragraph 9 of Schedule 2 to, the Criminal Justice Act 1987 (c. 38), section 131 of the Criminal Justice Act 1988

(a) to secure that the defendant surrenders to custody;
(b) to secure that the defendant does not commit an offence while on bail;
(c) to secure that the defendant does not interfere with witnesses or otherwise obstruct the course of justice whether in relation to the defendant or any other person;
(d) for the defendant's own protection or, if a child or young person, for the defendant's welfare or in the defendant's own interests;
(e) to secure the defendant's availability for the purpose of enabling enquiries or a report to be made to assist the court in dealing with the defendant for the offence;
(f) to secure that before the time appointed for surrender to custody the defendant attends an interview with a legal representative.

Under section 3 of the Bail Act 1976, a person granted bail in criminal proceedings is under a duty to surrender to custody as required by that bail. Under section 6 of the Act, such a person who fails without reasonable cause so to surrender commits an offence and, under section 7, may be arrested.

Exceptions to the general right to bail are listed in Schedule 1 to the Bail Act 1976[48]*. They differ according to the category of offence concerned. Under section 4(2B) of the 1976 Act*[49]*, in an extradition case there is no general right to bail where the defendant is alleged to have been convicted in the territory requesting extradition.*

Under Part I of Schedule 1 to the 1976 Act, where the offence is punishable with imprisonment, and is not one that can be tried only in a magistrates' court, or in an extradition case—

(a) the defendant need not be granted bail if the court is satisfied that—
  (i) there are substantial grounds for believing that, if released on bail (with or without conditions), the defendant would fail to surrender to custody, would commit an offence, or would interfere with witnesses or otherwise obstruct the course of justice,
  (ii) there are substantial grounds for believing that, if released on bail (with or without conditions), the defendant would commit an offence by engaging in conduct that would, or would be likely to, cause physical or mental injury to an associated person (within the meaning of section 33 of the Family Law Act 1996[50]*), or cause that person to fear injury,*
  (iii) the defendant should be kept in custody for his or her own protection or welfare, or
  (iv) it has not been practicable, for want of time since the institution of the proceedings, to obtain sufficient information for the court to take the decisions required;
(b) the defendant need not be granted bail if it appears to the court that the defendant was on bail at the time of the offence (this exception does not apply in an extradition case);
(c) the defendant need not be granted bail if, having been released on bail in the case on a previous occasion, the defendant since has been arrested for breach of bail;
(d) the defendant need not be granted bail if in custody pursuant to a sentence;
(e) the defendant need not be granted bail if it appears to the court that it would be impracticable to complete enquiries or a report for which the case is to be adjourned without keeping the defendant in custody;

(c. 33), sections 27 and 168 of, and paragraph 12 of Schedule 9 and Schedule 11 to, the Criminal Justice and Public Order Act 1994 (c. 33), sections 54 and 120 of, and paragraph 37 of Schedule 8 and Schedule 10 to, the Crime and Disorder Act 1998 (c. 37), paragraph 51 of Schedule 9 to the Powers of Criminal Courts (Sentencing) Act 2000 (c. 6), section 131 of the Criminal Justice and Police Act 2001 (c. 16), sections 13 and 19 of, and paragraph 48 of Schedule 3 and Schedule 37 to, the Criminal Justice Act 2003 (c. 44), paragraphs 33 and 34 of Schedule 21 to the Legal Services Act 2007 (c. 29) and paragraphs 1 and 2 of Schedule 11, paragraphs 1 and 2 of Schedule 12, to the Criminal Justice and Immigration Act 2008 (c. 4) and paragraphs 1 to 4 of Schedule 11, and paragraphs 14 and 15 of Schedule 12, to the Legal Aid, Sentencing and Punishment of Offenders Act 2012 (c. 10).

48 1976 c. 63; Schedule 1 was amended by section 34 of the Mental Health (Amendment) Act 1982 (c. 51), sections 153, 154 and 155 of the Criminal Justice Act 1988 (c. 33), paragraph 22 of Schedule 11 to the Criminal Justice Act 1991 (c. 53), section 26 of the Criminal Justice and Public Order Act 1994 (c. 33), paragraph 38 of Schedule 8 to the Crime and Disorder Act 1998 (c. 37), paragraph 54 of Schedule 9 to the Powers of Criminal Courts (Sentencing) Act 2000 (c. 6), sections 129 and 137 of, and Schedule 7 to, the Criminal Justice and Police Act 2001 (c. 16), section 198 of the Extradition Act 2003 (c. 41), sections 13, 14, 15, 19 and 20 of, and paragraphs 20 and 23 of Schedule 32 and paragraphs 1 and 3 of Schedule 36 to, the Criminal Justice Act 2003 (c. 44), paragraph 40 of the Schedule to S.I. 2005/886, paragraph 78 of Schedule 16, and Schedule 17, to the Armed Forces Act 2006 (c. 52), paragraphs 1, 4, 5 and 6 of Schedule 12 to the Criminal Justice and Immigration Act 2008 (c. 4), section 114 of the Coroners and Justice Act 2009 (c. 25) and paragraphs 10 to 31 of Schedule 11, and paragraphs 14 and 17 of Schedule 12, to the Legal Aid, Sentencing and Punishment of Offenders Act 2012 (c. 10).

49 1976 c. 63; section 4(2B) was inserted by section 198 of the Extradition Act 2003 (c. 41) and amended by paragraph 34 of Schedule 13 to the Police and Justice Act 2006 (c. 48).

50 1996 c. 27; section 33 was amended by section 82 of, and paragraph 4 of Schedule 9 to, the Civil Partnership Act 2004 (c. 33).

(f) the defendant may not be granted bail if charged with murder, unless the court is of the opinion that there is no significant risk of the defendant committing an offence while on bail that would, or would be likely to, cause physical or mental injury to some other person;
(g) the defendant in an extradition case need not be granted bail if he or she was on bail on the date of the alleged offence and that offence is not one that could be tried only in a magistrates' court if it were committed in England or Wales.

Exceptions (a)(i), (b) and (c) do not apply where—

(a) the defendant is 18 or over;
(b) the defendant has not been convicted of an offence in those proceedings; and
(c) it appears to the court that there is no real prospect that the defendant will be sentenced to a custodial sentence in those proceedings.

In deciding whether an exception to the right to bail applies the court must have regard to any relevant consideration, including—

(a) the nature and seriousness of the offence, and the probable method of dealing with the defendant for it;
(b) the character, antecedents, associations and community ties of the defendant;
(c) the defendant's record of fulfilling obligations imposed under previous grants of bail; and
(d) except where the case is adjourned for enquires or a report, the strength of the evidence of the defendant having committed the offence.

Under Part IA of Schedule 1 to the 1976 Act, where the offence is punishable with imprisonment, and is one that can be tried only in a magistrates' court—

(a) the defendant need not be granted bail if it appears to the court that—
(i) having previously been granted bail in criminal proceedings, the defendant has failed to surrender as required and, in view of that failure, the court believes that, if released on bail (with or without conditions), the defendant would fail to surrender to custody, or
(ii) the defendant was on bail on the date of the offence and the court is satisfied that there are substantial grounds for believing that, if released on bail (with or without conditions), the defendant would commit an offence while on bail;
(b) the defendant need not be granted bail if the court is satisfied that—
(i) there are substantial grounds for believing that, if released on bail (with or without conditions), the defendant would commit an offence while on bail by engaging in conduct that would, or would be likely to, cause physical or mental injury to some other person, or cause some other person to fear such injury,
(ii) the defendant should be kept in custody for his or her own protection or welfare, or
(iii) it has not been practicable, for want of time since the institution of the proceedings, to obtain sufficient information for the court to take the decisions required;
(c) the defendant need not be granted bail if in custody pursuant to a sentence;
(d) the defendant need not be granted bail if, having been released on bail in the case on a previous occasion, the defendant since has been arrested for breach of bail, and the court is satisfied that there are substantial grounds for believing that, if released on bail (with or without conditions), the defendant would fail to surrender to custody, would commit an offence, or would interfere with witnesses or otherwise obstruct the course of justice.

Exceptions (a) and (d) do not apply where—

(a) the defendant is 18 or over;
(b) the defendant has not been convicted of an offence in those proceedings; and
(c) it appears to the court that there is no real prospect that the defendant will be sentenced to a custodial sentence in those proceedings.

Under Part II of Schedule 1 to the 1976 Act, where the offence is not punishable with imprisonment—

(a) the defendant need not be granted bail if it appears to the court that having previously been granted bail in criminal proceedings, the defendant has failed to surrender as required and, in view of that failure, the court believes that, if released on bail (with or without conditions), the defendant would fail to surrender to custody;
(b) the defendant need not be granted bail if the court is satisfied that the defendant should be kept in custody for his or her own protection or welfare;
(c) the defendant need not be granted bail if in custody pursuant to a sentence;

(d) *the defendant need not be granted bail if, having been released on bail in the case on a previous occasion, the defendant since has been arrested for breach of bail, and the court is satisfied that there are substantial grounds for believing that, if released on bail (with or without conditions), the defendant would fail to surrender to custody, would commit an offence, or would interfere with witnesses or otherwise obstruct the course of justice;*

(e) *the defendant need not be granted bail if, having been released on bail in the case on a previous occasion, the defendant since has been arrested for breach of bail, and the court is satisfied that there are substantial grounds for believing that, if released on bail (with or without conditions), the defendant would commit an offence while on bail by engaging in conduct that would, or would be likely to, cause physical or mental injury to an associated person (within the meaning of section 33 of the Family Law Act 1996), or to cause that person to fear such injury.*

Exceptions (a) and (d) apply only where—

(a) *the defendant is under 18; and*

(b) *the defendant has been convicted in those proceedings.*

Further exceptions to the general right to bail are set out in section 25 of the Criminal Justice and Public Order Act 1994[51]*, under which a defendant charged with murder, attempted murder, manslaughter, rape or another sexual offence specified in that section, and who has been previously convicted of such an offence, may be granted bail only if there are exceptional circumstances which justify it.*

Criminal Practice Directions Part 14 Bail and Custody Time Limits

CPD.14A **CPD III Custody and bail 14A: Bail Before Sending for Trial**

14A.1 Before the Crown Court can deal with an application under CrimPR 14.8 by a defendant after a magistrates' court has withheld bail, it must be satisfied that the magistrates' court has issued a certificate, under section 5(6A) of the Bail Act 1976, that it heard full argument on the application for bail before it refused the application. The certificate of full argument is produced by the magistrates' court's computer system, Libra, as part of the GENORD (General Form of Order). Two hard copies are produced, one for the defence and one for the prosecution. (Some magistrates' courts may also produce a manual certificate which will usually be available from the justices' legal adviser at the conclusion of the hearing; the GENORD may not be produced until the following day.) Under CrimPR 14.4(4), the magistrates' court officer will provide the defendant with a certificate that the court heard full argument. However, it is the responsibility of the defence, as the applicant in the Crown Court, to ensure that a copy of the certificate of full argument is provided to the Crown Court as part of the application (CrimPR 14.8(3)(e)). The applicant's solicitors should attach a copy of the certificate to the bail application form. If the certificate is not enclosed with the application form, it will be difficult to avoid some delay in listing.

Venue

14A.2 Applications should be made to the court to which the defendant will be, or would have been, sent for trial. In the event of an application in a purely summary case, it should be made to the Crown Court centre which normally receives Class 3 work. The hearing will be listed as a chambers matter, unless a judge has directed otherwise.

CPD.14B **CPD III Custody and bail 14B: Bail: Failure to Surrender and Trials in Absence**

14B.1 The failure of defendants to comply with the terms of their bail by not surrendering, or not doing so at the appointed time, undermines the administration of justice and disrupts proceedings. The resulting delays impact on victims, witnesses and other court users and also waste costs. A defendant's failure to surrender affects not only the case with which he or she is concerned, but also the court's ability to administer justice more generally, by damaging the confidence of victims, witnesses and the public in the effectiveness of the court system and the judiciary. It is,

[51] 1994 c. 33; section 25 was amended by section 56 of the Crime and Disorder Act 1998 (c. 37), paragraph 160 of Schedule 9 to the Powers of Criminal Courts (Sentencing) Act 2000 (c. 6), paragraph 32 of Schedule 6 to the Sexual Offences Act 2003 (c. 42), paragraph 67 of Schedule 32 and Schedule 37 to the Criminal Justice Act 2003 (c. 44), article 16 of S.I. 2008/1779, paragraph 3 of Schedule 17, and Schedule 23, to the Coroners and Justice Act 2009 (c. 25) and paragraph 33 of Schedule 11 to the Legal Aid, Sentencing and Punishment of Offenders Act 2012 (c. 10).

therefore, most important that defendants who are granted bail appreciate the significance of the obligation to surrender to custody in accordance with the terms of their bail and that courts take appropriate action, if they fail to do so.

14B.2 A defendant who will be unable for medical reasons to attend court in accordance with his or her bail must obtain a certificate from his or her general practitioner or another appropriate medical practitioner such as the doctor with care of the defendant at a hospital. This should be obtained in advance of the hearing and conveyed to the court through the defendant's legal representative. In order to minimise the disruption to the court and to others, particularly witnesses if the case is listed for trial, the defendant should notify the court through his legal representative as soon as his inability to attend court becomes known.

14B.3 Guidance has been produced by the British Medical Association and the Crown Prosecution Service on the roles and responsibilities of medical practitioners when issuing medical certificates in criminal proceedings. Judges and magistrates should seek to ensure that this guidance is followed. However, it is a matter for each individual court to decide whether, in any particular case, the issued certificate should be accepted. Without a medical certificate or if an unsatisfactory certificate is provided, the court is likely to consider that the defendant has failed to surrender to bail.

14B.4 If a defendant fails to surrender to his or her bail there are at least four courses of action for the courts to consider taking:

(a) imposing penalties for the failure to surrender;
(b) revoking bail or imposing more stringent conditions;
(c) conducting trials in the absence of the defendant; and
(d) ordering that some or all of any sums of money lodged with the court as a security or pledged by a surety as a condition on the grant of bail be forfeit.

The relevant sentencing guideline is the Definitive Guideline Fail to Surrender to Bail. Under section 125(1) of the Coroners and Justice Act 2009, for offences committed on or after 6 April 2010, the court must follow the relevant guideline unless it would be contrary to the interests of justice to do so. The guideline can be obtained from the Sentencing Council's website: https://www.sentencingcouncil.org.uk/

CPD III Custody and bail 14C: Penalties for Failure to Surrender **CPD.14C**

Initiating Proceedings — Bail granted by a police officer

14C.1 When a person has been granted bail by a police officer to attend court and subsequently fails to surrender to custody, the decision whether to initiate proceedings for a section 6(1) or section 6(2) offence will be for the police/prosecutor and proceedings are commenced in the usual way.

14C.2 The offence in this form is a summary offence although section 6(10) to (14) of the Bail Act 1976, inserted by section 15(3) of the Criminal Justice Act 2003, disapplies section 127 of the Magistrates' Courts Act 1980 and provides for alternative time limits for the commencement of proceedings. The offence should be dealt with on the first appearance after arrest, unless an adjournment is necessary, as it will be relevant in considering whether to grant bail again.

Initiating Proceedings — Bail granted by a court

14C.3 Where a person has been granted bail by a court and subsequently fails to surrender to custody, on arrest that person should normally be brought as soon as appropriate before the court at which the proceedings in respect of which bail was granted are to be heard. (There is no requirement to lay an information within the time limit for a Bail Act offence where bail was granted by the court).

14C.4 Given that bail was granted by a court, it is more appropriate that the court itself should initiate the proceedings by its own motion although the prosecutor may invite the court to take proceedings, if the prosecutor considers proceedings are appropriate.

Timing of disposal

14C.5 Courts should not, without good reason, adjourn the disposal of a section 6(1) or section 6(2) Bail Act 1976 offence (failure to surrender) until the conclusion of the proceedings in respect of which bail was granted but should deal with defendants as soon as is practicable. In deciding what is practicable, the court must take into account when the proceedings in respect of which bail was granted are expected to conclude, the seriousness of the offence for which the defendant is already being prosecuted, the type of penalty that might be imposed for the Bail Act offence and the original offence, as well as any other relevant circumstances.

14C.6 If the Bail Act offence is adjourned alongside the substantive proceedings, then it is still necessary to consider imposing a separate penalty at the trial. In addition, bail should usually be revoked in the meantime. Trial in the absence of the defendant is not a penalty for the Bail Act offence and a separate penalty may be imposed for the Bail Act offence.

Conduct of Proceedings

14C.7 Proceedings under section 6 of the Bail Act 1976 may be conducted either as a summary offence or as a criminal contempt of court. Where proceedings are commenced by the police or prosecutor, the prosecutor will conduct the proceedings and, if the matter is contested, call the evidence. Where the court initiates proceedings, with or without an invitation from the prosecutor, the court may expect the assistance of the prosecutor, such as in cross-examining the defendant, if required.

14C.8 The burden of proof is on the defendant to prove that he had reasonable cause for his failure to surrender to custody (section 6(3) of the Bail Act 1976).

Sentencing for a Bail Act offence

14C.9 A defendant who commits an offence under section 6(1) or section 6(2) of the Bail Act 1976 commits an offence that stands apart from the proceedings in respect of which bail was granted. The seriousness of the offence can be reflected by an appropriate and generally separate penalty being imposed for the Bail Act offence.

14C.10 As noted above, there is a sentencing guideline on sentencing offenders for Bail Act offences and this must be followed unless it would be contrary to the interests of justice to do so. Where the appropriate penalty is a custodial sentence, consecutive sentences should be imposed unless there are circumstances that make this inappropriate.

Arrest for breach of bail

14C.11 A defendant who has been released on bail but subsequently arrested for breach of a bail condition, or for failure to surrender to the court, actual or anticipated, must be brought before a magistrates' court (or a Crown Court judge, if the defendant is charged with murder) as soon as practicable and in any event within 24 hours of arrest. This does not apply to a defendant who is arrested within 24 hours of the next court hearing which that defendant is due to attend: such a defendant must be produced at that hearing instead. The period of 24 hours does not include Sunday, Christmas Day or Good Friday: see section 7 of the Bail Act 1976.

14C.12 Paragraphs II 7A.2 to 7A.8 of these Practice Directions apply to such a defendant as they do to one charged and brought before the court under section 46 of the Police and Criminal Evidence Act 1984, except for the requirements listed at paragraph II 7A.5(a)(i) and (ii) (requirements for confirmation of charge and preparation of case file), which must be read as if they required confirmation that (i) the allegation or allegations of breach of bail have been reduced to writing, and (ii) that allegation or those allegations, and any supporting documents, are complete and available. If the requirements of paragraph 7A.5, as thus read, are met, then the court before which the defendant is brought should take all the appropriate next steps in the case, including the taking of the defendant's plea; allocation and sending for trial, if applicable; and, if possible, sentencing; and should do so even if the defendant had been released on bail by a different court.

Voluntary attendance at a court after failure to attend

14C.13 The court may consider taking any of the following courses of action where

(i) a defendant has failed to attend a court at the appointed time, (ii) a warrant has been issued for the defendant's arrest for that failure, and (iii) the defendant subsequently attends voluntarily at some other time, or indicates a wish to do so, for example by making telephone enquiries of court staff:

- (a) if the defendant is present, the court may arrange for the execution there and then of the warrant;
- (b) if the defendant is present, the court may deal there and then with the case as if consequent on the execution of the warrant;
- (c) the court may arrange a resumed hearing in the defendant's case at the next convenient opportunity, while warning the defendant that the warrant remains liable to be executed in the meantime; and
- (d) the court may withdraw the warrant and arrange a resumed hearing in the defendant's case at the next convenient opportunity. The court should not withdraw an outstanding warrant unless the defendant provides evidence of an established current residential address, a telephone number and, if available, an email or other established electronic address.

14C.14 If an outstanding warrant is executed there and then, or if the court decides to deal at once with the defendant as if consequent on arrest, then paragraphs 14C.11 and 14C.12 apply and, consequently, paragraphs II 7A.2 to 7A.8 of these Practice Directions. However, if the defendant has not been arrested then the designated officer's delegate is under no such statutory duty as otherwise would apply to make efforts to accommodate the defendant's case and no step should be taken that disadvantages other cases awaiting hearing that day. In particular, it is only in exceptional circumstances that efforts should be made to accommodate a defendant who attends voluntarily and unexpectedly at a court building on any day other than a weekday on which a court is sitting at that building, or later than 12 noon on any such day.

14C.15 If an outstanding warrant for the defendant's arrest for failure to attend is either executed or withdrawn, court staff must ensure that this is recorded promptly in national police records.

CPD III Custody and bail 14D: Relationship between the Bail Act Offence and Further Remands on Bail or in Custody CPD.14D

14D.1 The court at which the defendant is produced should, where practicable and legally permissible, arrange to have all outstanding cases brought before it (including those from different courts) for the purpose of progressing matters and dealing with the question of bail. This is likely to be practicable in the magistrates' court where cases can easily be transferred from one magistrates' court to another. Practice is likely to vary in the Crown Court. If the defendant appears before a different court, for example because he is charged with offences committed in another area, and it is not practicable for all matters to be concluded by that court then the defendant may be remanded on bail or in custody, if appropriate, to appear before the first court for the outstanding offences to be dealt with.

14D.2 When a defendant has been convicted of a Bail Act offence, the court should review the remand status of the defendant, including the conditions of that bail, in respect of all outstanding proceedings against the defendant.

14D.3 Failure by the defendant to surrender or a conviction for failing to surrender to bail in connection with the main proceedings will be significant factors weighing against the re-granting of bail.

14D.4 Whether or not an immediate custodial sentence has been imposed for the Bail Act offence, the court may, having reviewed the defendant's remand status, also remand the defendant in custody in the main proceedings.

CPD III Custody and bail 14E: Trials in Absence CPD.14E

14E.1 Paragraphs VI 24C and 25B of these Practice Directions (Trial adjournment in magistrates' courts; Trial adjournment in the Crown Court) include guidance on the circumstances in which the court should proceed with or adjourn a trial from which the defendant absents himself or herself voluntarily.

CPD III Custody and bail 14F: Forfeiture of Monies Lodged as Security or Pledged by a Surety/ Estreatment of Recognisances CPD.14F

14F.1 A surety undertakes to forfeit a sum of money if the defendant fails to surrender as required. Considerable care must be taken to explain that obligation and the consequences before a surety is taken. This system, in one form or another, has great antiquity. It is immensely valuable. A court concerned that a defendant will fail to surrender will not normally know that defendant personally, nor indeed much about him. When members of the community who do know the defendant say they trust him to surrender and are prepared to stake their own money on that trust, that can have a powerful influence on the decision of the court as to whether or not to grant bail. There are two important side-effects. The first is that the surety will keep an eye on the defendant, and report to the authorities if there is a concern that he will abscond. In those circumstances, the surety can withdraw. The second is that a defendant will be deterred from absconding by the knowledge that if he does so then his family or friends who provided the surety will lose their money. In the experience of the courts, it is comparatively rare for a defendant to fail to surrender when meaningful sureties are in place.

14F.2 Any surety should have the opportunity to make representations to the defendant to surrender himself, in accordance with their obligations.

14F.3 The court should not wait or adjourn a decision on estreatment of sureties or securities until such time, if any, that the bailed defendant appears before the court. It is possible that any defendant who apparently absconds may have a defence of reasonable cause to the allegation of failure to surrender. If that happens, then any surety or security estreated would be returned. The reason for proceeding is that the defendant may never surrender, or may not surrender for many years. The court should still consider the sureties' obligations if that happens. Moreover, the longer the matter is delayed the more probable it is that the personal circumstances of the sureties will change.

14F.4 The court should follow the procedure at CrimPR 14.15. Before the court makes a decision, it should give the sureties the opportunity to make representations, either in person, through counsel or by statement.

14F.5 The court has discretion to forfeit the whole sum, part only of the sum, or to remit the sum. The starting point is that the surety is forfeited in full. It would be unfortunate if this valuable method of allowing a defendant to remain at liberty were undermined. Courts would have less confidence in the efficacy of sureties. It is also important to note that a defendant who absconds without in any way forewarning his sureties does not thereby release them from any or all of their responsibilities. Even if a surety does his best, he remains liable for the full amount, except at the discretion of the court. However, all factors should be taken into account and the following are noted for guidance only:

i) The presence or absence of culpability is a factor, but is not in itself a reason to reduce or set aside the obligations entered into by the surety.
ii) The means of a surety, and in particular changed means, are relevant.
iii) The court should forfeit no more than is necessary, in public policy, to maintain the integrity and confidence of the system of taking sureties.

CPD.14G **CPD III Custody and bail 14G: Bail During Trial**

14G.1 The following should be read subject to the Bail Act 1976.

14G.2 Once a trial has begun the further grant of bail, whether during the short adjournment or overnight, is in the discretion of the trial judge or trial Bench. It may be a proper exercise of this discretion to refuse bail during the short adjournment if the accused cannot otherwise be segregated from witnesses and jurors.

14G.3 An accused who was on bail while on remand should not be refused bail during the trial unless, in the opinion of the court, there are positive reasons to justify this refusal. Such reasons might include:

(a) that a point has been reached where there is a real danger that the accused will abscond, either because the case is going badly for him, or for any other reason;
(b) that there is a real danger that he may interfere with witnesses, jurors or co-defendants.

14G.4 Once the jury has returned a guilty verdict or a finding of guilt has been made, a further renewal of bail should be decided in the light of the gravity of the offence, any friction between co-defendants and the likely sentence to be passed in all the circumstances of the case.

CPD.14H **CPD III Custody and bail 14H: Crown Court Judge's Certification of Fitness to Appeal and Applications to the Crown Court for Bail Pending Appeal**

14H.1 The trial or sentencing judge may grant a certificate of fitness for appeal (see, for example, sections 1(2) (b) and 11(1A) of the Criminal Appeal Act 1968); the judge in the Crown Court should only certify cases in exceptional circumstances. The Crown Court judge should use the Criminal Appeal Office Form C (Crown Court Judge's Certificate of fitness for appeal) which is available to court staff on the HMCTS intranet.

14H.2 The judge may well think it right to encourage the defendant's advocate to submit to the court, and serve on the prosecutor, before the hearing of the application, a draft of the grounds of appeal which he will ask the judge to certify on Form C.

14H.3 The first question for the judge is then whether there exists a particular and cogent ground of appeal. If there is no such ground, there can be no certificate; and if there is no certificate there can be no bail. A judge should not grant a certificate with regard to sentence merely in the light of mitigation to which he has, in his opinion, given due weight, nor in regard to conviction on a ground where he considers the chance of a successful appeal is not substantial. The judge should bear in mind that, where a certificate is refused, application may be made to the Court of Appeal for leave to appeal and for bail; it is expected that certificates will only be granted in exceptional circumstances.

14H.4 Defence advocates should note that the effect of a grant of a certificate is to remove the need for leave to appeal to be granted by the Court of Appeal. It does not in itself commence the appeal. The completed Form C will be sent by the Crown Court to the Criminal Appeal Office; it is not copied to the parties. The procedures in CrimPR Part 39 should be followed.

14H.5 Bail pending appeal to the Court of Appeal (Criminal Division) may be granted by the trial or sentencing judge if they have certified the case as fit for appeal (see sections 81(1)(f) and 81(1B) of the Senior Courts Act 1981). Bail can only be granted in the Crown Court within 28 days of the conviction or sentence which is to be the subject of the appeal and may not be granted if an application for bail has already been made to the Court of Appeal. The procedure for bail to be granted by a judge of the Crown Court pending an appeal is governed by CrimPR Part 14. The Crown Court judge should use the Criminal Appeal Office Form BC (Crown Court Judge's Order granting bail) which is available to court staff on the HMCTS intranet.

14H.6 The length of the period which might elapse before the hearing of any appeal is not relevant to the grant of a certificate; but, if the judge does decide to grant a certificate, it may be one factor in the decision whether or not to grant bail. If bail is granted, the judge should consider imposing a condition of residence in line with the practice in the Court of Appeal (Criminal Division).

Criminal Procedure Rules Part 15 Disclosure

When this Part applies **R15.1**

15.1 This Part applies in a magistrates' court and in the Crown Court where Parts I and II of the Criminal Procedure and Investigations Act 1996 apply.

[Note. A summary of the disclosure requirements of the Criminal Procedure and Investigations Act 1996 is at the end of this Part.]

Prosecution disclosure **R15.2**

15.2 (1) This rule applies in the Crown Court where, under section 3 of the Criminal Procedure and Investigations Act 1996[1], the prosecutor—
(a) discloses prosecution material to the defendant; or
(b) serves on the defendant a written statement that there is no such material to disclose.
(2) The prosecutor must at the same time so inform the court officer.

[Note. See section 3 of the Criminal Procedure and Investigations Act 1996 and paragraph 10 of the Code of Practice accompanying the Criminal Procedure and Investigations Act 1996 (Code of Practice) Order 2015[2].]

Prosecutor's application for public interest ruling **R15.3**

15.3 (1) This rule applies where—
(a) without a court order, the prosecutor would have to disclose material; and
(b) the prosecutor wants the court to decide whether it would be in the public interest to disclose it.
(2) The prosecutor must—
(a) apply in writing for such a decision; and
(b) serve the application on—
(i) the court officer,
(ii) any person who the prosecutor thinks would be directly affected by disclosure of the material, and
(iii) the defendant, but only to the extent that serving it on the defendant would not disclose what the prosecutor thinks ought not be disclosed.
(3) The application must—
(a) describe the material, and explain why the prosecutor thinks that—
(i) it is material that the prosecutor would have to disclose,
(ii) it would not be in the public interest to disclose that material, and
(iii) no measure such as the prosecutor's admission of any fact, or disclosure by summary, extract or edited copy, adequately would protect both the public interest and the defendant's right to a fair trial;
(b) omit from any part of the application that is served on the defendant anything that would disclose what the prosecutor thinks ought not be disclosed (in which case, paragraph (4) of this rule applies); and
(c) explain why, if no part of the application is served on the defendant.
(4) Where the prosecutor serves only part of the application on the defendant, the prosecutor must—
(a) mark the other part, to show that it is only for the court; and
(b) in that other part, explain why the prosecutor has withheld it from the defendant.
(5) Unless already done, the court may direct the prosecutor to serve an application on—
(a) the defendant; and
(b) any other person who the court considers would be directly affected by the disclosure of the material.
(6) The court must determine the application at a hearing which—
(a) must be in private, unless the court otherwise directs; and
(b) if the court so directs, may take place, wholly or in part, in the defendant's absence.
(7) At a hearing at which the defendant is present—
(a) the general rule is that the court must consider, in the following sequence—
(i) representations first by the prosecutor and any other person served with the application, and then by the defendant, in the presence of them all, and then
(ii) further representations by the prosecutor and any such other person in the defendant's absence; but
(b) the court may direct other arrangements for the hearing.

[1] 1996 c. 25; section 3 was amended by section 82 of, and paragraph 7 of Schedule 4 to, the Regulation of Investigatory Powers Act 2000 (c. 23) and section 32 and section 331 of, and paragraphs 20 and 21 of Schedule 36 to, the Criminal Justice Act 2003 (c. 44).
[2] S.I. 2015/861.

(8) The court may only determine the application if satisfied that it has been able to take adequate account of—
(a) such rights of confidentiality as apply to the material; and
(b) the defendant's right to a fair trial.
(9) Unless the court otherwise directs, the court officer—
(a) must not give notice to anyone other than the prosecutor—
(i) of the hearing of an application under this rule, unless the prosecutor served the application on that person, or
(ii) of the court's decision on the application; and
(b) may—
(i) keep a written application or representations, or
(ii) arrange for the whole or any part to be kept by some other appropriate person, subject to any conditions that the court may impose.

[Note. The court's power to order that it is not in the public interest to disclose material is provided for by sections 3(6), 7(6) (where the investigation began between 1st April, 1997 and 3rd April, 2005) and 7A(8) (where the investigation began on or after 4th April, 2005) of the Criminal Procedure and Investigations Act 1996[3].

See also sections 16 and 19 of the 1996 Act[4].*]*

R15.4 **Defence disclosure**

15.4 (1) This rule applies where—
(a) under section 5 or 6 of the Criminal Procedure and Investigations Act 1996[5], the defendant gives a defence statement; and
(b) under section 6C of the 1996 Act[6], the defendant gives a defence witness notice.
(2) The defendant must serve such a statement or notice on—
(a) the court officer; and
(b) the prosecutor.

[Note. The Practice Direction sets out forms of—

(a) defence statement; and
(b) defence witness notice.

Under section 5 of the 1996 Act, in the Crown Court the defendant must give a defence statement. Under section 6 of the Act, in a magistrates' court the defendant may give such a statement but need not do so.

Under section 6C of the 1996 Act, in the Crown Court and in magistrates' courts the defendant must give a defence witness notice indicating whether he or she intends to call any witnesses (other than him or herself) and, if so, identifying them.]

R15.5 **Defendant's application for prosecution disclosure**

15.5 (1) This rule applies where the defendant—
(a) has served a defence statement given under the Criminal Procedure and Investigations Act 1996; and
(b) wants the court to require the prosecutor to disclose material.
(2) The defendant must serve an application on—
(a) the court officer; and
(b) the prosecutor.
(3) The application must—
(a) describe the material that the defendant wants the prosecutor to disclose;
(b) explain why the defendant thinks there is reasonable cause to believe that—
(i) the prosecutor has that material, and
(ii) it is material that the Criminal Procedure and Investigations Act 1996 requires the prosecutor to disclose; and

[3] 1996 c. 25; section 7 was repealed by sections 331 and 332 of, and paragraphs 20 and 25 of Schedule 36 and Part 3 of Schedule 37 to, the Criminal Justice Act 2003 (c. 44), with transitional provisions for certain offences in article 2 of S.I. 2005/1817. Section 7A was inserted by section 37 of the Criminal Justice Act 2003 (c. 44).

[4] 1996 c. 25; section 16 was amended by section 331 of, and paragraphs 20 and 32 of Schedule 36 to, the Criminal Justice Act 2003 (c. 44). Section 19 was amended by section 109 of, and paragraph 377 of Schedule 8 to, the Courts Act 2003 (c. 39), section 331 of, and paragraphs 20 and 34 of Schedule 36 to, the Criminal Justice Act 2003 (c. 44) and section 15 of, and paragraph 251 of Schedule 4 to, the Constitutional Reform Act 2005 (c. 4).

[5] 1996 c. 25; section 5 was amended by section 33 of, and paragraph 66 of Schedule 3, paragraphs 20 and 23 of Schedule 36 and Parts 3 and 4 of Schedule 37 to, the Criminal Justice Act 2003 (c. 44). It was further amended by section 119 of, and paragraph 126 of Schedule 8 to, the Crime and Disorder Act 1998 (c. 37) in respect of certain proceedings only.

[6] 1996 c. 25; section 6C was inserted by section 34 of the Criminal Justice Act 2003 (c. 44).

(c) ask for a hearing, if the defendant wants one, and explain why it is needed.

(4) The court may determine an application under this rule—

(a) at a hearing, in public or in private; or

(b) without a hearing.

(5) The court must not require the prosecutor to disclose material unless the prosecutor—

(a) is present; or

(b) has had at least 10 business days in which to make representations.

[Note. The Practice Direction sets out a form of application for use in connection with this rule.

Under section 8 of the Criminal Procedure and Investigations Act 1996[7]*, a defendant may apply for prosecution disclosure only if the defendant has given a defence statement.]*

Review of public interest ruling **R15.6**

15.6 (1) This rule applies where the court has ordered that it is not in the public interest to disclose material that the prosecutor otherwise would have to disclose, and—

(a) the defendant wants the court to review that decision; or

(b) the Crown Court reviews that decision on its own initiative.

(2) Where the defendant wants the court to review that decision, the defendant must—

(a) serve an application on—

(i) the court officer, and

(ii) the prosecutor; and

(b) in the application—

(i) describe the material that the defendant wants the prosecutor to disclose, and

(ii) explain why the defendant thinks it is no longer in the public interest for the prosecutor not to disclose it.

(3) The prosecutor must serve any such application on any person who the prosecutor thinks would be directly affected if that material were disclosed.

(4) The prosecutor, and any such person, must serve any representations on—

(a) the court officer; and

(b) the defendant, unless to do so would in effect reveal something that either thinks ought not be disclosed.

(5) The court may direct—

(a) the prosecutor to serve any such application on any person who the court considers would be directly affected if that material were disclosed; and

(b) the prosecutor and any such person to serve any representations on the defendant.

(6) The court must review a decision to which this rule applies at a hearing which—

(a) must be in private, unless the court otherwise directs; and

(b) if the court so directs, may take place, wholly or in part, in the defendant's absence.

(7) At a hearing at which the defendant is present—

(a) the general rule is that the court must consider, in the following sequence—

(i) representations first by the defendant, and then by the prosecutor and any other person served with the application, in the presence of them all, and then

(ii) further representations by the prosecutor and any such other person in the defendant's absence; but

(b) the court may direct other arrangements for the hearing.

(8) The court may only conclude a review if satisfied that it has been able to take adequate account of—

(a) such rights of confidentiality as apply to the material; and

(b) the defendant's right to a fair trial.

[Note. The court's power to review a public interest ruling is provided for by sections 14 and 15 of the Criminal Procedure and Investigations Act 1996[8]*. Under section 14 of the Act, a magistrates' court may reconsider an order for non-disclosure only if a defendant applies. Under section 15, the Crown Court may do so on an application, or on its own initiative.*

See also sections 16 and 19 of the 1996 Act.]

[7] 1996 c. 25; section 8 was amended by section 82 of, and paragraph 7 of Schedule 4 to, the Regulation of Investigatory Powers Act 2000 (c. 23) and section 38 of the Criminal Justice Act 2003 (c. 44).

[8] 1996 c. 25; section 14 was amended by section 331 of, and paragraphs 20 and 30 of Schedule 36 to, the Criminal Justice Act 2003 (c. 44) and section 15 was amended by section 331 of, and paragraphs 20 and 31 of Schedule 36 to, the Criminal Justice Act 2003 (c. 44).

R15.7 **Defendant's application to use disclosed material**

15.7 (1) This rule applies where a defendant wants the court's permission to use disclosed prosecution material—
(a) otherwise than in connection with the case in which it was disclosed; or
(b) beyond the extent to which it was displayed or communicated publicly at a hearing.
(2) The defendant must serve an application on—
(a) the court officer; and
(b) the prosecutor.
(3) The application must—
(a) specify what the defendant wants to use or disclose; and
(b) explain why.
(4) The court may determine an application under this rule—
(a) at a hearing, in public or in private; or
(b) without a hearing.
(5) The court must not permit the use of such material unless—
(a) the prosecutor has had at least 20 business days in which to make representations; and
(b) the court is satisfied that it has been able to take adequate account of any rights of confidentiality that may apply to the material.

[Note. The court's power to allow a defendant to use disclosed material is provided for by section 17 of the Criminal Procedure and Investigations Act 1996[9].]

R15.8 **Unauthorised use of disclosed material**

15.8 (1) This rule applies where a person is accused of using disclosed prosecution material in contravention of section 17 of the Criminal Procedure and Investigations Act 1996.
(2) A party who wants the court to exercise its power to punish that person for contempt of court must comply with the rules in Part 48 (Contempt of court).
(3) The court must not exercise its power to forfeit material used in contempt of court unless—
(a) the prosecutor; and
(b) any other person directly affected by the disclosure of the material.
is present, or has had at least 14 days in which to make representations.

[Under section 18 of the 1996 Act, the court can punish for contempt of court any other use of disclosed prosecution material. See also section 19 of the 1996 Act.]

R15.9 **Court's power to vary requirements under this Part**

15.9 The court may—
(a) shorten or extend (even after it has expired) a time limit under this Part;
(b) allow a defence statement, or a defence witness notice, to be in a different written form to one set out in the Practice Direction, as long as it contains what the Criminal Procedure and Investigations Act 1996 requires;
(c) allow an application under this Part to be in a different form to one set out in the Practice Direction, or to be presented orally; and
(d) specify the period within which—
(i) any application under this Part must be made, or
(ii) any material must be disclosed, on an application to which rule 15.5 applies (Defendant's application for prosecution disclosure).

Summary of disclosure requirements of Criminal Procedure and Investigations Act 1996

The Criminal Procedure and Investigations Act 1996 came into force on 1st April, 1997. It does not apply where the investigation began before that date. With effect from 4th April, 2005, the Criminal Justice Act 2003 made changes to the 1996 Act that do not apply where the investigation began before that date.

In some circumstances, the prosecutor may be required to disclose material to which the 1996 Act does not apply: see sections 1 and 21[10].

[9] 1996 c. 25; section 17 was amended by section 331 of, and paragraphs 20 and 33 of Schedule 36 to, the Criminal Justice Act 2003 (c. 44).

[10] 1996 c. 25; section 1 was amended by section 119 of, and paragraph 125 of Schedule 8 to, the Crime and Disorder Act 1998 (c. 37), paragraph 66 of Schedule 3 and Part 4 of Schedule 37 to the Criminal Justice Act 2003 (c. 44) and paragraph 37 of Schedule 17 to the Crime and Courts Act 2013 (c. 22). It was amended in respect of certain proceedings only by section 119 of, and paragraph 125(a) of Schedule 8 to, the Crime and Disorder Act 1998 (c. 37). It is further amended by section 9 of the Sexual Offences (Protected Material) Act 1997 (c. 39), with effect from a date to be appointed. Section 21 was amended by paragraph 66 of Schedule 3 to the Criminal Justice Act 2003 (c. 44).

Part I of the 1996 Act contains sections 1 to 21A. Part II, which contains sections 22 to 27, requires an investigator to record information relevant to an investigation that is obtained during its course. See also the Criminal Procedure and Investigations Act 1996 (Code of Practice) (No. 2) Order 1997[11], *the Criminal Procedure and Investigations Act 1996 (Code of Practice) Order 2005*[12] *and the Criminal Procedure and Investigations Act 1996 (Code of Practice) Order 2015*[13] *issued under sections 23 to 25 of the 1996 Act.*

Prosecution disclosure

Where the investigation began between 1st April, 1997, and 3rd April, 2005, sections 3 and 7 of the 1996 Act require the prosecutor—

(a) to disclose material not previously disclosed that in the prosecutor's opinion might undermine the case for the prosecution against the defendant—
(i) in a magistrates' court, as soon as is reasonably practicable after the defendant pleads not guilty, and
(ii) in the Crown Court, as soon as is reasonably practicable after the case is committed or transferred for trial, or after the evidence is served where the case is sent for trial; and
(b) as soon as is reasonably practicable after service of the defence statement, to disclose material not previously disclosed that might be reasonably expected to assist the defendant's case as disclosed by that defence statement; or in either event
(c) if there is no such material, then to give the defendant a written statement to that effect.

Where the investigation began on or after 4th April, 2005, sections 3 and 7A of the 1996 Act[14] *require the prosecutor—*

(a) to disclose prosecution material not previously disclosed that might reasonably be considered capable of undermining the case for the prosecution against the defendant or of assisting the case for the defendant—
(i) in a magistrates' court, as soon as is reasonably practicable after the defendant pleads not guilty, or
(ii) in the Crown Court, as soon as is reasonably practicable after the case is committed or transferred for trial, or after the evidence is served where the case is sent for trial, or after a count is added to the indictment; and in either case
(b) if there is no such material, then to give the defendant a written statement to that effect; and after that
(c) in either court, to disclose any such material—
(i) whenever there is any, until the court reaches its verdict or the prosecutor decides not to proceed with the case, and
(ii) in particular, after the service of the defence statement.

Sections 2 and 3 of the 1996 Act define material, and prescribe how it must be disclosed.

In some circumstances, disclosure is prohibited by section 17 of the Regulation of Investigatory Powers Act 2000.

The prosecutor must not disclose material that the court orders it would not be in the public interest to disclose: see sections 3(6), 7(6) and 7A(8) of the 1996 Act.

Sections 12 and 13 of the 1996 Act prescribe the time for prosecution disclosure. Under paragraph 10 of the Code of Practice accompanying the Criminal Procedure and Investigations Act 1996 (Code of Practice) Order 2015, in a magistrates' court the prosecutor must disclose any material due to be disclosed at the hearing where a not guilty plea is entered, or as soon as possible following a formal indication from the accused or representative that a not guilty plea will be entered at that hearing.

See also sections 1, 4 and 10 of the 1996 Act.

Defence disclosure

Under section 5 of the 1996 Act[15], *in the Crown Court the defendant must give a defence statement. Under section 6 of the Act, in a magistrates' court the defendant may give such a statement but need not do so.*

[11] S.I. 1997/1033; this Order was revoked by S.I. 2005/985.
[12] S.I. 2005/985.
[13] S.I. 2015/861.
[14] 1996 c. 25; section 3 was amended by section 82 of, and paragraph 7 of Schedule 4 to, the Regulation of Investigatory Powers Act 2000 (c. 23) and section 32 and section 331 of, and paragraphs 20 and 21 of Schedule 36 to, the Criminal Justice Act 2003 (c. 44). Section 7A was inserted by section 37 of the Criminal Justice Act 2003 (c. 44).
[15] 1996 c. 25; section 5 was amended by section 33 of, and paragraph 66 of Schedule 3, paragraphs 20 and 23 of Schedule 36 and Parts 3 and 4 of Schedule 37 to, the Criminal Justice Act 2003 (c. 44). It was further amended by section 119 of, and paragraph 126 of Schedule 8 to, the Crime and Disorder Act 1998 (c. 37) in respect of certain proceedings only.

Under section 6C of the 1996 Act[16]*, in the Crown Court and in magistrates' courts the defendant must give a defence witness notice indicating whether he or she intends to call any witnesses (other than him or herself) and, if so, identifying them.*

The time for service of a defence statement is prescribed by section 12 of the 1996 Act[17] *and by the Criminal Procedure and Investigations Act 1996 (Defence Disclosure Time Limits) Regulations 2011*[18]*. It is—*

(a) in a magistrates' court, not more than 14 days after the prosecutor—
 (i) discloses material under section 3 of the 1996 Act, or
 (ii) serves notice that there is no such material to disclose;
(b) in the Crown Court, not more than 28 days after either of those events, if the prosecution evidence has been served on the defendant.

The requirements for the content of a defence statement are set out in—

(a) section 5 of the 1996 Act, where the investigation began between 1st April, 1997 and 3rd April, 2005;
(b) section 6A of the 1996 Act[19]*, where the investigation began on or after 4th April, 2005. See also section 6E of the Act*[20]*.*

Where the investigation began between 1st April, 1997 and 3rd April, 2005, the defence statement must—

(a) set out in general terms the nature of the defence;
(b) indicate the matters on which the defendant takes issue with the prosecutor, and, in respect of each, explain why;
(c) if the defence statement discloses an alibi, give particulars, including—
 (i) the name and address of any witness whom the defendant believes can give evidence in support (that is, evidence that the defendant was in a place, at a time, inconsistent with having committed the offence),
 (ii) where the defendant does not know the name or address, any information that might help identify or find that witness.

Where the investigation began on or after 4th April, 2005, the defence statement must—

(a) set out the nature of the defence, including any particular defences on which the defendant intends to rely;
(b) indicate the matters of fact on which the defendant takes issue with the prosecutor, and, in respect of each, explain why;
(c) set out particulars of the matters of fact on which the defendant intends to rely for the purposes of the defence;
(d) indicate any point of law that the defendant wants to raise, including any point about the admissibility of evidence or about abuse of process, and any authority relied on; and
(e) if the defence statement discloses an alibi, give particulars, including—
 (i) the name, address and date of birth of any witness whom the defendant believes can give evidence in support (that is, evidence that the defendant was in a place, at a time, inconsistent with having committed the offence),
 (ii) where the defendant does not know any of those details, any information that might help identify or find that witness.

The time for service of a defence witness notice is prescribed by section 12 of the 1996 Act and by the Criminal Procedure and Investigations Act 1996 (Defence Disclosure Time Limits) Regulations 2011. The time limits are the same as those for a defence statement.

A defence witness notice that identifies any proposed defence witness (other than the defendant) must—

(a) give the name, address and date of birth of each such witness, or as many of those details as are known to the defendant when the notice is given;

[16] 1996 c. 25; section 6C was inserted by section 34 of the Criminal Justice Act 2003 (c. 44).
[17] 1996 c. 25; section 12 was amended by sections 331 of, and paragraphs 20 and 28 of Schedule 36 to, the Criminal Justice Act 2003 (c. 44).
[18] S.I. 2011/209.
[19] 1996 c. 25; section 6A was inserted by section 33 of the Criminal Justice Act 2003 (c. 44) and amended by section 60 of the Criminal Justice and Immigration Act 2008 (c. 4).
[20] 1996 c. 25; section 6E was inserted by section 36 of the Criminal Justice Act 2003 (c. 44).

(b) *provide any information in the defendant's possession which might be of material assistance in identifying or finding any such witness in whose case any of the details mentioned in paragraph (a) are not known to the defendant when the notice is given; and*

(c) *amend any earlier such notice, if the defendant—*

(i) *decides to call a person not included in an earlier notice as a proposed witness,*

(ii) *decides not to call a person so included, or*

(iii) *discovers any information which the defendant would have had to include in an earlier notice, if then aware of it.*

Under section 11 of the 1996 Act[21], *if a defendant—*

(a) *fails to disclose what the Act requires;*

(b) *fails to do so within the time prescribed;*

(c) *at trial, relies on a defence, or facts, not mentioned in the defence statement;*

(d) *at trial, introduces alibi evidence without having given in the defence statement—*

(i) *particulars of the alibi, or*

(ii) *the details of the alibi witness, or witnesses, required by the Act; or*

(e) *at trial, calls a witness not identified in a defence witness notice,*

then the court or another party at trial may comment on that, and the court may draw such inferences as appear proper in deciding whether the defendant is guilty.

Under section 6E(2) of the 1996 Act, if before trial in the Crown Court it seems to the court that section 11 may apply, then the court must warn the defendant.

Criminal Practice Directions Part 15 Disclosure

CPD IV Disclosure 15A: Disclosure of Unused Material CPD.15A

15A.1 Disclosure is a vital part of the preparation for trial, both in the magistrates' courts and in the Crown Court. All parties must be familiar with their obligations, in particular under the Criminal Procedure and Investigations Act 1996 as amended and the Code issued under that Act, and must comply with the relevant judicial protocol and guidelines from the Attorney-General. These documents have recently been revised and the new guidance will be issued shortly as *Judicial Protocol on the Disclosure of Unused Material in Criminal Cases* and the *Attorney-General's Guidelines on Disclosure*. The new documents should be read together as complementary, comprehensive guidance. They will be available electronically on the respective websites.

15A.2 In addition, certain procedures are prescribed under CrimPR Part 15 and these should be followed. The notes to Part 15 contain a useful summary of the requirements of the CPIA 1996 as amended.

Criminal Procedure Rules Part 16 Written Witness Statements

When this Part applies R16.1

16.1 This Part applies where a party wants to introduce a written witness statement in evidence under section 9 of the Criminal Justice Act 1967[1].

[Note. Under section 9 of the Criminal Justice Act 1967, if the conditions specified in that section are met the written statement of a witness is admissible in evidence to the same extent as if that witness gave evidence in person.]

Content of written witness statement R16.2

16.2 The statement must contain—

(a) at the beginning—

(i) the witness' name, and

[21] 1996 c. 25; section 11 was substituted by section 39 of the Criminal Justice Act 2003 (c. 44) and amended by section 60(2) of the Criminal Justice and Immigration Act 2008 (c. 4).

[1] 1967 c. 80; section 9 was amended by section 56 of, and paragraph 49 of Schedule 8 to, the Courts Act 1971 (c. 23), section 168 of, and paragraph 6 of Schedule 9 to, the Criminal Justice and Public Order Act 1994 (c. 33), section 69 of the Criminal Procedure and Investigations Act 1996 (c. 25), regulation 9 of, and paragraph 4 of Schedule 5 to, S.I. 2001/1090, paragraph 43 of Schedule 3 and Part 4 of Schedule 37 to the Criminal Justice Act 2003 (c. 44), section 26 of, and paragraph 7 of Schedule 2 to, the Armed Forces Act 2011 (c. 18) and section 80 of the Deregulation Act 2015 (c. 20). It is further amended by section 72 of, and paragraph 55 of Schedule 5 to, the Children and Young Persons Act 1969 (c. 54) and section 65 of, and paragraph 1 of Schedule 4 to, the Courts Act 2003 (c. 39), with effect from dates to be appointed.

(ii) the witness' age, if under 18;
(b) a declaration by the witness that—
(i) it is true to the best of the witness' knowledge and belief, and
(ii) the witness knows that if it is introduced in evidence, then it would be an offence wilfully to have stated in it anything that the witness knew to be false or did not believe to be true;
(c) if the witness cannot read the statement, a signed declaration by someone else that that person read it to the witness; and
(d) the witness' signature.

[Note. The Practice Direction sets out a form of written statement for use in connection with this rule.]

R16.3 **Reference to exhibit**

16.3 Where the statement refers to a document or object as an exhibit, it must identify that document or object clearly.

[Note. See section 9(7) of the Criminal Justice Act 1967[2].]

R16.4 **Written witness statement in evidence**

16.4 (1) A party who wants to introduce in evidence a written witness statement must—
(a) before the hearing at which that party wants to introduce it, serve a copy of the statement on—
(i) the court officer, and
(ii) each other party; and
(b) at or before that hearing, serve on the court officer the statement or an authenticated copy.
(2) If that party relies on only part of the statement, that party must mark the copy in such a way as to make that clear.
(3) A prosecutor must serve on a defendant, with the copy of the statement, a notice—
(a) of the right to object to the introduction of the statement in evidence instead of the witness giving evidence in person;
(b) of the time limit for objecting under this rule; and
(c) that if the defendant does not object in time, the court—
(i) can nonetheless require the witness to give evidence in person, but
(ii) may decide not to do so.
(4) A party served with a written witness statement who objects to its introduction in evidence must—
(a) serve notice of the objection on—
(i) the party who served it, and
(ii) the court officer; and
(b) serve the notice of objection not more than 5 business days after service of the statement unless—
(i) the court extends that time limit, before or after the statement was served,
(ii) rule 24.8 (Written guilty plea: special rules) applies, in which case the time limit is the later of 5 business days after service of the statement or 5 business days before the hearing date, or
(iii) rule 24.9 (Single justice procedure: special rules) applies, in which case the time limit is 15 business days after service of the statement.
(5) The court may exercise its power to require the witness to give evidence in person—
(a) on application by any party; or
(b) on its own initiative.
(6) A party entitled to receive a copy of a statement may waive that entitlement by so informing—
(a) the party who would have served it; and
(b) the court.

[Note. The Practice Direction sets out a form of written witness statement and a form of notice for use in connection with this rule.

Under section 9(2A) of the Criminal Justice Act 1967[3], Criminal Procedure Rules may prescribe the period within which a party served with a written witness statement must object to its introduction in evidence, subject to a minimum period of 7 days from its service.

2 1967 c. 80.
3 1967 c. 80; section 9(2A) was inserted by section 80 of the Deregulation Act 2015 (c. 20).

Under section 133 of the Criminal Justice Act 2003[4], where a statement in a document is admissible as evidence in criminal proceedings, the statement may be proved by producing either (a) the document, or (b) (whether or not the document exists) a copy of the document or of the material part of it, authenticated in whatever way the court may approve. By section 134 of the 2003 Act, 'document' means anything in which information of any description is recorded.]

CRIMINAL PRACTICE DIRECTIONS PART 16 WRITTEN WITNESS STATEMENTS

CPD V Evidence 16A: Evidence by Written Statement CPD.16A

16A.1 Where the prosecution proposes to tender written statements in evidence under section 9 of the Criminal Justice Act 1967, it will frequently be necessary for certain statements to be edited. This will occur either because a witness has made more than one statement whose contents should conveniently be reduced into a single, comprehensive statement, or where a statement contains inadmissible, prejudicial or irrelevant material. Editing of statements must be done by a Crown Prosecutor (or by a legal representative, if any, of the prosecutor if the case is not being conducted by the Crown Prosecution Service) and not by a police officer.

Composite statements

16A.2 A composite statement giving the combined effect of two or more earlier statements must be prepared in compliance with the requirements of section 9 of the 1967 Act; and must then be signed by the witness.

Editing single statements

16A.3 There are two acceptable methods of editing single statements. They are:

(a) By marking copies of the statement in a way which indicates the passages on which the prosecution will not rely. This merely indicates that the prosecution will not seek to adduce the evidence so marked. The original signed statement to be tendered to the court is not marked in any way.

The marking on the copy statement is done by lightly striking out the passages to be edited, so that what appears beneath can still be read, or by bracketing, or by a combination of both. It is not permissible to produce a photocopy with the deleted material obliterated, since this would be contrary to the requirement that the defence and the court should be served with copies of the signed original statement.

Whenever the striking out/bracketing method is used, it will assist if the following words appear at the foot of the frontispiece or index to any bundle of copy statements to be tendered:

'The prosecution does not propose to adduce evidence of those passages of the attached copy statements which have been struck out and/or bracketed (nor will it seek to do so at the trial unless a notice of further evidence is served)'.

(b) By obtaining a fresh statement, signed by the witness, which omits the offending material, applying the procedure for composite statements above.

16A.4 In most cases where a single statement is to be edited, the striking out/bracketing method will be the more appropriate, but the taking of a fresh statement is preferable in the following circumstances:

(a) When a police (or other investigating) officer's statement contains details of interviews with more suspects than are eventually charged, a fresh statement should be prepared and signed, omitting all details of interview with those not charged except, insofar as it is relevant, for the bald fact that a certain named person was interviewed at a particular time, date and place.

(b) When a suspect is interviewed about more offences than are eventually made the subject of charges, a fresh statement should be prepared and signed, omitting all questions and answers about the uncharged offences unless either they might appropriately be taken into consideration, or evidence about those offences is admissible on the charges preferred. It may, however, be desirable to replace the omitted questions and answers with a phrase such as: '*After referring to some other matters, I then said, "........."*', so as to make it clear that part of the interview has been omitted.

(c) A fresh statement should normally be prepared and signed if the only part of the original on which the prosecution is relying is only a small proportion of the whole, although it remains desirable to use the alternative method if there is reason to believe that the defence might itself wish to rely, in mitigation or for any other purpose, on at least some of those parts which the prosecution does not propose to adduce.

[4] 2003 c. 44.

Criminal Procedure Rules and Criminal Practice Directions

(d) When the passages contain material which the prosecution is entitled to withhold from disclosure to the defence.

16A.5 Prosecutors should also be aware that, where statements are to be tendered under section 9 of the 1967 Act in the course of summary proceedings, there will be a need to prepare fresh statements excluding inadmissible or prejudicial material, rather than using the striking out or bracketing method.

16A.6 Whenever a fresh statement is taken from a witness and served in evidence, the earlier, unedited statement(s) becomes unused material and should be scheduled and reviewed for disclosure to the defence in the usual way.

CPD.16B **CPD V Evidence 16B: Video Recorded Evidence in Chief**

16B.1 The procedure for making an application for leave to admit into evidence video recorded evidence in chief under section 27 of the Youth Justice and Criminal Evidence Act 1999 is given in CrimPR Part 18.

16B.2 Where a court, on application by a party to the proceedings or of its own motion, grants leave to admit a video recording in evidence under section 27(1) of the 1999 Act, it may direct that any part of the recording be excluded (section 27(2) and (3)). When such direction is given, the party who made the application to admit the video recording must edit the recording in accordance with the judge's directions and send a copy of the edited recording to the appropriate officer of the Crown Court and to every other party to the proceedings.

16B.3 Where a video recording is to be adduced during proceedings before the Crown Court, it should be produced and proved by the interviewer, or any other person who was present at the interview with the witness at which the recording was made. The applicant should ensure that such a person will be available for this purpose, unless the parties have agreed to accept a written statement in lieu of attendance by that person.

16B.4 Once a trial has begun, if, by reason of faulty or inadequate preparation or for some other cause, the procedures set out above have not been properly complied with and an application is made to edit the video recording, thereby necessitating an adjournment for the work to be carried out, the court may, at its discretion, make an appropriate award of costs.

CPD.16C **CPD V Evidence 16C: Evidence of Audio and Video Recorded Interviews**

16C.1 The interrogation of suspects is primarily governed by Code C, one of the Codes of Practice under the Police and Criminal Evidence Act 1984 ('PACE'). Under that Code, interviews must normally be contemporaneously recorded. Under PACE Code E, interviews conducted at a police station concerning an indictable offence must normally be audio-recorded. In practice, most interviews are audio-recorded under Code E, or video-recorded under Code F, and it is best practice to do so. The questioning of terrorism suspects is governed separately by Code H. The Codes are available electronically on the Home Office website.

16C.2 Where a record of the interview is to be prepared, this should be in accordance with the current national guidelines, as envisaged by Note 5A of Code E.

16C.3 If the prosecution wishes to rely on the defendant's interview in evidence, the prosecution should seek to agree the record with the defence. Both parties should have received a copy of the audio or video recording, and can check the record against the recording. The record should be edited (see below) if inadmissible matters are included within it and, in particular if the interview is lengthy, the prosecution should seek to shorten it by editing or summary.

16C.4 If the record is agreed there is usually no need for the audio or video recording to be played in court. It is a matter for the discretion of the trial judge, but usual practice is for edited copies of the record to be provided to the court, and to the jury if there is one, and for the prosecution advocate to read the interview with the interviewing officer or the officer in the case, as part of the officer's evidence in chief, the officer reading the interviewer and the advocate reading the defendant and defence representative. In the magistrates' court, the Bench sometimes retire to read the interview themselves, and the document is treated as if it had been read aloud in court. This is permissible, but CrimPR 24.5 should be followed.

16C.5 Where the prosecution intends to adduce the interview in evidence, and agreement between the parties has not been reached about the record, sufficient notice must be given to allow consideration of any amendment to the record, or the preparation of any transcript of the interview, or any editing of a recording for the purpose of playing it in court. To that end, the following practice should be followed:

(a) Where the defence is unable to agree a record of interview or transcript (where one is already available) the prosecution should be notified at latest at the Plea and Case Management Hearing ('PCMH'), with a view to securing agreement to amend. The notice should specify the part to which objection is taken, or the part omitted which the defence consider should be included. A copy of the notice should be supplied to the court within the period specified above. The PCMH form inquires about the admissibility of the defendant's interview and shortening by editing or summarising for trial.

(b) If agreement is not reached and it is proposed that the audio or video recording or part of it be played in court, notice should be given to the prosecution by the defence as ordered at the PCMH, in order that the advocates for the parties may agree those parts of the audio or video recording that should not be adduced and that arrangements may be made, by editing or in some other way, to exclude that material. A copy of the notice should be supplied to the court.

(c) Notice of any agreement reached should be supplied to the court by the prosecution, as soon as is practicable.

16C.6 Alternatively, if, the prosecution advocate proposes to play the audio or video recording or part of it, the prosecution should at latest at the PCMH, notify the defence and the court. The defence should notify the prosecution and the court within 14 days of receiving the notice, if they object to the production of the audio or video recording on the basis that a part of it should be excluded. If the objections raised by the defence are accepted, the prosecution should prepare an edited recording, or make other arrangements to exclude the material part; and should notify the court of the arrangements made.

16C.7 If the defendant wishes to have the audio or video recording or any part of it played to the court, the defence should provide notice to the prosecution and the court at latest at the PCMH. The defence should also, at that time, notify the prosecution of any proposals to edit the recording and seek the prosecution's agreement to those amendments.

16C.8 Whenever editing or amendment of a record of interview or of an audio or video recording or of a transcript takes place, the following general principles should be followed:

(i) Where a defendant has made a statement which includes an admission of one or more other offences, the portion relating to other offences should be omitted unless it is or becomes admissible in evidence;

(ii) Where the statement of one defendant contains a portion which exculpates him or her and partly implicates a co-defendant in the trial, the defendant making the statement has the right to insist that everything relevant which is exculpatory goes before the jury. In such a case the judge must be consulted about how best to protect the position of the co-defendant.

16C.9 If it becomes necessary for either party to access the master copy of the audio or video recording, they should give notice to the other party and follow the procedure in PACE Code E at section 6.

16C.10 If there is a challenge to the integrity of the master recording, notice and particulars should be given to the court and to the prosecution by the defence as soon as is practicable. The court may then, at its discretion, order a case management hearing or give such other directions as may be appropriate.

16C.11 If an audio or video recording is to be adduced during proceedings before the Crown Court, it should be produced and proved in a witness statement by the interviewing officer or any other officer who was present at the interview at which the recording was made. The prosecution should ensure that the witness is available to attend court if required by the defence in the usual way.

16C.12 It is the responsibility of the prosecution to ensure that there is a person available to operate any audio or video equipment needed during the course of the proceedings. Subject to their other responsibilities, the court staff may be able to assist.

16C.13 If either party wishes to present audio or video evidence, that party must ensure, in advance of the hearing, that the evidence is in a format that is compatible with the court's equipment, and that the material to be used does in fact function properly in the relevant court room.

16C.14 In order to avoid the necessity for the court to listen to or watch lengthy or irrelevant material before the relevant part of a recording is reached, counsel shall indicate to the equipment operator those parts of a recording which it may be necessary to play. Such an indication should, so far as possible, be expressed in terms of the time track or other identifying process used by the interviewing police force and should be given in time for the operator to have located those parts by the appropriate point in the trial.

16C.15 Once a trial has begun, if, by reason of faulty preparation or for some other cause, the procedures above have not been properly complied with, and an application is made to amend the record of interview or transcript or to edit the recording, as the case may be, thereby making necessary an adjournment for the work to be carried out, the court may make at its discretion an appropriate award of costs.

16C.16 Where a case is listed for hearing on a date which falls within the time limits set out above, it is the responsibility of the parties to ensure that all the necessary steps are taken to comply with this Practice Direction within such shorter period as is available.

Criminal Procedure Rules Part 17 Witness Summonses, Warrants and Orders

R17.1 **When this Part applies**

17.1 (1) This Part applies in magistrates' courts and in the Crown Court where—
(a) a party wants the court to issue a witness summons, warrant or order under—
(i) section 97 of the Magistrates' Courts Act 1980[1],
(ii) paragraph 4 of Schedule 3 to the Crime and Disorder Act 1998[2],
(iii) section 2 of the Criminal Procedure (Attendance of Witnesses) Act 1965[3], or
(iv) section 7 of the Bankers' Books Evidence Act 1879[4];
(b) the court considers the issue of such a summons, warrant or order on its own initiative as if a party had applied; or
(c) one of those listed in rule 17.7 wants the court to withdraw such a summons, warrant or order.
(2) A reference to a 'witness' in this Part is a reference to a person to whom such a summons, warrant or order is directed.

[Note. A magistrates' court may require the attendance of a witness to give evidence or to produce in evidence a document or thing by a summons, or in some circumstances a warrant for the witness' arrest, under section 97 of the Magistrates' Courts Act 1980 or under paragraph 4 of Schedule 3 to the Crime and Disorder Act 1998. The Crown Court may do so under sections 2, 2D, 3 and 4 of the Criminal Procedure (Attendance of Witnesses) Act 1965. Either court may order the production in evidence of a copy of an entry in a banker's book without the attendance of an officer of the bank, under sections 6 and 7 of the Bankers' Books Evidence Act 1879. See section 2D of the Criminal Procedure (Attendance of Witnesses) Act 1965 for the Crown Court's power to issue a witness summons on the court's own initiative.

See Part 3 for the court's general powers to consider an application and to give directions.]

R17.2 **Issue etc. of summons, warrant or order with or without a hearing**

17.2 (1) The court may issue or withdraw a witness summons, warrant or order with or without a hearing.
(2) A hearing under this Part must be in private unless the court otherwise directs.

[Note. If rule 17.5 applies, a person served with an application for a witness summons will have an opportunity to make representations about whether there should be a hearing of that application before the witness summons is issued.]

R17.3 **Application for summons, warrant or order: general rules**

17.3 (1) A party who wants the court to issue a witness summons, warrant or order must apply as soon as practicable after becoming aware of the grounds for doing so.
(2) A party applying for a witness summons or order must—
(a) identify the proposed witness;
(b) explain—
(i) what evidence the proposed witness can give or produce,
(ii) why it is likely to be material evidence, and
(iii) why it would be in the interests of justice to issue a summons, order or warrant as appropriate.

[1] 1980 c. 43; section 97 was amended by sections 13 and 14 of, and paragraph 7 of Schedule 2 to, the Contempt of Court Act 1981 (c. 47), section 31 of, and paragraph 2 of Schedule 4 to, the Criminal Justice (International Co-operation) Act 1990 (c. 5), sections 17 and 65 of, and paragraph 6 of Schedule 3 and Part I of Schedule 4 to, the Criminal Justice Act 1991 (c. 53), section 51 of the Criminal Procedure and Investigations Act 1996 (c. 25) and section 169 of the Serious Organised Crime and Police Act 2005 (c. 15).
[2] 1998 c. 37; paragraph 4 of Schedule 3 was amended by paragraphs 15, 20, 68 and 72 of Schedule 3 to the Criminal Justice Act 2003 (c. 44), section 169 of the Serious Organised Crime and Police Act 2005 (c. 15), article 3 of, and paragraphs 35 and 37 of the Schedule to, S.I. 2004/2035 and article 2 of, and paragraph 61 of the Schedule to, S.I. 2005/886.
[3] 1965 c. 69; section 2 was substituted, together with sections 2 A to 2E, by section 66 of the Criminal Procedure and Investigations Act 1996 (c. 25) and amended by section 119 of, and paragraph 8 of Schedule 8 to, the Crime and Disorder Act 1998 (c. 37), section 109 of, and paragraph 126 of Schedule 8 to, the Courts Act 2003 (c. 39), paragraph 42 of Schedule 3 and Part 4 of Schedule 37 to the Criminal Justice Act 2003 (c. 44), section 169 of the Serious Organised Crime and Police Act 2005 (c. 15) and paragraph 33 of Schedule 17 to the Crime and Courts Act 2013 (c. 22).
[4] 1879 c. 11; section 6 has been amended; none is relevant to these rules.

(3) A party applying for an order to be allowed to inspect and copy an entry in bank records must—
(a) identify the entry;
(b) explain the purpose for which the entry is required; and
(c) propose—
(i) the terms of the order, and
(ii) the period within which the order should take effect, if 3 days from the date of service of the order would not be appropriate.
(4) The application may be made orally unless—
(a) rule 17.5 applies; or
(b) the court otherwise directs.
(5) The applicant must serve any order made on the witness to whom, or the bank to which, it is directed.

[Note. The court may issue a warrant for a witness' arrest if that witness fails to obey a witness summons directed to him: see section 97(3) of the Magistrates' Courts Act 1980, paragraph 4(5) of Schedule 3 to the Crime and Disorder Act 1998 and section 4 of the Criminal Procedure (Attendance of Witnesses) Act 1965. Before a magistrates' court may issue a warrant under section 97(3) of the 1980 Act, the witness must first be paid or offered a reasonable amount for costs and expenses.]

Written application: form and service R17.4

17.4 (1) An application in writing under rule 17.3 must be in the form set out in the Practice Direction, containing the same declaration of truth as a witness statement.
(2) The party applying must serve the application—
(a) in every case, on the court officer and as directed by the court; and
(b) as required by rule 17.5, if that rule applies.

[Note. Declarations of truth in witness statements are required by section 9 of the Criminal Justice Act 1967[5]. Section 89 of the 1967 Act[6] makes it an offence to make a written statement under section 9 of that Act which the person making it knows to be false or does not believe to be true.]

Application for summons to produce a document, etc.: special rules R17.5

17.5 (1) This rule applies to an application under rule 17.3 for a witness summons requiring the proposed witness—
(a) to produce in evidence a document or thing; or
(b) to give evidence about information apparently held in confidence, that relates to another person.
(2) The application must be in writing in the form required by rule 17.4.
(3) The party applying must serve the application—
(a) on the proposed witness, unless the court otherwise directs; and
(b) on one or more of the following, if the court so directs—
(i) a person to whom the proposed evidence relates, and
(ii) another party.
(4) The court must not issue a witness summons where this rule applies unless—
(a) everyone served with the application has had at least 10 business days in which to make representations, including representations about whether there should be a hearing of the application before the summons is issued; and
(b) the court is satisfied that it has been able to take adequate account of the duties and rights, including rights of confidentiality, of the proposed witness and of any person to whom the proposed evidence relates.
(5) This rule does not apply to an application for an order to produce in evidence a copy of an entry in bank records.

[Note. Under section 2A of the Criminal Procedure (Attendance of Witnesses) Act 1965[7]), a witness summons to produce a document or thing issued by the Crown Court may require the witness to produce it for inspection by the applicant before producing it in evidence.]

[5] 1967 c. 80; section 9 was amended by section 56 of, and paragraph 49 of Schedule 8 to, the Courts Act 1971 (c. 23), section 168 of, and paragraph 6 of Schedule 9 to, the Criminal Justice and Public Order Act 1994 (c. 33), section 69 of the Criminal Procedure and Investigations Act 1996 (c. 25), regulation 9 of, and paragraph 4 of Schedule 5 to, S.I. 2001/1090, paragraph 43 of Schedule 3 and Part 4 of Schedule 37 to the Criminal Justice Act 2003 (c. 44), section 26 of, and paragraph 7 of Schedule 2 to, the Armed Forces Act 2011 (c. 18) and section 80 of the Deregulation Act 2015 (c. 20). It is further amended by section 72 of, and paragraph 55 of Schedule 5 to, the Children and Young Persons Act 1969 (c. 54) and section 65 of, and paragraph 1 of Schedule 4 to, the Courts Act 2003 (c. 39), with effect from dates to be appointed.
[6] 1967 c. 80; section 89 was amended by section 154 of, and Schedule 9 to, the Magistrates' Courts Act 1980 (c. 43).
[7] 1965 c. 69; section 2A was substituted, together with sections 2, 2 B, 2D and 2E, for existing section 2 by section 66(1) and (2) of the Criminal Procedure and Investigations Act 1996 (c. 25).

R17.6 **Application for summons to produce a document, etc.: court's assessment of relevance and confidentiality**

17.6 (1) This rule applies where a person served with an application for a witness summons requiring the proposed witness to produce in evidence a document or thing objects to its production on the ground that—
(a) it is not likely to be material evidence; or
(b) even if it is likely to be material evidence, the duties or rights, including rights of confidentiality, of the proposed witness or of any person to whom the document or thing relates, outweigh the reasons for issuing a summons.
(2) The court may require the proposed witness to make the document or thing available for the objection to be assessed.
(3) The court may invite—
(a) the proposed witness or any representative of the proposed witness; or
(b) a person to whom the document or thing relates or any representative of such a person, to help the court assess the objection.

R17.7 **Application to withdraw a summons, warrant or order**

17.7 (1) The court may withdraw a witness summons, warrant or order if one of the following applies for it to be withdrawn—
(a) the party who applied for it, on the ground that it no longer is needed;
(b) the witness, on the grounds that he was not aware of any application for it, and—
(i) he cannot give or produce evidence likely to be material evidence, or
(ii) even if he can, his duties or rights, including rights of confidentiality, or those of any person to whom the evidence relates, outweigh the reasons for the issue of the summons, warrant or order; or
(c) any person to whom the proposed evidence relates, on the grounds that he was not aware of any application for it, and—
(i) that evidence is not likely to be material evidence, or
(ii) even if it is, his duties or rights, including rights of confidentiality, or those of the witness, outweigh the reasons for the issue of the summons, warrant or order.
(2) A person applying under the rule must—
(a) apply in writing as soon as practicable after becoming aware of the grounds for doing so, explaining why he wants the summons, warrant or order to be withdrawn; and
(b) serve the application on the court officer and as appropriate on—
(i) the witness,
(ii) the party who applied for the summons, warrant or order, and
(iii) any other person who he knows was served with the application for the summons, warrant or order.
(3) Rule 17.6 applies to an application under this rule that concerns a document or thing to be produced in evidence.

[Note. See sections 2B, 2C and 2E of the Criminal Procedure (Attendance of Witnesses) Act 1965[8] *for the Crown Court's powers to withdraw a witness summons, including the power to order costs.]*

R17.8 **Court's power to vary requirements under this Part**

17.8 (1) The court may—
(a) shorten or extend (even after it has expired) a time limit under this Part; and
(b) where a rule or direction requires an application under this Part to be in writing, allow that application to be made orally instead.
(2) Someone who wants the court to allow an application to be made orally under paragraph (1)(b) of this rule must—
(a) give as much notice as the urgency of his application permits to those on whom he would otherwise have served an application in writing; and
(b) in doing so explain the reasons for the application and for wanting the court to consider it orally.

[8] 1965 c. 69; sections 2B, 2C and 2E were substituted with section 2 and 2A, for the existing section 2 by section 66(1) and (2) of the Criminal Procedure and Investigations Act 1996 (c. 25) and amended by section 109 of, and paragraph 126 of Schedule 8 to, the Courts Act 2003 (c. 39).

CRIMINAL PRACTICE DIRECTIONS PART 17 WITNESS SUMMONSES, WARRANTS AND ORDERS

CPD V Evidence 17A: Wards of Court and Children Subject to Current Family Proceedings CPD.17A

17A.1 Where police wish to interview a child who is subject to current family proceedings, leave of the Family Court is only required where such an interview may lead to a child disclosing information confidential to those proceedings and not otherwise available to the police under Working Together to Safeguard Children (March 2013), a guide to inter-agency working to safeguard and promote the welfare of children: www.workingtogetheronline.co.uk/chapters/contents.html

17A.2 Where exceptionally the child to be interviewed or called as a witness in criminal proceedings is a Ward of Court then the leave of the court which made the wardship order will be required.

17A.3 Any application for leave in respect of any such child must be made to the court in which the relevant family proceedings are continuing and must be made on notice to the parents, any actual carer (e.g., relative or foster parent) and, in care proceedings, to the local authority and the guardian. In private proceedings the Family Court Reporter (if appointed) should be notified.

17A.4 If the police need to interview the child without the knowledge of another party (usually a parent or carer), they may make the application for leave without giving notice to that party.

17A.5 Where leave is given the order should ordinarily give leave for any number of interviews that may be required. However, anything beyond that actually authorised will require a further application.

17A.6 Exceptionally the police may have to deal with complaints by or allegations against such a child immediately without obtaining the leave of the court as, for example:
(a) a serious offence against a child (like rape) where immediate medical examination and collection of evidence is required; or
(b) where the child is to be interviewed as a suspect.

When any such action is necessary, the police should, in respect of each and every interview, notify the parents and other carer (if any) and the Family Court Reporter (if appointed). In care proceedings the local authority and guardian should be notified. The police must comply with all relevant Codes of Practice when conducting any such interview.

17A.7 The Family Court should be appraised of the position at the earliest reasonable opportunity by one of the notified parties and should thereafter be kept informed of any criminal proceedings.

17A.8 No evidence or document in the family proceedings or information about the proceedings should be disclosed into criminal proceedings without the leave of the Family Court.

CRIMINAL PROCEDURE RULES PART 18 MEASURES TO ASSIST A WITNESS OR DEFENDANT TO GIVE EVIDENCE OR OTHERWISE PARTICIPATE

General rules

When this Part applies R18.1

18.1 This Part applies—
(a) where the court can give a direction (a 'special measures direction'), under section 19 of the Youth Justice and Criminal Evidence Act 1999[1], on an application or on its own initiative, for any of the following measures—
(i) preventing a witness from seeing the defendant (section 23 of the 1999 Act),
(ii) allowing a witness to give evidence by live link (section 24 of the 1999 Act[2]),
(iii) hearing a witness' evidence in private (section 25 of the 1999 Act[3]),
(iv) dispensing with the wearing of wigs and gowns (section 26 of the 1999 Act),
(v) admitting video recorded evidence (sections 27 and 28 of the 1999 Act[4]),
(vi) questioning a witness through an intermediary (section 29 of the 1999 Act[5]),
(vii) using a device to help a witness communicate (section 30 of the 1999 Act);
(b) where the court can vary or discharge such a direction, under section 20 of the 1999 Act[6];

1 1999 c. 23.

2 1999 c. 23; section 24 was amended by paragraph 385 of Schedule 8 to, and Schedule 10 to, the Courts Act 2003 (c. 39) and section 102(1) of the Coroners and Justice Act 2009 (c. 25).

3 1999 c. 23; section 25 was amended by paragraphs 1 and 3 of the Schedule to S.I. 2013/554 and section 46 of the Modern Slavery Act 2015 (c. 30).

4 1999 c. 23; section 27 was amended by paragraph 384 of Schedule 8 to the Courts Act 2003 (c. 39), paragraph 73 of Schedule 3 and Part 4 of Schedule 37 to the Criminal Justice Act 2003 (c. 44) and sections 102(2), 103(1), (3), (4) and (5), 177(1) and (2) and 178 of, and paragraph 73 of Schedule 21, paragraph 23 of Schedule 22 and Part 3 of Schedule 23 to, the Coroners and Justice Act 2009 (c. 25).

5 1999 c. 23; section 29 was amended by paragraph 384(d) of Schedule 8 to the Courts Act 2003 (c. 39).

6 1999 c. 23; section 20(6) was amended by paragraph 384(a) of Schedule 8 to the Courts Act 2003 (c. 39).

(c) where the court can give, vary or discharge a direction (a 'defendant's evidence direction') for a defendant to give evidence—
  (i) by live link, under section 33A of the 1999 Act[7], or
  (ii) through an intermediary, under sections 33BA and 33BB of the 1999 Act[8];
(d) where the court can—
  (i) make a witness anonymity order, under section 86 of the Coroners and Justice Act 2009[9], or
  (ii) vary or discharge such an order, under section 91, 92 or 93 of the 2009 Act;
(e) where the court can give or discharge a direction (a 'live link direction'), on an application or on its own initiative, for a witness to give evidence by live link under—
  (i) section 32 of the Criminal Justice Act 1988[10], or
  (ii) sections 51 and 52 of the Criminal Justice Act 2003[11];
(f) (i) appoint an intermediary to facilitate a defendant's effective participation in that defendant's trial, when the defendant gives evidence or at any other time, or
  (ii) vary or discharge such an appointment; and
(g) where the court can exercise any other power it has to give, make, vary, rescind, discharge or revoke a direction for a measure to help a witness to give evidence or to help a defendant to participate in that defendant's trial.

[Note. At the end of this Part there is a summary of the circumstances in which a witness or defendant may be eligible for the assistance of one of the measures to which this Part applies.]

R18.2 Meaning of 'witness'

18.2 In this Part, 'witness' means anyone (other than a defendant) for whose benefit an application, direction or order is made.

R18.3 Meaning of 'intermediary' and 'intermediary's report'

18.3 In this part:
(a) 'intermediary' means a person who is—
  (i) approved by the court for the purposes of section 29 of the Youth Justice and Criminal Evidence Act 1999[12] (Examination of witness through intermediary),
  (ii) approved by the court for the purposes of section 33BA of the 1999 Act[13] (Examination of accused through intermediary),
  (iii) asked to assess a defendant's communication needs, or
  (iv) appointed by the court to facilitate a defendant's effective participation in the trial, when the defendant gives evidence or at any other time, where otherwise that defendant's communication needs would impede such participation; and
(b) a reference to 'an intermediary's report' means a report by such a person which complies with rule 18.32.

R18.4 Making an application for a direction or order

18.4 A party who wants the court to exercise its power to give or make a direction or order must—
(a) apply in writing as soon as reasonably practicable, and in any event not more than—
  (i) 20 business days after the defendant pleads not guilty, in a magistrates' court, or
  (ii) 10 business days after the defendant pleads not guilty, in the Crown Court; and
(b) serve the application on—
  (i) the court officer, and
  (ii) each other party.

[7] 1999 c. 23; section 33A was inserted by section 47 of the Police and Justice Act 2006 (c. 48).
[8] 1999 c. 23; sections 33BA and 33BB are inserted by section 104 of the Coroners and Justice Act 2009 (c. 25), with effect from a date to be appointed.
[9] 2009 c. 25.
[10] 1988 c. 33; section 32 was amended by section 55 of the Criminal Justice Act 1991 (c. 53), section 29 of, and paragraph 16 of Schedule 2 to, the Criminal Appeal Act 1995 (c. 35), section 62 of the Criminal Procedure and Investigations Act 1996 (c. 25), section 67 of, and Schedule 6 and paragraph 3 of Schedule 7 to, the Youth Justice and Criminal Evidence Act 1999 (c. 23) and paragraphs 24 and 26 of the Schedule to S.I. 2004/2035.
[11] 2003 c. 44.
[12] 1999 c. 23; section 29 was amended by paragraph 384 of Schedule 8 to the Courts Act 2003 (c. 39).
[13] 1999 c. 23; section 33BA is inserted by section 104(1) of the Coroners and Justice Act 2009 (c. 25), with effect from a date to be appointed.

[Note. See also rule 18.10 (Content of application for a special measures direction), rule 18.15 (Content of application for a defendant's evidence direction), rule 18.19 (Content and conduct of application for a witness anonymity order) rule 18.24 (Content of application for a live link direction) and rule 18.27 ((Appointment of intermediary to facilitate a defendant's participation.

The Practice Direction sets out forms for use in connection with—

(a) an application under rule 18.10 for a special measures direction;
(b) an application under rule 18.24 for a live link direction (otherwise than as a special measures direction).]

Decisions and reasons R18.5

18.5 (1) A party who wants to introduce the evidence of a witness who is the subject of an application, direction or order must—
(a) inform the witness of the court's decision as soon as reasonably practicable; and
(b) explain to the witness the arrangements that as a result will be made for him or her to give evidence.
(2) The court must—
(a) promptly determine an application; and
(b) allow a party sufficient time to comply with the requirements of—
(i) paragraph (1), and
(ii) the code of practice issued under section 32 of the Domestic Violence, Crime and Victims Act 2004[14].
(3) The court must announce, at a hearing in public before the witness gives evidence or the defendant's trial begins (as the case may be), the reasons for a decision—
(a) to give, make, vary or discharge
(i) a special measures direction for a witness, or
(ii) a direction to help a defendant to participate in that defendant's trial; or
(b) to refuse to do so.
(4) Where the court can give, vary or rescind a live link direction the court must—
(a) announce the reasons for a decision not to give such a direction; and
(b) in the case of a live link direction for a sentencing hearing, announce the reasons for a decision to rescind that direction.
(5) Where the court gives a direction for everyone taking part in a hearing to do so by live link the court must announce the reasons for a decision—
(a) not to direct that the proceedings are to be broadcast, within the meaning of section 85A of the Courts Act 2003[15] (Enabling the public to see and hear proceedings); or
(b) not to direct that a recording of the proceedings is to be made, within the meaning of that section of that Act

[Note. See sections 20(5), 33A(8) and 33BB(4) of the Youth Justice and Criminal Evidence Act 1999[16]*, sections 57B(6), 57E(8) and 57F(9) of the Crime and Disorder Act 1998 and section 51(8) of the Criminal Justice Act 2003.*

Under section 32 of the Domestic Violence, Crime and Victims Act 2004, the Secretary of State for Justice must issue a code of practice as to the services to be provided by specified persons to a victim of criminal conduct.]

Under section 85A of the Courts Act 2003, if the court directs that proceedings are to be conducted wholly by live video or live audio link the court may direct (i) that the proceedings are to be broadcast for the purpose of enabling members of the public to see and hear, or to hear, those proceedings (as the case may be), and (ii) that a recording of the proceedings is to be made for the purpose of enabling the court to keep an audio-visual, or audio, record of the proceedings (as the case may be).]

Court's power to vary requirements under this Part R18.6

18.6 (1) The court may—
(a) shorten or extend (even after it has expired) a time limit under this Part; and
(b) allow an application or representations to be made in a different form to one set out in the Practice Direction, or to be made orally.
(2) A person who wants an extension of time must—

[14] 2004 c. 28; section 32 was amended by article 8 of, and paragraph 10 of the Schedule to, S.I. 2007/2128.
[15] 2003 c. 39; section 85A was temporarily inserted by section 55 of, and paragraph 1 of Schedule 25 to, the Coronavirus Act 2020 (c. 7).
[16] 1999 c. 23; section 20 was amended by paragraph 384(a) of Schedule 8 to the Courts Act 2003 (c. 39). Section 33A was inserted by section 47 of the Police and Justice Act 2006 (c. 48). Section 33BB is inserted by section 104 of the Coroners and Justice Act 2009 (c. 25), with effect from a date to be appointed.

(a) apply when serving the application or representations for which it is needed; and
(b) explain the delay.

R18.7 Custody of documents

18.7 Unless the court otherwise directs, the court officer may—
(a) keep a written application or representations; or
(b) arrange for the whole or any part to be kept by some other appropriate person, subject to any conditions that the court may impose.

R18.8 Exercise of court's powers

18.8 The court may decide whether to give, vary or discharge a special measures direction—
(a) at a hearing, in public or in private, or without a hearing; and
(b) in a party's absence, if that party—
(i) applied for the direction, variation or discharge, or
(ii) has had at least 10 business days in which to make representations.

R18.9 Special measures direction without application

18.9 (1) This rule applies where—
(a) a party notifies the court that a witness is eligible for assistance under section 16 or section 17 of the Youth Justice and Criminal Evidence Act 1999;
(b) the notice is given at—
(i) a preparation for trial hearing in a magistrates' court, or
(ii) a plea and trial preparation hearing in the Crown Court; and
(c) no other party opposes the giving of a special measures direction for the benefit of that witness.
(2) The court may exercise its power to give a special measures direction without requiring an application under rule 18.10.
(3) The party who gives the notice must—
(a) provide any information that the court may need to assess—
(i) the measure or measures likely to maximise so far as practicable the quality of the witness' evidence, and
(ii) the witness' own views; and
(b) where a direction provides for video recorded evidence to be admitted under section 27 or section 28 of the Youth Justice and Criminal Evidence Act 1999, as soon as reasonably practicable serve such evidence on—
(i) the court officer, and
(ii) each other party.

[Note. Under sections 21 and 22 of the Youth Justice and Criminal Evidence Act 1999, a 'child witness' is one who is under 18, and a 'qualifying witness' is one who was a child witness when interviewed.

Under those sections, the 'primary rule' requires the court to give a direction—

(a) for the evidence of a child witness or of a qualifying witness to be admitted—
(b) by means of a video recording of an interview with the witness, in the place of examination-in-chief, and
(c) after that, by live link; or
(d) if one or both of those measures is not taken, for the witness while giving evidence to be screened from seeing the defendant.

The primary rule always applies unless—

(a) the witness does not want it to apply, and the court is satisfied that to omit a measure usually required by that rule would not diminish the quality of the witness' evidence; or
(b) the court is satisfied that to direct one of the measures usually required by that rule would not be likely to maximise, so far as practicable, the quality of the witness' evidence.]

R18.10 Content of application for a special measures direction

18.10 An applicant for a special measures direction must—
(a) explain how the witness is eligible for assistance;
(b) explain why special measures would be likely to improve the quality of the witness' evidence;
(c) propose the measure or measures that in the applicant's opinion would be likely to maximise, so far as practicable, the quality of that evidence;
(d) report any views that the witness has expressed about—
(i) his or her eligibility for assistance,
(ii) the likelihood that special measures would improve the quality of his or her evidence, and
(iii) the measure or measures proposed by the applicant;

(e) in a case in which a child witness or a qualifying witness does not want the primary rule to apply, provide any information that the court may need to assess the witness' views;
(f) in a case in which the applicant proposes that the witness should give evidence by live link—
(i) identify someone to accompany the witness while the witness gives evidence,
(ii) name that person, if possible, and
(iii) explain why that person would be an appropriate companion for the witness, including the witness' own views;
(g) in a case in which the applicant proposes the admission of video recorded evidence, identify—
(i) the date and duration of the recording, and
(ii) which part the applicant wants the court to admit as evidence, if the applicant does not want the court to admit all of it;
(h) attach any other material on which the applicant relies; and
(i) if the applicant wants a hearing, ask for one, and explain why it is needed.

[Note. The Practice Direction sets out a form of application for use in connection with this rule.]

Application to vary or discharge a special measures direction R18.11

18.11 (1) A party who wants the court to vary or discharge a special measures direction must—
(a) apply in writing, as soon as reasonably practicable after becoming aware of the grounds for doing so; and
(b) serve the application on—
(i) the court officer, and
(ii) each other party.
(2) The applicant must—
(a) explain what material circumstances have changed since the direction was given (or last varied, if applicable);
(b) explain why the direction should be varied or discharged; and
(c) ask for a hearing, if the applicant wants one, and explain why it is needed.

[Note. Under section 20 of the Youth Justice and Criminal Evidence Act 1999, the court can vary or discharge a special measures direction—
(a) on application, if there has been a material change of circumstances; or
(b) on the court's own initiative.]

Application containing information withheld from another party R18.12

18.12 (1) This rule applies where—
(a) an applicant serves an application for a special measures direction, or for its variation or discharge; and
(b) the application includes information that the applicant thinks ought not be revealed to another party.
(2) The applicant must—
(a) omit that information from the part of the application that is served on that other party;
(b) mark the other part to show that, unless the court otherwise directs, it is only for the court; and
(c) in that other part, explain why the applicant has withheld that information from that other party.
(3) Any hearing of an application to which this rule applies—
(a) must be in private, unless the court otherwise directs; and
(b) if the court so directs, may be, wholly or in part, in the absence of a party from whom information has been withheld.
(4) At any hearing of an application to which this rule applies—
(a) the general rule is that the court must consider, in the following sequence—
(i) representations first by the applicant and then by each other party, in all the parties' presence, and then
(ii) further representations by the applicant, in the absence of a party from whom information has been withheld; but
(b) the court may direct other arrangements for the hearing.

[Note. See section 20 of the Youth Justice and Criminal Evidence Act 1999.]

Representations in response R18.13

18.13 (1) This rule applies where a party wants to make representations about—
(a) an application for a special measures direction;
(b) an application for the variation or discharge of such a direction; or
(c) a direction, variation or discharge that the court proposes on its own initiative.

(2) Such a party must—
(a) serve the representations on—
(i) the court officer, and
(ii) each other party;
(b) do so not more than 10 business days after, as applicable—
(i) service of the application, or
(ii) notice of the direction, variation or discharge that the court proposes; and
(c) ask for a hearing, if that party wants one, and explain why it is needed.
(3) Where representations include information that the person making them thinks ought not be revealed to another party, that person must—
(a) omit that information from the representations served on that other party;
(b) mark the information to show that, unless the court otherwise directs, it is only for the court; and
(c) with that information include an explanation of why it has been withheld from that other party.
(4) Representations against a special measures direction must explain, as appropriate—
(a) why the witness is not eligible for assistance;
(b) if the witness is eligible for assistance, why—
(i) no special measure would be likely to improve the quality of the witness' evidence,
(ii) the proposed measure or measures would not be likely to maximise, so far as practicable, the quality of the witness' evidence, or
(iii) the proposed measure or measures might tend to inhibit the effective testing of that evidence; and
(c) in a case in which the admission of video recorded evidence is proposed, why it would not be in the interests of justice for the recording, or part of it, to be admitted as evidence.
(5) Representations against the variation or discharge of a special measures direction must explain why it should not be varied or discharged.

[Note. Under sections 21 and 22 of the Youth Justice and Criminal Evidence Act 1999, where the witness is a child witness or a qualifying witness the special measures that the court usually must direct must be treated as likely to maximise, so far as practicable, the quality of the witness' evidence, irrespective of representations to the contrary.]

Defendant's evidence directions

R18.14 Exercise of court's powers

18.14 The court may decide whether to give, vary or discharge a defendant's evidence direction—
(a) at a hearing, in public or in private, or without a hearing; and
(b) in a party's absence, if that party—
(i) applied for the direction, variation or discharge, or
(ii) has had at least 10 business days in which to make representations.

R18.15 Content of application for a defendant's evidence direction

18.15 An applicant for a defendant's evidence direction must—
(a) explain how the proposed direction meets the conditions prescribed by the Youth Justice and Criminal Evidence Act 1999;
(b) in a case in which the applicant proposes that the defendant give evidence by live link—
(i) identify a person to accompany the defendant while the defendant gives evidence, and
(ii) explain why that person is appropriate; and
(c) ask for a hearing, if the applicant wants one, and explain why it is needed.

[Note. See sections 33A and 33BA of the Youth Justice and Criminal Evidence Act 1999.]

R18.16 Application to vary or discharge a defendant's evidence direction

18.16 (1) A party who wants the court to vary or discharge a defendant's evidence direction must—
(a) apply in writing, as soon as reasonably practicable after becoming aware of the grounds for doing so; and
(b) serve the application on—
(i) the court officer, and
(ii) each other party.
(2) The applicant must—
(a) on an application to discharge a live link direction, explain why it is in the interests of justice to do so;
(b) on an application to discharge a direction for an intermediary, explain why it is no longer necessary in order to ensure that the defendant receives a fair trial;
(c) on an application to vary a direction for an intermediary, explain why it is necessary for the

direction to be varied in order to ensure that the defendant receives a fair trial; and
(d) ask for a hearing, if the applicant wants one, and explain why it is needed.

[Note. See sections 33A(7) and 33BB of the Youth Justice and Criminal Evidence Act 1999.]

Representations in response **R18.17**

18.17 (1) This rule applies where a party wants to make representations about—
(a) an application for a defendant's evidence direction;
(b) an application for the variation or discharge of such a direction; or
(c) a direction, variation or discharge that the court proposes on its own initiative.
(2) Such a party must—
(a) serve the representations on—
(i) the court officer, and
(ii) each other party;
(b) do so not more than 10 business days after, as applicable—
(i) service of the application, or
(ii) notice of the direction, variation or discharge that the court proposes; and
(c) ask for a hearing, if that party wants one, and explain why it is needed.
(3) Representations against a direction, variation or discharge must explain why the conditions prescribed by the Youth Justice and Criminal Evidence Act 1999 are not met.

Witness anonymity orders

Exercise of court's powers **R18.18**

18.18 (1) The court may decide whether to make, vary or discharge a witness anonymity order—
(a) at a hearing (which must be in private, unless the court otherwise directs), or without a hearing (unless any party asks for one); and
(b) in the absence of a defendant.
(2) The court must not exercise its power to make, vary or discharge a witness anonymity order, or to refuse to do so—
(a) before or during the trial, unless each party has had an opportunity to make representations;
(b) on an appeal by the defendant to which applies Part 34 (Appeal to the Crown Court) or Part 39 (Appeal to the Court of Appeal about conviction or sentence), unless in each party's case—
(i) that party has had an opportunity to make representations, or
(ii) the appeal court is satisfied that it is not reasonably practicable to communicate with that party;
(c) after the trial and any such appeal are over, unless in the case of each party and the witness—
(i) each has had an opportunity to make representations, or
(ii) the court is satisfied that it is not reasonably practicable to communicate with that party or witness.

Content and conduct of application for a witness anonymity order **R18.19**

18.19 (1) An applicant for a witness anonymity order must—
(a) include in the application nothing that might reveal the witness' identity;
(b) describe the measures proposed by the applicant;
(c) explain how the proposed order meets the conditions prescribed by section 88 of the Coroners and Justice Act 2009[17];
(d) explain why no measures other than those proposed will suffice, such as—
(i) an admission of the facts that would be proved by the witness,
(ii) an order restricting public access to the trial,
(iii) reporting restrictions, in particular under sections 45, 45A or 46 of the Youth Justice and Criminal Evidence Act 1999[18],
(iv) a direction for a special measure under section 19 of the Youth Justice and Criminal Evidence Act 1999,
(v) introduction of the witness' written statement as hearsay evidence, under section 116 of the Criminal Justice Act 2003[19], or
(vi) arrangements for the protection of the witness;
(e) attach to the application—

[17] 2009 c. 25.
[18] 1999 c. 23; section 45A was inserted by section 78 of the Criminal Justice and Courts Act 2015 (c. 2).
[19] 2003 c. 44.

(i) a witness statement setting out the proposed evidence, edited in such a way as not to reveal the witness' identity,
(ii) where the prosecutor is the applicant, any further prosecution evidence to be served, and any further prosecution material to be disclosed under the Criminal Procedure and Investigations Act 1996, similarly edited, and
(iii) any defence statement that has been served, or as much information as may be available to the applicant that gives particulars of the defence; and

(f) ask for a hearing, if the applicant wants one.

(2) At any hearing of the application, the applicant must—
(a) identify the witness to the court, unless at the prosecutor's request the court otherwise directs; and
(b) present to the court, unless it otherwise directs—
(i) the unedited witness statement from which the edited version has been prepared,
(ii) where the prosecutor is the applicant, the unedited version of any further prosecution evidence or material from which an edited version has been prepared, and
(iii) such further material as the applicant relies on to establish that the proposed order meets the conditions prescribed by section 88 of the 2009 Act.

(3) At any such hearing—
(a) the general rule is that the court must consider, in the following sequence—
(i) representations first by the applicant and then by each other party, in all the parties' presence, and then
(ii) information withheld from a defendant, and further representations by the applicant, in the absence of any (or any other) defendant; but
(b) the court may direct other arrangements for the hearing.

(4) Before the witness gives evidence, the applicant must identify the witness to the court—
(a) if not already done;
(b) without revealing the witness' identity to any other party or person; and
(c) unless at the prosecutor's request the court otherwise directs.

R18.20 Duty of court officer to notify the Director of Public Prosecutions

18.20 The court officer must notify the Director of Public Prosecutions of an application, unless the prosecutor is, or acts on behalf of, a public authority.

R18.21 Application to vary or discharge a witness anonymity order

18.21 (1) A party who wants the court to vary or discharge a witness anonymity order, or a witness who wants the court to do so when the case is over, must—
(a) apply in writing, as soon as reasonably practicable after becoming aware of the grounds for doing so; and
(b) serve the application on—
(i) the court officer, and
(ii) each other party.

(2) The applicant must—
(a) explain what material circumstances have changed since the order was made (or last varied, if applicable);
(b) explain why the order should be varied or discharged, taking account of the conditions for making an order; and
(c) ask for a hearing, if the applicant wants one.

(3) Where an application includes information that the applicant thinks might reveal the witness' identity, the applicant must—
(a) omit that information from the application that is served on a defendant;
(b) mark the information to show that it is only for the court and the prosecutor (if the prosecutor is not the applicant); and
(c) with that information include an explanation of why it has been withheld.

(4) Where a party applies to vary or discharge a witness anonymity order after the trial and any appeal are over, the party who introduced the witness' evidence must serve the application on the witness.

[Note. Under sections 91, 92 and 93 of the Coroners and Justice Act 2009, the court can vary or discharge a witness anonymity order—

(a) on an application, if there has been a material change of circumstances since it was made or previously varied; or
(b) on the court's own initiative, unless the trial and any appeal are over.]

Representations in response R18.22

18.22 (1) This rule applies where a party or, where the case is over, a witness, wants to make representations about—
(a) an application for a witness anonymity order;
(b) an application for the variation or discharge of such an order; or
(c) a variation or discharge that the court proposes on its own initiative.
(2) Such a party or witness must—
(a) serve the representations on—
(i) the court officer, and
(ii) each other party;
(b) do so not more than 10 business days after, as applicable—
(i) service of the application, or
(ii) notice of the variation or discharge that the court proposes; and
(c) ask for a hearing, if that party or witness wants one.
(3) Where representations include information that the person making them thinks might reveal the witness' identity, that person must—
(a) omit that information from the representations served on a defendant;
(b) mark the information to show that it is only for the court (and for the prosecutor, if relevant); and
(c) with that information include an explanation of why it has been withheld.
(4) Representations against a witness anonymity order must explain why the conditions for making the order are not met.
(5) Representations against the variation or discharge of such an order must explain why it would not be appropriate to vary or discharge it, taking account of the conditions for making an order.
(6) A prosecutor's representations in response to an application by a defendant must include all information available to the prosecutor that is relevant to the conditions and considerations specified by sections 88 and 89 of the Coroners and Justice Act 2009.

Live link directions

[Note. The rules in this Section do not apply to an application for a special measures direction allowing a witness to give evidence by live link: as to which, see rules 18.8 to 18.13.]

Exercise of court's powers R18.23

18.23 The court may decide whether to give or discharge a live link direction—
(a) at a hearing, in public or in private, or without a hearing; and
(b) in a party's absence, if that party—
(i) applied for the direction or discharge, or
(ii) has had at least 10 business days in which to make representations in response to an application by another party.

Content of application for a live link direction R18.24

18.24 An applicant for a live link direction must—
(a) unless the court otherwise directs, identify the place from which the witness will give evidence;
(b) if that place is in the United Kingdom, explain why it would be in the interests of the efficient or effective administration of justice for the witness to give evidence by live link;
(c) if the applicant wants the witness to be accompanied by another person while giving evidence—
(i) name that person, if possible, and
(ii) explain why it is appropriate for the witness to be accompanied; and
(d) ask for a hearing, if the applicant wants one, and explain why it is needed.

[Note. See section 32 of the Criminal Justice Act 1988[20] *and section 51 of the Criminal Justice Act 2003.*

The Practice Direction sets out a form of application for use in connection with this rule.]

[20] 1988 c. 33; section 32 was amended by section 55 of the Criminal Justice Act 1991 (c. 53), section 29 of, and paragraph 16 of Schedule 2 to, the Criminal Appeal Act 1995 (c. 35), sections 67 and 68 of, and Schedule 6 to, the Youth Justice and Criminal Evidence Act 1999 (c. 23) and article 3 of, and paragraph 26 of the Schedule to, S.I. 2004/2035. It is temporarily omitted by section 87 of, and paragraph 10 of Schedule 23 to, the Coronavirus Act 2020 (c. 7).

R18.25 **Application to discharge a live link direction**

18.25 (1) A party who wants the court to discharge a live link direction must—
(a) apply in writing, as soon as reasonably practicable after becoming aware of the grounds for doing so; and
(b) serve the application on—
(i) the court officer, and
(ii) each other party.
(2) The applicant must—
(a) explain what material circumstances have changed since the direction was given;
(b) explain why it is in the interests of justice to discharge the direction; and
(c) ask for a hearing, if the applicant wants one, and explain why it is needed.
(3) An applicant for the variation or revocation of a European investigation order made on an application under rule 18.24 must demonstrate that the applicant is, as the case may be—
(a) the person who applied for the order;
(b) a prosecuting authority; or
(c) any other person affected by the order.
(4) Where the court varies or revokes such an order, the court officer must promptly notify the appropriate authority in the participating State in which the measure or measures are to be carried out.

[Note. See section 32(4) of the Criminal Justice Act 1988[21] *and section 52(3) of the Criminal Justice Act 2003*[22]*.]*

R18.26 **Representations in response**

18.26 (1) This rule applies where a party wants to make representations about an application for a live link direction or for the discharge of such a direction.
(2) Such a party must—
(a) serve the representations on—
(i) the court officer, and
(ii) each other party;
(b) do so not more than 10 business days after service of the application; and—
(c) ask for a hearing, if that party wants one, and explain why it is needed.
(3) Representations against a direction or discharge must explain, as applicable, why the conditions prescribed by the Criminal Justice Act 1988 or the Criminal Justice Act 2003 are not met.

Intermediary for a Defendant

R18.27 **Appointment of intermediary to facilitate a defendant's participation**

18.27 (1) The court must exercise its power to appoint an intermediary to facilitate a defendant's effective participation in the trial where—
(a) the defendant's ability to participate is likely to be diminished by reason of—
(i) age, if the defendant is under 18, or
(ii) mental disorder (as defined in section 1(2) of the Mental Health Act 1983[23]), a significant impairment of intelligence and social functioning, or a physical disability or disorder; and
(b) the appointment is necessary for that purpose.
(2) In determining whether such an appointment is necessary, who to appoint and the duration or purpose of the appointment, the court must have regard to—
(a) the defendant's communication needs as reported to the court;
(b) the recommendations in any intermediary's report received by the court;
(c) any views that the defendant has expressed about—
(i) receiving the assistance of an intermediary,
(ii) other measures or arrangements to facilitate the defendant's effective participation in the trial;
(d) the likely impact of the defendant's age, if under 18, level of intellectual ability or social functioning on the ability to—

[21] 1988 c. 33; section 32(4) was amended by article 3 of, and paragraph 26 of the Schedule to, S.I. 2004/2035.
[22] 2003 c. 44; section 52 is temporarily omitted by section 87 of, and paragraph 2 of Schedule 23 to, the Coronavirus Act 2020 (c. 7).
[23] 1983 c. 20; section 1(2) was amended by sections 1, 55 and 56 of, and Schedule 11 to, the Mental Health Act 2007 (c. 12).

(i) give evidence, and
(ii) understand what is said and done by the court and other participants;
(e) the likely impact on such participation and on such understanding of any mental disorder or other significant impairment of intelligence or social functioning;
(f) the adequacy of arrangements for questioning the defendant in the absence of an intermediary;
(g) any assistance that the defendant has received in the past—
(i) while giving evidence in legal proceedings,
(ii) while being questioned during the investigation of an alleged offence, or
(iii) as a defendant in a criminal case;
(h) any assessment of the defendant's health by a mental health practitioner acting independently of the parties to assist the court;
(i) any expert medical opinion that the court may have received; and
(j) any other matter that the court thinks relevant.

(3) The court may exercise its power to appoint an intermediary—
(a) for the duration of every hearing that the defendant is due to attend;
(b) for the duration of any specified such hearing or hearings, or for the duration of a specified part of such a hearing; or
(c) for a specified purpose during a hearing.

(4) Unless the court otherwise directs, the appointment of an intermediary extends to facilitating the defendant's communication with that defendant's legal representatives for the duration and for the purpose of the appointment.

(5) The court may decide whether to appoint an intermediary to facilitate a defendant's effective participation in the trial and whether to vary or discharge any such appointment—
(a) on application or on the court's own initiative;
(b) at a hearing, in public or in private, or without a hearing; and
(c) in a party's absence, if that party—
(i) applied for the appointment, variation or discharge, or
(ii) has had at least 10 business days in which to make representations.

(6) The court must not exercise its power to vary or discharge a direction for the appointment of an intermediary unless satisfied that—
(a) since the direction was made—
(i) the defendant's communication needs have changed materially, or
(ii) any other material circumstance has changed materially; and
(b) the defendant will be able to participate effectively in the trial despite the variation or discharge of the direction.

Application to vary or discharge the appointment of an intermediary for a defendant **R18.28**

18.28 (1) A party who wants the court to vary or discharge the appointment of an intermediary to facilitate a defendant's effective participation in the trial must—
(a) apply in writing, as soon as reasonably practicable after becoming aware of the grounds for doing so; and
(b) serve the application on—
(i) the court officer, and
(ii) each other party.

(2) The applicant must—
(a) explain how the criteria listed in rule 18.27(7) are met (variation or discharge of appointment); and
(b) ask for a hearing, if the applicant wants one, and explain why it is needed.

Representations in response to application or proposal **R18.29**

18.29 (1) This rule applies where a party wants to make representations about—
(a) an application or proposal for the appointment of an intermediary to facilitate a defendant's effective participation in the trial; or
(b) an application or proposal for the variation or discharge of such an appointment.

(2) Such a party must—
(a) serve the representations on—
(i) the court officer, and
(ii) each other party;

(b) do so not more than 10 business days after, as applicable—
(i) service of the application, or
(ii) notice of the appointment, variation or discharge that the court proposes; and
(c) ask for a hearing, if that party wants one, and explain why it is needed.
(3) Representations against such an appointment, variation or discharge must explain why the criteria that apply are not met.

Duties of Intermediaries

R18.30 **Intermediary's duty to the court**

18.30 (1) This rule applies to an intermediary who accepts—
(a) approval by the court for the purposes of section 29 of the Youth Justice and Criminal Evidence Act 1999[24] (Examination of witness through intermediary);
(b) approval by the court for the purposes of section 33BA of the 1999 Act[25] (Examination of accused through intermediary); or
(c) appointment by the court to facilitate a defendant's effective participation in the trial, when the defendant gives evidence or at any other time.
(2) The intermediary must help the court to achieve the overriding objective—
(a) to the best of the intermediary's skill and understanding by—
(i) communicating to the witness or defendant (as the case may be) questions put to them,
(ii) communicating to the questioner and the court the replies, and
(iii) explaining such questions and answers so that they can be understood;
(b) by assessing continually the witness' or the defendant's (as the case may be) ability to participate effectively and intervening if necessary;
(c) where the intermediary is appointed to facilitate a defendant's effective participation, by explaining to the defendant, in terms the defendant can understand, what is said and done by the court and other participants; and
(d) by actively assisting the court in fulfilling its duties under rule 3.2 (Case management; The duty of the court) and rule 3.9 (Case management; Ground rules hearing), in particular by—
(i) complying with directions made by the court, and
(ii) at once informing the court of any significant failure (by the intermediary or another) to take any step required by such a direction.
(3) This duty overrides any obligation to the witness or to the defendant (as the case may be), or to the person by whom the intermediary is paid.

Declaration by intermediary

R18.31 18.31 (1) This rule applies where—
(a) a video recorded interview with a witness is conducted through an intermediary; or
(b) the court directs the examination of a witness or defendant through an intermediary.
(2) The intermediary must make a declaration—
(a) before such an interview begins; and
(b) before the examination begins (even if such an interview with the witness was conducted through the same intermediary).
(3) The declaration must be in these terms, or in any corresponding terms that the intermediary declares to be binding—

"I swear by Almighty God [*or* I solemnly, sincerely and truly declare and affirm] that I shall faithfully communicate questions and answers and make true explanation of all matters and things required of me according to the best of my skill and understanding."

Content of intermediary's report

R18.32 18.32 (1) An intermediary's report must, in every case—
(a) give details of the intermediary's qualifications, relevant experience and any accreditation;
(b) identify the commissioner of the report;

[24] 1999 c. 23; section 29 was amended by paragraph 384 of Schedule 8 to the Courts Act 2003 (c. 39).
[25] 1999 c. 23; section 33BA is inserted by section 104(1) of the Coroners and Justice Act 2009 (c. 25), with effect from a date to be appointed.

(c) identify those from whom the intermediary has obtained information material to the report;
(d) list the documents received or inspected by the intermediary which contained such information and give an indication of their content;
(e) give the date or dates on which the intermediary met the witness or defendant, as the case may be, for the purpose of preparing the report;
(f) describe the nature and duration of the intermediary's assessment, or assessments, of the witness or defendant;
(g) by reference to examples drawn from the intermediary's assessment of the witness or defendant explain why in this particular case intermediary assistance is necessary;
(h) include an evaluation of—
 (i) the impact of any condition or conditions which, whether in isolation or together, may adversely affect the witness' or the defendant's ability to communicate, and
 (ii) the extent, if any, to which that impact may be exacerbated by the trial;
(i) if the intermediary is not able to reach an evaluation without qualifying it, state the qualification;
(j) report the views of the witness or defendant, as the case may be, on receiving the assistance of an intermediary;
(k) include in a summary of the intermediary's conclusions any recommendation, with reasons, for—
 (i) the approval or appointment of an intermediary,
 (ii) the manner and duration of any questioning of the witness or defendant, as the case may be, and
 (iii) arrangements for the way in which the intermediary, if approved or appointed, should participate; and
(l) contain a statement that the intermediary—
 (i) understands an intermediary's duty to the court, and
 (ii) will comply with that duty if approved or appointed.

(2) Where the intermediary is asked to evaluate a defendant's communication needs the report must also—
(a) include an evaluation of the extent to which any measures or arrangements beside the appointment of an intermediary will facilitate the defendant's effective participation in the trial; and
(b) in the summary of the intermediary's conclusions include any recommendation, with reasons, for—
 (i) the duration and purpose of any appointment of an intermediary, and
 (ii) other measures or arrangements to help the defendant to participate effectively in the trial

Summary of eligibility for measures to which this Part applies

Special measures direction

Under section 16 of the Youth Justice and Criminal Evidence Act 1999[26]*, a witness is eligible for the assistance of a special measures direction given under section 19 of that Act if—*

(a) the witness is under 18; or
(b) the witness has—
 (i) a mental disorder, or a significant impairment of intelligence and social functioning, or
 (ii) a physical disability or disorder

and the court considers that the completeness, coherence and accuracy (the 'quality') of evidence given by the witness is likely to be diminished by reason of those circumstances.

Under section 17 of the 1999([27]*) Act, a witness is eligible for such assistance if—*

(a) the court is satisfied that the quality of evidence given by the witness is likely to be diminished because of his or her fear or distress in connection with giving evidence, taking account particularly of—
 (i) the circumstances of the offence,
 (ii) the witness' age, social and cultural background, ethnic origins, domestic and employment circumstances, religious beliefs or political opinions,

[26] 1999 c. 23.
[27] 1999 c. 23; section 17 was amended by section 99 of the Coroners and Justice Act 2009 (c. 25), paragraphs 1 and 2 of the Schedule to S.I. 2013/554 and section 46 of the Modern Slavery Act 2015 (c. 30).

(iii) any behaviour towards the witness on the part of the defendant, the defendant's family or associates, or any other potential defendant or witness, and
(iv) the witness' own views;
(b) the witness is the complainant in respect of a sexual offence, and has not declined such assistance; or
(c) the offence is one of a list of offences involving weapons, and the witness has not declined such assistance.

Section 28 of the 1999 Act (video recorded cross-examination or re-examination) is not yet in force. With that exception, all the special measures listed in rule 18.1 potentially are available where the witness is eligible for assistance under section 16 of the Act. Those numbered (i) to (v) are available where the witness is eligible for assistance under section 17.

As a general rule, but with exceptions, the court must give a special measures direction—
(a) under section 21 or 22 of the 1999 Act[28], where the witness—
(i) is under 18, or
(ii) was under that age when interviewed whether or not an application for a direction is made;
(b) under section 22A of the 1999 Act[29], where an application is made in the Crown Court for the evidence of a witness who is the complainant of a sexual offence to be admitted by means of a video recording of an interview with the witness in the place of examination-in-chief.

Defendant's evidence direction

Under section 33A of the 1999 Act[30], the court can allow a defendant to give evidence by live link, or (when the Coroners and Justice Act 2009 comes into force) under section 33BA[31] can allow a defendant to give evidence through an intermediary, if—
(a) the defendant—
(i) is under 18, and the defendant's ability to participate effectively as a witness giving oral evidence is compromised by his or her level of intellectual ability or social functioning; or
(ii) suffers from a mental disorder or some other significant impairment of intelligence and social functioning and cannot participate effectively as a witness giving oral evidence for that reason;
(b) the use of a live link—
(i) would enable the defendant to participate more effectively, and
(ii) is in the interests of justice;
(c) the examination of the defendant through an intermediary is necessary to ensure that the defendant receives a fair trial.

Witness anonymity order

Under section 86 of the Coroners and Justice Act 2009[32], a witness anonymity order is an order that specifies measures to be taken to ensure that the identity of a witness is not disclosed, such as withholding the witness' name from materials disclosed to a party to the proceedings, the use of a pseudonym, the screening of the witness from view, the modulation of the witness' voice, and the prohibition of questions that might reveal his or her identity. Before making such an order, the court must—
(a) be satisfied that three conditions prescribed by the Act are met (section 88 of the 2009 Act); and
(b) have regard to considerations specified by the Act (section 89 of the 2009 Act).

Live link direction

Under section 32 of the Criminal Justice Act 1988, the court can allow a witness who is outside the United Kingdom to give evidence by live link—
(a) in proceedings in a youth court, or on appeal from such proceedings; or
(b) at a trial in the Crown Court, or on appeal from such a trial.

[28] 1999 c. 23; sections 21 and 22 were amended by sections 98, 100 and 178 of, and Part 3 of Schedule 23 to, the Coroners and Justice Act 2009 (c. 25).
[29] 1999 c. 23; section 22A was inserted by section 101 of the Coroners and Justice Act 2009 (c. 25).
[30] 1999 c. 23; section 33A was inserted by section 47 of the Police and Justice Act 2006 (c. 48).
[31] 1999 c. 23; section 33BA is inserted by section 104 of the Coroners and Justice Act 2009 (c. 25), with effect from a date to be appointed.
[32] 2009 c. 25.

Under section 51 of the Criminal Justice Act 2003, on an application or on its own initiative, the court can allow a witness who is in the United Kingdom, but outside the building in which the proceedings are held, to give evidence by live link. The court must be satisfied that that is in the interests of the efficient or effective administration of justice.

If a witness is eligible for the assistance of a special measures direction (as to which, see the note above), the court can allow the witness to give evidence by live link under sections 19 and 24 of the 1999 Act[33]. *See rules 18.8 to 18.13.]*

Intermediary for a defendant

In order to ensure the defendant's effective participation in his or her trial the court has an inherent power to appoint an intermediary to facilitate that participation, including during the giving of evidence by the defendant.

Criminal Practice Directions Part 18 Measures to Assist a Witness or Defendant to Give Evidence or Otherwise Participate

CPD V Evidence 18A: Measures to Assist a Witness or Defendant to give Evidence CPD.18A

18A.1 For special measures applications, the procedures at CrimPR Part 18 should be followed. However, assisting a vulnerable witness to give evidence is not merely a matter of ordering the appropriate measure. Further directions about vulnerable people in the courts, ground rules hearings and intermediaries are given in paragraphs I 3D to 3G.

18A.2 Special measures need not be considered or ordered in isolation. The needs of the individual witness should be ascertained, and a combination of special measures may be appropriate. For example, if a witness who is to give evidence by live link wishes, screens can be used to shield the live link screen from the defendant and the public, as would occur if screens were being used for a witness giving evidence in the court room.

CPD V Evidence 18B: Witnesses giving Evidence by Live Link CPD.18B

18B.1 A special measures direction for the witness to give evidence by live link may also provide for a specified person to accompany the witness (CrimPR 18.10(f)). In determining who this should be, the court must have regard to the wishes of the witness. The presence of a supporter is designed to provide emotional support to the witness, helping reduce the witness's anxiety and stress and contributing to the ability to give best evidence. It is preferable for the direction to be made well before the trial begins and to ensure that the designated person is available on the day of the witness's testimony so as to provide certainty for the witness.

18B.2 An increased degree of flexibility is appropriate as to who can act as supporter. This can be anyone known to and trusted by the witness who is not a party to the proceedings and has no detailed knowledge of the evidence in the case. The supporter may be a member of the Witness Service but need not be an usher or court official. Someone else may be appropriate.

18B.3 The usher should continue to be available both to assist the witness and the witness supporter, and to ensure that the court's requirements are properly complied with in the live link room.

18B.4 In order to be able to express an informed view about special measures, the witness is entitled to practise speaking using the live link (and to see screens in place). Simply being shown the room and equipment is inadequate for this purpose.

18B.5 If, with the agreement of the court, the witness has chosen not to give evidence by live link but to do so in the court room, it may still be appropriate for a witness supporter to be selected in the same way, and for the supporter to sit alongside the witness while the witness is giving evidence.

CPD V Evidence 18C: Visually Recorded Interviews: Memory Refreshing and Watching at a Different Time from the Trial Court CPD.18C

18C.1 Witnesses are entitled to refresh their memory from their statement or visually recorded interview. The court should enquire at the PTPH or other case management hearing about arrangements for memory refreshing. The witness's first viewing of the visually recorded interview can be distressing or distracting. It should not be seen for the first time immediately before giving evidence. Depending upon the age and vulnerability of the witness several competing issues have to be

[33] 1999 c. 23; section 24 was amended by paragraph 385 of Schedule 8 to, and Schedule 10 to, the Courts Act 2003 (c. 39) and section 102(1) of the Coroners and Justice Act 2009 (c. 25).

considered and it may be that the assistance of the intermediary is needed to establish exactly how memory refreshing should be managed.

18C.2 If the interview is ruled inadmissible, the court must decide what constitutes an acceptable alternative method of memory refreshing.

18C.3 Decisions about how, when and where refreshing should take place should be court-led and made on a case-by-case basis in respect of each witness. General principles to be addressed include:

i. the venue for viewing. The delicate balance between combining the court familiarisation visit and watching the DVD, and having them on two separate occasions, needs to be considered in respect of each witness as combining the two may lead to 'information overload'. Refreshing need not necessarily take place within the court building but may be done, for example, at the police ABE suite;

ii. requiring that any viewing is monitored by a person (usually the officer in the case) who will report to the court about anything said by the witness;

iii. whether it is necessary for the witness to see the DVD more than once for the purpose of refreshing. The court will need to ask the advice of the intermediary, if any, with respect to this;

iv. arrangements, if the witness will not watch the DVD at the same time as the trial bench or judge and jury, for the witness to watch it before attending to be cross examined, (depending upon their ability to retain information this may be the day before).

18C.4 There is no legal requirement that the witness should watch the interview at the same time as the trial bench or jury. Increasingly, this is arranged to occur at a different time, with the advantages that breaks can be taken as needed without disrupting the trial, and cross-examination starts while the witness is fresh. An intermediary may be present to facilitate communication but should not act as the independent person designated to take a note and report to the court if anything is said.

18C.5 Where the viewing takes place at a different time from that of the trial bench or jury, the witness is sworn (or promises) just before cross-examination and, unless the judge otherwise directs:

(a) it is good practice for the witness to be asked by the prosecutor, (or the judge/magistrate if they so direct), in appropriate language if, and when, he or she has watched the recording of the interview;

(b) if, in watching the recording of the interview or otherwise the witness has indicated that there is something he or she wishes to correct or to add then it is good practice for the prosecutor (or the judge/magistrate if they so direct) to deal with that before cross-examination provided that proper notice has been given to the defence.

CPD.18D **CPD V Evidence 18D: Witness Anonymity Orders**

18D.1 This direction supplements CrimPR 18.18 to 18.22, which governs the procedure to be followed on an application for a witness anonymity order. The court's power to make such an order is conferred by the Coroners and Justice Act 2009 (in this section, 'the Act'); section 87 of the Act provides specific relevant powers and obligations.

18D.2 As the Court of Appeal stated in *R v Mayers and Others* [2008] EWCA Crim 2989, [2009] 1 WLR 1915, [2009] 1 Cr App R 30 and emphasised again in *R v Donovan and Kafunda* [2012] EWCA Crim 2749, unreported, 'a witness anonymity order is to be regarded as a special measure of the last practicable resort': Lord Chief Justice, Lord Judge. In making such an application, the prosecution's obligations of disclosure 'go much further than the ordinary duties of disclosure' (*R v Mayers*); reference should be made to the Judicial Protocol on Disclosure, see paragraph IV 15A.1.

Case management

18D.3 Where such an application is proposed, with the parties' active assistance the court should set a realistic timetable, in accordance with the duties imposed by CrimPR 3.2 and 3.3. Where possible, the trial judge should determine the application, and any hearing should be attended by the parties' trial advocates.

Service of evidence and disclosure of prosecution material pending an application

18D.4 Where the prosecutor proposes an application for a witness anonymity order, it is not necessary for that application to have been determined before the proposed evidence is served. In most cases, an early indication of what that evidence will be if an order is made will be consistent with a party's duties under CrimPR 1.2 and 3.3. The prosecutor should serve with the other prosecution evidence a witness statement setting out the proposed evidence, redacted in such a way as to prevent disclosure of the witness' identity, as permitted by section 87(4) of the Act.

Likewise the prosecutor should serve with other prosecution material disclosed under the Criminal Procedure and Investigations Act 1996 any such material appertaining to the witness, similarly redacted.

The application

18D.5 An application for a witness anonymity order should be made as early as possible and within the period for which CrimPR 18.3 provides. The application, and any hearing of it, must comply with the requirements of that rule and with those of rule 18.19. In accordance with CrimPR 1.2 and 3.3, the applicant must provide the court with all available information relevant to the considerations to which the Act requires a court to have regard.

Response to the application

18D.6 A party upon whom an application for a witness anonymity order is served must serve a response in accordance with CrimPR 18.22. That period may be extended or shortened in the court's discretion: CrimPR 18.5.

18D.7 To avoid the risk of injustice, a respondent, whether the Prosecution or a defendant, must actively assist the court. If not already done, a respondent defendant should serve a defence statement under section 5 or 6 of the Criminal Procedure and Investigations Act 1996, so that the court is fully informed of what is in issue. When a defendant makes an application for a witness anonymity order the prosecutor should consider the continuing duty to disclose material under section 7A of the Criminal Procedure and Investigations Act 1996; therefore a prosecutor's response should include confirmation that that duty has been considered. Great care should be taken to ensure that nothing disclosed contains anything that might reveal the witness' identity. A respondent prosecutor should provide the court with all available information relevant to the considerations to which the Act requires a court to have regard, whether or not that information falls to be disclosed under the 1996 Act.

Determination of the application

18D.8 All parties must have an opportunity to make oral representations to the court on an application for a witness anonymity order: section 87(6) of the Act. However, a hearing may not be needed if none is sought: CrimPR 18.18(1) (a). Where, for example, the witness is an investigator who is recognisable by the defendant but known only by an assumed name, and there is no likelihood that the witness' credibility will be in issue, then the court may indicate a provisional decision and invite representations within a defined period, usually 14 days, including representations about whether there should be a hearing. In such a case, where the parties do not object the court may make an order without a hearing. Or where the court provisionally considers an application to be misconceived, an applicant may choose to withdraw it without requiring a hearing. Where the court directs a hearing of the application then it should allow adequate time for service of the representations in response.

18D.9 The hearing of an application for a witness anonymity order usually should be in private: CrimPR 18.18(1)(a), and before the trial judge wherever possible. The court has power to hear a party in the absence of a defendant and that defendant's representatives: section 87(7) of the Act and rule 18.18(1)(b). In the Crown Court, a recording of the proceedings will be made, in accordance with CrimPR 5.5. The Crown Court officer must treat such a recording in the same way as the recording of an application for a public interest ruling. It must be kept in secure conditions, and the arrangements made by the Crown Court officer for any transcription must impose restrictions that correspond with those under CrimPR 5.5(2).

18D.10 The hearing of an application for a witness anonymity order usually should be in private: CrimPR 18.18(1)(a). The court has power to hear a party in the absence of a defendant and that defendant's representatives: section 87(7) of the Act and rule 18.18(1)(b). In the Crown Court, a recording of the proceedings will be made, in accordance with CrimPR 5.5. The Crown Court officer must treat such a recording in the same way as the recording of an application for a public interest ruling. It must be kept in secure conditions, and the arrangements made by the Crown Court officer for any transcription must impose restrictions that correspond with those under CrimPR 5.5(2).

18D.11 Where confidential supporting information is presented to the court before the last stage of the hearing, the court may prefer not to read that information until that last stage.

18D.12 The court may adjourn the hearing at any stage, and should do so if its duty under CrimPR 3.2 so requires.

18D.13 On a prosecutor's application, the court is likely to be assisted by the attendance of a senior investigator or other person of comparable authority who is familiar with the case.

18D.14 During the last stage of the hearing it is essential that the court test thoroughly the information supplied in confidence in order to satisfy itself that the conditions prescribed by the Act are met. At that stage, if the court concludes that this is the only way in which it can satisfy itself as to a relevant condition or consideration, exceptionally it may invite the applicant to present the proposed witness to be questioned by the court. Any such questioning should be carried out at such a time, and the witness brought to the court in such a way, as to prevent disclosure of his or her identity.

18D.15 The court may ask the Attorney General to appoint special counsel to assist. However, it must be kept in mind that, 'Such an appointment will always be exceptional, never automatic; a course of last and never first resort. It should not be ordered unless and until the trial judge is satisfied that no other course will adequately meet the overriding requirement of fairness to the defendant': *R v H* [2004] UKHL 3, [2004] 2 AC 134 (at paragraph 22), [2004] 2 Cr App R 10. Whether to accede to such a request is a matter for the Attorney General, and adequate time should be allowed for the consideration of such a request.

18D.16 The Court of Appeal in *R v Mayers* 'emphasise[d] that all three conditions, A, B and C, must be met before the jurisdiction to make a witness anonymity order arises. Each is mandatory. Each is distinct.' The Court also noted that if there is more than one anonymous witness in a case any link, and the nature of any link, between the witnesses should be investigated: 'questions of possible improper collusion between them, or cross-contamination of one another, should be addressed.'

18D.17 Following a hearing the court should announce its decision on an application for a witness anonymity order in the parties' presence and in public: CrimPR 18.4(2). The court should give such reasons as it is possible to give without revealing the witness' identity. In the Crown Court, the court will be conscious that reasons given in public may be reported and reach the jury. Consequently, the court should ensure that nothing in its decision or its reasons could undermine any warning it may give jurors under section 90(2) of the Act. A record of the reasons must be kept. In the Crown Court, the announcement of those reasons will be recorded.

18D.18 Should the judge grant the anonymity then the following should be considered by the judge with the assistance of the court staff, so that the practical arrangements (confidentially recorded) are in place to ensure that the witness's anonymity is not compromised:

i. Any pre-trial visit by the anonymous witness;
ii. How the witness will enter and leave the court building;
iii. Where the witness will wait until they give evidence;
iv. Provision for prosecution counsel to speak to the anonymous witness at court before they give evidence;
v. Provision for the anonymous witness to see their statement or view their ABEs;
vi. How the witness will enter and leave the court room;
vii. Provisions to disguise the identity of the anonymous witness whilst they give evidence (voice modulation and screens);
viii. Provisions for the anonymous witness to have any breaks required;
ix. Provisions to protect the anonymity of the witness in the event of an emergency such as a security alert.

Order

18D.19 Where the court makes a witness anonymity order, it is essential that the measures to be taken are clearly specified in a written record of that order approved by the court and issued on its behalf. An order made in a magistrates' court must be recorded in the court register, in accordance with CrimPR 5.4.

18D.20 Should the application for anonymity be refused, consideration will be given as to whether the witness to whom the application related can be compelled to give evidence despite any risk to their safety and what special measures could support them to give their evidence.

18D.21 Self-evidently, the written record of the order must not disclose the identity of the witness to whom it applies. However, it is essential that there be maintained some means of establishing a clear correlation between witness and order, and especially where in the same proceedings witness anonymity orders are made in respect of more than one witness, specifying different measures in respect of each. Careful preservation of the application for the order, including the confidential part, ordinarily will suffice for this purpose.

Discharge or variation of the order

18D.22 Section 91 of the Act allows the court to discharge or vary a witness anonymity order: on application, if there has been a material change of circumstances since the order was made or since any previous variation of it; or on its own initiative. CrimPR 18.21 allows the parties to apply for the variation of a pre-trial direction where circumstances have changed.

18D.23 The court should keep under review the question of whether the conditions for making an order are met. In addition, consistently with the parties' duties under CrimPR 1.2 and 3.3, it is incumbent on each, and in particular on the applicant for the order, to keep the need for it under review.

18D.24 Where the court considers the discharge or variation of an order, the procedure that it adopts should be appropriate to the circumstances. As a general rule, that procedure should approximate to the procedure for determining an application for an order. The court may need to hear further representations by the applicant for the order in the absence of a respondent defendant and that defendant's representatives.

Arrangements at trial

18D.25 At trial the greatest possible care must be taken to ensure that nothing will compromise the witness' anonymity. Detailed arrangements may have been proposed by the applicant under CrimPR 18.19(1)(b) and directed by the court on determining the application for the order. Such arrangements must take account of the layout of the courtroom and of the means of access for the witness, for the defendant or defendants, and for members of the public. The risk of a chance encounter between the witness and someone who may recognise him or her, either then or subsequently, must be rigorously excluded. Subject to contrary direction by the trial judge, the court staff and those accompanying the witness must adopt necessary measures to ensure that the witness is neither seen nor heard by anyone whose observation would, or might, render nugatory the court's order. Further HMCTS guidance for court staff can be found in Guidance for Criminal Courts for England and Wales for Anonymous/Protected Witnesses.

Retention of confidential material

18D.26 If retained by the court, confidential material must be stored in secure conditions by the court officer. Alternatively, subject to such directions as the court may give, such material may be committed to the safe keeping of the applicant or any other appropriate person in exercise of the powers conferred by CrimPR 18.6. If the material is released to any such person, the court should ensure that it will be available to the court at trial.

CPD V Evidence 18E: Use of s. 28 Youth Justice and Criminal Evidence Act 1999; Pre-recording of Cross-examination and Re-examination for Witnesses Captured by s. 16 YJCEA 1999 **CPD.18E**

18E.1 When Section 28 of the Youth Justice and Criminal Evidence Act 1999 (s.28 YJCEA 1999) is bought into force by Statutory Instrument for a particular Crown Court, under that S.I., a witness will be eligible for special measures under s.28 if

i. he or she is under the age of 18 at the time of the special measures determination; or

ii. he or she suffers from a mental disorder within the meaning of the Mental Health Act 1983, or has a significant impairment of intelligence and social functioning, or has a physical disability or a physical disorder, and the quality of his or her evidence is likely to be diminished as a consequence.

18E.2 This process is governed by the Criminal Procedure Rules and careful attention should be paid to the court's case management powers and the obligations on the parties. Advocates should also refer to the annex of this practice direction which contains further detailed guidance on ground rules hearings.

18E.3 The Resident Judge may appoint a judicial lead from full time judges at the court centre who will be responsible for monitoring and supervision of the scheme. The Plea and Trial Preparation Hearing (PTPH) must be conducted by a full time judge authorised by the Resident Judge to sit on that class of case and who has been authorised to deal with s.28 YJCEA 1999 cases by the Resident Judge.

18E.4 Reference should be made to the joint protocol agreed between the police and the Crown Prosecution Service.

18E.5 Witnesses eligible for special measures under s.28 YJCEA 1999 should be identified by the police. The police and Crown Prosecution Service should discuss, with the witness or with the witness' parent or carer, special measures available and the witness' needs, such that the most appropriate package of special measures can be identified. This may include use of a Registered Intermediary. See Criminal Practice Directions of 2015 (CPD) General matters 3D: Vulnerable people in the courts and 3F: Intermediaries.

18E.6 For access to special measures under s.28 YJCEA 1999, the witness' interview must be recorded in accordance with the Achieving Best Evidence ('ABE') guidance which is available on the Ministry of Justice website.

18E.7 For timetabling of the case, it is imperative that the investigators and prosecutor commence the disclosure process at the start of the investigation. The *Judicial Protocol on Disclosure of Unused Material in Criminal Proceedings* (November 2013) must be followed, and if applicable, the *2013 Protocol and Good Practice Model on Disclosure of information in cases of alleged child abuse and linked criminal and care directions*. Local Implementation Teams (LITs) should encourage all appropriate agencies to endorse and follow both the Protocol and the Good Practice Model. LITs should monitor compliance and issues should initially be raised at the LITs.

The first hearing in the magistrates' court

18E.8 Initial details of the prosecution case must be served in accordance with Part 8 of the Rules.

18E.9 The prosecutor must formally notify the court at the first hearing that the case is eligible for special measures under s.28 YJCEA 1999.

18E.10 At the hearing the court must follow part 9 of the Rules (Allocation) and refer to the Sentencing Council's guideline on Allocation. This practice direction applies only where the defendant indicates a not guilty plea or does not indicate a plea, and the case is sent for trial in the Crown Court, either with or without allocation.

18E.11 If the case is to be sent to the Crown Court, the prosecutor should inform the court and the defence if not already notified that the prosecution will seek special measures including under s.28 YJCEA 1999.

18E.12 In any case that is sent to the Crown Court for trial in which the prosecution has notified the court of its intention to make an application for special measures under s.28 of the YJCEA 1999 the timetable is that as established by the Better Case Management initiative. The Court must be mindful of its duties under Parts 1 and 3 of the Rules to manage the case effectively. Wherever the Crown Prosecution Service will seek a s.28 YJCEA 1999 special measures direction this should, where possible, be listed for PTPH within 28 days of the date of sending from the magistrates' court. Section 10.2 of *A protocol between the Association of Chief Police Officers, the Crown Prosecution Service and Her Majesty's Courts and Tribunals Service to expedite cases involving witnesses under 10 years* does not apply.

18E.13 From the point of grant of the s.28 YJCEA 1999 special measures application, timescales provided by section 8.6 of *A protocol between the Association of Chief Police Officers, the Crown Prosecution Service and Her Majesty's Courts and Tribunals Service to expedite cases involving witnesses under 10 years* will cease to apply and the case should be managed in accordance with the timescales established in this practice direction.

Before the PTPH hearing in the Crown Court

18E.14 On being notified of the sending of the case by the magistrates' court, the case should be flagged as a s.28 case and referred to the Resident Judge or the judicial lead at that Crown Court, according to instructions issued by the Resident Judge.

18E.15 A transcript of the ABE interview and the application for special measures, including under s.28 YJCEA 1999, must be served on the Court and defence at least 7 days prior to the PTPH. The report of any Registered Intermediary must be served with the application for special measures.

18E.16 Any defence representations about the application for special measures must be served before the PTPH, within 28 days from the first hearing at the magistrates' court, when notice was first given of the application.

Plea and Trial Preparation Hearing

18E.17 The s.28 YJCEA 1999 part of the PTPH form should, on enquiry of the parties, be completed by the judge during the hearing. Orders should be recorded on the form, and uploaded onto the Digital Case System (DCS) as the record of orders made by the court. Any unrepresented defendant should be served with a paper copy of the orders.

18E.18 A plea should be taken and recorded and the defence required to identify the issues. The detail of a defence statement is not required at this stage, but the defence should identify the core issues in dispute.

The application

18E.19 The judge may hear submissions from the advocates and will rule on the application. If it is refused (see the assumptions to be applied by the courts in s.21 and s.22 of the YJCEA 1999), this practice direction ceases to apply.

18E.20 If the application is granted, the judge should make orders and give directions for preparation for the recorded cross-examination and re-examination hearing and advance preparation for the trial, including for disclosure of unused material. The correct and timely application of the Criminal Procedure and Investigations Act 1996 ('CPIA 1996') will be vital and close attention should be paid to the *2013 Protocol and Good Practice Model on Disclosure* (November 2013), above.

18E.21 The orders made are likely to include:

i. Service of the prosecution evidence within 50 days of sending;
ii. Directions for service of defence witness requirements;
iii. Service of initial disclosure; under the CPIA 1996, as soon as reasonably practical; in this context, this should be interpreted as being simultaneous with the service of the prosecution evidence, i.e. within 50 days of sending for both bail and custody cases. This will be within 3 weeks of the PTPH;
iv. Orders on disclosure material held by a third party;
v. Service of the defence statement; under the CPIA 1996, this must be served within 28 days of the prosecutor serving or purporting to serve initial disclosure;
vi. Any editing of the ABE interview;
vii. Fixing a date for a ground rules hearing, about one week prior to the recorded cross-examination and re-examination hearing, see CPD General matters 3E: Ground rules hearings to plan questioning of a vulnerable witness or defendant;
viii. Service of the Ground Rules Hearing Form by the defence advocate;
ix. Making arrangements for the witness to refresh his or her memory by viewing the recorded examination-in-chief ('ABE interview'), see CPD Evidence 18C: Visually recorded interviews: memory refreshing and watching at a different time from the jury;
x. Making arrangements for the recorded cross-examination and re-examination hearing under s.28, including fixing a date, time and location;
xi. Other special measures;
xii. Directions for any further directions hearing whether at the conclusion of the recorded cross-examination and re-examination hearing or subsequently;
xiii. Fixing a date for trial.

18E.22 The timetable should ensure the prosecution evidence and initial disclosure are served swiftly. The ground rules hearing will usually be soon after the deadline for service of the defence statement, the recorded cross-examination and re-examination hearing about one week later. However, there must be time afforded for any further disclosure of unused material following service of the defence statement and for determination of any application under s.8 of the CPIA 1996. Subject to judicial discretion applications for extensions of time for service of disclosure by either party should generally be refused.

18E.23 Where the defendant may be unfit to plead, a timetable for s.28 should usually still be set, taking into account extra time needed for the obtaining of medical reports, save in cases where it is indicated that it is unlikely that there would be a trial if the defendant is found fit.

18E.24 As far as possible, without diminishing the defendant's right to a fair trial, the timing and duration of the recorded cross-examination should take into account the needs of the witness. For a young child, the hearing should usually be in the morning and conclude before lunch time.

18E.25 An application for a witness summons to obtain material held by a third party, should be served in advance of the PTPH and determined at that hearing, or as soon as reasonably practicable thereafter. The timetable should accommodate any consequent hearings or applications, but it is imperative parties are prompt to obtain third party disclosure material. The prosecution must make the court and the defence aware of any difficulty as soon as it arises. As noted above, the *2013 Protocol and Good Practice Model on Disclosure of information in cases of alleged child abuse and linked criminal and care directions hearings* should be followed, if applicable. Engagement with the Protocol is to be overseen by LITs. A single point of contact in each relevant agency can facilitate speedy disclosure.

18E.26 The needs of other witnesses should not be neglected. Witness and intermediary availability dates should be available for the PTPH.

Prior to ground rules hearing and hearing under section 28

18E.27 It is imperative parties abide by orders made at the PTPH, including the completion and service of the Ground Rules Hearing Form by the defence advocate. Delays or failures must be reported to the judge as soon as they arise; this is the responsibility of each legal representative. If ordered, the lead lawyer for the prosecution and defence must provide a weekly update to the court Case Progression Officer, copied to the judge and parties, detailing the progress and any difficulties or delays in complying with orders. The court may order a further case management hearing if necessary.

18E.28 Any applications under s.100 of the Criminal Justice Act 2003 ('CJA 2003') (non-defendant's bad character) or under s.41 of the YJCEA 1999 (evidence or cross-examination about complainants sexual behaviour) or any other application which may affect the cross-examination must be made promptly, and responses submitted in time for the judge to rule on the application at the ground rules hearing. Parts 21 and 22 of the Rules apply to applications under s.100 and s.41 respectively.

18E.29 The witness' court familiarisation visit must take place, including an opportunity to practice on the live link/recording facilities, see the Code of Practice for Victims of Crime, October 2013, Chapter 3, paragraph 1.22. The witness must have the opportunity to view his or her ABE interview to refresh his or her memory. It may or may not be appropriate for this to take place on the day of the court visit: CPD Evidence 18C must be followed.

18E.30 When the court has deemed that the case is suitable for the witness to give evidence from a remote site then a familiarisation visit should take place at that site. At the ground rules hearing the judge and advocates should consider appropriate arrangements for them to talk to the witness before the cross examination hearing.

18E.31 Applications to vary or discharge a special measures declaration must comply with Rule 18.11. Although the need for prompt action will make case preparation tight.

Ground rules hearing

18E.32 Advocates should master the toolkits available through The Advocate's Gateway. These provide guidance on questioning a vulnerable witness, see CPD General matters 3D and the annex to this practice direction.

18E.33 Any appointed Registered Intermediary must attend the ground rules hearing, see CPD General matters 3E.2.

18E.34 The defence advocate at the ground rules hearing must be she or he who will conduct the recorded cross-examination. See listing and allocation below on continuity of counsel and release from other cases.

18E.35 Topics for discussion and agreement at the ground rules hearing will depend on the individual needs of the witness, and an intermediary may provide advance indications. CPD General matters 3E must be followed. Topics that will need discussion in every case will include:

i. the overall length of cross-examination;
ii. cross-examination by a single advocate in a multi-handed case;
iii. any restrictions on the advocate's usual duty to 'put the defence case'.

18E.36 It may be helpful to discuss at this stage how any limitations on questioning will be explained to the jury.

18E.37 At the ground rules hearing, the judge should:

i. rule on any application under s.100 of the CJA 2003 or s.41 of the YJCEA 1999, or other applications that may affect the cross-examination;
ii. decide how the witness may view exhibits or documents;
iii. review progress in complying with orders made at the preliminary hearing and make any necessary orders.

Recording of cross-examination and re-examination: hearing under s.28

18E.38 At the hearing, the witness will be cross-examined and re-examined, if required, via the live link from the court room to the witness suite (unless provision has been made for the use of a remote link) and the examination will be recorded. It is the responsibility of the designated court clerk to ensure in advance that all of the equipment is working and to contact the provider's Service Desk if support is required. Any other special measures must be in place and any intermediary or supporter should sit in the live link room with the witness. The intermediary's role is transparent and therefore must be visible and audible to the judge and advocates at the cross-examination and in the subsequent replaying.

18E.39 The judge, advocates and parties, including the defendant will usually assemble in the court room for the hearing. In some cases the judge and advocates may be in the witness suite with the witness, for example when questioning a very young child or where the witness has a particular communication need. The court will decide this on a case-by-case basis. The defendant should be able to communicate with his or her representatives and should be able to hear the witness via the live link and see the proceedings: s.28 (2). Whether the witness is screened or not will depend on the other special measures ordered, for example screens may have been ordered under s.23 YJCEA 1999.

18E.40 On the admission of the public or media to the hearing, please see below.

18E.41 At the conclusion of the hearing, the judge will issue further orders, such as for the editing of the recorded cross-examination and may set a timetable for progress.

18E.42 Under s.28(4) YJCEA 1999, the judge, on application of any parties or on the court's own motion may direct that the recorded examination is not admitted into evidence, despite any previous direction. Such direction must be given promptly, preferably immediately after the conclusion of the examination.

18E.43 Without exception, editing of the ABE interview/examination-in-chief or recorded cross-examination is precluded without an order of the court.

18E.44 The ability to record simultaneously from a court and a witness room and to play back the recording at trial will be provided in all Crown Courts as an additional facility within the existing Justice Video Service (JVS). Courts will book recording slots with the Service Desk who will launch the recording at the scheduled time when the court is ready. Recordings will be stored in a secure data centre with backup and resiliency, for authorised access.

After the recording

18E.45 Following the recording the judge should review compliance with orders and progress towards preparation for trial, make any further orders necessary and confirm the date of the trial. Any further orders made by the judge should be recorded and uploaded onto the relevant section of the DCS.

18E.46 If the defendant enters a guilty plea, the judge should proceed towards sentence, making any appropriate orders, such as for a Pre-Sentence Report and setting a date for sentencing. Any reduction for a guilty plea shall reflect the day of the recorded cross-examination as the first day of trial; the Sentencing Council guideline on guilty plea reductions should be applied.

Preparation for trial

18E.47 Parties must notify the court promptly if any difficulties arise or any orders are not complied with. The court may order a further case management hearing (FCMH).

18E.48 In accordance with orders, either after recorded cross-examination or at the FCMH, necessary editing of the ABE interview/examination-in-chief and/or the recorded cross-examination must be done only on the order of the court. Any editing must be done promptly.

18E.49 Recorded cross-examinations and re-examinations will be stored securely by the service provider so as to be accessible to the advocates and the court. It will not usually be necessary to obtain a transcript of the recorded cross-examination, but if it is difficult to comprehend, a transcript should be obtained and served. The ground rules hearing form outlines questions to the witness that might be completed electronically by the judge during cross-examination forming a contemporaneous note of the hearing, served on the parties as an agreed record.

18E.50 Editing, authorised by the judge, is to be submitted by the court to the Service Desk, who produce an edited copy. The master and all edited copy versions are retained in the secure data centre from where they can be accessed. Courts book playback timeslots with the Service Desk for the trial date. The court may authorise parties to view playback at JVS endpoints, by submitting a request form to the Service Desk. Access for those so authorised is via the Quickcode (recording ID) and a security PIN (password) on the courtroom touch panel or remote control.

18E.51 No further cross-examination or re-examination of the witness may take place unless the criteria in section 28(6) are satisfied and the judge makes a further special measures direction under section 28(5). Any such further examination must be recorded via live link as described above.

18E.52 Section 28(6) of the YJCEA 1999 provides as follows:

(6) *The court may only give such a further direction if it appears to the court—*

(a) *that the proposed cross-examination is sought by a party to the proceedings as a result of that party having become aware, since the time when the original recording was made in pursuance of subsection (1), of a matter which that party could not with reasonable diligence have ascertained by then, or*

(b) *that for any other reason it is in the interests of justice to give the further direction.*

18E.53 Any application under section 28(5) must be in writing and be served on the court and the prosecution at least 28 days before the date of trial. The application must specify:

i. the topics on which further cross-examination is sought;
ii. the material or matter of which the defence has become aware since the original recording;
iii. why it was not possible for the defence to have obtained the material or ascertained the matter earlier; and
iv. the expected impact on the issues before the court at trial.

18E.54 The prosecution should respond in writing within 7 days of the application. The judge may determine the application on the papers or order a hearing. Any further cross-examination ordered must be recorded via live link in advance of the trial and served on the court and the parties.

Trial

18E.55 In accordance with the judge's directions, the ABE interview/examination-in-chief and the recorded cross-examination and re-examination, edited as directed, should be played to the jury at the appropriate point within the trial.

18E.56 The jury should not usually receive transcripts of the recordings, and if they do these should be removed from the jury as soon as the recording has been played, see CPD Trial 26L.2.

18E.57 If the matter was not addressed at the ground rules hearing, the judge should discuss with the advocates how any limitations on questioning should be explained to the jury before summing-up.

After conclusion of trial

18E.58 Immediately after the trial, the ABE interview/examination-in-chief and the recorded cross-examination and re-examination should be stored securely on the cloud.

Listing and allocation

18E.59 **Advocates:** It is the responsibility of the defence advocate, on accepting the brief, to ensure that he or she is available for both the ground rules hearing and the hearing under section 28; continuity at trial is obligatory except in exceptional circumstances. The judge and list office will make whatever reasonable arrangements are possible to achieve this, assisted by the Resident Judge where necessary.

18E.60 When the timetable for the case is being set, advocates must have their up to date availability with them (in so far as is possible). When an advocate who is part-heard in another trial at a different Crown Court centre finds themselves in difficulties in attending either the ground rules hearing, s.28 hearing itself or the trial where s.28 has been utilised, they must inform the Resident Judges of both courts as soon as practicable. The Resident Judges must resolve any conflict with the advocate's availability. The starting point should be that the case involving s.28 hearing takes priority. However, due consideration should also be given to custody time limits, other issues which make either case particularly complex or sensitive, high profile cases and anything else that the judges should take into consideration in the interests of justice.

18E.61 **Judicial:** All PTPHs must be listed before judges who have been authorised to deal with s.28 cases by the Resident Judge at the relevant court centre. The nominated lead judge (if there is one) or Resident Judge may allocate individual cases to one of the judges in the court centre identified to deal with the case if necessary. The Resident Judge, lead judge or allocated judge may make directions in the case if required.

18E.62 It is essential that the ground rules hearing and the s. 28 YJCEA 1999 hearing are before the same judge. Once the s.28 hearing has taken place, any judge, in accordance with CPD XIII Listing E, including recorders, can deal with the trial.

18E.63 LITs should be established with all relevant agencies represented by someone of sufficient seniority. Their task will be to monitor the operation of the scheme and compliance with this practice direction and other relevant protocols.

18E.64 **Listing:** Due to the limited availability of recording facilities, the hearing held under section 28 must take precedence over other hearings. Section 28 hearings should be listed as the first matter in the morning and will usually conclude before lunch time. Ground rules hearings may be held at any time, including towards the end of the court day, to accommodate the advocates and intermediary (if there is one) and to minimise disruption to other trials.

Public, including media access, and reporting restrictions

18E.65 Open justice is an essential principle of the common law. However, certain automatic statutory restrictions may apply, and the judge may consider it appropriate in the specific circumstances of a case to make an order applying discretionary restrictions. CPD Preliminary proceedings 16B must be followed and the templates published by the Judicial College (available on LMS) should be used. The parties to the proceedings, and interested parties such as the media, should have the opportunity to make representations before an order is made.

18E.66 The statutory powers most likely to be available to the judge are listed below. The judge should consider the specific statutory requirements necessary for the making of the particular order carefully, and the order made must be in writing.

a) Provisions to exclude the public from hearings:
   i. Section 37 of the Children and Young Persons Act 1933, applicable to witnesses under 18;
   ii. Section 25 of the YJCEA 1999, applicable to the evidence of a child or vulnerable adult in sexual offences cases.

b) Automatic reporting restrictions:
   i. Section 1 of the Sexual Offences (Amendment) Act 1992, applicable to the complainant in any sex offence case.
c) Discretionary reporting restrictions:
   i. Section 45 of the YJCEA 1999, applicable to under 18s concerned in criminal proceedings;
   ii. Section 46 of the YJCEA 1999, applicable to an adult witness whose evidence would be diminished by fear or distress.
d) Postponement of fair and accurate reports under section 4(2) of the Contempt of Court Act 1981.

18E.67 Note that public access to information held by the court is now the subject of Rule 5.8 and CPD General matters 5B that must be followed.

Annex for section 28 ground rules hearings at the Crown Court when dealing with witnesses under s.16 YJCEA 1999

Introduction

1. This annex is designed to assist all advocates in their preparation for cross-examination of vulnerable witnesses.
2. Adherence to the principles below will avoid interruption during the pre-recorded cross-examination and reduce any ordered editing.
3. Issues concerning the vulnerable witness and the nature of the cross-examination will be addressed by the judge at the Ground Rules Hearing (GRH).
4. In appropriate cases and in particular where the witness is of very young years or suffers from a disability or disorder it is expected that the advocate will have prepared his or her cross-examination in writing for consideration by the court.
5. It is thus incumbent on the Defence to ensure that full instructions have been taken prior to the GRH.

Required preparation prior to the GRH

6. All advocates should be familiar with the relevant toolkits, available through **The Advocates Gateway** www.theadvocatesgateway.org/toolkits which provide guidance on questioning a vulnerable witness. A synopsis of this guidance, which advocates should have read prior to any GRH, is included in this annex.

Attendance at, and procedure during, the GRH

7. In preparation for trial, courts must take every reasonable step to facilitate the participation of witnesses and defendants CPR 3.8(4) (d). The court should order that the defendant attends the GRH.
8. The defence advocate must complete and submit the Ground Rules Hearing form by the time and date ordered at the PTPH.
9. The hearing facilitates the judge's duty to control questioning if and when necessary.
10. The hearing enables the court to ensure its process is adapted to enable the witness to give his or her best evidence whilst ensuring the defendant's right to a fair trial is not diminished. Accordingly the ground rules and the nature of the questioning of the witness by the advocate (and limitations imposed if necessary in accordance with principles above) will be discussed.
11. Prior to the hearing it is necessary for both advocates and the judge to have viewed the ABE evidence.
12. The judge will state what ground rules will apply. The advocates must comply with them.
13. Any intermediary must attend the GRH. It is the responsibility of those instructing the intermediary to ensure this.
14. The defendant's advocate attending the hearing must be the same advocate who will be conducting the recorded cross-examination (and the subsequent trial, if any).
15. Any intermediary for the witness should only be warned for the GRH and the section 28 hearing they are assisting with. An Intermediary should not be instructed unless available to attend the GRH and the section 28 hearings ordered by the court.
16. Topics for discussion and agreement at the GRH will depend on the individual needs of the witness. CPD I General Matters 3E must be followed.
17. Topics of discussion at the hearing will include the length of cross-examination and any restrictions on the advocate's usual duty to 'put the defence case'. As was made plain by the Vice President of the Court of Appeal Criminal Division in *Regina v Lubemba and Pooley* 2014 EWCA Crim 2064, advocates cannot insist upon any supposed right 'to put one's case' or previous inconsistent statements to a vulnerable witness. If there is a right to 'put one's case' it must be modified for young or vulnerable witnesses. It is perfectly possible to ensure the jury are made aware of the defence case and of significant inconsistencies without intimidation or distressing a witness. It is expected that all advocates will be familiar with and have read this case.

18. At the GRH counsel need to agree with the judge how and when the matters referred to in paragraph 11 will be explained to the jury. This explanation will normally be done by the judge, but may exceptionally, and only with the permission of the judge, be explained by counsel. If there is no agreement the judge will rule on it.
19. A Section 28 Defence GRH form should be completed as far as possible prior to attendance at the GRH before the judge.
20. Rulings will be made on any application under section 100 of the CJA 2003 or section 41 of the YCEA 1999, and on any other application that may affect the conduct of the cross examination. Any ruling will be included in the trial practice note.
21. A review will take place of the progress made by the parties in complying with the orders made at the PTPH and the court will make any other necessary orders.
22. Additional information can be found in the Inns of Court College of Advocacy training document 'Advocacy and the vulnerable: 20 principles of questioning' at the following link: www.icca.ac.uk/images/download/advocacy-and-the-vulnerable/20-principles-of-questioning.pdf. This document is part of a suite of training materials available to assist advocates in dealing with questioning vulnerable victims in the criminal justice system.

Court of Appeal guidance

In a series of decisions the Court of Appeal has made it clear that there has to be a different and fresh approach to the cross-examination of, in particular, children of tender years, and witnesses who are vulnerable as a result of mental incapacity. The following propositions have support in decisions on appeal: (*R v B 2010 EWCA Crim 4*; *R v F 2013 EWCA Crim 424*; *Wills v R 2011 EWCA Crim 1938*; *R v Edwards 2011 EWCA Crim 3028*; *R v Watts 2010 EWCA Crim 1824*; *R v W and M 2010 EWCA Crim 1926*)

'The reality of questioning children of tender years is that direct challenge that he or she is wrong or lying could lead to confusion and, worse, to capitulation which the child does not, in reality, accept.

Capitulation is not a consequence of unreliability but a function of the youngster's age. Experience has shown that young children are scared of disagreeing with a mature adult whom they do not wish to confront.

It is common, in the trial of an adult, to hear, once the nursery slopes of cross-examination have been skied, the assertion "you were never punched or kicked, as you have suggested, were you?"

It was precisely that approach which the Court is anxious to avoid. Such an approach risks confusion in the minds of the witness whose evidence was bound to take centre stage, and it is difficult to see how it can be helpful. We struggle to understand how the defendant's right to a fair trial was in any way compromised simply because Mr X was not allowed to ask the question "Simon did not punch you in the way you suggest?"

The overriding objective. The Criminal Procedure Rules objective is that criminal cases be dealt with justly. Dealing with a criminal case justly includes dealing with the case efficiently and expeditiously in ways that take account of the gravity of the offence alleged and the complexity of what is in issue.

In our collective experience the age of a witness is not determinative of his or her ability to give truthful and accurate evidence. Like adults some children will provide truthful and accurate testimony, and some will not. However children are not miniature adults, but children, and to be treated for what they are, not what they will, in the years ahead, grow to be.

There is undoubtedly a danger of a child witness wishing simply to please.

There is undoubtedly a danger of a child witness assenting to what is put rather than disagreeing during the questioning process in an endeavour to bring that process to a speedier conclusion.

It is particularly important in the case of a child witness to keep a question short and simple, and even more important than it is with an adult witness to avoid questions which are rolled up and contain, inadvertently two or three questions at once. It is generally recognised that, particularly with child witnesses, short and untagged questions are best at eliciting the evidence. By untagged we mean questions that do not contain a statement of the answer which is sought. That said, when it comes to directly contradicting a particular statement and inviting the witness to face a directly contradictory suggestion, it may often be difficult to examine otherwise.

No doubt if a way can be found of engaging the witness to tell the story, and the content then differs from what had been said before, that will be a yet better indication that the original account is wrong. But that is difficult to achieve and indeed may itself have the disadvantage of prolonging the child's time giving evidence. Even then there may be no guarantee as to which account is the more reliable.

Most of the questions which produced the answers which were chiefly relied upon, unlike many others, constituted the putting of direct suggestions with an indication of the answer "this happened didn't it?" Or "this didn't happen, did it?" The consequence of that is that it can be very difficult to tell whether the child is truly changing her account or simply taking the line of least resistance.

At the same time the right of the defendant to a fair trial must be undiminished. When the issue is whether the child is lying or mistaken, when claiming that the defendant behaved indecently towards him or her, it should not be over problematic for the advocate to formulate short, simple questions, which put the essential elements of the defendant's case to the witness, and fully ventilate before the jury the areas of evidence which bear on the child's credibility.

Aspects of evidence which undermine or are believed to undermine the child's credibility must, of course, be revealed to the jury. However it is not necessarily appropriate for them to form the subject matter of detailed cross-examination of the child, and the advocate may have to forego much of the kind of contemporary cross-examination which consists of no more than comment on matters which will be before the jury, in any event, from different sources.

Notwithstanding some of the difficulties; when all is said and done, the witness whose cross-examination is in contemplation is a child, sometimes very young, and it should not take very lengthy cross examination to demonstrate, when it is the case, that the child may indeed be fabricating, or fantasising, or imagining, or reciting a well-rehearsed untruthful script, learned by rote; or simply just suggestible, or contaminated by or in collusion with others to make false allegations, or making assertions in language which is beyond his or her level of comprehension; and are therefore likely to be derived from another source. Comment on the evidence, including comment on evidence which may bear adversely on the credibility of the child, should be addressed after the child has finished giving evidence. Clear limitations have to be imposed on the cross-examination of vulnerable young complainants.'

CRIMINAL PROCEDURE RULES PART 19 EXPERT EVIDENCE

When this Part applies R19.1

19.1 (1) This Part applies where a party wants to introduce expert opinion evidence.
(2) A reference to an 'expert' in this Part is a reference to a person who is required to give or prepare expert evidence for the purpose of criminal proceedings, including evidence required to determine fitness to plead or for the purpose of sentencing.

[Note. Expert medical evidence may be required to determine fitness to plead under section 4 of the Criminal Procedure (Insanity) Act 1964[1]*. It may be required also under section 11 of the Powers of Criminal Courts (Sentencing) Act 2000*[2]*, under Part III of the Mental Health Act 1983*[3] *or under Part 12 of the Criminal Justice Act 2003*[4]*. Those Acts contain requirements about the qualification of medical experts.]*

Expert's duty to the court R19.2

19.2 (1) An expert must help the court to achieve the overriding objective—
(a) by giving opinion which is—
(i) objective and unbiased, and
(ii) within the expert's area or areas of expertise; and
(b) by actively assisting the court in fulfilling its duty of case management under rule 3.2, in particular by—
(i) complying with directions made by the court, and
(iii) at once informing the court of any significant failure (by the expert or another) to take any step required by such a direction.
(2) This duty overrides any obligation to the person from whom the expert receives instructions or by whom the expert is paid.
(3) This duty includes obligations—
(a) to define the expert's area or areas of expertise—
(i) in the expert's report, and
(ii) when giving evidence in person;

[1] 1964 c. 84; section 4 was substituted, together with section 4A, for section 4 as originally enacted, by section 2 of the Criminal Procedure (Insanity and Unfitness to Plead) Act 1991 (c. 25), and amended by section 22 of the Domestic Violence, Crime and Victims Act 2004 (c. 28).
[2] 2000 c. 6.
[3] 1983 c. 20.
[4] 2003 c. 44.

Criminal Procedure Rules and Criminal Practice Directions

(b) when giving evidence in person, to draw the court's attention to any question to which the answer would be outside the expert's area or areas of expertise;
(c) inform all parties and the court if the expert's opinion changes from that contained in a report served as evidence or given in a statement; and
(d) to disclose to the party for whom the expert's evidence is commissioned anything—
(i) of which the expert is aware, and
(ii) of which that party, if aware of it, would be required to give notice under rule 19.3(3)(c).

[Note. The Practice Direction lists examples of matters that should be disclosed under this rule and rule 19.3(3)(c).]

R19.3 **Introduction of expert evidence**

19.3 (1) A party who wants another party to admit as fact a summary of an expert's conclusions must serve that summary—
(a) on the court officer and on each party from whom that admission is sought; and
(b) as soon as practicable after the defendant whom it affects pleads not guilty.
(2) A party on whom such a summary is served must—
(a) serve a response stating—
(i) which, if any, of the expert's conclusions are admitted as fact, and
(ii) where a conclusion is not admitted, what are the disputed issues concerning that conclusion; and
(b) serve the response—
(i) on the court officer and on the party who served the summary, and
(ii) as soon as practicable, and in any event not more than 10 business days after service of the summary.
(3) A party who wants to introduce expert evidence otherwise than as admitted fact must—
(a) serve a report by the expert which complies with rule 19.4 (Content of expert's report) on—
(i) the court officer, and
(ii) each other party;
(b) serve the report as soon as practicable, and in any event with any application in support of which that party relies on that evidence;
(c) serve with the report notice of anything of which the party serving it is aware which might reasonably be thought capable of—
(i) undermining the reliability of the expert's opinion, or
(ii) detracting from the credibility or impartiality of the expert; and
(d) if another party so requires, give that party a copy of, or a reasonable opportunity to inspect—
(i) a record of any examination, measurement, test or experiment on which the expert's findings and opinion are based, or that were carried out in the course of reaching those findings and opinion, and
(ii) anything on which any such examination, measurement, test or experiment was carried out.
(4) Unless the parties otherwise agree or the court directs, a party may not—
(a) introduce expert evidence if that party has not complied with paragraph (3); or
(b) introduce in evidence an expert report if the expert does not give evidence in person.

[Note. A party who accepts another party's expert's conclusions may admit them as fact under section 10 of the Criminal Justice Act 1967[5]*.*

Under section 81 of the Police and Criminal Evidence Act 1984[6]*, and under section 20(3) of the Criminal Procedure and Investigations Act 1996*[7]*, Criminal Procedure Rules may require the disclosure of expert evidence before it is introduced as part of a party's case and prohibit its introduction without the court's permission, if it was not disclosed as required.*

[5] 1967 c. 80.
[6] 1984 c. 60; section 81 was amended by section 109(1) of, and paragraph 286 of Schedule 8 to, the Courts Act 2003 (c. 39).
[7] 1996 c. 25; section 20(3) was amended by section 109(1) of, and paragraph 378 of Schedule 8 to, the Courts Act 2003 (c. 39).

Under section 30 of the Criminal Justice Act 1988[8]*, an expert report is admissible in evidence whether or not the person who made it gives oral evidence, but if that person does not give oral evidence then the report is admissible only with the court's permission.]*

Content of expert's report R19.4

19.4 (1) Where rule 19.3(3) applies, an expert's report must—
(a) give details of the expert's qualifications, relevant experience and accreditation;
(b) give details of any literature or other information which the expert has relied on in making the report;
(c) contain a statement setting out the substance of all facts given to the expert which are material to the opinions expressed in the report, or upon which those opinions are based;
(d) make clear which of the facts stated in the report are within the expert's own knowledge;
(e) where the expert has based an opinion or inference on a representation of fact or opinion made by another person for the purposes of criminal proceedings (for example, as to the outcome of an examination, measurement, test or experiment)—
(i) identify the person who made that representation to the expert,
(ii) give the qualifications, relevant experience and any accreditation of that person, and
(iii) certify that that person had personal knowledge of the matters stated in that representation;
(f) where there is a range of opinion on the matters dealt with in the report—
(i) summarise the range of opinion, and
(ii) give reasons for the expert's own opinion;
(g) if the expert is not able to give an opinion without qualification, state the qualification;
(h) include such information as the court may need to decide whether the expert's opinion is sufficiently reliable to be admissible as evidence;
(i) contain a summary of the conclusions reached;
(j) contain a statement that the expert understands an expert's duty to the court, and has complied and will continue to comply with that duty; and
(k) contain the same declaration of truth as a witness statement.

[Note. Part 16 contains rules about written witness statements. Declarations of truth in witness statements are required by section 9 of the Criminal Justice Act 1967[9]*. Evidence of examinations etc. on which an expert relies may be admissible under section 127 of the Criminal Justice Act 2003*[10]*.]*

Expert to be informed of service of report R19.5

19.5 A party who serves on another party or on the court a report by an expert must, at once, inform that expert of that fact.

Pre-hearing discussion of expert evidence R19.6

19.6 (1) This rule applies where more than one party wants to introduce expert evidence.
(2) The court may direct the experts to—
(a) discuss the expert issues in the proceedings; and
(b) prepare a statement for the court of the matters on which they agree and disagree, giving their reasons.
(3) Except for that statement, the content of that discussion must not be referred to without the court's permission.
(4) A party may not introduce expert evidence without the court's permission if the expert has not complied with a direction under this rule.

[8] 1988 c. 33; section 30 was amended by section 47 of, and paragraph 32 of Schedule 1 to, the Criminal Procedure and Investigations Act 1996 (c. 25) and paragraph 60 of Schedule 3 and Schedule 37 to the Criminal Justice Act 2003 (c. 44).
[9] 1967 c. 80; section 9 was amended by section 56 of, and paragraph 49 of Schedule 8 to, the Courts Act 1971 (c. 23), section 168 of, and paragraph 6 of Schedule 9 to, the Criminal Justice and Public Order Act 1994 (c. 33), section 69 of the Criminal Procedure and Investigations Act 1996 (c. 25), regulation 9 of, and paragraph 4 of Schedule 5 to, S.I. 2001/1090, paragraph 43 of Schedule 3 and Part 4 of Schedule 37 to the Criminal Justice Act 2003 (c. 44), section 26 of, and paragraph 7 of Schedule 2 to, the Armed Forces Act 2011 (c. 18) and section 80 of the Deregulation Act 2015 (c. 20). It is further amended by section 72 of, and paragraph 55 of Schedule 5 to, the Children and Young Persons Act 1969 (c. 54) and section 65 of, and paragraph 1 of Schedule 4 to, the Courts Act 2003 (c. 39), with effect from dates to be appointed.
[10] 2003 c. 44; section 127 was amended by article 3 of, and paragraphs 45 and 50 of the Schedule to, S.I. 2004/2035.

[Note. At a pre-trial hearing, a court may make binding rulings about the admissibility of evidence and about questions of law under section 9 of the Criminal Justice Act 1987[11]*; sections 31 and 40 of the Criminal Procedure and Investigations Act 1996*[12]*; and section 8A of the Magistrates' Courts Act 1980*[13]*.]*

R19.7 **Court's power to direct that evidence is to be given by a single joint expert**

19.7 (1) Where more than one defendant wants to introduce expert evidence on an issue at trial, the court may direct that the evidence on that issue is to be given by one expert only.

(2) Where the co-defendants cannot agree who should be the expert, the court may—
(a) select the expert from a list prepared or identified by them; or
(b) direct that the expert be selected in another way.

R19.8 **Instructions to a single joint expert**

19.8 (1) Where the court gives a direction under rule 19.7 for a single joint expert to be used, each of the co-defendants may give instructions to the expert.

(2) A co-defendant who gives instructions to the expert must, at the same time, send a copy of the instructions to each other co-defendant.

(3) The court may give directions about—
(a) the payment of the expert's fees and expenses; and
(b) any examination, measurement, test or experiment which the expert wishes to carry out.

(4) The court may, before an expert is instructed, limit the amount that can be paid by way of fees and expenses to the expert.

(5) Unless the court otherwise directs, the instructing co-defendants are jointly and severally liable for the payment of the expert's fees and expenses.

R19.9 **Application to withhold information from another party**

19.9 (1) This rule applies where—
(a) a party introduces expert evidence under rule 19.3(3);
(b) the evidence omits information which it otherwise might include because the party introducing it thinks that that information ought not be revealed to another party; and
(c) the party introducing the evidence wants the court to decide whether it would be in the public interest to withhold that information.

(2) The party who wants to introduce the evidence must—
(a) apply for such a decision; and
(b) serve the application on—
(i) the court officer, and
(ii) the other party, but only to the extent that serving it would not reveal what the applicant thinks ought to be withheld.

(3) The application must—
(a) identify the information;
(b) explain why the applicant thinks that it would be in the public interest to withhold it; and
(c) omit from the part of the application that is served on the other party anything that would reveal what the applicant thinks ought to be withheld.

(4) Where the applicant serves only part of the application on the other party, the applicant must—
(a) mark the other part, to show that it is only for the court; and
(b) in that other part, explain why the applicant has withheld it from the other party.

(5) The court may—
(a) direct the applicant to serve on the other party any part of the application which has been withheld; and
(b) determine the application at a hearing or without a hearing.

(6) Any hearing of an application to which this rule applies—
(a) must be in private, unless the court otherwise directs; and

[11] 1987 c. 38; section 9 was amended by section 170 of, and Schedule 16 to, the Criminal Justice Act 1988 (c. 33), section 6 of the Criminal Justice Act 1993 (c. 36), sections 72, 74 and 80 of, and paragraph 3 of Schedule 3 and Schedule 5 to, the Criminal Procedure and Investigations Act 1996 (c. 25), sections 45 and 310 of, and paragraphs 18, 52 and 54 of Schedule 36 and Part 3 of Schedule 37 to, the Criminal Justice Act 2003 (c. 44), article 3 of, and paragraphs 21 and 23 of S.I. 2004/2035, section 59 of, and paragraph 1 of Schedule 11 to, the Constitutional Reform Act 2005 (c. 4) and Part 10 of Schedule 10 to the Protection of Freedoms Act 2012 (c. 9). The amendment made by section 45 of the Criminal Justice Act 2003 (c. 44) is in force for certain purposes; for remaining purposes it has effect from a date to be appointed.

[12] 1996 c. 25; section 31 was amended by sections 310, 331 and 332 of, and paragraphs 20, 36, 65 and 67 of Schedule 36 and Schedule 37 to, the Criminal Justice Act 2003 (c. 44).

[13] 1980 c. 43; section 8A was inserted by section 45 of, and Schedule 3 to, the Courts Act 2003 (c. 39) and amended by SI 2006/2493 and paragraphs 12 and 14 of Schedule 5 to the Legal Aid, Sentencing and Punishment of Offenders Act 2012 (c. 10).

(b) if the court so directs, may be, wholly or in part, in the absence of the party from whom information has been withheld.

(7) At any hearing of an application to which this rule applies—

(a) the general rule is that the court must consider, in the following sequence—

(i) representations first by the applicant and then by the other party, in both parties' presence, and then

(ii) further representations by the applicant, in the absence of the party from whom information has been withheld; but

(b) the court may direct other arrangements for the hearing.

Court's power to vary requirements under this Part R19.10

19.10 (1) The court may extend (even after it has expired) a time limit under this Part.

(2) A party who wants an extension of time must—

(a) apply when serving the report, summary or notice for which it is required; and

(b) explain the delay.

Criminal Practice Directions Part 19 Expert Evidence

CPD V Evidence 19A: Expert Evidence CPD.19A

19A.1 Expert opinion evidence is admissible in criminal proceedings at common law if, in summary, (i) it is relevant to a matter in issue in the proceedings; (ii) it is needed to provide the court with information likely to be outside the court's own knowledge and experience; and (iii) the witness is competent to give that opinion.

19A.2 Legislation relevant to the introduction and admissibility of such evidence includes section 30 of the Criminal Justice Act 1988, which provides that an expert report shall be admissible as evidence in criminal proceedings whether or not the person making it gives oral evidence, but that if he or she does not give oral evidence then the report is admissible only with the leave of the court; and CrimPR Part 19, which in exercise of the powers conferred by section 81 of the Police and Criminal Evidence Act 1984 and section 20 of the Criminal Procedure and Investigations Act 1996 requires the service of expert evidence in advance of trial in the terms required by those rules.

19A.3 In the Law Commission report entitled 'Expert Evidence in Criminal Proceedings in England and Wales', report number 325, published in March, 2011, the Commission recommended a statutory test for the admissibility of expert evidence. However, in its response the government declined to legislate. The common law, therefore, remains the source of the criteria by reference to which the court must assess the admissibility and weight of such evidence; and CrimPR 19.4 lists those matters with which an expert's report must deal, so that the court can conduct an adequate such assessment.

19A.4 In its judgment in *R v Dlugosz and Others* [2013] EWCA Crim 2, the Court of Appeal observed (at paragraph 11): 'It is essential to recall the principle which is applicable, namely in determining the issue of admissibility, the court must be satisfied that there is a sufficiently reliable scientific basis for the evidence to be admitted. If there is then the court leaves the opposing views to be tested before the jury.' Nothing at common law precludes assessment by the court of the reliability of an expert opinion by reference to substantially similar factors to those the Law Commission recommended as conditions of admissibility, and courts are encouraged actively to enquire into such factors.

19A.5 Therefore factors which the court may take into account in determining the reliability of expert opinion, and especially of expert scientific opinion, include:

(a) the extent and quality of the data on which the expert's opinion is based, and the validity of the methods by which they were obtained;

(b) if the expert's opinion relies on an inference from any findings, whether the opinion properly explains how safe or unsafe the inference is (whether by reference to statistical significance or in other appropriate terms);

(c) if the expert's opinion relies on the results of the use of any method (for instance, a test, measurement or survey), whether the opinion takes proper account of matters, such as the degree of precision or margin of uncertainty, affecting the accuracy or reliability of those results;

(d) the extent to which any material upon which the expert's opinion is based has been reviewed by others with relevant expertise (for instance, in peer-reviewed publications), and the views of those others on that material;

(e) the extent to which the expert's opinion is based on material falling outside the expert's own field of expertise;

(f) the completeness of the information which was available to the expert, and whether the expert took account of all relevant information in arriving at the opinion (including information as to the context of any facts to which the opinion relates);

(g) if there is a range of expert opinion on the matter in question, where in the range the expert's own opinion lies and whether the expert's preference has been properly explained; and
(h) whether the expert's methods followed established practice in the field and, if they did not, whether the reason for the divergence has been properly explained.

19A.6 In addition, in considering reliability, and especially the reliability of expert scientific opinion, the court should be astute to identify potential flaws in such opinion which detract from its reliability, such as:
(a) being based on a hypothesis which has not been subjected to sufficient scrutiny (including, where appropriate, experimental or other testing), or which has failed to stand up to scrutiny;
(b) being based on an unjustifiable assumption;
(c) being based on flawed data;
(d) relying on an examination, technique, method or process which was not properly carried out or applied, or was not appropriate for use in the particular case; or
(e) relying on an inference or conclusion which has not been properly reached.

19A.7 To assist in the assessment described above, CrimPR 19.3(3)(c) requires a party who introduces expert evidence to give notice of anything of which that party is aware which might reasonably be thought capable of undermining the reliability of the expert's opinion, or detracting from the credibility or impartiality of the expert; and CrimPR 19.2(3)(d) requires the expert to disclose to that party any such matter of which the expert is aware. Examples of matters that should be disclosed pursuant to those rules include (this is not a comprehensive list), both in relation to the expert and in relation to any corporation or other body with which the expert works, as an employee or in any other capacity:
(a) any fee arrangement under which the amount or payment of the expert's fees is in any way dependent on the outcome of the case (see also the declaration required by paragraph 19B.1 of these directions);
(b) any conflict of interest of any kind, other than a potential conflict disclosed in the expert's report (see also the declaration required by paragraph 19B.1 of these directions);
(c) adverse judicial comment;
(d) any case in which an appeal has been allowed by reason of a deficiency in the expert's evidence;
(e) any adverse finding, disciplinary proceedings or other criticism by a professional, regulatory or registration body or authority, including the Forensic Science Regulator;
(f) any such adverse finding or disciplinary proceedings against, or other such criticism of, others associated with the corporation or other body with which the expert works which calls into question the quality of that corporation's or body's work generally;
(g) conviction of a criminal offence in circumstances that suggest:
  (i) a lack of respect for, or understanding of, the interests of the criminal justice system (for example, perjury; acts perverting or tending to pervert the course of public justice),
  (ii) dishonesty (for example, theft or fraud), or
  (iii) a lack of personal integrity (for example, corruption or a sexual offence);
(h) lack of an accreditation or other commitment to prescribed standards where that might be expected;
(i) a history of failure or poor performance in quality or proficiency assessments;
(j) a history of lax or inadequate scientific methods;
(k) a history of failure to observe recognised standards in the expert's area of expertise;
(l) a history of failure to adhere to the standards expected of an expert witness in the criminal justice system.

19A.8 In a case in which an expert, or a corporation or body with which the expert works, has been criticised without a full investigation, for example by adverse comment in the course of a judgment, it would be reasonable to expect those criticised to supply information about the conduct and conclusions of any independent investigation into the incident, and to explain what steps, if any, have been taken to address the criticism.

19A.9 The rules require disclosure of that of which the expert, or the party who introduces the expert evidence, is aware. The rules do not require persistent or disproportionate enquiry, and courts will recognise that there may be occasions on which neither the expert nor the party has been made aware of criticism. Nevertheless, where matters ostensibly within the scope of the disclosure obligations come to the attention of the court without their disclosure by the party who introduces the evidence then that party, and the expert, should expect a searching examination of the circumstances by the court; and, subject to what emerges, the court may exercise its power under section 81 of the Police and Criminal Evidence Act 1984 or section 20 of the Criminal Procedure and Investigations Act 1996 to exclude the expert evidence.

CPD V Evidence 19B: Statements of Understanding and Declarations of Truth in Expert Reports

19B.1 The statement and declaration required by CrimPR 19.4(j), (k) should be in the following terms, or in terms substantially the same as these: CPD.19B

'I (name) DECLARE THAT:

1. I understand that my duty is to help the court to achieve the overriding objective by giving independent assistance by way of objective, unbiased opinion on matters within my expertise, both in preparing reports and giving oral evidence. I understand that this duty overrides any obligation to the party by whom I am engaged or the person who has paid or is liable to pay me. I confirm that I have complied with and will continue to comply with that duty.
2. I confirm that I have not entered into any arrangement where the amount or payment of my fees is in any way dependent on the outcome of the case.
3. I know of no conflict of interest of any kind, other than any which I have disclosed in my report.
4. I do not consider that any interest which I have disclosed affects my suitability as an expert witness on any issues on which I have given evidence.
5. I will advise the party by whom I am instructed if, between the date of my report and the trial, there is any change in circumstances which affect my answers to points 3 and 4 above.
6. I have shown the sources of all information I have used.
7. I have exercised reasonable care and skill in order to be accurate and complete in preparing this report.
8. I have endeavoured to include in my report those matters, of which I have knowledge or of which I have been made aware, that might adversely affect the validity of my opinion. I have clearly stated any qualifications to my opinion.
9. I have not, without forming an independent view, included or excluded anything which has been suggested to me by others including my instructing lawyers.
10. I will notify those instructing me immediately and confirm in writing if for any reason my existing report requires any correction or qualification.
11. I understand that:
    (a) my report will form the evidence to be given under oath or affirmation;
    (b) the court may at any stage direct a discussion to take place between experts;
    (c) the court may direct that, following a discussion between the experts, a statement should be prepared showing those issues which are agreed and those issues which are not agreed, together with the reasons;
    (d) I may be required to attend court to be cross-examined on my report by a cross-examiner assisted by an expert.
    (e) I am likely to be the subject of public adverse criticism by the judge if the Court concludes that I have not taken reasonable care in trying to meet the standards set out above.
12. I have read Part 19 of the Criminal Procedure Rules and I have complied with its requirements.
13. I confirm that I have acted in accordance with the code of practice or conduct for experts of my discipline, namely [*identify the code*].
14. [For Experts instructed by the Prosecution only] I confirm that I have read guidance contained in a booklet known as *Disclosure: Experts' Evidence and Unused Material* which details my role and documents my responsibilities, in relation to revelation as an expert witness. I have followed the guidance and recognise the continuing nature of my responsibilities of disclosure. In accordance with my duties of disclosure, as documented in the guidance booklet, I confirm that:
    (a) I have complied with my duties to record, retain and reveal material in accordance with the Criminal Procedure and Investigations Act 1996, as amended;
    (b) I have compiled an Index of all material. I will ensure that the Index is updated in the event I am provided with or generate additional material;
    (c) in the event my opinion changes on any material issue, I will inform the investigating officer, as soon as reasonably practicable and give reasons.

I confirm that the contents of this report are true to the best of my knowledge and belief and that I make this report knowing that, if it is tendered in evidence, I would be liable to prosecution if I have wilfully stated anything which I know to be false or that I do not believe to be true.'

CPD V Evidence 19C: Pre-Hearing Discussion of Expert Evidence

CPD.19C **19C.1.** To assist the court in the preparation of the case for trial, parties must consider, with their experts, at an early stage, whether there is likely to be any useful purpose in holding an experts' discussion and, if so, when. Under CrimPR 19.6 such pre-trial discussions are not compulsory unless directed by the court. However, such a direction is listed in the magistrates' courts Preparation for Effective Trial form and in the Crown Court Plea and Trial Preparation Hearing form as one to be given by default, and therefore the court can be expected to give such a direction in every case unless persuaded otherwise. Those standard directions include a timetable to which the parties must adhere unless it is varied.

19C.2. The purpose of discussions between experts is to agree and narrow issues and in particular to identify:

(a) the extent of the agreement between them;
(b) the points of and short reasons for any disagreement;
(c) action, if any, which may be taken to resolve any outstanding points of disagreement; and
(d) any further material issues not raised and the extent to which these issues are agreed.

19C.3. Where the experts are to meet, that meeting conveniently may be conducted by telephone conference or live link; and experts' meetings always should be conducted by those means where that will avoid unnecessary delay and expense.

19C.4. Where the experts are to meet, the parties must discuss and if possible agree whether an agenda is necessary, and if so attempt to agree one that helps the experts to focus on the issues which need to be discussed. The agenda must not be in the form of leading questions or hostile in tone. The experts may not be required to avoid reaching agreement, or to defer reaching agreement, on any matter within the experts' competence.

19C.5. If the legal representatives do attend:

(a) they should not normally intervene in the discussion, except to answer questions put to them by the experts or to advise on the law; and
(b) the experts may if they so wish hold part of their discussions in the absence of the legal representatives.

19C.6. A statement must be prepared by the experts dealing with paragraphs 19C.2(a)–(d) above. Individual copies of the statements must be signed or otherwise authenticated by the experts, in manuscript or by electronic means, at the conclusion of the discussion, or as soon thereafter as practicable, and in any event within 5 business days. Copies of the statements must be provided to the parties no later than 10 business days after signing.

19C.7. Experts must give their own opinions to assist the court and do not require the authority of the parties to sign a joint statement. The joint statement should include a brief re-statement that the experts recognise their duties, which should be in the following terms, or in terms substantially the same as these:

'We each DECLARE THAT:

1. We individually here re-state the Expert's Declaration contained in our respective reports that we understand our overriding duties to the court, have complied with them and will continue to do so.
2. We have neither jointly nor individually been instructed to, nor has it been suggested that we should, avoid reaching agreement, or defer reaching agreement, on any matter within our competence.'

19C.8. If an expert significantly alters an opinion, the joint statement must include a note or addendum by that expert explaining the change of opinion.

Criminal Procedure Rules Part 20 Hearsay Evidence

R20.1 **When this Part applies**

20.1 This Part applies in a magistrates' court and in the Crown Court where a party wants to introduce hearsay evidence, within the meaning of section 114 of the Criminal Justice Act 2003[1]

[Note. Under section 114 of the Criminal Justice Act 2003, a statement not made in oral evidence is admissible as evidence of any matter stated if—

(a) a statutory provision makes it admissible;
(b) a rule of law preserved by section 118 makes it admissible;
(c) the parties agree to it being admissible; or
(d) it is in the interests of justice for it to be admissible.

[1] 2003 c. 44.

Under section 115 of the Act—

(a) a "statement" means any representation of fact or opinion, by any means, and includes a representation in pictorial form; and
(b) a "matter stated" is something stated by someone with the apparent purpose of—
(c) causing another person to believe it, or
(d) causing another person, or a machine, to act or operate on the basis that the matter is as stated.]

Notice to introduce hearsay evidence **R20.2**

20.2 (1) This rule applies where a party wants to introduce hearsay evidence for admission under any of the following sections of the Criminal Justice Act 2003—
(a) section 114(1)(d) (evidence admissible in the interests of justice);
(b) section 116 (evidence where a witness is unavailable);
(c) section 117(1)(c)[2] (evidence in a statement prepared for the purposes of criminal proceedings);
(d) section 121 (multiple hearsay).
(2) That party must—
(a) serve notice on—
(i) the court officer, and
(ii) each other party;
(b) in the notice—
(i) identify the evidence that is hearsay,
(ii) set out any facts on which that party relies to make the evidence admissible,
(iii) explain how that party will prove those facts if another party disputes them, and
(iv) explain why the evidence is admissible; and
(c) attach to the notice any statement or other document containing the evidence that has not already been served.
(3) A prosecutor who wants to introduce such evidence must serve the notice not more than—
(a) 20 business days after the defendant pleads not guilty, in a magistrates' court; or
(b) 10 business days after the defendant pleads not guilty, in the Crown Court.
(4) A defendant who wants to introduce such evidence must serve the notice as soon as reasonably practicable.
(5) A party entitled to receive a notice under this rule may waive that entitlement by so informing—
(a) the party who would have served it; and
(b) the court.

[Note. The Practice Direction sets out a form of notice for use in connection with this rule.

The sections of the Criminal Justice Act 2003 listed in this rule set out the conditions on which hearsay evidence may be admitted under them.

If notice is not given as this rule requires, then under section 132(5) of the 2003 Act—

(a) the evidence is not admissible without the court's permission;
(b) if the court gives permission, it may draw such inferences as appear proper from the failure to give notice; and
(c) the court may take the failure into account in exercising its powers to order costs.

This rule does not require notice of hearsay evidence that is admissible under any of the following sections of the 2003 Act—

(a) section 117 (business and other documents), otherwise than as required by rule 20.2(1)(c);
(b) section 118 (preservation of certain common law categories of admissibility);
(c) section 119 (inconsistent statements);
(d) section 120[3] (other previous statements of witness); or
(e) section 127[4] (expert evidence: preparatory work): but see Part 19 for the procedure where a party wants to introduce such evidence.]

[2] 2003 c. 44; section 117 was amended by regulation 4 of, and paragraph 8 of Schedule 3 to, S.I. 2017/730 and section 10 of the Crime (Overseas Production Orders) Act 2019 (c. 5).
[3] 2003 c. 44; section 120 was amended by sections 112 and 178 of, and Schedule 23 to, the Coroners and Justice Act 2009 (c. 25).
[4] 2003 c. 44; section 127 was amended by article 3 of, and paragraphs 45 and 50 of the Schedule to, S.I. 2004/2035.

R20.3 Opposing the introduction of hearsay evidence

20.3 (1) This rule applies where a party objects to the introduction of hearsay evidence.
(2) That party must—
(a) apply to the court to determine the objection;
(b) serve the application on—
(i) the court officer, and
(ii) each other party;
(c) serve the application as soon as reasonably practicable, and in any event not more than 10 business days after—
(i) service of notice to introduce the evidence under rule 20.2,
(ii) service of the evidence to which that party objects, if no notice is required by that rule, or
(iii) the defendant pleads not guilty
whichever of those events happens last; and
(d) in the application, explain—
(i) which, if any, facts set out in a notice under rule 20.2 that party disputes,
(ii) why the evidence is not admissible, and
(iii) any other objection to the evidence.
(3) The court—
(a) may determine an application—
(i) at a hearing, in public or in private, or
(ii) without a hearing;
(b) must not determine the application unless the party who served the notice—
(i) is present, or
(ii) has had a reasonable opportunity to respond;
(c) may adjourn the application; and
(d) may discharge or vary a determination where it can do so under—
(i) section 8B of the Magistrates' Courts Act 1980[5] (ruling at pre-trial hearing in a magistrates' court), or
(ii) section 9 of the Criminal Justice Act 1987[6], or section 31 or 40 of the Criminal Procedure and Investigations Act 1996[7] (ruling at preparatory or other pre-trial hearing in the Crown Court).

R20.4 Unopposed hearsay evidence

20.4 (1) This rule applies where—
(a) a party has served notice to introduce hearsay evidence under rule 20.2; and
(b) no other party has applied to the court to determine an objection to the introduction of the evidence.
(2) The court must treat the evidence as if it were admissible by agreement.

[Note. Under section 132(4) of the Criminal Justice Act 2003, rules may provide that evidence is to be treated as admissible by agreement of the parties if notice to introduce that evidence has not been opposed.]

R20.5 Court's power to vary requirements under this Part

20.5 (1) The court may—
(a) shorten or extend (even after it has expired) a time limit under this Part;
(b) allow an application or notice to be in a different form to one set out in the Practice Direction, or to be made or given orally; and
(c) dispense with the requirement for notice to introduce hearsay evidence.
(2) A party who wants an extension of time must—
(a) apply when serving the application or notice for which it is needed; and
(b) explain the delay.

[5] 1980 c. 43; section 8B was inserted by section 45 of, and Schedule 3 to, the Courts Act 2003 (c. 39) and amended by paragraph 51 of Schedule 3, and Part 4 of Schedule 37, to the Criminal Justice Act 2003 (c. 44).
[6] 1987 c. 38; section 9 was amended by section 170 of, and Schedule 16 to, the Criminal Justice Act 1988 (c. 33), section 6 of the Criminal Justice Act 1993 (c. 36), sections 72, 74 and 80 of, and paragraph 3 of Schedule 3 and Schedule 5 to, the Criminal Procedure and Investigations Act 1996 (c. 25), sections 45 and 310 of, and paragraphs 18, 52 and 54 of Schedule 36 and Part 3 of Schedule 37 to, the Criminal Justice Act 2003 (c. 44), article 3 of, and paragraphs 21 and 23 of S.I. 2004/2035, section 59 of, and paragraph 1 of Schedule 11 to, the Constitutional Reform Act 2005 (c. 4) and Part 10 of Schedule 10 to the Protection of Freedoms Act 2012 (c. 9). The amendment made by section 45 of the Criminal Justice Act 2003 (c. 44) is in force for certain purposes; for remaining purposes it has effect from a date to be appointed.
[7] 1996 c. 25; section 31 was amended by sections 310, 331 and 332 of, and paragraphs 20, 36, 65 and 67 of Schedule 36 and Schedule 37 to, the Criminal Justice Act 2003 (c. 44).

Criminal Procedure Rules Part 21 Evidence of Bad Character

When this Part applies **R21.1**

21.1 This Part applies in a magistrates' court and in the Crown Court where a party wants to introduce evidence of bad character within the meaning of section 98 of the Criminal Justice Act 2003[1]

[Note. Under section 98 of the Criminal Justice Act 2003, evidence of a person's bad character means evidence of, or of a disposition towards, misconduct on that person's part, other than evidence that—

(a) has to do with the alleged facts of the offence; or
(b) is evidence of misconduct in connection with the investigation or prosecution.

Under section 100(1) of the Criminal Justice Act 2003, evidence of a non-defendant's bad character is admissible if—

(a) it is important explanatory evidence;
(b) it has substantial probative value in relation to a matter which—
(i) is a matter in issue in the proceedings, and
(ii) is of substantial importance in the context of the case as a whole; or
(c) all parties to the proceedings agree to the evidence being admissible.

The section explains requirements (a) and (b). Unless the parties agree to the evidence being admissible, it may not be introduced without the court's permission.

Under section 101(1) of the Criminal Justice Act 2003, evidence of a defendant's bad character is admissible if—

(a) all parties to the proceedings agree to the evidence being admissible;
(b) the evidence is introduced by the defendant, or is given in answer to a question asked by the defendant in cross-examination which was intended to elicit that evidence;
(c) it is important explanatory evidence;
(d) it is relevant to an important matter in issue between the defendant and the prosecution;
(e) it has substantial probative value in relation to an important matter in issue between the defendant and a co-defendant;
(f) it is evidence to correct a false impression given by the defendant; or
(g) the defendant has made an attack on another person's character.

Sections 102 to 106 of the Act supplement those requirements. The court must not admit evidence under (d) or (g) if, on an application by the defendant, the court concludes that to do so would be unfair.]

Content of application or notice **R21.2**

21.2 (1) A party who wants to introduce evidence of bad character must—
(a) make an application under rule 21.3, where it is evidence of a non-defendant's bad character;
(b) give notice under rule 21.4, where it is evidence of a defendant's bad character.
(2) An application or notice must—
(a) set out the facts of the misconduct on which that party relies,
(b) explain how that party will prove those facts (whether by certificate of conviction, other official record, or other evidence), if another party disputes them, and
(c) explain why the evidence is admissible.

[Note. The Practice Direction sets out forms of application and notice for use in connection with rules 21.3 and 21.4.

The fact that a person was convicted of an offence may be proved under—

(a) section 73 of the Police and Criminal Evidence Act 1984[2] (conviction in the United Kingdom); or
(b) section 7 of the Evidence Act 1851[3] (conviction outside the United Kingdom).

See also sections 117 and 118 of the Criminal Justice Act 2003 (admissibility of evidence contained in business and other documents).

Under section 10 of the Criminal Justice Act 1967[4], a party may admit a matter of fact.]

[1] 2003 c. 44.
[2] 1984 c. 60; section 73 was amended by section 90(1) of, and paragraphs 125 and 128 of Schedule 13 to, the Access to Justice Act 1999 (c. 22) and paragraph 285 of Schedule 8 to, the Courts Act 2003 (c. 39).
[3] 1851 c. 99.
[4] 1967 c. 80.

R21.3 **Application to introduce evidence of a non-defendant's bad character**

21.3 (1) This rule applies where a party wants to introduce evidence of the bad character of a person other than the defendant.

(2) That party must serve an application to do so on—
(a) the court officer; and
(b) each other party.

(3) The applicant must serve the application—
(a) as soon as reasonably practicable; and in any event
(b) not more than 10 business days after the prosecutor discloses material on which the application is based (if the prosecutor is not the applicant).

(4) A party who objects to the introduction of the evidence must—
(a) serve notice on—
(i) the court officer, and
(ii) each other party
not more than 10 business days after service of the application; and
(b) in the notice explain, as applicable—
(i) which, if any, facts of the misconduct set out in the application that party disputes,
(ii) what, if any, facts of the misconduct that party admits instead,
(iii) why the evidence is not admissible, and
(iv) any other objection to the application.

(5) The court—
(a) may determine an application—
(i) at a hearing, in public or in private, or
(ii) without a hearing;
(b) must not determine the application unless each party other than the applicant—
(i) is present, or
(ii) has had at least 10 business days in which to serve a notice of objection;
(c) may adjourn the application; and
(d) may discharge or vary a determination where it can do so under—
(i) section 8B of the Magistrates' Courts Act 1980[5] (ruling at pre-trial hearing in a magistrates' court), or
(ii) section 9 of the Criminal Justice Act 1987[6], or section 31 or 40 of the Criminal Procedure and Investigations Act 1996[7] (ruling at preparatory or other pre-trial hearing in the Crown Court).

[Note. The Practice Direction sets out a form of application for use in connection with this rule.

See also rule 21.5 (reasons for decisions must be given in public).]

R21.4 **Notice to introduce evidence of a defendant's bad character**

21.4 (1) This rule applies where a party wants to introduce evidence of a defendant's bad character.

(2) A prosecutor or co-defendant who wants to introduce such evidence must serve notice on—
(a) the court officer; and
(b) each other party.

(3) A prosecutor must serve any such notice not more than—
(a) 20 business days after the defendant pleads not guilty, in a magistrates' court; or
(b) 10 business days after the defendant pleads not guilty, in the Crown Court.

(4) A co-defendant who wants to introduce such evidence must serve the notice—
(a) as soon as reasonably practicable; and in any event
(b) not more than 10 business days after the prosecutor discloses material on which the notice is based.

(5) A party who objects to the introduction of the evidence identified by such a notice must—
(a) apply to the court to determine the objection;

[5] 1980 c. 43; section 8B was inserted by section 45 of, and Schedule 3 to, the Courts Act 2003 (c. 39) and amended by paragraph 51 of Schedule 3, and Part 4 of Schedule 37, to the Criminal Justice Act 2003 (c. 44).

[6] 1987 c. 38; section 9 was amended by section 170 of, and Schedule 16 to, the Criminal Justice Act 1988 (c. 33), section 6 of the Criminal Justice Act 1993 (c. 36), sections 72, 74 and 80 of, and paragraph 3 of Schedule 3 and Schedule 5 to, the Criminal Procedure and Investigations Act 1996 (c. 25), sections 45 and 310 of, and paragraphs 18, 52 and 54 of Schedule 36 and Part 3 of Schedule 37 to, the Criminal Justice Act 2003 (c. 44), article 3 of, and paragraphs 21 and 23 of S.I. 2004/2035, section 59 of, and paragraph 1 of Schedule 11 to, the Constitutional Reform Act 2005 (c. 4) and Part 10 of Schedule 10 to the Protection of Freedoms Act 2012 (c. 9). The amendment made by section 45 of the Criminal Justice Act 2003 (c. 44) is in force for certain purposes; for remaining purposes it has effect from a date to be appointed.

[7] 1996 c. 25; section 31 was amended by sections 310, 331 and 332 of, and paragraphs 20, 36, 65 and 67 of Schedule 36 and Schedule 37 to, the Criminal Justice Act 2003 (c. 44).

(b) serve the application on—
(i) the court officer, and
(ii) each other party
not more than 10 business days after service of the notice; and
(c) in the application explain, as applicable—
(i) which, if any, facts of the misconduct set out in the notice that party disputes,
(ii) what, if any, facts of the misconduct that party admits instead,
(iii) why the evidence is not admissible,
(iv) why it would be unfair to admit the evidence, and
(v) any other objection to the notice.
(6) The court—
(a) may determine such an application—
(i) at a hearing, in public or in private, or
(ii) without a hearing;
(b) must not determine the application unless the party who served the notice—
(i) is present, or
(ii) has had a reasonable opportunity to respond;
(c) may adjourn the application; and
(d) may discharge or vary a determination where it can do so under—
(i) section 8B of the Magistrates' Courts Act 1980 (ruling at pre-trial hearing in a magistrates' court), or
(ii) section 9 of the Criminal Justice Act 1987, or section 31 or 40 of the Criminal Procedure and Investigations Act 1996 (ruling at preparatory or other pre-trial hearing in the Crown Court).
(7) A party entitled to receive such a notice may waive that entitlement by so informing—
(a) the party who would have served it; and
(b) the court.
(8) A defendant who wants to introduce evidence of his or her own bad character must—
(a) give notice, in writing or orally—
(i) as soon as reasonably practicable, and in any event
(ii) before the evidence is introduced, either by the defendant or in reply to a question asked by the defendant of another party's witness in order to obtain that evidence; and
(b) in the Crown Court, at the same time give notice (in writing, or orally) of any direction about the defendant's character that the defendant wants the court to give the jury under rule 25.14 (Directions to the jury and taking the verdict).

[Note. The Practice Direction sets out a form of notice for use in connection with this rule.

See also rule 21.5 (reasons for decisions must be given in public).

If notice is not given as this rule requires, then under section 111(4) of the Criminal Justice Act 2003 the court may take the failure into account in exercising its powers to order costs.]

Reasons for decisions **R21.5**

21.5 The court must announce at a hearing in public (but in the absence of the jury, if there is one) the reasons for a decision—
(a) to admit evidence as evidence of bad character, or to refuse to do so; or
(b) to direct an acquittal or a retrial under section 107 of the Criminal Justice Act 2003.

[Note. See section 110 of the Criminal Justice Act 2003.]

Court's power to vary requirements under this Part **R21.6**

21.6 (1) The court may—
(a) shorten or extend (even after it has expired) a time limit under this Part;
(b) allow an application or notice to be in a different form to one set out in the Practice Direction, or to be made or given orally; and
(c) dispense with a requirement for notice to introduce evidence of a defendant's bad character.
(2) A party who wants an extension of time must—
(a) apply when serving the application or notice for which it is needed; and
(b) explain the delay.

CRIMINAL PRACTICE DIRECTIONS PART 21 EVIDENCE OF BAD CHARACTER

CPD.21A **CPD V Evidence 21A: Spent Convictions**

21A.1 The effect of section 4(1) of the Rehabilitation of Offenders Act 1974 is that a person who has become a rehabilitated person for the purpose of the Act in respect of a conviction (known as a 'spent' conviction) shall be treated for all purposes in law as a person who has not committed, or been charged with or prosecuted for, or convicted of or sentenced for, the offence or offences which were the subject of that conviction.

21A.2 Section 4(1) of the 1974 Act does not apply, however, to evidence given in criminal proceedings: section 7(2)(a). During the trial of a criminal charge, reference to previous convictions (and therefore to spent convictions) can arise in a number of ways. The most common is when a bad character application is made under the Criminal Justice Act 2003. When considering bad character applications under the 2003 Act, regard should always be had to the general principles of the Rehabilitation of Offenders Act 1974.

21A.3 On conviction, the court must be provided with a statement of the defendant's record for the purposes of sentence. The record supplied should contain all previous convictions, but those which are spent should, so far as practicable, be marked as such. No one should refer in open court to a spent conviction without the authority of the judge, which authority should not be given unless the interests of justice so require. When passing sentence the judge should make no reference to a spent conviction unless it is necessary to do so for the purpose of explaining the sentence to be passed.

CRIMINAL PROCEDURE RULES PART 22 EVIDENCE OF A COMPLAINANT'S PREVIOUS SEXUAL BEHAVIOUR

R22.1 **When this Part applies**

22.1 This Part applies in a magistrates' court and in the Crown Court where—

(i) section 41 of the Youth Justice and Criminal Evidence Act 1999[1] prohibits the introduction of evidence or cross-examination about any sexual behaviour of the complainant of a sexual offence, and

(ii) despite that prohibition, a defendant wants to introduce such evidence or to cross-examine a witness about such behaviour.

[Note. Section 41 of the Youth Justice and Criminal Evidence Act 1999 prohibits evidence or cross-examination about the sexual behaviour of a complainant of a sexual offence, subject to exceptions.

See also—

(a) section 42 of the 1999 Act[2], which among other things defines 'sexual behaviour' and 'sexual offence';

(b) section 34, which prohibits cross-examination by a defendant in person of the complainant of a sexual offence (Part 23 contains relevant rules).]

R22.2 **Exercise of court's powers**

22.2 The court—

(a) must determine an application under rule 22.4 (Application for permission to introduce evidence or cross-examine)—

(i) at a hearing in private, and

(ii) in the absence of the complainant;

(b) must not determine the application unless—

(i) each party other than the applicant is present, or has had at least 10 business days in which to make representations, and

(ii) the court is satisfied that it has been able to take adequate account of the complainant's rights;

(c) may adjourn the application; and

(d) may discharge or vary a determination where it can do so under—

(i) section 8B of the Magistrates' Courts Act 1980[3] (ruling at pre-trial hearing in a magistrates' court), or

[1] 1999 c. 23.

[2] 1999 c. 23; section 42 was amended by paragraph 73 of Schedule 3 and Schedule 37 to the Criminal Justice Act 2003 (c. 44).

[3] 1980 c. 43; section 8B was inserted by section 45 of, and Schedule 3 to, the Courts Act 2003 (c. 39) and amended by paragraph 51 of Schedule 3, and Part 4 of Schedule 37, to the Criminal Justice Act 2003 (c. 44).

(ii) section 9 of the Criminal Justice Act 1987[4], or section 31 or 40 of the Criminal Procedure and Investigations Act 1996[5] (ruling at preparatory or other pre-trial hearing in the Crown Court).

[Note. See also section 43 of the Youth Justice and Criminal Evidence Act 1999[6], which among other things requires an application under section 41 of the Act to be heard in private and in the absence of the complainant.

At a pre-trial hearing a court may make binding rulings about the admissibility of evidence and about questions of law under sections 31 and 40 of the Criminal Procedure and Investigations Act 1996[7] and section 8A of the Magistrates' Courts Act 1980[8].]

Decisions and reasons **R22.3**

22.3 (1) A prosecutor who wants to introduce the evidence of a complainant in respect of whom the court allows the introduction of evidence or cross-examination about any sexual behaviour must—

(a) inform the complainant of the court's decision as soon as reasonably practicable; and

(b) explain to the complainant any arrangements that as a result will be made for him or her to give evidence.

(2) The court must—

(a) promptly determine an application; and

(b) allow the prosecutor sufficient time to comply with the requirements of—

(i) paragraph (1), and

(ii) the code of practice issued under section 32 of the Domestic Violence, Crime and Victims Act 2004[9].

(3) The court must announce at a hearing in public—

(a) the reasons for a decision to allow or refuse an application under rule 22.4; and

(b) if it allows such an application, the extent to which evidence may be introduced or questions asked.

[Note. Under section 43 of the Youth Justice and Criminal Evidence Act 1999—

(a) the reasons for the court's decision on an application must be given in open court; and

(b) the court must state in open court the extent to which evidence may be introduced or questions asked.]

Application for permission to introduce evidence or cross-examine **R22.4**

22.4. (1) A defendant who wants to introduce evidence or cross-examine a witness about any sexual behaviour of the complainant must—

(a) serve an application for permission to do so on—

(i) the court officer, and

(ii) each other party; and

(b) serve the application—

(i) as soon as reasonably practicable after becoming aware of the grounds for doing so, and in any event

[4] 1987 c. 38; section 9 was amended by section 170 of, and Schedule 16 to, the Criminal Justice Act 1988 (c. 33), section 6 of the Criminal Justice Act 1993 (c. 36), sections 72, 74 and 80 of, and paragraph 3 of Schedule 3 and Schedule 5 to, the Criminal Procedure and Investigations Act 1996 (c. 25), sections 45 and 310 of, and paragraphs 18, 52 and 54 of Schedule 36 and Part 3 of Schedule 37 to, the Criminal Justice Act 2003 (c. 44), article 3 of, and paragraphs 21 and 23 of S.I. 2004/2035, section 59 of, and paragraph 1 of Schedule 11 to, the Constitutional Reform Act 2005 (c. 4) and Part 10 of Schedule 10 to the Protection of Freedoms Act 2012 (c. 9). The amendment made by section 45 of the Criminal Justice Act 2003 (c. 44) is in force for certain purposes; for remaining purposes it has effect from a date to be appointed.

[5] 1996 c. 25; section 31 was amended by sections 310, 331 and 332 of, and paragraphs 20, 36, 65 and 67 of Schedule 36 and Schedule 37 to, the Criminal Justice Act 2003 (c. 44).

[6] 1999 c. 23; section 43(3) was amended by section 109(1) of, and paragraph 384(g) of Schedule 8 to, the Courts Act 2003 (c. 39).

[7] 1996 c. 25; section 31 was amended by sections 310, 331 and 332 of, and paragraphs 20, 36, 65 and 67 of Schedule 36 and Schedule 37 to, the Criminal Justice Act 2003 (c. 44).

[8] 1980 c. 43; section 8A was inserted by section 45 of, and Schedule 3 to, the Courts Act 2003 (c. 39) and amended by SI 2006/2493 and paragraphs 12 and 14 of Schedule 5 to the Legal Aid, Sentencing and Punishment of Offenders Act 2012 (c. 10).

[9] 2004 c. 28; section 32 was amended by article 8 of, and paragraph 10 of the Schedule to, S.I. 2007/2128.

(ii) not more than 10 business days after the prosecutor discloses material on which the application is based.

(2) The application must—

(a) identify the issue to which the defendant says the complainant's sexual behaviour is relevant;

(b) give particulars of—

(i) any evidence that the defendant wants to introduce, and

(ii) any questions that the defendant wants to ask;

(c) identify the exception to the prohibition in section 41 of the Youth Justice and Criminal Evidence Act 1999 on which the defendant relies; and

(d) give the name and date of birth of any witness whose evidence about the complainant's sexual behaviour the defendant wants to introduce.

R22.5 **Application containing information withheld from another party**

22.5. (1) This rule applies where—

(a) an applicant serves an application under rule 22.4 (Application for permission to introduce evidence or cross-examine); and

(b) the application includes information that the applicant thinks ought not be revealed to another party.

(2) The applicant must—

(a) omit that information from the part of the application that is served on that other party;

(b) mark the other part to show that, unless the court otherwise directs, it is only for the court; and

(c) in that other part, explain why the applicant has withheld that information from that other party.

(3) If the court so directs, the hearing of an application to which this rule applies may be, wholly or in part, in the absence of a party from whom information has been withheld.

(4) At the hearing of an application to which this rule applies—

(a) the general rule is that the court must consider, in the following sequence—

(i) representations first by the applicant and then by each other party, in all the parties' presence, and then

(ii) further representations by the applicant, in the absence of a party from whom information has been withheld; but

(b) the court may direct other arrangements for the hearing.

[Note. See section 43(3)(c) of the Youth Justice and Criminal Evidence Act 1999.]

R22.6 **Representations in response**

22.6. (1) This rule applies where a party wants to make representations about—

(a) an application under rule 22.4 (Application for permission to introduce evidence or cross-examine); or

(b) a proposed variation or discharge of a decision allowing such an application.

(2) Such a party must—

(a) serve the representations on—

(i) the court officer, and

(ii) each other party; and

(b) do so not more than 10 business days after, as applicable—

(i) service of the application, or

(ii) notice of the proposal to vary or discharge.

(3) Where representations include information that the person making them thinks ought not be revealed to another party, that person must—

(a) omit that information from the representations served on that other party;

(b) mark the information to show that, unless the court otherwise directs, it is only for the court; and

(c) with that information include an explanation of why it has been withheld from that other party.

(4) Representations against an application under rule 22.4 must explain the grounds of objection.

(5) Representations against the variation or discharge of a decision must explain why it should not be varied or discharged.

R22.7 **Special measures, etc. for a witness**

22.7 (1) This rule applies where the court allows an application under rule 22.4 (Application for permission to introduce evidence or cross-examine).

(2) Despite the time limits in rule 18.4 (Making an application for a direction or order)—
(a) a party may apply for a special measures direction or for the variation of an existing special measures direction not more than 10 business days after the court's decision; and
(b) the court may shorten the time for opposing that application.
(3) Where the court allows the cross-examination of a witness, the court must give directions for the appropriate treatment and questioning of that witness in accordance with rule 3.8(6) and (7) (setting ground rules for the conduct of questioning).

[Note. Special measures to improve the quality of evidence given by certain witnesses may be directed by the court under section 19 of the Youth Justice and Criminal Evidence Act 1999 and varied under section 20[10]*. An application for a special measures direction may be made by a party under Part 18 or the court may make a direction on its own initiative. Rule 18.13(2) sets the usual time limit (10 business days) for opposing a special measures application.]*

Court's power to vary requirements under this Part **R22.8**

22.8. The court may shorten or extend (even after it has expired) a time limit under this Part.

Criminal Practice Directions Part 22 Evidence of a Complainant's Previous Sexual Behaviour

CPD V Evidence 22A: Use of Ground Rules Hearing when Dealing with S.41 Youth Justice and Criminal Evidence Act 1999 (YJCEA 1999) Evidence of Complainant's Previous Sexual Behaviour **CPD.22A**

The Application

22A.1 When a defendant wishes to introduce evidence, or cross-examine about the previous sexual behaviour of the complainant, then it is imperative that the timetable and procedure as laid down in the Criminal Procedure Rules Part 22 is followed. The application must be submitted in writing as soon as reasonably practicable and not more than 14 days after the prosecutor has disclosed material on which the application is based. Should the prosecution wish to make any representations then these should be served on the court and other parties not more than 14 days after receiving the application.

22A.2 The application must clearly state the issue to which the defendant says the complainant's sexual behaviour is relevant and the reasons why it should be admitted. It must outline the evidence which the defendant wants to introduce and articulate the questions which it is proposed should be asked. The application must identify the statutory exception to the prohibition in section 41 YJCEA 1999 on which the defendant relies and give the name and date of birth of any witness whose evidence about the complainant's sexual behaviour the defendant wants to introduce.

The Hearing

22A.3 When determining the application, the judge should examine the questions with the usual level of scrutiny expected at a ground rules hearing. For each question that it is sought to put to a witness, or evidence it is sought to adduce, the defence should identify clearly for the judge the suggested relevance it has to an issue in the case. In order for the judge to rule on which evidence can be adduced or questions put, the defence must set out individual questions for the judge; merely identifying a topic is not sufficient for this type of application. The judge should make it clear that if the application is granted then no other questions on this topic will be allowed to be asked, unless with the express permission of the court.

22A.4 The application should be dealt with in private and in the absence of the complainant, but the judge must state in open court, without the jury or complainant present, the reasons for the decision, and if leave is granted, the extent of the questions or evidence that is allowed.

Late applications

22A.5 Late applications should be considered with particular scrutiny especially if there is a suggestion of tactical thinking behind the timing of the application and/or when the application is based on material that has been available for some time. If consideration of a late application has the potential to disrupt the timetabling of witnesses, then the judge will need to take account of the potential impact of delay upon a witness who is due to give evidence. If necessary, the judge may defer consideration of any such application until later in the trial.

22A.6 By analogy, following the approach adopted by the Court of Appeal in *R v Musone* [2007] 1 WLR 2467, the trial judge is entitled to refuse the application where (s)he is satisfied that the applicant is seeking to manipulate the court process so as to prevent the respondent from being able to

[10] 1999 c. 23; section 20(6) was amended by paragraph 384(a) of Schedule 8 to the Courts Act 2003 (c. 39).

prepare an adequate response. This may be the only remedy available to the court to ensure that the fairness of the trial is upheld and will be particularly relevant when the application is made on the day of trial.

22A.7 Where the application has been granted in good time before the trial, the complainant is entitled to be made aware that such evidence is part of the defence case.

At the trial

22A.8 Advocates should be reminded that the questioning must be conducted in an appropriate manner. Any aggressive, repetitive and oppressive questioning will be stopped by the judge. Judges should intervene and stop any attempts to refer to evidence that might have been adduced under section 41, but for which no leave has been given and/or should have formed the basis of a section 41 application, but did not do so. When evidence about the complainant's previous sexual behaviour is referred to without an application, the judge may be required to consider whether the impact of that happening is so prejudicial to the overall fairness of the trial that the trial should be stopped and a re-trial should be ordered, should the impact not be capable of being ameliorated by way of jury direction.

Criminal Procedure Rules Part 23 Restriction on Cross-Examination by a Defendant

General rules

R23.1 **When this Part applies**

23.1 This Part applies where—

(a) a defendant may not cross-examine in person a witness because of section 34 or section 35 of the Youth Justice and Criminal Evidence Act 1999[1] (Complainants in proceedings for sexual offences; Child complainants and other child witnesses); or

(b) the court can prohibit a defendant from cross-examining in person a witness under section 36 of that Act[2] (Direction prohibiting accused from cross-examining particular witness).

[Note. Under section 34 of the Youth Justice and Criminal Evidence Act 1999, no defendant charged with a sexual offence may cross-examine in person a witness who is the complainant, either—

(a) in connection with that offence; or

(b) in connection with any other offence (of whatever nature) with which that defendant is charged in the proceedings.

Under section 35 of the 1999 Act, no defendant charged with an offence listed in that section may cross-examine in person a protected witness, either—

(a) in connection with that offence; or

(b) in connection with any other offence (of whatever nature) with which that defendant is charged in the proceedings.

A 'protected witness' is one who—

(a) either is the complainant or is alleged to have been a witness to the commission of the offence; and

(b) either is a child, within the meaning of section 35, or is due to be cross-examined after giving evidence in chief—

(i) by means of a video recording made when the witness was a child, or

(ii) in any other way when the witness was a child.

Under section 36 of the 1999 Act, where neither section 34 nor section 35 applies the court may give a direction prohibiting the defendant from cross-examining, or further cross-examining, in person a witness, on application by the prosecutor or on the court's own initiative. See also rules 23.3 to 23.7.]

R23.2 **Appointment of advocate to cross-examine witness**

23.2 (1) This rule applies where a defendant may not cross-examine in person a witness in consequence of—

(a) the prohibition imposed by section 34 or section 35 of the Youth Justice and Criminal Evidence Act 1999; or

(b) a prohibition imposed by the court under section 36 of the 1999 Act.

[1] 1999 c. 23; section 35 was amended by sections 139 and 140 of, and paragraph 41 of Schedule 6 and Schedule 7 to, the Sexual Offences Act 2003 (c. 42), section 148 of, and paragraphs 35 and 36 of Schedule 26 to, the Criminal Justice and Immigration Act 2008 (c. 4) and section 105 of the Coroners and Justice Act 2009 (c. 25).

[2] 1999 c. 23.

(2) The court must, as soon as practicable, explain in terms the defendant can understand (with help, if necessary)—
(a) the prohibition and its effect;
(b) that if the defendant will not be represented by a lawyer with a right of audience in the court for the purposes of the case then the defendant is entitled to arrange for such a lawyer to cross-examine the witness on his or her behalf;
(c) that the defendant must notify the court officer of the identity of any such lawyer, with details of how to contact that person, by no later than a date set by the court; and
(d) that if the defendant does not want to make such arrangements, or if the defendant gives no such notice by that date, then—
(i) the court must decide whether it is necessary in the interests of justice to appoint such a lawyer to cross-examine the witness in the defendant's interests, and
(ii) if the court decides that that is necessary, the court will appoint a lawyer chosen by the court who will not be responsible to the defendant.

(3) Having given those explanations, the court must—
(a) ask whether the defendant wants to arrange for a lawyer to cross-examine the witness, and set a date by when the defendant must notify the court officer of the identity of that lawyer if the answer to that question is 'yes'; and
(b) if the answer to that question is 'no', or if by the date set the defendant has given no such notice—
(i) decide whether it is necessary in the interests of justice for the witness to be cross-examined by an advocate appointed to represent the defendant's interests, and
(ii) if the court decides that that is necessary, give directions for the appointment of such an advocate.

(4) The court may give the explanations and ask the questions required by this rule—
(a) at a hearing, in public or in private; or
(b) without a hearing, by written notice to the defendant.

(5) The court may extend (even after it has expired) the time limit that it sets under paragraph (3)(a)—
(a) on application by the defendant; or
(b) on its own initiative.

(6) Paragraphs (7), (8), (9) and (10) apply where the court appoints an advocate.

(7) The directions that the court gives under paragraph (3)(b)(ii) must provide for the supply to the advocate of a copy of—
(a) all material served by one party on the other, whether before or after the advocate's appointment, to which applies—
(i) Part 8 (Initial details of the prosecution case),
(ii) in the Crown Court, rule 3.19 (service of prosecution evidence in a case sent for trial),
(iii) Part 16 (Written witness statements),
(iv) Part 19 (Expert evidence),
(v) Part 20 (Hearsay evidence),
(vi) Part 21 (Evidence of bad character), or
(vii) Part 22 (Evidence of a complainant's previous sexual behaviour);
(b) any material disclosed, given or served, whether before or after the advocate's appointment, which is—
(i) prosecution material disclosed to the defendant under section 3 (Initial duty of prosecutor to disclose) or section 7A (Continuing duty of prosecutor to disclose) of the Criminal Procedure and Investigations Act 1996[3],
(ii) a defence statement given by the defendant under section 5 (Compulsory disclosure by accused) or section 6 (Voluntary disclosure by accused) of the 1996 Act[4],
(iii) a defence witness notice given by the defendant under section 6C of that Act[5] (Notification of intention to call defence witnesses), or

[3] 1996 c. 25; section 3 was amended by section 82 of, and paragraph 7 of Schedule 4 to, the Regulation of Investigatory Powers Act 2000 (c. 23), section 32 of, and paragraphs 20 and 21 of Schedule 36 to, the Criminal Justice Act 2003 (c. 44) and section 271 of, and paragraph 39 of Schedule 10 to, the Investigatory Powers Act 2016 (c. 25). Section 7A was inserted by section 37 of the Criminal Justice Act 2003 (c. 44) and was amended by section 271 of, and paragraph 39 of Schedule 10 to, the Investigatory Powers Act 2016 (c. 25).

[4] 1996 c. 25; section 5 was amended by section 119 of, and paragraph 126 of Schedule 8 to, the Crime and Disorder Act 1998 (c. 37), in respect of certain proceedings only, and by section 33 of, and paragraph 66 of Schedule 3, paragraphs 20 and 23 of Schedule 36 and Parts 3 and 4 of Schedule 37 to, the Criminal Justice Act 2003 (c. 44). Section 6 was amended by paragraphs 20 and 24 of Schedule 36 and Part 3 of Schedule 37 to the Criminal Justice Act 2003 (c. 44).) For transitional provisions and savings see paragraph (2) of Schedule 2 to S.I. 2005/950.

[5] 1996 c. 25; section 6C was inserted by section 34 of the Criminal Justice Act 2003 (c. 44).

(iv) an application by the defendant under section 8 of that Act[6] (Application by accused for disclosure);

(c) any case management questionnaire prepared for the purposes of the trial or, as the case may be, the appeal; and

(d) all case management directions given by the court for the purposes of the trial or the appeal.

(8) Where the defendant has given a defence statement—

(a) section 8(2) of the Criminal Procedure and Investigations Act 1996 is modified to allow the advocate, as well as the defendant, to apply for an order for prosecution disclosure under that subsection if the advocate has reasonable cause to believe that there is prosecution material concerning the witness which is required by section 7A of the Act to be disclosed to the defendant and has not been; and

(b) rule 15.5 (Defendant's application for prosecution disclosure) applies to an application by the advocate as it does to an application by the defendant.

(9) Before receiving evidence the court must establish, with the active assistance of the parties and of the advocate, and in the absence of any jury in the Crown Court—

(a) what issues will be the subject of the advocate's cross-examination; and

(b) whether the court's permission is required for any proposed question, for example where Part 21 or Part 22 applies.

(10) The appointment terminates at the conclusion of the cross-examination of the witness.

[Note. See section 38 of the Youth Justice and Criminal Evidence Act 1999[7]*. Under section 38(8) the references in that section to a 'legal representative' are to a representative who is an advocate within the meaning of rule 2.2.*

Under section 38(7) of the 1999 Act, where the court appoints an advocate Criminal Procedure Rules may apply with modifications any of the provisions of Part I of the Criminal Procedure and Investigations Act 1996. A summary of the disclosure requirements of the 1996 Act is at the end of Part 15 (Disclosure). Under section 5 of that Act, in the Crown Court the defendant must give a defence statement. Under section 6, in a magistrates' court the defendant may give such a statement but need not do so. Under section 6C, in the Crown Court and in magistrates' courts the defendant must give a defence witness notice indicating whether he or she intends to call any witnesses (other than him or herself) and, if so, identifying them. Under section 8 a defendant may apply for prosecution disclosure only if the defendant has given a defence statement.]

Application to prohibit cross-examination

R23.3 **Exercise of court's powers**

23.3 (1) The court may decide whether to impose or discharge a prohibition against cross-examination under section 36 of the Youth Justice and Criminal Evidence Act 1999—

(a) at a hearing, in public or in private, or without a hearing; and

(b) in a party's absence, if that party—

(i) applied for the prohibition or discharge, or

(ii) has had at least 10 business days in which to make representations.

(2) The court must announce, at a hearing in public before the witness gives evidence, the reasons for a decision—

(a) to impose or discharge such a prohibition; or

(b) to refuse to do so.

[Note. See section 37 of the Youth Justice and Criminal Evidence Act 1999[8]*.]*

R23.4 **Application to prohibit cross-examination**

23.4 (1) This rule applies where under section 36 of the Youth Justice and Criminal Evidence Act 1999 the prosecutor wants the court to prohibit the cross-examination of a witness by a defendant in person.

(2) The prosecutor must—

(a) apply in writing, as soon as reasonably practicable after becoming aware of the grounds for doing so; and

(b) serve the application on—

(i) the court officer,

(ii) the defendant who is the subject of the application, and

(iii) any other defendant, unless the court otherwise directs.

[6] 1996 c. 25; section 8 was amended by section 82 of, and paragraph 7 of Schedule 4 to, the Regulation of Investigatory Powers Act 2000 (c. 23), section 38 of the Criminal Justice Act 2003 (c. 44) and section 271 of, and paragraph 39 of Schedule 10 to, the Investigatory Powers Act 2016 (c. 25).

[7] 1999 c. 23; section 38 was amended by section 109 of, and paragraph 384(f) of Schedule 8 to, the Courts Act 2003 (c. 39).

[8] 1999 c. 23; section 37 was amended by section 109 of, and paragraph 384(e) of Schedule 8 to, the Courts Act 2003 (c. 39).

(3) The application must—
(a) report any views that the witness has expressed about whether he or she is content to be cross-examined by the defendant in person;
(b) identify—
(i) the nature of the questions likely to be asked, having regard to the issues in the case,
(ii) any relevant behaviour of the defendant at any stage of the case, generally and in relation to the witness,
(iii) any relationship, of any nature, between the witness and the defendant,
(iv) any other defendant in the case who is subject to such a prohibition in respect of the witness, and
(v) any special measures direction made in respect of the witness, or for which an application has been made;
(c) explain why the quality of evidence given by the witness on cross-examination—
(i) is likely to be diminished if no such prohibition is imposed, and
(ii) would be likely to be improved if it were imposed; and
(d) explain why it would not be contrary to the interests of justice to impose the prohibition.

[Note. The Practice Direction sets out a form of application for use in connection with this rule.]

Application to discharge prohibition imposed by the court **R23.5**

23.5 (1) A party who wants the court to discharge a prohibition against cross-examination which the court imposed under section 36 of the Youth Justice and Criminal Evidence Act 1999 must—
(a) apply in writing, as soon as reasonably practicable after becoming aware of the grounds for doing so; and
(b) serve the application on—
(i) the court officer, and
(ii) each other party.
(2) The applicant must—
(a) explain what material circumstances have changed since the prohibition was imposed; and
(b) ask for a hearing, if the applicant wants one, and explain why it is needed.

[Note. Under section 37 of the Youth Justice and Criminal Evidence Act 1999, the court can discharge a prohibition against cross-examination which it has imposed—
(a) on application, if there has been a material change of circumstances; or
(b) on its own initiative.]

Application containing information withheld from another party **R23.6**

23.6 (1) This rule applies where—
(a) an applicant serves an application for the court to impose a prohibition against cross-examination, or for the discharge of such a prohibition; and
(b) the application includes information that the applicant thinks ought not be revealed to another party.
(2) The applicant must—
(a) omit that information from the part of the application that is served on that other party;
(b) mark the other part to show that, unless the court otherwise directs, it is only for the court; and
(c) in that other part, explain why the applicant has withheld that information from that other party.
(3) Any hearing of an application to which this rule applies—
(a) must be in private, unless the court otherwise directs; and
(b) if the court so directs, may be, wholly or in part, in the absence of a party from whom information has been withheld.
(4) At any hearing of an application to which this rule applies—
(a) the general rule is that the court must consider, in the following sequence—
(i) representations first by the applicant and then by each other party, in all the parties' presence, and then
(ii) further representations by the applicant, in the absence of a party from whom information has been withheld; but
(b) the court may direct other arrangements for the hearing.

[Note. See section 37 of the Youth Justice and Criminal Evidence Act 1999.]

R23.7 **Representations in response**

23.7 (1) This rule applies where a party wants to make representations about—
(a) an application under rule 23.4 for a prohibition against cross-examination;
(b) an application under rule 23.5 for the discharge of such a prohibition; or
(c) a prohibition or discharge that the court proposes on its own initiative.
(2) Such a party must—
(a) serve the representations on—
(i) the court officer, and
(ii) each other party;
(b) do so not more than 10 business days after, as applicable—
(i) service of the application, or
(ii) notice of the prohibition or discharge that the court proposes; and
(c) ask for a hearing, if that party wants one, and explain why it is needed.
(3) Representations against a prohibition must explain in what respect the conditions for imposing it are not met.
(4) Representations against the discharge of a prohibition must explain why it should not be discharged.
(5) Where representations include information that the person making them thinks ought not be revealed to another party, that person must—
(a) omit that information from the representations served on that other party;
(b) mark the information to show that, unless the court otherwise directs, it is only for the court; and
(c) with that information include an explanation of why it has been withheld from that other party.

R23.8 **Court's power to vary requirements**

23.8 (1) The court may—
(a) shorten or extend (even after it has expired) a time limit under rule 23.4 (Application to prohibit cross-examination), rule 23.5 (Application to discharge prohibition imposed by the court) or rule 23.7 (Representations in response); and
(b) allow an application or representations required by any of those rules to be made in a different form to one set out in the Practice Direction, or to be made orally.
(2) A person who wants an extension of time must—
(a) apply when serving the application or representations for which it is needed; and
(b) explain the delay.

CRIMINAL PRACTICE DIRECTIONS PART 23 CROSS-EXAMINATION ADVOCATES

CPD.23A **CPD V Evidence 23A: Cross-Examination Advocates**

Provisional appointment of advocate

23A.1 At the first hearing in the court in the case, and in a magistrates' court in particular, there may be occasions on which a defendant has engaged no legal representative, within the meaning of the Criminal Procedure Rules, for the purposes of the case generally, but still intends to do so – for example, where he or she has made an application for legal aid which has yet to be determined. Where the defendant nonetheless has identified a prospective legal representative who has a right of audience in the court; where the court is satisfied that that representative will be willing to cross-examine the relevant witness or witnesses in the interests of the defendant should it transpire that the defendant will not be represented for the purposes of the case generally; and if the court is in a position there and then to make, contingently, the decision required by section 38(3) of the Youth Justice and Criminal Evidence Act 1999 ('the court must consider whether it is necessary in the interests of justice for the witness to be cross-examined by a legal representative appointed to represent the interests of the accused'); then the court may appoint that representative under section 38(4) of the 1999 Act contingently, the appointment to come into effect only if, and when, it is established that the defendant will not be represented for the purposes of the case generally.

23A.2 Where such a provisional appointment is made it is essential that the role and status of the representative is clearly established at the earliest possible opportunity. The court's directions under CrimPR 23.2(3) should require the defendant to notify the court officer, by the date set by the court, whether:

(i) the defendant will be represented by a legal representative for the purposes of the case generally, and if so by whom (in which event the court's provisional appointment has no effect);

(ii) the defendant will not be represented for the purposes of the case generally, but the defendant and the legal representative provisionally appointed by the court remain content with that provisional appointment (in which event the court's provisional appointment takes effect); or

(iii) the defendant will not be represented for the purposes of the case generally, but will arrange for a lawyer to cross-examine the relevant witness or witnesses on his or her behalf, giving that lawyer's name and contact details.

If in the event the defendant fails to give notice by the due date then, unless it is apparent that she or he will, in fact, be represented for the purposes of the case generally, the court may decide to confirm the provisional appointment and proceed accordingly.

Supply of case papers

23A.3 For the advocate to fulfil the duty imposed by the appointment, and to achieve a responsible, professional and appropriate treatment both of the defendant and of the witness, it is essential for the advocate to establish what is in issue. To that end, it is likewise essential for the advocate to have been supplied with the material listed in CrimPR 23.2(7).

23A.4 In the Crown Court, much of this this can be achieved most conveniently by giving the advocate access to the Crown Court Digital Case System. However, material disclosed by the prosecutor to the defendant under section 3 or section 7A of the Criminal Procedure and Investigations Act 1996 is not stored in that system and therefore must be supplied to the advocate either by the defendant or by the prosecutor. In the latter case, the prosecutor reasonably may omit from the copies supplied to the advocate any material that can have no bearing on the cross-examination for which the advocate has been appointed – the medical or social services records of another witness, for example.

23A.5 In a magistrates' court, pending the introduction of comparable electronic arrangements:

i. in some instances the advocate may have received the relevant material at a point at which he or she was acting as the defendant's legal representative subject to a restriction on the purpose or duration of that appointment notified under CrimPR 46.2(5) – for example, pending the outcome of an application for legal aid.

ii. in some instances the defendant may be able to provide spare copies of relevant material. Where that material has been disclosed by the prosecutor under section 3 or section 7A of the Criminal Procedure and Investigations Act 1996 then its supply to the advocate by the defendant is permitted by section 17(2)(a) of the 1996 Act (exception to the prohibition against further disclosure where that further disclosure is 'in connection with the proceedings for whose purposes [the defendant] was given the object or allowed to inspect it').

iii. in some instances the prosecutor may be able to supply the relevant material, or some of it, at no, or minimal, expense by electronic means.

iv. in the event that, unusually, none of those sources of supply is available, then the court's directions under CrimPR 23.2(3) should require the court officer to provide copies from the court's own records, as if the advocate were a party and had applied under CrimPR 5.7.

Obtaining information and observations from the defendant

23A.6 Advocates and courts should keep in mind section 38(5) of the 1999 Act, which provides 'A person so appointed shall not be responsible to the accused.' The advocate therefore cannot and should not take instructions from the defendant, in the usual sense; and to avoid any misapprehension in that respect, either by the defendant or by others, some advocates may prefer to avoid direct oral communication with the defendant before, and even perhaps during, the trial.

23A.7 However, as remarked above at paragraph 23A.3, for the advocate to fulfil the duty imposed by the appointment it is essential for him or her to establish what is in issue; which may require communication with the defendant both before and at the trial as well as a thorough examination of the case papers. CrimPR 23.2(7)(a) in effect requires the advocate to have identified the issues on which the cross-examination of the witness is expected to proceed before the court begins to receive prosecution evidence, and to have taken part in their discussion with the court. To that end, communication with the defendant may be necessary.

Extent of cross-examination advocate's appointment

23A.8 In *Abbas v Crown Prosecution Service* [2015] EWHC 579 (Admin); [2015] 2 Cr.App.R. 11 the Divisional Court observed:

> 'The role of a section 38 advocate is, undoubtedly, limited to the proper performance of their duty as a cross examiner of a particular witness. Sections 36 and 38 are all about protecting vulnerable witnesses from cross examination by the accused. Therefore, it should not be thought that an advocate appointed under section 38 has a free ranging remit to conduct the trial on the accused's behalf. Their professional duty and their statutory duty would be to

ensure that they are in a position properly to conduct the cross examination. Their duties might include therefore applications to admit bad character of the witness and or applications for disclosure of material relevant to the cross examination. That is as far as one can go. All these matters must be entirely fact specific. The important thing to note is that the section 38 advocate must ensure that s/he performs his/her duties in accordance with the words of the statute. It means also that their appointment comes to an end, under section 38, at the conclusion of the cross examination, save to the extent that the court otherwise determines. Technically the lawyer no longer has a role in the proceedings thereafter. However, if the lawyer is prepared to stay and assist the defendant on a pro bono basis, I see nothing in the Act and no logical reason why the court should oblige them to leave. The advocate may well prove beneficial to the efficient and fair resolution of the proceedings. The aim of the legislation as I have said is simply to stop the accused cross examining the witness. It is not to prevent the person appointed to cross examine from playing any other part in the trial.'

23A.9 Advocates will be alert to, and courts should keep in mind, the extent of the remuneration available to a cross-examination advocate, in assessing the amount of which the court has only a limited role: see section 19(3) of the Prosecution of Offences Act 1985, which empowers the Lord Chancellor to make regulations authorising payments out of central funds 'to cover the proper fee or costs of a legal representative appointed under section 38(4) of the Youth Justice and Criminal Evidence Act 1999 and any expenses properly incurred in providing such a person with evidence or other material in connection with his appointment', and also sections 19(3ZA) and 20(1A)(d) of the 1985 Act and the Costs in Criminal Cases (General) Regulations 1986, as amended.

23A.10 Advocates and courts must be alert, too, to the possibility that were an advocate to agree to represent a defendant generally at trial, for no payment save that to which such regulations entitled him or her, then the statutory condition precedent for the appointment might be removed and the appointment in consequence withdrawn.

CRIMINAL PROCEDURE RULES PART 24 TRIAL AND SENTENCE IN A MAGISTRATES' COURT

R24.1 **When this Part applies**

24.1 (1) This Part applies in a magistrates' court where the court tries a case or the defendant pleads guilty.

(2) Where the defendant is under 18, in this Part—

(a) a reference to convicting the defendant includes a reference to finding the defendant guilty of an offence; and

(b) a reference to sentence includes a reference to an order made on a finding of guilt.

[Note. A magistrates' court's powers to try an allegation of an offence are contained in section 2 of the Magistrates' Courts Act 1980[1]*. In relation to a defendant under 18, they are contained in sections 45, 46 and 48 of the Children and Young Persons Act 1933*[2]*.*

See also section 18 of the Children and Young Persons Act 1963[3]*), section 47 of the Crime and Disorder Act 1998*[4] *and section 27 of the Sentencing Act 2020*[5]*.*

[1] 1980 c. 43; section 2 was substituted by section 44 of the Courts Act 2003 (c. 39) and amended by section 41 of, and paragraph 51 of Schedule 3 to, the Criminal Justice 2003 (c. 44).

[2] 1933 c. 12; section 45 was substituted by section 50 of the Courts Act 2003 (c. 39) and amended by section 15 of, and paragraph 20 of Schedule 4 to, the Constitutional Reform Act 2005 (c. 4); section 46 was amended by section 46 of, and Schedule 7 to, the Justices of the Peace Act 1949 (c. 101), section 72 of, and paragraph 4 of Schedule 5 to, the Children and Young Persons Act 1969 (c. 54), section 154 of, and paragraph 6 of Schedule 7 to, the Magistrates' Courts Act 1980 (c. 43), sections 68 and 100 of, and paragraph 1 of Schedule 8 and paragraph 40 of Schedule 11 to, the Criminal Justice Act 1991 (c. 53) and section 109 of, and paragraph 74 of Schedule 8 to, the Courts Act 2003 (c. 39); and section 48 was amended by section 79 of, and Schedule 9 to, the Criminal Justice Act 1948 (c. 58), section 132 of, and Schedule 6 to, the Magistrates' Courts Act 1952 (c. 55), section 64 of, and paragraph 12 of Schedule 3 and Schedule 5 to, the Children and Young Persons Act 1963 (c. 37), sections 72, 79 and 83 of, and Schedules 6, 9 and 10 to, the Children and Young Persons Act 1969 (c. 54), sections 68 and 100 of, and paragraph 1 of Schedule 8 and paragraph 40 of Schedule 11 to, the Criminal Justice Act 1991 (c. 53), section 106 of, and Schedule 15 to, the Access to Justice Act 1999 (c. 22) and section 109 of, and paragraph 75 of Schedule 8 to, the Courts Act 2003 (c. 39).

[3] 1963 c. 37; section 18 was amended by section 100 of, and paragraph 40 of Schedule 11 to, the Criminal Justice Act 1991 (c. 53) and section 168 of, and paragraph 5 of Schedule 9 to, the Criminal Justice and Public Order Act 1994 (c. 33).

[4] 1998 c. 37; section 47 was amended by section 165 of, and Schedule 12 to, the Powers of Criminal Courts (Sentencing) Act 2000 (c. 6), section 332 of, and Schedule 37 to, the Criminal Justice Act 2003 (c. 44) and article 2 of, and paragraph 59 of the Schedule to S.I. 2005/886.

[5] 2000 c. 6; section 9 was amended by article 2 of, and paragraph 63 of the Schedule to S.I. 2005/886.

The exercise of the court's powers is affected by—

- *(a) the classification of the offence (and the general rule, subject to exceptions, is that a magistrates' court must try—*
  - *(i) an offence classified as one that can be tried only in a magistrates' court (in other legislation, described as triable only summarily), and*
  - *(ii) an offence classified as one that can be tried either in a magistrates' court or in the Crown Court (in other legislation, described as triable either way) that has been allocated for trial in a magistrates' court); and*
- *(b) the defendant's age (and the general rule, subject to exceptions, is that an allegation of an offence against a defendant under 18 must be tried in a magistrates' court sitting as a youth court, irrespective of the classification of the offence and without allocation for trial there).*

Under sections 10, 14, 27A, 121 and 148 of the Magistrates' Courts Act 1980[6] *and the Justices of the Peace Rules 2016*[7]*, the court—*

- *(a) must comprise at least two but not more than three justices, or a District Judge (Magistrates' Courts) (but a single member can adjourn the hearing);*
- *(b) must not include any member who adjudicated at a hearing to which rule 44.2 applies (defendant's declaration of no knowledge of hearing);*
- *(c) when reaching a verdict, must not include any member who was absent from any part of the hearing;*
- *(d) when passing sentence, need not include any of the members who reached the verdict (but may do so).*

Under section 16A of the Magistrates' Courts Act 1980[8]*, the court may comprise a single justice where—*

- *(a) the offence charged is a summary offence not punishable with imprisonment;*
- *(b) the defendant was at least 18 years old when charged;*
- *(c) the court is satisfied that specified documents giving notice of the procedure under that section and containing other specified information have been served on the defendant; and*
- *(d) the defendant has not served notice of an intention to plead not guilty, or of a desire not to be tried in accordance with that section.*

Under section 45 of the Children and Young Persons Act 1933[9] *and under the Justices of the Peace Rules 2016, where the court is a youth court comprising justices each member must be authorised to sit as a member of that youth court.*

Under section 150 of the Magistrates' Courts Act 1980[10]*, where two or more justices are present one may act on behalf of all.*

Section 59 of the Children and Young Persons Act 1933[11] *requires that—*

- *(a) the expressions 'conviction' and 'sentence' must not be used by a magistrates' court dealing with a defendant under 18; and*
- *(b) a reference in legislation to a defendant who is convicted, to a conviction, or to a sentence, must be read as including a reference to a defendant who is found guilty of an offence, a finding of guilt, or an order made on a finding of guilt, respectively.*

Under section 14 of the Magistrates' Courts Act 1980, proceedings which begin with a summons or requisition will become void if the defendant, at any time during or after the trial, makes a statutory declaration that he or she did not know of them until a date after the trial began. See rule 44.2.

[6] 1980 c. 43; section 10 was amended by section 59 of, and paragraph 1 of Schedule 9 to, the Criminal Justice Act 1982 (c. 48), section 68 of, and paragraph 6 of Schedule 8 to, the Criminal Justice Act 1991 (c. 53) and section 47 of the Crime and Disorder Act 1998 (c. 37). Section 14 was amended by section 109 of, and paragraph 205 of Schedule 8 to, the Courts Act 2003 (c. 39). Section 27A was inserted by section 46 of the Courts Act 2003 (c. 39). Section 121 was amended by section 61 of the Criminal Justice Act 1988 (c. 33), section 92 of, and paragraph 8 of Schedule 11 to, the Children Act 1989 (c. 41), section 109 of, and paragraph 237 of Schedule 8 and Schedule 10 to, the Courts Act 2003 (c. 39). Section 148 was amended by section 109 of, and paragraph 248 of Schedule 8 to, the Courts Act 2003 (c. 39).

[7] S.I. 2016/709.

[8] 1980 c. 43; section 16A was inserted by section 48 of the Criminal Justice and Courts Act 2015 (c. 2).

[9] 1933 c. 12; section 45 was substituted by section 50 of the Courts Act 2003 (c. 39) and amended by section 15 of, and paragraph 20 of Schedule 4 to, the Constitutional Reform Act 2005 (c. 4).

[10] 1980 c. 43; section 150 has been amended but none is relevant to the note to this rule.

[11] 1933 c. 12; section 59 was amended by sections 79 and 83 of, and Schedules 9 and 10 to, the Criminal Justice Act 1948 (c. 58) and section 18 of the Costs in Criminal Cases Act 1952 (c. 48).

Under section 142 of the Magistrates' Courts Act 1980—

(a) where a defendant is convicted by a magistrates' court, the court may order that the case should be heard again by different justices; and
(b) the court may vary or rescind an order which it has made when dealing with a convicted defendant,

if in either case it appears to the court to be in the interests of justice to do so. See rule 44.3.

See also Part 32 (Breach, revocation and amendment of community and other orders). Rule 32.4 (Procedure on application by responsible officer) applies rules in this Part to the procedure with which that rule deals.]

R24.2 General rules

24.2 (1) Where this Part applies—
(a) the general rule is that the hearing must be in public; but
(b) the court may exercise any power it has to—
(i) impose reporting restrictions,
(ii) withhold information from the public, or
(iii) order a hearing in private; and
(c) unless the court otherwise directs, only the following may attend a hearing in a youth court—
(i) the parties and their legal representatives,
(ii) a defendant's parents, guardian or other supporting adult,
(iii) a witness,
(iv) anyone else directly concerned in the case, and
(v) a representative of a news-gathering or reporting organisation.
(2) Unless already done, the justices' legal adviser or the court must—
(a) read the allegation of the offence to the defendant;
(b) explain, in terms the defendant can understand (with help, if necessary)—
(i) the allegation, and
(ii) what the procedure at the hearing will be;
(c) ask whether the defendant has been advised about the potential effect on sentence of a guilty plea;
(d) ask whether the defendant pleads guilty or not guilty; and
(e) take the defendant's plea.
(3) The court may adjourn the hearing—
(a) at any stage, to the same or to another magistrates' court; or
(b) to a youth court, where the court is not itself a youth court and the defendant is under 18.
(4) Paragraphs (1) and (2) of this rule do not apply where the court tries a case under rule 24.9 (Single justice procedure: special rules).

[Note. See sections 10, 16A, 27A, 29 and 121 of the Magistrates' Courts Act 1980[12] *and sections 46 and 47 of the Children and Young Persons Act 1933.*

Where the case has been allocated for trial in a magistrates' court, part of the procedure under rule 24.2(2) will have taken place.

Part 6 contains rules about reporting, etc. restrictions. For a list of the court's powers to impose reporting and access restrictions, see the note to rule 6.1.

Under section 34A of the Children and Young Persons Act 1933[13]*, the court—*

(a) may require the defendant's parents or guardian to attend court with the defendant, where the defendant is under 18; and
(b) must do so, where the defendant is under 16, unless satisfied that that would be unreasonable.

Part 7 contains rules about (among other things) the issue of a summons to a parent or guardian.

Part 46 (Representatives) contains rules allowing a parent, guardian or other supporting adult to help a defendant under 18.]

[12] 1980 c. 43; section 29 was amended by sections 68 and 100 of, and paragraph 6 of Schedule 8 and paragraph 40 of Schedule 11 to, the Criminal Justice Act 1991 (c. 53), section 168 of, and paragraph 41 of Schedule 10 to, the Criminal Justice and Public Order Act 1994 (c. 33) and section 41 of, and paragraph 51 of Schedule 3 to, the Criminal Justice Act 2003 (c. 44). Section 16A was inserted by section 48 of the Criminal Justice and Courts Act 2015 (c. 2).
[13] 1933 c. 12; section 34A was inserted by section 56 of the Criminal Justice Act 1991 (c. 53) and amended by section 107 of, and paragraph 1 of Schedule 5 to, the Local Government Act 2000 (c. 22).

Procedure on plea of not guilty **R24.3**

24.3 (1) This rule applies—
(a) if the defendant has—
(i) entered a plea of not guilty, or
(ii) not entered a plea; or
(b) if, in either case, it appears to the court that there may be grounds for making a hospital order without convicting the defendant.
(2) If a not guilty plea was taken on a previous occasion, the justices' legal adviser or the court must ask the defendant to confirm that plea.
(3) In the following sequence—
(a) the prosecutor may summarise the prosecution case, concisely identifying the relevant law, outlining the facts and indicating the matters likely to be in dispute;
(b) to help the members of the court to understand the case and resolve any issue in it, the court may invite the defendant concisely to identify what is in issue;
(c) the prosecutor must introduce the evidence on which the prosecution case relies;
(d) at the conclusion of the prosecution case, on the defendant's application or on its own initiative, the court—
(i) may acquit on the ground that the prosecution evidence is insufficient for any reasonable court properly to convict, but
(ii) must not do so unless the prosecutor has had an opportunity to make representations;
(e) the justices' legal adviser or the court must explain, in terms the defendant can understand (with help, if necessary)—
(i) the right to give evidence, and
(ii) the potential effect of not doing so at all, or of refusing to answer a question while doing so;
(f) the defendant may introduce evidence;
(g) a party may introduce further evidence if it is then admissible (for example, because it is in rebuttal of evidence already introduced);
(h) the prosecutor may make final representations in support of the prosecution case, where—
(i) the defendant is represented by a legal representative, or
(ii) whether represented or not, the defendant has introduced evidence other than his or her own; and
(i) the defendant may make final representations in support of the defence case.
(4) Where a party wants to introduce evidence or make representations after that party's opportunity to do so under paragraph (3), the court—
(a) may refuse to receive any such evidence or representations; and
(b) must not receive any such evidence or representations after it has announced its verdict.
(5) If the court—
(a) convicts the defendant; or
(b) makes a hospital order instead of doing so,
it must give sufficient reasons to explain its decision.
(6) If the court acquits the defendant, it may—
(a) give an explanation of its decision; and
(b) exercise any power it has to make—
(i) a behaviour order,
(ii) a costs order.

[Note. See section 9 of the Magistrates' Courts Act 1980[14].

Under section 37(3) of the Mental Health Act 1983[15]*, if the court is satisfied that the defendant did the act or made the omission alleged, then it may make a hospital order without convicting the defendant.*

Under section 35 of the Criminal Justice and Public Order Act 1994[16]*, the court may draw such inferences as appear proper from a defendant's failure to give evidence, or refusal without good cause to answer a question while doing so. The procedure set out in rule 24.3(3)(e) is prescribed by that section.*

[14] 1980 c. 43.
[15] 1983 c. 20; section 37(3) was amended by sections 1 and 55 of, and paragraphs 1 and 7 of Schedule 1 and Schedule 11 to, the Mental Health Act 2007 (c. 12). 37(3) was amended by sections 1 and 55 of, and paragraphs 1 and 7 of Schedule 1 and Schedule 11 to, the Mental Health Act 2007 (c. 12).
[16] 1994 c. 33; section 35 was amended by sections 35 and 120 of, and Schedule 10 to, the Crime and Disorder Act 1998 (c. 37). The Criminal Justice Act 2003 (c. 44) amendment to section 35 is not relevant to procedure in magistrates' courts.

The admissibility of evidence that a party introduces is governed by rules of evidence.

Section 2 of the Criminal Procedure Act 1865[17] *and section 3 of the Criminal Evidence Act 1898*[18] *restrict the circumstances in which the prosecutor may make final representations without the court's permission.*

See rule 24.11 for the procedure if the court convicts the defendant.

Part 31 contains rules about behaviour orders.]

R24.4 **Evidence of a witness in person**

24.4 (1) This rule applies where a party wants to introduce evidence by calling a witness to give that evidence in person.

(2) Unless the court otherwise directs—

(a) a witness waiting to give evidence must not wait inside the courtroom, unless that witness is—

(i) a party, or

(ii) an expert witness;

(b) a witness who gives evidence in the courtroom must do so from the place provided for that purpose; and

(c) a witness' address must not be announced unless it is relevant to an issue in the case.

(3) Unless other legislation otherwise provides, before giving evidence a witness must take an oath or affirm.

(4) In the following sequence—

(a) the party who calls a witness must ask questions in examination-in-chief;

(b) every other party may ask questions in cross-examination; and

(c) the party who called the witness may ask questions in re-examination.

(5) If other legislation so permits, at any time while giving evidence a witness may refer to a record of that witness' recollection of events.

(6) The justices' legal adviser or the court may—

(a) ask a witness questions; and in particular

(b) where the defendant is not represented, ask any question necessary in the defendant's interests.

[Note. Section 53 of the Youth Justice and Criminal Evidence Act 1999[19] *provides that everyone is competent to give evidence in criminal proceedings unless unable to understand questions put or give intelligible answers. See also section 1 of the Criminal Evidence Act 1898*[20].

Sections 1, 3, 5 and 6 of the Oaths Act 1978[21] *provide for the taking of oaths and the making of affirmations, and for the words that must be used. Section 28 of the Children and Young Persons Act 1963*[22] *provides that in a youth court, and where a witness in any court is under 18, an oath must include the words 'I promise' in place of the words 'I swear'. Under sections 55 and 56 of the Youth Justice and Criminal Evidence Act 1999, a person may give evidence without taking an oath, or making an affirmation, where that person (i) is under 14 or (ii) has an insufficient appreciation of the solemnity of the occasion and of the particular responsibility to tell the truth which is involved in taking an oath.*

The questions that may be put to a witness—

(a) by a party are governed by rules of evidence, for example—

(i) the rule that a question must be relevant to what is in issue,

(ii) the rule that the party who calls a witness must not ask that witness a leading question about what is in dispute, and

(iii) the rule that a party who calls a witness may contradict that witness only in limited circumstances (see section 3 of the Criminal Procedure Act 1865)[23];

[17] 1865 c. 18; section 2 was amended by section 10(2) of, and Part III of Schedule 3 to, the Criminal Law Act 1967 (c. 58).

[18] 1898 c. 36; section 3 was amended by section 1(2) of the Criminal Procedure (Right of Reply) Act 1964 (c. 34).

[19] 1999 c. 23.

[20] 1898 c. 36; section 1 was amended by section 1 of the Criminal Evidence Act 1979 (c. 16), section 78 of, and Schedule 16 to, the Criminal Justice Act 1982 (c. 48), sections 80(9) and 119(2) of, and Schedule 7 to, the Police and Criminal Evidence Act 1984 (c. 60), sections 31 and 168 of, and paragraph 2 of Schedule 10, and Schedule 11 to, the Criminal Justice and Public Order Act 1994 (c. 33), section 67 of, and paragraph 1 of Schedule 4, and Schedule 6 to, the Youth Justice and Criminal Evidence Act 1999 (c. 23) and sections 331 and 332 of, and paragraph 80 of Schedule 36, and Part 5 of Schedule 37 to, the Criminal Justice Act 2003 (c. 44).

[21] 1978 c. 19.

[22] 1963 c. 37; section 28 was amended by section 2 of the Oaths Act 1978 (c. 19) and section 100 of, and paragraph 40 of Schedule 11 to, the Criminal Justice Act 1991 (c. 53).

[23] 1865 c. 18.

(b) by the justices' legal adviser or the court are in their discretion, but that is subject to—
(i) rules of evidence, and
(ii) rule 1.3 (the application by the court of the overriding objective).

Under sections 34, 35 and 36 of the Youth Justice and Criminal Evidence Act 1999[24]*, a defendant who is not represented may not cross-examine a witness where—*

(a) the defendant is charged with a sexual offence against the witness;
(b) the defendant is charged with a sexual offence, or one of certain other offences, and the witness is a child; or
(c) the court prohibits the defendant from cross-examining the witness.

Part 23 contains rules relevant to restrictions on cross-examination.

Under section 139 of the Criminal Justice Act 2003[25]*, a witness may refresh his or her memory by referring to a record made before the hearing, either contained in a document made or verified by the witness, or in the transcript of a sound recording, if—*

(a) the witness states that it records his or her recollection of events at that earlier time; and
(b) that recollection is likely to have been significantly better when the record was made than at the time of the hearing.

In some circumstances, a witness may give evidence in accordance with special measures directed by the court under section 19 of the Youth Justice and Criminal Evidence Act 1999[26]*, or by live link under section 32 of the Criminal Justice Act 1988*[27] *or section 51 of the Criminal Justice Act 2003. Part 18 contains relevant rules.]*

Evidence of a witness in writing **R24.5**

24.5 (1) This rule applies where a party wants to introduce in evidence the written statement of a witness to which applies—
(a) Part 16 (Written witness statements);
(b) Part 19 (Expert evidence); or
(c) Part 20 (Hearsay evidence).
(2) If the court admits such evidence—
(a) the court must read the statement; and
(b) unless the court otherwise directs, if any member of the public, including any reporter, is present, each relevant part of the statement must be read or summarised aloud.

[Note. See Parts 16, 19 and 20, and the other legislation to which those Parts apply. The admissibility of evidence that a party introduces is governed by rules of evidence.]

Evidence by admission **R24.6**

24.6 (1) This rule applies where—
(a) a party introduces in evidence a fact admitted by another party; or
(b) parties jointly admit a fact.
(2) Unless the court otherwise directs, a written record must be made of the admission.

[Note. See section 10 of the Criminal Justice Act 1967[28]*. The admissibility of evidence that a party introduces is governed by rules of evidence.]*

Procedure on plea of guilty **R24.7**

24.7 (1) This rule applies if—
(a) the defendant pleads guilty; and
(b) the court is satisfied that the plea represents a clear acknowledgement of guilt.
(2) The court may convict the defendant without receiving evidence.

[Note. See section 9 of the Magistrates' Courts Act 1980[29]*.]*

24 1999 c. 23; section 35 was amended by sections 139 and 140 of, and paragraph 41 of Schedule 6 and Schedule 7 to, the Sexual Offences Act 2003 (c. 42) and section 148 of, and paragraphs 35 and 36 of Schedule 26 to, the Criminal Justice and Immigration Act 2008 (c. 4).
25 2003 c. 44.
26 1999 c. 23.
27 1988 c. 33; section 32 was amended by section 55 of the Criminal Justice Act 1991 (c. 53), section 29 of, and paragraph 16 of Schedule 2 to, the Criminal Appeal Act 1995 (c. 35), section 62 of the Criminal Procedure and Investigations Act 1996 (c. 25), section 67 of, and Schedule 6 and paragraph 3 of Schedule 7 to, the Youth Justice and Criminal Evidence Act 1999 (c. 23) and paragraphs 24 and 26 of the Schedule to S.I. 2004/2035.
28 1967 c. 80.
29 1980 c. 43.

R24.8 **Written guilty plea: special rules**

24.8 (1) This rule applies where—

(a) the offence alleged—

(i) can be tried only in a magistrates' court, and

(ii) is not one specified under section 12(1)(a) of the Magistrates' Courts Act 1980[30];

(b) the defendant is at least 16 years old;

(c) the prosecutor has served on the defendant—

(i) the summons or requisition,

(ii) the material listed in paragraph (2) on which the prosecutor relies to set out the facts of the offence,

(iii) the material listed in paragraph (3) on which the prosecutor relies to provide the court with information relevant to sentence,

(iv) a notice that the procedure set out in this rule applies, and

(v) a notice for the defendant's use if the defendant wants to plead guilty without attending court; and

(d) the prosecutor has served on the court officer—

(i) copies of those documents, and

(ii) a certificate of service of those documents on the defendant.

(2) The material that the prosecutor must serve to set out the facts of the offence is—

(a) a summary of the evidence on which the prosecution case is based;

(b) any—

(i) written witness statement to which Part 16 (Written witness statements) applies, or

(ii) document or extract setting out facts; or

(c) any combination of such a summary, statement, document or extract.

(3) The material that the prosecutor must serve to provide information relevant to sentence is—

(a) details of any previous conviction of the defendant which the prosecutor considers relevant, other than any conviction listed in the defendant's driving record;

(b) if applicable, a notice that the defendant's driving record will be made available to the court; and

(c) a notice containing or describing any other information about the defendant, relevant to sentence, which will be made available to the court.

(4) A defendant who wants to plead guilty without attending court must, before the hearing date specified in the summons or requisition—

(a) serve a notice of guilty plea on the court officer; and

(b) include with that notice—

(i) any representations that the defendant wants the court to consider, and

(ii) a statement of the defendant's assets and other financial circumstances.

(5) A defendant who wants to withdraw such a notice must notify the court officer in writing before the hearing date.

(6) If the defendant does not withdraw the notice before the hearing date, then on or after that date—

(a) to establish the facts of the offence and other information about the defendant relevant to sentence, the court may take account only of—

(i) information contained in a document served by the prosecutor under paragraph (1),

(ii) any previous conviction listed in the defendant's driving record, where the offence is under the Road Traffic Regulation Act 1984[31], the Road Traffic Act 1988[32], the Road Traffic (Consequential Provisions) Act 1988[33] or the Road Traffic (Driver Licensing and Information Systems) Act 1989[34],

(iii) any other information about the defendant, relevant to sentence, of which the prosecutor served notice under paragraph (1), and

[30] 1980 c. 43; section 12(1)(a) was amended by sections 308 and 332 of, and Part 12 of Schedule 37 to, the Criminal Justice Act 2003 (c. 44).

[31] 1984 c. 27.

[32] 1988 c. 52.

[33] 1988 c. 54.

[34] 1989 c. 22.

(iv) any representations and any other information served by the defendant under paragraph (4)

and rule 24.11(3) to (9) inclusive must be read accordingly;

(b) unless the court otherwise directs, the prosecutor need not attend; and

(c) the court may accept such a guilty plea and pass sentence in the defendant's absence.

(7) With the defendant's agreement, the court may deal with the case in the same way as under paragraph (6) where the defendant is present and—

(a) has served a notice of guilty plea under paragraph (4); or

(b) pleads guilty there and then.

[Note. The procedure set out in this rule is prescribed by sections 12 and 12A of the Magistrates' Courts Act 1980[35]*. Under section 12(1)(a), the Secretary of State can specify offences to which the procedure will not apply. None has been specified.*

Under section 1 of the Magistrates' Courts Act 1980[36] *a justice of the peace may issue a summons requiring a defendant to attend court to answer an allegation of an offence. Under section 29 of the Criminal Justice Act 2003*[37] *a prosecutor authorised under that section may issue a written charge alleging an offence and a requisition requiring a defendant to attend court. Part 7 contains relevant rules.*

For the court's power, where this rule applies, to take account of a previous conviction listed in a defendant's driving record, see section 13(3A) of the Road Traffic Offenders Act 1988[38]*.*

The Practice Direction sets out forms of notice for use in connection with this rule.]

Single justice procedure: special rules **R24.9**

24.9 (1) This rule applies where—

(a) the offence alleged—

(i) can be tried only in a magistrates' court, and

(ii) is not one punishable with imprisonment;

(b) the defendant is at least 18 years old;

(c) the prosecutor has served on the defendant—

(i) a written charge,

(ii) the material listed in paragraph (2) on which the prosecutor relies to set out the facts of the offence,

(iii) the material listed in paragraph (3) on which the prosecutor relies to provide the court with information relevant to sentence,

(iv) a notice that the procedure set out in this rule applies,

(v) a notice for the defendant's use if the defendant wants to plead guilty,

(vi) a notice for the defendant's use if the defendant wants to plead guilty but wants the case dealt with at a hearing by a court comprising more than one justice, and

(vii) a notice for the defendant's use if the defendant wants to plead not guilty; and

(d) the prosecutor has served on the court officer—

(i) copies of those documents, and

(ii) a certificate of service of those documents on the defendant.

(2) The material that the prosecutor must serve to set out the facts of the offence is—

(a) a summary of the evidence on which the prosecution case is based;

[35] 1980 c. 43; section 12 was amended by section 45 of, and paragraph 1 of Schedule 5 to, the Criminal Justice and Public Order Act 1994 (c. 33), section 1 of the Magistrates' Courts (Procedure) Act 1998 (c. 15), section 109 of, and paragraph 203 of Schedule 8 to, the Courts Act 2003 (c. 39), section 308 of, and Part 12 of Schedule 37 to, the Criminal Justice Act 2003 (c. 44) and section 81 of the Deregulation Act 2015 (c. 20). Section 12A was inserted by section 45 of, and paragraph 2 of Schedule 5 to, the Criminal Justice and Public Order Act 1994 (c. 33) and amended by section 109 of, and paragraph 204 of Schedule 8 to, the Courts Act 2003 (c. 39).

[36] 1980 c. 43; section 1 was amended by section 68 of, and paragraph 6 of Schedule 8 to, the Criminal Justice Act 1991 (c. 53), sections 43 and 109 of, and Schedule 10 to, the Courts Act 2003 (c. 39), section 31 of, and paragraph 12 of Schedule 7 to, the Criminal Justice Act 2003 (c. 44) and section 153 of the Police Reform and Social Responsibility Act 2011. It is further amended by paragraphs 7 and 8 of Schedule 36 to, the Criminal Justice Act 2003 (c. 44), with effect from a date to be appointed.

[37] 2003 c. 44; section 29 has been brought into force for certain purposes only (see S.I. 2007/1999, 2008/1424, 2009/2879, 2010/3005, 2011/2188, 2012/825 and 2014/633). It was amended by section 50 of, and paragraph 130 of Schedule 4 to, the Commissioners for Revenue and Customs Act 2005 (c. 11), section 59 of, and paragraph 196 of Schedule 4 to, the Serious Organised Crime and Police Act 2005 (c. 15), section 15 of, and paragraph 187 of Schedule 8 to, the Crime and Courts Act 2013 (c. 22), S.I. 2014/834 and section 46 of the Criminal Justice and Courts Act 2015 (c. 2).

[38] 1988 c. 53; section 13(3A) was inserted by section 2 of the Magistrates' Courts (Procedure) Act 1998 (c. 15).

(b) any—
(i) written witness statement to which Part 16 (Written witness statements) applies, or
(ii) document or extract setting out facts; or
(c) any combination of such a summary, statement, document or extract.

(3) The material that the prosecutor must serve to provide information relevant to sentence is—
(a) details of any previous conviction of the defendant which the prosecutor considers relevant, other than any conviction listed in the defendant's driving record;
(b) if applicable, a notice that the defendant's driving record will be made available to the court; and
(c) a notice containing or describing any other information about the defendant, relevant to sentence, which will be made available to the court.

(4) Not more than 15 business days after service on the defendant of the documents listed in paragraph (1)(c)—
(a) a defendant who wants to plead guilty must serve a notice to that effect on the court officer and include with that notice—
(i) any representations that the defendant wants the court to consider, and
(ii) a statement of the defendant's assets and other financial circumstances;
(b) a defendant who wants to plead guilty but wants the case dealt with at a hearing by a court comprising more than one justice must serve a notice to that effect on the court officer; and
(c) a defendant who wants to plead not guilty must serve a notice to that effect on the court officer.

(5) If within 15 business days of service on the defendant of the documents listed in paragraph (1)(c) the defendant serves a notice to plead guilty under paragraph (4)(a)—
(a) the court officer must arrange for the court to deal with the case in accordance with that notice; and
(b) the time for service of any other notice under paragraph (4) expires at once.

(6) If within 15 business days of service on the defendant of the documents listed in paragraph (1)(c) the defendant wants to withdraw a notice which he or she has served under paragraph (4)(b) (notice to plead guilty at a hearing) or under paragraph (4)(c) (notice to plead not guilty), the defendant must—
(a) serve notice of that withdrawal on the court officer; and
(b) serve any substitute notice under paragraph (4).

(7) Paragraph (8) applies where by the date of trial the defendant has not—
(a) served notice under paragraph (4)(b) or (c) of wanting to plead guilty at a hearing, or wanting to plead not guilty; or
(b) given notice to that effect under section 16B(2) of the Magistrates' Courts Act 1980[39].

(8) Where this paragraph applies—
(a) the court may try the case in the parties' absence and without a hearing;
(b) the court may accept any guilty plea of which the defendant has given notice under paragraph (4)(a); and
(c) to establish the facts of the offence and other information about the defendant relevant to sentence, the court may take account only of—
(i) information contained in a document served by the prosecutor under paragraph (1),
(ii) any previous conviction listed in the defendant's driving record, where the offence is under the Road Traffic Regulation Act 1984, the Road Traffic Act 1988, the Road Traffic (Consequential Provisions) Act 1988 or the Road Traffic (Driver Licensing and Information Systems) Act 1989,
(iii) any other information about the defendant, relevant to sentence, of which the prosecutor served notice under paragraph (1), and
(iv) any representations and any other information served by the defendant under paragraph (4)(a)

and rule 24.11(3) to (9) inclusive must be read accordingly.

(9) Paragraph (10) applies where—
(a) the defendant serves on the court officer a notice under paragraph (4)(b) or (c); or
(b) the court which tries the defendant under paragraph (8) adjourns the trial for the defendant to attend a hearing by a court comprising more than one justice.

[39] 1980 c. 43; section 16B was inserted by section 48 of the Criminal Justice and Courts Act 2015 (c. 2).

(10) Where this paragraph applies, the court must exercise its power to issue a summons and—
(a) the rules in Part 7 apply (Starting a prosecution in a magistrates' court) as if the prosecutor had just served an application for a summons to be issued in the same terms as the written charge;
(b) the rules in Part 8 (Initial details of the prosecution case) apply as if the documents served by the prosecutor under paragraph (1) had been served under that Part; and
(c) except for rule 24.8 (Written guilty plea: special rules) and this rule, the rules in this Part apply.

[Note. The procedure set out in this rule is prescribed by sections 16A to 16D of the Magistrates' Courts Act 1980[40] *and section 29 of the Criminal Justice Act 2003*[41]*. Under section 16A of the 1980 Act, the court may comprise a single justice. Under section 29 of the 2003 Act, a prosecutor authorised under that section may issue a written charge alleging an offence and a single justice procedure notice. Part 7 contains relevant rules.*

Under section 1 of the Magistrates' Courts Act 1980[42]*) a justice of the peace may issue a summons requiring a defendant to attend court to answer an allegation of an offence. Under sections 16C and 16D of the 1980 Act, a justice may issue a summons requiring a defendant to attend court in the circumstances listed in rule 24.9(9).*

For the court's power, where this rule applies, to take account of—
(a) information contained or described in a document served by the prosecutor under rule 24.9(1), see section 16F of the Magistrates' Courts Act 1980[43]*;*
(b) a previous conviction listed in a defendant's driving record, see section 13(3A) of the Road Traffic Offenders Act 1988[44]*.*

The Practice Direction sets out forms of notice for use in connection with this rule.]

Application to withdraw a guilty plea **R24.10**

24.10 (1) This rule applies where the defendant wants to withdraw a guilty plea.
(2) The defendant must apply to do so—
(a) as soon as practicable after becoming aware of the reasons for doing so; and
(b) before sentence.
(3) Unless the court otherwise directs, the application must be in writing and the defendant must serve it on—
(a) the court officer; and
(b) the prosecutor.
(4) The application must—
(a) explain why it would be unjust not to allow the defendant to withdraw the guilty plea;
(b) identify—
(i) any witness that the defendant wants to call, and
(ii) any other proposed evidence; and
(c) say whether the defendant waives legal professional privilege, giving any relevant name and date.

Procedure if the court convicts **R24.11**

24.11 (1) This rule applies if the court convicts the defendant.
(2) The court—
(a) may exercise its power to require—
(i) a statement of the defendant's financial circumstances,
(ii) a pre-sentence report; and
(b) may (and in some circumstances must) remit the defendant to a youth court for sentence where—
(i) the defendant is under 18, and

[40] 1980 c. 43; sections 16A to 16D were inserted by section 48 of the Criminal Justice and Courts Act 2015 (c. 2).
[41] 2003 c. 44; section 29 has been brought into force for certain purposes only (see S.I. 2007/1999, 2008/1424, 2009/2879, 2010/3005, 2011/2188, 2012/825 and 2014/633). It was amended by section 50 of, and paragraph 130 of Schedule 4 to, the Commissioners for Revenue and Customs Act 2005 (c. 11), section 59 of, and paragraph 196 of Schedule 4 to, the Serious Organised Crime and Police Act 2005 (c. 15), section 15 of, and paragraph 187 of Schedule 8 to, the Crime and Courts Act 2013 (c. 22), S.I. 2014/834 and section 46 of the Criminal Justice and Courts Act 2015 (c. 2).
[42] 1980 c. 43; section 1 was amended by section 68 of, and paragraph 6 of Schedule 8 to, the Criminal Justice Act 1991 (c. 53), sections 43 and 109 of, and Schedule 10 to, the Courts Act 2003 (c. 39), section 31 of, and paragraph 12 of Schedule 7 to, the Criminal Justice Act 2003 (c. 44) and section 153 of the Police Reform and Social Responsibility Act 2011. It is further amended by paragraphs 7 and 8 of Schedule 36 to, the Criminal Justice Act 2003 (c. 44), with effect from a date to be appointed.
[43] 1980 c. 43; section 16F was inserted by section 48 of the Criminal Justice and Courts Act 2015 (c. 2).
[44] 1988 c. 53; section 13(3A) was inserted by section 2 of the Magistrates' Courts (Procedure) Act 1998 (c. 15).

(ii) the convicting court is not itself a youth court.

(3) The prosecutor must—
(a) summarise the prosecution case, if the sentencing court has not heard evidence;
(b) identify any offence to be taken into consideration in sentencing;
(c) provide information relevant to sentence, including any statement of the effect of the offence on the victim, the victim's family and others; and
(d) where it is likely to assist the court, identify any other matter relevant to sentence, including—
(i) the legislation applicable,
(ii) any sentencing guidelines, or guideline cases,
(iii) aggravating and mitigating features affecting the defendant's culpability and the harm which the offence caused, was intended to cause or might forseeably have caused, and
(iv) the effect of such of the information listed in paragraph (2)(a) as the court may need to take into account.

(4) The defendant must provide details of financial circumstances—
(a) in any form required by the court officer;
(b) by any date directed by the court or by the court officer.

(5) Where the defendant pleads guilty but wants to be sentenced on a different basis to that disclosed by the prosecution case—
(a) the defendant must set out that basis in writing, identifying what is in dispute;
(b) the court may invite the parties to make representations about whether the dispute is material to sentence; and
(c) if the court decides that it is a material dispute, the court must—
(i) invite such further representations or evidence as it may require, and
(ii) decide the dispute.

(6) Where the court has power to order the endorsement of the defendant's driving record, or power to order the defendant to be disqualified from driving—
(a) if other legislation so permits, a defendant who wants the court not to exercise that power must introduce the evidence or information on which the defendant relies;
(b) the prosecutor may introduce evidence; and
(c) the parties may make representations about that evidence or information.

(7) Before the court passes sentence—
(a) the court must—
(i) give the defendant an opportunity to make representations and introduce evidence relevant to sentence, and
(ii) where the defendant is under 18, give the defendant's parents, guardian or other supporting adult, if present, such an opportunity as well; and
(b) the justices' legal adviser or the court must elicit any further information relevant to sentence that the court may require.

(8) If the court requires more information, it may exercise its power to adjourn the hearing for not more than—
(a) 3 weeks at a time, if the defendant will be in custody; or
(b) 4 weeks at a time.

(9) When the court has taken into account all the evidence, information and any report available, the court must—
(a) as a general rule, pass sentence there and then;
(b) when passing sentence, explain the reasons for deciding on that sentence, unless neither the defendant nor any member of the public, including any reporter, is present;
(c) when passing sentence, explain to the defendant its effect, the consequences of failing to comply with any order or pay any fine, and any power that the court has to vary or review the sentence, unless—
(i) the defendant is absent, or
(ii) the defendant's ill-health or disorderly conduct makes such an explanation impracticable;
(d) give any such explanation in terms the defendant, if present, can understand (with help, if necessary); and
(e) consider exercising any power it has to make a costs or other order.

(10) Despite the general rule—
(a) the court must adjourn the hearing if the defendant is absent, the case started with a summons, requisition or single justice procedure notice, and either—
(i) the court considers passing a custodial sentence (where it can do so), or

(ii) the court considers imposing a disqualification (unless it has already adjourned the hearing to give the defendant an opportunity to attend); and

(b) the court may exercise any power it has to—

(i) commit the defendant to the Crown Court for sentence (and in some cases it must do so), or

(ii) defer sentence for up to 6 months.

[Note. See sections 9, 10 and 11 of the Magistrates' Courts Act 1980[45]*, and sections 31, 52, 59, 63, 124, 125 and 126 of the Sentencing Act 2020*[46]*.*

Under section 11(3A) of the 1980 Act, a custodial sentence passed in the defendant's absence does not take effect until the defendant is brought before the court.

Under sections 57D and 57E of the Crime and Disorder Act 1998[47]*, the court may require a defendant to attend a sentencing hearing by live link.*

Under section 35 of the Sentencing Act 2020[48]*, the court may require a defendant who is an individual to provide a statement of assets and other financial circumstances if the defendant—*

(a) serves notice of guilty plea, where rule 24.8 (Written guilty plea: special rules) applies; or

(b) is convicted.

Under section 20A of the Criminal Justice Act 1991[49]*, it is an offence for a defendant knowingly or recklessly to make a false or incomplete statement of assets or other financial circumstances, or to fail to provide such a statement, in response to a request by a court officer on behalf of the court.*

Under section 30 of the Sentencing Act 2020[50]*, the general rule (subject to exceptions) is that the court must obtain and consider a pre-sentence report—*

(a) where it is considering a custodial sentence or a community sentence;

(b) where it thinks the defendant may pose a significant risk of causing serious harm to the public by further offending.

Under section 32(3) of the Sentencing Act 2020[51]*, where the court obtains a written pre-sentence report about a defendant who is under 18, it may direct that information in it must be withheld, if it would be likely to create a risk of significant harm to the defendant.*

For the circumstances in which a magistrates' court may (and, in some cases, must) remit the defendant to a youth court for sentence, section 25 of the Sentencing Act 2020[52]*.*

The Sentencing Council may issue sentencing guidelines under section 120 of the Coroners and Justice Act 2009[53]*.*

[45] 1980 c. 43; section 10 was amended by section 59 of, and paragraph 1 of Schedule 9 to, the Criminal Justice Act 1982 (c. 48), section 68 of, and paragraph 6 of Schedule 8 to, the Criminal Justice Act 1991 (c. 53) and section 47 of the Crime and Disorder Act 1998 (c. 37). Section 11 was amended by section 123 of, and paragraph 1 of Schedule 8 to, the Criminal Justice Act 1988 (c. 33), section 168 of, and paragraph 39 of Schedule 10 to, the Criminal Justice and Public Order Act 1994 (c. 33), section 119 of, and paragraph 39 of Schedule 8 to, the Crime and Disorder Act 1998 (c. 37), section 304 of, and paragraphs 25 and 26 of Schedule 32 to, the Criminal Justice Act 2003 (c. 44) and section 54 of the Criminal Justice and Immigration Act 2008 (c. 4).

[46] 2003 c. 44; section 143 was amended by section 378 of, and paragraph 216 of Schedule 16 to the Armed Forces Act 2006 (c. 52). Section 158 was amended by section 64 of, and Part 4 of Schedule 5 to, the Children Act 2004 (c. 31), article 3 of, and paragraph 19 of Schedule 1 to, S.I. 2008/912 and section 12 of the Criminal Justice and Immigration Act 2008 (c. 4). Section 164 was amended by section 14 of the Domestic Violence, Crime and Victims Act 2004 (c. 28). Section 174 was substituted by section 64 of the Legal Aid, Sentencing and Punishment of Offenders Act 2012 (c. 10).

[47] 1998 c. 37; sections 57A to 57E were substituted for section 57 as originally enacted by section 45 of the Police and Justice Act 2006 (c. 48), and amended by sections 106, 109 and 178 of, and Part 3 of Schedule 23 to, the Coroners and Justice Act 2009 (c. 25).

[48] 2003 c. 44; section 162 was amended by paragraph 24 of Schedule 16 to the Crime and Courts Act 2013 (c. 22).

[49] 1991 c. 53; section 20A was inserted by section 168 of, and paragraph 43 of Schedule 9 to, the Criminal Justice and Public Order Act 1994 (c. 33) and amended by sections 95 and 109 of, and paragraph 350 of Schedule 8 to, the Courts Act 2003 (c. 39) and section 44 of, and paragraph 26 of Schedule 16 to, the Crime and Courts Act 2013 (c. 22).

[50] 2003 c. 44; section 156 was amended by sections 6 and 149 of, and paragraphs 71 and 77 of Schedule 4 and Part 1 of Schedule 28 to, the Criminal Justice and Immigration Act 2008 (c. 4) and paragraphs 8 and 13 of Schedule 19, and paragraphs 20 and 22 of Schedule 21, to the Legal Aid, Sentencing and Punishment of Offenders Act 2012 (c. 10).

[51] 2003 c. 44; section 159 was amended by section 208 of, and paragraphs 145 and 147 of Schedule 21 to, the Legal Services Act 2007 (c. 29).

[52] 2000 c. 6; section 8 was amended by section 41 of, and paragraph 74 of Schedule 3 to, the Criminal Justice Act 2003 (c. 44) and article 2 of, and paragraph 62 of the Schedule to S.I. 2005/886).

[53] 2009 c. 25.

For the circumstances in which a court may (and, in some cases, must) order the endorsement of a defendant's driving record, or the disqualification of a defendant from driving, see sections 34, 35 and 44 of the Road Traffic Offenders Act 1988[54]*. Under that legislation, in some circumstances the court has discretion not to make such an order. See also rule 29.1.*

The evidence that may be introduced is subject to rules of evidence.

In addition to the specific powers to which this rule applies, the court has a general power to adjourn a trial: see rule 24.2.

Under section 52(4) of the Sentencing Act 2020[55]*, Criminal Procedure Rules may prescribe cases in which there do not apply the court's usual duties to give reasons and explanations. Written notice of the effect of some sentences is required by rule 28.2 (Notice of requirements of suspended sentence or community, etc. order), rule 28.3 (Notification requirements) and rule 30.2 (notice of fine or other financial order).*

For the circumstances in which a magistrates' court may (and, in some cases, must) commit a defendant to the Crown Court for sentence, sections 14, 15, 16, 17, 18, 19 and 20 of the Sentencing Act 2020[56]*.*

Under section 3 of the Sentencing Act 2020[57]*, if (among other things) the defendant consents, the court may defer sentence for up to 6 months, for the purpose of allowing it to take account of the defendant's conduct after conviction, or any change in the defendant's circumstances.]*

R24.12 Procedure where a party is absent

24.12 (1) This rule—
(a) applies where a party is absent; but
(b) does not apply where—
(i) the defendant has served a notice of guilty plea under rule 24.8 (Written guilty plea: special rules), or
(ii) the court tries a case under rule 24.9 (Single justice procedure: special rules).

(2) Where the prosecutor is absent, the court may—
(a) if it has received evidence, deal with the case as if the prosecutor were present; and
(b) in any other case—
(i) enquire into the reasons for the prosecutor's absence, and
(ii) if satisfied there is no good reason, exercise its power to dismiss the allegation.

(3) Where the defendant is absent the general rule is that the court must proceed as if the defendant were present, and had pleaded not guilty (unless a plea already has been taken) but the general rule—
(a) does not apply if the defendant is under 18;
(b) is subject to the court being satisfied that—
(i) any summons or requisition was served on the defendant a reasonable time before the hearing, or
(ii) in a case in which the hearing has been adjourned, the defendant had reasonable notice of where and when it would resume; and
(c) is subject also to rule 24.11(10)(a) (restrictions on passing sentence in the defendant's absence).

(4) Where the defendant is absent, the court—

[54] 1988 c. 53; section 34 was amended by section 29 of the Road Traffic Act 1991 (c. 40), section 3 of the Aggravated Vehicle-Taking Act 1992 (c. 11), section 165 of, and paragraph 121 of Schedule 9 to, the Powers of Criminal Courts (Sentencing) Act 2000 (c. 6), sections 56 and 107 of, and Schedule 8 to, the Police Reform Act 2002 (c. 30), section 25 of the Road Safety Act 2006 (c. 49), article 2 of S.I. 2007/3480, paragraphs 2 and 5 of Schedule 27 to the Legal Aid, Sentencing and Punishment of Offenders Act 2012 (c. 10), section 56 of, and paragraphs 9 and 12 of Schedule 22 to, the Crime and Courts Act 2013 (c. 22) and section 177 of, and paragraph 90 of Schedule 21 to, the Coroners and Justice Act 2009 (c. 25). Section 35 was amended by section 48 of, and paragraph 95 of Schedule 4 to, the Road Traffic Act 1991 (c. 40), section 165 of, and paragraph 122 of Schedule 9 to, the Powers of Criminal Courts (Sentencing) Act 2000 (c. 6) and section 177 of, and 90 of Schedule 21 to, the Coroners and Justice Act 2009 (c. 25). Section 44 was amended by regulations 2 and 3 of, and paragraph 10 of Schedule 2 to, S.I. 1990/144 and sections 9, 10 and 59 of, and Schedule 7 to, the Road Safety Act 2006 (c. 49).

[55] 2003 c. 44; section 174 was substituted by section 64 of the Legal Aid, Sentencing and Punishment of Offenders Act 2012 (c. 10).

[56] 2000 c. 6; sections 3, 4 and 6 were amended, and sections 3A, 3B, 3C and 4A inserted, by paragraphs 21, 22A, 23, 24, 25 and 28 of Schedule 3 to the Criminal Justice Act 2003 (c. 44). Section 3A was amended by section 53 of, and paragraphs 1 and 9 of Schedule 13 to, the Criminal Justice and Immigration Act 2008 (c. 4) and paragraphs 7 and 8 of Schedule 21 to the Legal Aid, Sentencing and Punishment of Offenders Act 2012 (c. 10). Section 3C was amended by paragraphs 7 and 9 of Schedule 21 to the Legal Aid, Sentencing and Punishment of Offenders Act 2012 (c. 10). Section 6 was further amended by paragraphs 90 and 91 of Schedule 32, and Parts 7 and 9 of Schedule 37, to the Criminal Justice Act 2003 (c. 44).

[57] 2000 c. 6; section 1 was substituted, together with sections 1A to 1D, by section 278 of, and paragraph 1 of Schedule 23 to, the Criminal Justice Act 2003 (c. 44) and amended by article 3 of, and paragraph 14 of Schedule 1 to, S.I. 2008/912.

(a) must exercise its power to issue a warrant for the defendant's arrest and detention in the terms required by rule 13.3(3) (Terms of a warrant for detention or imprisonment), if it passes a custodial sentence; and
(b) may exercise its power to issue a warrant for the defendant's arrest in any other case, if it does not apply the general rule in paragraph (3) of this rule about proceeding in the defendant's absence.

[Note. See sections 11, 15 and 16 of the Magistrates' Courts Act 1980[58]*.*

Under section 27 of the 1980 Act, where a magistrates' court dismisses an allegation of an offence classified as one that can be tried either in a magistrates' court or in the Crown Court (in other legislation, described as triable either way), that dismissal has the same effect as an acquittal in the Crown Court.

Under section 11 of the 1980 Act, the court may pass a custodial sentence in the defendant's absence if the case started with the defendant's arrest and charge (and not with a summons or requisition). Section 11(3A) requires that, in that event, the defendant must be brought before the court before being taken to a prison or other institution to begin serving that sentence: see also rule 13.3. Under section 7(1) of the Bail Act 1976[59]*, the court has power to issue a warrant for the arrest of a defendant released on bail who has failed to attend court when due to do so.*

Under section 13 of the 1980 Act[60]*, the court has power to issue a warrant for the arrest of an absent defendant, instead of proceeding, where—*
(1) the case started with—
(a) the defendant's arrest and charge, or
(b) a summons or requisition, if—
(i) the court is satisfied that that summons or requisition was served on the defendant a reasonable time before the hearing, or
(ii) the defendant was present when the hearing was arranged; and
(2) the offence is punishable with imprisonment; or
(3) the defendant has been convicted and the court considers imposing a disqualification.]

Provision of documents for the court **R24.13**

24.13 (1) A party who introduces a document in evidence, or who otherwise uses a document in presenting that party's case, must provide a copy for—
(a) each other party;
(b) any witness that party wants to refer to that document;
(c) the court; and
(d) the justices' legal adviser.
(2) Unless the court otherwise directs, on application or on its own initiative, the court officer must provide for the court—
(a) any copy received under paragraph (1) before the hearing begins; and
(b) a copy of the court officer's record of—
(i) information supplied by each party for the purposes of case management, including any revision of information previously supplied,
(ii) each pre-trial direction for the management of the case,
(iii) any pre-trial decision to admit evidence,
(iv) any pre-trial direction about the giving of evidence, and
(v) any admission to which rule 24.6 applies.
(3) Where rule 24.8 (Written guilty plea: special rules) applies, the court officer must provide for the court—
(a) each document served by the prosecutor under rule 24.8(1)(d);
(b) the defendant's driving record, where the offence is under the Road Traffic Regulation Act 1984[61], the Road Traffic Act 1988[62], the Road Traffic (Consequential Provisions) Act 1988[63] or the Road Traffic (Driver Licensing and Information Systems) Act 1989[64];

[58] 1980 c. 43; section 14 was amended by section 109 of, and paragraph 205 of Schedule 8 to, the Courts Act 2003 (c. 39).
[59] 1976 c. 63.
[60] 1980 c. 43; section 13 was amended by section 45 of, and paragraph 3 of Schedule 5 to, the Criminal Justice and Public Order Act 1994 (c. 33), section 48 of the Criminal Procedure and Investigations Act 1996 (c. 25), section 3 of the Magistrates' Courts (Procedure) Act 1998 (c. 15), sections 31 and 332 of, and Part 12 of Schedule 37 to, the Criminal Justice Act 2003 (c. 44) and sections 54 and 149 of, and Part 4 of Schedule 28 to, the Criminal Justice and Immigration Act 2008 (c. 4).
[61] 1984 c. 27.
[62] 1988 c. 52.
[63] 1988 c. 54.
[64] 1989 c. 22.

(c) any other information about the defendant, relevant to sentence, of which the prosecutor served notice under rule 24.8(1); and
(d) the notice of guilty plea and any representations and other information served by the defendant under rule 24.8(4).

(4) Where the court tries a case under rule 24.9 (Single justice procedure: special rules), the court officer must provide for the court—
(a) each document served by the prosecutor under rule 24.9(1)(d);
(b) the defendant's driving record, where the offence is under the Road Traffic Regulation Act 1984, the Road Traffic Act 1988, the Road Traffic (Consequential Provisions) Act 1988 or the Road Traffic (Driver Licensing and Information Systems) Act 1989;
(c) any other information about the defendant, relevant to sentence, of which the prosecutor served notice under rule 24.9(1); and
(d) any notice, representations and other information served by the defendant under rule 29.9(4)(a).

[Note. A written witness statement to which Part 16 applies may only be introduced in evidence if there has been no objection within the time limit to which rule 16.4 refers.

An expert report to which Part 19 applies may only be introduced in evidence if it has been served in accordance with rule 19.3.

See also rule 20.3 for the procedure where a party objects to the introduction of hearsay evidence, including such evidence in a document, and rules 21.3 and 21.4 for the procedure where a party objects to the introduction of evidence of bad character.

A direction about the giving of evidence may be made on an application to which Part 18 applies (Measures to assist a witness or defendant to give evidence).]

R24.14 **Duty of justices' legal adviser**

24.14 (1) A justices' legal adviser must attend the court and carry out the duties listed in this rule, as applicable, unless the court—
(a) includes a District Judge (Magistrates' Courts); and
(b) otherwise directs.

(2) A justices' legal adviser must—
(a) before the hearing begins, by reference to what is provided for the court under rule 24.13 (Provision of documents for the court) draw the court's attention to—
(i) what the prosecutor alleges,
(ii) what the parties say is agreed,
(iii) what the parties say is in dispute, and
(iv) what the parties say about how each expects to present the case, especially where that may affect its duration and timetabling;
(b) whenever necessary, give the court legal advice and—
(i) if necessary, attend the members of the court outside the courtroom to give such advice, but
(ii) inform the parties (if present) of any such advice given outside the courtroom; and
(c) assist the court, where appropriate, in the formulation of its reasons and the recording of those reasons.

(3) A justices' legal adviser must—
(a) assist an unrepresented defendant; and
(b) assist the court by—
(i) making a note of the substance of any oral evidence or representations, to help the court recall that information,
(ii) if the court rules inadmissible part of a written statement introduced in evidence, marking that statement in such a way as to make that clear,
(iii) ensuring that an adequate record is kept of the court's decisions and the reasons for them, and
(iv) making any announcement, other than of the verdict or sentence.

(4) Where the defendant has served a notice of guilty plea to which rule 24.8 (Written guilty plea: special rules) applies, a justices' legal adviser must—
(a) unless the court otherwise directs, if any member of the public, including any reporter, is present, read aloud to the court—
(i) the material on which the prosecutor relies to set out the facts of the offence and to provide information relevant to sentence (or summarise any written statement included in that material, if the court so directs), and
(ii) any written representations by the defendant; and

(b) otherwise, draw the court's attention to—
(i) what the prosecutor alleges, and any significant features of the material listed in paragraph (4)(a)(i), and
(ii) any written representations by the defendant.

(5) Where the court tries a case under rule 24.9 (Single justice procedure: special rules), a justices' legal adviser must draw the court's attention to—
(a) what the prosecutor alleges, and any significant features of the material on which the prosecutor relies to prove the alleged offence and to provide information relevant to sentence; and
(b) any representations served by the defendant.

[Note. Section 28 of the Courts Act 2003[65] provides for the functions of a justices' legal adviser. See also sections 12 and 16A of the Magistrates' Courts Act 1980[66].

Under section 12(7ZA) of the 1980 Act[67], Criminal Procedure Rules may specify which of the documents listed in section 12(7) of that Act[68], if any, must be read aloud, and may require them to be read aloud only in circumstances specified in the rules.]

Duty of court officer and custodian **R24.15**

24.15 (1) The court officer must—
(a) serve on each party notice of where and when an adjourned hearing will resume, unless—
(i) the party was present when that was arranged,
(ii) the defendant has served a notice of guilty plea to which rule 24.8 (Written guilty plea: special rules) applies, and the adjournment is for not more than 4 weeks, or
(iii) the court tries a case under rule 24.9 (Single justice procedure: special rules), and the adjourned trial will resume under that rule;
(b) if the reason for the adjournment was to postpone sentence, include that reason in any such notice to the defendant;
(c) unless the court otherwise directs, make available to the parties any written report to which rule 24.11 (Procedure if the court convicts) applies;
(d) where the court has ordered a defendant to provide information under section 25 of the Road Traffic Offenders Act 1988[69], serve on the defendant notice of that order unless the defendant was present when it was made;
(e) serve on the prosecutor—
(i) any notice of guilty plea to which rule 24.8 (Written guilty plea: special rules) applies, and
(ii) any declaration served under rule 44.2 (Statutory declaration of ignorance of proceedings) that the defendant did not know about the case;
(f) serve on the prosecutor notice of any hearing date arranged in consequence of such a declaration, unless—
(i) the prosecutor was present when that was arranged, or
(ii) the court otherwise directs;
(g) serve on the prosecutor—
(i) notice of any hearing date arranged in consequence of the issue of a summons under rule 24.9 (Single justice procedure: special rules), and in that event
(ii) any notice served by the defendant under rule 24.9(2)(b) or (c);
(h) record the court's reasons for not proceeding in the defendant's absence where rule 24.12(3)(a) applies; and
(i) give the court such other assistance as it requires.

[65] 2003 c. 39; section 28 was amended by section 15 of, and paragraphs 308 and 327 of Schedule 4 to, the Constitutional Reform Act 2005 (c. 4).
[66] 1980 c. 43; section 12 was amended by section 45 of, and paragraph 1 of Schedule 5 to, the Criminal Justice and Public Order Act 1994 (c. 33), section 1 of the Magistrates' Courts (Procedure) Act 1998 (c. 15), section 109 of, and paragraph 203 of Schedule 8 to, the Courts Act 2003 (c. 39), section 308 of, and Part 12 of Schedule 37 to, the Criminal Justice Act 2003 (c. 44) and section 81 of the Deregulation Act 2015 (c. 20). Section 16A was inserted by section 48 of the Criminal Justice and Courts Act 2015 (c. 2).
[67] 1980 c. 43; section 12(7ZA) was inserted by section 81 of the Deregulation Act 2015 (c. 20).
[68] 1980 c. 43; section 12(7) was amended by section 81 of the Deregulation Act 2015 (c. 20).
[69] 1988 c. 53; section 25 was amended by section 90 of, and paragraphs 140 and 142 of Schedule 13 to, the Access to Justice Act 1999 (c. 22), section 165 of, and paragraph 118 of Schedule 9 to, the Powers of Criminal Courts (Sentencing) Act 2000 (c. 6) and section 109 of, and paragraph 311 of Schedule 8 to, the Courts Act 2003 (c. 39).

(2) Where the court passes a sentence of immediate imprisonment or detention, or orders a suspended sentence of imprisonment to take effect, by this rule—
(a) the court requires the defendant to provide, in writing or orally, his or her nationality; and
(b) the custodian must obtain that information and record it

[Note. See sections 10, 11 and 12 of the Magistrates' Courts Act 1980[70]*.*

Under section 25 of the Road Traffic Offenders Act 1988, where the court does not know a defendant's sex or date of birth, then on convicting the defendant of an offence involving obligatory or discretionary disqualification, the court must order the defendant to provide that information.

Under Part 5, the magistrates' court officer must record details of a case and of the court's decisions.]

Under section 86A of the Courts Act 2003[71]*, Criminal Procedure Rules must specify stages of proceedings at which the court must require the information to which rule 24.15(2) refers. A person commits an offence if, without reasonable excuse, that person fails to comply with such a requirement, whether by providing false or incomplete information or by providing no information.]*

Criminal Practice Directions Part 24 Trial and Sentence in a Magistrates' Court

CPD.24A **CPD VI Trial 24A: Role of the Justices' Clerk/Legal Adviser**

24A.1 The role of the justices' clerk/legal adviser is a unique one, which carries with it independence from direction when undertaking a judicial function and when advising magistrates. These functions must be carried out in accordance with the Bangalore Principles of Judicial Conduct (judicial independence, impartiality, integrity, propriety, ensuring fair treatment and competence and diligence). More specifically, duties must be discharged in accordance with the relevant professional Code of Conduct and the Legal Adviser Competence Framework.

24A.2 A justices' clerk is responsible for:
(a) the legal advice tendered to the justices within the area;
(b) the performance of any of the functions set out below by any member of his staff acting as justices' legal adviser;
(c) ensuring that competent advice is available to justices when the justices' clerk is not personally present in court; and
(d) ensuring that advice given at all stages of proceedings and powers exercised (including those delegated to justices' legal advisers) take into account the court's duty to deal with cases justly and actively to manage the case.

24A.3 Where a person other than the justices' clerk (a justices' legal adviser), who is authorised to do so, performs any of the functions referred to in this direction, he or she will have the same duties, powers and responsibilities as the justices' clerk. The justices' legal adviser may consult the justices' clerk, or other person authorised by the justices' clerk for that purpose, before tendering advice to the bench. If the justices' clerk or that person gives any advice directly to the bench, he or she should give the parties or their advocates an opportunity of repeating any relevant submissions, prior to the advice being given.

24A.4 When exercising judicial powers, a justices' clerk or legal adviser is acting in exactly the same capacity as a magistrate. The justices' clerk may delegate powers to a justices' legal adviser in accordance with the relevant statutory authority. The scheme of delegation must be clear and in writing, so that all justices' legal advisers are certain of the extent of their powers. Once a power is delegated, judicial discretion in an individual case lies with the justices' legal adviser exercising the power. When exercise of a power does not require the consent of the parties, a justices' clerk or legal adviser may deal with and decide a contested issue or may refer that issue to the court.

24A.5 It shall be the responsibility of the justices' clerk or legal adviser to provide the justices with any advice they require to perform their functions justly, whether or not the advice has been requested, on:
(a) questions of law;
(b) questions of mixed law and fact;
(c) matters of practice and procedure;

[70] 1980 c. 43; section 10 was amended by section 59 of, and paragraph 1 of Schedule 9 to, the Criminal Justice Act 1982 (c. 48), section 68 of, and paragraph 6 of Schedule 8 to, the Criminal Justice Act 1991 (c. 53) and section 47 of the Crime and Disorder Act 1998 (c. 37).

[71] 2003 c. 39; section 86A was inserted by section 162 of the Policing and Crime Act 2016 (c. 3).

(d) the process to be followed at sentence and the matters to be taken into account, together with the range of penalties and ancillary orders available, in accordance with the relevant sentencing guidelines;
(e) any relevant decisions of the superior courts or other guidelines;
(f) the appropriate decision-making structure to be applied in any given case; and
(g) other issues relevant to the matter before the court.

24A.6 In addition to advising the justices, it shall be the justices' legal adviser's responsibility to assist the court, where appropriate, as to the formulation of reasons and the recording of those reasons.

24A.7 The justices' legal adviser has a duty to assist an unrepresented defendant, see CrimPR 9.4(3)(a), 14.3(2)(a) and 24.15(3)(a), in particular when the court is making a decision on allocation, bail, at trial and on sentence.

24A.8 Where the court must determine allocation, the legal adviser may deal with any aspect of the allocation hearing save for the decision on allocation, indication of sentence and sentence.

24A.9 When a defendant acting in person indicates a guilty plea, the legal adviser must explain the procedure and inform the defendant of their right to address the court on the facts and to provide details of their personal circumstances in order that the court can decide the appropriate sentence.

24A.10 When a defendant indicates a not guilty plea but has not completed the relevant sections of the Magistrates' Courts Trial Preparation Form, the legal adviser must either ensure that the Form is completed or, in appropriate cases, assist the court to obtain and record the essential information on the form.

24A.11 Immediately prior to the commencement of a trial, the legal adviser must summarise for the court the agreed and disputed issues, together with the way in which the parties propose to present their cases. If this is done by way of pre-court briefing, it should be confirmed in court or agreed with the parties.

24A.12 A justices' clerk or legal adviser must not play any part in making findings of fact, but may assist the bench by reminding them of the evidence, using any notes of the proceedings for this purpose, and clarifying the issues which are agreed and those which are to be determined.

24A.13 A justices' clerk or legal adviser may ask questions of witnesses and the parties in order to clarify the evidence and any issues in the case. A legal adviser has a duty to ensure that every case is conducted justly.

24A.14 When advising the justices, the justices' clerk or legal adviser, whether or not previously in court, should:
(a) ensure that he is aware of the relevant facts; and
(b) provide the parties with an opportunity to respond to any advice given.

24A.15 At any time, justices are entitled to receive advice to assist them in discharging their responsibilities. If they are in any doubt as to the evidence which has been given, they should seek the aid of their legal adviser, referring to his notes as appropriate. This should ordinarily be done in open court. Where the justices request their adviser to join them in the retiring room, this request should be made in the presence of the parties in court. Any legal advice given to the justices other than in open court should be clearly stated to be provisional; and the adviser should subsequently repeat the substance of the advice in open court and give the parties the opportunity to make any representations they wish on that provisional advice. The legal adviser should then state in open court whether the provisional advice is confirmed or, if it is varied, the nature of the variation.

24A.16 The legal adviser is under a duty to assist unrepresented parties, whether defendants or not, to present their case, but must do so without appearing to become an advocate for the party concerned. The legal adviser should also ensure that members of the court are aware of obligations under the Victims' Code.

24A.17 The role of legal advisers in fine default proceedings, or any other proceedings for the enforcement of financial orders, obligations or penalties, is to assist the court. They must not act in an adversarial or partisan manner, such as by attempting to establish wilful refusal or neglect or any other type of culpable behaviour, to offer an opinion on the facts, or to urge a particular course of action upon the justices. The expectation is that a legal adviser will ask questions of the defaulter to elicit information which the justices will require to make an adjudication, such as the explanation for the default. A legal adviser may also advise the justices as to the options open to them in dealing with the case.

24A.18 The performance of a legal adviser is subject to regular appraisal. For that purpose the appraiser may be present in the justices' retiring room. The content of the appraisal is confidential, but the fact that an appraisal has taken place, and the presence of the appraiser in the retiring room, should be briefly explained in open court.

CPD.24B **CPD VI Trial 24B: Identification for the Court of the Issues in the Case**

24B.1 CrimPR 3.11(a) requires the court, with the active assistance of the parties, to establish what are the disputed issues in order to manage the trial. To that end, the purpose of the prosecutor's summary of the prosecution case is to explain briefly, in the prosecutor's own terms, what the case is about, including any relevant legislation or case law relevant to the particular case. It will not usually be necessary, or helpful, to present a detailed account of all the prosecution evidence due to be introduced.

24B.2 CrimPR 24.3(3)(b) provides for a defendant, or his or her advocate, immediately after the prosecution opening to set out the issues in the defendant's own terms, if invited to do so by the court. The purpose of any such identification of issues is to provide the court with focus as to what it is likely to be called upon to decide, so that the members of the court will be alert to those issues from the outset and can evaluate the prosecution evidence that they hear accordingly.

24B.3 The parties should keep in mind that, in most cases, the members of the court already will be aware of what has been declared to be in issue. The court will have access to any written admissions and to information supplied for the purposes of case management: CrimPR 24.13(2). The court's legal adviser will have drawn the court's attention to what is alleged and to what is understood to be in dispute: CrimPR 24.15(2). If a party has nothing of substance to add to that, then he or she should say so. The requirement to be concise will be enforced and the exchange with the court properly may be confined to enquiry and confirmation that the court's understanding of those allegations and issues is correct. Nevertheless, for the defendant to be offered an opportunity to identify issues at this stage may assist even if all he or she wishes to announce, or confirm, is that the prosecution is being put to proof.

24B.4 The identification of issues at the case management stage will have been made without the risk that they would be used at trial as statements of the defendant admissible in evidence against the defendant, provided the advocate follows the letter and the spirit of the Criminal Procedure Rules. The court may take the view that a party is not acting in the spirit of the Criminal Procedure Rules in seeking to ambush the other party or raising late and technical legal arguments that were not previously raised as issues. No party that seeks to ambush the other at trial should derive an advantage from such a course of action. The court may also take the view that a defendant is not acting in the spirit of the Criminal Procedure Rules if he or she refuses to identify the issues and puts the prosecutor to proof at the case management stage. In both such circumstances the court may limit the proceedings on the day of trial in accordance with CrimPR 3.11(d). In addition any significant divergence from the issues identified at case management at this late stage may well result in the exercise of the court's powers under CrimPR 3.5(6), the powers to impose sanctions.

CPD.24C **CPD VI Trial 24C: Trial Adjournment in Magistrates' Courts**

24C.1 Courts are entitled to expect the parties and other participants to adhere to CrimPR 1.2 (The duty of the participants in a criminal case) and to prepare accordingly for the trial to proceed on the date arranged. The court will expect communication between the parties and with the court regarding any issues which are likely to affect the effectiveness of any trial: CrimPR 3.2(2)(b)-(e). In particular, any revision of the information provided in the preparation for effective trial form must be reported to the court and each other party well in advance of the trial, not at trial or shortly before; and in considering any application to adjourn a trial the court will regard as especially significant any failure in this respect. Any communication should clearly identify the issue and any direction sought. and should require reference to a legal adviser or case progression officer. The parties and other participants are entitled to expect the court and its staff to adhere to CrimPR 1.3 (The application by the court of the overriding objective) and to conduct its business accordingly. If relevant Criminal Procedure Rules, Criminal Practice Directions and judicial directions for trial preparation are followed, an effective trial on the date arranged will be the result.

24C.2 In some circumstances during preparation for trial it will become apparent to a party that a trial will not be required. It is in the interests of victims, witnesses, defendants, the court and legal representatives that these decisions are made at the earliest opportunity and that the other party, or parties, and the court are notified immediately. The requirements for an application to vacate a trial fixture are set out at paragraphs 24C.30 to 24C.32 beneath.

24C.3 Where a defendant who previously has pleaded not guilty decides to enter a guilty plea, notice of that decision, and the basis of plea, should be given to the prosecution and court as soon as possible so that a decision can be taken about the need for witnesses to attend (but caution should be exercised before the witnesses' attendance is dispensed with, and usually it will be advisable to set a date for the plea to be taken in advance of the date already set for trial). The sooner that notice of such a plea is given, the greater the reduction in sentence the defendant can expect. The court will expect an explanation for the change of plea to assess the level of credit to be applied.

24C.4 Where a party is unable to comply with a direction within the time set by the court, and that failure will have implications for preparation by another party or for the likelihood of the trial proceeding within the time allocated, the party concerned should advise each other party and the court immediately of the failure and of the anticipated date for compliance: CrimPR 1.2(1)(c) and 3.10(2)(d). Parties are encouraged to communicate with each other to agree alternative dates consistent with maintaining the trial fixture: CrimPR 3.7.

Application to adjourn on day of trial

General principles

24C.5 The court is entitled to expect that trials will start on time with all case management issues dealt with in advance of the trial date. Early engagement between the parties and communication with the court should mean that it is rare for applications to adjourn trials to be made on the day of trial, except in circumstances that could not have been foreseen. However, there will be occasions on which, on the day set for trial, the court is invited without prior warning to adjourn to another day in consequence of an event or events said to make it unjust to proceed as planned; and in some circumstances it may have been necessary to arrange to hear a contested application to adjourn a trial on the very date on which that trial is due to begin (though before making such arrangements the court should have kept in mind the need to make time available for other cases, too, where the time available for the trial will be abbreviated by the time required to hear the application to adjourn it).

24C.6 Section 10 of the Magistrates' Courts Act 1980 confers a discretionary power to adjourn, and see also CrimPR 24.2(3). The following directions codify and restate procedural principles established in a long line of judgments of the senior courts, to some of which they refer. Therefore these directions supersede those judgments and it is to these directions that magistrates' courts must refer in the first instance.

24C.7 The starting point is that the trial should proceed. The basic approach was explained by Gross LJ in *Director of Public Prosecutions v Petrie* [2015] EWHC 48 (Admin):

> '*... successive initiatives ... have repeatedly exhorted the magistracy and District Bench to case manage robustly and to resist the granting of adjournments. Although there are of course instances where the interests of justice require the grant of an adjournment, this should be a course of last rather than first resort – and after other alternatives have been considered. ... It is essential that parties to proceedings in a magistrates' court should proceed on the basis of a need to get matters right first time; any suggestion of a culture readily permitting an opportunity to correct failures of preparation should be firmly dispelled.*'

24C.8 A magistrates' court may keep in mind that, if appropriate, the court's decision may be re-opened (see CrimPR 24.18), and that avenues of appeal by way of rehearing or of review are open to the parties, including in a case in which it is later discovered that the court has acted on a material mistake of fact (see *R (Director of Public Prosecutions) v Sunderland Magistrates' Court, R (Kharaghan) v City of London Magistrates' Court* [2018] EWHC 229 (Admin)). The court should not be deterred from a prompt and robust determination therefore. Only if there are compelling reasons for doing so will the High Court interfere with the court's exercise of its discretion.

24C.9 In general, the relevant principles relating to trial adjournment are these:

- the court's duty is to deal justly with the case, which includes doing justice between the parties.
- the court must have regard to the need for expedition. Delay is generally inimical to the interests of justice and brings the criminal justice system into disrepute. Proceedings in a magistrates' court should be simple and speedy.
- applications for adjournments should be rigorously scrutinised and the court must have a clear reason for adjourning. To do this, the court must review the history of the case.
- where the prosecutor asks for an adjournment the court must consider not only the interest of the defendant in getting the matter dealt with without delay but also the public interest in ensuring that criminal charges are adjudicated upon thoroughly, with the guilty convicted as well as the innocent acquitted.
- with a more serious charge the public interest that there be a trial will carry greater weight. It is, however, reasonable for the court to expect that parties should have given especially careful attention to the preparation of trials involving serious offences or where the trial has significant implications for victims or witnesses.

- where the defendant asks for an adjournment the court must consider whether he or she will be able to present the defence fully without and, if not, the extent to which his or her ability to do so is compromised.
- the court must consider the consequences of an adjournment and its impact on the ability of witnesses and defendants accurately to recall events.
- the impact of adjournment on other cases. The relisting of one case almost inevitably delays or displaces the hearing of others. The length of the hearing and the extent of delay in other cases will need to be considered.

The relevance of fault

24C.10 As the starting point is that the trial should proceed, a consequence of doing so without adjournment may be that the prosecutor is unable to prove the prosecution case, or that the defendant is unable to explore an issue. That may be a just consequence of inadequate preparation. Even in the absence of fault on the part of either party it may not be in the interests of justice to adjourn, notwithstanding that an imperfect trial may be the result.

24C.11 The reason why the adjournment is required should be examined and if it arises through the fault of the applicant for that adjournment then that weighs against its grant, carrying weight in accordance with the gravity of the fault. For the purposes of this paragraph, the prosecutor and those who investigated the case usually should be treated as one.

24C.12 If the applicant was at fault, was it serious? A fault will be serious if the relevant act or omission has been repeated, especially where it has caused a previous adjournment, or where there is no reasonable explanation for that act or omission. The more serious the default, the less willing the court will be to adjourn.

24C.13 Where a party has been at fault, did the other party, if aware of it, draw attention to that fault promptly and explicitly? CrimPR 1.2(1)(c) imposes a collective responsibility on participants promptly to draw attention to a significant failure to take a required procedural step. CrimPR 3.10(2)(d) requires each party promptly to inform the court and the other parties of anything that may affect the date or duration of the trial or significantly affect the progress of the case in any other way. If no such action has been taken by a party who could have done so then the court may look less favourably on any application by that same party to adjourn, and especially if that application reasonably might have been made before the trial date.

Length of adjournment

24C.14 Were an adjournment granted, for how long would it need to be? The shorter the necessary adjournment, the less objectionable it will be – although much will depend on the ability of the court to accommodate it without undue impact on other cases. Courts must make every effort to make the adjournment as short as possible, for example by using time vacated by another trial or by conducting the hearing at another court house. In some cases it may be possible to achieve a just outcome by a short adjournment to later on the same day.

24C.15 If the reason for the application to adjourn is that the applicant party seeks more time in which to raise or explore an issue, has that party reasonable grounds for its late identification despite the requirements of CrimPR 3.3(1) read with 3.2(2) (early identification of issues)? In the absence of such grounds, that failure will constitute a fault for the purposes of these directions.

Particular grounds of applications to adjourn trials

24C.16 The following paragraphs identify some particular factors which may need to be taken into account in addition to those identified in paragraphs 24C.5 – 24C15.

Absence of defendant

24C.17 If a defendant has attained the age of 18 years, the court shall proceed in his absence unless it appears to the court to be contrary to the interests of justice to do so: section 11 of the Magistrates' Courts Act 1980. In marked contrast to the position in the Crown Court, in magistrates' courts proceeding in the absence of a defendant is the default position where the defendant is aware of the date of trial and no acceptable reason is offered for that absence. The court is not obliged to investigate if no reason is offered. In assessing where the interests of justice lie the court will take into account all factors, including such reasons for absence as may be offered; the reliability of the information supplied in support of those reasons; the date on which the reasons for absence became known to the defendant; and what action the defendant thereafter took in response. Where the defendant provides a medical note to excuse his or her non-attendance the court must consider 5C of these Practice Directions (issue of medical certificates) and give reasons if deciding to proceed notwithstanding.

24C.18 If the court does not proceed to trial in the absence of the defendant it is required by the 1980 Act to give its reasons, which must be specific to the case: section 11(7), and see also CrimPR 24.16(h).

24C.19 Where a defendant is under 18, there is no presumption that the court should proceed in absence. In deciding whether it is in the interests of justice to proceed the court should take into account:

- that trial in absence can and sometimes does result in acquittal and that it is in nobody's interests to delay an acquittal;
- that if convicted the defendant can ask that the conviction be re-opened in the interests of justice, for example if absence was involuntary;
- that if convicted the defendant has a right to a rehearing on appeal to the Crown Court;
- the age, vulnerability, or experience of the defendant;
- whether a parent or guardian is present, whether a parent or guardian ordinarily would be required to attend and whether such a person has attended a previous hearing;
- the interests of any co-defendant in the case proceeding;
- the interests of witnesses who have attended, including the age of any such witness;
- the nature of the evidence and whether memories of relevant evidence are liable to fade;
- how soon an adjourned trial can be accommodated in the court list.

When proceeding in absence or adjourning the court must give its reasons.

Absence of witness

24C.20 Where the court is asked to adjourn because a witness has failed to attend, the court must:

- rigorously investigate the steps taken to secure that witness' attendance, the reasons given for absence and the likelihood of the witness attending should the case be adjourned;
- consider the relevance of the witness to the case, and whether the witness' statement can be agreed or admitted, in whole or part, as hearsay, including under section 114(1)(d) of the Criminal Justice Act 2003;
- in the case of a defence witness, consider whether proper notice has been given of the intention to call that witness;
- consider whether an absent witness can be heard later in the trial;
- where other witnesses have attended and the court has determined that the absent witness is required, consider hearing those witnesses who are present and adjourning the case part-heard, provided the next hearing can be held conveniently in a matter of days or weeks, not months, to avoid having to recall all the witnesses.

Failure to serve evidence in time

24C.21 It should rarely be the case that an application to adjourn based on a failure to serve evidence is made on the day of trial. The court is entitled to expect that evidence will have been served in good time and in accordance with the directions of the court. The court should consider whether the party who complains of the failure had drawn attention to it: CrimPR 1.2(1)(c) and 3.10(2)(d), and see paragraphs 24C.10 – 24C.13 above.

24C.22 The court must conduct a rigorous inquiry into the nature of the evidence and must consider whether any of what is sought has been served, and if so when; the volume and the significance of what is sought; and the time likely to be needed for its consideration. In particular, the court must satisfy itself that any material still sought is relevant and that the party seeking it has a right to it. In some circumstances a failure to serve evidence can be addressed by refusing to admit it instead of by adjourning the trial to allow it to be served: see *R v Boardman* [2015] EWCA Crim 175; [2015] 1 Cr. App. R. 33; [2015] Crim. L.R. 451.

Failure to comply with disclosure obligations

24C.23 The parties' disclosure obligations arise from the Criminal Procedure and Investigations Act 1996. The procedure to comply with those duties is set out at CrimPR Part 15. Disclosure is not a trial issue. It should have been resolved by the parties complying with their statutory obligations and with the Rules in advance of the trial.

24C.24 Where a defendant complains of a prosecution failure to disclose material that ought to have been disclosed the court must first establish whether either party is applying for an adjournment as a result. If an adjournment is sought, the court should consider whether the matter can be resolved by the giving of disclosure immediately. If it cannot, the court should consider whether the parties have complied with their obligations under CrimPR 3.3 and under the provisions listed in paragraph 24C.1 above, and should consider the relevance of fault.

24C.25 If the prosecutor has complied or purported to comply with his or her initial disclosure obligations, no further material is disclosable and consequently no application to adjourn should be entertained unless the defendant has served a defence statement in accordance with section 6 of the Criminal Procedure and Investigations Act 1996 and CrimPR 15.4.

24C.26 If the defendant has served a defence statement and asks for further disclosure, in consequence of the prosecutor's allegedly inadequate response or in consequence of a failure to respond at all, the court has no power to entertain an application for that further disclosure unless it is made pursuant to section 8 of the Criminal Procedure and Investigations Act 1996 and CrimPR 15.5. The court should consider hearing such an application immediately, provided that there is sufficient time available for the application itself and then for the defence to consider any material disclosed in consequence of it.

Managing trials within available court time

24C.27 Where there is a risk of a trials being adjourned for lack of court time the court or legal adviser must assess the priority to be assigned to each trial listed for hearing that day based on the needs of the parties, whether the case has been adjourned before and the seriousness of the offence; giving priority to any cases in which the defendant is in custody by reason only of a trial due to be heard that day. Where more than one court is sitting to deal with trials, liaison between courtrooms should occur to determine the potential for all listed trials to be heard through movement of cases. Where a case is moved from one courtroom to another and as a result is assigned to a different advocate, the court must allow the fresh advocate adequate time in which to prepare. Courts should always begin a trial by reviewing the need for witnesses and the timetable set during pre-trial case management. The court will be slow to adjourn a trial until it is clear that all other trials assessed as having an equal or higher priority for hearing that day will be effective.

24C.28 The court is entitled to expect that parties will present their case within the time set during pre-trial case management. In entertaining additional applications for which no time has been allowed the court must keep in mind the expectation that the trial will be completed within the allocated time with minimal impact on other cases.

24C.29 While it is preferable to complete a trial on the date allocated, there will be occasions on which it is appropriate to adjourn part-heard, particularly where it is possible to hear the majority of witnesses. If necessary future listings will be moved to accommodate the hearing.

Applications to vacate trials

24C.30 To make the best use of the court's and the parties' time it is expected that applications to vacate trials will be made promptly and in writing, in advance of the date of trial. Any application should be served on each other party at the same time as it is served on the court. As a general rule, such an application will be dealt with outside the courtroom under CrimPR 3.5. An application to vacate a trial will be considered in accordance with the same principles as those identified in paragraphs 24C.5 – 24C.26 of these Directions.

24C.31 Given the binding nature of any decision on an application to vacate and refix a trial, absent a change of circumstances, it is incumbent on the parties to provide full and accurate information to the court to enable it to assess where the interests of justice lie: see *R (on the application of F and another) v Knowsley Magistrates Court* [2006] EWHC 695 (Admin); *R (Jones) v South East Surrey Local Justice Area* [2010] EWHC 916 (Admin), (2010) 174 JP 342; *DPP v Woods* [2017] EWHC 1070 (Admin). Any application should, as a minimum, include (as should, as appropriate, any response):

- the reason for the application;
- a chronology of the case, recording the dates of compliance with any directions and of communication between the parties;
- an assessment of the interests of justice, addressing the factors identified in these Practice Directions and indicating the likely effect should the court conclude that the trial should proceed on the date fixed;
- any restrictions on the future availability of witnesses;
- any likely changes to the number of witnesses or the way in which the evidence will be presented and any impact on the trial time estimate.

24C.32 On receipt of an application each other party should serve that party's response on the court and on the applicant within 2 business days unless the court otherwise directs. Any request for the matter to be determined at a hearing should be served with the application to vacate the trial or with the response to that application, as the case may be, together with the reasons for that request, to enable the court to decide whether a hearing is needed.

Criminal Procedure Rules Part 25 Trial and Sentence in the Crown Court

[Note. Part 3 contains rules about case management that apply during preparation for trial and at trial. The rules in this Part must be read in conjunction with those rules.]

When this Part applies **R25.1**

25.1 This Part applies in the Crown Court where the court tries a case or the defendant pleads guilty.

[Note. The Crown Court's powers to try an allegation of an offence are contained in sections 45 and 46 of the Senior Courts Act 1981[1]*.*

The exercise of the court's powers is affected by—

(a) the classification of the offence (and the general rule, subject to exceptions, is that the Crown Court must try—
(i) an offence classified as one that can be tried only in the Crown Court (in other legislation, described as triable only on indictment), and
(ii) an offence classified as one that can be tried either in a magistrates' court or in the Crown Court (in other legislation, described as triable either way) that has been allocated for trial in the Crown Court); and

(b) the defendant's age (and the general rule is that an allegation of an offence against a defendant under 18 must be tried in a magistrates' court sitting as a youth court, irrespective of the classification of the offence and without allocation for trial there, unless the offence is—
(i) one of homicide,
(ii) one for which a convicted adult could be imprisoned for 14 years or more,
(iii) one of certain specified offences involving firearms, or
(iv) one of certain specified sexual offences).

See sections 17 and 24 of the Magistrates' Courts Act 1980[2]*) and section 51A of the Crime and Disorder Act 1998*[3]*.*

Under section 34A of the Children and Young Persons Act 1933[4]*, the court—*

(a) may require the defendant's parents or guardian to attend court with the defendant, where the defendant is under 18; and
(b) must do so, where the defendant is under 16,

unless satisfied that that would be unreasonable. Part 46 (Representatives) contains rules allowing a parent, guardian or other supporting adult to help a defendant under 18.]

General powers and requirements **R25.2**

25.2 (1) Where this Part applies, the general rule is that—
(a) the trial must be in public, but that is subject to the court's power to—
(i) impose a restriction on reporting what takes place at a public hearing, or public access to what otherwise would be a public hearing,
(ii) withhold information from the public during a public hearing, or
(iii) order a trial in private;
(b) the court must not proceed if the defendant is absent, unless the court is satisfied that—
(i) the defendant has waived the right to attend, and
(ii) the trial will be fair despite the defendant's absence; and
(c) the court must not sentence the defendant to imprisonment or detention unless—
(i) the defendant has a legal representative,

[1] 1981 c. 54.
[2] 1980 c. 43; section 24 was amended by paragraph 47 of Schedule 14 to the Criminal Justice Act 1982 (c. 48), sections 17, 68 and 101 of, and paragraph 6 of Schedule 8 and Schedule 13 to, the Criminal Justice Act 1991 (c. 53), paragraph 40 of Schedule 10, and Schedule 11, to the Criminal Justice and Public Order Act 1994 (c. 33), sections 47 and 119 of, and paragraph 40 of Schedule 8, to the Crime and Disorder Act 1998 (c. 37), paragraph 64 of Schedule 9 to the Powers of Criminal Courts (Sentencing) Act 2000 (c. 6), section 42 of, and paragraphs 1 and 9 of Schedule 3, and Part 4 of Schedule 37, to the Criminal Justice Act 2003 (c. 44) and sections 49 and 65 of, and paragraph 1 of Schedule 1 and Schedule 5 to, the Violent Crime Reduction Act 2006 (c. 38).
[3] 1998 c. 37; section 51A was inserted by paragraphs 15 and 18 of Schedule 3 to the Criminal Justice Act 2003 (c. 44) and amended by section 49 of, and paragraph 5 of Schedule 1 to, the Violent Crime Reduction Act 2006 (c. 38) and paragraph 6 of Schedule 21 to the Legal Aid, Sentencing and Punishment of Offenders Act 2012 (c. 10).
[4] 1933 c. 12; section 34A was inserted by section 56 of the Criminal Justice Act 1991 (c. 53) and amended by section 107 of, and paragraph 1 of Schedule 5 to, the Local Government Act 2000 (c. 22).

(ii) the defendant has been sentenced to imprisonment or detention on a previous occasion in the United Kingdom, or
(iii) the defendant could have been represented under legal aid but is not because section 226(7), (8) of the Sentencing Act 2020[5] applies to him or her.

(2) Before proceeding to trial the court must—
(a) obtain the prosecutor's confirmation, in writing or orally, that the indictment on which the defendant is about to be tried sets out—
(i) a statement of each offence that the prosecutor wants the court to try, and
(ii) such particulars of the conduct constituting the commission of each such offence as the prosecutor relies upon to make clear what is alleged;
(b) ensure that the defendant is correctly identified by that indictment;
(c) satisfy itself that there has been explained to the defendant, in terms the defendant can understand (with help, if necessary), each allegation in that indictment against him or her; and
(d) invite any objection to the terms or validity of that indictment.

(3) The court may adjourn the trial at any stage.

See section 226(7), (8) of the Sentencing Act 2020, which applies to a defendant if—

(a) representation was made available to the defendant for the purposes of the proceedings under Part 1 of the Legal Aid, Sentencing and Punishment of Offenders Act 2012 but was withdrawn because of the defendant's conduct or because it appeared that the defendant's financial resources were such that he or she was not eligible for such representation;
(b) the defendant applied for such representation and the application was refused because it appeared that the defendant's financial resources were such that he or she was not eligible for such representation; or
(c) having been informed of the right to apply for such representation and having had the opportunity to do so, the defendant refused or failed to apply.

Part 6 contains rules about reporting, etc. restrictions. For a list of the court's powers to impose reporting and access restrictions, see the note to rule 6.1.

Part 10 contains rules about the content and service of indictments. Under section 2(6ZA) of the Administration of Justice (Miscellaneous Provisions) Act 1933[6], no objection to the indictment may be taken after the trial commences by reason of any failure to observe those rules.]

R25.3 **Application for ruling on procedure, evidence or other question of law**

25.3 (1) This rule applies to an application—
(a) about—
(i) case management, or any other question of procedure, or
(ii) the introduction or admissibility of evidence, or any other question of law; and
(b) that has not been determined before the trial begins.

(2) The application is subject to any other rule that applies to it (for example, as to the time and form in which the application must be made).

(3) Unless the court otherwise directs, the application must be made, and the court's decision announced, in the absence of the jury (if there is one).

[Note. See also rule 3.21 (Pre-trial hearings in the Crown Court: general rules).]

R25.4 **Procedure on plea of guilty**

25.4 (1) This rule applies if—
(a) the defendant pleads guilty to an offence; and
(b) the court is satisfied that the plea represents a clear acknowledgement of guilt.

(2) The court need not receive evidence unless rule 25.16(4) applies (determination of facts for sentencing).

[Note. See also rule 3.32 (Arraigning the defendant on the indictment).]

R25.5 **Application to vacate a guilty plea**

25.5 (1) This rule applies where a party wants the court to vacate a guilty plea.

(2) Such a party must—
(a) apply in writing—
(i) as soon as practicable after becoming aware of the grounds for doing so, and

[5] 2000 c. 6; section 83(3) was amended by section 4 of the Criminal Defence Service Act 2006 (c. 9) and section 39 of, and paragraphs 52 and 53 of Schedule 5 to, the Legal Aid, Sentencing and Punishment of Offenders Act 2012 (c. 10).
[6] 1933 c. 36; section 2(6ZA) was inserted by section 116 of the Coroners and Justice Act 2009 (c. 25).

(ii) in any event, before the final disposal of the case, by sentence or otherwise; and
(b) serve the application on—
(i) the court officer, and
(ii) the prosecutor.
(3) Unless the court otherwise directs, the application must—
(a) explain why it would be unjust for the guilty plea to remain unchanged;
(b) indicate what, if any, evidence the applicant wishes to call;
(c) identify any proposed witness; and
(d) indicate whether legal professional privilege is waived, specifying any material name and date.

Selecting the jury **R25.6**

25.6 (1) This rule—
(a) applies where—
(i) the defendant pleads not guilty,
(ii) the defendant declines to enter a plea and the court treats that as a not guilty plea, or
(iii) the court determines that the defendant is not fit to be tried; but
(b) does not apply where—
(i) the court orders a trial without a jury because of a danger of jury tampering or where jury tampering appears to have taken place, or
(ii) the court tries without a jury counts on an indictment after a trial of sample counts with a jury.
(2) The court must select a jury to try the case from the panel, or part of the panel, of jurors summoned by the Lord Chancellor to attend at that time and place.
(3) Where it appears that too few jurors to constitute a jury will be available from among those so summoned, the court—
(a) may exercise its own power to summon others in the court room, or in the vicinity, up to the number likely to be required, and add their names to the panel summoned by the Lord Chancellor; but
(b) must inform the parties, if they are absent when the court exercises that power.
(4) The court must select the jury by drawing at random each juror's name from among those so summoned and—
(a) announcing each name so drawn; or
(b) announcing an identifying number assigned by the court officer to that person, where the court is satisfied that that is necessary.
(5) If too few jurors to constitute a jury are available from the panel after all their names have been drawn, the court may—
(a) exercise its own power to summon others in the court room, or in the vicinity, up to the number required; and
(b) announce—
(i) the name of each person so summoned, or
(ii) an identifying number assigned by the court officer to that person, where the court is satisfied that that is necessary.
(6) The jury the court selects—
(a) must comprise no fewer than 12 jurors; and
(b) may comprise as many as 14 jurors to begin with, where the court expects the trial to last for more than 4 weeks.
(7) Where the court selects a jury comprising more than 12 jurors, the court must explain to them that—
(a) the purpose of selecting more than 12 jurors to begin with is to fill any vacancy or vacancies caused by the discharge of any of the first 12 before the prosecution evidence begins;
(b) any such vacancy or vacancies will be filled by the extra jurors in order of their selection from the panel;
(c) the court will discharge any extra juror or jurors remaining by no later than the beginning of the prosecution evidence; and
(d) any juror who is discharged for that reason then will be available to be selected for service on another jury, during the period for which that juror has been summoned.
(8) Each of the 12 or more jurors the court selects—
(a) must take an oath or affirm; and
(b) becomes a full jury member until discharged.
(9) The oath or affirmation must be in these terms, or in any corresponding terms that the juror declares to be binding on him or her—

'I swear by Almighty God [*or* I do solemnly, sincerely and truly declare and affirm] that I will faithfully try the defendant and give a true verdict according to the evidence.'

[Note. See sections 2, 5, 6, and 11 of the Juries Act 1974[7]*. See also rule 38.7 (Discharging jurors).*

Under sections 44 and 46 of the Criminal Justice Act 2003[8]*, the court may try a case without a jury where there is a danger of jury tampering, or where jury tampering appears to have taken place. Under section 17 of the Domestic Violence, Crime and Victims Act 2004*[9]*, the court may try sample counts with a jury and other counts without a jury. Part 3 (preparation for trial in the Crown Court) contains rules about an application for such a trial.*

Sections 1, 3, 4, 5 and 6 of the Oaths Act 1978[10] *provide for the taking of oaths and the making of affirmations, and for the words that must be used.*

Part 26 contains other rules about jurors.]

R25.7 Discharging jurors

25.7 (1) The court may exercise its power to discharge a juror at any time—
(a) after the juror completes the oath or affirmation; and
(b) before the court discharges the jury.
(2) No later than the beginning of the prosecution evidence, if the jury then comprises more than 12 jurors the court must discharge any in excess of 12 in reverse order of their selection from the panel.
(3) The court may exercise its power to discharge the jury at any time—
(a) after each juror has completed the oath or affirmation; and
(b) before the jury has delivered its verdict on each offence charged in the indictment.
(4) The court must exercise its power to discharge the jury when, in respect of each offence charged in the indictment, either—
(a) the jury has delivered its verdict on that offence; or
(b) the court has discharged the jury from reaching a verdict.

[Note. See sections 16 and 18 of the Juries Act 1974[11]*.]*

R25.8 Objecting to jurors

25.8 (1) A party who objects to the panel of jurors must serve notice explaining the objection on the court officer and on the other party before the first juror's name or number is drawn.
(2) A party who objects to the selection of an individual juror must—
(a) tell the court of the objection—
(i) after the juror's name or number is announced, and
(ii) before the juror completes the oath or affirmation; and
(b) explain the objection.
(3) A prosecutor who exercises the prosecution right without giving reasons to prevent the court selecting an individual juror must announce the exercise of that right before the juror completes the oath or affirmation.
(4) The court must determine an objection under paragraph (1) or (2)—
(a) at a hearing, in public or in private; and
(b) in the absence of the jurors, unless the court otherwise directs.

[Note. See section 29 of the Juries Act 1825[12] *and section 12 of the Juries Act 1974*[13]*.]*

[7] 1974 c. 23; section 2 was amended by section 61 of the Administration of Justice Act 1982 (c. 53) and Part 10 of Schedule 37 to the Criminal Justice Act 2003 (c. 44). Section 5 was amended by section 15 of, and paragraphs 77 and 78 of Schedule 4 to, the Constitutional Reform Act 2005 (c. 4). Section 6 was amended by paragraph 45 of Schedule 15 to the Criminal Justice Act 1988 (c. 33). Section 11 was amended by section 58 of, and paragraph 8 of Schedule 10 and Schedule 11 to, the Domestic Violence, Crime and Victims Act 2004 (c. 28).
[8] 2003 c. 44.
[9] 2004 c. 28.
[10] 1978 c. 19.
[11] 1974 c. 23; section 16 was amended by sections 121 and 170 of, and Schedule 16 to, the Criminal Justice Act 1988 (c. 33).
[12] 1825 c. 50; section 29 was amended by section 40 of, and paragraph 3 of Schedule 4 to, the Courts Act 1971 (c. 23). There are other amendments not relevant to this rule.
[13] 1974 c. 23; section 12 was amended by section 170 of, and Schedule 16 to, the Criminal Justice Act 1988 (c. 33).

Procedure on plea of not guilty R25.9

25.9 (1) This rule applies where—
(a) the defendant pleads not guilty; or
(b) the defendant declines to enter a plea and the court treats that as a not guilty plea.

(2) In the following sequence—
(a) where there is a jury, the court must—
(i) inform the jurors of each offence charged in the indictment to which the defendant pleads not guilty, and
(ii) explain to the jurors that it is their duty, after hearing the evidence, to decide whether the defendant is guilty or not guilty of each offence;
(b) the prosecutor may summarise the prosecution case, concisely outlining the facts and the matters likely to be in dispute;
(c) where there is a jury, to help the jurors to understand the case and resolve any issue in it the court may—
(i) invite the defendant concisely to identify what is in issue, if necessary in terms approved by the court, and
(ii) if the defendant declines to do so, direct that the jurors be given a copy of any defence statement served under rule 15.4 (Defence disclosure), edited if necessary to exclude any reference to inappropriate matters or to matters evidence of which would not be admissible;
(d) the prosecutor must introduce the evidence on which the prosecution case relies;
(e) subject to paragraph (3), at the end of the prosecution evidence, on the defendant's application or on its own initiative, the court—
(i) may direct the jury (if there is one) to acquit on the ground that the prosecution evidence is insufficient for any reasonable court properly to convict, but
(ii) must not do so unless the prosecutor has had an opportunity to make representations;
(f) subject to paragraph (4), at the end of the prosecution evidence, the court must ask whether the defendant intends to give evidence in person and, if the answer is 'no', then the court must satisfy itself that there has been explained to the defendant, in terms the defendant can understand (with help, if necessary)—
(i) the right to give evidence in person, and
(ii) that if the defendant does not give evidence in person, or refuses to answer a question while giving evidence, the court may draw such inferences as seem proper;
(g) the defendant may summarise the defence case, if he or she intends to call at least one witness other than him or herself to give evidence in person about the facts of the case;
(h) in this order (or in a different order, if the court so directs) the defendant may—
(i) give evidence in person,
(ii) call another witness, or witnesses, to give evidence in person, and
(iii) introduce any other evidence;
(i) a party may introduce further evidence if it is then admissible (for example, because it is in rebuttal of evidence already introduced);
(j) the prosecutor may make final representations, where—
(i) the defendant has a legal representative,
(ii) the defendant has called at least one witness, other than the defendant him or herself, to give evidence in person about the facts of the case, or
(iii) the court so permits; and
(k) the defendant may make final representations.

(3) Paragraph (2)(e) does not apply in relation to a charge of murder, manslaughter, attempted murder, or causing harm contrary to section 18 or 20 of the Offences against the Person Act 1861[14] until the court has heard all the evidence (including any defence evidence), where the defendant is charged with—
(a) any of those offences; and
(b) an offence of causing or allowing a child or vulnerable adult to die or to suffer serious physical harm, contrary to section 5 of the Domestic Violence, Crime and Victims Act 2004[15].

[14] 1861 c. 100; section 18 was amended by the Statute Law Revision Act 1892 (c. 19), the Statute Law Revision (No 2) Act 1893 (c. 54) and section 10 of, and Part III of Schedule 3 to, the Criminal Law Act 1967 (c. 58). Section 20 was amended by the Statute Law Revision Act 1892 (c. 19).

[15] 2004 c. 28; section 5 was amended by section 1 of the Domestic Violence, Crime and Victims (Amendment) Act 2012 (c. 4).

(4) Paragraph (2)(f) does not apply where it appears to the court that, taking account of all the circumstances, the defendant's physical or mental condition makes it undesirable for the defendant to give evidence in person.

(5) Where there is more than one defendant, this rule applies to each in the order their names appear in the indictment, or in an order directed by the court.

(6) Unless the jury (if there is one) has retired to consider its verdict, the court may allow a party to introduce evidence, or make representations, after that party's opportunity to do so under paragraph (2).

(7) Unless the jury has already reached a verdict on a count, the court may exercise its power to—
  (a) discharge the jury from reaching a verdict on that count;
  (b) direct the jury to acquit the defendant on that count; or
  (c) invite the jury to convict the defendant, if the defendant pleads guilty to the offence charged by that count.

[Note. See also rule 3.32 (Arraigning the defendant on the indictment).

Under section 6E of the Criminal Procedure and Investigations Act 1996[16]*, the court may make the direction for which rule 25.9(2)(c)(ii) provides, on application or on the court's own initiative.*

The admissibility of evidence that a party introduces is governed by rules of evidence.

Under section 35 of the Criminal Justice and Public Order Act 1994[17]*, the court may draw such inferences as appear proper from a defendant's failure to give evidence, or refusal without good cause to answer a question while doing so. The procedure set out in rule 25.9(2)(f) and (4) is prescribed by that section.*

Section 2 of the Criminal Evidence Act 1898[18] *restricts the circumstances in which the defendant may summarise the defence case before introducing evidence.*

Section 79 of the Police and Criminal Evidence Act 1984[19] *requires a defendant who wishes to give evidence in person to do so before calling any other witness, unless the court otherwise permits.*

Section 2 of the Criminal Procedure Act 1865[20] *and section 3 of the Criminal Evidence Act 1898*[21] *restrict the circumstances in which the prosecutor may make final representations without the court's permission. See also section 1 of the Criminal Procedure (Right of Reply) Act 1964*[22].

The procedure set out in rule 25.9(3) is prescribed by sections 6 and 6A of the Domestic Violence, Crime and Victims Act 2004[23].

Under section 17 of the Criminal Justice Act 1967[24]*, the court may direct the jury to acquit where the prosecutor offers no evidence.*

See rule 25.14 for the procedure on taking the verdict and rule 25.16 for the procedure if the court convicts the defendant.]

R25.10 Defendant unfit to plead

25.10 (1) This rule applies where—
  (a) it appears to the court, on application or on its own initiative, that the defendant may not be fit to be tried; and
  (b) the defendant has not by then been acquitted of each offence charged by the indictment.

(2) The court—
  (a) must exercise its power to decide, without a jury, whether the defendant is fit to be tried; but
  (b) may postpone the exercise of that power until immediately before the opening of the defence case.

[16] 1996 c. 25; section 6E was inserted by section 36 of the Criminal Justice Act 2003 (c. 44).
[17] 1994 c. 33; section 35 was amended by sections 35 and 120 of, and Schedule 10 to, the Crime and Disorder Act 1998 (c. 37) and paragraphs 62 and 63 of Schedule 36 to the Criminal Justice Act 2003 (c. 44).
[18] 1898 c. 36.
[19] 1984 c. 60.
[20] 1865 c. 18; section 2 was amended by section 10(2) of, and Part III of Schedule 3 to, the Criminal Law Act 1967 (c. 58).
[21] 1898 c. 36; section 3 was amended by section 1(2) of the Criminal Procedure (Right of Reply) Act 1964 (c. 34).
[22] 1964 c. 34; section 1 was amended by section 1 of, and the Schedule to, the Statute Law (Repeals) Act 1974 (c. 22).
[23] 2004 c. 28; section 6 was amended by section 3 of, and paragraphs 7 and 8 of the Schedule to, the Domestic Violence, Crime and Victims (Amendment) Act 2012 (c. 4) and section 6A was inserted by section 2 of that Act.
[24] 1967 c. 80; section 17 was amended by paragraph 42 of Schedule 36 to the Criminal Justice Act 2003 (c. 44).

(3) Where the court determines that the defendant is not fit to be tried—
(a) the court must exercise its power to appoint a person to put the case for the defence, taking account of all the circumstances and in particular—
(i) the willingness and suitability (including the qualifications and experience) of that person,
(ii) the nature and complexity of the case,
(iii) any advantage of continuity of representation, and
(iv) the defendant's wishes and needs;
(b) the court must select a jury, if none has been selected yet; and
(c) rule 25.9 (Procedure on plea of not guilty) applies, if the steps it lists have not already been taken, except that—
(i) everything which that rule requires to be done by the defendant may be done instead by the person appointed to put the case for the defence,
(ii) under rule 25.9(2)(a), the court must explain to the jurors that their duty is to decide whether or not the defendant did the act or made the omission charged as an offence, not whether the defendant is guilty of that offence, and
(iii) rule 25.9(2)(e) does not apply (warning of consequences of defendant not giving evidence).

[Note. See sections 4 and 4A of the Criminal Procedure (Insanity) Act 1964[25].

Under section 4 of the 1964 Act, the court must not determine the defendant's fitness to be tried except on the evidence of two or more registered medical practitioners, at least one of whom is approved as having special experience in the diagnosis or treatment of mental disorder. Under section 4A, if satisfied that the defendant did the act or made the omission charged as an offence the jury must make a finding to that effect, and if not so satisfied must acquit the defendant.]

Evidence of a witness in person **R25.11**

25.11 (1) This rule applies where a party wants to introduce evidence by calling a witness to give that evidence in person.
(2) Unless the court otherwise directs—
(a) a witness waiting to give evidence must not wait inside the courtroom, unless that witness is—
(i) a party, or
(ii) an expert witness;
(b) a witness who gives evidence in the courtroom must do so from the place provided for that purpose; and
(c) a witness' address—
(i) must not be given in public unless the address is relevant to an issue in the case, and
(ii) may be given in writing to the court, parties and jury.
(3) Unless other legislation otherwise provides, before giving evidence a witness must take an oath or affirm.
(4) In the following sequence—
(a) the party who calls a witness may ask questions in examination-in-chief;
(b) if the witness gives evidence for the prosecution—
(i) the defendant, if there is only one, may ask questions in cross-examination, or
(ii) subject to the court's directions, each defendant, if there is more than one, may ask such questions, in the order their names appear in the indictment or as directed by the court;
(c) if the witness gives evidence for a defendant—
(i) subject to the court's directions, each other defendant, if there is more than one, may ask questions in cross-examination, in the order their names appear in the indictment or as directed by the court, and
(ii) the prosecutor may ask such questions; and
(d) the party who called the witness may ask questions in re-examination arising out of any cross-examination.
(5) If other legislation so permits, at any time while giving evidence a witness may refer to a record of that witness' recollection of events.
(6) The court may—
(a) ask a witness questions; and in particular

[25] 1964 c. 84; sections 4 and 4A were substituted for section 4 as originally enacted by section 2 of the Criminal Procedure (Insanity and Unfitness to Plead) Act 1991 (c. 25), and amended by section 22 of the Domestic Violence, Crime and Victims Act 2004 (c. 28).

(b) where the defendant is not represented, ask a witness any question necessary in the defendant's interests.

[Note. Section 53 of the Youth Justice and Criminal Evidence Act 1999[26] *provides that everyone is competent to give evidence in criminal proceedings unless unable to understand questions put or give intelligible answers. See also section 1 of the Criminal Evidence Act 1898*[27].

Sections 1, 3, 5 and 6 of the Oaths Act 1978[28] *provide for the taking of oaths and the making of affirmations, and for the words that must be used. Section 28 of the Children and Young Persons Act 1963*[29] *provides that in a youth court, and where a witness in any court is under 18, an oath must include the words 'I promise' in place of the words 'I swear'. Under sections 55 and 56 of the Youth Justice and Criminal Evidence Act 1999, a person may give evidence without taking an oath, or making an affirmation, where that person (i) is under 14 or (ii) has an insufficient appreciation of the solemnity of the occasion and of the particular responsibility to tell the truth which is involved in taking an oath.*

The questions that may be put to a witness—

(a) by a party are governed by rules of evidence, for example—
(i) the rule that a question must be relevant to what is in issue,
(ii) the rule that the party who calls a witness must not ask that witness a leading question about what is in dispute, and
(iii) the rule that a party who calls a witness may contradict that witness only in limited circumstances (see section 3 of the Criminal Procedure Act 1865)[30]*;*
(b) by the court are in its discretion, but that is subject to—
(i) rules of evidence, and
(ii) rule 1.3 (the application by the court of the overriding objective).

Under sections 34, 35 and 36 of the Youth Justice and Criminal Evidence Act 1999[31]*, a defendant who is not represented may not cross-examine a witness where—*

(a) the defendant is charged with a sexual offence against the witness;
(b) the defendant is charged with a sexual offence, or one of certain other offences, and the witness is a child; or
(c) the court prohibits the defendant from cross-examining the witness.

Part 23 contains rules relevant to restrictions on cross-examination.

Under section 139 of the Criminal Justice Act 2003[32]*, a witness may refresh his or her memory by referring to a record made earlier, either contained in a document made or verified by the witness, or in the transcript of a sound recording, if—*

(a) the witness states that it records his or her recollection of events at that earlier time; and
(b) that recollection is likely to have been significantly better when the record was made than by the time the witness gives evidence in person.

In some circumstances, a witness may give evidence in accordance with special measures directed by the court under section 19 of the Youth Justice and Criminal Evidence Act 1999[33]*, or by live link under section 32 of the Criminal Justice Act 1988*[34] *or section 51 of the Criminal Justice Act 2003. Part 18 contains relevant rules.]*

[26] 1999 c. 23.
[27] 1898 c. 36; section 1 was amended by section 1 of the Criminal Evidence Act 1979 (c. 16), section 78 of, and Schedule 16 to, the Criminal Justice Act 1982 (c. 48), sections 80(9) and 119(2) of, and Schedule 7 to, the Police and Criminal Evidence Act 1984 (c. 60), sections 31 and 168 of, and paragraph 2 of Schedule 10, and Schedule 11 to, the Criminal Justice and Public Order Act 1994 (c. 33), section 67 of, and paragraph 1 of Schedule 4, and Schedule 6 to, the Youth Justice and Criminal Evidence Act 1999 (c. 23) and sections 331 and 332 of, and paragraph 80 of Schedule 36, and Part 5 of Schedule 37 to, the Criminal Justice Act 2003 (c. 44).
[28] 1978 c. 19.
[29] 1963 c. 37; section 28 was amended by section 2 of the Oaths Act 1978 (c. 19) and section 100 of, and paragraph 40 of Schedule 11 to, the Criminal Justice Act 1991 (c. 53).
[30] 1865 c. 18.
[31] 1999 c. 23; section 35 was amended by sections 139 and 140 of, and paragraph 41 of Schedule 6 and Schedule 7 to, the Sexual Offences Act 2003 (c. 42) and section 148 of, and paragraphs 35 and 36 of Schedule 26 to, the Criminal Justice and Immigration Act 2008 (c. 4).
[32] 2003 c. 44.
[33] 1999 c. 23.
[34] 1988 c. 33; section 32 was amended by section 55 of the Criminal Justice Act 1991 (c. 53), section 29 of, and paragraph 16 of Schedule 2 to, the Criminal Appeal Act 1995 (c. 35), section 62 of the Criminal Procedure and Investigations Act 1996 (c. 25), section 67 of, and Schedule 6 and paragraph 3 of Schedule 7 to, the Youth Justice and Criminal Evidence Act 1999 (c. 23) and paragraphs 24 and 26 of the Schedule to S.I. 2004/2035.

Evidence of a witness in writing R25.12

25.12 (1) This rule applies where a party wants to introduce in evidence the written statement of a witness to which applies—
(a) Part 16 (Written witness statements);
(b) Part 19 (Expert evidence); or
(c) Part 20 (Hearsay evidence).
(2) If the court admits such evidence each relevant part of the statement must be read or summarised aloud, unless the court otherwise directs.

[Note. See Parts 16, 19 and 20, and the other legislation to which those Parts apply. The admissibility of evidence that a party introduces is governed by rules of evidence.

A written witness statement to which Part 16 applies may only be introduced in evidence if there has been no objection within the time limit to which rule 16.4 refers.

An expert report to which Part 19 applies may only be introduced in evidence if it has been served in accordance with rule 19.3.

Rule 20.3 provides for opposing the introduction of hearsay evidence, including such evidence in a document.

Where a witness gives evidence in person, a previous written statement by that witness may be admissible as evidence under section 119 (Inconsistent statements) or under section 120 (Other previous statements of witnesses) of the Criminal Justice Act 2003.]

Evidence by admission R25.13

25.13 (1) This rule applies where—
(a) a party introduces in evidence a fact admitted by another party; or
(b) parties jointly admit a fact.
(2) Unless the court otherwise directs, a written record must be made of the admission.

[Note. See section 10 of the Criminal Justice Act 1967[35]*. The admissibility of evidence that a party introduces is governed by rules of evidence.]*

Directions to the jury and taking the verdict R25.14

25.14 (1) This rule applies where there is a jury.
(2) The court must give the jury directions about the relevant law at any time at which to do so will assist jurors to evaluate the evidence.
(3) After following the sequence in rule 25.9 (Procedure on plea of not guilty), the court must—
(a) summarise for the jury, to such extent as is necessary, the evidence relevant to the issues they must decide;
(b) give the jury such questions, if any, as the court invites jurors to answer in coming to a verdict;
(c) direct the jury to retire to consider its verdict;
(d) if necessary, recall the jury
(i) to answer jurors' questions, or
(ii) to give directions, or further directions, about considering and delivering its verdict or verdicts, including, if appropriate, directions about reaching a verdict by a majority;
(e) in a case in which the jury is required to return a single verdict—
(i) recall the jury (unless already recalled) when it informs the court that it has reached its verdict, and
(ii) direct the delivery of that verdict there and then;
(f) in a case in which the jury is required to return two or more verdicts—
(i) recall the jury (unless already recalled) when it informs the court that it has reached a verdict or verdicts, and
(ii) ask the jury whether its members all agree on every verdict required;
(g) if the answer to that question is 'yes', direct the delivery of each of those verdicts there and then; and
(h) if the answer to that question is 'no'—
(i) direct the delivery there and then of any unanimous verdict that has been reached, or
(ii) postpone the taking of any such verdict while the jury considers each other verdict required.
(4) The court may give the jury directions, questions or other assistance in writing.

[35] 1967 c. 80.

(5) When the court directs the jury to deliver its verdict or verdicts, the court must ask the foreman chosen by the jury, in respect of each count—
(a) whether the jury has reached a verdict on which all the jurors agree;
(b) if so, whether that verdict is guilty or not guilty;
(c) if not, where the jury has deliberated for at least 2 hours and if the court decides to invite a majority verdict, then—
(i) whether at least 10 (of 11 or 12 jurors), or 9 (of 10 jurors), agreed on a verdict,
(ii) if so, is that verdict guilty or not guilty, and
(iii) if (and only if) such a verdict is guilty, how many jurors agreed to that verdict and how many disagreed.

(6) Where evidence has been given that the defendant was insane, so as not to be responsible for the act or omission charged as the offence, then under paragraph (5)(b) the court must ask whether the jury's verdict is guilty, not guilty, or not guilty by reason of insanity.

[Note. Under section 17 of the Juries Act 1974[36]*, the court may accept the verdict of a majority, as long as the jury has had at least 2 hours for deliberation.*

Under section 6 of the Criminal Law Act 1967, the jury may convict a defendant of an offence other than one charged by the indictment if that offence is proved by the evidence.

The verdict to which rule 25.14(6) refers is provided for by section 2 of the Trial of Lunatics Act 1883[37]*. The evidence required before such a verdict may be reached is prescribed by section 1 of the Criminal Procedure (Insanity and Unfitness to Plead) Act 1991*[38]*.]*

R25.15 **Conviction or acquittal without a jury**

25.15 (1) This rule applies where—
(a) the court tries the case without a jury; and
(b) after following the sequence in rule 25.9 (Procedure on plea of not guilty).

(2) In respect of each count, the court must give reasons for its decision to convict or acquit.

[Note. Under sections 44 and 46 of the Criminal Justice Act 2003[39]*, the court may try a case without a jury where there is a danger of jury tampering, or where jury tampering appears to have taken place. Under section 17 of the Domestic Violence, Crime and Victims Act 2004*[40]*, the court may try sample counts with a jury and other counts without a jury. Part 3 (preparation for trial in the Crown Court) contains rules about an application for such a trial.]*

R25.16 **Procedure if the court convicts**

25.16 (1) This rule applies where, in respect of any count in the indictment—
(a) the defendant pleads guilty; or
(b) the court convicts the defendant.

(2) The court may exercise its power—
(a) if the defendant is an individual—
(i) to require a pre-sentence report,
(ii) to commission a medical report,
(iii) to require a statement of the defendant's assets and other financial circumstances;
(b) if the defendant is a corporation, to require such information as the court directs about the defendant's corporate structure and financial resources;
(c) to adjourn sentence pending—
(i) receipt of any such report, statement or information,
(ii) the verdict in a related case.

(3) The prosecutor must—
(a) summarise the prosecution case, if the sentencing court has not heard evidence;
(b) identify in writing any offence that the prosecutor proposes should be taken into consideration in sentencing;
(c) provide information relevant to sentence, including—
(i) any previous conviction of the defendant, and the circumstances where relevant,
(ii) any statement of the effect of the offence on the victim, the victim's family or others; and

[36] 1974 c. 23.
[37] 1883 c. 38; section 2 was amended by section 17 of, and Schedule 2 to, the Criminal Lunatics Act 1884 (c. 64) and sections 1 and 8 of the Criminal Procedure (Insanity) Act 1964 (c. 84).
[38] 1991 c. 25.
[39] 2003 c. 44.
[40] 2004 c. 28.

(d) identify any other matter relevant to sentence, including—
(i) the legislation applicable,
(ii) any sentencing guidelines, or guideline cases,
(iii) aggravating and mitigating features affecting the defendant's culpability and the harm which the offence caused, was intended to cause or might forseeably have caused, and
(iv) the effect of such of the information listed in paragraph (2) as the court may need to take into account.

(4) Where the defendant pleads guilty, the court may give directions for determining the facts on the basis of which sentence must be passed if—
(a) the defendant wants to be sentenced on a basis agreed with the prosecutor; or
(b) in the absence of such agreement, the defendant wants to be sentenced on the basis of different facts to those disclosed by the prosecution case.

(5) Where the court has power to order the endorsement of the defendant's driving record, or power to order the defendant to be disqualified from driving—
(a) if other legislation so permits, a defendant who wants the court not to exercise that power must introduce the evidence or information on which the defendant relies;
(b) the prosecutor may introduce evidence; and
(c) the parties may make representations about that evidence or information.

(6) Before passing sentence—
(a) the court must give the defendant an opportunity to make representations and introduce evidence relevant to sentence;
(b) where the defendant is under 18, the court may give the defendant's parents, guardian or other supporting adult, if present, such an opportunity as well; and
(c) if the court requires more information, it may exercise its power to adjourn the hearing.

(7) When the court has taken into account all the evidence, information and any report available, the court must—
(a) as a general rule, pass sentence at the earliest opportunity;
(b) when passing sentence—
(i) explain the reasons,
(ii) explain to the defendant its effect, the consequences of failing to comply with any order or pay any fine, and any power that the court has to vary or review the sentence, unless the defendant is absent or the defendant's ill-health or disorderly conduct makes such an explanation impracticable, and
(iii) give any such explanation in terms the defendant, if present, can understand (with help, if necessary); and
(c) deal with confiscation, costs and any behaviour order.

(8) The general rule is subject to the court's power to defer sentence for up to 6 months.

[Note. See sections 31, 52, 59, 63, 124, 125 and 126 of the Sentencing Act 2020.

Under sections 57D and 57E of the Crime and Disorder Act 1998[41]*, the court may require a defendant to attend a sentencing hearing by live link.*

Under section 30 of the Sentencing Act 2020, the general rule (subject to exceptions) is that the court must obtain and consider a pre-sentence report—

(a) where it is considering a custodial sentence or a community sentence;
(b) where it thinks the defendant may pose a significant risk of causing serious harm to the public by further offending.

Under section 32(3) of the Sentencing Act 2020, where the court obtains a written pre-sentence report about a defendant who is under 18, it may direct that information in it must be withheld, if it would be likely to create a risk of significant harm to the defendant.

Rule 28.8 of these Rules applies to commissions for medical reports.

Under section 35 of the Sentencing Act 2020, the court may require a defendant who is an individual to provide a statement of assets and other financial circumstances if the defendant is convicted.

[41] 1998 c. 37; sections 57A to 57E were substituted for section 57 as originally enacted by section 45 of the Police and Justice Act 2006 (c. 48), and amended by sections 106, 109 and 178 of, and Part 3 of Schedule 23 to, the Coroners and Justice Act 2009 (c. 25). Section 57A was further amended by paragraphs 36 and 39 of Schedule 12 to the Legal Aid, Sentencing and Punishment of Offenders Act 2012 (c. 10).

Under section 20A of the Criminal Justice Act 1991[42], it is an offence for a defendant knowingly or recklessly to make a false or incomplete statement of assets or other financial circumstances, or to fail to provide such a statement, in response to a request by a court officer on behalf of the court.

The Sentencing Council may issue sentencing guidelines under section 120 of the Coroners and Justice Act 2009[43].

For the circumstances in which a court may (and, in some cases, must) order the endorsement of a defendant's driving record, or the disqualification of a defendant from driving, see sections 34, 35 and 44 of the Road Traffic Offenders Act 1988[44]. Under that legislation, in some circumstances the court has discretion not to make such an order. See also rule 29.1.

The evidence that may be introduced is subject to rules of evidence.

In addition to the specific powers to which this rule applies, the court has a general power to adjourn a trial: see rule 25.2.

Part 28 contains rules about sentencing procedure in special cases. Part 31 contains rules about behaviour orders. Part 33 contains rules about confiscation and related orders. Part 45 contains rules about costs.

Under section 3 of the Sentencing Act 2020[45], if (among other things) the defendant consents, the court may defer sentence for up to 6 months, for the purpose of allowing it to take account of the defendant's conduct after conviction, or any change in the defendant's circumstances.]

R25.17 **Provision of documents for the court**

25.17 (1) Unless the court otherwise directs, a party who introduces a document in evidence, or who otherwise uses a document in presenting that party's case, must provide a copy for—
(a) each other party;
(b) any witness that party wants to refer to the document; and
(c) the court.

(2) If the court so directs, a party who introduces or uses a document for such a purpose must provide a copy for the jury.

(3) Unless the court otherwise directs, on application or on its own initiative, the court officer must provide for the court—
(a) any copy received under paragraph (1) before the trial begins; and
(b) a copy of the court officer's record of—
(i) information supplied by each party for the purposes of case management, including any revision of information previously supplied,
(ii) each pre-trial direction for the management of the case,
(iii) any pre-trial decision to admit evidence,
(iv) any pre-trial direction about the giving of evidence, and
(v) any admission to which rule 25.13 (Evidence by admission) applies; and
(c) any other document served on the court officer for the use of the court.

R25.18 **Duty of court officer and custodian**

25.18 (1) The court officer must—
(a) serve on each party notice of where and when an adjourned hearing will resume, unless that party was present when that was arranged;
(b) if the reason for the adjournment was to postpone sentence, include that reason in any such notice to the defendant;

[42] 1991 c. 53; section 20A was inserted by section 168 of, and paragraph 43 of Schedule 9 to, the Criminal Justice and Public Order Act 1994 (c. 33) and amended by sections 95 and 109 of, and paragraph 350 of Schedule 8 to, the Courts Act 2003 (c. 39) and section 44 of, and paragraph 26 of Schedule 16 to, the Crime and Courts Act 2013 (c. 22).
[43] 2009 c. 25.
[44] 1988 c. 53; section 34 was amended by section 29 of the Road Traffic Act 1991 (c. 40), section 3 of the Aggravated Vehicle-Taking Act 1992 (c. 11), section 165 of, and paragraph 121 of Schedule 9 to, the Powers of Criminal Courts (Sentencing) Act 2000 (c. 6), sections 56 and 107 of, and Schedule 8 to, the Police Reform Act 2002 (c. 30), section 25 of the Road Safety Act 2006 (c. 49), article 2 of S.I. 2007/3480, paragraphs 2 and 5 of Schedule 27 to the Legal Aid, Sentencing and Punishment of Offenders Act 2012 (c. 10), section 56 of, and paragraphs 9 and 12 of Schedule 22 to, the Crime and Courts Act 2013 (c. 22) and section 177 of, and paragraph 90 of Schedule 21 to, the Coroners and Justice Act 2009 (c. 25). Section 35 was amended by section 48 of, and paragraph 95 of Schedule 4 to, the Road Traffic Act 1991 (c. 40), section 165 of, and paragraph 122 of Schedule 9 to, the Powers of Criminal Courts (Sentencing) Act 2000 (c. 6) and section 177 of, and 90 of Schedule 21 to, the Coroners and Justice Act 2009 (c. 25). Section 44 was amended by regulations 2 and 3 of, and paragraph 10 of Schedule 2 to, S.I. 1990/144 and sections 9, 10 and 59 of, and Schedule 7 to, the Road Safety Act 2006 (c. 49).
[45] 2000 c. 6; section 1 was substituted, together with sections 1A to 1D, for this section by section 278 of, and paragraph 1 of Schedule 23 to, the Criminal Justice Act 2003 (c. 44).

(c) unless the court otherwise directs, make available to the parties any written report to which rule 25.16(2) applies (pre-sentence and medical reports);
(d) where the court has ordered a defendant to provide information under section 25 of the Road Traffic Offenders Act 1988[46], serve on the defendant notice of that order unless the defendant was present when it was made;
(e) give the court such other assistance as it requires, including—
(i) selecting jurors from the panel summoned by the Lord Chancellor, under rule 25.6 (Selecting the jury),
(ii) taking the oaths or affirmations of jurors and witnesses, under rules 25.6 and 25.11 (Evidence of a witness in person),
(iii) informing the jurors of the offence or offences charged in the indictment, and of their duty, under rule 25.9 (Procedure on plea of not guilty),
(iv) recording the date and time at which the court gives the jury oral directions under rule 25.14(2) (directions about the law),
(v) recording the date and time at which the court gives the jury any written directions, questions or other assistance under rule 25.14(4), and
(vi) asking the jury foreman to deliver the verdict, under rule 25.14(5).

(2) Where the court passes a sentence of immediate imprisonment or detention, or orders a suspended sentence of imprisonment to take effect, by this rule—
(a) the court requires the defendant to provide, in writing or orally, his or her nationality; and
(b) the custodian must obtain that information and record it

[Note. See also section 82 of the Senior Courts Act 1981[47] (Duties of officers of Crown Court).

Under Part 5, the court officer must—

(a) record details of a case and of the court's decisions; and
(b) give public notice of specified details about a trial, including by such arrangements as the Lord Chancellor directs.

Under section 25 of the Road Traffic Offenders Act 1988, where the court does not know a defendant's sex or date of birth, then on convicting the defendant of an offence involving obligatory or discretionary disqualification, the court must order the defendant to provide that information.

Under section 86A of the Courts Act 2003, Criminal Procedure Rules must specify stages of proceedings at which the court must require the information to which rule 25.18(2) refers. A person commits an offence if, without reasonable excuse, that person fails to comply with such a requirement, whether by providing false or incomplete information or by providing no information.]

Criminal Practice Directions Part 25 Trial and Sentence in the Crown Court

CPD VI Trial 25A: Identification for the Jury of the Issues in the Case CPD.25A

25A.1 CrimPR 3.11(a) requires the court, with the active assistance of the parties, to establish what are the disputed issues in order to manage the trial. To that end, prosecution opening speeches are invaluable. They set out for the jury the principal issues in the trial, and the evidence which is to be introduced in support of the prosecution case. They should clarify, not obfuscate. The purpose of the prosecution opening is to help the jury understand what the case concerns, not necessarily to present a detailed account of all the prosecution evidence due to be introduced.

25A.2 CrimPR 25.9(2)(c) provides for a defendant, or his or her advocate, to set out the issues in the defendant's own terms (subject to superintendence by the court), immediately after the prosecution opening. Any such identification of issues at this stage is not to be treated as a substitute for or extension of the summary of the defence case which can be given later, under CrimPR 25.9(2)(g). Its purpose is to provide the jury with focus as to the issues that they are likely to be called upon to decide, so that jurors will be alert to those issues from the outset and can evaluate the prosecution evidence that they hear accordingly. For that purpose, the defendant is not confined to what is included in the defence statement (though any divergence from the defence statement will expose the defendant to adverse comment or inference), and for the defendant to

[46] 1988 c. 53; section 25 was amended by section 90 of, and paragraphs 140 and 142 of Schedule 13 to, the Access to Justice Act 1999 (c. 22), section 165 of, and paragraph 118 of Schedule 9 to, the Powers of Criminal Courts (Sentencing) Act 2000 (c. 6) and section 109 of, and paragraph 311 of Schedule 8 to, the Courts Act 2003 (c. 39).
[47] 1981 c. 54; section 82 was amended by section 15 of, and paragraphs 114 and 135 of Schedule 4 to, the Constitutional Reform Act 2005 (c. 4) and sections 116 and 178 of, and Part 3 of Schedule 3 to, the Coroners and Justice Act 2009 (c. 25).

take the opportunity at this stage to identify the issues may assist even if all he or she wishes to announce is that the prosecution is being put to proof.

25A.3 To identify the issues for the jury at this stage also provides an opportunity for the judge to give appropriate directions about the law; for example, as to what features of the prosecution evidence they should look out for in a case in which what is in issue is the identification of the defendant by an eye-witness. Giving such directions at the outset is another means by which the jury can be helped to focus on the significant features of the evidence, in the interests of a fair and effective trial.

25A.4 A defendant is not entitled to identify issues at this stage by addressing the jury unless the court invites him or her to do so. Given the advantages described above, usually the court should extend such an invitation but there may be circumstances in which, in the court's judgment, it furthers the overriding objective not to do so. Potential reasons for denying the defendant the opportunity at this stage to address the jury about the issues include (i) that the case is such that the issues are apparent; (ii) that the prosecutor has given a fair, accurate and comprehensive account of the issues in opening, rendering repetition superfluous; and (iii) where the defendant is not represented, that there is a risk of the defendant, at this early stage, inflicting injustice on him or herself by making assertions to the jury to such an extent, or in such a manner, as is unfairly detrimental to his or her subsequent standing.

25A.5 Whether or not there is to be a defence identification of issues, and, if there is, in what manner and in what terms it is to be presented to the jury, are questions that must be resolved in the absence of the jury and that should be addressed at the opening of the trial.

25A.6 Even if invited to identify the issues by addressing the jury, the defendant is not obliged to accept the invitation. However, where the court decides that it is important for the jury to be made aware of what the defendant has declared to be in issue in the defence statement then the court may require the jury to be supplied with copies of the defence statement, edited at the court's direction if necessary, in accordance with section 6E(4) of the Criminal Procedure and Investigations Act 1996.

CPD.25B **CPD VI Trial 25B: Trial Adjournment in the Crown Court**

25B.1 A defendant has a right, in general, to be present and to be represented at his trial. However, a defendant may choose not to exercise those rights, such as by voluntarily absenting himself and failing to instruct his lawyers adequately so that they can represent him.

25B.2 The court has a discretion as to whether a trial should take place or continue in the defendant's absence and must exercise its discretion with due regard for the interests of justice. The overriding concern must be to ensure that such a trial is as fair as circumstances permit and leads to a just outcome. If the defendant's absence is due to involuntary illness or incapacity it would very rarely be right to exercise the discretion in favour of commencing or continuing the trial.

25B.3 Proceeding in the absence of a defendant is a step which ought normally to be taken only if it is unavoidable. The court must exercise its discretion as to whether a trial should take place or continue in the defendant's absence with the utmost care and caution. Due regard should be had to the judgment of Lord Bingham in *R v Jones (Anthony William)* [2002] UKHL 5, [2003] 1 A.C. 1, [2002] 2 Cr. App. R. 9. Circumstances to be taken into account before proceeding include:

i) the conduct of the defendant,
ii) the disadvantage to the defendant,
iii) the public interest, taking account of the inconvenience and hardship to witnesses, and especially to any complainant, of a delay; if the witnesses have attended court and are ready to give evidence, that will weigh in favour of continuing with the trial,
iv) the effect of any delay,
v) whether the attendance of the defendant could be secured at a later hearing, and
vii) the likely outcome if the defendant is found guilty.

Even if the defendant is voluntarily absent, it is still generally desirable that he or she is represented.

Criminal Procedure Rules Part 26 Jurors

R26.1 **Appeal against officer's refusal to excuse or postpone jury service**

26.1 (1) This rule applies where a person summoned for jury service in the Crown Court, the High Court or the county court wants to appeal against a refusal by an officer on the Lord Chancellor's behalf—

(a) to excuse that person from such service; or
(b) to postpone the date on which that person is required to attend for such service.

(2) The appellant must appeal to the court to which the appellant has been summoned.

(3) The appellant must—
(a) apply in writing, as soon as reasonably practicable; and
(b) serve the application on the court officer.

(4) The application must—
(a) attach a copy of—
(i) the jury summons, and
(ii) the refusal to excuse or postpone which is under appeal; and
(b) explain why the court should excuse the appellant from jury service, or postpone its date, as appropriate.

(5) The court to which the appeal is made—
(a) may extend the time for appealing, and may allow the appeal to be made orally;
(b) may determine the appeal at a hearing in public or in private, or without a hearing;
(c) may adjourn any hearing of the appeal; but
(d) must not determine an appeal unless the appellant has had a reasonable opportunity to make representations in person.

[Note. See sections 9 and 9A of the Juries Act 1974[1]*.*

Where a person summoned for jury service—

(a) fails to attend as required; or
(b) after attending as required, when selected under rule 25.6—
(i) is not available, or
(ii) is unfit for jury service by reason of drink or drugs

that conduct may be punished as if it were a contempt of court. See section 20 of the Juries Act 1974 and rules 48.5 to 48.8 (contempt of court). The maximum penalty which the court can impose is a fine of £1,000.]

Excusal from jury service by court **R26.2**

26.2 At any time before a juror completes the oath or affirmation, the court may exercise its power to excuse him or her from jury service for lack of capacity to act effectively as a juror because of an insufficient understanding of English—
(a) on the court's own initiative, or where the court officer refers the juror to the court; and
(b) after enquiry of the juror.

[Note. See section 10 of the Juries Act 1974[2]*.]*

Provision of information for jurors **R26.3**

26.3 The court officer must arrange for each juror to receive—
(a) by such means as the Lord Chancellor directs, general information about jury service and about a juror's responsibilities;
(b) written notice of the prohibitions against—
(i) research by a juror into the case,
(ii) disclosure by a juror of any such research to another juror during the trial,
(iii) conduct by a juror which suggests that that juror intends to try the case otherwise than on the evidence, and
(iv) disclosure by a juror of the deliberations of the jury; and
(c) written warning that breach of those prohibitions is an offence, for which the penalty is imprisonment or a fine or both, and may be a contempt of court.

[Note. See sections 20A, 20B, 20C and 20D of the Juries Act 1974[3]*.*

The Practice Direction sets out a form of notice for use in connection with this rule.]

Assessment of juror's availability for long trial, etc. **R26.4**

26.4 (1) The court may invite each member of a panel of jurors to provide such information, by such means and at such a time as the court directs, about—
(a) that juror's availability to try a case expected to last for longer than the juror had expected to serve; and

[1] 1974 c. 23; section 9 was amended by paragraphs 1, 3, 4, 5 and 6 of Schedule 33, and Part 10 of Schedule 37, to the Criminal Justice Act 2003 (c. 44) and paragraph 172 of Schedule 8 to the Courts Act 2003 (c. 39). Section 9A was inserted by section 120 of the Criminal Justice Act 1988 (c. 33) and amended by paragraphs 1, 7, 8, 9, 10 and 11 of Schedule 33 to the Criminal Justice Act 2003 (c. 44) and paragraph 172 of Schedule 8 to the Courts Act 2003 (c. 39).

[2] 1974 c. 23; section 10 was amended by section 168 of, and Schedule 11 to, the Criminal Justice and Public Order Act 1994 (c. 33) and sections 65 and 109 of, and paragraph 4 of Schedule 4 and Schedule 10 to, the Courts Act 2003 (c. 39).

[3] 1974 c. 23; sections 20A, 20B, 20C and 20D were inserted by sections 71, 72, 73 and 74 respectively of the Criminal Justice and Courts Act 2015 (c. 2).

(b) any association of that juror with, or any knowledge by that juror of—
(i) a party or witness, or
(ii) any other person, or any place, of significance to the case.

(2) Where jurors provide information under this rule, the court may postpone the selection of the jury to try a case to allow each juror an opportunity to review and amend that information before that selection.

(3) Using that information, the court may exercise its power to excuse a juror from selection as a member of the jury to try a case, but the court must not—
(a) excuse a juror without allowing the parties an opportunity to make representations; or
(b) refuse to excuse a juror without allowing that juror such an opportunity.

R26.5 **Surrender of electronic communication devices by jurors**

26.5 (1) This rule applies where the court can order the members of a jury to surrender for a specified period any electronic communication devices that they possess.

(2) The court may make such an order—
(a) on application; or
(b) on its own initiative.

(3) A party who wants the court to make such an order must—
(a) apply as soon as reasonably practicable;
(b) notify each other party;
(c) specify for what period any device should be surrendered; and
(d) explain why—
(i) the proposed order is necessary or expedient in the interest of justice, and
(ii) the terms of the proposed order are a proportionate means of safeguarding those interests.

[Note. See section 15A of the Juries Act 1974[4].]

CRIMINAL PRACTICE DIRECTIONS PART 26 JURORS

CPD.26A **CPD VI Trial 26A: Juries: introduction**

26A.1 Jury service is an important public duty which individual members of the public are chosen at random to undertake. As the Court has acknowledged: 'Jury service is not easy; it never has been. It involves a major civic responsibility' (*R v Thompson* [2010] EWCA Crim 1623, [9] per Lord Judge CJ, [2011] 1 WLR 200, [2010] 2 Cr App R 27).

Provision of information to prospective jurors

26A.2 HMCTS provide every person summoned as a juror with information about the role and responsibilities of a juror. Prospective jurors are provided with a pamphlet, 'Your Guide to Jury Service', and may also view the film 'Your Role as a Juror' online at any time on the Ministry of Justice YouTube site www.youtube.com/watch?v=JP7slp-X9Pc. There is also information at https://www.gov.uk/jury-service/overview

CPD.26B **CPD VI Trial 26B: Juries: Preliminary Matters Arising before Jury Service Commences**

26B.1 The effect of section 321 of the Criminal Justice Act 2003 was to remove certain categories of persons from those previously ineligible for jury service (the judiciary and others concerned with the administration of justice) and certain other categories ceased to be eligible for excusal as of right, (such as members of Parliament and medical professionals). The normal presumption is that everyone, unless ineligible or disqualified, will be required to serve when summoned to do so.

Excusal and deferral

26B.2 The jury summoning officer is empowered to defer or excuse individuals in appropriate circumstances and in accordance with the HMCTS *Guidance for summoning officers when considering deferral and excusal applications* (2009): https://assets.publishing.service.gov.uk/government/uploads/system/uploads/attachment_data/file/228867/9780108508400.pdf

Appeals from officer's refusal to excuse or postpone jury service

26B.3 CrimPR 26.1 governs the procedure for a person's appeal against a summoning officer's decision in relation to excusal or deferral of jury service.

Provision of information at court

26B.4 The court officer is expected to provide relevant further information to jurors on their arrival in the court centre.

[4] 1974 c. 23; section 15A was inserted by section 69 of the Criminal Justice and Courts Act 2015 (c. 2).

CPD VI Trial 26C: Juries: Eligibility CPD.26C

English language ability

26C.1 Under the Juries Act 1974 section 10, a person summoned for jury service who applies for excusal on the grounds of insufficient understanding of English may, where necessary, be brought before the judge.

26C.2 The court may exercise its power to excuse any person from jury service for lack of capacity to act effectively as a juror because of an insufficient understanding of English.

26C.3 The judge has the discretion to stand down jurors who are not competent to serve by reason of a personal disability: *R v Mason* [1981] QB 881, (1980) 71 Cr App R 157; *R v Jalil* [2008] EWCA Crim 2910, [2009] 2 Cr App R (S.) 40.

Jurors with professional and public service commitments

26C.4 The legislative change in the Criminal Justice Act 2003 means that more individuals are eligible to serve as jurors, including those previously excused as of right or ineligible. Judges need to be vigilant to the need to exercise their discretion to adjourn a trial, excuse or discharge a juror should the need arise.

26C.5 Whether or not an application has already been made to the jury summoning officer for deferral or excusal, it is also open to the person summoned to apply to the court to be excused. Such applications must be considered with common sense and according to the interests of justice. An explanation should be required for an application being much later than necessary.

Serving police officers, prison officers or employees of prosecuting agencies

26C.6 A judge should always be made aware at the stage of jury selection if any juror in waiting is in these categories. The juror summons warns jurors in these categories that they will need to alert court staff.

26C.7 In the case of police officers an inquiry by the judge will have to be made to assess whether a police officer may serve as a juror. Regard should be had to: whether evidence from the police is in dispute in the case and the extent to which that dispute involves allegations made against the police; whether the potential juror knows or has worked with the officers involved in the case; whether the potential juror has served or continues to serve in the same police units within the force as those dealing with the investigation of the case or is likely to have a shared local service background with police witnesses in a trial.

26C.8 In the case of a serving prison officer summoned to a court, the judge will need to inquire whether the individual is employed at a prison linked to that court or is likely to have special knowledge of any person involved in a trial.

26C.9 The judge will need to ensure that employees of prosecuting authorities do not serve on a trial prosecuted by the prosecuting authority by which they are employed. They can serve on a trial prosecuted by another prosecuting authority: *R v Abdroikov* [2007] UKHL 37, [2007] 1 WLR 2679, [2008] 1 Cr App R 21; *Hanif v UK* [2011] ECHR 2247, (2012) 55 EHRR 16; *R v L* [2011] EWCA Crim 65, [2011] 1 Cr App R 27. Similarly, a serving police officer can serve where there is no particular link between the court and the station where the police officer serves.

26C.10 Potential jurors falling into these categories should be excused from jury service unless there is a suitable alternative court/trial to which they can be transferred.

CPD VI Trial 26D: Juries: Precautionary Measures before Swearing CPD.26D

26D.1 There should be a consultation with the advocates as to the questions, if any, it may be appropriate to ask potential jurors. Topics to be considered include:

a. the availability of jurors for the duration of a trial that is likely to run beyond the usual period for which jurors are summoned;
b. whether any juror knows the defendant or parties to the case;
c. whether potential jurors are so familiar with any locations that feature in the case that they may have, or come to have, access to information not in evidence;
d. in cases where there has been any significant local or national publicity, whether any questions should be asked of potential jurors.

26D.2 Judges should however exercise caution. At common law a judge has a residual discretion to discharge a particular juror who ought not to be serving, but this discretion can only be exercised to prevent an individual juror who is not competent from serving. It does not include a discretion to discharge a jury drawn from particular sections of the community or otherwise to influence the overall composition of the jury. However, if there is a risk that there is widespread local knowledge of the defendant or a witness in a particular case, the judge may, after hearing submissions from the advocates, decide to exclude jurors from particular areas to avoid the risk of jurors having or acquiring personal knowledge of the defendant or a witness.

Length of trial

26D.3 Where the length of the trial is estimated to be significantly longer than the normal period of jury service, it is good practice for the trial judge to enquire whether the potential jurors on the jury panel foresee any difficulties with the length and if the judge is satisfied that the jurors' concerns are justified, he may say that they are not required for that particular jury. This does not mean that the judge must excuse the juror from sitting at that court altogether, as it may well be possible for the juror to sit on a shorter trial at the same court.

Juror with potential connection to the case or parties

26D.4 Where a juror appears on a jury panel, it will be appropriate for a judge to excuse the juror from that particular case where the potential juror is personally concerned with the facts of the particular case, or is closely connected with a prospective witness. Judges need to exercise due caution as noted above.

CPD.26E **CPD VI Trial 26E: Juries: Swearing in Jurors**

Swearing Jury for trial

26E.1 All jurors shall be sworn or affirm. All jurors shall take the oath or affirmation in open court in the presence of one another. If, as a result of the juror's delivery of the oath or affirmation, a judge has concerns that a juror has such difficulties with language comprehension or reading ability that might affect that juror's capacity to undertake his or her duties, bearing in mind the likely evidence in the trial, the judge should make appropriate inquiry of that juror.

Form of oath or affirmation

26E.2 Each juror should have the opportunity to indicate to the court the Holy Book on which he or she wishes to swear. The precise wording will depend on his or her faith as indicated to the court.

26E.3 Any person who prefers to affirm shall be permitted to make a solemn affirmation instead. The wording of the affirmation is: 'I do solemnly, sincerely and truly declare and affirm that I will faithfully try the defendant and give a true verdict according to the evidence'.

CPD.26F **CPD VI Trial 26F: Juries: Ensuring an effective jury panel**

Adequacy of numbers

26F.1 By section 6 of the Juries Act 1974, if it appears to the court that a jury to try any issue before the court will be, or probably will be, incomplete, the court may, if the court thinks fit, require any persons who are in, or in the vicinity of, the court, to be summoned (without any written notice) for jury service up to the number needed (after allowing for any who may not be qualified under section 1 of the Act, and for excusals and challenges) to make up a full jury.

CPD.26G **CPD VI Trial 26G: Juries: Preliminary Instructions to Jurors**

26G.1 After the jury has been sworn and the defendant has been put in charge the judge will want to give directions to the jury on a number of matters.

26G.2 Jurors can be expected to follow the instructions diligently. As the Privy Council stated in *Taylor* [2013] UKPC 8, [2013] 1 WLR 1144:

> The assumption must be that the jury understood and followed the direction that they were given: … the experience of trial judges is that juries perform their duty according to law. … [T]he law proceeds on the footing that the jury, acting in accordance with the instructions given to them by the trial judge, will render a true verdict in accordance with the evidence. To conclude otherwise would be to underrate the integrity of the system of trial by jury and the effect on the jury of the instructions by the trial judge.

At the start of the trial

26G.3 Trial judges should instruct the jury on general matters which will include the time estimate for the trial and normal sitting hours. The jury will always need clear guidance on the following:

i. The need to try the case only on the evidence and remain faithful to their oath or affirmation;
ii. The prohibition on internet searches for matters related to the trial, issues arising or the parties;
iii. The importance of not discussing any aspect of the case with anyone outside their own number or allowing anyone to talk to them about it, whether directly, by telephone, through internet facilities such as Facebook or Twitter or in any other way;
iv. The importance of taking no account of any media reports about the case;
v. The collective responsibility of the jury. As the Lord Chief Justice made clear in *R v Thompson and Others* [2010] EWCA Crim 1623, [2011] 1 WLR 200, [2010] 2 Cr App R 27:
[T]here is a collective responsibility for ensuring that the conduct of each member is consistent with the jury oath and that the directions of the trial judge about the

discharge of their responsibilities are followed.... The collective responsibility of the jury for its own conduct must be regarded as an integral part of the trial itself.

vi. The need to bring any concerns, including concerns about the conduct of other jurors, to the attention of the judge at the time, and not to wait until the case is concluded. The point should be made that, unless that is done while the case is continuing, it may not be possible to deal with the problem at all.

Subsequent reminder of the jury instructions

26G.4 Judges should consider reminding jurors of these instructions as appropriate at the end of each day and in particular when they separate after retirement.

26G.5 Following the judge's direction to the jury, each member of the jury must be provided with a copy of the notice 'Your Legal Responsibilities as a Juror'. This notice outlines what is required of the juror during and after their time on the jury. It is not a substitute for the judge's direction, but is designed to reinforce what the judge has outlined in the direction. The court clerk should ensure a record is made of service of the notice. Jurors are advised to keep their copy of the notice with their summons and at the end of the trial, they are allowed to retain it for future information.

CPD VI Trial 26H: Juries: Discharge of a juror for personal reasons CPD.26H

26H.1 Where a juror unexpectedly finds him or herself in difficult professional or personal circumstances during the course of the trial, the juror should be encouraged to raise such problems with the trial judge. This might apply, for example, to a parent whose childcare arrangements unexpectedly fail, or a worker who is engaged in the provision of services the need for which can be critical, or a Member of Parliament who has deferred their jury service to an apparently more convenient time, but is unexpectedly called back to work for a very important reason. Such difficulties would normally be raised through a jury note in the normal manner.

26H.2 In such circumstances, the judge must exercise his or her discretion according to the interests of justice and the requirements of each individual case. The judge must decide for him or herself whether the juror has presented a sufficient reason to interfere with the course of the trial. If the juror has presented a sufficient reason, in longer trials it may well be possible to adjourn for a short period in order to allow the juror to overcome the difficulty.

26H.3 In shorter cases, it may be more appropriate to discharge the juror and to continue the trial with a reduced number of jurors. The power to do this is implicit in section 16(1) of the Juries Act 1974. In unusual cases (such as an unexpected emergency arising overnight) a juror need not be discharged in open court. The good administration of justice depends on the co-operation of jurors, who perform an essential public service. All such applications should be dealt with sensitively and sympathetically and the trial judge should always seek to meet the interests of justice without unduly inconveniencing any juror.

CPD VI Trial 26J: Juries: Views CPD.26J

26J.1 In each case in which it is necessary for the jury to view a location, the judge should produce ground rules for the view, after discussion with the advocates. The rules should contain details of what the jury will be shown and in what order and who, if anyone, will be permitted to speak and what will be said. The rules should also make provision for the jury to ask questions and receive a response from the judge, following submissions from the advocates, while the view is taking place.

CPD VI Trial 26K: Juries: Directions, Written Materials and Summing Up CPD.26K

Overview

26K.1 Sir Brian Leveson's *Review of Efficiency in Criminal Proceedings 2015* contained recommendations to improve the efficiency of jury trials including:

- Early provision of appropriate directions;
- Provision of a written route to verdict;
- Provision of a split summing up (a summing up delivered in two parts – the first part prior to the closing speeches and the second part afterwards); and
- Streamlining the summing up to help the jury focus on the issues.

The purpose of this practice direction, and the associated criminal procedure rules, is to give effect to these recommendations.

Record-keeping

26K.2 Full and accurate record-keeping is essential to enable the Registrar of Criminal Appeals to obtain transcripts in the event of an application or appeal to the Court of Appeal (Criminal Division).

26K.3 A court officer is required to record the date and time at which the court provides directions and written materials (CrimPR 25.18(e)(iv)–(v)).

26K.4 The judge should ensure that a court officer (such as a court clerk or usher) is present in court to record the information listed in paragraph 26K.5.

26K.5 A court officer should clearly record the:

- Date, time and subject of submissions and rulings relating to directions and written materials;
- Date, time and subject of directions and written materials provided prior to the summing up; and
- Date and time of the summing up, including both parts of a split summing up.

26K.6 A court officer should retain a copy of written materials on the court file or database.

26K.7 The parties should also record the information listed in paragraph 26K.5 and retain a copy of written materials. Where relevant to a subsequent application or appeal to the Court of Appeal (Criminal Division), the information listed in paragraph 26K.5 should be provided in the notice of appeal, and any written materials should be identified.

Early provision of appropriate directions

26K.8 The court is required to provide directions about the relevant law at any time that will assist the jury to evaluate the evidence (CrimPR 25.14(2)). The judge may provide an early direction prior to any evidence being called, prior to the evidence to which it relates or shortly thereafter.

26K.9 Where the judge decides it will assist the jury in:

- their approach to the evidence; and / or
- evaluating the evidence as they hear it

an early direction should be provided.

26K.10 For example:

- Where identification is in issue, an early *Turnbull* direction is likely to assist the jury in approaching the evidence with the requisite caution; and by having the relevant considerations in mind when listening to the evidence.
- Where special measures are to be used and / or ground rules will restrict the manner and scope of questioning, an early explanation may assist the jury in their approach to the evidence.
- An early direction may also assist the jury, by having the relevant approach, considerations and / or test in mind, when listening to:
  - Expert witnesses; and
  - Evidence of bad character;
  - Hearsay;
  - Interviews of co-defendants; and
  - Evidence involving legal concepts such as knowledge, dishonesty, consent, recklessness, conspiracy, joint enterprise, attempt, self-defence, excessive force, voluntary intoxication and duress.

Written route to verdict

26K.11 A route to verdict, which poses a series of questions that lead the jury to the appropriate verdict, may be provided by the court (CrimPR 25.14(3)(b)). Each question should tailor the law to the issues and evidence in the case.

26K.12 Save where the case is so straightforward that it would be superfluous to do so, the judge should provide a written route to verdict. It may be presented (on paper or digitally) in the form of text, bullet points, a flowchart or other graphic.

Other written materials

26K.13 Where the judge decides it will assist the jury, written materials should be provided. They may be presented (on paper or digitally) in the form of text, bullet points, a table, a flowchart or other graphic.

26K.14 For example, written materials may assist the jury in relation to a complex direction or where the case involves:

- A complex chronology;
- Competing expert evidence; or
- Differing descriptions of a suspect.

26K.15 Such written materials may be prepared by the judge or the parties at the direction of the judge. Where prepared by the parties at the direction of the judge, they will be subject to the judge's approval.

Split summing up and provision of appropriate directions prior to closing speeches

26K.16 Where the judge decides it will assist the jury when listening to the closing speeches, a split summing up should be provided. For example, the provision of appropriate directions prior to the closing speeches may avoid repetitious explanations of the law by the advocates.

26K.17 By way of illustration, such directions may include:

- Functions of the judge and jury;
- Burden and standard of proof;
- Separate consideration of counts;
- Separate consideration of defendants;
- Elements of offence(s);
- Defence(s);
- Route to verdict;
- Circumstantial evidence; and
- Inferences from silence.

Closing speeches

26K.18 The advocates closing speeches should be consistent with any directions and route to verdict already provided by the judge.

Summing up

26K.19 Prior to beginning or resuming the summing up at the conclusion of the closing speeches, the judge should briefly list (without repeating) any directions provided earlier in the trial. The purpose of this requirement is to provide a definitive account of all directions for the benefit of the Registrar of Criminal Appeals and the Court of Appeal (Criminal Division), in the event of an application or appeal.

26K.20 The court is required to summarise the evidence relevant to the issues to such extent as is necessary (CrimPR 25.14(3)(a)).

26K.21 To assist the jury to focus on the issues during retirement, save where the case is so straightforward that it would be superfluous to do so, the judge should provide:

- A reminder of the issues;
- A summary of the nature of the evidence relating to each issue;
- A balanced account of the points raised by the parties; and
- Any outstanding directions.

It is not necessary for the judge to recount all relevant evidence or to rehearse all of the significant points raised by the parties.

26K.22 At the conclusion of the summing up, the judge should provide final directions to the jury on the need:

- For unanimity (in respect of each count and defendant, where relevant);
- To dismiss any thoughts of majority verdicts until further direction; and
- To select a juror to chair their discussions and speak on their behalf to the court.

CPD VI Trial 26L: Juries: Jury access to exhibits and evidence in retirement **CPD.26L**

26L.1 At the end of the summing up it is also important that the judge informs the jury that any exhibits they wish to have will be made available to them.

26L.2 Judges should invite submissions from the advocates as to what material the jury should retire with and what material before them should be removed, such as the transcript of an ABE interview (which should usually be removed from the jury as soon as the recording has been played.)

26L.3 Judges will also need to inform the jury of the opportunity to view certain audio, DVD or CCTV evidence that has been played (excluding, for example ABE interviews). If possible, it may be appropriate for the jury to be able to view any such material in the jury room alone, such as on a sterile laptop, so that they can discuss it freely; this will be a matter for the judge's discretion, following discussion with counsel.

CPD VI Trial 26M: Juries: Jury Irregularities **CPD.26M**

26M.1 This practice direction replaces the protocol regarding jury irregularities issued by the President of the Queen's Bench Division in November 2012, and the subsequent practice direction, in light of sections 20A to 20D of the Juries Act 1974 and the associated repeal of section 8 of the Contempt of Court Act 1981 (confidentiality of jury's deliberations).

It applies to juries sworn on or after 13 April 2015.

26M.2 A jury irregularity is anything that may prevent one or more jurors from remaining faithful to their oath or affirmation to 'faithfully try the defendant and give a true verdict according to the evidence.' Jury irregularities take many forms. Some are clear-cut such as a juror conducting research about the case or an attempt to suborn or intimidate a juror. Others are less clear-cut — for example, when there is potential bias or friction between jurors.

26M.3 A jury irregularity may involve contempt of court and / or the commission of an offence by or in relation to a juror.

26M.4 Under the previous version of this practice direction, the Crown Court required approval from the Vice-President of the Court of Appeal (Criminal Division) (CACD) prior to providing a juror's details to the police for the purposes of an investigation into a jury irregularity. Such approval is no longer required. Provision of a juror's details to the police is now a matter for the Crown Court.

Jury Irregularity During Trial

26M.5 A jury irregularity that comes to light during a trial may impact on the conduct of the trial. It may also involve contempt of court and / or the commission of an offence by or in relation to a juror. **The primary concern of the judge should be the impact on the trial.**

26M.6 A jury irregularity should be drawn to the attention of the judge in the absence of the jury as soon as it becomes known.

26M.7 **When the judge becomes aware of a jury irregularity, the judge should follow the procedure set out below:**

STEP 1: **Consider isolating juror(s)**
STEP 2: **Consult with advocates**
STEP 3: **Consider appropriate provisional measures (which may include surrender / seizure of electronic communications devices and taking defendant into custody)**
STEP 4: **Seek to establish basic facts of jury irregularity**
STEP 5: **Further consult with advocates**
STEP 6: **Decide what to do in relation to conduct of trial**
STEP 7: **Consider ancillary matters (contempt in face of court and / or commission of criminal offence)**

STEP 1: Consider isolating juror(s)

26M.8 The judge should consider whether the juror(s) concerned should be isolated from the rest of the jury, particularly if the juror(s) may have conducted research about the case.

26M.9 If two or more jurors are concerned, the judge should consider whether they should also be isolated from each other, particularly if one juror has made an accusation against another.

STEP 2: Consult with advocates

26M.10 The judge should consult with the advocates and invite submissions about appropriate provisional measures (Step 3) and how to go about establishing the basic facts of the jury irregularity (Step 4).

26M.11 The consultation should be conducted

— in open court;
— in the presence of the defendant; and
— with all parties represented

unless there is good reason not to do so.

26M.12 If the jury irregularity involves a suspicion about the conduct of the defendant or another party, there may be good reason for the consultation to take place in the absence of the defendant or the other party. There may also be good reason for it to take place in private. If so, the proper location is in the court room, with DARTS recording, rather than in the judge's room.

26M.13 If the jury irregularity relates to the jury's deliberations, the judge should warn all those present that it is an offence to disclose, solicit or obtain information about a jury's deliberations (section 20D(1) of the Juries Act 1974 — see 26M.35 to 26M.38 regarding the offence and exceptions). This would include disclosing information about the jury's deliberations divulged in court during consultation with the advocates (Step 2 and Step 5) or when seeking to establish the basic facts of the jury irregularity (Step 4). The judge should emphasise that the advocates, court staff and those in the public gallery would commit the offence by explaining to another what is said in court about the jury's deliberations.

STEP 3: Consider appropriate provisional measures

26M.14 **The judge should consider appropriate provisional measures which may include surrender / seizure of electronic communications devices and taking the defendant into custody.**

Surrender / seizure of electronic communications devices

26M.15 The judge should consider whether to make an order under section 15A(1) of the Juries Act 1974 requiring the juror(s) concerned to surrender electronic communications devices, such as mobile telephones or smart phones.

26M.16 Having made an order for surrender, the judge may require a court security officer to search a juror to determine whether the juror has complied with the order. Section 54A of the Courts Act 2003 contains the court security officer's powers of search and seizure.

26M.17 Section 15A(5) of the Juries Act 1974 provides that it is contempt of court for a juror to fail to surrender an electronic communications device in accordance with an order for surrender (see paragraphs 26M.29 to 26M.30 regarding the procedure for dealing with such a contempt).

26M.18 Any electronic communications device surrendered or seized under these provisions should be kept safe by the court until returned to the juror or handed to the police as evidence.

Taking defendant into custody

26M.19 If the defendant is on bail, and the jury irregularity involves a suspicion about the defendant's conduct, the judge should consider taking the defendant into custody. If that suspicion involves an attempt to suborn or intimidate a juror, the defendant should be taken into custody.

STEP 4: SEEK TO ESTABLISH BASIC FACTS OF JURY IRREGULARITY

26M.20 The judge should seek to establish the basic facts of the jury irregularity for the purpose of determining how to proceed in relation to the conduct of the trial. The judge's enquiries may involve having the juror(s) concerned write a note of explanation and / or questioning the juror(s). The judge may enquire whether the juror(s) feel able to continue and remain faithful to their oath or affirmation. If there is questioning, each juror should be questioned separately, in the absence of the rest of the jury, unless there is good reason not to do so.

26M.21 In accordance with paragraphs 26M.10 to 26M.13, the enquiries should be conducted in open court; in the presence of the defendant; and with all parties represented unless there is good reason not to do so.

STEP 5: FURTHER CONSULT WITH ADVOCATES

26M.22 The judge should further consult with the advocates and invite submissions about how to proceed in relation to the conduct of the trial and what should be said to the jury (Step 6).

26M.23 In accordance with paragraphs 26M.10 to 26M.13, the consultation should be conducted in open court; in the presence of the defendant; and with all parties represented unless there is good reason not to do so.

STEP 6: DECIDE WHAT TO DO IN RELATION TO CONDUCT OF TRIAL

26M.24 When deciding how to proceed, the judge may take time to reflect.

26M.25 Considerations may include the stage the trial has reached. The judge should be alert to attempts by the defendant or others to thwart the trial. In cases of potential bias, the judge should consider whether a fair minded and informed observer would conclude that there was a real possibility that the juror(s) or jury would be biased (*Porter v Magill* [2001] UKHL 67, [2002] 2 AC 357).

26M.26 **In relation to the conduct of the trial, there are three possibilities:**

1. ***Take no action and continue with the trial***
   If so, the judge should consider what, if anything, to say to the jury. For example, the judge may reassure the jury nothing untoward has happened or remind them their verdict is a decision of the whole jury and that they should try to work together. Anything said should be tailored to the circumstances of the case.
2. ***Discharge the juror(s) concerned and continue with the trial***
   If so, the judge should consider what to say to the discharged juror(s) and the jurors who remain. All jurors should be warned not to discuss what has happened.
3. ***Discharge the whole jury***
   If so, the judge should consider what to say to the jury and they should be warned not to discuss what has happened.
   If the judge is satisfied that jury tampering has taken place, depending on the circumstances, the judge may continue the trial without a jury (section 46(3) of the Criminal Justice Act 2003) or order a new trial without a jury (section 46(5) of the Criminal Justice Act 2003). Alternatively, the judge may re-list the trial. If there is a real and present danger of jury tampering in the new trial, the prosecution may apply for a trial without a jury (section 44 of the Criminal Justice Act 2003).

STEP 7: Consider ancillary matters

26M.27 **A jury irregularity may also involve contempt in the face of the court and / or the commission of a criminal offence. The possibilities include the following:**

— **Contempt in the face of the court by a juror**

— **An offence by a juror or a non-juror under the Juries Act 1974**

Offences that may be committed by jurors are researching the case, sharing research, engaging in prohibited conduct or disclosing information about the jury's deliberations (sections 20A to 20D of the Juries Act 1974). Non-jurors may commit the offence of disclosing, soliciting or obtaining information about the jury's deliberations (section 20D of the Juries Act 1974).

— **An offence by juror or a non-juror other than under the Juries Act 1974** A juror may commit an offence such as assault or theft. A non-juror may commit an offence in relation to a juror such as attempting to pervert the course of justice — for example, if the defendant or another attempts to suborn or intimidate a juror.

Contempt in the face of the court by a juror

26M.28 If a juror commits contempt in the face of the court, the juror's conduct may also constitute an offence. If so, the judge should decide whether to deal with the juror summarily under the procedure for contempt in the face of the court or refer the matter to the Attorney General's Office or the police (see paragraphs 26M.31 and 26M.33).

26M.29 In the case of a *minor and clear* contempt in the face of the court, the judge may deal with the juror summarily. The judge should follow the procedure in CrimPR 48.5 to 48.8. The judge should also have regard to the practice direction regarding contempt of court issued in March 2015 (Practice Direction: Committal for Contempt of Court — Open Court), which emphasises the principle of open justice in relation to proceedings for contempt before all courts.

26M.30 If a juror fails to comply with an order for surrender of an electronic communications device (see paragraphs 26M.15 to 26M.18), the judge should deal with the juror summarily following the procedure for contempt in the face of the court.

Offence by a juror or non-juror under the Juries Act 1974

26M.31 If it appears that an offence under the Juries Act 1974 may have been committed by a juror or non-juror (and the matter has not been dealt with summarily under the procedure for contempt in the face of the court), **the judge** should contact the Attorney General's Office to consider a police investigation, setting out the position neutrally. The officer in the case should not be asked to investigate.

Contact details for the Attorney General's Office are set out at the end of this practice direction.

26M.32 If relevant to an investigation, any electronic communications device surrendered or seized pursuant to an order for surrender should be passed to the police as soon as practicable.

Offence by a juror or non-juror other than under the Juries Act 1974

26M.33 If it appears that an offence, other than an offence under the Juries Act 1974, may have been committed by a juror or non-juror (and the matter has not been dealt with summarily under the procedure for contempt in the face of the court), **the judge or a member of court staff** should contact the police setting out the position neutrally. The officer in the case should not be asked to investigate.

26M.34 If relevant to an investigation, any electronic communications device surrendered or seized pursuant to an order for surrender should be passed to the police as soon as practicable.

Other matters to consider

Jury deliberations

26M.35 **In light of the offence of disclosing, soliciting or obtaining information about a jury's deliberations (section 20D(1) of the Juries Act 1974), great care is required if a jury irregularity relates to the jury's deliberations.**

26M.36 *During the trial,* there are exceptions to this offence that enable the judge (and only the judge) to:

— Seek to establish the basic facts of a jury irregularity involving the jury's deliberations (Step 4); and

— Disclose information about the jury's deliberations to the Attorney General's Office if it appears that an offence may have been committed (Step 7).

26M.37 With regard to seeking to establish the basic facts of a jury irregularity involving the jury's deliberations (Step 4), it is to be noted that during the trial it is not an offence for the judge to disclose, solicit or obtain information about the jury's deliberations for the purposes of dealing with the case (sections 20E(2)(a) and 20G(1) of the Juries Act 1974).

26M.38 With regard to disclosing information about the jury's deliberations to the Attorney General's Office if it appears that an offence may have been committed (Step 7), it is to be noted that during the trial:

— It is not an offence for the judge to disclose information about the jury's deliberations for the purposes of an investigation by a relevant investigator into whether an offence or contempt of court has been committed by or in relation to a juror (section 20E(2)(b) of the Juries Act 1974); and

— A relevant investigator means a police force or the Attorney General (section 20E(5) of the Juries Act 1974).

Minimum number of jurors

26M.39 If it is decided to discharge one or more jurors (Step 6), a minimum of nine jurors must remain if the trial is to continue (section 16(1) of the Juries Act 1974).

Preparation of statement by judge

26M.40 If a jury irregularity occurs, and the trial continues, the judge should have regard to the remarks of Lord Hope in *R v Connors and Mirza* [2004] UKHL 2 at [127] and [128], [2004] 1 AC 1118, [2004] 2 Cr App R 8 and consider whether to prepare a statement that could be used in an application for leave to appeal or an appeal relating to the jury irregularity.

Jury Irregularity After Jury Discharged

26M.41 A jury irregularity that comes to light after the jury has been discharged may involve the commission of an offence by or in relation to a juror. It may also provide a ground of appeal.

26M.42 **A jury irregularity after the jury has been discharged may come to the attention of the:**

— **Trial judge or court**

— **Registrar of Criminal Appeals (the Registrar)**

— **Prosecution**

— **Defence**

Role of the trial judge or court

26M.43 The judge has no jurisdiction in relation to a jury irregularity that comes to light after the jury has been discharged (*R v Thompson and others* [2010] EWCA Crim 1623, [2011] 1 WLR 200, [2010] 2 Cr App R 27A). The jury will be deemed to have been discharged when all verdicts on all defendants have been delivered or when the jury has been discharged from giving all verdicts on all defendants.

26M.44 The judge will be *functus officio* in relation to a jury irregularity that comes to light during an adjournment between verdict and sentence. The judge should proceed to sentence unless there is good reason not to do so.

26M.45 In practice, a jury irregularity often comes to light when the judge or court receives a communication from a former juror.

26M.46 If a jury irregularity comes to the attention of a judge or court after the jury has been discharged, and regardless of the result of the trial, the judge or a member of court staff should contact the Registrar setting out the position neutrally. Any communication from a former juror should be forwarded to the Registrar.

Contact details for the Registrar are set out at the end of this practice direction.

Role of the Registrar

26M.47 If a jury irregularity comes to the attention of the Registrar after the jury has been discharged, and regardless of the result of the trial, the Registrar should consider if it appears that an offence may have been committed by or in relation to a juror. The Registrar should also consider if there may be a ground of appeal.

26M.48 When deciding how to proceed, particularly in relation to a communication from a former juror, the Registrar may seek the direction of the Vice-President of the Court of Appeal (Criminal Division) (CACD) or another judge of the CACD in accordance with instructions from the Vice-President.

26M.49 If it appears that an offence may have been committed by or in relation to a juror, the Registrar should contact the Private Office of the Director of Public Prosecutions to consider a police investigation.

26M.50 If there may be a ground of appeal, the Registrar should inform the defence.

26M.51 If a communication from a former juror is not of legal significance, the Registrar should respond explaining that no action is required. An example of such a communication is if it is restricted to a general complaint about the verdict from a dissenting juror or an expression of doubt or second thoughts.

Role of the prosecution

26M.52 If a jury irregularity comes to the attention of the prosecution after the jury has been discharged, which may provide a ground of appeal, they should notify the defence in accordance with their duties to act fairly and assist in the administration of justice (*R v Makin* [2004] EWCA Crim 1607, 148 SJLB 821).

Role of the defence

26M.53 If a jury irregularity comes to the attention of the defence after the jury has been discharged, which provides an arguable ground of appeal, an application for leave to appeal may be made.

Other matters to consider

Jury deliberations

26M.54 **In light of the offence of disclosing, soliciting or obtaining information about a jury's deliberations (section 20D(1) of the Juries Act 1974), great care is required if a jury irregularity relates to the jury's deliberations.**

26M.55 *After the jury has been discharged,* there are exceptions to this offence that enable a judge, a member of court staff, the Registrar, the prosecution and the defence to disclose information about the jury's deliberations if it appears that an offence may have been committed by or in relation to a juror or if there may be a ground of appeal.

26M.56 For example, it is to be noted that:

— After the jury has been discharged, it is not an offence for a person to disclose information about the jury's deliberations to defined persons if the person reasonably believes that an offence or contempt of court may have been committed by or in relation to a juror or the conduct of a juror may provide grounds of appeal (section 20F(1) (2) of the Juries Act 1974).

— The defined persons to whom such information may be disclosed are a member of a police force, a judge of the CACD, the Registrar of Criminal Appeals (the Registrar), a judge where the trial took place or a member of court staff where the trial took place who would reasonably be expected to disclose the information only to one of the aforementioned defined persons (section 20F(2) of the Juries Act 1974).

— After the jury has been discharged, it is not an offence for a judge of the CACD or the Registrar to disclose information about the jury's deliberations for the purposes of an investigation by a relevant investigator into whether an offence or contempt of court has been committed by or in relation to a juror or the conduct of a juror may provide grounds of appeal (section 20F(4) of the Juries Act 1974).

— A relevant investigator means a police force, the Attorney General, the Criminal Cases Review Commission (CCRC) or the Crown Prosecution Service (section 20F(10) of the Juries Act 1974).

Investigation by the Criminal Cases Review Commission (CCRC)

26M.57 If an application for leave to appeal, or an appeal, includes a ground of appeal relating to a jury irregularity, the Registrar may refer the case to the Full Court to decide whether to direct the CCRC to conduct an investigation under section 23A of the Criminal Appeal Act 1968.

26M.58 If the Court directs the CCRC to conduct an investigation, directions should be given as to the scope of the investigation.

Contact Details

Attorney General's Office

Contempt.SharedMailbox@attorneygeneral.gsi.gov.uk

Telephone: 020 7271 2492

The Registrar

penny.donnelly@hmcts.x.gsi.gov.uk (Secretary) or

criminalappealoffice.generaloffice@hmcts.gsi.gov.uk

Telephone: 020 7947 6103 (Secretary) or 020 7947 6011

CPD.26N **CPD VI Trial 26N: Open Justice**

26N.1 There must be freedom of access between advocate and judge. Any discussion must, however, be between the judge and the advocates on both sides. If an advocate is instructed by a solicitor who is in court, he or she, too, should be allowed to attend the discussion. This freedom of access is important because there may be matters calling for communication or discussion of such a nature that the advocate cannot, in the client's interest, mention them in open court, e.g. the advocate, by way of mitigation, may wish to tell the judge that reliable medical evidence shows that the defendant is suffering from a terminal illness and may not have long to live. It is imperative that, so far as possible, justice must be administered in open court. Advocates should, therefore, only ask to see the judge when it is felt to be really necessary. The judge must be careful only to treat such communications as private where, in the interests of justice, this is necessary. Where any such discussion takes place it should be recorded, preferably by audio recording.

CPD VI Trial 26P: Defendant's Right to Give or Not to Give Evidence **CPD.26P**

26P.1 At the conclusion of the evidence for the prosecution, section 35(2) of the Criminal Justice and Public Order Act 1994 requires the court to satisfy itself that the defendant is aware that the stage has been reached at which evidence can be given for the defence and that the defendant's failure to give evidence, or if he does so his failure to answer questions, without a good reason, may lead to inferences being drawn against him.

If the defendant is legally represented

26P.2 After the close of the prosecution case, if the defendant's representative requests a brief adjournment to advise his client on this issue the request should, ordinarily, be granted. When appropriate the judge should, in the presence of the jury, inquire of the representative in these terms:

> '*Have you advised your client that the stage has now been reached at which he may give evidence and, if he chooses not to do so or, having been sworn, without good cause refuses to answer any question, the jury may draw such inferences as appear proper from his failure to do so?*'

26P.3 If the representative replies to the judge that the defendant has been so advised, then the case shall proceed. If counsel replies that the defendant has not been so advised, then the judge shall direct the representative to advise his client of the consequences and should adjourn briefly for this purpose, before proceeding further.

If the defendant is not legally represented

26P.4 If the defendant is not represented, the judge shall, at the conclusion of the evidence for the prosecution, in the absence of the jury, indicate what he will say to him in the presence of the jury and ask if he understands and whether he would like a brief adjournment to consider his position.

26P.5 When appropriate, and in the presence of the jury, the judge should say to the defendant:

> '*Now is your chance to give evidence if you choose to do so. If you do give evidence it will be on oath [or affirmation], and you will be cross-examined like any other witness. If you do not give evidence the jury may hold it against you. If you do give evidence but refuse without good reason to answer the questions the jury may, as I have just explained, hold that against you. Do you now intend to give evidence?*'

CPD VI Trial 26Q: Majority Verdicts **CPD.26Q**

26Q.1 It is very important that all those trying indictable offences should, so far as possible, adopt a uniform practice when complying with section 17 of the Juries Act 1974, both in directing the jury in summing-up and also in receiving the verdict or giving further directions after retirement. So far as the summing-up is concerned, it is inadvisable for the judge, and indeed for advocates, to attempt an explanation of the section for fear that the jury will be confused. Before the jury retires, however, the judge should direct the jury in some such words as the following:

> '*As you may know, the law permits me, in certain circumstances, to accept a verdict which is not the verdict of you all. Those circumstances have not as yet arisen, so that when you retire I must ask you to reach a verdict upon which each one of you is agreed. Should, however, the time come when it is possible for me to accept a majority verdict, I will give you a further direction.*'

26Q.2 Thereafter, the practice should be as follows:
Should the jury return before two hours and ten minutes has elapsed since the last member of the jury left the jury box to go to the jury room (or such longer time as the judge thinks reasonable) (see section 17(4)), they should be asked:
(a) 'Have you reached a verdict upon which you are all agreed? Please answer "Yes" or "No".';
(b) (i) If unanimous, 'What is your verdict?';
 (ii) If not unanimous, the jury should be sent out again for further deliberation, with a further direction to arrive if possible at a unanimous verdict.

26Q.3 Should the jury return (whether for the first time or subsequently) or be sent for after the two hours and ten minutes (or the longer period) has elapsed, questions (a) and (b)(i) in the paragraph above should be put to them and, if it appears that they are not unanimous, they should be asked to retire once more and told they should continue to endeavour to reach a unanimous verdict but that, if they cannot, the judge will accept a majority verdict as in section 17(1).

26Q.4 When the jury finally return, they should be asked:
(a) 'Have at least ten (or nine as the case may be) of you agreed on your verdict?';
(b) If 'Yes', 'What is your verdict? Please only answer "Guilty" or "Not Guilty".';
(c) (i) If 'Not Guilty', accept the verdict without more ado;
(ii) If 'Guilty', 'Is that the verdict of you all, or by a majority?';
(d) If 'Guilty' by a majority, 'How many of you agreed to the verdict and how many dissented?'

26Q.5 At whatever stage the jury return, before question (a) is asked, the senior officer of the court present shall state in open court, for each period when the jury was out of court for the purpose of considering their verdict(s), the time at which the last member of the jury left the jury box to go to the jury room and the time of their return to the jury box; and will additionally state in open court the total of such periods.

26Q.6 The reason why section 17(3) is confined to a majority verdict of 'Guilty', and for the somewhat complicated procedure set out above, is to prevent it being known that a verdict of 'Not Guilty' is a majority verdict. If the final direction continues to require the jury to arrive, if possible, at a unanimous verdict and the verdict is received as specified, it will not be known for certain that the acquittal is not unanimous.

26Q.7 Where there are several counts (or alternative verdicts) left to the jury the above practice will, of course, need to be adapted to the circumstances. The procedure will have to be repeated in respect of each count (or alternative verdict), the verdict being accepted in those cases where the jury are unanimous and the further direction being given in cases in which they are not unanimous. The judge may exercise discretion in deciding when to record the unanimous verdict; the circumstances of the case may dictate that it is more desirable to give the majority direction before the recording of any unanimous verdicts. If so, then instead of being asked about each count in turn, the jury should be asked 'Have you reached verdicts upon which you are all agreed in respect of all defendants and/or all counts?'.

26Q.8 Should the jury in the end be unable to agree on a verdict by the required majority, the judge in his discretion will either ask them to deliberate further, or discharge them.

26Q.9 Section 17 will, of course, apply also to verdicts other than 'Guilty' or 'Not Guilty', e.g. to special verdicts under the Criminal Procedure (Insanity) Act 1964, following a finding by the judge that the defendant is unfit to be tried, and special verdicts on findings of fact. Accordingly, in such cases the questions to jurors will have to be suitably adjusted.

Criminal Procedure Rules Part 27 Retrial After Acquittal

General

R27.1 **When this Part applies**

27.1 (1) Rule 27.2 applies where, under section 54 of the Criminal Procedure and Investigations Act 1996[1], the Crown Court or a magistrates' court can certify for the High Court that interference or intimidation has been involved in proceedings leading to an acquittal.
(2) Rules 27.3 to 27.7 apply where, under section 77 of the Criminal Justice Act 2003[2], the Court of Appeal can—
(a) quash an acquittal for a serious offence and order a defendant to be retried; or
(b) order that an acquittal outside the United Kingdom is no bar to the defendant being tried in England and Wales,
if there is new and compelling evidence and it is in the interests of justice to make the order.

Application for certificate to allow order for retrial

R27.2 **Application for certificate**

27.2 (1) This rule applies where—
(a) a defendant has been acquitted of an offence;
(b) a person has been convicted of one of the following offences involving interference with or intimidation of a juror or a witness (or potential witness) in any proceedings which led to the defendant's acquittal—
(i) perverting the course of justice,
(ii) intimidation etc. of witnesses, jurors and others under section 51(1) of the Criminal Justice and Public Order Act 1994[3], or

[1] 1996 c. 25.
[2] 2003 c. 44.
[3] 1994 c. 33; section 51 was amended by section 29 of, and paragraph 19 of Schedule 2 to, the Criminal Appeal Act 1995 (c. 35), section 67 of, and paragraphs 21 and 22 of Schedule 4 to, the Youth Justice and Criminal Evidence Act 1999 (c. 23), paragraphs 62 and 64 of Schedule 36 to the Criminal Justice Act 2003 (c. 44), section 45 of, and paragraph 36 of Schedule 17

(iii) aiding, abetting, counselling, procuring, suborning or inciting another person to commit an offence under section 1 of the Perjury Act 1911[4]; and
(c) the prosecutor wants the court by which that person was convicted to certify for the High Court that there is a real possibility that, but for the interference or intimidation, the defendant would not have been acquitted.
(2) The prosecutor must—
(a) apply in writing as soon as practicable after that person's conviction; and
(b) serve the application on—
(i) the court officer, and
(ii) the defendant who was acquitted, if the court so directs.
(3) The application must—
(a) give details, with relevant facts and dates, of—
(i) the conviction for interference or intimidation, and
(ii) the defendant's acquittal; and
(b) explain—
(i) why there is a real possibility that, but for the interference or intimidation, the defendant would not have been acquitted, and
(ii) why it would not be contrary to the interests of justice to prosecute the defendant again for the offence of which he or she was acquitted, despite any lapse of time or other reason.
(4) The court may—
(a) extend the time limit under paragraph (2);
(b) allow an application to be in a different form to one set out in the Practice Direction, or to be made orally; and
(c) determine an application under this rule—
(i) at a hearing, in private or in public; or
(ii) without a hearing.
(5) If the court gives a certificate, the court officer must serve it on—
(a) the prosecutor; and
(b) the defendant who was acquitted.

[Note: See Section 54 of the Criminal Procedure and Investigations Act 1996 (Acquittals tainted by intimidation, etc.).

For the procedure on application to the High Court, see rules 77.6 to 77.15 of the Civil Procedure Rules 1998[5].]

Application to Court of Appeal to quash acquittal and order retrial

Application for reporting restriction pending application for order for retrial **R27.3**

27.3 (1) This rule applies where—
(a) no application has been made under rule 27.4 (Application for order for retrial);
(b) an investigation by officers has begun into an offence with a view to an application under that rule; and
(c) the Director of Public Prosecutions wants the Court of Appeal to make, vary or remove an order for a reporting restriction under section 82 of the Criminal Justice Act 2003 (Restrictions on publication in the interests of justice).
(2) The Director must—
(a) apply in writing; and
(b) serve the application on—
(i) the Registrar, and
(ii) the defendant, unless the court otherwise directs.
(3) The application must, as appropriate—
(a) explain why the Director wants the court to direct that it need not be served on the defendant until the application under rule 27.4 is served;
(b) specify the proposed terms of the order, and for how long it should last;
(c) explain why an order in the terms proposed is necessary; and
(d) explain why an order should be varied or removed.

to, the Crime and Courts Act 2013 (c. 22) and section 50 of, and paragraph 14 of Schedule 11 to, the Criminal Justice and Courts Act 2015 (c. 2). It is further amended by paragraph 11 of Schedule 36 to the Criminal Justice Act 2003 (c. 44), with effect from a date to be appointed.

4 1911 c.6.

5 S.I. 1998/3132; rules 77.6 to 77.15 were inserted by S.I. 2010/1953.

[Note: For other rules about reporting restrictions, see Part 6.]

R27.4 Application for order for retrial

27.4 (1) This rule applies where—
(a) a defendant has been acquitted—
(i) in the Crown Court, or on appeal from the Crown Court, of an offence listed in Part 1 of Schedule 5 to the Criminal Justice Act 2003[6] (qualifying offences), or
(ii) in proceedings elsewhere than in the United Kingdom of an offence under the law of that place, if what was alleged would have amounted to or included one of those listed offences; and
(b) with the Director of Public Prosecutions' written consent, a prosecutor wants the Court of Appeal to make an order, as the case may be—
(i) quashing the acquittal in the Crown Court and ordering the defendant to be retried for the offence, or
(ii) declaring whether the acquittal outside the United Kingdom is a bar to the defendant's trial in England and Wales and, if it is, whether that acquittal shall not be such a bar.

(2) Such a prosecutor must—
(a) apply in writing;
(b) serve the application on the Registrar; and
(c) not more than 2 business days later serve on the defendant who was acquitted—
(i) the application, and
(ii) a notice charging the defendant with the offence, unless the defendant has already been arrested and charged under section 87 of the Criminal Justice Act 2003[7] (arrest, under warrant or otherwise, and charge).

(3) The application must—
(a) give details, with relevant facts and dates, of the defendant's acquittal;
(b) explain—
(i) what new and compelling evidence there is against the defendant, and
(ii) why in all the circumstances it would be in the interests of justice for the court to make the order sought;
(c) include or attach any application for the following, with reasons—
(i) an order under section 80(6) of the Criminal Justice Act 2003[8] (Procedure and evidence) for the production of any document, exhibit or other thing which in the prosecutor's opinion is necessary for the determination of the application,
(ii) an order under that section for the attendance before the court of any witness who would be a compellable witness at the trial the prosecutor wants the court to order,
(iii) an order for a reporting restriction under section 82 of the Criminal Justice Act 2003[9] (Restrictions on publication in the interests of justice); and
(d) attach—
(i) written witness statements of the evidence on which the prosecutor relies as new and compelling evidence against the defendant,
(ii) relevant documents from the trial at which the defendant was acquitted, including a record of the offence or offences charged and of the evidence given, and
(iii) any other document or thing that the prosecutor thinks the court will need to decide the application.

[Note. See sections 75, 76, 77, 80 and 82 of the Criminal Justice Act 2003[10]. Under Part 1 of Schedule 5 to that Act, the qualifying offences include murder and other serious offences against the person, offences of importation and exportation of Class A drugs, offences of causing explosions and other serious damage, terrorism offences and war crimes and other international offences.

The time limit for serving an application on the defendant is prescribed by section 80(2) of the 2003 Act. It may be extended but not shortened.]

6 2003 c. 44; Part 1 of Schedule 5 was amended by section 26 of, and paragraph 3 of Schedule 2 to, the Corporate Manslaughter and Corporate Homicide Act 2007 (c. 19).
7 2003 c. 44.
8 2003 c. 44.
9 2003 c. 44.
10 2003 c. 44; section 76 was amended by S.I. 2012/1809.

Respondent's notice R27.5

27.5 (1) A defendant on whom a prosecutor serves an application may serve a respondent's notice, and must do so if the defendant wants to make representations to the court.

(2) Such a defendant must serve the respondent's notice on—
(a) the Registrar; and
(b) the prosecutor,
not more than 20 business days after service of the application.

(3) The respondent's notice must—
(a) give the date on which the respondent was served with the prosecutor's application;
(b) summarise any relevant facts not contained in that application;
(c) explain the defendant's grounds for opposing that application;
(d) include or attach any application for the following, with reasons—
(i) an extension of time within which to serve the respondent's notice,
(ii) bail pending the hearing of the prosecutor's application, if the defendant is in custody,
(iii) a direction to attend in person any hearing that the defendant could attend by live link, if the defendant is in custody,
(iv) an order under section 80(6) of the Criminal Justice Act 2003 (Procedure and evidence) for the production of any document, exhibit or other thing which in the defendant's opinion is necessary for the determination of the prosecutor's application, or
(v) an order under that section for the attendance before the court of any witness who would be a compellable witness at the trial the prosecutor wants the court to order; and
(e) attach or identify any other document or thing that the defendant thinks the court will need to decide the application.

Application to Crown Court for summons or warrant R27.6

27.6 (1) This rule applies where—
(a) the prosecutor has served on the Registrar an application under rule 27.4 (Application for order for retrial);
(b) the defendant is not in custody as a result of arrest under section 88 of the Criminal Justice Act 2003[11] (Bail and custody before application); and
(c) the prosecutor wants the Crown Court to issue—
(i) a summons requiring the defendant to appear before the Court of Appeal at the hearing of the prosecutor's application, or
(ii) a warrant for the defendant's arrest
under section 89 of the 2003 Act[12] (Bail and custody before hearing).

(2) The prosecutor must—
(a) apply in writing; and
(b) serve the application on the Crown Court officer.

(3) The application must—
(a) explain what the case is about, including a brief description of the defendant's acquittal, the new evidence and the stage that the application to the Court of Appeal has reached;
(b) specify—
(i) the decision that the prosecutor wants the Crown Court to make,
(ii) each offence charged, and
(iii) any relevant previous bail decision and the reasons given for it; and
(c) propose the terms of any suggested condition of bail.

[Note. Under section 87 of the Criminal Justice Act 2003[13], in the circumstances prescribed by that section a justice of the peace may issue a warrant for the arrest of the defendant who was acquitted and that defendant may be charged with an offence that is to be the subject of an application to the Court of Appeal under rule 27.4.

Under section 88 of the 2003 Act, in the circumstances prescribed by that section a defendant who has been arrested and charged must be brought before the Crown Court and that court must either grant bail for that defendant to attend the Court of Appeal on the hearing of an application under rule 27.4, or remand the defendant in custody.

[11] 2003 c. 44; section 88 is amended by section 148 of, and paragraphs 59 and 63 of Schedule 26 to, the Criminal Justice and Immigration Act 2008 (c. 4), with effect from a date to be appointed.
[12] 2003 c. 44.
[13] 2003 c. 44.

Under section 89 of the 2003 Act, where the prosecutor has made an application to the Court of Appeal under rule 27.4—

(a) if the defendant is in custody, the Crown Court must decide whether to remand him or her in custody to be brought before the Court of Appeal or to grant bail for that purpose; or

(b) if the defendant is not in custody, and if the prosecutor so applies, the Crown Court may either issue a summons for the defendant to attend the Court of Appeal or issue a warrant for the defendant's arrest.]

R27.7 **Application of other rules about procedure in the Court of Appeal**

27.7 On an application under rule 27.4 (Application for order for retrial)—

(a) the rules in Part 36 (Appeal to the Court of Appeal: general rules) apply with the necessary modifications;

(b) rules 39.8, 39.9 and 39.10 (bail and bail conditions in the Court of Appeal) apply as if the references in those rules to appeal included references to an application under rule 27.4; and

(c) rule 39.14 (Renewal or setting aside of order for retrial) applies as if the reference to section 7 of the Criminal Appeal Act 1968[14] were a reference to section 84 of the Criminal Justice Act 2003[15] (Retrial).

[Note. See also the notes to the rules listed in this rule.

For the powers of the Court of Appeal that may be exercised by one judge of that court or by the Registrar, and for the right to renew an application for directions to a judge or to the Court of Appeal, see the Criminal Justice Act 2003 (Retrial for Serious Offences) Order 2005[16] and rule 36.5 (Renewing an application refused by a judge or the Registrar).

For rules governing applications for reporting restrictions, see Part 6. For rules governing proceedings in the Crown Court about bail, see Part 14.]

Criminal Practice Directions: Sentencing

CPD.VII.A **CPD VII Sentencing A: Pleas of Guilty in the Crown Court**

A.1 Prosecutors and Prosecution Advocates should be familiar with and follow the Attorney-General's Guidelines on the Acceptance of Pleas and the Prosecutor's Role in the Sentencing Exercise.

CPD.VII.B **CPD VII Sentencing B: Determining the Factual Basis of Sentence**

Where a guilty plea is offered to less than the whole indictment and the prosecution is minded to accept pleas tendered to some counts or to lesser alternative counts.

B.1 In some cases, defendants wishing to plead guilty will simply plead guilty to all charges on the basis of the facts as alleged and opened by the prosecution, with no dispute as to the factual basis or the extent of offending. Alternatively a defendant may plead guilty to some of the charges brought; in such a case, the judge will consider whether that plea represents a proper plea on the basis of the facts set out by the papers.

B.2 Where the prosecution advocate is considering whether to accept a plea to a lesser charge, the advocate may invite the judge to approve the proposed course of action. In such circumstances, the advocate must abide by the decision of the judge.

B.3 If the prosecution advocate does not invite the judge to approve the acceptance by the prosecution of a lesser charge, it is open to the judge to express his or her dissent with the course proposed and invite the advocate to reconsider the matter with those instructing him or her.

B.4 In any proceedings where the judge is of the opinion that the course proposed by the advocate may lead to serious injustice, the proceedings may be adjourned to allow the following procedure to be followed:

(a) as a preliminary step, the prosecution advocate must discuss the judge's observations with the Chief Crown Prosecutor or the senior prosecutor of the relevant prosecuting authority as appropriate, in an attempt to resolve the issue;

(b) where the issue remains unresolved, the Director of Public Prosecutions or the Director of the relevant prosecuting authority should be consulted;

(c) in extreme circumstances the judge may decline to proceed with the case until the prosecuting authority has consulted with the Attorney General, as may be appropriate.

[14] 1968 c. 19; section 7 was amended by sections 43 and 170 of, and Schedule 16 to, the Criminal Justice Act 1988 (c. 33) and paragraph 44 of Schedule 36 to the Criminal Justice Act 2003 (c. 44).

[15] 2003 c. 44.

[16] 2003 S.I. 2005/679.

B.5 Prior to entering a plea of guilty, a defendant may seek an indication of sentence under the procedure set out in *R v Goodyear* [2005] EWCA Crim 888, [2005] 1 WLR 2532, [2005] 2 Cr App R 20; see below.

Where a guilty plea is offered on a limited basis

B.6 A defendant may put forward a plea of guilty without accepting all of the facts as alleged by the prosecution. The basis of plea offered may seek to limit the facts or the extent of the offending for which the defendant is to be sentenced. Depending on the view taken by the prosecution, and the content of the offered basis, the case will fall into one of the following categories:

(a) a plea of guilty upon a basis of plea agreed by the prosecution and defence;
(b) a plea of guilty on a basis signed by the defendant but in respect of which there is no or only partial agreement by the prosecution;
(c) a plea of guilty on a basis that contains within it matters that are purely mitigation and which do not amount to a contradiction of the prosecution case; or
(d) in cases involving serious or complex fraud, a plea of guilty upon a basis of plea agreed by the prosecution and defence accompanied by joint submissions as to sentence.

(a) A plea of guilty upon a basis of plea agreed by the prosecution and defence

B.7 The prosecution may reach an agreement with the defendant as to the factual basis on which the defendant will plead guilty, often known as an 'agreed basis of plea'. It is always subject to the approval of the court, which will consider whether it adequately and appropriately reflects the evidence as disclosed on the papers, whether it is fair and whether it is in the interests of justice.

B.8 *R v Underwood* [2004] EWCA Crim 2256, [2005] 1 Cr App R 13, [2005] 1 Cr App R (S) 90 outlines the principles to be applied where the defendant admits that he or she is guilty, but disputes the basis of offending alleged by the prosecution:

(a) The prosecution may accept and agree the defendant's account of the disputed facts or reject it in its entirety, or in part. If the prosecution accepts the defendant's basis of plea, it must ensure that the basis of plea is factually accurate and enables the sentencing judge to impose a sentence appropriate to reflect the justice of the case;
(b) In resolving any disputed factual matters, the prosecution must consider its primary duty to the court and must not agree with or acquiesce in an agreement which contains material factual disputes;
(c) If the prosecution does accept the defendant's basis of plea, it must be reduced to writing, be signed by advocates for both sides, and made available to the judge prior to the prosecution's opening;
(d) An agreed basis of plea that has been reached between the parties should not contain matters which are in dispute and any aspects upon which there is not agreement should be clearly identified;
(e) On occasion, the prosecution may lack the evidence positively to dispute the defendant's account, for example, where the defendant asserts a matter outside the knowledge of the prosecution. Simply because the prosecution does not have evidence to contradict the defendant's assertions does not mean those assertions should be agreed. In such a case, the prosecution should test the defendant's evidence and submissions by requesting a *Newton* hearing (*R v Newton* (1982) 77 Cr App R 13, (1982) 4 Cr App R (S) 388), following the procedure set out below;
(f) If it is not possible for the parties to resolve a factual dispute when attempting to reach a plea agreement under this part, it is the responsibility of the prosecution to consider whether the matter should proceed to trial, or to invite the court to hold a *Newton* hearing as necessary.

B.9 *R v Underwood* emphasises that, whether or not pleas have been 'agreed', the judge is not bound by any such agreement and is entitled of his or her own motion to insist that any evidence relevant to the facts in dispute (or upon which the judge requires further evidence for whatever reason) should be called. Any view formed by the prosecution on a proposed basis of plea is deemed to be conditional on the judge's acceptance of the basis of plea.

B.10 A judge is not entitled to reject a defendant's basis of plea absent a *Newton* hearing unless it is determined by the court that the basis is manifestly false and as such does not merit examination by way of the calling of evidence or alternatively the defendant declines the opportunity to engage in the process of the *Newton* hearing whether by giving evidence on his own behalf or otherwise.

(b) A plea of guilty on a basis signed by the defendant but in respect of which there is no or only partial agreement by the prosecution

B.11 Where the defendant pleads guilty, but disputes the basis of offending alleged by the prosecution and agreement as to that has not been reached, the following procedure should be followed:

(a) The defendant's basis of plea must be set out in writing, identifying what is in dispute and must be signed by the defendant;
(b) The prosecution must respond in writing setting out their alternative contentions and indicating whether or not they submit that a *Newton* hearing is necessary;
(c) The court may invite the parties to make representations about whether the dispute is material to sentence; and
(d) If the court decides that it is a material dispute, the court will invite such further representations or evidence as it may require and resolve the dispute in accordance with the principles set out in *R v Newton*.

B.12 Where the disputed issue arises from facts which are within the exclusive knowledge of the defendant and the defendant is willing to give evidence in support of his case, the defence advocate should be prepared to call the defendant. If the defendant is not willing to testify, and subject to any explanation which may be given, the judge may draw such inferences as appear appropriate.

B.13 The decision whether or not a *Newton* hearing is required is one for the judge. Once the decision has been taken that there will be a *Newton* hearing, evidence is called by the parties in the usual way and the criminal burden and standard of proof applies. Whatever view has been taken by the prosecution, the prosecutor should not leave the questioning to the judge, but should assist the court by exploring the issues which the court wishes to have explored. The rules of evidence should be followed as during a trial, and the judge should direct himself appropriately as the tribunal of fact. Paragraphs 6 to 10 of *Underwood* provide additional guidance regarding the *Newton* hearing procedure.

(c) A plea of guilty on a basis that contains within it matters that are purely mitigation and which do not amount to a contradiction of the prosecution case

B.14 A basis of plea should not normally set out matters of mitigation but there may be circumstances where it is convenient and sensible for the document outlining a basis to deal with facts closely aligned to the circumstances of the offending which amount to mitigation and which may need to be resolved prior to sentence. The resolution of these matters does not amount to a *Newton* hearing properly so defined and in so far as facts fall to be established the defence will have to discharge the civil burden in order to do so. The scope of the evidence required to resolve issues that are purely matters of mitigation is for the court to determine.

(d) Cases involving serious fraud — a plea of guilty upon a basis of plea agreed by the prosecution and defence accompanied by joint submissions as to sentence

B.15 This section applies when the prosecution and the defendant(s) to a matter before the Crown Court involving allegations of serious or complex fraud have agreed a basis of plea and seek to make submissions to the court regarding sentence.

B.16 Guidance for prosecutors regarding the operation of this procedure is set out in the 'Attorney General's Guidelines on Plea Discussions in Cases of Serious or Complex Fraud', which came into force on 5 May 2009 and is referred to in this direction as the 'Attorney General's Plea Discussion Guidelines'.

B.17 In this part—
(a) 'a plea agreement' means a written basis of plea agreed between the prosecution and defendant(s) in accordance with the principles set out in *R v Underwood*, supported by admissible documentary evidence or admissions under section 10 of the Criminal Justice Act 1967;
(b) 'a sentencing submission' means sentencing submissions made jointly by the prosecution and defence as to the appropriate sentencing authorities and applicable sentencing range in the relevant sentencing guideline relating to the plea agreement;
(c) 'serious or complex fraud' includes, but is not limited to, allegations of fraud where two or more of the following are present:
  (i) the amount obtained or intended to be obtained exceeded £500,000;
  (ii) there is a significant international dimension;
  (iii) the case requires specialised knowledge of financial, commercial, fiscal or regulatory matters such as the operation of markets, banking systems, trusts or tax regimes;
  (iv) the case involves allegations of fraudulent activity against numerous victims;
  (v) the case involves an allegation of substantial and significant fraud on a public body;
  (vi) the case is likely to be of widespread public concern;
  (vii) the alleged misconduct endangered the economic well-being of the United Kingdom, for example by undermining confidence in financial markets.

Procedure

B.18 The procedure regarding agreed bases of plea outlined above, applies with equal rigour to the acceptance of pleas under this procedure. However, because under this procedure the parties will have been discussing the plea agreement and the charges from a much earlier stage, it is vital that the judge is fully informed of all relevant background to the discussions, charges and the eventual basis of plea.

B.19 Where the defendant has not yet appeared before the Crown Court, the prosecutor must send full details of the plea agreement and sentencing submission(s) to the court, at least 7 days in advance of the defendant's first appearance. Where the defendant has already appeared before the Crown Court, the prosecutor must notify the court as soon as is reasonably practicable that a plea agreement and sentencing submissions under the Attorney General's Plea Discussion Guidelines are to be submitted. The court should set a date for the matter to be heard, and the prosecutor must send full details of the plea agreement and sentencing submission(s) to the court as soon as practicable, or in accordance with the directions of the court.

B.20 The provision to the judge of full details of the plea agreement requires sufficient information to be provided to allow the judge to understand the facts of the case and the history of the plea discussions, to assess whether the plea agreement is fair and in the interests of justice, and to decide the appropriate sentence. This will include, but is not limited to:

(i) the plea agreement;
(ii) the sentencing submission(s);
(iii) all of the material provided by the prosecution to the defendant in the course of the plea discussions;
(iv) relevant material provided by the defendant, for example documents relating to personal mitigation; and
(v) the minutes of any meetings between the parties and any correspondence generated in the plea discussions.

The parties should be prepared to provide additional material at the request of the court.

B.21 The court should at all times have regard to the length of time that has elapsed since the date of the occurrence of the events giving rise to the plea discussions, the time taken to interview the defendant, the date of charge and the prospective trial date (if the matter were to proceed to trial) so as to ensure that its consideration of the plea agreement and sentencing submissions does not cause any unnecessary further delay.

Status of plea agreement and joint sentencing submissions

B.22 Where a plea agreement and joint sentencing submissions are submitted, it remains entirely a matter for the court to decide how to deal with the case. The judge retains the absolute discretion to refuse to accept the plea agreement and to sentence otherwise than in accordance with the sentencing submissions made under the Attorney General's Plea Discussion Guidelines.

B.23 Sentencing submissions should draw the court's attention to any applicable range in any relevant guideline, and to any ancillary orders that may be applicable. Sentencing submissions should not include a specific sentence or agreed range other than the ranges set out in sentencing guidelines or authorities.

B.24 Prior to pleading guilty in accordance with the plea agreement, the defendant(s) may apply to the court for an indication of the likely maximum sentence under the procedure set out below (a '*Goodyear* indication').

B.25 In the event that the judge indicates a sentence or passes a sentence which is not within the submissions made on sentencing, the plea agreement remains binding.

B.26 If the defendant does not plead guilty in accordance with the plea agreement, or if a defendant who has pleaded guilty in accordance with a plea agreement, successfully applies to withdraw his plea under CrimPR 25.5, the signed plea agreement may be treated as confession evidence, and may be used against the defendant at a later stage in these or any other proceedings. Any credit for a timely guilty plea may be lost. The court may exercise its discretion under section 78 of the Police and Criminal Evidence Act 1984 to exclude any such evidence if it appears to the court that, having regard to all the circumstances, including the circumstances in which the evidence was obtained, the admission of the evidence would have such an adverse effect on the fairness of the proceedings that the court ought not to admit it.

B.27 Where a defendant has failed to plead guilty in accordance with a plea agreement, the case is unlikely to be ready for trial immediately. The prosecution may have been commenced earlier than it otherwise would have been, in reliance upon the defendant's agreement to plead guilty. This is likely to be a relevant consideration for the court in deciding whether or not to grant an application to adjourn or stay the proceedings to allow the matter to be prepared for trial in accordance with the protocol on the 'Control and Management of Heavy Fraud and other Complex Criminal Cases', or as required.

CPD.VII.C **CPD VII Sentencing C: Indications of Sentence: *R v Goodyear***

C.1 Prior to pleading guilty, it is open to a defendant in the Crown Court to request from the judge an indication of the maximum sentence that would be imposed if a guilty plea were to be tendered at that stage in the proceedings, in accordance with the guidance in *R v Goodyear* [2005] EWCA Crim 888, [2005] 1 WLR 2532, [2005] 2 Cr App R 20. The defence should notify the court and the prosecution of the intention to seek an indication in advance of any hearing.

C.2 Attention is drawn to the guidance set out in paragraphs 53 and following of *R v Goodyear*. The objective of the *Goodyear* guidelines is to safeguard against the creation or appearance of judicial pressure on a defendant. Any advance indication given should be the maximum sentence if a guilty plea were to be tendered at that stage of the proceedings only; the judge should not indicate the maximum possible sentence following conviction by a jury after trial. The judge should only give a *Goodyear* indication if one is requested by the defendant, although the judge can, in an appropriate case, remind the defence advocate of the defendant's entitlement to seek an advance indication of sentence.

C.3 Whether to give a *Goodyear* indication, and whether to give reasons for a refusal, is a matter for the discretion of the judge, to be exercised in accordance with the principles outlined by the Court of Appeal in that case. Such indications should normally not be given if there is a dispute as to the basis of plea unless the judge concludes that he or she can properly deal with the case without the need for a *Newton* hearing. If there is a basis of plea agreed by the prosecution and defence, it must be reduced into writing and a copy provided to the judge. As always, any basis of plea will be subject to the approval of the court. In cases where a dispute arises, the procedure in *R v Underwood* should be followed prior to the court considering a sentence indication further, as set out above. The judge should not become involved in negotiations about the acceptance of pleas or any agreed basis of plea, nor should a request be made for an indication of the different sentences that might be imposed if various different pleas were to be offered.

C.4 There should be no prosecution opening nor should the judge hear mitigation. However, during the sentence indication process the prosecution advocate is expected to assist the court by ensuring that the court has received all of the prosecution evidence, any statement from the victim about the impact of the offence, and any relevant previous convictions. Further, where appropriate, the prosecution should provide references to the relevant statutory powers of the court, relevant sentencing guidelines and authorities, and such other assistance as the court requires.

C.5 Attention is drawn to paragraph 70(d) of *Goodyear* which emphasises that the prosecution 'should not say anything which may create the impression that the sentence indication has the support or approval of the Crown.' This prohibition against the Crown indicating its approval of a particular sentence applies in all circumstances when a defendant is being sentenced, including when joint sentencing submissions are made.

C.6 An indication, once given, is, save in exceptional circumstances (such as arose in *R v Newman* [2010] EWCA Crim 1566, [2011] 1 Cr App R (S) 68), binding on the judge who gave it, and any other judge, subject to overriding statutory obligations such as those following a finding of 'dangerousness'. In circumstances where a judge proposes to depart from a *Goodyear* indication this must only be done in a way that does not give rise to unfairness (see *Newman*). However, if the defendant does not plead guilty, the indication will not thereafter bind the court.

C.7 If the offence is a specified offence such that the defendant might be liable to an assessment of 'dangerousness' in accordance with the Criminal Justice Act 2003 it is unlikely that the necessary material for such an assessment will be available. The court can still proceed to give an indication of sentence, but should state clearly the limitations of the indication that can be given.

C.8 A *Goodyear* indication should be given in open court in the presence of the defendant but any reference to the hearing is not admissible in any subsequent trial; and reporting restrictions should normally be imposed.

CPD.VII.D **CPD VII Sentencing D: Facts to be Stated on Pleas of Guilty**

D.1 To enable the press and the public to know the circumstances of an offence of which an accused has been convicted and for which he is to be sentenced, in relation to each offence to which an accused has pleaded guilty the prosecution shall state those facts in open court, before sentence is imposed.

CPD.VII.E **CPD VII Sentencing E: Concurrent and Consecutive Sentences**

E.1 Where a court passes on a defendant more than one term of imprisonment, the court should state in the presence of the defendant whether the terms are to be concurrent or consecutive. Should this not be done, the court clerk should ask the court, before the defendant leaves court, to do so.

E.2 If a defendant is, at the time of sentence, already serving two or more consecutive terms of imprisonment and the court intends to increase the total period of imprisonment, it should use the expression 'consecutive to the total period of imprisonment to which you are already subject' rather than 'at the expiration of the term of imprisonment you are now serving', as the defendant may not then be serving the last of the terms to which he is already subject.

E.3 The Sentencing Council has issued a definitive guideline on Totality which should be consulted. Under section 125(1) of the Coroners and Justice Act 2009, for offences committed after 6 April 2010, the guideline must be followed unless it would be contrary to the interests of justice to do so.

CPD VII Sentencing F: Victim Personal Statements **CPD.VII.F**

F.1 Victims of crime are invited to make a statement, known as a Victim Personal Statement ('VPS'). The statement gives victims a formal opportunity to say how a crime has affected them. It may help to identify whether they have a particular need for information, support and protection. The court will take the statement into account when determining sentence. In some circumstances, it may be appropriate for relatives of a victim to make a VPS, for example where the victim has died as a result of the relevant criminal conduct. The revised Code of Practice for Victims of Crime, published on 29 October 2013 gives further information about victims' entitlements within the criminal justice system, and the duties placed on criminal justice agencies when dealing with victims of crime.

F.2 When a police officer takes a statement from a victim, the victim should be told about the scheme and given the chance to make a VPS. The decision about whether or not to make a VPS is entirely a matter for the victim; no pressure should be brought to bear on their decision, and no conclusion should be drawn if they choose not to make such a statement. A VPS or a further VPS may be made (in proper s.9 form, see below) at any time prior to the disposal of the case. It will not normally be appropriate for a VPS to be made after the disposal of the case; there may be rare occasions between sentence and appeal when a further VPS may be necessary, for example, when the victim was injured and the final prognosis was not available at the date of sentence. However, VPS after disposal should be confined to presenting up to date factual material, such as medical information, and should be used sparingly.

F.3 If the court is presented with a VPS the following approach, subject to the further guidance given by the Court of Appeal in *R v Perkins*; *Bennett*; *Hall* [2013] EWCA Crim 323, [2013] Crim LR 533, should be adopted:

a) The VPS and any evidence in support should be considered and taken into account by the court, prior to passing sentence.
b) Evidence of the effects of an offence on the victim contained in the VPS or other statement, must be in proper form, that is a witness statement made under section 9 of the Criminal Justice Act 1967 or an expert's report; and served in good time upon the defendant's solicitor or the defendant, if he or she is not represented. Except where inferences can properly be drawn from the nature of or circumstances surrounding the offence, a sentencing court must not make assumptions unsupported by evidence about the effects of an offence on the victim. The maker of a VPS may be cross-examined on its content.
c) At the discretion of the court, the VPS may also be read aloud or played in open court, in whole or in part, or it may be summarised. If the VPS is to be read aloud, the court should also determine who should do so. In making these decisions, the court should take account of the victim's preferences, and follow them unless there is good reason not to do so; examples of this include the inadmissibility of the content or the potentially harmful consequences for the victim or others. Court hearings should not be adjourned solely to allow the victim to attend court to read the VPS. For the purposes of CPD I General matters 5B: Access to information held by the court, a VPS that is read aloud or played in open court in whole or in part should be considered as such, and no longer treated as a confidential document.
d) In all cases it will be appropriate for a VPS to be referred to in the course of the sentencing hearing and/or in the sentencing remarks.
e) The court must pass what it judges to be the appropriate sentence having regard to the circumstances of the offence and of the offender, taking into account, so far as the court considers it appropriate, the impact on the victim. The opinions of the victim or the victim's close relatives as to what the sentence should be are therefore not relevant, unlike the consequences of the offence on them. Victims should be advised of this. If, despite the advice, opinions as to sentence are included in the statement, the court should pay no attention to them.

CPD.VII.G **CPD VII Sentencing G: Families Bereaved by Homicide and other Criminal Conduct**

G.1 In cases in which the victim has died as a result of the relevant criminal conduct, the victim's family is not a party to the proceedings, but does have an interest in the case. Bereaved families have particular entitlements under the Code of Practice for Victims of Crime. All parties should have regard to the needs of the victim's family and ensure that the trial process does not expose bereaved families to avoidable intimidation, humiliation or distress.

G.2 In so far as it is compatible with family members' roles as witnesses, the court should consider the following measures:

a) Practical arrangements being discussed with the family and made in good time before the trial, such as seating for family members in the courtroom; if appropriate, in an alternative area, away from the public gallery;
b) Warning being given to families if the evidence on a certain day is expected to be particularly distressing;
c) Ensuring that appropriate use is made of the scheme for Victim Personal Statements, in accordance with the paragraphs above.

G.3 The sentencer should consider providing a written copy of the sentencing remarks to the family after sentence has been passed. Sentencers should tend in favour of providing such a copy, unless there is good reason not to do so, and the copy should be provided as soon as is reasonably practicable after the sentencing hearing.

CPD.VII.H **CPD VII Sentencing H: Community Impact Statements**

H.1 A community impact statement may be prepared by the police to make the court aware of particular crime trends in the local area and the impact of these on the local community.

H.2 Such statements must be in proper form, that is a witness statement made under section 9 of the Criminal Justice Act 1967 or an expert's report; and served in good time upon the defendant's solicitor or the defendant, if he is not represented.

H.3 The community impact statement and any evidence in support should be considered and taken into account by the court, prior to passing sentence. The statement should be referred to in the course of the sentencing hearing and/or in the sentencing remarks. Subject to the court's discretion, the contents of the statement may be summarised or read out in open court.

H.4 The court must pass what it judges to be the appropriate sentence having regard to the circumstances of the offence and of the offender, taking into account, so far as the court considers it appropriate, the impact on the local community. Opinions as to what the sentence should be are therefore not relevant. If, despite the advice, opinions as to sentence are included in the statement, the court should pay no attention to them.

H.5 Except where inferences can properly be drawn from the nature of or circumstances surrounding the offence, a sentencing court must not make assumptions unsupported by evidence about the effects of an offence on the local community.

H.6 It will not be appropriate for a Community Impact Statement to be made after disposal of the case but before an appeal.

CPD.VII.I **CPD VII Sentencing I: Impact Statements for Businesses**

I.1 Individual victims of crime are invited to make a statement, known as a Victim Personal Statement ('VPS'), see CPD VII Sentencing F. If a victim, or one of those others affected by a crime, is a business, enterprise or other body (including a charity or public body, for example a school or hospital), of any size, a nominated representative may make an Impact Statement for Business ('ISB'). The ISB gives a formal opportunity for the court to be informed how a crime has affected a business or other body. The court will take the statement into account when determining sentence. This does not prevent individual employees from making a VPS about the impact of the same crime on them as individuals. Indeed, the ISB should be about the impact on the business or other body exclusively, and the impact on any individual included within a VPS.

I.2 When a police officer takes statements about the alleged offence, he or she should also inform the business or other body about the scheme. An ISB may be made to the police at that time, or the ISB template may be downloaded from www.police.uk, completed and emailed or posted to the relevant police contact. Guidance on how to complete the form is available on www.police.uk and on the CPS website. There is no obligation to make an ISB.

I.3 An ISB or an updated ISB may be made (in proper s.9 form, see below) at any time prior to the disposal of the case. It will not be appropriate for an ISB to be made after disposal of the case but before an appeal.

I.4 A business or other body wishing to make an ISB should consider carefully who to nominate as the representative to make the statement on its behalf. A person making an ISB on behalf of such a business or body, the nominated representative, must be authorised to do so on its behalf, either by nature of their position, such as a director or owner or a senior official, or by having been suitably authorised, such as by the owner or Board of Directors or governing body. The nominated representative must also be in a position to give admissible evidence about the impact of the crime on the business or body. This will usually be through first hand personal knowledge, or using business documents (as defined in section 117 of the Criminal Justice Act 2003). The most appropriate person will vary depending on the nature of the crime, and the size and structure of the business or other body and may for example include a manager, director, chief executive or shop owner.

I.5 If the nominated representative leaves the business before the case comes to court, he or she will usually remain the representative, as the ISB made by him or her will still provide the best evidence of the impact of the crime, and he or she could still be asked to attend court. Nominated representatives should be made aware of the on-going nature of the role at the time of making the ISB.

I.6 If necessary a further ISB may be provided to the police if there is a change in circumstances. This could be made by an alternative nominated representative. However, the new ISB will usually supplement, not replace, the original ISB and again must contain admissible evidence. The prosecutor will decide which ISB to serve on the defence as evidence, and any ISB that is not served in evidence will be included in the unused material and considered for disclosure to the defence.

I.7 The ISB must be made in proper form, that is as a witness statement made under section 9 of the Criminal Justice Act 1967 or an expert's report; and served in good time upon the defendant's solicitor or the defendant, if he or she is not represented. The maker of an ISB can be cross-examined on its content.

I.8 The ISB and any evidence in support should be considered and taken into account by the court, prior to passing sentence. The statement should be referred to in the course of the sentencing hearing and/or in the sentencing remarks. Subject to the court's discretion, the contents of the statement may be summarised or read out in open court; the views of the business or body should be taken into account in reaching a decision.

I.9 The court must pass what it judges to be the appropriate sentence having regard to the circumstances of the offence and of the offender, taking into account, so far as the court considers it appropriate, the impact on the victims and others affected, including any business or other corporate victim. Opinions as to what the sentence should be are therefore not relevant. If, despite the advice, opinions as to sentence are included in the statement, the court should pay no attention to them.

I.10 Except where inferences can properly be drawn from the nature of or circumstances surrounding the offence, a sentencing court must not make assumptions unsupported by evidence about the effects of an offence on a business or other body.

CPD VII Sentencing J: Binding Over Orders and Conditional Discharges CPD.VII.J

J.1 This direction takes into account the judgments of the European Court of Human Rights in *Steel v United Kingdom* (1999) 28 EHRR 603, [1998] Crim LR 893 and in *Hashman and Harrup v United Kingdom* (2000) 30 EHRR 241, [2000] Crim LR 185. Its purpose is to give practical guidance, in the light of those two judgments, on the practice of imposing binding over orders. The direction applies to orders made under the court's common law powers, under the Justices of the Peace Act 1361, under section 1(7) of the Justices of the Peace Act 1968 and under section 115 of the Magistrates' Courts Act 1980. This direction also gives guidance concerning the court's power to bind over parents or guardians under section 150 of the Powers of Criminal Courts (Sentencing) Act 2000 and the Crown Court's power to bind over to come up for judgment. The court's power to impose a conditional discharge under section 12 of the Powers of Criminal Courts (Sentencing) Act 2000 is also covered by this direction.

Binding over to keep the peace

J.2 Before imposing a binding over order, the court must be satisfied so that it is sure that a breach of the peace involving violence, or an imminent threat of violence, has occurred or that there is a real risk of violence in the future. Such violence may be perpetrated by the individual who will be subject to the order or by a third party as a natural consequence of the individual's conduct.

J.3 In light of the judgment in *Hashman*, courts should no longer bind an individual over 'to be of good behaviour'. Rather than binding an individual over to 'keep the peace' in general terms, the court should identify the specific conduct or activity from which the individual must refrain.

Written order

J.4 When making an order binding an individual over to refrain from specified types of conduct or activities, the details of that conduct or those activities should be specified by the court in a written order, served on all relevant parties. The court should state its reasons for the making of the order, its length and the amount of the recognisance. The length of the order should be proportionate to the harm sought to be avoided and should not generally exceed 12 months.

Evidence

J.5 Sections 51 to 57 of the Magistrates' Courts Act 1980 set out the jurisdiction of the magistrates' court to hear an application made on complaint and the procedure which is to be followed. This includes a requirement under section 53 to hear evidence and the parties, before making any order. This practice should be applied to all cases in the magistrates' court and the Crown Court where the court is considering imposing a binding over order. The court should give the individual who would be subject to the order and the prosecutor the opportunity to make representations, both as to the making of the order and as to its terms. The court should also hear any admissible evidence the parties wish to call and which has not already been heard in the proceedings. Particularly careful consideration may be required where the individual who would be subject to the order is a witness in the proceedings.

J.6 Where there is an admission which is sufficient to found the making of a binding over order and/or the individual consents to the making of the order, the court should nevertheless hear sufficient representations and, if appropriate, evidence, to satisfy itself that an order is appropriate in all the circumstances and to be clear about the terms of the order.

J.7 Where there is an allegation of breach of a binding over order and this is contested, the court should hear representations and evidence, including oral evidence, from the parties before making a finding. If unrepresented and no opportunity has been given previously the court should give a reasonable period for the person said to have breached the binding over order to find representation.

Burden and standard of proof

J.8 The court should be satisfied so that it is sure of the matters complained of before a binding over order may be imposed. Where the procedure has been commenced on complaint, the burden of proof rests on the complainant. In all other circumstances, the burden of proof rests upon the prosecution.

J.9 Where there is an allegation of breach of a binding over order, the court should be satisfied on the balance of probabilities that the defendant is in breach before making any order for forfeiture of a recognisance. The burden of proof shall rest on the prosecution.

Recognisance

J.10 The court must be satisfied on the merits of the case that an order for binding over is appropriate and should announce that decision before considering the amount of the recognisance. If unrepresented, the individual who is made subject to the binding over order should be told he has a right of appeal from the decision.

J.11 When fixing the amount of recognisance, courts should have regard to the individual's financial resources and should hear representations from the individual or his legal representatives regarding finances.

J.12 A recognisance is made in the form of a bond giving rise to a civil debt on breach of the order.

Refusal to enter into a recognisance

J.13 If there is any possibility that an individual will refuse to enter a recognisance, the court should consider whether there are any appropriate alternatives to a binding over order (for example, continuing with a prosecution). Where there are no appropriate alternatives and the individual continues to refuse to enter into the recognisance, the court may commit the individual to custody. In the magistrates' court, the power to do so will derive from section 1(7) of the Justices of the Peace Act 1968 or, more rarely, from section 115(3) of the Magistrates' Courts Act 1980, and the court should state which power it is acting under; in the Crown Court, this is a common law power.

J.14 Before the court exercises a power to commit the individual to custody, the individual should be given the opportunity to see a duty solicitor or another legal representative and be represented in proceedings if the individual so wishes. Public funding should generally be granted to cover representation. In the Crown Court this rests with the Judge who may grant a Representation Order.

J.15 In the event that the individual does not take the opportunity to seek legal advice, the court shall give the individual a final opportunity to comply with the request and shall explain the consequences of a failure to do so.

Antecedents

J.16 Courts are reminded of the provisions of section 7(5) of the Rehabilitation of Offenders Act 1974 which excludes from a person's antecedents any order of the court 'with respect to any person otherwise than on a conviction'.

Binding over to come up for judgment

J.17 If the Crown Court is considering binding over an individual to come up for judgment, the court should specify any conditions with which the individual is to comply in the meantime and not specify that the individual is to be of good behaviour.

J.18 The Crown Court should, if the individual is unrepresented, explain the consequences of a breach of the binding over order in these circumstances.

Binding over of parent or guardian

J.19 Where a court is considering binding over a parent or guardian under section 150 of the Powers of Criminal Courts (Sentencing) Act 2000 to enter into a recognisance to take proper care of and exercise proper control over a child or young person, the court should specify the actions which the parent or guardian is to take.

Security for good behaviour

J.20 Where a court is imposing a conditional discharge under section 12 of the Powers of Criminal Courts (Sentencing) Act 2000, it has the power, under section 12(6) to make an order that a person who consents to do so give security for the good behaviour of the offender. When making such an order, the court should specify the type of conduct from which the offender is to refrain.

CPD VII Sentencing K: Committal for Sentence CPD.VII.K

K.1 CrimPR 28.10 applies when a case is committed to the Crown Court for sentence and specifies the information and documentation that must be provided by the magistrates' court. On a committal for sentence any reasons given by the magistrates for their decision should be included with the documents. All of these documents should be made available to the judge in the Crown Court if the judge requires them, in order to decide before the hearing questions of listing or representation or the like. They will also be available to the court during the hearing if it becomes necessary or desirable for the court to see what happened in the lower court.

CPD VII Sentencing L: Imposition of Life Sentences CPD.VII.L

L.1 Section 82A of the Powers of Criminal Courts (Sentencing) Act 2000 empowers a judge when passing a sentence of life imprisonment, where such a sentence is not fixed by law, to specify by order such part of the sentence ('the relevant part') as shall be served before the prisoner may require the Secretary of State to refer his case to the Parole Board. This is applicable to defendants under the age of 18 years as well as to adult defendants.

L.2 Thus the life sentence falls into two parts:

(a) the relevant part, which consists of the period of detention imposed for punishment and deterrence, taking into account the seriousness of the offence; and

(b) the remaining part of the sentence, during which the prisoner's detention will be governed by consideration of risk to the public.

L.3 The judge is not obliged by statute to make use of the provisions of section 82A when passing a life sentence. However, the judge should do so, save in the very exceptional case where the judge considers that the offence is so serious that detention for life is justified by the seriousness of the offence alone, irrespective of the risk to the public. In such a case, the judge should state this in open court when passing sentence.

L.4 In cases where the judge is to specify the relevant part of the sentence under section 82A, the judge should permit the advocate for the defendant to address the court as to the appropriate length of the relevant part. Where no relevant part is to be specified, the advocate for the defendant should be permitted to address the court as to the appropriateness of this course of action.

L.5 In specifying the relevant part of the sentence, the judge should have regard to the specific terms of section 82A and should indicate the reasons for reaching his decision as to the length of the relevant part.

CPD VII Sentencing M: Mandatory Life Sentences CPD.VII.M

M.1 The purpose of this section is to give practical guidance as to the procedure for passing a mandatory life sentence under section 269 and schedule 21 of the Criminal Justice Act 2003 ('the Act'). This direction also gives guidance as to the transitional arrangements under section 276 and schedule 22 of the Act. It clarifies the correct approach to looking at the practice of the Secretary of State prior to December 2002 for the purposes of schedule 22 of the Act, in the light of the judgment in ***R v***

Sullivan, Gibbs, Elener and Elener [2004] EWCA Crim 1762, [2005] 1 Cr App R 3, [2005] 1 Cr App R (S) 67.

M.2 Section 269 came into force on 18 December 2003. Under section 269, all courts passing a mandatory life sentence must either announce in open court the minimum term the prisoner must serve before the Parole Board can consider release on licence under the provisions of section 28 of the Crime (Sentences) Act 1997 (as amended by section 275 of the Act), or announce that the seriousness of the offence is so exceptionally high that the early release provisions should not apply at all (a 'whole life order').

M.3 In setting the minimum term, the court must set the term it considers appropriate taking into account the seriousness of the offence. In considering the seriousness of the offence, the court must have regard to the general principles set out in Schedule 21 of the Act as amended and any guidelines relating to offences in general which are relevant to the case and not incompatible with the provisions of Schedule 21. Although it is necessary to have regard to such guidance, it is always permissible not to apply the guidance if a judge considers there are reasons for not following it. It is always necessary to have regard to the need to do justice in the particular case. However, if a court departs from any of the starting points given in Schedule 21, the court is under a duty to state its reasons for doing so (section 270(2)(b) of the Act).

M.4 Schedule 21 states that the first step is to choose one of five starting points: 'whole life', 30 years, 25 years, 15 years or 12 years. Where the 15 year starting point has been chosen, judges should have in mind that this starting point encompasses a very broad range of murders. At paragraph 35 of *Sullivan*, the court found it should not be assumed that Parliament intended to raise all minimum terms that would previously have had a lower starting point, to 15 years.

M.5 Where the offender was 21 or over at the time of the offence, and the court takes the view that the murder is so grave that the offender ought to spend the rest of his life in prison, the appropriate starting point is a 'whole life order' (paragraph 4(1) of Schedule 21). The effect of such an order is that the early release provisions in section 28 of the Crime (Sentences) Act 1997 will not apply. Such an order should only be specified where the court considers that the seriousness of the offence (or the combination of the offence and one or more other offences associated with it) is exceptionally high. Paragraph 4(2) sets out examples of cases where it would normally be appropriate to take the 'whole life order' as the appropriate starting point.

M.6 Where the offender is aged 18 to 20 and commits a murder that is so serious that it would require a whole life order if committed by an offender aged 21 or over, the appropriate starting point will be 30 years. (Paragraph 5(2)(h) of Schedule 21).

M.7 Where a case is not so serious as to require a 'whole life order' but where the seriousness of the offence is particularly high and the offender was aged 18 or over when he committed the offence, the appropriate starting point is 30 years (paragraph 5(1) of Schedule 21). Paragraph 5(2) sets out examples of cases where a 30 year starting point would normally be appropriate (if they do not require a 'whole life order').

M.8 Where the offender was aged 18 or over when he committed the offence, took a knife or other weapon to the scene intending to commit any offence or have it available to use as a weapon, and used it in committing the murder, the offence is normally to be regarded as sufficiently serious for an appropriate starting point of 25 years (paragraph 5A of Schedule 21).

M.9 Where the offender was aged 18 or over when he committed the offence and the case does not fall within paragraph 4(1), 5(1) or 5A(1) of Schedule 21, the appropriate starting point is 15 years (see paragraph 6).

M.10 18 to 20 year olds are only the subject of the 30-year, 25-year and 15-year starting points.

M.11 The appropriate starting point when setting a sentence of detention during Her Majesty's pleasure for offenders aged under 18 when they committed the offence is always 12 years (paragraph 7 of Schedule 21).

M.12 The second step after choosing a starting point is to take account of any aggravating or mitigating factors which would justify a departure from the starting point. Additional aggravating factors (other than those specified in paragraphs 4(2), 5(2) and 5A) are listed at paragraph 10 of Schedule 21. Examples of mitigating factors are listed at paragraph 11 of Schedule 21. Taking into account the aggravating and mitigating features, the court may add to or subtract from the starting point to arrive at the appropriate punitive period.

M.13 The third step is that the court should consider the effect of section 143(2) of the Act in relation to previous convictions; section 143(3) of the Act where the offence was committed whilst the offender was on bail; and section 144 of the Act where the offender has pleaded guilty (paragraph 12 of Schedule 21). The court should then take into account what credit the offender would have received for a remand in custody under section 240 or 240ZA of the Act and/or for a remand on bail subject to a qualifying curfew condition under section 240A, but for the fact that the mandatory sentence is one of life imprisonment. Where the offender has been thus remanded in connection with the offence or a related offence, the court should have in mind that no credit will otherwise be given for this time when the prisoner is considered for early release. The appropriate time to take it into account is when setting the minimum term. The court should make any appropriate subtraction from the punitive period it would otherwise impose, in order to reach the minimum term.

M.14 Following these calculations, the court should have arrived at the appropriate minimum term to be announced in open court. As paragraph 9 of Schedule 21 makes clear, the judge retains ultimate discretion and the court may arrive at any minimum term from any starting point. The minimum term is subject to appeal by the offender under section 271 of the Act and subject to review on a reference by the Attorney-General under section 272 of the Act.

CPD VII Sentencing N: Transitional Arrangements for Sentences where the Offence was Committed before 18 December 2003 CPD.VII.N

N.1 Where the court is passing a sentence of mandatory life imprisonment for an offence committed before 18 December 2003, the court should take a fourth step in determining the minimum term in accordance with section 276 and Schedule 22 of the Act.

N.2 The purpose of those provisions is to ensure that the sentence does not breach the principle of non-retroactivity, by ensuring that a lower minimum term would not have been imposed for the offence when it was committed. Before setting the minimum term, the court must check whether the proposed term is greater than that which the Secretary of State would probably have notified under the practice followed by the Secretary of State before December 2002.

N.3 The decision in *Sullivan, Gibbs, Elener and Elener* [2004] EWCA Crim 1762, [2005] 1 Cr App R 3, [2005] 1 Cr App R (S) 67 gives detailed guidance as to the correct approach to this practice and judges passing mandatory life sentences where the murder was committed prior to 18 December 2003 are well advised to read that judgment before proceeding.

N.4 The practical result of that judgment is that in sentences where the murder was committed before 31 May 2002, the best guide to what would have been the practice of the Secretary of State is the letter sent to judges by Lord Bingham CJ on 10th February 1997, the relevant parts of which are set out below.

N.5 The practice of Lord Bingham, as set out in his letter of 10 February 1997, was to take 14 years as the period actually to be served for the 'average', 'normal' or 'unexceptional' murder. Examples of factors he outlined as capable, in appropriate cases, of mitigating the normal penalty were:

(1) Youth;
(2) Age (where relevant to physical capacity on release or the likelihood of the defendant dying in prison);
(3) [Intellectual disability or mental disorder];
(4) Provocation (in a non-technical sense), or an excessive response to a personal threat;
(5) The absence of an intention to kill;
(6) Spontaneity and lack of premeditation (beyond that necessary to constitute the offence: e.g., a sudden response to family pressure or to prolonged and eventually insupportable stress);
(7) Mercy killing;
(8) A plea of guilty, or hard evidence of remorse or contrition.

N.6 Lord Bingham then listed the following factors as likely to call for a sentence more severe than the norm:

(1) Evidence of planned, professional, revenge or contract killing;
(2) The killing of a child or a very old or otherwise vulnerable victim;
(3) Evidence of sadism, gratuitous violence, or sexual maltreatment, humiliation or degradation before the killing;
(4) Killing for gain (in the course of burglary, robbery, blackmail, insurance fraud, etc.);
(5) Multiple killings;
(6) The killing of a witness, or potential witness, to defeat the ends of justice;
(7) The killing of those doing their public duty (policemen, prison officers, postmasters, firemen, judges, etc.);
(8) Terrorist or politically motivated killings;
(9) The use of firearms or other dangerous weapons, whether carried for defensive or offensive reasons;
(10) A substantial record of serious violence;
(11) Macabre attempts to dismember or conceal the body.

N.7 Lord Bingham further stated that the fact that a defendant was under the influence of drink or drugs at the time of the killing is so common he would be inclined to treat it as neutral. But in the not unfamiliar case in which a couple, inflamed by drink, indulge in a violent quarrel in which one dies, often against a background of longstanding drunken violence, then he would tend to recommend a term somewhat below the norm.

N.8 Lord Bingham went on to say that given the intent necessary for proof of murder, the consequences of taking life and the understandable reaction of relatives to the deceased, a substantial term will almost always be called for, save perhaps in a truly venial case of mercy killing. While a recommendation of a punitive term longer than, say, 30 years will be very rare indeed, there should not be any upper limit. Some crimes will certainly call for terms very well in excess of the norm.

N.9 For the purposes of sentences where the murder was committed after 31 May 2002 and before 18 December 2003, the judge should apply the Practice Statement handed down on 31 May 2002 reproduced at paragraphs N.10 to N.20 below.

N.10 This Statement replaces the previous single normal tariff of 14 years by substituting a higher and a normal starting point of respectively 16 (comparable to 32 years) and 12 years (comparable to 24 years). These starting points have then to be increased or reduced because of aggravating or mitigating factors such as those referred to below. It is emphasised that they are no more than starting points.

The normal starting point of 12 years

N.11 Cases falling within this starting point will normally involve the killing of an adult victim, arising from a quarrel or loss of temper between two people known to each other. It will not have the characteristics referred to in paragraph N.13. Exceptionally, the starting point may be reduced because of the sort of circumstances described in the next paragraph.

N.12 The normal starting point can be reduced because the murder is one where the offender's culpability is significantly reduced, for example, because:
(a) the case came close to the borderline between murder and manslaughter; or
(b) the offender suffered from mental disorder, or from a mental disability which lowered the degree of his criminal responsibility for the killing, although not affording a defence of diminished responsibility; or
(c) the offender was provoked (in a non-technical sense) such as by prolonged and eventually unsupportable stress; or
(d) the case involved an over-reaction in self-defence; or
(e) the offence was a mercy killing.
These factors could justify a reduction to 8/9 years (equivalent to 16/18 years).

The higher starting point of 15/16 years

N.13 The higher starting point will apply to cases where the offender's culpability was exceptionally high, or the victim was in a particularly vulnerable position. Such cases will be characterised by a feature which makes the crime especially serious, such as:
(a) the killing was 'professional' or a contract killing;
(b) the killing was politically motivated;
(c) the killing was done for gain (in the course of a burglary, robbery etc.);
(d) the killing was intended to defeat the ends of justice (as in the killing of a witness or potential witness);
(e) the victim was providing a public service;
(f) the victim was a child or was otherwise vulnerable;
(g) the killing was racially aggravated;
(h) the victim was deliberately targeted because of his or her religion or sexual orientation;
(i) there was evidence of sadism, gratuitous violence or sexual maltreatment, humiliation or degradation of the victim before the killing;
(j) extensive and/or multiple injuries were inflicted on the victim before death;
(k) the offender committed multiple murders.

Variation of the starting point

N.14 Whichever starting point is selected in a particular case, it may be appropriate for the trial judge to vary the starting point upwards or downwards, to take account of aggravating or mitigating factors, which relate to either the offence or the offender, in the particular case.

N.15 Aggravating factors relating to the offence can include:
(a) the fact that the killing was planned;
(b) the use of a firearm;
(c) arming with a weapon in advance;
(d) concealment of the body, destruction of the crime scene and/or dismemberment of the body;
(e) particularly in domestic violence cases, the fact that the murder was the culmination of cruel and violent behaviour by the offender over a period of time.

N.16 Aggravating factors relating to the offender will include the offender's previous record and failures to respond to previous sentences, to the extent that this is relevant to culpability rather than to risk.

N.17 Mitigating factors relating to the offence will include:

(a) an intention to cause grievous bodily harm, rather than to kill;
(b) spontaneity and lack of pre-meditation.

N.18 Mitigating factors relating to the offender may include:
(a) the offender's age;
(b) clear evidence of remorse or contrition;
(c) a timely plea of guilty.

Very serious cases

N.19 A substantial upward adjustment may be appropriate in the most serious cases, for example, those involving a substantial number of murders, or if there are several factors identified as attracting the higher starting point present. In suitable cases, the result might even be a minimum term of 30 years (equivalent to 60 years) which would offer little or no hope of the offender's eventual release. In cases of exceptional gravity, the judge, rather than setting a whole life minimum term, can state that there is no minimum period which could properly be set in that particular case.

N.20 Among the categories of case referred to in paragraph N.13, some offences may be especially grave. These include cases in which the victim was performing his duties as a prison officer at the time of the crime, or the offence was a terrorist or sexual or sadistic murder, or involved a young child. In such a case, a term of 20 years and upwards could be appropriate.

N.21 In following this guidance, judges should bear in mind the conclusion of the Court in *Sullivan* that the general effect of both these statements is the same. While Lord Bingham does not identify as many starting points, it is open to the judge to come to exactly the same decision irrespective of which was followed. Both pieces of guidance give the judge a considerable degree of discretion.

CPD VII Sentencing P: Procedure for Announcing the Minimum Term in Open Court CPD.VII.P

P.1 Having gone through the three or four steps outlined above, the court is then under a duty, under section 270 of the Act, to state in open court, in ordinary language, its reasons for deciding on the minimum term or for passing a whole life order.

P.2 In order to comply with this duty, the court should state clearly the minimum term it has determined. In doing so, it should state which of the starting points it has chosen and its reasons for doing so. Where the court has departed from that starting point due to mitigating or aggravating features, it must state the reasons for that departure and any aggravating or mitigating features which have led to that departure. At that point, the court should also declare how much, if any, time is being deducted for time spent in custody and/or on bail subject to a qualifying curfew condition. The court must then explain that the minimum term is the minimum amount of time the prisoner will spend in prison, from the date of sentence, before the Parole Board can order early release. If it remains necessary for the protection of the public, the prisoner will continue to be detained after that date. The court should also state that where the prisoner has served the minimum term and the Parole Board has decided to direct release, the prisoner will remain on licence for the rest of his life and may be recalled to prison at any time.

P.3 Where the offender was 21 or over when he committed the offence and the court considers that the seriousness of the offence is so exceptionally high that a 'whole life order' is appropriate, the court should state clearly its reasons for reaching this conclusion. It should also explain that the early release provisions will not apply.

CPD VII Sentencing Q: Financial, Etc. Information Required for Sentencing CPD.VII.Q

Q.1 These directions supplement CrimPR 24.11 and 25.16, which set out the procedure to be followed where a defendant pleads guilty, or is convicted, and is to be sentenced. They are not concerned exclusively with corporate defendants, or with offences of an environmental, public health, health and safety or other regulatory character, but the guidance which they contain is likely to be of particular significance in such cases.

Q.2 The rules set out the prosecutor's responsibilities in all cases. Where the offence is of a character, or is against a prohibition, with which the sentencing court is unlikely to be familiar, those responsibilities are commensurately more onerous. The court is entitled to the greatest possible assistance in identifying information relevant to sentencing.

Q.3 In such a case, save where the circumstances are very straightforward, it is likely that justice will best be served by the submission of the required information in writing: see *R v Friskies Petcare (UK) Ltd* [2000] 2 Cr App R (S) 401. Though it is the prosecutor's responsibility to the court to prepare any such document, if the defendant pleads guilty, or indicates a guilty plea, then it is very highly desirable that such sentencing information should be agreed between the parties and jointly submitted. If agreement cannot be reached in all particulars, then the nature and extent of the disagreement should be indicated. If the court concludes that what is in issue is material to sentence, then it will give directions for resolution of the dispute, whether by hearing oral evidence or by other means. In every case, when passing sentence the sentencing court must make clear on what basis sentence is passed: in fairness to the defendant, and for the information of any other person, or court, who needs or wishes to understand the reasons for sentence.

Q.4 If so directed by or on behalf of the court, a defendant must supply accurate information about financial circumstances. In fixing the amount of any fine the court must take into account, amongst other considerations, the financial circumstances of the offender (whether an individual or other person) as they are known or as they appear to be. Before fixing the amount of fine when the defendant is an individual, the court must inquire into his financial circumstances. Where the defendant is an individual the court may make a financial circumstances order in respect of him. This means an order in which the court requires an individual to provide a statement as to his financial means, within a specified time. It is an offence, punishable with imprisonment, to fail to comply with such an order or for knowingly/recklessly furnishing a false statement or knowingly failing to disclose a material fact. The provisions of section 20A Criminal Justice Act 1991 apply to any person (thereby including a corporate organisation) and place the offender under a statutory duty to provide the court with a statement as to his financial means in response to an official request. There are offences for non-compliance, false statements or non-disclosure. It is for the court to decide how much information is required, having regard to relevant sentencing guidelines or guideline cases. However, by reference to those same guidelines and cases the parties should anticipate what the court will require, and prepare accordingly. In complex cases, and in cases involving a corporate defendant, the information required will be more extensive than in others. In the case of a corporate defendant, that information usually will include details of the defendant's corporate structure; annual profit and loss accounts, or extracts; annual balance sheets, or extracts; details of shareholders' receipts; and details of the remuneration of directors or other officers.

Q.5 In *R v F Howe and Son (Engineers) Ltd* [1999] 2 Cr App R (S) 37 the Court of Appeal observed: 'If a defendant company wishes to make any submission to the court about its ability to pay a fine it should supply copies of its accounts and any other financial information on which it intends to rely in good time before the hearing both to the court and to the prosecution. This will give the prosecution the opportunity to assist the court should the court wish it. Usually accounts need to be considered with some care to avoid reaching a superficial and perhaps erroneous conclusion. Where accounts or other financial information are deliberately not supplied the court will be entitled to conclude that the company is in a position to pay any financial penalty it is minded to impose. Where the relevant information is provided late it may be desirable for sentence to be adjourned, if necessary at the defendant's expense, so as to avoid the risk of the court taking what it is told at face value and imposing an inadequate penalty.'

Q.6 In the case of an individual, the court is likewise entitled to conclude that the defendant is able to pay any fine imposed unless the defendant has supplied financial information to the contrary. It is the defendant's responsibility to disclose to the court such information relevant to his or her financial position as will enable it to assess what he or she reasonably can afford to pay. If necessary, the court may compel the disclosure of an individual defendant's financial circumstances. In the absence of such disclosure, or where the court is not satisfied that it has been given sufficient reliable information, the court will be entitled to draw reasonable inferences as to the offender's means from evidence it has heard and from all the circumstances of the case.

CPD.VII.R

CPD VII Sentencing R: Medical Reports for Sentencing Purposes

General observations

R.1 CrimPR 24.11 and 25.16 concern standard sentencing procedures in magistrates' courts and in the Crown Court respectively. CrimPR 28.8 deals with the obtaining of medical reports for sentencing purposes.

R.2 Rule 28.8 governs the procedure to be followed where a report is commissioned at the instigation of the court. It is not a substitute for the prompt commissioning of a report or reports by a defendant or defendant's representatives where expert medical opinion is material to the defence case. In particular, the defendant's representatives may wish to obtain a medical report or reports wholly independently of the court. Nothing in these directions, therefore, should be read as discouraging the commissioning of a medical report before the case comes before the court, where such a report is expected to be material and where it is possible promptly to commission it. However, where such a report has been commissioned then if that report has not been received in time for sentencing and if the court agrees that it seems likely to be material, then the court should set a timetable for the reception of that report and should give directions for progress to be reviewed at intervals, adopting the timetable set out in these directions with such adaptations as are needed.

R.3 In assessing the likely materiality of an expert medical report for sentencing purposes the court will be assisted by the parties' representations; by the views expressed in any pre-sentence report that may have been prepared; and by the views of practitioners in local criminal justice mental health services, whose assistance is available to the court under local liaison arrangements.

R.4 Where the court requires the assistance of such a report then it is essential that there should be (i) absolute clarity about who is expected to do what, by when, and at whose expense; and (ii) judicial directions for progress with that report to be monitored and reviewed at prescribed intervals, following a timetable set by the court which culminates in the consideration of the report at a hearing. This is especially important where the report in question is a psychiatric assessment of the defendant for the preparation of which specific expertise may be required which is not readily available and because in some circumstances a second such assessment, by another medical practitioner, may be required.

Timetable for the commissioning, preparation and consideration of a report or reports

R.5 CrimPR 28.8 requires the court to set a timetable appropriate to the case for the preparation and reception of a report. In doing so the court will take account of such representations and other information that it receives, including information about the anticipated availability and workload of practitioners with the appropriate expertise. However, the timetable ought not be a protracted one. It is essential to keep in mind the importance of maintaining progress: in recognition of the defendant's rights and with respect for the interests of victims and witnesses, as required by CrimPR Part 1 (the overriding objective). In a magistrates' court account must be taken, too, of section 11 of the Powers of Criminal Courts (Sentencing) Act 2000, which limits the duration of each remand pending the preparation of a report to 3 weeks, where the defendant is to be in custody, and to 4 weeks if the defendant is to be on bail.

R.6 Subject, therefore, to contrary judicial direction the timetable set by the court should require:

(a) the convening of a hearing to consider the report no more than 6 – 8 weeks after the court makes its request;
(b) the prompt identification of an appropriate medical practitioner or practitioners, if not already identified by the court, and the despatch of a commission or commissions accordingly, within 2 business days of the court's decision to request a report;
(c) acknowledgement of a commission by its recipient, and acceptance or rejection of that commission, within 5 business days of its receipt;
(d) enquiries by court staff to confirm that the commission has been received, and to ascertain the action being taken in response, in the event that no acknowledgement is received within 10 business days of its despatch;
(e) delivery of the report within 5 weeks of the despatch of the commission;
(f) enquiries into progress by court staff in the event that no report is received within 5 weeks of the despatch of the commission.

R.7 The hearing that is convened for the court to consider the report, at 6 – 8 weeks after the court requests that report, should not be adjourned before it takes place save in exceptional circumstances and then only by explicit judicial direction the reasons for which must be recorded. If by the time of that hearing the report is available, as usually should be the case, then at that hearing the court can be expected to determine the issue in respect of which the report was commissioned and pass sentence. If by that time, exceptionally, the report is not available then the court should take the opportunity provided by that hearing to enquire into the reasons, give such directions as are appropriate, and if necessary adjourn the hearing to a fixed date for further consideration then. Where it is known in advance of that hearing that the report will not be available in time, the hearing may be conducted by live link or telephone: subject, in the defendant's case, to the same considerations as are identified at paragraph I.3N.6 of these Practice Directions. However, it rarely will be appropriate to dispense altogether with that hearing, or to make enquiries and give further directions without any hearing at all, in view of the arrangements for monitoring and review that the court already will have directed and which, by definition therefore, thus far will have failed to secure the report's timely delivery.

R.8 Where a requirement of the timetable set by the court is not met, or where on enquiry by court staff it appears that the timetable is unlikely to be met, and in any instance in which a medical practitioner who accepts a commission asks for more time, then court staff should not themselves adjust the timetable or accede to such a request but instead should seek directions from an appropriate judicial authority. Subject to local judicial direction, that will be, in the Crown Court, the judge assigned to the case or the resident judge and, in a magistrates' court, a District Judge (Magistrates' Courts) or justice of the peace assigned to the case, or the Justices' Clerk, an assistant clerk or other senior legal adviser. Even if the timetable is adjusted in consequence:

(a) the hearing convened to consider the report (that is, the hearing set for no more than 6 – 8 weeks after the court made its request) rarely should be adjourned before it takes place: see paragraph R.13 above;
(b) directions should be given for court staff henceforth to make regular enquiries into progress, at intervals of not more than 2 weeks, and to report the outcome to an appropriate judicial authority who will decide what further directions, if any, to give.

R.9 Any adjournment of a hearing convened to consider the report should be to a specific date: the hearing should not be adjourned generally, or to a date to be set in due course. The adjournment of such a hearing should not be for more than a further 6 – 8 weeks save in the most exceptional circumstances; and no more than one adjournment of the hearing should be allowed without obtaining written or oral representations from the commissioned medical practitioner explaining the reasons for the delay.

Commissioning a report

R.10 Guidance entitled 'Good practice guidance: commissioning, administering and producing psychiatric reports for sentencing' prepared for and published by the Ministry of Justice and HM Courts and Tribunals Service in September 2010 contains material that will assist court staff and those who are asked to prepare such reports:

http://www.ohrn.nhs.uk/resource/policy/GoodPracticeGuidePsychReports.pdf

That guidance includes standard forms of letters of instruction and other documents.

R.11 CrimPR 28.8 requires the commissioner of a report to explain why the court seeks the report and to include relevant information about the circumstances. The HMCTS Guidance contains forms for judicial use in the instruction of court staff, and guidance to court staff on the preparation of letters of instruction, where a report is required for sentencing purposes. Where a report is requested in a case involving manslaughter by reason of diminished responsibility, the report writer should have regard to the Sentencing Council's guideline on Manslaughter by reason of Diminished Responsibility. This should assist the report writer in providing the most helpful assessment to enable the court to determine the level of diminution involved in the case.

R.12 The commission should invite a practitioner who is unable to accept it promptly to nominate a suitably qualified substitute, if possible, and to transfer the commission to that person, reporting the transfer when acknowledging the court officer's letter. It is entirely appropriate for the commission to draw the recipient's attention to CrimPR 1.2 (the duty of the participants in a criminal case) and to CrimPR 19.2(1)(b) (the obligation of an expert witness to comply with directions made by a court and at once to inform the court of any significant failure, by the expert or another, to take any step required by such a direction).

R.13 Where the relevant legislation requires a second psychiatric assessment by a second medical practitioner, and where no commission already has been addressed to a second such practitioner, the commission may invite the person to whom it is addressed to nominate a suitably qualified second person and to pass a copy of the commission to that person forthwith.

Funding arrangements

R.14 Where a medical report has been, or is to be, commissioned by a party then that party is responsible for arranging payment of the fees incurred, even though the report is intended for the court's use. That must be made clear in that party's commission.

R.15 Where a medical report is requested by the court and commissioned by a party or by court staff at the court's direction then the commission must include (i) confirmation that the fees will be paid by HMCTS, (ii) details of how, and to whom, to submit an invoice or claim for fees, and (iii) notice of the prescribed rates of fees and of any legislative or other criteria applicable to the calculation of the fees that may be paid.

Remand in custody

R.16 Where the defendant who is to be examined will be remanded in custody then notice that directions have been given for a medical report or reports to be prepared must be included in the information given to the defendant's custodian, to ensure that the preparation of the report or reports can be facilitated. This is especially important where bail is withheld on the ground that it would be otherwise impracticable to complete the required report, and in particular where that is the only ground for withholding bail.

CPD.VII.S **CPD VII Sentencing S: Variation of Sentence**

S.1 Under section 142 of the Magistrates' Courts Act 1980, in some circumstances a magistrates' court may vary or rescind a sentence or other order that it has imposed or made if that appears to be in the interests of justice. Under section 155 of the Powers of Criminal Courts (Sentencing) Act 2000 the Crown Court may vary or rescind a sentence or order which it has imposed or made, within a period of 56 days beginning with the date of that sentence or order, or beginning with the date of another defendant's acquittal or sentencing in some circumstances (see CrimPR 28.4(1)(b)).

S.2 CrimPR 28.4(2) allows the court to exercise those powers at a hearing, in public or in private, or without a hearing. However, rule 28.4(4) confines the court's discretion to dispense with a hearing by requiring the defendant's presence, necessarily at a hearing, unless the variation is one proposed by the defendant, or the effect of the variation is such that the defendant is no more severely dealt with under the sentence as varied than before; or, if neither of those conditions is satisfied, where a hearing has been convened at which the defendant has had an opportunity to make representations, whether or not he or she in fact attends. Moreover, rule 28.4 requires service on the other party of any application to vary a sentence or order, in response to which that other party may wish to make such representations as general principles of law require to be heard. It follows that the circumstances in which a variation of sentence properly may be made without a hearing, consistently with the rule, will be confined to cases in which neither party objects to what is proposed and in which the consequences for the defendant of the variation will be neutral or benign.

S.3 In such a case usually there will be no other objection to the making of the variation without a hearing. Even in such a case, however, the court retains a discretion to convene a hearing, in the exercise of which discretion due regard must be had to the overriding objective and to the importance of dealing with criminal cases in public, in accordance with the principle of open justice. The application of that latter principle was described in *R v Cox* [2019] EWCA Crim 71; [2019] 4 WLR 88 at paragraphs 18–19 in these terms:

> 'As stated in cases such as *R v Pinkerton* [2017] 1 Cr App R(S) 47 at [8] (a case where there in fact was a downward adjustment of a concurrent custodial sentence which did not impact on the overall sentence) such alterations should be done openly "'so that justice may be seen to be done'". Likewise, in *R v Warren* [2017] 2 Cr App R(S) 5, the general desirability of re-sentencing taking place in the presence of the defendant and in court was stressed. Accordingly, whilst it is easy to understand the attractions of administrative convenience … and particularly perhaps where the sentencing judge is not a full-time judge based at a particular court centre, those administrative attractions should not be permitted routinely to prevail over the delivery of open justice.'

In reaching its decision the court therefore will take into account each of the relevant factors listed in CrimPR 1.1, and will be astute to distinguish between, on the one hand, the completion of details or the correction of errors of a quasi-administrative character and, on the other, a variation of sentence in which the determination will be a matter of legitimate public interest.

S.4 In any event, the making of the decision and the reasons for that decision always must be announced at a public hearing, even if only briefly and even if the parties are absent on that occasion: CrimPR 28.4(2)(b). While the decision itself must be made, and the reasons for that decision formulated, by the sentencing court itself (section 142(1) of the 1980 Act; section 155(4) of the 2000 Act), the public announcement may be made by a differently constituted court if it would be impracticable for the sentencing court to sit in public for the purpose within a reasonable time.

Criminal Procedure Rules Part 28 Sentencing Procedures in Special Cases

[Note. See also—

(a) Part 24, which contains rules about the general procedure on sentencing in a magistrates' court;
(b) Part 25, which contains rules about the general procedure on sentencing in the Crown Court;
(c) Part 29 (Road traffic penalties);
(d) Part 30 (Enforcement of fines and other orders for payment); and
(e) Part 32 (Breach, revocation and amendment of community and other orders).]

Reasons for not following usual sentencing requirements **R28.1**

28.1 (1) This rule applies where the court decides—
(a) not to follow a relevant sentencing guideline;
(b) not to make, where it could—
(i) a reparation order (unless it passes a custodial or community sentence),
(ii) a compensation order,
(iii) a slavery and trafficking reparation order, or
(iv) a travel restriction order;
(c) not to order, where it could—
(i) that a suspended sentence of imprisonment is to take effect,
(ii) the endorsement of the defendant's driving record, or
(iii) the defendant's disqualification from driving, for the usual minimum period or at all;
(d) to pass a lesser sentence than it otherwise would have passed because the defendant has assisted, or has agreed to assist, an investigator or prosecutor in relation to an offence.
(2) The court must explain why it has so decided, when it explains the sentence that it has passed.

(3) Where paragraph (1)(d) applies, the court must arrange for such an explanation to be given to the defendant and to the prosecutor in writing, if the court thinks that it would not be in the public interest to explain in public.

[Note. See sections 52, 54 and 55 of the Sentencing Act 2020[1]*; section 8(7) of the Modern Slavery Act 2015*[2]*; section 33(2) of the Criminal Justice and Police Act 2001*[3]*; paragraph 14(1) of Schedule 16 to the 2020 Act; section 47(1) of the Road Traffic Offenders Act 1988*[4]*; and section 74 of the 2020 Act.*

For the duty to explain the sentence the court has passed, see section 52(1) of the 2020 Act and rules 24.119 (procedure where a magistrates' court convicts) and 25.16(7) (procedure where the Crown Court convicts).

Under section 59 of the 2020 Act, the court when sentencing must follow any relevant sentencing guideline unless satisfied that to do so would be contrary to the interests of justice.

For the circumstances in which the court may make—

(a) a reparation or compensation order, see sections 110 and 134 of the 2020 Act[5]*;*
(b) a slavery and trafficking reparation order, see section 8 of the 2015 Act;
(c) a travel restriction order against a defendant convicted of drug trafficking, see sections 33 and 34 of the 2001 Act[6]*.]*

R28.2 Notice of requirements of suspended sentence and community, etc. orders

28.2 (1) This rule applies where the court—
(a) makes a suspended sentence order;
(b) imposes a requirement under—
(i) a community order,
(ii) a youth rehabilitation order, or
(iii) a suspended sentence order; or
(c) orders the defendant to attend meetings with a supervisor.

(2) The court officer must notify—
(a) the defendant of—
(i) the length of the sentence suspended by a suspended sentence order, and
(ii) the period of the suspension;
(b) the defendant and, where the defendant is under 14, an appropriate adult, of—
(i) any requirement or requirements imposed, and
(ii) the identity of any responsible officer or supervisor, and the means by which that person may be contacted;
(c) any responsible officer or supervisor, and, where the defendant is under 14, the appropriate qualifying officer (if that is not the responsible officer), of—
(i) the defendant's name, address and telephone number (if available),
(ii) the offence or offences of which the defendant was convicted, and
(iii) the requirement or requirements imposed; and
(d) the person affected, where the court imposes a requirement—
(i) for the protection of that person from the defendant, or
(ii) requiring the defendant to reside with that person.

(3) If the court imposes an electronic monitoring requirement, the monitor of which is not the responsible officer, the court officer must—
(a) notify the defendant and, where the defendant is under 16, an appropriate adult, of the monitor's identity, and the means by which the monitor may be contacted; and
(b) notify the monitor of—
(i) the defendant's name, address and telephone number (if available),
(ii) the offence or offences of which the defendant was convicted,
(iii) the place or places at which the defendant's presence must be monitored,
(iv) the period or periods during which the defendant's presence there must be monitored, and
(v) the identity of the responsible officer, and the means by which that officer may be contacted.

[1] 2020 c. 17.
[2] 2015 c. 30.
[3] 2001 c. 16.
[4] 1988 c. 53.
[5] 2009 c. 25; section 125 was repealed by section 413 of, and Schedule 28 to, the Sentencing Act 2020 (c. 17).
[6] 2001 c. 16; section 33 was amended by sections 39(3) and 39(4) of the Identity Cards Act 2006 (c. 15).

[Note. See sections 212(2) and 298(2) of the Sentencing Act 2020[7]*; section 190(2) of the 2020 Act*[8]*; and section 1A(7) of the Street Offences Act 1959*[9]*.*

For the circumstances in which the court may—

(a) make a suspended sentence order, see sections 264, 277, 286 and 288 of the 2020 Act[10]*;*
(b) make a community order (defined by section 200 of the 2020 Act), or a youth rehabilitation order (defined by section 173(1) of that Act), and for the identity and duties of responsible officers and qualifying officers, see generally Chapters 1 and 2 of Part 9 of the 2020 Act;
(c) order the defendant to attend meetings with a supervisor, see section 1(2A) of the Street Offences Act 1959[11]*.*

Under 174, 201 or 287 of the 2020 Act[12]*, the court may impose an electronic monitoring requirement to secure the monitoring of the defendant's compliance with certain other requirements (for example, a curfew or an exclusion).]*

Notification requirements **R28.3**

28.3 (1) This rule applies where, on a conviction, sentence or order, legislation requires the defendant—
(a) to notify information to the police; or;
(b) to be included in a barred list.
(2) The court must tell the defendant that such requirements apply, and under what legislation.

[Note. For the circumstances in which a defendant is required to notify information to the police, see—

(a) Part 2 of, and Schedule 3 to, the Sexual Offences Act 2003([13]*) (notification for the period specified by section 82 of the Act(*[14]*) after conviction, etc. of an offence listed in Schedule 3 and committed in the circumstances specified in that Schedule);*
(b) Part 4 of the Counter Terrorism Act 2008[15] *(notification after conviction of a specified offence of, or connected with, terrorism, for which a specified sentence is imposed).*

For the circumstances in which a defendant will be included in a barred list, see paragraphs 1, 2, 7, 8 and 24 of Schedule 3 to the Safeguarding Vulnerable Groups Act 2006[16]*. See also paragraph 25 of that Schedule*[17]*.*

These requirements are not part of the court's sentence.]

Variation of sentence **R28.4**

28.4 (1) This rule—
(a) applies where a magistrates' court or the Crown Court can vary or rescind a sentence or order, other than an order to which rule 44.3 applies (Setting aside a conviction or varying a costs etc. order); and
(b) authorises the Crown Court, in addition to its other powers, to do so within the period of 56 days beginning with another defendant's acquittal or sentencing where—
(i) defendants are tried separately in the Crown Court on the same or related facts alleged in one or more indictments, and
(ii) one is sentenced before another is acquitted or sentenced.
(2) The court—
(a) may exercise its power—
(i) on application by a party, or on its own initiative,
(ii) at a hearing, in public or in private, or without a hearing; and
(b) must announce, at a hearing in public—

[7] 2003 c. 44; section 219 was repealed by section 413 of, and Schedule 28 to, the Sentencing Act 2020 (c. 17).
[8] 2008 c. 4.
[9] 1959 c. 57; section 1A was inserted by section 17(1) and (3) of the Policing and Crime Act 2009 (c. 26).
[10] 2008 c. 4; Schedule 1 was repealed by section 413 of, and Schedule 28 to, the Sentencing Act 2020 (c. 17).
[11] 1959 c. 57; section 1(2A) was inserted by section 17(1) and (3) of the Policing and Crime Act 2009 (c. 26).
[12] 2008 c. 4.
[13] 2003 c. 42; Schedule 3 was amended by article 2 of S.I. 2007/296, section 63(2) of, and paragraph 63 of Schedule 6 to, the Serious Crimes Act 2007 (c. 27), section 148(1) of, and paragraphs 53 and 58 of Schedule 26 to, the Criminal Justice and Immigration Act 2008 (c. 4) and section 177(1) of, and paragraph 62 of Schedule 21 to, the Coroners and Justice Act 2009 (c. 25). Other amendments to Schedule 3 are not relevant to these Rules.
[14] 2003 c. 42; section 82 was amended by section 57 of the Violent Crime Reduction Act 2006 (c. 38).
[15] 2008 c. 28.
[16] 2006 c. 47; paragraphs 1, 2, 7 and 8 of Schedule 3 were amended by sections 81 and 89 of the Policing and Crime Act 2009 (c. 26). Paragraph 24 was amended by article 2 of S.I. 2008/3050.
[17] 2006 c. 47; paragraph 25 of Schedule 3 was amended by article 3 of S.I. 2008/3050 and section 81 of the Policing and Crime Act 2009 (c. 26).

(i) a decision to vary or rescind a sentence or order, or to refuse to do so, and
(ii) the reasons for that decision.
(3) A party who wants the court to exercise that power must—
(a) apply in writing as soon as reasonably practicable after—
(i) the sentence or order that that party wants the court to vary or rescind, or
(ii) where paragraph (1)(b) applies, the other defendant's acquittal or sentencing;
(b) serve the application on—
(i) the court officer, and
(ii) each other party; and
(c) in the application—
(i) explain why the sentence should be varied or rescinded,
(ii) specify the variation that the applicant proposes, and
(iii) if the application is late, explain why.
(4) The court must not exercise its power in the defendant's absence unless—
(a) the court makes a variation—
(i) which is proposed by the defendant, or
(ii) the effect of which is that the defendant is no more severely dealt with under the sentence as varied than before; or
(b) the defendant has had an opportunity to make representations at a hearing (whether or not the defendant in fact attends).
(5) The court may—
(a) extend (even after it has expired) the time limit under paragraph (3), unless the court's power to vary or rescind the sentence cannot be exercised; and
(b) allow an application to be made orally.
(6) For the purposes of the announcement required by paragraph (2)(b), the court need not comprise the same member or members as the court by which the decision to be announced was made.

[Note. Under section 142 of the Magistrates' Courts Act 1980[18]*, in some cases a magistrates' court can vary or rescind a sentence or other order that it has imposed or made, if that appears to be in the interests of justice. The power cannot be exercised if the Crown Court or the High Court has determined an appeal about that sentence or order. See also rule 44.3 (Setting aside a conviction or varying a costs etc. order), which governs the exercise by a magistrates' court of the power conferred by section 142 of the 1980 Act in the circumstances to which that rule applies.*

Under section 385 of the Sentencing Act 2020, the Crown Court can vary or rescind a sentence or other order that it has imposed or made. The power cannot be exercised—

(a) after the period of 56 days beginning with the sentence or order (but see the note below); or
(b) if an appeal or application for permission to appeal against that sentence or order has been determined.

Under section 385(7) of that Act, Criminal Procedure Rules can extend that period of 56 days where another defendant is tried separately in the Crown Court on the same or related facts alleged in one or more indictments.]

R28.5 Application to vary or discharge a compensation, etc. order

28.5 (1) This rule applies where on application by the defendant a magistrates' court can vary or discharge—
(a) a compensation order; or
(b) a slavery and trafficking reparation order.
(2) A defendant who wants the court to exercise that power must—
(a) apply in writing as soon as practicable after becoming aware of the grounds for doing so;
(b) serve the application on the magistrates' court officer;
(c) where the order was made in the Crown Court, serve a copy of the application on the Crown Court officer; and
(d) in the application, specify the order that the defendant wants the court to vary or discharge and explain (as applicable)—
(i) what civil court finding shows that the injury, loss or damage was less than it had appeared to be when the order was made,
(ii) in what circumstances the person for whose benefit the order was made has recovered the property for the loss of which it was made,

[18] 1980 c. 43; section 142 was amended by sections 26 and 29 of, and Schedule 3 to, the Criminal Appeal Act 1995 (c. 35).

(iii) why a confiscation order, unlawful profit order or slavery and trafficking reparation order makes the defendant now unable to pay compensation or reparation in full, or
(iv) in what circumstances the defendant's means have been reduced substantially and unexpectedly, and why they seem unlikely to increase for a considerable period.

(3) The court officer must serve a copy of the application on the person for whose benefit the order was made.
(4) The court must not vary or discharge the order unless—
(a) the defendant, and the person for whose benefit it was made, each has had an opportunity to make representations at a hearing (whether or not either in fact attends); and
(b) where the order was made in the Crown Court, the Crown Court has notified its consent.

[Note. For the circumstances in which—

(a) the court may make a compensation order, see section 133 of the Sentencing Act 2020;
(b) the court may make a slavery and trafficking reparation order, see section 8 of the Modern Slavery Act 2015[19]*;*
(c) a magistrates' court with power to enforce such an order may vary or discharge it under the 2020 Act, see section 143. (Under section 143(3), where the order was made in the Crown Court, the magistrates' court must first obtain the Crown Court's consent.)]

Application to remove, revoke or suspend a disqualification or restriction **R28.6**

28.6 (1) This rule applies where, on application by the defendant, the court can remove, revoke or suspend a disqualification or restriction included in a sentence (except a disqualification from driving).
(2) A defendant who wants the court to exercise such a power must—
(a) apply in writing, no earlier than the date on which the court can exercise the power;
(b) serve the application on the court officer; and
(c) in the application—
(i) specify the disqualification or restriction, and
(ii) explain why the defendant wants the court to remove, revoke or suspend it.
(3) The court officer must serve a copy of the application on the chief officer of police for the local justice area.

[Note. Part 29 contains rules about disqualification from driving. See in particular rule 29.2.

Part 34 (Appeal to the Crown Court) and Part 35 (Appeal to the High Court by case stated) contain rules about applications to suspend disqualifications pending appeal.

For the circumstances in which the court may—

(a) remove a disqualification from keeping a dog, see section 4(6) of the Dangerous Dogs Act 1991[20]*. The court may not consider an application made within 1 year of the disqualification; or, after that, within 1 year of any previous application that was refused.*
(b) revoke or suspend a travel restriction order against a defendant convicted of drug trafficking, see section 35 of the Criminal Justice and Police Act 2001[21]*). The court may not consider an application made within 2 years of the disqualification, in any case; or, after that, before a specified period has expired.]*

Application for a restitution order by the victim of a theft **R28.7**

28.7 (1) This rule applies where, on application by the victim of a theft, the court can order a defendant to give that person goods obtained with the proceeds of goods stolen in that theft.
(2) A person who wants the court to exercise that power if the defendant is convicted must—
(a) apply in writing as soon as practicable (without waiting for the verdict);
(b) serve the application on the court officer; and
(c) in the application—
(i) identify the goods, and
(ii) explain why the applicant is entitled to them.
(3) The court officer must serve a copy of the application on each party.
(4) The court must not determine the application unless the applicant and each party has had an opportunity to make representations at a hearing (whether or not each in fact attends).
(5) The court may—

[19] 2015 c. 30.
[20] 1991 c. 65; section 4(6) was amended by section 109(1) of, and paragraph 353 of Schedule 8 to, the Courts Act 2003 (c. 39).
[21] 2001 c. 16; section 35 was amended by sections 39(3) of the Identity Cards Act 2006 (c. 15).

Criminal Procedure Rules and Criminal Practice Directions

(a) extend (even after it has expired) the time limit under paragraph (2); and
(b) allow an application to be made orally.

[Note. For the circumstances in which the court may order—

(a) the return of stolen goods, see section 147 of the Sentencing Act 2020[22]*;*

(b) the defendant to give the victim of the theft goods that are not themselves the stolen goods but which represent their proceeds, see section 147(1)(b) of the 2020 Act.]

R28.8 **Directions for commissioning medical reports for sentencing purposes**

28.8 (1) This rule applies where for sentencing purposes the court requires—
(a) a medical examination of the defendant and a report; or
(b) information about the arrangements that could be made for the defendant where the court is considering—
(i) a hospital order, or
(ii) a guardianship order.

(2) The court must—
(a) identify each issue in respect of which the court requires expert medical opinion and the legislation applicable;
(b) specify the nature of the expertise likely to be required for giving such opinion;
(c) identify each party or participant by whom a commission for such opinion must be prepared, who may be—
(i) a party (or party's representative) acting on that party's own behalf,
(ii) a party (or party's representative) acting on behalf of the court, or
(iii) the court officer acting on behalf of the court;
(d) where there are available to the court arrangements with the National Health Service under which an assessment of a defendant's mental health may be prepared, give such directions as are needed under those arrangements for obtaining the expert report or reports required;
(e) where no such arrangements are available to the court, or they will not be used, give directions for the preparation of a commission or commissions for an expert report or expert reports, including—
(i) such directions as can be made about supplying the expert or experts with the defendant's medical records,
(ii) directions about the other information, about the defendant and about the offence or offences alleged to have been committed by the defendant, which is to be supplied to each expert, and
(iii) directions about the arrangements that will apply for the payment of each expert;
(f) set a timetable providing for—
(i) the date by which a commission is to be delivered to each expert,
(ii) the date by which any failure to accept a commission is to be reported to the court,
(iii) the date or dates by which progress in the preparation of a report or reports is to be reviewed by the court officer, and
(iv) the date by which each report commissioned is to be received by the court; and
(g) identify the person (each person, if more than one) to whom a copy of a report is to be supplied, and by whom.

(3) A commission addressed to an expert must—
(a) identify each issue in respect of which the court requires expert medical opinion and the legislation applicable;
(b) include—
(i) the information required by the court to be supplied to the expert,
(ii) details of the timetable set by the court, and
(iii) details of the arrangements that will apply for the payment of the expert;
(c) identify the person (each person, if more than one) to whom a copy of the expert's report is to be supplied; and
(d) request confirmation that the expert from whom the opinion is sought—
(i) accepts the commission, and
(ii) will adhere to the timetable.

[Note. See also rule 3.10 (directions for commissioning medical reports in connection with fitness to participate in the trial, etc.).

For sentencing purposes the court may request a medical examination of the defendant and a report under—

[22] 2020 (c. 17)

(a) section 35 of the Mental Health Act 1983[23]*, under which the court may order the defendant's detention in hospital to obtain a medical report;*

(b) section 36 of the 1983 Act[24]*, under which the Crown Court may order the defendant's detention in hospital instead of in custody pending trial or sentence;*

(c) section 37 of the 1983 Act[25]*, under which the court may order the defendant's detention and treatment in hospital, or make a guardianship order, instead of disposing of the case in another way (section 37(3) allows a magistrates' court to make such an order without convicting the defendant if satisfied that the defendant did the act or made the omission charged);*

(d) section 38 of the 1983 Act[26]*, under which the court may order the defendant's temporary detention and treatment in hospital instead of disposing of the case in another way;*

(e) section 232 of the Sentencing Act 2020[27]*, under which the court must usually obtain and consider a medical report before passing a custodial sentence if the defendant is, or appears to be, mentally disordered;*

(f) paragraphs 16 and 17 of Schedule 9 to the 2020 Act[28] *(in the case of a defendant aged 18 or over), or paragraphs 28 and 29 of Schedule 6 to that Act*[29] *(in the case of a defendant who is under 18), under which the court may impose a mental health treatment requirement.*

For the purposes of the legislation listed in (b), (c) and (d) above, the court requires the written or oral evidence of at least two registered medical practitioners, at least one of whom is approved as having special experience in the diagnosis or treatment of mental disorder. For the purposes of (a), (e) and (f), the court requires the evidence of one medical practitioner so approved.

Under section 11 of the Powers of Criminal Courts (Sentencing) Act 2000[30]*, a magistrates' court may adjourn a trial to obtain medical reports.*

Part 19 (Expert evidence) contains rules about the content of expert medical reports.

For the authorities from whom the court may require information about hospital treatment or guardianship, see sections 39 and 39A of the 1983 Act[31]*.*

The Practice Direction includes a timetable for the commissioning and preparation of a report or reports which the court may adopt with such adjustments as the court directs.

23 1983 c. 20; section 35 was amended by sections 1(4) and 10(1) and (2) of, and paragraphs 1 and 5 of Schedule 1 to, the Mental Health Act 2007 (c. 12) and section 208(1) of, and paragraphs 53 and 54 of Schedule 21 to, the Legal Services Act 2007 (c. 29).

24 1983 c. 20; section 36 was amended by sections 1(4), 5(1) and (2) and 10(1) and (3) of, and paragraphs 1 and 6 of Schedule 1 to, the Mental Health Act 2007 (c. 12) and section 208(1) of, and paragraphs 53 and 55 of Schedule 21 to, the Legal Services Act 2007 (c. 29).

25 1983 c. 20; section 37 was amended by sections 55 and 56 of, and paragraph 12 of Schedule 4 and Schedule 6 to, the Crime (Sentences) Act 1997 (c. 43), section 67 of, and paragraph 11 of Schedule 4 to, the Youth Justice and Criminal Evidence Act 1999 (c. 23), paragraph 90 of Schedule 9 to the Powers of Criminal Courts (Sentencing) Act 2000 (c. 6), section 304 of, and paragraphs 37 and 38 of Schedule 32 to, the Criminal Justice Act 2003 (c. 44), sections 49 and 65 of, and paragraph 2 of Schedule 1 and Schedule 5 to, the Violent Crime Reduction Act 2006 (c. 38), sections 1, 4, 10, 55 and paragraphs 1 and 7 of Schedule 1, and Part 1 of Schedule 11 to, the Mental Health Act 2007 (c. 12), sections 6 and 149 of, and paragraph 30 of Schedule 4, and Schedule 28 to, the Criminal Justice and Immigration Act 2008 (c. 4), sections 122 and 142 of, and paragraph 1 of Schedule 19 and paragraph 2 of Schedule 26 to, the Legal Aid, Sentencing and Punishment of Offenders Act 2012 (c. 10) and section 28 of, and paragraph 1 of Schedule 5 to, the Criminal Justice and Courts Act 2015 (c. 2). It is further amended by section 148 of, and paragraph 8 of Schedule 26 to, the Criminal Justice and Immigration Act 2008 (c. 4) with effect from a date to be appointed.

26 1983 c. 20; section 38 was amended by section 49(1) of the Crime (Sentences) Act 1997 (c. 43), sections 1(4) and 10(1) and (5) of, and paragraphs 1 and 8 of Schedule 1 to, the Mental Health Act 2007 (c. 12) and section 208(1) of, and paragraphs 53 and 56 of Schedule 21 to, the Legal Services Act 2007 (c. 29).

27 2020 (c. 17).

28 2003 c. 44; section 207 was amended by article 4(2) of, and paragraph 7 of Schedule 5 to, S.I. 2009/1182, article 14(a) and (b) of, and Part 1 of Schedule 5 to, S.I. 2010/813, section 72 of the Health and Social Care Act 2012 (c. 7), section 73 of the Legal Aid, Sentencing and Punishment of Offenders Act 2012 (c. 10) and section 62 of, and paragraph 48 of Schedule 5 to, the Children and Social Work Act 2017 (c. 16).

29 2020 (c. 17).

30 2000 c. 6.

31 1983 c. 20; section 39 was amended by sections 2(1) and 5(1) of, and paragraph 107 of Schedule 1 and Schedule 3 to, the Health Authorities Act 1995 (c. 17), section 2(5) of, and paragraphs 42 and 46 of Schedule 2 to, the National Health Service Reform and Health Care Professions Act 2002 (c. 17), section 31(1) and (2) of the Mental Health Act 2007 (c. 12), article 3 of, and paragraph 13 of the Schedule to, S.I. 2007/961 and section 55 of, and paragraphs 24 and 28 of Schedule 5 to, the Health and Social Care Act 2012 (c. 7). Section 39A was inserted by section 27(1) of the Criminal Justice Act 1991 (c. 53).

Payments to medical practitioners for reports and for giving evidence are governed by section 19(3) of the Prosecution of Offences Act 1985[32] *and by the Costs in Criminal Cases (General) Regulations 1986*[33], *regulation 17 (Determination of rates or scales of allowances payable out of central funds), regulation 20 (Expert witnesses, etc.) and regulation 25 (Written medical reports). The rates and scales of allowances payable under those Regulations are determined by the Lord Chancellor.]*

R28.9 **Information to be supplied on committal to custody or admission to hospital or guardianship**

28.9 (1) This rule applies where the court—
(a) orders the defendant's committal to custody on withholding bail or on sentencing;
(b) orders the defendant's detention and treatment in hospital; or
(c) makes a guardianship order.
(2) Where paragraph (1)(a) applies, unless the court otherwise directs the court officer must, as soon as practicable, serve on or make available to the custodian any psychiatric, psychological or other medical report about the defendant received by the court for the purposes of the case.
(3) Where paragraph (1)(b) or (c) applies, unless the court otherwise directs the court officer must, as soon as practicable, serve on or make available to (as applicable) the hospital or the guardian—
(a) a record of the court's order;
(b) such information as the court has received that appears likely to assist in treating or otherwise dealing with the defendant, including information about—
(i) the defendant's mental condition,
(ii) the defendant's other circumstances, and
(iii) the circumstances of the offence.

[Note. Rule 13.3 provides for the terms of a warrant for detention or imprisonment. Rule 13.4 provides for the information that such a warrant must contain.

For the circumstances in which the court may order the defendant's detention and treatment in hospital, see sections 35, 36, 37, 38 and 44 of the Mental Health Act 1983[34]. *For the circumstances in which the court may make a guardianship order, see the same section 37.]*

R28.10 **Information to be supplied on committal for sentence, etc.**

28.10 (1) This rule applies where a magistrates' court or the Crown Court convicts the defendant and—
(a) commits or adjourns the case to another court—
(i) for sentence, or
(ii) for the defendant to be dealt with for breach of a deferred sentence, a conditional discharge, or a suspended sentence of imprisonment, imposed by that other court;
(b) deals with a deferred sentence, a conditional discharge, or a suspended sentence of imprisonment, imposed by another court; or
(c) makes an order that another court is, or may be, required to enforce.
(2) Unless the convicting court otherwise directs, the court officer must, as soon as practicable—
(a) where paragraph (1)(a) applies, arrange the transmission from the convicting to the other court of a record of any relevant—
(i) certificate of conviction,
(ii) magistrates' court register entry,
(iii) decision about bail, for the purposes of section 5 of the Bail Act 1976[35],
(iv) note of evidence,
(v) statement or other document introduced in evidence,
(vi) medical or other report,

[32] 1985 c. 23; section 19(3) was amended by section 166 of the Criminal Justice Act 1988 (c. 33), section 7 of, and paragraph 8 of Schedule 3 to, the Criminal Procedure (Insanity and Unfitness to Plead) Act 1991 (c. 25), sections 40 and 67 of, and paragraph 4 of Schedule 7 to, the Youth Justice and Criminal Evidence Act 1999 (c. 23), section 165 of, and paragraph 99 of Schedule 9 to, the Powers of Criminal Courts (Sentencing) Act 2000 (c. 6) and section 378 of, and paragraph 107 of Schedule 16 to, the Armed Forces Act 2006 (c. 52).

[33] S.I. 1986/1335; regulation 17 was amended by regulations 2 and 13 of S.I. 2008/2448, regulation 20 was amended by regulations 2 and 14 of S.I. 2008/2448 and by regulations 4 and 7 of S.I. 2012/1804, and regulation 25 was amended by regulations 2 and 10 of S.I. 2009/2720.

[34] 1983 c. 20; section 44 was amended by sections 10, 40 and 55 of, and Part 8 of Schedule 11 to, the Mental Health Act 2007 (c. 12).

[35] 1976 c. 63; section 5 was amended by section 65 of, and Schedule 12 to, the Criminal Law Act 1977 (c. 45), section 60 of the Criminal Justice Act 1982 (c. 48), paragraph 1 of Schedule 3 to the Criminal Justice and Public Order Act 1994 (c. 33), paragraph 53 of Schedule 9 to the Powers of Criminal Courts (Sentencing) Act 2000 (c. 6), section 129(1) of the Criminal Justice and Police Act 2001 (c. 16), paragraph 182 of Schedule 8 to the Courts Act 2003 (c. 39), paragraph 48 of Schedule 3, paragraphs 1 and 2 of Schedule 36, and Parts 2, 4 and 12 of Schedule 37 to the Criminal Justice Act 2003 (c. 44) and section 208 of, and paragraphs 33 and 35 of Schedule 21 to, the Legal Services Act 2007 (c. 27).

(vii) representation order or application for such order, and
(viii) interim driving disqualification;
(b) where paragraph (1)(b) or (c) applies, arrange—
(i) the transmission from the convicting to the other court of notice of the convicting court's order, and
(ii) the recording of that order at the other court;
(c) in every case, notify the defendant and, where the defendant is under 14, an appropriate adult, of the location of the other court.

[Note. For the circumstances in which—

(a) a magistrates' court may (and, in some cases, must) commit the defendant to the Crown Court for sentence, see sections 14, 15, 16, 17, 18, 19 and 20 of the Sentencing Act 2020[36] and section 43 of the Mental Health Act 1983[37];

(b) a magistrates' court may adjourn the case to another magistrates' court for sentence, see section 10 of the Magistrates' Courts Act 1980[38] and section 28 of the 2020 Act[39];

(c) a magistrates' court or the Crown Court may (and, in some cases, must) adjourn the case to a youth court for sentence, see sections 25 and 26 of the 2020 Act[40];

(d) a youth court may adjourn the case to a magistrates' court for sentence, see section 27 of the 2020 Act[41];

(e) a magistrates' court may transfer a fine to be enforced to another court, see sections 89 and 90 of the 1980 Act[42].

For the court's powers where it convicts a defendant who is subject to a deferred sentence, a conditional discharge, or a suspended sentence of imprisonment, imposed by another court, see section 10 of, and Schedules 2 and 16 to, the 2020 Act[43].

Under section 132 of the 2020 Act[44], a fine imposed or other sum ordered to be paid in the Crown Court is enforceable by a magistrates' court specified in the order, or from which the case was committed or sent to the Crown Court.

See also sections 212(4), 298(4) and 190(4) of the 2020 Act[45]; and section 1A(9) of the Street Offences Act 1959[46].]

Application to review sentence because of assistance given or withheld **R28.11**

28.11 (1) This rule applies where the Crown Court can reduce or increase a sentence on application by a prosecutor in a case in which—
(a) since being sentenced, the defendant has assisted, or has agreed to assist, an investigator or prosecutor in relation to an offence; or
(b) since receiving a reduced sentence for agreeing to give such assistance, the defendant has failed to do so.
(2) A prosecutor who wants the court to exercise that power must—
(a) apply in writing as soon as practicable after becoming aware of the grounds for doing so;
(b) serve the application on—

36 2020 (c. 17).
37 1983 c. 20; section 43 was amended by paragraph 91 of Schedule 9 to the Powers of Criminal Courts (Sentencing) Act 2000 (c. 6) and paragraph 55 of Schedule 3, and Part 9 of Schedule 37, to the Criminal Justice Act 2003 (c. 44).
38 1980 c. 43; section 10 was amended by section 59 of, and paragraph 1 of Schedule 9 to, the Criminal Justice Act 1982 (c. 48), section 68 of, and paragraph 6 of Schedule 8 to, the Criminal Justice Act 1991 (c. 53) and section 47 of the Crime and Disorder Act 1998 (c. 37).
39 2020 (c. 17).
40 2020 (c. 17).
41 2020 (c. 17).
42 1980 c. 43; section 89 was amended by section 47 of the Criminal Justice and Public Order Act 1994 (c. 33), paragraphs 95 and 107 of Schedule 13 to the Access to Justice Act 1999 (c. 22), paragraph 225 of Schedule 8 to the Courts Act 2003 (c. 39) and articles 46 and 49 of S.I. 2006/1737. Section 90 was amended by section 47(2) of the Criminal Justice and Public Order Act 1994 (c. 33), paragraph 226 of Schedule 8 to the Courts Act 2003 (c. 39) and articles 46 and 50 of S.I. 2006/1737.
43 2020 (c. 17).
44 2020 (c. 17).
45 2020 (c. 17).
46 1959 c. 57; section 1A was inserted by section 17(1) and (3) of the Policing and Crime Act 2009 (c. 26).

(i) the court officer, and
(ii) the defendant; and
(c) in the application—
(i) explain why the sentence should be reduced, or increased, as appropriate, and
(ii) identify any other matter relevant to the court's decision, including any sentencing guideline or guideline case.

(3) The general rule is that the application must be determined by the judge who passed the sentence, unless that judge is unavailable.

(4) The court must not determine the application in the defendant's absence unless the defendant has had an opportunity to make representations at a hearing (whether or not the defendant in fact attends).

[Note. Under section 73 of the Serious Organised Crime and Police Act 2005[47]*, the Crown Court may pass a lesser sentence than it otherwise would have passed because the defendant has assisted, or has agreed to assist, an investigator or prosecutor in relation to an offence.*

Under sections 387 and 388 of the 2020 Act[48]*, where the Crown Court has sentenced a defendant a prosecutor may apply to the court—*

(a) to reduce the sentence, if the defendant subsequently assists, or agrees to assist, in the investigation or prosecution of an offence; or

(b) to increase a reduced sentence to that which the court otherwise would have passed, if the defendant agreed to give such assistance but subsequently has knowingly failed to do so.

Such an application may be made only where the defendant is still serving the sentence and the prosecutor thinks it is in the interests of justice to apply.]

CRIMINAL PROCEDURE RULES PART 29 ROAD TRAFFIC PENALTIES

[Note. Part 24 contains rules about the general procedure on sentencing in a magistrates' court. Part 25 contains corresponding rules for the Crown Court.]

R29.1 Representations about obligatory disqualification or endorsement

29.1 (1) This rule applies—

(a) where the court—
(i) convicts the defendant of an offence involving obligatory disqualification from driving and section 34(1) of the Road Traffic Offenders Act 1988[1] (Disqualification for certain offences) applies,
(ii) convicts the defendant of an offence where section 35 of the 1988 Act[2] (Disqualification for repeated offences) applies, or
(iii) convicts the defendant of an offence involving obligatory endorsement of the defendant's driving record and section 44 of the 1988 Act[3] (Orders for endorsement) applies;

(b) unless the defendant is absent.

(2) The court must explain, in terms the defendant can understand (with help, if necessary)—

(a) where paragraph (1)(a)(i) applies (obligatory disqualification under section 34)—
(i) that the court must order the defendant to be disqualified from driving for a minimum of 12 months (or 2 or 3 years, as the case may be, according to the offence and the defendant's driving record), unless the court decides that there are special reasons to order disqualification for a shorter period, or not to order disqualification at all, and
(ii) if applicable, that the period of disqualification will be reduced by at least 3 months if, by no later than 2 months before the end of the reduced period, the defendant completes an approved driving course;

47 2020 (c. 17).
48 2020 (c. 17).

1 1988 c. 53; section 34 was amended by section 29 of the Road Traffic Act 1991 (c. 40), section 3 of the Aggravated Vehicle-Taking Act 1992 (c. 11), section 165 of, and paragraph 121 of Schedule 9 to, the Powers of Criminal Courts (Sentencing) Act 2000 (c. 6), sections 56 and 107 of, and Schedule 8 to, the Police Reform Act 2002 (c. 30), section 25 of the Road Safety Act 2006 (c. 49), article 2 of S.I. 2007/3480, paragraphs 2 and 5 of Schedule 27 to the Legal Aid, Sentencing and Punishment of Offenders Act 2012 (c. 10), section 56 of, and paragraphs 9 and 12 of Schedule 22 to, the Crime and Courts Act 2013 (c. 22) and section 177 of, and paragraph 90 of Schedule 21 to, the Coroners and Justice Act 2009 (c. 25).
2 2005 c. 15.
3 2005 c. 15; section 74 was amended by article 13 of, and paragraphs 1 and 19 of Schedule 15 to, S.I. 2010/976.

(b) where paragraph (1)(a)(ii) applies (disqualification under section 35)—
  (i) that the court must order the defendant to be disqualified from driving for a minimum of 6 months (or 1 or 2 years, as the case may be, according to the defendant's driving record), unless, having regard to all the circumstances, the court decides to order disqualification for a shorter period, or not to order disqualification at all, and
  (ii) that circumstances of which the court cannot take account in making its decision are any that make the offence not a serious one; hardship (other than exceptional hardship); and any that during the last 3 years already have been taken into account by a court when ordering disqualification for less than the usual minimum period, or not at all, for repeated driving offences;

(c) where paragraph (1)(a)(iii) applies (obligatory endorsement), that the court must order the endorsement of the defendant's driving record unless the court decides that there are special reasons not to do so; and

(d) in every case, as applicable—
  (i) that the court already has received representations from the defendant about whether any such special reasons or mitigating circumstances apply and will take account of them, or
  (ii) that the defendant may make such representations now, on oath or affirmation.

(3) Unless the court already has received such representations from the defendant, before it applies rule 24.11 (magistrates' court procedure if the court convicts) or rule 25.16 (Crown Court procedure if the court convicts), as the case may be, the court must—
  (a) ask whether the defendant wants to make any such representations; and
  (b) if the answer to that question is 'yes', require the defendant to take an oath or affirm and make them.

[Note. For the circumstances in which the court—

(a) may, and in some cases must, order disqualification from driving under the Road Traffic Offenders Act 1988, see sections 26, 34, 35 and 36 of that Act[4]*;*

(b) may, for some reasons or in some circumstances, abbreviate or dispense with a period of disqualification otherwise required by the 1988 Act, see sections 34(1) and 35(1), (4) of that Act;

(c) must usually order endorsement, see sections 9, 44 and 96 of, and Schedule 2 to, the 1988 Act.

For the circumstances in which the period of a disqualification from driving must or may be extended where the court also imposes a custodial sentence, see sections 35A and 35B of the 1988 Act[5]*.*

For the circumstances in which the period of a disqualification from driving will be reduced if the defendant completes an approved driving course, see section 34A of the 1988 Act[6]*.]*

Application to remove a disqualification from driving R29.2

29.2 (1) This rule applies where, on application by the defendant, the court can remove a disqualification from driving.

(2) A defendant who wants the court to exercise that power must—
  (a) apply in writing, no earlier than the date on which the court can exercise the power;
  (b) serve the application on the court officer; and
  (c) in the application—

[4] 1988 c. 53; section 26 was substituted by section 25 of the Road Traffic Act 1991 (c. 40) and amended by paragraph 119 of Schedule 9 to the Powers of Criminal Courts (Sentencing) Act 2000 (c. 6), paragraphs 140 and 143 of Schedule 13 to the Access to Justice Act 1999 (c. 22), paragraph 2 of Schedule 2 to S.I. 1996/1974, paragraph 312 of Schedule 8 to the Courts Act 2003 (c. 39), paragraphs 32 and 34 of Schedule 5 to the Crime (International Co-operation) Act 2003 (c. 32) and sections 10 and 59 of, and paragraphs 30 and 32 of Schedule 3 and Schedule 7 to, the Road Safety Act 2006 (c. 49). Section 36 was substituted by section 32 of the Road Traffic Act 1991 (c. 40) and amended by paragraph 3 of Schedule 2 to S.I. 1996/1974, article 3 of S. I. 1998/1917, section 9(6) of, and paragraphs 2 and 7 of Schedule 7 to, the Road Safety Act 2006 (c. 49) and paragraphs 2 and 6 of Schedule 27 to the Legal Aid, Sentencing and Punishment of Offenders Act 2012 (c. 10). It is further amended by sections 10, 37 and 59 of, and paragraphs 30 and 39 of Schedule 3, and Schedule 7 to, the Road Safety Act 2006 (c. 49), with effect from a date to be appointed.

[5] 1988 c. 53; sections 35A and 35B were inserted by section 137 of, and paragraph 2 of Schedule 16 to, the Coroners and Justice Act 2009 (c. 25). Section 35A was amended by sections 89, 111 and 126 of, and paragraph 5 of Schedule 10, paragraph 1 of Schedule 14 and paragraph 4 of Schedule 21 to, the Legal Aid, Sentencing and Punishment of Offenders Act 2012 (c. 10) and sections 6 and 30 of, and paragraph 11 of Schedule 1 to, the Criminal Justice and Courts Act 2015 (c. 2).

[6] 1988 c. 53; section 34A was inserted by section 30 of the Road Traffic Act 1991 (c. 40). It was substituted by section 35 of the Road Safety Act 2006 (c. 49) for certain purposes, and for remaining purposes with effect from a date to be appointed. It is amended by section 177 of, and paragraphs 30 and 90 of Schedule 21 and paragraphs 30 and 31 of Schedule 22 to, the Coroners and Justice Act 2009 (c. 25), with effect from a date to be appointed.

(i) specify the disqualification, and
(ii) explain why the defendant wants the court to remove it.

(3) The court officer must serve a copy of the application on the chief officer of police for the local justice area.

[Note. For the circumstances in which the court may remove a disqualification from driving imposed under section 34 or 35 of the Road Traffic Offenders Act 1988, see section 42 of the Act[7]. The court may not consider an application made within 2 years of the disqualification, in any case; or, after that, before a specified period has expired.]

R29.3 Information to be supplied on order for endorsement of driving record, etc.

29.3 (1) This rule applies where the court—

(a) convicts the defendant of an offence involving obligatory endorsement, and orders there to be endorsed on the defendant's driving record (and on any counterpart licence, if other legislation requires)—
(i) particulars of the conviction,
(ii) particulars of any disqualification from driving that the court imposes, and
(iii) the penalty points to be attributed to the offence;
(b) disqualifies the defendant from driving for any other offence; or
(c) suspends or removes a disqualification from driving.

(2) The court officer must, as soon as practicable, serve on the Secretary of State notice that includes details of—

(a) where paragraph (1)(a) applies—
(i) the local justice area in which the court is acting,
(ii) the dates of conviction and sentence,
(iii) the offence, and the date on which it was committed,
(iv) the sentence, and
(v) the date of birth, and sex, of the defendant, where those details are available;
(b) where paragraph (1)(b) applies—
(i) the date and period of the disqualification, and
(ii) the power exercised by the court; and
(c) where paragraph (1)(c) applies—
(i) the date and period of the disqualification,
(ii) the date and terms of the order for its suspension or removal,
(iii) the power exercised by the court, and
(iv) where the court suspends the disqualification pending appeal, the court to which the defendant has appealed.

[Note. See sections 39(3), 42(5), 44A, 47 and 97A of the Road Traffic Offenders Act 1988[8].

Under section 25 of the 1988 Act[9], the court may order a defendant to disclose his or her date of birth, and sex, where that is not apparent (for example, where the defendant is convicted in his or her absence). Under section 27 of the 1988 Act[10], and under section 168 of the Sentencing Act 2020[11], the court may order a defendant to produce his or her driving licence, if not already produced.

For the circumstances in which the court—

(a) must usually order endorsement, see sections 9, 44 and 96 of, and Schedule 2 to, the 1988 Act;
(b) may, and in some cases must, order disqualification from driving under the 1988 Act, see sections 26, 34, 35 and 36 of that Act;

[7] 1988 c. 53; section 42 was amended by section 48 of, and paragraph 98 of Schedule 4 to, the Road Traffic Act 1991 (c. 40), sections 9, 10 and 59 of, and paragraphs 2 and 8 of Schedule 2, paragraphs 30 and 40 of Schedule 3 and Schedule 7 to, the Road Safety Act 2006 (c. 49) and paragraph 90 of Schedule 21 to the Coroners and Justice Act 2009 (c. 25).

[8] 1988 c. 53; section 44A was inserted by section 9(1) and (3) of the Road Safety Act 2006 (c. 49). Section 97A was inserted by section 8 of the Road Safety Act 2006 (c. 49).

[9] 1988 c. 53; section 25 was amended by section 90 of, and paragraphs 140 and 142 of Schedule 13 to, the Access to Justice Act 1999 (c. 22), section 165 of, and paragraph 118 of Schedule 9 to, the Powers of Criminal Courts (Sentencing) Act 2000 (c. 6) and section 109 of, and paragraph 311 of Schedule 8 to, the Courts Act 2003 (c. 39).

[10] 1988 c. 53; section 27 was amended by regulations 2 and 3 of, and paragraph 3 of Schedule 2 to, S.I. 1990/144, section 48 of, and paragraph 91 of Schedule 4 to, the Road Traffic Act 1991 (c. 40), paragraphs 140 and 144 of Schedule 13 to the Access to Justice Act 1999 (c. 22), paragraph 120 of Schedule 9 to the Powers of Criminal Courts (Sentencing) Act 2000 (c. 6), section 16 of the Child Support, Pensions and Social Security Act 2000 (c. 19), paragraph 313 of Schedule 8 to the Courts Act 2003 (c. 39) and section 10 of, and paragraphs 30 and 33 of Schedule 3 and Schedule 7 to, the Road Safety Act 2006 (c. 49). It is further amended by paragraphs 52 and 53 of Schedule 32 to the Criminal Justice Act 2003 (c. 44) and section 58 of, and Part 4 of Schedule 7 to, the Welfare Reform Act 2009 (c. 24), with effect from dates to be appointed.

[11] 2020 c. 17.

(c) *may order disqualification from driving under the 2020 Act, see sections 163 and 164 of that Act;*

(d) *may suspend a disqualification from driving pending appeal, see sections 39 and 40 of the 1988 Act*[12] *(Part 34 (Appeal to the Crown Court) and Part 35 (Appeal to the High Court by case stated) contain relevant rules);*

(e) *may remove a disqualification from driving imposed under section 34 or 35 of the 1988 Act, see section 42 of that Act (rule 29.2 applies).]*

Statutory declaration to avoid fine after fixed penalty notice **R29.4**

29.4 (1) This rule applies where—

(a) a chief officer of police, or the Secretary of State, serves on the magistrates' court officer a certificate registering, for enforcement as a fine, a sum payable by a defendant after failure to comply with a fixed penalty notice;

(b) the court officer notifies the defendant of the registration; and

(c) the defendant makes a statutory declaration with the effect that there become void—

(i) the fixed penalty notice, or any associated notice sent to the defendant as owner of the vehicle concerned, and

(ii) the registration and any enforcement proceedings.

(2) The defendant must serve that statutory declaration not more than 21 days after service of notice of the registration, unless the court extends that time limit.

(3) The court officer must—

(a) serve a copy of the statutory declaration on the person by whom the certificate was registered;

(b) cancel any endorsement on the defendant's driving record (and on any counterpart licence, if other legislation requires); and

(c) notify the Secretary of State of any such cancellation.

(4) A court officer may take the statutory declaration to which this rule refers if that officer—

(a) is a justices' legal adviser; or

(b) is nominated for the purpose by such a legal adviser.

[Note. See sections 72(1), (6), (6A), 73(1) and 74(2) of the Road Traffic Offenders Act 1988[13]*.*

For the circumstances in which—

(a) *a sum may be registered for enforcement as a fine after failure to comply with a fixed penalty notice, see sections 54, 55, 62, 63, 64, 70 and 71 of the 1988 Act*[14]*;*

(b) *the registration may become void on the making of a statutory declaration by the defendant, see sections 72 and 73 of the 1988 Act*[15]*).*

Section 2 of the Commissioners for Oaths Act 1889[16] *allows rules that regulate the procedure of a court to authorise the taking of a statutory declaration by an officer of that court.]*

[12] 1988 c. 53; section 40 was amended by sections 40 and 59 of, and paragraph 50 of Schedule 9 and paragraph 1 of Schedule 11 to, the Constitutional Reform Act 2005 (c.4).

[13] 1988 c. 53; section 72(1) was amended by paragraphs 140 and 151 of Schedule 13 to, the Access to Justice Act 1999 (c. 22).

[14] 1988 c. 53; section 54 was amended by regulations 2(2) and 3 of, and paragraph 15 of Schedule 2 to, S.I. 1990/144, sections 48 and 83 of, and paragraph 103 of Schedule 4 and Schedule 8 to, the Road Traffic Act 1991 (c. 40), sections 76 and 108 of the Police Reform Act 2002 (c. 30) and sections 5, 9(6), 10 and 59 of, and paragraphs 1, 3 and 9 of Schedule 1 to, and paragraphs 2 and 14 of Schedule 2 to, the Road Safety Act 2006 (c. 49). Section 62 was amended by section 5 of, and paragraphs 1 and 7 of Schedule 1 to, the Road Safety Act 2006 (c. 49). Section 63 was amended by section 5 of, and paragraphs 1 and 8 of Schedule 1 to, the Road Safety Act 2006 (c. 49). Section 70 was amended by section 109 of, and paragraph 316 of Schedule 8 to, the Courts Act 2003 (c. 39) and sections 5, 9(6) and 59 of, and paragraphs 1 and 12 of Schedule 1, paragraphs 2 and 21 of Schedule 2 and paragraph 7 to, the Road Safety Act 2006 (c. 49). Section 71 was amended by section 63 of, and paragraph 25(1) of Schedule 3 to, the Vehicle Excise and Registration Act 1994 (c. 22), sections 90(1) and 106 of, and paragraphs 140 and 150(1) and (2) of Schedule 13, and table 7 of Schedule 15 to, the Access to Justice Act 1999 (c. 22), section 109(1) of, and paragraph 317(1) and (2) of Schedule 8 to, the Courts Act 2003 (c. 39) and section 9(6) of, and paragraphs 2 and 22 of Schedule 2 to, the Road Safety Act 2006 (c. 49).

[15] 1988 c. 53; section 72 was amended by regulations 2(2) and 3 of, and paragraph 20 of Schedule 2 to S.I. 1990/144, section 90 of, and paragraphs 140 and 151 of Schedule 13 to, the Access to Justice Act 1999 (c. 22) and sections 5, 9 10 and 59 of, and paragraphs 1 and 13 of Schedule 1, paragraphs 2 and 23 of Schedule 2, paragraphs 30 and 50 of Schedule 3 and Schedule 7 to, the Road Safety Act 2006 (c. 49). Section 73 was amended by section 90 of, and paragraphs 140 and 151 of Schedule 13 to, the Access to Justice Act 1999 (c. 22) and sections 5 and 59 of, and paragraphs 1 and 14 of Schedule 1 and Schedule 7 to, the Road Safety Act 2006 (c. 49).

[16] 1889 c. 10; section 2 was amended by section 59 of, and paragraph 15 of Schedule 11 to, the Constitutional Reform Act 2005 (c. 4).

R29.5 Application for declaration about a course or programme certificate decision

29.5 (1) This rule applies where the court can declare unjustified—
(a) a course provider's failure or refusal to give a certificate of the defendant's satisfactory completion of an approved course; or
(b) a programme provider's giving of a certificate of the defendant's failure fully to participate in an approved programme.
(2) A defendant who wants the court to exercise that power must—
(a) apply in writing, not more than 20 business days after—
(i) the date by which the defendant was required to complete the course, or
(ii) the giving of the certificate of failure fully to participate in the programme;
(b) serve the application on the court officer; and
(c) in the application, specify the course or programme and explain (as applicable)—
(i) that the course provider has failed to give a certificate,
(ii) where the course provider has refused to give a certificate, why the defendant disagrees with the reasons for that decision, or
(iii) where the programme provider has given a certificate, why the defendant disagrees with the reasons for that decision.
(3) The court officer must serve a copy of the application on the course or programme provider.
(4) The court must not determine the application unless the defendant, and the course or programme provider, each has had an opportunity to make representations at a hearing (whether or not either in fact attends).

[Note. For the circumstances in which the court may reduce a road traffic penalty on condition that the defendant attend an approved course, or take part in an approved programme, see sections 30A, 34A and 34D of the Road Traffic Offenders Act 1988[17]*.*

Under sections 30B, 34B and 34E of the 1988 Act[18]*, the court that made the order, or the defendant's local magistrates' court, on application by the defendant may review a course or programme provider's decision that the defendant has not completed the course satisfactorily, or has not participated fully in the programme.]*

R29.6 Appeal against recognition of foreign driving disqualification

29.6 (1) This rule applies where—
(a) a Minister gives a disqualification notice under section 57 of the Crime (International Co-operation) Act 2003[19]; and
(b) the person to whom it is given wants to appeal under section 59 of the Act[20] to a magistrates' court.
(2) That person ('the appellant') must serve an appeal notice on—
(a) the court officer, at a magistrates' court in the local justice area in which the appellant lives; and
(b) the Minister, at the address given in the disqualification notice.
(3) The appellant must serve the appeal notice within the period for which section 59 of the 2003 Act provides.
(4) The appeal notice must—
(a) attach a copy of the disqualification notice;
(b) explain which of the conditions in section 56 of the 2003 Act[21] is not met, and why section 57 of the Act therefore does not apply; and

17 1988 c. 53; section 30A is inserted by section 34(1) and (3) of the Road Safety Act 2006 (c. 49), with effect from a date to be appointed. Section 34A was inserted by section 30 of the Road Traffic Act 1991 (c. 40). It is amended by section 177(1) and (2) of, and paragraphs 30 and 90(1) and (3) of Schedule 21 and paragraphs 30 and 31 of Schedule 22 to, the Coroners and Justice Act 2009 (c. 25), with effect from a date to be appointed. Section 34D is inserted by section 15(1) of the Road Safety Act 2006 (c. 49), with effect from a date to be appointed. It is amended by section 177(1) of, and paragraph 90(1) and (5) of Schedule 21 to, the Coroners and Justice Act 2009 (c. 25), with effect from a date to be appointed.

18 1988 c. 53; section 30B is inserted by section 34(1) and (3) of the Road Safety Act 2006 (c. 49), with effect from a date to be appointed. Section 34B was inserted by section 30 of the Road Traffic Act 1991 (c. 40) and amended by paragraphs 140, 145 and 146 of Schedule 13 and Part V of Schedule 15 to, the Access to Justice Act 1999 (c. 22). Section 34B is substituted by section 35 of the Road Safety Act 2006 (c. 49), with effect from a date to be appointed. Section 34E is inserted by section 15(1) of the Road Safety Act 2006 (c. 49), with effect from a date to be appointed.

19 2003 c. 32; section 57 is in force in relation only to an offence of which an offender has been convicted in Ireland. For remaining purposes, it will come into force on a date to be appointed.

20 2003 c. 32; section 59 is in force in relation only to an offence of which an offender has been convicted in Ireland. For remaining purposes, it will come into force on a date to be appointed. Section 59 was amended by article 2 of, and paragraph 97 of the Schedule to, S.I. 2005/886.

21 2003 c. 32; section 56 is in force in relation only to an offence of which an offender has been convicted in Ireland. For remaining purposes, it will come into force on a date to be appointed.

(c) include any application to suspend the disqualification, under section 60 of the Act[22].

(5) The Minister may serve a respondent's notice, and must do so if—
(a) the Minister wants to make representations to the court; or
(b) the court so directs.

(6) The Minister must—
(a) unless the court otherwise directs, serve any such respondent's notice not more than 14 days after—
(i) the appellant serves the appeal notice, or
(ii) a direction to do so; and
(b) in any such respondent's notice—
(i) identify the grounds of opposition on which the Minister relies,
(ii) summarise any relevant facts not already included in the disqualification and appeal notices, and
(iii) identify any other document that the Minister thinks the court will need to decide the appeal (and serve any such document with the notice).

(7) Where the court determines an appeal, the general rule is that it must do so at a hearing (which must be in public, unless the court otherwise directs).

(8) The court officer must serve on the Minister—
(a) notice of the outcome of the appeal;
(b) notice of any suspension of the disqualification; and
(c) the appellant's driving licence, if surrendered to the court officer.

[Note. Section 56 of the Crime (International Co-operation) Act 2003 sets out the conditions for recognition in the United Kingdom of a foreign driving disqualification, and provides that section 57 of the Act applies where they are met. Under section 57, the appropriate Minister may, and in some cases must, give the person concerned notice that he or she is disqualified in the UK, too, and for what period.

Under section 59 of the 2003 Act, that person may appeal to a magistrates' court. If the court is satisfied that section 57 of the Act does not apply in that person's case, the court must allow the appeal and notify the Minister. Otherwise, it must dismiss the appeal.

The time limit for appeal under section 59 of the 2003 Act is the end of the period of 21 days beginning with the day on which the Minister gives the notice under section 57. That period may be neither extended nor shortened.

Under section 60 of the 2003 Act, the court may suspend the disqualification, on such terms as it thinks fit.

Under section 63 of the 2003 Act[23], it is an offence for a person to whom the Minister gives a notice under section 57 not to surrender any licence that he or she holds, within the same period as for an appeal.]

Criminal Procedure Rules Part 30 Enforcement of Fines and Other Orders for Payment

[Note. Part 13 contains rules about warrants for arrest, detention or imprisonment, including such warrants issued for failure to pay fines, etc.

Part 24 contains rules about the procedure on sentencing in a magistrates' court.

Part 28 contains rules about the exercise of a magistrates' court's powers to enforce an order made by another court.]

When this Part applies R30.1

30.1 (1) This Part applies where a magistrates' court can enforce payment of—
(a) a fine, or a sum that legislation requires the court to treat as a fine; or
(b) any other sum that a court has ordered to be paid—
(i) on a conviction, or
(ii) on the forfeiture of a surety.

[22] 2003 c. 32; section 60 is in force in relation only to an offence of which an offender has been convicted in Ireland. For remaining purposes, it will come into force on a date to be appointed. Section 60 was amended by section 40(4) of, and paragraph 79 of Schedule 9 to, the Constitutional Reform Act 2005 (c. 4).

[23] 2003 c. 32; section 63 is in force in relation only to an offence of which an offender has been convicted in Ireland. For remaining purposes, it will come into force on a date to be appointed. It was amended by sections 10(12) and 59 of, and paragraphs 74 and 75 of Schedule 3, and Schedule 7 to, the Road Safety Act 2006 (c. 49).

(2) Rules 30.7 to 30.9 apply where the court, or a fines officer, issues a warrant for an enforcement agent to take control of a defendant's goods and sell them, using the procedure in Schedule 12 to the Tribunals, Courts and Enforcement Act 2007[1].

(3) In this Part—
(a) 'defendant' means anyone liable to pay a sum to which this Part applies;
(b) 'payment terms' means by when, and by what (if any) instalments, such a sum must be paid.

[Note. For the means by which a magistrates' court may enforce payment, see—

(a) Part 3 of the Magistrates' Courts Act 1980[2]; and
(b) Schedule 5 to the Courts Act 2003[3] and the Fines Collection Regulations 2006[4].

Under that Schedule and those Regulations, some enforcement powers may be exercised by a fines officer.

See also section 62 of, and Schedule 12 to, the Tribunals, Courts and Enforcement Act 2007. In that Act, a warrant to which this Part applies is described as 'a warrant of control'.]

R30.2 **Exercise of court's powers**

30.2 The court must not exercise its enforcement powers unless—
(a) the court officer has served on the defendant any collection order or other notice of—
(i) the obligation to pay,
(ii) the payment terms, and
(iii) how and where the defendant must pay; and
(b) the defendant has failed to comply with the payment terms.

[Note. See section 76 of the Magistrates' Courts Act 1980[5]; and paragraphs 12 and 13 of Schedule 5 to the Courts Act 2003[6].]

R30.3 **Duty to give receipt**

30.3 (1) This rule applies where the defendant makes a payment to—
(a) the court officer specified in an order or notice served under rule 30.2;
(b) another court officer;
(c) any—
(i) custodian of the defendant,
(ii) supervisor appointed to encourage the defendant to pay, or
(iii) responsible officer appointed under a community sentence or a suspended sentence of imprisonment; or
(d) a person executing a warrant to which rule 13.6 (warrants for arrest, detention or imprisonment that cease to have effect on payment) or this Part applies.

(2) The person receiving the payment must—
(a) give the defendant a receipt unless the method of payment generates an independent record (for example, a bank record); and
(b) as soon as practicable transmit the payment to the court officer specified in an order or notice served under rule 30.2, if the recipient is not that court officer.

[Note. For the effect of payment to a person executing a warrant to which rule 13.6 applies, see that rule and sections 79[7] and 125(1)[8] of the Magistrates' Courts Act 1980.

1 2007 c. 15.
2 1980 c. 43.
3 2003 c. 39; Schedule 5 was amended by articles 2, 4, 6, 7 and 8 of S.I. 2006/1737, section 62 of, and paragraphs 148 and 149 of Schedule 13 to, the Tribunals, Courts and Enforcement Act 2007 (c. 15), section 80 of the Criminal Justice and Immigration Act 2008 (c. 4), section 88 of the Legal Aid, Sentencing and Punishment of Offenders Act 2012 (c. 10), section 10 of, and paragraphs 24 and 27 of the Schedule to, the Prevention of Social Housing Fraud Act 2013 (c. 3), section 27 of the Crime and Courts Act 2013 (c. 22) and section 56 of the Criminal Justice and Courts Act 2015 (c. 2). It is further amended by section 26 of the Crime and Courts Act 2013 (c. 22) and paragraph 23 of Schedule 5 to the Modern Slavery Act 2015 (c. 30), with effect from dates to be appointed.
4 S.I. 2006/501.
5 1980 c. 43; section 76 was amended by section 7 of the Maintenance Enforcement Act 1991 (c. 17), section 78 of, and Schedule 16 to, the Criminal Justice Act 1982 (c. 48), and section 62(3) of, and paragraphs 45 and 46 of Schedule 13 to, the Tribunals, Courts and Enforcement Act 2007 (c. 15).
6 2003 c. 39; paragraph 13 was amended by articles 2, 4 and 15 of S.I. 2006/1737.
7 1980 c. 43; section 79 was amended by paragraph 219 of Schedule 8 to the Courts Act 2003 (c. 39) and section 62 of, and paragraphs 45, 47 and 48 of Schedule 13 to, the Tribunals, Courts and Enforcement Act 2007 (c. 15).
8 1980 c. 43; section 125 was amended by section 33 of the Police and Criminal Evidence Act 1984 (c. 60), section 65(1) of the Criminal Justice Act 1988 (c. 33), sections 95(1), 97(4) and 106 of, and Part V of Schedule 15 and Table (8) to, the Access to Justice Act 1999 (c. 22), section 109(1) of, and paragraph 238 of Schedule 8 to, the Courts Act 2003 (c. 39) and sections 62(3), 86 and 146 of and paragraphs 45 and 57 of Schedule 23 to, the Tribunals, Courts and Enforcement Act 2007 (c. 15).

For the circumstances in which the court may appoint a person to supervise payment, see section 88 of the 1980 Act[9]*.]*

Appeal against decision of fines officer R30.4

30.4 (1) This rule applies where—
(a) a collection order is in force;
(b) a fines officer makes a decision under one of these paragraphs of Schedule 5 to the Courts Act 2003—
(i) paragraph 22 (Application to fines officer for variation of order or attachment of earnings order, etc.),
(ii) paragraph 31[10] (Application to fines officer for variation of reserve terms), or
(iii) paragraph 37[11] (Functions of fines officer in relation to defaulters: referral or further steps notice); and
(c) the defendant wants to appeal against that decision.
(2) Unless the court otherwise directs, the defendant must—
(a) appeal in writing not more than 10 business days after the decision;
(b) serve the appeal on the court officer; and
(c) in the appeal—
(i) explain why a different decision should be made, and
(ii) specify the decision that the defendant proposes.
(3) Where the court determines an appeal the general rule is that it must do so at a hearing.

[Note. Under paragraph 12 of Schedule 5 to the Courts Act 2003, where a collection order is in force the court's powers to deal with the defendant's liability to pay the sum for which that order was made are subject to the provisions of that Schedule and to fines collection regulations.

For the circumstances in which a defendant may appeal against a decision to which this rule applies, see paragraphs 23, 32 and 37(9) of Schedule 5 to the 2003 Act[12]*. The time limit for appeal is prescribed by those paragraphs. It may be neither extended nor shortened.]*

Application to reduce a fine, vary payment terms or remit a courts charge R30.5

30.5 (1) This rule applies where—
(a) no collection order is in force; and the defendant wants the court to—
(i) reduce the amount of a fine, or
(ii) vary payment terms; or
(b) the defendant, a fines officer or an enforcement agent wants the court to remit a criminal courts charge.
(2) Unless the court otherwise directs, such a defendant, fines officer or enforcement agent must—
(a) apply in writing;
(b) serve the application on the court officer;
(c) if the application is to reduce a fine or vary payment terms, explain—
(i) what relevant circumstances have not yet been considered by the court, and
(ii) why the fine should be reduced, or the payment terms varied; and
(d) if the application is to remit a criminal courts charge, explain—
(i) how the circumstances meet the time limits and other conditions in section 50 of the Sentencing Act 2020[13], and
(ii) why the charge should be remitted.
(3) The court may determine an application—
(a) at a hearing, which may be in public or in private; or
(b) without a hearing.

[9] 1980 c. 43; section 88 was amended by paragraph 53 of Schedule 14 to the Criminal Justice Act 1982 (c. 48), paragraph 68 of Schedule 9 to the Powers of Criminal Courts (Sentencing) Act 2000 (c. 6) and section 62 of, and paragraphs 45 and 54 of Schedule 13 to, the Tribunals, Courts and Enforcement Act 2007 (c. 15). It is further amended by paragraphs 58 and 64 of Schedule 7 to the Criminal Justice and Court Services Act 2000 (c. 43) with effect from a date to be appointed.
[10] 2003 c. 39; paragraph 31 was amended by articles 2, 4 and 20 of S.I. 2006/1737.
[11] 2003 c. 39; paragraph 37 was amended by articles 2, 4 and 25(a) and (b) of S.I. 2006/1737.
[12] 2003 c. 39; paragraph 32 was amended by articles 2, 4 and 24(b) of S.I. 2006/1737.
[13] 2020 c. 17.

[Note. See sections 75, 85 and 85A of the Magistrates' Courts Act 1980[14]*, sections 50 and 127 of the Sentencing Act 2020*[15].

Under section 46 of the 2020 Act , a court must, at the times listed in sections 44 and 45 of that Act, order a defendant convicted of an offence to pay a charge in respect of relevant court costs. Under section 50 of the Act, a magistrates' court may remit the whole or part of such a charge, but—

(a) the court may do so only if it is satisfied that—
(i) the defendant has taken all reasonable steps to pay the charge, having regard to his or her personal circumstances, or
(ii) collection and enforcement of the charge is impracticable;
(b) the court may not do so at a time when the defendant is in prison; and
(c) the court may not do so unless the periods specified by regulations under section 21E all have expired.]

R30.6 **Claim to avoid fine after penalty notice**

30.6 (1) This rule applies where—
(a) a chief officer of police serves on the magistrates' court officer a certificate registering, for enforcement as a fine, a sum payable by a defendant after failure to comply with a penalty notice; and
(b) the court or a fines officer enforces the fine.
(2) A defendant who claims not to be the person to whom the penalty notice was issued must, unless the court otherwise directs—
(a) make that claim in writing; and
(b) serve it on the court officer.
(3) The court officer must—
(a) notify the chief officer of police by whom the certificate was registered; and
(b) refer the case to the court.
(4) Where such a claim is made—
(a) the general rule is that the court must adjourn the enforcement for 28 days and fix a hearing; but
(b) the court may make a different order.
(5) At any such hearing, the chief officer of police must introduce any evidence to contradict the defendant's claim.

[Note. See section 10 of the Criminal Justice and Police Act 2001[16].

For the circumstances in which a sum may be registered for enforcement as a fine after failure to comply with a penalty notice, see sections 8 and 9 of the 2001 Act[17]*.]*

R30.7 **Information to be included in a warrant of control**

30.7 (1) A warrant must identify—
(a) each person to whom it is directed;
(b) the defendant against whom it was issued;
(c) the sum for which it was issued and the reason that sum is owed;
(d) the court or fines officer who issued it, unless that is otherwise recorded by the court officer; and
(e) the court office for the court or fines officer who issued it.
(2) A person to whom a warrant is directed must record on it the date and time at which it is received.
(3) A warrant that contains an error is not invalid, as long as—

[14] 1980 c. 43; section 75 was amended by section 11 of, and paragraph 6 of Schedule 2 to, the Maintenance Enforcement Act 1991 (c. 17). Section 85 was substituted by section 61 of the Criminal Justice Act 1988 (c. 33) and amended by section 55 of, and paragraph 10(2) of Schedule 4 to, the Crime (Sentences) Act 1997 (c. 43), section 109(1) of, and paragraph 222 of Schedule 8 to, the Courts Act 2003 (c. 39) and section 179 of the Anti-social Behaviour, Crime and Policing Act 2014 (c. 12). It is further amended by paragraphs 25 and 28 of Schedule 32 to the Criminal Justice Act 2003 (c. 44) and section 26 of the Crime and Courts Act 2013 (c. 22), with effect from dates to be appointed. Section 85A was inserted by section 51(1) of the Criminal Justice Act 1982 (c. 48).

[15] 2020 (c. 17).

[16] 2001 c. 16; section 10 was amended by paragraphs 1 and 10 of Schedule 23 to the Legal Aid, Sentencing and Punishment of Offenders Act 2012 (c. 10).

[17] 2001 c. 16; section 8 was amended by section 109(1) of, and paragraph 399 of Schedule 8 to, the Courts Act 2003 (c. 39). Section 9 was amended by section 109(1) of, and paragraph 400(1) (2) (3) and (4) of Schedule 8 to, the Courts Act 2003 (c. 39).

(a) it was issued in respect of a lawful decision by the court or fines officer; and
(b) it contains enough information to identify that decision.

[Note. See sections 78 and 125ZA of the Magistrates' Courts Act 1980[18]*.]*

Warrant of control: application by enforcement agent for extension of time, etc. **R30.8**

30.8 (1) This rule applies where an enforcement agent wants the court to exercise a power under Schedule 12 to the Tribunals, Courts and Enforcement Act 2007[19], or under regulations made under that Schedule, to—
(a) shorten or extend a time limit;
(b) give the agent authority to—
(i) enter premises which the agent would not otherwise have authority to enter,
(ii) enter or remain on premises at a time at which the agent would not otherwise have authority to be there,
(iii) use reasonable force, in circumstances in which the agent would not otherwise have authority to use such force,
(iv) sell goods by a method which the agent would not otherwise have authority to use, or
(v) recover disbursements which the agent would not otherwise have authority to recover;
(c) specify the manner in which goods which have not been sold must be disposed of.

(2) Such an enforcement agent must—
(a) apply in writing;
(b) serve the application on the court officer; and
(c) pay any fee prescribed.

(3) The application must—
(a) identify the power that the agent wants the court to exercise;
(b) explain how the conditions for the exercise of that power are satisfied, including any condition that requires the agent to give another person notice of the application;
(c) specify those persons, if any, to whom the agent has given notice in accordance with such a condition; and
(d) propose the terms of the order that the agent wants the court to make.

(4) A person to whom the enforcement agent has given notice of an application and who wants to make representations to the court must—
(a) serve the representations on—
(i) the court officer,
(ii) the enforcement agent, and
(iii) any other person to whom the enforcement agent gave notice;
(b) do so as soon as reasonably practicable and in any event within such period as the court directs; and
(c) in the representations, propose the terms of the order that that person wants the court to make, and explain why.

(5) The court—
(a) must not determine an application unless any person to whom the enforcement agent gave notice—
(i) is present, or
(ii) has had a reasonable opportunity to respond; but
(b) subject to that, may determine an application—
(i) at a hearing, which must be in private unless the court otherwise directs, or
(ii) without a hearing.

[Note. See paragraphs 8, 15, 20, 21, 25, 31, 32 and 41 of Schedule 12 to the Tribunals, Courts and Enforcement Act 2007[20]*, regulations 6, 9, 13, 22, 25, 28, 29, 41 and 47 of the Taking Control of Goods Regulations 2013*[21] *and regulation 10 of the Taking Control of Goods (Fees) Regulations 2014*[22]*. Under paragraph 41 of that Schedule and regulation 41 of the 2013 Regulations, on an application for authority to sell*

[18] 1980 c. 43; section 78 was amended by sections 37 and 46 of the Criminal Justice Act 1982 (c. 48) and paragraph 219 of Schedule 8 to, the Courts Act 2003 (c. 39). Section 125ZA was inserted by section 68 of the Tribunals, Courts and Enforcement Act 2007 (c. 15).
[19] 2007 c. 15
[20] 2007 c. 15. Paragraph 31 of Schedule 12 was amended by section 25(1), (5) of the Crime and Courts Act 2013 (c. 22). Paragraphs 60 and 66 of Schedule 12 were amended by paragraph 52 of Schedule 9 to the Crime and Courts Act 2013 (c. 22).
[21] S.I. 2013/1894.
[22] S.I. 2014/1.

goods otherwise than by public auction the enforcement agent must give notice to a creditor of the defendant in the circumstances described in those provisions.]

R30.9 Warrant of control: application to resolve dispute

30.9 (1) This rule applies where a defendant's goods are sold using the procedure in Schedule 12 to the Tribunals, Courts and Enforcement Act 2007 and there is a dispute about—

(a) what share of the proceeds of those goods should be paid by the enforcement agent to a co-owner; or

(b) the fees or disbursements sought or recovered by the enforcement agent out of the proceeds.

(2) An enforcement agent, a defendant or a co-owner who wants the court to resolve the dispute must—

(a) apply in writing as soon as practicable after becoming aware of the grounds for doing so;

(b) serve the application on—

(i) the court officer,

(ii) each other party to the dispute, and

(iii) any other co-owner; and

(c) pay any fee prescribed.

(3) The application must—

(a) identify the warrant of control;

(b) specify the goods sold, the proceeds, and the fees and disbursements sought or recovered by the enforcement agent;

(c) identify the power that the applicant wants the court to exercise;

(d) specify the persons served with the application;

(e) explain the circumstances of the dispute; and

(f) propose the terms of the order that the applicant wants the court to make.

(4) A person served with an application who wants to make representations to the court must—

(a) serve the representations on—

(i) the court officer,

(ii) the applicant, and

(iii) any other person on whom the application was served;

(b) do so as soon as reasonably practicable and in any event within such period as the court directs; and

(c) in the representations, propose the terms of the order that that person wants the court to make, and explain why.

(5) The court—

(a) must determine an application at a hearing, which must be in private unless the court otherwise directs;

(b) must not determine an application unless each party—

(i) is present, or

(ii) has had a reasonable opportunity to attend.

[Note. See paragraph 50 of Schedule 12 to the Tribunals, Courts and Enforcement Act 2007[23], and regulations 15 and 16 of the Taking Control of Goods (Fees) Regulations 2014[24].]

Criminal Procedure Rules Part 31 Behaviour Orders

[Note. See Part 3 for the court's general powers to consider an application and to give directions.]

R31.1 When this Part applies

31.1 (1) This Part applies where a magistrates' court or the Crown Court can make, vary or revoke a civil order—

(a) as well as, or instead of, passing a sentence, or in any other circumstances in which other legislation allows the court to make such an order; and

(b) that requires someone to do, or not do, something

(2) A reference to a 'behaviour order' in this Part is a reference to any such order.

(3) A reference to 'hearsay evidence' in this Part is a reference to evidence consisting of hearsay within the meaning of section 1(2) of the Civil Evidence Act 1995[1].

[Note. In the circumstances set out in the Acts listed, the court can make a behaviour order—

23 2007 c. 15.
24 S.I. 2014/1.

1 1995 c. 38.

(a) on conviction, under—
(i) section 14A of the Football Spectators Act 1989[2] *(football banning orders),*
(ii) section 360 of the Sentencing Act 2020[3] *(restraining orders),*
(iii) sections 1C and 1D of the Crime and Disorder Act 1998[4] *(anti-social behaviour orders and interim anti-social behaviour orders),*
(iv) section 366 of the 2020 Act (parenting orders),
(v) section 345 of the 2020 Act (sexual harm prevention orders),
(vi) section 19 or 21 of the Serious Crime Act 2007[5] *(serious crime prevention orders),*
(vii) section 331 of the 2020 Act (criminal behaviour orders),
(viii) section 14 of the Modern Slavery Act 2015[6] *(slavery and trafficking prevention orders),*
(ix) section 19 of the Psychoactive Substances Act 2016[7] *(prohibition orders),*
(x) section 20 of the Immigration Act 2016[8] *(labour market enforcement orders),*
(xi) section 19 of the Offensive Weapons Act 2019[9] *(knife crime prevention orders);*
(b) on acquittal, under section 5A of the Protection from Harassment Act 1997[10] *(restraining orders on acquittal);*
(c) on the making of a finding of not guilty by reason of insanity, or a finding of disability, under section 14 of the Modern Slavery Act 2015 (slavery and trafficking prevention orders); and
(d) in proceedings for a genital mutilation offence, under paragraph 3 of Schedule 2 to the Female Genital Mutilation Act 2003[11] *(female genital mutilation protection orders).*

Section 1(2) of the Civil Evidence Act 1995 defines hearsay as meaning 'a statement made otherwise than by a person while giving oral evidence in the proceedings which is tendered as evidence of the matters stated'. Section 13 of that Act defines a statement as meaning 'any representation of fact or opinion, however made'.]

Behaviour orders: general rules **R31.2**

31.2 (1) The court must not make a behaviour order unless the person to whom it is directed has had an opportunity—
(a) to consider—
(i) what order is proposed and why, and
(ii) the evidence in support; and
(b) to make representations at a hearing (whether or not that person in fact attends).
(2) That restriction does not apply to making an interim behaviour order, but unless other legislation otherwise provides such an order has no effect unless the person to whom it is directed—
(a) is present when it is made; or
(b) is handed a document recording the order not more than 5 business days after it is made
(3) Where the court decides not to make, where it could—
(a) a football banning order; or
(b) a parenting order, after a person under 16 is convicted of an offence,
the court must announce, at a hearing in public, the reasons for its decision.

[Note. The Acts listed in the note to rule 31.1 impose requirements specific to each different type of behaviour order. Not all allow the court to make an interim behaviour order.

See section 14A(3) of the Football Spectators Act 1989[12]*, and section 366 of the Sentencing Act 2020.]*

[2] 1989 c. 37; section 14A was amended by section 1 of, and paragraphs 1 and 2 of Schedule 1 to, the Football (Disorder) Act 2000 (c. 25), section 86(5) of the Anti-Social Behaviour Act 2003 (c. 38), section 139(10) of the Serious Organised Crime and Police Act 2005 (c. 15) and sections 52(2) and 65 of, and paragraphs 1 and 2 of Schedule 3 and Schedule 5 to, the Violent Crime Reduction Act 2006 (c. 38).
[3] 2020 (c. 17).
[4] 1998 c. 37; section 1C was inserted by section 64 of the Police Reform Act 2002 (c. 30) and amended by sections 83 and 86 of the Anti-social Behaviour Act 2003 (c. 38), sections 139, 140, 141 and 174 of, and Part 2 of Schedule 17 to, the Serious Organised Crime and Police Act 2005 (c. 15) and sections 123 and 124 of the Criminal Justice and Immigration Act 2008 (c. 4). Section 1D was inserted by section 65 of the Police Reform Act 2002 (c. 30) and amended by section 139 of the Serious Organised Crime and Police Act 2005 (c. 15). Each section was repealed on 20th October, 2014, by section 181 of, and paragraph 24 of Schedule 11 to, the Anti-social Behaviour, Crime and Policing Act 2014 (c. 12), subject to the saving provisions of section 33 of that Act.
[5] 2007 c. 27; section 21 was amended by section 48 of the Serious Crime Act 2015 (c. 9).
[6] 2015 c. 30.
[7] 2016 c. 2.
[8] 2016 c. 19.
[9] 2019 c. 17; section 19 comes into force on a date to be appointed.
[10] 1997 c. 40; section 5A was inserted by section 12(5) of the Domestic Violence, Crime and Victims Act 2004 (c. 28).
[11] 2003 c. 31; Schedule 2 was inserted by section 73 of the Serious Crime Act 2015 (c. 9).
[12] 1989 c. 37; section 14A was substituted, together with sections 14 and 14B-14J, for the existing sections 14-17, by section 1 of, and paragraphs 1 and 2 of Schedule 1 to, the Football (Disorder) Act 2000 (c. 25).

R31.3 Application for behaviour order and notice of terms of proposed order: special rules

31.3 (1) This rule applies where—

(a) a prosecutor wants the court to make one of the following orders if the defendant is convicted—

(i) an anti-social behaviour order (but this rule does not apply to an application for an interim anti-social behaviour order),

(ii) a serious crime prevention order,

(iii) a criminal behaviour order,

(iv) a prohibition order; or

(v) a knife crime prevention order;

(b) a prosecutor proposes, on the prosecutor's initiative or at the court's request, a sexual harm prevention order if the defendant is convicted; or

(c) a prosecutor proposes a restraining order whether the defendant is convicted or acquitted.

(2) Where paragraph (1)(a) applies (order on application), the prosecutor must serve a notice of intention to apply for such an order on—

(a) the court officer;

(b) the defendant against whom the prosecutor wants the court to make the order; and

(c) any person on whom the order would be likely to have a significant adverse effect, as soon as practicable (without waiting for the verdict).

(3) A notice under paragraph (2) must—

(a) summarise the relevant facts;

(b) identify the evidence on which the prosecutor relies in support;

(c) attach any written statement that the prosecutor has not already served; and

(d) specify the order that the prosecutor wants the court to make.

(4) A defendant served with a notice under paragraph (2) must—

(a) serve notice of any evidence on which the defendant relies on—

(i) the court officer, and

(ii) the prosecutor,

as soon as practicable (without waiting for the verdict); and

(b) in the notice, identify that evidence and attach any written statement that has not already been served.

(5) Where paragraph (1)(b) applies (sexual harm prevention order proposed), the prosecutor must—

(a) serve a draft order on the court officer and on the defendant not less than 2 business days before the hearing at which the order may be made; and

(b) in the draft order specify those prohibitions which the prosecutor proposes as necessary for the purpose of—

(i) protecting the public or any particular members of the public from sexual harm from the defendant, or

(ii) protecting children or vulnerable adults generally, or any particular children or vulnerable adults, from sexual harm from the defendant outside the United Kingdom.

(6) Where paragraph (1)(c) applies (restraining order proposed), the prosecutor must—

(a) serve a draft order on the court officer and on the defendant as soon as practicable (without waiting for the verdict); and

(b) in the draft order specify—

(i) those prohibitions which, if the defendant is convicted, the prosecutor proposes for the purpose of protecting a person from conduct which amounts to harassment or will cause fear of violence, or

(ii) those prohibitions which, if the defendant is acquitted, the prosecutor proposes as necessary to protect a person from harassment by the defendant.

(7) Where the prosecutor wants the court to make an anti-social behaviour order, a criminal behaviour order or a prohibition order, the rules about special measures directions in Part 18 (Measures to assist a witness or defendant to give evidence) apply, but—

(a) the prosecutor must apply when serving a notice under paragraph (2); and

(b) the time limits in rule 18.4(a) do not apply.

[Note. The Practice Direction sets out a form of notice for use in connection with this rule.

The orders listed in rule 31.3(1)(a) may be made on application by the prosecutor. The orders to which rule 31.3(1)(b) and (c) apply require no application and may be made on the court's own initiative. Under section 8 of the Serious Crime Act 2007 a serious crime prevention order may be made only on an application by the Director of Public Prosecutions or the Director of the Serious Fraud Office. See also paragraphs 2, 7 and 13 of Schedule 2 to the 2007 Act.

Under section 1I of the Crime and Disorder Act 1998[13]*, on an application for an anti-social behaviour order the court may give a special measures direction under the Youth Justice and Criminal Evidence Act 1999. Under section 340 of the Sentencing Act 2020*[14] *the court may give such a direction on an application for a criminal behaviour order, and under section 33 of the Psychoactive Substances Act 2016*[15] *the court may do so in proceedings for a prohibition order.*

If a party relies on hearsay evidence, see also rules 31.6, 31.7, and 31.8.]

Evidence to assist the court: special rules **R31.4**

31.4 (1) This rule applies where the court can make on its own initiative—
(a) a football banning order;
(b) a restraining order; or
(c) an anti-social behaviour order.
(2) A party who wants the court to take account of evidence not already introduced must—
(a) serve notice on—
(i) the court officer, and
(ii) every other party,
as soon as practicable (without waiting for the verdict); and
(b) in the notice, identify that evidence; and
(c) attach any written statement containing such evidence.

[Note. If a party relies on hearsay evidence, see also rules 31.6, 31.7, and 31.8.]

Application to vary or revoke behaviour order **R31.5**

31.5 (1) The court may vary or revoke a behaviour order if—
(a) the legislation under which it is made allows the court to do so; and
(b) one of the following applies—
(i) the prosecutor,
(ii) the person to whom the order is directed,
(iii) any other person protected or affected by the order,
(iv) the relevant authority or responsible officer,
(v) the relevant Chief Officer of Police,
(vi) the Director of Public Prosecutions, or
(vii) the Director of the Serious Fraud Office.
(2) A person applying under this rule must—
(a) apply in writing as soon as practicable after becoming aware of the grounds for doing so, explaining—
(i) what material circumstances have changed since the order was made, and
(ii) why the order should be varied or revoked as a result; and
(b) serve the application on—
(i) the court officer,
(ii) as appropriate, the prosecutor or defendant, and
(iii) any other person listed in paragraph (1)(b), if the court so directs.
(3) A party who wants the court to take account of any particular evidence before making its decision must, as soon as practicable—
(a) serve notice on—
(i) the court officer,
(ii) as appropriate, the prosecutor or defendant, and
(iii) any other person listed in paragraph (1)(b) on whom the court directed the application to be served; and
(b) in that notice identify the evidence and attach any written statement that has not already been served.
(4) The court may decide an application under this rule with or without a hearing.
(5) But the court must not—
(a) dismiss an application under this rule unless the applicant has had an opportunity to make representations at a hearing (whether or not the applicant in fact attends); or
(b) allow an application under this rule unless everyone required to be served, by this rule or by the court, has had at least 10 business days in which to make representations, including representations about whether there should be a hearing.

[13] 1998 c. 37; section 1I was inserted by section 143 of the Serious Organised Crime and Police Act 2005 (c. 15) and amended by paragraph 72 of Schedule 21 and Part 3 of Schedule 23 to the Coroners and Justice Act 2009 (c. 25).
[14] 2014 c. 12.
[15] 2020 c. 17.

(6) The court officer must—
(a) serve the application on any person, if the court so directs; and
(b) give notice of any hearing to—
(i) the applicant, and
(ii) any person required to be served, by this rule or by the court.

[Note. The legislation that gives the court power to make a behaviour order may limit the circumstances in which it may be varied or revoked and may require a hearing. Under section 22E of the Serious Crime Act 2007[16], where a person already subject to a serious crime prevention order is charged with a serious offence or with an offence of failing to comply with the order, the court may vary the order so that it continues in effect until that prosecution concludes.

Under section 26 of the Offensive Weapons Act 2019[17], where the court has made a knife crime prevention order the court may require the applicant and the defendant to attend one or more review hearings to consider whether the order should be varied or discharged. Where a requirement or prohibition imposed by the knife crime prevention order is to have effect after the end of one year from the date the order is made, the court must convene such a review on a specified date within the last 4 weeks of that year.

If a party relies on hearsay evidence, see also rules 31.6, 31.7 and 31.8.]

R31.6 **Notice of hearsay evidence**

31.6 (1) A party who wants to introduce hearsay evidence must—
(a) serve notice on—
(i) the court officer, and
(ii) every other party directly affected; and
(b) in that notice—
(i) explain that it is a notice of hearsay evidence,
(ii) identify that evidence,
(iii) identify the person who made the statement which is hearsay, or explain why if that person is not identified, and
(iv) explain why that person will not be called to give oral evidence.
(2) A party may serve one notice under this rule in respect of more than one notice and more than one witness.

[Note. For the time within which to serve a notice of hearsay evidence, see rule 31.3(2) to (4), rule 31.4(2) and rule 31.5(3). See also the requirement in section 2 of the Civil Evidence Act 1995 for reasonable and practicable notice of a proposal to introduce hearsay evidence.

Rules 31.6, 31.7 and 31.8 broadly correspond with rules 3, 4 and 5 of the Magistrates' Courts (Hearsay Evidence in Civil Proceedings) Rules 1999[18], which apply in civil proceedings in magistrates' courts. Rule 3 of the 1999 Rules however includes a time limit, which may be varied by the court, or a justices' legal adviser, of 21 days before the date fixed for the hearing, for service of a hearsay notice.]

R31.7 **Cross-examination of maker of hearsay statement**

31.7 (1) This rule applies where a party wants the court's permission to cross-examine a person who made a statement which another party wants to introduce as hearsay.
(2) The party who wants to cross-examine that person must—
(a) apply in writing, with reasons, not more than 5 business days after service of the notice of hearsay evidence; and
(b) serve the application on—
(i) the court officer,
(ii) the party who served the hearsay evidence notice, and
(iii) every party on whom the hearsay evidence notice was served.
(3) The court may decide an application under this rule with or without a hearing.
(4) But the court must not—
(a) dismiss an application under this rule unless the applicant has had an opportunity to make representations at a hearing (whether or not the applicant in fact attends); or
(b) allow an application under this rule unless everyone served with the application has had at least 5 business days in which to make representations, including representations about whether there should be a hearing.

[Note. See also section 3 of the Civil Evidence Act 1995.]

[16] 2007 c. 27; section 22E was inserted by section 49 of the Serious Crime Act 2015 (c. 9).
[17] 2019 c. 17; section 26 comes into force on a date to be appointed.
[18] S.I. 1999/681, amended by S.I. 2005/617.

Credibility and consistency of maker of hearsay statement R31.8

31.8 (1) This rule applies where a party wants to challenge the credibility or consistency of a person who made a statement which another party wants to introduce as hearsay.

(2) The party who wants to challenge the credibility or consistency of that person must—

(a) serve notice of intention to do so on—

(i) the court officer, and

(ii) the party who served the notice of hearsay evidence

not more than 5 business days after service of that hearsay evidence notice; and

(b) in the notice, identify any statement or other material on which that party relies.

(3) The party who served the hearsay notice—

(a) may call that person to give oral evidence instead; and

(b) if so, must serve notice of intention to do so on—

(i) the court officer, and

(ii) every party on whom the hearsay notice was served

not more than 5 business days after service of the notice under paragraph (2).

[Note. Section 5(2) of the Civil Evidence Act 1995 describes the procedure for challenging the credibility of the maker of a statement of which hearsay evidence is introduced. See also section 6 of that Act. The 1995 Act does not allow the introduction of evidence of a previous inconsistent statement otherwise than in accordance with sections 5, 6 and 7 of the Criminal Procedure Act 1865[19].]

Court's power to vary requirements under this Part R31.9

31.9 Unless other legislation otherwise provides, the court may—

(a) shorten a time limit or extend it (even after it has expired);

(b) allow a notice or application to be given in a different form, or presented orally.

Criminal Procedure Rules Part 32 Breach, Revocation and Amendment of Community and Other Orders

When this Part applies R32.1

32.1 This Part applies where—

(a) the person responsible for a defendant's compliance with an order to which applies—

(i) Schedule 5, 7, 10 or 16 to the Sentencing Act 2020[1], or

(ii) the Schedule to the Street Offences Act 1959[2],

wants the court to deal with that defendant for failure to comply;

(b) one of the following wants the court to exercise any power it has to revoke or amend such an order—

(i) the responsible officer or supervisor,

(ii) the defendant, or

(iii) where the legislation allows, a person affected by the order; or

(c) the court considers exercising on its own initiative any power it has to revoke or amend such an order.

[Note. In the Sentencing Act 2020—

(a) Schedule 5 deals with the breach, revocation and amendment of reparation orders;

(b) Schedule 7 deals with the breach, revocation and amendment of youth rehabilitation orders;

(c) Schedule 10 deals with the breach, revocation and amendment of community orders; and

(d) Schedule 16 deals with the breach or amendment of suspended sentence orders, and the effect of a further conviction.]

Application by responsible officer or supervisor R32.2

32.2 (1) This rule applies where—

(a) the responsible officer or supervisor wants the court to—

[19] 1865 c. 18; section 6 was amended by section 10 of the Decimal Currency Act 1969 (c. 19), section 90 of, and paragraph 3 of Schedule 13 to, the Access to Justice Act 1999 (c. 22), section 109 of, and paragraph 47 of Schedule 8 to, the Courts Act 2003 (c. 39) and paragraph 79 of Schedule 36 and Schedule 37 to the Criminal Justice Act 2003 (c. 44). It is further amended by section 119 of, and Schedule 7 to, the Police and Criminal Evidence Act 1984 (c. 60), with effect from a date to be appointed.

[1] 2020 c. 17.

[2] 1959 c. 57; Schedule: Orders under section 1(2A) was inserted by section 17(1) and (4) of the Policing and Crime Act 2009 (c. 26).

(i) deal with a defendant for failure to comply with an order to which this Part applies, or
(ii) revoke or amend such an order; or
(b) the court considers exercising on its own initiative any power it has to—
(i) revoke or amend such an order, and
(ii) summon the defendant to attend for that purpose.

(2) Rules 7.2 to 7.4, which deal, among other things, with starting a prosecution in a magistrates' court, apply—
(a) as if—
(i) a reference in those rules to an allegation of an offence included a reference to an allegation of failure to comply with an order to which this Part applies, and
(ii) a reference to the prosecutor included a reference to the responsible officer or supervisor; and
(b) with the necessary consequential modifications.

R32.3 **Application by defendant or person affected**

32.3 (1) This rule applies where—
(a) the defendant wants the court to exercise any power it has to revoke or amend an order to which this Part applies; or
(b) where the legislation allows, a person affected by such an order wants the court to exercise any such power.

(2) That defendant, or person affected, must—
(a) apply in writing, explaining why the order should be revoked or amended; and
(b) serve the application on—
(i) the court officer,
(ii) the responsible officer or supervisor, and
(iii) as appropriate, the defendant or the person affected.

R32.4 **Procedure on application by responsible officer or supervisor**

32.4 (1) Except for rules 24.8 (Written guilty plea; special rules) and 24.9 (Single justice procedure: special rules), the rules in Part 24, which deal with the procedure at a trial in a magistrates' court, apply—
(a) as if—
(i) a reference in those rules to an allegation of an offence included a reference to an allegation of failure to comply with an order to which this Part applies,
(ii) a reference to the court's verdict included a reference to the court's decision to revoke or amend such an order, or to exercise any other power it has to deal with the defendant, and
(iii) a reference to the court's sentence included a reference to the exercise of any such power; and
(b) with the necessary consequential modifications.

(2) The court officer must serve on each party any order revoking or amending an order to which this Part applies.

Criminal Procedure Rules Part 33 Confiscation and Related Proceedings

General rules

R33.1 **Interpretation**

33.1 In this Part: words and expressions used have the same meaning as in Part 2 of the Proceeds of Crime Act 2002 and:

'document' means anything in which information of any description is recorded;

'hearsay evidence' means evidence consisting of hearsay within the meaning of section 1(2) of the Civil Evidence Act 1995[1];

'restraint proceedings' means proceedings under sections 42 and 58(2) and (3) of the Proceeds of Crime Act 2002[2];

[1] 1995 c. 38.

[2] 2002 c. 29; section 42 was amended by sections 74(2) and 92 of, and paragraphs 1 and 23 of Schedule 8, and Schedule 14 to, the Serious Crime Act 2007 (c. 27). Section 58(2) was amended by section 62(3) of, and paragraphs 142 and 143 of Schedule 13 to, the Tribunals, Courts and Enforcement Act 2007 (c. 15).

'receivership proceedings' means proceedings under sections 48, 49, 50, 51, 54(4), 59(2) and (3), 62 and 63 of the 2002 Act[3];

'witness statement' means a written statement signed by a person which contains the evidence, and only that evidence, which that person would be allowed to give orally.

Calculation of time R33.2

33.2 (1) This rule shows how to calculate any period of time for doing any act which is specified by this Part for the purposes of any proceedings under Part 2 of the Proceeds of Crime Act 2002 or by an order of the Crown Court in restraint proceedings or receivership proceedings.

(2) A period of time expressed as a number of days shall be computed as clear days.

(3) In this rule 'clear days' means that in computing the number of days—

(a) the day on which the period begins; and

(b) if the end of the period is defined by reference to an event, the day on which that event occurs,

are not included.

(4) Where the specified period is 5 days or less and includes a day which is not a business day that day does not count.

Court office closed R33.3

33.3 When the period specified by this Part, or by an order of the Crown Court under Part 2 of the Proceeds of Crime Act 2002, for doing any act at the court office falls on a day on which the office is closed, that act shall be in time if done on the next day on which the court office is open.

Application for registration of Scottish or Northern Ireland order R33.4

33.4 (1) This rule applies to an application for registration of an order under article 6 of the Proceeds of Crime Act 2002 (Enforcement in different parts of the United Kingdom) Order 2002[4].

(2) The application may be made without notice.

(3) The application must be in writing and may be supported by a witness statement which must—

(a) exhibit the order or a certified copy of the order; and

(b) to the best of the witness's ability, give full details of the realisable property located in England and Wales in respect of which the order was made and specify the person holding that realisable property.

(4) If the court registers the order, the applicant must serve notice of the registration on—

(a) any person who holds realisable property to which the order applies; and

(b) any other person whom the applicant knows to be affected by the order.

(5) The permission of the Crown Court under rule 33.10 (Service outside the jurisdiction) is not required to serve the notice outside England and Wales.

Application to vary or set aside registration R33.5

33.5 (1) An application to vary or set aside registration of an order under article 6 of the Proceeds of Crime Act 2002 (Enforcement in different parts of the United Kingdom) Order 2002 may be made to the Crown Court by—

(a) any person who holds realisable property to which the order applies; and

(b) any other person affected by the order.

(2) The application must be in writing and may be supported by a witness statement.

(3) The application and any witness statement must be lodged with the Crown Court.

(4) The application must be served on the person who applied for registration at least 7 days before the date fixed by the court for hearing the application, unless the Crown Court specifies a shorter period.

(5) No property in England and Wales may be realised in pursuance of the order before the Crown Court has decided the application.

Register of orders R33.6

33.6 (1) The Crown Court must keep, under the direction of the Lord Chancellor, a register of the orders registered under article 6 of the Proceeds of Crime Act 2002 (Enforcement in different parts of the United Kingdom) Order 2002.

[3] 2002 c. 29; sections 49, 62 and 63 were amended by sections 74 and 82(1) of, and paragraphs 1, 29 and 30 of Schedule 8 to, the Serious Crime Act (c. 27). Section 59(2) was amended by section 62(3) of, and paragraphs 142 and 144 of Schedule 13 to, the Tribunals, Courts and Enforcement Act 2007 (c. 15).

[4] S.I. 2002/3133.

(2) The register must include details of any variation or setting aside of a registration under rule 33.5 and of any execution issued on a registered order.

(3) If the person who applied for registration of an order which is subsequently registered notifies the Crown Court that the court which made the order has varied or discharged the order, details of the variation or discharge, as the case may be, must be entered in the register.

R33.7 **Statements of truth**

33.7 (1) Any witness statement required to be served by this Part must be verified by a statement of truth contained in the witness statement.

(2) A statement of truth is a declaration by the person making the witness statement to the effect that the witness statement is true to the best of his knowledge and belief and that he made the statement knowing that, if it were tendered in evidence, he would be liable to prosecution if he wilfully stated in it anything which he knew to be false or did not believe to be true.

(3) The statement of truth must be signed by the person making the witness statement.

(4) If the person making the witness statement fails to verify the witness statement by a statement of truth, the Crown Court may direct that it shall not be admissible as evidence.

R33.8 **Use of witness statements for other purposes**

33.8 (1) Except as provided by this rule, a witness statement served in proceedings under Part 2 of the Proceeds of Crime Act 2002 may be used only for the purpose of the proceedings in which it is served.

(2) Paragraph (1) does not apply if and to the extent that—

(a) the witness gives consent in writing to some other use of it;

(b) the Crown Court gives permission for some other use; or

(c) the witness statement has been put in evidence at a hearing held in public.

R33.9 **Service of documents**

33.9 (1) Rule 49.1 (Notice required to accompany process served outside the United Kingdom and translations) shall not apply in restraint proceedings and receivership proceedings.

(2) An order made in restraint proceedings or receivership proceedings may be enforced against the defendant or any other person affected by it notwithstanding that service of a copy of the order has not been effected in accordance with Part 4 if the Crown Court is satisfied that the person had notice of the order by being present when the order was made.

R33.10 **Service outside the jurisdiction**

33.10 (1) Where this Part requires a document to be served on someone who is outside England and Wales, it may be served outside England and Wales with the permission of the Crown Court.

(2) Where a document is to be served outside England and Wales it may be served by any method permitted by the law of the country in which it is to be served.

(3) Nothing in this rule or in any court order shall authorise or require any person to do anything in the country where the document is to be served which is against the law of that country.

(4) Where this Part requires a document to be served a certain period of time before the date of a hearing and the recipient does not appear at the hearing, the hearing must not take place unless the Crown Court is satisfied that the document has been duly served.

R33.11 **Certificates of service**

33.11 (1) Where this Part requires that the applicant for an order in restraint proceedings or receivership proceedings serve a document on another person, the applicant must lodge a certificate of service with the Crown Court within 7 days of service of the document.

(2) The certificate must state—

(a) the method of service;

(b) the date of service; and

(c) if the document is served under rule 4.9 (Service by another method), such other information as the court may require when making the order permitting service by that method.

(3) Where a document is to be served by the Crown Court in restraint proceedings and receivership proceedings and the court is unable to serve it, the court must send a notice of non-service stating the method attempted to the party who requested service.

External requests and orders R33.12

33.12 (1) The rules in this Part and in Part 42 (Appeal to the Court of Appeal in confiscation and related proceedings) apply with the necessary modifications to proceedings under the Proceeds of Crime Act 2002 (External Requests and Orders) Order 2005[5] in the same way that they apply to corresponding proceedings under Part 2 of the Proceeds of Crime Act 2002[6].

(2) This table shows how provisions of the 2005 Order correspond with provisions of the 2002 Act.

Article of the Proceeds of Crime Act 2002 (External Requests and Orders) Order 2005	*Section of the Proceeds of Crime Act 2002*
8	41
9	42
10	43
11	44
15	48
16	49
17	58
23	31
27	50
28	51
41	62
42	63
44	65
45	66

Confiscation proceedings

Statements in connection with confiscation orders R33.13

33.13 (1) This rule applies where—
(a) the court can make a confiscation order; and
(b) the prosecutor asks the court to make such an order, or the court decides to make such an order on its own initiative.

(2) Within such periods as the court directs—
(a) if the court so orders, the defendant must give such information, in such manner, as the court directs;
(b) the prosecutor must serve a statement of information relevant to confiscation on the court officer and the defendant; and
(c) if the court so directs—
(i) the defendant must serve a response notice on the court officer and the prosecutor, and
(ii) the parties must identify what is in dispute.

(3) Where it appears to the court that a person other than the defendant holds, or may hold, an interest in property held by the defendant which property is likely to be realised or otherwise used to satisfy a confiscation order—
(a) the court must not determine the extent of the defendant's interest in that property unless that other person has had a reasonable opportunity to make representations; and
(b) the court may order that other person to give such information, in such manner and within such a period, as the court directs.

(4) The court may—
(a) shorten or extend a time limit which it has set;
(b) vary, discharge or supplement an order which it has made; and
(c) postpone confiscation proceedings without a hearing.

(5) A prosecutor's statement of information must—
(a) identify the maker of the statement and show its date;
(b) identify the defendant in respect of whom it is served;

[5] S.I. 2005/3181.
[6] 2002 c. 29.

(c) specify the conviction which gives the court power to make the confiscation order, or each conviction if more than one;
(d) if the prosecutor believes the defendant to have a criminal lifestyle, include such matters as the prosecutor believes to be relevant in connection with deciding—
(i) whether the defendant has such a lifestyle,
(ii) whether the defendant has benefited from his or her general criminal conduct,
(iii) the defendant's benefit from that conduct, and
(iv) whether the court should or should not make such assumptions about the defendant's property as legislation permits;
(e) if the prosecutor does not believe the defendant to have a criminal lifestyle, include such matters as the prosecutor believes to be relevant in connection with deciding—
(i) whether the defendant has benefited from his or her particular criminal conduct, and
(ii) the defendant's benefit from that conduct; and
(f) in any case, include such matters as the prosecutor believes to be relevant in connection with deciding—
(i) whether to make a determination about the extent of the defendant's interest in property in which another person holds, or may hold, an interest, and
(ii) what determination to make, if the court decides to make one.

(6) A defendant's response notice must—
(a) indicate the extent to which the defendant accepts the allegations made in the prosecutor's statement of information; and
(b) so far as the defendant does not accept an allegation, give particulars of any matters on which the defendant relies, in any manner directed by the court.

(7) The court must satisfy itself that there has been explained to the defendant, in terms the defendant can understand (with help, if necessary)—
(a) that if the defendant accepts to any extent an allegation in a prosecutor's statement of information, then the court may treat that as conclusive for the purposes of deciding whether the defendant has benefited from general or particular criminal conduct, and if so by how much;
(b) that if the defendant fails in any respect to comply with a direction to serve a response notice, then the court may treat that as acceptance of each allegation to which the defendant has not replied, except the allegation that the defendant has benefited from general or particular criminal conduct; and
(c) that if the defendant fails without reasonable excuse to comply with an order to give information, then the court may draw such inference as it believes is appropriate.

[Note. Under section 6 of the Proceeds of Crime Act 2002[7]*, where a defendant is convicted of an offence the Crown Court must (with some exceptions)—*

(a) decide whether the defendant has 'a criminal lifestyle', within the meaning of the Act, or has benefited from particular criminal conduct;
(b) decide the 'recoverable amount', within the meaning of the Act; and
(c) make a confiscation order requiring the defendant to pay that amount.

Under section 14 of the 2002 Act[8]*, unless exceptional circumstances apply the court may postpone confiscation proceedings for a maximum of 2 years from the date of conviction, or until the end of a period of 3 months following the determination of an appeal by the defendant against conviction, if that is later.*

Under section 16 of the 2002 Act[9]*, where the Crown Court is considering confiscation the prosecutor must give the court a statement of information which the prosecutor believes to be relevant to what the court must decide, within such period as the court directs. Under section 17 of the Act*[10]*, where the prosecutor gives such a statement the court may order the defendant to respond and, if the defendant does not do so, then the court may treat the defendant as accepting the prosecutor's allegations. Under section 18*[11]*, for the purpose of obtaining information*

[7] 2002 c. 29; section 6 was amended by paragraph 75 of Schedule 3 to the Criminal Justice Act 2003 (c. 44), section 74(2) of, and paragraphs 1 and 2 of Schedule 8 to, the Serious Crime Act 2007 (c. 27) and section 10 of, and paragraphs 11 and 12 of the Schedule to, the Prevention of Social Housing Fraud Act 2013 (c. 3).

[8] 2002 c. 29; section 14 was amended by section 74(2) of, and paragraphs 1 and 4 of Schedule 8 to, the Serious Crime Act 2007 (c. 27).

[9] 2002 c. 29; section 16 was amended by section 74(2) of, and paragraphs 1 and 5 of Schedule 8 to, the Serious Crime Act 2007 (c. 27) and section 2 of the Serious Crime Act 2015 (c. 9).

[10] 2002 c. 29; section 17 was amended by section 74(2) of, and paragraphs 1 and 6 of Schedule 8 to, the Serious Crime Act 2007 (c. 27).

[11] 2002 c. 29; section 18 was amended by section 74(2) of, and paragraphs 1 and 7 of Schedule 8 to, the Serious Crime Act 2007 (c. 27).

to help it in carrying out its functions the court may at any time order the defendant to give it information specified in the order and, if the defendant does not do so, then the court may draw such inference as it believes appropriate. Under section 18A[12]*, for the purpose of obtaining information to help it to determine the extent of the defendant's interest in property the court may at any time order a person who the court thinks may hold an interest in that property to give it information specified in the order and, if that person does not do so, then the court may draw such inference as it believes appropriate.*

Under section 27 of the 2002 Act[13]*, special provisions apply where the defendant absconds.*

Under section 97 of the Serious Organised Crime and Police Act 2005[14]*, the Secretary of State may by order provide for confiscation orders to be made by magistrates' courts.]*

Application for compliance order **R33.14**

33.14 (1) This rule applies where—
(a) the prosecutor wants the court to make a compliance order after a confiscation order has been made;
(b) the prosecutor or a person affected by a compliance order wants the court to vary or discharge the order.
(2) Such a prosecutor or person must—
(a) apply in writing; and
(b) serve the application on—
(i) the court officer, and
(ii) as appropriate, the prosecutor and any person who is affected by the compliance order (or who would be affected if it were made), unless the court otherwise directs.
(3) The application must—
(a) specify—
(i) the confiscation order, and
(ii) the compliance order, if it is an application to vary or discharge that order;
(b) if it is an application for a compliance order—
(i) specify each measure that the prosecutor proposes to ensure that the confiscation order is effective, including in particular any restriction or prohibition on the defendant's travel outside the United Kingdom, and
(ii) explain why each such measure is appropriate;
(c) if it is an application to vary or discharge a compliance order, as appropriate—
(i) specify any proposed variation, and
(ii) explain why it is appropriate for the order to be varied or discharged;
(d) attach any material on which the applicant relies;
(e) propose the terms of the order; and
(f) ask for a hearing, if the applicant wants one, and explain why it is needed.
(4) A person who wants to make representations about the application must—
(a) serve the representations on—
(i) the court officer, and
(ii) the applicant;
(b) do so as soon as reasonably practicable after service of the application;
(c) attach any material on which that person relies; and
(d) ask for a hearing, if that person wants one, and explain why it is needed.
(5) The court—
(a) may determine the application at a hearing (which must be in private unless the court otherwise directs), or without a hearing; and
(b) may dispense with service on any person of a prosecutor's application for a compliance order if, in particular—
(i) the application is urgent, or
(ii) there are reasonable grounds for believing that to give notice of the application would cause the dissipation of property that otherwise would be available to satisfy the confiscation order.

[Note. See section 13A of the Proceeds of Crime Act 2002[15]*.]*

[12] 2002 c. 29; section 18A was inserted by section 2 of the Serious Crime Act 2015 (c. 9).
[13] 2002 c. 29; section 27 was amended by paragraph 75 of Schedule 3 to the Criminal Justice Act 2003 (c. 44) and section 74 of, and paragraphs 1 and 14 of Schedule 8 to, the Serious Crime Act 2007 (c. 27).
[14] 2005 c. 15; section 97 was amended by S.I. 2010/976.
[15] 2002 c. 29; section 13A was inserted by section 7 of the Serious Crime Act 2015 (c. 9).

R33.15 **Application for reconsideration**

33.15 (1) This rule applies where the prosecutor wants the court, in view of fresh evidence—
(a) to consider making a confiscation order where the defendant was convicted but no such order was considered;
(b) to reconsider a decision that the defendant had not benefited from criminal conduct; or
(c) to reconsider a decision about the amount of the defendant's benefit.
(2) The application must—
(a) be in writing and give—
(i) the name of the defendant,
(ii) the date on which and the place where any relevant conviction occurred,
(iii) the date on which and the place where any relevant confiscation order was made or varied,
(iv) details of any slavery and trafficking reparation order made by virtue of any relevant confiscation order,
(v) the grounds for the application, and
(vi) an indication of the evidence available to support the application; and
(b) where the parties are agreed on the terms of the proposed order include, in one or more documents—
(i) a draft order in the terms proposed, and
(ii) evidence of the parties' agreement.
(3) The application must be served on—
(a) the court officer; and
(b) the defendant.
(4) The court—
(a) may determine the application without a hearing where the parties are agreed on the terms of the proposed order; but
(b) must determine the application at a hearing in any other case.
(5) Where this rule or the court requires the application to be heard, the court officer must arrange for the court to hear it no sooner than the eighth day after it was served unless the court otherwise directs.

[Note. See sections 19, 20 and 21 of the Proceeds of Crime Act 2002[16] *and section 10 of the Modern Slavery Act 2015*[17]*.]*

R33.16 **Application for new calculation of available amount**

33.16 (1) This rule applies where the prosecutor or a receiver wants the court to make a new calculation of the amount available for confiscation.
(2) The application—
(a) must be in writing and may be supported by a witness statement;
(b) must identify any slavery and trafficking reparation order made by virtue of the confiscation order; and
(c) where the parties are agreed on the terms of the proposed order, must include in one or more documents—
(i) a draft order in the terms proposed, and
(ii) evidence of the parties' agreement.
(3) The application and any witness statement must be served on the court officer.
(4) The application and any witness statement must be served on—
(a) the defendant;
(b) the receiver, if the prosecutor is making the application and a receiver has been appointed; and
(c) the prosecutor, if the receiver is making the application,
(5) The court—
(a) may determine the application without a hearing where the parties are agreed on the terms of the proposed order; but
(b) must determine the application at a hearing in any other case.

[16] 2002 c. 29; sections 19, 20 and 21 were amended by section 74(2) of, and paragraph 1 and paragraphs 8, 9 and 10 respectively, of Schedule 8 to, the Serious Crime Act 2007 (c. 27). Sections 19 and 20 were further amended by paragraphs 16 and 17 of Schedule 5 to the Modern Slavery Act 2015 (c. 30).
[17] 2015 c. 30.

(6) Where this rule or the court requires the application to be heard, the court officer must arrange for the court to hear it no sooner than the eighth day after it was served unless the court otherwise directs.

[Note. See section 22 of the Proceeds of Crime Act 2002[18] *and section 10 of the Modern Slavery Act 2015.]*

Variation of confiscation order due to inadequacy of available amount **R33.17**

33.17 (1) This rule applies where the defendant, the prosecutor or a receiver wants the court to vary a confiscation order because the amount available is inadequate.

(2) The application—

(a) must be in writing and may be supported by a witness statement;

(b) must identify any slavery and trafficking reparation order made by virtue of the confiscation order; and

(c) where the parties are agreed on the terms of the proposed order, must include in one or more documents—

(i) a draft order in the terms proposed, and

(ii) evidence of the parties' agreement.

(3) The application and any witness statement must be served on the court officer.

(4) The application and any witness statement must be served on—

(a) the prosecutor;

(b) the defendant, if the receiver is making the application; and

(c) the receiver, if the defendant is making the application and a receiver has been appointed.

(5) The court—

(a) may determine the application without a hearing where the parties are agreed on the terms of the proposed order; but

(a) must determine the application at a hearing in any other case.

(6) Where this rule or the court requires the application to be heard, the court officer must arrange for the court to hear it no sooner than the eighth day after it was served unless the court otherwise directs.

[Note. See section 23 of the Proceeds of Crime Act 2002[19] *and section 10 of the Modern Slavery Act 2015.]*

Application by magistrates' court officer to discharge confiscation order **R33.18**

33.18 (1) This rule applies where a magistrates' court officer wants the court to discharge a confiscation order because the amount available is inadequate or the sum outstanding is very small.

(2) The application must be in writing and give details of—

(a) the confiscation order;

(b) any slavery and trafficking reparation order made by virtue of the confiscation order;

(c) the amount outstanding under the order; and

(d) the grounds for the application.

(3) The application must be served on—

(a) the defendant;

(b) the prosecutor; and

(c) any receiver.

(4) The court may determine the application without a hearing unless a person listed in paragraph (3) indicates, within 7 days after the application was served, that he or she would like to make representations.

(5) If the court makes an order discharging the confiscation order, the court officer must, at once, send a copy of the order to—

(a) the magistrates' court officer who applied for the order;

(b) the defendant;

(c) the prosecutor; and

(d) any receiver.

[Note. See sections 24 and 25 of the Proceeds of Crime Act 2002[20] *and section 10 of the Modern Slavery Act 2015.]*

[18] 2002 c. 29; section 22 was amended by section 74(2) of, and paragraph 11 of Schedule 8 to, the Serious Crime Act 2007 (c. 27).

[19] 2002 c. 29; section 23 was amended by section 74(2) of, and paragraph 12 of Schedule 8 to, the Serious Crime Act 2007 (c. 27) and section 8 of the Serious Crime Act 2015 (c. 9).

[20] 2002 c. 29; sections 24 and 25 were amended by section 109(1) of, and paragraphs 406(a) and 406(b), respectively, of Schedule 8 to, the Courts Act 2003 (c. 39).

R33.19 **Application for variation of confiscation order made against an absconder**

33.19 (1) This rule applies where the defendant wants the court to vary a confiscation order made while the defendant was an absconder.

(2) The application must be in writing and supported by a witness statement which must give details of—

(a) the confiscation order;

(b) any slavery and trafficking reparation order made by virtue of the confiscation order;

(c) the circumstances in which the defendant ceased to be an absconder;

(d) the defendant's conviction of the offence or offences concerned; and

(e) the reason why the defendant believes the amount required to be paid under the confiscation order was too large.

(3) The application and witness statement must be served on the court officer.

(4) The application and witness statement must be served on the prosecutor at least 7 days before the date fixed by the court for hearing the application, unless the court specifies a shorter period.

[Note. See section 29 of the Proceeds of Crime Act 2002[21] *and section 10 of the Modern Slavery Act 2015.]*

R33.20 **Application for discharge of confiscation order made against an absconder**

33.20 (1) This rule applies where the defendant wants the court to discharge a confiscation order made while the defendant was an absconder and—

(a) the defendant since has been tried and acquitted of each offence concerned; or

(b) the prosecution has not concluded or is not to proceed.

(2) The application must be in writing and supported by a witness statement which must give details of—

(a) the confiscation order;

(b) the date on which the defendant ceased to be an absconder;

(c) the acquittal of the defendant if he or she has been acquitted of the offence concerned; and

(d) if the defendant has not been acquitted of the offence concerned—

(i) the date on which the defendant ceased to be an absconder,

(ii) the date on which the proceedings taken against the defendant were instituted and a summary of steps taken in the proceedings since then, and

(iii) any indication that the prosecutor does not intend to proceed against the defendant.

(3) The application and witness statement must be served on the court officer.

(4) The application and witness statement must be served on the prosecutor at least 7 days before the date fixed by the court for hearing the application, unless the court specifies a shorter period.

(5) If the court orders the discharge of the confiscation order, the court officer must serve notice on any other court responsible for enforcing the order.

[Note. See section 30 of the Proceeds of Crime Act 2002[22]*.]*

R33.21 **Application for increase in term of imprisonment in default**

33.21 (1) This rule applies where —

(a) a court varies a confiscation order; and

(b) the prosecutor wants the court in consequence to increase the term of imprisonment to be served in default of payment.

(2) The application must be made in writing and give details of—

(a) the name and address of the defendant;

(b) the confiscation order;

(c) the grounds for the application; and

(d) the enforcement measures taken, if any.

(3) On receipt of the application, the court officer must—

(a) at once, send to the defendant and any other court responsible for enforcing the order, a copy of the application; and

(b) fix a time, date and place for the hearing and notify the applicant and the defendant of that time, date and place.

(4) If the court makes an order increasing the term of imprisonment in default, the court officer must, at once, send a copy of the order to—

(a) the applicant;

(b) the defendant;

[21] 2002 c. 29.
[22] 2002 c. 29.

(c) where the defendant is in custody at the time of the making of the order, the person having custody of the defendant; and
(d) any other court responsible for enforcing the order.

[Note. See section 39(5) of the Proceeds of Crime Act 2002[23].]

Compensation—general R33.22

33.22 (1) This rule applies where a person who held realisable property wants the court to award compensation for loss suffered in consequence of anything done in relation to that property in connection with confiscation proceedings.
(2) The application must be in writing and may be supported by a witness statement.
(3) The application and any witness statement must be served on the court officer.
(4) The application and any witness statement must be served on—
(a) the person alleged to be in default; and
(b) the person or authority by whom the compensation would be payable,
at least 7 days before the date fixed by the court for hearing the application, unless the court directs otherwise.

[Note. See section 72 of the Proceeds of Crime Act 2002[24].]

Compensation—confiscation order made against absconder R33.23

33.23 (1) This rule applies where—
(a) the court varies or discharges a confiscation order made against an absconder;
(b) a person who held realisable property suffered loss as a result of the making of that confiscation order; and
(c) that person wants the court to award compensation for that loss.
(2) The application must be in writing and supported by a witness statement which must give details of—
(a) the confiscation order;
(b) the variation or discharge of the confiscation order;
(c) the realisable property to which the application relates; and
(d) the loss suffered by the applicant as a result of the confiscation order.
(3) The application and witness statement must be served on the court officer.
(4) The application and witness statement must be served on the prosecutor at least 7 days before the date fixed by the court for hearing the application, unless the court specifies a shorter period.

[Note. See section 73 of the Proceeds of Crime Act 2002[25].]

Payment of money held or detained in satisfaction of confiscation order R33.24

33.24 (1) An order under section 67 of the Proceeds of Crime Act 2002[26] requiring the payment of money to a magistrates' court officer ('a payment order') shall—
(a) be directed to—
(i) the bank or building society concerned, where the money is held in an account maintained with that bank or building society, or
(ii) the person on whose authority the money is detained, in any other case;
(b) name the person against whom the confiscation order has been made;
(c) state the amount which remains to be paid under the confiscation order;
(d) state the name and address of the branch at which the account in which the money ordered to be paid is held and the sort code of that branch, if the sort code is known;
(e) state the name in which the account in which the money ordered to be paid is held and the account number of that account, if the account number is known;
(f) state the amount which the bank or building society is required to pay to the court officer under the payment order;
(g) give the name and address of the court officer to whom payment is to be made; and
(h) require the bank or building society to make payment within a period of 7 days beginning

[23] 2002 c. 29; section 39(5) was amended by section 74(2) of, and paragraphs 1 and 21(2) of Schedule 8 to, the Serious Crime Act 2007 (c. 27).
[24] 2002 c. 29; section 72 was amended by section 50(6) of, and paragraph 97 of Schedule 4 to, the Commissioners for Revenue and Customs Act 2005 (c. 11), section 61 of the Policing and Crime Act 2009 (c. 26) and sections 15 and 55 of, and paragraphs 108 and 114 of Schedule 8 and paragraphs 14 and 19 of Schedule 21 to, the Crime and Courts Act 2013 (c. 22).
[25] 2002 c. 29.
[26] 2002 c. 29; section 67 was amended by section 109 of, and paragraph 409 of Schedule 8 to, the Courts Act 2003 (c. 39), section 74 of, and paragraph 33 of Schedule 8 to, the Serious Crime Act 2007 (c. 27), section 14 of the Serious Crime Act 2015 (c. 9) and section 26 of the Criminal Finances Act 2017 (c. 22).

on the day on which the payment order is made, unless it appears to the court that a longer or shorter period would be appropriate in the particular circumstances.

(2) In this rule 'confiscation order' has the meaning given to it by section 88(6) of the Proceeds of Crime Act 2002.

R33.25 **Application to realise seized property**

33.25 (1) This rule applies where—

(a) property is held by a defendant against whom a confiscation order has been made;
(b) the property has been seized by or produced to an officer; and
(c) an officer who is entitled to apply wants a magistrates' court—
(i) to make an order under section 67A of the Proceeds of Crime Act 2002[27] authorising the realisation of the property towards satisfaction of the confiscation order, or
(ii) to determine any storage, insurance or realisation costs in respect of the property which may be recovered under section 67B of the 2002 Act[28].

(2) Such an officer must—
(a) apply in writing; and
(b) serve the application on—
(i) the court officer, and
(ii) any person whom the applicant believes would be affected by an order.

(3) The application must—
(a) specify the property;
(b) explain—
(i) the applicant's entitlement to apply,
(ii) how the proposed realisation meets the conditions prescribed by section 67A of the 2002 Act, and
(iii) how any storage, etc. costs have been calculated;
(c) attach any material on which the applicant relies; and
(d) propose the terms of the order.

(4) The court may—
(a) determine the application at a hearing, or without a hearing;
(b) consider an application made orally instead of in writing; and
(c) consider an application which has not been served on a person likely to be affected by an order.

(5) If the court authorises the realisation of the property, the applicant must—
(a) notify any person affected by the order who was absent when it was made; and
(b) serve on the court officer a list of those so notified.

[Note. Under section 67A of the Proceeds of Crime Act 2002, one of the officers listed in section 41A of the Act may apply to a magistrates' court for authority to realise property seized by such an officer if—

(a) a confiscation order has been made against the owner of the property;
(b) no receiver has been appointed in relation to that property; and
(c) any period allowed for payment of the confiscation order has expired.

Under section 67B of the 2002 Act, if a magistrates' court makes an order under section 67A then on the same or a subsequent occasion the court may determine an amount which may be recovered by the applicant in respect of reasonable costs incurred in storing or insuring the property, or realising it.]

R33.26 **Appeal about decision on application to realise seized property**

33.26 (1) This rule applies where on an application under rule 33.25 for an order authorising the realisation of property—

(a) a magistrates' court decides not to make such an order and an officer who is entitled to apply wants to appeal against that decision to the Crown Court, under section 67C(1) of the Proceeds of Crime Act 2002[29];
(b) a magistrates' court makes such an order and a person who is affected by that decision, other than the defendant against whom the confiscation order was made, wants to appeal against it to the Crown Court, under section 67C(2) of the 2002 Act; or
(c) a magistrates' court makes a decision about storage, etc. costs and an officer who is entitled to apply wants to appeal against that decision to the Crown Court, under section 67C(4) of the 2002 Act.

[27] 2002 c. 29; section 67A was inserted by section 58 of the Policing and Crime Act 2009 (c. 26) and amended by section 14 of the Serious Crime Act 2015 (c. 9).
[28] 2002 c. 29; section 67B was inserted by section 58 of the Policing and Crime Act 2009 (c. 26).
[29] 2002 c. 29; section 67C was inserted by section 58 of the Policing and Crime Act 2009 (c. 26).

(2) The appellant must serve an appeal notice—
(a) on the Crown Court officer and on any other party; and
(b) not more than 21 days after the magistrates' court's decision, or, if applicable, service of notice under rule 33.25(5).
(3) The appeal notice must—
(a) specify the decision under appeal;
(b) where paragraph (1)(a) applies, explain why the property should be realised;
(c) in any other case, propose the order that the appellant wants the court to make, and explain why.
(4) Rule 34.11 (Constitution of the Crown Court) applies on such an appeal.

[Note. Under section 67C of the Proceeds of Crime Act 2002, an officer entitled to apply for an order under section 67A or 67B of that Act (authority to realise seized property towards satisfaction of a confiscation order; determination of storage, etc. costs) may appeal against a refusal to make an order, or against a costs determination; and a person affected by an order, other than the owner, may appeal against the order.]

Application for direction about surplus proceeds R33.27

33.27 (1) This rule applies where—
(a) on an application under rule 33.25, a magistrates' court has made an order authorising an officer to realise property;
(b) an officer so authorised holds proceeds of that realisation;
(c) the confiscation order has been fully paid; and
(d) the officer, or a person who had or has an interest in the property represented by the proceeds, wants a magistrates' court or the Crown Court to determine under section 67D of the Proceeds of Crime Act 2002[30]—
(i) to whom the remaining proceeds should be paid, and
(ii) in what amount or amounts.
(2) Such a person must—
(a) apply in writing; and
(b) serve the application on—
(i) the court officer, and
(ii) as appropriate, the officer holding the proceeds, or any person to whom such proceeds might be paid.
(3) The application must—
(a) specify the property which was realised;
(b) explain the applicant's entitlement to apply;
(c) describe the distribution proposed by the applicant and explain why that is proposed;
(d) attach any material on which the applicant relies; and
(e) ask for a hearing, if the applicant wants one, and explain why it is needed.
(4) A person who wants to make representations about the application must—
(a) serve the representations on—
(i) the court officer,
(ii) the applicant, and
(iii) any other person to whom proceeds might be paid;
(b) do so as soon as reasonably practicable after service of the application;
(c) attach any material on which that person relies; and
(d) ask for a hearing, if that person wants one, and explain why it is needed.
(5) The court—
(a) must not determine the application unless the applicant and each person on whom it was served—
(i) is present, or
(ii) has had an opportunity to attend or to make representations; but
(b) subject to that, may determine the application—
(i) at a hearing (which must be in private unless the court otherwise directs), or without a hearing,
(ii) in the absence of any party to the application.

[Note. Under section 67D of the Proceeds of Crime Act 2002, a magistrates' court or the Crown Court may determine to whom, and in what proportions, any surplus proceeds of realisation must be distributed. Once a magistrates' court has made such a determination, the Crown Court may not do so, and vice versa.]

30 2002 c. 29; section 67D was inserted by section 58 of the Policing and Crime Act 2009 (c. 26).

Seizure and detention proceedings

R33.28 Application for approval to seize property or to search

33.28 (1) This rule applies where an officer who is entitled to apply wants the approval of a magistrates' court, under section 47G of the Proceeds of Crime Act 2002[31]—
(a) to seize property, under section 47C of that Act[32]; or
(b) to search premises or a person or vehicle for property to be seized, under section 47D, 47E or 47F of that Act[33].
(2) Such an officer must—
(a) apply in writing; and
(b) serve the application on the court officer.
(3) The application must—
(a) explain—
(i) the applicant's entitlement to apply, and
(ii) how the proposed seizure meets the conditions prescribed by sections 47B, 47C and, if applicable, 47D, 47E or 47F of the 2002 Act[34];
(b) if applicable, specify any premises, person or vehicle to be searched;
(c) attach any material on which the applicant relies; and
(d) propose the terms in which the applicant wants the court to give its approval.
(4) The court—
(a) must determine the application—
(i) at a hearing, which must be in private unless the court otherwise directs, and
(ii) in the applicant's presence; but
(b) may consider an application made orally instead of in writing.

[Note. Under section 47C of the Proceeds of Crime Act 2002, if any of the conditions listed in section 47B of the Act are met then one of the officers listed in section 47A may seize property other than cash or exempt property, as defined in the section, if that officer has reasonable grounds for suspecting that—

(a) the property may otherwise be made unavailable for satisfying any confiscation order that has been or may be made against a defendant; or
(b) the value of the property may otherwise be diminished as a result of conduct by the defendant or any other person.

Under sections 47D, 47E and 47F of the 2002 Act, such an officer may search premises, a person or a vehicle, respectively, for such property, on the conditions listed in those sections.

By sections 47C(6), 47D(2), 47E(4), 47F(6) and 47G of the 2002 Act, such an officer may seize property, and may search for it, only with the approval of a magistrates' court or, if that is impracticable, the approval of a senior officer (as defined by section 47G), unless in the circumstances it is not practicable to obtain the approval of either.]

R33.29 Application to extend detention period

33.29 (1) This rule applies where an officer who is entitled to apply, or the prosecutor, wants a magistrates' court to make an order, under section 47M of the Proceeds of Crime Act 2002[35], extending the period for which seized property may be detained.
(2) Such an officer or prosecutor must—
(a) apply in writing; and
(b) serve the application on—
(i) the court officer, and
(ii) any person whom the applicant believes would be affected by an order.
(3) The application must—
(a) specify—
(i) the property to be detained, and
(ii) whether the applicant wants it to be detained for a specified period or indefinitely;

[31] 2002 c. 29; section 47G was inserted by section 55 of the Policing and Crime Act 2009 (c. 26) and amended by section 55 of, and paragraphs 14 and 17 of Schedule 21 to, the Crime and Courts Act 2013 (c. 22) and section 13 of the Serious Crime Act 2015 (c. 9).
[32] 2002 c. 29; section 47C was inserted by section 55 of the Policing and Crime Act 2009 (c. 26) and amended by section 55 of, and paragraphs 14 and 16 of Schedule 21 to, the Crime and Courts Act 2013
[33] 2002 c. 29; sections 47D, 47E and 47F were inserted by section 55 of the Policing and Crime Act 2009 (c. 26).
[34] 2002 c. 29; section 47B was inserted by section 55 of the Policing and Crime Act 2009 (c. 26) and amended by section 13 of the Serious Crime Act 2015 (c. 9).
[35] 2002 c. 29; section 47M was inserted by section 55 of the Policing and Crime Act 2009 (c. 26) and amended by section 55 of, and paragraphs 14 and 18 of Schedule 21 to, the Crime and Courts Act 2013 (c. 22).

(b) explain—
(i) the applicant's entitlement to apply, and
(ii) how the proposed detention meets the conditions prescribed by section 47M of the 2002 Act;
(c) attach any material on which the applicant relies; and
(d) propose the terms of the order.
(4) The court—
(a) must determine the application—
(i) at a hearing, which must be in private unless the court otherwise directs, and
(ii) in the applicant's presence; but
(b) may—
(i) consider an application made orally instead of in writing,
(ii) require service of the application on the court officer after it has been heard, instead of before.
(5) If the court extends the period for which the property may be detained, the applicant must—
(a) notify any person affected by the order who was absent when it was made; and
(b) serve on the court officer a list of those so notified.

[Note. Under section 47M of the Proceeds of Crime Act 2002, one of the officers listed in that section, or the prosecutor, may apply to a magistrates' court for an order extending the period of 48 hours for which, under section 47J of the Act[36]*, property seized under section 47C may be detained.*

On an application to which this rule applies, hearsay evidence within the meaning of section 1(2) of the Civil Evidence Act 1995 is admissible: see section 47Q of the 2002 Act[37]*.]*

Application to vary or discharge order for extended detention **R33.30**

33.30 (1) This rule applies where an officer who is entitled to apply, the prosecutor, or a person affected by an order to which rule 33.29 applies, wants a magistrates' court to vary or discharge that order, under section 47N of the Proceeds of Crime Act 2002[38].
(2) Such a person must—
(a) apply in writing; and
(b) serve the application on—
(i) the court officer, and
(ii) as appropriate, the applicant for the order, or any person affected by the order.
(3) The application must—
(a) specify the order and the property detained;
(b) explain—
(i) the applicant's entitlement to apply,
(ii) why it is appropriate for the order to be varied or discharged,
(iii) if applicable, on what grounds the court must discharge the order;
(c) attach any material on which the applicant relies;
(d) if applicable, propose the terms of any variation; and
(e) ask for a hearing, if the applicant wants one, and explain why it is needed.
(4) A person who wants to make representations about the application must—
(a) serve the representations on—
(i) the court officer, and
(ii) the applicant;
(b) do so as soon as reasonably practicable after service of the application;
(c) attach any material on which that person relies; and
(d) ask for a hearing, if that person wants one, and explain why it is needed.
(5) The court—
(a) must not determine the application unless the applicant and each person on whom it was served—
(i) is present, or
(ii) has had an opportunity to attend or to make representations; but
(b) subject to that, may determine the application—
(i) at a hearing (which must be in private unless the court otherwise directs), or without a hearing,
(ii) in the absence of any party to the application.

[36] 2002 c. 29; section 47J was inserted by section 55 of the Policing and Crime Act 2009 (c. 26).
[37] 2002 c. 29; section 47Q was inserted by section 55 of the Policing and Crime Act 2009 (c. 26).
[38] 2002 c. 29; section 47N was inserted by section 55 of the Policing and Crime Act 2009 (c. 26).

[Note. Under section 47N of the Proceeds of Crime Act 2002, one of the officers listed in section 47M of the Act, the prosecutor, or a person affected by an order under section 47M, may apply to a magistrates' court for the order to be varied or discharged. Section 47N(3) lists the circumstances in which the court must discharge such an order.

On an application to which this rule applies, hearsay evidence within the meaning of section 1(2) of the Civil Evidence Act 1995 is admissible: see section 47Q of the 2002 Act.]

R33.31 Appeal about property detention decision

33.31 (1) This rule applies where—
(a) on an application under rule 33.29 for an order extending the period for which property may be detained—
(i) a magistrates' court decides not to make such an order, and
(ii) an officer who is entitled to apply for such an order, or the prosecutor, wants to appeal against that decision to the Crown Court under section 47O(1) of the Proceeds of Crime Act 2002[39];
(b) on an application under rule 33.30 to vary or discharge an order under rule 33.29—
(i) a magistrates' court determines the application, and
(ii) a person who is entitled to apply under that rule wants to appeal against that decision to the Crown Court under section 47O(2) of the 2002 Act.
(2) The appellant must serve an appeal notice—
(a) on the Crown Court officer and on any other party; and
(b) not more than 21 days after the magistrates' court's decision, or, if applicable, service of notice under rule 33.29(5).
(3) The appeal notice must—
(a) specify the decision under appeal;
(b) where paragraph (1)(a) applies, explain why the detention period should be extended;
(c) where paragraph (1)(b) applies, propose the order that the appellant wants the court to make, and explain why.
(4) Rule 34.11 (Constitution of the Crown Court) applies on such an appeal.

[Note. Under section 47O of the Proceeds of Crime Act 2002, one of those entitled to apply for an order under section 47M of that Act (extension of detention of property) may appeal against a refusal to make an order, and one of those entitled to apply for the variation or discharge of such an order, under section 47N of that Act, may appeal against the decision on such an application.

On an appeal to which this rule applies, hearsay evidence within the meaning of section 1(2) of the Civil Evidence Act 1995 is admissible: see section 47Q of the 2002 Act.]

Restraint and receivership proceedings: rules that apply generally

R33.32 Taking control of goods and forfeiture

33.32 (1) This rule applies to applications under sections 58(2) and (3) and 59(2) and (3) of the Proceeds of Crime Act 2002[40] for leave of the Crown Court to take control of goods or levy distress against property, or to exercise a right of forfeiture by peaceable re-entry in relation to a tenancy, in circumstances where the property or tenancy is the subject of a restraint order or a receiver has been appointed in respect of the property or tenancy.
(2) The application must be made in writing to the Crown Court.
(3) The application must be served on—
(a) the person who applied for the restraint order or the order appointing the receiver; and
(b) any receiver appointed in respect of the property or tenancy,
at least 7 days before the date fixed by the court for hearing the application, unless the Crown Court specifies a shorter period.

R33.33 Joining of applications

33.33 An application for the appointment of a management receiver or enforcement receiver under rule 33.56 may be joined with—
(a) an application for a restraint order under rule 33.51; and
(b) an application for the conferral of powers on the receiver under rule 33.57.

[39] 2002 c. 29; section 47O was inserted by section 55 of the Policing and Crime Act 2009 (c. 26).
[40] 2002 c. 29; section 58(2) was amended by section 62(3) of, and paragraphs 142 and 143 of Schedule 13 of the Tribunals, Courts and Enforcement Act 2007 (c. 15).

Applications to be dealt with in writing R33.34

33.34 Applications in restraint proceedings and receivership proceedings are to be dealt with without a hearing, unless the Crown Court orders otherwise.

Business in chambers R33.35

33.35 Restraint proceedings and receivership proceedings may be heard in chambers.

Power of court to control evidence R33.36

33.36 (1) When hearing restraint proceedings and receivership proceedings, the Crown Court may control the evidence by giving directions as to—
(a) the issues on which it requires evidence;
(b) the nature of the evidence which it requires to decide those issues; and
(c) the way in which the evidence is to be placed before the court.
(2) The court may use its power under this rule to exclude evidence that would otherwise be admissible.
(3) The court may limit cross-examination in restraint proceedings and receivership proceedings.

Evidence of witnesses R33.37

33.37 (1) The general rule is that, unless the Crown Court orders otherwise, any fact which needs to be proved in restraint proceedings or receivership proceedings by the evidence of a witness is to be proved by their evidence in writing.
(2) Where evidence is to be given in writing under this rule, any party may apply to the Crown Court for permission to cross-examine the person giving the evidence.
(3) If the Crown Court gives permission under paragraph (2) but the person in question does not attend as required by the order, his evidence may not be used unless the court gives permission.

Witness summons R33.38

33.38 (1) Any party to restraint proceedings or receivership proceedings may apply to the Crown Court to issue a witness summons requiring a witness to—
(a) attend court to give evidence; or
(b) produce documents to the court.
(2) Rule 17.3 (Application for summons, warrant or order: general rules) applies to an application under this rule as it applies to an application under section 2 of the Criminal Procedure (Attendance of Witnesses) Act 1965[41].

Hearsay evidence R33.39

33.39 Section 2(1) of the Civil Evidence Act 1995[42] (duty to give notice of intention to rely on hearsay evidence) does not apply to evidence in restraint proceedings and receivership proceedings.

Disclosure and inspection of documents R33.40

33.40 (1) This rule applies where, in the course of restraint proceedings or receivership proceedings, an issue arises as to whether property is realisable property.
(2) The Crown Court may make an order for disclosure of documents.
(3) Part 31 of the Civil Procedure Rules 1998[43] as amended from time to time shall have effect as if the proceedings were proceedings in the High Court.

Court documents R33.41

33.41 (1) Any order which the Crown Court issues in restraint proceedings or receivership proceedings must—
(a) state the name and judicial title of the person who made it;
(b) bear the date on which it is made; and
(c) be sealed by the Crown Court.
(2) The Crown Court may place the seal on the order—
(a) by hand; or
(b) by printing a facsimile of the seal on the order whether electronically or otherwise.
(3) A document purporting to bear the court's seal shall be admissible in evidence without further proof.

[41] 1965 c. 69; section 2 was substituted, together with sections 2 A to 2E, by section 66 of the Criminal Procedure and Investigations Act 1996 (c. 25) and amended by section 119 of, and paragraph 8 of Schedule 8 to, the Crime and Disorder Act 1998 (c. 37), section 109 of, and paragraph 126 of Schedule 8 to, the Courts Act 2003 (c. 39), paragraph 42 of Schedule 3 and Part 4 of Schedule 37 to the Criminal Justice Act 2003 (c. 44), section 169 of the Serious Organised Crime and Police Act 2005 (c. 15) and paragraph 33 of Schedule 17 to the Crime and Courts Act 2013 (c. 22).
[42] 1995 c. 38.
[43] S.I. 1998/3132; amending instruments relevant to this Part are S.I. 2000/221 and 2001/4015.

R33.42 **Consent orders**

33.42 (1) This rule applies where all the parties to restraint proceedings or receivership proceedings agree the terms in which an order should be made.
(2) Any party may apply for a judgment or order in the terms agreed.
(3) The Crown Court may deal with an application under paragraph (2) without a hearing.
(4) Where this rule applies—
(a) the order which is agreed by the parties must be drawn up in the terms agreed;
(b) it must be expressed as being 'By Consent'; and
(c) it must be signed by the legal representative acting for each of the parties to whom the order relates or by the party if he is a litigant in person.
(5) Where an application is made under this rule, then the requirements of any other rule as to the procedure for making an application do not apply.

R33.43 **Slips and omissions**

33.43 (1) The Crown Court may at any time correct an accidental slip or omission in an order made in restraint proceedings or receivership proceedings.
(2) A party may apply for a correction without notice.

R33.44 **Supply of documents from court records**

33.44 (1) No document relating to restraint proceedings or receivership proceedings may be supplied from the records of the Crown Court for any person to inspect or copy unless the Crown Court grants permission.
(2) An application for permission under paragraph (1) must be made on notice to the parties to the proceedings.

R33.45 **Disclosure of documents in criminal proceedings**

33.45 (1) This rule applies where—
(a) proceedings for an offence have been started in the Crown Court and the defendant has not been either convicted or acquitted on all counts; and
(b) an application for a restraint order under section 42(1) of the Proceeds of Crime Act 2002 has been made.
(2) The judge presiding at the proceedings for the offence may be supplied from the records of the Crown Court with documents relating to restraint proceedings and any receivership proceedings.
(3) Such documents must not otherwise be disclosed in the proceedings for the offence.

R33.46 **Preparation of documents**

33.46 (1) Every order in restraint proceedings or receivership proceedings must be drawn up by the Crown Court unless—
(a) the Crown Court orders a party to draw it up;
(b) a party, with the permission of the Crown Court, agrees to draw it up; or
(c) the order is made by consent under rule 33.42.
(2) The Crown Court may direct that—
(a) an order drawn up by a party must be checked by the Crown Court before it is sealed; or
(b) before an order is drawn up by the Crown Court, the parties must lodge an agreed statement of its terms.
(3) Where an order is to be drawn up by a party—
(a) he must lodge it with the Crown Court no later than 7 days after the date on which the court ordered or permitted him to draw it up so that it can be sealed by the Crown Court; and
(b) if he fails to lodge it within that period, any other party may draw it up and lodge it.
(4) Nothing in this rule shall require the Crown Court to accept a document which is illegible, has not been duly authorised, or is unsatisfactory for some other similar reason.

R33.47 **Order for costs**

33.47 (1) This rule applies where the Crown Court is deciding whether to make an order for costs in restraint proceedings or receivership proceedings.
(2) The court has discretion as to—
(a) whether costs are payable by one party to another;
(b) the amount of those costs; and
(c) when they are to be paid.

(3) If the court decides to make an order about costs—
(a) the general rule is that the unsuccessful party must be ordered to pay the costs of the successful party; but
(b) the court may make a different order.
(4) In deciding what order (if any) to make about costs, the court must have regard to all of the circumstances, including—
(a) the conduct of all the parties; and
(b) whether a party has succeeded on part of an application, even if he has not been wholly successful.
(5) The orders which the court may make include an order that a party must pay—
(a) a proportion of another party's costs;
(b) a stated amount in respect of another party's costs;
(c) costs from or until a certain date only;
(d) costs incurred before proceedings have begun;
(e) costs relating to particular steps taken in the proceedings;
(f) costs relating only to a distinct part of the proceedings; and
(g) interest on costs from or until a certain date, including a date before the making of an order.
(6) Where the court would otherwise consider making an order under paragraph (5)(f), it must instead, if practicable, make an order under paragraph (5)(a) or (c).
(7) Where the court has ordered a party to pay costs, it may order an amount to be paid on account before the costs are assessed.

[Note. See section 52 of the Senior Courts Act 1981[44].]

Assessment of costs **R33.48**

33.48 (1) Where the Crown Court has made an order for costs in restraint proceedings or receivership proceedings it may either—
(a) make an assessment of the costs itself; or
(b) order assessment of the costs under rule 45.11.
(2) In either case, the Crown Court or the assessing authority, as the case may be, must—
(a) only allow costs which are proportionate to the matters in issue; and
(b) resolve any doubt which it may have as to whether the costs were reasonably incurred or reasonable and proportionate in favour of the paying party.
(3) The Crown Court or the assessing authority, as the case may be, is to have regard to all the circumstances in deciding whether costs were proportionately or reasonably incurred or proportionate and reasonable in amount.
(4) In particular, the Crown Court or the assessing authority must give effect to any orders which have already been made.
(5) The Crown Court or the assessing authority must also have regard to—
(a) the conduct of all the parties, including in particular, conduct before, as well as during, the proceedings;
(b) the amount or value of the property involved;
(c) the importance of the matter to all the parties;
(d) the particular complexity of the matter or the difficulty or novelty of the questions raised;
(e) the skill, effort, specialised knowledge and responsibility involved;
(f) the time spent on the application; and
(g) the place where and the circumstances in which work or any part of it was done.

Time for complying with an order for costs **R33.49**

33.49 A party to restraint proceedings or receivership proceedings must comply with an order for the payment of costs within 14 days of—
(a) the date of the order if it states the amount of those costs;
(b) if the amount of those costs is decided later under rule 45.11, the date of the assessing authority's decision; or
(c) in either case, such later date as the Crown Court may specify.

[44] 1981 c. 54; section 52 was amended by section 31 of, and Part II of Schedule 1 to, the Prosecution of Offences Act 1985 (c. 23), section 4 of the Courts and Legal Services Act 1990 (c. 41), article 3 and paragraphs 11 and 12(a) of the Schedule to S.I. 2004/2035 and section 59 of, and paragraph 26 of Schedule 11 to, the Constitutional Reform Act 2005 (c. 4). The Act's title was amended by section 59(5) of, and paragraph 1 of Schedule 11 to, the Constitutional Reform Act 2005 (c. 4).

R33.50 **Application of costs rules**

33.50 Rules 33.47, 33.48 and 33.49 do not apply to the assessment of costs in proceedings to the extent that section 11 of the Access to Justice Act 1999[45] applies and provisions made under that Act make different provision.

Restraint proceedings

R33.51 **Application for restraint order or ancillary order**

33.51 (1) This rule applies where the prosecutor, or an accredited financial investigator, makes an application under section 42 of the Proceeds of Crime Act 2002[46] for—
(a) a restraint order, under section 41(1) of the 2002 Act; or
(b) an ancillary order, under section 41(7) of that Act, for the purpose of ensuring that a restraint order is effective.

(2) The application may be made without notice if the application is urgent or if there are reasonable grounds for believing that giving notice would cause the dissipation of realisable property which is the subject of the application.

(3) An application for a restraint order must be in writing and supported by a witness statement which must—
(a) give the grounds for the application;
(b) to the best of the witness' ability, give full details of the realisable property in respect of which the applicant is seeking the order and specify the person holding that realisable property;
(c) include the proposed terms of the order.

(4) An application for an ancillary order must be in writing and supported by a witness statement which must—
(a) give the grounds for, and full details of, the application;
(b) include, if appropriate—
(i) any request for an order for disclosure of documents to which rule 33.40 applies (Disclosure and inspection of documents),
(ii) the identity of any person whom the applicant wants the court to examine about the extent or whereabouts of realisable property,
(iii) a list of the main questions that the applicant wants to ask any such person, and
(iv) a list of any documents to which the applicant wants to refer such a person; and
(c) include the proposed terms of the order.

(5) An application for a restraint order and an application for an ancillary order may (but need not) be made at the same time and contained in the same documents.

(6) An application by an accredited financial investigator must include a statement that, under section 68 of the 2002 Act[47], the applicant has authority to apply.

R33.52 **Restraint and ancillary orders**

33.52 (1) The Crown Court may make a restraint order subject to exceptions, including, but not limited to, exceptions for reasonable living expenses and reasonable legal expenses, and for the purpose of enabling any person to carry on any trade, business or occupation.

(2) But the Crown Court must not make an exception for legal expenses where this is prohibited by section 41(4) of the Proceeds of Crime Act 2002.

(3) An exception to a restraint order may be made subject to conditions.

(4) The Crown Court must not require the applicant for a restraint order to give any undertaking relating to damages sustained as a result of the restraint order by a person who is prohibited from dealing with realisable property by the restraint order.

(5) The Crown Court may require the applicant for a restraint order to give an undertaking to pay the reasonable expenses of any person, other than a person who is prohibited from dealing with realisable property by the restraint order, which are incurred in complying with the restraint order.

(6) An order must include a statement that disobedience of the order, either by a person to whom the order is addressed, or by another person, may be contempt of court and the order must include details of the possible consequences of being held in contempt of court.

[45] 1999 c. 22; section 11 was repealed by section 39 of, and paragraph 51 of Schedule 5 to, the Legal Aid, Sentencing and Punishment of Offenders Act 2012 (c. 10) with saving and transitional provisions made by regulations 6, 7 and 8 of S.I. 2013/534.

[46] 2002 c. 29; section 42 was amended by sections 74(2) and 92 of, and paragraphs 1 and 23 of Schedule 8, and Schedule 14 to, the Serious Crime Act 2007 (c. 27) and section 12 of the Serious Crime Act 2015 (c. 9).

[47] 2002 c. 29; section 68 was amended by section 50 of the Commissioners for Revenue and Customs Act 2005 (c. 11).

(7) Unless the Crown Court otherwise directs, an order made without notice has effect until the court makes an order varying or discharging it.

(8) The applicant for an order must—

(a) serve copies of the order and of the witness statement made in support of the application on the defendant and any person who is prohibited by the order from dealing with realisable property; and

(b) notify any person whom the applicant knows to be affected by the order of its terms.

Application for discharge or variation of restraint or ancillary order by a person affected by the order **R33.53**

33.53 (1) This rule applies where a person affected by a restraint order makes an application to the Crown Court under section 42(3) of the Proceeds of Crime Act 2002 to discharge or vary the restraint order or any ancillary order made under section 41(7) of the Act.

(2) The application must be in writing and may be supported by a witness statement.

(3) The application and any witness statement must be lodged with the Crown Court.

(4) The application and any witness statement must be served on the person who applied for the restraint order and any person who is prohibited from dealing with realisable property by the restraint order (if he is not the person making the application) at least 2 days before the date fixed by the court for hearing the application, unless the Crown Court specifies a shorter period.

Application for variation of restraint or ancillary order by the person who applied for the order **R33.54**

33.54 (1) This rule applies where the applicant for a restraint order makes an application under section 42(3) of the Proceeds of Crime Act 2002 to the Crown Court to vary the restraint order or any ancillary order made under section 41(7) of the 2002 Act (including where the court has already made a restraint order and the applicant is seeking to vary the order in order to restrain further realisable property).

(2) The application may be made without notice if the application is urgent or if there are reasonable grounds for believing that giving notice would cause the dissipation of realisable property which is the subject of the application.

(3) The application must be in writing and must be supported by a witness statement which must—

(a) give the grounds for the application;

(b) where the application is for the inclusion of further realisable property in a restraint order give full details, to the best of the witness's ability, of the realisable property in respect of which the applicant is seeking the order and specify the person holding that realisable property;

(c) where the application is to vary an ancillary order, include, if appropriate—

(i) any request for an order for disclosure of documents to which rule 33.40 applies (Disclosure and inspection of documents),

(ii) the identity of any person whom the applicant wants the court to examine about the extent or whereabouts of realisable property,

(iii) a list of the main questions that the applicant wants to ask any such person, and

(iv) a list of any documents to which the applicant wants to refer such a person; and

(d) include the proposed terms of the variation.

(4) An application by an accredited financial investigator must include a statement that, under section 68 of the 2002 Act, the applicant has authority to apply.

(5) The application and witness statement must be lodged with the Crown Court.

(6) Except where, under paragraph (2), notice of the application is not required to be served, the application and witness statement must be served on any person who is prohibited from dealing with realisable property by the restraint order at least 2 days before the date fixed by the court for hearing the application, unless the Crown Court specifies a shorter period.

(7) If the court makes an order for the variation of a restraint or ancillary order, the applicant must serve copies of the order and of the witness statement made in support of the application on—

(a) the defendant;

(b) any person who is prohibited from dealing with realisable property by the restraint order (whether before or after the variation); and

(c) any other person whom the applicant knows to be affected by the order.

Application for discharge of restraint or ancillary order by the person who applied for the order **R33.55**

33.55 (1) This rule applies where the applicant for a restraint order makes an application under section 42(3) of the Proceeds of Crime Act 2002 to discharge the order or any ancillary order made under section 41(7) of the 2002 Act.

(2) The application may be made without notice.

(3) The application must be in writing and must state the grounds for the application.

(4) If the court makes an order for the discharge of a restraint or ancillary order, the applicant must serve copies of the order on—

(a) the defendant;

(b) any person who is prohibited from dealing with realisable property by the restraint order (whether before or after the discharge); and

(c) any other person whom the applicant knows to be affected by the order.

Receivership proceedings

R33.56 Application for appointment of a management or an enforcement receiver

33.56 (1) This rule applies to an application for the appointment of a management receiver under section 48(1) of the Proceeds of Crime Act 2002[48] and an application for the appointment of an enforcement receiver under section 50(1) of the 2002 Act.

(2) The application may be made without notice if—

(a) the application is joined with an application for a restraint order under rule 33.51 (Application for restraint order or ancillary order);

(b) the application is urgent; or

(c) there are reasonable grounds for believing that giving notice would cause the dissipation of realisable property which is the subject of the application.

(3) The application must be in writing and must be supported by a witness statement which must—

(a) give the grounds for the application;

(b) give full details of the proposed receiver;

(c) to the best of the witness' ability, give full details of the realisable property in respect of which the applicant is seeking the order and specify the person holding that realisable property;

(d) where the application is made by an accredited financial investigator, include a statement that, under section 68 of the 2002 Act, the applicant has authority to apply; and

(e) if the proposed receiver is not a person falling within section 55(8) of the 2002 Act[49] and the applicant is asking the court to allow the receiver to act—

(i) without giving security, or

(ii) before he has given security or satisfied the court that he has security in place,

explain the reasons why that is necessary.

(4) Where the application is for the appointment of an enforcement receiver, the applicant must provide the Crown Court with a copy of the confiscation order made against the defendant.

(5) The application and witness statement must be lodged with the Crown Court.

(6) Except where, under paragraph (2), notice of the application is not required to be served, the application and witness statement must be lodged with the Crown Court and served on—

(a) the defendant;

(b) any person who holds realisable property to which the application relates; and

(c) any other person whom the applicant knows to be affected by the application,

at least 7 days before the date fixed by the court for hearing the application, unless the Crown Court specifies a shorter period.

(7) If the court makes an order for the appointment of a receiver, the applicant must serve copies of the order and of the witness statement made in support of the application on—

(a) the defendant;

(b) any person who holds realisable property to which the order applies; and

(c) any other person whom the applicant knows to be affected by the order.

R33.57 Application for conferral of powers on a management receiver or an enforcement receiver

33.57 (1) This rule applies to an application for the conferral of powers on a management receiver under section 49(1) of the Proceeds of Crime Act 2002 or an enforcement receiver under section 51(1) of the 2002 Act.

(2) The application may be made without notice if the application is to give the receiver power to take possession of property and—

(a) the application is joined with an application for a restraint order under rule 33.51 (Application for restraint order or ancillary order);

(b) the application is urgent; or

(c) there are reasonable grounds for believing that giving notice would cause the dissipation of the property which is the subject of the application.

[48] 2002 c. 29.

[49] 2002 c. 29; section 55(8) was amended by section 51(1) and (2) of the Policing and Crime Act 2009 (c. 26).

(3) The application must be made in writing and supported by a witness statement which must—
(a) give the grounds for the application;
(b) give full details of the realisable property in respect of which the applicant is seeking the order and specify the person holding that realisable property;
(c) where the application is made by an accredited financial investigator, include a statement that, under section 68 of the 2002 Act, the applicant has authority to apply; and
(d) where the application is for power to start, carry on or defend legal proceedings in respect of the property, explain—
(i) what proceedings are concerned, in what court, and
(ii) what powers the receiver will ask that court to exercise.

(4) Where the application is for the conferral of powers on an enforcement receiver, the applicant must provide the Crown Court with a copy of the confiscation order made against the defendant.

(5) The application and witness statement must be lodged with the Crown Court.

(6) Except where, under paragraph (2), notice of the application is not required to be served, the application and witness statement must be served on—
(a) the defendant;
(b) any person who holds realisable property in respect of which a receiver has been appointed or in respect of which an application for a receiver has been made;
(c) any other person whom the applicant knows to be affected by the application; and
(d) the receiver (if one has already been appointed),
at least 7 days before the date fixed by the court for hearing the application, unless the Crown Court specifies a shorter period.

(7) If the court makes an order for the conferral of powers on a receiver, the applicant must serve copies of the order on—
(a) the defendant;
(b) any person who holds realisable property in respect of which the receiver has been appointed; and
(c) any other person whom the applicant knows to be affected by the order.

Applications for discharge or variation of receivership orders, and applications for other orders R33.58

33.58 (1) This rule applies to applications under section 62(3) of the Proceeds of Crime Act 2002 for orders (by persons affected by the action of receivers) and applications under section 63(1) of the 2002 Act[50] for the discharge or variation of orders relating to receivers.

(2) The application must be made in writing and lodged with the Crown Court.

(3) The application must be served on the following persons (except where they are the person making the application)—
(a) the person who applied for appointment of the receiver;
(b) the defendant;
(c) any person who holds realisable property in respect of which the receiver has been appointed;
(d) the receiver; and
(e) any other person whom the applicant knows to be affected by the application,
at least 7 days before the date fixed by the court for hearing the application, unless the Crown Court specifies a shorter period.

(4) If the court makes an order for the discharge or variation of an order relating to a receiver under section 63(2) of the 2002 Act, the applicant must serve copies of the order on any persons whom he knows to be affected by the order.

Sums in the hands of receivers R33.59

33.59 (1) This rule applies where the amount payable under a confiscation order has been fully paid and any sums remain in the hands of an enforcement receiver.

(2) The receiver must make an application to the Crown Court for directions as to the distribution of the sums in his hands.

(3) The application and any evidence which the receiver intends to rely on in support of the application must be served on—
(a) the defendant; and
(b) any other person who held (or holds) interests in any property realised by the receiver,
at least 7 days before the date fixed by the court for hearing the application, unless the Crown Court specifies a shorter period.

50 2002 c. 29; section 63(1) was amended by section 74(2) of, and paragraphs 1 and 30 of Schedule 8 to, the Serious Crime Act 2007 (c. 27).

(4) If any of the provisions listed in paragraph (5) (provisions as to the vesting of funds in a trustee in bankruptcy) apply, then the Crown Court must make a declaration to that effect.

(5) These are the provisions—

(a) section 82 of the Bankruptcy (Scotland) Act 2016[51];

(b) section 306B of the Insolvency Act 1986[52]; and

(c) article 279B of the Insolvency (Northern Ireland) Order 1989[53].

R33.60 **Security**

33.60 (1) This rule applies where the Crown Court appoints a receiver under section 48 or 50 of the Proceeds of Crime Act 2002 and the receiver is not a person falling within section 55(8) of the 2002 Act[54] (and it is immaterial whether the receiver is a permanent or temporary member of staff or on secondment from elsewhere).

(2) The Crown Court may direct that before the receiver begins to act, or within a specified time, he must either—

(a) give such security as the Crown Court may determine; or

(b) file with the Crown Court and serve on all parties to any receivership proceedings evidence that he already has in force sufficient security,

to cover his liability for his acts and omissions as a receiver.

(3) The Crown Court may terminate the appointment of a receiver if he fails to—

(a) give the security; or

(b) satisfy the court as to the security he has in force,

by the date specified.

R33.61 **Remuneration**

33.61 (1) This rule applies where the Crown Court appoints a receiver under section 48 or 50 of the Proceeds of Crime Act 2002 and the receiver is not a person falling within section 55(8) of the 2002 Act (and it is immaterial whether the receiver is a permanent or temporary member of staff or on secondment from elsewhere).

(2) The receiver may only charge for his services if the Crown Court—

(a) so directs; and

(b) specifies the basis on which the receiver is to be remunerated.

(3) Unless the Crown Court orders otherwise, in determining the remuneration of the receiver, the Crown Court shall award such sum as is reasonable and proportionate in all the circumstances and which takes into account—

(a) the time properly given by him and his staff to the receivership;

(b) the complexity of the receivership;

(c) any responsibility of an exceptional kind or degree which falls on the receiver in consequence of the receivership;

(d) the effectiveness with which the receiver appears to be carrying out, or to have carried out, his duties; and

(e) the value and nature of the subject matter of the receivership.

(4) The Crown Court may refer the determination of a receiver's remuneration to be ascertained by the taxing authority of the Crown Court and rules 45.11 (Assessment and re-assessment) to 45.14 (Application for an extension of time) shall have effect as if the taxing authority was ascertaining costs.

(5) A receiver appointed under section 48 of the 2002 Act is to receive his remuneration by realising property in respect of which he is appointed, in accordance with section 49(2)(d) of the 2002 Act.

(6) A receiver appointed under section 50 of the 2002 Act is to receive his remuneration by applying to the magistrates' court officer for payment under section 55(4)(b) of the 2002 Act[55].

R33.62 **Accounts**

33.62 (1) The Crown Court may order a receiver appointed under section 48 or 50 of the Proceeds of Crime Act 2002 to prepare and serve accounts.

[51] 2016 asp 21.

[52] 1986 c. 45; section 306B was inserted by section 456 of, and paragraphs 1 and 16 of Schedule 11 to, the Proceeds of Crime Act 2002 (c. 29).

[53] S.I. 1989/2405 (N.I. 19); article 279B was inserted by section 456 of, and paragraph 20(3) of Schedule 11 to, the Proceeds of Crime Act 2002 (c. 29).

[54] 2002 c. 29; section 55(8) was amended by section 51(1) and (2) of the Policing and Crime Act 2009 (c. 26).

[55] 2002 c. 29; section 55(4)(b) was amended by paragraph 408 of Schedule 8 to, the Courts Act 2003 (c. 39).

(2) A party to receivership proceedings served with such accounts may apply for an order permitting him to inspect any document in the possession of the receiver relevant to those accounts.

(3) Any party to receivership proceedings may, within 14 days of being served with the accounts, serve notice on the receiver—
(a) specifying any item in the accounts to which he objects;
(b) giving the reason for such objection; and
(c) requiring the receiver within 14 days of receipt of the notice, either—
(i) to notify all the parties who were served with the accounts that he accepts the objection, or
(ii) if he does not accept the objection, to apply for an examination of the accounts in relation to the contested item.

(4) When the receiver applies for the examination of the accounts he must at the same time lodge with the Crown Court–
(a) the accounts; and
(b) a copy of the notice served on him under this section of the rule.

(5) If the receiver fails to comply with paragraph (3)(c) of this rule, any party to receivership proceedings may apply to the Crown Court for an examination of the accounts in relation to the contested item.

(6) At the conclusion of its examination of the accounts the court must certify the result.

Non-compliance by receiver R33.63

33.63 (1) If a receiver appointed under section 48 or 50 of the Proceeds of Crime Act 2002 fails to comply with any rule, practice direction or direction of the Crown Court, the Crown Court may order him to attend a hearing to explain his non-compliance.

(2) At the hearing, the Crown Court may make any order it considers appropriate, including—
(a) terminating the appointment of the receiver;
(b) reducing the receiver's remuneration or disallowing it altogether; and
(c) ordering the receiver to pay the costs of any party.

Proceedings under the Criminal Justice Act 1988 and the Drug Trafficking Act 1994

[Note. The relevant provisions of the 1988 and 1994 Acts were repealed on 24th March 2003, but they continue to have effect in respect of proceedings for offences committed before that date.]

Statements, etc. relevant to making confiscation orders R33.64

33.64 (1) Where a prosecutor or defendant—
(a) serves on the magistrates' court officer any statement or other document under section 73 of the Criminal Justice Act 1988[56] in any proceedings in respect of an offence listed in Schedule 4 to that Act; or
(b) serves on the Crown Court officer any statement or other document under section 11 of the Drug Trafficking Act 1994[57] or section 73 of the 1988 Act in any proceedings in respect of a drug trafficking offence or in respect of an offence to which Part VI of the 1988 Act applies,

that party must serve a copy as soon as practicable on the defendant or the prosecutor, as the case may be.

(2) Any statement tendered by the prosecutor to the magistrates' court under section 73 of the 1988 Act or to the Crown Court under section 11(1) of the 1994 Act or section 73(1A) of the 1988 Act must include the following particulars—
(a) the name of the defendant;
(b) the name of the person by whom the statement is made and the date on which it was made;
(c) where the statement is not tendered immediately after the defendant has been convicted, the date on which and the place where the relevant conviction occurred; and
(d) such information known to the prosecutor as is relevant to the determination as to whether or not the defendant has benefited from drug trafficking or relevant criminal conduct and to the assessment of the value of any proceeds of drug trafficking or, as the case may be, benefit from relevant criminal conduct.

[56] 1988 c. 33; section 73 and Schedule 4 were repealed, with savings, by paragraphs 1 and 17 of Schedule 11 and Schedule 12 to, the Proceeds of Crime Act 2002 (c. 29).
[57] 1994 c. 37; section 11 was repealed, with savings, by paragraphs 1 and 25 of Schedule 11 and Schedule 12 to, the Proceeds of Crime Act 2002 (c. 29).

(3) Where, in accordance with section 11(7) of the 1994 Act or section 73(1C) of the 1988 Act, the defendant indicates in writing the extent to which he or she accepts any allegation contained within the prosecutor's statement, the defendant must serve a copy of that reply on the court officer.

(4) Expressions used in this rule have the same meanings as in the 1994 Act or, where appropriate, the 1988 Act.

R33.65 **Postponed determinations**

33.65 (1) Where an application is made by the defendant or the prosecutor—

(a) to a magistrates' court under section 72A(5)(a) of the Criminal Justice Act 1988[58] asking the court to exercise its powers under section 72A(4) of that Act; or

(b) to the Crown Court under section 3(5)(a) of the Drug Trafficking Act 1994[59] asking the Court to exercise its powers under section 3(4) of that Act, or under section 72A(5)(a) of the 1988 Act asking the court to exercise its powers under section 72A(4) of the 1988 Act,

the application must be in writing and the applicant must serve a copy on the prosecutor or the defendant, as the case may be.

(2) A party served with a copy of an application under paragraph (1) must, within 28 days of the date of service, notify the applicant and the court officer, in writing, whether or not that party opposes the application, giving reasons for any opposition.

(3) After the expiry of the period referred to in paragraph (2), the court may determine an application under paragraph (1) —

(a) without a hearing; or

(b) at a hearing at which the parties may be represented.

R33.66 **Confiscation orders—revised assessments**

33.66 (1) Where the prosecutor makes an application under section 13, 14 or 15 of the Drug Trafficking Act 1994[60] or section 74A, 74B or 74C of the Criminal Justice Act 1988[61], the application must be in writing and a copy must be served on the defendant.

(2) The application must include the following particulars—

(a) the name of the defendant;

(b) the date on which and the place where any relevant conviction occurred;

(c) the date on which and the place where any relevant confiscation order was made or, as the case may be, varied;

(d) the grounds on which the application is made; and

(e) an indication of the evidence available to support the application.

R33.67 **Application to the Crown Court to discharge or vary order to make material available**

33.67 (1) Where an order under section 93H of the Criminal Justice Act 1988[62] (order to make material available) or section 55 of the Drug Trafficking Act 1994[63] (order to make material available) has been made by the Crown Court, any person affected by it may apply in writing to the court officer for the order to be discharged or varied, and on hearing such an application the court may discharge the order or make such variations to it as the court thinks fit.

(2) Subject to paragraph (3), where a person proposes to make an application under paragraph (1) for the discharge or variation of an order, that person must give a copy of the application, not later than 48 hours before the making of the application—

(a) to a constable at the police station specified in the order; or

(b) to the office of the appropriate officer who made the application, as specified in the order,

in either case together with a notice indicating the time and place at which the application for discharge or variation is to be made.

58 1988 c. 33; section 72A was inserted by section 28 of the Criminal Justice Act 1993 (c. 36) and repealed, with savings, by sections 456 and 457 of, and paragraphs 1 and 17 of Schedule 11, and Schedule 12 to, the Proceeds of Crime Act 2002 (c. 29).

59 1994 c. 37; section 3 was repealed, with savings, by paragraphs 1 and 25 of Schedule 11 and Schedule 12 to, the Proceeds of Crime Act 2002 (c. 29).

60 1994 c. 37; sections 13, 14 and 15 were repealed, with savings, by paragraphs 1 and 25 of Schedule 11 and Schedule 12 to, the Proceeds of Crime Act 2002 (c. 29).

61 1988 c. 33; sections 74A, 74B and 74C were inserted by the Proceeds of Crime Act 1995 (c. 11), sections 5, 6 and 7 respectively, and repealed, with savings by paragraphs 1 and 17 of Schedule 11 and Schedule 12 to, the Proceeds of Crime Act 2002 (c. 29).

62 1988 c. 33; section 93H was inserted by section 11 of the Proceeds of Crime Act 1995 (c. 11) and repealed, with savings, by paragraphs 1 and 17 of Schedule 11 and Schedule 12 to, the Proceeds of Crime Act 2002 (c. 29).

63 1994 c. 37; section 55 was amended by paragraphs 1 and 25 of Schedule 11 and Schedule 12 to, the Proceeds of Crime Act 2002 (c. 29) and by paragraph 364 of Schedule 8 to the Courts Act 2003 (c. 39).

(3) The court may direct that paragraph (2) need not be complied with if satisfied that the person making the application has good reason to seek a discharge or variation of the order as soon as possible and it is not practicable to comply with that paragraph.

(4) In this rule:

'constable' includes a person commissioned by the Commissioners for Her Majesty's Revenue and Customs;

'police station' includes a place for the time being occupied by Her Majesty's Revenue and Customs.

Application to the Crown Court for increase in term of imprisonment in default of payment R33.68

33.68 (1) This rule applies to applications made, or that have effect as made, to the Crown Court under section 10 of the Drug Trafficking Act 1994[64] and section 75A of the Criminal Justice Act 1988[65] (interest on sums unpaid under confiscation orders).

(2) Notice of an application to which this rule applies to increase the term of imprisonment or detention fixed in default of payment of a confiscation order by a person ('the defendant') must be made by the prosecutor in writing to the court officer.

(3) A notice under paragraph (2) shall—
- (a) state the name and address of the defendant;
- (b) specify the grounds for the application;
- (c) give details of the enforcement measures taken, if any; and
- (d) include a copy of the confiscation order.

(4) On receiving a notice under paragraph (2), the court officer must—
- (a) forthwith send to the defendant and the magistrates' court required to enforce payment of the confiscation order under section 140(1) of the Powers of Criminal Courts (Sentencing) Act 2000[66], a copy of the said notice; and
- (b) notify in writing the applicant and the defendant of the date, time and place appointed for the hearing of the application.

(5) Where the Crown Court makes an order pursuant to an application mentioned in paragraph (1) above, the court officer must send forthwith a copy of the order—
- (a) to the applicant;
- (b) to the defendant;
- (c) where the defendant is at the time of the making of the order in custody, to the person having custody of him or her; and
- (d) to the magistrates' court mentioned in paragraph (4)(a).

Drug trafficking—compensation on acquittal in the Crown Court R33.69

33.69 Where the Crown Court cancels a confiscation order under section 22(2) of the Drug Trafficking Act 1994[67], the Crown Court officer must serve notice to that effect on the High Court officer and on the court officer of the magistrates' court which has responsibility for enforcing the order.

Contempt proceedings

Application to punish for contempt of court R33.70

33.70 (1) This rule applies where a person is accused of disobeying—
- (a) a compliance order made for the purpose of ensuring that a confiscation order is effective;
- (b) a restraint order; or
- (c) an ancillary order made for the purpose of ensuring that a restraint order is effective.

(2) An applicant who wants the Crown Court to exercise its power to punish that person for contempt of court must comply with the rules in Part 48 (Contempt of court).

64 1994 c. 37; section 10 was repealed, with savings, by paragraphs 1 and 25 of Schedule 11 and Schedule 12 to, the Proceeds of Crime Act 2002 (c. 29).

65 1988 c. 33; section 75A was inserted by section 9 of the Proceeds of Crime Act 1995 (c. 11) and repealed, with savings, by paragraphs 1 and 17 of Schedule 11 and Schedule 12 to, the Proceeds of Crime Act 2002 (c. 29).

66 2000 c. 6; section 140 was amended by paragraphs 74 of Schedule 3 and Part 4 of Schedule 37 to the Criminal Justice Act 2003 (c. 44) and section 40(4) of, and paragraph 69 of Schedule 9 to, the Constitutional Reform Act 2005 (c. 4). It is further amended by sections 74 and 75 of, and paragraphs 160 and 194 of Schedule 8 to, the Criminal Justice and Court Services Act 2000 (c. 43) with effect from a date to be appointed.

67 1994 c. 37; section 22 was repealed, with savings, by paragraphs 1 and 25 of Schedule 11 and Schedule 12 to, the Proceeds of Crime Act 2002 (c. 29).

[Note. The Crown Court has inherent power to punish for contempt of court a person who disobeys its order: see section 45 of the Senior Courts Act 1981[68].]

Criminal Procedure Rules Part 34 Appeal to the Crown Court

R34.1 When this Part applies

34.1 (1) This Part applies where—

(a) a defendant wants to appeal under—

(i) section 108 of the Magistrates' Courts Act 1980[1],

(ii) section 45 of the Mental Health Act 1983[2],

(iii) paragraph 10 of Schedule 3 to the Powers of Criminal Courts (Sentencing) Act 2000[3], or paragraphs 9(8) or 13(5) of Schedule 8 to the Criminal Justice Act 2003[4],

(iv) section 42 of the Counter Terrorism Act 2008[5];

(b) the Criminal Cases Review Commission refers a defendant's case to the Crown Court under section 11 of the Criminal Appeal Act 1995[6];

(c) a prosecutor wants to appeal under—

(i) section 14A(5A) of the Football Spectators Act 1989[7], or

(ii) section 147(3) of the Customs and Excise Management Act 1979[8]; or

(d) a person wants to appeal under—

(i) section 1 of the Magistrates' Courts (Appeals from Binding Over Orders) Act 1956[9],

(ii) section 12(5) of the Contempt of Court Act 1981[10],

(iii) regulation 3C or 3H of the Costs in Criminal Cases (General) Regulations 1986[11],

(iv) section 22 of the Football Spectators Act 1989[12],

(v) section 10(4) or (5) of the Crime and Disorder Act 1998[13] or

(vi) section 28(5)(b) of the Offensive Weapons Act 2019[14].

(2) A reference to an 'appellant' in this Part is a reference to such a party or person.

[Note. An appeal to the Crown Court is by way of re-hearing: see section 79(3) of the Senior Courts Act 1981[15]. For the powers of the Crown Court on an appeal, see section 48 of that Act.

68 1981 c. 54. The Act's title was amended by section 59(5) of, and paragraph 1 of Schedule 11 to, the Constitutional Reform Act 2005 (c. 4).

1 1980 c. 43; section 108 was amended by sections 66(2) and 78 of, and Schedule 16 to, the Criminal Justice Act 1982 (c. 48), section 23(3) of the Football Spectators Act 1989 (c. 37), section 101(2) of, and Schedule 13 to, the Criminal Justice Act 1991 (c. 53), sections 119 and 120(2) of, and paragraph 43 of Schedule 8 and Schedule 10 to, the Crime and Disorder Act 1998 (c. 37), section 7(2) of the Football (Offences and Disorder) Act 1999 (c. 21), section 165(1) of, and paragraph 71 of Schedule 9 to, the Powers of Criminal Courts (Sentencing) Act 2000 (c. 6), section 1 of, and Schedule 3 to, the Football (Disorder) Act 2000 (c. 25), section 58(1) of, and paragraph 10 of Schedule 10 to, the Domestic Violence, Crime and Victims Act 2004 (c. 28), section 52(2) of, and paragraph 14 of Schedule 3 to, the Violent Crime Reduction Act 2006 (c. 38) and section 64 of, and paragraph 10 of Schedule 3 to, the Animal Welfare Act 2006 (c. 45).

2 1983 c. 20.

3 2000 c. 6.

4 2003 c. 44.

5 2008 c. 28.

6 1995 c. 35.

7 1989 c. 37; section 14A(5A) was inserted by section 52 of, and paragraphs 1 and 3 of Schedule 3 to, the Violent Crime Reduction Act 2006 (c. 38).

8 1979 c. 2.

9 1956 c. 44; section 1 was amended by Part 1 of Schedule 7 to, the Criminal Justice Act 1967 (c. 80), Part 1 of Schedule 9 to, the Courts Act 1971 (c. 23) and Schedule 9 to, the Magistrates' Courts Act 1980 (c. 43).

10 1981 c. 49; section 12(5) was amended by section 165(1) of, and paragraph 83 of Schedule 9 to, the Powers of Criminal Courts (Sentencing) Act 2000 (c. 6).

11 S.I. 1986/1335; regulation 3C was inserted by regulation 2 of The Costs in Criminal Cases (General) (Amendment) Regulations 1991 (SI 1991/789) and amended by regulation 5 of The Costs in Criminal Cases (General) (Amendment) Regulations 2004 (SI 2004/2408). Regulation 3H was inserted by regulation 7 of The Costs in Criminal Cases (General) (Amendment) Regulations 2004 (S.I. 2004/2408).

12 1989 c. 37; section 22 was amended by section 5 of the Football (Offences and Disorder) Act 1999 (c. 21), section 1 of, and paragraphs 9 – 11 and 17 of Schedule 2 to, the Football (Disorder) Act 2000 (c. 25) and section 109(1) and (3) of, and paragraph 335 of Schedule 8, and Schedule 10 to, the Courts Act 2003 (c. 39).

13 1998 c. 37; section 10 was amended by section 15 of, and paragraphs 276 and 277 of Schedule 4 to, the Constitutional Reform Act 2005 (c. 4), section 41 of the Crime and Security Act 2010 (c. 17) and section 17 of, and paragraph 52 of Schedule 9 to, the Crime and Courts Act 2013 (c. 22).

14 2019 c. 17; section 28 comes into force on a date to be appointed.

15 1981 c. 54. The Act's title was amended by section 59(5) of, and paragraph 1 of Schedule 11 to, the Constitutional Reform Act 2005 (c. 4).

A defendant may appeal from a magistrates' court to the Crown Court—

(a) *under section 108 of the Magistrates' Courts Act 1980, against sentence after a guilty plea and after a not guilty plea against conviction, against a finding of guilt or against sentence;*
(b) *under section 45 of the Mental Health Act 1983, where the magistrates' court makes a hospital order or guardianship order without convicting the defendant;*
(c) *under paragraph 10 of Schedule 3 to the Powers of Criminal Courts (Sentencing) Act 2000, or under paragraphs 9(8) or 13(5) of Schedule 8 to the Criminal Justice Act 2003, where the magistrates' court revokes a community order and deals with the defendant in another way;*
(d) *under section 42 of the Counter Terrorism Act 2008, where the magistrates' court decides that an offence has a terrorist connection.*

See section 13 of the Criminal Appeal Act 1995[16] *for the circumstances in which the Criminal Cases Review Commission may refer a conviction or sentence to the Crown Court.*

Under section 14A(5A) of the Football Spectators Act 1989, a prosecutor may appeal to the Crown Court against a failure by a magistrates' court to make a football banning order.

Under section 147(3) of the Customs and Excise Management Act 1979, a prosecutor may appeal to the Crown Court against any decision of a magistrates' court in proceedings for an offence under any Act relating to customs or excise.

Under section 1 of the Magistrates' Courts (Appeals from Binding Over Orders) Act 1956, a person bound over to keep the peace or be of good behaviour by a magistrates' court may appeal to the Crown Court.

Under section 12(5) of the Contempt of Court Act 1981, a person detained, committed to custody or fined by a magistrates' court for insulting a member of the court or another participant in the case, or for interrupting the proceedings, may appeal to the Crown Court.

Under regulation 3C of the Costs in Criminal Cases (General) Regulations 1986, a legal representative against whom a magistrates' court makes a wasted costs order under section 19A of the Prosecution of Offences Act 1985 and regulation 3B may appeal against that order to the Crown Court.

Under regulation 3H of the Costs in Criminal Cases (General) Regulations 1986, a third party against whom a magistrates' court makes a costs order under section 19B of the Prosecution of Offences Act 1985 and regulation 3F may appeal against that order to the Crown Court.

Under section 22 of the Football Spectators Act 1989, any person aggrieved by the decision of a magistrates' court making a football banning order may appeal to the Crown Court.

Under section 10(4) or (5) of the Crime and Disorder Act 1998, a person in respect of whom a magistrates' court makes a parenting order may appeal against that order to the Crown Court.

Under section 28(5)(b) of the Offensive Weapons Act 2019 an applicant to a magistrates' court for the variation, renewal or discharge of a knife crime prevention order made by that court, or a respondent to such an application, may appeal to the Crown Court against the decision of the magistrates' court.]

Service of appeal and respondent's notices **R34.2**

34.2 (1) An appellant must serve an appeal notice on—
(a) the magistrates' court officer; and
(b) every other party.

(2) The appellant must serve the appeal notice—
(a) as soon after the decision appealed against as the appellant wants; but
(b) not more than 15 business days after—
(i) sentence or the date sentence is deferred, whichever is earlier, if the appeal is against conviction or against a finding of guilt,
(ii) sentence, if the appeal is against sentence, or
(iii) the order or failure to make an order about which the appellant wants to appeal, in any other case.

(3) The appellant must serve with the appeal notice any application for the following, with reasons—
(a) an extension of the time limit under this rule, if the appeal notice is late;
(b) bail pending appeal, if the appellant is in custody; or
(c) the suspension of any disqualification imposed or order made in the case, where the magistrates' court or the Crown Court can order such a suspension pending appeal.

[16] 1995 c. 35; section 13 was amended by section 321 of, and paragraph 3 of Schedule 11 to, the Armed Forces Act 2006 (c.52).

(4) Where both the magistrates' court and the Crown Court can grant bail or suspend a disqualification or order pending appeal, an application must indicate by which court the appellant wants the application determined.

(5) Where the appeal is against conviction or against a finding of guilt, unless the respondent agrees that the court should allow the appeal—

(a) the respondent must serve a respondent's notice on—

(i) the Crown Court officer; and

(ii) the appellant; and

(b) the respondent must serve that notice not more than 15 business days after service of the appeal notice.

[Note. Under section 1(1) of the Powers of Criminal Courts (Sentencing) Act 2000[17]*, a magistrates' court may defer passing sentence for up to 6 months.*

Under section 113 of the Magistrates' Courts Act 1980[18]*, the magistrates' court may grant an appellant bail pending appeal. Under section 81(1)(b) of the Senior Courts Act 1981*[19]*, the Crown Court also may do so. See also rule 14.7.*

Under section 39 of the Road Traffic Offenders Act 1988[20]*, a court which has made an order disqualifying a person from driving may suspend the disqualification pending appeal. Under section 40 of the 1988 Act*[21]*, the appeal court may do so. See also rule 29.2.*

Under section 129 of the Licensing Act 2003[22]*, a court which has made an order to forfeit or suspend a personal licence issued under that Act may suspend the order pending appeal. Under section 130 of the 2003 Act*[23]*, the appeal court may do so.]*

R34.3 **Form of appeal and respondent's notices**

34.3 (1) The appeal notice must—

(a) specify—

(i) the conviction or finding of guilt,

(ii) the sentence, or

(iii) the order, or the failure to make an order

about which the appellant wants to appeal;

(b) summarise the issues;

(c) in an appeal against conviction or against a finding of guilt, to the best of the appellant's ability and to assist the court in fulfilling its duty under rule 3.2 (the court's duty of case management)—

(i) identify the witnesses who gave oral evidence in the magistrates' court,

(ii) identify the witnesses who gave written evidence in the magistrates' court,

(iii) identify the prosecution witnesses whom the appellant will want to question if they are called to give oral evidence in the Crown Court,

(iv) identify the likely defence witnesses,

(v) give notice of any special arrangements or other measures that the appellant thinks are needed for witnesses,

(vi) explain whether the issues in the Crown Court differ from the issues in the magistrates' court, and if so how, and

(vii) say how long the trial lasted in the magistrates' court and how long the appeal is likely to last in the Crown Court;

(d) in an appeal against a sentence, order or failure to make an order—

(i) identify any circumstances, report or other information of which the appellant wants the court to take account, and

(ii) explain the significance of those circumstances or that information to what is in issue;

(e) in an appeal against a finding that the appellant insulted someone or interrupted

17 2000 c. 6.

18 1980 c. 43; section 113 was amended by section 168 of, and paragraph 44 of Schedule 10 to, the Criminal Justice and Public Order Act 1994 (c. 33) and section 165 of, and paragraph 72 of Schedule 9 to, the Powers of Criminal Courts (Sentencing) Act 2000 (c. 6).

19 1981 c.54.

20 1988 c. 53.

21 1988 c. 53; section 40 was amended by sections 40 and 59 of, and paragraph 50 of Schedule 9 and paragraph 1 of Schedule 11 to, the Constitutional Reform Act 2005 (c.4).

22 2003 c. 17.

23 2003 c. 17; section 130 was amended by sections 40 and 59 of, and paragraph 78 of Schedule 9 and paragraph 1 of Schedule 11 to, the Constitutional Reform Act 2005 (c. 4).

proceedings in the magistrates' court, attach—
(i) the magistrates' court's written findings of fact, and
(ii) the appellant's response to those findings;
(f) say whether the appellant has asked the magistrates' court to reconsider the case; and
(g) include a list of those on whom the appellant has served the appeal notice.
(2) A respondent's notice must—
(a) give the date on which the respondent was served with the appeal notice; and
(b) to assist the court in fulfilling its duty under rule 3.2—
(i) identify the witnesses who gave oral evidence in the magistrates' court,
(ii) identify the witnesses who gave written evidence in the magistrates' court,
(iii) identify the prosecution witnesses whom the respondent intends to call to give oral evidence in the Crown Court,
(iv) give notice of any special arrangements or other measures that the respondent thinks are needed for witnesses,
(v) explain whether the issues in the Crown Court differ from the issues in the magistrates' court, and if so how, and
(vi) say how long the trial lasted in the magistrates' court and how long the appeal is likely to last in the Crown Court.
(3) Paragraph (4) applies in an appeal against conviction or against a finding of guilt where in the magistrates' court a party to the appeal—
(a) introduced in evidence material to which applies—
(i) Part 16 (Written witness statements),
(ii) Part 19 (Expert evidence),
(iii) Part 20 (Hearsay evidence),
(iv) Part 21 (Evidence of bad character), or
(v) Part 22 (Evidence of a complainant's previous sexual behaviour); or
(b) made an application to which applies—
(i) Part 17 (Witness summonses, warrants and orders),
(ii) Part 18 (Measures to assist a witness or defendant to give evidence), or
(iii) Part 23 (Restriction on cross-examination by a defendant).
(4) If such a party wants to reintroduce that material or to renew that application in the Crown Court that party must include a notice to that effect in the appeal or respondent's notice, as the case may be.

[Note. The Practice Direction sets out forms of appeal and respondent's notices for use in connection with this rule.

In some cases, a magistrates' court can reconsider a conviction, sentence or other order and make a fresh decision. See section 142 of the Magistrates' Courts Act 1980[24].

See also rule 3.13 (Conduct of a trial or an appeal).]

Duty of magistrates' court officer **R34.4**

34.4 (1) The magistrates' court officer must—
(a) arrange for the magistrates' court to hear as soon as practicable any application to that court under rule 34.2(3)(c) (suspension of disqualification or order pending appeal); and
(b) as soon as practicable notify the Crown Court officer of the service of the appeal notice and make available to that officer—
(i) the appeal notice and any accompanying application served by the appellant,
(ii) details of the parties including their addresses, and
(iii) a copy of each magistrates' court register entry relating to the decision under appeal and to any application for bail or for the suspension of a disqualification or order pending appeal.
(2) Where the appeal is against conviction or against a finding of guilt, the magistrates' court officer must make available to the Crown Court officer as soon as practicable—
(a) all material served on the magistrate's court officer to which applies—
(i) Part 8 (Initial details of the prosecution case),
(ii) Part 16 (Written witness statements),
(iii) Part 17 (Witness summonses, warrants and orders),
(iv) Part 18 (Measures to assist a witness or defendant to give evidence),
(v) Part 19 (Expert evidence),
(vi) Part 20 (Hearsay evidence),

[24] 1980 c. 43; section 142 was amended by sections 26 and 29 of, and Schedule 3 to, the Criminal Appeal Act 1995 (c. 35).

(vii) Part 21 (Evidence of bad character),
(viii) Part 22 (Evidence of a complainant's previous sexual behaviour), or
(ix) Part 23 (Restriction on cross-examination by a defendant);
(b) any case management questionnaire prepared for the purposes of the trial;
(c) all case management directions given by the magistrates' court for the purposes of the trial; and
(d) any other document, object or information for which the Crown Court officer asks.

(3) Where the appeal is against sentence, the magistrates' court officer must make available to the Crown Court officer as soon as practicable any report received for the purposes of sentencing.

(4) Unless the magistrates' court otherwise directs, the magistrates' court officer—
(a) must keep any document or object exhibited in the proceedings in the magistrates' court, or arrange for it to be kept by some other appropriate person, until at least—
(i) 6 weeks after the conclusion of those proceedings, or
(ii) the conclusion of any proceedings in the Crown Court that begin within that 6 weeks; but
(b) need not keep such a document if—
(i) the document that was exhibited is a copy of a document retained by the party who produced it, and
(ii) what was in evidence in the magistrates' court was the content of that document.

[Note. See also section 133 of the Criminal Justice Act 2003[25] *(Proof of statements in documents).]*

R34.5 Duty of person keeping exhibit

34.5 A person who, under arrangements made by the magistrates' court officer, keeps a document or object exhibited in the proceedings in the magistrates' court must—
(a) keep that exhibit until—
(i) 6 weeks after the conclusion of those proceedings, or
(ii) the conclusion of any proceedings in the Crown Court that begin within that 6 weeks, unless the magistrates' court or the Crown Court otherwise directs; and
(b) provide the Crown Court with any such document or object for which the Crown Court officer asks, within such period as the Crown Court officer may require.

R34.6 Reference by the Criminal Cases Review Commission

34.6 (1) The Crown Court officer must, as soon as practicable, serve a reference by the Criminal Cases Review Commission on—
(a) the appellant;
(b) every other party; and
(c) the magistrates' court officer.

(2) The appellant may serve an appeal notice on—
(a) the Crown Court officer; and
(b) every other party,
not more than 15 business days later.

(3) The Crown Court must treat the reference as the appeal notice if the appellant does not serve an appeal notice.

R34.7 Preparation for appeal

34.7 (1) The Crown Court may conduct a preparation for appeal hearing (and if necessary more than one such hearing) where—
(a) it is necessary to conduct such a hearing in order to give directions for the effective determination of the appeal; or
(b) such a hearing is required to set ground rules for the conduct of the questioning of a witness or appellant.

(2) Where under rule 34.3(4) a party gives notice to reintroduce material or to renew an application first introduced or made in the magistrates' court—
(a) no other notice or application to the same effect otherwise required by these Rules need be served; and
(b) any objection served by the other party in the magistrates' court is treated as renewed unless within 15 business days that party serves notice withdrawing it.

(3) Paragraphs (4) and (5) apply where—
(a) the appeal is against conviction or against a finding of guilt;
(b) a party wants to introduce material or make an application under a Part of these Rules listed in rule 34.3(3); and

[25] 2003 c. 44.

(c) that party gives no notice of reintroduction or renewal under rule 34.3(4) (whether because the conditions for giving such a notice are not met or for any other reason).

(4) Such a party must serve the material, notice or application required by that Part not more than 21 days after service of the appeal notice.

(5) Subject to paragraph (4), the requirements of that Part apply (for example, as to the form in which a notice must be given or an application made and as to the time and form in which such a notice or application may be opposed).

Hearings and decisions R34.8

34.8 (1) The Crown Court as a general rule must hear in public an appeal or reference to which this part applies, but—

(a) may order any hearing to be in private; and

(b) where a hearing is about a public interest ruling, must hold that hearing in private.

(2) The Crown Court officer must give as much notice as reasonably practicable of every hearing to—

(a) the parties;

(b) any party's custodian; and

(c) any other person whom the Crown Court requires to be notified.

(3) The Crown Court officer must serve every decision on—

(a) the parties;

(b) any other person whom the Crown Court requires to be served; and

(c) the magistrates' court officer and any party's custodian, where the decision determines an appeal.

(4) But where a hearing or decision is about a public interest ruling, the Crown Court officer must not—

(a) give notice of that hearing to; or

(b) serve that decision on,

anyone other than the prosecutor who applied for that ruling, unless the court otherwise directs.

[Note. See also Part 15 (Disclosure).]

Abandoning an appeal R34.9

34.9 (1) The appellant—

(a) may abandon an appeal without the Crown Court's permission, by serving a notice of abandonment on—

(i) the magistrates' court officer,

(ii) the Crown Court officer, and

(iii) every other party

before the hearing of the appeal begins; but

(b) after the hearing of the appeal begins, may only abandon the appeal with the Crown Court's permission.

(2) A notice of abandonment must be signed by or on behalf of the appellant.

(3) Where an appellant who is on bail pending appeal abandons an appeal—

(a) the appellant must surrender to custody as directed by the magistrates' court officer; and

(b) any conditions of bail apply until then.

[Note. The Practice Direction sets out a form of notice of abandonment for use in connection with this rule. Where an appellant abandons an appeal to the Crown Court, both the Crown Court and the magistrates' court have power to make a costs order against that appellant in favour of the respondent: see section 52 of the Senior Courts Act 1981[26] and section 109 of the Magistrates' Courts Act 1980[27]. Part 45 contains rules about costs on abandoning an appeal.]

Court's power to vary requirements under this Part R34.10

34.10 The Crown Court may—

(a) shorten or extend (even after it has expired) a time limit under this Part;

(b) allow an appellant to vary an appeal notice that that appellant has served;

[26] 1981 c. 54; section 52 was amended by section 31(5) of, and Part II of Schedule 1 to, the Prosecution of Offences Act 1985 (c. 23), section 4 of the Courts and Legal Services Act 1990 (c. 41), article 3 of, and paragraphs 11 and 12(a) of the Schedule to, S.I. 2004/2035, and section 59(5) of, and paragraph 26(1) and (2) of Schedule 11 to, the Constitutional Reform Act 2005 (c. 4). The Act's title was amended by section 59(5) of, and paragraph 1 of Schedule 11 to, the Constitutional Reform Act 2005 (c. 4).

[27] 1980 c. 43; section 109(2) was amended by section 109(1) of, and paragraph 234 of Schedule 8 to, the Courts Act 2003 (c. 39).

(c) direct that an appeal notice be served on any person; and
(d) allow an appeal notice or a notice of abandonment to be in a different form to one set out in the Practice Direction, or to be presented orally.

R34.11 **Constitution of the Crown Court**

34.11 (1) On the hearing of an appeal the general rule is that—
(a) the Crown Court must comprise—
(i) a judge of the High Court, a Circuit judge, a Recorder or a qualifying judge advocate, and
(ii) no less than two and no more than four justices of the peace, none of whom took part in the decision under appeal; and
(b) if the appeal is from a youth court, each justice of the peace must be qualified to sit as a member of a youth court.
(2) Despite the general rule—
(a) the Crown Court may include only one justice of the peace if—
(i) the presiding judge decides that otherwise the start of the appeal hearing will be delayed unreasonably, or
(ii) one or more of the justices of the peace who started hearing the appeal is absent; and
(b) the Crown Court may comprise only a judge of the High Court, a Circuit judge, a Recorder or a qualifying judge advocate if—
(i) the appeal is against conviction, under section 108 of the Magistrates' Courts Act 1980[28], and
(ii) the respondent agrees that the court should allow the appeal, under section 48(2) of the Senior Courts Act 1981[29].
(3) Before the hearing of an appeal begins and after that hearing ends—
(a) the Crown Court may comprise only a judge of the High Court, a Circuit judge, a Recorder or a qualifying judge advocate; and
(b) so constituted, the court may, among other things, exercise the powers to which apply—
(i) the rules in this Part and in Part 3 (Case management), and
(ii) rule 35.2 (stating a case for the opinion of the High Court, or refusing to do so).

[Note. See sections 73 and 74 of the Senior Courts Act 1981[30] *(which allow rules of court to provide for the constitution of the Crown Court in proceedings on appeal), section 45 of the Children and Young Persons Act 1933*[31] *and section 9 of the Courts Act 2003*[32]*. Under section 8(1A) of the Senior Courts Act 1981*[33]*, a qualifying judge advocate may not exercise the jurisdiction of the Crown Court on an appeal from a youth court.]*

CRIMINAL PRACTICE DIRECTIONS PART 34 APPEAL TO THE CROWN COURT

CPD.34A **CPD IX Appeal 34A: Appeals to the Crown Court**

34A.1 On an appeal against conviction CrimPR 34.3 requires the appellant and respondent to supply information needed for the effective case management of the appeal, but allows the Crown Court to relieve the appellant – not the respondent – of that obligation, in whole or part.

34A.2 The court is most likely to exercise that discretion in an appellant's favour where he or she is not represented and is unable, without assistance, to provide reliable such information. The notes to

28 1980 c. 43; section 108 was amended by sections 66(2) and 78 of, and Schedule 16 to, the Criminal Justice Act 1982 (c. 48), section 23(3) of the Football Spectators Act 1989 (c. 37), section 101(2) of, and Schedule 13 to, the Criminal Justice Act 1991 (c. 53), sections 119 and 120(2) of, and paragraph 43 of Schedule 8 and Schedule 10 to, the Crime and Disorder Act 1998 (c. 37), section 7(2) of the Football (Offences and Disorder) Act 1999 (c. 21), section 165(1) of, and paragraph 71 of Schedule 9 to, the Powers of Criminal Courts (Sentencing) Act 2000 (c. 6), section 1 of, and Schedule 3 to, the Football (Disorder) Act 2000 (c. 25), section 58(1) of, and paragraph 10 of Schedule 10 to, the Domestic Violence, Crime and Victims Act 2004 (c. 28), section 52(2) of, and paragraph 14 of Schedule 3 to, the Violent Crime Reduction Act 2006 (c. 38), section 64 of, and paragraph 10 of Schedule 3 to, the Animal Welfare Act 2006 (c. 45) and section 54 of, and paragraphs 2 and 4 of Schedule 12 to, the Criminal Justice and Courts Act 2015 (c. 2).

29 1981 c. 54; section 48(2) was amended by section 156 of the Criminal Justice Act 1988 (c. 33).

30 1981 c. 54; section 73 was amended by article 3 of, and paragraphs 11 and 12 of the Schedule to, S.I. 2004/2035 and section 26 of, and paragraph 2 of Schedule 2 to, the Armed Forces Act 2011 (c. 18). Section 74 was amended by sections 79 and 106 of, and Table (4) of Part V of Schedule 15 to, the Access to Justice Act 1999 (c. 22), article 3 of, and paragraphs 11 and 12 of the Schedule to S.I. 2004/2035, section 15 of, and paragraphs 114 and 133 of Schedule 4 to, the Constitutional Reform Act 2005 (c. 4) and section 26 of, and paragraph 3 of Schedule 2 to, the Armed Forces Act 2011 (c. 18). The Act's title was amended by section 59(5) of, and paragraph 1 of Schedule 11 to, the Constitutional Reform Act 2005 (c. 4).

31 1933 c. 12; section 45 was substituted by section 50 of the Courts Act 2003 (c. 39) and amended by section 15 of, and paragraph 20 of Schedule 4 to, the Constitutional Reform Act 2005 (c. 4).

32 2003 c. 39.

33 1981 c. 54; section 8(1A) was inserted by paragraph 1 of Schedule 2 to the Armed Forces Act 2011 (c. 18).

the standard form of appeal notice invite the appellant to answer the relevant questions in that form to the extent that he or she is able, explaining that while the appellant may not be able to answer all those questions nevertheless any answers that can be given will assist in making arrangements for the hearing of the appeal. Where an appellant uses the prescribed form of easy read appeal notice the court usually should assume that the appellant will not be able to supply case management information, and that form contains no questions corresponding with those in the standard appeal notice. In such a case relevant information will be supplied by the respondent in the respondent's notice and may be gleaned from material obtained from magistrates' court records by Crown Court staff.

CPD IX Appeal 34B: Appeal to the Crown Court: Information from the Magistrates' Court **CPD.34B**

34B.1 CrimPR 34.4 applies when a defendant appeals to the Crown Court against conviction or sentence and specifies the information and documentation that must be made available by the magistrates' court.

34B.2 In all cases magistrates' court staff must ensure that Crown Court staff are notified of the appeal as soon as practicable: CrimPR 34.4(2)(b). In most cases Crown Court staff will be able to obtain the other information required by CrimPR 34.4(3) or (4) by direct access to the electronic records created by magistrates' court staff. However, if such access is not available then alternative arrangements must be made for the transfer of such information to Crown Court staff by electronic means. Paper copies of documents should be created and sent only as a last resort.

34B.3 On an appeal against conviction, the reasons given by the magistrates for their decision should not be included with the documents; the appeal hearing is not a review of the magistrates' court's decision but a re-hearing. There is no requirement for the Notice of Appeal form to be redacted in any way; the judge and magistrates presiding over the rehearing will base their decision on the evidence presented during the re-hearing itself.

34B.4 On an appeal solely against sentence, the magistrates' court's reasons and factual finding leading to the finding of guilt should be included, but any reasons for the sentence imposed should be omitted as the Crown Court will be conducting a fresh sentencing exercise. Whilst reasons for the sentence imposed are not necessary for the re-hearing, the Notice of Appeal form may include references to the sentence that is being appealed. There is no requirement to redact this before the form is given to the judge and magistrates hearing the appeal.

Criminal Procedure Rules Part 35 Appeal to the High Court by Case Stated

When this Part applies **R35.1**

35.1 This Part applies where a person wants to appeal to the High Court by case stated—

(a) under section 111 of the Magistrates' Courts Act 1980, against a decision of a magistrates' court; or

(b) under section 28 of the Senior Courts Act 1981, against a decision of the Crown Court.

[Note. Under section 111 of the Magistrates' Courts Act 1980, 'any person who was a party to any proceeding before a magistrates' court or is aggrieved by the conviction, order, determination or other proceeding of the court may question the proceeding on the ground that it is wrong in law or is in excess of jurisdiction by applying to the justices composing the court to state a case for the opinion of the High Court on the question of law or jurisdiction involved'.

Under section 28 of the Senior Courts Act 1981, 'any order, judgment or other decision of the Crown Court may be questioned by any party to the proceedings, on the ground that it is wrong in law or is in excess of jurisdiction, by applying to the Crown Court to have a case stated by that court for the opinion of the High Court.'

Under section 28A of the 1981 Act[1]*, the High Court may 'reverse, affirm or amend the determination in respect of which the case has been stated; or remit the matter to the magistrates' court, or the Crown Court, with the opinion of the High Court, and may make such other order … as it thinks fit.' Under that section, the High Court also may send the case back for amendment, if it thinks fit.]*

Application to state a case **R35.2**

35.2 (1) A party who wants the court to state a case for the opinion of the High Court must—

(a) apply in writing, not more than 21 days after the decision against which the applicant wants to appeal; and

[1] 1981 c. 54; section 28A was inserted by section 1 of, and paragraph 9 of Schedule 2 to, the Statute Law (Repeals) Act 1993 (c. 50), and amended by section 61 of the Access to Justice Act 1999 (c. 22) and section 40 of, and paragraph 36 of Schedule 9 to, the Constitutional Reform Act 2005 (c. 4).

(b) serve the application on—
(i) the court officer, and
(ii) each other party.
(2) The application must—
(a) specify the decision in issue;
(b) specify the proposed question or questions of law or jurisdiction on which the opinion of the High Court will be asked;
(c) indicate the proposed grounds of appeal; and
(d) include or attach any application for the following, with reasons—
(i) if the application is to the Crown Court, an extension of time within which to apply to state a case,
(ii) bail pending appeal, or
(iii) the suspension of any disqualification imposed in the case, where the court can order such a suspension pending appeal.
(3) A party who wants to make representations about the application must—
(a) serve the representations on—
(i) the court officer, and
(ii) each other party; and
(b) do so not more than 10 business days after service of the application.
(4) The court may determine the application without a hearing.
(5) If the court decides not to state a case, the court officer must serve on each party—
(a) notice of that decision; and
(b) the court's written reasons for that decision, if not more than 15 business days later the applicant asks for those reasons.

[Note. The time limit for applying to a magistrates' court to state a case is prescribed by section 111(2) of the Magistrates' Courts Act 1980. It may be neither extended nor shortened.

Under section 113 of the Magistrates' Courts Act 1980[2]*, the magistrates' court may grant an appellant bail pending appeal. Under section 81(1)(d) of the Senior Courts Act 1981*[3]*, the Crown Court may do so. See also rule 14.7.*

Where Part 34 (Appeal to the Crown Court) applies, an application to which this rule applies may be determined by a judge of the High Court, a Circuit judge, a Recorder or a qualifying judge advocate without justices of the peace: see rule 34.11 (Constitution of the Crown Court).

Under section 39 of the Road Traffic Offenders Act 1988[4]*, a court which has made an order disqualifying a person from driving may suspend the disqualification pending appeal. See also rule 29.2.*

The Practice Direction sets out a form of application for use in connection with this rule.]

R35.3 **Preparation of case stated**

35.3 (1) This rule applies where the court decides to state a case for the opinion of the High Court.
(2) The court officer must serve on each party notice of—
(a) the decision to state a case, and
(b) any recognizance ordered by the court.
(3) Unless the court otherwise directs, not more than 15 business days after the court's decision to state a case—
(a) in a magistrates' court, the court officer must serve a draft case on each party; or
(b) in the Crown Court, the applicant must serve a draft case on the court officer and each other party.
(4) The draft case must—
(a) specify the decision in issue;
(b) specify the question(s) of law or jurisdiction on which the opinion of the High Court will be asked;
(c) include a succinct summary of—
(i) the nature and history of the proceedings,
(ii) the court's relevant findings of fact, and
(iii) the relevant contentions of the parties; and

[2] 1980 c. 43; section 113 was amended by section 168 of, and paragraph 44 of Schedule 10 to, the Criminal Justice and Public Order Act 1994 (c. 33) and section 165 of, and paragraph 72 of Schedule 9 to, the Powers of Criminal Courts (Sentencing) Act 2000 (c. 6).
[3] 1981 c.54.
[4] 1988 c. 53.

(d) if a question is whether there was sufficient evidence on which the court reasonably could reach a finding of fact—
(i) specify that finding, and
(ii) include a summary of the evidence on which the court reached that finding.
(5) Except to the extent that paragraph (4)(d) requires, the draft case must not include an account of the evidence received by the court.
(6) A party who wants to make representations about the content of the draft case, or to propose a revised draft, must—
(a) serve the representations, or revised draft, on—
(i) the court officer, and
(ii) each other party; and
(b) do so not more than 15 business days after service of the draft case.
(7) The court must state the case not more than 15 business days after the time for service of representations under paragraph (6) has expired.
(8) A case stated for the opinion of the High Court must—
(a) comply with paragraphs (4) and (5); and
(b) identify—
(i) the court that stated it, and
(ii) the court office for that court.
(9) The court officer must serve the case stated on each party.

[Note. Under section 114 of the Magistrates' Courts Act 1980[5]*, a magistrates' court need not state a case until the person who applied for it has entered into a recognizance to appeal promptly to the High Court. The Crown Court has a corresponding inherent power.*

Under section 121(6) of the 1980 Act, the magistrates' court which states a case need not include all the members of the court which took the decision questioned.

For the procedure on appeal to the High Court, see Part 52 of the Civil Procedure Rules 1998[6] *and the associated Practice Direction.]*

Duty of justices' legal adviser R35.4

35.4 (1) This rule applies—
(a) only in a magistrates' court; and
(b) unless the court—
(i) includes a District Judge (Magistrates' Courts), and
(ii) otherwise directs.
(2) A justices' legal adviser must—
(a) give the court legal advice; and
(b) if the court so requires, assist it by—
(i) preparing and amending the draft case, and
(ii) completing the case stated.

Court's power to vary requirements under this Part R35.5

35.5 (1) The court may shorten or extend (even after it has expired) a time limit under this Part.
(2) A person who wants an extension of time must—
(a) apply when serving the application, representations or draft case for which it is needed; and
(b) explain the delay.

[Note. See also rule 35.2(2)(d)(i) and the note to rule 35.2.]

Criminal Procedure Rules Part 36 Appeal to the Court of Appeal: General Rules

When this Part applies R36.1

36.1 (1) This Part applies to all the applications, appeals and references to the Court of Appeal to which Parts 37, 38, 39, 40, 41 and 43 apply.
(2) In this Part and in those, unless the context makes it clear that something different is meant, 'court' means the Court of Appeal or any judge of that court.

[5] 1980 c. 43; section 114 was amended by section 90 of, and paragraphs 95 and 113 of Schedule 13 to, the Access to Justice Act 1999 (c. 22) and section 109 of, and paragraph 235 of Schedule 8 to, the Courts Act 2003 (c. 39).
[6] S.I. 1998/3132; Part 52 was inserted by S.I. 2000/221 and amended by paragraph 1 of Schedule 11 to the Constitutional Reform Act 2005 (c. 4) and S.I. 2003/2113, 2003/3361, 2006/3435, 2007/2204 and 2009/2092.

[Note. See rule 2.2 for the usual meaning of 'court'.

Under section 53 of the Senior Courts Act 1981[1]*, the criminal division of the Court of Appeal exercises jurisdiction in the appeals and references to which Parts 37, 38, 39, 40 and 41 apply.*

Under section 55 of that Act[2] *, the Court of Appeal must include at least two judges, and for some purposes at least three.*

For the powers of the Court of Appeal that may be exercised by one judge of that court or by the Registrar, see sections 31, 31A, 31B, 31C and 44 of the Criminal Appeal Act 1968[3]*; section 49 of the Criminal Justice Act 2003*[4]*; the Criminal Justice Act 2003 (Mandatory Life Sentences: Appeals in Transitional Cases) Order 2005*[5]*; the Serious Organised Crime and Police Act 2005 (Appeals under section 74) Order 2006*[6]*; the Serious Crime Act 2007 (Appeals under Section 24) Order 2008*[7]*; and the power conferred by section 53(4) of the 1981 Act.]*

R36.2 **Case management in the Court of Appeal**

36.2 (1) The court and the parties have the same duties and powers as under Part 3 (Case management).

(2) The Registrar—

(a) must fulfil the duty of active case management under rule 3.2; and

(b) in fulfilling that duty may exercise any of the powers of case management under—

(i) rule 3.5 (the court's general powers of case management),

(ii) rule 3.12(3) (requiring a certificate of readiness), and

(iii) rule 3.13 (requiring a party to identify intentions and anticipated requirements) subject to the directions of the court.

(3) The Registrar must nominate a case progression officer under rule 3.4.

R36.3 **Power to vary requirements**

36.3 The court or the Registrar may—

(a) shorten a time limit or extend it (even after it has expired) unless that is inconsistent with other legislation;

(b) allow a party to vary any notice that that party has served;

(c) direct that a notice or application be served on any person; and

(d) allow a notice or application to be in a different form, or presented orally.

[Note. The time limit for serving an appeal notice—

(a) under section 18 of the Criminal Appeal Act 1968[8] *on an appeal against conviction or sentence, and*

(b) under section 18A of that Act[9] *on an appeal against a finding of contempt of court*

[1] 1981 c. 54. The Act's title was amended by section 59(5) of, and paragraph 1 of Schedule 11 to, the Constitutional Reform Act 2005 (c. 4).

[2] 1981 c. 54; section 55 was amended by section 170 of, and paragraph 80 of Schedule 15 to, the Criminal Justice Act 1988 (c. 33), section 52 of the Criminal Justice and Public Order Act 1994 (c. 33) and section 58 of the Domestic Violence, Crime and Victims Act 2004 (c. 28). It is further amended by section 40 of, and paragraph 36 of Schedule 9 to, the Constitutional Reform Act 2005 (c. 4).

[3] 1968 c. 19; section 31 was amended by section 21 of, and Schedule 2 to, the Costs in Criminal Cases Act 1973 (c. 14), section 24 of, and paragraph 10 of Schedule 6 to, the Road Traffic Act 1974 (c. 50), section 29 of the Criminal Justice Act 1982 (c. 48), section 170 of, and paragraphs 20, 29 and 30 of Schedule 15 to, the Criminal Justice Act 1988 (c. 33), section 4 of, and paragraph 4 of Schedule 3 to, the Road Traffic (Consequential Provisions) Act 1988 (c. 54), section 198 of, and paragraphs 38 and 40 of Schedule 6 to, the Licensing Act 2003 (c. 17), section 87 of the Courts Act 2003 (c. 39), paragraphs 86, 87 and 88 of Schedule 36 to the Criminal Justice Act 2003 (c. 44), section 48 of the Police and Justice Act 2006 (c. 48), section 47 of, and paragraphs 1, 9 and 11 of Schedule 8 to, the Criminal Justice and Immigration Act 2008 (c. 4) and section 177 of, and paragraph 69 of Schedule 21 to, the Coroners and Justice Act 2009 (c. 25). It is further amended by section 67 of, and paragraph 4 of Schedule 4 to, the Youth Justice and Criminal Evidence Act 1999 (c. 23), with effect from a date to be appointed. Section 31A was inserted by section 6 of the Criminal Appeal Act 1995 (c. 35) and amended by sections 87 and 109 of, and Schedule 10 to, the Courts Act 2003 (c. 39) and section 331 of, and paragraphs 86 and 88 of Schedule 36 to, the Criminal Justice Act 2003 (c. 44). Section 31B was inserted by section 87 of the Courts Act 2003 (c. 39). Section 31C was inserted by section 87 of the Courts Act 2003 (c. 39) and amended by sections 47 and 149 of, and paragraphs 1 and 12 of Schedule 8 and part 3 of Schedule 28 to, the Criminal Justice and Immigration Act 2008 (c. 4). Section 44 was amended by section 24(2) of, and paragraph 11 of Schedule 6 to, the Road Traffic Act 1974 (c. 50), section 170(1) of, and paragraphs 20 and 31 of the Criminal Justice Act 1988 (c. 33), section 4 of, and paragraph 4(2) of the Road Traffic (Consequential Provisions) Act 1988 (c. 54) and section 198(1), and paragraphs 38 and 41 of Schedule 6 to, the Licensing Act 2003 (c. 17).

[4] 2003 c. 44.

[5] S.I. 2005/2798.

[6] S.I. 2006/2135.

[7] S.I. 2008/1863.

[8] 1968 c. 19.

[9] 1968 c. 19; section 18A was inserted by section 170 of, and paragraphs 20 and 25 of Schedule 15 to, the Criminal Justice Act 1988 (c. 33).

may be extended but not shortened: see rule 39.2.

The time limit for serving an application for permission to refer a sentencing case under section 36 of the Criminal Justice Act 1988[10] *may be neither extended nor shortened: see rule 41.2(4).*

The time limits in rule 43.2 for applying to the Court of Appeal for permission to appeal or refer a case to the Supreme Court may be extended or shortened only as explained in the note to that rule.]

Application for extension of time **R36.4**

36.4 A person who wants an extension of time within which to serve a notice or make an application must—

(a) apply for that extension of time when serving that notice or making that application; and
(b) give the reasons for the application for an extension of time.

Renewing an application refused by a judge or the Registrar **R36.5**

36.5 (1) This rule applies where a party with the right to do so wants to renew—
(a) to a judge of the Court of Appeal an application refused by the Registrar; or
(b) to the Court of Appeal an application refused by a judge of that court.
(2) That party must—
(a) renew the application in the form set out in the Practice Direction, signed by or on behalf of the applicant; and
(b) serve the renewed application on the Registrar not more than 10 business days after—
(i) the refusal of the application that the applicant wants to renew; or
(ii) the Registrar serves that refusal on the applicant, if the applicant was not present in person or by live link when the original application was refused.

[Note. The time limit of 10 business days under this rule is reduced to 5 business days where Parts 37, 38 or 40 apply: see rules 37.7, 38.10 and 40.7.

For the right to renew an application to a judge or to the Court of Appeal, see sections 31(3), 31C and 44 of the Criminal Appeal Act 1968, the Criminal Justice Act 2003 (Mandatory Life Sentences: Appeals in Transitional Cases) Order 2005[11]*, the Serious Organised Crime and Police Act 2005 (Appeals under section 74) Order 2006*[12] *and the Serious Crime Act 2007 (Appeals under Section 24) Order 2008.*

A party has no right under section 31C of the 1968 Act to renew to the Court of Appeal an application for procedural directions refused by a judge, but in some circumstances a case management direction might be varied: see rule 3.6.

If an applicant does not renew an application that a judge has refused, including an application for permission to appeal, the Registrar will treat it as if it had been refused by the Court of Appeal.

Under section 22 of the Criminal Appeal Act 1968[13]*, the Court of Appeal may direct that an appellant who is in custody is to attend a hearing by live link.]*

Hearings **R36.6**

36.6 (1) The general rule is that the Court of Appeal must hear in public—
(a) an application, including an application for permission to appeal; and
(b) an appeal or reference,
but it may order any hearing to be in private.
(2) Where a hearing is about a public interest ruling, that hearing must be in private unless the court otherwise directs.
(3) Where the appellant wants to appeal against an order restricting public access to a trial, the court—
(a) may decide without a hearing—
(i) an application, including an application for permission to appeal, and
(ii) an appeal; but

[10] 1988 c. 33; section 36 was amended by section 272 of, and paragraphs 45 and 46 of Schedule 32 and paragraph 96 of Schedule 36 to, the Criminal Justice Act 2003 (c. 44), sections 49 and 65 of, and paragraph 3 of Schedule 1 and Schedule 5 to, the Violent Crime Reduction Act 2006 (c. 38), section 40 of, and paragraph 48 of Schedule 9 to, the Constitutional Reform Act 2005 (c. 4), sections 46, 148 and 149 of, and paragraphs 22 and 23 of Schedule 26 and Part 3 of Schedule 28 to, the Criminal Justice and Immigration Act 2008 (c. 4), paragraph 2 of Schedule 19 and paragraphs 4 and 5 of Schedule 26 to the Legal Aid, Sentencing and Punishment of Offenders Act 2012 (c. 10) and section 28 of, and paragraph 2 of Schedule 5 to, the Criminal Justice and Courts Act 2015 (c. 2). It is further amended by section 46 of the Criminal Justice and Immigration Act 2008 (c. 4) with effect from a date to be appointed.
[11] S.I. 2005/2798.
[12] S.I. 2006/2135.
[13] 1968 c. 19; section 22 was amended by section 48 of the Police and Justice Act 2006 (c. 48).

(b) must announce its decision on such an appeal at a hearing in public.

(4) Where the appellant wants to appeal or to refer a case to the Supreme Court, the court—
(a) may decide without a hearing an application—
(i) for permission to appeal or to refer a sentencing case, or
(ii) to refer a point of law; but
(b) must announce its decision on such an application at a hearing in public.

(5) Where a party wants the court to reopen the determination of an appeal—
(a) the court—
(i) must decide the application without a hearing, as a general rule, but
(ii) may decide the application at a hearing; and
(b) need not announce its decision on such an application at a hearing in public.

(6) A judge of the Court of Appeal and the Registrar may exercise any of their powers—
(a) at a hearing in public or in private; or
(b) without a hearing.

[Note. For the procedure on an appeal against an order restricting public access to a trial, see Part 40.

For the procedure on an application to reopen the determination of an appeal, see rule 36.15.]

R36.7 Notice of hearings and decisions

36.7 (1) The Registrar must give as much notice as reasonably practicable of every hearing to—
(a) the parties;
(b) any party's custodian;
(c) any other person whom the court requires to be notified; and
(d) the Crown Court officer, where Parts 37, 38 or 40 apply.

(2) The Registrar must serve every decision on—
(a) the parties;
(b) any other person whom the court requires to be served; and
(c) the Crown Court officer and any party's custodian, where the decision determines an appeal or application for permission to appeal.

(3) But where a hearing or decision is about a public interest ruling, the Registrar must not—
(a) give notice of that hearing to; or
(b) serve that decision on,
anyone other than the prosecutor who applied for that ruling, unless the court otherwise directs.

R36.8 Duty of Crown Court officer

36.8 (1) The Crown Court officer must—
(a) where electronic arrangements have been made to receive and store information and documents for the Crown Court, as soon as practicable ensure that all such material is available to the Registrar in accordance with those arrangements; and
(b) provide the Registrar with any document, object or information for which the Registrar asks, within such period as the Registrar may require.

(2) Where someone may appeal to the Court of Appeal, the Crown Court officer must keep any document or object exhibited in the proceedings in the Crown Court, or arrange for it to be kept by some other appropriate person, until—
(a) 6 weeks after the conclusion of those proceedings; or
(b) the conclusion of any appeal proceedings that begin within that 6 weeks,
unless the court, the Registrar or the Crown Court otherwise directs.

(3) Where Part 37 applies (Appeal to the Court of Appeal against ruling at preparatory hearing), the Crown Court officer must as soon as practicable serve on the appellant a transcript or note of—
(a) each order or ruling against which the appellant wants to appeal; and
(b) the decision by the Crown Court judge on any application for permission to appeal.

(4) Where Part 38 applies (Appeal to the Court of Appeal against ruling adverse to prosecution), the Crown Court officer must as soon as practicable serve on the appellant a transcript or note of—
(a) each ruling against which the appellant wants to appeal;
(b) the decision by the Crown Court judge on any application for permission to appeal; and
(c) the decision by the Crown Court judge on any request to expedite the appeal.

(5) Where Part 39 applies (Appeal to the Court of Appeal about conviction or sentence), the Crown Court officer must as soon as practicable serve on or make available to the Registrar—
(a) any Crown Court judge's certificate that the case is fit for appeal;
(b) the decision on any application at the Crown Court centre for bail pending appeal;
(c) such of the Crown Court case papers as the Registrar requires; and

(d) such transcript of the Crown Court proceedings as the Registrar requires.

(6) Where Part 40 applies (Appeal to the Court of Appeal about reporting or public access) and an order is made restricting public access to a trial, the Crown Court officer must—

(a) immediately notify the Registrar of that order, if the appellant has given advance notice of intention to appeal; and

(b) as soon as practicable provide the applicant for that order with a transcript or note of the application.

[Note. See also section 87(4) of the Senior Courts Act 1981[14] *and rules 5.5 (Recording and transcription of proceedings in the Crown Court), 36.9 (duty of person transcribing record of proceedings in the Crown Court) and 36.10 (Duty of person keeping exhibit).]*

Duty of person transcribing proceedings in the Crown Court **R36.9**

36.9 A person who transcribes a recording of proceedings in the Crown Court under arrangements made by the Crown Court officer must provide the Registrar with any transcript for which the Registrar asks, within such period as the Registrar may require.

[Note. See also section 32 of the Criminal Appeal Act 1968[15] *and rule 5.5 (Recording and transcription of proceedings in the Crown Court).]*

Duty of person keeping exhibit **R36.10**

36.10 A person who under arrangements made by the Crown Court officer keeps a document or object exhibited in the proceedings in the Crown Court must—

(a) keep that exhibit until—

(i) 6 weeks after the conclusion of the Crown Court proceedings, or

(ii) the conclusion of any appeal proceedings that begin within that 6 weeks,

unless the court, the Registrar or the Crown Court otherwise directs; and

(b) provide the Registrar with any such document or object for which the Registrar asks, within such period as the Registrar may require.

[Note. See also rule 36.8(2) (Duty of Crown Court officer).]

Registrar's duty to provide copy documents for appeal or reference **R36.11**

36.11 Unless the court otherwise directs, for the purposes of an appeal or reference—

(a) the Registrar must—

(i) provide a party with a copy of any document or transcript held by the Registrar for such purposes, or

(ii) allow a party to inspect such a document or transcript,

on payment by that party of any charge fixed by the Treasury; but

(b) the Registrar must not provide a copy or allow the inspection of—

(i) a document provided only for the court and the Registrar, or

(ii) a transcript of a public interest ruling or of an application for such a ruling.

[Note. Section 21 of the Criminal Appeal Act 1968 requires the Registrar to collect, prepare and provide documents needed by the court.]

Declaration of incompatibility with a Convention right **R36.12**

36.12 (1) This rule applies where a party—

(a) wants the court to make a declaration of incompatibility with a Convention right under section 4 of the Human Rights Act 1998[16]; or

(b) raises an issue that the Registrar thinks may lead the court to make such a declaration.

(2) The Registrar must serve notice on—

(a) the relevant person named in the list published under section 17(1) of the Crown Proceedings Act 1947[17]; or

(b) the Treasury Solicitor, if it is not clear who is the relevant person.

[14] 1981 c. 54; section 87(4) was amended by articles 2 and 3 of, and paragraphs 11 and 17 of the Schedule to, S.I. 2004/2035.

[15] 1968 c. 19.

[16] 1998 c. 42; section 4 was amended by section 40 of, and paragraph 66 of Schedule 9 to, the Constitutional Reform Act 2005 (c. 4) and section 67 of, and paragraph 43 of Schedule 6 to, the Mental Capacity Act 2005 (c. 9).

[17] 1987 c. 38; section 9 was amended by section 170 of, and Schedule 16 to, the Criminal Justice Act 1988 (c. 33), section 6 of the Criminal Justice Act 1993 (c. 36), sections 72, 74 and 80 of, and paragraph 3 of Schedule 3 and Schedule 5 to, the Criminal Procedure and Investigations Act 1996 (c. 25), sections 45 and 310 of, and paragraphs 18, 52 and 54 of Schedule 36 and Part 3 of Schedule 37 to, the Criminal Justice Act 2003 (c. 44), article 3 of, and paragraphs 21 and 23 of S.I. 2004/2035, section 59 of, and paragraph 1 of Schedule 11 to, the Constitutional Reform Act 2005 (c. 4) and Part 10 of Schedule 10 to the Protection of Freedoms Act 2012 (c. 9). The amendment made by section 45 of the Criminal Justice Act 2003 (c. 44) is in force for certain purposes; for remaining purposes it has effect from a date to be appointed.

(3) That notice must include or attach details of—
(a) the legislation affected and the Convention right concerned;
(b) the parties to the appeal; and
(c) any other information or document that the Registrar thinks relevant.
(4) A person who has a right under the 1998 Act to become a party to the appeal must—
(a) serve notice on—
(i) the Registrar, and
(ii) the other parties,
if that person wants to exercise that right; and
(b) in that notice—
(i) indicate the conclusion that that person invites the court to reach on the question of incompatibility, and
(ii) identify each ground for that invitation, concisely outlining the arguments in support.
(5) The court must not make a declaration of incompatibility—
(a) less than 15 business days after the Registrar serves notice under paragraph (2); and
(b) without giving any person who serves a notice under paragraph (4) an opportunity to make representations at a hearing.

R36.13 **Abandoning an appeal**

36.13 (1) This rule applies where an appellant wants to—
(a) abandon—
(i) an application to the court for permission to appeal, or
(ii) an appeal; or
(b) reinstate such an application or appeal after abandoning it.
(2) The appellant—
(a) may abandon such an application or appeal without the court's permission by serving a notice of abandonment on—
(i) the Registrar, and
(ii) any respondent
before any hearing of the application or appeal; but
(b) at any such hearing, may only abandon that application or appeal with the court's permission.
(3) A notice of abandonment must be in the form set out in the Practice Direction, signed by or on behalf of the appellant.
(4) On receiving a notice of abandonment the Registrar must—
(a) date it;
(b) serve a dated copy on—
(i) the appellant,
(ii) the appellant's custodian, if any,
(iii) the Crown Court officer, and
(iv) any other person on whom the appellant or the Registrar served the appeal notice; and
(c) treat the application or appeal as if it had been refused or dismissed by the Court of Appeal.
(5) An appellant who wants to reinstate an application or appeal after abandoning it must—
(a) apply in writing, with reasons; and
(b) serve the application on the Registrar.

[Note. The Court of Appeal has power only in exceptional circumstances to allow an appellant to reinstate an application or appeal that has been abandoned.]

R36.14 **Grounds of appeal and opposition**

36.14 (1) If the court gives permission to appeal then unless the court otherwise directs the decision indicates that—
(a) the appellant has permission to appeal on every ground identified by the appeal notice; and
(b) the court finds reasonably arguable each ground on which the appellant has permission to appeal.
(2) If the court gives permission to appeal but not on every ground identified by the appeal notice the decision indicates that—
(a) at the hearing of the appeal the court will not consider representations that address any ground thus excluded from argument; and

(b) an appellant who wants to rely on such an excluded ground needs the court's permission to do so.

(3) An appellant who wants to rely at the hearing of an appeal on a ground of appeal excluded from argument by a judge of the Court of Appeal when giving permission to appeal must—
(a) apply for permission to do so, with reasons, and identify each such ground;
(b) serve the application on—
(i) the Registrar, and
(ii) any respondent; and
(c) serve the application not more than 10 business days after—
(i) the giving of permission to appeal, or
(ii) the Registrar serves notice of that decision on the applicant, if the applicant was not present in person or by live link when permission to appeal was given.

(4) Paragraph (5) applies where one of the following Parts applies—
(a) Part 37 (Appeal to the Court of Appeal against ruling at preparatory hearing);
(b) Part 38 (Appeal to the Court of Appeal against ruling adverse to prosecution);
(c) Part 39 (Appeal to the Court of Appeal about conviction or sentence); or
(d) Part 40 (Appeal to the Court of Appeal about reporting or public access restriction).

(5) An appellant who wants to rely on a ground of appeal not identified by the appeal notice must—
(a) apply for permission to do so and identify each such ground;
(b) in respect of each such ground—
(i) explain why it was not included in the appeal notice, and
(ii) where Part 39 applies, comply with rule 39.3(2);
(c) serve the application on—
(i) the Registrar, and
(ii) any respondent; and
(d) serve the application—
(i) as soon as reasonably practicable, and in any event
(ii) at the same time as serving any renewed application for permission to appeal which relies on that ground.

(6) Paragraph (7) applies where a party wants to abandon—
(a) a ground of appeal on which that party has permission to appeal; or
(b) a ground of opposition identified in a respondent's notice.

(7) Such a party must serve notice on—
(a) the Registrar; and
(b) each other party,
before any hearing at which that ground will be considered by the court.

[Note. In some legislation, including the Criminal Appeal Act 1968, permission to appeal is described as 'leave to appeal'.

Under rule 36.5 (Renewing an application refused by a judge or the Registrar), if permission to appeal is refused the application for such permission may be renewed within the time limit (10 business days) set by that rule.]

Reopening the determination of an appeal **R36.15**

36.15 (1) This rule applies where—
(a) a party wants the court to reopen a decision which determines an appeal or reference to which this Part applies (including a decision on an application for permission to appeal or refer); or
(b) the Registrar refers such a decision to the court for the court to consider reopening it.

(2) Such a party must—
(a) apply in writing for permission to reopen that decision, as soon as practicable after becoming aware of the grounds for doing so; and
(b) serve the application on the Registrar.

(3) The application must—
(a) specify the decision which the applicant wants the court to reopen; and
(b) explain—
(i) why it is necessary for the court to reopen that decision in order to avoid real injustice,
(ii) how the circumstances are exceptional and make it appropriate to reopen the decision notwithstanding the rights and interests of other participants and the importance of finality,
(iii) why there is no alternative effective remedy among any potentially available, and
(iv) any delay in making the application.

(4) The Registrar—
(a) may invite a party's representations on—
(i) an application to reopen a decision, or
(ii) a decision that the Registrar has referred, or intends to refer, to the court; and
(b) must do so if the court so directs.
(5) A party invited to make representations must serve them on the Registrar within such period as the Registrar directs.
(6) The court must not reopen a decision to which this rule applies unless each other party has had an opportunity to make representations.

[Note. The Court of Appeal has power only in exceptional circumstances to reopen a decision to which this rule applies.]

Criminal Procedure Rules Part 37 Appeal to the Court of Appeal against Ruling at Preparatory Hearing

R37.1 **When this Part applies**

37.1 (1) This Part applies where a party wants to appeal under—
(a) section 9(11) of the Criminal Justice Act 1987[1] or section 35(1) of the Criminal Procedure and Investigations Act 1996[2]; or
(b) section 47(1) of the Criminal Justice Act 2003[3].
(2) A reference to an 'appellant' in this Part is a reference to such a party.

[Note. Under section 9(11) of the Criminal Justice Act 1987 (which applies to serious or complex fraud cases) and under section 35(1) of the Criminal Procedure and Investigations Act 1996 (which applies to other complex, serious or long cases) a party may appeal to the Court of Appeal against an order made at a preparatory hearing in the Crown Court.

Under section 47(1) of the Criminal Justice Act 2003 a party may appeal to the Court of Appeal against an order in the Crown Court that because of jury tampering a trial will continue without a jury or that there will be a new trial without a jury.

Part 3 contains rules about preparatory hearings.

The rules in Part 36 (Appeal to the Court of Appeal: general rules) also apply where this Part applies.]

R37.2 **Service of appeal notice**

37.2 (1) An appellant must serve an appeal notice on—
(a) the Crown Court officer;
(b) the Registrar; and
(c) every party directly affected by the order or ruling against which the appellant wants to appeal.
(2) The appellant must serve the appeal notice not more than 5 business days after—
(a) the order or ruling against which the appellant wants to appeal; or
(b) the Crown Court judge gives or refuses permission to appeal.

R37.3 **Form of appeal notice**

37.3 (1) An appeal notice must be in the form set out in the Practice Direction.
(2) The appeal notice must—
(a) specify each order or ruling against which the appellant wants to appeal;
(b) identify each ground of appeal on which the appellant relies, numbering them consecutively (if there is more than one) and concisely outlining each argument in support;
(c) summarise the relevant facts;
(d) identify any relevant authorities;
(e) include or attach any application for the following, with reasons—
(i) permission to appeal, if the appellant needs the court's permission,
(ii) an extension of time within which to serve the appeal notice, or
(iii) a direction to attend in person a hearing that the appellant could attend by live link, if the appellant is in custody;

[1] 1947 c. 44; section 17 was amended by article 3(2) of S.I. 1968/1656.
[2] 1996 c. 25; section 35(1) was amended by section 45 of the Criminal Justice Act 2003 (c. 44). The amendment is in force for certain purposes, for remaining purposes it has effect from a date to be appointed. Section 35 was also amended by paragraphs 65 and 69 of Schedule 36 to the Criminal Justice Act 2003 (c. 44) and section 59 of, and paragraph 1 of Schedule 11 to, the Constitutional Reform Act 2005 (c. 4) and Part 10 of Schedule 10 to the Protection of Freedoms Act 2012 (c. 9).
[3] 2003 c. 44.

(f) include a list of those on whom the appellant has served the appeal notice;
(g) attach—
  (i) a transcript or note of each order or ruling against which the appellant wants to appeal,
  (ii) all relevant skeleton arguments considered by the Crown Court judge,
  (iii) any written application for permission to appeal that the appellant made to the Crown Court judge,
  (iv) a transcript or note of the decision by the Crown Court judge on any application for permission to appeal, and
  (v) any other document or thing that the appellant thinks the court will need to decide the appeal and include or attach an electronic link to each such document that has been made available to the Registrar under rule 36.8(1)(a) (Duty of Crown Court officer); and
(h) include or attach—
  (i) an electronic copy of any authority identified under paragraph (2)(d), or
  (ii) if two or more such authorities are identified, electronic copies of each together in a single electronic document.

[Note. An appellant needs the court's permission to appeal in every case to which this Part applies unless the Crown Court judge gives permission.]

Crown Court judge's permission to appeal **R37.4**

37.4 (1) An appellant who wants the Crown Court judge to give permission to appeal must—
(a) apply orally, with reasons, immediately after the order or ruling against which the appellant wants to appeal; or
(b) apply in writing and serve the application on—
  (i) the Crown Court officer, and
  (ii) every party directly affected by the order or ruling
not more than 2 business days after that order or ruling.
(2) A written application must include the same information (with the necessary adaptations) as an appeal notice.

[Note. For the Crown Court judge's power to give permission to appeal, see section 9(11) of the Criminal Justice Act 1987, section 35(1) of the Criminal Procedure and Investigations Act 1996 and section 47(2) of the Criminal Justice Act 2003.]

Respondent's notice **R37.5**

37.5 (1) A party on whom an appellant serves an appeal notice may serve a respondent's notice, and must do so if—
(a) that party wants to make representations to the court; or
(b) the court so directs.
(2) Such a party must serve the respondent's notice on—
(a) the appellant;
(b) the Crown Court officer;
(c) the Registrar; and
(d) any other party on whom the appellant served the appeal notice.
(3) Such a party must serve the respondent's notice not more than 5 business days after—
(a) the appellant serves the appeal notice; or
(b) a direction to do so.
(4) The respondent's notice must be in the form set out in the Practice Direction.
(5) The respondent's notice must—
(a) give the date on which the respondent was served with the appeal notice;
(b) identify each ground of opposition on which the respondent relies, numbering them consecutively (if there is more than one), concisely outlining each argument in support and identifying the ground of appeal to which each relates;
(c) summarise any relevant facts not already summarised in the appeal notice;
(d) identify any relevant authorities;
(e) include or attach any application for the following, with reasons—
  (i) an extension of time within which to serve the respondent's notice, or
  (ii) a direction to attend in person any hearing that the respondent could attend by live link, if the respondent is in custody;
(f) identify any other document or thing that the respondent thinks the court will need to decide the appeal and include or attach an electronic link to each such document that has been made available to the Registrar under rule 36.8(1)(a) (Duty of Crown Court officer); and

(g) include or attach—
(i) an electronic copy of any authority identified under paragraph (5)(d), or
(ii) if two or more such authorities are identified, electronic copies of each together in a single electronic document

R37.6 **Powers of Court of Appeal judge**

37.6 A judge of the Court of Appeal may give permission to appeal as well as exercising the powers given by other legislation (including these Rules).

[Note. See section 31 of the Criminal Appeal Act 1968[4] and section 49 of the Criminal Justice Act 2003[5].]

R37.7 **Renewing applications**

37.7 Rule 36.5 (Renewing an application refused by a judge or the Registrar) applies with a time limit of 5 business days.

R37.8 **Right to attend hearing**

37.8 (1) A party who is in custody has a right to attend a hearing in public.
(2) The court or the Registrar may direct that such a party is to attend a hearing by live link.

[Note. See rule 36.6 (Hearings).]

Criminal Procedure Rules Part 38 Appeal to the Court of Appeal against Ruling Adverse to Prosecution

R38.1 **When this Part applies**

38.1 (1) This Part applies where a prosecutor wants to appeal under section 58(2) of the Criminal Justice Act 2003[1].
(2) A reference to an 'appellant' in this Part is a reference to such a prosecutor.

[Note. Under section 58(2) of the Criminal Justice Act 2003 a prosecutor may appeal to the Court of Appeal against a ruling in the Crown Court. See also sections 57 and 59 to 61 of the 2003 Act.

The rules in Part 36 (Appeal to the Court of Appeal: general rules) also apply where this Part applies.]

R38.2 **Decision to appeal**

38.2 (1) An appellant must tell the Crown Court judge of any decision to appeal—
(a) immediately after the ruling against which the appellant wants to appeal; or
(b) on the expiry of the time to decide whether to appeal allowed under paragraph (2).
(2) If an appellant wants time to decide whether to appeal—
(a) the appellant must ask the Crown Court judge immediately after the ruling; and
(b) the general rule is that the judge must not require the appellant to decide there and then but instead must allow until the next business day.

[Note. If the ruling against which the appellant wants to appeal is a ruling that there is no case to answer, the appellant may appeal against earlier rulings as well: see section 58(7) of the Criminal Justice Act 2003.

Under section 58(8) of the 2003 Act the appellant must agree that a defendant directly affected by the ruling must be acquitted if the appellant (a) does not get permission to appeal or (b) abandons the appeal.

The Crown Court judge may give permission to appeal and may expedite the appeal: see rules 38.5 and 38.6.]

R38.3 **Service of appeal notice**

38.3 (1) An appellant must serve an appeal notice on—
(a) the Crown Court officer;
(b) the Registrar; and

[4] 1968 c. 19; section 31 was amended by section 21 of, and Schedule 2 to, the Costs in Criminal Cases Act 1973 (c. 14), section 24 of, and paragraph 10 of Schedule 6 to, the Road Traffic Act 1974 (c. 50), section 29 of the Criminal Justice Act 1982 (c. 48), section 170 of, and paragraphs 20, 29 and 30 of Schedule 15 to, the Criminal Justice Act 1988 (c. 33), section 4 of, and paragraph 4 of Schedule 3 to, the Road Traffic (Consequential Provisions) Act 1988 (c. 54), section 198 of, and paragraphs 38 and 40 of Schedule 6 to, the Licensing Act 2003 (c. 17), section 87 of the Courts Act 2003 (c. 39), paragraphs 86, 87 and 88 of Schedule 36 to the Criminal Justice Act 2003 (c. 44), section 48 of the Police and Justice Act 2006 (c. 48), section 47 of, and paragraphs 1, 9 and 11 of Schedule 8 to, the Criminal Justice and Immigration Act 2008 (c. 4) and section 177 of, and paragraph 69 of Schedule 21 to, the Coroners and Justice Act 2009 (c. 25). It is further amended by section 67 of, and paragraph 4 of Schedule 4 to, the Youth Justice and Criminal Evidence Act 1999 (c. 23), with effect from a date to be appointed.

[5] 2003 c. 44.

[1] 2003 c. 44.

(c) every defendant directly affected by the ruling against which the appellant wants to appeal.

(2) The appellant must serve the appeal notice not later than—

(a) the next business day after telling the Crown Court judge of the decision to appeal, if the judge expedites the appeal; or

(b) 5 business days after telling the Crown Court judge of that decision, if the judge does not expedite the appeal.

[Note. If the ruling against which the appellant wants to appeal is a public interest ruling, see rule 38.8.]

Form of appeal notice R38.4

38.4 (1) An appeal notice must be in the form set out in the Practice Direction.

(2) The appeal notice must—

(a) specify each ruling against which the appellant wants to appeal;

(b) identify each ground of appeal on which the appellant relies, numbering them consecutively (if there is more than one) and concisely outlining each argument in support;

(c) summarise the relevant facts;

(d) identify any relevant authorities;

(e) include or attach any application for the following, with reasons—

(i) permission to appeal, if the appellant needs the court's permission,

(ii) an extension of time within which to serve the appeal notice,

(iii) expedition of the appeal, or revocation of a direction expediting the appeal;

(f) include a list of those on whom the appellant has served the appeal notice;

(g) attach—

(i) a transcript or note of each ruling against which the appellant wants to appeal,

(ii) all relevant skeleton arguments considered by the Crown Court judge,

(iii) any written application for permission to appeal that the appellant made to the Crown Court judge,

(iv) a transcript or note of the decision by the Crown Court judge on any application for permission to appeal,

(v) a transcript or note of the decision by the Crown Court judge on any request to expedite the appeal, and

(vi) any other document or thing that the appellant thinks the court will need to decide the appeal and include or attach an electronic link to each such document that has been made available to the Registrar under rule 36.8(1)(a) (Duty of Crown Court officer);

(h) include or attach—

(i) an electronic copy of any authority identified under paragraph (5)(d), or

(ii) if two or more such authorities are identified, electronic copies of each together in a single electronic document

(i) include or attach—

(i) an electronic copy of any authority identified under paragraph (2)(d), or

(ii) if two or more such authorities are identified, electronic copies of each together in a single electronic document; and

(j) attach a form of respondent's notice for any defendant served with the appeal notice to complete if that defendant wants to do so.

[Note. An appellant needs the court's permission to appeal unless the Crown Court judge gives permission: see section 57(4) of the Criminal Justice Act 2003. For 'respondent's notice' see rule 38.7.]

Crown Court judge's permission to appeal R38.5

38.5 (1) An appellant who wants the Crown Court judge to give permission to appeal must—

(a) apply orally, with reasons, immediately after the ruling against which the appellant wants to appeal; or

(b) apply in writing and serve the application on—

(i) the Crown Court officer, and

(ii) every defendant directly affected by the ruling

on the expiry of the time allowed under rule 38.2 to decide whether to appeal.

(2) A written application must include the same information (with the necessary adaptations) as an appeal notice.

(3) The Crown Court judge must allow every defendant directly affected by the ruling an opportunity to make representations.

(4) The general rule is that the Crown Court judge must decide whether or not to give permission to appeal on the day that the application for permission is made.

[Note. For the Crown Court judge's power to give permission to appeal, see section 57(4) of the Criminal Justice Act 2003.

Rule 38.5(3) does not apply where the appellant wants to appeal against a public interest ruling: see rule 38.8(5).]

R38.6 Expediting an appeal

38.6 (1) An appellant who wants the Crown Court judge to expedite an appeal must ask, giving reasons, on telling the judge of the decision to appeal.

(2) The Crown Court judge must allow every defendant directly affected by the ruling an opportunity to make representations.

(3) The Crown Court judge may revoke a direction expediting the appeal unless the appellant has served the appeal notice.

[Note. For the Crown Court judge's power to expedite the appeal, see section 59 of the Criminal Justice Act 2003.

Rule 38.6(2) does not apply where the appellant wants to appeal against a public interest ruling: see rule 38.8(5).]

R38.7 Respondent's notice

38.7 (1) A defendant on whom an appellant serves an appeal notice may serve a respondent's notice, and must do so if—

(a) the defendant wants to make representations to the court; or

(b) the court so directs.

(2) Such a defendant must serve the respondent's notice on—

(a) the appellant;

(b) the Crown Court officer;

(c) the Registrar; and

(d) any other defendant on whom the appellant served the appeal notice.

(3) Such a defendant must serve the respondent's notice—

(a) not later than the next business day after—

(i) the appellant serves the appeal notice, or

(ii) a direction to do so

if the Crown Court judge expedites the appeal; or

(b) not more than 5 business days after—

(i) the appellant serves the appeal notice, or

(ii) a direction to do so

if the Crown Court judge does not expedite the appeal.

(4) The respondent's notice must be in the form set out in the Practice Direction.

(5) The respondent's notice must—

(a) give the date on which the respondent was served with the appeal notice;

(b) identify each ground of opposition on which the respondent relies, numbering them consecutively (if there is more than one), concisely outlining each argument in support and identifying the ground of appeal to which each relates;

(c) summarise any relevant facts not already summarised in the appeal notice;

(d) identify any relevant authorities;

(e) include or attach any application for the following, with reasons—

(i) an extension of time within which to serve the respondent's notice, or

(ii) a direction to attend in person any hearing that the respondent could attend by live link, if the respondent is in custody; and

(f) identify any other document or thing that the respondent thinks the court will need to decide the appeal.

R38.8 Public interest ruling

38.8 (1) This rule applies where the appellant wants to appeal against a public interest ruling.

(2) The appellant must not serve on any defendant directly affected by the ruling—

(a) any written application to the Crown Court judge for permission to appeal; or

(b) an appeal notice,

if the appellant thinks that to do so in effect would reveal something that the appellant thinks ought not be disclosed.

(3) The appellant must not include in an appeal notice—

(a) the material that was the subject of the ruling; or

(b) any indication of what sort of material it is,

if the appellant thinks that to do so in effect would reveal something that the appellant thinks ought not be disclosed.

(4) The appellant must serve on the Registrar with the appeal notice an annex—
(a) marked to show that its contents are only for the court and the Registrar;
(b) containing whatever the appellant has omitted from the appeal notice, with reasons; and
(c) if relevant, explaining why the appellant has not served the appeal notice.
(5) Rules 38.5(3) and 38.6(2) do not apply.

[Note. Rules 38.5(3) and 38.6(2) require the Crown Court judge to allow a defendant to make representations about (i) giving permission to appeal and (ii) expediting an appeal.]

Powers of Court of Appeal judge **R38.9**

38.9 A judge of the Court of Appeal may—
(a) give permission to appeal;
(b) revoke a Crown Court judge's direction expediting an appeal; and
(c) where an appellant abandons an appeal, order a defendant's acquittal, his release from custody and the payment of his costs,

as well as exercising the powers given by other legislation (including these Rules).

Renewing applications **R38.10**

38.10 Rule 36.5 (Renewing an application refused by a judge or the Registrar) applies with a time limit of 5 business days.

Right to attend hearing **R38.11**

38.11 (1) A respondent who is in custody has a right to attend a hearing in public.
(2) The court or the Registrar may direct that such a respondent is to attend a hearing by live link.

[Note. See rule 36.6 (Hearings).]

Criminal Procedure Rules Part 39 Appeal to the Court of Appeal about Conviction or Sentence

When this Part applies **R39.1**

39.1 (1) This Part applies where—
(a) a defendant wants to appeal under—
(i) Part 1 of the Criminal Appeal Act 1968[1],
(ii) section 274(3) of the Criminal Justice Act 2003[2],
(iii) paragraph 14 of Schedule 22 to the Criminal Justice Act 2003[3], or
(iv) section 42 of the Counter-Terrorism Act 2008[4];
(b) the Criminal Cases Review Commission refers a case to the Court of Appeal under section 9 of the Criminal Appeal Act 1995[5];
(c) a prosecutor wants to appeal to the Court of Appeal under section 14A(5A) of the Football Spectators Act 1989[6];
(d) a party wants to appeal under section 389 of the Sentencing Act 2020[7];
(e) a person found in contempt of court wants to appeal under section 13 of the Administration of Justice Act 1960[8] and section 18A of the Criminal Appeal Act 1968[9]; or
(f) a person wants to appeal to the Court of Appeal under—
(i) section 24 of the Serious Crime Act 2007[10],

[1] 1968 c. 19.
[2] 2003 c. 44; section 274 was amended by section 40 of, and paragraph 82 of Schedule 9 to, the Constitutional Reform Act 2005 (c. 4).
[3] 2003 c. 44; paragraph 14 of Schedule 22 was amended by section 40 of, and paragraph 82 of Schedule 9 and paragraph 1 of Schedule 11 to, the Constitutional Reform Act 2005 (c. 4).
[4] 2008 c. 28.
[5] 1995 c. 35; section 9 was amended by section 58 of, and paragraph 31 of Schedule 10 to, the Domestic Violence, Crime and Victims Act 2004 (c. 28).
[6] 1989 c. 37; section 14A(5A) was inserted by section 52 of, and paragraphs 1 and 3 of Schedule 3 to, the Violent Crime Reduction Act 2006 (c. 38).
[7] 2020 c. 17.
[8] 1960 c. 65; section 13 was amended paragraph 40 of Schedule 8 to, the Courts Act 1971 (c. 23), Schedule 5 to, the Criminal Appeal Act 1968 (c. 19), paragraph 36 of Schedule 7 to, the Magistrates' Courts Act 1980 (c. 43), Schedule 7 to, the Supreme Court Act 1981 (c. 54), paragraph 25 of Schedule 2 to, the County Courts Act 1984 (c. 28), Schedule 15 to, the Access to Justice Act 1999 (c. 22), paragraph 13 of Schedule 9 to the Constitutional Reform Act 2005 (c. 4) and paragraph 45 of Schedule 16 to, the Armed Forces Act 2006 (c. 52).
[9] 1968 c. 19; section 18A was inserted by section 170 of, and paragraphs 20 and 25 of Schedule 15 to, the Criminal Justice Act 1988 (c. 33).
[10] 2007 c. 27.

(ii) section 28(5)(a) of the Offensive Weapons Act 2019[11], or
(iii) regulation 3C or 3H of the Costs in Criminal Cases (General) Regulations 1986[12].

(2) A reference to an 'appellant' in this Part is a reference to such a party or person.

[Note. Under Part 1 (sections 1 to 32) of the Criminal Appeal Act 1968, a defendant may appeal against—

(a) a conviction (section 1 of the 1968 Act[13]);
(b) a sentence (sections 9 and 10 of the 1968 Act[14]);
(c) a verdict of not guilty by reason of insanity (section 12 of the 1968 Act);
(d) a finding of disability or a finding that the defendant did the act or made the omission charged as an offence (section 15 of the 1968 Act[15];
(e) a hospital order, interim hospital order or supervision order under section 5 or 5A of the Criminal Procedure (Insanity) Act 1964[16] (section 16A of the 1968 Act[17]).

See section 50 of the 1968 Act[18] for the meaning of 'sentence'.

Under section 274(3) of the 2003 Act, a defendant sentenced to life imprisonment outside the United Kingdom, and transferred to serve the sentence in England and Wales, may appeal against the minimum term fixed by a High Court judge under section 321 of the 2020 Act or under section 269 of the 2003 Act.

Under paragraph 14 of Schedule 22 to the Criminal Justice Act 2003 a defendant sentenced to life imprisonment may appeal against the minimum term fixed on review by a High Court judge in certain cases.

Under section 42 of the Counter Terrorism Act 2008 a defendant may appeal against a decision of the Crown Court that an offence has a terrorist connection.

See section 13 of the Criminal Appeal Act 1995[19] for the circumstances in which the Criminal Cases Review Commission may refer a conviction, sentence, verdict or finding to the Court of Appeal.

Under section 14A(5A) of the Football Spectators Act 1989 a prosecutor may appeal against a failure by the Crown Court to make a football banning order.

[11] 2019 c. 17; section 28 comes into force on a date to be appointed.
[12] S.I. 1986/1335; regulation 3C was inserted by regulation 2 of The Costs in Criminal Cases (General) (Amendment) Regulations 1991 (SI 1991/789) and amended by regulation 5 of The Costs in Criminal Cases (General) (Amendment) Regulations 2004 (SI 2004/2408). Regulation 3H was inserted by regulation 7 of The Costs in Criminal Cases (General) (Amendment) Regulations 2004 (SI 2004/2408).
[13] 1968 c. 19; section 1 was amended by section 154 of, and paragraph 71 of Schedule 7 to, the Magistrates' Courts Act 1980 (c. 43), paragraph 44 of Schedule 3 to the Criminal Justice Act 2003 (c. 44), section 1 of the Criminal Appeal Act 1995 (c. 35) and section 47 of, and paragraphs 1 and 2 of Schedule 8 to, the Criminal Justice and Immigration Act 2008 (c. 4).
[14] 1968 c. 19; section 9 was amended by section 170 of, and paragraph 21 of Schedule 15 to, the Criminal Justice Act 1988 (c. 33), section 119 of, and paragraph 12 of Schedule 8 to, the Crime and Disorder Act 1998 (c. 37), section 58 of the Access to Justice Act 1999 (c. 22) and section 271 of, and paragraph 44 of Schedule 3 and Schedule 37 to, the Criminal Justice Act 2003 (c. 44). Section 10 was amended by section 56 of, and paragraph 57 of Schedule 8 to, the Courts Act 1971 (c. 23), section 77 of, and paragraph 23 of Schedule 14 to, the Criminal Justice Act 1982 (c. 48), section 170 of, and paragraphs 20 and 22 of Schedule 15 and Schedule 16 to, the Criminal Justice Act 1988 (c. 33), section 100 of, and paragraph 3 of Schedule 11 to, the Criminal Justice Act 1991 (c. 53), sections 119 and 120 of, and paragraph 13 of Schedule 8 and Schedule 10 to, the Crime and Disorder Act 1998 (c. 37), section 58 of the Access to Justice Act 1999 (c. 22), section 67 of, and paragraph 4 of Schedule 4 and Schedule 6 to, the Youth Justice and Criminal Evidence Act 1999 (c. 23), sections 304, 319 and 322 of, and paragraphs 7 and 8 of Schedule 32 and Schedule 37 to, the Criminal Justice Act 2003 (c. 44) and section 6(2) of, and paragraph 4 of Schedule 4 to, the Criminal Justice and Immigration Act 2008 (c. 4).
[15] 1968 c. 19; section 15 was amended by section 7 of, and paragraph 2 of Schedule 3 to, the Criminal Procedure (Insanity and Unfitness to Plead) Act 1991 (c. 25), section 1 of the Criminal Appeal Act 1995 (c. 35) and section 58 of, and paragraph 4 of Schedule 10 to, the Domestic Violence, Crime and Victims Act 2004 (c. 28) and section 47 of, and paragraphs 1 and 5 of Schedule 8 to, the Criminal Justice and Immigration Act 2008 (c. 4).
[16] 1964 c. 84; section 5 was substituted, and section 5A inserted, by section 24 of the Domestic Violence, Crime and Victims Act 2004 (c. 28). Section 5A was amended by section 15 of the Mental Health Act 2007 (c. 12).
[17] 1968 c. 19; section 16A was inserted by section 25 of the Domestic Violence, Crime and Victims Act 2004 (c. 28).
[18] 1968 c. 19; section 50 was amended by section 66 of the Criminal Justice Act 1982 (c. 48), sections 100 and 101 of, and paragraph 4 of Schedule 11 and Schedule 13 to, the Criminal Justice Act 1991 (c. 53), section 79 of, and Schedule 5 to, the Criminal Justice Act 1993 (c. 36), section 65 of, and Schedule 1 to, the Drug Trafficking Act 1994 (c. 37), section 7 of the Football (Offences and Disorder) Act 1999 (c. 21), section 24 of, and paragraph 3 of Schedule 4 to, the Access to Justice Act 1999 (c. 22), section 165 of, and paragraph 30 of Schedule 9 to, the Powers of Criminal Courts (Sentencing) Act 2000 (c. 6), section 1 of, and Schedule 3 to, the Football (Disorder) Act 2000 (c. 25), section 456 of, and paragraphs 1 and 4 of Schedule 11 to, the Proceeds of Crime Act 2002 (c. 43), section 198 of, and paragraphs 38 and 42 of Schedule 6 to, the Licensing Act 2003 (c. 17), section 52 of, and paragraph 14 of Schedule 3 to, the Violent Crime Reduction Act 2006 (c. 38), paragraph 3 of Schedule 5 to the Legal Aid, Sentencing and Punishment of Offenders Act 2012 (c. 10) and section 85 of, and paragraph 3 of Schedule 4 to, the Serious Crime Act 2015 (c. 9). It is further amended by section 55 of, and paragraph 6 of Schedule 4 to, the Crime (Sentences) Act 1997 (c. 43), with effect from a date to be appointed.
[19] 1995 c. 35; section 13 was amended by section 321 of, and paragraph 3 of Schedule 11 to, the Armed Forces Act 2006 (c. 52).

Under section 389 of the 2020 Act a prosecutor or defendant may appeal against a review by a Crown Court judge of a sentence that was reduced because the defendant assisted the investigator or prosecutor.

Under section 13 of the Administration of Justice Act 1960 a person in respect of whom an order or decision is made by the Crown Court in the exercise of its jurisdiction to punish for contempt of court may appeal to the Court of Appeal.

Under section 24 of the Serious Crime Act 2007 a person who is the subject of a serious crime prevention order, or the relevant applicant authority, may appeal to the Court of Appeal against a decision of the Crown Court in relation to that order. In addition, any person who was given an opportunity to make representations in the proceedings by virtue of section 9(4) of the Act may appeal to the Court of Appeal against a decision of the Crown Court to make, vary or not vary a serious crime prevention order.

Under section 28(5)(a) of the Offensive Weapons Act 2019 an applicant to the Crown Court for the variation, renewal or discharge of a knife crime prevention order made by that court, or a respondent to such an application, may appeal to the Court of Appeal against the decision of the Crown Court.

Under regulation 3C of the Costs in Criminal Cases (General) Regulations 1986, a legal representative against whom the Crown Court makes a wasted costs order under section 19A of the Prosecution of Offences Act 1985[20] *and regulation 3B may appeal against that order to the Court of Appeal.*

Under regulation 3H of the Costs in Criminal Cases (General) Regulations 1986, a third party against whom the Crown Court makes a costs order under section 19B of the Prosecution of Offences Act 1985[21] *and regulation 3F may appeal against that order to the Court of Appeal.*

The rules in Part 36 (Appeal to the Court of Appeal: general rules) also apply where this Part applies.]

Service of appeal notice R39.2

39.2 (1) The appellant must serve an appeal notice on the Registrar—
- (a) not more than 28 days after—
  - (i) the conviction, verdict, or finding,
  - (ii) the sentence,
  - (iii) the order (subject to paragraph (b)), or the failure to make an order, or
  - (iv) the minimum term review decision under section 274(3) of, or paragraph 14 of Schedule 22 to, the Criminal Justice Act 2003

  about which the appellant wants to appeal;
- (b) not more than 15 business days after the order in a case in which the appellant appeals against a wasted or third party costs order; and
- (c) not more than 20 business days after the Registrar serves notice that the Criminal Cases Review Commission has referred a conviction to the court.

(2) Unless the appeal notice includes grounds of appeal prepared by the person who was appointed to put the case for the defence under rule 25.10 (Defendant unfit to plead), paragraphs (3), (4) and (5) of this rule apply where the appeal is about—
- (a) a finding of disability under section 4 of the Criminal Procedure (Insanity) Act 1964[22],
- (b) a finding under section 4A of the 1964 Act that the defendant did the act or made the omission charged as an offence; or
- (c) a hospital order, interim hospital order or supervision order made under section 5 or 5A of the 1964 Act[23];

(3) The Registrar must refer the appeal notice to a judge of the Court of Appeal for the judge to give or refuse to give procedural directions under section 31B of the Criminal Appeal Act 1968[24].

(4) The judge may—
- (a) give such procedural directions as the case requires where the appeal notice includes grounds of appeal that the judge considers reasonably arguable; or
- (b) refuse to give such directions, in any other case.

(5) Such procedural directions may include—
- (a) a direction for the appointment of a person to put the case for the appellant on appeal;

20 1985 c. 23; section 19A was inserted by section 111 of the Courts and Legal Services Act 1990 (c. 41).
21 1985 c. 23; section 19B was inserted by section 93 of the Courts Act 2003 (c. 39).
22 1964 c. 84; section 4 was substituted, together with section 4A, for section 4 as originally enacted, by section 2 of the Criminal Procedure (Insanity and Unfitness to Plead) Act 1991 (c. 25), and amended by section 22 of the Domestic Violence, Crime and Victims Act 2004 (c. 28).
23 1964 c. 84; section 5 was substituted, and section 5A inserted, by section 24 of the Domestic Violence, Crime and Victims Act 2004 (c. 28). Section 5A was amended by section 15 of the Mental Health Act 2007 (c. 12).
24 1968 c. 19; section 31B was inserted by section 87 of the Courts Act 2003 (c. 39).

(b) a direction to commission medical evidence; and
(c) a direction for the reference of the case to the judge again to give, or to refuse to give, further directions.

[Note. The time limit for serving an appeal notice (a) on an appeal under Part 1 of the Criminal Appeal Act 1968 and (b) on an appeal against a finding of contempt of court is prescribed by sections 18 and 18A of the Criminal Appeal Act 1968. It may be extended, but not shortened.

For service of a reference by the Criminal Cases Review Commission, see rule 39.5.

[Under section 31C of the 1968 Act[25] *a party has no right to renew to the Court of Appeal an application for procedural directions refused by a judge.]*

R39.3 **Form of appeal notice**

39.3 (1) An appeal notice must—
(a) specify—
(i) the conviction, verdict, or finding,
(ii) the sentence, or
(iii) the order, or the failure to make an order about which the appellant wants to appeal;
(b) identify each ground of appeal on which the appellant relies (and see paragraph (2));
(c) identify the transcript that the appellant thinks the court will need, if the appellant wants to appeal against a conviction;
(d) identify the relevant sentencing powers of the Crown Court, if sentence is in issue;
(e) include or attach any application for the following, with reasons—
(i) permission to appeal, if the appellant needs the court's permission,
(ii) an extension of time within which to serve the appeal notice,
(iii) bail pending appeal,
(iv) a direction to attend in person a hearing that the appellant could attend by live link, if the appellant is in custody,
(v) the introduction of evidence, including hearsay evidence and evidence of bad character,
(vi) an order requiring a witness to attend court,
(vii) a direction for special measures for a witness,
(viii)a direction for special measures for the giving of evidence by the appellant, or
(ix) the suspension of any disqualification imposed, or order made, in the case, where the Court of Appeal can order such a suspension pending appeal;
(f) identify any other document or thing that the appellant thinks the court will need to decide the appeal and include or attach an electronic link to each such document that has been made available to the Registrar under rule 36.8(1)(a) (Duty of Crown Court officer); and
(g) include or attach—
(i) an electronic copy of any authority identified by the grounds of appeal (see paragraph (2)(f)), or
(ii) if two or more such authorities are identified, electronic copies of each together in a single electronic document.

(2) The grounds of appeal must—
(a) include in no more than the first two pages a summary of the grounds that makes what then follows easy to understand;
(b) in each ground of appeal identify the event or decision to which that ground relates;
(c) in each ground of appeal summarise the facts relevant to that ground, but only to the extent necessary to make clear what is in issue;
(d) concisely outline each argument in support of each ground;
(e) number each ground consecutively, if there is more than one;
(f) identify any relevant authority and—
(i) state the proposition of law that the authority demonstrates, and
(ii) identify the parts of the authority that support that proposition; and
(a) where the Criminal Cases Review Commission refers a case to the court, explain how each ground of appeal relates (if it does) to the reasons for the reference.

[Note. The Practice Direction sets out forms of appeal notice for use in connection with this rule.

In some legislation, including the Criminal Appeal Act 1968, permission to appeal is described as 'leave to appeal'.

[25] 1968 c. 19; section 31C was inserted by section 87 of the Courts Act 2003 (c. 39) and amended by sections 47 and 149 of, and paragraphs 1 and 12 of Schedule 8 and part 3 of Schedule 28 to, the Criminal Justice and Immigration Act 2008 (c. 4).

An appellant needs the court's permission to appeal in every case to which this Part applies, except where—

(a) the Criminal Cases Review Commission refers the case;
(b) the appellant appeals against—
(i) an order or decision made in the exercise of jurisdiction to punish for contempt of court, or
(ii) a wasted or third party costs order; or
(c) the Crown Court judge certifies under sections 1(2)(a), 11(1A), 12(b), 15(2)(b) or 16A(2)(b) of the Criminal Appeal Act 1968([26]), under section 81(1B) of the Senior Courts Act 1981[27], under section 14A(5B) of the Football Spectators Act 1989[28], or under section 24(4) of the Serious Crime Act 2007, that a case is fit for appeal.

A judge of the Court of Appeal may give permission to appeal under section 31 of the Criminal Appeal Act 1968[29].

See also rules 39.7 (Introducing evidence) and 39.8 (Application for bail, or to suspend a disqualification or order, pending appeal or retrial).]

Crown Court judge's certificate that case is fit for appeal **R39.4**

39.4 (1) An appellant who wants the Crown Court judge to certify that a case is fit for appeal must either—
(a) apply orally, with reasons, immediately after there occurs—
(i) the conviction, verdict, or finding,
(ii) the sentence, or
(iii) the order, or the failure to make an order
about which the appellant wants to appeal; or
(b) apply in writing and serve the application on the Crown Court officer not more than 10 business days after that occurred.
(2) A written application must include the same information (with the necessary adaptations) as an appeal notice.

[Note. The Crown Court judge may certify that a case is fit for appeal under sections 1(2)(b), 11(1A), 12(b), 15(2)(b) or 16A(2)(b) of the Criminal Appeal Act 1968, under section 81(1B) of the Senior Courts Act 1981, under section 14A(5B) of the Football Spectators Act 1989 or under section 24(4) of the Serious Crime Act 2007.

See also rule 39.2 (service of appeal notice required in all cases).]

Reference by Criminal Cases Review Commission **R39.5**

39.5 (1) The Registrar must serve on the appellant a reference by the Criminal Cases Review Commission.
(2) The court must treat that reference as the appeal notice if the appellant does not serve such a notice under rule 39.2.

Respondent's notice **R39.6**

39.6 (1) The Registrar—
(a) may serve an appeal notice on any party directly affected by the appeal; and
(b) must do so if the Criminal Cases Review Commission refers a conviction, verdict, finding or sentence to the court.
(2) Such a party may serve a respondent's notice, and must do so if—
(a) that party wants to make representations to the court; or
(b) the court or the Registrar so directs.

[26] 1968 c. 19; section 11(1A) was inserted by section 29 of the Criminal Justice Act 1982 (c. 48) and amended by section 47 of, and paragraphs 1 and 3 of Schedule 8 to, the Criminal Justice and Immigration Act 2008 (c. 4).
[27] 1981 c. 54; section 81(1B) was inserted by sections 29 and 60 of the Criminal Justice Act 1982 (c. 48). The Act's title was amended by section 59(5) of, and paragraph 1 of Schedule 11 to, the Constitutional Reform Act 2005 (c. 4).
[28] 1989 c. 37; section 14A(5B) was inserted by section 52 of, and paragraphs 1 and 3 of Schedule 3 to, the Violent Crime Reduction Act 2006 (c. 38).
[29] 1968 c. 19; section 31 was amended by section 21 of, and Schedule 2 to, the Costs in Criminal Cases Act 1973 (c. 14), section 24 of, and paragraph 10 of Schedule 6 to, the Road Traffic Act 1974 (c. 50), section 29 of the Criminal Justice Act 1982 (c. 48), section 170 of, and paragraphs 20, 29 and 30 of Schedule 15 to, the Criminal Justice Act 1988 (c. 33), section 4 of, and paragraph 4 of Schedule 3 to, the Road Traffic (Consequential Provisions) Act 1988 (c. 54), section 198 of, and paragraphs 38 and 40 of Schedule 6 to, the Licensing Act 2003 (c. 17), section 87 of the Courts Act 2003 (c. 39), paragraphs 86, 87 and 88 of Schedule 36 to the Criminal Justice Act 2003 (c. 44), section 48 of the Police and Justice Act 2006 (c. 48), section 47 of, and paragraphs 1, 9 and 11 of Schedule 8 to, the Criminal Justice and Immigration Act 2008 (c. 4) and section 177 of, and paragraph 69 of Schedule 21 to, the Coroners and Justice Act 2009 (c. 25). It is further amended by section 67 of, and paragraph 4 of Schedule 4 to, the Youth Justice and Criminal Evidence Act 1999 (c. 23), with effect from a date to be appointed.

(3) Such a party must serve the respondent's notice on—
(a) the appellant;
(b) the Registrar; and
(c) any other party on whom the Registrar served the appeal notice.
(4) Such a party must serve the respondent's notice—
(a) not more than 10 business days after the Registrar serves—
(i) the appeal notice, or
(ii) a direction to do so; or
(b) not more than 20 business days after the Registrar serves notice that the Commission has referred a conviction.
(5) The respondent's notice must be in the form set out in the Practice Direction.
(6) The respondent's notice must—
(a) give the date on which the respondent was served with the appeal notice;
(b) identify each ground of opposition on which the respondent relies, numbering them consecutively (if there is more than one), concisely outlining each argument in support and identifying the ground of appeal to which each relates;
(c) identify the relevant sentencing powers of the Crown Court, if sentence is in issue;
(d) summarise any relevant facts not already summarised in the appeal notice;
(e) identify any relevant authorities;
(f) include or attach any application for the following, with reasons—
(i) an extension of time within which to serve the respondent's notice,
(ii) bail pending appeal,
(iii) a direction to attend in person a hearing that the respondent could attend by live link, if the respondent is in custody,
(iv) the introduction of evidence, including hearsay evidence and evidence of bad character,
(v) an order requiring a witness to attend court, or
(vi) a direction for special measures for a witness;
(g) identify any other document or thing that the respondent thinks the court will need to decide the appeal and include or attach an electronic link to each such document that has been made available to the Registrar under rule 36.8(1)(a) (Duty of Crown Court officer); and
(h) include or attach—
(i) an electronic copy of any authority identified under paragraph (6)(e), or
(ii) if two or more such authorities are identified, electronic copies of each together in a single electronic document.

[Note. The Practice Direction sets out the circumstances in which the Registrar usually will serve a defendant's appeal notice on the prosecutor.

See also rule 39.7 (Introducing evidence).]

R39.7 **Introducing evidence**

39.7 (1) The following Parts apply with such adaptations as the court or the Registrar may direct—
(a) Part 16 (Written witness statements);
(b) Part 18 (Measures to assist a witness or defendant to give evidence);
(c) Part 19 (Expert evidence);
(d) Part 20 (Hearsay evidence);
(e) Part 21 (Evidence of bad character); and
(f) Part 22 (Evidence of a complainant's previous sexual behaviour).
(2) But the general rule is that—
(a) a respondent who opposes an appellant's application or notice to which one of those Parts applies must do so in the respondent's notice, with reasons;
(b) an appellant who opposes a respondent's application or notice to which one of those Parts applies must serve notice, with reasons, on—
(i) the Registrar, and
(ii) the respondent
not more than 10 business days after service of the respondent's notice; and
(c) the court or the Registrar may give directions with or without a hearing.
(3) A party who wants the court to order the production of a document, exhibit or other thing connected with the proceedings must—
(a) identify that item; and
(b) explain—
(i) how it is connected with the proceedings,

(ii) why its production is necessary for the determination of the case, and
(iii) to whom it should be produced (the court, appellant or respondent, or any two or more of them).

(4) A party who wants the court to order a witness to attend to be questioned must—
(a) identify the proposed witness;
(b) explain—
(i) what evidence the proposed witness can give,
(ii) why that evidence is capable of belief,
(iii) if applicable, why that evidence may provide a ground for allowing the appeal,
(iv) on what basis that evidence would have been admissible in the case which is the subject of the application for permission to appeal or appeal, and
(v) why that evidence was not introduced in that case; and
(c) where the court can exercise a power to which Part 18 (Measures to assist a witness or defendant to give evidence) applies, provide any information that the court may need to assess—
(i) the measure or measures likely to maximise so far as practicable the quality of the witness' evidence, and
(ii) the witness' own views.

(5) Where the court orders a witness to attend to be questioned, the witness must attend the hearing of the application for permission to appeal or of the appeal, as applicable, unless the court otherwise directs.

(6) Where the court orders a witness to attend to be questioned before an examiner on the court's behalf, the court must identify the examiner and may give directions about—
(a) the time and place, or times and places, at which that questioning must be carried out;
(b) the manner in which that questioning must be carried out, in particular as to—
(i) the service of any report, statement or questionnaire in preparation for the questioning,
(ii) the sequence in which the parties may ask questions, and
(iii) if more than one witness is to be questioned, the sequence in which those witnesses may be questioned; and
(c) the manner in which, and when, a record of the questioning must be submitted to the court.

(7) Where the court orders the questioning of a witness before an examiner, the court may delegate to that examiner the giving of directions under paragraph (6)(a), (b) and (c).

[Note. An application to introduce evidence or for directions about evidence must be included in, or attached to, an appeal notice or a respondent's notice: see rules 39.3(1)(e)(v), (vi) and 39.6(6)(f)(iv), (v).

Under section 23 of the Criminal Appeal Act 1968[30]*, the Court of Appeal may order the production of a document, exhibit or other thing, may order a witness to attend to be examined before the court and may allow the introduction of evidence that was not introduced at trial. Under section 23(4), if it thinks it necessary or expedient in the interests of justice the court may order the examination of a witness to be conducted before any judge, court officer or other person, and allow the admission of a record of that examination as evidence before the court.]*

Application for bail, or to suspend a disqualification or order, pending appeal or retrial **R39.8**

39.8 (1) This rule applies where—
(a) a party wants to make an application to the court about bail pending appeal or retrial; or
(b) an appellant wants to apply to the court to suspend a disqualification or order pending appeal.

(2) That party must serve an application in the form set out in the Practice Direction on—
(a) the Registrar, unless the application is with the appeal notice; and
(b) the other party.

(3) The court must not decide such an application without giving the other party an opportunity to make representations, including, in the case of a bail application, representations about any condition or surety proposed by the applicant.

[30] 1968 c. 19; section 23 was amended by sections 4 and 29 of, and paragraph 4 of Schedule 2 to, the Criminal Appeal Act 1995 (c. 35), section 48 of the Police and Justice Act 2006 (c. 48) and section 47 of, and paragraphs 1 and 10 of Schedule 8 to, the Criminal Justice and Immigration Act 2008 (c. 4).

[Note. See section 19 of the Criminal Appeal Act 1968[31]*, and section 3(8) of the Bail Act 1976*[32] *An application about bail or about the conditions of bail may be made either by an appellant or respondent.*

Under section 81(1) of the Senior Courts Act 1981[33]*, a Crown Court judge may grant bail pending appeal only (a) if that judge gives a certificate that the case is fit for appeal (see rule 39.4) and (b) not more than 28 days after the conviction or sentence against which the appellant wants to appeal.*

Under section 39 of the Road Traffic Offenders Act 1988[34]*, a court which has made an order disqualifying a person from driving may suspend the disqualification pending appeal. Under section 40 of the 1988 Act*[35]*, the appeal court may do so. See also rule 29.2.*

Under section 129 of the Licensing Act 2003[36]*, a court which has made an order to forfeit or suspend a personal licence issued under that Act may suspend the order pending appeal. Under section 130 of the 2003 Act*[37]*, the appeal court may do so.]*

R39.9 Conditions of bail pending appeal or retrial

39.9 (1) This rule applies where the court grants a party bail pending appeal or retrial subject to any condition that must be met before that party is released.

(2) The court may direct how such a condition must be met.

(3) The Registrar must serve a certificate in the form set out in the Practice Direction recording any such condition and direction on—

(a) that party;

(b) that party's custodian; and

(c) any other person directly affected by any such direction.

(4) A person directly affected by any such direction need not comply with it until the Registrar serves that person with that certificate.

(5) Unless the court otherwise directs, if any such condition or direction requires someone to enter into a recognizance it must be—

(a) in the form set out in the Practice Direction and signed before—

(i) the Registrar,

(ii) the custodian, or

(iii) someone acting with the authority of the Registrar or custodian;

(b) copied immediately to the person who enters into it; and

(c) served immediately by the Registrar on the appellant's custodian or vice versa, as appropriate.

(6) Unless the court otherwise directs, if any such condition or direction requires someone to make a payment, surrender a document or take some other step—

(a) that payment, document or step must be made, surrendered or taken to or before—

(i) the Registrar,

(ii) the custodian, or

(iii) someone acting with the authority of the Registrar or custodian; and

(b) the Registrar or the custodian, as appropriate, must serve immediately on the other a statement that the payment, document or step has been made, surrendered or taken, as appropriate.

(7) The custodian must release the appellant where it appears that any condition ordered by the court has been met.

[31] 1968 c. 19; section 19 was substituted by section 29 of the Criminal Justice Act 1982 (c. 48) and was amended by section 170 of, and paragraphs 20 and 26 of Schedule 15 to, the Criminal Justice Act 1988 (c. 33), section 168 of, and paragraph 22 of Schedule 10 to, the Criminal Justice and Public Order Act 1994 (c. 33) and section 59 of, and paragraph 1 of Schedule 11 to, the Constitutional Reform Act 2005 (c. 4).

[32] 1976 c. 63; section 3(8) was amended by section 65 of, and Schedule 12 to, the Criminal Law Act 1977 (c. 45) and paragraph 48 of Schedule 3 to the Criminal Justice Act 2003 (c. 44).

[33] 1981 c. 54; section 81(1) was amended by sections 29 and 60 of the Criminal Justice Act 1982 (c. 48), section 15 of, and paragraph 2 of Schedule 12 to, the Criminal Justice Act 1987 (c. 38), section 168 of, and paragraph 19 of Schedule 9 and paragraph 48 of Schedule 10 to, the Criminal Justice and Public Order Act 1994 (c. 33), section 119 of, and paragraph 48 of Schedule 8 and Schedule 10 to, the Crime and Disorder Act 1998 (c. 37), section 165 of, and paragraph 87 of Schedule 9 and Schedule 12 to, the Powers of Criminal Courts (Sentencing) Act 2000 (c. 6), paragraph 54 of Schedule 3, paragraph 4 of Schedule 36 and Part 4 of Schedule 37 to the Criminal Justice Act 2003 (c. 44), articles 2 and 6 of S.I. 2004/1033 and section 177(1) of, and paragraph 76 of Schedule 21 to, the Coroners and Justice Act 2009 (c. 25).

[34] 1988 c. 53.

[35] 1988 c. 53; section 40 was amended by sections 40 and 59 of, and paragraph 50 of Schedule 9 and paragraph 1 of Schedule 11 to, the Constitutional Reform Act 2005 (c.4).

[36] 2003 c. 17.

[37] 2003 c. 17; section 130 was amended by sections 40 and 59 of, and paragraph 78 of Schedule 9 and paragraph 1 of Schedule 11 to, the Constitutional Reform Act 2005 (c. 4).

(8) For the purposes of section 5 of the Bail Act 1976[38] (record of decision about bail), the Registrar must keep a copy of—
(a) any certificate served under paragraph (3);
(b) a notice of hearing given under rule 36.7(1); and
(c) a notice of the court's decision served under rule 36.7(2).
(9) Where the court grants bail pending retrial the Registrar must serve on the Crown Court officer copies of the documents kept under paragraph (8).

Forfeiture of a recognizance given as a condition of bail **R39.10**

39.10 (1) This rule applies where—
(a) the court grants a party bail pending appeal or retrial; and
(b) the bail is subject to a condition that that party provides a surety to guarantee that he will surrender to custody as required; but
(c) that party does not surrender to custody as required.
(2) The Registrar must serve notice on—
(a) the surety; and
(b) the prosecutor,
of the hearing at which the court may order the forfeiture of the recognizance given by that surety.
(3) The court must not forfeit a surety's recognizance—
(a) less than 5 business days after the Registrar serves notice under paragraph (2); and
(b) without giving the surety an opportunity to make representations at a hearing.

[Note. If the purpose for which a recognizance is entered is not fulfilled, that recognizance may be forfeited by the court. If the court forfeits a surety's recognizance, the sum promised by that person is then payable to the Crown.]

Right to attend hearing **R39.11**

39.11 A party who is in custody has a right to attend a hearing in public unless—
(a) it is a hearing preliminary or incidental to an appeal, including the hearing of an application for permission to appeal;
(b) it is the hearing of an appeal and the court directs that—
(i) the appeal involves a question of law alone, and
(ii) for that reason the appellant has no permission to attend; or
(c) that party is in custody in consequence of—
(i) a verdict of not guilty by reason of insanity, or
(ii) a finding of disability.

[Note. See rule 36.6 (Hearings) and section 22 of the Criminal Appeal Act 1968[39]. There are corresponding provisions in the Criminal Justice Act 2003 (Mandatory Life Sentences: Appeals in Transitional Cases) Order 2005[40], the Serious Organised Crime and Police Act 2005 (Appeals under section 74) Order 2006[41] and the Serious Crime Act 2007 (Appeals under Section 24) Order 2008[42]. Under section 22 of the 1968 Act and corresponding provisions in those Orders, the court may direct that an appellant who is in custody is to attend a hearing by live link.]

Power to vary determination of appeal against sentence **R39.12**

39.12 (1) This rule applies where the court decides an appeal affecting sentence in a party's absence.
(2) The court may vary such a decision if it did not take account of something relevant because that party was absent.
(3) A party who wants the court to vary such a decision must—
(a) apply in writing, with reasons; and
(b) serve the application on the Registrar not more than 5 business days after—
(i) the decision, if that party was represented at the appeal hearing, or
(ii) the Registrar serves the decision, if that party was not represented at that hearing.

[38] 1976 c. 63; section 5 was amended by section 65 of, and Schedule 12 to, the Criminal Law Act 1977 (c. 45), section 60 of the Criminal Justice Act 1982 (c. 48), paragraph 1 of Schedule 3 to the Criminal Justice and Public Order Act 1994 (c. 33), paragraph 53 of Schedule 9 to the Powers of Criminal Courts (Sentencing) Act 2000 (c. 6), section 129(1) of the Criminal Justice and Police Act 2001 (c. 16), paragraph 182 of Schedule 8 to the Courts Act 2003 (c. 39), paragraph 48 of Schedule 3, paragraphs 1 and 2 of Schedule 36, and Parts 2, 4 and 12 of Schedule 37 to the Criminal Justice Act 2003 (c. 44) and section 208 of, and paragraphs 33 and 35 of Schedule 21 to, the Legal Services Act 2007 (c. 27).
[39] 1968 c. 19; section 22 was amended by section 48 of the Police and Justice Act 2006 (c. 48).
[40] S.I. 2005/2798.
[41] S.I. 2006/2135.
[42] S.I. 2008/1863.

[Note. Section 22(3) of the Criminal Appeal Act 1968 allows the court to sentence in an appellant's absence. There are corresponding provisions in the Criminal Justice Act 2003 (Mandatory Life Sentences: Appeals in Transitional Cases) Order 2005 and in the Serious Organised Crime and Police Act 2005 (Appeals under Section 74) Order 2006.]

R39.13 **Directions about re-admission to hospital on dismissal of appeal**

39.13 (1) This rule applies where—

(a) an appellant subject to—

(i) an order under section 37(1) of the Mental Health Act 1983[43] (detention in hospital on conviction), or

(ii) an order under section 5(2) of the Criminal Procedure (Insanity) Act 1964[44] (detention in hospital on finding of insanity or disability)

has been released on bail pending appeal; and

(b) the court—

(i) refuses permission to appeal,

(ii) dismisses the appeal, or

(iii) affirms the order under appeal.

(2) The court must give appropriate directions for the appellant's—

(a) re-admission to hospital; and

(b) if necessary, temporary detention pending re-admission.

R39.14 **Renewal or setting aside of order for retrial**

39.14 (1) This rule applies where—

(a) a prosecutor wants a defendant to be arraigned more than 2 months after the court ordered a retrial under section 7 of the Criminal Appeal Act 1968[45]; or

(b) a defendant wants such an order set aside after 2 months have passed since it was made.

(2) That party must apply in writing, with reasons, and serve the application on—

(a) the Registrar;

(b) the other party.

[Note. Section 8(1) and (1A) of the Criminal Appeal Act 1968[46] set out the criteria for making an order on an application to which this rule applies.]

Criminal Practice Directions Part 39 Appeal to the Court of Appeal about Conviction or Sentence

CPD.39A **CPD IX Appeal 39A: Appeals Against Conviction and Sentence — The Provision of Notice to the Prosecution**

39A.1 When an appeal notice served under CrimPR 39.2 is received by the Registrar of Criminal Appeals, the Registrar will notify the relevant prosecution authority, giving the case name, reference number and the trial or sentencing court.

39A.2 If the court or the Registrar directs, or invites, the prosecution authority to serve a respondent's notice under CrimPR 39.6, prior to the consideration of leave, the Registrar will also at that time serve on the prosecution authority the appeal notice containing the grounds of appeal and the transcripts, if available. If the prosecution authority is not directed or invited to serve a respondent's notice but wishes to do so, the authority should request the grounds of appeal and any existing transcript from the Criminal Appeal Office. Any respondent's notice received prior to the consideration of leave will be made available to the single judge.

39A.3 The Registrar of Criminal Appeals will notify the relevant prosecution authority in the event that:

(a) leave to appeal against conviction or sentence is granted by the single Judge; or

(b) the single Judge or the Registrar refers an application for leave to appeal against conviction or sentence to the Full Court for determination; or

(c) there is to be a renewed application for leave to appeal against sentence only.

[43] 1983 c. 20; section 37(1) was amended by section 55 of, and paragraph 12 of Schedule 4 to, the Crime (Sentences) Act 1997 (c. 43) and section 304 of, and paragraphs 37 and 38 of Schedule 32 to, the Criminal Justice Act 2003 (c. 44).

[44] 1964 c. 84.

[45] 1968 c.19; section 7 was amended by sections 43 and 170 of, and Schedule 16 to, the Criminal Justice Act 1988 (c. 33) and section 331 of, and paragraph 44 of Schedule 36 to, the Criminal Justice Act 2003 (c. 44).

[46] 1968 c.19; section 8(1) was amended by section 56 of, and Part IV of Schedule 11 to, the Courts Act 1971 (c. 23) and section 43 of the Criminal Justice Act 1988 (c. 33). Section 8(1A) was inserted by section 43(4) of the Criminal Justice Act 1988 (c. 33).

If the prosecution authority has not yet been served with the appeal notice and transcript, the Registrar will serve these with the notification, and if leave is granted, the Registrar will also serve the authority with the comments of the single judge.

39A.4 The prosecution should notify the Registrar without delay if they wish to be represented at the hearing. The prosecution should note that the Registrar will not delay listing to await a response from the Prosecution as to whether they wish to attend. Prosecutors should note that occasionally, for example, where the single Judge fixes a hearing date at short notice, the case may be listed very quickly.

39A.5 If the prosecution wishes to be represented at any hearing, the notification should include details of Counsel instructed and a time estimate. An application by the prosecution to remove a case from the list for Counsel's convenience, or to allow further preparation time, will rarely be granted.

39A.6 There may be occasions when the Court of Appeal Criminal Division will grant leave to appeal to an unrepresented applicant and proceed forthwith with the appeal in the absence of the appellant and Counsel. The prosecution should not attend any hearing at which the appellant is unrepresented. *Nasteska v The former Yugoslav Republic of Macedonia (Application No.23152/05)* As a Court of Review, the Court of Appeal Criminal Division would expect the prosecution to have raised any specific matters of relevance with the sentencing Judge in the first instance.

39A.7 Where there is a renewed application for leave to appeal against a sentence imposed for an offence involving a fatality, the Crown Prosecution Service has indicated that it wishes to be represented at all sentence appeals in order to ensure that they are in a position, if appropriate, to make representations as to the impact of the offence upon the victim and their family. In those circumstances, if the court is minded to grant the application for leave to appeal the court should consider adjourning the hearing of the appeal to allow prosecution counsel to attend and for the victim's family to be notified and attend if they so wish.

CPD IX Appeal 39B: Listing of Appeals against Conviction and Sentence in the Court of Appeal Criminal Division (CACD) **CPD.39B**

39B.1 Arrangements for the fixing of dates for the hearing of appeals will be made by the Criminal Appeal Office Listing Officer, under the superintendence of the Registrar of Criminal Appeals who may give such directions as he deems necessary.

39B.2 Where possible, regard will be had to an advocate's existing commitments. However, in relation to the listing of appeals, the Court of Appeal takes precedence over all lower courts, including the Crown Court. Wherever practicable, a lower court will have regard to this principle when making arrangements to release an advocate to appear in the Court of Appeal. In case of difficulty the lower court should communicate with the Registrar. In general an advocate's commitment in a lower court will not be regarded as a good reason for failing to accept a date proposed for a hearing in the Court of Appeal.

39B.3 Similarly when the Registrar directs that an appellant should appear by video link, the prison must give precedence to video-links to the Court of Appeal over video-links to the lower courts, including the Crown Court.

39B.4 The copy of the Criminal Appeal Office summary provided to advocates will contain the summary writer's time estimate for the whole hearing including delivery of judgment. It will also contain a time estimate for the judges' reading time of the core material. The Listing Officer will rely on those estimates, unless the advocate for the appellant or the Crown provides different time estimates to the Listing Officer, in writing, within 7 days of the receipt of the summary by the advocate. Where the time estimates are considered by an advocate to be inadequate, or where the estimates have been altered because, for example, a ground of appeal has been abandoned, it is the duty of the advocate to inform the Court promptly, in which event the Registrar will reconsider the time estimates and inform the parties accordingly.

39B.5 The following target times are set for the hearing of appeals. Target times will run from the receipt of the appeal by the Listing Officer, as being ready for hearing.

39B.6

Nature of Appeal:	*From Receipt by Listing Officer to Fixing of Hearing Date:*	*From Fixing of Hearing Date to Hearing:*	*Total Time From Receipt by Listing Officer to Hearing:*
Sentence Appeal	14 days	14 days	28 days
Conviction Appeal	21 days	42 days	63 days
Conviction Appeal where witness to attend	28 days	52 days	80 days

39B.7 Where legal vacations impinge, these periods may be extended. Where expedition is required, the Registrar may direct that these periods be abridged.

39B.8 'Appeal' includes an application for leave to appeal which requires an oral hearing.

CPD.39C **CPD IX Appeal 39C: Appeal Notices Containing Grounds of Appeal**

39C.1 The requirements for the service of notices of appeal and the time limits for doing so are as set out in CrimPR Part 39. The Court must be provided with an appeal notice as a single document which sets out the grounds of appeal. Advocates should not provide the Court with an advice addressed to lay or professional clients. Any appeal notice or grounds of appeal served on the Court will usually be provided to the respondent.

39C.2 Advocates should not settle grounds unless they consider that they are properly arguable. Grounds should be carefully drafted; the court is not assisted by grounds of appeal which are not properly set out and particularised in accordance with CrimPR 39.3. The grounds must:

i. be concise; and
ii. be presented in A4 page size and portrait orientation, in not less than 12 point font and in 1.5 line spacing.

Appellants and advocates should keep in mind the powers of the court and the Registrar to return for revision, within a directed period, grounds that do not comply with the rule or with these directions, including grounds that are so prolix or diffuse as to render them incomprehensible. They should keep in mind also the court's powers to refuse permission to appeal on any ground that is so poorly presented as to render it unarguable and thus to exclude it from consideration by the court: see CrimPR 36.14. Should leave to amend the grounds be granted, it is most unlikely that further grounds will be entertained.

39C.3 Where the appellant wants to appeal against conviction, transcripts must be identified in accordance with CrimPR 39.3(1)(c). This includes specifying the date and time of transcripts in the notice of appeal. Accordingly, the date and time of the summing up should be provided, including both parts of a split summing-up. Where relevant, the date and time of additional transcripts (such as rulings or early directions) should be provided. Similarly, any relevant written materials (such as route to verdict) should be identified.

39C.4 Where the appellant wants to rely on a ground of appeal that is not identified by the appeal notice, an application under CrimPR 36.14(5) is required. In *R v James and Others* [2018] EWCA Crim 285 the Court of Appeal identified as follows the considerations that obtain and the criteria that the court will apply on any such application:

(a) as a general rule all the grounds of appeal that an appellant wishes to advance should be lodged with the appeal notice, subject to their being perfected on receipt of transcripts from the Registrar.
(b) the application for permission to appeal under section 31 of the Criminal Appeal Act 1968 is an important stage in the process. It may not be treated lightly or its determination in effect ignored merely because fresh representatives would have done or argued things differently to their predecessors. Fresh grounds advanced by fresh representatives must be particularly cogent.
(c) as well as addressing the factors material to the determination of an application for an extension of time within which to renew an application for permission to appeal, if that is required, on an application under CrimPR 36.14(5) the appellant or his or her representatives must address directly the factors which the court is likely to consider relevant when deciding whether to allow the substitution or addition of grounds of appeal. Those factors include (but this list is not exhaustive):
    (i) the extent of the delay in advancing the fresh ground or grounds;
    (ii) the reasons for that delay;
    (iii) whether the facts or issues the subject of the fresh ground were known to the appellant's representatives when they advised on appeal;
    (iv) the interests of justice and the overriding objective in Part 1 of the Criminal Procedure Rules.
(d) on the assumption that an appellant will have received advice on appeal from his or her trial advocate, who will have settled the grounds of appeal in the original appeal notice or who will have advised that there are no reasonably arguable grounds to challenge the safety of the conviction:
    (i) fresh representatives should comply with the duty of due diligence explained in *McCook* [2014] EWCA Crim 734. Waiver of privilege by the appellant is very likely to be required.
    (ii) once the trial lawyers have responded, the fresh representatives should again consider with great care their duty to the court and whether the proposed fresh grounds should be advanced as reasonably arguable and particularly cogent.

(iii) the Registrar will obtain, before the determination of the application under CrimPR 36.14(5), transcripts relevant to the fresh grounds and, where required, a respondents' notice relating to the fresh grounds.

(e) while an application under CrimPR 36.14(5) will not require "exceptional leave", and hence the demonstration of substantial injustice should it not be granted, the hurdle for the applicant is a high one nonetheless. Representatives should remind themselves of the provisions of paragraph 39C.2 above.

(f) permission to renew out of time an application for permission to appeal is not given unless the applicant can persuade the court that very good reasons exist. If that application to renew out of time is accompanied by an application to vary the grounds of appeal, the hurdle will be higher still.

(g) any application to substitute or add grounds will be considered by a fully constituted court and at a hearing, not on the papers.

(h) on any renewal of an application for permission to appeal accompanied by an application under CrimPR 36.14(5), if the court refuses those applications it has the power to make a loss of time order or an order for costs in line with *R v Gray and Others* [2014] EWCA Crim 2372. By analogy with *R v Kirk* [2015] EWCA Crim 1764 (where the court refused an extension of time) the court has the power to order payment of the costs of obtaining the respondent's notice and any additional transcripts.

Direct Lodgement

39C.5 With effect from 1st October 2018, Forms NG and Grounds of Appeal which are covered by Part 39 of the Criminal Procedure Rules (appeal to the Court of Appeal about conviction or sentence) are to be lodged directly with the Criminal Appeal Office and not with the Crown Court where the appellant was convicted or sentenced. This Practice Direction must be read alongside the detailed guidance notes that have been produced to accompany the new forms. They are available: https://www.justice.gov.uk/courts/procedure-rules/criminal/forms

From this date the Crown Court will no longer accept Forms NG and will return them to the sender. Forms NG and Grounds of Appeal should only be lodged once. They should, where possible, be lodged by email. Applications should not be lodged directly onto the Digital Case System. Applications must be lodged at the following address: criminalappealoffice.applications@hmcts.x.gsi.gov.uk

If you do not have access to an email account, you should post Form NG and the Grounds of Appeal to:

The Registrar, Criminal Appeal Office, Royal Courts of Justice, Strand, London WC2A 2LL.

Once an application has been effectively lodged, the Registrar will confirm receipt within 7 days.

Service

39C.6 Legal representatives should make sure they provide their secure email address for the purposes of correspondence and service of document. The date of service for new applications lodged by email will be the day on which it is sent, if that day is a business day and if sent no later than 2:30pm on that day, otherwise the date of service will be on the next business day after it was sent.

Completing the Form NG

39C.7 All applications must be compliant with the relevant Criminal Procedure Rules, particularly those in Part 39. A separate Form NG should be completed for each substantive application which is being made. Each application (conviction, sentence and confiscation order) has its own Form NG and must be drafted and lodged as a stand-alone application.

CPD IX Appeal 39D: Respondents' Notices **CPD.39D**

39D.1 The requirements for the service of respondents' notices and the time limits for doing so are as set out in Part 39 of the Criminal Procedure Rules. Any respondent's notice served should be in accordance with Rule 39.6. The Court does not require a response to the respondent's notice.

CPD IX Appeal 39E: Loss of Time **CPD.39E**

39E.1 Both the Court and the single judge have power, in their discretion, under the Criminal Appeal Act 1968 sections 29 and 31, to direct that part of the time during which an applicant is in custody after lodging his notice of application for leave to appeal should not count towards sentence. When leave to appeal has been refused by the single judge, it is necessary to consider the reasons given by the single judge before making a decision whether to renew the application. Where an application devoid of merit has been refused by the single judge he may indicate that the Full Court should consider making a direction for loss of time on renewal of the application-.However, the Full Court may make such a direction whether or not such an indication has been given by the single judge.

39E.2 The case of *R v Gray and Others* [2014] EWCA Crim 2372 makes clear 'that unmeritorious renewal applications took up a wholly disproportionate amount of staff and judicial resources in preparation and hearing time. They also wasted significant sums of public money… . The more time the Court of Appeal Office and the judges spent on unmeritorious applications, the longer the waiting times were likely to be… . The only means the court has of discouraging unmeritorious applications which waste precious time and resources is by using the powers given to us by Parliament in the Criminal Appeal Act 1968 and the Prosecution of Offenders Act 1985.'

39E.3 Further, applicants and counsel are reminded of the warning given by the Court of Appeal in *R v Hart and Others* [2006] EWCA Crim 3239, [2007] 1 Cr. App. R. 31, [2007] 2 Cr. App. R. (S.) 34 and should 'heed the fact that this court is prepared to exercise its power … . The mere fact that counsel has advised that there are grounds of appeal will not always be a sufficient answer to the question as to whether or not an application has indeed been brought which was totally without merit.'

39E.4 Where the Single Judge has not indicated that the Full Court should consider making a Loss of Time Order because the defendant has already been released, the case of *R v Terence Nolan* [2017] EWCA Crim 2449 indicates that the Single Judge should consider what, if any, costs have been incurred by the Registrar and the Prosecution and should make directions accordingly. Reference should be made to the relevant Costs Division of the Criminal Practice Direction.

CPD.39F **CPD IX Appeal 39F: Skeleton Arguments**

39F.1 Advocates should always ensure that the court, and any other party as appropriate, has a single document containing all of the points that are to be argued. The appeal notice must comply with the requirements of CrimPR 39.3. In cases of an appeal against conviction, advocates must serve a skeleton argument when the appeal notice does not sufficiently outline the grounds of the appeal, particularly in cases where a complex or novel point of law has been raised. In an appeal against sentence it may be helpful for an advocate to serve a skeleton argument when a complex issue is raised.

39F.2 The appellant's skeleton argument, if any, must be served no later than 21 days before the hearing date, and the respondent's skeleton argument, if any, no later than 14 days before the hearing date, unless otherwise directed by the Court.

39F.3 Paragraphs XII D.17 to D.23 of these Practice Directions set out the general requirements for skeleton arguments. A skeleton argument, if provided, should contain a numbered list of the points the advocate intends to argue, grouped under each ground of appeal, and stated in no more than one or two sentences. It should be as succinct as possible. Advocates should ensure that the correct Criminal Appeal Office number and the date on which the document was served appear at the beginning of any document and that their names are at the end.

39F.4 A skeleton argument must comply with the requirements of these Practice Directions and, if applicable, of the court. The Criminal Appeal Office may refuse to accept service of a document that fails to comply and instead return that document to the advocate for amendment.

CPD.39G **CPD IX Appeal 39G: Criminal Appeal Office Summaries**

39G.1 To assist the Court, the Criminal Appeal Office prepares summaries of the cases coming before it. These are entirely objective and do not contain any advice about how the Court should deal with the case or any view about its merits. They consist of two Parts.

39G.2 Part I, which is provided to all of the advocates in the case, generally contains:

(a) particulars of the proceedings in the Crown Court, including representation and details of any co-accused;
(b) particulars of the proceedings in the Court of Appeal (Criminal Division);
(c) the facts of the case, as drawn from the transcripts, appeal notice, respondent's notice, witness statements and/or the exhibits;
(d) the submissions and rulings, summing up and sentencing remarks.

39G.3 The contents of the summary are a matter for the professional judgment of the writer, but an advocate wishing to suggest any significant alteration to Part I should write to the Registrar of Criminal Appeals. If the Registrar does not agree, the summary and the letter will be put to the Court for decision. The Court will not generally be willing to hear oral argument about the content of the summary.

39G.4 Advocates may show Part I of the summary to their professional or lay clients (but to no one else) if they believe it would help to check facts or formulate arguments, but summaries are not to be copied or reproduced without the permission of the Criminal Appeal Office; permission for this will not normally be given in cases involving children, or sexual offences, or where the Crown Court has made an order restricting reporting.

39G.5 Unless a judge of the High Court or the Registrar of Criminal Appeals gives a direction to the contrary, in any particular case involving material of an explicitly salacious or sadistic nature, Part

I will also be supplied to appellants who seek to represent themselves before the Full Court, or who renew to the full court their applications for leave to appeal against conviction or sentence.

39G.6 Part II, which is supplied to the Court alone, contains:
(a) a summary of the grounds of appeal; and
(b) in appeals against sentence (and applications for such leave), summaries of the antecedent histories of the parties and of any relevant pre-sentence, medical or other reports.

39G.7 All of the source material is provided to the Court and advocates are able to draw attention to anything in it which may be of particular relevance.

CPD IX Appeal 39H: Criminal Appeal Office Bundles & Indexes for Full Court Hearings CPD.39H

39H.1 To assist the full Court, the Criminal Appeal Office will, in most instances, prepare indexed bundles containing the documents and material which the Registrar considers necessary to understand and determine the appeal for each member of the constitution.

39H.2 The Registrar will not provide bundles where a party or the parties have been directed to prepare and lodge indexed bundles, or where an advocate has lodged indexed bundles of their own volition. Where an appellant who is not privately represented is directed to lodge indexed bundles, a Representation Order will usually be granted by the Court or the Registrar for this purpose.

39H.3 Where bundles are prepared by the Criminal Appeal Office, a copy of the index will be provided to the appellant, or if the appellant is represented, to the advocate. If the advocate or appellant considers that there is additional material which it is necessary to include in the bundle, they must notify the Registrar of this in writing.

39H.4 Where indexed bundles are lodged in response to a direction to do so, or of an advocate's own volition, unless otherwise directed, four copies of the indexed bundle should be lodged with the Registrar in good time before the hearing and in accordance with any direction as to the time by which they should be lodged. The bundles should contain only documents and material which are necessary for the proper understanding of, and determination of, the issues involved in the appeal. The index and order of documents/material in the bundles should follow the order of the Registrar's template *Index to Judge's Bundles* available from the Registrar on request.

Criminal Procedure Rules Part 40 Appeal to the Court of Appeal about Reporting or Public Access Restriction

When this Part applies R40.1

40.1 (1) This Part applies where a person directly affected by an order to which section 159(1) of the Criminal Justice Act 1988[1] applies wants to appeal against that order.
(2) A reference to an 'appellant' in this Part is a reference to such a party.

[Note. Section 159(1) of the Criminal Justice Act 1988 gives a 'person aggrieved' (in this Part described as a person directly affected) a right of appeal to the Court of Appeal against a Crown Court judge's order—

(a) under section 4 or 11 of the Contempt of Court Act 1981[2];
(b) under section 58(7) of the Criminal Procedure and Investigations Act 1996[3];
(c) restricting public access to any part of a trial for reasons of national security or for the protection of a witness or other person; or
(d) restricting the reporting of any part of a trial.

See also Part 6 (Reporting, etc. restrictions) and Part 18 (Measures to assist a witness or defendant to give evidence).

The rules in Part 36 (Appeal to the Court of Appeal: general rules) also apply where this Part applies.]

Service of appeal notice R40.2

40.2 (1) An appellant must serve an appeal notice on—
(a) the Crown Court officer;
(b) the Registrar;
(c) the parties; and
(d) any other person directly affected by the order against which the appellant wants to appeal.
(2) The appellant must serve the appeal notice not later than—

[1] 1988 c. 33; section 159(1) was amended by section 61 of the Criminal Procedure and Investigations Act 1996 (c. 25).
[2] 1981 c. 49; section 4 was amended by section 57 of the Criminal Procedure and Investigations Act 1996 (c. 25), section 16 of, and Schedule 2 to, the Defamation Act 1996 (c. 31), paragraph 53 of Schedule 3 to the Criminal Justice Act 2003 (c. 44) and the Statute Law (Repeals) Act 2004 (c. 14).
[3] 1996 c. 25.

(a) the next business day after an order restricting public access to the trial; or
(b) 10 business days after an order restricting reporting of the trial.

R40.3 **Form of appeal notice**

40.3 (1) An appeal notice must be in the form set out in the Practice Direction.
(2) The appeal notice must—
(a) specify the order against which the appellant wants to appeal;
(b) identify each ground of appeal on which the appellant relies, numbering them consecutively (if there is more than one) and concisely outlining each argument in support;
(c) summarise the relevant facts;
(d) identify any relevant authorities;
(e) include or attach, with reasons—
(i) an application for permission to appeal,
(ii) any application for an extension of time within which to serve the appeal notice,
(iii) any application for a direction to attend in person a hearing that the appellant could attend by live link, if the appellant is in custody,
(iv) any application for permission to introduce evidence, and
(v) a list of those on whom the appellant has served the appeal notice;
(f) attach any document or thing that the appellant thinks the court will need to decide the appeal and include or attach an electronic link to each such document that has been made available to the Registrar under rule 36.8(1)(a) (Duty of Crown Court officer); and
(g) include or attach—
(i) an electronic copy of any authority identified under paragraph (2)(d), or
(ii) if two or more such authorities are identified, electronic copies of each together in a single electronic document.

[Note. An appellant needs the court's permission to appeal in every case to which this Part applies.

A Court of Appeal judge may give permission to appeal under section 31(2B) of the Criminal Appeal Act 1968[4]*.]*

R40.4 **Advance notice of appeal against order restricting public access**

40.4 (1) This rule applies where the appellant wants to appeal against an order restricting public access to a trial.
(2) The appellant may serve advance written notice of intention to appeal against any such order that may be made.
(3) The appellant must serve any such advance notice—
(a) on—
(i) the Crown Court officer,
(ii) the Registrar,
(iii) the parties, and
(iv) any other person who will be directly affected by the order against which the appellant intends to appeal, if it is made; and
(b) not more than 5 business days after the Crown Court officer displays notice of the application for the order.
(4) The advance notice must include the same information (with the necessary adaptations) as an appeal notice.
(5) The court must treat that advance notice as the appeal notice if the order is made.

R40.5 **Duty of applicant for order restricting public access**

40.5 (1) This rule applies where the appellant wants to appeal against an order restricting public access to a trial.
(2) The party who applied for the order must serve on the Registrar—
(a) a transcript or note of the application for the order; and
(b) any other document or thing that that party thinks the court will need to decide the appeal.
(3) That party must serve that transcript or note and any such other document or thing as soon as practicable after—

[4] 1968 c. 19; section 31(2B) was inserted by section 170 of, and paragraphs 20 and 30 of Schedule 15 to, the Criminal Justice Act 1988 (c. 33).

(a) the appellant serves the appeal notice; or
(b) the order, where the appellant served advance notice of intention to appeal.

Respondent's notice on appeal against reporting restriction **R40.6**

40.6 (1) This rule applies where the appellant wants to appeal against an order restricting the reporting of a trial.
(2) A person on whom an appellant serves an appeal notice may serve a respondent's notice, and must do so if—
(a) that person wants to make representations to the court; or
(b) the court so directs.
(3) Such a person must serve the respondent's notice on—
(a) the appellant;
(b) the Crown Court officer;
(c) the Registrar;
(d) the parties; and
(e) any other person on whom the appellant served the appeal notice.
(4) Such a person must serve the respondent's notice not more than 3 business days after—
(a) the appellant serves the appeal notice; or
(b) a direction to do so.
(5) The respondent's notice must be in the form set out in the Practice Direction.
(6) The respondent's notice must—
(a) give the date on which the respondent was served with the appeal notice;
(b) identify each ground of opposition on which the respondent relies, numbering them consecutively (if there is more than one), concisely outlining each argument in support and identifying the ground of appeal to which each relates;
(c) summarise any relevant facts not already summarised in the appeal notice;
(d) identify any relevant authorities;
(e) include or attach any application for the following, with reasons—
(i) an extension of time within which to serve the respondent's notice,
(ii) a direction to attend in person any hearing that the respondent could attend by live link, if the respondent is in custody,
(iii) permission to introduce evidence; and
(f) identify any other document or thing that the respondent thinks the court will need to decide the appeal and include or attach an electronic link to each such document that has been made available to the Registrar under rule 36.8(1)(a) (Duty of Crown Court officer); and
(g) include or attach—
(i) an electronic copy of any authority identified under paragraph (6)(d), or
(ii) if two or more such authorities are identified, electronic copies of each together in a single electronic document.

Renewing applications **R40.7**

40.7 Rule 36.5 (Renewing an application refused by a judge or the Registrar) applies with a time limit of 5 business days.

Right to introduce evidence **R40.8**

40.8 No person may introduce evidence without the court's permission.

[Note. Section 159(4) of the Criminal Justice Act 1988 entitles the parties to give evidence, subject to procedure rules.]

Right to attend hearing **R40.9**

40.9 (1) A party who is in custody has a right to attend a hearing in public of an appeal against an order restricting the reporting of a trial.
(2) The court or the Registrar may direct that such a party is to attend a hearing by live link.

[Note. See rule 36.6 (Hearings). The court may decide an application and an appeal without a hearing where the appellant wants to appeal against an order restricting public access to a trial: rule 36.6(3).]

Criminal Procedure Rules Part 41 Reference to the Court of Appeal of Point of Law or Unduly Lenient Sentencing

R41.1 **When this Part applies**

41.1 This Part applies where the Attorney General wants to—
(a) refer a point of law to the Court of Appeal under section 36 of the Criminal Justice Act 1972[1]; or
(b) refer a sentencing case to the Court of Appeal under section 36 of the Criminal Justice Act 1988[2].

[Note. Under section 36 of the Criminal Justice Act 1972, where a defendant is acquitted in the Crown Court the Attorney General may refer to the Court of Appeal a point of law in the case.

Under section 36 of the Criminal Justice Act 1988, if the Attorney General thinks the sentencing of a defendant in the Crown Court is unduly lenient he may refer the case to the Court of Appeal: but only if the sentence is one to which Part IV of the 1988 Act applies, and only if the Court of Appeal gives permission. See also section 35 of the 1988 Act[3] and the Criminal Justice Act 1988 (Reviews of Sentencing) Order 2006[4].

The rules in Part 36 (Appeal to the Court of Appeal: general rules) also apply where this Part applies.]

R41.2 **Service of notice of reference and application for permission**

41.2. (1) The Attorney General must serve any notice of reference and any application for permission to refer a sentencing case on—
(a) the Registrar; and
(b) the defendant.
(2) Where the Attorney General refers a point of law—
(a) the Attorney must give the Registrar details of—
(i) the defendant affected,
(ii) the date and place of the relevant Crown Court decision, and
(iii) the relevant verdict and sentencing; and
(b) the Attorney must give the defendant notice that—
(i) the outcome of the reference will not make any difference to the outcome of the trial, and
(ii) the defendant may serve a respondent's notice.
(3) Where the Attorney General applies for permission to refer a sentencing case, the Attorney must give the defendant notice that—
(a) the outcome of the reference may make a difference to that sentencing, and in particular may result in a more severe sentence; and
(b) the defendant may serve a respondent's notice.
(4) The Attorney General must serve an application for permission to refer a sentencing case on the Registrar not more than 28 days after the last of the sentences in that case.

[Note. The time limit for serving an application for permission to refer a sentencing case is prescribed by paragraph 1 of Schedule 3 to the Criminal Justice Act 1988[5]. It may be neither extended nor shortened.]

R41.3 **Form of notice of reference and application for permission**

41.3 (1) A notice of reference and an application for permission to refer a sentencing case must give the year and number of that reference or that case.
(2) A notice of reference of a point of law must—
(a) specify the point of law in issue and indicate the opinion that the Attorney General invites the court to give;
(b) identify each ground for that invitation, numbering them consecutively (if there is more

[1] 1972 c. 71; section 36 was amended by section 31 of, and paragraph 8 of Schedule 1 to, the Prosecution of Offences Act 1985 (c. 23) and section 40 of, and paragraph 23 of Schedule 9 to, the Constitutional Reform Act 2005 (c. 4).
[2] 1988 c. 33; section 36 was amended by section 272 of, and paragraphs 45 and 46 of Schedule 32 and paragraph 96 of Schedule 36 to, the Criminal Justice Act 2003 (c. 44), sections 49 and 65 of, and paragraph 3 of Schedule 1 and Schedule 5 to, the Violent Crime Reduction Act 2006 (c. 38), section 40 of, and paragraph 48 of Schedule 9 to, the Constitutional Reform Act 2005 (c. 4), sections 46, 148 and 149 of, and paragraphs 22 and 23 of Schedule 26 and Part 3 of Schedule 28 to, the Criminal Justice and Immigration Act 2008 (c. 4), paragraph 2 of Schedule 19 and paragraphs 4 and 5 of Schedule 26 to the Legal Aid, Sentencing and Punishment of Offenders Act 2012 (c. 10) and section 28 of, and paragraph 2 of Schedule 5 to, the Criminal Justice and Courts Act 2015 (c. 2). It is further amended by section 46 of the Criminal Justice and Immigration Act 2008 (c. 4) with effect from a date to be appointed.
[3] 1988 c. 33; section 35(3) was amended by section 168 of, and paragraph 34 of Schedule 9 to, the Criminal Justice and Public Order Act 1994 (c. 33).
[4] S.I. 2006/1116.
[5] 1988 c. 33.

than one) and concisely outlining each argument in support;
(c) exclude any reference to the defendant's name and any other reference that may identify the defendant;
(d) summarise the relevant facts; and
(e) identify any relevant authorities.

(3) An application for permission to refer a sentencing case must—
(a) give details of—
(i) the defendant affected,
(ii) the date and place of the relevant Crown Court decision, and
(iii) the relevant verdict and sentencing;
(b) explain why that sentencing appears to the Attorney General unduly lenient, concisely outlining each argument in support; and
(c) include the application for permission to refer the case to the court.

(4) A notice of reference of a sentencing case must—
(a) include the same details and explanation as the application for permission to refer the case;
(b) summarise the relevant facts; and
(c) identify any relevant authorities.

(5) Where the court gives the Attorney General permission to refer a sentencing case, it may treat the application for permission as the notice of reference.

(6) A notice of reference must include or attach—
(a) an electronic link to each material document that has been made available to the Registrar under rule 36.8(1)(a) (Duty of Crown Court officer); and
(b) an electronic copy of any authority identified under paragraph (2)(e) or (4)(c), or if two or more such authorities are identified then electronic copies of each together in a single electronic document.

Respondent's notice **R41.4**

41.4 (1) A defendant on whom the Attorney General serves a notice of reference or an application for permission to refer a sentencing case may serve a respondent's notice, and must do so if—
(a) the defendant wants to make representations to the court; or
(b) the court so directs.

(2) Such a defendant must serve the respondent's notice on—
(a) the Attorney General; and
(b) the Registrar.

(3) Such a defendant must serve the respondent's notice—
(a) where the Attorney General refers a point of law, not more than 20 business days after—
(i) the Attorney serves the reference, or
(ii) a direction to do so; or
(b) where the Attorney General applies for permission to refer a sentencing case, not more than 10 business days after—
(i) the Attorney serves the application, or
(ii) a direction to do so.

(4) Where the Attorney General refers a point of law, the respondent's notice must—
(a) give the date on which the respondent was served with the notice of reference;
(b) identify each ground of opposition on which the respondent relies, numbering them consecutively (if there is more than one), concisely outlining each argument in support and identifying the Attorney General's ground or reason to which each relates;
(c) summarise any relevant facts not already summarised in the reference;
(d) identify any relevant authorities; and
(e) include or attach any application for the following, with reasons—
(i) an extension of time within which to serve the respondent's notice,
(ii) permission to attend a hearing that the respondent does not have a right to attend, or
(iii) a direction to attend in person a hearing that the respondent could attend by live link, if the respondent is in custody.

(5) Where the Attorney General applies for permission to refer a sentencing case, the respondent's notice must—
(a) give the date on which the respondent was served with the application;
(b) say if the respondent wants to make representations at the hearing of the application or reference; and
(c) include or attach any application for the following, with reasons—
(i) an extension of time within which to serve the respondent's notice,
(ii) permission to attend a hearing that the respondent does not have a right to attend, or

(iii) a direction to attend in person a hearing that the respondent could attend by live link, if the respondent is in custody.

(6) A respondent's notice must include or attach—

(a) an electronic link to each material document that has been made available to the Registrar under rule 36.8(1)(a) (Duty of Crown Court officer); and

(b) an electronic copy of any authority identified under paragraph (4)(d), or if two or more such authorities are identified then electronic copies of each together in a single electronic document.

R41.5 Variation or withdrawal of notice of reference or application for permission

41.5 (1) This rule applies where the Attorney General wants to vary or withdraw—

(a) a notice of reference; or

(b) an application for permission to refer a sentencing case.

(2) The Attorney General—

(a) may vary or withdraw the notice or application without the court's permission by serving notice on—

(i) the Registrar, and

(ii) the defendant

before any hearing of the reference or application; but

(b) at any such hearing, may only vary or withdraw that notice or application with the court's permission.

R41.6 Right to attend hearing

41.6 (1) A respondent who is in custody has a right to attend a hearing in public unless it is a hearing preliminary or incidental to a reference, including the hearing of an application for permission to refer a sentencing case.

(2) The court or the Registrar may direct that such a respondent is to attend a hearing by live link.

[Note. See rule 36.6 (Hearings) and paragraphs 6 and 7 of Schedule 3 to the Criminal Justice Act 1988. Under paragraph 8 of that Schedule, the Court of Appeal may sentence in the absence of a defendant whose sentencing is referred.]

R41.7 Anonymity of defendant on reference of point of law

41.7 Where the Attorney General refers a point of law, the court must not allow anyone to identify the defendant during the proceedings unless the defendant gives permission.

Criminal Procedure Rules Part 42 Appeal to the Court of Appeal in Confiscation and Related Proceedings

General rules

R42.1 Extension of time

42.1 (1) An application to extend the time limit for giving notice of application for permission to appeal under Part 2 of the Proceeds of Crime Act 2002[1] must—

(a) be included in the notice of appeal; and

(b) state the grounds for the application.

(2) The parties may not agree to extend any date or time limit set by this Part or by the Proceeds of Crime Act 2002 (Appeals under Part 2) Order 2003[2].

R42.2 Other applications

42.2 Rules 39.3(2)(h) (Form of appeal notice) applies in relation to an application—

(a) by a party to an appeal under Part 2 of the Proceeds of Crime Act 2002 that, under article 7 of the Proceeds of Crime Act 2002 (Appeals under Part 2) Order 2003, a witness be ordered to attend or that the evidence of a witness be received by the Court of Appeal; or

(b) by the defendant to be given permission by the court to be present at proceedings for which permission is required under article 6 of the 2003 Order,

as it applies in relation to applications under Part I of the Criminal Appeal Act 1968[3] and the form in which rules 39.3 requires notice to be given may be modified as necessary.

1 2002 c. 29.
2 S.I. 2003/82.
3 1968 c. 19.

Examination of witness by court R42.3

42.3 Rule 36.7 (Notice of hearings and decisions) applies in relation to an order of the court under article 7 of the Proceeds of Crime Act 2002 (Appeals under Part 2) Order 2003 to require a person to attend for examination as it applies in relation to such an order of the court under Part I of the Criminal Appeal Act 1968.

Supply of documentary and other exhibits R42.4

42.4 Rule 36.11 (Registrar's duty to provide copy documents for appeal or reference) applies in relation to an appellant or respondent under Part 2 of the Proceeds of Crime Act 2002 as it applies in relation to an appellant and respondent under Part I of the Criminal Appeal Act 1968.

Registrar's power to require information from court of trial R42.5

42.5 The Registrar may require the Crown Court to provide the Court of Appeal with any assistance or information which it requires for the purposes of exercising its jurisdiction under Part 2 of the Proceeds of Crime Act 2002, the Proceeds of Crime Act 2002 (Appeals under Part 2) Order 2003 or this Part.

Hearing by single judge R42.6

42.6 Rule 36.6(6) (Hearings) applies in relation to a judge exercising any of the powers referred to in article 8 of the Proceeds of Crime Act 2002 (Appeals under Part 2) Order 2003[4] or the powers in rules 42.12(3) and (4) (Respondent's notice), 42.15(2) (Notice of appeal) and 42.16(6) (Respondent's notice), as it applies in relation to a judge exercising the powers referred to in section 31(2) of the Criminal Appeal Act 1968[5].

Determination by full court R42.7

42.7 Rule 36.5 (Renewing an application refused by a judge or the Registrar) applies where a single judge has refused an application by a party to exercise in that party's favour any of the powers listed in article 8 of the Proceeds of Crime Act 2002 (Appeals under Part 2) Order 2003, or the power in rule 42.12(3) or (4) as it applies where the judge has refused to exercise the powers referred to in section 31(2) of the Criminal Appeal Act 1968.

Notice of determination R42.8

42.8 (1) This rule applies where a single judge or the Court of Appeal has determined an application or appeal under the Proceeds of Crime Act 2002 (Appeals under Part 2) Order 2003 or under Part 2 of the Proceeds of Crime Act 2002.

(2) The Registrar must, as soon as practicable, serve notice of the determination on all of the parties to the proceedings.

(3) Where a single judge or the Court of Appeal has disposed of an application for permission to appeal or an appeal under section 31 of the 2002 Act[6], the Registrar must also, as soon as practicable, serve the order on a court officer of the court of trial and any magistrates' court responsible for enforcing any confiscation order which the Crown Court has made.

Record of proceedings and transcripts R42.9

42.9 Rule 5.5 (Recording and transcription of proceedings in the Crown Court) and rule 36.9 (Duty of person transcribing proceedings in the Crown Court) apply in relation to proceedings in respect of which an appeal lies to the Court of Appeal under Part 2 of the Proceeds of Crime Act 2002 as they apply in relation to proceedings in respect of which an appeal lies to the Court of Appeal under Part I of the Criminal Appeal Act 1968.

Appeal to the Supreme Court R42.10

42.10 (1) An application to the Court of Appeal for permission to appeal to the Supreme Court under Part 2 of the Proceeds of Crime Act 2002 must be made—

(a) orally after the decision of the Court of Appeal from which an appeal lies to the Supreme Court; or

(b) in the form set out in the Practice Direction, in accordance with article 12 of the Proceeds of Crime Act 2002 (Appeals under Part 2) Order 2003 and served on the Registrar.

(2) The application may be abandoned at any time before it is heard by the Court of Appeal by serving notice in writing on the Registrar.

[4] S.I. 2003/82.

[5] 1968 c. 19; section 31(2) was amended by section 21 of, and Schedule 2 to, the Costs in Criminal Cases Act 1973 (c. 14), section 29 of the Criminal Justice Act 1982 (c. 48), section 170 of, and paragraphs 20 and 29 of Schedule 15 to, the Criminal Justice Act 1988 (c. 33), section 87 of the Courts Act 2003 (c. 39) and section 48 of the Police and Justice Act 2006 (c. 48).

[6] 2002 c. 29; section 31 was amended by section 74 of, and paragraphs 1 and 16 of Schedule 8 to, the Serious Crime Act 2007 (c. 27).

(3) Rule 36.6(6) (Hearings) applies in relation to a single judge exercising any of the powers referred to in article 15 of the 2003 Order, as it applies in relation to a single judge exercising the powers referred to in section 31(2) of the Criminal Appeal Act 1968.
(4) Rules 36.5 (Renewing an application refused by a judge or the Registrar) applies where a single judge has refused an application by a party to exercise in that party's favour any of the powers listed in article 15 of the 2003 Order as they apply where the judge has refused to exercise the powers referred to in section 31(2) of the 1968 Act.
(5) The form in which rule 36.5(2) requires an application to be made may be modified as necessary.

Confiscation: appeal by prosecutor or person with interest in property

R42.11 **Notice of appeal**

42.11 (1) Where an appellant wishes to apply to the Court of Appeal for permission to appeal under section 31 of the Proceeds of Crime Act 2002[7], the appellant must serve a notice of appeal in the form set out in the Practice Direction on—
(a) the Crown Court officer; and
(b) the defendant.
(2) When the notice of a prosecutor's appeal about a confiscation order is served on the defendant, it must be accompanied by a respondent's notice in the form set out in the Practice Direction for the defendant to complete and a notice which—
(a) informs the defendant that the result of an appeal could be that the Court of Appeal would increase a confiscation order already imposed, make a confiscation order itself or direct the Crown Court to hold another confiscation hearing;
(b) informs the defendant of any right under article 6 of the Proceeds of Crime Act 2002 (Appeals under Part 2) Order 2003[8] to be present at the hearing of the appeal, although in custody;
(c) invites the defendant to serve any notice on the Registrar —
(i) to apply to the Court of Appeal for permission to be present at proceedings for which such permission is required under article 6 of the 2003 Order, or
(ii) to present any argument to the Court of Appeal on the hearing of the application or, if permission is given, the appeal, and whether the defendant wishes to present it in person or by means of a legal representative;
(d) draws to the defendant's attention the effect of rule 42.4 (Supply of documentary and other exhibits); and
(e) advises the defendant to consult a solicitor as soon as possible.
(3) The appellant must provide the Crown Court officer with a certificate of service stating that the appellant has served the notice of appeal on the defendant in accordance with paragraph (1) or explaining why it has not been possible to do so.

R42.12 **Respondent's notice**

42.12 (1) This rule applies where a defendant is served with a notice of appeal under rule 42.11.
(2) If the defendant wishes to oppose the application for permission to appeal, the defendant must, not more than 10 business days after service of the notice of appeal, serve on the Registrar and on the appellant a notice in the form set out in the Practice Direction—
(a) stating the date on which the notice of appeal was served;
(b) summarising the defendant's response to the arguments of the appellant; and
(c) specifying the authorities which the defendant intends to cite.
(3) The time for giving notice under this rule may be extended by the Registrar, a single judge or by the Court of Appeal.
(4) Where the Registrar refuses an application under paragraph (3) for the extension of time, the defendant is entitled to have the application determined by a single judge.
(5) Where a single judge refuses an application under paragraph (3) or (4) for the extension of time, the defendant is entitled to have the application determined by the Court of Appeal.

R42.13 **Amendment and abandonment of appeal**

42.13 (1) The appellant may amend a notice of appeal served under rule 42.11 or abandon an appeal under section 31 of the Proceeds of Crime Act 2002—
(a) without the permission of the court at any time before the Court of Appeal has begun hearing the appeal; and

[7] 2002 c. 29; section 31 was amended by section 74 of, and paragraphs 1 and 16 of Schedule 8 to, the Serious Crime Act 2007 (c. 27) and section 3 of the Serious Crime Act 2015 (c. 9).
[8] S.I. 2003/82.

(b) with the permission of the court after the Court of Appeal has begun hearing the appeal, by serving notice in writing on the Registrar.

(2) Where the appellant serves a notice abandoning an appeal under paragraph (1), the appellant must send a copy of it to—

(a) the defendant;

(b) a court officer of the court of trial; and

(c) the magistrates' court responsible for enforcing any confiscation order which the Crown Court has made.

(3) Where the appellant serves a notice amending a notice of appeal under paragraph (1), the appellant must send a copy of it to the defendant.

(4) Where an appeal is abandoned under paragraph (1), the application for permission to appeal or appeal must be treated, for the purposes of section 85 of the 2002 Act (Conclusion of proceedings), as having been refused or dismissed by the Court of Appeal.

Appeal about compliance, restraint or receivership order

Permission to appeal **R42.14**

42.14 (1) Permission to appeal to the Court of Appeal under section 13B, section 43 or section 65 of the Proceeds of Crime Act 2002[9] may only be given where—

(a) the Court of Appeal considers that the appeal would have a real prospect of success; or

(b) there is some other compelling reason why the appeal should be heard.

(2) An order giving permission to appeal may limit the issues to be heard and be made subject to conditions.

Notice of appeal **R42.15**

42.15 (1) Where an appellant wishes to apply to the Court of Appeal for permission to appeal under section 13B, 43 or 65 of the Proceeds of Crime Act 2002 Act, the appellant must serve a notice of appeal in the form set out in the Practice Direction on the Crown Court officer.

(2) Unless the Registrar, a single judge or the Court of Appeal directs otherwise, the appellant must serve the notice of appeal, accompanied by a respondent's notice in the form set out in the Practice Direction for the respondent to complete, on—

(a) each respondent;

(b) any person who holds realisable property to which the appeal relates; and

(c) any other person affected by the appeal

as soon as practicable and in any event not later than 5 business days after the notice of appeal is served on the Crown Court officer.

(3) The appellant must serve the following documents with the notice of appeal—

(a) four additional copies of the notice of appeal for the Court of Appeal;

(b) four copies of any skeleton argument;

(c) one sealed copy and four unsealed copies of any order being appealed;

(d) four copies of any witness statement or affidavit in support of the application for permission to appeal;

(e) four copies of a suitable record of the reasons for judgment of the Crown Court; and

(f) four copies of the bundle of documents used in the Crown Court proceedings from which the appeal lies.

(4) Where it is not possible to serve all of the documents referred to in paragraph (3), the appellant must indicate which documents have not yet been served and the reasons why they are not currently available.

(5) The appellant must provide the Crown Court officer with a certificate of service stating that the notice of appeal has been served on each respondent in accordance with paragraph (2) and including full details of each respondent or explaining why it has not been possible to effect service.

Respondent's notice **R42.16**

42.16 (1) This rule applies to an appeal under section 13B, 43 or 65 of the Proceeds of Crime Act 2002.

(2) A respondent may serve a respondent's notice on the Registrar.

(3) A respondent who—

(a) is seeking permission to appeal from the Court of Appeal; or

(b) wishes to ask the Court of Appeal to uphold the decision of the Crown Court for reasons different from or additional to those given by the Crown Court,

must serve a respondent's notice on the Registrar.

[9] 2002 c. 29; section 65 was amended by section 74 of, and paragraphs 1 and 32 of Schedule 8 to, the Serious Crime Act 2007 (c. 27). Section 13B was inserted by section 7 of the Serious Crime Act 2015 (c. 9).

(4) A respondent's notice must be in the form set out in the Practice Direction and where the respondent seeks permission to appeal to the Court of Appeal it must be requested in the respondent's notice.

(5) A respondent's notice must be served on the Registrar not later than 10 business days after—

(a) the date the respondent is served with notification that the Court of Appeal has given the appellant permission to appeal; or

(b) the date the respondent is served with notification that the application for permission to appeal and the appeal itself are to be heard together.

(6) Unless the Registrar, a single judge or the Court of Appeal directs otherwise, the respondent serving a respondent's notice must serve the notice on the appellant and any other respondent—

(a) as soon as practicable; and

(b) in any event not later than 5 business days,

after it is served on the Registrar.

R42.17 **Amendment and abandonment of appeal**

42.17 (1) The appellant may amend a notice of appeal served under rule 42.15 or abandon an appeal under section 13B, 43 or 65 of the Proceeds of Crime Act 2002—

(a) without the permission of the court at any time before the Court of Appeal has begun hearing the appeal; and

(b) with the permission of the court after the Court of Appeal has begun hearing the appeal,

by serving notice in writing on the Registrar.

(2) Where the appellant serves a notice under paragraph (1), the appellant must send a copy of it to each respondent.

R42.18 **Stay**

42.18 Unless the Court of Appeal or the Crown Court orders otherwise, an appeal under section 13B, 43 or 65 of the Proceeds of Crime Act 2002 does not operate as a stay of any order or decision of the Crown Court.

R42.19 **Striking out appeal notices and setting aside or imposing conditions on permission to appeal**

42.19 (1) The Court of Appeal may—

(a) strike out the whole or part of a notice of appeal served under rule 42.15; or

(b) impose or vary conditions upon which an appeal under section 13B, 43 or 65 of the Proceeds of Crime Act 2002 may be brought.

(2) The Court of Appeal may only exercise its powers under paragraph (1) where there is a compelling reason for doing so.

(3) Where a party is present at the hearing at which permission to appeal was given, that party may not subsequently apply for an order that the Court of Appeal exercise its powers under paragraph (1)(b).

R42.20 **Hearing of appeals**

42.20 (1) This rule applies to appeals under section 13B, 43 or 65 of the Proceeds of Crime Act 2002.

(2) Every appeal must be limited to a review of the decision of the Crown Court unless the Court of Appeal considers that in the circumstances of an individual appeal it would be in the interests of justice to hold a re-hearing.

(3) The Court of Appeal may allow an appeal where the decision of the Crown Court was—

(a) wrong; or

(b) unjust because of a serious procedural or other irregularity in the proceedings in the Crown Court.

(4) The Court of Appeal may draw any inference of fact which it considers justified on the evidence.

(5) At the hearing of the appeal a party may not rely on a matter not contained in that party's notice of appeal unless the Court of Appeal gives permission.

Criminal Procedure Rules Part 43 Appeal or Reference to the Supreme Court

When this Part applies **R43.1**

43.1 (1) This Part applies where—

(a) a party wants to appeal to the Supreme Court after—

(i) an application to the Court of Appeal to which Part 27 applies (Retrial following acquittal), or

(ii) an appeal to the Court of Appeal to which applies Part 37 (Appeal to the Court of Appeal against ruling at preparatory hearing), Part 38 (Appeal to the Court of Appeal against ruling adverse to prosecution), or Part 39 (Appeal to the Court of Appeal about conviction or sentence); or

(b) a party wants to refer a case to the Supreme Court after a reference to the Court of Appeal to which Part 41 applies (Reference to the Court of Appeal of point of law or unduly lenient sentencing).

(2) A reference to an 'appellant' in this Part is a reference to such a party.

[Note. Under section 33 of the Criminal Appeal Act 1968[1]*, a party may appeal to the Supreme Court from a decision of the Court of Appeal on—*

(a) an application to the court under section 76 of the Criminal Justice Act 2003[2] *(prosecutor's application for retrial after acquittal for serious offence). See also Part 27.*

(b) an appeal to the court under—

(i) section 9 of the Criminal Justice Act 1987[3] *or section 35 of the Criminal Procedure and Investigations Act 1996*[4] *(appeal against order at preparatory hearing). See also Part 37.*

(ii) section 47 of the Criminal Justice Act 2003[5] *(appeal against order for non-jury trial after jury tampering.) See also Part 37.*

(iii) Part 9 of the Criminal Justice Act 2003[6] *(prosecutor's appeal against adverse ruling). See also Part 38.*

(iv) Part 1 of the Criminal Appeal Act 1968[7] *(defendant's appeal against conviction, sentence, etc.). See also Part 39.*

Under section 13 of the Administration of Justice Act 1960[8]*, a person found to be in contempt of court may appeal to the Supreme Court from a decision of the Court of Appeal on an appeal to the court under that section. See also Part 39.*

Under article 12 of the Criminal Justice Act 2003 (Mandatory Life Sentence: Appeals in Transitional Cases) Order 2005[9]*, a party may appeal to the Supreme Court from a decision of the Court of Appeal on an appeal*

[1] 1968 c. 19; section 33 was amended by section 152 of, and Schedule 5 to, the Supreme Court Act 1981 (c. 54), section 15 of, and paragraph 3 of Schedule 2 to, the Criminal Justice Act 1987 (c. 38), section 36(1)(a) of the Criminal Procedure and Investigations Act 1996 (c. 25), section 456 of, and paragraphs 1 and 4 of Schedule 11 to, the Proceeds of Crime Act 2002 (c. 29), sections 47, 68 and 81 of the Criminal Justice Act 2003 (c. 44), by section 40 of, and paragraph 16 of Schedule 9 to, the Constitutional Reform Act 2005 (c. 4) and sections 74 and 92 of, and paragraph 144 of Schedule 8, and Schedule 14 to, the Serious Crime Act 2007 (c. 27).

[2] 2003 c. 44.

[3] 1987 c. 38; section 9 was amended by section 170 of, and Schedule 16 to, the Criminal Justice Act 1988 (c. 33), section 6 of the Criminal Justice Act 1993 (c. 36), sections 72, 74 and 80 of, and paragraph 3 of Schedule 3 and Schedule 5 to, the Criminal Procedure and Investigations Act 1996 (c. 25), sections 45 and 310 of, and paragraphs 18, 52 and 54 of Schedule 36 and Part 3 of Schedule 37 to, the Criminal Justice Act 2003 (c. 44), article 3 of, and paragraphs 21 and 23 of S.I. 2004/2035, section 59 of, and paragraph 1 of Schedule 11 to, the Constitutional Reform Act 2005 (c. 4) and Part 10 of Schedule 10 to the Protection of Freedoms Act 2012 (c. 9). The amendment made by section 45 of the Criminal Justice Act 2003 (c. 44) is in force for certain purposes; for remaining purposes it has effect from a date to be appointed.

[4] 1996 c. 25; section 35(1) was amended by section 45 of the Criminal Justice Act 2003 (c. 44). The amendment is in force for certain purposes, for remaining purposes it has effect from a date to be appointed. Section 35 was also amended by paragraphs 65 and 69 of Schedule 36 to the Criminal Justice Act 2003 (c. 44) and section 59 of, and paragraph 1 of Schedule 11 to, the Constitutional Reform Act 2005 (c. 4) and Part 10 of Schedule 10 to the Protection of Freedoms Act 2012 (c. 9).

[5] 2003 c. 44; section 47 was amended by section 59(5) of, and paragraph 1(2) of Schedule 11 to, the Constitutional Reform Act 2005 (c. 4).

[6] 2003 c. 44.

[7] 1968 c. 19.

[8] 1960 c. 65; section 13 was amended paragraph 40 of Schedule 8 to, the Courts Act 1971 (c. 23), Schedule 5 to, the Criminal Appeal Act 1968 (c. 19), paragraph 36 of Schedule 7 to, the Magistrates' Courts Act 1980 (c. 43), Schedule 7 to, the Supreme Court Act 1981 (c. 54), paragraph 25 of Schedule 2 to, the County Courts Act 1984 (c. 28), Schedule 15 to, the Access to Justice Act 1999 (c. 22), paragraph 13 of Schedule 9 to the Constitutional Reform Act 2005 (c. 4) and paragraph 45 of Schedule 16 to, the Armed Forces Act 2006 (c. 52).

[9] S.I. 2005/2798.

to the court under paragraph 14 of Schedule 22 to the Criminal Justice Act 2003[10] *(appeal against minimum term review decision). See also Part 39.*

Under article 15 of the Serious Organised Crime and Police Act 2005 (Appeals under Section 74) Order 2006[11]*, a party may appeal to the Supreme Court from a decision of the Court of Appeal on an appeal to the court under section 74 of the Serious Organised Crime and Police Act 2005*[12] *(appeal against sentence review decision). See also Part 39.*

Under section 24 of the Serious Crime Act 2007[13]*, a party may appeal to the Supreme Court from a decision of the Court of Appeal on an appeal to that court under that section (appeal about a serious crime prevention order). See also Part 39.*

Under section 36(3) of the Criminal Justice Act 1972[14]*, the Court of Appeal may refer to the Supreme Court a point of law referred by the Attorney General to the court. See also Part 41.*

Under section 36(5) of the Criminal Justice Act 1988[15]*, a party may refer to the Supreme Court a sentencing decision referred by the Attorney General to the court. See also Part 41.*

Under section 33(3) of the Criminal Appeal Act 1968, there is no appeal to the Supreme Court—

(a) from a decision of the Court of Appeal on an appeal under section 14A(5A) of the Football Spectators Act 1989[16] *(prosecutor's appeal against failure to make football banning order). See Part 39.*

(b) from a decision of the Court of Appeal on an appeal under section 159(1) of the Criminal Justice Act 1988[17] *(appeal about reporting or public access restriction). See Part 40.*

The rules in Part 36 (Appeal to the Court of Appeal: general rules) also apply where this Part applies.]

R43.2 Application for permission or reference

43.2 (1) An appellant must—

(a) apply orally to the Court of Appeal—

(i) for permission to appeal or to refer a sentencing case, or

(ii) to refer a point of law

immediately after the court gives the reasons for its decision; or

(b) apply in writing and serve the application on the Registrar and every other party not more than—

(i) 14 days after the court gives the reasons for its decision if that decision was on a sentencing reference to which Part 41 applies (Attorney General's reference of sentencing case), or

(ii) 28 days after the court gives those reasons in any other case.

(2) An application for permission to appeal or to refer a sentencing case must—

(a) identify the point of law of general public importance that the appellant wants the court to certify is involved in the decision; and

(b) give reasons why—

(i) that point of law ought to be considered by the Supreme Court, and

(ii) the court ought to give permission to appeal.

(3) An application to refer a point of law must give reasons why that point ought to be considered by the Supreme Court.

(4) An application must include or attach any application for the following, with reasons—

(a) an extension of time within which to make the application for permission or for a reference;

[10] 2003 c. 44; paragraph 14 of Schedule 22 was amended by section 40 of, and paragraph 82 of Schedule 9 and paragraph 1 of Schedule 11 to, the Constitutional Reform Act 2005 (c. 4).

[11] S.I. 2006/2135.

[12] 2005 c. 15.

[13] 2007 c. 27.

[14] 1972 c. 71; section 36(3) was amended by section 40 of, and paragraph 23 of Schedule 9 to, the Constitutional Reform Act 2005 (c. 4).

[15] 1988 c. 33; section 36(5) was amended by section 40(4) of, and paragraph 48(1) and (2) of Schedule 9 to, the Constitutional Reform Act 2005 (c. 4).

[16] 1989 c. 37; section 14A(5A) was inserted by section 52 of, and paragraphs 1 and 3 of Schedule 3 to, the Violent Crime Reduction Act 2006 (c. 38).

[17] 1988 c. 33; section 159(1) was amended by section 61 of the Criminal Procedure and Investigations Act 1996 (c. 25).

(b) bail pending appeal; or

(c) permission to attend any hearing in the Supreme Court, if the appellant is in custody.

(5) A written application must be in the form set out in the Practice Direction.

[Note. In some legislation, including the Criminal Appeal Act 1968, permission to appeal is described as 'leave to appeal'.

Under the provisions listed in the note to rule 43.1, except section 36(3) of the Criminal Justice Act 1972 (Attorney General's reference of point of law), an appellant needs permission to appeal or to refer a sentencing case. Under those provisions, the Court of Appeal must not give permission unless it first certifies that—

(a) a point of law of general public importance is involved in the decision, and

(b) it appears to the court that the point is one which the Supreme Court ought to consider.

If the Court of Appeal gives such a certificate but refuses permission, an appellant may apply for such permission to the Supreme Court.

Under section 36(3) of the Criminal Justice Act 1972 an appellant needs no such permission. The Court of Appeal may refer the point of law to the Supreme Court, or may refuse to do so.

For the power of the court or the Registrar to shorten or extend a time limit, see rule 36.3. The time limit in this rule—

(a) for applying for permission to appeal under section 33 of the Criminal Appeal Act 1968 (28 days) is prescribed by section 34 of that Act[18]. That time limit may be extended but not shortened by the court. But it may be extended on an application by a prosecutor only after an application to which Part 27 applies (Retrial after acquittal).

(b) for applying for permission to refer a case under section 36(5) of the Criminal Justice Act 1988 (Attorney General's reference of sentencing decision: 14 days) is prescribed by paragraph 4 of Schedule 3 to that Act. That time limit may be neither extended nor shortened.

(c) for applying for permission to appeal under article 12 of the Criminal Justice Act 2003 (Mandatory Life Sentence: Appeals in Transitional Cases) Order 2005 (28 days) is prescribed by article 13 of that Order. That time limit may be extended but not shortened.

(d) for applying for permission to appeal under article 15 of the Serious Organised Crime and Police Act 2005 (Appeals under Section 74) Order 2006 (28 days) is prescribed by article 16 of that Order. That time limit may be extended but not shortened.

For the power of the Court of Appeal to grant bail pending appeal to the Supreme Court, see—

(a) section 36 of the Criminal Appeal Act 1968[19];

(b) article 18 of the Serious Organised Crime and Police Act 2005 (Appeals under Section 74) Order 2006[20].

For the right of an appellant in custody to attend a hearing in the Supreme Court, see—

(a) section 38 of the Criminal Appeal Act 1968[21];

(b) paragraph 9 of Schedule 3 to the Criminal Justice Act 1988[22];

(c) article 15 of the Criminal Justice Act 2003 (Mandatory Life Sentences: Appeals in Transitional Cases) Order 2005[23];

(d) article 20 of the Serious Organised Crime and Police Act 2005 (Appeals under Section 74) Order 2006[24].]

[18] 1968 c. 19; section 34 was amended by section 88 of the Courts Act 2003 (c. 39), section 81 of the Criminal Justice Act 2003 (c. 44), and section 40(4) of, and paragraph 16 of Schedule 9 to, the Constitutional Reform Act 2005 (c. 4).

[19] 1968 c. 19; section 36 was amended by section 12 of, and paragraph 43 of Schedule 2 to, the Bail Act 1976 (c. 63), section 15 of, and paragraph 4 of Schedule 2 to, the Criminal Justice Act 1987 (c. 38), section 168 of, and paragraph 23 of Schedule 10 to, the Criminal Justice and Public Order Act 1994 (c. 33), section 36 of the Criminal Procedure and Investigations Act 1996 (c. 25), sections 47 and 68 of the Criminal Justice Act 2003 (c. 44) and section 40 of, and paragraph 16 of Schedule 9 to, the Constitutional Reform Act 2005 (c. 4).

[20] S.I. 2006/2135.

[21] 1968 c. 19; section 38 was amended by section 81 of the Criminal Justice Act 2003 (c. 44), and section 40(4) of, and paragraph 16 of Schedule 9 to, the Constitutional Reform Act 2005 (c. 4).

[22] 1988 c. 33; paragraph 9 of Schedule 3 was amended by section 40 of, and paragraph 48 of Schedule 9 to, the Constitutional Reform Act 2005 (c. 4).

[23] S.I. 2005/2798.

[24] S.I. 2006/2135.

R43.3 **Determination of detention pending appeal, etc.**

43.3 On an application for permission to appeal, the Court of Appeal must—
(a) decide whether to order the detention of a defendant who would have been liable to be detained but for the decision of the court; and
(b) determine any application for—
(i) bail pending appeal,
(ii) permission to attend any hearing in the Supreme Court, or
(iii) a representation order.

[Note. For the liability of a defendant to be detained pending a prosecutor's appeal to the Supreme Court and afterwards, see—
(a) section 37 of the Criminal Appeal Act 1968[25];
(b) article 19 of the Serious Organised Crime and Police Act 2005 (Appeals under Section 74) Order 2006[26].

For the grant of legal aid for proceedings in the Supreme Court, see sections 14, 16 and 19 of the Legal Aid, Sentencing and Punishment of Offenders Act 2012[27].]

R43.4 **Bail pending appeal**

43.4 Rules 39.8 (Application for bail pending appeal or retrial), 39.9 (Conditions of bail pending appeal or re-trial) and 39.10 (Forfeiture of a recognizance given as a condition of bail) apply.

Criminal Procedure Rules Part 44 Reopening a Case in a Magistrates' Court

R44.1 **When this Part applies**

44.1 (1)
(a) under section 14 or section 16E of the Magistrates' Courts Act 1980[1], the defendant makes a statutory declaration of not having found out about the case until after the trial began; or
(b) under section 142 of the 1980 Act[2], the court can—
(i) set aside a conviction, or
(ii) vary or rescind a costs order, or an order to which Part 31 applies (Behaviour orders).

R44.2 **Statutory declaration of ignorance of proceedings**

44.2 (1) This rule applies where—
(a) the case started with—
(i) an application for a summons,
(ii) a written charge and requisition, or
(iii) a written charge and single justice procedure notice; and
(b) under section 14 or section 16E of the Magistrates' Courts Act 1980[3], the defendant makes a statutory declaration of not having found out about the case until after the trial began.

(2) The defendant must—
(a) serve such a declaration on the court officer —
(i) not more than 21 days after the date of finding out about the case, or
(ii) with an explanation for the delay, if serving it more than 21 days after that date; and
(b) serve with the declaration one of the following, as appropriate, if the case began with a written charge and single justice procedure notice—
(i) a notice under rule 24.9(4)(a) (notice of guilty plea), with any representations that the defendant wants the court to consider and a statement of the defendant's assets and other financial circumstances, as required by that rule,

[25] 1968 c. 19; section 37 was amended by section 65(1) of, and paragraph 39 of Schedule 3 to, the Mental Health (Amendment) Act 1982 (c. 51), section 148 of, and paragraph 23 of Schedule 4 to, the Mental Health Act 1983 (c. 20), section 58(1) of, and paragraph 5 of Schedule 10 to, the Domestic Violence, Crime and Victims Act 2004 (c. 28), section 40 of, and paragraph 16 of Schedule 9 to, the Constitutional Reform Act 2005 (c. 4) and section 47 of, and paragraphs 1 and 13 of Schedule 8 to, the Criminal Justice and Immigration Act 2008 (c. 4).
[26] S.I. 2006/2135.
[27] 2012 c. 10.
[1] 1980 c. 43; section 14 was amended by section 109 of, and paragraph 205 of Schedule 8 to, the Courts Act 2003 (c. 39). Section 16E was inserted by section 48 of the Criminal Justice and Courts Act 2015 (c. 2).
[2] 1980 c. 43; section 142 was amended by sections 26 and 29 of, and Schedule 3 to, the Criminal Appeal Act 1995 (c. 35).
[3] 1980 c. 43; section 14 was amended by section 109 of, and paragraph 205 of Schedule 8 to, the Courts Act 2003 (c. 39). Section 16E was inserted by section 48 of the Criminal Justice and Courts Act 2015 (c. 2).

(ii) a notice under rule 24.9(4)(b) (notice of intention to plead guilty at a hearing before a court comprising more than one justice), or
(iii) a notice under rule 24.9(4)(c) (notice of intention to plead not guilty).

(3) The court may extend that time limit, even after it has expired—
(a) at a hearing, in public or in private; or
(b) without a hearing.

(4) Where the defendant serves such a declaration, in time or with an extension of time in which to do so, and the case began with a summons or requisition—
(a) the court must treat the summons or requisition and all subsequent proceedings as void (but not the application for the summons or the written charge with which the case began);
(b) if the defendant is present when the declaration is served, the rules in Part 24 (Trial and sentence in a magistrates' court) apply as if the defendant had been required to attend the court on that occasion; and
(c) if the defendant is absent when the declaration is served—
(i) the rules in Part 7 apply (Starting a prosecution in a magistrates' court) as if the prosecutor had just served an application for a summons in the same terms as the original application or written charge;
(ii) the court may exercise its power to issue a summons in accordance with those rules; and
(iii) except for rule 24.8 (Written guilty plea: special rules), the rules in Part 24 then apply.

(5) Where the defendant serves such a declaration, in time or with an extension of time in which to do so, and the case began with a single justice procedure notice—
(a) the court must treat the single justice procedure notice and all subsequent proceedings as void (but not the written charge with which the case began);
(b) rule 24.9 (Single justice procedure: special rules) applies as if the defendant had served the notice required by paragraph (2)(b) of this rule within the time allowed by rule 24.9(4); and
(c) where that notice is under rule 24.9(4)(b) (notice of intention to plead guilty at a hearing before a court comprising more than one justice) or under rule 24.9(4)(c) (notice of intention to plead not guilty), then—
(i) if the defendant is present when the declaration is served, the rules in this Part apply as if the defendant had been required to attend the court on that occasion, or
(ii) if the defendant is absent when the declaration is served, paragraph (6) of this rule applies.

(6) Where this paragraph applies, the court must exercise its power to issue a summons and—
(a) the rules in Part 7 apply (Starting a prosecution in a magistrates' court) as if the prosecutor had just served an application for a summons in the same terms as the written charge;
(b) except for rule 24.8 (Written guilty plea: special rules) and rule 24.9 (Single justice procedure: special rules), the rules in Part 24 apply.

(7) A court officer may take the statutory declaration to which this rule refers if that officer—
(a) is a justices' legal adviser; or
(b) is nominated for the purpose by such a legal adviser.

[Note. Under sections 14 and 16E of the Magistrates' Courts Act 1980, proceedings which begin with a summons, requisition or single justice procedure notice will become void if the defendant, at any time during or after the trial, makes a statutory declaration that he or she did not know of them until a date after the trial began.

Under section 14(3) or section 16E(9) of the 1980 Act, the court which decides whether or not to extend the time limit for serving a declaration under this rule may comprise a single justice.

Section 2 of the Commissioners for Oaths Act 1889[4] *allows rules that regulate the procedure of a court to authorise the taking of a statutory declaration by an officer of that court.*

The Practice Direction sets out a form of declaration for use in connection with this rule.]

Setting aside a conviction or varying a costs, etc. order **R44.3**

44.3 (1) This rule applies where under section 142 of the Magistrates' Courts Act 1980[5], the court can—
(a) set aside a conviction, or

[4] 1889 c. 10; section 2 was amended by section 59 of, and paragraph 15 of Schedule 11 to, the Constitutional Reform Act 2005 (c. 4).

[5] 1980 c. 43; section 142 was amended by sections 26 and 29 of, and Schedule 3 to, the Criminal Appeal Act 1995 (c. 35).

(b) vary or rescind—
(i) a costs order, or
(ii) an order to which Part 31 applies (Behaviour orders).

(2) The court may exercise its power—
(a) on application by a party, or on its own initiative; and
(b) at a hearing, in public or in private, or without a hearing.

(3) The court must not exercise its power in a party's absence unless—
(a) the court makes a decision proposed by that party;
(b) the court makes a decision to which that party has agreed in writing; or
(c) that party has had an opportunity to make representations at a hearing (whether or not that party in fact attends).

(4) A party who wants the court to exercise its power must—
(a) apply in writing as soon as reasonably practicable after the conviction or order that that party wants the court to set aside, vary or rescind;
(b) serve the application on—
(i) the court officer, and
(ii) each other party; and
(c) in the application—
(i) explain why, as appropriate, the conviction should be set aside, or the order varied or rescinded,
(ii) specify any variation of the order that the applicant proposes,
(iii) identify any witness that the defendant wants to call, and any other proposed evidence,
(iv) say whether the defendant waives legal professional privilege, giving any relevant name and date, and
(v) if the application is late, explain why.

(5) The court may—
(a) extend (even after it has expired) the time limit under paragraph (4), unless the court's power to set aside the conviction, or vary the order, can no longer be exercised; and
(b) allow an application to be made orally.

[Note. Under section 142 of the Magistrates' Courts Act 1980—

(a) where a defendant is convicted by a magistrates' court, the court may order that the case should be heard again by different justices; and

(b) the court may vary or rescind an order which it has made when dealing with a convicted defendant,

if in either case it appears to the court to be in the interests of justice to do so.

The power cannot be exercised if the Crown Court or the High Court has determined an appeal about that conviction or order.

See also rule 28.4 (Variation of sentence), which applies to an application under section 142 of the 1980 Act to vary or rescind a sentence.]

Criminal Practice Directions Part 44 Request to the European Court for a Preliminary Ruling

CPD.44A **CPD IX Appeal 44A: References to the European Court of Justice**

44A.1 Further to rule 44.3 of the Criminal Procedure Rules, the order containing the reference shall be filed with the Senior Master of the Queen's Bench Division of the High Court for onward transmission to the Court of Justice of the European Union. The order should be marked for the attention of Mrs Isaac and sent to the Senior Master:
c/o Queen's Bench Division Associates Dept
Room WG03
Royal Courts of Justice
Strand
London
WC2A 2LL

44A.2 There is no longer a requirement that the relevant court file be sent to the Senior Master. The parties should ensure that all appropriate documentation is sent directly to the European Court at the following address:
The Registrar
Court of Justice of the European Union

Kirchberg
L-2925 Luxemburg

44A.3 There is no prescribed form for use but the following details must be included in the back sheet to the order:

i. Solicitor's full address;
ii. Solicitor's and Court references;
iii. Solicitor's e-mail address.

44A.4 The European Court of Justice regularly updates its Recommendation to national courts and tribunals in relation to the initiation of preliminary ruling proceedings. The current Recommendation is 2012/C 338/01: eurlex.europa.eu/LexUriServ/LexUriServ.do?uri=OJ:C:2012:338:0001:0006:EN:PDF

44A.5 The referring court may request the Court of Justice of the European Union to apply its urgent preliminary ruling procedure where the referring court's proceedings relate to a person in custody. For further information see Council Decision 2008/79/EC [2008] OJ L24/42: http://eurlex.europa.eu/LexUriServ/LexUriServ.do?uri=OJ:L:2008:024:0042:0043:EN:PDF

44A.6 Any such request must be made in a document separate from the order or in a covering letter and must set out:

iv. The matters of fact and law which establish the urgency;
v. The reasons why the urgent preliminary ruling procedure applies; and
vi. In so far as possible, the court's view on the answer to the question referred to the Court of Justice of the European Union for a preliminary ruling.

44A.7 Any request to apply the urgent preliminary ruling procedure should be filed with the Senior Master as described above.

Criminal Procedure Rules Part 45 Costs

General rules

When this Part applies **R45.1**

45.1 (1) This Part applies where the court can make an order about costs under—

(a) Part II of the Prosecution of Offences Act 1985[1] and Part II, IIA or IIB of The Costs in Criminal Cases (General) Regulations 1986[2];
(b) section 109 of the Magistrates' Courts Act 1980[3];
(c) section 52 of the Senior Courts Act 1981[4] and rule 45.6 or rule 45.7;
(d) section 8 of the Bankers Books Evidence Act 1879[5];
(e) section 2C(8) of the Criminal Procedure (Attendance of Witnesses) Act 1965[6];
(f) section 36(5) of the Criminal Justice Act 1972[7];
(g) section 159(5) and Schedule 3, paragraph 11, of the Criminal Justice Act 1988[8];
(h) section 14H(5) of the Football Spectators Act 1989[9];
(i) section 4(7) of the Dangerous Dogs Act 1991[10];
(j) Part 3 of the Serious Crime Act 2007 (Appeals under Section 24) Order 2008[11]; or
(k) Part 1 or 2 of the Extradition Act 2003[12].

(2) In this Part, 'costs' means—

(a) the fees payable to a legal representative;

[1] 1985 c. 23.
[2] S.I. 1986/1335.
[3] 1980 c. 43; section 109(2) was amended by section 109 of, and paragraph 234 of Schedule 8 to, the Courts Act 2003 (c. 39).
[4] 1981 c. 54. The Act's title was amended by section 59(5) of, and paragraph 1 of Schedule 11 to, the Constitutional Reform Act 2005 (c. 4).
[5] 1879 c. 11.
[6] 1965 c. 69; section 2C was substituted with section 2, 2A, 2B, 2D and 2E, for the existing section 2 by section 66(1) and (2) of the Criminal Procedure and Investigations Act 1996 (c. 25).
[7] 1972 c. 71; section 36(5) was amended by section 40 of, and paragraph 23 of Schedule 9 to, the Constitutional Reform Act 2005 (c. 4).
[8] 1988 c. 33; paragraph 11 of Schedule 3 was amended by section 40 of, and paragraph 48 of Schedule 9 to, the Constitutional Reform Act 2005 (c. 4) and paragraph 11 and Part 4 of Schedule 7 to the Legal Aid, Sentencing and Punishment of Offenders Act 2012 (c. 10).
[9] 1989 c. 37; section 14H was substituted, together with sections 14, 14A-14G and 14J, for existing sections 14-17, by section 1 of, and paragraphs 1 and 2 of Schedule 1 to, the Football (Disorder) Act 2000 (c. 25).
[10] 1991 c. 65.
[11] S.I. 2008/1863.
[12] 2003 c. 41.

(b) the disbursements paid by a legal representative; and
(c) any other expenses incurred in connection with the case.

[Note. A costs order can be made under—

(a) section 16 of the Prosecution of Offences Act 1985[13] (defence costs), for the payment out of central funds of a defendant's costs (see rule 45.4);
(b) section 17 of the Prosecution of Offences Act 1985[14] (prosecution costs), for the payment out of central funds of a private prosecutor's costs (see rule 45.4);
(c) section 18 of the Prosecution of Offences Act 1985[15] (award of costs against accused), for the payment by a defendant of another person's costs (see rules 45.5 and 45.6);
(d) section 19(1) of the Prosecution of Offences Act 1985[16] and regulation 3 of the Costs in Criminal Cases (General) Regulations 1986, for the payment by a party of another party's costs incurred as a result of an unnecessary or improper act or omission by or on behalf of the first party (see rule 45.8);
(e) section 19A of the Prosecution of Offences Act 1985[17] (costs against legal representatives, etc.)—
  (i) for the payment by a legal representative of a party's costs incurred as a result of an improper, unreasonable or negligent act or omission by or on behalf of the representative, or
  (ii) disallowing the payment to that representative of such costs (see rule 45.9);
(f) section 19B of the Prosecution of Offences Act 1985[18] (provision for award of costs against third parties) and regulation 3F of the Costs in Criminal Cases (General) Regulations 1986[19], for the payment by a person who is not a party of a party's costs where there has been serious misconduct by the non-party (see rule 45.10);
(g) section 109 of the Magistrates' Courts Act 1980, section 52 of the Senior Courts Act 1981 and rule 45.6, for the payment by an appellant of a respondent's costs on abandoning an appeal to the Crown Court (see rule 45.6);
(h) section 52 of the Senior Courts Act 1981 and—
  (i) rule 45.6, for the payment by a party of another party's costs on an appeal to the Crown Court in any case not covered by (c) or (g),
  (ii) rule 45.7, for the payment by a party of another party's costs on an application to the Crown Court about the breach or variation of a deferred prosecution agreement, or on an application to lift the suspension of a prosecution after breach of such an agreement;
(i) section 8 of the Bankers Books Evidence Act 1879, for the payment of costs by a party or by the bank against which an application for an order is made (see rule 45.7);
(j) section 2C(8) of the Criminal Procedure (Attendance of Witnesses) Act 1965, for the payment by the applicant for a witness summons of the costs of a party who applies successfully under rule 17.7 to have it withdrawn (see rule 45.7);
(k) section 36(5) of the Criminal Justice Act 1972 or Schedule 3, paragraph 11, of the Criminal Justice Act 1988, for the payment out of central funds of a defendant's costs on a reference by the Attorney General of—
  (i) a point of law, or
  (ii) an unduly lenient sentence
  (see rule 45.4);
(l) section 159(5) of the Criminal Justice Act 1988, for the payment by a person of another person's costs on an appeal about a reporting or public access restriction (see rule 45.6);

[13] 1985 c. 23; section 16 was amended by section 15 of, and paragraphs 14 and 15 of Schedule 2 to, the Criminal Justice Act 1987 (c. 38), section 150 of, and paragraph 103 of Schedule 15 to, the Criminal Justice Act 1988 (c. 33), section 7 of, and paragraph 7 of Schedule 3 to, the Criminal Procedure (Insanity and Unfitness to Plead) Act 1991 (c. 25), sections 69 and 312 of, and paragraph 57 of Schedule 3, and Part 4 of Schedule 37, to the Criminal Justice Act 2003 (c. 44), section 58 of, and Schedule 11 to, the Domestic Violence, Crime and Victims Act 2004 (c. 28), section 40 of, and paragraph 23 of Schedule 9 to, the Constitutional Reform Act 2005 (c. 4) and paragraphs 1 and 2 and Part 4 of Schedule 7 to the Legal Aid, Sentencing and Punishment of Offenders Act 2012 (c. 10).
[14] 1985 c. 23; section 17 was amended by section 40 of, and paragraph 41 of Schedule 9 to, the Constitutional Reform Act 2005 (c. 4) and paragraphs 1 and 4 and Part 4 of Schedule 7 to the Legal Aid, Sentencing and Punishment of Offenders Act 2012 (c. 10).
[15] 1985 c. 23; section 18 was amended by section 15 of, and paragraph 16 of Schedule 2 to, the Criminal Justice Act 1987 (c. 38), section 168 of, and paragraph 26 of Schedule 9 to, the Criminal Justice and Public Order Act 1994 (c. 33), sections 69 and 312 of the Criminal Justice Act 2003 (c. 44) and section 40 of, and paragraph 41 of Schedule 9 to, the Constitutional Reform Act 2005 (c. 4).
[16] 1985 c. 23.
[17] 1985 c. 23; section 19A was inserted by section 111 of the Courts and Legal Services Act 1990 (c. 41).
[18] 1985 c. 23; section 19B was inserted by section 93 of the Courts Act 2003 (c. 39).
[19] S.I. 1986/1335; regulation 3F was inserted by regulation 7 of S.I. 2004/2408 and amended by regulations 2 and 5 of S.I. 2008/2448.

(m) section 14H(5) of the Football Spectators Act 1989, for the payment by a defendant of another person's costs on an application to terminate a football banning order (see rule 45.7);
(n) section 4(7) of the Dangerous Dogs Act 1991, for the payment by a defendant of another person's costs on an application to terminate a disqualification for having custody of a dog (see rule 45.7);
(o) article 14 of the Serious Crime Act 2007 (Appeals under Section 24) Order 2008[20], corresponding with section 16 of the Prosecution of Offences Act 1985 (see rule 45.4);
(p) article 15 of the Serious Crime Act 2007 (Appeals under Section 24) Order 2008, corresponding with section 18 of the Prosecution of Offences Act 1985 (see rule 45.6);
(q) article 16 of the Serious Crime Act 2007 (Appeals under Section 24) Order 2008, corresponding with an order under section 19(1) of the 1985 Act (see rule 45.8);
(r) article 17 of the Serious Crime Act 2007 (Appeals under Section 24) Order 2008, corresponding with an order under section 19A of the 1985 Act (see rule 45.9);
(s) article 18 of the Serious Crime Act 2007 (Appeals under Section 24) Order 2008, corresponding with an order under section 19B of the 1985 Act (see rule 45.10);
(t) section 60 or 133 of the Extradition Act 2003 (costs where extradition ordered) for the payment by a defendant of another person's costs (see rule 45.4); or
(u) section 61 or 134 of the Extradition Act 2003[21] (costs where discharge ordered) for the payment out of central funds of a defendant's costs (see rule 45.4).

See also the Criminal Costs Practice Direction.

Part 39 (Appeal to the Court of Appeal about conviction or sentence) contains rules about appeals against costs orders made in the Crown Court under the legislation listed in (c) above.

Part 34 (Appeal to the Crown Court) and Part 39 (Appeal to the Court of Appeal about conviction or sentence) contain rules about appeals against costs orders made under the legislation listed in (e) and (f) above.

As to costs in restraint or receivership proceedings under Part 2 of the Proceeds of Crime Act 2002[22], see rules 33.47 to 33.50.

A costs order can be enforced—
(a) against a defendant, under section 41(1) or (3) of the Administration of Justice Act 1970[23];
(b) against a prosecutor, under section 41(2) or (3) of the Administration of Justice Act 1970;
(c) against a representative, under regulation 3D of the Costs in Criminal Cases (General) Regulations 1986[24] or article 18 of the Serious Crime Act 2007 (Appeals under Section 24) Order 2008;
(d) against a non-party, under regulation 3I of the Costs in Criminal Cases (General) Regulations 1986[25] or article 31 of the Serious Crime Act 2007 (Appeals under Section 24) Order 2008[26].

See also section 58, section 150(1) and Part III of the Magistrates' Courts Act 1980[27] and Schedule 5 to the Courts Act 2003[28].]

Costs orders: general rules **R45.2**

45.2 (1) The court must not make an order about costs unless each party and any other person directly affected—
(a) is present; or
(b) has had an opportunity—
(i) to attend, or
(ii) to make representations.

[20] S.I. 2008/1863.
[21] 2003 c. 41; sections 61 and 134 were amended by paragraphs 12, 13 and 16 and Part 4 of Schedule 7 to the Legal Aid, Sentencing and Punishment of Offenders Act 2012 (c. 10).
[22] 2002 c. 29.
[23] 1970 c. 31; section 41(3) was amended by section 62 of, and paragraph 35 of Schedule 13 to the Tribunals, Courts and Enforcement Act 2007 (c. 15) and section 17 of, and paragraph 52 of Schedule 9 to, the Crime and Courts Act 2013 (c. 22).
[24] S.I. 1986/1335; regulation 3D was inserted by article 2 of S.I. 1991/789 and amended by regulation 6 of S.I. 2004/2408.
[25] S.I. 1986/1335; regulation 3I was inserted by regulation 7 of S.I. 2004/2408.
[26] S.I. 2008/1863.
[27] 1980 c. 43; section 58 was amended by section 33 of, and paragraph 80 of Schedule 2 to, the Family Law Reform Act 1987 (c. 42); a relevant amendment was made to section 150(1) by paragraph 250 of Schedule 8, and Schedule 10 to, the Courts Act 2003 (c. 39).
[28] 2003 c. 39; Schedule 5 was amended by articles 2, 4, 6, 7 and 8 of S.I. 2006/1737, section 62 of, and paragraphs 148 and 149 of Schedule 13 to, the Tribunals, Courts and Enforcement Act 2007 (c. 15), section 80 of the Criminal Justice and Immigration Act 2008 (c. 4), section 88 of the Legal Aid, Sentencing and Punishment of Offenders Act 2012 (c. 10), section 10 of, and paragraphs 24 and 27 of the Schedule to, the Prevention of Social Housing Fraud Act 2013 (c. 3), section 27 of the Crime and Courts Act 2013 (c. 22) and section 56 of the Criminal Justice and Courts Act 2015 (c. 2). It is further amended by section 26 of the Crime and Courts Act 2013 (c. 22) and paragraph 23 of Schedule 5 to the Modern Slavery Act 2015 (c. 30), with effect from dates to be appointed.

(2) The court may make an order about costs—
(a) at a hearing in public or in private; or
(b) without a hearing.
(3) In deciding what order, if any, to make about costs, the court must have regard to all the circumstances, including—
(a) the conduct of all the parties; and
(b) any costs order already made.
(4) If the court makes an order about costs, it must—
(a) specify who must, or must not, pay what, to whom; and
(b) identify the legislation under which the order is made, where there is a choice of powers.
(5) The court must give reasons if it—
(a) refuses an application for a costs order; or
(b) rejects representations opposing a costs order.
(6) If the court makes an order for the payment of costs—
(a) the general rule is that it must be for an amount that is sufficient reasonably to compensate the recipient for costs—
(i) actually, reasonably and properly incurred, and
(ii) reasonable in amount; but
(b) the court may order the payment of—
(i) a proportion of that amount,
(ii) a stated amount less than that amount,
(iii) costs from or until a certain date only,
(iv) costs relating only to particular steps taken, or
(v) costs relating only to a distinct part of the case.
(7) On an assessment of the amount of costs, relevant factors include—
(a) the conduct of all the parties;
(b) the particular complexity of the matter or the difficulty or novelty of the questions raised;
(c) the skill, effort, specialised knowledge and responsibility involved;
(d) the time spent on the case;
(e) the place where and the circumstances in which work or any part of it was done; and
(f) any direction or observations by the court that made the costs order.
(8) If the court orders a party to pay costs to be assessed under rule 45.11, it may order that party to pay an amount on account.
(9) An order for the payment of costs takes effect when the amount is assessed, unless the court exercises any power it has to order otherwise.

[Note. Under the powers to which apply rule 45.8 (Costs resulting from unnecessary or improper act, etc.) and rule 45.9 (Costs against a legal representative), specified conduct must be established for such orders to be made.

The amount recoverable under a costs order may be affected by the legislation under which the order is made. See, for example, section 16A of the Prosecution of Offences Act 1985[29]*.*

Under section 141 of the Powers of Criminal Courts (Sentencing) Act 2000[30] *and section 75 of the Magistrates' Courts Act 1980*[31]*, the Crown Court and magistrates' court respectively can allow time for payment, or payment by instalments.]*

R45.3 Court's power to vary requirements

45.3 (1) Unless other legislation otherwise provides, the court may—
(a) extend a time limit for serving an application or representations under rules 45.4 to 45.10, even after it has expired; and
(b) consider an application or representations—
(i) made in a different form to one set out in the Practice Direction, or
(ii) made orally instead of in writing.
(2) A person who wants an extension of time must—
(a) apply when serving the application or representations for which it is needed; and
(b) explain the delay.

[29] 1985 c. 23; section 16A was inserted by paragraphs 1 and 3 and Part 4 of Schedule 7 to the Legal Aid, Sentencing and Punishment of Offenders Act 2012 (c. 10).
[30] 2000 c. 6.
[31] 1980 c. 43, section 75 was amended by section 11 of, and paragraph 6 of Schedule 2 to, the Maintenance Enforcement Act 1991 (c. 17).

[Note. The time limit for applying for a costs order may be affected by the legislation under which the order is made. See, for example, sections 19(1), (2) and 19A of the Prosecution of Offences Act 1985[32]*, regulation 3 of the Costs in Criminal Cases (General) Regulations 1986*[33] *and rules 45.8(4)(a) and 45.9(4)(a).]*

Costs out of central funds

Costs out of central funds **R45.4**

45.4 (1) This rule applies where the court can order the payment of costs out of central funds.
(2) In this rule, costs—
(a) include—
(i) on an appeal, costs incurred in the court that made the decision under appeal, and
(ii) at a retrial, costs incurred at the initial trial and on any appeal; but
(b) do not include costs met by legal aid.
(3) The court may make an order—
(a) on application by the person who incurred the costs; or
(b) on its own initiative.
(4) Where a person wants the court to make an order that person must apply as soon as practicable and—
(a) outline the type of costs and the amount claimed, if that person wants the court to direct an assessment; or
(b) specify the amount claimed, if that person wants the court to assess the amount itself.
(5) The general rule is that the court must make an order, but—
(a) the court may decline to make a defendant's costs order if, for example—
(i) the defendant is convicted of at least one offence, or
(ii) the defendant's conduct led the prosecutor reasonably to think the prosecution case stronger than it was; and
(b) the court may decline to make a prosecutor's costs order if, for example, the prosecution was started or continued unreasonably.
(6) If the court makes an order—
(a) the court may direct an assessment under, as applicable—
(i) Part III of the Costs in Criminal Cases (General) Regulations 1986[34], or
(ii) Part 3 of the Serious Crime Act 2007 (Appeals under Section 24) Order 2008[35];
(b) the court may assess the amount itself in a case in which either—
(i) the recipient agrees the amount, or
(ii) the court decides to allow a lesser sum than that which is reasonably sufficient to compensate the recipient for expenses properly incurred in the proceedings; and
(c) an order for the payment of a defendant's costs which includes an amount in respect of fees payable to a legal representative, or disbursements paid by a legal representative, must include a statement to that effect.
(7) If the court directs an assessment, the order must specify any restriction on the amount to be paid that the court considers appropriate.
(8) If the court assesses the amount itself, it must do so subject to any restriction on the amount to be paid that is imposed by regulations made by the Lord Chancellor.

[Note. See also rule 45.2.

An order for the payment of costs out of central funds can be made—

(a) for a defendant—
(i) on acquittal,
(ii) where a prosecution does not proceed,
(iii) where the Crown Court allows any part of a defendant's appeal from a magistrates' court,
(iv) where the Court of Appeal allows any part of a defendant's appeal from the Crown Court,

[32] 1985 c. 23; section 19 was amended by section 166 of the Criminal Justice Act 1988 (c. 33), section 45 of, and Schedule 6 to, the Legal Aid Act 1988 (c. 34), section 7 of, and paragraph 8 of Schedule 3 to, the Criminal Procedure (Insanity and Unfitness to Plead) Act 1991 (c. 25), section 24 of, and paragraphs 27 and 28 of Schedule 4 to, the Access to Justice Act 1999 (c. 22), sections 40 and 67 of, and paragraph 4 of Schedule 7 to, the Youth Justice and Criminal Evidence Act 1999 (c. 23), section 165 of, and paragraph 99 of Schedule 9 to, the Powers of Criminal Courts (Sentencing) Act 2000 (c. 6), section 378 of, and paragraph 107 of Schedule 16 to, the Armed Forces Act 2006 (c. 52), section 6 of, and paragraph 32 of Schedule 4 and paragraphs 1 and 5 of Schedule 27 to, the Criminal Justice and Immigration Act 2008 (c. 4) and paragraphs 22 and 23 of Schedule 5, and paragraphs 1 and 5 and Part 4 of Schedule 7, to the Legal Aid, Sentencing and Punishment of Offenders Act 2012 (c. 10). Section 19A was inserted by section 111 of the Courts and Legal Services Act 1990 (c. 41).
[33] S.I. 1986/1335; regulation 3 was amended by regulations 2 and 3 of S.I. 2008/2448.
[34] S.I. 1986/1335; relevant amending instruments are S.I. 1999/2096 and S.I. 2008/2448.
[35] S.I. 2008/1863.

(v) where the Court of Appeal decides a prosecutor's appeal under Part 37 (Appeal to the Court of Appeal against ruling at preparatory hearing) or Part 38 (Appeal to the Court of Appeal against ruling adverse to prosecution),
(vi) where the Court of Appeal decides a reference by the Attorney General under Part 41 (Reference to the Court of Appeal of point of law or unduly lenient sentence),
(vii) where the Court of Appeal decides an appeal by someone other than the defendant about a serious crime prevention order, or
(viii) where the defendant is discharged under Part 1 or 2 of the Extradition Act 2003;

(See section 16 of the Prosecution of Offences Act 1985 and regulation 14 of the Costs in Criminal Cases (General) Regulations 1986[36]; section 36(5) of the Criminal Justice Act 1972 and paragraph 11 of Schedule 3 to the Criminal Justice Act 1988; article 14 of the Serious Crime Act 2007 (Appeals under Section 24) Order 2008; and sections 61 and 134 of the Extradition Act 2003.)

(b) for a private prosecutor, in proceedings in respect of an offence that must or may be tried in the Crown Court;

(See section 17 of the Prosecution of Offences Act 1985 and regulation 14 of the Costs in Criminal Cases (General) Regulations 1986.)

(c) for a person adversely affected by a serious crime prevention order, where the Court of Appeal—
(i) allows an appeal by that person about that order, or
(ii) decides an appeal about that order by someone else.

(See article 14 of the Serious Crime Act 2007 (Appeals under Section 24) Order 2008.)

Where the court makes an order for the payment of a defendant's costs out of central funds—

(a) the general rule is that the order may not require the payment of any amount in respect of fees payable to a legal representative, or disbursements paid by a legal representative (including expert witness costs), but if the defendant is an individual then an order may require payment of such an amount in a case—
(i) in a magistrates' court, including in an extradition case,
(ii) in the Crown Court, on appeal from a magistrates' court,
(iii) in the Crown Court, where the defendant has been sent for trial, the High Court gives permission to serve a draft indictment or the Court of Appeal orders a retrial and the defendant has been found financially ineligible for legal aid, or
(iv) in the Court of Appeal, on an appeal against a verdict of not guilty by reason of insanity, or against a finding under the Criminal Procedure (Insanity) Act 1964[37], or on an appeal under section 16A of the Criminal Appeal Act 1968[38] (appeal against order made in cases of insanity or unfitness to plead); and

(b) any such amount may not exceed an amount specified by regulations made by the Lord Chancellor.

(See section 16A of the Prosecution of Offences Act 1985[39], sections 62A, 62B, 135A and 135B of the Extradition Act 2003[40] and regulations 4A and 7 of the Costs in Criminal Cases (General) Regulations 1986[41].)]

Payment of costs by one party to another

R45.5 Costs on conviction and sentence, etc.

45.5 (1) This rule applies where the court can order a defendant to pay the prosecutor's costs if the defendant is—
(a) convicted or found guilty;
(b) dealt with in the Crown Court after committal for sentence there;
(c) dealt with for breach of a sentence; or
(d) in an extradition case—
(i) ordered to be extradited, under Part 1 of the Extradition Act 2003,

[36] S.I. 1986/1335; regulation 14 was amended by regulations 2 and 11 of S.I. 2008/2448.
[37] 1964 c. 84.
[38] 1968 c. 19; section 16A was inserted by section 25 of the Domestic Violence, Crime and Victims Act 2004 (c. 28).
[39] 1985 c. 23; section 16A was inserted by paragraphs 1 and 3 and Part 4 of Schedule 7 to the Legal Aid, Sentencing and Punishment of Offenders Act 2012 (c. 10).
[40] 2003 c. 41; sections 62A and 62B were inserted by paragraphs 12 and 15 and Part 4 of Schedule 7 to the Legal Aid, Sentencing and Punishment of Offenders Act 2012 (c. 10) and sections 135A and 135B were inserted by paragraphs 12 and 18 and Part 4 of that Schedule.
[41] S.I. 1986/1335; regulation 4A was inserted by regulations 4 and 5 of S.I. 2012/1804. Regulation 7 was substituted by regulations 4 and 6 of S.I. 2012/1804 and amended by S.I. 2013/2830.

(ii) sent for extradition to the Secretary of State, under Part 2 of that Act, or
(iii) unsuccessful on an appeal by the defendant to the High Court, or on an application by the defendant for permission to appeal from the High Court to the Supreme Court.

(2) The court may make an order—
(a) on application by the prosecutor; or
(b) on its own initiative.

(3) Where the prosecutor wants the court to make an order—
(a) the prosecutor must—
(i) apply as soon as practicable, and
(ii) specify the amount claimed; and
(b) the general rule is that the court must make an order if it is satisfied that the defendant can pay;

(4) A defendant who wants to oppose an order must make representations as soon as practicable.

(5) If the court makes an order, it must assess the amount itself.

[Note. See—

(a) rule 45.2;
(b) section 18 of the Prosecution of Offences Act 1985[42] *and regulation 14 of the Costs in Criminal Cases (General) Regulations 1986; and*
(c) sections 60 and 133 of the Extradition Act 2003.

Under section 18(4) and (5) of the 1985 Act, if a magistrates' court—

(a) imposes a fine, a penalty, forfeiture or compensation that does not exceed £5—
(i) the general rule is that the court will not make a costs order against the defendant, but
(ii) the court may do so;
(b) fines a defendant under 18, no costs order against the defendant may be for more than the fine.

Part 39 (Appeal to the Court of Appeal about conviction or sentence) contains rules about appeal against a Crown Court costs order to which this rule applies.]

Costs on appeal **R45.6**

45.6 (1) This rule—
(a) applies where a magistrates' court, the Crown Court or the Court of Appeal can order a party to pay another person's costs on an appeal, or an application for permission to appeal; and
(b) authorises the Crown Court, in addition to its other powers, to order a party to pay another party's costs on an appeal to that court, except on an appeal under—
(i) section 108 of the Magistrates' Courts Act 1980[43], or
(ii) section 45 of the Mental Health Act 1983[44].

(2) In this rule, costs include—
(a) costs incurred in the court that made the decision under appeal; and
(b) costs met by legal aid.

(3) The court may make an order—
(a) on application by the person who incurred the costs; or
(b) on its own initiative.

(4) A person who wants the court to make an order must—
(a) apply as soon as practicable;
(b) notify each other party;
(c) specify—
(i) the amount claimed, and

[42] 1985 c. 23; section 18 was amended by section 15 of, and paragraph 16 of Schedule 2 to, the Criminal Justice Act 1987 (c. 38), section 168 of, and paragraph 26 of Schedule 9 to, the Criminal Justice and Public Order Act 1994 (c. 33), sections 69 and 312 of the Criminal Justice Act 2003 (c. 44) and section 40 of, and paragraph 41 of Schedule 9 to, the Constitutional Reform Act 2005 (c. 4).

[43] 1980 c. 43; section 108 was amended by sections 66(2) and 78 of, and Schedule 16 to, the Criminal Justice Act 1982 (c. 48), section 23(3) of the Football Spectators Act 1989 (c. 37), section 101(2) of, and Schedule 13 to, the Criminal Justice Act 1991 (c. 53), sections 119 and 120(2) of, and paragraph 43 of Schedule 8 and Schedule 10 to, the Crime and Disorder Act 1998 (c. 37), section 7(2) of the Football (Offences and Disorder) Act 1999 (c. 21), section 165(1) of, and paragraph 71 of Schedule 9 to, the Powers of Criminal Courts (Sentencing) Act 2000 (c. 6), section 1 of, and Schedule 3 to, the Football (Disorder) Act 2000 (c. 25), section 58(1) of, and paragraph 10 of Schedule 10 to, the Domestic Violence, Crime and Victims Act 2004 (c. 28), section 52(2) of, and paragraph 14 of Schedule 3 to, the Violent Crime Reduction Act 2006 (c. 38) and section 64 of, and paragraph 10 of Schedule 3 to, the Animal Welfare Act 2006 (c. 45).

[44] 1983 c. 20.

(ii) against whom; and

(d) where an appellant abandons an appeal to the Crown Court by serving a notice of abandonment—

(i) apply in writing not more than 10 business days later, and

(ii) serve the application on the appellant and on the Crown Court officer.

(5) A party who wants to oppose an order must—

(a) make representations as soon as practicable; and

(b) where the application was under paragraph (4)(d), serve representations on the applicant, and on the Crown Court officer, not more than 5 business days after it was served.

(6) Where the application was under paragraph (4)(d), the Crown Court officer may—

(a) submit it to the Crown Court; or

(b) serve it on the magistrates' court officer, for submission to the magistrates' court.

(7) If the court makes an order, it may direct an assessment under rule 45.11, or assess the amount itself where—

(a) the appellant abandons an appeal to the Crown Court;

(b) the Crown Court decides an appeal, except an appeal under—

(i) section 108 of the Magistrates' Courts Act 1980, or

(ii) section 45 of the Mental Health Act 1983; or

(c) the Court of Appeal decides an appeal to which Part 40 applies (Appeal to the Court of Appeal about reporting or public access restriction).

(8) If the court makes an order in any other case, it must assess the amount itself.

[Note. See also rule 45.2.

A magistrates' court can order an appellant to pay a respondent's costs on abandoning an appeal to the Crown Court.

The Crown Court can order—

(a) the defendant to pay the prosecutor's costs on dismissing a defendant's appeal—

(i) against conviction or sentence, under section 108 of the Magistrates' Courts Act 1980, or

(ii) where the magistrates' court makes a hospital order or guardianship order without convicting the defendant, under section 45 of the Mental Health Act 1983; and

(b) one party to pay another party's costs on deciding any other appeal to which Part 34 (Appeal to the Crown Court) applies.

The Court of Appeal can order—

(a) the defendant to pay another person's costs on dismissing a defendant's appeal or application to which Part 37 (Appeal to the Court of Appeal against ruling at preparatory hearing), Part 39 (Appeal to the Court of Appeal about conviction or sentence) or Part 43 (Appeal or reference to the Supreme Court) applies;

(b) the defendant to pay another person's costs on allowing a prosecutor's appeal to which Part 38 (Appeal to the Court of Appeal against ruling adverse to the prosecution) applies;

(c) the appellant to pay another person's costs on dismissing an appeal or application by a person affected by a serious crime prevention order;

(d) one party to pay another party's costs on deciding an appeal to which Part 40 (Appeal to the Court of Appeal about reporting or public access restriction) applies.

See section 109 of the Magistrates' Courts Act 1980[45]*; section 52 of the Senior Courts Act 1981*[46] *(which allows rules of court to authorise the Crown Court to order costs); section 18 of the Prosecution of Offences Act 1985; section 159(5) of the Criminal Justice Act 1988*[47]*; and article 15 of the Serious Crime Act 2007 (Appeals under Section 24) Order 2008*[48]*.]*

R45.7 Costs on an application

45.7 (1) This rule—

(a) applies where the court can order a party to pay another person's costs in a case in which—

(i) the court decides an application for the production in evidence of a copy of a bank record,

[45] 1980 c. 43; section 109(2) was amended by section 109 of, and paragraph 234 of Schedule 8 to, the Courts Act 2003 (c. 39).

[46] 1981 c. 54. The Act's title was amended by section 59(5) of, and paragraph 1 of Schedule 11 to, the Constitutional Reform Act 2005 (c. 4).

[47] 1988 c. 33.

[48] S.I. 2008/1863.

(ii) a magistrates' court or the Crown Court decides an application to terminate a football banning order,
(iii) a magistrates' court or the Crown Court decides an application to terminate a disqualification for having custody of a dog,
(iv) the Crown Court allows an application to withdraw a witness summons, or
(v) the Crown Court decides an application relating to a deferred prosecution agreement under rule 11.5 (breach), rule 11.6 (variation) or rule 11.7 (lifting suspension of prosecution); and
(b) authorises the Crown Court, in addition to its other powers, to order a party to pay another party's costs on an application to that court under rule 11.5, 11.6 or 11.7.
(2) The court may make an order—
(a) on application by the person who incurred the costs; or
(b) on its own initiative.
(3) A person who wants the court to make an order must—
(a) apply as soon as practicable;
(b) notify each other party; and
(c) specify—
(i) the amount claimed, and
(ii) against whom.
(4) A party who wants to oppose an order must make representations as soon as practicable.
(5) If the court makes an order, it may direct an assessment under rule 45.11, or assess the amount itself.

[Note. See—

(a) rule 45.2;
(b) section 8 of the Bankers Books Evidence Act 1879[49]*;*
(c) section 14H(5) of the Football Spectators Act 1989[50]*;*
(d) section 2C(8) of the Criminal Procedure (Attendance of Witnesses) Act 1965[51]*; and*
(e) section 4(7) of the Dangerous Dogs Act 1991[52]*.*

Section 52 of the Senior Courts Act 1981 allows rules of court to authorise the Crown Court to order costs.]

Costs resulting from unnecessary or improper act, etc. **R45.8**

45.8 (1) This rule applies where the court can order a party to pay another party's costs incurred as a result of an unnecessary or improper act or omission by or on behalf of the first party.
(2) In this rule, costs include costs met by legal aid.
(3) The court may make an order—
(a) on application by the party who incurred such costs; or
(b) on its own initiative.
(4) A party who wants the court to make an order must—
(a) apply in writing as soon as practicable after becoming aware of the grounds for doing so and in any event no later than the end of the case;
(b) serve the application on—
(i) the court officer (or, in the Court of Appeal, the Registrar), and
(ii) each other party; and
(c) in that application specify—
(i) the party by whom costs should be paid,
(ii) the relevant act or omission,
(iii) the reasons why that act or omission meets the criteria for making an order,
(iv) the amount claimed, and
(v) those on whom the application has been served.
(5) Where the court considers making an order on its own initiative, it must—
(a) identify the party against whom it proposes making the order; and
(b) specify—
(i) the relevant act or omission,
(ii) the reasons why that act or omission meets the criteria for making an order, and
(iii) with the assistance of the party who incurred the costs, the amount involved.

[49] 1879 c. 11.
[50] 1989 c. 37; section 14H was substituted, together with sections 14, 14A-14G and 14J, for existing sections 14-17, by section 1 of, and paragraphs 1 and 2 of Schedule 1 to, the Football (Disorder) Act 2000 (c. 25).
[51] 1965 c. 69; section 2C was substituted with section 2, 2A, 2B, 2D and 2E, for the existing section 2 by section 66(1) and (2) of the Criminal Procedure and Investigations Act 1996 (c. 25).
[52] 1991 c. 65.

(6) A party who wants to oppose an order must—
(a) make representations as soon as practicable; and
(b) in reply to an application, serve representations on the applicant and on the court officer (or Registrar) not more than 5 business days after it was served.
(7) If the court makes an order, it must assess the amount itself.
(8) To help assess the amount, the court may direct an enquiry by—
(a) the Lord Chancellor, where the assessment is by a magistrates' court or by the Crown Court; or
(b) the Registrar, where the assessment is by the Court of Appeal.
(9) In deciding whether to direct such an enquiry, the court must have regard to all the circumstances including—
(a) any agreement between the parties about the amount to be paid;
(b) the amount likely to be allowed;
(c) the delay and expense that may be incurred in the conduct of the enquiry; and
(d) the particular complexity of the assessment, or the difficulty or novelty of any aspect of the assessment.
(10) If the court directs such an enquiry—
(a) paragraphs (3) to (8) inclusive of rule 45.11 (Assessment and re-assessment) apply as if that enquiry were an assessment under that rule (but rules 45.12 (Appeal to a costs judge) and 45.13 (Appeal to a High Court judge) do not apply);
(b) the authority that carries out the enquiry must serve its conclusions on the court officer as soon as reasonably practicable after following that procedure; and
(c) the court must then assess the amount to be paid.

[Note. See—

(a) rule 45.2;
(b) section 19(1) of the Prosecution of Offences Act 1985[53] *and regulation 3 of the Costs in Criminal Cases (General) Regulations 1986*[54]*; and*
(c) article 16 of the Serious Crime Act 2007 (Appeals under Section 24) Order 2008[55]*.*

Under section 19(1), (2) of the 1985 Act and regulation 3(1) of the 1986 Regulations, the court's power to make a costs order to which this rule applies can only be exercised during the proceedings.

Under regulation 3(5) of the 1986 Regulations, if a magistrates' court fines a defendant under 17, no costs order to which this rule applies may be for more than the fine.

The Criminal Costs Practice Direction sets out a form of application for use in connection with this rule.]

Other costs orders

R45.9 Costs against a legal representative

45.9 (1) This rule applies where—
(a) a party has incurred costs—
(i) as a result of an improper, unreasonable or negligent act or omission by a legal or other representative or representative's employee, or
(ii) which it has become unreasonable for that party to have to pay because of such an act or omission occurring after those costs were incurred; and
(b) the court can—
(i) order the representative responsible to pay such costs, or
(ii) prohibit the payment of costs to that representative.
(2) In this rule, costs include costs met by legal aid.
(3) The court may make an order—
(a) on application by the party who incurred such costs; or
(b) on its own initiative.
(4) A party who wants the court to make an order must—
(a) apply in writing as soon as practicable after becoming aware of the grounds for doing so and in any event no later than the end of the case;
(b) serve the application on—
(i) the court officer (or, in the Court of Appeal, the Registrar),
(ii) the representative responsible,

[53] 1985 c. 23.
[54] S.I. 1986/1335; regulation 3 was amended by regulations 2 and 3 of S.I. 2008/2448.
[55] S.I. 2008/1863.

(iii) each other party, and
(iv) any other person directly affected; and
(c) in that application specify—
(i) the representative responsible,
(ii) the relevant act or omission,
(iii) the reasons why that act or omission meets the criteria for making an order,
(iv) the amount claimed, and
(v) those on whom the application has been served.

(5) Where the court considers making an order on its own initiative, it must—
(a) identify the representative against whom it proposes making that order; and
(b) specify—
(i) the relevant act or omission,
(ii) the reasons why that act or omission meets the criteria for making an order, and
(iii) with the assistance of the party who incurred the costs, the amount involved.

(6) A representative who wants to oppose an order must—
(a) make representations as soon as practicable; and
(b) in reply to an application, serve representations on the applicant and on the court officer (or Registrar) not more than 5 business days after it was served.

(7) If the court makes an order—
(a) the general rule is that it must do so without waiting until the end of the case, but it may postpone making the order; and
(b) it must assess the amount itself.

(8) To help assess the amount, the court may direct an enquiry by—
(a) the Lord Chancellor, where the assessment is by a magistrates' court or by the Crown Court; or
(b) the Registrar, where the assessment is by the Court of Appeal.

(9) In deciding whether to direct such an enquiry, the court must have regard to all the circumstances including—
(a) any agreement between the parties about the amount to be paid;
(b) the amount likely to be allowed;
(c) the delay and expense that may be incurred in the conduct of the enquiry; and
(d) the particular complexity of the assessment, or the difficulty or novelty of any aspect of the assessment.

(10) If the court directs such an enquiry—
(a) paragraphs (3) to (8) inclusive of rule 45.11 (Assessment and re-assessment) apply as if that enquiry were an assessment under that rule (but rules 45.12 (Appeal to a costs judge) and 45.13 (Appeal to a High Court judge) do not apply);
(b) the authority that carries out the enquiry must serve its conclusions on the court officer as soon as reasonably practicable after following that procedure; and
(c) the court must then assess the amount to be paid.

(11) Instead of making an order, the court may make adverse observations about the representative's conduct for use in an assessment where—
(a) a party's costs are—
(i) to be met by legal aid, or
(ii) to be paid out of central funds; or
(b) there is to be an assessment under rule 45.11.

[Note. See—
(a) rule 45.2;
(b) section 19A of the Prosecution of Offences Act 1985[56]*;*
(c) article 17 of the Serious Crime Act 2007 (Appeals under Section 24) Order 2008[57]*.*

Under section 19A(1) of the 1985 Act, the court's power to make a costs order to which this rule applies can only be exercised during the proceedings.

The Criminal Costs Practice Direction sets out a form of application for use in connection with this rule.

Part 34 (Appeal to the Crown Court) and Part 39 (Appeal to the Court of Appeal about conviction or sentence) contain rules about appeals against a costs order to which this rule applies.]

56 1985 c. 23; section 19A was inserted by section 111 of the Courts and Legal Services Act 1990 (c. 41).
57 S.I. 2008/1863.

R45.10 Costs against a third party

45.10 (1) This rule applies where—
(a) there has been serious misconduct by a person who is not a party; and
(b) the court can order that person to pay a party's costs.
(2) In this rule, costs include costs met by legal aid.
(3) The court may make an order—
(a) on application by the party who incurred the costs; or
(b) on its own initiative.
(4) A party who wants the court to make an order must—
(a) apply in writing as soon as practicable after becoming aware of the grounds for doing so;
(b) serve the application on—
(i) the court officer (or, in the Court of Appeal, the Registrar),
(ii) the person responsible,
(iii) each other party, and
(iv) any other person directly affected; and
(c) in that application specify—
(i) the person responsible,
(ii) the relevant misconduct,
(iii) the reasons why the criteria for making an order are met,
(iv) the amount claimed, and
(v) those on whom the application has been served.
(5) Where the court considers making an order on its own initiative, it must—
(a) identify the person against whom it proposes making that order; and
(b) specify—
(i) the relevant misconduct,
(ii) the reasons why the criteria for making an order are met, and
(iii) with the assistance of the party who incurred the costs, the amount involved.
(6) A person who wants to oppose an order must—
(a) make representations as soon as practicable; and
(b) in reply to an application, serve representations on the applicant and on the court officer (or Registrar) not more than 5 business days after it was served.
(7) If the court makes an order—
(a) the general rule is that it must do so at the end of the case, but it may do so earlier; and
(b) it must assess the amount itself.
(8) To help assess the amount, the court may direct an enquiry by—
(a) the Lord Chancellor, where the assessment is by a magistrates' court or by the Crown Court; or
(b) the Registrar, where the assessment is by the Court of Appeal.
(9) In deciding whether to direct such an enquiry, the court must have regard to all the circumstances including—
(a) any agreement between the parties about the amount to be paid;
(b) the amount likely to be allowed;
(c) the delay and expense that may be incurred in the conduct of the enquiry; and
(d) the particular complexity of the assessment, or the difficulty or novelty of any aspect of the assessment.
(10) If the court directs such an enquiry—
(a) paragraphs (3) to (8) inclusive of rule 45.11 (Assessment and re-assessment) apply as if that enquiry were an assessment under that rule (but rules 45.12 (Appeal to a costs judge) and 45.13 (Appeal to a High Court judge) do not apply);
(b) the authority that carries out the enquiry must serve its conclusions on the court officer as soon as reasonably practicable after following that procedure; and
(c) the court must then assess the amount to be paid.

[Note. See—

(a) rule 45.2;
(b) section 19B of the Prosecution of Offences Act 1985 and regulation 3F of the Costs in Criminal Cases (General) Regulations 1986; and
(c) article 18 of the Serious Crime Act 2007 (Appeals under Section 24) Order 2008.

The Criminal Costs Practice Direction sets out a form of application for use in connection with this rule.

Part 34 (Appeal to the Crown Court) and Part 39 (Appeal to the Court of Appeal about conviction or sentence) contain rules about appeals against a costs order to which this rule applies.]

Assessment of costs

Assessment and re-assessment **R45.11**

45.11 (1) This rule applies where the court directs an assessment under—
(a) rule 33.48 (Confiscation and related proceedings—restraint and receivership proceedings; rules that apply generally — assessment of costs);
(b) rule 45.6 (Costs on appeal); or
(c) rule 45.7 (Costs on an application).
(2) The assessment must be carried out by the relevant assessing authority, namely—
(a) the Lord Chancellor, where the direction was given by a magistrates' court or by the Crown Court; or
(b) the Registrar, where the direction was given by the Court of Appeal.
(3) The party in whose favour the court made the costs order ('the applicant') must—
(a) apply for an assessment—
(i) in writing, in any form required by the assessing authority, and
(ii) not more than 3 months after the costs order; and
(b) serve the application on—
(i) the assessing authority, and
(ii) the party against whom the court made the costs order ('the respondent').
(4) The applicant must—
(a) summarise the work done;
(b) specify—
(i) each item of work done, giving the date, time taken and amount claimed,
(ii) any disbursements or expenses, including the fees of any advocate, and
(iii) any circumstances of which the applicant wants the assessing authority to take particular account; and
(c) supply—
(i) receipts or other evidence of the amount claimed, and
(ii) any other information or document for which the assessing authority asks, within such period as that authority may require.
(5) A respondent who wants to make representations about the amount claimed must—
(a) do so in writing; and
(b) serve the representations on the assessing authority, and on the applicant, not more than 15 business days after service of the application.
(6) The assessing authority must—
(a) if it seems likely to help with the assessment, obtain any other information or document;
(b) resolve in favour of the respondent any doubt about what should be allowed; and
(c) serve the assessment on the parties.
(7) Where either party wants the amount allowed to be re-assessed—
(a) that party must—
(i) apply to the assessing authority, in writing and in any form required by that authority,
(ii) serve the application on the assessing authority, and on the other party, not more than 15 business days after service of the assessment,
(iii) explain the objections to the assessment,
(iv) supply any additional supporting information or document, and
(v) ask for a hearing, if that party wants one;
(b) a party who wants to make representations about an application for re-assessment must—
(i) do so in writing,
(ii) serve the representations on the assessing authority, and on the other party, not more than 15 business days after service of the application, and
(iii) ask for a hearing, if that party wants one; and
(c) the assessing authority—
(i) must arrange a hearing, in public or in private, if either party asks for one,
(ii) subject to that, may re-assess the amount allowed with or without a hearing,
(iii) must re-assess the amount allowed on the initial assessment, taking into account the reasons for disagreement with that amount and any other representations,
(iv) may maintain, increase or decrease the amount allowed on the assessment,
(v) must serve the re-assessment on the parties, and
(vi) must serve reasons on the parties, if not more than 15 business days later either party asks for such reasons.
(8) A time limit under this rule may be extended even after it has expired—
(a) by the assessing authority, or
(b) by the Senior Costs Judge, if the assessing authority declines to do so.

R45.12 **Appeal to a costs judge**

45.12 (1) This rule applies where—
(a) the assessing authority has re-assessed the amount allowed under rule 45.11; and
(b) either party wants to appeal against that amount.
(2) That party must—
(a) serve an appeal notice on—
(i) the Senior Costs Judge,
(ii) the other party, and
(iii) the assessing authority
not more than 15 business days after service of the written reasons for the re-assessment;
(b) explain the objections to the re-assessment;
(c) serve on the Senior Costs Judge with the appeal notice—
(i) the applications for assessment and re-assessment,
(ii) any other information or document considered by the assessing authority,
(iii) the assessing authority's written reasons for the re-assessment, and
(iv) any other information or document for which a costs judge asks, within such period as the judge may require; and
(d) ask for a hearing, if that party wants one.
(3) A party who wants to make representations about an appeal must—
(a) serve representations in writing on—
(i) the Senior Costs Judge, and
(ii) the applicant
not more than 15 business days after service of the appeal notice; and
(b) ask for a hearing, if that party wants one.
(4) Unless a costs judge otherwise directs, the parties may rely only on—
(a) the objections to the amount allowed on the initial assessment; and
(b) any other representations and material considered by the assessing authority.
(5) A costs judge—
(a) must arrange a hearing, in public or in private, if either party asks for one;
(b) subject to that, may determine an appeal with or without a hearing;
(c) may—
(i) consult the assessing authority,
(ii) consult the court which made the costs order, and
(iii) obtain any other information or document;
(d) must reconsider the amount allowed by the assessing authority, taking into account the objections to the re-assessment and any other representations;
(e) may maintain, increase or decrease the amount allowed on the re-assessment;
(f) may provide for the costs incurred by either party to the appeal; and
(g) must serve reasons for the decision on—
(i) the parties, and
(ii) the assessing authority.
(6) A costs judge may extend a time limit under this rule, even after it has expired.

[Note. The Criminal Costs Practice Direction sets out a form for use in connection with this rule.]

R45.13 **Appeal to a High Court judge**

45.13 (1) This rule applies where—
(a) a costs judge has determined an appeal under rule 45.12; and
(b) either party wants to appeal against the amount allowed.
(2) A party who wants to appeal—
(a) may do so only if a costs judge certifies that a point of principle of general importance was involved in the decision on the review; and
(b) must apply in writing for such a certificate and serve the application on—
(i) the costs judge, and
(ii) the other party
not more than 15 business days after service of the decision on the review.
(3) That party must—
(a) appeal to a judge of the High Court attached to the Queen's Bench Division as if it were an appeal from the decision of a master under Part 52 of the Civil Procedure Rules 1998[58]; and

[58] S.I. 1998/3132.

(b) serve the appeal not more than 15 business days after service of the costs judge's certificate under paragraph (2).

(4) A High Court judge—

(a) may extend a time limit under this rule even after it has expired;

(b) has the same powers and duties as a costs judge under rule 45.12; and

(c) may hear the appeal with one or more assessors.

[Note. See also section 70 of the Senior Courts Act 1981[59].]

Application for an extension of time R45.14

45.14 A party who wants an extension of time under rule 45.11, 45.12 or 45.13 must—

(a) apply in writing;

(b) explain the delay; and

(c) attach the application, representations or appeal for which the extension of time is needed.

Criminal Practice Directions Part 45 Costs

CPD X CrimPR Part 45 Costs CPD.45

Reference should be made to the Practice Direction (Costs in Criminal Proceedings) 2015.

Criminal Procedure Rules Part 46 Representatives

Functions of representatives and supporters R46.1

46.1 (1) Under these Rules, anything that a party may or must do may be done—

(a) by a legal representative on that party's behalf;

(b) by a person with the corporation's written authority, where that corporation is a defendant; or

(c) with the help of a parent, guardian or other suitable supporting adult where that party is a defendant—

(i) who is under 18, or

(ii) whose understanding of what the case involves is limited

unless other legislation (including a rule) otherwise requires.

(2) A member, officer or employee of a prosecutor may, on the prosecutor's behalf—

(a) serve on the magistrates' court officer, or present to a magistrates' court, an application for a summons or warrant under section 1 of the Magistrates' Courts Act 1980[1]; or

(b) issue a written charge and requisition, or single justice procedure notice, under section 29 of the Criminal Justice Act 2003[2].

[Note. See also section 122 of the Magistrates' Courts Act 1980[3]. A party's legal representative must be entitled to act as such under section 13 of the Legal Services Act 2007[4].

Section 33(6) of the Criminal Justice Act 1925[5], section 46 of the Magistrates' Courts Act 1980[6] and Schedule 3 to that Act[7] provide for the representation of a corporation.

59 1981 c. 54. The Act's title was amended by section 59(5) of, and paragraph 1 of Schedule 11 to, the Constitutional Reform Act 2005 (c. 4).

1 1980 c. 43; section 1 was amended by section 68 of, and paragraph 6 of Schedule 8 to, the Criminal Justice Act 1991 (c. 53), sections 43 and 109 of, and Schedule 10 to, the Courts Act 2003 (c. 39), section 31 of, and paragraph 12 of Schedule 7 to, the Criminal Justice Act 2003 (c. 44) and section 153 of the Police Reform and Social Responsibility Act 2011. It is further amended by paragraphs 7 and 8 of Schedule 36 to, the Criminal Justice Act 2003 (c. 44), with effect from a date to be appointed.

2 2003 c. 44; section 29 has been brought into force for certain purposes only (see S.I. 2007/1999, S.I. 2008/1424 and S.I. 2009/2879). It was amended by section 50 of, and paragraph 130 of Schedule 4 to, the Commissioners for Revenue and Customs Act 2005 (c. 11) and section 59 of, and paragraph 196 of Schedule 4 to, the Serious Organised Crime and Police Act 2005 (c. 15).

3 1980 c. 43; section 122 was amended by section 125(3) of, and paragraph 25 of Schedule 18 to, the Courts and Legal Services Act 1990 (c. 41).

4 2007 c. 29.

5 1925 c. 86.

6 1980 c. 43.

7 1980 c. 43; Schedule 3 was amended by sections 25(2) and 101(2) of, and Schedule 13 to, the Criminal Justice Act 1991 (c. 53), section 47 of, and paragraph 13 of Schedule 1 to, the Criminal Procedure and Investigations Act 1996 (c. 25) (in relation to proceedings begun on or after 1 April 1997) and paragraph 51 of Schedule 3, and Part 4 of Schedule 37, to the Criminal Justice Act 2003 (c. 44).

Sections 3 and 6 of the Prosecution of Offences Act 1985[8] *make provision about the institution of prosecutions.*

Section 223 of the Local Government Act 1972[9] *allows a member or officer of a local authority on that authority's behalf to prosecute or defend a case before a magistrates' court, and to appear in and to conduct any proceedings before a magistrates' court.*

Part 7 contains rules about starting a prosecution.]

R46.2 **Notice of appointment, etc. of legal representative: general rules**

46.2 (1) This rule applies—
(a) in relation to—
(i) a party who does not have legal aid for the purposes of a case, and
(ii) a party to an extradition case in the High Court, whether that party has legal aid or not;
(b) where such a party—
(i) appoints a legal representative for the purposes of the case, or
(ii) dismisses such a representative, with or without appointing another; and
(c) where a legal representative for such a party withdraws from the case.

(2) Where paragraph (1)(b) applies, that party must give notice of the appointment or dismissal to—
(a) the court officer;
(b) each other party; and
(c) where applicable, the legal representative who has been dismissed,
as soon as practicable and in any event within 5 business days.

(3) Where paragraph (1)(c) applies, that legal representative must—
(a) as soon as practicable give notice to—
(i) the court officer,
(ii) the party whom he or she has represented, and
(iii) each other party; and
(b) where that legal representative has represented the defendant in an extradition case in the High Court, include with the notice—
(i) confirmation that the defendant has notice of when and where the appeal hearing will take place and of the need to attend, if the defendant is on bail,
(ii) details sufficient to locate the defendant, including details of the custodian and of the defendant's date of birth and custody reference, if the defendant is in custody, and
(iii) details of any arrangements likely to be required by the defendant to facilitate his or her participation in consequence of the representative's withdrawal, including arrangements for interpretation.

(4) Any such notice—
(a) may be given orally if—
(i) it is given at a hearing, and
(ii) it specifies no restriction under paragraph (5)(b) (restricted scope of appointment); but
(b) must be in writing in any other case

[8] 1985 c. 23; section 3 was amended by section 15 of, and paragraph 13 of Schedule 2 to, the Criminal Justice Act 1987 (c. 38), paragraph 39 of Schedule 7 to the Police Act 1996 (c. 16), section 134 of, and paragraph 48 of Schedule 9 to, the Police Act 1997 (c. 50), section 164 of the Immigration and Asylum Act 1999 (c. 33), paragraph 10 of Schedule 7 to the Police Reform Act 2002 (c. 30), sections 86 and 92 of, and Schedule 3 to, the Anti-social Behaviour Act 2003 (c. 38), section 190 of the Extradition Act 2003 (c. 41), section 7 of the Asylum and Immigration (Treatment of Claimants, etc) Act 2004 (c. 19), section 40 of, and paragraph 41 of Schedule 9 to, the Constitutional Reform Act 2005 (c. 4), sections 59, 140 and 174 of, and paragraph 47 of Schedule 4 and Part 2 of Schedule 17 to, the Serious Organised Crime and Police Act 2005 (c. 15), sections 7, 8 and 52 of, and paragraph 15 of Schedule 3 to, the Violent Crime Reduction Act 2006 (c. 38), section 74 of, and paragraph 149 of Schedule 8 to, the Serious Crime Act 2007 (c. 27), paragraph 171 of Schedule 16 to the Police Reform and Social Responsibility Act 2011 (c. 13), section 15 of, and paragraph 30 of Schedule 8 to, the Crime and Courts Act 2013 (c. 22) and article 3 of, and paragraphs 1 and 2 of the Schedule to, S.I. 2014/834.

[9] 1972 c. 70; section 223 was amended by paragraph 9 of Schedule 3 to the Solicitors Act 1974 (c. 47), section 134 of, and Schedule 10 to, the Police Act 1977 (c. 50), section 84 of, and paragraph 21 of Schedule 14 to, the Local Government Act 1985 (c. 51), section 237 of, and Schedule 13 to, the Education Reform Act 1988 (c. 40), section 120 of, and paragraph 17 of Schedule 22 and Schedule 24 to, the Environment Act 1995 (c. 25), paragraph 1 of Schedule 7 to the Police Act 1996 (c. 16), paragraphs 1 and 13 of Schedule 13 to the Local Government and Public Involvement in Health Act 2007 (c. 28), section 208 of, and paragraph 28 of Schedule 21 to, the Legal Services Act 2007 (c. 29), paragraphs 10 and 24 of Schedule 6 to the Local Democracy, Economic Development and Construction Act 2009 (c. 20), paragraphs 100 and 109 of Schedule 16 to the Police Reform and Social Responsibility Act 2011 (c. 13) and article 2 of, and paragraphs 1 and 2 of the Schedule to, S.I. 2001/3719.

(5) A notice of the appointment of a legal representative—
(a) must identify—
(i) the legal representative who has been appointed, with details of how to contact that representative, and
(ii) all those to whom the notice is given;
(b) may specify a restriction, or restrictions, on the purpose or duration of the appointment; and
(c) if it specifies any such restriction, may nonetheless provide that documents may continue to be served on the represented party at the representative's address until—
(i) further notice is given under this rule, or
(ii) that party obtains legal aid for the purposes of the case.
(6) A legal representative who is dismissed by a party or who withdraws from representing a party must, as soon as practicable, make available to that party such documents in the representative's possession as have been served on that party.

Application to change legal representative: legal aid **R46.3**

46.3 (1) This rule applies in a magistrates' court, the Crown Court and the Court of Appeal.—
(a) in relation to a party who has legal aid for the purposes of a case; and
(b) where such a party wants to select a legal representative in place of the representative named in the legal aid representation order.
(2) Such a party must—
(a) apply in writing as soon as practicable after becoming aware of the grounds for doing so; and
(b) serve the application on—
(i) the court officer, and
(ii) the legal representative named in the legal aid representation order.
(3) The application must—
(a) explain what the case is about, including what offences are alleged, what stage it has reached and what is likely to be in issue at trial;
(b) explain how and why the applicant chose the legal representative named in the legal aid representation order;
(c) if an advocate other than that representative has been instructed for the applicant, explain whether the applicant wishes to replace that advocate;
(d) explain, giving relevant facts and dates—
(i) in what way, in the applicant's opinion, there has been a breakdown in the relationship between the applicant and the current representative such that neither the individual representing the applicant nor any colleague of his or hers any longer can provide effective representation, or
(ii) what other compelling reason, in the applicant's opinion, means that neither the individual representing the applicant nor any colleague of his or hers any longer can provide effective representation;
(e) give details of any previous application by the applicant to replace the legal representative named in the legal aid representation order;
(f) state whether the applicant—
(i) waives the legal professional privilege attaching to the applicant's communications with the current representative, to the extent required to allow that representative to respond to the matters set out in the application, or
(ii) declines to waive that privilege and acknowledges that the court may draw such inferences as it thinks fit in consequence;
(g) explain how and why the applicant has chosen the proposed new representative;
(h) include or attach a statement by the proposed new representative which—
(i) confirms that that representative is eligible and willing to conduct the case for the applicant,
(ii) confirms that that representative can and will meet the current timetable for the case, including any hearing date or dates that have been set, if the application succeeds, and
(iii) explains what, if any, dealings that representative has had with the applicant before the present case; and
(i) ask for a hearing, if the applicant wants one, and explain why it is needed.
(4) The legal representative named in the legal aid representation order must—
(a) respond in writing no more than 5 business days after service of the application; and
(b) serve the response on—
(i) the court officer,
(ii) the applicant, and
(iii) the proposed new representative.

(5) The response must—
(a) explain which, if any, of the matters set out in the application the current representative disputes;
(b) explain, as appropriate, giving relevant facts and dates—
(i) whether, and if so in what way, in the current representative's opinion, there has been a breakdown in the relationship with the applicant such that neither the individual representing the applicant nor any colleague of his or hers any longer can provide effective representation,
(ii) whether, in the current representative's opinion, there is some other compelling reason why neither the individual representing the applicant nor any colleague of his or hers any longer can provide effective representation, and if so what reason,
(iii) whether the current representative considers there to be a duty to withdraw from the case in accordance with professional rules of conduct, and if so the nature of that duty, and
(iv) whether the current representative no longer is able to represent the applicant through circumstances outside the representative's control, and if so the particular circumstances that render the representative unable to do so;
(c) explain what, if any, dealings the current representative had had with the applicant before the present case; and
(d) ask for a hearing, if the current representative wants one, and explain why it is needed.
(6) The court may determine the application—
(a) without a hearing, as a general rule; or
(b) at a hearing, which must be in private unless the court otherwise directs.
(7) Unless the court otherwise directs, any hearing must be in the absence of each other party and each other party's representative and advocate (if any).
(8) If the court allows the application, as soon as practicable—
(a) the current representative must make available to the new representative such documents in the current representative's possession as have been served on the applicant party; and
(b) the new representative must serve notice of appointment on each other party.
(9) Paragraph (10) applies where—
(a) the court refuses the application;
(b) in response to that decision—
(i) the applicant declines further representation by the current representative or asks for legal aid to be withdrawn, or
(ii) the current representative declines further to represent the applicant; and
(c) the court in consequence withdraws the applicant's legal aid.
(10) The court officer must serve notice of the withdrawal of legal aid on—
(a) the applicant; and
(b) the current representative.

[Note. Under sections 16 and 19 of the Legal Aid, Sentencing and Punishment of Offenders Act 2012[10] *and Part 2 of the Criminal Legal Aid (Determinations by a Court and Choice of Representative) Regulations 2013*[11]*, a court before which criminal proceedings take place may determine whether an individual qualifies for legal aid representation in accordance with the 2012 Act.*

Under regulation 13 of the 2013 Regulations, in relation to any proceedings involving co-defendants a represented person must select a representative who is also instructed by a co-defendant unless there is, or there is likely to be, a conflict of interest between the two defendants.

Under regulation 14 of the 2013 Regulations, once a representative has been selected the person who is represented has no right to select another in the place of the first unless the court so decides, in the circumstances set out in the regulation.

Under regulation 9 of the 2013 Regulations, if a represented person declines to accept representation on the terms offered or requests that legal aid representation is withdrawn, or if the current representative declines to continue to represent that person, the court may withdraw legal aid.

See also regulation 11 of the 2013 Regulations, which requires that an application under regulation 14 (among others) must be made by the represented person, must be in writing and must specify the grounds.

The Practice Direction sets out forms of application and response for use in connection with this rule.]

[10] 2012 c. 10.
[11] S.I. 2013/614.

Criminal Procedure Rules Part 47 Investigation Orders and Warrants

Section 1: general rules

When this Part applies R47.1

47.1 This Part applies to the exercise of the powers listed in each of rules 47.4, 47.24, 47.35, 47.42, 47.46, 47.51, 47.54, 47.59 and 47.63

Meaning of 'court', 'applicant' and 'respondent' R47.2

47.2 In this Part—

(a) a reference to the 'court' includes a reference to any justice of the peace or judge who can exercise a power to which this Part applies;

(b) 'applicant' means a person who, or an authority which, can apply for an order or warrant to which this Part applies; and

(c) 'respondent' means any person—

(i) against whom such an order is sought or made, or

(ii) on whom an application for such an order is served.

Documents served on the court officer R47.3

47.3 (1) Unless the court otherwise directs, the court officer may—

(a) keep a written application; or

(b) arrange for the whole or any part to be kept by some other appropriate person, subject to any conditions that the court may impose.

(2) Where the court makes an order when the court office is closed, the applicant must, not more than 72 hours later, serve on the court officer—

(a) a copy of the order; and

(b) any written material that was submitted to the court.

(3) Where the court issues a warrant—

(a) the applicant must return it to the court officer as soon as practicable after it has been executed, and in any event not more than 3 months after it was issued (unless other legislation otherwise provides); and

(b) the court officer must—

(i) keep the warrant for 12 months after its return, and

(ii) during that period, make it available for inspection by the occupier of the premises to which it relates, if that occupier asks to inspect it.

[Note. See section 16(10) of the Police and Criminal Evidence Act 1984[1]*.]*

Section 2: investigation orders

When this Section applies R47.4

47.4 This Section applies where—

(a) a Circuit judge can make, vary or discharge an order for the production of, or for giving access to, material under paragraph 4 of Schedule 1 to the Police and Criminal Evidence Act 1984[2], other than material that consists of or includes journalistic material;

(b) for the purposes of a terrorist investigation, a Circuit judge can make, vary or discharge—

(i) an order for the production of, or for giving access to, material, or for a statement of its location, under paragraphs 5 and 10 of Schedule 5 to the Terrorism Act 2000[3],

(ii) an explanation order, under paragraphs 10 and 13 of Schedule 5 to the 2000 Act[4], or

(iii) a customer information order, under paragraphs 1 and 4 of Schedule 6 to the 2000 Act[5];

[1] 1984 c. 60; section 16(10) was substituted by section 114 of the Serious Organised Crime and Police Act 2005 (c. 15).

[2] 1984 c. 60; paragraph 4 of Schedule 1 was amended by section 65 of, and paragraph 6 of Schedule 4 to, the Courts Act 2003 (c. 39).

[3] 2000 c. 11; paragraph 5 of Schedule 5 is amended by section 65 of, and paragraph 9 of Schedule 4 to, the Courts Act 2003 (c. 39), with effect from a date to be appointed. Paragraph 10 of Schedule 5 was amended by section 109(1) of, and paragraph 389 of Schedule 8 to, the Courts Act 2003 (c. 39) and it is further amended by section 65 of, and paragraph 9 of Schedule 4 to, the Courts Act 2003 (c. 39), with effect from a date to be appointed.

[4] 2000 c. 11; paragraph 13 of Schedule 5 was amended by section 65 of, and paragraph 9 of Schedule 4 to, the Courts Act 2003 (c. 39) and section 41(3)(d) of the Criminal Finances Act 2017 (c. 22).

[5] 2000 c. 11; paragraph 1 of Schedule 6 was amended by section 3 of, and paragraph 6 of Schedule 2 to, the Anti-terrorism, Crime and Security Act 2001 (c. 24). Paragraph 4 of Schedule 6 was amended by section 109(1) of, and paragraph 390 of Schedule 8 to, the Courts Act 2003 (c. 39).

(c) for the purposes of—
  (i) a terrorist investigation, a Circuit judge can make, and the Crown Court can vary or discharge, an account monitoring order, under paragraphs 2 and 4 of Schedule 6A to the 2000 Act[6], or
  (ii) a terrorist financing investigation, a judge entitled to exercise the jurisdiction of the Crown Court can make, and the Crown Court can vary or discharge, a disclosure order, under paragraphs 9 and 14 of Schedule 5A to the 2000 Act[7];

(d) for the purposes of an investigation to which Part 8 of the Proceeds of Crime Act 2002[8] or the Proceeds of Crime Act 2002 (External Investigations) Order 2014[9] applies, a Crown Court judge can make, and the Crown Court can vary or discharge—
  (i) a production order, under sections 345 and 351 of the 2002 Act[10] or under articles 6 and 12 of the 2014 Order,
  (ii) an order to grant entry, under sections 347 and 351 of the 2002 Act or under articles 8 and 12 of the 2014 Order,
  (iii) a disclosure order, under sections 357 and 362 of the 2002 Act[11] or under articles 16 and 21 of the 2014 Order,
  (iv) a customer information order, under sections 363 and 369 of the 2002 Act[12] or under articles 22 and 28 of the 2014 Order, or
  (v) an account monitoring order, under sections 370, 373 and 375 of the 2002[13] Act or under articles 29, 32 and 34 of the 2014 Order;

(e) in connection with an extradition request, a Circuit judge can make an order for the production of, or for giving access to, material under section 157 of the Extradition Act 2003[14].

(f) a magistrates' court can make a further information order under section 22B of the Terrorism Act 2000[15] in connection with—
  (i) an investigation into whether a person is involved in the commission of an offence under any of sections 15 to 18 of the 2000 Act[16],
  (ii) determining whether such an investigation should be started, or
  (iii) identifying terrorist property or its movement or use; and

6 2000 c. 11; Schedule 6A was inserted by section 3 of, and paragraph 1(1) and (3) of Part 1 of Schedule 2 to, the Anti-terrorism, Crime and Security Act 2001 (c. 24). Paragraph 4 was amended by section 41(5)(c) of the Criminal Finances Act 2017 (c. 22).

7 2000 c. 11; Schedule 5A was inserted by Schedule 2 to the Criminal Finances Act 2017 (c. 22).

8 2002 c. 29.

9 S.I. 2014/1893.

10 2002 c. 29; section 345 was amended by section 75 of the Serious Crime Act 2007 (c. 27), section 169 of, and paragraphs 1 and 6 of Schedule 19 to, the Coroners and Justice Act 2009 (c. 25) and section 49 of, and paragraphs 1 and 4 of Schedule 19 to, the Crime and Courts Act 2013 (c. 22). Section 351 was amended by sections 74 and 77 of, and paragraphs 103 and 104 of Schedule 8 and paragraphs 1 and 6 of Schedule 10 to, the Serious Crime Act 2007 (c. 27), section 169 of, and paragraphs 1 and 9 of Schedule 19 to, the Coroners and Justice Act 2009 (c. 25), sections 66 and 112 of, and Part 5 of Schedule 8 to, the Policing and Crime Act 2009 (c. 26), sections 15 and 55 of, and paragraphs 108 and 136 of Schedule 8 and paragraphs 14 and 30 of Schedule 21 to, the Crime and Courts Act 2013 (c.22) and section 224 of, and paragraphs 1 and 11 of Schedule 48 to, the Finance Act 2013 (c. 29).

11 2002 c. 29; section 357 was amended by sections 74 and 77 of, and paragraphs 103 and 108 of Schedule 8 and paragraphs 1 and 10 of Schedule 10 to, the Serious Crime Act 2007 (c. 27), section 169 of, and paragraphs 1 and 13 of Schedule 19 to, the Coroners and Justice Act 2009 (c. 25), sections 15, 49 and 55 of, and paragraphs 108 and 139 of Schedule 8, paragraphs 1 and 8 of Schedule 19 and paragraphs 14 and 34 of Schedule 21 to, the Crime and Courts Act 2013 (c. 22) and article 3 of, and paragraphs 19 and 27 of Schedule 2 to, SI 2014/834. Section 362 was amended by section 74 of, and paragraphs 103 and 110 of Schedule 8 to, the Serious Crime Act 2007 (c. 27), section 169 of, and paragraphs 1 and 15 of Schedule 19 to, the Coroners and Justice Act 2009 (c. 25) and section 15 of, and paragraphs 108 and 140 of Schedule 8 to, the Crime and Courts Act 2013 (c. 22).

12 2002 c. 29; section 363 was amended by section 77 of, and paragraphs 1 and 11 of Schedule 10 to, the Serious Crime Act 2007 (c. 27), section 169 of, and paragraphs 1 and 16 of Schedule 19 to, the Coroners and Justice Act 2009 (c. 25) and section 49 of, and paragraphs 1 and 10 of Schedule 19 to, the Crime and Courts Act 2013 (c. 22). Section 369 was amended by section 74 of, and paragraphs 103 and 111 of Schedule 8 to, the Serious Crime Act 2007 (c. 27), sections 15 and 55 of, and paragraphs 108 and 141 of Schedule 8, and paragraphs 14 and 35 of Schedule 21 to, the Crime and Courts Act 2013 (c. 22) and section 224 of, and paragraphs 1 and 14 of Schedule 48 to, the Finance Act 2013 (c. 29).

13 2002 c. 29; section 370 was amended by section 77 of, and paragraphs 1 and 12 of Schedule 10 to, the Serious Crime Act 2007 (c. 27), section 169 of, and paragraphs 1 and 17 of Schedule 19 to, the Coroners and Justice Act 2009 (c. 25) and section 49 of, and paragraphs 1 and 12 of Schedule 19 to, the Crime and Courts Act 2013 (c. 22). Section 375 was amended by section 74 of, and paragraphs 103 and 112 of Schedule 8 to, the Serious Crime Act 2007 (c. 27), sections 15 and 55 of, and paragraphs 108 and 142 of Schedule 8 and paragraphs 14 and 36 of Schedule 21 to, the Crime and Courts Act 2013 (c. 22) and section 224 of, and paragraphs 1 and 15 of Schedule 48 to, the Finance Act 2013 (c. 29).

14 2003 c. 41; section 157 was amended by section 174 of the Anti-social Behaviour, Crime and Policing Act 2014 (c. 12).

15 2000 c. 11; section 22B was inserted by section 37 of the Criminal Finances Act 2017 (c. 22).

16 2000 c. 11; section 17A was inserted by section 42 of the Counter-Terrorism and Security Act 2015 (c. 6).

(g) a magistrates' court can make a further information order under section 339ZH of the Proceeds of Crime Act 2002[17] in connection with—
   (i) an investigation into whether a person is engaged in money laundering,
   (ii) determining whether such an investigation should be started, or
   (iii) an investigation into money laundering by an authority in a country outside the United Kingdom.

[Note. In outline, the orders to which these rules apply are—

(a) under the Police and Criminal Evidence Act 1984, a production order requiring a person to produce or give access to material, other than material that consists of or includes journalistic material;

(b) for the purposes of a terrorist investigation under the Terrorism Act 2000—
   (i) an order requiring a person to produce, give access to, or state the location of material,
   (ii) an explanation order, requiring a person to explain material obtained under a production, etc. order,
   (iii) a customer information order, requiring a financial institution to provide information about an account holder,
   (iv) an account monitoring order, requiring a financial institution to provide specified information, for a specified period, about an account held at that institution;

(c) for the purposes of a terrorist financing investigation under the Terrorism Act 2000, a disclosure order, requiring a person to provide information or documents, or to answer questions;

(d) for the purposes of an investigation to which Part 8 of the Proceeds of Crime Act 2002 or the Proceeds of Crime Act 2002 (External Investigations) Order 2014 applies—
   (i) a production order, requiring a person to produce or give access to material,
   (ii) an order to grant entry, requiring a person to allow entry to premises so that a production order can be enforced,
   (iii) a disclosure order, requiring a person to provide information or documents, or to answer questions,
   (iv) a customer information order, requiring a financial institution to provide information about an account holder,
   (v) an account monitoring order, requiring a financial institution to provide specified information, for a specified period, about an account held at that institution;

(e) in connection with extradition proceedings, a production order requiring a person to produce or give access to material;

(f) under the Terrorism Act 2000, a further information order requiring a person to provide information related to a matter arising from a disclosure under section 21A of that Act[18] *(Failure to disclose: regulated sector) or under the law of a country outside the United Kingdom which corresponds with Part III of that Act (Terrorist property);*

(g) under the Proceeds of Crime Act 2002, a further information order requiring a person to provide information related to a matter arising from a disclosure under Part 7 of that Act (Money laundering) or under the law of a country outside the United Kingdom which corresponds with that Part of that Act.

These rules do not apply to an application for a production order under the Police and Criminal Evidence Act 1984 requiring a person to produce or give access to journalistic material: see paragraph 15A of Schedule 1 to the Act[19]*.*

For all the relevant terms under which these orders can be made, see the provisions listed in rule 47.4.

Under section 8 of the Senior Courts Act 1981[20]*, a High Court judge, a Circuit judge, a Recorder, a qualifying judge advocate and a District Judge (Magistrates' Courts) each may act as a Crown Court judge.*

When the relevant provisions of the Courts Act 2003 come into force, a District Judge (Magistrates' Courts) will have the same powers as a Circuit judge under the Police and Criminal Evidence Act 1984 and under the Terrorism Act 2000.

[17] 2002 c. 29; section 339ZH was inserted by section 12 of the Criminal Finances Act 2017 (c. 22).

[18] 2000 c. 11; section 21A was inserted by section 3 of, and paragraph 5 of Schedule 2 to, the Anti-terrorism, Crime and Security Act 2001 (c. 24) and amended by regulation 2 of, and paragraphs 1 and 3 of Schedule 1 to, S.I. 2007/3398, section 59 of, and paragraphs 125 and 128 of, the Serious Organised Crime and Police Act 2005 (c. 15) and section 15 of, and paragraphs 67 and 72 of Schedule 8 to, the Crime and Courts Act 2013 (c. 22).

[19] 1984 c. 60; paragraph 15A of Schedule 1 was inserted by section 82 of the Deregulation Act 2015 (c. 20).

[20] 1981 c. 54; section 8 was amended by sections 65 and 109 of, and paragraph 259 of Schedule 8 to, the Courts Act 2003 (c. 39) and paragraph 1 of Schedule 2 to the Armed Forces Act 2011 (c. 18). The 1981 Act's title was amended by section 59(5) of, and paragraph 1 of Schedule 11 to, the Constitutional Reform Act 2005 (c. 4).

Under section 66 of the Courts Act 2003[21]*, in criminal cases a High Court judge, a Circuit judge, a Recorder and a qualifying judge advocate each has the powers of a justice of the peace who is a District Judge (Magistrates' Courts).*

By section 341 of the Proceeds of Crime Act 2002[22]*, an investigation under Part 8 of the Act may be—*

- *(a) an investigation into (i) whether a person has benefited from criminal conduct, (ii) the extent or whereabouts of such benefit, (iii) the available amount in respect of that person, or (iv) the extent or whereabouts of realisable property available for satisfying a confiscation order made in respect of that person ('a confiscation investigation');*
- *(b) an investigation into whether a person has committed a money laundering offence ('a money laundering investigation');*
- *(c) an investigation into whether property is recoverable property or associated property (as defined by section 316 of the 2002 Act*[23]*), or into who holds the property or its extent or whereabouts ('a civil recovery investigation');*
- *(d) an investigation into the derivation of cash detained under the 2002 Act, or into whether such cash is intended to be used in unlawful conduct ('a detained cash investigation');*
- *(e) an investigation into the derivation of property detained under the 2002 Act, or into whether such property is intended to be used in unlawful conduct ('a detained property investigation');*
- *(f) an investigation into the derivation of money held in an account in relation to which an account freezing order made under the 2002 Act has effect, or into whether such money is intended to be used in unlawful conduct ('a frozen funds investigation');*
- *(g) an investigation for the purposes of Part 7 of the Coroners and Justice Act 2009(*[24]*) (criminal memoirs, etc.) into whether a person is a qualifying offender or has obtained exploitation proceeds from a relevant offence, or into the value of any benefits derived by such a person from such an offence or the amount available ('an exploitation proceeds investigation').*

Under section 343 of the Proceeds of Crime Act 2002[25]*—*

- *(a) any Crown Court judge may make an order to which this Section applies for the purposes of a confiscation investigation, a money laundering investigation, a detained cash investigation, a detained property investigation or a frozen funds investigation;*
- *(b) only a High Court judge may make such an order for the purposes of a civil recovery investigation or an exploitation proceeds investigation (and these rules do not apply to an application to such a judge in such a case).*

As well as governing procedure on an application to the Crown Court, under the following provisions rules may govern the procedure on an application to an individual judge—

- *(a) paragraph 15A of Schedule 1 to the Police and Criminal Evidence Act 1984;*
- *(b) paragraph 10 of Schedule 5, paragraph 14 of Schedule 5A, paragraph 4 of Schedule 6 and paragraph 5 of Schedule 6A to the Terrorism Act 2000; and*
- *(c) sections 351, 362, 369, 375 and 446 of the Proceeds of Crime Act 2002.]*

R47.5 Exercise of court's powers

47.5 (1) Subject to paragraphs (2), (3) and (4), the court may determine an application for an order, or to vary or discharge an order—

(a) at a hearing (which must be in private unless the court otherwise directs), or without a hearing; and

[21] 2003 c. 39; section 66 was amended by paragraph 6 of Schedule 2 to the Armed Forces Act 2011 (c. 18) and sections 17 and 21 of, and paragraphs 83 and 90 of Schedule 10 and paragraph 4 of Schedule 14 to, the Crime and Courts Act 2013 (c. 22).

[22] 2002 c. 29; section 341 was amended by section 75 of the Serious Crime Act 2007 (c. 27), section 169 of, and paragraphs 1 and 2 of Schedule 19 to, the Coroners and Justice Act 2009 (c. 25) and section 112 of, and paragraphs 99 and 110 of Schedule 7 to, the Policing and Crime Act 2009 (c. 26), section 49 of, and paragraphs 1, 2, 24 and 25 of Schedule 19 to, the Crime and Courts Act 2013 (c.22) and sections 38 and 85 of, and paragraph 55 of Schedule 4 to, the Serious Crime Act 2015 (c. 9).

[23] 2002 c. 29; section 316 was amended by paragraph 78 of Schedule 36 to the Criminal Justice Act 2003 (c. 44), section 109 of, and paragraphs 4 and 22 of Schedule 6 to, the Serious Organised Crime and Police Act 2005 (c. 15), section 74 of, and paragraphs 85 and 91 of Schedule 8 to, the Serious Crime Act 2007 (c. 27), article 12 of, and paragraphs 47 and 65 of Schedule 14 to, S.I. 2010/976, sections 15 and 48 of, and paragraphs 108 and 121 of Schedule 8 to, the Crime and Courts Act 2013 (c. 22), article 3 of, and paragraphs 19 and 25 of Schedule 2 to, SI 2014/834, section 85 of, and paragraph 54 of Schedule 4 to, the Serious Crime Act 2015 (c. 9) and article 8 of SI 2015/798.

[24] 2009 c. 25.

[25] 2002 c. 29; section 343 was amended by section 77 of, and paragraphs 1 and 3 of Schedule 10 to, the Serious Crime Act 2007 (c. 27), section 169 of, and paragraphs 1 and 4 of Schedule 19 to, the Coroners and Justice Act 2009 (c. 25) and sections 66 and 112 of, and Part 5 of Schedule 8 to, the Policing and Crime Act 2009 (c. 26).

(b) in the absence of—
(i) the applicant,
(ii) any respondent
(iii) any other person affected by the order.

(2) The court must not determine such an application in the applicant's absence if—
(a) the applicant asks for a hearing; or
(b) it appears to the court that—
(i) the proposed order may infringe legal privilege, within the meaning of section 10 of the Police and Criminal Evidence Act 1984[26], section 348 or 361 of the Proceeds of Crime Act 2002[27] or article 9 of the Proceeds of Crime Act 2002 (External Investigations) Order 2014[28],
(ii) the proposed order may require the production of excluded material, within the meaning of section 11 of the 1984 Act, or
(iii) for any other reason the application is so complex or serious as to require the court to hear the applicant.

(3) The court must not determine such an application in the absence of any respondent or other person affected, unless—
(a) the absentee has had at least 2 business days in which to make representations; or
(b) the court is satisfied that—
(i) the applicant cannot identify or contact the absentee,
(ii) it would prejudice the investigation if the absentee were present,
(iii) it would prejudice the investigation to adjourn or postpone the application so as to allow the absentee to attend, or
(iv) the absentee has waived the opportunity to attend.

(4) The court must not determine such an application in the absence of any respondent who, if the order sought by the applicant were made, would be required to produce or give access to journalistic material, unless that respondent has waived the opportunity to attend.

(5) The court officer must arrange for the court to hear such an application no sooner than 2 business days after it was served, unless—
(a) the court directs that no hearing need be arranged; or
(b) the court gives other directions for the hearing.

(6) The court must not determine an application unless satisfied that sufficient time has been allowed for it.

(7) If the court so directs, the parties to an application may attend a hearing by live link or telephone.

(8) The court must not make, vary or discharge an order unless the applicant states, in writing or orally, that to the best of the applicant's knowledge and belief—
(a) the application discloses all the information that is material to what the court must decide; and
(b) the content of the application is true.

(9) Where the statement required by paragraph (8) is made orally—
(a) the statement must be on oath or affirmation, unless the court otherwise directs; and
(b) the court must arrange for a record of the making of the statement.

(10) The court may—
(a) shorten or extend (even after it has expired) a time limit under this Section;
(b) dispense with a requirement for service under this Section (even after service was required); and
(c) consider an application made orally instead of in writing.

(11) A person who wants an extension of time must—
(a) apply when serving the application for which it is needed; and
(b) explain the delay.

Application for order: general rules **R47.6**

47.6 (1) This rule applies to each application for an order to which this Section applies.
(2) The applicant must—
(a) apply in writing and serve the application on the court officer;
(b) demonstrate that the applicant is entitled to apply, for example as a constable or under legislation that applies to other officers;

[26] 1984 c. 60.
[27] 2002 c. 29; section 361 was amended by section 74 of, and paragraphs 103 and 109 of Schedule 8 to, the Serious Crime Act 2007 (c. 27).
[28] S.I. 2014/1893.

Criminal Procedure Rules and Criminal Practice Directions

(c) give the court an estimate of how long the court should allow—
(i) to read the application and prepare for any hearing, and
(ii) for any hearing of the application;
(d) attach a draft order in the terms proposed by the applicant;
(e) serve notice of the application on the respondent if any, unless the court otherwise directs; and
(f) serve the application on any respondent to such extent, if any, as the court directs.
(3) A notice served on a respondent must—
(a) specify the material or information in respect of which the application is made; and
(b) identify—
(i) the power that the applicant invites the court to exercise, and
(ii) the conditions for the exercise of that power which the applicant asks the court to find are met.
(4) The applicant must serve any order made on a respondent.

R47.7 Application containing information withheld from a respondent or other person

47.7 (1) This rule applies where an application includes information that the applicant thinks ought to be revealed only to the court.
(2) The application must—
(a) identify that information; and
(b) explain why that information ought not to be served on a respondent or other person.
(3) At a hearing of an application to which this rule applies—
(a) the general rule is that the court must consider, in the following sequence—
(i) representations first by the applicant and then by the respondent if any and any other person, in the presence of them all, and then
(ii) further representations by the applicant, in the others' absence; but
(b) the court may direct other arrangements for the hearing.

R47.8 Application to vary or discharge an order

47.8 (1) This rule applies where one of the following wants the court to vary or discharge an order to which a rule in this Section refers—
(a) an applicant;
(b) a respondent; or
(c) a person affected by the order.
(2) That applicant, respondent or person affected must—
(a) apply in writing as soon as practicable after becoming aware of the grounds for doing so;
(b) serve the application on—
(i) the court officer, and
(ii) the respondent, applicant, or any person known to be affected, as applicable;
(c) explain why it is appropriate for the order to be varied or discharged;
(d) propose the terms of any variation; and
(e) ask for a hearing, if one is wanted, and explain why it is needed.

R47.9 Application to punish for contempt of court

47.9 (1) This rule applies where a person is accused of disobeying—
(a) a production order made under paragraph 4 of Schedule 1 to the Police and Criminal Evidence Act 1984;
(b) a production etc. order made under paragraph 5 of Schedule 5 to the Terrorism Act 2000;
(c) an explanation order made under paragraph 13 of that Schedule;
(d) an account monitoring order made under paragraph 2 of Schedule 6A to that Act;
(e) a production order made under section 345 of the Proceeds of Crime Act 2002 or article 6 of the Proceeds of Crime Act 2002 (External Investigations) Order 2014;
(f) an account monitoring order made under section 370 of the 2002 Act or article 29 of the 2014 Order; or
(g) a production order made under section 157 of the Extradition Act 2003.
(2) An applicant who wants the court to exercise its power to punish that person for contempt of court must comply with the rules in Part 48 (Contempt of court).

[Note. The Crown Court has power to punish for contempt of court a person who disobeys its order. See paragraphs 10(1) and 13(5) of Schedule 5, and paragraph 6(1) of Schedule 6A, to the Terrorism Act 2000; sections 351(7) and 375(6) of the Proceeds of Crime Act 2002 and articles 12(6) and 34(5) of the Proceeds of Crime Act 2002 (External Investigations) Order 2014; and section 45 of the Senior Courts Act 1981[29].

[29] 1981 c. 54. The Act's title was amended by section 59(5) of, and paragraph 1 of Schedule 11 to, the Constitutional Reform Act 2005 (c. 4).

A Circuit judge has power to punish a person who disobeys a production order under the Police and Criminal Evidence Act 1984 as if that were a contempt of the Crown Court: see paragraph 15 of Schedule 1 to the Act[30].

Disobedience to an explanation order, to a disclosure order or to a customer information order under the Terrorism Act 2000 is an offence: see paragraph 14 of Schedule 5, paragraph 11 of Schedule 5A and paragraph 1(3) of Schedule 6, to the Act.

Disobedience to a disclosure order or to a customer information order under the Proceeds of Crime Act 2002 or under the Proceeds of Crime Act 2002 (External Investigations) Order 2014 is an offence: see sections 359 and 366 of the Act and articles 18 and 25 of the Order. Under section 342 of the Act[31] *and under article 5 of the Order, subject to the exceptions for which those provide it is an offence to make a disclosure likely to prejudice an investigation or to interfere with documents relevant to it.*

If a person fails to comply with a further information order under the Terrorism Act 2000 or under the Proceeds of Crime Act 2002 the magistrates' court may order that person to pay an amount not exceeding £5,000, which order may be enforced as if the sum due had been adjudged to be paid by a conviction: see section 22B(8), (9) of the Terrorism Act 2000[32] *and section 339ZH((8), (9) of the Proceeds of Crime Act 2002*[33]*.]*

Orders under the Police and Criminal Evidence Act 1984

Application for a production order under the Police and Criminal Evidence Act 1984 **R47.10**

47.10 (1) This rule applies where an applicant wants the court to make an order to which rule 47.4(a) refers.

(2) As well as complying with rule 47.6 (Application for order: general rules), the application must, in every case—
(a) specify the offence under investigation (and see paragraph (3)(a));
(b) describe the material sought;
(c) identify the respondent;
(d) specify the premises on which the material is believed to be, or explain why it is not reasonably practicable to do so;
(e) explain the grounds for believing that the material is on the premises specified, or (if applicable) on unspecified premises of the respondent;
(f) specify the set of access conditions on which the applicant relies (and see paragraphs (3) and (4)); and
(g) propose—
(i) the terms of the order, and
(ii) the period within which it should take effect.

(3) Where the applicant relies on paragraph 2 of Schedule 1 to the Police and Criminal Evidence Act 1984[34] ('the first set of access conditions': general power to gain access to special procedure material), the application must—
(a) specify the indictable offence under investigation;
(b) explain the grounds for believing that the offence has been committed;
(c) explain the grounds for believing that the material sought—
(i) is likely to be of substantial value to the investigation (whether by itself, or together with other material),
(ii) is likely to be admissible evidence at trial for the offence under investigation, and
(iii) does not consist of or include items subject to legal privilege or excluded material;
(d) explain what other methods of obtaining the material—
(i) have been tried without success, or
(ii) have not been tried because they appeared bound to fail; and
(e) explain why it is in the public interest for the respondent to produce the material, having regard to—
(i) the benefit likely to accrue to the investigation if the material is obtained, and
(ii) the circumstances under which the respondent holds the material.

[30] 1984 c. 60; paragraph 15 of Schedule 1 was amended by section 65 of, and paragraph 6 of Schedule 4 to, the Courts Act 2003 (c. 39).
[31] 2002 c. 29; section 342 was amended by section 77 of, and paragraphs 1 and 2 of Schedule 10 to, the Serious Crime Act 2007 (c. 27), regulation 3 of, and paragraphs 1 and 8 of Schedule 2 to, S.I. 2007/3398 and section 169 of, and paragraphs 1 and 3 of Schedule 19 to, the Coroners and Justice Act 2009 (c. 25).
[32] 2000 c. 11; section 22B was inserted by section 37 of the Criminal Finances Act 2017 (c. 22).
[33] 2002 c. 29; section 339ZH was inserted by section 12 of the Criminal Finances Act 2017 (c. 22).
[34] 1984 c. 60; paragraph 2 of Schedule 1 was amended by sections 111 and 113 of, and paragraph 43 of Schedule 7 to, the Serious Organised Crime and Police Act 2005 (c. 15).

(4) Where the applicant relies on paragraph 3 of Schedule 1 to the Police and Criminal Evidence Act 1984[35] ('the second set of access conditions': use of search warrant power to gain access to excluded or special procedure material), the application must—
   (a) state the legislation under which a search warrant could have been issued, had the material sought not been excluded or special procedure material (in this paragraph, described as 'the main search power');
   (b) include or attach the terms of the main search power;
   (c) explain how the circumstances would have satisfied any criteria prescribed by the main search power for the issue of a search warrant; and
   (d) explain why the issue of such a search warrant would have been appropriate.

[Note. See paragraphs 1 to 4 of Schedule 1 to the Police and Criminal Evidence Act 1984[36]. The applicant for an order must be a constable. Sections 10, 11 and 14 of the 1984 Act[37] define 'items subject to legal privilege', 'excluded material' and 'special procedure material'. The period within which an order takes effect must be specified in the order and, unless the court considers a longer period appropriate, must be 7 days from the date of the order.

See also the code of practice for searches of premises by police officers and the seizure of property found by police officers on persons or premises issued under section 66 of the Police and Criminal Evidence Act 1984[38].

The Practice Direction sets out forms of application, notice and order for use in connection with this rule.]

Orders under the Terrorism Act 2000

R47.11 **Application for an order under the Terrorism Act 2000**

47.11 (1) This rule applies where an applicant wants the court to make one of the orders to which rule 47.4(b) and (c) refers.
(2) As well as complying with rule 47.6 (Application for order: general rules), the application must—
   (a) specify the offence under investigation;
   (b) explain how the investigation constitutes a terrorist investigation or terrorist financing investigation, as appropriate, within the meaning of the Terrorism Act 2000;[39]
   (c) identify any respondent; and
   (d) give the information required by whichever of rules 47.12 to 47.16 applies.

R47.12 **Content of application for a production etc. order under the Terrorism Act 2000**

47.12 (1) As well as complying with rules 47.6 and 47.11, an applicant who wants the court to make an order for the production of, or for giving access to, material, or for a statement of its location, must—
   (a) describe that material;
   (b) explain why the applicant thinks the material is—
      (i) in the respondent's possession, custody or power, or
      (ii) expected to come into existence and then to be in the respondent's possession, custody or power within 28 days of the order;
   (c) explain how the material constitutes or contains excluded material or special procedure material;
   (d) confirm that none of the material is expected to be subject to legal privilege;
   (e) explain why the material is likely to be of substantial value to the investigation;
   (f) explain why it is in the public interest for the material to be produced, or for the applicant to be given access to it, having regard to—
      (i) the benefit likely to accrue to the investigation if it is obtained, and
      (ii) the circumstances in which the respondent has the material, or is expected to have it; and

35 1984 c. 60; paragraph 3 of Schedule 1 was amended by section 113 of the Serious Organised Crime and Police Act 2005 (c. 15).

36 1984 c. 60; paragraphs 1 and 4 of Schedule 1 were amended by section 65 of, and paragraph 6 of Schedule 4 to, the Courts Act 2003 (c. 39).

37 1984 c. 60; section 14 was amended by section 1177 of, and paragraph 193 of Schedule 1 to, the Corporation Tax Act 2010 (c. 4).

38 1984 c. 60; section 66 was amended by section 57 of the Criminal Justice and Court Services Act 2000 (c. 43), sections 110 and 174 of, and Schedule 17 to, the Serious Organised Crime and Police Act 2005 (c. 15) and section 115 of, and paragraph 21 of Schedule 9 to, the Protection of Freedoms Act 2012 (c. 9).

39 2000 c. 11.

(g) propose—
(i) the terms of the order, and
(ii) the period within which it should take effect.

(2) An applicant who wants the court to make an order to grant entry in aid of a production order must—
(a) specify the premises to which entry is sought;
(b) explain why the order is needed; and
(c) propose the terms of the order.

[Note. See paragraphs 5 to 9 of Schedule 5 to the Terrorism Act 2000[40]. The applicant for a production, etc. order must be an 'appropriate officer' as defined by paragraph 5(6) of that Schedule. Where the applicant is a counter-terrorism financial investigator the application must be for the purposes of an investigation relating to 'terrorist property' as defined by section 14 of the 2000 Act. Under paragraphs 5 and 7 of Schedule 5 to that Act a production order may require a specified person—

(a) to produce to an appropriate officer within a specified period for seizure and retention any material which that person has in his or her possession, custody or power and to which the application relates; to give an appropriate officer access to any such material within a specified period; and to state to the best of that person's knowledge and belief the location of material to which the application relates if it is not in, and it will not come into, his or her possession, custody or power within the period specified; or

(b) where such material is expected to come into existence within the period of 28 days beginning with the date of the order, to notify a named appropriate officer as soon as is reasonably practicable after any material to which the application relates comes into that person's possession, custody or power, and then to produce that material to an appropriate officer; to give an appropriate officer access to it; and to state to the best of that person's knowledge and belief the location of material to which the application relates if it is not in, and it will not come into, his or her possession, custody or power within that period of 28 days.

Under paragraph 4 of Schedule 5 to the 2000 Act, 'legal privilege', 'excluded material' and 'special procedure material' mean the same as under sections 10, 11 and 14 of the Police and Criminal Evidence Act 1984.

The period within which an order takes effect must be specified in the order and, unless the court otherwise directs, must be—

(a) where the respondent already has the material, 7 days from the date of the order; or
(b) where the respondent is expected to have the material within 28 days, 7 days from the date the respondent notifies the applicant of its receipt.

The Practice Direction sets out forms of application, notice and order for use in connection with this rule.]

Content of application for a disclosure order or further information order under the Terrorism Act 2000 **R47.13**

47.13 (1) As well as complying with rules 47.6 and 47.11, an applicant who wants the court to make a disclosure order must—
(a) explain why the applicant thinks that—
(i) a person has committed an offence under any of sections 15 to 18 of the Terrorism Act 2000[41], or
(ii) property described in the application is terrorist property within the meaning of section 14 of the 2000 Act[42];
(b) describe in general terms the information that the applicant wants a person to provide;
(c) confirm that none of the information is—
(i) expected to be subject to legal privilege, or
(ii) excluded material;
(d) explain why the information is likely to be of substantial value to the investigation;
(e) explain why it is in the public interest for the information to be provided, having regard to the benefit likely to accrue to the investigation if it is obtained; and
(f) propose the terms of the order.

(2) As well as complying with rule 47.6, an applicant who wants the court to make a further information order must—

40 2000 c. 11; paragraphs 5, 6 and 7 of Schedule 5 were amended by section 65 of, and paragraph 9 of Schedule 4 to, the Courts Act 2003 (c. 39) and section 41 of the Criminal Finances Act 2017 (c. 22).
41 2000 c. 11; section 17A was inserted by section 42 of the Counter-Terrorism and Security Act 2015 (c. 6).
42 2000 c. 11.

Criminal Procedure Rules and Criminal Practice Directions

(a) identify the respondent from whom the information is sought and explain—
 (i) whether the respondent is the person who made the disclosure to which the information relates or is otherwise carrying on a business in the regulated sector within the meaning of Part 1 of Schedule 3A to the 2000 Act[43], and
 (ii) why the applicant thinks that the information is in the possession, or under the control, of the respondent;
(b) specify or describe the information that the applicant wants the respondent to provide;
(c) where the information sought relates to a disclosure of information by someone under section 21A of the 2000 Act[44] (Failure to disclose: regulated sector), explain—
 (i) how the information sought relates to a matter arising from that disclosure,
 (ii) how the information would assist in investigating whether a person is involved in the commission of an offence under any of sections 15 to 18 of that Act[45], or in determining whether an investigation of that kind should be started, or in identifying terrorist property or its movement or use, and
 (iii) why it is reasonable in all the circumstances for the information to be provided;
(d) where the information sought relates to a disclosure made under a requirement of the law of a country outside the United Kingdom which corresponds with Part III of the 2000 Act (Terrorist property), and an authority in that country which investigates offences corresponding with sections 15 to 18 of that Act has asked the National Crime Agency for information in connection with that disclosure, explain—
 (i) how the information sought relates to a matter arising from that disclosure,
 (ii) why the information is likely to be of substantial value to the authority that made the request in determining any matter in connection with the disclosure, and
 (iii) why it is reasonable in all the circumstances for the information to be provided;
(e) confirm that none of the information is expected to be subject to legal privilege; and
(f) propose the terms of the order, including—
 (i) how the respondent must provide the information required, and
 (ii) the date by which the information must be provided.

(3) Rule 47.8 (Application to vary or discharge an order) does not apply to a further information order.
(4) Paragraph (5) applies where a party to an application for a further information order wants to appeal to the Crown Court from the decision of the magistrates' court.
(5) The appellant must—
 (a) serve an appeal notice—
  (i) on the Crown Court officer and on the other party,
  (ii) not more than 15 business days after the magistrates' court's decision; and
 (b) in the appeal notice, explain, as appropriate, why the Crown Court should (as the case may be) make, discharge or vary a further information order.
(6) Rule 34.11 (Constitution of the Crown Court) applies on such an appeal.

[Note. See sections 22B, 22D and 22E of, and Schedule 5A to, the Terrorism Act 2000[46]*.*

Under paragraph 9(6) of Schedule 5A to the 2000 Act the applicant for a disclosure order must be an 'appropriate officer', as defined by paragraph 5, who is, or who is authorised to apply by, a police officer of at least the rank of superintendent.

Under section 22B(12) of the 2000 Act the applicant for a further information order must be 'a law enforcement officer', as defined by section 22B(14), who is, or who is authorised to apply by, a 'senior law enforcement officer', defined by section 22B(14) as a police officer of at least the rank of superintendent, the Director General of the National Crime Agency or an officer of that Agency authorised by the Director General for that purpose.

[43] 2000 c. 11; Part 1 of Schedule 3A was inserted by section 3 of, and paragraph 5 of Schedule 2 to, the Anti-terrorism, Crime and Security Act 2001 (c. 24), substituted by article 2 of S.I. 2007/3288 and amended by articles 3 and 6 of, and paragraph 25 of Schedule 1 to, S.I. 2008/948, sections 183 and 237 of, and paragraph 1 of Schedule 18 and Part 29 of Schedule 25 to, the Localism Act 2011 (c. 20), regulation 79 of, and paragraph 3 of Schedule 4 to, S.I. 2011/99, article 2 of S.I. 2011/2701, article 2 of S.I. 2012/2299, article 2 of S.I. 2012/1534, regulation 46 of, and paragraph 40 of Schedule 2 to, S.I. 2013/3115, section 151 of, and paragraph 73 of Schedule 4 to, the Co-operative and Community Benefit Societies Act 2014 (c. 14), regulation 59 of, and paragraph 21 of Schedule 1 to, S.I. 2015/575, regulation 12 of S.I. 2016/680, regulation 2 of, and paragraph 11 of the Schedule to, S.I. 2017/80, regulation 109 of, and paragraph 4 of Schedule 7 to, S.I. 2017/692 and regulation 50 of, and paragraph 6 of Schedule 4 to, S.I. 2017/701.

[44] 2000 c. 11; section 21A was inserted by section 3 of, and paragraph 5 of Schedule 2 to, the Anti-terrorism, Crime and Security Act 2001 (c. 24) and amended by regulation 2 of, and paragraphs 1 and 3 of Schedule 1 to, S.I. 2007/3398, section 59 of, and paragraphs 125 and 128 of, the Serious Organised Crime and Police Act 2005 (c. 15) and section 15 of, and paragraphs 67 and 72 of Schedule 8 to, the Crime and Courts Act 2013 (c. 22).

[45] 2000 c. 11; section 17A was inserted by section 42 of the Counter-Terrorism and Security Act 2015 (c. 6).

[46] 2000 c. 11; sections 22B, 22D and 22E were inserted by section 37 to the Criminal Finances Act 2017 (c. 22). Schedule 5A was inserted by Schedule 2 to the Criminal Finances Act 2017 (c. 22).

Section 14 of the 2000 Act[47] *defines terrorist property as money or other property which is likely to be used for the purposes of terrorism; proceeds of the commission of terrorism; and proceeds of acts carried out for the purposes of terrorism. Sections 15 to 18 of the Act create offences of fund raising for the purposes of terrorism; use or possession of property for the purposes of terrorism; funding terrorism; making an insurance payment in response to a terrorist demand; and facilitating the retention or control of terrorist property.*

A disclosure order can require a lawyer to provide a client's name and address.

Under section 21A of the 2000 Act[48] *a person engaged in a business in the regulated sector commits an offence where the conditions listed in that section are met and that person does not disclose, in the manner required by that section, knowledge or a suspicion that another person has committed or attempted to commit an offence under any of sections 15 to 18 in Part III of the Act. Part III of the Act also contains other disclosure provisions.*

The Practice Direction sets out forms of application, notice and order for use in connection with this rule.]

Content of application for an explanation order under the Terrorism Act 2000 R47.14

47.14 As well as complying with rules 47.6 and 47.11, an applicant who wants the court to make an explanation order must—
(a) identify the material that the applicant wants the respondent to explain;
(b) confirm that the explanation is not expected to infringe legal privilege; and
(c) propose the terms of the order.

[Note. See paragraph 13 of Schedule 5 to the Terrorism Act 2000[49]*. The applicant for an explanation order may be a constable or, where the application concerns material produced to a counter-terrorism financial investigator, such an investigator.*

An explanation order can require a lawyer to provide a client's name and address.

The Practice Direction sets out forms of application, notice and order for use in connection with this rule.]

Content of application for a customer information order under the Terrorism Act 2000 R47.15

47.15 As well as complying with rules 47.6 and 47.11, an applicant who wants the court to make a customer information order must—
(a) explain why it is desirable for the purposes of the investigation to trace property said to be terrorist property within the meaning of the Terrorism Act 2000;
(b) explain why the order will enhance the effectiveness of the investigation; and
(c) propose the terms of the order.

[Note. See Schedule 6 to the Terrorism Act 2000. The applicant for a customer information order must be a police officer of at least the rank of superintendent.

'Customer information' is defined by paragraph 7 of Schedule 6 to the 2000 Act. 'Terrorist property' is defined by section 14 of the Act.

The Practice Direction sets out forms of application, notice and order for use in connection with this rule.]

Content of application for an account monitoring order under the Terrorism Act 2000 R47.16

47.16 As well as complying with rules 47.6 and 47.11, an applicant who wants the court to make an account monitoring order must—
(a) specify—
  (i) the information sought,
  (ii) the period during which the applicant wants the respondent to provide that information (to a maximum of 90 days), and
  (iii) where, when and in what manner the applicant wants the respondent to provide that information;
(b) explain why it is desirable for the purposes of the investigation to trace property said to be terrorist property within the meaning of the Terrorism Act 2000;
(c) explain why the order will enhance the effectiveness of the investigation; and
(d) propose the terms of the order.

[47] 2000 c. 11.

[48] 2000 c. 11; section 21A was inserted by section 3 of, and paragraph 5 of Schedule 2 to, the Anti-terrorism, Crime and Security Act 2001 (c. 24) and amended by regulation 2 of, and paragraphs 1 and 3 of Schedule 1 to, S.I. 2007/3398, section 59 of, and paragraphs 125 and 128 of, the Serious Organised Crime and Police Act 2005 (c. 15) and section 15 of, and paragraphs 67 and 72 of Schedule 8 to, the Crime and Courts Act 2013 (c. 22).

[49] 2000 c. 11; paragraph 13 of Schedule 5 was amended by section 65 of, and paragraph 9 of Schedule 4 to, the Courts Act 2003 (c. 39) and section 41(3)(d) of the Criminal Finances Act 2017 (c. 22).

[Note. See Schedule 6A to the Terrorism Act 2000[50]*. The applicant for an account monitoring order may be a police officer or a counter-terrorism financial investigator.*

'Terrorist property' is defined by section 14 of the Act.

The Practice Direction sets out forms of application, notice and order for use in connection with this rule.]

Orders under the Proceeds of Crime Act 2002

R47.17 Application for an order under the Proceeds of Crime Act 2002

47.17 (1) This rule applies where an applicant wants the court to make one of the orders to which rule 47.4(d) refers.

(2) As well as complying with rule 47.6 (Application for order: general rules), the application must—

(a) identify—
   (i) any respondent, and
   (ii) the person or property the subject of the investigation;

(b) in the case of an investigation in the United Kingdom, explain why the applicant thinks that—
   (i) the person under investigation has benefited from criminal conduct, in the case of a confiscation investigation, or committed a money laundering offence, in the case of a money laundering investigation, or
   (ii) in the case of a detained cash investigation, a detained property investigation or a frozen funds investigation, the cash or property involved, or the money held in the frozen account, was obtained through unlawful conduct or is intended to be used in unlawful conduct;

(c) in the case of an investigation outside the United Kingdom, explain why the applicant thinks that—
   (i) there is an investigation by an overseas authority which relates to a criminal investigation or to criminal proceedings (including proceedings to remove the benefit of a person's criminal conduct following that person's conviction), and
   (ii) the investigation is into whether property has been obtained as a result of or in connection with criminal conduct, or into the extent or whereabouts of such property; and

(d) give the additional information required by whichever of rules 47.18 to 47.22 applies.

[Note. See also the code of practice for those exercising functions as officers and investigators issued under section 377 of the 2002 Act[51]*, and the code of practice for prosecutors and others issued under section 377A of that Act*[52]*.]*

R47.18 Content of application for a production order under the Proceeds of Crime Act 2002

47.18 As well as complying with rules 47.6 and 47.17, an applicant who wants the court to make an order for the production of, or for giving access to, material, must—

(a) describe that material;

(b) explain why the applicant thinks the material is in the respondent's possession or control;

(c) confirm that none of the material is—
   (i) expected to be subject to legal privilege, or
   (ii) excluded material;

(d) explain why the material is likely to be of substantial value to the investigation;

(e) explain why it is in the public interest for the material to be produced, or for the applicant to be given access to it, having regard to—
   (i) the benefit likely to accrue to the investigation if it is obtained, and
   (ii) the circumstances in which the respondent has the material; and

(f) propose—
   (i) the terms of the order, and
   (ii) the period within which it should take effect, if 7 days from the date of the order would not be appropriate.

[50] 2000 c. 11; Schedule 6A was inserted by section 3 of, and paragraph 1(1) and (3) of Part 1 to, the Anti-terrorism, Crime and Security Act 2001 (c. 24) and amended by section 41(1), (5) of the Criminal Finances Act 2017 (c. 22).

[51] 2002 c. 29; section 377 was amended by section 74 of, and paragraphs 103 and 114 of Schedule 8 to, the Serious Crime Act 2007 (c. 27), article 12 of, and paragraphs 47 and 67 of Schedule 14 to, SI 2010/976, sections 15 and 55 of, and paragraphs 108 and 143 of Schedule 8 and paragraphs 14 and 37 of Schedule 21 to, the Crime and Courts Act 2013 (c. 22) and section 224 of, and paragraphs 1 and 17 of Schedule 48 to, the Finance Act 2013 (c. 29).

[52] 2002 c. 29; section 377A was inserted by section 74 of, and paragraphs 103 and 115 of Schedule 8 to, the Serious Crime Act 2007 (c. 27) and amended by article 3 of, and paragraphs 19 and 28 of Schedule 2 to, SI 2014/834.

[Note. See sections 345 to 350 of the Proceeds of Crime Act 2002[53] and articles 6 to 11 of the Proceeds of Crime Act 2002 (External Investigations) Order 2014[54]. Under those provisions—

(a) 'excluded material' means the same as under section 11 of the Police and Criminal Evidence Act 1984; and
(b) 'legal privilege' is defined by section 348 of the 2002 Act.

A Crown Court judge may make a production order for the purposes of a confiscation investigation, a money laundering investigation, a detained cash investigation, a detained property investigation or a frozen funds investigation.

The applicant for a production order must be an 'appropriate officer' as defined by section 378(1), (4) and (5) of the 2002 Act[55] and article 2(1) of the 2014 Order.

The Practice Direction sets out forms of application, notice and order for use in connection with this rule.]

Content of application for an order to grant entry under the Proceeds of Crime Act 2002 **R47.19**

47.19 An applicant who wants the court to make an order to grant entry in aid of a production order must—
(a) specify the premises to which entry is sought;
(b) explain why the order is needed; and
(c) propose the terms of the order.

[Note. See section 347 of the Proceeds of Crime Act 2002 and article 8 of the Proceeds of Crime Act 2002 (External Investigations) Order 2014. The applicant for an order to grant entry must be an 'appropriate officer' as defined by section 378(1), (4) and (5) of the Act and article 2(1) of the 2014 Order.]

Content of application for a disclosure order or further information order under the Proceeds of Crime Act 2002 **R47.20**

47.20 (1) As well as complying with rules 47.6 and 47.17, an applicant who wants the court to make a disclosure order must—
(a) describe in general terms the information that the applicant wants a person to provide;
(b) confirm that none of the information is—
(i) expected to be subject to legal privilege, or
(ii) excluded material;
(c) explain why the information is likely to be of substantial value to the investigation;
(d) explain why it is in the public interest for the information to be provided, having regard to the benefit likely to accrue to the investigation if it is obtained; and
(e) propose the terms of the order.

(2) As well as complying with rule 47.6, an applicant who wants the court to make a further information order must—
(a) identify the respondent from whom the information is sought and explain—
(i) whether the respondent is the person who made the disclosure to which the information relates or is otherwise carrying on a business in the regulated sector within the meaning of Part 1 of Schedule 9 to the Proceeds of Crime Act 2002[56], and
(ii) why the applicant thinks that the information is in the possession, or under the control, of the respondent;

[53] 2002 c. 29; sections 345 and 346 were amended by section 75 of the Serious Crime Act 2007 (c. 27), section 169 of, and paragraphs 1, 6 and 7 of Schedule 19 to, the Coroners and Justice Act 2009 (c. 25) and section 49 of, and paragraphs 1, 4 and 5 of Schedule 19 to, the Crime and Courts Act 2013 (c. 22). Section 350 was amended by section 77 of, and paragraphs 1 and 5 of Schedule 10 to, the Serious Crime Act 2007 (c. 27), section 169 of, and paragraphs 1 and 8 of Schedule 19 to, the Coroners and Justice Act 2009 (c. 25) and sections 66 and 112 of, and Schedule 8 to, the Policing and Crime Act 2009 (c. 26).

[54] S.I. 2014/1893.

[55] 2002 c. 29; section 378 was amended by section 59 of, and paragraphs 168 and 175 of Schedule 4 to, the Serious Organised Crime and Police Act 2005 (c. 15), sections 74, 77 and 80 of, and paragraphs 103 and 116 of Schedule 8 and paragraphs 1 and 13 of Schedule 10 to, the Serious Crime Act 2007 (c. 27), sections 15, 49 and 55 of, and paragraphs 108 and 144 of Schedule 8 and paragraphs 1, 24, 27, 29 and 30 of Schedule 19 to, the Crime and Courts Act 2013 (c. 22) and section 224 of, and paragraphs 1 and 18 of Schedule 48 to, the Finance Act 2013 (c. 29).

[56] 2002 c. 29; Part 1 of Schedule 9 was substituted by articles 2 and 3 of S.I. 2007/3287 and amended by sections 183 and 237 of, and paragraph 2 of Schedule 18 and Part 29 of Schedule 25 to, the Localism Act 2011 (c. 20), regulation 79 of, and paragraph 3 of Schedule 4 to, S.I. 2011/99, article 3 of S.I. 2011/2701, article 3 of S.I. 2012/1534, article 3 of S.I. 2012/2299, regulation 46 of, and paragraph 41 of Schedule 2 to, S.I. 2013/3115, section 151 of, and paragraph 81 of Schedule 4 to, the Co-operative and Community Benefit Societies Act 2014 (c. 14), regulation 59 of, and paragraph 23 of Schedule 1 to, S.I. 2015/575, regulation 14 of S.I. 2016/680, regulation 2 of, and paragraph 13 of the Schedule to, S.I. 2017/80, regulation 109 of, and paragraph 6 of Schedule 7 to, S.I. 2017/692 and regulation 50 of, and paragraph 7 of Schedule 4 to, S.I. 2017/701.

(b) specify or describe the information that the applicant wants the respondent to provide;
(c) where the information sought relates to a disclosure of information under Part 7 of the Proceeds of Crime Act 2002 (Money laundering), explain—
(i) how the information sought relates to a matter arising from that disclosure,
(ii) how the information would assist in investigating whether a person is engaged in money laundering or in determining whether an investigation of that kind should be started, and
(iii) why it is reasonable in all the circumstances for the information to be provided;
(d) where the information sought relates to a disclosure made under a requirement of the law of a country outside the United Kingdom which corresponds with Part 7 of the 2002 Act, and an authority in that country which investigates money laundering has asked the National Crime Agency for information in connection with that disclosure, explain—
(i) how the information sought relates to a matter arising from that disclosure,
(ii) why the information is likely to be of substantial value to the authority that made the request in determining any matter in connection with the disclosure, and
(iii) why it is reasonable in all the circumstances for the information to be provided;
(e) confirm that none of the information is expected to be subject to legal privilege; and
(f) propose the terms of the order, including—
(i) how the respondent must provide the information required, and
(ii) the date by which the information must be provided.

(3) Rule 47.8 (Application to vary or discharge an order) does not apply to a further information order.
(4) Paragraph (5) applies where a party to an application for a further information order wants to appeal to the Crown Court from the decision of the magistrates' court.
(5) The appellant must—
(a) serve an appeal notice on the Crown Court officer and on the other party not more than 15 business days after the magistrates' court's decision; and
(b) in the appeal notice, explain, as appropriate, why the Crown Court should (as the case may be) make, discharge or vary a further information order.
(6) Rule 34.11 (Constitution of the Crown Court) applies on such an appeal.

[Note. See sections 339ZH, 339ZJ, 339ZK, 357, 358 and 361 of the Proceeds of Crime Act 2002([57]) *and articles 16, 17 and 20 of the Proceeds of Crime Act 2002 (External Investigations) Order 2014*[58].

Where the 2002 Act applies, a Crown Court judge may make a disclosure order for the purposes of a confiscation investigation or a money laundering investigation.

The applicant for a disclosure order must be a 'relevant authority' as defined by section 357(7) of the 2002 Act, or an 'appropriate officer' as defined by article 2(1) of the 2014 Order where the Order applies. Under section 362(6) of the Act[59]*, a relevant authority who under section 357(7) is an 'appropriate officer' (as defined by section 378(1), (4) and (5)*[60]*) may apply only if that person is, or is authorised to do so by, a 'senior appropriate officer' (as defined by section 378(2)).*

[57] 2002 c. 29; sections 339ZH, 339ZJ and 339ZK were inserted by section 12 of the Criminal Finances Act 2017 (c. 22). Section 357 was amended by sections 74 and 77 of, and paragraphs 103 and 108 of Schedule 8 and paragraphs 1 and 10 of Schedule 10 to, the Serious Crime Act 2007 (c. 27), section 169 of, and paragraphs 1 and 13 of Schedule 19 to, the Coroners and Justice Act 2009 (c. 25), sections 15, 49 and 55 of, and paragraphs 108 and 139 of Schedule 8, paragraphs 1 and 8 of Schedule 19 and paragraphs 14 and 34 of Schedule 21 to, the Crime and Courts Act 2013 (c. 22) and article 3 of, and paragraphs 19 and 27 of Schedule 2 to, SI 2014/834 and section 7(2) of, and paragraph 51 of Schedule 5 to, the Criminal Finances Act 2017 (c. 22). Section 358 was amended by section 169 of, and paragraphs 1 and 14 of Schedule 19 to, the Coroners and Justice Act 2009 (c. 25), section 49(a) of, and paragraphs 1 and 9 of Schedule 19 to, the Crime and Courts Act 2013 (c. 22) and section 7(3) of the Criminal Finances Act 2017 (c. 22). Section 361 was amended by section 74 of, and paragraphs 103 and 109 of Schedule 8 to, the Serious Crime Act 2007 (c. 27).

[58] S.I. 2014/1893.

[59] 2002 c. 29; section 362 was amended by section 74 of, and paragraphs 103 and 110 of Schedule 8 to, the Serious Crime Act 2007 (c. 27), section 169 of, and paragraphs 1 and 15 of Schedule 19 to, the Coroners and Justice Act 2009 (c. 25) and section 15 of, and paragraphs 108 and 140 of Schedule 8 to, the Crime and Courts Act 2013 (c. 22). It is further amended by section 7(4) of the Criminal Finances Act 2017 (c. 22), with effect from a date to be appointed.

[60] 2002 c. 29; section 378 was amended by section 59 of, and paragraphs 168 and 175 of Schedule 4 to, the Serious Organised Crime and Police Act 2005 (c. 15), sections 74, 77 and 80 of, and paragraphs 103 and 116 of Schedule 8 and paragraphs 1 and 13 of Schedule 10 to, the Serious Crime Act 2007 (c. 27), sections 15, 49 and 55 of, and paragraphs 108 and 144 of Schedule 8 and paragraphs 1, 24, 27, 29 and 30 of Schedule 19 to, the Crime and Courts Act 2013 (c. 22) and section 224 of, and paragraphs 1 and 18 of Schedule 48 to, the Finance Act 2013 (c. 29). It is further amended by paragraph 25 of Schedule 1, and paragraph 59 of Schedule 5, to the Criminal Finances Act 2017 (c. 22), with effect from dates to be appointed.

Under section 339ZH(1), (12) the applicant for a further information order must be the Director General of the National Crime Agency or an officer of that Agency authorised by the Director General for that purpose.

A disclosure order can require a lawyer to provide a client's name and address.

Under sections 330, 331 and 332 in Part 7 of the 2002 Act[61] *a person engaged in a business in the regulated sector commits an offence where the conditions listed in any of those sections are met and that person does not disclose, in the manner required by the relevant section, knowledge or a suspicion that another person is engaged in money laundering.*

The Practice Direction sets out forms of application, notice and order for use in connection with this rule.]

Content of application for a customer information order under the Proceeds of Crime Act 2002 **R47.21**

47.21 As well as complying with rules 47.6 and 47.17, an applicant who wants the court to make a customer information order must—

(a) explain why customer information about the person under investigation is likely to be of substantial value to that investigation;

(b) explain why it is in the public interest for the information to be provided, having regard to the benefit likely to accrue to the investigation if it is obtained; and

(c) propose the terms of the order.

[Note. See sections 363, 364, 365 and 368 of the Proceeds of Crime Act 2002[62] *and articles 22, 23, 24 and 27 of the Proceeds of Crime Act 2002 (External Investigations) Order 2014.*

A Crown Court judge may make a customer information order for the purposes of a confiscation investigation or a money laundering investigation.

The applicant for a customer information order must be an 'appropriate officer' as defined by section 378(1), (4) and (5) of the 2002 Act and article 2(1) of the 2014 Order.

'Customer information' is defined by section 364 of the 2002 Act and article 2(1) of the 2014 Order.

The Practice Direction sets out forms of application, notice and order for use in connection with this rule.]

Content of application for an account monitoring order under the Proceeds of Crime Act 2002 **R47.22**

47.22 As well as complying with rules 47.6 and 47.17, an applicant who wants the court to make an account monitoring order for the provision of account information must—

(a) specify—

(i) the information sought,

(ii) the period during which the applicant wants the respondent to provide that information (to a maximum of 90 days), and

(iii) when and in what manner the applicant wants the respondent to provide that information;

(b) explain why the information is likely to be of substantial value to the investigation;

(c) explain why it is in the public interest for the information to be provided, having regard to the benefit likely to accrue to the investigation if it is obtained; and

(d) propose the terms of the order.

[Note. See sections 370, 371 and 374 of the Proceeds of Crime Act 2002[63] *and articles 29, 30 and 33 of the Proceeds of Crime Act 2002 (External Investigations) Order 2014.*

[61] 2002 c. 29; section 330 was amended by sections 102, 104, 105, 106 and 174 of, and Schedule 17 to, the Serious Organised Crime and Police Act 2005 (c. 15), article 2 of S.I. 2006/308, regulation 3 of, and paragraphs 1 and 2 of Schedule 2 to, S.I. 2007/3398 and section 15 of, and paragraphs 108 and 129 of Schedule 8 to, the Crime and Courts Act 2013 (c. 22). Section 331 was amended by sections 102 and 104 of the Serious Organised Crime and Police Act 2005 (c. 15) and section 15 of, and paragraphs 108 and 130 of Schedule 8 to, the Crime and Courts Act 2013 (c. 22). Section 332 was amended by sections 102 and 104 of the Serious Organised Crime and Police Act 2005 (c. 15) and section 15 of, and paragraphs 108 and 131 of Schedule 8 to, the Crime and Courts Act 2013 (c. 22).

[62] 2002 c. 29; section 363 was amended by section 77 of, and paragraphs 1 and 11 of Schedule 10 to, the Serious Crime Act 2007 (c. 27), section 169 of, and paragraphs 1 and 16 of Schedule 19 to, the Coroners and Justice Act 2009 (c. 25) and section 49 of, and paragraphs 1 and 10 of Schedule 19 to, the Crime and Courts Act 2013 (c. 22). Section 364 was amended by section 107 of the Serious Organised Crime and Police Act 2005 (c. 27) and article 2(1) of and paragraph 196 of Schedule 1 to, S.I. 2009/1941.

[63] 2002 c. 29; section 370 was amended by section 77 of, and paragraphs 1 and 12 of Schedule 10 to, the Serious Crime Act 2007 (c. 27), section 169 of, and paragraphs 1 and 17 of Schedule 19 to, the Coroners and Justice Act 2009 (c. 25) and section 49 of, and paragraphs 1 and 12 of Schedule 19 to, the Crime and Courts Act 2013 (c. 22).

Where the 2002 Act applies, a Crown Court judge may make an account monitoring order for the purposes of a confiscation investigation, a money laundering investigation, a detained cash investigation, a detained property investigation or a frozen funds investigation.

The applicant for an account monitoring order must be an 'appropriate officer' as defined by section 378(1), (4) and (5) of the 2002 Act and article 2(1) of the 2014 Order.

'Account information' is defined by section 370 of the 2002 Act and article 29(3) of the 2014 Order.

The Practice Direction sets out forms of application, notice and order for use in connection with this rule.]

Orders under the Extradition Act 2003

R47.23 **Application for a production order under the Extradition Act 2003**

47.23 (1) This rule applies where an applicant wants the court to make an order to which rule 47.4(e) refers.

(2) As well as complying with rule 47.6 (Application for order: general rules), the application must—

(a) identify the person whose extradition is sought;
(b) specify the extradition offence of which that person is accused;
(c) identify the respondent; and
(d) describe the special procedure or excluded material sought.

(3) In relation to the person whose extradition is sought, the application must explain the grounds for believing that—

(a) that person has committed the offence for which extradition is sought;
(b) that offence is an extradition offence; and
(c) that person is in the United Kingdom or is on the way to the United Kingdom.

(4) In relation to the material sought, the application must—

(a) specify the premises on which the material is believed to be;
(b) explain the grounds for believing that—
  (i) the material is on those premises,
  (ii) the material consists of or includes special procedure or excluded material, and
  (iii) the material would be likely to be admissible evidence at a trial in England and Wales for the offence for which extradition is sought;
(c) explain what other methods of obtaining the material—
  (i) have been tried without success, or
  (ii) have not been tried because they appeared bound to fail; and
(d) explain why it is in the public interest for the respondent to produce or give access to the material.

(5) The application must propose—

(a) the terms of the order, and
(b) the period within which it should take effect.

[Note. See sections 157 and 158 of the Extradition Act 2003[64]*. Under those provisions—*

(c) 'special procedure material' means the same as under section 14 of the Police and Criminal Evidence Act 1984; and
(d) 'excluded material' means the same as under section 11 of the 1984 Act.

The applicant for a production order must be a constable.

The period within which an order takes effect must be specified in the order and, unless the court considers a longer period appropriate, must be 7 days from the date of the order.]

Section 3: investigation warrants

R47.24 **When this Section applies**

47.24 This Section applies where—

(a) a justice of the peace can issue a warrant under—
  (i) section 8 of the Police and Criminal Evidence Act 1984[65] or,
  (ii) section 2 of the Criminal Justice Act 1987[66];
(b) a Circuit judge can issue a warrant under—

[64] 2003 c. 41; section 157 was amended by section 174 of the Anti-social Behaviour, Crime and Policing Act 2014 (c. 12).

[65] 1984 c. 60; section 8 was amended by paragraph 80 of Schedule 14 to the Immigration and Asylum Act 1999 (c. 33), sections 111, 113 and 114 of, and paragraph 43 of Schedule 7 to, the Serious Organised Crime and Police Act 2005 (c. 15) and section 86 of the Finance Act 2007 (c. 11).

[66] 1987 c. 38; section 2 was amended by sections 143 and 170 of, and paragraph 113 of Schedule 15 to, the Criminal Justice Act 1988 (c. 33), section 164 of the Criminal Justice and Public Order Act 1994 (c. 33), paragraph 20 of Schedule 3 to the

(i) paragraph 12 of Schedule 1 to the Police and Criminal Evidence Act 1984[67],
(ii) paragraph 11 of Schedule 5 to the Terrorism Act 2000[68], or
(iii) section 160 of the Extradition Act 2003;[69]

(c) a Crown Court judge can issue a warrant under—
(i) section 352 of the Proceeds of Crime Act 2002[70], or
(ii) article 13 of the Proceeds of Crime Act 2002 (External Investigations) Order 2014[71]; and

(d) a court to which these Rules apply can issue a warrant to search for and seize articles or persons under a power not listed in paragraphs (a), (b) or (c).

[Note. In outline, the warrants to which these rules apply are—

(a) under the Police and Criminal Evidence Act 1984, a warrant authorising entry to, and the search of, premises for material, articles or persons;
(b) under the Criminal Justice Act 1987, a warrant authorising entry to, and the search of, premises for documents sought by the Director of the Serious Fraud Office;
(c) under the Terrorism Act 2000, a warrant authorising entry to, and the search of, premises for material sought for the purposes of a terrorist investigation;
(d) under the Proceeds of Crime Act 2002 or under the Proceeds of Crime Act 2002 (External Investigations) Order 2014, a warrant authorising entry to, and the search of, premises for material sought for the purposes of a confiscation investigation, a money laundering investigation, a detained cash investigation or an external investigation;
(e) under the Extradition Act 2003, a warrant authorising entry to, and the search of, premises for material sought in connection with the prosecution of a person whose extradition has been requested;
(f) under other Acts, comparable warrants.

For all the relevant terms under which such warrants can be issued, see the provisions listed in this rule.

Under section 8 of the Senior Courts Act 1981[72]*, a High Court judge, a Circuit judge, a Recorder, a qualifying judge advocate and a District Judge (Magistrates' Courts) each may act as a Crown Court judge.*

When the relevant provisions of the Courts Act 2003 come into force, a District Judge (Magistrates' Courts) will have the same powers as a Circuit judge under the Police and Criminal Evidence Act 1984 and under the Terrorism Act 2000.

Under section 66 of the Courts Act 2003[73]*, in criminal cases a High Court judge, a Circuit judge, a Recorder and a qualifying judge advocate each has the powers of a justice of the peace who is a District Judge (Magistrates' Courts).*

As well as governing procedure on an application to a magistrates' court or the Crown Court, under the following provisions rules may govern the procedure on an application to an individual Circuit or Crown Court judge—

(a) paragraph 15A of Schedule 1 to the Police and Criminal Evidence Act 1984[74]*;*
(b) paragraph 11 of Schedule 5 to the Terrorism Act 2000;

Youth Justice and Criminal Evidence Act 1999 (c. 23), paragraph 23 of Schedule 2 to the Criminal Justice and Police Act 2001 (c. 16), paragraphs 11 and 12 of Schedule 5 to the Crime (International Co-operation) Act 2003 (c. 32) and section 12 of, and paragraphs 11, 12 and 13 of Schedule 1 to, the Criminal Justice Act 2003 (c. 44).

[67] 1984 c. 60; paragraph 12 of Schedule 1 was amended by section 65 of, and paragraph 6 of Schedule 4 to, the Courts Act 2003 (c. 39) and section 113 of the Serious Organised Crime and Police Act 2005 (c. 15).

[68] 2000 c. 11; paragraph 11 of Schedule 5 was amended by section 26 of the Terrorism Act 2006 (c. 11) and section 82 of the Deregulation Act 2015 (c. 20). It is further amended by section 65 of, and paragraph 9 of Schedule 4 to, the Courts Act 2003 (c. 39), with effect from a date to be appointed.

[69] 2003 c. 41; section 160 was amended by section 174 of the Anti-social Behaviour, Crime and Policing Act 2014 (c. 12).

[70] 2002 c. 29; section 352 was amended by sections 74, 76, 77 and 80 of, and paragraphs 103 and 105 of Schedule 8 and paragraphs 1 and 7 of Schedule 10 to, the Serious Crime Act 2007 (c. 27), section 169 of, and paragraphs 1 and 10 of Schedule 19 to, the Coroners and Justice Act 2009 (c. 25), sections 15, 49 and 55 of, and paragraphs 108 and 137 of Schedule 8, paragraphs 1 and 6 of Schedule 19 and paragraphs 14 and 31 of Schedule 21 to, the Crime and Courts Act 2013 (c. 22), section 224 of, and paragraphs 1 and 12 of Schedule 48 to, the Finance Act 2013 (c. 29), article 3 of, and paragraphs 19 and 26 of Schedule 2 to, SI 2014/834 and section 82 of the Deregulation Act 2015 (c. 20).

[71] S.I. 2014/1893.

[72] 1981 c. 54; section 8 was amended by sections 65 and 109 of, and paragraph 259 of Schedule 8 to, the Courts Act 2003 (c. 39) and paragraph 1 of Schedule 2 to the Armed Forces Act 2011 (c. 18). The 1981 Act's title was amended by section 59(5) of, and paragraph 1 of Schedule 11 to, the Constitutional Reform Act 2005 (c. 4).

[73] 2003 c. 39; section 66 was amended by paragraph 6 of Schedule 2 to the Armed Forces Act 2011 (c. 18) and sections 17 and 21 of, and paragraphs 83 and 90 of Schedule 10 and paragraph 4 of Schedule 14 to, the Crime and Courts Act 2013 (c. 22).

[74] 1984 c. 60; paragraph 15A of Schedule 1 was inserted by section 82 of the Deregulation Act 2015 (c. 20).

(c) *section 352 of the Proceeds of Crime Act 2002; and*
(d) *section 160 of the Extradition Act 2003.]*

For a list of the types of investigation under Part 8 of the Proceeds of Crime Act 2002 and a list of the powers of judges in respect of each type, see the note to rule 47.4 (Section 2: Investigation orders; When this Section applies.]

R47.25 **Exercise of court's powers**

47.25 (1) The court must determine an application for a warrant—
(a) at a hearing, which must be in private unless the court otherwise directs;
(b) in the presence of the applicant; and
(c) in the absence of any person affected by the warrant, including any person in occupation or control of premises which the applicant wants to search.
(2) If the court so directs, the applicant may attend the hearing by live link or telephone.
(3) The court must not determine an application unless satisfied that sufficient time has been allowed for it.
(4) The court must not determine an application unless the applicant confirms, on oath or affirmation, that to the best of the applicant's knowledge and belief—
(a) the application discloses all the information that is material to what the court must decide, including any circumstances that might reasonably be considered capable of undermining any of the grounds of the application; and
(b) the content of the application is true.
(5) If the court requires the applicant to answer a question about an application—
(a) the applicant's answer must be on oath or affirmation;
(b) the court must arrange for a record of the gist of the question and reply; and
(c) if the applicant cannot answer to the court's satisfaction, the court may—
(i) specify the information the court requires, and
(ii) give directions for the presentation of any renewed application.
(6) Unless to do so would be inconsistent with other legislation, on an application the court may issue—
(a) a warrant in respect of specified premises;
(b) a warrant in respect of all premises occupied or controlled by a specified person;
(c) a warrant in respect of all premises occupied or controlled by a specified person which specifies some of those premises; or
(d) more than one warrant—
(i) each one in respect of premises specified in the warrant,
(ii) each one in respect of all premises occupied or controlled by a person specified in the warrant (whether or not such a warrant also specifies any of those premises), or
(iii) at least one in respect of specified premises and at least one in respect of all premises occupied or controlled by a specified person (whether or not such a warrant also specifies any of those premises).

[Note. See section 15 of the Police and Criminal Evidence Act 1984[75] *and section 2(4) of the Criminal Justice Act 1987*[76]*. Not all the powers to which the rules in this Section apply permit the issue of a warrant in respect of all premises occupied or controlled by a specified person: see, for example, rule 47.32 (Application for warrant under section 352 of the Proceeds of Crime Act 2002).]*

R47.26 **Application for warrant: general rules**

47.26 (1) This rule applies to each application to which this Section applies.
(2) The applicant must—
(a) apply in writing;
(b) serve the application on—
(i) the court officer, or
(ii) if the court office is closed, the court;
(c) demonstrate that the applicant is entitled to apply, for example as a constable or under legislation that applies to other officers;
(d) give the court an estimate of how long the court should allow—
(i) to read and prepare for the application, and
(ii) for the hearing of the application; and
(e) tell the court when the applicant expects any warrant issued to be executed.

[75] 1984 c. 60; section 15 was amended by sections 113 and 114 of the Serious Organised Crime and Police Act 2005 (c. 15) and article 7 of S.I. 2005/3496.
[76] 1987 c. 38.

(3) The application must disclose anything known or reported to the applicant that might reasonably be considered capable of undermining any of the grounds of the application.

(4) Where the application includes information that the applicant thinks should not be supplied under rule 5.7 (Supply to a party of information or documents from records or case materials) to a person affected by a warrant, the applicant may—

(a) set out that information in a separate document, marked accordingly; and

(b) in that document, explain why the applicant thinks that that information ought not to be supplied to anyone other than the court.

(5) The application must include—

(a) a declaration by the applicant that to the best of the applicant's knowledge and belief—

(i) the application discloses all the information that is material to what the court must decide, including anything that might reasonably be considered capable of undermining any of the grounds of the application, and

(ii) the content of the application is true; and

(b) a declaration by an officer senior to the applicant that the senior officer has reviewed and authorised the application.

(6) The application must attach a draft warrant or warrants in the terms proposed by the applicant.

Information to be included in a warrant **R47.27**

47.27 (1) A warrant must identify—

(a) the person or description of persons by whom it may be executed;

(b) any person who may accompany a person executing the warrant;

(c) so far as practicable, the material, documents, articles or persons to be sought;

(d) the legislation under which it was issued;

(e) the name of the applicant;

(f) the court that issued it, unless that is otherwise recorded by the court officer;

(g) the court office for the court that issued it; and

(h) the date on which it was issued.

(2) A warrant must specify—

(a) either—

(i) the premises to be searched, where the application was for authority to search specified premises, or

(ii) the person in occupation or control of premises to be searched, where the application was for authority to search any premises occupied or controlled by that person; and

(b) the number of occasions on which specified premises may be searched, if more than one.

(3) A warrant must include, by signature, initial, or otherwise, an indication that it has been approved by the court that issued it.

(4) Where a warrant comprises more than a single page, each page must include such an indication.

(5) A copy of a warrant must include a prominent certificate that it is such a copy.

[Note. See sections 15 and 16 of the Police and Criminal Evidence Act 1984[77]*. Not all the powers to which the rules in this Section apply permit the issue of a warrant in respect of all premises occupied or controlled by a specified person: see, for example, rule 47.32 (Application for warrant under section 352 of the Proceeds of Crime Act 2002).]*

Application for warrant under section 8 of the Police and Criminal Evidence Act 1984 **R47.28**

47.28 (1) This rule applies where an applicant wants a magistrates' court to issue a warrant or warrants under section 8 of the Police and Criminal Evidence Act 1984[78].

(2) As well as complying with rule 47.26, the application must—

(a) specify the offence under investigation (and see paragraph (3));

(b) so far as practicable, identify the material sought (and see paragraph (4));

(c) specify the premises to be searched (and see paragraphs (5) and (6));

(d) state whether the applicant wants the premises to be searched on more than one occasion (and see paragraph (7)); and

(e) state whether the applicant wants other persons to accompany the officers executing the warrant or warrants (and see paragraph (8)).

[77] 1984 c. 60; section 16 was amended by paragraph 281 of Schedule 8 to the Courts Act 2003 (c. 39), section 2 of the Criminal Justice Act 2003 (c. 44), sections 113 and 114 of the Serious Organised Crime and Police Act 2005 (c. 15) and article 8 of S.I. 2005/3496.

[78] 1984 c. 60; section 8 was amended by paragraph 80 of Schedule 14 to the Immigration and Asylum Act 1999 (c. 33), sections 111, 113 and 114 of, and paragraph 43 of Schedule 7 to, the Serious Organised Crime and Police Act 2005 (c. 15) and section 86 of the Finance Act 2007 (c. 11).

(3) In relation to the offence under investigation, the application must—
   (a) state whether that offence is—
      (i) an indictable offence, or
      (ii) a relevant offence as defined in section 28D of the Immigration Act 1971[79]; and
   (b) explain the grounds for believing that the offence has been committed.

(4) In relation to the material sought, the application must explain the grounds for believing that that material—
   (a) is likely to be of substantial value to the investigation (whether by itself, or together with other material);
   (b) is likely to be admissible evidence at trial for the offence under investigation; and
   (c) does not consist of or include items subject to legal privilege, excluded material or special procedure material.

(5) In relation to premises which the applicant wants to be searched and can specify, the application must—
   (a) specify each set of premises;
   (b) in respect of each set of premises, explain the grounds for believing that material sought is on those premises; and
   (c) in respect of each set of premises, explain the grounds for believing that—
      (i) it is not practicable to communicate with any person entitled to grant entry to the premises,
      (ii) it is practicable to communicate with such a person but it is not practicable to communicate with any person entitled to grant access to the material sought,
      (iii) entry to the premises will not be granted unless a warrant is produced, or
      (iv) the purpose of a search may be frustrated or seriously prejudiced unless a constable arriving at the premises can secure immediate entry to them.

(6) In relation to premises which the applicant wants to be searched but at least some of which the applicant cannot specify, the application must—
   (a) explain the grounds for believing that—
      (i) because of the particulars of the offence under investigation it is necessary to search any premises occupied or controlled by a specified person, and
      (ii) it is not reasonably practicable to specify all the premises which that person occupies or controls which might need to be searched;
   (b) specify as many sets of premises as is reasonably practicable;
   (c) in respect of each set of premises, whether specified or not, explain the grounds for believing that material sought is on those premises; and
   (d) in respect of each specified set of premises, explain the grounds for believing that—
      (i) it is not practicable to communicate with any person entitled to grant entry to the premises,
      (ii) it is practicable to communicate with such a person but it is not practicable to communicate with any person entitled to grant access to the material sought,
      (iii) entry to the premises will not be granted unless a warrant is produced, or
      (iv) the purpose of a search may be frustrated or seriously prejudiced unless a constable arriving at the premises can secure immediate entry to them.

(7) In relation to any set of premises which the applicant wants to be searched on more than one occasion, the application must—
   (a) explain why it is necessary to search on more than one occasion in order to achieve the purpose for which the applicant wants the court to issue the warrant; and
   (b) specify any proposed maximum number of occasions.

(8) In relation to any set of premises which the applicant wants to be searched by the officers executing the warrant with other persons authorised by the court, the application must—
   (a) identify those other persons, by function or description; and
   (b) explain why those persons are required.

[Note. Under section 8 of the Police and Criminal Evidence Act 1984, where there are reasonable grounds for believing that an indictable offence has been committed a constable may apply to a justice of the peace for a warrant authorising a search for evidence on specified premises, or on the premises of a specified person. Under section 8(6) of the 1984 Act, section 8 applies also in relation to relevant offences as defined in section 28D(4) of the Immigration Act 1971 (some of which are not indictable offences).

[79] 1971 c. 77; section 28D was inserted by section 131 of the Immigration and Asylum Act 1999 (c. 33) and amended by sections 144 and 150 of the Nationality, Immigration and Asylum Act 2002 (c. 41).

Under section 23 of the 1984 Act[80], *'premises' includes any place, and in particular any vehicle, vessel, aircraft or hovercraft, any offshore installation, any renewable energy installation and any tent or moveable structure.*

Under section 16(3) of the 1984 Act[81], *entry and search under a warrant must be within 3 months from the date of its issue.*

See also the code of practice for the search of premises issued under section 66 of the 1984 Act[82].

The Practice Direction sets out forms of application and warrant for use in connection with this rule.]

Application for warrant under section 2 of the Criminal Justice Act 1987 **R47.29**

47.29 (1) This rule applies where an applicant wants a magistrates' court to issue a warrant or warrants under section 2 of the Criminal Justice Act 1987[83].

(2) As well as complying with rule 47.26, the application must—
- (a) describe the investigation being conducted by the Director of the Serious Fraud Office and include—
  - (i) an explanation of what is alleged and why, and
  - (ii) a chronology of relevant events;
- (b) specify the document, documents or description of documents sought by the applicant (and see paragraphs (3) and (4)); and
- (c) specify the premises which the applicant wants to be searched (and see paragraph (5)).

(3) In relation to each document or description of documents sought, the application must—
- (a) explain the grounds for believing that each such document—
  - (i) relates to a matter relevant to the investigation, and
  - (ii) could not be withheld from disclosure or production on grounds of legal professional privilege; and
- (b) explain the grounds for believing that—
  - (i) a person has failed to comply with a notice by the Director to produce the document or documents,
  - (ii) it is not practicable to serve such a notice, or
  - (iii) the service of such a notice might seriously impede the investigation.

(4) In relation to any document or description of documents which the applicant wants to be preserved but not seized under a warrant, the application must—
- (a) specify the steps for which the applicant wants the court's authority in order to preserve and prevent interference with the document or documents; and
- (b) explain why such steps are necessary.

(5) In respect of each set of premises which the applicant wants to be searched, the application must explain the grounds for believing that a document or description of documents sought by the applicant is on those premises.

(6) If the court so directs, the applicant must make available to the court material on which is based the information given under paragraph (2).

[Note. Under section 2 of the Criminal Justice Act 1987, where the Director of the Serious Fraud Office is investigating a case of serious or complex fraud a member of that Office may apply to a justice of the peace for a warrant authorising a search of specified premises for documents relating to any matter relevant to the investigation. Under section 66 of the Courts Act 2003[84], *a Circuit judge can exercise the power to issue a warrant.*

Under section 16(3) of the Police and Criminal Evidence Act 1984, entry and search under a warrant must be within 3 months from the date of its issue.

The Practice Direction sets out forms of application and warrant for use in connection with this rule.]

[80] 1984 c. 60; section 23 was amended by sections 103 and 197 of, and Part 1 of Schedule 23 to, the Energy Act 2004 (c. 20).

[81] 1984 c. 60; section 16(3) was amended by section 114 of the Serious Organised Crime and Police Act 2005 (c. 15).

[82] 1984 c. 60; section 66 was amended by section 57 of the Criminal Justice and Court Services Act 2000 (c. 43), sections 110 and 174 of, and Schedule 17 to, the Serious Organised Crime and Police Act 2005 (c. 15) and section 115 of, and paragraph 21 of Schedule 9 to, the Protection of Freedoms Act 2012 (c. 9).

[83] 1987 c. 38; section 2 was amended by sections 143 and 170 of, and paragraph 113 of Schedule 15 to, the Criminal Justice Act 1988 (c. 33), section 164 of the Criminal Justice and Public Order Act 1994 (c. 33), paragraph 20 of Schedule 3 to the Youth Justice and Criminal Evidence Act 1999 (c. 23), paragraph 23 of Schedule 2 to the Criminal Justice and Police Act 2001 (c. 16), paragraphs 11 and 12 of Schedule 5 to the Crime (International Co-operation) Act 2003 (c. 32) and section 12 of, and paragraphs 11, 12 and 13 of Schedule 1 to, the Criminal Justice Act 2003 (c. 44).

[84] 2003 c. 39; section 66 was amended by paragraph 6 of Schedule 2 to the Armed Forces Act 2011 (c. 18) and sections 17 and 21 of, and paragraphs 83 and 90 of Schedule 10 and paragraph 4 of Schedule 14 to, the Crime and Courts Act 2013 (c. 22).

R47.30 **Application for warrant under paragraph 12 of Schedule 1 to the Police and Criminal Evidence Act 1984**

47.30 (1) This rule applies where an applicant wants a Circuit judge to issue a warrant or warrants under paragraph 12 of Schedule 1 to the Police and Criminal Evidence Act 1984[85].

(2) As well as complying with rule 47.26, the application must—
(a) specify the offence under investigation (and see paragraph (3)(a));
(b) specify the set of access conditions on which the applicant relies (and see paragraphs (3) and (4));
(c) so far as practicable, identify the material sought;
(d) specify the premises to be searched (and see paragraphs (6) and (7)); and
(e) state whether the applicant wants other persons to accompany the officers executing the warrant or warrants (and see paragraph (8)).

(3) Where the applicant relies on paragraph 2 of Schedule 1 to the Police and Criminal Evidence Act 1984[86] ('the first set of access conditions': general power to gain access to special procedure material), the application must—
(a) specify the indictable offence under investigation;
(b) explain the grounds for believing that the offence has been committed;
(c) explain the grounds for believing that the material sought—
(i) is likely to be of substantial value to the investigation (whether by itself, or together with other material),
(ii) is likely to be admissible evidence at trial for the offence under investigation, and
(iii) does not consist of or include items subject to legal privilege or excluded material;
(d) explain what other methods of obtaining the material—
(i) have been tried without success, or
(ii) have not been tried because they appeared bound to fail; and
(e) explain why it is in the public interest to obtain the material, having regard to—
(i) the benefit likely to accrue to the investigation if the material is obtained, and
(ii) the circumstances under which the material is held.

(4) Where the applicant relies on paragraph 3 of Schedule 1 to the Police and Criminal Evidence Act 1984[87] ('the second set of access conditions': use of search warrant power to gain access to excluded or special procedure material), the application must—
(a) state the legislation under which a search warrant could have been issued, had the material sought not been excluded or special procedure material (in this paragraph, described as 'the main search power');
(b) include or attach the terms of the main search power;
(c) explain how the circumstances would have satisfied any criteria prescribed by the main search power for the issue of a search warrant; and
(d) explain why the issue of such a search warrant would have been appropriate.

(5) Where the applicant relies on the second set of access conditions and on an assertion that a production order made under paragraph 4 of Schedule 1 to the 1984 Act[88] in respect of the material sought has not been complied with—
(a) the application must—
(i) identify that order and describe its terms, and
(ii) specify the date on which it was served; but
(b) the application need not comply with paragraphs (6) or (7).

(6) In relation to premises which the applicant wants to be searched and can specify, the application must (unless paragraph (5) applies)—
(a) specify each set of premises;
(b) in respect of each set of premises, explain the grounds for believing that material sought is on those premises; and
(c) in respect of each set of premises, explain the grounds for believing that—
(i) it is not practicable to communicate with any person entitled to grant entry to the premises,
(ii) it is practicable to communicate with such a person but it is not practicable to communicate with any person entitled to grant access to the material sought,

85 1984 c. 60; paragraph 12 of Schedule 1 was amended by section 65 of, and paragraph 6 of Schedule 4 to, the Courts Act 2003 (c. 39) and section 113 of the Serious Organised Crime and Police Act 2005 (c. 15).
86 1984 c. 60; paragraph 2 of Schedule 1 was amended by sections 111 and 113 of, and paragraph 43 of Schedule 7 to, the Serious Organised Crime and Police Act 2005 (c. 15).
87 1984 c. 60; paragraph 3 of Schedule 1 was amended by section 113 of the Serious Organised Crime and Police Act 2005 (c. 15).
88 1984 c. 60; paragraph 4 of Schedule 1 was amended by section 65 of, and paragraph 6 of Schedule 4 to, the Courts Act 2003 (c. 39).

(iii) the material sought contains information which is subject to a restriction on disclosure or an obligation of secrecy contained in an enactment and is likely to be disclosed in breach of the restriction or obligation if a warrant is not issued, or
(iv) service of notice of an application for a production order under paragraph 4 of Schedule 1 to the 1984 Act may seriously prejudice the investigation.

(7) In relation to premises which the applicant wants to be searched but at least some of which the applicant cannot specify, the application must (unless paragraph (5) applies)—
(a) explain the grounds for believing that—
(i) because of the particulars of the offence under investigation it is necessary to search any premises occupied or controlled by a specified person, and
(ii) it is not reasonably practicable to specify all the premises which that person occupies or controls which might need to be searched;
(b) specify as many sets of premises as is reasonably practicable;
(c) in respect of each set of premises, whether specified or not, explain the grounds for believing that material sought is on those premises; and
(d) in respect of each specified set of premises, explain the grounds for believing that—
(i) it is not practicable to communicate with any person entitled to grant entry to the premises,
(ii) it is practicable to communicate with such a person but it is not practicable to communicate with any person entitled to grant access to the material sought,
(iii) the material sought contains information which is subject to a restriction on disclosure or an obligation of secrecy contained in an enactment and is likely to be disclosed in breach of the restriction or obligation if a warrant is not issued, or
(iv) service of notice of an application for a production order under paragraph 4 of Schedule 1 to the 1984 Act may seriously prejudice the investigation.

(8) In relation to any set of premises which the applicant wants to be searched by the officers executing the warrant with other persons authorised by the court, the application must—
(a) identify those other persons, by function or description; and
(b) explain why those persons are required.

[Note. Under paragraph 12 of Schedule 1 to the Police and Criminal Evidenced Act 1984, where the conditions listed in that paragraph and, if applicable, in paragraphs 12A and 14 of that Schedule[89] *are fulfilled a constable may apply to a Circuit judge for a warrant authorising a search for evidence consisting of special procedure material or, in some cases, excluded material on specified premises or on the premises of a specified person.*

Under section 16(3) of the 1984 Act[90]*, entry and search under a warrant must be within 3 months from the date of its issue.*

See also the code of practice for the search of premises issued under section 66 of the 1984 Act.

The Practice Direction sets out forms of application and warrant for use in connection with this rule.]

Application for warrant under paragraph 11 of Schedule 5 to the Terrorism Act 2000 **R47.31**

47.31 (1) This rule applies where an applicant wants a Circuit judge to issue a warrant or warrants under paragraph 11 of Schedule 5 to the Terrorism Act 2000[91].

(2) As well as complying with rule 47.26, the application must—
(a) specify the offence under investigation;
(b) explain how the investigation constitutes a terrorist investigation within the meaning of the Terrorism Act 2000;
(c) so far as practicable, identify the material sought (and see paragraph (4));
(d) specify the premises to be searched (and see paragraph (5)); and
(e) state whether the applicant wants other persons to accompany the officers executing the warrant or warrants (and see paragraph (6)).

[89] 1984 c. 60; paragraph 12A of Schedule 1 was inserted by section 113 of the Serious Organised Crime and Police Act 2005 (c. 15). Paragraph 14 of Schedule 1 was amended by sections 113 and 174 of, and Schedule 17 to, the Serious Organised Crime and Police Act 2005 (c. 15).

[90] 1984 c. 60; section 16(3) was amended by section 114 of the Serious Organised Crime and Police Act 2005 (c. 15).

[91] 2000 c. 11; paragraph 11 of Schedule 5 was amended by section 26 of the Terrorism Act 2006 (c. 11) and section 82 of the Deregulation Act 2015 (c. 20). It is further amended by section 65 of, and paragraph 9 of Schedule 4 to, the Courts Act 2003 (c. 39), with effect from a date to be appointed.

(3) Where the applicant relies on an assertion that a production order made under paragraph 5 of Schedule 5 to the 2000 Act[92] in respect of material on the premises has not been complied with—
(a) the application must—
(i) identify that order and describe its terms, and
(ii) specify the date on which it was served; but
(b) the application need not comply with paragraphs (4) or (5)(b).
(4) In relation to the material sought, unless paragraph (3) applies the application must explain the grounds for believing that—
(a) the material consists of or includes excluded material or special procedure material but does not include items subject to legal privilege;
(b) the material is likely to be of substantial value to a terrorist investigation (whether by itself, or together with other material); and
(c) it is not appropriate to make an order under paragraph 5 of Schedule 11 to the 2000 Act in relation to the material because—
(i) it is not practicable to communicate with any person entitled to produce the material,
(ii) it is not practicable to communicate with any person entitled to grant access to the material or entitled to grant entry to premises to which the application for the warrant relates, or
(iii) a terrorist investigation may be seriously prejudiced unless a constable can secure immediate access to the material.
(5) In relation to the premises which the applicant wants to be searched, the application must—
(a) specify—
(i) where paragraph (3) applies, the respondent and any premises to which the production order referred, or
(ii) in any other case, one or more sets of premises, or any premises occupied or controlled by a specified person (which may include one or more specified sets of premises);
(b) unless paragraph (3) applies, in relation to premises which the applicant wants to be searched but cannot specify, explain why—
(i) it is necessary to search any premises occupied or controlled by the specified person, and
(ii) it is not reasonably practicable to specify all the premises which that person occupies or controls which might need to be searched; and
(c) explain the grounds for believing that material sought is on those premises.
(6) In relation to any set of premises which the applicant wants to be searched by the officers executing the warrant with other persons authorised by the court, the application must—
(a) identify those other persons, by function or description; and
(b) explain why those persons are required.

[Note. Under paragraph 11 of Schedule 5 to the Terrorism Act 2000, where the conditions listed in that paragraph and in paragraph 12 of that Schedule[93] are fulfilled a constable may apply to a Circuit judge for a warrant authorising a search for material consisting of excluded material or special procedure material on specified premises or on the premises of a specified person.

Under section 16(3) of the 1984 Act, entry and search under a warrant must be within 3 months from the date of its issue.

See also the code of practice for the search of premises issued under section 66 of the 1984 Act.

The Practice Direction sets out forms of application and warrant for use in connection with this rule.]

R47.32 **Application for warrant under section 352 of the Proceeds of Crime Act 2002**

47.32 (1) This rule applies where an applicant wants a Crown Court judge to issue a warrant or warrants under—
(a) section 352 of the Proceeds of Crime Act 2002[94]; or

[92] 2000 c. 11; paragraph 5 of Schedule 5 is amended by section 65 of, and paragraph 9 of Schedule 4 to, the Courts Act 2003 (c. 39), with effect from a date to be appointed.
[93] 2000 c. 11; paragraph 12 of Schedule 5 was amended by Section 26 of the Terrorism Act 2006 (c. 11). It is further amended by section 65 of, and paragraph 9 of Schedule 4 to, the Courts Act 2003 (c. 39), with effect from a date to be appointed.
[94] 2002 c. 29; section 352 was amended by sections 74, 76, 77 and 80 of, and paragraphs 103 and 105 of Schedule 8 and paragraphs 1 and 7 of Schedule 10 to, the Serious Crime Act 2007 (c. 27), section 169 of, and paragraphs 1 and 10 of Schedule 19 to, the Coroners and Justice Act 2009 (c. 25), sections 15, 49 and 55 of, and paragraphs 108 and 137 of Schedule 8,

(b) article 13 of the Proceeds of Crime Act 2002 (External Investigations) Order 2014[95].

(2) As well as complying with rule 47.26, the application must—

(a) explain whether the investigation is a confiscation investigation, a money laundering investigation, a detained cash investigation, a detained property investigation, a frozen funds investigation or an external investigation;

(b) in the case of an investigation in the United Kingdom, explain why the applicant suspects that—

(i) the person under investigation has benefited from criminal conduct, in the case of a confiscation investigation, or committed a money laundering offence, in the case of a money laundering investigation, or

(ii) in the case of a detained cash investigation, a detained property investigation or a frozen funds investigation, the cash or property involved, or the money held in the frozen account, was obtained through unlawful conduct or is intended to be used in unlawful conduct;

(c) in the case of an investigation outside the United Kingdom, explain why the applicant believes that—

(i) there is an investigation by an overseas authority which relates to a criminal investigation or to criminal proceedings (including proceedings to remove the benefit of a person's criminal conduct following that person's conviction), and

(ii) the investigation is into whether property has been obtained as a result of or in connection with criminal conduct, or into the extent or whereabouts of such property;

(d) indicate what material is sought (and see paragraphs (4) and (5));

(e) specify the premises to be searched (and see paragraph (6)); and

(f) state whether the applicant wants other persons to accompany the officers executing the warrant or warrants (and see paragraph (7)).

(3) Where the applicant relies on an assertion that a production order made under sections 345 and 351 of the 2002 Act[96] or under articles 6 and 12 of the 2014 Order has not been complied with—

(a) the application must—

(i) identify that order and describe its terms,

(ii) specify the date on which it was served, and

(iii) explain the grounds for believing that the material in respect of which the order was made is on the premises specified in the application for the warrant; but

(b) the application need not comply with paragraphs (4) or (5).

(4) Unless paragraph (3) applies, in relation to the material sought the application must—

(a) specify the material; or

(b) give a general description of the material and explain the grounds for believing that it relates to the person, cash, property or money under investigation and—

(i) in the case of a confiscation investigation, relates to the question whether that person has benefited from criminal conduct, or to any question about the extent or whereabouts of that benefit,

(ii) in the case of a money laundering investigation, relates to the question whether that person has committed a money laundering offence,

(iii) in the case of a detained cash investigation, a detained property investigation or a frozen funds investigation into the derivation of cash, property or money, relates to the question whether that cash, property or money is recoverable property,

paragraphs 1 and 6 of Schedule 19 and paragraphs 14 and 31 of Schedule 21 to, the Crime and Courts Act 2013 (c. 22), section 224 of, and paragraphs 1 and 12 of Schedule 48 to, the Finance Act 2013 (c. 29), article 3 of, and paragraphs 19 and 26 of Schedule 2 to, SI 2014/834 and section 82 of the Deregulation Act 2015 (c. 20).

[95] S.I. 2014/1893.

[96] 2002 c. 29; section 345 was amended by section 75 of the Serious Crime Act 2007 (c. 27), section 169 of, and paragraphs 1 and 6 of Schedule 19 to, the Coroners and Justice Act 2009 (c. 25) and section 49 of, and paragraphs 1 and 4 of Schedule 19 to, the Crime and Courts Act 2013 (c. 22). Section 351 was amended by sections 74 and 77 of, and paragraphs 103 and 104 of Schedule 8 and paragraphs 1 and 6 of Schedule 10 to, the Serious Crime Act 2007 (c. 27), section 169 of, and paragraphs 1 and 9 of Schedule 19 to, the Coroners and Justice Act 2009 (c. 25), sections 66 and 112 of, and Part 5 of Schedule 8 to, the Policing and Crime Act 2009 (c. 26), sections 15 and 55 of, and paragraphs 108 and 136 of Schedule 8 and paragraphs 14 and 30 of Schedule 21 to, the Crime and Courts Act 2013 (c.22) and section 224 of, and paragraphs 1 and 11 of Schedule 48 to, the Finance Act 2013 (c. 29).

(iv) in the case of a detained cash investigation, a detained property investigation or a frozen funds investigation into the intended use of cash, property or money, relates to the question whether that cash, property or money is intended by any person to be used in unlawful conduct, or

(v) in the case of an investigation outside the United Kingdom, relates to that investigation.

(5) Unless paragraph (3) applies, in relation to the material sought the application must explain also the grounds for believing that—

(a) the material consists of or includes special procedure material but does not include excluded material or privileged material;

(b) the material is likely to be of substantial value to the investigation (whether by itself, or together with other material); and

(c) it is in the public interest for the material to be obtained, having regard to—

(i) other potential sources of information, and

(ii) the benefit likely to accrue to the investigation if the material is obtained.

(6) In relation to the premises which the applicant wants to be searched, unless paragraph (3) applies the application must—

(a) explain the grounds for believing that material sought is on those premises;

(b) if the application specifies the material sought, explain the grounds for believing that it is not appropriate to make a production order under sections 345 and 351 of the 2002 Act or under articles 6 and 12 of the 2014 Order because—

(i) it is not practicable to communicate with any person against whom the production order could be made,

(ii) it is not practicable to communicate with any person who would be required to comply with an order to grant entry to the premises, or

(iii) the investigation might be seriously prejudiced unless an appropriate person is able to secure immediate access to the material; and

(c) if the application gives a general description of the material sought, explain the grounds for believing that—

(i) it is not practicable to communicate with any person entitled to grant entry to the premises,

(ii) entry to the premises will not be granted unless a warrant is produced, or

(iii) the investigation might be seriously prejudiced unless an appropriate person arriving at the premises is able to secure immediate access to them.

(7) In relation to any set of premises which the applicant wants to be searched by those executing the warrant with other persons authorised by the court, the application must—

(a) identify those other persons, by function or description; and

(b) explain why those persons are required.

[Note. Under section 352 of the Proceeds of Crime Act 2002 where there is a confiscation investigation, a money laundering investigation, a detained cash investigation, a detained property investigation or a frozen funds investigation, an 'appropriate officer' within the meaning of that section may apply to a Crown Court judge for a warrant authorising a search for special procedure material on specified premises, on the conditions listed in that section and in section 353 of the Act[97]*.*

Under article 13 of the Proceeds of Crime Act 2002 (External Investigations) Order 2014, where there is an external investigation an 'appropriate officer' within the meaning of that article may apply to a Crown Court judge for a warrant authorising a search for special procedure material on specified premises, on the conditions listed in that article and in article 14 of the Order.

Under section 16(3) of the 1984 Act[98]*, as applied by article 3 of the Proceeds of Crime Act 2002 (Application of Police and Criminal Evidence Act 1984) Order 2015*[99]*, entry and search under a warrant must be within 3 months from the date of its issue.*

See also the code of practice for the search of premises issued under section 66 of the 1984 Act.

The Practice Direction sets out forms of application and warrant for use in connection with this rule.]

[97] 2002 c. 29; section 353 was amended by sections 74, 76, 77 and 80 of, and paragraphs 103 and 106 of Schedule 8 and paragraphs 1 and 8 of Schedule 10 to, the Serious Crime Act 2007 (c. 27), section 169 of, and paragraphs 1 and 11 of Schedule 19 to, the Coroners and Justice Act 2009 (c. 25), sections 15, 49 and 55 of, and paragraphs 108 and 138 of Schedule 8, paragraphs 1 and 7 of Schedule 19 and paragraphs 14 and 32 of Schedule 21 to, the Crime and Courts Act 2013 (c. 22), section 224 of, and paragraphs 1 and 13 of Schedule 48 to, the Finance Act 2013 (c. 29) and section 38 of the Serious Crime Act 2015 (c. 9) and paragraph 48 of Schedule 5 to the Criminal Finances Act 2017 (c. 22).

[98] 1984 c. 60; section 16(3) was amended by section 114 of the Serious Organised Crime and Police Act 2005 (c. 15).

[99] S.I. 2015/759.

Application for warrant under section 160 of the Extradition Act 2003 R47.33

47.33 (1) This rule applies where an applicant wants a Circuit judge to issue a warrant or warrants under section 160 of the Extradition Act 2003[100].

(2) As well as complying with rule 47.26, the application must—

(a) identify the person whose extradition is sought (and see paragraph (3));

(b) specify the extradition offence of which that person is accused;

(c) specify the material, or description of material, sought (and see paragraph (4)); and

(d) specify the premises to be searched (and see paragraph (5)).

(3) In relation to the person whose extradition is sought, the application must explain the grounds for believing that—

(a) that person has committed the offence for which extradition is sought;

(b) that offence is an extradition offence; and

(c) that person is in the United Kingdom or is on the way to the United Kingdom.

(4) In relation to the material sought, the application must explain the grounds for believing that—

(a) the material consists of or includes special procedure or excluded material; and

(b) the material would be likely to be admissible evidence at a trial in England and Wales for the offence for which extradition is sought.

(5) In relation to the premises which the applicant wants to search, the application must explain the grounds for believing that—

(a) material sought is on those premises; and

(b) one or more of the following conditions is satisfied, namely—

(i) it is not practicable to communicate with any person entitled to grant entry to the premises,

(ii) it is practicable to communicate with such a person but it is not practicable to communicate with any person entitled to grant access to the material sought, or

(iii) the material contains information which is subject to a restriction on disclosure or an obligation of secrecy contained in an enactment and is likely to be disclosed in breach of the restriction or obligation if a warrant is not issued.

(6) In relation to any set of premises which the applicant wants to be searched by the officers executing the warrant with other persons authorised by the court, the application must—

(a) identify those other persons, by function or description; and

(b) explain why those persons are required.

[Note. Under section 160 of the Extradition Act 2003, where a person's extradition is sought a constable may apply to a Circuit judge for a warrant authorising a search for special procedure material or excluded material on specified premises, on the conditions listed in that section.

Under section 16(3) of the 1984 Act, entry and search under a warrant must be within 3 months from the date of its issue.

See also the code of practice for the search of premises issued under section 66 of the 1984 Act.]

Application for warrant under any other power R47.34

47.34 (1) This rule applies—

(a) where an applicant wants a court to issue a warrant or warrants under a power (in this rule, 'the relevant search power') to which rule 47.24(d) (other powers) refers; but

(b) subject to any inconsistent provision in legislation that applies to the relevant search power.

(2) As well as complying with rule 47.26, the application must—

(a) demonstrate the applicant's entitlement to apply;

(b) identify the relevant search power (and see paragraph (3));

(c) so far as practicable, identify the articles or persons sought (and see paragraph (4));

(d) specify the premises to be searched (and see paragraphs (5) and (6));

(e) state whether the applicant wants the premises to be searched on more than one occasion, if the relevant search power allows (and see paragraph (7)); and

(f) state whether the applicant wants other persons to accompany the officers executing the warrant or warrants, if the relevant search power allows (and see paragraph (8)).

(3) The application must—

(a) include or attach the terms of the relevant search power; and

(b) explain how the circumstances satisfy the criteria prescribed by that power for making the application.

[100] 2003 c. 41; section 160 was amended by section 174 of the Anti-social Behaviour, Crime and Policing Act 2014 (c. 12).

(4) In relation to the articles or persons sought, the application must explain how they satisfy the criteria prescribed by the relevant search power about such articles or persons.
(5) In relation to premises which the applicant wants to be searched and can specify, the application must—
(a) specify each set of premises; and
(b) in respect of each, explain how the circumstances satisfy any criteria prescribed by the relevant search power—
(i) for asserting that the articles or persons sought are on those premises, and
(ii) for asserting that the court can exercise its power to authorise the search of those particular premises.
(6) In relation to premises which the applicant wants to be searched but at least some of which the applicant cannot specify, the application must—
(a) explain how the relevant search power allows the court to authorise such searching;
(b) specify the person who occupies or controls such premises;
(c) specify as many sets of such premises as is reasonably practicable;
(d) explain why—
(i) it is necessary to search more premises than those specified, and
(ii) it is not reasonably practicable to specify all the premises which the applicant wants to be searched;
(e) in respect of each set of premises, whether specified or not, explain how the circumstances satisfy any criteria prescribed by the relevant search power for asserting that the articles or persons sought are on those premises; and
(f) in respect of each specified set of premises, explain how the circumstances satisfy any criteria prescribed by the relevant search power for asserting that the court can exercise its power to authorise the search of those premises.
(7) In relation to any set of premises which the applicant wants to be searched on more than one occasion, the application must—
(a) explain how the relevant search power allows the court to authorise such searching;
(b) explain why the applicant wants the premises to be searched more than once; and
(c) specify any proposed maximum number of occasions.
(8) In relation to any set of premises which the applicant wants to be searched by the officers executing the warrant with other persons authorised by the court, the application must—
(a) identify those other persons, by function or description; and
(b) explain why those persons are required.

[Note. See, among other provisions, sections 15 and 16 of the Police and Criminal Evidence Act 1984[101]*, which apply to an application by a constable under any Act for a warrant authorising the search of specified premises, or the search of premises of a specified person, and to the execution of such a warrant. Unless other legislation otherwise provides, under section 16(3) of the 1984 Act entry and search under a warrant must be within 3 months from the date of its issue.*

The Practice Direction sets out forms of application and warrant for use in connection with this rule.]

Section 4: orders for the retention or return of property

R47.35 When this Section applies

47.35 (1) This Section applies where—
(a) under section 1 of the Police (Property) Act 1897[102], a magistrates' court can—
(i) order the return to the owner of property which has come into the possession of the police or the National Crime Agency in connection with an investigation of a suspected offence, or
(ii) make such order with respect to such property as the court thinks just, where the owner cannot be ascertained; and
(b) a Crown Court judge can—
(i) order the return of seized property under section 59(4) of the Criminal Justice and Police Act 2001[103], or

[101] 1984 c. 60; section 15 was amended by sections 113 and 114 of the Serious Organised Crime and Police Act 2005 (c. 15) and article 7 of S.I. 2005/3496. Section 16 was amended by paragraph 281 of Schedule 8 to the Courts Act 2003 (c. 39), section 2 of the Criminal Justice Act 2003 (c. 44), sections 113 and 114 of the Serious Organised Crime and Police Act 2005 (c. 15) and article 8 of S.I. 2005/3496.
[102] 1897 c. 30; section 1 was amended by sections 33 and 36 of, and Part III of Schedule 3 to, the Theft Act 1968 (c. 60), section 58 of the Criminal Justice Act 1972 (c. 71), section 192 of, and Part I of Schedule 5 to, the Consumer Credit Act 1974 (c. 39), the Statute Law (Repeals) Act 1989 (c. 43) and section 4 of the Police (Property) Act 1997 (c. 30).
[103] 2001 c. 16.

(ii) order the examination, retention, separation or return of seized property under section 59(5) of the Act.

(2) In this Section, a reference to a person with 'a relevant interest' in seized property means someone from whom the property was seized, or someone with a proprietary interest in the property, or someone who had custody or control of it immediately before it was seized.

Exercise of court's powers R47.36

47.36 (1) The court may determine an application for an order—

(a) at a hearing (which must be in private unless the court otherwise directs), or without a hearing; and

(b) in a party's absence, if that party—

(i) applied for the order, or

(ii) has had at least 10 business days in which to make representations.

(2) The court officer must arrange for the court to hear such an application no sooner than 10 business days after it was served, unless—

(a) the court directs that no hearing need be arranged; or

(b) the court gives other directions for the hearing.

(3) If the court so directs, the parties to an application may attend a hearing by live link or telephone.

(4) The court may—

(a) shorten or extend (even after it has expired) a time limit under this Section;

(b) dispense with a requirement for service under this Section (even after service was required); and

(c) consider an application made orally instead of in writing.

(5) A person who wants an extension of time must—

(a) apply when serving the application or representations for which it is needed; and

(b) explain the delay.

Application for an order under section 1 of the Police (Property) Act 1897 R47.37

47.37 (1) This rule applies where an applicant wants the court to make an order to which rule 47.35(1)(a) refers.

(2) The applicant must apply in writing and serve the application on—

(a) the court officer; and

(b) as appropriate—

(i) the officer who has the property,

(ii) any person who appears to be its owner.

(3) The application must—

(a) explain the applicant's interest in the property (either as a person who claims to be its owner or as an officer into whose possession the property has come);

(b) specify the direction that the applicant wants the court to make, and explain why; and

(c) include or attach a list of those on whom the applicant has served the application.

[Note. Under section 1 of the Police (Property) Act 1897, the owner of property which has come into the possession of the police or the National Crime Agency in connection with the investigation of a suspected offence can apply to a magistrates' court for an order for its delivery to the claimant.]

Application for an order under section 59 of the Criminal Justice and Police Act 2001 R47.38

47.38 (1) This rule applies where an applicant wants the court to make an order to which rule 47.35(1)(b) refers.

(2) The applicant must apply in writing and serve the application on—

(a) the court officer; and

(b) as appropriate—

(i) the person who for the time being has the seized property,

(ii) each person whom the applicant knows or believes to have a relevant interest in the property.

(3) In each case, the application must—

(a) explain the applicant's interest in the property (either as a person with a relevant interest, or as possessor of the property in consequence of its seizure, as appropriate);

(b) explain the circumstances of the seizure of the property and identify the power that was exercised to seize it (or which the person seizing it purported to exercise, as appropriate); and

(c) include or attach a list of those on whom the applicant has served the application.

(4) On an application for an order for the return of property under section 59(4) of the Criminal Justice and Police Act 2001, the application must explain why any one or more of these applies—
(a) there was no power to make the seizure;
(b) the property seized is, or contains, an item subject to legal privilege which is not an item that can be retained lawfully in the circumstances listed in section 54(2) of the Act[104];
(c) the property seized is, or contains, excluded or special procedure material which is not material that can be retained lawfully in the circumstances listed in sections 55 and 56 of the Act; or
(d) the property seized is, or contains, something taken from premises under section 50 of the Act, or from a person under section 51 of the Act, in the circumstances listed in those sections and which cannot lawfully be retained on the conditions listed in the Act.

(5) On an application for an order for the examination, retention, separation or return of property under section 59(5) of the 2001 Act, the application must—
(a) specify the direction that the applicant wants the court to make, and explain why;
(b) if applicable, specify each requirement of section 53(2) of the Act (examination and return of property) which is not being complied with; and
(c) if applicable, explain why the retention of the property by the person who now has it would be justified on the grounds that, even if it were returned, it would immediately become appropriate for that person to get it back under—
(i) a warrant for its seizure, or
(ii) a production order made under paragraph 4 of Schedule 1 to the Police and Criminal Evidence Act 1984[105], section 20BA of the Taxes Management Act 1970[106] or paragraph 5 of Schedule 5 to the Terrorism Act 2000[107].

[Note. Under section 59 of the Criminal Justice and Police Act 2001, a person with a 'relevant interest' (see rule 47.35(2)) in seized property can apply in the circumstances listed in the Act to a Crown Court judge for an order for its return. A person who has the property in consequence of its seizure can apply for an order authorising its retention. Either can apply for an order relating to the examination of the property.]

R47.39 Application containing information withheld from another party

47.39 (1) This rule applies where—
(a) an applicant serves an application to which rule 47.37 (Application for an order under section 1 of the Police (Property) Act 1897) or rule 47.38 (Application for an order under section 59 of the Criminal Justice and Police Act 2001) applies; and
(b) the application includes information that the applicant thinks ought not be revealed to another party.

(2) The applicant must—
(a) omit that information from the part of the application that is served on that other party;
(b) mark the other part to show that, unless the court otherwise directs, it is only for the court; and
(c) in that other part, explain why the applicant has withheld that information from that other party.

(3) If the court so directs, any hearing of an application to which this rule applies may be, wholly or in part, in the absence of a party from whom information has been withheld.

(4) At any hearing of an application to which this rule applies—
(a) the general rule is that the court must consider, in the following sequence—
(i) representations first by the applicant and then by each other party, in all the parties' presence, and then
(ii) further representations by the applicant, in the absence of a party from whom information has been withheld; but
(b) the court may direct other arrangements for the hearing.

104 2001 c. 16; section 55 was amended by sections 456 and 457 of, and paragraphs 1 and 40 of Schedule 11 and Schedule 12 to, the Proceeds of Crime Act 2002 (c. 29). Section 56 was amended by article 364 of SI 2001/3649, section 12 of, and paragraph 14 of Schedule 1 to, the Criminal Justice Act 2003 (c. 44) and article 2 of, and paragraph 189 of Schedule 1 to, S.I. 2009/1941.

105 1984 c. 60; paragraph 4 of Schedule 1 was amended by section 65 of, and paragraph 6 of Schedule 4 to, the Courts Act 2003 (c. 39).

106 1970 c. 9; section 20BA was inserted by section 149 of the Finance Act 2000 (c. 17).

107 2000 c. 11; paragraph 5 of Schedule 5 is amended by section 65 of, and paragraph 9 of Schedule 4 to, the Courts Act 2003 (c. 39), with effect from a date to be appointed.

Representations in response R47.40

47.40 (1) This rule applies where a person wants to make representations about an application under rule 47.37 or rule 47.38.

(2) Such a person must—

(a) serve the representations on—

(i) the court officer, and

(ii) the applicant and any other party to the application;

(b) do so not more than 10 business days after service of the application; and

(c) ask for a hearing, if that person wants one.

(3) Representations in opposition to an application must explain why the grounds on which the applicant relies are not met.

(4) Where representations include information that the person making them thinks ought not be revealed to another party, that person must—

(a) omit that information from the representations served on that other party;

(b) mark the information to show that, unless the court otherwise directs, it is only for the court; and

(c) with that information include an explanation of why it has been withheld from that other party.

Application to punish for contempt of court R47.41

47.41 (1) This rule applies where a person is accused of disobeying an order under section 59 of the Criminal Justice and Police Act 2001.

(2) A person who wants the court to exercise its power to punish that person for contempt of court must comply with the rules in Part 48 (Contempt of court).

[Note. A Crown Court judge has power to punish a person who disobeys an order under section 59 of the 2001 Act as if that were a contempt of the Crown Court: see section 59(9) of the Act.]

Section 5: orders for the retention of fingerprints, etc.

When this Section applies R47.42

47.42 This Section applies where—

(a) a District Judge (Magistrates' Court) can make an order under—

(i) section 63F(7) or 63R(6) of the Police and Criminal Evidence Act 1984[108], or

(ii) paragraph 20B(5) or 20G(6) of Schedule 8 to the Terrorism Act 2000[109]; and

(b) the Crown Court can determine an appeal under—

(i) section 63F(10) of the Police and Criminal Evidence Act 1984, or

(ii) paragraph 20B(8) of Schedule 8 to the Terrorism Act 2000.

[Note. Under the Police and Criminal Evidence Act 1984 or under the Terrorism Act 2000, an order may be made extending the period during which fingerprints, DNA profiles or samples may be retained by the police.]

Exercise of court's powers R47.43

47.43 (1) The court must determine an application under rule 47.44, and an appeal under rule 47.45—

(a) at a hearing, which must be in private unless the court otherwise directs; and

(b) in the presence of the applicant or appellant.

(2) The court must not determine such an application or appeal unless any person served under those rules—

(a) is present; or

(b) has had an opportunity—

(i) to attend, or

(ii) to make representations.

Application to extend retention period R47.44

47.44 (1) This rule applies where a magistrates' court can make an order extending the period for which there may be retained material consisting of—

(a) fingerprints taken from a person—

[108] 1984 c. 60; section 63D was inserted by section 1 of the Protection of Freedoms Act 2012 (c. 9). Section 63R was inserted by section 14 of that Act.

[109] 2000 c. 11; paragraph 20B of Schedule 8 was inserted by section 19 of, and paragraph 1 of Schedule 1 to, the Protection of Freedoms Act 2012 (c. 9) (for certain purposes, and for remaining purposes with effect from a date to be appointed) and amended by section 181 of, and paragraph 125 of Schedule 11 to, the Anti-social Behaviour, Crime and Policing Act 2014 (c. 12). Paragraph 20G of Schedule 8 was inserted by section 19 of, and paragraph 1 of Schedule 1 to, the Protection of Freedoms Act 2012 (c. 9) for certain purposes, and for remaining purposes with effect from a date to be appointed.

(i) under a power conferred by Part V of the Police and Criminal Evidence Act 1984[110],
(ii) with that person's consent, in connection with the investigation of an offence by the police, or
(iii) under a power conferred by Schedule 8 to the Terrorism Act 2000[111] in relation to a person detained under section 41 of that Act;
(b) a DNA profile derived from a DNA sample so taken; or
(c) a sample so taken.

(2) A chief officer of police who wants the court to make such an order must—
(a) apply in writing—
(i) within the period of 3 months ending on the last day of the retention period, where the application relates to fingerprints or a DNA profile, or
(ii) before the expiry of the retention period, where the application relates to a sample;
(b) in the application—
(i) identify the material,
(ii) state when the retention period expires,
(iii) give details of any previous such application relating to the material, and
(iv) outline the circumstances in which the material was acquired;
(c) serve the application on the court officer, in every case; and
(d) serve the application on the person from whom the material was taken, where—
(i) the application relates to fingerprints or a DNA profile, or
(ii) the application is for the renewal of an order extending the retention period for a sample.

(3) An application to extend the retention period for fingerprints or a DNA profile must explain why that period should be extended.

(4) An application to extend the retention period for a sample must explain why, having regard to the nature and complexity of other material that is evidence in relation to the offence, the sample is likely to be needed in any proceedings for the offence for the purposes of—
(a) disclosure to, or use by, a defendant; or
(b) responding to any challenge by a defendant in respect of the admissibility of material that is evidence on which the prosecution proposes to rely.

(5) On an application to extend the retention period for fingerprints or a DNA profile, the applicant must serve notice of the court's decision on any respondent where—
(a) the court makes the order sought; and
(b) the respondent was absent when it was made.

[Note. See rule 47.42(a). The powers to which rule 47.44 applies may be exercised only by a District Judge (Magistrates' Courts).

The time limits for making an application under this rule are prescribed by sections 63F(8) and 63R(8) of the Police and Criminal Evidence Act 1984[112], and by paragraphs 20B(6) and 20G(8) of Schedule 8 to the Terrorism Act 2000[113]. They may be neither extended nor shortened.

Sections 63D and 63R of the 1984 Act[114], and paragraphs 20A and 20G of Schedule 8 to the 2000 Act[115], provide for the circumstances in which there must be destroyed the material to which this rule applies.

Section 63F of the 1984 Act, and paragraph 20B of Schedule 8 to the 2000 Act, provide for the circumstances in which fingerprints and DNA profiles may be retained instead of being destroyed. Under section 63F(7) and paragraph 20B(5), a chief officer of police to whom those provisions apply may apply for an order extending the statutory retention period of 3 years by up to another 2 years.

110 1984 c. 60.

111 2000 c. 11.

112 1984 c. 60; section 63F was inserted by section 3 of the Protection of Freedoms Act 2012 (c. 9). Section 63R was inserted by section 14 of that Act.

113 2000 c. 11; paragraph 20B of Schedule 8 was inserted by section 19 of, and paragraph 1 of Schedule 1 to, the Protection of Freedoms Act 2012 (c. 9) (for certain purposes, and for remaining purposes with effect from a date to be appointed) and amended by section 181 of, and paragraph 125 of Schedule 11 to, the Anti-social Behaviour, Crime and Policing Act 2014 (c. 12). Paragraph 20G of Schedule 8 was inserted by section 19 of, and paragraph 1 of Schedule 1 to, the Protection of Freedoms Act 2012 (c. 9) for certain purposes, and for remaining purposes with effect from a date to be appointed.

114 1984 c. 60; section 63D was inserted by section 1 of the Protection of Freedoms Act 2012 (c. 9).

115 2000 c. 11; paragraph 20A of Schedule 8 was inserted by section 19 of, and paragraph 1 of Schedule 1 to, the Protection of Freedoms Act 2012 (c. 9) for certain purposes, and for remaining purposes with effect from a date to be appointed.

Section 63R of the 1984 Act and paragraph 20G of Schedule 8 to the 2000 Act provide for the circumstances in which samples taken from a person may be retained instead of being destroyed. Under section 63R(6) of the 1984 Act and paragraph 20G(6) of Schedule 8 to the 2000 Act, a chief officer of police to whom those provisions apply may apply for an order to retain a sample for up to 12 months after the date on which it would otherwise have to be destroyed. Under section 63R(9) and paragraph 20G(9), such an order may be renewed, on one or more occasions, for a further period of not more than 12 months from the end of the period when the order would otherwise cease to have effect.]

Appeal **R47.45**

47.45 (1) This rule applies where, under rule 47.44, a magistrates' court determines an application relating to fingerprints or a DNA profile and—
(a) the person from whom the material was taken wants to appeal to the Crown Court against an order extending the retention period; or
(b) a chief officer of police wants to appeal to the Crown Court against a refusal to make such an order.
(2) The appellant must—
(a) serve an appeal notice—
(i) on the Crown Court officer and on the other party, and
(ii) not more than 15 business days after the magistrates' court's decision, or, if applicable, service of notice under rule 47.44(5); and
(b) in the appeal notice, explain, as appropriate, why the retention period should, or should not, be extended.
(3) Rule 34.11 (Constitution of the Crown Court) applies on such an appeal.

[Note. Under section 63F(10) of the Police and Criminal Evidence Act 1984, and under paragraph 20B(8) of Schedule 8 to the Terrorism Act 2000, the person from whom fingerprints were taken, or from whom a DNA profile derives, may appeal to the Crown Court against an order extending the retention period; and a chief officer of police may appeal to the Crown Court against the refusal of such an order.]

Section 6: investigation anonymity orders under the Coroners and Justice Act 2009

When this Section applies **R47.46**

47.46 This Section applies where—
(a) a justice of the peace can make or discharge an investigation anonymity order, under sections 76 and 80(1) of the Coroners and Justice Act 2009[116]; and
(b) a Crown Court judge can determine an appeal against—
(i) a refusal of such an order, under section 79 of the 2009 Act, or
(ii) a decision on an application to discharge such an order, under section 80(6) of the 2009 Act.

[Note. Under the Coroners and Justice Act 2009, an investigation anonymity order may be made prohibiting the disclosure of information that identifies, or might identify, a specified person as someone who is, or was, willing to assist the investigation of an offence of murder or manslaughter caused by a gun or knife.]

Exercise of court's powers **R47.47**

47.47 (1) The court may determine an application for an investigation anonymity order, and any appeal against the refusal of such an order—
(a) at a hearing (which must be in private unless the court otherwise directs); or
(b) without a hearing.
(2) The court must determine an application to discharge an investigation anonymity order, and any appeal against the decision on such an application—
(a) at a hearing (which must be in private unless the court otherwise directs); and
(b) in the presence of the person specified in the order, unless—
(i) that person applied for the discharge of the order,
(ii) that person has had an opportunity to make representations, or
(iii) the court is satisfied that it is not reasonably practicable to communicate with that person.
(3) The court may consider an application or an appeal made orally instead of in writing.

Application for an investigation anonymity order **R47.48**

47.48 (1) This rule applies where an applicant wants a magistrates' court to make an investigation anonymity order.
(2) The applicant must—

116 2009 c. 25.

(a) apply in writing;
(b) serve the application on the court officer;
(c) identify the person to be specified in the order, unless—
(i) the applicant wants the court to determine the application at a hearing, or
(ii) the court otherwise directs;
(d) explain how the proposed order meets the conditions prescribed by section 78 of the Coroners and Justice Act 2009[117];
(e) say if the applicant intends to appeal should the court refuse the order;
(f) attach any material on which the applicant relies; and
(g) propose the terms of the order.

(3) At any hearing of the application, the applicant must—
(a) identify to the court the person to be specified in the order, unless—
(i) the applicant has done so already, or
(ii) the court otherwise directs; and
(b) unless the applicant has done so already, inform the court if the applicant intends to appeal should the court refuse the order.

[Note. See section 77 of the Coroners and Justice Act 2009.]

R47.49 Application to discharge an investigation anonymity order

47.49 (1) This rule applies where one of the following wants a magistrates' court to discharge an investigation anonymity order—
(a) an applicant; or
(b) the person specified in the order.

(2) That applicant or the specified person must—
(a) apply in writing as soon as practicable after becoming aware of the grounds for doing so;
(b) serve the application on—
(i) the court officer, and as applicable
(ii) the applicant for the order, and
(iii) the specified person;
(c) explain—
(i) what material circumstances have changed since the order was made, or since any previous application was made to discharge it, and
(ii) why it is appropriate for the order to be discharged; and
(d) attach—
(i) a copy of the order, and
(ii) any material on which the applicant relies.

(3) A party must inform the court if that party intends to appeal should the court discharge the order.

[Note. See section 80 of the Coroners and Justice Act 2009.]

R47.50 Appeal

47.50 (1) This rule applies where one of the following ('the appellant') wants to appeal to the Crown Court—
(a) the applicant for an investigation anonymity order, where a magistrates' court has refused to make the order; or
(b) a party to an application to discharge such an order, where a magistrates' court has decided that application.

(2) The appellant must—
(a) serve on the Crown Court officer a copy of the application to the magistrates' court; and
(b) where the appeal concerns a discharge decision, notify each other party,

not more than 15 business days after the decision against which the appellant wants to appeal.

(3) The Crown Court must hear the appeal without justices of the peace.

[Note. See sections 79 and 80(6) of the Coroners and Justice Act 2009, and section 74 of the Senior Courts Act 1981[118].]

117 2009 c. 25.

118 1981 c. 54; section 74 was amended by sections 79 and 106 of, and Table (4) of Part V of Schedule 15 to, the Access to Justice Act 1999 (c. 22), article 3 of, and paragraphs 11 and 12 of the Schedule to S.I. 2004/2035 and section 15 of, and paragraphs 114 and 133 of Schedule 4 to, the Constitutional Reform Act 2005 (c. 4). The Act's title was amended by section 59(5) of, and paragraph 1 of Schedule 11 to, the Constitutional Reform Act 2005 (c. 4).

Section 7: investigation approval orders under the Regulation of Investigatory Powers Act 2000

When this Section applies

R47.51

47.51 This Section applies where a justice of the peace can make an order approving—

(a) the grant or renewal of an authorisation, or the giving or renewal of a notice, under section 23A of the Regulation of Investigatory Powers Act 2000[119]; and

(b) the grant or renewal of an authorisation under section 32A of the 2000 Act[120].

[Note. Under the Regulation of Investigatory Powers Act 2000, an order may be made approving a local authority officer's authorisation for the obtaining of information about the use of postal or telecommunications services, or for the use of surveillance or of a 'covert human intelligence source'.]

Exercise of court's powers

R47.52

47.52 (1) Rule 47.5 (Investigation orders; Exercise of court's powers) applies, subject to sections 23B(2) and 32B(2) of the Regulation of Investigatory Powers Act 2000[121].

(2) Where a magistrates' court refuses to approve the grant, giving or renewal of an authorisation or notice, the court must not exercise its power to quash that authorisation or notice unless the applicant has had at least 2 business days from the date of the refusal in which to make representations.

[Note. Under sections 23B(2) and 32B(2) of the Regulation of Investigatory Powers Act 2000, the applicant is not required to give notice of an application to any person to whom the authorisation or notice relates, or to such a person's legal representatives. See also sections 23B(3) and 32B(3) of the 2000 Act.]

Application for approval for authorisation or notice

R47.53

47.53 (1) This rule applies where an applicant wants a magistrates' court to make an order approving—

(a) under sections 23A and 23B of the Regulation of Investigatory Powers Act 2000[122]—

(i) an authorisation to obtain or disclose communications data, under section 22(3) of the 2000 Act[123], or

(ii) a notice that requires a postal or telecommunications operator if need be to obtain, and in any case to disclose, communications data, under section 22(4) of the 2000 Act; or

(b) under sections 32A and 32B of the Regulation of Investigatory Powers Act 2000[124], an authorisation for—

(i) the carrying out of directed surveillance, under section 28 of the 2000 Act, or

(ii) the conduct or use of a covert human intelligence source, under section 29 of the 2000 Act[125].

(2) The applicant must—

(a) apply in writing and serve the application on the court officer;

(b) attach the authorisation or notice which the applicant wants the court to approve;

(c) attach such other material (if any) on which the applicant relies to satisfy the court—

(i) as required by section 23A(3) and (4) of the 2000 Act, in relation to communications data,

(ii) as required by section 32A(3) and (4) of the 2000 Act, in relation to directed surveillance, or

(iii) as required by section 32A(5) and (6), and, if relevant, section 43(6A), of the 2000 Act[126], in relation to a covert human intelligence source; and

(d) propose the terms of the order.

[Note. See also rule 47.5, under which the court may—

(a) exercise its powers in the parties' absence; and

(b) consider an application made orally.

[119] 2000 c. 23; section 23A was inserted by section 37 of the Protection of Freedoms Act 2012 (c. 9).

[120] 2000 c. 23; section 32A was inserted by section 38 of the Protection of Freedoms Act 2012 (c. 9).

[121] 2000 c. 23; section 23B was inserted by section 37 and section 32B by section 38 of the Protection of Freedoms Act 2012 (c. 9).

[122] 2000 c. 23; sections 23A and 23B were inserted by section 37 of the Protection of Freedoms Act 2012 (c. 9).

[123] 2000 c. 23; section 22 was amended by section 112 of, and paragraphs 12 and 13 of Schedule 7 to, the Policing and Crime Act 2009 (c. 26).

[124] 2000 c. 23; sections 32A and 32B were inserted by section 38 of the Protection of Freedoms Act 2012 (c. 9).

[125] 2000 c. 23; section 29 was amended by section 8 of the Policing and Crime Act 2009 (c. 26).

[126] 2000 c. 23; section 43(6A) was inserted by section 38 of the Protection of Freedoms Act 2012 (c. 9).

Under section 23A(3) to (5) of the Regulation of Investigatory Powers Act 2000, on an application for an order approving an authorisation or notice concerning communications data (as defined in section 21 of the Act[127]), the court must be satisfied that—

- *(a) the person who granted or renewed the authorisation, or who gave or renewed the notice, was entitled to do so;*
- *(b) the grant, giving or renewal met any prescribed restrictions or conditions;*
- *(c) at the time the authorisation or notice was granted, given or renewed, as the case may be, there were reasonable grounds for believing that to obtain or disclose the data described in the authorisation or notice was—*
  - *(i) necessary, for the purpose of preventing or detecting crime or preventing disorder, and*
  - *(ii) proportionate to what was sought to be achieved by doing so; and*
- *(d) there remain reasonable grounds for believing those things, at the time the court considers the application.*

The Regulation of Investigatory Powers (Communications Data) Order 2010[128] specifies the persons who are entitled to grant, give or renew an authorisation or notice concerning such data, and for what purpose each may do so.

Under section 32A(3) and (4) of the Regulation of Investigatory Powers Act 2000, on an application for an order approving an authorisation concerning directed surveillance (as defined in section 26 of the Act[129]), the court must be satisfied that—

- *(a) the person who granted the authorisation was entitled to do so;*
- *(b) the grant met any prescribed restrictions or conditions;*
- *(c) at the time the authorisation was granted there were reasonable grounds for believing that the surveillance described in the authorisation was—*
  - *(i) necessary, for the purpose of preventing or detecting crime or preventing disorder, and*
  - *(ii) proportionate to what was sought to be achieved by it; and*
- *(d) there remain reasonable grounds for believing those things, at the time the court considers the application.*

Under section 32A(5) and (6) of the Regulation of Investigatory Powers Act 2000, on an application for an order approving an authorisation of the conduct or use of a covert human intelligence source (as defined in section 26 of the Act), the court must be satisfied that—

- *(a) the person who granted the authorisation was entitled to do so;*
- *(b) the grant met any prescribed restrictions or conditions;*
- *(c) at the time the authorisation was granted there were reasonable grounds for believing that the conduct or use of a covert human intelligence source described in the authorisation was—*
  - *(i) necessary, for the purpose of preventing or detecting crime or preventing disorder, and*
  - *(ii) proportionate to what was sought to be achieved by it; and*
- *(d) there remain reasonable grounds for believing those things, at the time the court considers the application.*

Under section 43(6A) of the 2000 Act, on an application to approve the renewal of such an authorisation the court in addition must—

- *(a) be satisfied that, since the grant or latest renewal of the authorisation, a review has been carried out of the use made of the source, of the tasks given to him or her and of the information obtained; and*
- *(b) consider the results of that review.*

The Regulation of Investigatory Powers (Directed Surveillance and Covert Human Intelligence Sources) Order 2010[130] specifies the persons who are entitled to grant an authorisation concerning such surveillance or such a source, and for what purpose each may do so.

Under sections 23B(2) and 32B(2) of the 2000 Act, the applicant is not required to give notice of an application to any person to whom the authorisation or notice relates, or to such a person's legal representatives.]

[127] 2000 c. 23; section 21 was amended by section 88 of, and paragraphs 5 and 7 of Schedule 12 to, the Serious Crime Act 2007 (c. 27).

[128] S.I. 2010/480.

[129] 2000 c. 23; section 26 was amended by section 406 of, and paragraph 161 of Schedule 17 to, the Communications Act 2003 (c. 21).

[130] S.I. 2010/521.

Section 8: orders for access to documents, etc. under the Criminal Appeal Act 1995

When this Section applies R47.54

47.54 This Section applies where the Crown Court can order a person to give the Criminal Cases Review Commission access to a document or other material under section 18A of the Criminal Appeal Act 1995[131].

[Note. Under section 18A of the Criminal Appeal Act 1995, on an application by the Criminal Cases Review Commission the court may order that the Commission be given access to a document or material in a person's possession or control if the court thinks that that document or material may assist the Commission in the exercise of any of their functions.]

Exercise of court's powers R47.55

47.55 (1) Subject to paragraphs (2), (3) and (4), the court may determine an application by the Criminal Cases Review Commission for an order—
- (a) at a hearing (which must be in private unless the court otherwise directs), or without a hearing; and
- (b) in the absence of—
  - (i) the Commission,
  - (ii) the respondent, and
  - (iii) any other person affected by the order.

(2) The court must not determine such an application in the Commission's absence if—
- (a) the Commission asks for a hearing; or
- (b) it appears to the court that the application is so complex or serious as to require the court to hear the Commission.

(3) The court must not determine such an application in the absence of any respondent or other person affected, unless—
- (a) the absentee has had at least 2 business days in which to make representations; or
- (b) the court is satisfied that—
  - (i) the Commission cannot identify or contact the absentee,
  - (ii) it would prejudice the exercise of the Commission's functions to adjourn or postpone the application so as to allow the absentee to attend, or
  - (iii) the absentee has waived the opportunity to attend.

(4) The court must not determine such an application in the absence of any respondent who, if the order sought by the Commission were made, would be required to produce or give access to journalistic material, unless that respondent has waived the opportunity to attend.

(5) The court officer must arrange for the court to hear such an application no sooner than 2 business days after it was served, unless—
- (a) the court directs that no hearing need be arranged; or
- (b) the court gives other directions for the hearing.

(6) The court must not determine an application unless satisfied that sufficient time has been allowed for it.

(7) If the court so directs, the parties to an application may attend a hearing by live link or telephone.

(8) The court must not make an order unless an officer of the Commission states, in writing or orally, that to the best of that officer's knowledge and belief—
- (a) the application discloses all the information that is material to what the court must decide; and
- (b) the content of the application is true.

(9) Where the statement required by paragraph (8) is made orally—
- (a) the statement must be on oath or affirmation, unless the court otherwise directs; and
- (b) the court must arrange for a record of the making of the statement.

(10) The court may shorten or extend (even after it has expired) a time limit under this Section.

Application for an order for access R47.56

47.56 (1) Where the Criminal Cases Review Commission wants the court to make an order for access to a document or other material, the Commission must—
- (a) apply in writing and serve the application on the court officer;
- (b) give the court an estimate of how long the court should allow—
  - (i) to read the application and prepare for any hearing, and
  - (ii) for any hearing of the application;
- (c) attach a draft order in the terms proposed by the Commission; and
- (d) serve the application and draft order on the respondent.

[131] 1995 c. 35; section 18A was inserted by section 1 of the Criminal Cases Review Commission (Information) Act 2016 (c. 17).

(2) The application must—
(a) identify the respondent;
(b) describe the document, or documents, or other material sought;
(c) explain the reasons for thinking that—
(i) what is sought is in the respondent's possession or control, and
(ii) access to what is sought may assist the Commission in the exercise of any of their functions; and
(d) explain the Commission's proposals for—
(i) the manner in which the respondent should give access, and
(ii) the period within which the order should take effect.
(3) The Commission must serve any order made on the respondent.

[Note. Under section 18A(3) of the Criminal Appeal Act 1995, the court may give directions for the manner in which access to a document or other material must be given, and may direct that the Commission must be allowed to take away such a document or material, or to make copies. Under section 18A(4) of the Act, the court may direct that the respondent must not destroy, damage or alter a document or other material before the direction is withdrawn by the court.]

R47.57 Application containing information withheld from a respondent or other person

47.57 (1) This rule applies where—
(a) the Criminal Cases Review Commission serves an application under rule 47.56 (Application for an order for access); and
(b) the application includes information that the Commission thinks ought not be revealed to a recipient.
(2) The Commission must—
(a) omit that information from the part of the application that is served on that recipient;
(b) mark the other part, to show that it is only for the court; and
(c) in that other part, explain why the Commission has withheld it from that recipient.
(3) A hearing of an application to which this rule applies may take place, wholly or in part, in the absence of that recipient and any other person.
(4) At a hearing of an application to which this rule applies—
(a) the general rule is that the court must consider, in the following sequence—
(i) representations first by the Commission and then by the other parties, in the presence of them all, and then
(ii) further representations by the Commission, in the others' absence; but
(b) the court may direct other arrangements for the hearing.

R47.58 Application to punish for contempt of court

47.58 (1) This rule applies where a person is accused of disobeying an order for access made under section 18A of the Criminal Appeal Act 1995.
(2) An applicant who wants the court to exercise its power to punish that person for contempt of court must comply with the rules in Part 48 (Contempt of court).

[Note. The Crown Court has power to punish for contempt of court a person who disobeys its order. See section 45 of the Senior Courts Act 1981[132].]

Section 9: European investigation orders

Section 9: order for the extension of a moratorium period under the Proceeds of Crime Act 2002

R47.59 When this Section applies

47.59 (1) This Section applies where the Crown Court can extend a moratorium period under section 336A of the Proceeds of Crime Act 2002[133].
(2) In this Section, 'respondent' means, as well as a person within the meaning of rule 47.2(c), an 'interested person' within the meaning of section 336D of the 2002 Act[134].

132 1981 c. 54. The Act's title was amended by section 59(5) of, and paragraph 1 of Schedule 11 to, the Constitutional Reform Act 2005 (c. 4).
133 2002 c. 29; section 336A was inserted by section 10 of the Criminal Finances Act 2017 (c. 22).
134 2002 c. 29; section 336D was inserted by section 10 of the Criminal Finances Act 2017 (c. 22).

[Note. Under section 336A of the Proceeds of Crime Act 2002, the Crown Court may extend a moratorium period under section 335 or section 336 of the Act[135] *by up to 31 days beginning with the day after the day on which the period otherwise would end.*

Under sections 335 and 336 of the 2002 Act, a moratorium period is the period of 31 days starting with the day on which consent to the doing of an act is refused by a constable, a customs officer or the Director General of the National Crime Agency. The act to which those sections refer is one that would be an offence under section 327, 328 or 329 of the 2002 Act (money laundering offences) but for the making of a disclosure within the meaning of section 338 to such an officer in relation to that act. On the expiry of the moratorium period the person who made the disclosure will be treated as having the relevant officer's consent to the doing of the act and so will commit no offence by doing it.

The Crown Court may extend a moratorium period more than once, but the total period of extension may not exceed 186 days beginning with the day after the day on which the first 31 day period ended.

Under section 336D(3) of the 2002 Act, 'interested person' means the person who made the disclosure and any other person who appears to the person making an application under rule 47.61 to have an interest in the property that is the subject of that disclosure.]

Exercise of court's powers **R47.60**

47.60 (1) The court may determine an application to which rule 47.61 (Application for extension of moratorium period) applies—
- (a) at a hearing (which must be in private unless the court otherwise directs), or without a hearing; and
- (b) in the absence of—
  - (i) the applicant, and
  - (ii) a respondent.

(2) The court must not determine such an application in the applicant's absence if the applicant asks for a hearing.

(3) The court must not determine such an application in the absence of a respondent unless—
- (a) the absentee has had at least 2 business days in which to make representations; or
- (b) the court is satisfied that—
  - (i) the applicant cannot identify or contact the absentee,
  - (ii) it would prejudice the investigation if the absentee were present,
  - (iii) it would prejudice the investigation to adjourn or postpone the application so as to allow the absentee to attend, or
  - (iv) the absentee has waived the opportunity to attend.

(4) The court officer must arrange for the court to hear such an application no sooner than 2 business days after notice of the application was served, unless—
- (a) the court directs that no hearing need be arranged; or
- (b) the court gives other directions for the hearing.

(5) If the court so directs, the parties to an application may attend a hearing by live link or telephone.

(6) The court must not extend a moratorium period unless the applicant states, in writing or orally, that to the best of the applicant's knowledge and belief—
- (a) the application discloses all the information that is material to what the court must decide; and
- (b) the content of the application is true.

(7) Where the statement required by paragraph (6) is made orally—
- (a) the statement must be on oath or affirmation, unless the court otherwise directs; and
- (b) the court must arrange for a record of the making of the statement.

(8) The court may—
- (a) shorten or extend (even after it has expired) a time limit imposed by this rule;
- (b) dispense with a requirement for service under this Section (even after service was required); and
- (c) consider an application made orally instead of in writing.

[135] 2002 c. 29; section 335 was amended by section 10 of the Criminal Finances Act 2017 (c. 22). Section 336 was amended by paragraphs 168 and 173 of Schedule 4 to the Serious Organised Crime and Police Act 2005 (c. 15), paragraphs 108 and 133 of Schedule 8 to the Crime and Courts Act 2013 (c .22) and section 10 of the Criminal Finances Act 2017 (c. 22).

R47.61 Application for extension of moratorium period

47.61 (1) This rule applies where an applicant wants the court to extend a moratorium period.
(2) The applicant must—
(a) apply in writing before the date on which the moratorium period otherwise would end;
(b) demonstrate that the applicant is entitled to apply as a senior officer within the meaning of section 336D of the Proceeds of Crime Act 2002;
(c) serve the application on the court officer;
(d) serve notice on each respondent that an application has been made; and
(e) serve the application on each respondent to such extent, if any, as the court directs.
(3) The application must specify—
(a) the disclosure in respect of which the application is made;
(b) the date on which the moratorium period began;
(c) the date and period of any previous extension of that period; and
(d) the date on which that period is due to end.
(4) The application must—
(a) describe the investigation being carried out in relation to that disclosure; and
(b) explain the grounds for believing that—
(i) the investigation is being conducted diligently and expeditiously,
(ii) further time is needed for conducting the investigation, and
(iii) it would be reasonable in all the circumstances for the moratorium period to be extended.
(5) A respondent who objects to the application must—
(a) serve notice of the objection on—
(i) the court officer, and
(ii) the applicant,
not more than 2 business days after service of notice of the application; and
(b) in that notice explain the grounds of the objection.
(6) The applicant must serve any order made on each respondent.

[Note. The Practice Direction sets out forms of application and notice of objection for use in connection with this rule.

Under section 336D of the Proceeds of Crime Act 2002, 'senior officer' means the Director General of the National Crime Agency or an authorised officer of that Agency, a police officer of at least the rank of inspector, an officer of HM Revenue and Customs or an immigration officer of equivalent rank, a senior member of the Financial Conduct Authority, the Director of the Serious Fraud Office or an authorised member of that Office, or an accredited financial investigator.

The time limit for making an application is prescribed by section 336A(3) of the Proceeds of Crime Act 2002. It may be neither extended nor shortened. Under section 336B(2) of the Act[136] *the court must determine the application as soon as reasonably practicable. Under section 336C*[137]*, where an application is made and not determined before the moratorium period otherwise would expire then that period is extended until (i) the application is determined, or (ii) the expiry of 31 days beginning with the day after the day on which that period expired, whichever occurs first.]*

R47.62 Application containing information withheld from a respondent

47.62 (1) This rule applies where an application to extend a moratorium period includes an application to withhold information from a respondent.
(2) The applicant must—
(a) omit that information from any part of the application that is served on the respondent;
(b) mark the other part to show that, unless the court otherwise directs, it is only for the court; and
(c) in that other part, explain the grounds for believing that the disclosure of that information would have one or more of the following results—
(i) evidence of an offence would be interfered with or harmed,
(ii) the gathering of information about the possible commission of an offence would be interfered with,

[136] 2002 c. 29; section 336B was inserted by section 10 of the Criminal Finances Act 2017 (c. 22).
[137] 2002 c. 29; section 336C was inserted by section 10 of the Criminal Finances Act 2017 (c. 22).

(iii) a person would be interfered with or physically injured,
(iv) the recovery of property under this Act would be hindered, or
(v) national security would be put at risk.

(3) At any hearing of an application to which this rule applies—
(a) the court must first determine the application to withhold information, in the respondent's absence and that of any legal representative of the respondent; and
(b) if the court allows the application to withhold information, then in the following sequence—
(i) the court must consider representations first by the applicant and then by the respondent, in the presence of both, and
(ii) the court may consider further representations by the applicant in the respondent's absence and that of any legal representative of the respondent.

(4) If the court refuses an application to withhold information from the respondent, the applicant may withdraw the application to extend the moratorium period.

[Note. See section 336B of the Proceeds of Crime Act 2002.]

Section 10: orders for access to electronic data under the Crime (Overseas Production Orders) Act 2019

When this Section applies R47.63

47.63 (1) This Section applies where the Crown Court can make an overseas production order under section 1 of the Crime (Overseas Production Orders) Act 2019.[138]

(2) In this Section, a reference to a person affected by such an order includes a person by whom or on whose behalf there is stored any journalistic data specified or described in the application for that order.

[Note. Under section 1 of the Crime (Overseas Production Orders) Act 2019, on an application by an appropriate officer (defined by section 2 of the Act) a Crown Court judge may order a person (in these rules, 'the respondent') to produce or give access to electronic data (by section 3, 'data stored electronically'), other than excepted such data, where, among other criteria listed in sections 1 and 4 of the Act, the judge is satisfied that—

(a) there are reasonable grounds for believing that—
(i) an indictable offence has been committed and proceedings in respect of the offence have been instituted or the offence is being investigated, or
(ii) the order is sought for the purposes of a terrorist investigation within the meaning of the Terrorism Act 2000; and
(b) there are reasonable grounds for believing that the respondent operates in, or is based in, a country or territory outside the United Kingdom which is a party to, or which participates in, a designated international co-operation arrangement.

Section 3 of the 2019 Act defines 'excepted electronic data' as data stored electronically that is (a) an item subject to legal privilege, or (b) a personal record within the meaning of section 3(7) (medical, etc. records) which (i) was created in circumstances giving rise to a continuing obligation of confidence to an individual who can be identified from that record, or (ii) is held subject to a restriction on disclosure, or an obligation of secrecy, contained in an enactment. Where the respondent against whom an overseas production order is sought is a telecommunications operator, within the meaning of the Investigatory Powers Act 2016, 'excepted electronic data' also includes communications data within the meaning of the 2016 Act. Where the investigation in aid of which an overseas production order is sought is a terrorist investigation other than a terrorist financing investigation within the meaning of the Terrorism Act 2000, 'excepted electronic data' does not include a confidential personal record.

Section 12 of the Act defines 'journalistic data' as electronic data that (a) was created or acquired for the purposes of journalism and (b) is stored by or on behalf of a person who created or acquired it for those purposes.]

Exercise of court's powers R47.64

47.64 (1) Subject to paragraphs (2), (3) and (4), the court may determine an application under rule 47.68 for an overseas production order, or an application under rule 47.69 to vary or revoke an order—
(a) at a hearing (which must be in private unless the court otherwise directs), or without a hearing; and
(b) in the absence of—

[138] 2019 c. 5.

(i) the applicant,
(ii) the respondent, and
(iii) any other person affected by the order.

(2) The court must not determine such an application in the applicant's absence if—
(a) the applicant asks for a hearing; or
(b) it appears to the court that—
(i) the proposed order may require the production of excepted electronic data, within the meaning of section 3 of the Crime (Overseas Production Orders) Act 2019, or
(ii) for any other reason the application is so complex or serious as to require the court to hear the applicant.

(3) The court must not determine such an application in the absence of any respondent or other person affected unless—
(a) the absentee has had at least 2 business days in which to make representations; or
(b) the court is satisfied that—
(i) the applicant cannot identify or contact the absentee,
(ii) it would prejudice the investigation if the absentee were present,
(iii) where journalistic data is sought, it would prejudice the investigation of another indictable offence or another terrorist investigation if the absentee were present,
(iv) it would prejudice the investigation to adjourn or postpone the application so as to allow the absentee to attend, or
(v) the absentee has waived the opportunity to attend.

(4) The court must not determine such an application in the absence of any respondent who, if the order sought by the applicant were made, would be required to produce or give access to journalistic data, unless that respondent has waived the opportunity to attend.

(5) The court officer must arrange for the court to hear such an application no sooner than 2 business days after notice of the application was served, unless—
(a) the court directs that no hearing need be arranged; or
(b) the court gives other directions for the hearing.

(6) The court must not determine an application unless satisfied that sufficient time has been allowed for it.

(7) If the court so directs, the parties to an application may attend a hearing by live link or telephone.

(8) The court must not make, vary or revoke an order unless the applicant states, in writing or orally, that to the best of the applicant's knowledge and belief—
(a) the application discloses all the information that is material to what the court must decide; and
(b) the content of the application is true.

(9) Where the statement required by paragraph (8) is made orally—
(a) the statement must be on oath or affirmation, unless the court otherwise directs; and
(b) the court must arrange for a record of the making of the statement.

(10) The court may—
(a) shorten or extend (even after it has expired) a time limit under this Section;
(b) dispense with a requirement for service under this Section (even after service was required); and
(c) consider an application made orally instead of in writing.

(11) A person who wants an extension of time must—
(a) apply when serving the application for which it is needed; and
(b) explain the delay.

R47.65 Application for order

47.65 (1) An applicant who wants the court to make an overseas production order must—
(a) apply in writing and serve the application on the court officer;
(b) demonstrate that the applicant is entitled to apply;
(c) give the court an estimate of how long the court should allow—
(i) to read the application and prepare for any hearing, and
(ii) for any hearing of the application;
(d) attach a draft order in the terms proposed by the applicant;
(e) serve notice of the application on the respondent and on any other person affected by the order, unless the court otherwise directs; and

(f) serve the application on the respondent and on any such other person to such extent, if any, as the court directs.

(2) A notice served on the respondent and on any other person affected by the order must—
(a) specify or describe the electronic data in respect of which the application is made; and
(b) identify—
(i) the power that the applicant invites the court to exercise, and
(ii) the conditions for the exercise of that power which the applicant asks the court to find are met.

(3) The application must—
(a) specify the designated international co-operation arrangement by reference to which the application is made;
(b) identify the respondent;
(c) explain the grounds for believing that the respondent operates in, or is based in, a country or territory outside the United Kingdom which is a party to, or participates in, that designated international co-operation arrangement;
(d) specify or describe the electronic data in respect of which the order is sought;
(e) explain the grounds for believing that the electronic data sought does not consist of or include excepted electronic data;
(f) briefly describe the investigation for the purposes of which the electronic data is sought and explain—
(i) the grounds for believing that an indictable offence has been committed which is under investigation or in respect of which proceedings have begun, or
(ii) how the investigation constitutes a terrorist investigation within the meaning of the Terrorism Act 2000;
(g) explain the grounds for believing that the respondent has possession or control of all or part of the electronic data sought;
(h) explain the grounds for believing that the electronic data sought is likely to be of substantial value to the investigation, or to the proceedings (as the case may be), whether by itself or together with other material;
(i) where paragraph (3)(f)(i) applies, explain the grounds for believing that all or part of the electronic data sought is likely to be relevant evidence in respect of the offence concerned;
(j) explain the grounds for believing that it is in the public interest for the respondent to produce or give access to the electronic data sought, having regard to—
(i) the benefit likely to accrue to the investigation, or to the proceedings (as the case may be), if that data is obtained, and
(ii) the circumstances under which the respondent has possession or control of any of that data;
(k) specify—
(i) the person, or the description of person, to whom the applicant wants the court to order that electronic data must be produced or made accessible, and
(ii) the period by the end of which the applicant wants the court to order that that electronic data must be produced or made accessible (which must be a period of 7 days beginning with the day on which the order is served on the respondent, unless the court otherwise directs); and
(l) where the applicant wants the court to include a non-disclosure requirement in the order—
(i) explain why such a requirement would be appropriate, and
(ii) specify or describe when the applicant wants that requirement, if ordered, to expire.

(4) In the event that an overseas production order is made, the applicant must serve the order on the Secretary of State for service on the respondent.

(5) Where notice of the application was served on a respondent, in the event that the application is dismissed or abandoned the applicant must—
(a) promptly so notify that respondent; and
(b) where the application is dismissed, promptly inform that respondent if the court nonetheless orders that for a period that respondent must not—
(i) conceal, destroy, alter or dispose of any of the electronic data specified or described in the application, or
(ii) disclose the making of the application or its contents to any person.

[Note. See sections 1, 2, 4 and 5 of the Crime (Overseas Production Orders) Act 2019.

Under section 8 of the 2019 Act, an overseas production order may include a non-disclosure requirement obliging the respondent not to disclose the making of the order or its contents to any person except with the court's permission or with the written permission of the applicant (or an equivalent appropriate officer).

Under section 9 of the Act, an overseas production order may be served only by the Secretary of State.

Under section 12 of the Act, if there are reasonable grounds for believing that the electronic data specified or described in the application consists of or includes journalistic data then unless the judge otherwise directs notice of the application must be served on (a) the person against whom the overseas production order is sought and (b) if different, the person by whom, or on whose behalf, the journalistic data is stored. The criteria for making such a direction correspond with those listed in rule 47.64(3)(b).

Under section 13 of the Act, following service of notice of an application for an overseas production order the respondent must not conceal, destroy, alter or dispose of any of the electronic data specified or described in the application, or disclose the making of the application or its contents to any person, except with the court's permission or with the written permission of the applicant (or an equivalent appropriate officer). Those obligations are superseded if an order is made. If the application is abandoned or dismissed, those obligations cease unless, in the event of dismissal, the court otherwise orders.

Section 14 of the Act provides for the means of service of notices and orders.

The Practice Direction sets out forms of application, notice and order for use in connection with this rule.]

R47.66 **Application to vary or revoke an order**

47.66 (1) The orders to which this rule applies are—
- (a) an overseas production order;
- (b) an order under section 8(4) of the Crime (Overseas Production Orders) Act 2019 maintaining an unexpired non-disclosure requirement;
- (c) an order under section 13(3) of the 2019 Act maintaining a duty not to conceal, destroy, alter or dispose of electronic data, and not to disclose the making or content of an application for an overseas production order; and
- (d) an order under section 13(4)(b) of the Act maintaining a duty not to conceal, destroy, alter or dispose of electronic data.

(2) This rule applies where one of the following wants the court to vary, to further vary or to revoke an order listed in paragraph (1)—
- (a) the applicant for that order, or an equivalent appropriate officer;
- (b) the respondent;
- (c) another person affected by the order; or
- (d) the Secretary of State.

(3) The applicant for the variation or revocation must—
- (a) apply in writing as soon as practicable after becoming aware of the grounds for doing so;
- (b) serve the application on—
  - (i) the court officer, and
  - (ii) as applicable, the applicant for the order, the respondent, any other person known to be affected and the Secretary of State; and
- (c) ask for a hearing, if one is wanted, and explain why it is needed.

(4) Where the applicant wants the court to vary, or further vary, an overseas production order, the application must—
- (a) specify or describe the electronic data in respect of which the varied order is sought (which may include electronic data not specified or described in the original order);
- (b) satisfy or, as the case may be, continue to satisfy, the requirements of rule 47.65(3)(a) and (c) to (i) (which may be done by reference to the original application); and
- (c) meet the requirements of rule 47.65(3)(j).

(5) Where the applicant wants the court to revoke an overseas production order, the application must—
- (a) explain why revocation is appropriate;
- (b) if the applicant wants the court, despite revocation, to maintain the requirement that for a period the respondent must not conceal, destroy, alter or dispose of any of the electronic data specified or described in the order—
  - (i) explain why it would be appropriate to maintain that requirement, and
  - (ii) specify or describe when the applicant wants that requirement, if maintained, to expire; and

(c) if the order includes an unexpired non-disclosure requirement that the applicant wants the court, despite revocation, to maintain—
(i) explain why it would be appropriate to maintain that requirement, and
(ii) specify or describe when the applicant wants that requirement, if maintained, to expire.

(6) Where the applicant wants the court to vary, to further vary or to revoke an order under section 8(4), section 13(3) or section 13(4)(b) of the 2019 Act the application must—
(a) explain—
(i) what material circumstances have changed since the order was made, and
(ii) why the order should be varied or revoked, as the case may be, as a result; and
(b) if applicable, specify the variation proposed.

[Note. See sections 7, 11(1) and 18(2) of the Crime (Overseas Production Orders) Act 2019.

Under section 8(4) of the 2019 Act, where the court revokes an overseas production order which includes an unexpired non-disclosure requirement the court may order that the respondent is to remain subject to that requirement for a defined period.

Under section 13(3) of the Act, where the court dismisses an application for an overseas production order then the duty under section 13(1)(a) not to conceal, destroy, alter or dispose of any of the electronic data specified or described in the application, and under section 13(1)(b) not to disclose the making of the application or its contents to any person except with the court's permission or with the written permission of the applicant (or an equivalent appropriate officer), ceases to apply unless the court orders that a person served with notice of the application is to remain subject to that duty for a defined period.

Under section 13(4)(b) of the Act, where the court revokes an overseas production order before it is served then the duty under section 13(1)(a) not to conceal, destroy, alter or dispose of any of the electronic data specified or described in the application for the order ceases to apply unless the court orders that a person served with notice of the application is to remain subject to that duty for a defined period.]

Application containing information withheld from a respondent or other person R47.67

47.67 (1) This rule applies where an application under rule 47.65 or 47.66 includes information that the applicant thinks ought to be revealed only to the court.

(2) The application must—
(a) identify that information; and
(b) explain why that information ought not to be served on the respondent or another person.

(3) At a hearing of an application to which this rule applies—
(a) the general rule is that the court must consider, in the following sequence—
(i) representations first by the applicant and then by the respondent and any other person, in the presence of them all, and then
(ii) further representations by the applicant, in the others' absence; but
(b) the court may direct other arrangements for the hearing.

Application to punish for contempt of court R47.68

47.68 (1) This rule applies where a person is accused of disobeying an order made by the court under the Crime (Overseas Production Orders) Act 2019.

(2) An applicant who wants the court to exercise its power to punish that person for contempt of court must comply with the rules in Part 48 (Contempt of court).

[Note. The Crown Court has power to punish for contempt of court a person who disobeys its order: see section 45 of the Senior Courts Act 1981[139]*. Under section 11(4) of the Crime (Overseas Production Orders) Act 2019, an order made by a judge under the Act has effect as if it were an order of the Crown Court.]*

[139] 1981 c. 54. The Act's title was amended by section 59(5) of, and paragraph 1 of Schedule 11 to, the Constitutional Reform Act 2005 (c. 4).

CRIMINAL PRACTICE DIRECTIONS PART 47 INVESTIGATION ORDERS AND WARRANTS

CPD.47A **CPD XI Other Proceedings 47A: Investigation Orders and Warrants**

47A.1 Powers of entry, search and seizure, and powers to obtain banking and other confidential information, are among the most intrusive that investigators can exercise. Every application must be carefully scrutinised with close attention paid to what the relevant statutory provision requires of the applicant and to what it permits. CrimPR Part 47 must be followed, and the prescribed forms (retaining the Notes for Guidance section) must be used. These are designed to prompt applicants, and the courts, to deal with all of the relevant criteria.

47A.2 The issuing of a warrant or the making of such an order is never to be treated as a formality and it is therefore essential that the judge or magistrate considering the application is given, and must take, sufficient time for the purpose. The prescribed forms require the applicant to provide a time estimate, and listing officers and justices' legal advisers should take account of these.

47A.3 Applicants for orders and warrants owe the court duties of candour and truthfulness. On any application made without notice to the respondent, and so on all applications for search warrants, the duty of frank and complete disclosure is especially onerous. The applicant must draw the court's attention to any information that is unfavourable to the application. The existence of unfavourable information will not necessarily lead to the application being refused; it will be a matter for the court what weight to place on each piece of information. As Hughes LJ made clear in *Re Stanford International Limited*[1] 'In effect a prosecutor seeking an *ex parte* order must put on his defence hat and ask himself what, if he was representing the defendant or a third party with a relevant interest, he would be saying to the judge, and, having answered that question, that is what he must tell the judge'. This is, as Aitkins LJ recognised, 'a heavy burden but a vital safeguard. Full details must be given[2].'

47A.4 Where an applicant supplements an application with additional oral or written information, on questioning by the court or otherwise, it is essential that the court keeps an adequate record. What is needed will depend upon the circumstances. The Rules require that a record of the 'gist' be retained. The purpose of such a record is to allow the sufficiency of the court's reasons for its decision subsequently to be assessed. The gravity of such decisions requires that their exercise should be susceptible to scrutiny and to explanation by reference to all of the information that was taken into account.

47A.5 The forms that accompany CrimPR Part 47 provide for the most frequently encountered applications. The included Notes for Guidance summarise for the applicant and the court the relevant criteria for making and considering an application. However, there are some hundreds of powers of entry, search and seizure, supplied by a corresponding number of legislative provisions. In any criminal matter, if there is no form designed for the particular warrant or order sought, the forms should still be used, as far as is practicable, and adapted as necessary. The applicant should pay particular attention to the specific legislative requirements for the granting of such an application to ensure that the court has all of the necessary information, and, if the court might be unfamiliar with the legislation, should provide a copy of the relevant provisions. Applicants must comply with the duties of candour and truthfulness, and include in their application the declarations required by the Rules and must make disclosure of any unfavourable information to the court.

CPD.47B **CPD XI Other Proceedings 47B: Investigation Orders and Warrants in the Crown Court**

47B.1 This section covers applications made under:

(i) Schedule 1 Police and Criminal Evidence Act 1984 (PACE);
(ii) Section 2 Criminal Justice Act 1987;
(iii) Drug Trafficking Act 1994;
(iv) Part 8 of the Proceeds of Crime Act 2002;
(v) Section 5 Coroners and Justice Act 2009;
(vi) Terrorism Act 2000.

It does NOT cover applications under the Extradition Act 2003.

Crown Court Centres

47B.2 Investigators must give careful consideration to which Crown Court centre is most appropriate to hear the application. In all cases, the application must explain the rationale for choosing the particular court centre. Relevant considerations will usually be:

[1] [2010] EWCA Civ 137 at para 159.

[2] *R (On the Application of S, F and L) v Chief Constable of the British Transport Police and Southwark Crown Court* [2013] EWHC 2189 (Admin) at [45 (d)].

(i) where any subsequent proceedings are likely to be commenced;
(ii) where a main suspect has some geographical connection; and/or
(iii) where, in broad terms, the offending has taken place.

A court centre should not be chosen simply because it is most convenient or proximate to the investigator's location. Any dispute over the proper venue for an application should be determined by the relevant Presiding Judges.

47B.3 Where the investigation is complex, lengthy and/or involves multiple suspects all applications should be made to one court centre. To ensure consistency, all subsequent applications arising out of the same or any connected investigation should be made to the same court centre and, where practicable, the same judge.

47B.4 Judges can refuse to determine applications and request they be resubmitted (if necessary to another court) where:
(i) the application is not in the proper form;
(ii) there is an inaccurate reading time estimate; and/or
(iii) there is insufficient justification for the application to be made at that court centre.

Dealing with applications without a hearing

47B.5 The court must not determine an application in the applicant's absence in the circumstances set out in CrimPR 47.5(2); or in the absence of any respondent in the circumstances set out in CrimPR 47.5(3) and (4).

47B.6 When permitted by the rules, and where the application has been sufficiently completed and submitted on the correct form, there is a presumption that the application will be dealt with without a hearing. The judge is always entitled to require a hearing to clarify omissions or ambiguity on the application, or for any other reason.

47B.7 It will often not be appropriate for a court to deal with an application without a hearing in the following situations:
(i) where the investigation involved covert activity or the application is based on material gathered covertly;
(ii) where the application is based on material which is especially sensitive and/or where it will be necessary to ensure the security at court of the material produced in support of the application;
(iii) where the case may result in substantial local and/or national public interest;
(iv) where the application is particularly lengthy, serious or complex.

47B.8 Applications should be sent electronically to the designated secure email address at the relevant court centre.

47B.9 A judge considering an application without a hearing will subject the application to the usual intense level of scrutiny ensuring that the relevant statutory requirements have been met. If the judge is not so satisfied then the judge will refuse the application, require further information to be served or adjourn it for a hearing in court, which can be carried out via live link or telephone, where permitted by the Rules. The Court will inform the applicant of the outcome and make the necessary arrangements for any additional hearings that may be required. There is no requirement for any order to be signed by the judge with a 'wet ink' signature. The applicant will be notified electronically of any orders that are made.

47B.10 Applications considered without a hearing will be determined by a judge as soon as practicable. Approved orders will be returned electronically to the applicant and an electronic copy must be securely saved by the court. If there is a particular urgency with any application, that fact should be made clear to the court when it is served and the judge should expedite it where possible.

Listing

47B.11 To assist the listing process, the applicant must supply a realistic estimate of the reading time required when the application is served. This estimate should be provided in the application and in the covering email to which it is attached. The covering email should also stipulate whether there have been any previous applications in the same or any connected investigation and provide the name of the judge who granted any previous Orders.

47B.12 Where the judge has decided that a hearing is required to determine or further consider the application, the expectation is that this hearing should usually take place by live link or telephone.[3] Where the judge directs a hearing at court, any additional material relied on by the

[3] Although the court cannot receive evidence by telephone, information in support of the application can be given on oath bythis means.

applicant must be brought to court on the day of the hearing. Any additional material should not be retained by the court once the application has been determined, but must be taken away by the applicant at the end of the hearing.[4]

47B.13 When listing such hearings consideration should be given to Division XIII Listing of these practice directions which states at A.1 that listing is a judicial responsibility and function. G.3(1) of that division envisages that such applications will be completed by 10.30am or start after 4.30pm so as not to interfere with trials. This general direction does not prevent a judge from considering applications outside of these times where other court business allows.

47B.14 However, as paragraph G.8 of Division XIII Listing makes clear, along with the relevant case law, that the search powers in PACE constitute 'a serious inroad upon the liberty of the subject. The responsibility for ensuring that the procedure is not abused lies with circuit judges. It is of cardinal importance that circuit judges should be scrupulous in discharging that responsibility.'[5] Accordingly, there must be adequate time allowed for the judge to read carefully the application and all the supporting evidence supplied with it. The judge will require sufficient time to enable a short judgment to be given, where necessary so that in the event of challenge in the Administrative Court there is an explanation of the reasons for the decision for that court to consider.

DARTS Recording

47B.15 Hearings in court are required to be recorded whether on DARTS or some other secure method such as on a hand-held machine. Determination of the method of recording is a matter for the judge.

[4] Generally, there are no secure storage at facilities at court centres where sensitive material can be safely left.
[5] *per* Lloyd LJ *R v Maidstone Crown Court, ex p Waitt* [1988] Crim LR 384.

Criminal Procedure Rules Part 48 Contempt of Court

General rules

R48.1 When this Part applies

48.1 (1) This Part applies where the court can deal with a person for conduct—
(a) in contempt of court; or
(b) in contravention of the legislation to which rules 48.5 and 48.9 refer.
(2) In this Part, 'respondent' means any such person.

[Note. For the court's powers to punish for contempt of court, see the notes to rules 48.5 and 48.9.]

R48.2 Exercise of court's power to deal with contempt of court

48.2 (1) The court must determine at a hearing—
(a) an enquiry under rule 48.8; and
(b) an allegation under rule 48.9.
(2) The court must not proceed in the respondent's absence unless—
(a) the respondent's behaviour makes it impracticable to proceed otherwise; or
(b) the respondent has had at least 10 business days' notice of the hearing, or was present when it was arranged.
(3) If the court hears part of an enquiry or allegation in private, it must announce at a hearing in public—
(a) the respondent's name;
(b) in general terms, the nature of any conduct that the respondent admits, or the court finds proved; and
(c) any punishment imposed.

R48.3 Notice of suspension of imprisonment by Court of Appeal or Crown Court

48.3 (1) This rule applies where—
(a) the Court of Appeal or the Crown Court suspends an order of imprisonment for contempt of court; and
(b) the respondent is absent when the court does so.
(2) The respondent must be served with notice of the terms of the court's order—
(a) by any applicant under rule 48.9; or
(b) by the court officer, in any other case.

[Note. By reason of sections 15 and 45 of the Senior Courts Act 1981[1]*, the Court of Appeal and the Crown Court each has an inherent power to suspend imprisonment for contempt of court, on conditions, or for a period, or both.]*

Application to discharge an order for imprisonment **R48.4**

48.4 (1) This rule applies where the court can discharge an order for a respondent's imprisonment for contempt of court.

(2) A respondent who wants the court to discharge such an order must—

(a) apply in writing, unless the court otherwise directs, and serve any written application on—

(i) the court officer, and

(ii) any applicant under rule 48.9 on whose application the respondent was imprisoned;

(b) in the application—

(i) explain why it is appropriate for the order for imprisonment to be discharged, and

(ii) give details of any appeal, and its outcome; and

(c) ask for a hearing, if the respondent wants one.

[Note. By reason of sections 15 and 45 of the Senior Courts Act 1981, the Court of Appeal and the Crown Court each has an inherent power to discharge an order for a respondent's imprisonment for contempt of court in failing to comply with a court order.

Under section 97(4) of the Magistrates' Courts Act 1980[2]*, a magistrates' court can discharge an order for imprisonment if the respondent gives evidence.*

Under section 12(4) of the Contempt of Court Act 1981[3]*, a magistrates' court can discharge an order for imprisonment made under that section.]*

Contempt of court by obstruction, disruption, etc.

Initial procedure on obstruction, disruption etc. **R48.5**

48.5 (1) This rule applies where the court observes, or someone reports to the court—

(a) in the Court of Appeal or the Crown Court, obstructive, disruptive, insulting or intimidating conduct, in the courtroom or in its vicinity, or otherwise immediately affecting the proceedings;

(b) in the Crown Court, a contravention of—

(i) section 3 of the Criminal Procedure (Attendance of Witnesses) Act 1965[4] (disobeying a witness summons); or

(ii) section 20 of the Juries Act 1974[5] (disobeying a jury summons);

(c) in a magistrates' court, a contravention of—

(i) section 97(4) of the Magistrates' Courts Act 1980 (refusing to give evidence), or

(ii) section 12 of the Contempt of Court Act 1981[6] (insulting or interrupting the court, etc.);

(d) a contravention of section 9 of the Contempt of Court Act 1981[7] (without the court's permission, recording the proceedings, etc.); or

(e) any other conduct with which the court can deal as, or as if it were, a criminal contempt of court, except failure to surrender to bail under section 6 of the Bail Act 1976[8].

[1] 1981 c. 54.

[2] 1980 c. 43; section 97(4) was amended by sections 13 and 14 of, and paragraph 7 of Schedule 2 to, the Contempt of Court Act 1981 (c. 47) and section 17 of, and paragraph 6 of Schedule 3 and Part I of Schedule 4 to, the Criminal Justice Act 1991 (c. 53).

[3] 1981 c. 49.

[4] 1965 c. 69; section 3 was amended by section 56 of, and Part IV of Schedule 11 to, the Courts Act 1971 (c. 23) and sections 65 and 66 of the Criminal Procedure and Investigations Act 1996 (c. 25).

[5] 1974 c. 23; section 20 was amended by sections 37, 38 and 46 of the Criminal Justice Act 1982 (c. 48), section 170(1) of, and paragraph 46 of Schedule 15 to, the Criminal Justice Act 1988 (c. 33), paragraph 28 of Schedule 10 to, the Criminal Justice and Public Order Act 1994 (c. 33) and paragraphs 1 and 14 of Schedule 33 to, the Criminal Justice Act 2003 (c. 44).

[6] 1981 c. 49; section 12 was amended by section 78 of, and Schedule 16 to, the Criminal Justice Act 1982 (c. 48), section 17(3) of, and Part I of Schedule 4 to, the Criminal Justice Act 1991 (c. 53); section 65(3) and (4) of, and paragraph 6(4) of Schedule 3 to, the Criminal Justice Act 1993 (c. 36) and section 165 of, and paragraph 83 of Schedule 9 to, the Powers of Criminal Courts (Sentencing) Act 2000 (c. 6).

[7] 1981 c. 49.

[8] 1976 c. 63; section 6 was amended by sections 37, 38 and 46 of the Criminal Justice Act 1982 (c. 48), section 109 of, and paragraph 184 of Schedule 8 to, the Courts Act 2003 (c. 39) and section 15 of, and paragraph 48(1), (4) of Schedule 3 to, the Criminal Justice Act 2003 (c. 44).

(2) Unless the respondent's behaviour makes it impracticable to do so, the court must—
(a) explain, in terms the respondent can understand (with help, if necessary)—
(i) the conduct that is in question,
(ii) that the court can impose imprisonment, or a fine, or both, for such conduct,
(iii) (where relevant) that the court has power to order the respondent's immediate temporary detention, if in the court's opinion that is required,
(iv) that the respondent may explain the conduct,
(v) that the respondent may apologise, if he or she so wishes, and that this may persuade the court to take no further action, and
(vi) that the respondent may take legal advice; and
(b) allow the respondent a reasonable opportunity to reflect, take advice, explain and, if he or she so wishes, apologise.
(3) The court may then—
(a) take no further action in respect of that conduct;
(b) enquire into the conduct there and then; or
(c) postpone that enquiry (if a magistrates' court, only until later the same day).

[Note. The conduct to which this rule applies is sometimes described as 'criminal' contempt of court.

By reason of sections 15 and 45 of the Senior Courts Act 1981, the Court of Appeal and the Crown Court each has an inherent power to imprison (for a maximum of 2 years), or fine (to an unlimited amount), or both, a respondent for contempt of court for the conduct listed in paragraph (1)(a), (b), (d) or (e). See also section 14 of the Contempt of Court Act 1981[9]*.*

Under section 97(4) of the Magistrates' Courts Act 1980, and under sections 12 and 14 of the Contempt of Court Act 1981, a magistrates' court can imprison (for a maximum of 1 month), or fine (to a maximum of £2,500), or both, a respondent who contravenes a provision listed in paragraph (1)(c) or (d). Section 12(1) of the 1981 Act allows the court to deal with any person who—

(a) wilfully insults the justice or justices, any witness before or officer of the court or any solicitor or counsel having business in the court, during his or their sitting or attendance in court or in going to or returning from the court; or
(b) wilfully interrupts the proceedings of the court or otherwise misbehaves in court.

Under section 89 of the Powers of Criminal Courts (Sentencing) Act 2000[10]*, no respondent who is under 21 may be imprisoned for contempt of court. Under section 108 of that Act*[11]*, a respondent who is at least 18 but under 21 may be detained if the court is of the opinion that no other method of dealing with him or her is appropriate. Under section 14(2A) of the Contempt of Court Act 1981*[12]*, a respondent who is under 17 may not be ordered to attend an attendance centre.*

[9] 1981 c. 49; section 14 was amended by sections 77 and 78 of, and paragraph 60 of Schedule 14 and Schedule 16 to, the Criminal Justice Act 1982 (c. 48), section 65 of, and paragraphs 59 and 60 of Schedule 3 to, the Mental Health (Amendment) Act 1982 (c. 51), section 148 of, and paragraph 57 of Schedule 4 to, the Mental Health Act 1983 (c. 20), section 1 of the County Courts (Penalties for Contempt) Act 1983 (c. 45), section 17 of, and Parts 1 and V of Schedule 4 to, the Criminal Justice Act 1991 (c. 53), section 65 of, and paragraph 6 of Schedule 3 to, the Criminal Justice Act 1993 (c. 36), section 165 of, and paragraph 84 of Schedule 9 to, the Powers of Criminal Courts (Sentencing) Act 2000 (c. 6), section 1 of, and paragraph 19 of Schedule 1 to, the Mental Health Act 2007 (c. 12) and section 17 of, and paragraph 52 of Schedule 9 and paragraph 53 of Schedule 10 to, the Crime and Courts Act 2013 (c. 22). It is further amended by sections 6 and 149 of, and paragraph 25 of Schedule 4 and Part 1 of Schedule 28 to, the Criminal Justice and Immigration Act 2008 (c. 4), with effect from a date to be appointed.

[10] 2000 c. 6; section 89 was amended by paragraph 74 of Schedule 3, and Part 4 of Schedule 37, to the Criminal Justice Act 2003 (c. 44). It is further amended by section 74 of, and paragraphs 160 and 180 of Schedule 7 to, the Criminal Justice and Court Services Act 2000 (c. 43) with effect from a date to be appointed.

[11] 2000 c. 6; section 108 is repealed by sections 74 and 75 of, and paragraphs 160 and 188 of Schedule 7 and Schedule 8 to, the Criminal Justice and Court Services Act 2000 (c. 43), with effect from a date to be appointed.

[12] 1981 c. 49; section 14 was amended by section 65(1) of, and paragraphs 59 and 60 of Schedule 3 to, the Mental Health (Amendment) Act 1982 (c. 51), section 148 of, and paragraph 57 of Schedule 4 to, the Mental Health Act 1983 (c. 20), section 17(3) of, and Parts 1 and V of Schedule 4 to, the Criminal Justice Act 1991 (c. 53), section 65(3) and (4) of, and paragraph 6(5) of Schedule 3 to, the Criminal Justice Act 1993 (c. 36), section 165(1) of, and paragraph 84 of Schedule 9 to, the Powers of Criminal Courts (Sentencing) Act 2000 (c. 6), section 1(4) of, and paragraph 19 of Schedule 1 to, the Mental Health Act 2007 (c. 12) and section 17 of, and paragraph 52 of Schedule 9 and paragraph 53 of Schedule 10 to, the Crime and Courts Act 2013 (c. 22). It is further amended by sections 6(2) and 149 of, and paragraph 25 of Schedule 4 and Part 1 of Schedule 28 to, the Criminal Justice and Immigration Act 2008 (c. 4), with effect from a date to be appointed.

Under section 258 of the Criminal Justice Act 2003[13]*, a respondent who is imprisoned for contempt of court must be released unconditionally after serving half the term.*

Under sections 14, 15 and 16 of the Legal Aid, Sentencing and Punishment of Offenders Act 2012[14]*, the respondent may receive advice and representation in "proceedings for contempt committed, or alleged to have been committed, by an individual in the face of the court".*

By reason of sections 15 and 45 of the Senior Courts Act 1981, the Court of Appeal and the Crown Court each has an inherent power temporarily to detain a respondent, for example to restore order, when dealing with obstructive, disruptive, insulting or intimidating conduct. Under section 12(2) of the Contempt of Court Act 1981[15]*, a magistrates' court can temporarily detain a respondent until later the same day on a contravention of that section.*

Part 14 contains rules about bail.]

Review after temporary detention **R48.6**

48.6 (1) This rule applies in a case in which the court has ordered the respondent's immediate temporary detention for conduct to which rule 48.5 applies.
(2) The court must review the case—
(a) if a magistrates' court, later the same day; or
(b) in the Court of Appeal or the Crown Court, no later than the next business day.
(3) On the review, the court must—
(a) unless the respondent is absent, repeat the explanations required by rule 48.5(2)(a); and
(b) allow the respondent a reasonable opportunity to reflect, take advice, explain and, if he or she so wishes, apologise.
(4) The court may then—
(a) take no further action in respect of the conduct;
(b) if a magistrates' court, enquire into the conduct there and then; or
(c) if the Court of Appeal or the Crown Court—
(i) enquire into the conduct there and then, or
(ii) postpone the enquiry, and order the respondent's release from such detention in the meantime.

Postponement of enquiry **R48.7**

48.7 (1) This rule applies where the Court of Appeal or the Crown Court postpones the enquiry.
(2) The court must arrange for the preparation of a written statement containing such particulars of the conduct in question as to make clear what the respondent appears to have done.
(3) The court officer must serve on the respondent—
(a) that written statement;
(b) notice of where and when the postponed enquiry will take place; and
(c) a notice that—
(i) reminds the respondent that the court can impose imprisonment, or a fine, or both, for contempt of court, and
(ii) warns the respondent that the court may pursue the postponed enquiry in the respondent's absence, if the respondent does not attend.

Procedure on enquiry **R48.8**

48.8 (1) At an enquiry, the court must—
(a) ensure that the respondent understands (with help, if necessary) what is alleged, if the enquiry has been postponed from a previous occasion;
(b) explain what the procedure at the enquiry will be; and
(c) ask whether the respondent admits the conduct in question.
(2) If the respondent admits the conduct, the court need not receive evidence.
(3) If the respondent does not admit the conduct, the court must consider—
(a) any statement served under rule 48.7;
(b) any other evidence of the conduct;
(c) any evidence introduced by the respondent; and
(d) any representations by the respondent about the conduct.
(4) If the respondent admits the conduct, or the court finds it proved, the court must—

[13] 2003 c. 44; section 258 was amended by article 3 of S.I. 2005/643, section 34 of the Police and Justice Act 2006 (c. 4) and sections 117 and 121 of, and paragraphs 1 and 5 of Schedule 17 and paragraphs 1 and 8 of Schedule 20 to, the Legal Aid, Sentencing and Punishment of Offenders Act 2012 (c. 10).
[14] 2012 c. 10.
[15] 1981 c. 49; section 12(2) was amended by Part 1 of Schedule 4 to the Criminal Justice Act 1991 (c. 53).

(a) before imposing any punishment for contempt of court, give the respondent an opportunity to make representations relevant to punishment;
(b) explain, in terms the respondent can understand (with help, if necessary)—
(i) the reasons for its decision, including its findings of fact, and
(ii) the punishment it imposes, and its effect; and
(c) if a magistrates' court, arrange for the preparation of a written record of those findings.
(5) The court that conducts an enquiry—
(a) need not include the same member or members as the court that observed the conduct; but
(b) may do so, unless that would be unfair to the respondent.

Contempt of court by failure to comply with court order, etc.

R48.9 Initial procedure on failure to comply with court order, etc.

48.9 (1) This rule applies where—
(a) a party, or other person directly affected, alleges—
(i) in the Crown Court, a failure to comply with an order to which applies rule 33.70 (compliance order, restraint order or ancillary order), rule 47.9 (certain investigation orders under the Police and Criminal Evidence Act 1984[16], the Terrorism Act 2000[17], the Proceeds of Crime Act 2002[18], the Proceeds of Crime Act 2002 (External Investigations) Order 2014[19] and the Extradition Act 2003[20]), rule 47.41 (order for retention or return of property under section 59 of the Criminal Justice and Police Act 2001[21]) or rule 47.58 (order for access under section 18A of the Criminal Appeal Act 1995[22]),
(ii) in the Court of Appeal or the Crown Court, any other conduct with which that court can deal as a civil contempt of court, or
(iii) in the Crown Court or a magistrates' court, unauthorised use of disclosed prosecution material under section 17 of the Criminal Procedure and Investigations Act 1996[23]; or
(b) the court deals on its own initiative with conduct to which paragraph (1)(a) applies.
(2) Such a party or person must—
(a) apply in writing and serve the application on the court officer; and
(b) serve on the respondent—
(i) the application, and
(ii) notice of where and when the court will consider the allegation (not less than 10 business days after service).
(3) The application must—
(a) identify the respondent;
(b) explain that it is an application for the respondent to be dealt with for contempt of court;
(c) contain such particulars of the conduct in question as to make clear what is alleged against the respondent; and
(d) include a notice warning the respondent that the court—
(i) can impose imprisonment, or a fine, or both, for contempt of court, and
(ii) may deal with the application in the respondent's absence, if the respondent does not attend the hearing.
(4) A court which acts on its own initiative under paragraph (1)(b) must—
(a) arrange for the preparation of a written statement containing the same information as an application; and
(b) arrange for the service on the respondent of—
(i) that written statement, and
(ii) notice of where and when the court will consider the allegation (not less than 10 business days after service).

[Note. The conduct to which this rule applies is sometimes described as 'civil' contempt of court.

16 1984 c. 60.
17 2000 c. 11.
18 2002 c. 29.
19 S.I. 2014/1893.
20 2003 c. 41.
21 2001 c. 16; section 59 was amended by section 82 of the Deregulation Act 2015 (c. 20).
22 1995 c. 35; section 18A was inserted by section 1 of the Criminal Cases Review Commission (Information) Act 2016 (c. 17).
23 1996 c. 25; section 17 was amended by section 331 of, and paragraphs 20 and 33 of Schedule 36 to, the Criminal Justice Act 2003 (c. 44).

By reason of section 45 of the Senior Courts Act 1981[24], the Crown Court has an inherent power to imprison (for a maximum of 2 years), or fine (to an unlimited amount), or both, a respondent for conduct in contempt of court by failing to comply with a court order or an undertaking given to the court.

Under section 18 of the Criminal Procedure and Investigations Act 1996—[25]

(a) the Crown Court can imprison (for a maximum of 2 years), or fine (to an unlimited amount), or both;

(b) a magistrates' court can imprison (for a maximum of 6 months), or fine (to a maximum of £5,000), or both,

a person who uses disclosed prosecution material in contravention of section 17 of that Act. See also rule 15.8.

Under section 89 of the Powers of Criminal Courts (Sentencing) Act 2000, no respondent who is under 21 may be imprisoned for contempt of court. Under section 108 of that Act, a respondent who is at least 18 but under 21 may be detained if the court is of the opinion that no other method of dealing with him or her is appropriate. Under section 14(2A) of the Contempt of Court Act 1981, a respondent who is under 17 may not be ordered to attend an attendance centre.

Under section 258 of the Criminal Justice Act 2003, a respondent who is imprisoned for contempt of court must be released unconditionally after serving half the term.

The Practice Direction sets out a form of application for use in connection with this rule.

The rules in Part 4 require that an application under this rule must be served by handing it to the person accused of contempt of court unless the court otherwise directs.]

Procedure on hearing **R48.10**

48.10 (1) At the hearing of an allegation under rule 48.9, the court must—
(a) ensure that the respondent understands (with help, if necessary) what is alleged;
(b) explain what the procedure at the hearing will be; and
(c) ask whether the respondent admits the conduct in question.
(2) If the respondent admits the conduct, the court need not receive evidence.
(3) If the respondent does not admit the conduct, the court must consider—
(a) the application or written statement served under rule 48.9;
(b) any other evidence of the conduct;
(c) any evidence introduced by the respondent; and
(d) any representations by the respondent about the conduct.
(4) If the respondent admits the conduct, or the court finds it proved, the court must—
(a) before imposing any punishment for contempt of court, give the respondent an opportunity to make representations relevant to punishment;
(b) explain, in terms the respondent can understand (with help, if necessary)—
(i) the reasons for its decision, including its findings of fact, and
(ii) the punishment it imposes, and its effect; and
(c) in a magistrates' court, arrange for the preparation of a written record of those findings.

Introduction of written witness statement or other hearsay **R48.11**

48.11 (1) Where rule 48.9 applies, an applicant or respondent who wants to introduce in evidence the written statement of a witness, or other hearsay, must—
(a) serve a copy of the statement, or notice of other hearsay, on—
(i) the court officer, and
(ii) the other party; and
(b) serve the copy or notice—
(i) when serving the application under rule 48.9, in the case of an applicant, or
(ii) not more than 5 business days after service of that application or of the court's written statement, in the case of the respondent.
(2) Such service is notice of that party's intention to introduce in evidence that written witness statement, or other hearsay, unless that party otherwise indicates when serving it.
(3) A party entitled to receive such notice may waive that entitlement.

[24] 1981 c. 54.
[25] 1996 c. 25.

[Note. On an application under rule 48.9, hearsay evidence is admissible under the Civil Evidence Act 1995. Section 1(2) of the 1995 Act[26] *defines hearsay as meaning 'a statement made otherwise than by a person while giving oral evidence in the proceedings which is tendered as evidence of the matters stated'. Section 13 of the Act*[27] *defines a statement as meaning 'any representation of fact or opinion, however made'.*

Under section 2 of the 1995 Act[28]*, a party who wants to introduce hearsay in evidence must give reasonable and practicable notice, in accordance with procedure rules, unless the recipient waives that requirement.]*

R48.12 **Content of written witness statement**

48.12 (1) This rule applies to a written witness statement served under rule 48.11.

(2) Such a written witness statement must contain a declaration by the person making it that it is true to the best of that person's knowledge and belief.

[Note. By reason of sections 15 and 45 of the Senior Courts Act 1981[29]*, the Court of Appeal and the Crown Court each has an inherent power to imprison (for a maximum of 2 years), or fine (to an unlimited amount), or both, for contempt of court a person who, in a written witness statement to which this rule applies, makes, or causes to be made, a false statement without an honest belief in its truth. See also section 14 of the Contempt of Court Act 1981*[30]*.]*

R48.13 **Content of notice of other hearsay**

48.13 (1) This rule applies to a notice of hearsay, other than a written witness statement, served under rule 48.11.

(2) Such a notice must—

(a) set out the evidence, or attach the document that contains it; and

(b) identify the person who made the statement that is hearsay.

R48.14 **Cross-examination of maker of written witness statement or other hearsay**

48.14 (1) This rule applies where a party wants the court's permission to cross-examine a person who made a statement which another party wants to introduce as hearsay.

(2) The party who wants to cross-examine that person must—

(a) apply in writing, with reasons; and

(b) serve the application on—

(i) the court officer, and

(ii) the party who served the hearsay.

(3) A respondent who wants to cross-examine such a person must apply to do so not more than 5 business days after service of the hearsay by the applicant.

(4) An applicant who wants to cross-examine such a person must apply to do so not more than 3 business days after service of the hearsay by the respondent.

(5) The court—

(a) may decide an application under this rule without a hearing; but

(b) must not dismiss such an application unless the person making it has had an opportunity to make representations at a hearing.

[Note. See also section 3 of the Civil Evidence Act 1995[31]*.]*

R48.15 **Credibility and consistency of maker of written witness statement or other hearsay**

48.15 (1) This rule applies where a party wants to challenge the credibility or consistency of a person who made a statement which another party wants to introduce as hearsay.

(2) The party who wants to challenge the credibility or consistency of that person must—

(a) serve notice of intention to do so on—

26 1995 c. 38.

27 1995 c. 38.

28 1995 c. 38.

29 1981 c. 54.

30 1981 c. 49; section 14 was amended by sections 77 and 78 of, and paragraph 60 of Schedule 14 and Schedule 16 to, the Criminal Justice Act 1982 (c. 48), section 65 of, and paragraphs 59 and 60 of Schedule 3 to, the Mental Health (Amendment) Act 1982 (c. 51), section 148 of, and paragraph 57 of Schedule 4 to, the Mental Health Act 1983 (c. 20), section 1 of the County Courts (Penalties for Contempt) Act 1983 (c. 45), section 17 of, and Parts 1 and V of Schedule 4 to, the Criminal Justice Act 1991 (c. 53), section 65 of, and paragraph 6 of Schedule 3 to, the Criminal Justice Act 1993 (c. 36), section 165 of, and paragraph 84 of Schedule 9 to, the Powers of Criminal Courts (Sentencing) Act 2000 (c. 6), section 1 of, and paragraph 19 of Schedule 1 to, the Mental Health Act 2007 (c. 12) and section 17 of, and paragraph 52 of Schedule 9 and paragraph 53 of Schedule 10 to, the Crime and Courts Act 2013 (c. 22). It is further amended by sections 6 and 149 of, and paragraph 25 of Schedule 4 and Part 1 of Schedule 28 to, the Criminal Justice and Immigration Act 2008 (c. 4), with effect from a date to be appointed.

31 1995 c. 38.

(i) the court officer, and
(ii) the party who served the hearsay; and
(b) in it, identify any statement or other material on which that party relies.
(3) A respondent who wants to challenge such a person's credibility or consistency must serve such a notice not more than 5 business days after service of the hearsay by the applicant.
(4) An applicant who wants to challenge such a person's credibility or consistency must serve such a notice not more than 3 business days after service of the hearsay by the respondent.
(5) The party who served the hearsay—
(a) may call that person to give oral evidence instead; and
(b) if so, must serve notice of intention to do so on—
(i) the court officer, and
(ii) the other party
as soon as practicable after service of the notice under paragraph (2).

[Note. Section 5(2) of the Civil Evidence Act 1995[32] *describes the procedure for challenging the credibility of the maker of a statement of which hearsay evidence is introduced. See also section 6 of that Act*[33]*.*

The 1995 Act does not allow the introduction of evidence of a previous inconsistent statement otherwise than in accordance with sections 5, 6 and 7 of the Criminal Procedure Act 1865[34]*.]*

Magistrates' courts' powers to adjourn, etc. **R48.16**

48.16 (1) This rule applies where a magistrates' court deals with unauthorised disclosure of prosecution material under sections 17 and 18 of the Criminal Procedure and Investigations Act 1996[35].
(2) The sections of the Magistrates' Courts Act 1980 listed in paragraph (3) apply as if in those sections—
(a) 'complaint' and 'summons' each referred to an application or written statement under rule 48.9;
(b) 'complainant' meant an applicant; and
(c) 'defendant' meant the respondent.
(3) Those sections are—
(a) section 51[36] (issue of summons on complaint);
(b) section 54[37] (adjournment);
(c) section 55[38] (non-appearance of defendant);
(d) section 97(1)[39] Superscript footnote number (summons to witness);
(e) section 121(1)[40] (constitution and place of sitting of court); and
(f) section 123[41] (defect in process).
(4) Section 127 of the 1980 Act[42] (limitation of time) does not apply.

[Note. Under section 19(3) of the Criminal Procedure and Investigations Act 1996[43]*, Criminal Procedure Rules may contain provisions equivalent to those contained in Schedule 3 to the Contempt of Court Act 1981*[44] *(which allows magistrates' courts in cases of contempt of court to use certain powers such courts possess in other cases).]*

Court's power to vary requirements **R48.17**

48.17 (1) The court may shorten or extend (even after it has expired) a time limit under rule 48.11, 48.14 or 48.15.

[32] 1995 c. 38.
[33] 1995 c. 38.
[34] 1865 c. 18; section 6 was amended by section 10 of the Decimal Currency Act 1969 (c. 19), section 90 of, and paragraph 3 of Schedule 13 to, the Access to Justice Act 1999 (c. 22), section 109 of, and paragraph 47 of Schedule 8 to, the Courts Act 2003 (c. 39) and paragraph 79 of Schedule 36 and Schedule 37 to the Criminal Justice Act 2003 (c. 44). It is further amended by section 119 of, and Schedule 7 to, the Police and Criminal Evidence Act 1984 (c. 60), with effect from a date to be appointed.
[35] 1996 c. 25; section 17 was amended by section 331 of, and paragraphs 20 and 33 of Schedule 36 to, the Criminal Justice Act 2003 (c. 44).
[36] 1980 c. 43; section 51 was substituted by section 47(1) of the Courts Act 2003 (c. 39).
[37] 1980 c. 43.
[38] 1980 c. 43.
[39] 1980 c. 43; section 97(1) was substituted by section 169(2) of the Serious Organised Crime and Police Act 2005 (c. 15).
[40] 1980 c. 43.
[41] 1980 c. 43.
[42] 1980 c. 43.
[43] 1996 c. 25; section 19(3) was amended by section 109 of, and paragraph 377 of Schedule 8 to, the Courts Act 2003 (c. 39) and section 15 of, and paragraph 251 of Schedule 4 to, the Constitutional Reform Act 2005 (c. 4).
[44] 1981 c. 49; Schedule 3 has been amended but the amendment is not relevant to this rule.

(2) A person who wants an extension of time must—
(a) apply when serving the statement, notice or application for which it is needed; and
(b) explain the delay.

CRIMINAL PRACTICE DIRECTIONS PART 48 CONTEMPT OF COURT

CPD.48A **CPD XI Other proceedings 48A: Contempt in the Face of the Magistrates' Court**

General

48A.1 The procedure to be followed in cases of contempt of court is given in CrimPR Part 48. The magistrates' courts' power to deal with contempt in the face of the court is contained within section 12 of the Contempt of Court Act 1981. Magistrates' courts also have the power to punish a witness who refuses to be sworn or give evidence under section 97(4) of the Magistrates' Courts Act 1980.

Contempt consisting of wilfully insulting anyone specified in section 12 or interrupting proceedings

48A.2 In the majority of cases, an apology and a promise as to future conduct should be sufficient for the court to order a person's release. However, there are likely to be certain cases where the nature and seriousness of the misconduct requires the court to consider using its powers, under section 12(2) of the Contempt of Court Act 1981, either to fine or to order the person's committal to custody.

Imposing a penalty for contempt

48A.3 The court should allow the person a further opportunity to apologise for his or her contempt, and should follow the procedure at CrimPR 48.8(4). The court should consider whether it is appropriate to release the person or whether it must exercise its powers to fine the person or to commit the person to custody under section 12(2) of the 1981 Act. In deciding how to deal with the person, the court should have regard to the period for which he or she has been detained, whether the conduct was admitted and the seriousness of the contempt. Any period of committal to custody should be for the shortest period of time commensurate with the interests of preserving good order in the administration of justice.

CRIMINAL PROCEDURE RULES PART 49 INTERNATIONAL CO-OPERATION

R49.1 **Notice required to accompany process served outside the United Kingdom and translations**

49.1 (1) The notice which by virtue of section 3(4)(b) of the Crime (International Co-operation) Act 2003[1] (general requirements for service of process) must accompany any process served outside the United Kingdom must give the information specified in paragraphs (2) and (4) below.

(2) The notice must—
(a) state that the person required by the process to appear as a party or attend as a witness can obtain information about his rights in connection therewith from the relevant authority; and
(b) give the particulars specified in paragraph (4) about that authority.

(3) The relevant authority where the process is served—
(a) at the request of the prosecuting authority, is that authority; or
(b) at the request of the defendant or the prosecutor in the case of a private prosecution, is the court by which the process is served.

(4) The particulars referred to in paragraph (2) are—
(a) the name and address of the relevant authority, together with its telephone and fax numbers and e-mail address; and
(b) the name of a person at the relevant authority who can provide the information referred to in paragraph (2)(a), together with his telephone and fax numbers and e-mail address.

(5) The magistrates' court or Crown Court officer must send, together with any process served outside the United Kingdom—
(a) any translation which is provided under section 3(3)(b) of the 2003 Act; and
(b) any translation of the information required to be given by this rule which is provided to him.

(6) In this rule 'process' has the same meaning as in section 51(3) of the 2003 Act.

[1] 2003 c. 32.

Proof of service outside the United Kingdom R49.2

49.2 (1) A statement in a certificate given by or on behalf of the Secretary of State—
(a) that process has been served on any person under section 4(1) of the Crime (International Co-operation) Act 2003 (service of process otherwise than by post);
(b) of the manner in which service was effected; and
(c) of the date on which process was served;
shall be admissible as evidence of any facts so stated.
(2) In this rule 'process' has the same meaning as in section 51(3) of the 2003 Act.

Supply of copy of notice of request for assistance abroad R49.3

49.3 Where a request for assistance under section 7 of the Crime (International Co-operation) Act 2003 is made by a justice of the peace or a judge exercising the jurisdiction of the Crown Court and is sent in accordance with section 8(1) of the 2003 Act, the magistrates' court or Crown Court officer shall send a copy of the letter of request to the Secretary of State as soon as practicable after the request has been made.

Persons entitled to appear and take part in proceedings before a nominated court, and exclusion of the public R49.4

49.4 A court nominated under section 15(1) of the Crime (International Co-operation) Act 2003 (nominating a court to receive evidence) may—
(a) determine who may appear or take part in the proceedings under Schedule 1 to the 2003 Act before the court and whether a party to the proceedings is entitled to be legally represented; and
(b) direct that the public be excluded from those proceedings if it thinks it necessary to do so in the interests of justice.

Record of proceedings to receive evidence before a nominated court R49.5

49.5 (1) Where a court is nominated under section 15(1) of the Crime (International Co-operation) Act 2003 the magistrates' court or Crown Court officer shall enter in an overseas record—
(a) details of the request in respect of which the notice under section 15(1) of the 2003 Act was given;
(b) the date on which, and place at which, the proceedings under Schedule 1 to the 2003 Act in respect of that request took place;
(c) the name of any witness who gave evidence at the proceedings in question;
(d) the name of any person who took part in the proceedings as a legal representative or an interpreter;
(e) whether a witness was required to give evidence on oath or (by virtue of section 5 of the Oaths Act 1978[2]) after making a solemn affirmation; and
(f) whether the opportunity to cross-examine any witness was refused.
(2) When the court gives the evidence received by it under paragraph 6(1) of Schedule 1 to the 2003 Act to the court or authority that made the request or to the territorial authority for forwarding to the court or authority that made the request, the magistrates' court or Crown Court officer shall send to the court, authority or territorial authority (as the case may be) a copy of an extract of so much of the overseas record as relates to the proceedings in respect of that request.

[Note. As to the keeping of an overseas record, see rule 49.9.]

Interpreter for the purposes of proceedings involving a television or telephone link R49.6

49.6 (1) This rule applies where a court is nominated under section 30(3) (hearing witnesses in the UK through television links) or section 31(4) (hearing witnesses in the UK by telephone) of the Crime (International Co-operation) Act 2003.
(2) Where it appears to the justices' legal adviser or the Crown Court officer that the witness to be heard in the proceedings under Part 1 or 2 of Schedule 2 to the 2003 Act ('the relevant proceedings') is likely to give evidence in a language other than English, he shall make arrangements for an interpreter to be present at the proceedings to translate what is said into English.
(3) Where it appears to the justices' legal adviser or the Crown Court officer that the witness to be heard in the relevant proceedings is likely to give evidence in a language other than that in which the proceedings of the court referred to in section 30(1) or, as the case may be, 31(1) of the 2003 Act ('the external court') will be conducted, he shall make arrangements for an

[2] 1978 c. 19.

interpreter to be present at the relevant proceedings to translate what is said into the language in which the proceedings of the external court will be conducted.

(4) Where the evidence in the relevant proceedings is either given in a language other than English or is not translated into English by an interpreter, the court shall adjourn the proceedings until such time as an interpreter can be present to provide a translation into English.

(5) Where a court in Wales understands Welsh—
(a) paragraph (2) does not apply where it appears to the justices' legal adviser or Crown Court officer that the witness in question is likely to give evidence in Welsh;
(b) paragraph (4) does not apply where the evidence is given in Welsh; and
(c) any translation which is provided pursuant to paragraph (2) or (4) may be into Welsh instead of English.

R49.7 **Record of television link hearing before a nominated court**

49.7 (1) This rule applies where a court is nominated under section 30(3) of the Crime (International Co-operation) Act 2003.

(2) The magistrates' court or Crown Court officer shall enter in an overseas record—
(a) details of the request in respect of which the notice under section 30(3) of the 2003 Act was given;
(b) the date on which, and place at which, the proceedings under Part 1 of Schedule 2 to that Act in respect of that request took place;
(c) the technical conditions, such as the type of equipment used, under which the proceedings took place;
(d) the name of the witness who gave evidence;
(e) the name of any person who took part in the proceedings as a legal representative or an interpreter; and
(f) the language in which the evidence was given.

(3) As soon as practicable after the proceedings under Part 1 of Schedule 2 to the 2003 Act took place, the magistrates' court or Crown Court officer shall send to the external authority that made the request a copy of an extract of so much of the overseas record as relates to the proceedings in respect of that request.

[Note. As to the keeping of an overseas record, see rule 49.9.]

R49.8 **Record of telephone link hearing before a nominated court**

49.8 (1) This rule applies where a court is nominated under section 31(4) of the Crime (International Co-operation) Act 2003.

(2) The magistrates' court or Crown Court officer shall enter in an overseas record—
(a) details of the request in respect of which the notice under section 31(4) of the 2003 Act was given;
(b) the date, time and place at which the proceedings under Part 2 of Schedule 2 to the 2003 Act took place;
(c) the name of the witness who gave evidence;
(d) the name of any interpreter who acted at the proceedings; and
(e) the language in which the evidence was given.

[Note. As to the keeping of an overseas record, see rule 49.9.]

R49.9 **Overseas record**

49.9 (1) The overseas records of a magistrates' court shall be part of the register (within the meaning of section 150(1) of the Magistrates' Courts Act 1980[3]).

(2) The overseas records of any court shall not be open to inspection by any person except—
(a) as authorised by the Secretary of State; or
(b) with the leave of the court.

[Note. As to the making of court records, see rule 5.4.]

R49.10 **Overseas freezing orders**

49.10 (1) This rule applies where a court is nominated under section 21(1) of the Crime (International Co-operation) Act 2003[4] to give effect to an overseas freezing order.

(2) Where the Secretary of State serves a copy of such an order on the court officer—
(a) the general rule is that the court must consider the order no later than the next business day; but

[3] 1980 c. 43; a relevant amendment was made to section 150(1) by paragraph 250 of Schedule 8, and Schedule 10 to, the Courts Act 2003 (c. 39).

[4] 2003 c. 32.

(b) exceptionally, the court may consider the order later than that, though not more than 5 business days after service.

(3) The court must not consider the order unless—

(a) it is satisfied that the chief officer of police for the area in which the evidence is situated has had notice of the order; and

(b) that chief officer of police has had an opportunity to make representations, at a hearing if that officer wants.

(4) The court may consider the order—

(a) without a hearing; or

(b) at a hearing, in public or in private.

[Note. Under sections 20, 21 and 22 of the Crime (International Co-operation) Act 2003, a court nominated by the Secretary of State must consider an order, made by a court or other authority in a country outside the United Kingdom, the purpose of which is to protect evidence in the United Kingdom which may be used in proceedings or an investigation in that other country pending the transfer of that evidence to that country. The court may decide not to give effect to such an order only if—

(a) were the person whose conduct is in question to be charged with the offence to which the order relates, a previous conviction or acquittal would entitle that person to be discharged; or

(b) giving effect to the order would be incompatible with a Convention right, within the meaning of the Human Rights Act 1998.]

Overseas forfeiture orders **R49.11**

49.11 (1) This rule applies where—

(a) the Crown Court can—

(i) make a restraint order under article 5 of the Criminal Justice (International Co-operation) Act 1990 (Enforcement of Overseas Forfeiture Orders) Order 2005[5], or

(ii) give effect to an external forfeiture order under article 19 of that Order;

(b) the Director of Public Prosecutions or the Director of the Serious Fraud Office receives—

(i) a request for the restraint of property to which article 3 of the 2005 Order applies, or

(ii) a request to give effect to an external forfeiture order to which article 15 of the Order applies; and

(c) the Director wants the Crown Court to—

(i) make such a restraint order, or

(ii) give effect to such a forfeiture order.

(2) The Director must—

(a) apply in writing;

(b) serve the application on the court officer; and

(c) serve the application on the defendant and on any other person affected by the order, unless the court is satisfied that—

(i) the application is urgent, or

(ii) there are reasonable grounds for believing that to give notice of the application would cause the dissipation of the property which is the subject of the application.

(3) The application must—

(a) identify the property the subject of the application;

(b) identify the person who is or who may become the subject of such a forfeiture order;

(c) explain how the requirements of the 2005 Order are satisfied, as the case may be—

(i) for making a restraint order, or

(ii) for giving effect to a forfeiture order;

(d) where the application is to give effect to a forfeiture order, include an application to appoint the Director as the enforcement authority; and

(e) propose the terms of the Crown Court order.

(4) If the court allows the application, it must—

(a) where it decides to make a restraint order—

(i) specify the property the subject of the order,

(ii) specify the person or persons who are prohibited from dealing with that property,

(iii) specify any exception to that prohibition, and

(iv) include any ancillary order that the court believes is appropriate to ensure that the restraint order is effective; and

(b) where it decides to give effect to a forfeiture order, exercise its power to—

(i) direct the registration of the order as an order of the Crown Court,

[5] S.I. 2005/3180.

(ii) give directions for notice of the order to be given to any person affected by it, and
(iii) appoint the applicant Director as the enforcement authority.

(5) Paragraph (6) applies where a person affected by an order, or the Director, wants the court to vary or discharge a restraint order or cancel the registration of a forfeiture order.

(6) Such a person must—
(a) apply in writing as soon as practicable after becoming aware of the grounds for doing so;
(b) serve the application on the court officer and, as applicable—
(i) the other party, and
(ii) any other person who will or may be affected;
(c) explain why it is appropriate, as the case may be—
(i) for the restraint order to be varied or discharged, or
(ii) for the registration of the forfeiture order to be cancelled;
(d) propose the terms of any variation; and
(e) ask for a hearing, if one is wanted, and explain why it is needed.

(7) The court may—
(a) consider an application
(i) at a hearing, which must be in private unless the court otherwise directs, or
(ii) without a hearing; and
(b) allow an application to be made orally.

[Note. Under article 19 of the Criminal Justice (International Co-operation) Act 1990 (Enforcement of Overseas Forfeiture Orders) Order 2005, on the application of the Director of Public Prosecutions or the Director of the Serious Fraud Office the Crown Court may give effect to an order made by a court in a country outside the United Kingdom for the forfeiture and destruction, or other disposal, of any property in respect of which an offence has been committed in that country, or which was used or intended for use in connection with the commission of such an offence (described in the Order as an 'external forfeiture order').

Under article 5 of the 2005 Order, on the application of the Director of Public Prosecutions or the Director of the Serious Fraud Office the Crown Court may make a restraint order prohibiting any specified person from dealing with property, for the purpose of facilitating the enforcement of such a forfeiture order which has yet to be made.]

Criminal Procedure Rules Part 50 Extradition

Section 1: general rules

R50.1 **When this Part applies**

50.1 (1) This Part applies to extradition under Part 1 or Part 2 of the Extradition Act 2003[1].

(2) Section 2 of this Part applies to proceedings in a magistrates' court, and in that Section—
(a) rules 50.3 to 50.7, 50.15 and 50.16 apply to extradition under Part 1 of the Act;
(b) rules 50.3, 50.4 and 50.8 to 50.16 apply to extradition under Part 2 of the Act.

(3) Section 3 of this Part applies where—
(a) a party wants to appeal to the High Court against an order by the magistrates' court or by the Secretary of State; and
(b) a party to an appeal to the High Court wants to appeal further to the Supreme Court under—
(i) section 32 of the Act (appeal under Part 1 of the Act), or
(ii) section 114 of the Act (appeal under Part 2 of the Act).

(4) Section 4 of this Part applies to proceedings in a magistrates' court under—
(a) sections 54 and 55 of the Act (Request for consent to other offence being dealt with; Questions for decision at consent hearing); and
(b) sections 56 and 57 of the Act (Request for consent to further extradition to category 1 territory; Questions for decision at consent hearing).

(5) In this Part, and for the purposes of this Part in other rules—
(a) 'magistrates' court' means a District Judge (Magistrates' Courts) exercising the powers to which Section 2 of this Part applies;
(b) 'presenting officer' means an officer of the National Crime Agency, a police officer, a prosecutor or other person representing an authority or territory seeking the extradition of a defendant; and
(c) 'defendant' means a person arrested under Part 1 or Part 2 of the Extradition Act 2003.

[Note. The Extradition Act 2003 provides for the extradition of a person accused or convicted of a crime to the territory within which that person is accused, was convicted or is to serve a sentence.

[1] 2003 c. 41.

Under Part 1 of the Act (sections 1 to 68), the magistrates' court may give effect to a warrant for arrest issued by an authority in a territory designated for the purposes of that Part.

Under Part 2 of the Act (sections 69 to 141), the magistrates' court and the Secretary of State may give effect to a request for extradition made under a treaty between the United Kingdom and the requesting territory.

Under sections 67 and 139 of the Extradition Act 2003[2]*, a District Judge (Magistrates' Courts) must be designated for the purposes of the Act to exercise the powers to which Section 2 of this Part applies.*

There are rights of appeal to the High Court from decisions of the magistrates' court and of the Secretary of State: see Section 3 of this Part.]

Further objective in extradition proceedings **R50.2**

50.2 When exercising a power to which this Part applies, as well as furthering the overriding objective, in accordance with rule 1.3, the court must have regard to the importance of—
(a) mutual confidence and recognition between judicial authorities in the United Kingdom and in requesting territories; and
(b) the conduct of extradition proceedings in accordance with international obligations, including obligations to deal swiftly with extradition requests.

Section 2: extradition proceedings in a magistrates' court

Exercise of magistrates' court's powers **R50.3**

50.3 (1) The general rule is that the magistrates' court must exercise its powers at a hearing in public, but—
(a) that is subject to any power the court has to—
(i) impose reporting restrictions,
(ii) withhold information from the public, or
(iii) order a hearing in private; and
(b) despite the general rule the court may, without a hearing—
(i) give any directions to which rule 50.4 applies (Case management in the magistrates' court and duty of court officer), or
(ii) determine an application which these Rules allow to be determined by a magistrates' court without a hearing in a case to which this Part does not apply.
(2) If the court so directs, a party may attend by live link any hearing except an extradition hearing under rule 50.6 or 50.13.
(3) Where the defendant is absent from a hearing—
(a) the general rule is that the court must proceed as if the defendant—
(i) were present, and
(ii) opposed extradition on any ground of which the court has been made aware;
(b) the general rule does not apply if the defendant is under 18;
(c) the general rule is subject to the court being satisfied that—
(i) the defendant had reasonable notice of where and when the hearing would take place,
(ii) the defendant has been made aware that the hearing might proceed in his or her absence, and
(iii) there is no good reason for the defendant's absence; and
(d) the general rule does not apply but the court may exercise its powers in the defendant's absence where—
(i) the court discharges the defendant,
(ii) the defendant is represented and the defendant's presence is impracticable by reason of his or her ill health or disorderly conduct, or
(iii) on an application under rule 50.32 (Application for consent to deal with another offence or for consent to further extradition), the defendant is represented or the defendant's presence is impracticable by reason of his or her detention in the territory to which he or she has been extradited.
(4) The court may exercise its power to adjourn—
(a) if either party asks, or on its own initiative; and
(b) in particular—
(i) to allow there to be obtained information that the court requires,
(ii) following a provisional arrest under Part 1 of the Extradition Act 2003, pending receipt of the warrant,

[2] 2003 c. 41; sections 67 and 139 were amended by section 15 of, and paragraphs 352 and 353 of Schedule 4 to, the Constitutional Reform Act 2005 (c. 4) and section 42 of, and paragraph 15 of Schedule 13 to, the Police and Justice Act 2006 (c. 48).

Criminal Procedure Rules and Criminal Practice Directions

(iii) following a provisional arrest with a warrant under Part 2 of the Act, pending receipt of the extradition request,
(iv) following a provisional arrest without a warrant under Part 2 of the Act, pending receipt of evidence or information required by the court,
(v) if the court is informed that the defendant is serving a custodial sentence in the United Kingdom,
(vi) if it appears to the court that the defendant is not fit to be extradited, unless the court discharges the defendant for that reason,
(vii) where a court dealing with a warrant to which Part 1 of the Act applies is informed that another such warrant has been received in the United Kingdom,
(viii) where a court dealing with a warrant to which Part 1 of the Act applies is informed of a request for the temporary transfer of the defendant to the territory to which the defendant's extradition is sought, or a request for the defendant to speak to the authorities of that territory, or
(ix) during a hearing to which rule 50.32 applies (Application for consent to deal with another offence or for consent to further extradition).

(5) The court must exercise its power to adjourn if informed that the defendant has been charged with an offence in the United Kingdom.
(6) The general rule is that, before exercising a power to which this Part applies, the court must give each party an opportunity to make representations, unless that party is absent without good reason.
(7) The court may—
(a) shorten a time limit or extend it (even after it has expired), unless that is inconsistent with other legislation;
(b) direct that a notice or application be served on any person; and
(c) allow a notice or application to be in a different form to one set out in the Practice Direction, or to be presented orally.
(8) A party who wants an extension of time within which to serve a notice or make an application must—
(a) apply for that extension of time when serving that notice or making that application; and
(b) give the reasons for the application for an extension of time.

[Note. See sections 8A, 8B, 9, 21B, 22, 23, 25 and 44 of the Extradition Act 2003[3] *(powers in relation to extradition under Part 1 of the Act) and sections 76A, 76B, 77, 88, 89 and 91 of the Act*[4] *(powers in relation to extradition under Part 2 of the Act). Under sections 9 and 77 of the Act, at the extradition hearing the court has the same powers (as nearly as may be) as a magistrates' court would have if the proceedings were the summary trial of an allegation against the defendant: see also rule 24.12(3) (Trial and sentence in a magistrates' court; procedure where the defendant is absent).*

Under sections 206A to 206C of the 2003 Act[5]*, the court may require a defendant to attend by live link a preliminary hearing to which rule 50.5, 50.9 or 50.11 applies, any hearing for the purposes of rule 50.12 and the hearing to which rule 50.32 applies.*

Part 6 contains rules about reporting and access restrictions.

Part 14 contains rules about bail. Rules 14.2(3) and 14.7(7)(c) allow an application to be determined without a hearing in the circumstances to which those rules apply.

The principal time limits are prescribed by the Extradition Act 2003: see rule 50.16.]

R50.4 **Case management in the magistrates' court and duty of court officer**

50.4 (1) The magistrates' court and the parties have the same duties and powers as under Part 3 (Case management), subject to—
(a) rule 50.2 (Special objective in extradition proceedings); and

[3] 2003 c. 41; sections 8A and 8B were inserted by section 69 of the Policing and Crime Act 2009 (c. 26). Sections 9 and 44 were amended by paragraph 16 of Schedule 13 to the Police and Justice Act 2006 (c. 48). Section 21B was inserted by section 159 of the Anti-social Behaviour, Crime and Policing Act 2014 (c. 12). Section 22 was amended by section 71 of the Policing and Crime Act 2009 (c. 26). Section 23 was amended by paragraph 7 of Schedule 13 to the Police and Justice Act 2006 (c. 48) and section 71 of the Policing and Crime Act 2009 (c. 26).

[4] 2003 c. 41; sections 76A and 76B were inserted by section 70 of the Policing and Crime Act 2009 (c. 26). Section 77 was amended by paragraph 16 of Schedule 13 to the Police and Justice Act 2006 (c. 48). Section 88 was amended by section 71 of the Policing and Crime Act 2009 (c. 26). Section 89 was amended by paragraph 7 of Schedule 13 to the Police and Justice Act 2006 (c. 48) and section 71 of the Policing and Crime Act 2009 (c. 26).

[5] 2003 c. 41; sections 206A, 206B and 206C were inserted by section 78 of the Policing and Crime Act 2009 (c. 26).

(b) paragraph (2) of this rule.

(2) Rule 3.6 (Application to vary a direction) does not apply to a decision to extradite or discharge.

(3) Where this rule applies, active case management by the court includes—

(a) if the court requires information from the authorities in the requesting territory—

(i) nominating a court officer, the designated authority which certified the arrest warrant where Part 1 of the Extradition Act 2003 Act applies, a party or other person to convey that request to those authorities, and

(ii) in a case in which the terms of that request need to be prepared in accordance with directions by the court, giving such directions accordingly; and

(b) giving such directions as are required where, under section 21B of the Extradition Act 2003[6], the parties agree—

(i) to the temporary transfer of the defendant to the requesting territory, or

(ii) that the defendant should speak with representatives of an authority in that territory.

(4) Where this rule applies, active assistance by the parties includes—

(a) applying for any direction needed as soon as reasonably practicable; and

(b) concisely explaining the reasons for any application for the court to direct—

(i) the preparation of a request to which paragraph (3)(a) applies, or

(ii) the making of arrangements to which paragraph (3)(b) applies.

(5) Where this rule applies, active assistance by the presenting officer includes—

(a) taking reasonable steps to ensure that the defendant will be able to understand (with help, if necessary)—

(i) what is alleged by the warrant, if Part 1 of the 2003 Act applies, or

(ii) the content of the extradition request, if Part 2 of the Act applies; and

(b) providing in writing identification of the equivalent offence or offences under the law of England and Wales for the conduct being relied on if—

(i) this is raised for the defence as an issue and the court considers it necessary to identify the equivalent offence or offences in writing, or

(ii) the defendant is not represented.

(6) The court officer must—

(a) as soon as practicable, serve notice of the court's decision to extradite or discharge—

(i) on the defendant,

(ii) on the designated authority which certified the arrest warrant, where Part 1 of the 2003 Act applies, and

(iii) on the Secretary of State, where Part 2 of the Act applies; and

(b) give the court such assistance as it requires.

[Note. Part 3 contains rules about case management which apply at an extradition hearing and during preparation for that hearing. This rule must be read in conjunction with those rules.

Under section 21B of the Extradition Act 2003 (Request for temporary transfer etc.), where Part 1 of the Act applies, and in the circumstances described in that section, the parties may agree to the defendant's temporary transfer to the requesting territory, or may agree that the defendant will speak to representatives of an investigating, prosecuting or judicial authority in that territory. On the making by a party of a request to such effect the court must if necessary adjourn the proceedings for 7 days while the other party considers it. If the parties then agree to proceed with the proposed transfer or discussion the court must adjourn the proceedings for however long seems necessary.]

Extradition under Part 1 of the Extradition Act 2003

Preliminary hearing after arrest **R50.5**

50.5 (1) This rule applies where the defendant is first brought before the court after—

(a) arrest under a warrant to which Part 1 of the Extradition Act 2003 applies; or

(b) provisional arrest under Part 1 of the Act.

(2) The presenting officer must—

(a) serve on the court officer—

(i) the arrest warrant, and

(ii) a certificate, given by the authority designated by the Secretary of State, that the warrant was issued by an authority having the function of issuing such warrants in the territory to which the defendant's extradition is sought; or

(b) apply at once for an extension of time within which to serve that warrant and that certificate.

(3) An application under paragraph (2)(b) must—

[6] 2003 c. 41; section 21B was inserted by section 159 of the Anti-social Behaviour, Crime and Policing Act 2014 (c. 12).

(a) explain why the requirement to serve the warrant and certificate at once could not reasonably be complied with; and
(b) include—
(i) any written material in support of that explanation, and
(ii) representations about bail pending service of those documents.
(4) When the presenting officer serves the warrant and certificate, in the following sequence the court must—
(a) decide whether the defendant is the person in respect of whom the warrant was issued;
(b) explain, in terms the defendant can understand (with help, if necessary)—
(i) the allegation made in the warrant, and
(ii) that the defendant may consent to extradition, and how that may be done and with what effect;
(c) give directions for an extradition hearing to begin—
(i) no more than 21 days after the defendant's arrest, or
(ii) if either party so applies, at such a later date as the court decides is in the interests of justice;
(d) consider any ancillary application, including an application about bail pending the extradition hearing; and
(e) give such directions as are required for the preparation and conduct of the extradition hearing.

[Note. See sections 4, 6, 7 and 8 of the Extradition Act 2003[7]*.*

Under section 6 of the Act, following a provisional arrest pending receipt of a warrant the defendant must be brought before the court within 48 hours, and the warrant and certificate must be served within that same period. If they are not so served, the court may extend the time for service by a further 48 hours.

Under section 45 of the Act[8]*, a defendant's consent to extradition must be given before the court, must be recorded in writing, and is irrevocable. Consent may not be given unless the defendant has a legal representative with him or her when giving consent, or the defendant has failed or refused to apply for legal aid, or legal aid has been refused or withdrawn.*

Part 14 contains rules about bail.]

R50.6 **Extradition hearing**

50.6 (1) This rule applies at the extradition hearing arranged by the court under rule 50.5.
(2) In the following sequence, the court must decide—
(a) whether the offence specified in the warrant is an extradition offence;
(b) whether a bar to extradition applies, namely—
(i) the rule against double jeopardy,
(ii) absence of prosecution decision,
(iii) extraneous considerations,
(iv) the passage of time,
(v) the defendant's age,
(vi) speciality,
(vii) earlier extradition or transfer to the United Kingdom, or
(viii) forum;
(c) where the warrant alleges that the defendant is unlawfully at large after conviction, whether conviction was in the defendant's presence and if not—
(i) whether the defendant was absent deliberately, and
(ii) if the defendant was not absent deliberately, whether the defendant would be entitled to a retrial (or to a review of the conviction, amounting to a retrial);
(d) whether extradition would be—
(i) compatible with the defendant's human rights, and
(ii) proportionate;
(e) whether it would be unjust or oppressive to extradite the defendant because of his or her physical or mental condition;
(f) after deciding each of (a) to (e) above, before progressing to the next, whether to order the

[7] 2003 c. 41; section 6 was amended by section 77 of the Policing and Crime Act 2009 (c. 26). Section 7 was amended by paragraph 16 of Schedule 13 to the Police and Justice Act 2006 (c. 48) and section 77 of the Policing and Crime Act 2009 (c. 26). Section 8 was amended by paragraph 16 of Schedule 13 to the Police and Justice Act 2006 (c. 48) and section 155 of the Anti-social Behaviour, Crime and Policing Act 2014 (c. 12).

[8] 2003 c. 41; section 45 was amended by paragraphs 62 and 63 of Schedule 5 to the Legal Aid, Sentencing and Punishment of Offenders Act 2012 (c. 10) and section 163 of the Anti-social Behaviour, Crime and Policing Act 2014 (c. 12).

defendant's discharge, and
(g) whether to order the temporary transfer of the defendant to the territory to which the defendant's extradition is sought.

(3) If the court discharges the defendant, the court must consider any ancillary application, including an application about—
(a) reporting restrictions; or
(b) costs.

(4) If the court does not discharge the defendant, the court must—
(a) exercise its power to order the defendant's extradition;
(b) explain, in terms the defendant can understand (with help, if necessary), that the defendant may appeal to the High Court within the next 7 days; and
(c) consider any ancillary application, including an application about—
(i) bail pending extradition,
(ii) reporting restrictions, or
(iii) costs.

(5) If the court orders the defendant's extradition, the court must order its postponement where—
(a) the defendant has been charged with an offence in the United Kingdom; or
(b) the defendant has been sentenced to imprisonment or detention in the United Kingdom.

[Note. See sections 10, 11, 20, 21, 21B, 25, 26, 36A, 36B, 64 and 65 of the Extradition Act 2003[9]*.*

Part 6 contains rules about reporting restrictions. Part 45 contains rules about costs.]

Discharge where warrant withdrawn R50.7

50.7 (1) This rule applies where the authority that certified the warrant gives the court officer notice that the warrant has been withdrawn—
(a) after the start of the hearing under rule 50.5; and
(b) before the court orders the defendant's extradition or discharge.

(2) The court must exercise its power to discharge the defendant.

[Note. See section 41 of the Extradition Act 2003.]

Extradition under Part 2 of the Extradition Act 2003

Issue of arrest warrant R50.8

50.8 (1) This rule applies where the Secretary of State serves on the court officer—
(a) an extradition request to which Part 2 of the Extradition Act 2003 applies;
(b) a certificate given by the Secretary of State that the request was received in the way approved for the request; and
(c) a copy of any Order in Council which applies to the request.

(2) In the following sequence, the court must decide—
(a) whether the offence in respect of which extradition is requested is an extradition offence; and
(b) whether there is sufficient evidence, or (where the Secretary of State has so ordered, for this purpose) information, to justify the issue of a warrant of arrest.

(3) The court may issue an arrest warrant—
(a) without giving the parties an opportunity to make representations; and
(b) without a hearing, or at a hearing in public or in private.

[Note. See sections 70, 71, 137 and 138 of the Extradition Act 2003[10]*.]*

Preliminary hearing after arrest R50.9

50.9 (1) This rule applies where a defendant is first brought before the court after arrest under a warrant to which rule 50.8 applies.

(2) In the following sequence, the court must—
(a) explain, in terms the defendant can understand (with help, if necessary)—

[9] 2003 c. 41; section 11 was amended by paragraphs 3 and 4 of Schedule 13 to the Police and Justice Act 2006 (c. 48), paragraphs 1 and 2 of Schedule 20 to the Crime and Courts Act 2013 (c. 22) and sections 156, 157, 158 and 181 of, and paragraph 104 of Schedule 11 to, the Anti-social Behaviour, Crime and Policing Act 2014 (c. 12). Section 21 was amended by paragraph 16 of Schedule 13 to the Police and Justice Act 2006 (c. 48). Section 21B was inserted by section 159 of the Anti-social Behaviour, Crime and Policing Act 2014 (c. 12), section 26 was amended by section 160 of that Act, sections 36A and 36B were inserted by section 161 of that Act and sections 64 and 65 were substituted by section 164 of that Act.

[10] 2003 c. 41; section 70 was amended by paragraphs 1 and 17 of Schedule 13 to the Police and Justice Act 2006 (c. 48). Section 71 was amended by paragraph 202 of Schedule 16 to the Armed Forces Act 2006 (c. 52). Section 137 was amended by sections 164 and 181 of, and paragraph 117 of Schedule 11 to, the Anti-social Behaviour, Crime and Policing Act 2014 (c. 12). Section 138 was amended by sections 164 and 181 of, and paragraph 118 of Schedule 11 to, the 2014 Act.

(i) the content of the extradition request, and
(ii) that the defendant may consent to extradition, and how that may be done and with what effect;
(b) arrange for an extradition hearing to begin—
(i) no more than 2 months later, or
(ii) if either party so applies, at such a later date as the court decides is in the interests of justice;
(c) consider any ancillary application, including an application about bail pending the extradition hearing; and
(d) give any direction as is appropriate to the needs of the case about the introduction of evidence at the extradition hearing.

[Note. See sections 72 and 75 of the Extradition Act 2003[11].

Under section 127 of the 2003 Act[12] *a defendant's consent to extradition must be given before the court, must be recorded in writing, and is irrevocable. Consent may not be given unless the defendant has a legal representative with him or her when giving consent, or the defendant has failed or refused to apply for legal aid, or legal aid has been refused or withdrawn.*

Part 14 contains rules about bail.]

R50.10 **Issue of provisional arrest warrant**

50.10 (1) This rule applies where a presenting officer wants a justice of the peace to issue a provisional arrest warrant under Part 2 of the Extradition Act 2003, pending receipt of an extradition request.
(2) The presenting officer must—
(a) serve an application for a warrant on the court officer; and
(b) verify that application on oath or affirmation.
(3) In the following sequence, the justice must decide—
(a) whether the alleged offence is an extradition offence; and
(b) whether there is sufficient evidence, or (where the Secretary of State has so ordered, for this purpose) information, to justify the issue of a warrant of arrest.

[Note. See sections 73, 137 and 138 of the Extradition Act 2003[13]*.]*

R50.11 **Preliminary hearing after provisional arrest**

50.11 (1) This rule applies where a defendant is first brought before the court after arrest—
(a) under a provisional arrest warrant to which rule 50.10 applies; or
(b) under section 74A of the Extradition Act 2003[14], without a warrant.
(2) Where paragraph (1)(b) applies the court must first—
(a) on the basis of such evidence or information as is produced to the court, decide whether a warrant to which rule 50.10 applies would be issued if the defendant were not already under arrest; and
(b) if no such warrant would be issued, order the defendant's discharge.
(3) Unless the court orders the defendant's discharge under paragraph (2), the court must—
(a) explain, in terms the defendant can understand (with help, if necessary)—
(i) the allegation in respect of which the defendant has been arrested, and
(ii) that the defendant may consent to extradition, and how that may be done and with what effect; and
(b) consider any ancillary application, including an application about bail pending receipt of the extradition request.

[Note. See sections 74, 74A, 74B, 74C, 74D and 74E of the Extradition Act 2003[15]*. Under section 127 of the Act, a defendant's consent to extradition must be given before the court, must be recorded in writing, and is irrevocable. Consent may not be given unless the defendant has a legal representative with him or her when giving consent, or the defendant has failed or refused to apply for legal aid, or legal aid has been refused or withdrawn.]*

[11] 2003 c. 41; section 72 was amended by paragraph 16 of Schedule 13 to the Police and Justice Act 2006 (c. 48).
[12] 2003 c. 41; section 127 was amended by paragraphs 62 and 64 of Schedule 5 to the Legal Aid, Sentencing and Punishment of Offenders Act 2012 (c. 10).
[13] 2003 c. 41; section 73 was amended by paragraph 203 of Schedule 16 to the Armed Forces Act 2006 (c. 52). Section 137 was amended by sections 164 and 181 of, and paragraph 117 of Schedule 11 to, the Anti-social Behaviour, Crime and Policing Act 2014 (c. 12). Section 138 was amended by sections 164 and 181 of, and paragraph 118 of Schedule 11 to, the 2014 Act.
[14] 2003 c. 41; section 74A was inserted by paragraphs 1 and 2 of the Schedule to the Extradition (Provisional Arrest) Act 2020 (c. 18).
[15] 2003 c. 41; sections 74B, 74C, 74D and 74E were inserted by paragraphs 1 and 2 of the Schedule to the Extradition (Provisional Arrest) Act 2020 (c. 18).

Arrangement of extradition hearing after provisional arrest R50.12

50.12 (1) This rule applies when the Secretary of State serves on the court officer—
(a) a request for extradition in respect of which a defendant has been arrested—
(i) under a provisional arrest warrant to which rule 50.10 applies, or
(ii) under section 74A of the Extradition Act 2003, without a warrant;
(b) a certificate given by the Secretary of State that the request was received in the way approved for the request; and
(c) a copy of any Order in Council which applies to the request.
(2) Unless a time limit for service of the request has expired, the court must—
(a) give directions for an extradition hearing to begin—
(i) no more than 2 months after service of the request, or
(ii) if either party so applies, at such a later date as the court decides is in the interests of justice;
(b) consider any ancillary application, including an application about bail pending the extradition hearing; and
(c) give such directions as are required for the preparation and conduct of the extradition hearing.

[Note. See section 76 of the Extradition Act 2003.]

Extradition hearing R50.13

50.13 (1) This rule applies at the extradition hearing directed under rule 50.9 or rule 50.12.
(2) In the following sequence, the court must decide—
(a) whether the documents served on the court officer by the Secretary of State include—
(i) those listed in rule 50.8(1) or rule 50.12(1), as the case may be,
(ii) particulars of the person whose extradition is requested,
(iii) particulars of the offence specified in the request, and
(iv) as the case may be, a warrant for the defendant's arrest, or a certificate of the defendant's conviction and (if applicable) sentence, issued in the requesting territory;
(b) whether the defendant is the person whose extradition is requested;
(c) whether the offence specified in the request is an extradition offence;
(d) whether the documents served on the court officer by the Secretary of State have been served also on the defendant;
(e) whether a bar to extradition applies, namely—
(i) the rule against double jeopardy,
(ii) extraneous considerations,
(iii) the passage of time,
(iv) hostage-taking considerations, or
(v) forum;
(f) where the request accuses the defendant of an offence, whether there is evidence which would be sufficient to make a case requiring an answer by the defendant if the extradition proceedings were a trial (unless the Secretary of State has otherwise ordered, for this purpose);
(g) where the request accuses the defendant of being unlawfully at large after conviction, whether the defendant was—
(i) convicted in his or her presence, or
(ii) absent deliberately;
(h) where the request accuses the defendant of being unlawfully at large after conviction, and the defendant was absent but not deliberately—
(i) whether the defendant would be entitled to a retrial (or to a review of the conviction amounting to a retrial), and
(ii) if so, whether there is evidence which would be sufficient to make a case requiring an answer by the defendant if the extradition proceedings were a trial (unless the Secretary of State has otherwise ordered, for this purpose);
(i) whether extradition would be compatible with the defendant's human rights;
(j) whether it would be unjust or oppressive to extradite the defendant because of his or her physical or mental condition; and
(k) after deciding each of (a) to (j) above, before progressing to the next, whether to order the defendant's discharge.
(3) If the court discharges the defendant, the court must consider any ancillary application, including an application about—
(a) reporting restrictions; or
(b) costs.

(4) If the court does not discharge the defendant, the court must—
(a) exercise its power to send the case to the Secretary of State to decide whether to extradite the defendant;
(b) explain, in terms the defendant can understand (with help, if necessary), that—
(i) the defendant may appeal to the High Court not more than 14 days after being informed of the Secretary of State's decision, and
(ii) any such appeal brought before the Secretary of State's decision has been made will not be heard until after that decision; and
(c) consider any ancillary application, including an application about—
(i) bail pending extradition,
(ii) reporting restrictions, or
(iii) costs.
(5) If the Secretary of State orders the defendant's extradition, the court must order its postponement where—
(a) the defendant has been charged with an offence in the United Kingdom; or
(b) the defendant has been sentenced to imprisonment or detention in the United Kingdom.

[Note. See sections 78, 79, 84, 85, 86, 87, 91, 92, 137 and 138 of the Extradition Act 2003[16].

Part 6 contains rules about reporting restrictions. Part 45 contains rules about costs.]

R50.14 **Discharge where extradition request withdrawn**

50.14 (1) This rule applies where the Secretary of State gives the court officer notice that the extradition request has been withdrawn—
(a) after the start of the hearing under rule 50.9 or 50.11; and
(b) before the court—
(i) sends the case to the Secretary of State to decide whether to extradite the defendant, or
(ii) discharges the defendant.
(2) The court must exercise its power to discharge the defendant.

[Note. See section 122 of the Extradition Act 2003.]

Evidence at extradition hearing

R50.15 **Introduction of additional evidence**

50.15 (1) Where a party wants to introduce evidence at an extradition hearing under the law that would apply if that hearing were a trial, the relevant Part of these Rules applies with such adaptations as the court directs.
(2) If the court admits as evidence the written statement of a witness—
(a) each relevant part of the statement must be read or summarised aloud; or
(b) the court must read the statement and its gist must be summarised aloud.
(3) If a party introduces in evidence a fact admitted by another party, or the parties jointly admit a fact, a written record must be made of the admission.

[Note. The admissibility of evidence that a party introduces is governed by rules of evidence.
Under section 202 of the Extradition Act 2003[17]*, the court may receive in evidence—*

(a) a warrant to which Part 1 of the Act applies;
(b) any other document issued in a territory to which Part 1 of the Act applies, if the document is authenticated as required by the Act;
(c) a document issued in a territory to which Part 2 of the Act applies, if the document is authenticated as required by the Act.

Under sections 84 and 86 of the Act, which apply to evidence, if required, at an extradition hearing to which Part 2 of the Act applies, the court may accept as evidence of a fact a statement by a person in a document if oral evidence by that person of that fact would be admissible, and the statement was made to a police officer, or to someone else responsible for investigating offences or charging offenders.

[16] 2003 c. 41; section 79 was amended by paragraphs 4 and 5 of Schedule 20 to the Crime and Courts Act 2013 (c. 22). Section 103 was amended by section 160 of the Anti-social Behaviour, Crime and Policing Act 2014 (c. 12). Section 118A and 118B were inserted by section 161 of the 2014 Act. Section 137 was amended by sections 164 and 181 of, and paragraph 117 of Schedule 11 to, the 2014 Act. Section 138 was amended by sections 164 and 181 of, and paragraph 118 of Schedule 11 to, the 2014 Act.
[17] 2003 c. 41; section 202 was amended by paragraph 26 of Schedule 13 to the Police and Justice Act 2006 (c. 48).

Under section 205 of the Act, section 9 (proof by written witness statement) and section 10 (proof by formal admission) of the Criminal Justice Act 1967[18] apply to extradition proceedings as they apply in relation to proceedings for an offence.]

Discharge after failure to comply with a time limit

Defendant's application to be discharged **R50.16**

50.16 (1) This rule applies where a defendant wants to be discharged—

(a) because of a failure—

(i) to give the defendant a copy of any warrant under which the defendant is arrested as soon as practicable after arrest,

(ii) to bring the defendant before the court as soon as practicable after arrest under a warrant,

(iii) to bring the defendant before the court no more than 48 hours after provisional arrest under Part 1 of the Extradition Act 2003;

(iv) to give the defendant a copy of any certificate enabling provisional arrest without a warrant under section 74A of the 2003 Act as soon as practicable after arrest, or

(v) to bring the defendant before the court as soon as practicable after arrest under that section;

(b) because of a defect in a certificate enabling arrest without a warrant under section 74A of the 2003 Act;

(c) because there were no reasonable grounds on which there could have been issued a certificate enabling arrest without a warrant under section 74A of the 2003 Act;

(d) following the expiry of a time limit for—

(i) service of a warrant to which Part 1 of the 2003 Act applies, after provisional arrest under that Part of the Act (48 hours, under section 6 of the Act[19], unless the court otherwise directs),

(ii) service of an extradition request to which Part 2 of the Act applies, after provisional arrest under that Part of the Act (45 days, under section 74 of the Act[20], unless the Secretary of State has otherwise ordered for this purpose),

(iii) receipt of an undertaking that the defendant will be returned to complete a sentence in the United Kingdom, where the court required such an undertaking (21 days, under section 37 of the Act[21]),

(iv) making an extradition order, after the defendant has consented to extradition under Part 1 of the Act (10 days, under section 46 of the Act[22]),

(v) extradition, where an extradition order has been made under Part 1 of the Act and any appeal by the defendant has failed (10 days, under sections 35, 36 and 47 of the Act[23], unless the court otherwise directs),

(vi) extradition, where an extradition order has been made under Part 2 of the Act and any appeal by the defendant has failed (28 days, under sections 117 and 118 of the Act[24]),

(vii) the resumption of extradition proceedings, where those proceedings were adjourned pending disposal of another extradition claim which has concluded (21 days, under section 180 of the Act),

(viii) extradition, where extradition has been deferred pending the disposal of another extradition claim which has concluded (21 days, under section 181 of the Act), or

[18] 1967 c. 80; section 9 was amended by section 56 of, and paragraph 49 of Schedule 8 to, the Courts Act 1971 (c. 23), section 168 of, and paragraph 6 of Schedule 9 to, the Criminal Justice and Public Order Act 1994 (c. 33), section 69 of the Criminal Procedure and Investigations Act 1996 (c. 25), regulation 9 of, and paragraph 4 of Schedule 5 to, S.I. 2001/1090, paragraph 43 of Schedule 3 and Part 4 of Schedule 37 to the Criminal Justice Act 2003 (c. 44), section 26 of, and paragraph 7 of Schedule 2 to, the Armed Forces Act 2011 (c. 18) and section 80 of the Deregulation Act 2015 (c. 20). It is further amended by section 72 of, and paragraph 55 of Schedule 5 to, the Children and Young Persons Act 1969 (c. 54) and section 65 of, and paragraph 1 of Schedule 4 to, the Courts Act 2003 (c. 39), with effect from dates to be appointed.

[19] 2003 c. 41; section 6 was amended by section 77 of the Policing and Crime Act 2009 (c. 26).

[20] 2003 c. 41; section 74 was amended by paragraph 16 of Schedule 13 to the Police and Justice Act 2006 (c. 48).

[21] 2003 c. 41; section 37 was amended by paragraphs 9 and 10 of Schedule 13 to the Police and Justice Act 2006 (c. 48).

[22] 2003 c. 41; section 46 was amended by paragraph 16 of Schedule 13 to the Police and Justice Act 2006 (c. 48).

[23] 2003 c. 41; section 35 was amended by paragraph 9 of Schedule 13 to the Police and Justice Act 2006 (c. 48). Section 36 was amended by section 40 of, and paragraph 81 of Schedule 9 to, the Constitutional Reform Act 2005 (c. 4).

[24] 2003 c. 41; section 118 was amended by section 40 of, and paragraph 81 of Schedule 9 to, the Constitutional Reform Act 2005 (c. 4).

(ix) re-extradition, where the defendant has been returned to the United Kingdom to serve a sentence before serving a sentence overseas (as soon as practicable, under section 187 of the Act[25]); or

(e) because an extradition hearing does not begin on the date arranged by the court.

(2) Unless the court otherwise directs—

(a) such a defendant must apply in writing and serve the application on—

(i) the magistrates' court officer,

(ii) the High Court officer, where paragraph (1)(d)(v) applies, and

(iii) the prosecutor;

(b) the application must explain the grounds on which it is made; and

(c) the court officer must arrange a hearing as soon as practicable, and in any event no later than the second business day after an application is served.

[Note. See sections 4(4) & (5), 6(6) & (7), 8(7) & (8)[26], 35(5), 36(8), 37(7), 46(8)[27], 47(4), 72(5) & (6), 74(5), (6) & (10), 74D(10), 75(4),76(5), 117(3), 118(7), 180(4) & (5), 181(4) & (5) and 187(3) of the Extradition Act 2003.]

Section 3: appeal to the High Court

[Note. Under Part 1 of the Extradition Act 2003—

(a) a defendant may appeal to the High Court against an order for extradition made by the magistrates' court; and

(b) the authority requesting the defendant's extradition may appeal to the High Court against an order for the defendant's discharge,

(see sections 26 and 28 of the Act[28].

Under Part 2 of the 2003 Act—

(a) a defendant may appeal to the High Court against an order by the magistrates' court sending a case to the Secretary of State for a decision whether to extradite the defendant;

(b) a defendant may appeal to the High Court against an order for extradition made by the Secretary of State; and

(c) the territory requesting the defendant's extradition may appeal to the High Court against an order for the defendant's discharge by the magistrates' court or by the Secretary of State,

(see sections 103, 105, 108 and 110 of the Act[29].

In each case the appellant needs the High Court's permission to appeal (in the 2003 Act, described as 'leave to appeal').]

R50.17 **Exercise of the High Court's powers**

50.17 (1) The general rule is that the High Court must exercise its powers at a hearing in public, but—

(a) that is subject to any power the court has to—

(i) impose reporting restrictions,

(ii) withhold information from the public, or

(iii) order a hearing in private;

(b) despite the general rule, the court may determine without a hearing—

(i) an application for the court to consider out of time an application for permission to appeal to the High Court,

(ii) an application for permission to appeal to the High Court (but a renewed such application must be determined at a hearing),

(iii) an application for permission to appeal from the High Court to the Supreme Court,

(iv) an application for permission to reopen a decision under rule 50.27 (Reopening the determination of an appeal), or

(v) an application concerning bail; and

(c) despite the general rule the court may, without a hearing—

(i) give case management directions,

25 2003 c. 41; section 187 was amended by paragraph 15 of Schedule 13 to the Police and Justice Act 2006 (c. 48).

26 2003 c. 41; section 8 was amended by paragraph 16 of Schedule 13 to the Police and Justice Act 2006 (c. 48).

27 2003 c. 41; section 46 was amended by paragraph 16 of Schedule 13 to the Police and Justice Act 2006 (c. 48).

28 2003 c. 41; sections 26 and 28 were amended by section 160 of the Anti-social Behaviour, Crime and Policing Act 2014 (c. 12).

29 2003 c. 41; section 108 was amended by paragraphs 10 and 12 of Schedule 20 to the Crime and Courts Act 2013 (c. 22). Section 108 was further amended, and sections 103, 105 and 110 were amended, by section 160 of the Anti-social Behaviour, Crime and Policing Act 2014 (c. 12).

(ii) reject a notice or application and, if applicable, dismiss an application for permission to appeal, where rule 50.31 (Payment of High Court fees) applies and the party who served the notice or application fails to comply with that rule, or
(iii) make a determination to which the parties have agreed in writing.

(2) If the High Court so directs, a party may attend a hearing by live link.

(3) The general rule is that where the High Court exercises its powers at a hearing it may do so only if the defendant attends, in person or by live link, but, despite the general rule, the court may exercise its powers in the defendant's absence if—
(a) the defendant waives the right to attend;
(b) subject to any appeal to the Supreme Court, the result of the court's order would be the discharge of the defendant; or
(c) the defendant is represented and—
(i) the defendant is in custody, or
(ii) the defendant's presence is impracticable by reason of his or her ill health or disorderly conduct.

(4) If the High Court gives permission to appeal to the High Court—
(a) unless the court otherwise directs, the decision indicates that the appellant has permission to appeal on every ground identified by the appeal notice;
(b) unless the court otherwise directs, the decision indicates that the court finds reasonably arguable each ground on which the appellant has permission to appeal; and
(c) the court must give such directions as are required for the preparation and conduct of the appeal, including a direction as to whether the appeal must be heard by a single judge of the High Court or by a divisional court.

(5) If the High Court decides without a hearing an application for permission to appeal from the High Court to the Supreme Court, the High Court must announce its decision at a hearing in public.

(6) The High Court may—
(a) shorten a time limit or extend it (even after it has expired), unless that is inconsistent with other legislation;
(b) allow or require a party to vary or supplement a notice that that party has served;
(c) direct that a notice or application be served on any person; and
(d) allow a notice or application to be in a different form to one set out in the Practice Direction, or to be presented orally.

(7) A party who wants an extension of time within which to serve a notice or make an application must—
(a) apply for that extension of time when serving that notice or making that application; and
(b) give the reasons for the application for an extension of time.

[Note. The time limits for serving an appeal notice are prescribed by the Extradition Act 2003: see rule 50.19.]

Case management in the High Court R50.18

50.18 (1) The High Court and the parties have the same duties and powers as under Part 3 (Case management), subject to—
(a) rule 50.2 (Special objective in extradition proceedings); and
(b) paragraph (3) of this rule.

(2) A master of the High Court, a deputy master, or a court officer nominated for the purpose by the Lord Chief Justice—
(a) must fulfil the duty of active case management under rule 3.2, and in fulfilling that duty may exercise any of the powers of case management under—
(i) rule 3.5 (the court's general powers of case management),
(ii) rule 3.12(3) (requiring a certificate of readiness), and
(iii) rule 3.13 (requiring a party to identify intentions and anticipated requirements)
subject to the directions of a judge of the High Court; and
(b) must nominate a case progression officer under rule 3.4.

(3) Rule 3.6 (Application to vary a direction) does not apply to a decision to give or to refuse—
(a) permission to appeal; or
(b) permission to reopen a decision under rule 50.27 (Reopening the determination of an appeal).

R50.19 **Service of appeal notice**

50.19 (1) A party who wants to appeal to the High Court must serve an appeal notice on—

(a) in every case—

(i) the High Court officer,

(ii) the other party, and

(iii) the Director of Public Prosecutions, unless the Director already has the conduct of the proceedings;

(b) the designated authority which certified the arrest warrant, where Part 1 of the Extradition Act 2003 applies; and

(c) the Secretary of State, where the appeal is against—

(i) an order by the Secretary of State, or

(ii) an order by the magistrates' court sending a case to the Secretary of State.

(2) A defendant who wants to appeal must serve the appeal notice—

(a) not more than 7 days after the day on which the magistrates' court makes an order for the defendant's extradition, starting with that day, where that order is under Part 1 of the Extradition Act 2003; or

(b) not more than 14 days after the day on which the Secretary of State informs the defendant of the Secretary of State's decision, starting with that day, where under Part 2 of the Act—

(i) the magistrates' court sends the case to the Secretary of State for a decision whether to extradite the defendant, or

(ii) the Secretary of State orders the defendant's extradition.

(3) An authority or territory seeking the defendant's extradition which wants to appeal against an order for the defendant's discharge must serve the appeal notice—

(a) not more than 7 days after the day on which the magistrates' court makes that order, starting with that day, if the order is under Part 1 of the Extradition Act 2003;

(b) not more than 14 days after the day on which the magistrates' court makes that order, starting with that day, if the order is under Part 2 of the Act; or

(c) not more than 14 days after the day on which the Secretary of State informs the territory's representative of the Secretary of State's order, starting with that day, where the order is under Part 2 of the Act.

[Note. See sections 26, 28, 103, 105, 108 and 110 of the Extradition Act 2003[30]*. The time limits for serving an appeal notice are prescribed by those sections. They may be neither shortened nor extended, but—*

(a) if a defendant applies out of time for permission to appeal to the High Court the court must not for that reason refuse to consider the application if the defendant did everything reasonably possible to ensure that the notice was given as soon as it could be; and

(b) a defendant may apply out of time for permission to appeal to the High Court on human rights grounds against an order for extradition made by the Secretary of State.

Under section 3 of the Prosecution of Offences Act 1985[31]*, the Director of Public Prosecutions may conduct extradition proceedings (but need not do so).]*

R50.20 **Form of appeal notice**

50.20 (1) An appeal notice constitutes—

(a) an application to the High Court for permission to appeal to that court; and

(b) an appeal to that court, if the court gives permission.

(2) An appeal notice must be in writing.

[30] 2003 c. 41; section 108 was amended by paragraphs 10 and 12 of Schedule 20 to the Crime and Courts Act 2013 (c. 22). Section 108 was further amended, and sections 26, 28, 103, 105 and 110 were amended, by section 160 of the Anti-social Behaviour, Crime and Policing Act 2014 (c. 12).

[31] 1985 c. 23; section 3 was amended by section 15 of, and paragraph 13 of Schedule 2 to, the Criminal Justice Act 1987 (c. 38), paragraph 39 of Schedule 7 to the Police Act 1996 (c. 16), section 134 of, and paragraph 48 of Schedule 9 to, the Police Act 1997 (c. 50), section 164 of the Immigration and Asylum Act 1999 (c. 33), paragraph 10 of Schedule 7 to the Police Reform Act 2002 (c. 30), sections 86 and 92 of, and Schedule 3 to, the Anti-social Behaviour Act 2003 (c. 38), section 190 of the Extradition Act 2003 (c. 41), section 7 of the Asylum and Immigration (Treatment of Claimants, etc) Act 2004 (c. 19), section 40 of, and paragraph 41 of Schedule 9 to, the Constitutional Reform Act 2005 (c. 4), sections 59, 140 and 174 of, and paragraph 47 of Schedule 4 and Part 2 of Schedule 17 to, the Serious Organised Crime and Police Act 2005 (c. 15), sections 7, 8 and 52 of, and paragraph 15 of Schedule 3 to, the Violent Crime Reduction Act 2006 (c. 38), section 74 of, and paragraph 149 of Schedule 8 to, the Serious Crime Act 2007 (c. 27), paragraph 171 of Schedule 16 to the Police Reform and Social Responsibility Act 2011 (c. 13), section 15 of, and paragraph 30 of Schedule 8 to, the Crime and Courts Act 2013 (c. 22) and article 3 of, and paragraphs 1 and 2 of the Schedule to, S.I. 2014/834.

(3) In every case, the appeal notice must—
(a) specify—
(i) the date of the defendant's arrest under Part 1 or Part 2 of the Extradition Act 2003, and
(ii) the decision about which the appellant wants to appeal, including the date of that decision;
(b) identify each ground of appeal on which the appellant relies;
(c) summarise the relevant facts;
(d) identify any document or other material that the appellant thinks the court will need to decide the appeal; and
(e) include or attach a list of those on whom the appellant has served the appeal notice.
(4) If a defendant serves an appeal notice after the expiry of the time limit specified in rule 50.19 (Service of appeal notice)—
(a) the notice must—
(i) explain what the defendant did to ensure that it was served as soon as it could be, and
(ii) include or attach such evidence as the defendant relies upon to support that explanation; and
(b) where the appeal is on human rights grounds against an order for extradition made by the Secretary of State, the notice must explain why—
(i) the appeal is necessary to avoid real injustice, and
(ii) the circumstances are exceptional and make it appropriate to consider the appeal.
(5) Unless the High Court otherwise directs, the appellant may amend the appeal notice—
(a) by serving on those listed in rule 50.19(1) the appeal notice as so amended; and
(b) not more than 10 business days after service of the appeal notice.
(6) Where the appeal is against an order by the magistrates' court—
(a) if the grounds of appeal are that the magistrates' court ought to have decided differently a question of fact or law at the extradition hearing, the appeal notice must—
(i) identify that question,
(ii) explain what decision the magistrates' court should have made, and why, and
(iii) explain why the magistrates' court would have been required not to make the order under appeal, if that question had been decided differently; and
(b) if the grounds of appeal are that there is an issue which was not raised at the extradition hearing, or that evidence is available which was not available at the extradition hearing, the appeal notice must—
(i) identify that issue or evidence,
(ii) explain why it was not then raised or available,
(iii) explain why that issue or evidence would have resulted in the magistrates' court deciding a question differently at the extradition hearing, and
(iv) explain why, if the court had decided that question differently, the court would have been required not to make the order it made.
(7) Where the appeal is against an order by the Secretary of State—
(a) if the grounds of appeal are that the Secretary of State ought to have decided differently a question of fact or law, the appeal notice must—
(i) identify that question,
(ii) explain what decision the Secretary of State should have made, and why, and
(iii) explain why the Secretary of State would have been required not to make the order under appeal, if that question had been decided differently; and
(b) if the grounds of appeal are that there is an issue which was not raised when the case was being considered by the Secretary of State, or that information is available which was not then available, the appeal notice must—
(i) identify that issue or information,
(ii) explain why it was not then raised or available,
(iii) explain why that issue or information would have resulted in the Secretary of State deciding a question differently, and
(iv) explain why, if the Secretary of State had decided that question differently, the order under appeal would not have been made.

[Note. The Practice Direction sets out a form of appeal notice for use in connection with this rule.]

R50.21 **Respondent's notice**

50.21 (1) A party on whom an appellant serves an appeal notice under rule 50.19 may serve a respondent's notice, and must do so if—
(a) that party wants to make representations to the High Court; or
(b) the court so directs.
(2) Such a party must serve any such notice on—
(a) the High Court officer;
(b) the appellant;
(c) the Director of Public Prosecutions, unless the Director already has the conduct of the proceedings; and
(d) any other person on whom the appellant served the appeal notice.
(3) Such a party must serve any such notice, as appropriate—
(a) not more than 10 business days after—
(i) service on that party of an amended appeal notice under rule 50.20(5) (Form of appeal notice), or
(ii) the expiry of the time for service of any such amended appeal notice
whichever of those events happens first; and
(b) not more than 5 business days after service on that party of—
(i) an appellant's notice renewing an application for permission to appeal, or
(ii) a direction to serve a respondent's notice.
(4) A respondent's notice must—
(a) give the date or dates on which the respondent was served with, as appropriate—
(i) the appeal notice,
(ii) the appellant's notice renewing the application for permission to appeal, or
(iii) the direction to serve a respondent's notice;
(b) identify each ground of opposition on which the respondent relies and the ground of appeal to which each such ground of opposition relates;
(c) summarise any relevant facts not already summarised in the appeal notice; and
(d) identify any document or other material that the respondent thinks the court will need to decide the appeal.

[Note. Under rule 50.17, the High Court may extend or shorten the time limit under this rule.]

R50.22 **Renewing an application for permission to appeal, restoring excluded grounds, etc.**

50.22 (1) This rule—
(a) applies where the High Court—
(i) refuses permission to appeal to the High Court, or
(ii) gives permission to appeal to the High Court but not on every ground identified by the appeal notice; but
(b) does not apply where—
(i) a defendant applies out of time for permission to appeal to the High Court, and
(ii) the court for that reason refuses to consider that application.
(2) Unless the court refuses permission to appeal at a hearing, the appellant may renew the application for permission by serving notice on—
(a) the High Court officer;
(b) the respondent; and
(c) any other person on whom the appellant served the appeal notice,
not more than 5 business days after service of notice of the court's decision on the appellant.
(3) If the court refuses permission to appeal, the renewal notice must explain the grounds for the renewal.
(4) If the court gives permission to appeal but not on every ground identified by the appeal notice the decision indicates that—
(a) at the hearing of the appeal the court will not consider representations that address any ground thus excluded from argument; and
(b) an appellant who wants to rely on such an excluded ground needs the court's permission to do so.
(5) An appellant who wants to rely at the hearing of an appeal on a ground of appeal excluded from argument must—
(a) apply in writing, with reasons, and identify each such ground;
(b) serve the application on—

(i) the High Court officer, and
(ii) the respondent; and
(c) serve the application not more than 5 business days after—
(i) the giving of permission to appeal, or
(ii) the High Court officer serves notice of that decision on the applicant, if the applicant was not present in person or by live link when permission to appeal was given.

(6) Paragraph (7) applies where a party wants to abandon—
(a) a ground of appeal on which that party has permission to appeal; or
(b) a ground of opposition identified in a respondent's notice.

(7) Such a party must serve notice on—
(a) the High Court officer; and
(b) each other party,

before any hearing at which that ground will be considered by the court.

[Note. Under rule 50.17 (Exercise of the High Court's powers), the High Court may extend or shorten the time limits under this rule.

Rule 50.19 (Service of appeal notice) and the note to that rule set out the time limits for appeal.]

Appeal hearing **R50.23**

50.23 (1) Unless the High Court otherwise directs, where the appeal to the High Court is under Part 1 of the Extradition Act 2003 the hearing of the appeal must begin no more than 40 days after the defendant's arrest.

(2) Unless the High Court otherwise directs, where the appeal to the High Court is under Part 2 of the 2003 Act the hearing of the appeal must begin no more than 76 days after the later of—
(a) service of the appeal notice; or
(b) the day on which the Secretary of State informs the defendant of the Secretary of State's order, in a case in which—
(i) the appeal is by the defendant against an order by the magistrates' court sending the case to the Secretary of State, and
(ii) the appeal notice is served before the Secretary of State decides whether the defendant should be extradited.

(3) If the effect of the decision of the High Court on the appeal is that the defendant is to be extradited—
(a) the High Court must consider any ancillary application, including an application about—
(i) bail pending extradition,
(ii) reporting restrictions, or
(iii) costs; and
(b) the High Court is the appropriate court to order a postponement of the defendant's extradition where—
(i) the defendant has been charged with an offence in the United Kingdom, or
(ii) the defendant has been sentenced to imprisonment or detention in the United Kingdom.

(4) If the effect of the decision of the High Court on the appeal is that the defendant is discharged, the High Court must consider any ancillary application, including an application about—
(a) reporting restrictions; or
(b) costs.

[Note. Under sections 31 and 113 of the Extradition Act 2003[32]*, if the appeal hearing does not begin within the period prescribed by this rule or ordered by the High Court the appeal must be taken to have been dismissed by decision of the High Court.*

Under section 103 of the Extradition Act 2003[33]*, a defendant's appeal against an order by the magistrates' court sending the case to the Secretary of State must not be heard until after the Secretary of State has decided whether to order the defendant's extradition.*

Part 6 contains rules about reporting restrictions. Part 45 contains rules about costs.

[32] 2003 c. 41.
[33] 2003 c. 41; section 103 was amended by section 160 of the Anti-social Behaviour, Crime and Policing Act 2014 (c. 12).

See sections 36A, 36B, 118A and 118B Extradition Act 2003[34]*. Where there is an appeal against an order for extradition, rules may provide that the appeal court may exercise the power under those sections to postpone the extradition.]*

R50.24 **Early termination of appeal: order by consent, etc.**

50.24 (1) This rule applies where—

(a) an appellant has served an appeal notice under rule 50.19; and

(b) the High Court—

(i) has not determined the application for permission to appeal, or

(ii) where the court has given permission to appeal, has not determined the appeal.

(2) Where the warrant or extradition request with which the appeal is concerned is withdrawn—

(a) the party or person so informing the court must serve on the High Court officer—

(i) notice to that effect by the authority or territory requesting the defendant's extradition,

(ii) details of how much of the warrant or extradition request remains outstanding, if any, and of any other warrant or extradition request outstanding in respect of the defendant,

(iii) details of any bail condition to which the defendant is subject, if the defendant is on bail, and

(iv) details sufficient to locate the defendant, including details of the custodian and of the defendant's date of birth and custody reference, if the defendant is in custody; and

(b) paragraph (5) applies but only to the extent that the parties want the court to deal with an ancillary matter.

(3) Where a defendant with whose discharge the appeal is concerned consents to extradition, paragraph (5) applies but only to the extent that the parties want the court to—

(a) give directions for that consent to be given to the magistrates' court or to the Secretary of State, as the case may be; or

(b) deal with an ancillary matter.

(4) Paragraph (5) applies where the parties want the court to make a decision on which they are agreed—

(a) determining the application for permission to appeal or the appeal, as the case may be;

(b) specifying the date on which that application or appeal is to be treated as discontinued; and

(c) determining an ancillary matter, including costs, if applicable.

(5) The parties must serve on the High Court officer, in one or more documents—

(a) a draft order in the terms proposed;

(b) evidence of each party's agreement to those terms; and

(c) concise reasons for the request that the court make the proposed order.

[Note. Under sections 42 and 124 of the Extradition Act 2003[35]*, where an appeal is pending in the High Court and the court is informed that the relevant warrant or extradition request has been withdrawn the court must—*

(a) order the defendant's discharge and quash the extradition order or decision, where the defendant has appealed against extradition;

(b) dismiss the application for permission to appeal or the appeal, as the case may be, where the authority or territory requesting the defendant's extradition has appealed against the defendant's discharge.

Under sections 45 and 127 of the 2003 Act[36]*, a defendant in respect of whom no extradition order or decision has been made may give consent to extradition in the magistrates' court, or may give such consent to the Secretary of State if the case has been sent there.*

34 2003 c. 41; sections 36A, 36B, 118A and 118B were inserted by section 161 of the Anti-social Behaviour, Crime and Policing Act 2014 (c. 12).

35 2003 c. 41; sections 42 and 124 were amended by article 3 of S.I. 2015/992.

36 2003 c. 41; sections 45 was amended by section 39 of, and paragraphs 62 and 63 of Schedule 5 to, the Legal Aid, Sentencing and Punishment of Offenders Act 2012 (c. 10) and section 163 of the Anti-social Behaviour, Crime and Policing Act 2014 (c. 12). Section 127 was amended by section 39 of, and paragraphs 62 and 64 of Schedule 5 to, the Legal Aid, Sentencing and Punishment of Offenders Act 2012 (c. 10).

Where the effect of the High Court's decision is that the defendant is to be extradited, sections 36 and 118 of the Act[37] *set time limits for extradition after the end of the case.*

Part 45 contains rules about costs.]

Application for permission to appeal to the Supreme Court **R50.25**

50.25 (1) This rule applies where a party to an appeal to the High Court wants to appeal to the Supreme Court.

(2) Such a party must—

(a) apply orally to the High Court for permission to appeal immediately after the court's decision; or

(b) apply in writing and serve the application on the High Court officer and every other party not more than 14 days after that decision.

(3) Such a party must—

(a) identify the point of law of general public importance that the appellant wants the High Court to certify is involved in the decision;

(b) serve on the High Court officer a statement of that point of law; and

(c) give reasons why—

(i) that point of law ought to be considered by the Supreme Court, and

(ii) the High Court ought to give permission to appeal.

(4) As well as complying with paragraph (3), a defendant's application for permission to appeal to the Supreme Court must include or attach any application for the following, with reasons—

(a) bail pending appeal; or

(b) permission to attend any hearing in the Supreme Court, if the appellant is in custody.

[Note. See sections 32 and 114 of the Extradition Act 2003[38]*. Those sections prescribe the time limit for serving an application for permission to appeal to the Supreme Court. It may be neither shortened nor extended.]*

Determination of detention pending appeal to the Supreme Court against discharge **R50.26**

50.26 On an application for permission to appeal to the Supreme Court against a decision of the High Court which, but for that appeal, would have resulted in the defendant's discharge, the High Court must—

(a) decide whether to order the detention of the defendant; and

(b) determine any application for—

(i) bail pending appeal,

(ii) permission to attend any hearing in the Supreme Court, or

(iii) a representation order.

[Note. See sections 33A and 115A of the Extradition Act 2003[39]*.*

For the grant of legal aid for proceedings in the Supreme Court, see sections 14, 16 and 19 of the Legal Aid, Sentencing and Punishment of Offenders Act 2012[40]*.]*

Reopening the determination of an appeal **R50.27**

50.27 (1) This rule applies where a party wants the High Court to reopen a decision of that court which determines an appeal or an application for permission to appeal.

(2) Such a party must—

(a) apply in writing for permission to reopen that decision, as soon as practicable after becoming aware of the grounds for doing so; and

(b) serve the application on the High Court officer and every other party.

(3) The application must—

(a) specify the decision which the applicant wants the court to reopen; and

(b) give reasons why—

(i) it is necessary for the court to reopen that decision in order to avoid real injustice,

(ii) the circumstances are exceptional and make it appropriate to reopen the decision, and

(iii) there is no alternative effective remedy.

[37] 2003 c. 41; sections 36 and 118 were amended by section 40 of, and paragraph 81 of Schedule 9 to, the Constitutional Reform Act 2005 (c. 4).

[38] 2003 c. 41; sections 32 and 114 were amended by paragraph 81 of Schedule 9 to the Constitutional Reform Act 2005 (c. 4) and section 42 of, and paragraph 8 of Schedule 13 to, the Police and Justice Act 2006 (c. 48).

[39] 2003 c. 41; sections 33A and 115A were inserted by section 42 of, and paragraphs 8 and 35 of Schedule 13 to, the Police and Justice Act 2006 (c. 48).

[40] 2012 c. 10.

(4) The court must not give permission to reopen a decision unless each other party has had an opportunity to make representations.

R50.28 Declaration of incompatibility with a Convention right

50.28 (1) This rule applies where a party—

(a) wants the High Court to make a declaration of incompatibility with a Convention right under section 4 of the Human Rights Act 1998[41]; or

(b) raises an issue that appears to the High Court may lead to the court making such a declaration.

(2) If the High Court so directs, the High Court officer must serve notice on—

(a) the relevant person named in the list published under section 17(1) of the Crown Proceedings Act 1947[42]; or

(b) the Treasury Solicitor, if it is not clear who is the relevant person.

(3) That notice must include or attach details of—

(a) the legislation affected and the Convention right concerned;

(b) the parties to the appeal; and

(c) any other information or document that the High Court thinks relevant.

(4) A person who has a right under the 1998 Act to become a party to the appeal must—

(a) serve notice on—

(i) the High Court officer, and

(ii) the other parties,

if that person wants to exercise that right; and

(b) in that notice—

(i) indicate the conclusion that that person invites the High Court to reach on the question of incompatibility, and

(ii) identify each ground for that invitation, concisely outlining the arguments in support.

(5) The High Court must not make a declaration of incompatibility—

(a) less than 15 business days after the High Court officer serves notice under paragraph (2); and

(b) without giving any person who serves a notice under paragraph (4) an opportunity to make representations at a hearing.

R50.29 Duties of court officers

50.29 (1) The magistrates' court officer must—

(a) keep any document or object exhibited in the proceedings in the magistrates' court, or arrange for it to be kept by some other appropriate person, until—

(i) 6 weeks after the conclusion of those proceedings, or

(ii) the conclusion of any proceedings in the High Court that begin within that 6 weeks;

(b) provide the High Court with any document, object or information for which the High Court officer asks, within such period as the High Court officer may require; and

(c) arrange for the magistrates' court to hear as soon as practicable any application to that court for bail pending appeal.

(2) A person who, under arrangements made by the magistrates' court officer, keeps a document or object exhibited in the proceedings in the magistrates' court must—

(a) keep that exhibit until—

(i) 6 weeks after the conclusion of those proceedings, or

(ii) the conclusion of any proceedings in the High Court that begin within that 6 weeks,

unless the magistrates' court or the High Court otherwise directs; and

(b) provide the High Court with any such document or object for which the High Court officer asks, within such period as the High Court officer may require.

(3) The High Court officer must—

(a) give as much notice as reasonably practicable of each hearing to—

(i) the parties,

(ii) the defendant's custodian, if any, and

(iii) any other person whom the High Court requires to be notified;

(b) serve a record of each order or direction of the High Court on—

(i) the parties,

(ii) any other person whom the High Court requires to be notified;

[41] 1998 c. 42; section 4 was amended by section 40 of, and paragraph 66 of Schedule 9 to, the Constitutional Reform Act 2005 (c. 4) and section 67 of, and paragraph 43 of Schedule 6 to, the Mental Capacity Act 2005 (c. 9).

[42] 1947 c. 44; section 17 was amended by article 3(2) of S.I. 1968/1656.

(c) if the High Court's decision determines an appeal or application for permission to appeal, serve a record of that decision on—
   (i) the defendant's custodian, if any,
   (ii) the magistrates' court officer, and
   (iii) the designated authority which certified the arrest warrant, where Part 1 of the Extradition Act 2003 applies;
(d) where rule 50.24 applies (Early termination of appeal: order by consent, etc.), arrange for the High Court to consider the document or documents served under that rule; and
(e) treat the appeal as if it had been dismissed by the High Court where—
   (i) the hearing of the appeal does not begin within the period required by rule 50.23 (Appeal hearing) or ordered by the High Court, or
   (ii) on an appeal by a requesting territory under section 105 of the Extradition Act 2003[43], the High Court directs the magistrates' court to decide a question again and the magistrates' court comes to the same conclusion as it had done before.

[Note. See section 106 of the Extradition Act 2003[44].]

Constitution of the High Court R50.30

50.30 (1) A master of the High Court or a deputy master, may exercise any power of the High Court to which the rules in this Section apply, except the power to—
(a) give or refuse permission to appeal;
(b) determine an appeal;
(c) reopen a decision which determines an appeal or an application for permission to appeal;
(d) grant or withhold bail; or
(e) impose or vary a condition of bail.

(2) Despite paragraph (1), such a master or deputy master may exercise one of the powers listed in paragraph (1)(a), (b), (d) or (e) if making a decision to which the parties have agreed in writing.

(3) A renewed application for permission to appeal to the High Court may be determined by—
(a) a single judge of the High Court other than the judge who first refused permission, or
(b) a divisional court.

(4) An appeal may be determined by—
(a) a single judge of the High Court; or
(b) a divisional court.

[Note. See sections 19 and 66 of the Senior Courts Act 1981[45].]

Payment of High Court fees R50.31

50.31 (1) This rule applies where a party serves on the High Court officer a notice or application in respect of which a court fee is payable under legislation that requires the payment of such a fee.

(2) Such a party must pay the fee, or satisfy the conditions for any remission of the fee, when so serving the notice or application.

(3) If such a party fails to comply with paragraph (2), then unless the High Court otherwise directs—
(a) the High Court officer must serve on that party a notice requiring payment of the fee due, or satisfaction of the conditions for any remission of that fee, within a period specified in the notice;
(b) that party must comply with such a requirement; and
(c) until the expiry of the period specified in the notice, the High Court must not exercise its power—
   (i) to reject the notice or application in respect of which the fee is payable, or
   (ii) to dismiss an application for permission to appeal, in consequence of rejecting an appeal notice.

[43] 2003 c. 41; section 105 was amended by section 160 of the Anti-social Behaviour, Crime and Policing Act 2014 (c. 12).
[44] 2003 c. 41; section 106 was amended by section 42 of, and paragraph 8 of Schedule 13 to, the Police and Justice Act 2006 (c. 48).
[45] 1981 c. 54.

[Note. Section 92 of the Courts Act 2003[46] *and the Civil Proceedings Fees Order 2008*[47] *require the payment of High Court fees in cases to which this Section of this Part applies. Article 5 and Schedule 2 to the 2008 Order provide for the remission of such fees in some cases.]*

Section 4: post-extradition proceedings

R50.32 Application for consent to deal with another offence or for consent to further extradition

50.32 (1) This rule applies where—

(a) a defendant has been extradited to a territory under Part 1 of the Extradition Act 2003[48]; and

(b) the court officer receives from the authority designated by the Secretary of State a request for the court's consent to—

(i) the defendant being dealt with in that territory for an offence other than one in respect of which the extradition there took place, or

(ii) the defendant's further extradition from there to another such territory for an offence.

(2) The presenting officer must serve on the court officer—

(a) the request; and

(b) a certificate given by the designated authority that the request was made by a judicial authority with the function of making such requests in the territory to which the defendant was extradited.

(3) The court must—

(a) give directions for service by a party or other person on the defendant of notice that the request for consent has been received, unless satisfied that it would not be practicable for such notice to be served;

(b) give directions for a hearing to consider the request to begin—

(i) no more than 21 days after the request was received by the designated authority, or

(ii) at such a later date as the court decides is in the interests of justice; and

(c) give such directions as are required for the preparation and conduct of that hearing.

(4) At the hearing directed under paragraph (3), in the following sequence the court must decide—

(a) whether the consent requested is required, having regard to—

(i) any opportunity given for the defendant to leave the requesting territory after extradition which the defendant did not take within 45 days of arrival there,

(ii) if the defendant did not take such an opportunity, any requirements for consent imposed by the law of the requesting territory or by arrangements between that territory and the United Kingdom where the request is for consent to deal with the defendant in that territory for another offence, and

(iii) if the defendant did not take such an opportunity, any requirements for consent imposed by arrangements between the requesting territory and the United Kingdom where the request is for consent to extradite the defendant to another territory for an offence; and

(b) if such consent is required, then—

(i) whether the offence in respect of which consent is requested is an extradition offence, and

(ii) if it is, whether the court would order the defendant's extradition under sections 11 to 25 of the Extradition Act 2003 (bars to extradition and other considerations) were the defendant in the United Kingdom and the court was considering extradition for that offence.

(5) The court must give directions for notice of its decision to be conveyed to the authority which made the request.

(6) Rules 50.3 (Exercise of magistrates' court's powers) and 50.4 (Case management in the magistrates' court and duty of court officer) apply on an application under this rule.

[Note. See sections 54, 55, 56 and 57 of the Extradition Act 2003[49]*.]*

46 2003 c. 39; section 92 was amended by sections 15 and 59 of, and paragraphs 308 and 345 of Schedule 4 and paragraph 4 of Schedule 11 to, the Constitutional Reform Act 2005 (c. 4) and section 17 of, and paragraph 40 of Schedule 9 and paragraphs 83 and 95 of Schedule 10 to, the Crime and Courts Act 2013.

47 S. I. 2008/1053; amended by S.I. 2013/1410, 2013/2302, 2014/874.

48 2003 c. 41.

49 2003 c. 41.

Criminal Practice Directions Part 50 Extradition

CPD XI Other Proceedings 50A: Extradition: General Matters and Management of the Appeal CPD.50A

General matters: expedition at all times

50A.1 Compliance with these directions is essential to ensure that extradition proceedings are dealt with expeditiously, both in accordance with the spirit of the Council Framework Decision of 13 June 2002 on the European Arrest Warrant and surrender procedures between Member States and the United Kingdom's other treaty obligations. It is of the utmost importance that orders which provide directions for the proper management and progress of cases are obeyed so that the parties can fulfil their duty to assist the court in furthering the overriding objective and in making efficient use of judicial resources. To that end:

(i) the court may, and usually should, give case management directions, which may be based on a model, but adapted to the needs of the individual case, requiring the parties to supply case management information, consistently with the overriding objective of the Criminal Procedure Rules and compatibly with the parties' entitlement to legal professional and litigation privilege;

(ii) a defendant whose extradition is requested must expect to be required to identify what he or she intends to put in issue so that directions can be given to achieve a single, comprehensive and effective extradition hearing at the earliest possible date;

(iii) where the issues are such that further information from the requesting authority or state is needed then it is essential that the request is formulated clearly and in good time, in terms to which the parties can expect to contribute but which terms must be approved by the court, in order that those to whom the request is addressed will be able to understand what is sought, and why, and so can respond promptly;

(iv) where such a request or other document, including a formal notice to the defendant of a post-extradition consent request, requires transmission to an authority or other person in a requesting state or other place outside the UK, it is essential that clear and realistic directions for the transmission are given, identifying who is to be responsible and to what timetable, having regard to the capacity of the proposed courier. Once given, such directions must be promptly complied with and the court at once informed if difficulties are encountered.

(v) any skeleton argument must comply with the requirements of these Practice Directions and, if applicable, of the court. (Paragraphs XII D.17 to D.23 set out the general requirements for skeleton arguments. Paragraphs XI 50E.1 to 50E.7 set out some special requirements that apply in an extradition appeal to the High Court.)

General guidance under s. 2(7A) Extradition Act 2003 (as amended by the Anti-Social Behaviour, Crime and Policing Act 2014)

50A.2 When proceeding under section 21A of the Act and considering under subsection (3)(a) of the Act the seriousness of the conduct alleged to constitute the extradition offence, the judge will determine the issue on the facts of each case as set out in the warrant, subject to the guidance in paragraph 50A.3 below.

50A.3 In any case where the conduct alleged to constitute the offence falls into one of the categories in the table at paragraph 50A.5 below, unless there are exceptional circumstances, the judge should generally determine that extradition would be disproportionate. It would follow under the terms of s. 21A(4)(b) of the Act that the judge must order the person's discharge.

50A.4 The exceptional circumstances referred to above in paragraph 50A.3 will include:

i. Vulnerable victim
ii. Crime committed against someone because of their disability, gender-identity, race, religion or belief, or sexual orientation
iii. Significant premeditation
iv. Multiple counts
v. Extradition also sought for another offence
vi. Previous offending history

50A.5 The table is as follows:

Category of offence	Examples
Minor **theft** — (not robbery/ burglary or theft from the person)	Where the theft is of a low monetary value and there is a low impact on the victim or indirect harm to others, for example: (a) Theft of an item of food from a supermarket (b) Theft of a small amount of scrap metal from company premises (c) Theft of a very small sum of money
Minor financial offences (**forgery, fraud** and **tax** offences)	Where the sums involved are small and there is a low impact on the victim and / or low indirect harm to others, for example: (a) Failure to file a tax return or invoices on time (b) Making a false statement in a tax return (c) Dishonestly applying for a tax refund (d) Obtaining a bank loan using a forged or falsified document (e) Non-payment of child maintenance
Minor **road traffic, driving** and related offences	Where no injury, loss or damage was incurred to any person or property, for example: (a) Driving whilst using a mobile phone (b) Use of a bicycle whilst intoxicated
Minor **public order** offences	Where there is no suggestion the person started the trouble, and the offending behaviour was for example: (a) Non-threatening verbal abuse of a law enforcement officer or government official (b) Shouting or causing a disturbance, without threats (c) Quarrelling in the street, without threats
Minor **criminal damage**, (other than by fire)	For example, breaking a window
Possession of controlled substance (other than one with a high capacity for harm such as heroin, cocaine, LSD or crystal meth)	Where it was possession of a very small quantity and intended for personal use

CPD.50B **CPD XI Other Proceedings 50B Management of the Appeal to the High Court**

50B.1 Applications for permission to appeal to the High Court under the Extradition Act 2003 must be started in the Administrative Court of the Queen's Bench Division at the Royal Courts of Justice in London.

50.B.2 A Lord Justice of Appeal appointed by the Lord Chief Justice will have responsibility to assist the President of the Queen's Bench Division with overall supervision of extradition appeals.

Definitions

50B.3 Where appropriate 'appeal' includes 'application for permission to appeal'.

50B.4 'EAW' means European Arrest Warrant.

50B.5 A 'nominated legal officer of the court' is a court officer assigned to the Administrative Court Office who is a barrister or solicitor and who has been nominated for the purpose by the Lord Chief Justice under CrimPR 50.18 and 50.30.

Forms

50B.6 The forms are to be used in the High Court, in accordance with the CrimPR 50.19, 50.20, 50.21 and 50.22.

50B.7 The forms may be amended or withdrawn from time to time, or new forms added, under the authority of the Lord Chief Justice: see CrimPD I 5A.

Management of the Appeal

50B.8 Where it is not possible for the High Court to begin to hear the appeal in accordance with time limits contained in Crim PR 50.23(1) and (2), the Court may extend the time limit if it believes it to be in the interests of justice to do so and may do so even after the time limit has expired.

50B.9 The power to extend those time limits may be exercised by a Lord Justice of Appeal, a Single Judge of the High Court, a Master of the Administrative Court or a nominated legal officer of the court.

50B.10 Case Management directions setting down a timetable may be imposed upon the parties by a Lord Justice of Appeal, a Single Judge of the High Court, a Master of the Administrative Court or a nominated legal officer of the court. For the court's constitution and relevant powers and duties see section 4 of the Senior Courts Act 1981 and CrimPR 50.18 and 50.30.

Listing of Oral, Renewal Hearings and Substantive Hearings

50B.11 Arrangements for the fixing of dates for hearings will be made by a Listing Officer of the Administrative Court under the direction of the Judge with overall responsibility for supervision of extradition appeals.

50B.12 A Lord Justice of Appeal, a Single Judge of the High Court, a Master of the Administrative Court or a nominated legal officer of the court may give such directions to the Listing Officer as they deem necessary with regard to the fixing of dates, including as to whether cases in the same/related proceedings or raising the same or similar issues should be heard together or consecutively under the duty imposed by Crim PR 1.1(2)(e). Parties must alert the nominated legal officer of the court for the need for such directions.

50B.13 Save in exceptional circumstances, regard will not be given to an advocate's existing commitments. This is in accordance with the spirit of the legislation that extradition matters should be dealt with expeditiously. Extradition matters are generally not so complex that an alternative advocate cannot be instructed.

50B.14 If a party disagrees with the time estimate given by the Court, they must inform the Listing Office within 5 business days of the notification of the listing and they must provide a time estimate of their own.

Expedited appeals

50B.15 The Court may direct that the hearing of an appeal be expedited.

50B.16 The Court will deal with requests for an expedited appeal without a hearing. Requests for expedition must be made in writing, either within the appeal notice, or by application notice, clearly marked with the Administrative Court reference number, which must be lodged with the Administrative Court Office or emailed to the appropriate email address: administrativecourt office.crimex@hmcts.x.gsi.gov.uk and notice must be given to the other parties.

50B.17 Any requests for an expedited appeal made to an out of hours Judge must be accompanied by:

i) A detailed chronology;

ii) Reasons why the application could not be made within Court hours;

iii) Any Orders or Judgments made in the proceedings.

Amendment to Notices

50B.18 Amendment to Notice of Appeal requiring permission

(i) Subject to Crim PR 50.20(5), an appeal notice may not be amended without the permission of the Court: CrimPR 50.17(6)(b);

(ii) An application for permission to amend made before permission to appeal has been considered will be determined without a hearing;

(iii) An application for permission to amend after permission to appeal has been granted and any submissions in opposition will normally be dealt with at the hearing unless there is any risk that the hearing may have to be adjourned. If there is any risk that the application to amend may lead the other party to seek time to answer the proposed amendment, the application must be made as soon as practicable and well in advance of the hearing. A failure to make immediate applications for such an amendment is likely to result in refusal.

(iv) Legal representatives or the appellant, if acting in person, must

a. Inform the Court at the time they make the application if the existing time estimate is affected by the proposed amendment; and

b. Attempt to agree any revised time estimate no later than 5 business days after service of the application.

(v) where the appellant wishes to restore grounds of appeal excluded on the grant of permission to appeal, the procedure is governed by CrimPR 50.22.

50B.19 Amendment to Respondent's Notice

(i) A respondent's notice may not be amended without the permission of the Court: CrimPR 50.17(6)(b);

(ii) An application for permission to amend made before permission to appeal has been considered will be determined without a hearing.

(iii) An application for permission to amend after permission to appeal has been granted and any submissions in opposition will normally be dealt with at the hearing unless there is any risk that the hearing may have to be adjourned. If there is any risk that the application to amend may require the other party to seek time to answer the proposed amendment, the application must be made as soon as practicable and well in advance of the hearing. A failure to make immediate applications for such an amendment is likely to result in refusal.

(iv) Legal representatives or the appellant, if acting in person, must

a. Inform the Court at the time they make the application if the existing time estimate is affected by the proposed amendment; and

b. Attempt to agree any revised time estimate no later than 5 business days after service of the application.

Use of Live-Links

50B.20 When a party acting in person is in custody, the Court office will request the institution to use live-link for attendance at any oral or renewal hearing or substantive appeal. The institution must give precedence to all such applications in the High Court over live-links to the lower courts, including the Crown Court.

Interpreters

50B.21 It is the responsibility of the Court Listing Officer to ensure the attendance of an accredited interpreter when an unrepresented party in extradition proceedings is acting in person and does not understand or speak English.

50B.22 Where a party who does not understand or speak English is legally represented it is the responsibility of his/her solicitors to instruct an interpreter if required for any hearing in extradition proceedings.

Disposing of applications and appeals by way of consent

50B.23 CrimPR 50.24 governs the submission of Consent Orders and lists the essential requirements for such orders. Any Consent Order, the effect of which will be to allow extradition to proceed, must specify the date on which the appeal proceedings are to be treated as discontinued, for the purposes of section 36 or 118, as the case may be, of the Extradition Act 2003: whether that is to be the date on which the order is made or some later date. A Consent Order may be approved by a Lord Justice of Appeal, a Single Judge of the High Court or, under CrimPR 50.30(2), a nominated legal officer of the court. The order may, but need not, be pronounced in open court: CrimPR 50.17(1)(c)(iii). Once approved, the order will be sent to the parties and to any other person as required by CrimPR 50.29(3)(b), (c).

50B.24 A consent order to allow an appeal brought under s.28 of the Extradition Act 2003 must provide—

(i) for the quashing of the decision of the District Judge in Westminster Magistrates' Court discharging the Requested Person;

(ii) for the matter to be remitted to the District Judge to hold fresh extradition proceedings;

(iii) for any ancillary matter, such as bail or costs.

50B.25 A consent order to allow an appeal brought under s.110 of the Extradition Act 2003 must provide—

(i) for the quashing of the decision of the Secretary of State for the Home Department not to order extradition;

(ii) for the matter to be remitted to the Secretary of State to make a fresh decision on whether or not to order extradition;

(iii) for any ancillary matter, such as bail or costs.

50B.26 (a) a Consent Order is intended to dispose of an application for permission to appeal which has not yet been considered by the court, the order must make clear by what means that will be achieved, bearing in mind that an application for permission which is refused without a hearing can be renewed under CrimPR 50.22(2). If the parties intend to exclude the possibility of renewal the order should declare either (i) that the time limit under rule 50.22(2) is reduced to nil, or (ii) permission to appeal is given and the appeal determined on the other terms of the order.

(b) one of the parties is a child or protected party, the documents served under CrimPR 50.24(5) must include an opinion from the advocate acting on behalf of the child or protected party and, in the case of a protected party, any relevant documents prepared for the Court of Protection.

Fees

50B.27 Applications to extend representation orders do not attract any fee.

50B.28 Fees are payable for all other applications in accordance with the current Fees Order.

CPD XI Other Proceedings 50C: Extradition: Representation Orders CPD.50C

50C.1 Representation orders may be granted by a Lord Justice of Appeal, a Single Judge of the High Court, a Master of the Administrative Court or a nominated legal officer of the court upon a properly completed CRM14 being lodged with the Court. A representation order will cover junior advocate and solicitors for the preparation of the Notice of Appeal to determination of the appeal.

50C.2 Applications to extend representation orders may be granted by a Lord Justice of Appeal, a Single Judge of the High Court, a Master of the Administrative Court or a nominated Court Officer who may direct a case management hearing before a Lord Justice of Appeal, a Single Judge, or a Master of the Administrative Court. Since these applications do not attract a fee, parties may lodge them with the Court by attaching them to an email addressed to the nominated legal officer of the court.

50C.3 Applications to extend representation orders to cover the instruction of Queen's Counsel to appear either alone or with junior advocate must be made in writing, either by letter or application notice, clearly marked with the Administrative Court reference number, which must be lodged with the Administrative Court Office or emailed to the appropriate email address: administrativecourtoffice.crimex@hmcts.x.gsi.gov.uk.

The request must:

(i) identify the substantial novel or complex issues of law or fact in the case;
(ii) explain why these may only be adequately presented by a Queen's Counsel;
(iii) state whether a Queen's Counsel has been instructed on behalf of the respondent;
(iv) explain any delay in making the request;
(v) be supported by advice from junior advocate or Queen's Counsel.

50C.4 Applications for prior authority to cover the cost of obtaining expert evidence must be made in writing, either by letter, clearly marked with the Administrative Court reference number, which must be sent or emailed to the Administrative Court Office.

The request must:

(i) confirm that the evidence sought has not been considered in any previous appeals determined by the appellate courts;
(ii) explain why the evidence was not called at the extradition hearing in Westminster Magistrates' Court and what evidence can be produced to support that;
(iii) explain why the new evidence would have resulted in the District Judge deciding a question at the extradition hearing differently and whether, if so, the District Judge would have been required to make a different order as to discharge of the requested person;
(iv) explain why the evidence was not raised when the case was being considered by the Secretary of State for the Home Department or information was available that was not available at that time;
(v) explain why the new evidence would have resulted in the Secretary of State deciding a question differently, and if the question had been decided differently, the Secretary of State would not have ordered the person's extradition;
(vi) state when the need for the new evidence first became known;
(vii) explain any delay in making the request;
(viii) explain what relevant factual, as opposed to expert evidence, is being given by whom to create the factual basis for the expert's opinion;
(ix) explain why this particular area of expertise is relevant: for example why a child psychologist should be appointed as opposed to a social worker;
(x) state whether the requested person has capacity;
(xi) set out a full breakdown of all costs involved including any VAT or other tax payable, including alternative quotes or explaining why none are available;
(xii) provide a list of all previous extensions of the representation order and the approval of expenditure to date;
(xiii) provide a timetable for the production of the evidence and its anticipated effect on the time estimate and hearing date;
(xiv) set out the level of compliance to date with any directions order.

50C.5 Experts must have direct personal experience of and proven expertise in the issue on which a report is sought; it is only if they do have such experience and it is relevant, that they can give evidence of what they have observed.

50C.6 Where an order is granted to extend a representation order to obtain further evidence it will still be necessary for the party seeking to rely on the new evidence to satisfy the Court hearing the application for permission or the substantive appeal that the evidence obtained should be admitted having regard to sections 27(4) and 29(4) of the Extradition Act 2003 and the judgment in *Szombathely City Court v Fenyvesi* [2009] EWHC 231 (Admin).

50C.7 Applications to extend representation for the translation of documents must be made in writing, either by letter, clearly marked with the Administrative Court reference number, which must be sent to Administrative Court Office, The Royal Courts of Justice, Strand, London, WC2A 2LL or emailed to the appropriate email address: administrativecourtoffice.crimex@hmcts.x.gsi.gov.uk

The request should:

(i) explain the importance of the document for which a translation is being sought and the justification for obtaining it;
(ii) explain what it is believed the contents of the document is and the issues it will assist the court to address in hearing the appeal;
(iii) confirm that the evidence sought has not been considered in any previous appeals determined by the appellate courts;
(iv) confirm that the evidence sought was not called at the extradition hearing in the Westminster Magistrates' Court;
(v) explain why the evidence sought would have resulted in the District Judge deciding a question at the extradition hearing differently and whether, if so, the District Judge would have been required to make a different order as to discharge of the requested person;
(vi) confirm that the new evidence was not raised when the case was being considered by the Secretary of State for the Home Department;
(vii) explain why the new evidence sought would have resulted in the Secretary of State deciding a question differently, and if the question had been decided differently, the Secretary of State would not have ordered the person's extradition;
(viii) confirm when the need for the new evidence first became known;
(ix) explain any delay in making the request;
(x) explain fully the evidential basis for incurring the expenditure;
(xi) explain why the appellant cannot produce the evidence himself or herself in the form of a statement of truth;
(xii) set out a full breakdown of all costs involved including any VAT or other tax payable and the Legal Aid Agency contractual rates;
(xiii) provide a list of all previous extensions of the representation order and the expenditure to date.

50C.8 Where an order is made to extend representation to cover the cost of the translation of documents it will still be necessary for the party seeking to rely on the documents as evidence to satisfy the Court that it should be admitted at the hearing of the appeal having regard to sections 27(4) and 29(4) of the Extradition Act 2003 and the judgment in *Szombathely City Court v Fenyvesi* [2009] EWHC 231 (Admin).

CPD.50D CPD XI Other Proceedings 50D: Extradition: Applications, etc

Extension or abridgement of time

50D.1 (i) Any party who seeks extension or abridgment of time for the service of documents, evidence or skeleton arguments must apply to the High Court on the appropriate form and pay the appropriate fee.
(ii) Applications for extension or abridgment of time may be determined by a Lord Justice of Appeal, a Single Judge of the High Court, a Master of the Administrative Court or a nominated legal officer of the court.
(iii) Applications for extension of time must include a witness statement setting out the reasons for non-compliance with any previous order and the proposed timetable for compliance.
(iv) Any application made to an out of hours Judge must be accompanied with:
   a. A detailed chronology;
   b. Reasons why the application could not be made within Court hours;
   c. Any Orders or Judgments made in the proceedings

Representatives

50D.2 CrimPR Part 46 applies.

50D.3 Where under CrimPR 46.2(1)(c) a legal representative withdraws from the case then that representative should satisfy him or herself that the defendant is aware of the time and date of the appeal hearing and of the need to attend, by live link if the court has so directed. If the legal representative has any reason to doubt that the defendant is so aware then he or she should promptly notify the Administrative Court Office.

Application to adjourn

50D.4 Where a hearing date has been fixed, any application to vacate the hearing must be made on the appropriate form. A fee is required for the application if it is made within 14 days of the hearing date. The application must:

(i) explain the reasons why an application is being made to vacate the hearing;
(ii) detail the views of the other parties to the appeal;
(iii) include a draft order with the application notice.

50D.5 If the parties both seek an adjournment then the application must be submitted for consideration by a Lord Justice of Appeal, a Single Judge of the High Court or a Master of the Administrative Court. Exceptional circumstances must be shown if a date for the hearing has been fixed or the adjournment will result in material delay to the determination of the appeal.

50D.6 An application to adjourn following a compromise agreement must be supported by evidence justifying exceptional circumstances and why it is in compliance with the overriding objective.

Variation of directions

50D.7 Where parties are unable to comply with any order of the court they must apply promptly to vary directions before deadlines for compliance have expired and seek further directions. An application to vary directions attracts a fee and the application notice, to be submitted on the appropriate form, must:

(i) provide full and proper explanations for why the current and existing directions have not been complied with;
(ii) detail the views of the other parties to the appeal;
(iii) include a draft order setting out in full the timetable and directions as varied i.e. a superseding order which stands alone.

50D.8 A failure to make the application prior to the expiry of the date specified in the order will generally result in the refusal of the application unless good reasons are shown.

Application to certify a point of law of general public importance

50D.9 Where an application is made under CrimPR 50.25(2)(b) the application must be made on the appropriate form accompanied by the relevant fee.

50D.10 Any response to the application must be made within 10 business days.

50D.11 Where an application to certify is granted but permission to appeal to the Supreme Court is refused, it shall be for those representing the Requested Person to apply for an extension of the Representation Order to cover proceedings in the Supreme Court, if so advised.

50D.12 The representation order may be extended by a Lord Justice of Appeal, a Single Judge of the High Court, a Master of the Administrative Court or a nominated legal officer of the court.

50D.13 The result of the application to certify a point of law of general public importance and permission to appeal to the Supreme Court may be notified in advance to the legal representatives but legal representatives must not communicate it to the Requested Person until 1 hour before the pronouncement is made in open court.

50D.14 There shall be no public announcement of the result until after it has been formally pronounced.

Application to reopen the determination of an appeal

50D.15 An application under CrimPR 50.27 to reopen an appeal must be referred to the court that determined the appeal, but may if circumstances require be considered by a judge or judges other than those who determined the original appeal.

Application to extend required period for removal pursuant to section 36 of the Extradition Act 2003

50D.16 Where an application is made for an extension of the required period within which to extradite a Requested Person it must be accompanied by:

(i) a witness statement explaining why it is not possible to remove the Requested Person within the required period and the proposed timetable for removal;
(ii) a draft order.

50D.17 The application to extend time may be made before or after the expiry of the required period for extradition, but the court will scrutinise with particular care an application made after its expiry.

50D.18 Where extensions of time are sought for the same reason in respect of a number of Requested Persons who are due to be extradited at the same time, a single application may be made to the court listing each of the Requested Persons for whom an extension is sought.

50D.19 The application may be determined by a Lord Justice of Appeal, a Single Judge of the High Court, a Master of the Administrative listing those persons may be granted.

Application for directions ancillary to a discharge pursuant to section 42 or 124 of the Extradition Act 2003

50D.20 Where the High Court is informed that the warrant or extradition request has been withdrawn then unless ancillary matters are dealt with by Consent Order an application notice must be issued seeking any such directions. The notice of discharge of a Requested Person must be accompanied by:

(i) the notification by the requesting state that the EAW has been withdrawn together with a translation of the same;
(ii) a witness statement containing:
  a. details of whether the withdrawn EAW is the only EAW outstanding in respect of the Requested Person;
  b. details of other EAWs outstanding in respect of the Requested Person and the stage which the proceedings have reached;
  c. whether only part of the EAW has been withdrawn;
  d. details of any bail conditions;
  e. details of any institution in which the Requested Person is being detained, the Requested Person's prison number and date of birth.

50D.21 The order for discharge may be made by a Lord Justice of Appeal, a Single Judge of the High Court, a Master of the Administrative Court or a nominated legal officer of the court.

50D.22 It is the responsibility of the High Court to serve the approved order on the appropriate institution and Westminster Magistrates' Court.

CPD.50E **CPD XI Other Proceedings 50E: Extradition: Court Papers**

Skeleton arguments

50E.1 The Court on granting permission to appeal or directing an oral hearing for permission to appeal will give directions as to the filing of skeleton arguments. Strict compliance is required with all time limits.

50E.2 A skeleton argument must:

(a) not normally exceed 25 pages (excluding front sheets and back sheets) and be concise;
(b) be printed on A4 paper in not less than 12 point font and 1.5 line spacing;
(c) define the issues in the appeal;
(d) be set out in numbered paragraphs;
(e) be cross-referenced to any relevant document in the bundle;
(f) be self-contained and not incorporate by reference material from previous skeleton arguments;
(g) not include extensive quotations from documents or authorities.

50E.3 Where it is necessary to refer to an authority, the skeleton argument must

(a) state the proposition of law the authority demonstrates; and
(b) identify but not quote the parts of the authority that support the proposition.

50E.4 If more than one authority is cited in support of a given proposition, the skeleton argument must briefly state why.

50E.5 A chronology of relevant events will be necessary in most appeals.

50E.6 Where a skeleton argument has been prepared in respect of an application for permission to appeal, the same skeleton argument may be relied upon in the appeal upon notice being given to the Court or a replacement skeleton may be lodged not less than 10 business days before the hearing of the appeal.

50E.7 At the hearing the Court may refuse to hear argument on a point not included in a skeleton argument filed within the prescribed time.

Bundles

50E.8 The bundle for the hearing should be agreed by the parties save where the Requested Person is acting in person. In those circumstances the Court expects the Requesting State to prepare the bundle.

50E.9 The bundle must be paginated and indexed.

50E.10 Subject to any order made by the Court, the following documents must be included in the appeal bundle:
- (i) a copy of the appellant's notice;
- (ii) a copy of any respondent's notice;
- (iii) a copy of any appellant's or respondent's skeleton argument;
- (iv) a copy of the order under appeal;
- (v) a copy of any order made by the Court in the exercise of its case management powers;
- (vi) any judgment of the Court made in a previous appeal involving the party or parties which is relevant to the present proceedings.
- (vii) where the bundle of papers reaches more than 200 pages, the parties should agree a core appeal bundle which must contain (i)–(vi) above.

50E.11 The Bundle should only contain relevant documents and must not include duplicate documents.

50E.12 Bundles lodged with the Court will not be returned to the parties but will be destroyed in the confidential waste system at the conclusion of the proceedings and without further notification.

CPD XI Other Proceedings 50F: Extradition: Consequences of Non Compliance with Directions **CPD.50F**

50F.1 Failure to comply with these directions will lead to applications for permission and appeals being dealt with on the material available to the Court at the time when the decision is made.

50F.2 Judges dealing with extradition appeals will seek full and proper explanations for any breaches of the rules and the provisions of this Practice Direction.

50F.3 If no good explanation can be given immediately by counsel or solicitors, the senior partner or the departmental head responsible is likely to be called to court to explain any failure to comply with a court order. Where counsel or solicitors fail to obey orders of the Court and are unable to provide proper and sufficient reasons for their disobedience they may anticipate the matter being formally referred to the President of the Queen's Bench Division with a recommendation that the counsel or solicitors involved be reported to their professional bodies.

50F.4 The court may also refuse to admit any material or any evidence not filed in compliance with the order for Directions or outside a time limit specified by the court.

50F.5 A failure to comply with the time limits or other requirements for skeleton arguments will have the consequences specified in 50E.7.

Criminal Practice Directions: General Application

CPD XII General Application A: Court Dress **CPD.XII.A**

A.1 In magistrates' courts, advocates appear without robes or wigs. In all other courts, Queen's Counsel wear a short wig and a silk (or stuff) gown over a court coat with bands, junior counsel wear a short wig and stuff gown with bands. Solicitors and other advocates authorised under the Courts and Legal Services Act 1990 wear a black solicitor's gown with bands; they may wear short wigs in circumstances where they would be worn by Queen's Counsel or junior counsel.

A.2 High Court Judges hearing criminal cases may wear the winter criminal robe year-round. However, scarlet summer robes may be worn.

CPD XII General Application B: Modes of Address and Titles of Judges and Magistrates **CPD.XII.B**

Modes of Address

B.1 The following judges, when sitting in court, should be addressed as 'My Lord' or 'My Lady', as the case may be, whatever their personal status:
- (a) Judges of the Court of Appeal and of the High Court;
- (b) any Circuit Judge sitting as a judge of the Court of Appeal (Criminal Division) or the High Court under section 9(1) of the Senior Courts Act 1981;
- (c) any judge sitting at the Central Criminal Court;
- (d) any Senior Circuit Judge who is an Honorary Recorder.

B.2 Subject to the paragraph above, Circuit Judges, qualifying judge advocates, Recorders and Deputy Circuit Judges should be addressed as 'Your Honour' when sitting in court.
District Judges (Magistrates' Courts) should be addressed as 'Sir [or Madam]' or 'Judge' when sitting in Court.
Magistrates in court should be addressed through the Chairperson as 'Sir [or Madam]' or collectively as 'Your Worships'.

Description

B.3 In cause lists, forms and orders members of the judiciary should be described as follows:

(a) Circuit Judges, as 'His [or Her] Honour Judge A'.

When the judge is sitting as a judge of the High Court under section 9(1) of the Senior Courts Act 1981, the words 'sitting as a judge of the High Court' should be added;

(b) Recorders, as 'Mr [or Mrs, Ms or Miss] Recorder B'.

This style is appropriate irrespective of any honour or title which the recorder might possess, but if in any case it is desired to include an honour or title, the alternative description, 'Sir CD, Recorder' or 'The Lord D, Recorder' may be used;

(c) Deputy Circuit Judges, as 'His [or Her] Honour EF, sitting as a Deputy Circuit Judge';

(d) qualifying judge advocates, as 'His [or Her] Honour GH, sitting as a qualifying judge advocate.';

(e) District Judges (Magistrates' Courts), as 'District Judge (Magistrates' Courts) J'.

CPD.XII.C **CPD XII General Application C: Availability of Judgments Given in the Court of Appeal and the High Court**

C.1 For cases in the High Court, reference should be made to Practice Direction 40E, the supplementary Practice Direction to the Civil Procedure Rules Part 40.

C.2 For cases in the Court of Appeal (Criminal Division), the following provisions apply.

Availability of reserved judgments before handing down, corrections and applications consequential on judgment

C.3 Where judgment is to be reserved the Presiding Judge may, at the conclusion of the hearing, invite the views of the parties' legal representatives as to the arrangements to be made for the handing down of the judgment.

C.4 Unless the court directs otherwise, the following provisions apply where the Presiding Judge is satisfied that the judgment will attract no special degree of confidentiality or sensitivity.

C.5 The court will provide a copy of the draft judgment to the parties' legal representatives about three working days before handing down, or at such other time as the court may direct. Every page of every judgment which is made available in this way will be marked 'Unapproved judgment: No permission is granted to copy or use in court.' The draft is supplied in confidence and on the conditions that:

(a) neither the draft judgment nor its substance will be disclosed to any other person or used in the public domain; and

(b) no action will be taken (other than internally) in response to the draft judgment, before the judgment is handed down.

C.6 Unless the parties' legal representatives are told otherwise when the draft judgment is circulated, any proposed corrections to the draft judgment should be sent to the clerk of the judge who prepared the draft (or to the associate, if the judge has no clerk) with a copy to any other party's legal representatives, by 12 noon on the day before judgment is handed down.

C.7 If, having considered the draft judgment, the prosecution will be applying to the Court for a retrial or either party wishes to make any other application consequent on the judgment, the judge's clerk should be informed with a time estimate for the application by 12 noon on the day before judgment is handed down. This will enable the court to make appropriate listing arrangements and notify advocates to attend if the court so requires. There is no fee payable to advocates who attend the hand down hearing if not required to do so by the court. If either party is considering applying to the Court to certify a point for appeal to the Supreme Court, it would assist if the judge's clerk could be informed at the same time, although this is not obligatory as under section 34 of the Criminal Appeal Act 1968, the time limit for such applications is 28 days.

Communication to the parties including the defendant or the victim

C.8 The contents are not to be communicated to the parties, including to the defendant, respondent or the victim (defined as a person entitled to receive services under the Code of Practice for Victims of Crime) until two hours before the listed time for pronouncement of judgment.

C.9 Judges may permit more information about the result of a case to be communicated on a confidential basis to the parties including to the defendant, respondent or the victim at an earlier stage if good reason is shown for making such a direction.

C.10 If, for any reason, the parties' legal representatives have special grounds for seeking a relaxation of the usual condition restricting disclosure to the parties, a request for relaxation of the condition may be made informally through the judge's clerk (or through the associate, if the judge has no clerk).

C.11 If the parties or their legal representatives are in any doubt about the persons to whom copies of the draft judgment may be distributed they should enquire of the judge or Presiding Judge.

C.12 Any breach of the obligations or restrictions in this section or failure to take reasonable steps to ensure compliance may be treated as contempt of court.

Restrictions on disclosure or reporting

C.13 Anyone who is supplied with a copy of the handed-down judgment, or who reads it in court, will be bound by any direction which the court may have given in a child case under section 39 of the Children and Young Persons Act 1933 or section 45 or 45A of the Youth Justice and Criminal Evidence Act 1999, or any other form of restriction on disclosure, or reporting, of information in the judgment.

C.14 Copies of the approved judgment can be ordered from the official shorthand writers, on payment of the appropriate fee. Judgments identified as of legal or public interest will generally be made available on the website managed by BAILLI: http://www.bailii.org/

CPD XII General Application D: Citation of Authority and Provision of Copies of Judgments to the Court **CPD.XII.D**

D.1 This Practice Direction applies to all criminal matters before the Court of Appeal (Criminal Division), the Crown Court and the magistrates' courts. In relation to those matters only, Practice Direction (Citation of Authorities) [2012] 1 WLR 780 is hereby revoked.

Citation of authority

D.2 In *R v Erskine; R v Williams* [2009] EWCA Crim 1425, [2010] 1 WLR 183, (2009) 2 Cr App R 29 the Lord Chief Justice stated:

75. The essential starting point, relevant to any appeal against conviction or sentence, is that, adapting the well known aphorism of Viscount Falkland in 1641: if it is not necessary to refer to a previous decision of the court, it is necessary not to refer to it. Similarly, if it is not necessary to include a previous decision in the bundle of authorities, it is necessary to exclude it. That approach will be rigidly enforced.

76. It follows that when the advocate is considering what authority, if any, to cite for a proposition, only an authority which establishes the principle should be cited. Reference should not be made to authorities which do no more than either (a) illustrate the principle or (b) restate it.

78. Advocates must expect to be required to justify the citation of each authority relied on or included in the bundle. The court is most unlikely to be prepared to look at an authority which does no more than illustrate or restate an established proposition.

80. . . .In particular, in sentencing appeals, where a definitive Sentencing Guidelines Council guideline is available there will rarely be any advantage in citing an authority reached before the issue of the guideline, and authorities after its issue which do not refer to it will rarely be of assistance. In any event, where the authority does no more than uphold a sentence imposed at the Crown Court, the advocate must be ready to explain how it can assist the court to decide that a sentence is manifestly excessive or wrong in principle.

D.3 Advocates should only cite cases when it is necessary to do so; when the case identifies or represents a principle or the development of a principle. In sentencing appeals, other cases are rarely helpful, providing only an illustration, and this is especially true if there is a sentencing guideline. Unreported cases should only be cited in exceptional circumstances, and the advocate must expect to explain why such a case has been cited.

D.4 Advocates should not assume that because a case cited to the court is not referred to in the judgment the court has not considered it; it is more likely that the court was not assisted by it.

D.5 When an authority is to be cited, whether in written or oral submissions, the advocate should always provide the neutral citation followed by the law report reference.

D.6 The following practice should be followed:

i) Where a judgment is reported in the Official Law Reports (A.C., Q.B., Ch., Fam.) published by the Incorporated Council of Law Reporting for England and Wales or the Criminal Appeal Reports or the Criminal Appeal Reports (Sentencing) one of those two series of reports must be cited; either is equally acceptable. However, where a judgment is reported in the Criminal Appeal Reports or the Criminal Appeal Reports (Sentencing) that reference must be given in addition to any other reference. Other series of reports and official transcripts of judgment may only be used when a case is not reported, or not yet reported, in the Official Law Reports or the Criminal Appeal Reports or the Criminal Appeal Reports (Sentencing).

ii) If a judgment is not reported in the Official Law Reports, the Criminal Appeal Reports or the Criminal Appeal Reports (Sentencing), but it is reported in an authoritative series of reports which contains a headnote and is made by individuals holding a Senior Courts qualification (for the purposes of section 115 of the Courts and Legal Services Act 1990), that report should be cited.

iii) Where a judgment is not reported in any of the reports referred to above, but is reported in other reports, they may be cited.

iv) Where a judgment has not been reported, reference may be made to the official transcript if that is available, not the handed-down text of the judgment, as this may have been subject to late revision after the text was handed down. Official transcripts may be obtained from, for instance, BAILLI (http://www.bailii.org/).

D.7 In the majority of cases, it is expected that all references will be to the Official Law Reports and the Criminal Appeal Reports or the Criminal Appeal Reports (Sentencing); it will be rare for there to be a need to refer to any other reports. An unreported case should not be cited unless it contains a relevant statement of legal principle not found in reported authority, and it is expected that this will only occur in exceptional circumstances.

Provision of copies of judgments to the Court

D.8 The paragraphs below specify whether or not copies should be provided to the court. Authorities should not be included for propositions not in dispute. If more than one authority is to be provided, the copies should be presented in paginated and tagged bundles.

D.9 If required, copies of judgments should be provided either by way of a photocopy of the published report or by way of a copy of a reproduction of the judgment in electronic form that has been authorised by the publisher of the relevant series, but in any event:

i) the report must be presented to the court in an easily legible form (a 12-point font is preferred but a 10 or 11-point font is acceptable); and

ii) the advocate presenting the report must be satisfied that it has not been reproduced in a garbled form from the data source.

In any case of doubt the court will rely on the printed text of the report (unless the editor of the report has certified that an electronic version is more accurate because it corrects an error contained in an earlier printed text of the report).

D.10 If such a copy is unavailable, a printed transcript such as from BAILLI may be included.

Provision of copies to the Court of Appeal (Criminal Division)

D.11 Advocates must provide to the Registrar of Criminal Appeals, with their appeal notice, respondent's notice or skeleton argument, a list of authorities upon which they wish to rely in their written or oral submissions. The list of authorities should contain the name of the applicant, appellant or respondent and the Criminal Appeal Office number where known. The list should include reference to the relevant paragraph numbers in each authority. An updated list can be provided if a new authority is issued, or in response to a respondent's notice or skeleton argument. From time to time, the Registrar may issue guidance as to the style or content of lists of authorities, including a suggested format; this guidance should be followed by all parties. The latest guidance is available from the Criminal Appeal Office.

D.12 If the case cited is reported in the Official Law Reports, the Criminal Appeal Reports or the Criminal Appeal Reports (Sentencing), the law report reference must be given after the neutral citation, and the relevant paragraphs listed, but copies should not be provided to the court.

D.13 If, exceptionally, reference is made to a case that is not reported in the Official Law Reports, the Criminal Appeal Reports or the Criminal Appeal Reports (Sentencing), three copies must be provided to the Registrar with the list of authorities and the relevant appeal notice or respondent's notice (or skeleton argument, if provided). The relevant passages of the authorities should be marked or sidelined.

Provision of copies to the Crown Court and the magistrates' courts

D.14 When the court is considering routine applications, it may be sufficient for the court to be referred to the applicable legislation or to one of the practitioner texts. However, it is the responsibility of the advocate to ensure that the court is provided with the material that it needs properly to consider any matter.

D.15 If it would assist the court to consider any authority, the directions at paragraphs D.2 to D.7 above relating to citation will apply and a list of authorities should be provided.

D.16 Copies should be provided by the party seeking to rely upon the authority in accordance with CrimPR 24.13. This Rule is applicable in the magistrates' courts, and in relation to the provision of authorities, should also be followed in the Crown Court since courts often do not hold library stock (see CrimPR 25.17). Advocates should comply with paragraphs D.8 to D.10 relating to the provision of copies to the court.

D.17 The court may give directions for the preparation of skeleton arguments. Such directions will provide for the time within which skeleton arguments must be served and for the issues which they must address. Such directions may provide for the number of pages, or the number of words, to which a skeleton argument is to be confined. Any such directions displace the following to the extent of any inconsistency. Subject to that, however, a skeleton argument must:

i. not normally exceed 15 pages (excluding front sheets and back sheets) and be concise;

ii. be presented in A4 page size and portrait orientation, in not less than 12 point font and in 1.5 line spacing;
iii. define the issues;
iv. be set out in numbered paragraphs;
v. be cross-referenced to any relevant document in any bundle prepared for the court;
vi. be self-contained and not incorporate by reference material from previous skeleton arguments;
vii. not include extensive quotations from documents or authorities.

D.18 Where it is necessary to refer to an authority, the skeleton argument must:
i. state the proposition of law the authority demonstrates; and
ii. identify but not quote the parts of the authority that support the proposition.

D.19 If more than one authority is cited in support of a given proposition, the skeleton argument must briefly state why.

D.20 A chronology of relevant events will be necessary in most cases.

D.21 There are directions at paragraphs I 3C.3 and 3C.4 of these Practice Directions that apply to the service of skeleton arguments in support of, and in opposition to, an application to stay an indictment on the grounds of abuse of process; and directions at paragraphs IX 39F.1 to 39F.3 that apply to the service of skeleton arguments in the Court of Appeal. Where a skeleton argument has been prepared in respect of an application for permission to appeal, the same skeleton argument may be relied upon in the appeal upon notice being given to the court, or a replacement skeleton may be served to the timetable set out in those paragraphs.

D.22 At the hearing the court may refuse to hear argument on a point unless it is included in a skeleton argument which (i) is served within the required time, and (ii) complies with the requirements of these Practice Directions (as varied, if applicable, by direction of the court). Any application for a variation, or further variation, of those requirements must give reasons, and such an application must accompany any skeleton argument that does not comply.

D.23 In *R v James, R v Selby* [2016] EWCA Crim 1639; [2017] Crim.L.R. 228 the Court of Appeal observed (at paragraphs 52 to 54):

'Legal documents of unnecessary and too often of excessive length offer very little assistance to the court. In *Tombstone Ltd v Raja* [2008] EWCA Civ 1441, [2009] 1 WLR 1143 Mummery LJ said:

"Practitioners … are well advised to note the risk of the court's negative reaction to unnecessarily long written submissions. The skeleton argument procedure was introduced to assist the court, as well as the parties, by improving preparations for, and the efficiency of, adversarial oral hearings, which remain central to this court's public role… . An unintended and unfortunate side effect of the growth in written advocacy… has been that too many practitioners, at increased cost to their clients and diminishing assistance to the court, burden their opponents and the court with written briefs."

He might have penned those remarks had he been sitting in these two cases, and many more, in this Division.

In *Standard Bank PLC v Via Mat International* [2013] EWCA Civ 490, [2013] 2 All ER (Comm) 1222 the excessive length of court documents prompted:

"It is important that both practitioners and their clients understand that skeleton arguments are not intended to serve as vehicles for extended advocacy and that in general a short, concise skeleton is both more helpful to the court and more likely to be persuasive than a longer document which seeks to develop every point which the advocate would wish to make in oral argument."

No area of law is exempt from the requirement to produce careful and concise documents: *Tchenquiz v Director of the Serious Fraud Office* [2014] EWCA Civ 1333, [2015] 1 WLR 838, paragraph 10.'

CPD XII General application E: Preparation of Judgments: Neutral Citation CPD.XII.E

E.1 Since 11 January 2001 every judgment of the Court of Appeal, and of the Administrative Court, and since 14 January 2002 every judgment of the High Court, has been prepared and issued as approved with single spacing, paragraph numbering (in the margins) and no page numbers. In courts with more than one judge, the paragraph numbering continues sequentially through each judgment and does not start again at the beginning of each judgment. Indented paragraphs are not numbered. A unique reference number is given to each judgment. For judgments of the Court of Appeal, this number is given by the official shorthand writers, Merrill Legal Solutions (Tel: 020 7421 4000 ext.4036). For judgments of the High Court, it is provided by the Courts Recording and Transcription Unit at the Royal Courts of Justice. Such a number will also be furnished, on request to the Courts Recording and Transcription Unit, Royal Courts of Justice, Strand, London WC2A 2LL (Tel: 020 7947 7820), (e-mail: rcj.cratu@hmcts.gsi.gov.uk) for High Court judgments delivered outside London.

E.2 Each Court of Appeal judgment starts with the year, followed by EW (for England and Wales), then CA (for Court of Appeal), followed by Civ or Crim and finally the sequential number. For example, '*Smith v Jones* [2001] EWCA Civ 10'.

E.3 In the High Court, represented by HC, the number comes before the divisional abbreviation and, unlike Court of Appeal judgments, the latter is bracketed: (Ch), (Pat), (QB), (Admin), (Comm), (Admlty), (TCC) or (Fam), as appropriate. For example, '[2002] EWHC 123 (Fam)', or '[2002] EWHC 124 (QB)', or '[2002] EWHC 125 (Ch)'.

E.4 This 'neutral citation', as it is called, is the official number attributed to the judgment and must always be used at least once when the judgment is cited in a later judgment. Once the judgment is reported, this neutral citation appears in front of the familiar citation from the law reports series. Thus: '*Smith v Jones* [2001] EWCA Civ 10; [2001] QB 124; [2001] 2 All ER 364', etc.

E.5 Paragraph numbers are referred to in square brackets. When citing a paragraph from a High Court judgment, it is unnecessary to include the descriptive word in brackets: (Admin), (QB), or whatever. When citing a paragraph from a Court of Appeal judgment, however, 'Civ' or 'Crim' is included. If it is desired to cite more than one paragraph of a judgment, each numbered paragraph should be enclosed with a square bracket. Thus paragraph 59 in *Green v White* [2002] EWHC 124 (QB) would be cited: '*Green v White* [2002] EWHC 124 at [59]'; paragraphs 30 – 35 in *Smith v Jones* would be '*Smith v Jones* [2001] EWCA Civ 10 at [30] – [35]'; similarly, where a number of paragraphs are cited: '*Smith v Jones* [2001] EWCA Civ 10 at [30], [35] and [40 – 43]'.

E.6 If a judgment is cited more than once in a later judgment, it is helpful if only one abbreviation is used, e.g., '*Smith v Jones*' or 'Smith's case', but preferably not both (in the same judgment).

CPD.XII.F **CPD XII General application F: Citation of Hansard**

F.1 Where any party intends to refer to the reports of Parliamentary proceedings as reported in the Official Reports of either House of Parliament ('Hansard') in support of any such argument as is permitted by the decisions in *Pepper v Hart* [1993] AC 593 and *Pickstone v Freemans PLC* [1989] AC 66, or otherwise, he must, unless the court otherwise directs, serve upon all other parties and the court copies of any such extract, together with a brief summary of the argument intended to be based upon such extract. No other report of Parliamentary proceedings may be cited.

F.2 Unless the court otherwise directs, service of the extract and summary of the argument shall be effected not less than 5 clear working days before the first day of the hearing, whether or not it has a fixed date. Advocates must keep themselves informed as to the state of the lists where no fixed date has been given. Service on the court shall be effected by sending three copies to the Registrar of Criminal Appeals, Royal Courts of Justice, Strand, London, WC2A 2LL or to the court manager of the relevant Crown Court centre, as appropriate. If any party fails to do so, the court may make such order (relating to costs or otherwise) as is, in all the circumstances, appropriate.

Criminal Practice Directions Listing

CPD.XIII.A **CPD XIII Listing A: Judicial Responsibility for Listing and Key Principles**

Listing as a judicial responsibility and function

A.1 Listing is a judicial responsibility and function. The purpose is to ensure that all cases are brought to a hearing or trial in accordance with the interests of justice, that the resources available for criminal justice are deployed as effectively as possible, and that cases are heard by an appropriate judge or bench with the minimum of delay.

A.2 The agreement reached between the Lord Chief Justice and the Secretary of State for Constitutional Affairs and Lord Chancellor set out in a statement to the House of Lords on 26 January 2004 ('the Concordat'), states that judges, working with HMCTS, are responsible for deciding on the assignment of cases to particular courts and the listing of those cases before particular judges. Therefore:

(a) The Presiding Judges of each circuit have the overall responsibility for listing at all courts, Crown and magistrates', on their circuit;

(b) Subject to the supervision of the Presiding Judges, the Resident Judge at each Crown Court has the general responsibility within his or her court centre for the allocation of criminal judicial work, to ensure the just and efficient despatch of the business of the court or group of courts. This includes overseeing the deployment of allocated judges at the court or group, including the distribution of work between all the judges allocated to that court. A Resident Judge must appoint a deputy or deputies to exercise his or her functions when he or she is absent from his or her court centre. See also paragraph A.5: Discharge of judicial responsibilities;

(c) The listing officer in the Crown Court is responsible for carrying out the day-to-day operation of listing practice under the direction of the Resident Judge. The listing officer at each Crown Court centre has one of the most important functions at that Crown Court and makes a vital contribution to the efficient running of that Crown Court and to the efficient operation of the administration of criminal justice;

(d) In the magistrates' courts, the Judicial Business Group, subject to the supervision of the Presiding Judges of the circuit, is responsible for determining the listing practice in that area. The day-to-day operation of that listing practice is the responsibility of the justices' clerk with the assistance of the listing officer.

Key principles of listing

A.3 When setting the listing practice, the Resident Judge or the Judicial Business Group should take into account principles a-j:

(a) Ensure the timely trial of cases and resolution of other issues (such as confiscation) so that justice is not delayed. The following factors are relevant:
   i. In general, each case should be tried within as short a time of its arrival in the court as is consistent with the interests of justice, the needs of victims and witnesses, and with the proper and timely preparation by the prosecution and defence of their cases in accordance with the directions and timetable set;
   ii. Priority should be accorded to the trial of young defendants, and cases where there are vulnerable or young witnesses. In *R v Barker* [2010] EWCA Crim 4, the Lord Chief Justice highlighted 'the importance to the trial and investigative process of keeping any delay in a case involving a child complainant to an irreducible minimum';
   iii. Custody time limits (CTLs) should be observed, see CPD XIII Listing F;
   iv. Every effort must be made to avoid delay in cases in which the defendant is on bail;

(b) Ensure that in the magistrates' court unless impracticable, non-custody anticipated guilty plea cases are listed 14 days after charge, and non-custody anticipated not guilty pleas are listed 28 days after charge;

(c) Provide, when possible, for certainty and/or as much advance notice as possible, of the trial date; and take all reasonable steps to ensure that the trial date remains fixed;

(d) Ensure that a judge or bench with any necessary authorisation and of appropriate experience is available to try each case and, wherever desirable and practicable, there is judicial continuity, including in relation to post-trial hearings;

(e) Strike an appropriate balance in the use of resources, by taking account of:
   i. The efficient deployment of the judiciary in the Crown Court and the magistrates' courts taking into account relevant sitting requirements for magistrates. See CPD XIII Annex 1 for information to support judicial deployment in the magistrates' courts;
   ii. The proper use of the courtrooms available at the court;
   iii. The provision in long and/or complex cases for adequate reading time for the judiciary;
   iv. The facilities in the available courtrooms, including the security needs (such as a secure dock), size and equipment, such as video and live link facilities;
   v. The proper use of those who attend the Crown Court as jurors;
   vi. The availability of legal advisers in the magistrates' courts;
   vii. The need to return those sentenced to custody as soon as possible after the sentence is passed, and to facilitate the efficient operation of the prison escort contract;

(f) Provide where practicable:
   i. the defendant and the prosecution with the advocate of their choice where this does not result in any delay to the trial of the case; and,
   ii. for the efficient deployment of advocates, lawyers and associate prosecutors of the Crown Prosecution Service, and other prosecuting authorities, and of the resources available to the independent legal profession, for example by trying to group certain cases together;

(g) Meet the need for special security measures for category A and other high-risk defendants;

(h) Ensure that proper time (including judicial reading time) is afforded to hearings in which the court is exercising powers that impact on the rights of individuals, such as applications for investigative orders or warrants;

(i) Consider the significance of ancillary proceedings, such as confiscation hearings, and the need to deal with such hearings promptly and, where possible, for such hearings to be conducted by the trial judge;

(j) Provide for government initiatives or projects approved by the Lord Chief Justice.

A.4 Although the listing practice at each Crown Court centre and magistrates' court will take these principles into account, the listing practice adopted will vary from court to court depending particularly on the number of courtrooms and the facilities available, the location and the workload, its volume and type.

Discharge of judicial responsibilities

A.5 The Resident Judge of each court is responsible for:
i. ensuring that good practice is implemented throughout the court, such that all hearings commence on time;
ii. ensuring that the causes of trials that do not proceed on the date originally fixed are examined to see if there is any systemic issue;
iii. monitoring the general performance of the court and the listing practices;
iv. monitoring the timeliness of cases and reporting any cases of serious concern to the Presiding Judge;
v. maintaining and reviewing annually a list of Recorders, qualifying judge advocates and Deputy Circuit Judges authorised to hear appeals from the magistrates' courts unless such a list is maintained by the Presiding Judge.

A.6 The Judicial Business Group for each clerkship subject to the overall jurisdiction of the Presiding Judge is responsible for:
i. monitoring the workload and anticipated changes which may impact on listing policies;
ii. ensuring that any listing practice meets the needs of the system as a whole.

CPD.XIII.B **CPD XIII Listing B: Classification**

B.1 The classification structure outlined below is solely for the purposes of trial in the Crown Court. The structure has been devised to accommodate practical administrative functions and is not intended to reflect a hierarchy of the offences therein.

Offences are classified as follows:

Class 1: A:
i. Murder;
ii. Attempted Murder;
iii. Manslaughter;
iv. Infanticide;
v. Child destruction (section 1(1) of the Infant Life (Preservation) Act 1929);
vi. Abortion (section 58 of the Offences against the Person Act 1861);
vii. Assisting a suicide;
viii. Cases including section 5 of the Domestic Violence, Crime and Victims Act 2004, as amended (if a fatality has resulted);
ix. Soliciting, inciting, encouraging or assisting, attempting or conspiring to commit any of the above offences or assisting an offender having committed such an offence.

Class 1: B:
i. Genocide;
ii. Torture, hostage-taking and offences under the War Crimes Act 1991;
iii. Offences under ss. 51 and 52 International Criminal Courts Act 2001;
iv. An offence under section 1 of the Geneva Conventions Act 1957;
v. Terrorism offences (where offence charged is indictable only and took place during an act of terrorism or for the purposes of terrorism as defined in s.1 of the Terrorism Act 2000);
vi. Piracy, under the Merchant Shipping and Maritime Security Act 1997;
vii. Treason;
viii. An offence under the Official Secrets Acts;
ix. Incitement to disaffection;
x. Soliciting, inciting, encouraging or assisting, attempting or conspiring to commit any of the above offences or assisting an offender having committed such an offence.

Class 1: C:
i. Prison mutiny, under the Prison Security Act 1992;
ii. Riot in the course of serious civil disturbance;
iii. Serious gang related crime resulting in the possession or discharge of firearms, particularly including a campaign of firebombing or extortion, especially when accompanied by allegations of drug trafficking on a commercial scale;
iv. Complex sexual offence cases in which there are many complainants (often under age, in care or otherwise particularly vulnerable) and/or many defendants who are alleged to have systematically groomed and abused them, often over a long period of time;
v. Cases involving people trafficking for sexual, labour or other exploitation and cases of human servitude;
vi. Soliciting, inciting, encouraging or assisting, attempting or conspiring to commit any of the above offences or assisting an offender having committed such an offence.

Class 1: D:
- i. Causing death by dangerous driving;
- ii. Causing death by careless driving;
- iii. Causing death by unlicensed, disqualified or uninsured driving;
- iv. Any Health and Safety case resulting in a fatality or permanent serious disability;
- v. Any other case resulting in a fatality or permanent serious disability;
- vi. Soliciting, inciting, encouraging or assisting, attempting or conspiring to commit any of the above offences or assisting an offender having committed such an offence.

Class 2: A
- i. Arson with intent to endanger life or reckless as to whether life was endangered;
- ii. Cases in which explosives, firearms or imitation firearms are used or carried or possessed;
- iii. Kidnapping or false imprisonment (without intention to commit a sexual offence but charged on the same indictment as a serious offence of violence such as under section 18 or section 20 of the Offences Against the Person Act 1861);
- iv. Cases in which the defendant is a police officer, member of the legal profession or a high profile or public figure;
- v. Cases in which the complainant or an important witness is a high profile or public figure;
- vi. Riot otherwise than in the course of serious civil disturbance;
- vii. Child cruelty;
- viii. Cases including section 5 of the Domestic Violence, Crime and Victims Act 2004, as amended (if no fatality has resulted);
- ix. Soliciting, inciting, encouraging or assisting, attempting or conspiring to commit any of the above offences or assisting an offender having committed such an offence.

Class 2: B
- i. Any sexual offence, with the exception of those included in Class 1C;
- ii. Kidnapping or false imprisonment (with intention to commit a sexual offence or charged on the same indictment as a sexual offence);
- iii. Soliciting, inciting, encouraging or assisting, attempting or conspiring to commit any of the above offences or assisting an offender having committed such an offence.

Class 2: C:
- i. Serious, complex fraud;
- ii. Serious and/or complex money laundering;
- iii. Serious and/or complex bribery;
- iv. Corruption;
- v. Complex cases in which the defendant is a corporation (including cases for sentence as well as for trial);
- vi. Any case in which the defendant is a corporation with a turnover in excess of £1bn (including cases for sentence as well as for trial);
- vii. Soliciting, inciting, encouraging or assisting, attempting or conspiring to commit any of the above offences or assisting an offender having committed such an offence.

Class 3: All other offences not listed in the classes above.

Deferred Prosecution Agreements

B.2 Cases coming before the court under section 45 [of] and Schedule 17 [to] the Crime and Courts Act 2013 must be referred to the President of the Queen's Bench Division who will allocate the matter to a judge from a list of judges approved by the Lord Chief Justice. Only the allocated judge may thereafter hear any matter or make any decision in relation to that case.

Criminal Cases Review Commission

B.3 Where the CCRC refers a case upon conviction from the magistrates' courts to the Crown Court, this shall be dealt with at a Crown Court centre designated by the Senior Presiding Judge.

CPD XIII Listing C: Referral of Cases in the Crown Court to the Resident Judge and to the Presiding Judges **CPD.XIII.C**

C.1 This Practice Direction specifies:
- (a) cases which must be referred to a Presiding Judge for release; and
- (b) cases which must be referred to the Resident Judge before being assigned to a judge, Recorder or qualifying judge advocate to hear.

It is applicable to all Crown Courts, but its application may be modified by the Senior Presiding Judge or the Presiding Judges, with the approval of the Senior Presiding Judge, through the provision of further specific guidance to Resident Judges in relation to the allocation and management of the work at their court.

C.2 This Practice Direction does not prescribe the way in which the Resident Judge gives directions as to listing policy to the listing officer; its purpose is to ensure that there is appropriate judicial control over the listing of cases. However, the Resident Judge must arrange with the listing officers a satisfactory means of ensuring that all cases listed at their court are listed before judges, Recorders or qualifying judge advocates of suitable seniority and experience, subject to the requirements of this Practice Direction. The Resident Judge should ensure that listing officers are made aware of the contents and importance of this Practice Direction, and that listing officers develop satisfactory procedures for referral of cases to him or her.

C.3 In order to assist the Resident Judge and the listing officer, all cases sent to the Crown Court should where possible include a brief case summary prepared by the prosecution. The prosecutor should ensure that any factors that make the case complex, or would lead it to be referred to the Resident Judge or a Presiding Judge are highlighted. The defence may also send submissions to the court, again highlighting any areas of complexity or any other factors that might assist in the case being allocated to an appropriate judge.

Cases in the Crown Court to be referred to the Resident Judge

C.4 All cases in Class 1A, 1B, 1C, 1D, 2A and 2C must be referred to the Resident Judge as must any case which appears to raise particularly complex, sensitive or serious issues.

C.5 Resident Judges should give guidance to the judges and staff of their respective courts as to which Class 2B cases should be referred to them following consultation with the Senior Presiding Judge. This will include any cases that may be referred to the Presiding Judge, see below. Class 2B cases to be referred to the Resident Judge are likely to be identified by the list officer, or by the judge at the first hearing in the Crown Court. Any appeal against conviction and/or sentence from a Youth Court involving a Class 2B case must be brought to the attention of the Resident Judge as soon as practicable. Where not provided with the appeal papers, the list officer must obtain a full summary of the prosecution case so as to allow an informed allocation decision to be made.

C.6 Once a case has been referred to the Resident Judge, the Resident Judge should refer the case to the Presiding Judge, following the guidance below, or allocate the case to an appropriate category of judge, and if possible to a named judge.

Cases in the Crown Court to be referred to a Presiding Judge

C.7 All cases in Class 1A, 1B and 1C must be referred by the Resident Judge to a Presiding Judge, as must a case in any class which is:

i. An usually grave or complex case or one in which a novel and important point of law is to be raised;
ii. A case where it is alleged that the defendant caused more than 1 fatality;
iii. A non-fatal case of baby shaking where serious injury resulted;
iv. A case where the defendant is a police officer, or a member of the legal profession or a high profile figure;
v. A case which for any reason is likely to attract exceptional media attention;
vi. A case where a large organisation or corporation may, if convicted, be ordered to pay a very large fine;
vii. Any case likely to last more than three months.

C.8 Resident Judges are encouraged to refer any other case if they think it is appropriate to do so.

C.9 Presiding Judges and Resident Judges should agree a system for the referral of cases to the Presiding Judge, ideally by electronic means. The system agreed should include provision for the Resident Judge to provide the Presiding Judge with a brief summary of the case, a clear recommendation by the Resident Judge about the judges available to try the case and any other comments. A written record of the decision and brief reasons for it must be made and retained.

C.10 Once a case has been referred to the Presiding Judge, the Presiding Judge may retain the case for trial by a High Court Judge, or release the case back to the Resident Judge, either for trial by a named judge, or for trial by an identified category of judges, to be allocated by the Resident Judge.

CPD.XIII.D **CPD XIII Listing D: Authorisation of Judges**

D.1 Judges must be authorised by the Lord Chief Justice before they may hear certain types of case.

D.2 Judges (other than High Court Judges) to hear Class 1A cases must be authorised to hear such cases. Any judge previously granted a 'Class 1' or 'murder' authorisation is authorised to hear Class 1A cases. Judges previously granted an 'attempted murder' (including soliciting, incitement or conspiracy thereof) authorisation can only deal with these cases within Class 1A.

D.3 Judges (other than High Court Judges) to hear sexual offences cases in Class 1C or any case within Class 2B must be authorised to hear such cases. Any judge previously granted a 'Class 2' or 'serious sex offences' authorisation is authorised to hear sexual offences cases in Class 1C or 2B. It is a condition of the authorisation that it does not take effect until the judge has attended the relevant Judicial College course; the Resident Judge should check in the case of newly authorised judges that they have attended the course. Judges who have been previously authorised to try such cases should make every effort to ensure their training is up-to-date and maintained by attending the Serious Sexual Offences Seminar at least once every three years. See CPD XIII Annex 2 for guidance in dealing with sexual offences in the youth court.

D.4 Cases in the magistrates' courts involving the imposition of very large fines

i. Where a defendant appears before a magistrates' court for an either way offence, to which CPD XIII Annex 3 applies the case must be dealt with by a DJ (MC) who has been authorised to deal with such cases by the Chief Magistrate.

ii. The authorised DJ (MC) must first consider whether such cases should be allocated to the Crown Court or, where the defendant pleads guilty, committed for sentence under s. 3 Powers of [Criminal] Courts (Sentenc[ing]) Act 2000, and must do so when the DJ (MC) considers the offence or combination of offences so serious that the Crown Court should deal with the defendant had they been convicted on indictment.

iii. If an authorised DJ (MC) decides not to commit such a case the reasons must be recorded in writing to be entered onto the court register.

CPD XIII Listing E: Allocation of Business within the Crown Court **CPD.XIII.E**

E.1 Cases in Class 1A may only be tried by:

i. a High Court Judge, or

ii. a Circuit Judge, or Deputy High Court Judge, authorised to try such cases and provided that the Presiding Judge has released the case for trial by such a judge; or

iii. a Deputy Circuit Judge to whom the case has been specifically released by the Presiding Judge.

E.2 Cases in Class 1B may only be tried by:

i. a High Court Judge, or

ii. a Circuit Judge, or a Deputy High Court Judge, provided that the Presiding Judge has released the case for trial by such a judge; or

iii. a Deputy Circuit Judge to whom the case has been specifically released by the Presiding Judge.

E.3 Cases in Class 1C may only be tried by:

i. a High Court Judge, or

ii. a Circuit Judge, or a Deputy High Court Judge, or Deputy Circuit Judge, authorised to try such cases (if the case requires the judge to be authorised to hear sexual offences cases), provided that the Presiding Judge has released the case for trial by such a judge, or, if the case is a sexual offence, the Presiding Judge has assigned the case to that named judge.

See also CPD XIII Listing C.10.

E.4 Cases in Class 1D and 2A may be tried by:

i. a High Court Judge, or

ii. a Circuit Judge, or Deputy High Court Judge, or Deputy Circuit Judge, or a Recorder or a qualifying judge advocate, provided that either the Presiding Judge has released the case or the Resident Judge has allocated the case for trial by such a judge; with the exception that Class 2A i) cases may not be tried by a Recorder or qualifying judge advocate.

E.5 Cases in Class 2B may be tried by:

i. a High Court Judge, or

ii. a Circuit Judge, or Deputy High Court Judge, or Deputy Circuit Judge, or a Recorder or a qualifying judge advocate, authorised to try such cases and provided that either the Presiding Judge has released the case or the Resident Judge has allocated the case for trial by such a judge.

E.6 Cases in Class 2C may be tried by:

i. a High Court Judge, or

ii. a Circuit Judge, or Deputy High Court Judge, or Deputy Circuit Judge, or a Recorder or a qualifying judge advocate, with suitable experience (for example, with company accounts or other financial information) and provided that either the Presiding Judge has released the case or the Resident Judge has allocated the case for trial by such a judge.

E.7 Cases in Classes 1D, 2A and 2C will usually be tried by a Circuit Judge.

E.8 Cases in Class 3 may be tried by a High Court Judge, or a Circuit Judge, a Deputy Circuit Judge, a Recorder or a qualifying judge advocate. A case in Class 3 shall not be listed for trial by a High Court Judge except with the consent of a Presiding Judge.

E.9 If a case has been allocated to a judge, Recorder or qualifying judge advocate, the preliminary hearing should be conducted by the allocated judge if practicable, and if not, if possible by a judge of at least equivalent standing. PCMHs should only be heard by Recorders or qualifying judge advocates with the approval of the Resident Judge.

E.10 For cases in Class 1A, 1B or 1C, or any case that has been referred to the Presiding Judge, the preliminary hearing and PCMH must be conducted by a High Court Judge; by a Circuit Judge; or by a judge authorised by the Presiding Judges to conduct such hearings. In the event of a guilty plea before such an authorised judge, the case will be adjourned for sentencing and will immediately be referred to the Presiding Judge who may retain the case for sentence by a High Court Judge, or release the case back to the Resident Judge, either for sentence by a named judge, or for sentence by an identified category of judges, to be allocated by the Resident Judge.

E.11 Appeals from decisions of magistrates' courts shall be heard by:

i. a Resident Judge, or
ii. a Circuit Judge, nominated by the Resident Judge, or
iii. a Recorder or qualifying judge advocate or a Deputy Circuit Judge listed by the Presiding Judge to hear such appeals; or, if there is no such list nominated by the Resident Judge to hear such appeals;
iv. and, no less than two and no more than four justices of the peace, none of whom took part in the decision under appeal;
v. where no Circuit Judge or Recorder or qualifying judge advocate satisfying the requirements above is available, by a Circuit Judge, Recorder, qualifying judge advocate or Deputy Circuit Judge selected by the Resident Judge to hear a specific case or cases listed on a specific day.

E.12 Appeals from the youth court in relation to sexual offences shall be heard by:

i. A Resident Judge or;
ii. a Circuit Judge nominated by the Resident Judge who is authorised under D.3 to hear sexual offences in Class 1C or Class 2B;
iii. and no less than two and no more than four justices of the peace, none of whom took part in the decision under appeal. The justices of the peace must have undertaken specific training to deal with youth matters.
iv. No appeal against conviction and/or sentence from a Youth Court involving a Class 1C or Class 2B offence shall be heard by a Recorder save with the express permission of the Presiding Judge of the Circuit.

E.13 Allocation or committal for sentence following breach (such as a matter in which a community order has been made, or a suspended sentence passed), should, where possible, be listed before the judge who originally dealt with the matter or, if not, before a judge of the same or higher level.

E.14 Applications for removal of a driving disqualification should be made to the location of the Crown Court where the order of disqualification was made. Where possible, the matter should be listed before the judge who originally dealt with the matter or, if not, before a judge of the same or higher level.

CPD.XIII.F

CPD XIII Listing F: Listing of Trials, Custody Time Limits and Transfer of Cases

Estimates of trial length

F.1 Under the regime set out in the Criminal Procedure Rules, the parties will be expected to provide an accurate estimate of the length of trial at the hearing where the case is to be managed based on a detailed estimate of the time to be taken with each witness to be called, and accurate information about the availability of witnesses.

F.2 At the hearing the judge will ask the prosecution to clarify any custody time limit ('CTL') dates. The court clerk must ensure the CTL date is marked clearly on the court file or electronic file. When a case is subject to a CTL all efforts must be made at the first hearing to list the case within the CTL and the judge should seek to ensure this. Further guidance on listing CTL cases can be found below.

Cases that should usually have fixed trial dates

F.3 The cases where fixtures should be given will be set out in the listing practice applicable at the court, but should usually include the following:

i. Cases in classes 1A, 1B, 1C, 2B and 2C;
ii. Cases involving vulnerable and intimidated witnesses (including domestic violence cases), whether or not special measures have been ordered by the court;
iii. Cases where the witnesses are under 18 or have to come from overseas;
iv. Cases estimated to last more than a certain time — the period chosen will depend on the size of the centre and the available judges;
v. Cases where a previous fixed hearing has not been effective;
vi. Re-trials; and,
vii. Cases involving expert witnesses.

Custody Time Limits

F.4 Every effort must be made to list cases for trial within the CTL limits set by Parliament. The guiding principles are:

i. At the first hearing in the Crown Court, prosecution will inform the court when the CTL lapses.

ii. All efforts must be made to list the case within the CTL. The CTL may only be extended in accordance with s. 22 Prosecution of Offences Act 1985 and the Prosecution of Offences (Custody Time Limits) Regulations 1987.

iii. If suitable, given priority and listed on a date not less than 2 weeks before the CTL expires, the case may be placed in a warned list.

iv. The CTL must be kept under continual review by the parties, HMCTS and the Resident Judge.

v. If the CTL is at risk of being exceeded, an additional hearing should take place and should be listed before the Resident Judge or trial judge or other judge nominated by the Resident Judge.

vi. An application to extend the CTL in any case listed outside the CTL must be considered by the court whether or not it was listed with the express consent of the defence.

vii. Any application to extend CTLs must be considered as a matter of urgency. The reasons for needing the extension must be ascertained and fully explained to the court.

viii. Where courtroom or judge availability is an issue, the court must itself list the case to consider the extension of any CTL. The Delivery Director of the circuit must provide a statement setting out in detail what has been done to try to accommodate the case within the CTL.

ix. Where courtroom or judge availability is not in issue, but all parties and the court agree that the case will not be ready for trial before the expiration of the CTL, a date may be fixed outside the CTL. This may be done without prejudice to any application to extend the CTLs or with the express consent of the defence; this must be noted on the papers.

F.5 As legal argument may delay the swearing in of a jury, it is desirable to extend the CTL to a date later than the first day of the trial.

Re-trials ordered by the Court of Appeal

F.6 The Crown Court must comply with the directions of the Court of Appeal and cannot vary those directions without reference to the Court of Appeal.

F.7 In cases where a retrial is ordered by the Court of Appeal the CTL is 112 days starting from the date that the new indictment is preferred i.e. from the date that the indictment is delivered to the Crown Court. Court centres should check that CREST has calculated the dates correctly and that it has not used 182 days on cases that have previously been 'sent'.

Changes to the date of fixed cases

F.8 Once a trial date or window is fixed, it should not be vacated or moved without good reason. Under the Criminal Procedure Rules, parties are expected to be ready by the trial date.

F.9 The listing officer may, in circumstances determined by the Resident Judge, agree to the movement of the trial to a date to which the defence and prosecution both consent, provided the timely hearing of the case is not delayed. The prosecution will be expected to have consulted the witnesses before agreeing to any change.

F.10 In all other circumstances, requests to adjourn or vacate fixtures or trial windows must be referred to the Resident Judge for his or her personal attention; the Resident Judge may delegate the decision to a named deputy.

Transferring cases to another court

F.11 Transfer between courts on the same circuit must be agreed by the Resident Judges of each court, subject to guidance from the Presiding Judges of the circuit.

F.12 Transfer of trials between circuits must be agreed between the Presiding Judges and Delivery Directors of the respective circuits.

F.13 Transfers may be agreed either in specific cases or in accordance with general principles agreed between those cited above.

CPD XIII Listing G: Listing of Hearings other than Trials **CPD.XIII.G**

G.1 In addition to trials, the court's listing practice will have to provide court time for shorter matters, such as those listed below. These hearings are important, often either for setting the necessary case management framework for the proper and efficient preparation of cases for trial, or for determining matters that affect the rights of individuals. They must be afforded the appropriate level of resource that they require to be considered properly, and this may include judicial reading time as well as an appropriate length of hearing.

G.2 The applicant is responsible for notifying the court, and the other party if appropriate, and ensuring that the papers are served in good time, including a time estimate for judicial reading time and for the hearing. The applicant must endeavour to complete the application within the time estimate provided unless there are exceptional circumstances.

G.3 Hearings other than trials include the following:

i. Applications for search warrants and Production Orders, sufficient reading time must be provided, see G.8 below;
ii. Bail applications;
iii. Applications to vacate or adjourn hearings;
iv. Applications for dismissal of charges;
v. Preparation for trial hearings, plea and trial preparation hearings, and other pre-trial case management hearings;
vi. Applications for disclosure of further unused material under section 8 of CPIA 1996;
vii. Case progression or case management hearings;
viii. Applications in respect of sentence indications not sought at the PTPH;
ix. Sentences;
x. Civil applications under the Anti-Social Behaviour, Crime and Policing Act 2014;
xi. Breach proceedings (and see paragraph G.12 beneath);"
xii. Appeals from the magistrates' court: it is essential in all cases where witnesses are likely to be needed on the appeal to check availability before a date is fixed (and see paragraphs G.13 to G.15 beneath);
xiii. Appeals from the youth court: where the case involves a Class 2B offence then a directions hearing will be required before the re-hearing to consider special measures, ground rules and appropriate adjustments for the hearing of the trial.

G.4 Short hearings should not generally be listed before a judge such that they may delay the start or continuation of a trial at the Crown Court. It is envisaged that any such short hearing will be completed by 10.30am or start after 4.30pm.

G.5 Each Crown Court equipped with a video link with a prison must have in place arrangements for the conduct of PCMHs, other pre-trial hearings and sentencing hearings by video link.

Notifying sureties of hearing dates

G.6 Where a surety has entered into a recognizance in the magistrates' court in respect of a case allocated or sent to the Crown Court and where the bail order or recognizance refers to attendance at the first hearing in the Crown Court, the defendant should be reminded by the listing officer that the surety should attend the first hearing in the Crown Court in order to provide further recognizance. If attendance is not arranged, the defendant may be remanded in custody pending the recognisance being provided.

G.7 The Court should also notify sureties of the dates of the hearing at the Crown Court at which the defendant is ordered to appear in as far in advance as possible: see the observations of Parker LJ in *R v Crown Court at Reading ex p. Bello* [1992] 3 All ER 353.

Applications for Production Orders and Search Warrants

G.8 The use of production orders and search warrants involve the use of intrusive state powers that affect the rights and liberties of individuals. It is the responsibility of the court to ensure that those powers are not abused. To do so, the court must be presented with a properly completed application, on the appropriate form, which includes a summary of the investigation to provide the context for the order, a clear explanation of how the statutory requirements are fulfilled, and full and frank disclosure of anything that might undermine the basis for the application. Further directions on the proper making and consideration of such applications will be provided by Practice Direction. However, the complexity of the application must be taken into account in listing it such that the judge is afforded appropriate reading time and the hearing is given sufficient time for the issues to be considered thoroughly, and a short judgment given.

Confiscation and Related Hearings

G.9 Applications for restraint orders should be determined by the Resident Judge, or a judge nominated by the Resident Judge, at the Crown Court location at which they are lodged.

G.10 In order to prevent possible dissipation of assets of significant value, applications under the Proceeds of Crime Act 2002 should be considered urgent when lists are being fixed. In order to prevent potential prejudice, applications for the variation and discharge of orders, for the appointment of receivers, and applications to punish alleged breaches of orders as a contempt of court should similarly be treated as urgent and listed expeditiously.

Confiscation Hearings

G.11 It is important that confiscation hearings take place in good time after the defendant is convicted or sentenced.

Breach proceedings

G.12 As a general rule, proceedings to which CrimPR Part 32 applies (breach of community and other orders) should be brought in the court, and in case of the Crown Court at the Crown Court centre, at which the sentence was imposed, or in the magistrates' court at which the breach of a Crown Court order ordinarily would be dealt with. An exception to that general rule should be made, however, to reflect the application of CrimPR Part 1, the overriding objective, and the key listing principles at A above, where the defendant's home is significantly closer to another court with jurisdiction to determine the proceedings, in which case those proceedings should be brought in that court. If the court in which the breach proceedings are brought was not the sentencing court, or the magistrates' court for the Crown Court centre at which the sentence was passed, then the authority by which the proceedings are instituted must explain the reasons for choosing it. Any dispute over the proper venue for should be determined by the relevant Presiding Judges.

Appeals from magistrates' courts

G.13 As a general rule, the hearing in the Crown Court of an appeal to which CrimPR Part 34 applies (appeal against conviction or sentence from a magistrates' court) should take place at the Crown Court centre to which that magistrates' court ordinarily sends cases for trial or commits for sentence. This general rule applies irrespective of the location of the magistrates' court at which the case first began, if that was not the court at which the defendant was convicted, or sentenced, or both, because the reasons that led to the case being dealt with at a different magistrates' court may apply equally to the hearing of the appeal.

G.14 There are two exceptions to that general rule, however, each of which reflects the application of CrimPR Part 1, the overriding objective, and the key listing principles at A above. First, if on an appeal against conviction witnesses are required to give evidence in person then the appeal should be heard at the Crown Court centre which is the most conveniently situated for the majority of those witnesses. This exception is likely to apply where the defendant's conviction and sentence have been imposed at a magistrates' court distant from the place at which the offence occurred, perhaps because the defendant had failed to attend a hearing at the court for that area and subsequently was arrested for breach of bail and convicted and sentenced at another court. The information required of the parties to the appeal by CrimPR 34.3 and by the associated appeal forms will be essential to determining the most appropriate venue for the appeal. Second, where the appeal is against sentence only, or if, exceptionally, on an appeal against conviction no witnesses are required to give evidence in person, then then the appeal should be heard at the Crown Court centre which is the closest to the defendant's home. This exception is likely to apply where the defendant has been convicted and sentenced at a magistrates' court for the area in which the offence occurred but at a distance from the defendant's usual or present residence. This exception must not, however, be allowed to operate to the disadvantage of any victim of the offence who is expected to attend the sentencing in the Crown Court.

G.15 Once an appeal is submitted to the Crown Court, arrangements for its hearing, at that or at another Crown Court centre if appropriate, must be made by Crown Court staff under the direction of the Resident judge or Resident judges concerned. Any dispute over the proper venue for the appeal should be determined by the relevant Presiding Judges.

CPD XIII Annex 1: General Principles for the Deployment of the Judiciary in the Magistrates' Court CPD.XIII.x1

This distils the full deployment guidance issued in November 2012. The relevant sections dealing specifically with the allocation of work within the magistrates' court have been incorporated into this Practice Direction. It does not seek to replace the guidance in its entirety.

Presumptions

1. The presumptions which follow are intended to provide an acceptable and flexible framework establishing the deployment of the DJ (MC)s and magistrates. The system must be capable of adaptation to meet particular needs, whether of locality or caseload. In any event, the presumptions which follow are illustrative not exhaustive.
2. DJ(MC)s should generally (not invariably) be deployed in accordance with the following presumptions ('the Presumptions'):
   (a) Cases involving complex points of law and evidence.
   (b) Cases involving complex procedural issues.
   (c) Long cases (included on grounds of practicality).
   (d) Interlinked cases (given the need for consistency, together with their likely complexity and novelty).
   (e) Cases for which armed police officers are required in court, such as high end firearms cases.

(f) A share of the more routine business of the Court, including case management and pre-trial reviews, (for a variety of reasons, including the need for DJ(MC)s to have competence in all areas of work and the desirability of an equitable division of work between magistrates and DJ(MC)s, subject always to the interests of the administration of justice).
(g) Where appropriate, in supporting the training of magistrates.
(h) Occasionally, in mixed benches of DJ(MC)s and magistrates (with a particular view both to improving the case management skills of magistrates and to improving the culture of collegiality).
(i) In the short term tackling of particular local backlogs ('backlog busting'), sometimes in combination with magistrates from the local or (with the SPJ's approval) adjoining benches.

3. In accordance with current arrangements certain classes of cases necessarily require DJ(MC)s and have therefore been excluded from the above presumptions; these are as follows:
(a) Extradition;
(b) Terrorism;
(c) Prison Adjudications;
(d) Sex cases in the Youth Court as per Annex 2;
(e) Cases where the defendant is likely to be sentenced to a very large fine, see Annex 3;
(f) The Special Jurisdiction of the Chief Magistrate.

4. In formulating the Presumptions, the following considerations have been taken into account:
(a) The listing of cases is here, as elsewhere, a judicial function, see CPD XIII A.1. In the magistrates' courts the Judicial Business Group, subject to the supervision of the Presiding Judges of the circuit, is responsible for determining the day to day listing practice in that area. The day-to-day operation of that listing practice is the responsibility of the justices' clerk with the assistance of the listing officer.
(b) Equally, providing the training of magistrates is a responsibility of justices' clerks.
(c) It is best not to treat 'high profile' cases as a separate category but to consider their listing in the light of the principles and presumptions. The circumstances surrounding high profile cases do not permit ready generalisation, save that they are likely to require especially sensitive handling. Listing decisions involving such cases will often benefit from good communication at a local level between the justices' clerk, the DJ (MC) and the Bench Chairman.

Account must be taken of the need to maintain the competences of all members of the judiciary sitting in the magistrates' court.

5. The Special Jurisdiction of the Senior District Judge (Chief Magistrate) concerns cases which fall into the following categories:
i. cases with a terrorism connection;
ii. cases involving war crimes and crimes against humanity;
iii. matters affecting state security;
iv. cases brought under the Official Secrets Act;
v. offences involving royalty or parliament;
vi. offences involving diplomats;
vii. corruption of public officials;
viii. police officers charged with serious offences;
ix. cases of unusual sensitivity.

6. Where cases fall within the category of the Special Jurisdiction they must be heard by:-
i. the Senior District Judge (or if not available);
ii. the Deputy Senior District Judge (or if not available);
iii. a District Judge approved by the Senior District Judge or his/her deputy for the particular case.

7. Where a doubt may exist as to whether or not a case falls within the Special Jurisdiction, reference should always be made to the Senior District Judge or to the Deputy Senior District Judge for clarification.

CPD.XIII.x2 **CPD XIII Annex 2: Sexual Offences in the Youth Court**

Introduction

1. This annex sets out the procedure to be applied in the Youth Court in all cases involving allegations of sexual offences which are capable of being sent for trial at the Crown Court under the grave crime provisions.
2. This applies to all cases involving such charges, irrespective of the gravity of the allegation, the age of the defendant and / or the antecedent history of the defendant[1].

[1] So, for example, every allegation of sexual touching, under s3 of the Sexual Offences Act 2003, is covered by this protocol.

3. This does not alter the test[2] that the Youth Court must apply when determining whether a case is a 'grave crime'.
4. In the Crown Court, cases involving allegations of sexual offences frequently involve complex and sensitive issues and only those Circuit Judges and Recorders who have been specifically authorised and who have attended the appropriate Judicial College course may try this type of work.
5. A number of District Judges (Magistrates' Courts) have now undertaken training in dealing with these difficult cases and have been specifically authorised to hear cases involving serious sexual offences which fall short of requiring to be sent to the Crown Court ('an authorised DJ(MC)'). As such, a procedure similar to that of the Crown Court will now apply to allegations of sexual offences in the Youth Court.

Procedure

6. The determination of venue in the Youth Court is governed by section 51 Crime and Disorder Act 1998, which provides that the youth must be tried summarily unless charged with such a grave crime that long term detention is a realistic possibility[3], or that one of the other exceptions to this presumption arises.
7. Wherever possible such cases should be listed before an authorised DJ(MC), to decide whether the case falls within the grave crime provisions and should therefore be sent for trial. If jurisdiction is retained and the allegation involves actual, or attempted, penetrative activity, the case must be tried by an authorised DJ(MC). In all other cases, the authorised DJ(MC) must consider whether the case is so serious and / or complex that it must be tried by an authorised DJ(MC), or whether the case can be heard by any DJ(MC) or any Youth Court Bench.
8. If it is not practicable for an authorised DJ(MC) to determine venue, any DJ(MC) or any Youth Court Bench may consider that issue. If jurisdiction is retained, appropriate directions may be given but the case papers, including a detailed case summary and a note of any representations made by the parties, must be sent to an authorised DJ(MC) to consider. As soon as possible the authorised DJ(MC) must decide whether the case must be tried by an authorised DJ(MC) or whether the case is suitable to be heard by any DJ(MC) or any Youth Court Bench; however, if the case involves actual, or alleged, penetrative activity, the trial must be heard by an authorised DJ(MC).
9. Once an authorised DJ(MC) has decided that the case is one which must be tried by an authorised DJ(MC), and in all cases involving actual or alleged penetrative activity, all further procedural hearings should, so far as practicable, be heard by an authorised DJ(MC).

Cases remitted for sentence

10. All cases which are remitted for sentence from the Crown Court to the Youth Court should be listed for sentence before an authorised DJ(MC).

Arrangements for an authorised DJ(MC) to be appointed

11. Where a case is to be tried by an authorised DJ(MC) but no such Judge is available, the Bench Legal Adviser should contact the Chief Magistrates Office for an authorised DJ(MC) to be assigned.

CPD XIII Annex 3: Cases Involving Very Large Fines in the Magistrates' Court **CPD.XIII.x3**

1. This Annex applies when s. 85 Legal Aid, Sentencing and Punishment of Offenders Act 2012 comes into force and the magistrates' court has the power to impose a maximum fine of any amount.
2. An authorised DJ(MC) must deal with any allocation decision, trial and sentencing hearing in the following types of cases which are triable either way:
    a) Cases involving death or significant, life changing injury or a high risk of death or significant, life-changing injury;
    b) Cases involving substantial environmental damage or polluting material of a dangerous nature;
    c) Cases where major adverse effect on human health or quality of life, animal health or flora has resulted;
    d) Cases where major costs through clean up, site restoration or animal rehabilitation have been incurred;
    e) Cases where the defendant corporation has a turnover in excess of £10 million but does not exceed £250 million, and has acted in a deliberate, reckless or negligent manner;

[2] Set out in the Sentencing Guidelines Council's definitive guideline, entitled 'Overarching Principles — Sentencing Youths' Published by the Sentencing Guidelines Council in November 2009.
[3] Section 24(1) of the Magistrates Court Act 1980

f) Cases where the defendant corporation has a turnover in excess of £250 million;
g) Cases where the court will be expected to analyse complex company accounts;
h) High profile cases or ones of an exceptionally sensitive nature.

3. The prosecution agency must notify the justices' clerk where practicable of any case of the type mentioned in paragraph 2 of this Annex, no less than 7 days before the first hearing to ensure that an authorised DJ(MC) is available at the first hearing.
4. The justices' clerk shall contact the Office of the Chief Magistrate to ensure that an authorised DJ(MC) can be assigned to deal with such a case if there is not such a person available in the courthouse.
5. Where an authorised DJ(MC) is not appointed at the first hearing the court shall adjourn the case. The court shall ask the accused for an indication of his plea, but shall not allocate the case nor, if the accused indicates a guilty plea, sentence him, commit him for sentence, ask for a pre-sentence report or give any indication as to likely sentence that will be imposed. The justices' clerk shall ensure an authorised DJ(MC) is appointed for the following hearing.
6. When dealing with sentence, section 3 of the Powers of Criminal Courts (Sentenc[ing]) Act 2000 can be invoked where, despite the magistrates' court having maximum fine powers available to it, the offence or combination of offences make it so serious that the Crown Court should deal with it as though the person had been convicted on indictment.
7. An authorised DJ(MC) should consider allocating the case to the Crown Court or committing the accused for sentence.

CPD.XIII.x4 **CPD XIII Annex 4: Application This annex replaces the Protocol on the case management of Terrorism Cases issued in December 2006 by the President of the Queen's Bench Division**

1. This annex applies to 'terrorism cases'. For the purposes of this annex a case is a 'terrorism case' where:
   (a) one of the offences charged against any of the defendants is indictable only and it is alleged by the prosecution that there is evidence that it took place during an act of terrorism or for the purposes of terrorism as defined in s1 of the Terrorist Act 2000. This may include, but is not limited to:
      (i) murder;
      (ii) manslaughter;
      (iii) an offence under section 18 of the Offences against the Person Act 1861 (wounding with intent);
      (iv) an offence under section 23 or 24 of that Act (administering poison etc);
      (v) an offence under section 28 or 29 of that Act (explosives);
      (vi) an offence under section 2, 3 or 5 of the Explosive Substances Act 1883 (causing explosions);
      (vii) an offence under section 1(2) of the Criminal Damage Act 1971 (endangering life by damaging property);
      (viii) an offence under section 1 of the Biological Weapons Act 1974 (biological weapons);
      (ix) an offence under section 2 of the Chemical Weapons Act 1996 (chemical weapons);
      (x) an offence under section 56 of the Terrorism Act 2000 (directing a terrorist organisation);
      (xi) an offence under section 59 of that Act (inciting terrorism overseas);
      (xii) offences under (v), (vii) and (viii) above given jurisdiction by virtue of section 62 of that Act (terrorist bombing overseas); and
      (xiii) an offence under section 5 of the Terrorism Act 2006 (preparation of terrorism acts).
   (b) one of the offences charged is indictable only and includes an allegation by the prosecution of serious fraud that took place during an act of terrorism or for the purposes of terrorism as defined in s1 of the Terrorist Act 2000 and the prosecutor gives a notice under section 51B of the Crime and Disorder Act 1998 (Notices in serious or complex fraud cases);
   (c) one of the offences charged is indictable only, which includes an allegation that a defendant conspired, incited or attempted to commit an offence under sub paragraphs (1)(a) or (b) above; or
   (d) it is a case (which can be indictable only or triable either way) that a judge of the terrorism cases list (see paragraph 2(a) below) considers should be a terrorism case. In deciding whether a case not covered by subparagraphs (1)(a), (b) or (c) above should be a terrorism case, the judge may hear representations from the Crown Prosecution Service.

The terrorism cases list

2. (a) All terrorism cases, wherever they originate in England and Wales, will be managed in a list known as the 'terrorism cases list' by such judges of the High Court as are nominated by the President of the Queen's Bench Division.

(b) Such cases will be tried, unless otherwise directed by the President of the Queen's Bench Division, by a judge of the High Court as nominated by the President of the Queen's Bench Division.

3. The judges managing the terrorism cases referred to in paragraph 2(a) will be supported by the London and South Eastern Regional Co-ordinator's Office (the 'Regional Co-ordinator's Office'). An official of that office or an individual nominated by that office will act as the case progression officer for cases in that list for the purposes of CrimPR 3.4.

Procedure after charge

4. Immediately after a person has been charged in a terrorism case, anywhere in England and Wales, a representative of the Crown Prosecution Service will notify the person on the 24 hour rota for special jurisdiction matters at Westminster Magistrates' Court of the following information:
   (a) the full name of each defendant and the name of his solicitor of other legal representative, if known;
   (b) the charges laid;
   (c) the name and contact details of the Crown Prosecutor with responsibility for the case, if known; and
   (d) confirmation that the case is a terrorism case.
5. The person on the 24-hour rota will then ensure that all terrorism cases wherever they are charged in England and Wales are listed before the Chief Magistrate or other District Judge designated under the Terrorism Act 2000. Unless the Chief Magistrate or other District Judge designated under the Terrorism Act 2000 directs otherwise, the first appearance of all defendants accused of terrorism offences will be listed at Westminster Magistrates' Court.
6. In order to comply with section 46 of the Police and Criminal Evidence Act 1984, if a defendant in a terrorism case is charged at a police station within the local justice area in which Westminster Magistrates' Court is situated, the defendant must be brought before Westminster Magistrates' Court as soon as is practicable and in any event not later than the first sitting after he is charged with the offence. If a defendant in a terrorism case is charged in a police station outside the local justice area in which Westminster Magistrates' Court is situated, unless the Chief Magistrate or other designated judge directs otherwise, the defendant must be removed to that area as soon as is practicable. He must then be brought before Westminster Magistrates' Court as soon as is practicable after his arrival in the area and in any event not later than the first sitting of Westminster Magistrates' Court after his arrival in that area.
7. As soon as is practicable after charge a representative of the Crown Prosecution Service will also provide the Regional Listing Co-ordinator's Office with the information listed in paragraph 4 above.
8. The Regional Co-ordinator's Office will then ensure that the Chief Magistrate and the Legal Aid Agency have the same information.

Cases to be sent to the Crown Court under section 51 of the Crime and Disorder Act 1998

9. The court should ordinarily direct that the plea and trial preparation hearing should take place about 14 days after charge.
10. The sending magistrates' court should contact the Regional Listing Co-ordinator's Office who will be responsible for notifying the magistrates' court as to the relevant Crown Court to which to send the case.
11. In all terrorism cases, the magistrates' court case progression form for cases sent to the Crown Court under section 51 of the Crime and Disorder Act 1998 should not be used. Instead of the automatic directions set out in that form, the magistrates' court shall make the following directions to facilitate the preliminary hearing at the Crown Court:
    (a) three days prior to the preliminary hearing in the terrorism cases list, the prosecution must serve upon each defendant and the Regional Listing co-ordinator:
        (i) a preliminary summary of the case;
        (ii) the names of those who are to represent the prosecution, if known;
        (iii) an estimate of the length of the trial;
        (iv) a suggested provisional timetable which should generally include:
        - the general nature of further enquiries being made by the prosecution,
        - the time needed for the completion of such enquiries,
        - the time required by the prosecution to review the case,
        - a timetable for the phased service of the evidence,
        - the time for the provision by the Attorney General for his consent if necessary,
        - the time for service of the detailed defence case statement,
        - the date for the case management hearing, and
        - the estimated trial date;

(v) a preliminary statement of the possible disclosure issues setting out the nature and scale of the problem, including the amount of unused material, the manner in which the prosecution seeks to deal with these matters and a suggested timetable for discharging their statutory duty; and
(vi) any information relating to bail and custody time limits.
(b) one day prior to the preliminary hearing in the terrorist cases list, each defendant must serve in writing on the Regional Listing Co-ordinator and the prosecution:
(i) the proposed representation;
(ii) observations on the timetable; and
(iii) an indication of plea and the general nature of the defence.

Cases to be sent to the Crown Court after the prosecutor gives notice under section 51B of the Crime and Disorder Act 1998

12. If a terrorism case is to be sent to the Crown Court after the prosecutor gives a notice under section 51B of the Crime and Disorder Act 1998 the magistrates' court should proceed as in paragraphs 9-11 above.
13. When a terrorism case is so sent or transferred the case will go into the terrorism list and be managed by a judge as described in paragraph 2(a) above.

The plea and trial preparation hearing at the Crown Court

14. At the plea and trial preparation hearing, the judge will determine whether the case is one to remain in the terrorism list and if so, give directions setting the provisional timetable.
15. The Legal Aid Agency must attend the hearing by an authorised officer to assist the court.

Use of video links

16. Unless a judge otherwise directs, all Crown Court hearings prior to the trial will be conducted by video link for all defendants in custody.

Security

17. The police service and the prison service will provide the Regional Listing Co-ordinator's Office with an initial joint assessment of the security risks associated with any court appearance by the defendants within 14 days of charge. Any subsequent changes in circumstances or the assessment of risk which have the potential to impact upon the choice of trial venue will be notified to the Regional Listing Co-ordinator's Office immediately.

CPD.XIII.x5 **CPD XIII Annex 5: Management of cases from the organised crime division of the Crown Prosecution Service This annex replaces the guidance issued by the Senior Presiding Judge in January 2014**

1. The Organised Crime Division (OCD) of the CPS is responsible for prosecution of cases from the National Crime Agency (NCA). Typically, these cases involve more than one defendant, are voluminous and raise complex and specialised issues of law. It is recognised that if not closely managed, such cases have the potential to cost vast amounts of public money and take longer than necessary.
2. This annex applies to all cases handled by the OCD.

Designated court centres

3. Subject to the overriding discretion of the Presiding Judges of the circuit, OCD cases should normally be heard at Designated Court Centres (DCC). The process of designating court centres for this purpose has taken into account geographical factors and the size, security and facilities of those court centres. The designated court centres are:
(a) Northern Circuit: Manchester, Liverpool and Preston.
(b) North Eastern Circuit: Leeds, Newcastle and Sheffield.
(c) Western Circuit: Bristol and Winchester.
(d) South Eastern Circuit (not including London): Reading, Luton, Chelmsford, Ipswich, Maidstone, Lewes and Hove.
(e) South Eastern Circuit (London only): Southwark, Blackfriars, Kingston, Woolwich, Croydon and the Central Criminal Court.
(f) Midland Circuit: Birmingham, Leicester and Nottingham.
(g) Wales Circuit: Cardiff, Swansea and Mold.

Selection of designated court centres

4. If arrests are made in different parts of the country and the OCD seeks to have all defendants tried by one Crown Court, the OCD will, at the earliest opportunity, write to the relevant court cluster manager with a recommendation as to the appropriate designated

court centre, requesting that the decision be made by the relevant Presiding Judges. In the event that the designated court centre within one region is unable to accommodate a case, for example, as a result of a custody time limit expiry date, consideration may be given to transferring the case to a DCC in another region with the consent of the relevant Presiding Judges.

5. There will be a single point of contact person at the OCD for each HMCTS region, to assist listing co-ordinators.
6. The single contact person for each HMCTS region will be the relevant Cluster Manager, with the exception of the South Eastern Circuit, where the appropriate person will be the Regional Listing Co-ordinator.

Designation of the trial judge

7. The trial judge will be assigned by the Presiding Judge at the earliest opportunity, and in accordance with CPD XIII Listing E: Allocation of Business within the Crown Court. Where the trial judge is unable to continue with the case, all further pre-trial hearings should be by a single judge until a replacement has been assigned.

Procedure after charge

8. Within 24 hours of the laying of a charge, a representative of the OCD will notify the relevant Cluster Manager of the following information to enable an agreement to be reached between that Cluster Manager and the reviewing CPS lawyer before the first appearance as to the DCC to which the case should be sent:
   (a) the full name of each defendant and the name of his legal representatives, if known;
   (b) the charges laid; and
   (c) the name and contact details of the Crown Prosecutor with responsibility for the case.

Exceptions

9. Where it is not possible to have a case dealt with at a DCC, the OCD should liaise closely with the relevant Cluster Manager and the Presiding Judges to ensure that the cases are sent to the most appropriate court centre. This will, among other things, take into account the location of the likely source of the case, convenience of the witnesses, travelling distance for OCD staff and facilities at the court centres.
10. In the event that it is allocated to a non-designated court centre, the OCD should be permitted to make representations in writing to the Presiding Judges within 14 days as to why the venue is not suitable. The Presiding Judges will consider the reasons and, if necessary, hold a hearing. The CPS may renew their request at any stage where further reasons come to light that may affect the original decision on venue.
11. Nothing in this annex should be taken to remove the right of the defence to make representations as to the venue.

SENTENCING GUIDELINES

Sentencing Guidelines

Issued by the Sentencing Council SG0-1

This is an edited version of the sentencing guidelines, both those originally issued by the Sentencing Guidelines Council and those issued by the Sentencing Council for England and Wales which are now published direct to the Sentencing Council website: https://www.sentencingcouncil.org.uk/. By virtue of the Coroners and Justice Act 2009 (Commencement No. 4, Transitional and Saving Provisions) Order 2010 (SI 2010 No. 816), art. 7, guidelines issued by the SGC 'are to be treated as guidelines issued by the Sentencing Council'. For more on the status of guidelines and the duty of courts to follow them, see **E1.4** in the main work.

Crown Court and Magistrates' Court

The Sentencing Council produces sentencing guidelines for use in the Magistrates' Court and the Crown Court. The Overarching Guidelines are common to both. This section includes all of the Crown Court offence guidelines by offence type and many of these are also triable either way. For those offence guidelines which are included solely in the Magistrates' Court Sentencing Guidelines see **SG10**.

The application of sentencing principles during the Covid-19 emergency

On 23 June 2020 the Sentencing Council issued a statement on Covid-19 and the impact on conditions in prisons and the potentially heavier impact of custodial sentences on offenders and their families. The statement noted that well-established sentencing principles are familiar to judges and magistrates and were reaffirmed by the Lord Chief Justice when giving the judgment of the Court of Appeal in *Manning* [2020] EWCA Crim 592, [2020] 4 WLR 77, and that the purpose of the statement was to help to clarify the position for those less familiar with the principles or not involved in the criminal justice system.

In *Manning*, the Lord Chief Justice observed (at [41]) that the impact of the Covid-19 emergency on prisons is well-known, and continued as follows:

> The current conditions in prisons represent a factor which can properly be taken into account in deciding whether to suspend a sentence. In accordance with established principles, any court will take into account the likely impact of a custodial sentence upon an offender and, where appropriate, upon others as well. Judges and magistrates can, therefore, and in our judgment should, keep in mind that the impact of a custodial sentence is likely to be heavier during the current emergency than it would otherwise be. Those in custody are, for example, confined to their cells for much longer periods than would otherwise be the case—currently, 23 hours a day. They are unable to receive visits. Both they and their families are likely to be anxious about the risk of the transmission of Covid-19.
>
> 42. Applying ordinary principles, where a court is satisfied that a custodial sentence must be imposed, the likely impact of that sentence continues to be relevant to the further decisions as to its necessary length and whether it can be suspended. Moreover, sentencers can and should also bear in mind the Reduction in Sentence Guideline. That makes clear that a guilty plea may result in a different type of sentence or enable a magistrates' court to retain jurisdiction, rather than committing for sentence.

Throughout the sentencing process, and in considering all the circumstances of the individual case, the court must bear in mind the practical realities of the effects of the current health emergency. The court should consider whether increased weight should be given to mitigating factors, and should keep in mind that the impact of immediate imprisonment is likely to be particularly heavy for some groups of offenders or their families.

In addition, when applying the *Reduction in sentence for a guilty plea* guideline, the court must consider the exceptions in that guideline. The exceptions include whether there were particular circumstances affecting the defendant's ability to understand the allegations or to receive the advice necessary before pleading guilty, or where the defendant pleads guilty to, and is then convicted of, a different offence from that originally charged. In making these considerations, the court must keep in mind the practical difficulties of defendants accessing legal advice during the present emergency.

[For further information on Covid-19 see the Special Supplement.]

Treatment, Paragraph Numbering and Standard Steps by Offence Type SG0-2

This work uses 'SG1-1', 'SG1-2' (etc.) paragraph numbers as a cross-referencing aid for readers. The guidelines as provided by the Sentencing Council are not individually numbered and are presented as a group of Overarching Guidelines and a collection of individual offence guidelines associated with an offence type.

The following table lists the sentencing guidelines by type, the Effective From dates, and the paragraph at which the guidelines can be located:

Overarching Guidelines		**SG Effective From Date**	**BCP Paragraph**
Allocation		01 March 2016	SG1
Domestic Abuse		24 May 2018	SG6
General Guideline: Overarching Principles		01 October 2019	SG2
Imposition of Community and Custodial Sentences		01 February 2017	SG9
Offences Taken Into Consideration		11 June 2012	SG3
Reduction in Sentence for a Guilty Plea (First Hearing on or after 1 June 2017)		01 June 2017	SG5
Sentencing Children and Young People		01 June 2017	SG8
Sentencing Offenders with Mental Disorders, Developmental Disorders, or Neurological Impairments		01 October 2020	SG7
Totality		11 June 2012	SG4
Magistrates' Court Sentencing Guidelines			**SG10**
Offences on indictment or triable either way			
Offence Type	**Number of Guidelines**	**SG Effective From Date**	**BCP Paragraph**
Arson and Criminal Damage	7	01 October 2019	SG11
Assault Offences	6	13 June 2011	SG12
Attempted Murder	1	27 July 2009	SG13
Bladed Articles and Offensive Weapons	11 including one related to Sentencing Children and Young People	01 June 2018	SG14
Breach Offences	15	01 October 2018	SG15
Burglary Offences	4 including one related to Theft	16 January 2012	SG19
Causing Death by Driving	4	15 July 2008	SG22
Child Cruelty	4	01 January 2019	SG20
Dangerous Dog Offences	3	01 July 2016	SG21
Drug Offences	8	1 April 2021	SG35
Environmental Offences	12	01 July 2014	SG24
Fraud, Bribery, and Money Laundering Offences	19	01 October 2014	SG26
Health and Safety Offences	5	01 February 2016	SG28
Intimidatory Offences	7	01 October 2018	SG27
Manslaughter	4	01 November 2018	SG25
Public Order	6	01 January 2020	SG29
Robbery Offences	4 including one related to Sentencing Children and Young People	01 April 2016	SG30
Sexual Offences	54 including 4 related to Sentencing Children and Young People	01 April 2014	SG31
Terrorism Offences	17	27 April 2018	SG32
Theft Offences	5 including one related to Burglary	01 February 2016	SG33
Firearms Offences	8	1 January 2021	SG34

The following table of offences lists all of the offence specific guidelines in alphabetical order indicating where the standard steps apply.

Guideline	Assistance to prosecution step	Guilty plea step	Reasons step	Time on bail step
Abstracting electricity	3	4	7	8
Abuse of position of trust: sexual activity in the presence of a child/Abuse of position of trust: causing a child to watch a sexual act	3	4	8	9
Abuse of position of trust: sexual activity with a child/Abuse of position of trust: causing or inciting a child to engage in sexual activity	3	4	8	9
Administering a substance with intent	3	4	8	9
Affray	3	4	8	9
Aggravated burglary	3	4	8	9
Alcohol sale offences (Revised 2017)	3	4	7	n/a
Animal cruelty (Revised 2017)	3	4	7	8
Arranging or facilitating the commission of a child sex offence	n/a	n/a	n/a	n/a
Arson (criminal damage by fire)	3	4	8	9
Arson/criminal damage with intent to endanger life or reckless as to whether life endangered	3	4	8	9
Assault by penetration	3	4	8	9
Assault occasioning actual bodily harm/Racially or religiously aggravated ABH	3	4	8	9
Assault of a child under 13 by penetration	3	4	8	9
Assault on a police constable in execution of his duty	3	4	7	8
Assault with intent to resist arrest	3	4	8	9
Attempted murder	n/a	n/a	n/a	n/a
Benefit Fraud	3	4	7	8
Bladed articles and offensive weapons – possession	4	5	8	9
Bladed articles and offensive weapons – threats	4	5	8	9
Bladed articles and offensive weapons (possession and threats) – children and young people	n/a	4	n/a	n/a
Brakes defective	n/a	n/a	n/a	n/a
Brakes defective (over 3.5 tonnes)	n/a	n/a	n/a	n/a
Breach of a community order	n/a	n/a	n/a	n/a
Breach of a criminal behaviour order	3	4	7	8
Breach of a protective order (restraining and non-molestation orders)	3	4	7	8
Breach of a sexual harm prevention order	3	4	7	8
Breach of a suspended sentence order	n/a	n/a	n/a	n/a
Breach of disqualification from acting as a director	3	4	7	8
Breach of disqualification from keeping an animal	3	4	7	8
Breach of post-sentence supervision	n/a	n/a	n/a	n/a
Breach of supervision default order	n/a	n/a	n/a	n/a

Guideline	Assistance to prosecution step	Guilty plea step	Reasons step	Time on bail step
Breach offences (other)	n/a	n/a	n/a	n/a
Bribery	3	4	7	8
Care workers: sexual activity in the presence of a person with a mental disorder/Care workers: causing a person with a mental disorder to watch a sexual act	3	4	8	9
Care workers: sexual activity with a person with a mental disorder/Care workers: causing or inciting sexual activity	3	4	8	9
Careless Driving (drive without due care and attention) (Revised 2017)	3	4	7	n/a
Carrying a firearm in a public place	4	5	8	9
Causing a person to engage in sexual activity without consent	3	4	8	9
Causing death by careless driving when under the influence of drink or drugs, etc	n/a	n/a	n/a	n/a
Causing death by careless or inconsiderate driving	n/a	n/a	n/a	n/a
Causing death by dangerous driving	n/a	n/a	n/a	n/a
Causing death by driving: unlicensed, disqualified or uninsured drivers	n/a	n/a	n/a	n/a
Causing grievous bodily harm with intent to do grievous bodily harm/Wounding with intent to do GBH	3	4	8	9
Causing or allowing a child to suffer serious physical harm/Causing or allowing a child to die	3	4	9	10
Causing or inciting a child under 13 to engage in sexual activity	3	4	8	9
Causing or inciting prostitution for gain/Controlling prostitution for gain	3	4	8	9
Causing or inciting sexual exploitation of a child/Controlling a child in relation to sexual exploitation/Arranging or facilitating sexual exploitation of a child	3	4	8	9
Child sex offences committed by children or young persons (sections 9–12) (offender under 18)/Sexual activity with a child family member (offender under 18)/Inciting a child family member to engage in sexual activity (offender under 18)	n/a	n/a	n/a	n/a
Collection of terrorist information	3	4	7	8
Committing an offence with intent to commit a sexual offence	n/a	n/a	n/a	n/a
Common assault/Racially or religiously aggravated common assault	3	4	8	9
Communication network offences (Revised 2017)	3	4	7	8
Condition of vehicle/accessories/equipment involving danger of injury – buses/goods vehicles	n/a	n/a	n/a	n/a
Condition of vehicle/accessories/equipment involving danger of injury	n/a	n/a	n/a	n/a

Guideline	Assistance to prosecution step	Guilty plea step	Reasons step	Time on bail step
Controlling or coercive behaviour in an intimate or family relationship	3	4	7	8
Corporate manslaughter	5	6	9	n/a
Corporate offenders: fraud, bribery and money laundering	6	7	10	n/a
Criminal damage (other than by fire) value exceeding £5,000/Racially or religiously aggravated criminal damage	3	4	7	8
Criminal damage (other than by fire) value not exceeding £5,000/Racially or religiously aggravated criminal damage	3	4	7	8
Cruelty to a child – assault and ill treatment, abandonment, neglect and failure to protect	3	4	9	10
Dangerous driving	n/a	n/a	n/a	n/a
Dangerous parking	n/a	n/a	n/a	n/a
Disclosing private sexual images	3	4	7	8
Disorderly behaviour with intent to cause harassment, alarm or distress/Racially or religiously aggravated disorderly behaviour with intent to cause harassment, alarm or distress	3	4	8	9
Disorderly behaviour/Racially or religiously aggravated disorderly behaviour	3	4	7	8
Domestic burglary	3	4	8	9
Drive in reverse or wrong way on motorway	n/a	n/a	n/a	n/a
Drive in reverse or wrong way on slip road	n/a	n/a	n/a	n/a
Drive off carriageway (central reservation or hard shoulder)	n/a	n/a	n/a	n/a
Drive otherwise than in accordance with licence	n/a	n/a	n/a	n/a
Drive otherwise than in accordance with licence (where could be covered)	n/a	n/a	n/a	n/a
Drive whilst disqualified (Revised 2017)	3	4	7	8
Drug driving (guidance only)	n/a	n/a	n/a	n/a
Drug offences involving newer and less common drugs	n/a	n/a	n/a	n/a
Drugs – class A – fail to attend/remain for initial assessment	3	4	7	n/a
Drugs – class A – fail/refuse to provide a sample	3	4	7	n/a
Drunk and disorderly in a public place (Revised 2017)	3	4	7	n/a
Encouragement of terrorism	3	4	7	8
Engaging in sexual activity in the presence of a child/Causing a child to watch a sexual act	3	4	8	9
Engaging in sexual activity in the presence of a person with mental disorder impeding choice/Causing a person, with mental disorder impeding choice, to watch a sexual act	3	4	8	9

Guideline	Assistance to prosecution step	Guilty plea step	Reasons step	Time on bail step
Engaging in sexual activity in the presence procured by inducement, threat or deception, of a person with mental disorder/Causing a person with a mental disorder to watch a sexual act by inducement, threat or deception	3	4	8	9
Environmental offences (other)	n/a	n/a	n/a	n/a
Exceed permitted driving time/periods of duty	n/a	n/a	n/a	n/a
Excess Alcohol (drive/attempt to drive) (Revised 2017)	3	4	7	8
Excess Alcohol (in charge) (Revised 2017)	3	4	7	8
Exhaust defective	n/a	n/a	n/a	n/a
Exhaust emission	n/a	n/a	n/a	n/a
Explosive substances (terrorism only)	3	4	9	10
Exposure	3	4	8	9
Fail to comply with notification requirements	3	4	7	8
Fail to comply with police constable directing traffic	n/a	n/a	n/a	n/a
Fail to comply with traffic sign (e.g. give way sign, keep left sign, temporary signs)	n/a	n/a	n/a	n/a
Fail to comply with traffic sign (e.g. red traffic light, stop sign, double white lines, no entry sign)	n/a	n/a	n/a	n/a
Fail to co-operate with preliminary (roadside) breath test	n/a	n/a	n/a	n/a
Fail to give information of driver's identity as required	n/a	n/a	n/a	n/a
Fail to keep/return written record sheets	n/a	n/a	n/a	n/a
Fail to notify change of ownership to DVLA	n/a	n/a	n/a	n/a
Fail to produce insurance certificate	n/a	n/a	n/a	n/a
Fail to produce test certificate	n/a	n/a	n/a	n/a
Fail to provide specimen for analysis (drive/attempt to drive) (Revised 2017)	3	4	7	8
Fail to provide specimen for analysis (in charge) (Revised 2017)	3	4	7	8
Fail to stop when required by police constable	n/a	n/a	n/a	n/a
Fail to stop/report road accident (Revised 2017)	3	4	7	8
Fail to use appropriate child car seat	n/a	n/a	n/a	n/a
Failing to protect girl from risk of genital mutilation	3	4	8	9
Failure to disclose information about acts of terrorism	3	4	7	8
Failure to surrender to bail	3	4	7	8
Falsify or alter records with intent to deceive	n/a	n/a	n/a	n/a
Firearm, carrying in a public place	n/a	n/a	n/a	n/a
Firearms – possession by person prohibited	3	4	7	8
Firearms – possession of a prohibited weapon	4	5	8	9
Firearms – possession with intent – other offences	4	5	9	10

Guideline	Assistance to prosecution step	Guilty plea step	Reasons step	Time on bail step
Firearms – possession with intent to cause fear to violence	4	5	9	10
Firearms – possession with intent endanger life	4	5	9	10
Firearms – possession without certificate	3	4	7	8
Firearms – Transfer and manufacture	4	5	8	9
Football related offences (Revised 2017)	3	4	7	n/a
Fraud	3	4	7	8
Fraudulent evasion of a prohibition by bringing into or taking out of the UK a controlled drug	4	5	8	9
Funding terrorism	3	4	7	8
Going equipped for theft or burglary	3	4	7	8
Gross negligence manslaughter	3	4	8	9
Handling stolen goods	3	4	7	8
Harassment (fear of violence)/Stalking (fear of violence)/Racially or religiously aggravated harassment (fear of violence)/stalking (fear of violence)	3	4	8	9
Harassment/Stalking/Racially or religiously aggravated harassment/stalking	3	4	7	8
Identity documents – possess false/another's/improperly obtained	n/a	n/a	n/a	n/a
Importing or exporting a psychoactive substance	3	4	7	8
Individuals: Breach of duty of employer towards employees and non-employees/Breach of duty of self-employed to others/Breach of duty of employees at work/Breach of Health and Safety regulations/Secondary liability	4	5	8	9
Individuals: Breach of food safety and food hygiene regulations	4	5	8	9
Individuals: Unauthorised or harmful deposit, treatment or disposal etc of waste/Illegal discharges to air, land and water	7	8	11	12
Inducement, threat or deception to procure sexual activity with a person with a mental disorder/Causing a person with a mental disorder to engage in or agree to engage in sexual activity by inducement, threat or deception	3	4	8	9
Inflicting grievous bodily harm/Unlawful wounding/Racially or religiously aggravated GBH/Unlawful wounding	3	4	8	9
Keeping a brothel used for prostitution	3	4	7	8
Learner driver or excluded vehicle	n/a	n/a	n/a	n/a
Lights defective	n/a	n/a	n/a	n/a
Make U turn on motorway	n/a	n/a	n/a	n/a
Making Off Without Payment	3	4	7	8
Manslaughter by reason of diminished responsibility	6	7	10	11
Manslaughter by reason of loss of control	3	4	8	9
Meeting a child following sexual grooming	3	4	8	9

Guideline	Assistance to prosecution step	Guilty plea step	Reasons step	Time on bail step
Money laundering	3	4	7	8
Motoring offences appropriate for imposition of fine or discharge	n/a	n/a	n/a	n/a
No excise licence	n/a	n/a	n/a	n/a
No goods vehicle plating certificate	n/a	n/a	n/a	n/a
No goods vehicle test certificate	n/a	n/a	n/a	n/a
No insurance (Revised 2017)	3	4	7	n/a
No operators licence	n/a	n/a	n/a	n/a
No test certificate	n/a	n/a	n/a	n/a
Non-domestic burglary	3	4	8	9
Number of passengers or way carried involving danger of injury	n/a	n/a	n/a	n/a
Number of passengers or way carried involving danger of injury (over 3.5 tonnes)	n/a	n/a	n/a	n/a
Obstruct/resist a police constable in execution of duty (Revised 2017)	3	4	7	n/a
Organisations: Breach of duty of employer towards employees and non-employees/Breach of duty of self-employed to others/Breach of Health and Safety regulations	5	6	9	n/a
Organisations: Breach of food safety and food hygiene regulations	5	6	9	n/a
Organisations: Unauthorised or harmful deposit, treatment or disposal etc of waste/Illegal discharges to air, land and water	8	9	12	n/a
Overloading/exceeding axle weight	n/a	n/a	n/a	n/a
Overloading/exceeding axle weight (over 3.5 tonnes)	n/a	n/a	n/a	n/a
Owner or person in charge of a dog dangerously out of control in any place in England or Wales (whether or not a public place)	3	4	7	8
Owner or person in charge of a dog dangerously out of control in any place in England or Wales (whether or not a public place) where a person is injured	3	4	7	8
Owner or person in charge of a dog dangerously out of control in any place in England or Wales (whether or not a public place) where an assistance dog is injured or killed	3	4	7	8
Owner or person in charge of a dog dangerously out of control in any place in England or Wales (whether or not a public place) where death is caused	3	4	7	8
Paying for the sexual services of a child	3	4	8	9
Pelican/zebra crossing contravention	n/a	n/a	n/a	n/a
Permitting premises to be used	4	5	8	9
Position or manner in which load secured (not involving danger)	n/a	n/a	n/a	n/a
Position or manner in which load secured (not involving danger) (over 3.5 tonnes)	n/a	n/a	n/a	n/a

Guideline	Assistance to prosecution step	Guilty plea step	Reasons step	Time on bail step
Possession for terrorist purposes	3	4	9	10
Possession of a controlled drug	3	4	7	8
Possession of a prohibited dog/Breeding, selling, exchanging or advertising a prohibited dog	3	4	7	8
Possession of articles for use in frauds/Making or supplying articles for use in frauds	3	4	7	8
Possession of indecent photograph of child/ Indecent photographs of children	3	4	8	9
Preparation of terrorist acts	3	4	9	10
Producing a psychoactive substance	3	4	7	8
Production of a controlled drug/Cultivation of cannabis plant	4	5	8	9
Proscribed organisations – membership	3	4	7	8
Proscribed organisations – support	3	4	7	8
Racial hatred offences/Hatred against persons on religious grounds or grounds of sexual orientation	3	4	7	8
Railway fare evasion (Revised 2017)	3	4	7	n/a
Rape	3	4	8	9
Rape of a child under 13	3	4	8	9
Revenue fraud	3	4	7	8
Riot	3	4	8	9
Robbery – dwelling	3	4	8	9
Robbery – professionally planned commercial	3	4	8	9
Robbery – Sentencing children and young people	n/a	see next tab	n/a	n/a
Robbery – street and less sophisticated commercial	3	4	8	9
School non-attendance (Revised 2017)	3	4	7	n/a
Seat belt offences	n/a	n/a	n/a	n/a
Sex with an adult relative: penetration/Sex with an adult relative: consenting to penetration	3	4	8	9
Sexual activity in a public lavatory	3	4	7	n/a
Sexual activity with a child family member/ Inciting a child family member to engage in sexual activity	3	4	8	9
Sexual activity with a child/Causing or inciting a child to engage in sexual activity	3	4	8	9
Sexual activity with a person with a mental disorder impeding choice/Causing or inciting a person, with a mental disorder impeding choice, to engage in sexual activity	3	4	8	9
Sexual assault	3	4	8	9
Sexual assault of a child under 13	3	4	8	9
Sexual offences – historic	n/a	n/a	n/a	n/a
Sexual offences – Sentencing children and young people	n/a	see next tab	n/a	n/a
Speed limiter not used or incorrectly calibrated	n/a	n/a	n/a	n/a

Guideline	Assistance to prosecution step	Guilty plea step	Reasons step	Time on bail step
Speeding (Revised 2017)	3	4	7	n/a
Steering defective	n/a	n/a	n/a	n/a
Steering defective (over 3.5 tonnes)	n/a	n/a	n/a	n/a
Stop on hard shoulder	n/a	n/a	n/a	n/a
Supplying or offering to supply a controlled drug/Possession of a controlled drug with intent to supply it to another	4	5	8	9
Tachograph not used/not working	n/a	n/a	n/a	n/a
Taxi touting/soliciting for hire (Revised 2017)	3	4	7	n/a
Terrorism offences	n/a	n/a	n/a	n/a
Theft – general	3	4	7	8
Theft from a shop or stall	3	4	7	8
Threatening behaviour – fear or provocation of violence/Racially or religiously aggravated threatening behaviour – fear or provocation of violence	3	4	8	9
Threats to destroy or damage property	3	4	7	8
Threats to kill	3	4	8	9
Trade mark, unauthorised use of etc.	n/a	n/a	n/a	n/a
Trafficking people for sexual exploitation	3	4	8	9
Trespass with intent to commit a sexual offence	3	4	8	9
TV licence payment evasion (Revised 2017)	3	4	7	n/a
Tyres defective	n/a	n/a	n/a	n/a
Tyres defective – buses/goods vehicles	n/a	n/a	n/a	n/a
Unfit through drink or drugs (drive/attempt to drive) (Revised 2017)	3	4	7	8
Unfit through drink or drugs (in charge) (Revised 2017)	3	4	7	8
Unlawful act manslaughter	3	4	8	9
Use of mobile telephone	n/a	n/a	n/a	n/a
Vehicle in prohibited lane	n/a	n/a	n/a	n/a
Vehicle interference (Revised 2017)	3	4	7	8
Vehicle licence/registration fraud	n/a	n/a	n/a	n/a
Vehicle taking (aggravated). Damage caused to property other than the vehicle in accident or damage caused to vehicle	n/a	n/a	n/a	n/a
Vehicle taking (aggravated). Dangerous driving or accident causing injury	n/a	n/a	n/a	n/a
Vehicle taking, without consent (Revised 2017)	3	4	7	8
Violent disorder	3	4	8	9
Voyeurism	3	4	8	9
Walk on motorway, slip road or hard shoulder	n/a	n/a	n/a	n/a
Weight, position or distribution of load or manner in which load secured involving danger of injury	n/a	n/a	n/a	n/a

Guideline	Assistance to prosecution step	Guilty plea step	Reasons step	Time on bail step
Weight, position or distribution of load or manner in which load secured involving danger of injury (over 3.5 tonnes)	n/a	n/a	n/a	n/a
Witness intimidation	n/a	n/a	n/a	n/a

Equal Treatment Bench Book SG0-3

Guideline users should be aware that the *Equal Treatment Bench Book* covers important aspects of fair treatment and disparity of outcomes for different groups in the criminal justice system. It provides guidance which sentencers are encouraged to take into account wherever applicable, to ensure that there is fairness for all involved in court proceedings.

Applicability SG0-4

In accordance with section 120 of the Coroners and Justice Act 2009, the Sentencing Council issues definitive guidelines. They apply to all individual offenders aged 18 and older and organisations that are sentenced on or after the effective date of the guideline, regardless of the date of the offence. General principles to be considered in the sentencing of youths are in the Sentencing Council's definitive guideline, Overarching Principles—Sentencing Children and Young People [see **SG-8**].

Section 59(1) of the Sentencing Code provides that:

Every court –

1. must, in sentencing an offender, follow any sentencing guideline which is relevant to the offender's case, and
2. must, in exercising any other function relating to the sentencing of offenders, follow any sentencing guidelines which are relevant to the exercise of the function,

unless the court is satisfied that it would be contrary to the interests of justice to do so.

This guideline applies only to individual offenders aged 18 and older or organisations.

Following these guidelines SG0-5

When sentencing an offender, every court is under a statutory obligation to follow any relevant sentencing guideline unless it would be contrary to the interests of justice to do so (Sentencing Code, s.59(1)). If a court imposes a sentence outside the range indicated in an offence specific guideline, it is obliged to state its reasons for doing so (Sentencing Code, s.52(6)).

When to use these guidelines

- These guidelines apply to sentencing in a magistrates' court whatever the composition of the court. They cover offences for which sentences are frequently imposed in a magistrates' court when dealing with adult offenders.
- They also apply to allocation (mode of trial) decisions. When dealing with an either way offence for which there is no plea or an indication of a not guilty plea, these guidelines will be relevant to the allocation decision and should be consulted at this stage to assess the likely sentence. Reference should be made to the Allocation guideline.
- These guidelines apply also to the Crown Court when dealing with appeals against sentences imposed in a magistrates' court and when sentencing for summary only offences.

The offence guidelines include two structures: pre-Sentencing Council guidelines (created by the Sentencing Guidelines Council) and Sentencing Council guidelines.

Using pre-Sentencing Council guidelines SG0-6

This section explains the key decisions involved in the sentencing process for SGC guidelines.

1. Assess offence seriousness (culpability and harm)

Offence seriousness is the starting point for sentencing under the Sentencing Code. The court's assessment of offence seriousness will:

Sentencing Guidelines

- determine which of the sentencing thresholds has been crossed;
- indicate whether a custodial, community or other sentence is the most appropriate;
- be the key factor in deciding the length of a custodial sentence, the onerousness of requirements to be incorporated in a community sentence and the amount of any fine imposed.

When considering the seriousness of any offence, the court must consider the offender's culpability in committing the offence and any harm which the offence caused, was intended to cause, or might foreseeably have caused (Sentencing Code, s.63). In using these guidelines, this assessment should be approached in two stages.

2. **Offence seriousness (culpability and harm)**

A. Identify the appropriate starting point

The guidelines set out examples of the nature of activity which may constitute the offence, progressing from less to more serious conduct, and provide a starting point based on a **first time offender pleading not guilty**. The guidelines also specify a sentencing range for each example of activity. Within the guidelines, a first time offender is a person who does not have a conviction which, by virtue of section 65 of the Sentencing Code, must be treated as an aggravating factor.

Sentencers should begin by considering which of the examples of offence activity corresponds most closely to the circumstances of the particular case in order to identify the appropriate starting point:

- where the starting point is a fine, this is indicated as band A, B or C;
- where the community sentence threshold is passed, the guideline sets out whether the starting point should be a low, medium or high level community order. For more information, see Imposition of Community and Custodial Sentences;
- where the starting point is a custodial sentence, see Imposition of Community and Custodial Sentence.

The Council's definitive guideline Overarching Principles: Seriousness, published 16 December 2004, identified four levels of culpability for sentencing purposes (intention, recklessness, knowledge and negligence). The starting points in the individual offence guidelines assume that culpability is at the highest level applicable to the offence (often, but not always, intention). Where a lower level of culpability is present, this should be taken into account.

B. Consider the effect of aggravating and mitigating factors

Once the starting point has been identified, the court can add to or reduce this to reflect any aggravating or mitigating factors that impact on the culpability of the offender and/or harm caused by the offence to reach a provisional sentence. Any factors contained in the description of the activity used to reach the starting point must not be counted again. The range is the bracket into which the provisional sentence will normally fall after having regard to factors which aggravate or mitigate the seriousness of the offence. However:

- the court is not precluded from going outside the range where the facts justify it;
- previous convictions which aggravate the seriousness of the current offence may take the provisional sentence beyond the range, especially where there are significant other aggravating factors present.

In addition, where an offender is being sentenced for multiple offences, the court's assessment of the totality of the offending may result in a sentence above the range indicated for the individual offences, including a sentence of a different type. See the definitive guideline on Totality for more information. The guidelines identify aggravating and mitigating factors which may be particularly relevant to each individual offence. These include some factors drawn from the general list of aggravating and mitigating factors in the Council's definitive guideline (see 'seriousness' link above). In each case, sentencers should have regard to the full list, which includes the factors that, by statute, make an offence more serious:

- offence committed while on bail for other offences;
- offence was racially or religiously aggravated;
- offence was motivated by, or demonstrates, hostility based on the victim's sexual orientation (or presumed sexual orientation);
- offence was motivated by, or demonstrates, hostility based on the victim being (or being presumed to be) transgender;
- offence was motivated by, or demonstrates, hostility based on the victim's disability (or presumed disability);
- offender has previous convictions that the court considers can reasonably be treated as aggravating factors having regard to their relevance to the current offence and the time that has elapsed since conviction.

While the lists in the offence guidelines and other material referenced above, aim to identify the most common aggravating and mitigating factors, they are not intended to be exhaustive. Sentencers should always consider whether there are any other factors that make the offence more or less serious.

3. Form a preliminary view of the appropriate sentence, then consider offender mitigation

When the court has reached a provisional sentence based on its assessment of offence seriousness, it should take into account matters of offender mitigation. The issue of remorse should be taken into account at this point along with other mitigating features such as admissions to the police in interview.

4. Consider a reduction for a guilty plea

Reduction in sentence for a guilty plea, where first hearing is on or after 1 June 2017

[See SG5-3]

Reduction in sentence for a guilty plea, where first hearing is before 1 June 2017

The Council guideline Reduction in Sentence for a Guilty Plea, revised 2007, states that the punitive elements of the sentence should be reduced to recognise an offender's guilty plea. The reduction has no impact on sentencing decisions in relation to ancillary orders, including disqualification. The level of the reduction should reflect the stage at which the offender indicated a willingness to admit guilt and will be gauged on a sliding scale, ranging from a recommended one third (where the guilty plea was entered at the first reasonable opportunity), reducing to a recommended one quarter (where a trial date has been set) and to a recommended one tenth (for a guilty plea entered at the 'door of the court' or after the trial has begun). There is a presumption that the recommended reduction will be given unless there are good reasons for a lower amount. The application of the reduction may affect the type, as well as the severity, of the sentence. It may also take the sentence below the range in some cases. The court must state that it has reduced a sentence to reflect a guilty plea (Sentencing Code, s.52(7)). It should usually indicate what the sentence would have been if there had been no reduction as a result of the plea.

5. Consider ancillary orders, including compensation

Ancillary orders of particular relevance to individual offences are identified in the relevant guidelines. The court must always consider making a compensation order where the offending has resulted in personal injury, loss or damage. The court is required to give reasons if it decides not to make such an order (Sentencing Code, s.55).

- Ancillary orders – Magistrates' Court
- Ancillary orders – Crown Court Compendium, Part II Sentencing, S7

6. Decide sentence Give reasons

Review the total sentence to ensure that it is proportional to the offending behaviour and properly balanced. Sentencers must state reasons for the sentence passed in every case, including for any ancillary orders imposed (Sentencing Code, s.52). It is particularly important to identify any aggravating or mitigating factors, or matters of offender mitigation, that have resulted in a sentence more or less severe than the suggested starting point. If a court imposes a sentence of a different kind or outside the range indicated in the guidelines, it must state its reasons for doing so (Sentencing Code, s.52(6)). The court should also give its reasons for not making an order that has been canvassed before it or that it might have been expected to make.

USING SENTENCING COUNCIL GUIDELINES SG0-7

This section of the user guide explains the key decisions involved in the sentencing process for Sentencing Council guidelines.

STEP ONE: Determining the offence category

The decision making process includes a two-step approach to assessing seriousness. The first step is to determine the offence category by means of an assessment of the offender's culpability and the harm caused, or intended, by reference only to the factors set out at step one in each guideline. The contents are tailored for each offence and comprise the principal factual elements of the offence.

STEP TWO: Starting point and category range

The guidelines provide a starting point which applies to all offenders irrespective of plea or previous convictions. The guidelines also specify a category range for each offence category. The guidelines provide non-exhaustive lists of aggravating and mitigating factors relating to the context of the offence and to the offender. Sentencers should identify whether any combination of these, or other relevant factors, should result in an upward or downward adjustment from the starting point. In some cases, it may be appropriate to move outside the identified category range when reaching a provisional sentence.

This short video shows you how to use the expanded explanations in step two (start at 01:40). *https://youtu.be/CbYmouIMefU*

FURTHER STEPS

Having reached a provisional sentence, there are a number of further steps within the guidelines. These steps are clearly set out within each guideline and are tailored specifically for each offence in order to ensure that only the most appropriate guidance is included within each offence specific guideline. The further steps include:

- reduction for assistance to the prosecution;
- reduction for guilty pleas (the court should take account of any potential reduction for a guilty plea in accordance with section 73 of the Sentencing Code and the guideline for Reduction in Sentence for a Guilty Plea [see **SG5-12**]);
- where an offender is being sentenced for multiple offences – the court's assessment of the totality of the offending may result in a sentence above the range indicated for the individual offences, including a sentence of a different type (for more information, refer to the Totality guideline);
- compensation orders and/or ancillary orders appropriate to the case (Magistrates' court ancillary orders; Crown Court Compendium, Part II Sentencing, s.7);
- reasons for, and explain the effect of, the sentence.

Where there is no guideline for an offence, refer to the General guideline [See SG-2].

SG0-8 Expanded Explanations in Guidelines

The General guideline for sentencing offences that do not have a specific sentencing guideline, published by the Sentencing Council, came into force on 1 October 2019.

A set of expanded explanations are effective from the same day. These are now embedded in all existing offence specific guidelines. They add extra information to aggravating and mitigating factors to make it easier for courts to maintain consistency and transparency when sentencing. The expanded explanations will not change the factors in guidelines.

The expanded explanations are included at SG2-17.

PART 1 ALLOCATION

Determining whether Cases should be Dealt with by a Magistrates' Court or the Crown Court

SG1-1

Effective from: 1 March 2016

Venue for trial

It is important to ensure that all cases are tried at the appropriate level.

1. In general, either way offences should be tried summarily unless:
   - the outcome would clearly be a sentence in excess of the court's powers for the offence(s) concerned after taking into account personal mitigation and any potential reduction for a guilty plea; or
   - for reasons of unusual legal, procedural or factual complexity, the case should be tried in the Crown Court. This exception may apply in cases where a very substantial fine is the likely sentence. Other circumstances where this exception will apply are likely to be rare and case specific; the court will rely on the submissions of the parties to identify relevant cases.
2. In cases with no factual or legal complications the court should bear in mind its **power to commit for sentence after a trial** and **may retain jurisdiction** notwithstanding that the likely sentence might exceed its powers.
3. Cases may be tried summarily even where the defendant is subject to a Crown Court Suspended Sentence Order or Community Order.[1]
4. All parties should be asked by the court to make representations as to whether the case is suitable for summary trial. The court should refer to definitive guidelines (if any) to assess the likely sentence for the offence in the light of the facts alleged by the prosecution case, taking into account all aspects of the case including those advanced by the defence, including any personal mitigation to which the defence wish to refer.

Where the court decides that the case is suitable to be dealt with in the magistrates' court, it must warn the defendant that all sentencing options remain open and, if the defendant consents to summary trial and is convicted by the court or pleads guilty, the defendant may be committed to the Crown Court for sentence.

Committal for sentence

There is ordinarily no statutory restriction on committing an either way case for sentence following conviction. The general power of the magistrates' court to commit to the Crown Court for sentence after a finding that a case is suitable for summary trial and/or conviction continues to be available where the court is of the opinion 'that the offence or the combination of the offence and one or more offences associated with it was so serious that the Crown Court should have the power to deal with the offender in any way it could deal with him if he had been convicted on indictment'.[2]

However, where the court proceeds to the summary trial of certain offences relating to criminal damage, upon conviction there is no power to commit to the Crown Court for sentence.[3]

The court should refer to any definitive guideline to arrive at the appropriate sentence taking into account all of the circumstances of the case including personal mitigation and the appropriate guilty plea reduction.

In borderline cases the court should consider obtaining a pre-sentence report before deciding whether to commit to the Crown Court for sentence.

Where the offending is so serious that the court is of the opinion that the Crown Court should have the power to deal with the offender, the case should be committed to the Crown Court for sentence even if a community order may be the appropriate sentence (this will allow the Crown Court to deal with any breach of a community order, if that is the sentence passed).

Children and young people jointly charged with adults – interests of justice test

The proper venue for the trial of any child or young person is normally the youth court. Subject to statutory restrictions, that remains the case where a child or young person is charged jointly with an adult. This guideline does not provide information on the complex statutory framework for dealing with a youth jointly charged with an adult …

---

[1] The power to commit the case to the Crown Court to be dealt with under para.11(2) of Schedule 16 or para. 24 of Schedule 10 to the Sentencing Code can be exercised if the defendant is convicted.

[2] Sentencing Code s.14

[3] Magistrates' Courts Act 1980, s.3(4) and s.22

The following guidance must be applied in those cases where the interests of justice test falls to be considered:

1. If the adult is sent for trial to the Crown Court, the court should conclude that the child or young person must be tried separately in the youth court unless it is in the interests of justice for the child or young person and the adult to be tried jointly.
2. Examples of factors that should be considered when deciding whether it is in the interests of justice to send the child or young person to the Crown Court (rather than having a trial in the youth court) include:
   - whether separate trials will cause injustice to witnesses or to the case as a whole (consideration should be given to the provisions of sections 27 and 28 of the Youth Justice and Criminal Evidence Act 1999);
   - the age of the child or young person: the younger they are, the greater the desirability that they be tried in the youth court;
   - the age gap between the child or young person and the adult: a substantial gap in age militates in favour of the child or young person being tried in the youth court;
   - the lack of maturity of the child or young person;
   - the relative culpability of the child or young person compared with the adult and whether the alleged role played by the child or young person was minor;
   - the lack of previous convictions on the part of the child or young person.
3. The court should bear in mind that the youth court now has a general power to commit for sentence following conviction pursuant to Section 16 of the Sentencing Code. In appropriate cases this will permit the same court to sentence adults and child or young persons who have been tried separately.

Statutory framework

[Omitted. Sets out the MCA 1980, s. 19(1) to (4) (see **D6.21**) and the CAJA 2009, s. 125(1) (see **SG19-1**).]

PART 2 GENERAL GUIDELINE: OVERARCHING PRINCIPLES

APPLICABILITY SG2-1

[For the standard text on applicability see SG0-4]

Effective from: 1 October 2019

- For sentencing offences for which there is no offence specific sentencing guideline, and
- For use in conjunction with offence specific sentencing guidelines

APPLICABILITY SG2-2

Accompanying the General guideline are a set of expanded explanations which were effective from the same day. These are now embedded in all existing offence specific guidelines. They add extra information to aggravating and mitigating factors to make it easier for courts to maintain consistency and transparency when sentencing. The expanded explanations will not change the factors in guidelines.

The expanded explanations are included in this Part at SG2-17 following the General guideline.

STEP 1 Reaching a provisional sentence SG2-3

a) Where there is no definitive sentencing guideline for the offence, to arrive at a provisional sentence the court should take account of all of the following (if they apply):
   - the statutory maximum sentence (and if appropriate minimum sentence) for the offence;
   - sentencing judgments of the Court of Appeal (Criminal Division) for the offence; and
   - definitive sentencing guidelines for analogous offences.

The court will be assisted by the parties in identifying the above.

For the avoidance of doubt the court should **not** take account of any draft sentencing guidelines.

When considering definitive guidelines for analogous offences the court must apply these carefully, making adjustments for any differences in the statutory maximum sentence and in the elements of the offence. This will not be a merely arithmetical exercise.

b) Where possible the court should follow the stepped approach of sentencing guidelines to arrive at the sentence.

The seriousness of the offence is assessed by considering:

- the culpability [see SG2-18] of the offender

and

- the **harm [see SG2-19]** caused by the offending.

c) The initial assessment of harm and culpability should take no account of plea or previous convictions.

The court should consider which of the five purposes of sentencing (below) it is seeking to achieve through the sentence that is imposed. More than one purpose might be relevant and the importance of each must be weighed against the particular offence and offender characteristics when determining sentence. • The punishment of offenders • The reduction of crime (including its reduction by deterrence) • The reform and rehabilitation of offenders • The protection of the public • The making of reparation by offenders to persons affected by their offences

STEP 2 Aggravating and mitigating factors SG2-4

Once a provisional sentence is arrived at the court should take into account factors that may make the offence more serious and factors which may reduce seriousness or reflect personal mitigation.

- Identify whether a combination of these or other relevant factors should result in any upward or downward adjustment from the sentence arrived at so far.
- It is for the sentencing court to determine how much weight should be assigned to the aggravating and mitigating factors taking into account all of the circumstances of the offence and the offender.
- Not all factors that apply will necessarily influence the sentence.

- When sentencing an offence for which a **fixed penalty notice** was available the reason why the offender did not take advantage of the fixed penalty will be a relevant consideration. [see SG2-20]
- **If considering a fine – see information on fine band ranges below.**
- **If considering a community or custodial sentence refer also to the Imposition of community and custodial sentences definitive guideline [See SG9-2 for community orders and SG9-3 for custodial sentences] – see information on community orders and custodial sentences below.**

SG2-5 Fines

Fines	Starting point	Range
Fine Band A	50% of relevant weekly income	25 – 75% of relevant weekly income
Fine Band B	100% of relevant weekly income	75 – 125% of relevant weekly income
Fine Band C	150% of relevant weekly income	125 – 175% of relevant weekly income
Fine Band D	250% of relevant weekly income	200 – 300% of relevant weekly income
Fine Band E	400% of relevant weekly income	300 – 500% of relevant weekly income
Fine Band F	600% of relevant weekly income	500 – 700% of relevant weekly income

- The court should determine the appropriate level of fine in accordance with this guideline and section 125 of the Sentencing Code, which requires that the fine must reflect the seriousness of the offence and that the court must take into account the financial circumstances of the offender.
- Where possible, if a financial penalty is imposed, it should remove any economic benefit the offender has derived through the commission of the offence including:
  - o avoided costs;
  - o operating savings;
  - o any gain made as a direct result of the offence.
- The fine should meet, in a fair and proportionate way, the objectives of punishment, deterrence and the removal of gain derived through the commission of the offence; **it should not be cheaper to offend than to comply with the law.**
- In considering economic benefit, the court should avoid double recovery.
- Where the means of the offender are limited, priority should be given to compensation (where applicable) over payment of any other financial penalty.
- Where it is not possible to calculate or estimate the economic benefit, the court may wish to draw on information from the enforcing authorities about the general costs of operating within the law.
- When sentencing **organisations** the fine must be sufficiently substantial to have a real economic impact which will bring home to both management and shareholders the need to comply with the law. The court should ensure that the effect of the fine (particularly if it will result in closure of the business) is proportionate to the gravity of the offence.
- Obtaining financial information: It is for the offender to disclose to the court such data relevant to their financial position as will enable it to assess what they can reasonably afford to pay. If necessary, the court may compel the disclosure of an individual offender's financial circumstances pursuant to section 35 of the Sentencing Code. In the absence of such disclosure, or where the court is not satisfied that it has been given sufficient reliable information, the court will be entitled to draw reasonable inferences as to the offender's means from evidence it has heard and from all the circumstances of the case. In setting a fine, the court may conclude that the offender is able to pay any fine imposed unless the offender has supplied financial information to the contrary.

SG2-6 **Community Orders and Custodial Sentences**

[For the imposition of community orders, including the community orders table, see Imposition of Community and Custodial Sentences at **SG9-2**.

For the imposition of custodial sentences see Imposition of Community and Custodial Sentences at SG9-3.]

SG2-7

Factors increasing seriousness
(Factors are not listed in any particular order and are not exhaustive)

Statutory aggravating factors

- Previous convictions [See **SG2-21**], having regard to a) the **nature** of the offence to which the conviction relates and its **relevance** to the current offence; and b) the **time** that has elapsed since the conviction
- Offence committed whilst on bail [See **SG2-22**],
- Offence motivated by, or demonstrating hostility based on any of the following characteristics or presumed characteristics of the victim: religion, race, disability, sexual orientation, or transgender identity [See **SG2-23**],
- Offence was committed against an emergency worker acting in the exercise of functions as such a worker [See **SG2-24**],

Other aggravating factors

- Commission of offence whilst under the influence of alcohol or drugs [See **SG2-25**],
- Offence was committed as part of a group [See **SG2-26**],
- Offence involved use or threat of a weapon [See **SG2-27**],
- Planning of an offence [See **SG2-28**],
- Commission of the offence for financial gain [See **SG2-29**],
- High level of profit from the offence [See **SG2-30**],
- Abuse of trust or dominant position [See **SG2-31**],
- Restraint, detention or additional degradation of the victim [See **SG2-32**],
- Vulnerable victim [See **SG2-33**],
- Victim was providing a public service or performing a public duty at the time of the offence [See **SG2-34**],
- Other(s) put at risk of harm by the offending [See **SG2-35**],
- Offence committed in the presence of other(s) (especially children) [See **SG2-36**],
- Actions after the event including but not limited to attempts to cover up/conceal evidence [See **SG2-37**],
- Blame wrongly placed on other(s) [See **SG2-38**],
- Failure to respond to warnings or concerns expressed by others about the offender's behaviour [See **SG2-39**],
- Offence committed on licence or while subject to court order(s) [See **SG2-40**],
- Offence committed in custody [See **SG2-41**],
- Offences taken into consideration [See **SG2-42**],
- Offence committed in a domestic context [See **SG2-43**],
- Offence committed in a terrorist context [See **SG2-44**],
- Location and/or timing of offence [See **SG2-45**],
- Established evidence of community/wider impact [See **SG2-46**],
- Prevalence [See **SG2-47**],

SG2-8

Factors reducing seriousness or reflecting personal mitigation
(Factors are not listed in any particular order and are not exhaustive)

- No previous convictions or no relevant/recent convictions [See **SG2-48**],
- Good character and/or exemplary conduct [See **SG2-49**],
- Remorse [See **SG2-50**],
- Self-reporting [See **SG2-51**],
- Cooperation with the investigation/ early admissions [See **SG2-52**],
- Little or no planning [See **SG2-53**],
- The offender was in a lesser or subordinate role if acting with others/performed limited role under direction [See **SG2-54**],
- Involved through coercion, intimidation or exploitation [See **SG2-55**],
- Limited awareness or understanding of the offence [See **SG2-56**],
- Little or no financial gain [See **SG2-57**],
- Delay since apprehension [See **SG2-58**],
- Activity originally legitimate [See **SG2-59**],
- Age and/or lack of maturity [See **SG2-60**],

- Sole or primary carer for dependent relatives [See **SG2-61**],
- Physical disability or serious medical condition requiring urgent, intensive or long-term treatment [See **SG2-62**],
- Mental disorder or learning disability [See **SG2-63**],
- Determination and/or demonstration of steps having been taken to address addiction or offending behaviour [See **SG2-64**],

SG2-9 STEP 3 **Consider any factors which indicate a reduction for assistance to the prosecution**

The court should take into account section 74 of the Sentencing Code (reduction in sentence for assistance to prosecution) and any other rule of law by virtue of which an offender may receive a discounted sentence in consequence of assistance given (or offered) to the prosecutor or investigator.

SG2-10 STEP 4 **Reduction for guilty pleas**

The court should take account of any potential reduction for a guilty plea in accordance with section 73 of the Sentencing Code and the guideline for Reduction in Sentence for a Guilty Plea [see **SG5-1–SG5-12**].

SG2-11 STEP 5 **Dangerousness**

Where the offence is listed in Schedule 15, Schedule 18 and/or Schedule 19 of the Criminal Justice Act 2003

The court should consider:

1) whether having regard to the criteria contained in Chapter 6 of Part 10 of the Sentencing Code it would be appropriate to impose an extended sentence (sections 266 and 279) and

2) whether having regard to sections 273 and 283 of the Sentencing Code it would be appropriate to impose a life sentence.

When sentencing offenders to a life sentence under these provisions, the notional determinate sentence should be used as the basis for the setting of a minimum term.

SG2-12 STEP 6 **Special custodial sentence for certain offenders of particular concern**

Where the offence is listed in Schedule 13 of the Sentencing Code and the court does not impose a sentence of imprisonment for life or an extended sentence, but does impose a period of imprisonment, the term of the sentence must be equal to the aggregate of the appropriate custodial term and a further period of 1 year for which the offender is to be subject to a licence (sections 265 and 278 of the Sentencing Code).

See the **Crown Court Compendium, Part II Sentencing S4-3** for further details.

SG2-13 STEP 7 **Totality principle**

If sentencing an offender for more than one offence, or where the offender is already serving a sentence, consider whether the total sentence is just and proportionate to the overall offending behaviour in accordance with the Offences Taken into Consideration [see **SG3**] and **Totality** [see **SG4**] guidelines.

SG2-14 STEP 8 **Compensation and ancillary orders**

In all cases the court should consider whether to make compensation and/or other ancillary orders.

Where the offence involves a firearm, an imitation firearm or an offensive weapon the court may consider the criteria in section 19 of the Serious Crime Act 2007 for the imposition of a Serious Crime Prevention Order.

- **Ancillary orders – Magistrates' Court [SG10-5]**
- **Ancillary orders – Crown Court Compendium, Part II Sentencing, S7**

SG2-15 STEP 9 **Reasons**

Section 52 of the Sentencing Code imposes a duty to give reasons for, and explain the effect of, the sentence.

SG2-16 STEP 10 **Consideration for time spent on bail (tagged curfew)**

The court must consider whether to give credit for time spent on bail in accordance with section 240A of the Criminal Justice Act 2003 and section 325 of the Sentencing Code.

SG2-17 **Expanded explanations**

Effective date: October 1 2019

The following section sets out the text of the expanded explanations which accompany the General guideline. These are now embedded in all existing offence specific guidelines. They add extra information to aggravating and mitigating factors to make it easier for courts to maintain consistency and transparency when sentencing. The expanded explanations will not change the factors in guidelines.

Care should be taken to avoid double counting factors including those already taken into account in assessing culpability or harm or those inherent in the offence

Culpability SG2-18

Culpability is assessed with reference to the offender's role, level of intention and/or premeditation and the extent and sophistication of planning.

- The court should balance these factors to reach a fair assessment of the offender's overall culpability in all the circumstances of the case and the offender.
- The mere presence of a factor that is inherent in the offence should not be used in assessing culpability.
- Deliberate or gratuitous violence or damage to property, over and above what is needed to carry out the offence will normally indicate a higher level of culpability.
- For offences where there is no requirement for the offender to have any level of intention, recklessness, negligence, dishonesty, knowledge, understanding or foresight for the offence to be made out, the range of culpability **may** be inferred from the circumstances of the offence as follows:

Highest level	Deliberate – intentional act or omission
⇓	Reckless – acted or failed to act regardless of the foreseeable risk
	Negligent – failed to take steps to guard against the act or omission
Lowest level	Low/no culpability – act or omission with none of the above features

- For offences that require some level of culpability (eg intention, recklessness or knowledge) to be made out, the range of culpability will be narrower. Relevant factors **may** typically include but are not limited to:

Highest level	High level of planning/sophistication/leading role
⇓	Some planning/significant role
Lowest level	Little or no planning/minor role

- These models of assessing culpability will not be applicable to all offences.

Harm SG2-19

Harm – which the offence caused, was intended to cause or might foreseeably have caused

- There may be primary and secondary victims of an offence and, depending on the offence, victims may include one or more individuals, a community, the general public, the state, the environment and/or animal(s). In some cases there may not be an identifiable victim.
- An assessment of harm should generally reflect the overall impact of the offence upon the victim(s) and may include direct harm (including physical injury, psychological harm and financial loss) and consequential harm.
- When considering the value of property lost or damaged the court should also take account of any sentimental value to the victim(s) and any disruption caused to a victim's life, activities or business.
- When considering harm to animals or the environment relevant considerations will include the impact on rare or endangered species or sensitive locations, and any suffering caused.
- Where harm was intended but no harm or a lower level of harm resulted – the sentence will normally be assessed with reference to the level of harm intended.
- Where the harm caused is greater than that intended – the sentence will normally be assessed with reference to the level of harm suffered by the victim.
- Dealing with a risk of harm involves consideration of both the likelihood of harm occurring and the extent of it if it does.
- Risk of harm is less serious than the same actual harm. Where the offence has caused risk of harm but no (or less) actual harm the normal approach is to move down to the next category of harm. This may not be appropriate if either the likelihood or extent of potential harm is particularly high.
- A Victim Personal Statement (VPS) or other impact statement may assist the court in assessing harm, but the absence of a VPS or other impact statement should not be taken to indicate the absence of harm.
- The court should balance these characteristics to reach a fair assessment of harm in the context of the circumstances of the offence.

Highest level	Very serious harm caused to individual victim(s) or to wider public/environment etc
⇓	Serious harm caused OR high risk of very serious harm
	Significant harm caused OR high risk of serious harm
Lowest level	Low/no harm caused OR high risk significant harm

The table should be used in conjunction with the notes above and may not be applicable to all offences.

SG2-20 **Fixed Penalty Notice**

Penalty notices may be issued as an alternative to prosecution in respect of a range of offences. An admission of guilt is not a prerequisite to issuing a penalty notice. An offender who is issued with a penalty notice may nevertheless be prosecuted for the offence if he or she:

- asks to be tried for the offence; or
- fails to pay the penalty within the period stipulated in the notice and the prosecutor decides to proceed with charges.

In some cases of non-payment, the penalty is automatically registered and enforceable as a fine without need for recourse to the courts. This procedure applies to penalty notices for disorder and fixed penalty notices issued in respect of certain road traffic offences but not to fixed penalty notices issued for most other criminal offences.

When sentencing in cases in which a penalty notice was available:

- the fact that the offender did not take advantage of the penalty (whether that was by requesting a hearing or failing to pay within the specified timeframe) does not increase the seriousness of the offence and must not be regarded as an aggravating factor. The appropriate sentence must be determined in accordance with the sentencing principles set out in this guideline (including the amount of any fine, which must take an offender's financial circumstances into account), disregarding the availability of the penalty. In some cases this may result in a fine that is lower than the fixed penalty.
- where a penalty notice could not be offered or taken up for reasons unconnected with the offence itself, such as administrative difficulties outside the control of the offender, the starting point should be a fine equivalent to the amount of the penalty and no order of costs should be imposed. The offender should not be disadvantaged by the unavailability of the penalty notice in these circumstances.

Where an offender has had previous penalty notice(s), the fact that an offender has previously been issued with a penalty notice does not increase the seriousness of the current offence and must not be regarded as an aggravating factor. It may, however, properly influence the court's assessment of the offender's suitability for a particular sentence, so long as it remains within the limits established by the seriousness of the current offence.

SG2-21 **Previous convictions**

Guidance on the use of previous convictions

The following guidance should be considered when seeking to determine the degree to which previous convictions should aggravate sentence:

Section 143 of the Criminal Justice Act 2003 states that:

> In considering the seriousness of an offence ("the current offence") committed by an offender who has one or more previous convictions, the court must treat each previous conviction as an aggravating factor if (in the case of that conviction) the court considers that it can reasonably be so treated having regard, in particular, to—
> (a) the nature of the offence to which the conviction relates and its relevance to the current offence, and
> (b) the time that has elapsed since the conviction.

1. Previous convictions are considered at step two in the Council's offence-specific guidelines.
2. The primary significance of previous convictions (including convictions in other jurisdictions) is the extent to which they indicate trends in offending behaviour and possibly the offender's response to earlier sentences.
3. Previous convictions are normally **relevant** to the current offence when they are of a similar type.
4. Previous convictions of a type different from the current offence **may** be relevant where they are an indication of persistent offending or escalation and/or a failure to comply with previous court orders.
5. Numerous and frequent previous convictions might indicate an underlying problem (for example, an addiction) that could be addressed more effectively in the community and will not necessarily indicate that a custodial sentence is necessary.
6. If the offender received a non-custodial disposal for the previous offence, a court should not necessarily move to a custodial sentence for the fresh offence.